THE
BANTAM
CROSSWORD
DICTIONARY

"The highest percentage of most used
words of any crossword dictionary
ever compiled."

THE BANTAM CROSSWORD DICTIONARY

WALTER D. GLANZE, Editor

JEROME FRIED, Lexicographer

NAZARENO LA MARCA, Sr., Compiler

A Charles B. Bloch Book

BANTAM BOOKS

NEW YORK • TORONTO • LONDON • SYDNEY • AUCKLAND

Dedication
To Laura Borsten,
without whom this book would never have
happened

THE BANTAM CROSSWORD DICTIONARY
A Bantam Book / October 1979

ISBN 0-553-20730-X

Published simultaneously in the United States and Canada

Bantam Books are published by Bantam Books, Inc. Its trademark, consisting of the words "Bantam Books" and the portrayal of a rooster, is Registered in U.S. Patent and Trademark
Office and in other countries. Marca Registrada. Bantam
Books, Inc., 666 Fifth Avenue, New York, New York 10103.

PRINTED IN THE UNITED STATES OF AMERICA

20 19 18

CONTENTS

INTRODUCTION

THE BANTAM CROSSWORD DICTIONARY has been created for today's puzzle solver. It is modern, comprehensive, easy to use, and—well researched: The choice of cues and answers is not based on English dictionaries but is the result of 30 years of actual experience with crossword puzzles.

The alphabetical order of the cues is WORD BY WORD (telephone-book style), not letter for letter (dictionary style); for example, *anchor ring* precedes *anchorage.*

A logical and simple ARRANGEMENT of the answers has been adopted: (1) First, they are separated by part of speech, which permits the solver to decide if an -s (or -es) can be added to a noun, or an -ed or -ing to a verb. These groups are marked by periods. (2) The answers are then separated by the number of letters, the shortest first. These groups are marked by semicolons. (3) Answers of same length are then given in alphabetical order, separated by commas. (4) Each answer, whether a single word or a phrase, is printed as a solid word, the way it appears in the puzzle.

ABBREVIATIONS are kept to a minimum: pref., prefix; c.f., combining form; pert. to, pertaining to; poet., poetical. Also CROSS-REFERENCES have been minimized; the emphasis is on clarity right on the spot. There are NO FILL-IN definitions; such cues are either too simple (as "____ versa") or ambiguous (as "San ____"). Most important, this dictionary does not include gimmicky creations; all answers are LEGITIMATE WORDS.

Forty SPECIAL TABLES—from Books of the Bible to Wedding Anniversaries—are given in their respective alphabetical places.

There are two appendixes. (1) A unique LONG-WORD FINDER: All words of six to ten letters that appear in the book (about 22,000) are listed by word length and alphabetically in a special section. This novel approach to a word finder is more meaningful than the usual lists of three- to five-letter words, which are easy to guess. (2) Common words in SIX LANGUAGES: About 1,000 foreign words that are regulars in puzzles are given in a separate list, words such as *nein* and *oui* and *casa* and *vino.*

But tables and appendixes, useful as they may be, are secondary. The strength of this new dictionary is the fine choice of more than 50,000 cues, as well as the fresh way they are matched with over 160,000 answers. Everything in this book is as straightforward and usable as possible. Enjoy it. Be creative. Have fun.

CHARLES B. BLOCH

a priori / ILLATIVE; DEDUCTIVE

A in school / EXCELLENT

aardvark / ANTEATER

Aaron's brother / MOSES

Aaron's colleague / HUR

Aaron's magic wand / ROD

Aaron's nephew / HUR

Aaron's rod / MULLEIN

Aaron's sister / MIRIAM

Aaron's son / ABIHU, NADAB

abaca / HEMP; LUPIS; LINAGA

aback / ABAFT; BEHIND; BACKWARD

abacus / SOROBAN, SUANPAN, SWANPAN; CUPBOARD; CALCULATOR

abaft / AFT; ASTERN, BEHIND

abalone / ORMER; SEAEAR; HALIOTIS

abalone-shell money / ULLO; UHLLO

abandon / DROP, QUIT; CEASE, FORGO, LEAVE; ABJURE, DESERT

abandoned / BAD; SINFUL, WICKED

abandoned child / WAIF; FOUNDLING

abandonment / DESERTION

abase / SINK; LOWER; DEMEAN

abasement / SHAME; DEGRADATION

abash / AWE, COW; SHAME; HUMBLE

abashment / CHAGRIN; CONFUSION

abate / EBB; ALLAY, QUIET, RELAX

abatement / LETUP; DECREASE

abba / BISHOP, FATHER

abbe / ABBOT; CLERIC, PARSON

abbess / AMMA

abbey's superior / ABBE; ABBOT

abbot / ABBE

abbot's home / ABBEY; ABBACY

abbreviate / CUT; REDUCE; ABRIDGE

abbreviation / DIGEST; EPITOME

abbreviatory / CURTAILING

ABC's / ELEMENTS; PRINCIPIA

abdicate / CEDE; DEMIT; RESIGN

abdomen / WAME; BELLY, TUMMY

abdomen, pert. to / ALVINE; VENTRAL

abduct / PRESS; KIDNAP; SHANGHAI

abecedary / PRIMER

abed / ILL; SICK; ASLEEP; RETIRED

Abelard's wife / HELOISE

abele / POPLAR

Abel's assassin / CAIN

Abel's father / ADAM

Abel's mother / EVE

aberrant / STRAYING

aberration / LAPSE; DELIRIUM

abet / AID, EGG; BACK, HELP

abettor / ALLY; ACCESSORY

abeyance / DORMANCY, SUSPENSE

abhor / HATE; DETEST; ABOMINATE

abhorrent / VILE; ODIOUS

abide / BEAR, LIVE, STAY; AWAIT

abiding / STABLE; LASTING

abies / FIR

Abie's girl / ROSE

abigail / MAID

Abijah's son / ASA

ability / MIGHT, POWER, SKILL; TALENT; FACULTY; APTITUDE

abject / LOW; BASE, MEAN, VILE

abjection / HUMILIATION

abjure / DISAVOW; RENOUNCE

ablation / SURGERY

ablation, c.f. / ECTOMY

ablaze / AFIRE, EAGER; ARDENT

able / CLEVER; CAPABLE; COMPETENT

able to laugh / RISIBLE

able to pay / SOUND; SOLVENT

ablution / BATH, WASH, WUDU, WUZU

abnegate / DENY; REFUSE, REJECT

abnormal / ODD; IRREGULAR

abnormal growth / TUMOR; CANCER

aboard ship / ASEA

abode / HOME; DWELLING; RESIDENCE

abode of ancient harp / TARA

abode of the blissful / EDEN; DIXIE; AVALON, GOSHEN, HEAVEN; ARCADIA; PARADISE; COCKAIGNE, DIXIELAND

abode of dead / AALU; AARU; ARALU, HADES, ORCUS, SHEOL; AMENTI; CEMETERY

abode of fauna / HABITAT

abode of the gods / ASGARD, SUMERU; OLYMPUS

abolish / ANNUL; REPEAL; DESTROY

abolishment / EXTINCTION

abolition / ANNULMENT, REMISSION

abolitionist / LUNDY; GARRISON

aboma / BOA; CONSTRICTOR

abominable / BAD; FOUL; HORRID

abominable snowman / YETI

abominate / HATE; ABHOR; LOATHE

abomination / VICE; POLLUTION

aboon / ABOVE

aboriginal / FIRST; NATIVE; ORIGINAL, PRIMEVAL; INDIGENOUS

aboriginal American / ESKIMO, INDIAN
aborigine / NATIVE; BLACKFELLOW
aborigine of Antilles / CARIB, INERI; ARAWAK
abortion / FAILURE; MISCARRIAGE
abortive / VAIN; USELESS
abound / FLOW, TEEM; SWARM, SWELL
abounding / RIFE; REPLETE
about / AT, OF, ON, RE; NEAR; ANENT, CIRCA; AROUND, NEARLY
about, pref. / DE
about that / THEREOF
about this / HEREOF
about town / LOCAL
above / ON, UP; ATOP, ONTO, OVER, UPON; ABOON. CITED, NAMED
above, pref. / SUPER, SUPRA
above the ear / EPIOTIC
above and in contact with / ON
abrade / RUB; RASP, WEAR; CHAFE
abrading tool / FILE, RASP
Abraham's birthplace / UR
Abraham's bosom / HEAVEN
Abraham's brother / HARAN, NAHOR
Abraham's father / TERAH
Abraham's nephew / LOT
Abraham's son / ISAAC, MEDAN, SHUAH; ISHMAEL
Abraham's wife / HAGAR, SARAH
abrasion / FRICTION; ATTRITION
abrasive / BORT, HONE; EMERY; PUMICE; CORUNDUM
abraxas / GEM; CHARM; AMULET
abreast / EVEN; APACE
abri / SHED; DUGOUT
abridge / RAZEE; REDUCE; CURTAIL
abridged / DIGESTED; CONDENSED
abridgment / DIGEST, PRECIS
abroad / AFAR; WIDELY; OVERSEAS
abrogate / VOID; ANNUL; CANCEL
abrupt / CURT, RUDE, BLUFF, BLUNT, ROUGH, SHORT, STEEP
Absalom's cousin / AMASA
Absalom's sister / TAMAR
Absalom's slayer / JOAB
abscond / FLY; BOLT, FLEE; ELOIN
absconded / DECAMPED
absence / LACK; TRUANCY
absence of appetite / ASITIA
absent / OFF, OUT; AWAY, AWOL
absent-minded / RAPT; DISTRAIT
absinthe / GENIPI; WORMWOOD
absolute / PURE; SHEER, TOTAL
absolute property in land / ALOD
absolute ruler / MONARCH; DICTATOR

absolute superlative / ELATIVE
absolve / FREE; CLEAR; ACQUIT
absolve sins / SHRIVE; EXPIATE
absonant / HARSH; CONTRARY
absorb / MERGE; DEVOUR; CONSUME
absorbed / RAPT
absorbent substance / TOWEL; SPONGE; BLOTTER
abstain / FAST, STOP; AVOID
abstain from / ESCHEW; REFRAIN
abstemious / FRUGAL; ASCETIC
abstract / RECONDITE. PRECIS
abstract being / ENS; ENTIA
abstruse / DEEP; HIDDEN, OCCULT
absurd / MAD; COMIC, SILLY
abundance / FLOW; OODLES, PLENTY
abundant / FULL, RIFE; AMPLE
abuse / HARM, HURT; INJURE, MALIGN, REVILE, VILIFY; OUTRAGE
abusive / RUDE; ROUGH; INSULTING
abusive allegation / MUD; SLUR
abut / TOUCH; ADJOIN, BORDER
abutment / END; PIER; TERMINAL
abuzz / HUMMING
abyss / PIT; GULF, HELL; CHASM
Abyssinia / ETHIOPIA
Abyssinian / GEEZ; GALLA; ETHIOP
Abyssinian antelope / GERENUK
Abyssinian ape / GELADA
Abyssinian beer / TALLA
Abyssinian capital / ADDISABABA
Abyssinian cattle / GALLA, SANGA
Abyssinian grain / TEF
Abyssinian instrument / KRAC
Abyssinian monkey / WAAG; GRIVET
Abyssinian stew / WAT
Abyssinian thatched hut / TUKUL
Abyssinian title / RAS; NEGUS
Abyssinian toga / SHAMMA
Abyssinian tree / KOSO; CUSSO
Abyssinian tribesman / SHOA
Abyssinian weight / KASM, NATR
Abyssinian wolf / KABERU
acacia / BABUL; LOCUST, MIMOSA
acacia gum / AMRAD, CUTCH
academic / MOOT; SCHOLASTIC
academic achievement / DEGREE
academic cap / MORTARBOARD
academic gown / TOGA
academic year division / TERM; SEMESTER
academy / SCHOOL; INSTITUTE
acarid / MITE, TICK; CHIGGER
acarpous / BARREN; FRUITLESS
acaudal / TAILLESS
accede / AGREE; COMPLY; CONSENT
accelerate / PUSH, URGE; HURRY

accent / BROGUE, STRESS; EMPHASIS

accented / SFORZATO; SFORZANDO

accept / TAKE; ADMIT, AGREE

accept as one's own / ADOPT

accept as true / CREDIT; BELIEVE

accept as valid / ADMIT

access / WAY; ADIT, DOOR; ENTRY

accessible / EASY, OPEN

accession / ADDITION

accessory / ALLY; FRILL; GADGET

accident / SLIP; CHANCE, HAZARD

accidental / CASUAL; FORTUITOUS

accipitrine / HAWKLIKE; RAPTORIAL

acclaim / CLAP; PRAISE; APPLAUD. ECLAT; OVATION

acclamation / APPLAUSE, APPROVAL

acclimate / INURE; ACCUSTOM

acclivity / CLIMB, SLOPE, TALUS

accolade / AWARD, HONOR; DUBBING

accommodate / FIT; LEND; ADAPT

accompany / ATTEND, CONVOY

accompanying / WITH; ATTENDANT

accomplice / AID, PAL; ALLY, TOOL; SHILL; COLLEAGUE

accomplish / DO; ATTAIN; ACHIEVE

accomplished / ADROIT, CLEVER

accomplishment / DEED, FEAT

accord / AGREE, GRANT. UNISON

according to / ALA, PER; ALLA

according to Hoyle / CORRECT

accordingly / HENCE; CONSEQUENTLY

accost / HAIL; GREET; APPROACH

account / TAB; BILL, SAKE; STORY; RECITAL. HOLD, RATE; ESTEEM

account book / LEDGER

account received / ASSET

account rendered / BILL

accountable / LIABLE

accountant / CPA; AUDITOR

accounting notation / DEBIT; CREDIT

accouter / DRESS, EQUIP

accoutrements / ARMS; ARMOR

accredit / ACCEPT; AUTHORIZE

accredited / DEPUTED

accretion / GROWTH; ADDITION

accrue / ADD; ISSUE; FOLLOW

accumulate / PILE; AMASS, HOARD

accumulation / FUND, HEAP; STORE

accuracy / FIDELITY; PRECISION

accurate / JUST, NICE, TRUE

accursed / DOOMED, ODIOUS

accusation / CHARGE; INDICTMENT

accuse / BLAME; IMPUTE; CENSURE

accustom / DRILL, INURE, TRAIN

accustomed / WONT; USUAL

ace / JOT, ONE; UNIT; EXPERT; AVIATOR

acerb / ACID, SOUR, TART; HARSH

acerbate / EMBITTER, IRRITATE

acerbity / VENOM; RANCOR

acetic acid / VINEGAR

acetone / KETONE

acetose / SOUR, TART

ache / AIL; HURT, PAIN. PANG

achene / CYPSELA, UTRICLE

achieve / GET, WIN; GAIN; ATTAIN

achieved / DID; COMPLETED

achievement / DEED, FEAT, GEST

Achilles' adviser / NESTOR

Achilles' father / PELEUS

Achilles' friend / PATROCLUS

Achilles' horse / BALIOS; XANTHOS

Achilles' mother / THETIS

Achilles' slayer / PARIS

Achilles' tutor / CHIRON

Achilles' weak spot / HEEL

acid / SOUR; BITING, BITTER

acid berry / GOOSEBERRY

acid compound / THIAMID

acid condiment / VINEGAR

acid of fruits / MALIC

acid neutralizer / ALKALI; ANTACID

acid substance from grapes / TARTAR

acid-foaming yeast / TORULA

acidity / ACOR

acidulent / TART; PEEVISH

acidulous / SOUR; CRABBY

acknowledge / OWN; AVOW; ADMIT

acknowledge a greeting / BOW, NOD

acknowledge an offense / APOLOGIZE

acknowledged / UNDERSTOOD

acknowledgement / ADMISSION

acle / IRONWOOD

acme / TIP; APEX, PEAK; CREST

acolyte / NOVICE; ASSISTANT

acomia / BALDNESS

aconite / BIKH; WOLFBANE

acorn / CAMATA

acoustic / PHONIC

acquaint / TELL; IMPART; APPRISE

acquaintance / FRIEND; INTIMACY

acquainted / VERSANT; INFORMED

acquiesce / BOW; AGREE; CONCUR

acquire / GET, WIN; EARN, GAIN, MAKE, REAP

acquire knowledge / LEARN

acquire by labor / REAP; ATTAIN

acquire laboriously / EKE

acquire by seizure / PREEMPT

acquirement / ATTAINMENT

acquit / FREE; CLEAR; ABSOLVE

acreage for planting / FARM

acres / LAND; ESTATE
acrid / TART; ACERB; PUNGENT
acrimonious / KEEN; SHARP; BIT-ING, SEVERE; CAUSTIC; STING-ING
acrimony / VENOM; RANCOR
acrobat / GYMNAST, TUMBLER
acrobat of India / NAT
acrobat's costume / TIGHTS; LEO-TARD, MAILLOT
acrobat's spring / TRAMPOLINE
acrophobia / ALTOPHOBIA
acropolis / HEIGHT; CITADEL
across / OER; OVER; BEYOND
across, pref. / DIA; TRANS
act / DO; MAKE, MOVE; EMOTE, FEIGN; BEHAVE. LAW; DEED, FEAT
act in agreement / COACT; CONCUR
act of aid / HELP; SUCCOR
act of burning / ARSON
act of carrying / PORTAGE
act as chairman / PRESIDE
act of civility / BOW; CURTSY
act of coming in / ENTRANCE
act with dispatch / HURRY; HUS-TLE
act dispiritedly / MOPE, POUT
act of distributing cards / DEAL
act of god / MIRACLE; ACCIDENT
act hesitatingly / WAVER; FALTER
act of holding / RETENTION
act in law / RES
act of leaving / EXIT
act of omission / ELISION
act peculiarly / WANDER
act of repentance / PENANCE
act of selling / SALE, VEND
act of shunning / AVOIDANCE
act together / CONCERT; COOPER-ATE
act violently / ROW; RAGE
act of withdrawing / SECESSION
acted as doorkeeper / TILED
acting group / CAST; TROUPE
acting profession / STAGE
action / DEED; ENCOUNTER
action, pert. to / PRACTICAL
action to recover / REPLEVIN
action word / VERB
activate / STIR; AROUSE
active / BUSY, SPRY, YARE; AGILE
active consciousness / ATTENTION
active power / FORCE
activity / ACTION; CELERITY
actor / DOER; AGENT; MUMMER, PLAYER; HISTRIO; THESPIAN
actors, pert. to / THESPIAN
actor's aide / DRESSER
actor's hint / CUE
actor's part / ROLE
actors in a play / CAST

actor's speech / SIDE
actress / HEROINE, INGENUE
acts badly / HAMS
actual / REAL, TRUE; GENUINE
actually / INDEED, VERILY
actuate / MOVE, URGE; IMPEL
acuity / WIT; SHARPNESS
acumen / INSIGHT; SAGACITY
acuminate / SHARPEN. POINTED
acushla / DARLING; SWEETHEART
acute / KEEN; SHARP, SMART
acutely / DEEPLY; INTENSELY
acuteness / ACUITY, ACUMEN
ad lib / FREELY; EXTEMPORE
adage / SAW; AXIOM, MAXIM; BY-WORD, SAYING; PRECEPT, PROV-ERB
adagio / SLOWLY
Adah's husband / LAMECH
adamant / SET; FIRM. DIAMOND
adamantine / STONY; IMMOVABLE
adamites / MEN; NUDISTS
Adam's ale / WATER
Adam's apple / LARYNX
Adam's first mate / LILITH
Adam's needle / YUCCA
Adam's son / ABEL, CAIN, SETH
Adam's wife / EVE
adapt / FIT; SUIT; MATCH; CON-FORM
aday / daily
add / JOIN; AFFIX, TOTAL; ATTACH
add liquor to / LACE
add on / ANNEX; APPEND, ATTACH
add spices to / season
add a sweetener / SUGAR
add up / SUM, TOT; RECKON
added to / AND; MORE
addendum / ADDITION, APPENDIX
adder / ASP; VIPER
addict / FIEND; JUNKIE; TRIPPER
addicted / PRONE; HABITUATED
addiction / HABIT
addition / ADDENDUM
addition to amend / RIDER
addition of a syllable / PARAGOGE
additional / MORE, OVER; EXTRA
additional amount / MORE
additional territory / LEBENSRAUM
addle / SPOIL; MUDDLE
addleheaded / STUPID
address / SITE, TACT, TALK; SKILL; SPEECH. GREET; ACCOST
address an audience / ORATE
address of greeting / WELCOME
adduce / CITE, NAME; OFFER, QUOTE
adeem / REVOKE
adept / EXPERT, VERSED; SKILLED
adequate / DUE, FIT; ABLE; AMPLE
adhere / FIX; HOLD, JOIN; CLING
adhere closely / CLEAVE, FOLLOW

adhered / STUCK
adherence / DEVOTION; ATTACHMENT
adherent / IST, ITE; ALLY
adhesive / GUM; GLUE; PASTE; MUCILAGE. GUMMY; VISCOUS
adieu / GOODBY; FAREWELL
adipose / FAT; OBESE
adiposity / BULK; CORPULENCE
adit / STULM; ENTRANCE
adjacent / NEAR, NIGH; CLOSE
adjective suffix / IC; ENE, ENT, ESE, IAN, ILE, ITE, IVE, OUS
adjoin / ABUT; TOUCH, VERGE
adjoining / NEXT; ADJACENT
adjourn / DEFER; POSTPONE
adjudge / DEEM; AWARD; DECREE
adjudged unfit / CONDEMNED
adjudicate / FIND; DECIDE, SETTLE
adjugated / YOKED
adjunct / ADDITION; ACCESSORY
adjure / BEG; CHARGE; ENTREAT
adjust / FIX, SET; ADAPT, ALIGN
adjusted to pitch / TUNED
adjutant / AIDE; ARGALA; MARABOU
adminicle / AUXILIARY
administer / JUDGE, SERVE
administer punishment / CANE; SPANK
administration / REGIME
administrator / TRUSTEE
administrator in India / NABOB
admirable / FINE; SUPERB
admiration / REGARD, WONDER
admire / ESTEEM, REVERE; COMMEND
admire excessively / ADORE
admired / POPULAR
admirer / FAN; BEAU; SUITOR
admission / ACCESS, ENTREE
admission card / PASS; PERMIT, TICKET
admit / OWN; AVOW; AGREE, ALLOW
admonish / WARN; TEACH; EXHORT
admonition / ADVICE; CAUTION
ado / FUSS, STIR; HUBBUB
adolescence / TEENS; NONAGE
adolescent / LAD; YOUTH
adolescent boy / STRIPLING
Adonis' killer / BOAR
adopt / TAKE; ELECT; ACCEPT
adopted / CHOSE; ASSUMED
adopted food regimen / DIET
adoration / DULIA; WORSHIP
adore / LOVE; HONOR; HALLOW
adorn / DECK, GILD, STUD, TRIM
adorn with jewels / BEGEM
adorned / GRACED; BEDIGHT
adornment / ORNAMENT; DECORATION

Adriatic city / VENICE; TRIESTE
Adriatic cold wind / BORA
adrift / AFLOAT; UNCERTAIN
adroit / APT; ABLE, DEFT, NEAT; ADEPT, HANDY, QUICK; CLEVER
adulate / PRAISE; APPLAUD
adult / GROWN; MATURE; GROWNUP
adult female / WOMAN
adult insect / IMAGO
adult male / MAN
adulterate / DEBASE, DILUTE
adulterated / CORRUPT; VITIATED
adumbral / SHADY; SHADOW
advance / GAIN, GROW, LOAN, MOVE
advance guard / VAN
advanced / LEADING; PROMOTED
advanced study group / SEMINAR
advancement / STEP; PROGRESS
advancing the cause of / PROMOTING
advantage / USE; GAIN, GOOD
advantageous / USEFUL; BENEFICIAL
advent / ARRIVAL
adventitious / CASUAL; ACCIDENTAL
adventure / GEST; EVENT; HAZARD
adventure story / TALE, YARN
adventurer / GAMBLER; DAREDEVIL
adventurous / BOLD, RASH; DARING
adversary / FOE; ENEMY, RIVAL
adversary of man / DEVIL, SATAN
adverse / ANTI; HARMFUL; INIMICAL
adversity / ILL, WOE; TROUBLE
advertise / NOTIFY; ANNOUNCE
advertisement / AD; PLUG; NOTICE
advertising sign / POSTER
advice / COUNSEL; SUGGESTION
advisable / PRUDENT; EXPEDIENT
advise / WARM; INFORM; ADMONISH
advisedly / KNOWINGLY; DESIGNEDLY
adviser / COACH; MONITOR
advocate / LAWYER, SECOND; COUNSEL; ATTORNEY; PROPONENT. PLEAD
adytum / DEN; SHRINE; SANCTUM
Aeetes' daughter / MEDEA
Aeetes' kingdom / COLCHIS
Aegean island / IOS, NIO; SAMOS
aegis / SHIELD; PATRONAGE
Aeneas' admirer / DIDO
Aeneas' father / ANCHISES
Aeneas' friend / ACHATES
Aeneas' wife / CREUSA; LAVINIA
Aeneid's author / VERGIL, VIRGIL

Aeolus' invention / SAIL
aerate / CARBONATE
aerial / ANTENNA. AIRY, HIGH
aerial maneuver / LOOP, SPIN
aeriform fluid / GAS
aeronaut / AVIATOR; BALLOONIST
aeronautics / AVIATION
aerostat / BALLOON
aerugo / VERDIGRIS
aery / SPIRITUAL, VISIONARY
aesir / TIU, TYR; LOKI, ODIN, THOR, VALI; BRAGI; BALDER
afar / FAR; REMOTE; DISTANT
affable / CIVIL; POLITE, URBANE
affair / DEAL; EVENT; LIAISON
affair of honor / DUEL
affect / MOVE; FEIGN, TOUCH
affect deeply / IMPRESS
affect with feeling of dread / AWE
affect with fungus / MILDEW
affectation / POSE; PRETENSE
affected manners / AIRS
affected smile / SMIRK
affectedly modest person / PRUDE
affectedly shy / COY, MIM
affecting / MOVING; TOUCHING
affecting many / EPIDEMIC
affection / LOVE; LIKING
affectionate / FOND, KIND
affiance / ENGAGE; BETROTH
affidavit / OATH; DEPOSITION
affiliate / JOIN; ASSOCIATE
affinity / ACCORD; HARMONY
affirm / AVER; POSIT, SWEAR
affirmation / OATH; AVOWAL
affirmative / AY; AYE, YEA, YEP, YES; AMEN
affix / ADD; ANNEX; APPEND
affix name / SIGN
affix postage / STAMP
affix symbol / SEAL
afflatus / BREATH; INSPIRATION
afflict / AIL, TRY, VEX; HURT
afflicted / SMITTEN; TROUBLED
affliction / WOE; PAIN; GRIEF
affluence / PLENTY, RICHES
affluent / OPULENT; ABUNDANT
afflux / FLOW
afford / GIVE, LEND; GRANT, OFFER
affray / ROW; FEUD; BRAWL, MELEE
affright / COW; ALARM, APPAL
affront / VEX; GALL; PIQUE; INSULT, OFFEND; OUTRAGE. INJURY
Afghan cheese / KARUT
Afghan pony / YABU; YABOO
Afghanistan capital / KABUL
Afghanistan city / HERAT; GHAZNI
Afghanistan money / PUL; POOL; AMANIA; AFGHANI
Afghanistan mountain pass / KHYBER

Afghanistan mountains / HINDU-KUSH
Afghanistan native / TAJIK; DURANI; PASHTUN, PUKHTUN
Afghanistan prince / AMIR; AMEER
Afghanistan river / HELMAND
Afghanistan title / KHAN
afield / ASTRAY
afire / EAGER; AFLAME; BURNING
afloat / ASEA; AWASH; ABOARD
afoot / ASTIR
aforesaid / ABOVE; FORENAMED
aforethought / PREPENSE
afoul / ENMESHED; ENTANGLED
afraid / REDDE, TIMID; SCARED
afresh / ANEW
Africa and Asia, pert. to / AFRASIAN; AFROASIAN
African / NEGRO. See also South Africa
African anteater / AARDVARK, PANGOLIN
African antelope / GNU, KOB; BISA, GUIB, KOBE, KUDU, ORYX, PUKU, SUNI, TOPI, TORA; ADDAX, ELAND, NAKONG, NYALA, ORIBI; BOTIGO, DIKDIK, DUIKER, IMPALA, IMPOFO, KOODOO, LECHEE, LECHWE, POOKOO, RHEBOK; GAZELLE, GEMSBOK
African ape / CHIMP; GORILLA
African bird / OSTRICH, TOURACO
African boat / DHOW
African bread / KISRA
African bustard / KORI; KNORHAAN
African city / IFE; ORAN; ACCRA, CAIRO, DAKAR, LAGOS, TUNIS
African civet / GENET; MEERKAT
African clawed toad / XENOPUS
African cloth measure / JACKTAN
African cuckoo / TOURACO
African desert / ERG; NAMIB; SAHARA
African disease / NENTA; FRAMBESIA
African equine / ZEBRA
African expedition / TREK; SAFARI
African extinct equine / QUAGGA
African eye worm / LOA
African feline / LION; SERVAL
African fetish / JUJU; GRIGRI
African fly / KIVU; TSETSE
African fox / ASSE, CAMA; CAAMA; FENNEC
African fruit / FIG; DATE
African garment / KUTU, TOBE; JELAB; KAROSS; DASHIKI; DJELLABA
African gazelle / ADMI, CORA, DAMA, MOHR; ARIEL, KORIN, MHORR
African grass / FUNDI; MILLET
African grassland / VELD

African gum tree / BUMBO
African hemp / IFE
African honey badger / RATEL
African javelin / ASSEGAI
African jerky / BILTONG
African lake / CHAD, TANA; NYASA
African language family / BANTU
African lemur / GALAGO
African lemuroid / AYEAYE
African lizard / GECKO, SKINK
African loris / POTTO; BUSHBABY
African mammal / DAS; CAMEL, DAMAN, HIPPO, HYENA, MYRAX, OKAPI, RHINO; DASSIE, JACKAL; GIRAFFE, WARTHOG; ELEPHANT
African millet beer / POMBE
African monkey / MONA, WAAG; PATAS; GRIVET, GUENON, HUSSAR, MISNAS, VERVET; COLOBUS; TALAPOIN
African Moslem / MOOR
African mountain / KENYA
African mountains / ATLAS
African mud house / TEMBE
African musical instrument / GORA; GORAH, GOURA
African palm / DOOM
African pheasant / FRANCOLIN
African "piano" / SANZA
African pigeon / NAMAQUA
African Portuguese territory / ANGOLA; MOZAMBIQUE
African ravine / DONGA
African reed instrument / GORA
African region / CONGO, NUBIA
African religion / OBEAH; VOODOO
African reptile / CROCODILE
African river / NUN; JUBA, NILE, MELE; CONGO, NIGER, VOLTA; CALABAR, LIMPOPO, SENEGAL
African rodent / GUNDI; GERBIL
African seaport / DAKAR, TUNIS
African skunk / ZORILLA
African snake / ASP; ADDER, COBRA, MAMBA, VIPER; PYTHON
African soldier / SPAHI; ASKARI
African sorghum / IMPHEE
African soup ingredient / LALO
African stork / MARABOU
African tableland / KAROO; KARROO
African tallow / ROKA
African tree / BITO, COLA, SHEA; TARFA; BAOBAB
African village / BOMA, STAD; KRAAL
African weight / ROTI
African wild sheep / ARUI, UDAD; AOUDAD; FECHSTAL
African wood / EBONY; AVODIRE
Afrikaans / TAAL
aft / REAR; ASTERN
after / LATER; FOLLOWING

after cost / NET; PROFIT
after the manner of / AS; ALA
after a while / ANON, SOON
after-dinner candy / MINT
after-dinner drink / COGNAC
aftermath / ROWEN; ARRISH, EDDISH
afternoon / PM
afternoon nap / SIESTA
afternoon social / TEA
afterpiece / EXODE
aftersong / EPODE
afterward / LATER; SUBSEQUENTLY
again / BIS; ANEW, MORE, OVER; ENCORE, REPEAT
again, pref. / RE; ANA
against / CON; ANTI; CONTRA, VERSUS
against, pref. / ANTI, CATA, PARA
agalloch / AGAR, ALOE; GAROO
agama / LIZARD, TANTRA
Agamemnon's daughter / ELECTRA; IPHIGENIA
Agamemnon's father / ATREUS
Agamemnon's kingdom / MYCENAE
Agamemnon's son / ORESTES
agape / OPEN; YAWNING
agaric / BLEWITS
agate / ONYX; ACHATE, MARBLE
agave / ALOE, PITA; AMOLE; MAGUEY
agave fiber / PITA; ISTLE, SISAL
age / EON, ERA; DATE; PERIOD
aged / OLD; SENILE; SEASONED
aged, pert. to / GERIATRIC
agee / AWRY
ageless / ETERNAL
agency / FORCE, MEANS; RESOURCE
agency of Depression / NRA
agency of World War II / OPA
agenda / PROGRAM; SCHEDULE
agent / SPY; BROKER, DEPUTY
agglomerate / GATHER
agglutinant / CEMENT
aggrandize / EXALT; AUGMENT
aggravate / NAG; TEASE; ENRAGE
aggregate / BODY, HEAP, LUMP
aggregate amount / ALL, SUM; TOTAL
aggregate fruit / ETAERIO
aggregation / CONGERIES
aggregation of people / MOB; MASS
aggression / ATTACK; INVASION
aggressive / KEEN; PUSHING
aggrieve / PAIN; WRONG; INJURE
aghast / AGOG; AMAZED; TERRIFIED
agile / SPRY; ALERT, BRISK
agility / SPEED
agio / PREMIUM; DISCOUNT
agitate / JAR, VEX; FRET, GOAD

agitated / FEVERISH
agitation / ADO; STIR; DITHER
aglet / TAB, TAG; STUD
aglow / SHINING
agnail / WHITLOW
agname / ALIAS; AGNOMEN, EPITHET; NICKNAME
agnate / AKIN; ALLIED; RELATED
Agni's attribute / BOW
Agni's twin / INDRA
agnostic / SKEPTIC; NESCIENT
ago / GONE, PAST; SINCE
agog / AVID; EAGER
agonize / RACK; SUFFER; TORTURE
agony / WOE; PAIN, PANG; ANGUISH
agra / LOVE
Agra's monument / TAJMAHAL
agree / GEE; JIBE, SUIT; MATCH
agreeability / AMENITY
agreeable / MEET, NICE; PROPER
agreeable smell / AROMA; FRAGRANCE
agreement / YES; MISE, PACT; UNITY; ACCORD, ASSENT, TREATY
agricultural implement / HOE; PLOW; MOWER; HARROW, REAPER
agricultural machine / COMBINE, TRACTOR
agricultural tract / FARM; RANCH
agriculture / FARMING, TILLAGE
agriculture, pert. to / RUSTIC
agriculture, pref. / AGRO
agriculture goddess / CERES
agriculturist / FARMER; GARDENER
Agrippina's son / NERO
aground / BEACHED; STRANDED
agrypnia / INSOMNIA
agua / TOAD
ague / CHILL, FEVER
ague tree / SASSAFRAS
agueweed / BONESET
Ahab's daughter / ATHALIA
Ahab's obsession / WHALE
Ahab's quest / MOBYDICK
Ahab's wife / JEZEBEL
Ahasuerus' minister / HAMAN
Ahasuerus' wife / ESTHER, VASHTI
ahead / FORWARD. BEFORE
aid / ABET, HELP; ASSIST. RELIEF
aid to ships / RADAR, SONAR
aidant / HELPFUL
Aida's father / AMONASRO
Aida's lover / RADAMES
Aida's rival / AMNERIS
aide / HELPER; HENCHMAN
aigret / EGRET, PLUME
ail / HURT; SUFFER
ailing / ILL; SICK, SORE; UNWELL
ailment / MALADY; DISEASE

aim / END; BENT, GOAL, MARK
aimless / CASUAL; DESULTORY
aimless wanderer / VAGABOND
air / ARIA, CAST, LOOK, MIEN, SONG, TUNE; OZONE, VAPOR; BREEZE, MANNER. FAN; OPEN; EXPOSE
air, c.f. / AER; AERI; PNEUM
air, pert. to / AERIAL
air apparatus / FAN
air current / DRAFT; THERMAL
air hero / ACE
air mass edge / FRONT
air in motion / WIND
air passage / FLUE, VENT
air pressure meter / BAROMETER
air race marker / PYLON
air raid signal / ALERT, SIREN
air speed meter / ANEMOMETER
air spirit / SYLPH
air vehicle / KITE; PLANE; GLIDER; BALLOON
air voyage / HOP; FLIGHT
air-condition / COOL
aircraft / JET; BLIMP, PLANE
aircraft carrier / FLATTOP
aircraft flight record / LOG
air-driven / PNEUMATIC
air-drop / PARACHUTE
airedale / TERRIER
air-filled liquid film / BUBBLE
airman / AVIATOR
airplane / JET, MIG; GIRO, SPAD, ZERO; STUKA; BIPLANE; TRIPLANE
airplane control / JOYSTICK
airplane formation / ECHELON
airplane group / WING
airplane maneuver / BANK, DIVE, LOOP, SPIN
airplane operator / AVIATOR
airplane part / FLAP, NOSE, PROP, TAIL, WING; AILERON
airplane shed / HANGAR
airplane stabilizer / FIN
airplane target / DROGUE
airplane throttle / GUN
airplane transport / CARRIER
airplane wing part / AILERON
airplane without pilot / DRONE
airplane wood / BALSA
air-raid shelter / BUNKER
airship / BLIMP; DIRIGIBLE
airtight / HERMETIC
airy / LIGHT; BREEZY; ETHEREAL
ai's favorite tree / EMBAUBA
aisle / WALKWAY; CORRIDOR
ait / EYOT; ISLET
ajar / OPEN
Ajax's father / TELAMON
akin / SIB; AGNATE, ALLIED
akonge / BURBARK, BURBUSH

al / DYE
ala / AXIL, WING
Alabama capital / MONTGOMERY
Alabama city / MOBILE; GADSDEN
Alabama river / PEA; TOMBIGBEE
Alabama state bird / YELLOWHAM-
MER
Alabama state fish / TARPON
Alabama state flower / GOLDEN-
ROD
Alabama state nickname / COTTON
Alabama tribe / MOBILE; MUSKO-
GEE
alabaster / GYPSUM. MARMOREAL
alackaday / ALAS; ALACK
alacrity / HASTE, SPEED; VIVACITY
alameda / MALL, WALK
alamo / POPLAR
alan / HOUND
alang grass / COGON, KOGON
alar / WINGLIKE
alarm / BELL, FEAR; ALERT,
DREAD, SIREN; TERROR; WARN-
ING. SCARE
alarm signal / SIREN; TOCSIN
alas / AY; ACH, HEU, OCH, VAE
Alaska bay / PRUDHOE
Alaska bear / KODIAK
Alaska boat / KAYAK; BAIDARKA
Alaska cape / NOME
Alaska capital / SITKA; JUNEAU
Alaska city / NOME; SITKA
Alaska garment / PARKA
Alaska glacier / MUIR
Alaska island / KODIAK; PRIBILOF
Alaska islands / ALEUTIANS
Alaska mountain / BONA; MCKIN-
LEY
Alaska mountain pass / CHILKOOT
Alaska peninsula / UNGA; SEWARD
Alaska river / YUKON; COPPER
Alaska sable / SKUNK; RACCOON
Alaska state flower / FORGETME-
NOT
Alaska tribe / HAN; ALEUT, HAIDA
Alaska volcano / KATMAI; RE-
DOUBT
Alaska-Canada highway / ALCAN
Alaskan cod / WACHNA
alate / WINGED. LATELY
alb / TUNIC
Albania / SHQIPNI, SHQIPRI
Albania capital / TIRANA
Albanian city / DURAZZO, SCUTARI
Albanian dialect / GHEG, TOSK
Albanian money / LEK; QINT;
GROSH
Albanian river / DRIN; SEMENI
Albanian ruler / MPRET
albatross / GOONEY
albion / ENGLAND
albite / FELDSPAR; MOONSTONE

album / SCRAPBOOK
Alcestis' brother / ACASTUS
Alcestis' husband / ADMETUS
alchemist / PUFFER
alchemist's furnace / ATHANOR;
SOLUTORY
alchemist's still / AMBIX; ALEMBIC,
PELICAN
alchemist's stone / ELIXIR
alchemy / TRANSMUTATION
alchitran / TAR; PITCH
Alcinous' daughter / NAUSICAA
Alcinous' gardens / SCHERIA
Alcmene's son / HERCULES
alcohol / BOOZE, DRINK; LIQUOR
alcohol-burning furnace / ETNA
alcoholic / SOT; DRUNKARD
alcoholic beverage / GIN, RUM;
WINE; BRANDY, POSSET,
WHISKY
alcoholic drink / FLIP, SOUR;
JULEP, SLING, TODDY; MARTINI,
STINGER; COCKTAIL, HIGHBALL
Alcott character / JO; AMY, MEG;
BETH
alcove / APSE, NOOK; NICHE
alder / BIRCH
ale / MUM; EALE
ale mug / TOBY; STEIN
ale vinegar / ALEGAR
alee / SHELTERED
alehouse / TAVERN
alembic / STILL; RETORT
alert / SPRY; AGILE, AWAKE, BRISK
Aleutian island / ADAK, ATKA
alewife / SHAD; ALLICE; HERRING
Alexander's horse / BUCEPHALUS
Alexander's mother / OLYMPIAS
Alexander's successors / DIADOCHI
Alexander's victory / ISSUS
Alexander's wife / ROXANE
alfalfa / LUCERN; LUCERNE
alfresco / OPENAIR, OUTSIDE
alga / KELP, NORI, SCUM; WRACK
algarroba / CALDEN; MESQUITE
algebraic / FINITE
Algeria / NUMIDIA
Algeria capital / ALGIERS
Algerian cavalryman / SPAHI
Algerian city / BONE, ORAN
Algerian governor / DEY
Algerian money / DINAR
Algerian mountains / ATLAS
Algerian plain / TELL
Algerian plateau / AHAGGAR
Algeria's former name / NUMIDIA
Algiers district / KASBA; CASBAH
Algonquian Indian / FOX, SAC, WEA;
CREE, SAUX; MIAMI
Algonquin god / MANITOU
Ali Baba's word / SESAME
alias / See pen name

alias of Esther Johnson / STELLA
alibi / EXCUSE
alida / DIOPTER; THEODOLITE
alien / REMOTE; HOSTILE, STRANGE
alien in ancient Athens / METIC
alien in ancient Israel / GER
alienate / ESTRANGE, TRANSFER
alight / DESCEND; DISMOUNT
align / TRUE; DRESS; ADJUST
alike / AKIN, SAME, TWIN; EQUAL
aliment / DIET, FARE, FOOD, MEAT; BROMA; PABULUM; VICTUALS
alimony / ALLOWANCE
aline / TRUE; STRAIGHTEN
Ali's adoptive father / MOHAMMED
Ali's descendant / ALID; FATIMID
Ali's son / AHMED
Ali's wife / FATIMA
alive / VITAL; ACTIVE; SWARMING
alkali / LYE, REH; SODA, USAR
alkaline mineral / TRONA
alkaline solution / LYE
alkaline substance / LIME; ANTACID
alkaloid / CURARE, THEINE; CAFFEIN, COCAINE, CONIINE; CAFFEINE, MORPHINE, NICOTINE
alkaloid in mustard / SINAPINE
all / FULL, EVERY, TOTAL, WHOLE. QUITE; ENTIRE; TOTALLY. EVERYONE
all, c.f. / PAN; OMNI
all but / NIGH; ALMOST, NEARLY
all fours / SEVENUP
all get out / LIMIT; UTMOST
all hail / HEALTH; WELCOME
all hollow / COMPLETELY
all in / SPENT; POOPED
all out / COMPLETELY
all over / ENDED. EVERYWHERE
all possible / EVERY
all right / OK; OKAY
all set / READY
all wet / WRONG
all wool / REAL; GENUINE
allay / CALM, EASE; QUELL, QUIET
allege / SAY; AVER, CITE; STATE
alleged / SAID; QUOTED
alleged force / OD
allegiance / TIE; FEALTY, HOMAGE
allegory / PARABLE; APOLOGUE
allegro / GAY; BRISK, QUICK
allergy / ATOPY; ANTIPATHY
alleviate / EASE; ABATE, ALLAY
alley / MIB, MIG; LANE; PASSAGE
allheal / YARROW; VALERIAN
alliance / PACT; UNION; LEAGUE; COMPACT, ENTENTE; MARRIAGE
allice / SHAD; ALEWIFE
allied / ALIKE; AGNATE, JOINED
allied by nature / AKIN
allied to / NEXT

alligator / GATOR; CAIMAN, CAYMAN, JACARE; LAGARTO; CROCODILE
alligator pear / AVOCADO
all-knowing / OMNISCIENT
allocate / ALLOT; ASSIGN
allocate again / RELOCATE
allot / DEAL, GIVE, METE; SHARE
allotment / MEED; QUOTA; RATION
allotted place / POST; BERTH
allow / LET, OWN; BEAR; ABATE, ADMIT, GRANT, YIELD; ENDURE
allow use of / LEND
allowable / LAWFUL; SANCTIONED
allowable divergence / TOLERANCE
allowance / TARE, TRET; RATION
allowance for contingency / MARGIN
allowance for service / BONUS; PENSION
allowance for weight / TARE
allowed deduction / REBATE
allowing that / IF; ALTHOUGH
alloy / DEBASE; ADULTERATE
alloy of copper and tin / BRONZE
alloy of copper and zinc / BRASS
alloy used in dentistry / AMALGAM
alloy of iron / STEEL
alloy in jewelry / OROIDE
alloy used in kitchenware / PEWTER
alloy of nickel and steel / INVAR
alloy used for repair / SOLDER
alloy of tin / PEWTER
alloy of tin and zinc / OROIDE
all-powerful / OMNIPOTENT
allspice / PIMENTO
allude / HINT; IMPLY; ADVERT
allude to / MENTION
allure / COAX, LEAD, LURE, TOLE
alluring / INVITING; SEDUCTIVE
alluring woman / VAMP; SIREN
allusion / HINT; REFERENCE
alluvial clay / ADOBE
alluvial deposit / FAN; CONE; DELTA, GEEST; ALLUVIUM
alluvium / SILT; DETRITUS
ally / AIDE; HELPER; PARTNER
almanac / CALENDAR; EPHEMERIS
almighty / OMNIPOTENT. GOD
almond / AMYGDALA
almond confection / MARZIPAN
almond furnace / ALMAN
almond liqueur / RATAFIA
almond syrup / ORGEAT
almost / NEARLY
almost, pref. / PEN; PENE
alms / DOLE, GIFT; CHARITY
alms box / ARCA
almsgiver / ALMONER
almshouse / POORHOUSE
Aloadae slayer / APOLLO
alod / ALODIUM
aloe / AGAVE; TAMBAC

aloft / UP; ATOP, HIGH
alone / ONLY, SOLO; SINGLE
alone on stage / SOLA, SOLO
along / VIA; WITH; FORWARD
alongside / BY; ABREAST
aloof / APART; DISTANT; RESERVED
alose / SHAD
aloud / ORAL; AUDIBLY; VIVAVOCE
alow / BELOW, UNDER
alp / PEAK; PASTURE; MOUNTAIN
alpaca / PACO; LLAMA
alpha / ONE. CHIEF, FIRST
alpha and omega / EVERYTHING
alphabet / ABC; ABCS, OGAM
alphabetic character / RUNE; LETTER
alphabetical list / INDEX; CATALOGUE
alpine dress / DIRNDL
alpine goat / IBEX
alpine hut / CHALET
alpine instrument / ALPENHORN
alpine primrose / AURICULA
alpine wind / BORA; FOEHN
Alps, pert. to / ALPINE
Alps mountain / BLANC, EIGER
Alps pass / CENIS; SIMPLON
Alps river / RHONE
already / QUITE; BEFORE
Alsatian / SHEPHERD
also / AND, EKE, TOO; WITHAL
also called / ALIAS
also-ran / LOSER
alt / HIGH
altar / ARA; MENSA; CHANCEL
altar area of church / APSE
altar area of orthodox church / BEMA
altar boy / ACOLYTE
altar canopy / CIBORIUM
altar hanging / PALLA; DOSSAL
altar piece / ANCONA
altar screen / REREDOS
altar shelf / GRADIN; RETABLE
altar step / FOOTPACE; PREDELLA
altar vessel / PYX; PATEN; CHALICE; MONSTRANCE
alter / VARY; AMEND, EMEND
alter an animal / GELD, SPAY
alter ego / FRIEND; INTIMATE
alter a suit / BUSHEL
alteration / CHANGE; MODIFICATION
altercation / ROW; BRAWL, SCRAP
alternate / SUBSTITUTE. INTERCHANGE
alternative / OR; EITHER. PICK
althorn / SAXHORN; MELLOPHONE
although / IF; BUT, YET; EVEN
altitude / HEIGHT; EMINENCE
altitude meter / OROMETER
altogether / FULLY, QUITE. BUFF

alula / CALYPTER
alum / ASTRINGENT
aluminum alloy / DURAL
aluminum ore / BAUXITE
alumnus / GRAD; GRADUATE
alveary / BEEHIVE
always / AYE, EER; EVER; ALGATE
ama / CHALICE; CANDLENUT
amadou / PUNK; TINDER
amain / VIOLENTLY
Amalekite king / AGAG
amalgamate / MIX; FUSE; BLEND
amalgamation / UNION; LEAGUE
Amalthara's horn / CORNUCOPIA
amanita / AGARIC; DEATHCUP
amanuensis / COPYIST; SECRETARY
amaranth / COCKSCOMB
amaranthine / RED; UNFADING
amaryllis / AGAVE
amass / HEAP, PILE; GATHER
amass secretly / HOARD
amateur / HAM; TYRO; NOVICE
amative / EROTIC, LOVING
amaze / AWE; PERPLEX; ASTONISH
amazed / DAZED; AGHAST; CONFUSED
amazement / WONDER; SURPRISE
amazing / STRANGE; MIRACULOUS
amazing occurrence / MIRACLE
amazon / VIRAGO
Amazon cetacean / INIA
Amazon fish / CANDIRU, PIRANHA
Amazon mouth / PARA
Amazon port / MANAUS
Amazon queen / ANTIOPE; HIPPOLYTA
Amazon tribe / MURA; ANDOA
Amazon tributary / ICA; JARI, PARU; XINGU; TAPAJOZ
Amazons' conqueror / THESEUS
ambary / DA
ambassador / ENVOY; LEGATE
ambassador's case / PORTFOLIO
ambience / MILIEU
ambiguous / VAGUE; DELPHIC
ambit / BOUNDS; PERIMETER
ambition / AIM; GOAL; ASPIRATION
ambitious / PROUD; EMULOUS
amble / GAIT; STROLL
ambling horse / PADNAG
ambrosia / HONEY
ambrosial / FRAGRANT; DELICIOUS
ambry / CLOSET, PANTRY; STOREROOM
ambulant / WALKING
ambush / TRAP; WAYLAY; BUSHWHACK
ameliorate / AMEND; BETTER
amenable / OPEN; PLIANT
amend / ALTER, ATONE, EMEND

amend a manuscript / REVISE
amende honorable / APOLOGY
amendment / REVISION; ALTERA-
TION
amendment to document / RIDER
amends / REDRESS; ATONEMENT
amenity / CIVILITY, COURTESY
Amen's son / KHONSU
Amen's wife / MUT
ament / IDIOT; CATKIN, RACEME
amerce / FINE, LEVY; MULCT
American / see also United States
American / YANKEE. See also
South American
American aborigine / INDIAN;
AMERIND
American active volcano / KATMAI,
LASSEN
American aloe / AGAVE; MAGUEY
American aloe fiber / PITA, PITO
American apple / CRAB
American artist / PYLE; DAVIS;
WARHOL; RUSSELL; REMING-
TON
American author / ADE, BOK, POE,
ROE; BAUM, CERF, DANA, GREY,
HALE; HARTE, OHARA, PAINE,
POOLE, SETON, WYLIE, YERBY
American bear / KODIAK; GRIZZLY
American beauty / ROSE
American bird / TOWHEE
American brookline / SPEEDWELL
American buffalo / BISON
American canal / ERIE; PANAMA
American cartoonist / ARNO, NAST
American cataract / NIAGARA
American chameleon / ANOLE,
ANOLI
American cheese / CHEDDAR
American composer / IVES; FOOTE,
NEVIN; FOSTER; GERSHWIN
American congresswoman / RAN-
KIN
American coot / MUDHEN
American criminal organization /
SYNDICATE
American custom / YANKEEISM
American deer / MOOSE; WAPITI
American dramatist / AKINS,
BARRY, ODETS; CROUSE
American educator / MANN; DEWEY
American elk / WAPITI
American engineer / EADS; ROE-
BLING
American evangelist / GRAHAM,
SUNDAY; MCPHERSON
American explorer / BENT, BYRD,
KANE, PIKE; BOONE, CLARK,
LEWIS, PEARY; FREMONT
American feline / PUMA; BOBCAT,
COUGAR, JAGUAR, MARGAY

American feminist / CATT
American flag / OLDGLORY
American flycatcher / PHOEBE
American fries / HASHBROWN
American game / KENO; POKER;
BASEBALL
American general / DIX, LEE, ORD;
OTIS; CLARK, GRANT; GREENE
American gentian / COLUMBO
American germander / WOODSAGE
American grape / CATAWBA, NI-
AGARA
American hellebore / POKE
American holly / ASSI; YAPON
American humorist / ADE, DAY,
NYE; COBB, NASH, WARD;
TWAIN; ROGERS; LARDNER
American Indian / AHT, FOX, KAW,
OTO, SAC, UTE; CREE, ERIE,
HOPI, OTEE, OTOE; EWERS,
KERES, OSAGE, APACHE, MO-
HAVE, MOHAWK, ONEIDA, RED-
MAN; AMERIND, REDSKIN. See
also South American Indian
American Indian boat / BALSA,
CANOE; DUGOUT; PIRAGUA,
PIROGUE
American Indian ceremony / POT-
LATCH; MIDEWIWIN
American Indian clan symbol / TO-
TEM
American Indian currency / PEAG;
WAMPUM
American Indian deity / CHAC,
CHIA, IKTO, NAPI, TAMU; HAO-
KAH; MANITO; MANITOU, OLEL-
BIS; GLOOSCAP, MANABUSH;
MANABOZHO
American Indian dwelling / HUT;
TENT, TIPI; HOGAN, LODGE, TE-
PEE; TEEPEE, WIGWAM; WICKIUP
American Indian game / LACROSSE
American Indian guide / SCOUT
American Indian leader / CHIEF;
SACHEM; SAGAMORE; WERO-
WANCE
American Indian peace pipe / CAL-
UMET
American Indian religious group /
MIDE
American Indian shoe / PAC; MOC-
CASIN
American Indian smoking mixture /
KINNIKINICK
American Indian vehicle / TRA-
VOIS; TRAVOISE
American Indian village / PUEBLO;
RANCHERIA
American Indian war prize / COUP
American Indian warrior / BRAVE;
SANNUP

American Indian woman / SQUAW
American inventor / HOE; BELL, COLT, FELT, HOWE, IVES, LAKE, LAND, YALE; MORSE, TESLA; EDISON, SPERRY, WRIGHT
American jade / NEPHRITE; SERPENTINE; CALIFORNITE
American journalist / LUCE, REID; HEARST; SCRIPPS; PULITZER
American jurist / TANEY; HOLMES; MARSHALL
American larch / TAMARACK; HACKMATACK
American linden / BASSWOOD
American lion / PUMA
American lizard / ANOLE, ANOLI
American mandrake / MAYAPPLE
American marionette maker / SARG
American marsupial / OPOSSUM
American monetary unit / DOLLAR
American money / CENT, DIME; PENNY; DOLLAR, NICKEL; QUARTER
American national emblem / EAGLE
American nature writer / MUIR; BEEBE, SETON, TEALE; DITMARS
American nighthawk / PISK
American opera singer / ALDA; HOMER; FARRAR, TUCKER; STEVENS
American painter / BINO, WEST; HICKS, HOMER, MARIN, PEALE
American patriot / HALE, OTIS, ROSS; ALLEN, PAINE; REVERE
American plan / TABLEDHOTE
American poet / POE; TATE; BENET, FROST, GUEST, RILEY, STEIN; LANIER, LOWELL, MILLAY
American poplar / ASPEN
American president / ABE, CAL, IKE; TEDDY. See also president of the U.S.
American quail / COLIN; BOBWHITE
American reindeer / CARIBOU
American religious leader / YOUNG
American Revolution battle / CONCORD, COWPENS
American river / OHIO; TETON; PLATTE; GENESEE; ALLEGHENY
American saba / PINEMARTEN
American sculptor / BUFANO, CALDER, FRENCH; BORGLUM
American snake / RACER; HOGNOSE, RATTLER; MOCCASIN; COPPERHEAD
American socialist / DEBS
American songbird / CHAT; FINCH, VIREO; CHEWINK; BOBOLINK
American tiger / JAGUAR

American tree / ELM; WAHOO
American veteran / GI; VET
American vulture / CONDOR; BUZZARD
American widgeon / BALDPATE
American yew / HEMLOCK
amiable / LOVABLE, WINSOME
amicable / CORDIAL; FRIENDLY
amice / SCARF
amid / MID; AMONG
amide, pert. to / AMIC; AMIDIC
amidst / IN; AMONGST
amino acid / LYSINE, VALINE
amish / MENNONITE
amiss / AWRY; WRONG; ASTRAY
amity / PEACE; FRIENDSHIP
ammonia compound / AMIDE, AMINE
ammoniac plant / OSHAC
ammunition / AMMO, DATA, SHOT
ammunition storehouse / ARSENAL; MAGAZINE
ammunition wagon / CAISSON
amnesia / FUGUE; APHASIA
amnesty / PARDON
amnion / SAC; CAUL
amole / AGAVE, YUCCA
among / IN; MID; AMID
among, pref. / EPI
Amor / CUPID, PUTTO
amorous / FOND; ARDENT, EROTIC
amorous look / LEER, OGLE
amorphous / CHAOTIC; SHAPELESS
amorphous mass / BLOB
amort / LIFELESS
Amos' friend / ANDY
amount / SUM; WHOLE; QUANTITY
amount baked / BATCH
amount gained / NET; PROFIT
amount less than full / ULLAGE
amount of medicine / DOSE
amount offered / BID
amount owing / DEBT
amount staked / ANTE, MISE
ampersand / AND
amphetamine / BENNY, SPEED, UPPER
amphi / BOTH; ABOUT; AROUND
amphibian / EFT, OLM; FROG, NEWT, TOAD; AXOLOTL
amphibole / JADE; NEPHRITE
Amphion's wife / NIOBE
amphitheater / ARENA; CIRQUE
ample / ENOW, FULL; BROAD, LARGE
amplification / ENLARGEMENT
amplify / ADD, PAD; SWELL, WIDEN
amplifying device / LASER, MASER
amplitude / SIZE; RANGE, SWEEP
amputate / LOP; SEVER
amuck / AMOK; FRENZIED

amula / AMA; CHALICE
amulet / CHARM; MASCOT; PERI-APT; TALISMAN
amuse / DIVERT, REGALE; BE-GUILE
amusement / FUN; PLAY; SPORT; FROLIC; DELIGHT, PASTIME
amusing / COMIC, DROLL, WITTY
amusing play / FARCE; COMEDY
amusing story / JOKE, YARN
an / ANY, ONE; EACH
ana / BITS; MISCELLANY
anabasis / MARCH; EXPEDITION
anaconda / BOA; ABOMA
Anacreontic / GAY; CONVIVIAL
anadem / CHAPLET, GARLAND
anagram / LOGOGRIPH, SHUF-FLING
analects / ANA; MORSELS
analogous / ALIKE; SIMILAR
analogy / PARITY; COMPARISON
analysis / SYNOPSIS
analyze / ASSAY, SOLVE; DISSECT
analyze a sentence / PARSE
Ananias / LIAR
anarchist / RED; ANARCH
anarchy / CHAOS; DISORDER
anathema / BAN; CURSE
Anatolian goddess / MA; CYBELE
anatomical tube / DUCT; CANAL
anatomy / ANALYSIS, SKELETON
anatomy of tissue / HISTOLOGY
ancestor / SIRE; ELDER; ATAVUS
ancestor of the Hindus / MANU
ancestor of the Irish / ITH, MIL
ancestral / AVAL; AVITAL
ancestral spirit / LAR; ANITO
ancestry / RACE; LINEAGE
anchor / FIX, TIE; MOOR, WARP, CAT; KEDGE; GRAPNEL
anchor bill / PEE; PEAK
anchor chain / CABLE
anchor man / NEWSCASTER
anchor part / FLUKE
anchor ring / TORE; TORUS
anchorage / PORT; HARBOR
anchoret / EREMITE
ancient / OLD; AGED; EARLY, OLDEN; ANTIQUE, ARCHAIC, ARCHEAN
ancient Algerian city / HIPPO
ancient alphabetic character / RUNE
ancient Asia Minor city / EPHESUS
ancient Asia Minor region / IONIA
ancient Asian silk makers / SERES
ancient Asiatic country / ELAM; AK-KAD, MEDIA
ancient Aswan / SYENE
ancient biblical city / UR; TYRE
ancient celtic priest / DRUID
ancient Egyptian measure / KAT

ancient Egyptian ruler / PHARAOH
ancient flute / TIBIA
ancient galleys / BIREME; TRIREME
ancient game / MORA; COTTABUS
ancient Germanic fine / WERGELD, WERGILD; WEREGELD, WERE-GILD
ancient gold alloy / ASEM
ancient Greek coin / OBOL
ancient Greek flute / HEMIOPE
ancient Greek marker / STELE
ancient Greek merchant vessel / HOLCAD
ancient Greek Valhalla / LEUCE
ancient hair-do / TETE
ancient Hebrew liquid measure / BATH; EPHAH
ancient Hebrew musical instrument / SHOFAR; TIMBREL
ancient Hispania / IBERIA
ancient instrument of war / CELT; ONAGER
ancient invaders of India / SACAE
ancient Irishmen / MILESIANS
ancient Italian city / POMPEII
ancient Italian nation / ETRURIA
ancient knife / SKEAN, SKENE
ancient lyre / CITHARA
ancient measure of length / SPAN; CUBIT
ancient people of Britain / ICENI, PICTS; SILURES
ancient Persian / MEDE; ELAMITE
ancient Persian coil / DARIC
ancient Phoenician capital / TYRE
ancient porcelain / MURRA
ancient Roman citadel / ARX
ancient Romain coin / SESTERCE
ancient Roman garment / TOGA; STOLA
ancient Roman official / EDILE; PRETOR; PRAETOR, TRIBUNE
ancient string instrument / ASOR, LYRE, NEBEL, REBEC
ancient tree / OLIVE
ancient vehicle / ESSED
ancient war machine / ONAGER; CATAPULT
ancient weight / MINA; TALENT
ancillary / AUXILIARY, SECONDARY
ancon / ELBOW
and / TOO; ALSO; AMPERSAND
and not / NOR; NEITHER
and others / ETAL; ETALIA
and so / THUS
and so forth / ETCETERA
Andean / HIGH; PERUVIAN
Andean mountain sickness / SOR-OCHE
Andean rodent / ABROCOME
Andean ruminant / PUDU; LLAMA; ALPACA, VICUNA; GUANACO

Andes cold region / PUNA
Andes grass / ICHU
andiron / FIREDOG
Andorra's language / CATALAN
Andorra's mountains / PYRENEES
androgyne / EUNUCH; EPICENE
androgynous / EFFEMINATE
android / AUTOMATON
Andromeda's father / CEPHEUS
Andromeda's mother / CASSIOPEIA
Andromeda's rescuer / PERSEUS
Andy's friend / AMOS
anear / NEAR; CLOSE; NEARBY
anecdotes / ANA; TALES; STORIES
anele / ANOINT
anemia / CHLOROSIS
anemic / PALE; PALLID; BLOOD-LESS
anemone / POLYA; CROWFOOT
anent / RE; ABOUT; CONCERNING
anergia / INACTIVITY
anesthetic / GAS; ETHER; OPIATE
anet / DILL
anew / OVER; AGAIN; AFRESH
angel / POWER; CHERUB, SERAPH
angel of the Bible / GABRIEL, MICHAEL
angel of death / AZRAEL; SAMMAEL
angel guarding Eden / CHERUBIM
angel of healing / RAPHAEL
angel with the horn / GABRIEL
angel of mercy / NURSE
angel of the moon / MAH
angel who rebelled / EBLIS; LUCI-FER
angel of the sun / ABADDON
angelic / PURE; SERAPHIC
angelic doctor / AQUINAS
anger / IRE; BILE, FURY, GALL, RAGE, VEX; RILE; CHAFE, ROUSE
angle / HOOK, IDEA, NOOK, WORM; ELBOW; CORNER, SCHEME. FISH
angle of fault vein / HADE
angle iron / BRACE
angle of leaf and stalk / AXIL
angle formed by vaults / GROIN
angled pipe / TEE; ELBOW
angler / WALTON; FISHERMAN
angleworm / ESS; EARTHWORM
Anglian kingdom / DEIRA; MERCIA
Anglo-Indian money / ANNA; RU-PEE
Anglo-Saxon assembly / GEMOT
Anglo-Saxon crown tax / GELD
Anglo-Saxon court / GEMOT
Anglo-Saxon free servant / THANE
Anglo-Saxon god of peace / ING
Anglo-Saxon king / INE
Anglo-Saxon laborer / ESNE
Anglo-Saxon letter / EDH, ETH, YOK; YOGH; THORN
Anglo-Saxon money / ORA

Anglo-Saxon poet / SCOP
Angola capital / LUANDA
Angola exclave / CABINDA
Angola native / SONGO; CHOKWE
Angola plateau / BIE
angora fabric / CAMLET, MOHAIR
angora goat / CHAMAL
angry / HOT, MAD; SORE; IRATE
angry look / GLOWER
angry sound / SNORT
anguilloid / EELLIKE
anguish / WOE; PAIN, PANG; AGONY
anile / OLD; FEEBLE; CHILDISH
animal / BEAST, BRUTE; MAMMAL
animal backbone / CHINE, SPINE
animal of the Bible / REEM; BEHE-MOTH; LEVIATHAN
animal body / SOMA
animal doctor / VET, VETERINAR-IAN
animal enclosure / PEN; CAGE; CORRAL
animal fabulist / AESOP; BIDPAI
animal farm / RANCH
animal fat / LARD, SUET; ADEPS, ESTER; GREASE, TALLOW
animal leash / TETHER
animal lover / ZOOPHILE
animal magnetism / MESMERISM
animal of mixed parentage / MULE; HYBRID; MONGREL
animal mother / DAM
animal of myth / NAGA; HYDRA; DRAGON, SPHINX; UNICORN; BASILISK, CERBERUS, MINO-TAUR
animal park / ZOO; MENAGERIE
animal skin / FUR; HAIR, HIDE
animal sound / BARK, YELP; SNORT
animal trail / RUN; SLOT; SPOOR
animal trainer / TAMER
animalcule / AMEBA
animalism / SENSUALITY
animal-plant life / BIOTA
animals / FAUNA, STOCK
animals, pert. to / ZOIC
animals of an area / FAUNA
animal's neck hair / MANE
animal's stomach / MAW; CRAW
animate / GOAD, HEAT, URGE, WHET
animated / GAY; ALIVE; ACTIVE
animates / PEPS
animating principle / SOUL; ANIMA
animation / PEP, VIM; FORCE
anime / COPAL, ELEMI
animosity / ANGER, SPITE; MALICE
animus / PURPOSE; HOSTILITY
aniseed / ANISE
anklebone / TALUS; CUBOID, TAR-SUS

ankle-length robe / TALAR
anklets / SOCKS
anlage / BENT; BASIS; SOURCE
annals / ROLLS; ACCOUNT, ARCHIVE
Annam capital / HUE
Annapolis student / MIDDY, PLEBE
annatto seed / ACHIOTE
anneal / FUSE; TEMPER; TOUGHEN
annealing oven / LEER, LEHR; CAL-CAR
annelid / LURG; LEECH; NEREIS
annex / ADD; JOIN; APPEND. ELL
annihilate / END; KILL; ANNUL; CANCEL, EFFACE; DESTROY, NULLIFY
annotate / GLOSE; POSTIL
annotation / NOTE; GLOSS; RE-MARK
annotation in book / MEMO, NOTE
announce / STATE; BLAZON, HER-ALD
announce loudly / BLARE, BLAST
announcement / AD; BANNS; NO-TICE
announcer / DJ; EMCEE; REPORTER
annoy / IRK, NAG, TRY, VEX; RILE; HARRY, PEEVE, WORRY; BAD-GER
annoy pettily / TEASE
annoyance / BORE, PEST; PLAGUE
annual / YEARLY. YEARBOOK
annual grass / POA; DARNEL
annual potherb / SPINACH
annual service / ENCAENIA
annually recurring / ETESIAN
annuity / TONTINE
annul / UNDO, VOID; QUASH
annular / BANDED; RINGLIKE
annulment / DELETION; ABOLITION
anodyne / OPIATE; NARCOTIC
anoint / OIL; ANELE
anomalous / UNUSUAL; ABNOR-MAL
anomie / ANARCHY; CONFUSION
anon / SOON; BETIMES; PRES-ENTLY
anonymous / NAMELESS; AUTHOR-LESS
another time / AGAIN, LATER
ansate cross / ANKH
anserine bird / GOOSE
answer / REPLY; RETORT; SOLU-TION
answer affirmatively / NOD
answer a challenge / ACCEPT
answer negatively / DEMUR; RE-JECT
answer pertly / SASS
answer a purpose / SERVE
answer a thrust / PARRY

answerable / LIABLE; ACCOUNTA-BLE
ant / EMMET, KELEP; PISMIRE
ant, c.f. / MYRMECO
ant cow / APHID
ant egg / PUPA
ant queen / GYNE
anta / PIER; TAPIR
antagonism / ANIMOSITY, HOSTIL-ITY
antagonist / FOE; ENEMY, RIVAL
antagonistic / ANTI; ADVERSE
antarctic / FRIGID; ANTIPODAL
antarctic bird / PENGUIN
Antarctic explorer / BYRD, ROSS; SCOTT, HILLARY; AMUNDSEN
Antarctic penguin / ADELIE
Antarctic sea / ROSS; WEDDELL
Antarctic volcano / EREBUS
ante / BET; STAKE
anteater / MANIS; ECHIDNA, PAN-GOLIN, TAMANDUA
antecede / PRECEDE
antecedent / PRIOR. ANCESTOR
antelope / GNU, KOB, NYL; ASTE, BISA, CHOU, GUIB, KUDU, NGOR, ORYX, PUKU, SUNI, TORA; ADDAX, BEIRA, BEISA, BONGO, CHIRU, ELAND, GORAL, IPETE, NYALA, ORIBI, PALLA, SAIGA, SEROW; DIKDIK, LECHWE, NIL-GAI, PYGARG; CHAMOIS
antenna / PALP; AERIAL, FEELER
anterior / PRIOR; BEFORE, FORMER
anteroom / HALL; FOYER, LOBBY; VESTIBULE
anthem / HYMN; MOTET
anthology / ANA; COLLECTION
anthracite / COAL; GLANCE
anthrax / CHARBON, PUSTULE
anthropoid / APE, LAR; ORANG
anthropoid ape / KRA, LAR; BON-OBO, GIBBON, GORILLA, SIA-MANG; ORANGUTAN; CHIMPAN-ZEE
anti / AGAINST; OPPOSITE
antiaircraft fire / FLAK; ACKACK, ARCHIE
antiaircraft weapon / SAM; POM-POM
antibiotic / MYCIN; PENICILLIN
antic / DIDO; CAPER, PRANK
anticipate / HOPE; EXPECT
anticipate apprehensively / DREAD
anticlimax / BATHOS; LETDOWN
anticyclone / HIGH
antidote / CURE; BEZOAR, REMEDY
Antillean Indian / CARIB, INERI, TAINO; IGNERI, LUCAYO; CI-BONEY
Antilles island / CUBA; HAITI

antimacassar / TIDY; COVER, DOILY

antimony / KOHL; SURMA; KERMES

antipathy / DISLIKE; AVERSION

antiquated / PASSE; ARCHAIC

antique / OLD; AGED. RELIC

antiquity / AGE, ELD; YORE

antiseptic / DISINFECTANT

antisocial person / LONER

antithesis / CONTRAST; OPPOSITION

antithesis of wealth / ILLTH

antitoxin / SERUM

antler / DAG; HORN; SPIKE

antler point / BAY, BEZ; SNAG, TINE, TYND; PRONG

antlered animal / DEER, STAG; MOOSE; WAPITI; CARIBOU

antler's covering / VELVET

antrum / SINUS; CAVERN

Anubis / JACKAL

anvil / TEEST; STITHY

anvil of the ear / INCUS

anvil's projection / BEAK, HORN

anxiety / CARE; WORRY; CONCERN

anxious / EAGER; FEARFUL

any / ARY, FEW, ONI; SOME

any of several / AN; ONE

anybody / ONE; ANYONE

anything / ATALL, AUGHT

anything true / FACT

aorta / ARTERY

aoudad / ARUI; FECHSTAL

apace / FAST; QUICKLY

Apache alcoholic drink / TISWIN

Apache group / LIPAN; JICARILLA

Apache jacket / BIETLE

Apache war chief / MANGAS; CO-CHISE; GERONIMO

apart / ALOOF, ASIDE; ASUNDER

apart, pref. / SE; DIS

apartment / PAD; FLAT; ROOMS

apartment house / TENEMENT

apartment for women / HAREM; ZENANA; SERAGLIO

apathetic / COLD, DEAD, TAME; FRIGID; CALLOUS, PASSIVE

apathy / ENNUI; LETHARGY

ape / COPY, MIME, MOCK; MIMIC. SIMIAN; IMITATOR; ANTHROPOID

ape man / PITHECANTHROPUS

aper / MIMIC; COPYCAT

aperitif / STIMULANT

aperture / GAP; HOLE; RIFT

apex / TIP, TOP; ACME; APOGEE

apex, pert. to / APICAL

aphid / APHIS; ANTCOW

aphid secretion / HONEYDEW

aphorism / SAW; RULE; ADAGE,

GNOME, MAXIM; SAYING; PRECEPT

aphoristic / GNOMIC

Aphrodite / VENUS

Aphrodite's favorite / ARES

Aphrodite's husband / HEPHAESTUS

Aphrodite's mother / DIONE

Aphrodite's son / EROS; AENEAS

Aphrodite's title / CYPRIAN

aphtha / THRUSH

apiece / PER; EACH; SEVERALLY

apish / FOOLISH, FOPPISH

aplomb / COOL; POISE

apocalypse / REVELATION

apocope / CURTAILMENT

apocryphal / SPURIOUS; UN-AUTHENTIC, UNCANONICAL

apocryphal book / TOBIT; BARUCH, ESDRAS, JUDITH

apogee / ACME, APEX; CLIMAX

apogee's opposite / PERIGEE

Apollo / HELIOS, NOMIUS; PHOEBUS

Apollo's birthplace / DELOS

Apollo's festival / DELIA

Apollo's instrument / BOW; LUTE, LYRE

Apollo's mother / LETO; LATONA

Apollo's oracle / CLAROS, DELPHI

Apollo's paramour / ISSA; CYRENE, DAPHNE; CLYMENE, CORONIS

Apollo's plant / BAY; LAUREL

Apollo's priestess / SIBYL; PYTHIA

Apollo's servant / ABARIS

Apollo's sister / DIANA; ARTEMIS

Apollo's symbol / ARROW

Apollo's victim / OTUS; MIDAS

apologue / FABLE; ALLEGORY

apology / PLEA; AMENDS, EXCUSE

apoplexy / STROKE

apostate / HERETIC, TRAITOR; BETRAYER, RENEGADE

apostle / DISCIPLE. JOHN, JUDE, MARK, PAUL; JAMES, JUDAS, PETER, SIMON; ANDREW, PHILIP, THOMAS; DIDYMUS, MATTHEW; MATTHIAS, THADDEUS; BARTHOLOMEW

apostle of free trade / COBDEN

apostle to the Indians / ELIOT

apostle to the Indies / XAVIER

aposle of Ireland / PATRICK

apostle of Sweden / ANSCAR

apostle of the Sword / MOHAMMED

apostles' teaching / DIDACHE

apothecaries' weight / DRAM; GRAIN; SCRUPLE

apothecary / PHARMACIST

apothegm / SAW; AXIOM; APHORISM

appall / AWE, COW; DAUNT, SHOCK
appalling / TERRIBLE
apparatus / RIG; GEAR; OUTFIT
apparatus for pulping paper / MA-
CERATOR
apparel / GARB, SUIT; ARRAY,
DRESS, GUISE, HABIT; ATTIRE
apparent / OPEN; CLEAR, OVERT,
PLAIN; PATENT; EVIDENT
apparent contradiction / PARADOX
apparition / GHOST; VISION; EIDO-
LON, SPECTER; REVENANT
appeal / ASK; PLEAD; ENTREAT
appear / LOOK, LOOM; ARISE
appear to be / SEEM
appearance / AIR; MIEN; FRONT
appeared / CAME; ISSUED
appease / CALM, EASE, LULL; AL-
LAY, QUIET, STILL; PACIFY
appeaser / CONCILIATOR
appellation / NAME; STYLE, TITLE;
EPITHET
appellee / DEFENDANT
append / ADD; JOIN; AFFIX; AT-
TACH
appendage / TAB, TAG; TAIL
appendage of crustacean / PEDI-
PALP; CHELICERA
appendage of insect / LEG, WING;
CERCUS; ANTENNA, ELYTRON
appendage at leaf base / STIPULE
appended / SUBJOINED; ADDI-
TIONAL
appertain / BELONG, RELATE
appertaining / TOUCHING
appetite / GUSTO; HUNGER; CRAV-
ING, EDACITY, LONGING, STO-
MACH
appetizer / CANAPE; APERITIF
appetizing / SAVORY
appetizing condiment / SAUCE
applaud / CLAP; CHEER; PRAISE
applauder / FAN; ROOTER;
BOOSTER
applauders / CLAQUE
applauding word / OLE, RAH; VIVA;
BRAVO; ENCORE, HURRAH
applause / HAND; OVATION
apple / CRAB, POME
apple, pert. to / MALIC
apple acid / MALIC
apple center / CORE
apple dessert / PIE; DOWDY,
SLUMP, STRUDEL; FRITTER;
TURNOVER
apple and honey drink / CYSER
apple juice / CIDER
apple liquor / APPLEJACK
apple pulp / POMACE
apple seed / PIP
apple tree / SORB
apple variety / SPY; PIPPIN, RUS-

SET; BALDWIN, WINESAP; MC-
INTOSH; DELICIOUS
applelike fruit / POME; QUINCE
applesauce / BOSH; BALONEY
applicant / PETITIONER
application / USE, REQUEST
apply / ALLOT, TREAT; DEVOTE
apply friction / RUB; MASSAGE
apply oneself / PLY, TRY; ATTEND
apply remedies / TREAT
appoint / SET; NAME; EQUIP
appoint as agent / NAME; DEPU-
TIZE
appointed / DECREED; ORDAINED
appointed to arrive / DUE
appointed time / DAY; DATE, HOUR
appointment / DATE; TRYST
apportion / DEAL, DOLE, METE; AL-
LOT; ASSIGN
apportion scantily / STINT
apposite / FIT, MEET; GERMANE
appraisal / ESTIMATE; EVALUA-
TION
appraise / RATE; GAUGE, PRICE,
VALUE; ASSESS
appreciate / ENJOY, PRIZE, VALUE
appreciative / GRATEFUL, THANK-
FUL
apprehend / NAB; TAKE; CATCH,
GRASP, SEIZE; ARREST; CAP-
TURE
apprehend through senses / FEEL
apprehension / FEAR; ALARM,
DREAD
apprehensive / JUMPY, TIMID
apprentice / TYRO; NOVICE
apprise / TELL, WARN; ADVISE
approach / COME, NEAR; VERGE.
WAY; ADIT, MODE, PATH; AC-
CESS
approach more closely / CONVERGE
approachable / ACCESSIBLE
approaching / TO; TOWARD
approbation / ASSENT, PRAISE;
CONSENT, SUPPORT; APPROVAL
appropriate / APT, FIT; MEET;
PROPER; APPOSITE. USE; AP-
PLY
appropriated / TAKEN; PREEMPTED
approval / PERMIT; CONSENT.
OKAY
approve / OK; LIKE, OKAY, PASS;
ADMIT, FAVOR, VALUE; ADMIRE,
CONCUR, PRAISE, RATIFY, SEC-
OND
approximate / APPROACH
approximately / ABOUT; ROUGHLY
appurtenance / ACCESSORY
apricot cordial / PERSICO
April birthstone / DIAMOND; SAP-
PHIRE
apron / BIB; BRAT; PINAFORE

apropos / PAT; FITTING; OPPOR-
TUNE
apt / FIT, PAT; MEET; ADEPT,
PRONE, READY, SMART; BRIGHT,
CLEVER, LIKELY; FITTING
apteryx / KIWI
aptitude / BENT; FLAIR, SKILL
aptly / READILY; SUITABLY
aqua / WATER
aquamarine / BERYL
aquatic animal / EEL; FISH, NEWT;
POLYP; OPELET, SPONGE;
ANEMONE
aquatic athlete / DIVER; SURFER;
SWIMMER
aquatic bird / ERN; COOT, DUCK,
ERNE, GULL, SKUA, SMEE,
SMEW, SWAN, TERN; GOOSE,
SCAUP; FULMAR, GANNET, PE-
TREL, PUFFIN, SCOTER
aquatic mammal / ORC, SEI; SARO,
SEAL; OTTER, WHALE; BEAVER,
DUGONG, WALRUS; DOLPHIN,
MANATEE, MUSKRAT, NARWHAL,
RORQUAL
aquatic salamander / TRITON;
HELLBENDER
aquatic worm / NEREIS; PLANARIA
aqueduct / CANAL; CONDUIT
aqueous / WET; HUMID, MOIST
ara / ALTAR; MACAW
arab / TAD; GAMIN; SEMITE,
URCHIN; BEDOUIN, SARACEN
Arab country / UAR; IRAQ, OMAN;
EGYPT, LIBYA, QATAR, SYRIA,
SUDAN, YEMEN; JORDAN, KU-
WAIT; ALGERIA, BAHRAIN, LEB-
ANON, MOROCCO, TUNISIA;
SAUDIARABIA
Arab League capital / CAIRO
Arabia / ARABY
Arabian antelope / ORYX
Arabian camel / DROMEDARY
Arabian capital / SANA; RIYADH
Arabian chief / AMIR, EMIR; AM-
EER, EMEER, SAYID, SHEIK; SAY-
YID
Arabian city / ADEN, BEDA, BERA
Arabian cloak / ABA
Arabian cloth / ABA
Arabian country / IRAQ, NEJD; HE-
JAZ, YEMEN
Arabian deity / ALLAH, ALLAT
Arabian demon / GHUL; AFRIT, GE-
NIE, GHOUL, JINNI; AFREET, JIN-
NEE
Arabian devil / EBLIS
Arabian drink / BOSA; LEBAN
Arabian dust storm / SIMOOM
Arabian eye shadow / KOHL
Arabian garment / ABA; HAIK; CAF-
TAN, KAFTAN; BURNOOSE

Arabian gazelle / ARIEL
Arabian gulf / ADEN, OMAN
Arabian headband cord / AGAL
Arabian headdress / KAFFIYEH
Arabian holy city / MECCA; ME-
DINA
Arabian holy scripture / KORAN;
ALCORAN
Arabian holy war / JIHAD
Arabian ibex / JAAL
Arabian jasmine / BELA
Arabian judge / CADI
Arabian kingdom / IRAQ; JORDAN
Arabian language / ARABIC
Arabian letter / BA, BE, FA, FE, HA,
HE, RA, RE, SE, TA, TE,
YA, YE, ZA, ZE; AIN, AYN, DAD,
DAL, GAF, JIM, KAF, KEF, KHA,
KHE, LAM, MIM, NUN, QAF, SAD,
SIN, THA, WAN, ZAL; ALIF, DHAL,
SHIN; GHAIN, GHAYN
Arabian market / SUQ; SOOK,
SOUK; BAZAR; BAZAAR
Arabian measure / SAA
Arabian money / DINAR
Arabian monster bird / ROC; RUKH
Arabian Moslem / WAHABI;
SUNNITE
Arabian name / ALI
Arabian Nights character / HAR-
OUN, SINBAD; ALADDIN, ALI-
BABA
Arabian Nights translator / LANE;
BURTON
Arabian nomad / SLEB; BEDOUIN
Arabian peninsula / ADEN; SINAI
Arabian people / OMANI; YEMENI
Arabian pilgrim / HADJI, HAJJI
Arabian port / ADEN
Arabian prince / EMIR; SAYID; SAY-
YID, SHERIF; SHEREEF
Arabian raider / FEDAYEEN
Arabian ravine / WADI, WADY
Arabian religious body / ULEMA
Arabian "rose red city" / PETRA
Arabian sailboat / DHOW, SAIC
Arabian shrine / KAABA
Arabian stew / COUSCOUS
Arabian sultanate / OMAN
Arabian tambourine / TAAR; DAIRA
Arabian tea / KAT
Arabian vessel / DOW; DHOW
Arabian warrior / SARACEN
arabic acid / ARABIN
arabic script / NESKI
Arab's drugged trance / KEF
arachnid / MITE, TICK; SPIDER
arachnid's net / WEB
Aram / SYRIA
arara / MACAW
Araucanian Indian / AUCA
Arawak Indian / ARAUA, CAMPA

arbiter / JUDGE; UMPIRE; REFEREE
arbitrary / ABSOLUTE, DESPOTIC; IMPERIOUS, WHIMSICAL; CAPRICIOUS
arbitrary statement / DICTUM
arbitrate / JUDGE; ADJUST
arbor / BOWER; LATTICE, PERGOLA
arboreal mammal / LEMUR; RACCOON, TARSIER; SQUIRREL
arboreal marsupial / KOALA; OPOSSUM
arc / BOW; ARCH; CURVE
arc in the sky / RAINBOW
arcade / LOGGIA; GALLERY, PORTICO; COLONNADE
arcadian / RURAL; BUCOLIC
Arcadian huntress / ATALANTA
arcane / SECRET; CRYPTIC
arcanum / ELIXIR, SECRET; MYSTERY
arch / BOW; BEND, SPAN. CHIEF
arch over / SPAN
arch coming to a point / OGIVE
arch of the sky / COPE
archaeological mound / TELL, TEPE, TERP; BARROW
archaic / OLD; ANCIENT
archaic pronoun / YE; THY; THEE, THOU; THINE
archangel / URIEL; GABRIEL, MICHAEL, RAPHAEL
archbishop / PRELATE, PRIMATE; METROPOLITAN
archbishopric / PROVINCE
archean / OLD; ANCIENT
arched gallery / ARCADE
archenemy / DEVIL, SATAN
archer / BOWMAN; SAGITTARIUS
archer's implement / BOW; DART; ARROW
archer's target / BUTT, WAND
archetype / IDEAL, MODEL; PATTERN
archfiend / DEVIL, SATAN
architect / AUTHOR; PLANNER
architect's drawing / PLAN; EPURE, MODEL
architectural base / SOCLE; PLINTH
architectural column / TELAMON
architectural decoration / FRIEZE; PEDIMENT
architectural order / DORIC, IONIC, TUSCAN
architectural pier / ANTA; PILASTER
architectural school / BAUHAUS
archly / COYLY; ROGUISHLY
archness / SHYNESS; SHREWDNESS
arctic / POLAR; FRIGID
Arctic bird / AUK; BRANT; FULMAR
Arctic dog / HUSKY; SAMOYED

Arctic explorer / BYRD; DAVIS, PEARY; BERING, NANSEN
Arctic gulf / OB
Arctic hooded jacket / ANORAK
Arctic island / BANKS; GREENLAND
Arctic native / ESKIMO
Arctic navigator / ROSS
Arctic plain / TUNDRA
Arctic rodent / LEMMING
Arctic sandpiper / KNOT
Arctic sea / KARA; BARENTS
ardent / HOT; KEEN, WARM; EAGER, FIERY, RETHE, SHARP; FERVID
ardent affection / ADORATION
ardent partisan / FAN; DEVOTEE
ardent spirit / RUM; BRANDY; WHISKEY
ardor / DASH, ELAN, ZEAL; FERVOR
arduous / HARD; DIFFICULT
area / SITE; RANGE, SCOPE, SPACE
area, pert. to / AREAL; REGIONAL
area outside a city / COUNTRY, SUBURBS
area of swift current / RAPIDS; CASCADE
areca / BETEL
arena / OVAL, RINK; FIELD, FORUM; SPACE; CIRCUS; STADIUM
arenaceous / SANDY; GRITTY
areola / RING; DIMPLE; INTERSTICE
Ares / MARS
Ares' father / ZEUS
Ares' mother / ENYO, HERA
Ares' sister / ERIS
argent / SILVER. BRIGHT
Argentina capital / BUENOSAIRES
Argentine author / BORGES
Argentine cheese / GOYA, TAFI
Argentine city / CORDOBA, ROSARIO
Argentine cowboy / GAUCHO
Argentine dance / TANGO
Argentine estuary / LAPLATA
Argentine money / PESO
Argentine mountain / MAIPU
Argentine plain / CHACO, LLANO
Argentine region / PATAGONIA
Argentine river / PLATA; CHUBUT
Argentine tree / TALA
argol / TARTAR
argonaut / JASON; FORTYNINER
Argonauts' ship / ARGO
argot / CANT; SLANG; JARGON
argue / DEBATE; CONTEND, DISCUSS
argue legally / PLEAD
argument / ROW; SPAT; HASSLE
argument against / CON

argument for / PRO
argumentative / ERISTIC; FOREN-
SIC
argute / SHARP; SHRILL, SUBTLE
aria / AIR; SONG, TUNE
arid / DRY; SERE; XERIC; BARREN
arid, c.f. / XER; XERO
arid region / DESERT; BARRENS
Aries / RAM
aright / JUSTLY; RIGHTLY
Arikara Indian / REE
arioso / MELODIC; MELODIOUS
arise / FLY; RISE, SOAR; ISSUE
arista / AWN; BEARD; BRISTLE
aristocrat / PEER; NOBLE
aristocratic / TONY; PROUD;
TITLED; COURTLY, HAUGHTY
Arius' follower / ARIAN
Arizona capital / PHOENIX
Arizona city / MESA, YUMA; TUC-
SON
Arizona dam / HOOVER
Arizona Indian / HOPI, MOKI, PIMA,
YUMA; MOQUI; MOHAVE, PA-
PAGO
Arizona plateau / KAIBAB; MOGOL-
LON
Arizona river / GILA, SALT; VERDE
Arizona state flower / SAGUARO
Arizona state nickname / COPPER
Arizona state tree / PALOVERDE
Arkansas capital / LITTLEROCK
Arkansas river / RED; OUACHITA
Arkansas state bird / MOCKING-
BIRD
Arkansas state nickname / WON-
DER
Arkansas state tree / PINE
Ark's builder / NOE; NOAH
Ark's landing place / ARARAT
arm / FORTIFY, LIMB; BRANCH,
WEAPON
arm joint / ELBOW; SHOULDER
arm muscle / BICEPS, FLEXOR
arm of the sea / BAY; GULF; FIRTH,
FJORD, INLET
armada / FLOTILLA
armadillo / APAR, PEBA; TATOU
armadillo with six bands / PELUDO
armadillo with three bands / APAR;
MATACO
armbone / ULNA; RADIUS
armbone, pert. to / ULNAR
armed band / POSSE
armed fleet / NAVY; ARMADA
armed force / ARMY; TROOPS
armed with a gaff / HEELED
armed galley / BIREME, DROMON,
LEMBUS; TRIREME; CATA-
PHRACT
armed guard / SENTRY; VEDETTE
armed robber / BANDIT; BRIGAND

armed ship / MANOFWAR; BATTLE-
SHIP
armed ships, pert. to / NAVAL
armed strife / WAR; BATTLE
Armenia capital / ERIVAN
Armenian cheese / ZWIRN; TSCHIL
Armenian devil worshipers / YEZIDI
Armenian mountain / ARARAT
armhole / SCYE
armor / MAIL; PLATING
armor for arm / CANNON; VAM-
BRACE
armor bearer / SQUIRE; ARMIGER
armor for body / TACE; CULET,
TASSE; BYRNIE, CORIUM, LOR-
ICA, TASSET; CUIRASS, HAU-
BERK, PLACATE, SURCOAT;
CHAUSSES
armor for elbow / COUTER;
ROUNDEL
armor for face / BEVOR, VISOR
armor for foot / SABATON; SOLLE-
RET
armor for hand / GAUNTLET
armor for head / HELM; ARMET;
HELMET, MORION; BASCINET
armor for hips / CULET; TASSET
armor for horse / BARD; BARDE;
CRINET; CHANFRON
armor jacket / ACTON; AKETOUN;
HAQUETON
armor for knee / POLEYN
armor for leg / JAMB; GREAVE
armor for lower body / CULET
armor for neck / BUFFE; GORGET;
AVENTAIL
armor part for throat / GORGET
armor for shoulder / AILETTE;
PAULDRON; REREBRACE
armor skirt / TACE; TASSE; TASSET
armor for thigh / CUISH; TASLET
armored electrical cable / BX
armored vehicle / TANK
armory / ARSENAL
armpit / OXTER; AXILLA
arms / WEAPONS
arms storehouse / ARMORY; ARSE-
NAL; MAGAZINE
army / HOST; HORDE; LEGION
army, pert. to / MILITARY
army assistant / AIDE
army commissary / SUTLER
army engineer / SAPPER
army food / MESS
army group / CADRE, SQUAD; PLA-
TOON; REGIMENT, BATTALION
army life / CAMP
army officer / MAJOR; CAPTAIN,
COLONEL, GENERAL; LIEUTEN-
ANT
arnica / LINIMENT
aroid / ARUM

aroid food plant / TARO
aroma / ODOR; SCENT; FRA-
GRANCE
aromatic / BALMY, SPICY; REDO-
LENT
aromatic herb / DILL, MACE, MINT
aromatic herb root / GINSENG
aromatic perfume / INCENSE
aromatic plant / NARD; BASIL
aromatic resin / MYRRH; BALSAM
aromatic seasoning / SPICE
aromatic seed / ANISE, CUMIN
aromatic tree / BALSAM
arose / STOOD; EMERGED
Arouet / VOLTAIRE
around / ABOUT, CIRCA
around, pref. / AMBI, PERI
arouse / STIR, WAKE; ALARM,
PIQUE
aroused aversion / REPELLED
arow / ALINE; STRAIGHT
arquebus prop / CROC
arraign / ACCUSE, INDICT; IM-
PEACH
arrange / FIX, SET; FILE, PLAN,
RANK, SORT
arrange beforehand / PLAN
arrange hair / COIF, COMB; STYLE
arrange hangings / DRAPE
arrange in a line / ALIGN
arrange as a rope / BIGHT
arrange in succession / SERIATE
arrange terms / DEAL; NEGOTIATE
arrange troops / DEPLOY
arranged in rows / TIERED
arrangement / PLAN; ORDER,
SETUP
arrangement, c.f. / TAX; TAXI
arrangement, pert. to / TACTIC
arrangement of interwoven parts /
NET, WEB; MESH; FABRIC
arrangement of sails / RIG
arrangement of troops / RANK;
SQUARE; ECHELON
arrant / UTTER; FLAGRANT
arrant coward / POLTROON
array / DECK, GARB, RANK; DRESS
array troops / DEPLOY
arrears / DEBIT
arrest / NAB; HALT, HOLD, STAY,
STEM, STOP, TAKE; PINCH,
SEIZE; SECURE; CAPTURE
arret / EDICT; DECREE
arrive / COME; REACH
arrogance / PRIDE; CONCEIT
arrogant / RUDE; LOFTY; INSO-
LENT
arrogate / CLAIM; ASSUME
arrow / BARB, BOLT, DART; MIS-
SILE
arrow case / QUIVER
arrow poison / INEE, LOKI, UPAS;
URALI, URARE, URARI; ANTIAR,

CURARE, CURARI; HURUBUH,
WOORALI
arrow poison tree / UPAS
arrow shaft / STELE
arrow slot / NOCK
arrowroot / PIA; ARARU; MARANTA
arroyo / WASH; GULCH
arson, pert. to / INCENDIARY
art / WILE; CRAFT, GUILE, KNACK
art of dueling / DUELLO; FENCING
art gallery / SALON; MUSEUM
art of government / POLITICS
art patron / MECENAS; MAECENAS
art of writing well / RHETORIC;
PENMANSHIP; CALLIGRAPHY
Artemis / DIANA; PHOEBE
Artemis' mother / LETO
Artemis' twin / APOLLO
Artemis' victim / ORION
artery / AORTA
artery of neck / CAROTID
artful / SLY; WILY; CRAFTY,
SHREWD, SUBTLE
Arthurian lady / ENID; ELAINE
Arthur's capital / CAMELOT
Arthur's father / UTHER; PENDRA-
GON
Arthur's foster brother / KAY
Arthur's lance / RON
Arthur's last battle / CAMLAN
Arthur's queen / GUINEVERE
Arthur's shield / PRIDWIN
Arthur's slayer / MORDRED
Arthur's sword / CALIBURN;
EXCALIBUR
article / A; AN, YE; THE; ITEM
article of belief / CREDO, CREED,
TENET
article in document / CLAUSE
article of food / MEAT; VIAND
article of furniture / SOFA; CHAIR,
TABLE; SETTEE; DRESSER
article of jewelry / PIN; RING,
STUD; EARRING; BRACELET
article of value / CURIO; ANTIQUE
articulate / SPEAK, UTTER; ENUN-
CIATE, PRONOUNCE
articulated support / HINGE,
JOINT
artifice / ART; RUSE, WILE; CRAFT,
GUILE, TRICK
artificial / SHAM; FALSE, PASTE
artificial bait / LURE
artificial fishing fly / DUN; HARL,
HERL; NYMPH; HACKLE
artificial jewels / PASTE
artificial language / RO; IDO; NO-
VIAL; VOLAPUK; ESPERANTO
artificial light / BULB, LAMP
artificial teeth / DENTURE
artillery fire / BARRAGE
artisan / WORKER; MECHANIC;
CRAFTSMAN, OPERATIVE

artist / ACTOR; PAINTER; SCULP-TOR
artistic ability / KNACK; TALENT
artistic aspect / DECOR
artist's chalk / PASTEL
artist's crayon / CHARCOAL
artist's implement / BRUSH
artist's knife / SPATULA
artist's medium / OIL; CHALK; PEN-CIL
artist's plaster / GESSO
artist's stand / EASEL; TABORET
artist's workshop / STUDIO; ATEL-IER
artless / NAIF, OPEN; FRANK
arty / OVERORNATE
arum / ARROWROOT
arum plant / TARO; AROID, CALLA
as / QUA; LIKE, SAME; SINCE
as compared with / THAN, THUS
as far as / TO; UNTO
as long as / SO; WHILE
as it seems / THAT
as it stands / STA
asafetida / HING; LASER
Asa's father / ABIJAN
asbestos / ABISTON; CHRYSOTILE
ascend / RISE, SOAR; CLIMB, MOUNT
ascendant / RISING; SUPERIOR
ascended / AROSE
ascendency / SWAY; COMMAND, MASTERY; DOMINATION
ascending / ANABATIC, CLIMBING
ascending in expression / CLIMAC-TIC
ascent / RISE; SLOPE
ascertain / FIX, SEE; LEARN
ascertain direction of / ORIENT
ascertain the duration / TIME
ascertain size of / MEASURE
ascetic / YOGI; STOIC; ESSENE, HERMIT; RECLUSE
ascot / SCARF
ascribe / REFER; CHARGE, CREDIT
asea / MUDDLED; CONFUSED
ash / DUST; ROWAN; CINDER
ashen / WAN; PALE; LIVID
ashes / ASE; RESIDUE
ashy / GRAY; WHITE; PALLID
Asia / EAST; ORIENT
Asia Minor / ANATOLIA
Asia Minor kingdom / EOLIS; AEO-LIA, AEOLIS
Asian / KOREAN; CHINESE; JAPA-NESE. See also Asiatic
Asian alliance / SEATO
Asian cheese / CHHANA
Asian goat antelope / SEROW
Asian hemp / PUA
Asian narcotic / KEF; BANG, HASH, KAIF, KEEF, KIEF; BHANG; HASH-ISH

Asian spotted deer / AXIS
Asiatic / HUN; SERE; TATAR; CHI-NESE. See also Asian
Asiatic ape / GIBBON; ORANGUTAN
Asiatic bean / SOY
Asiatic bird / MYNAH; TRAGOPAN
Asiatic cattle / ZO; ZEBU
Asiatic civet / RASSE; BEARCAT, LINSANG; BINTURONG
Asiatic country / IRAN, IRAQ, SIAM; BURMA, CHINA, INDIA, KOREA, NEPAL, SYRIA, TIBET
Asiatic deer / MAHA; KAKAR, RATWA; HANGUL, SAMBAR; MUNTJAC
Asiatic desert / GOBI
Asiatic falcon / LUGGER, SHAHIN
Asiatic feline / LYNX; TIGER; LEOP-ARD
Asiatic fishhook money / LARI; LARIN; LARREE
Asiatic fowl / SAT; LANGSHAN
Asiatic fox / CORSAK; KARAGAN
Asiatic goat / JAGLA
Asiatic goat-antelope / SEROW
Asiatic hawk / SHIKRA
Asiatic lake / ARAL; BAIKAL
Asiatic lynx / CARACAL, SYAGUSH
Asiatic mammal / YAK; CAMEL
Asiatic monkey / LANGUR
Asiatic nomad / ARAB
Asiatic palm / NIPA; ARECA, BETEL
Asiatic peninsula / KOREA; ARABIA
Asiatic pepper / BETEL
Asiatic river / OB; ILI; AMUR, LENA, ONON; INDUS
Asiatic rodent / GERBIL
Asiatic sheep / ARGALI
Asiatic snake / KATUKA
Asiatic squirrel / JELERANG
Asiatic thrush / DYAL; SHAMA
Asiatic tree / ACLE, ASAK, ASOK, DITA; SIRIS
Asiatic wild goat / TUR; TAHR
Asiatic wild ox / ZEBU
Asiatic wind / SIMOON; MONSOON
aside / AWAY; APART; BESIDE
asinine / INANE, SILLY; STUPID
asininity / FATUITY
ask / BEG, BID; PRAY; SPEER
ask for alms / BEG
ask to come / INVITE
ask for contributions / SOLICIT
ask the cost / PRICE
ask for payment / DUN
askance / AWRY; SIDEWAYS
askew / WRY; AGEE, ALOP; ATILT
aslant / ATHWART
asleep / DORMANT
aslope / CANTED
asp / VIPER; SERPENT
aspect / AIR; LOOK, MIEN, VIEW
aspect of a situation / PHASE

aspen / ALAMO; POPLAR
asperate / ROUGH
asperge / SPRINKLE
asperity / RIGOR; ACERBITY
asperse / SLUR; BEFOUL, DEFAME
asphalt / TAR; PITCH; BITUMEN
asphyxia / SUFFOCATION
aspirant / CANDIDATE, AMBITIOUS
aspiration / AIM; HOPE, WISH
aspire / SEEK; COVET
asportation / ROBBERY
ass / FOOL, MULE; BURRO, KIANG, NINNY; DONKEY, ONAGER
assail / PELT; BESET; ACCOST
Assam silk / ERI; ERIA
Assamese gibbon / HOOLOCK
Assamese language / AO; AKA
Assamese tribe / AO; AHOM, AKAI, NAGA
assassin / BRAVO; KILLER, SLAYER
assault / RAID; STORM. ONSET
assault boat / LCI, LST
assayer / TESTER
assayer's cup / CUPEL
assegai / LANCE, SPEAR; JAVELIN
assemblage / BODY, HOST; GROUP
assemble / MASS, MEET; ERECT
assemble troops / MUSTER
assembling body / SESSION
assembly / DIET; AGORA, SYNOD; CAUCUS; COMPANY, COUNCIL; CONCLAVE, CONGRESS
assent / AGREE; ACCORD, ATTEST
assert / SAY; AVER, AVOW; CLAIM, POSIT, STATE
assert as fact / POSIT
assert positively / AFFIRM
assertion / DECLARATION
assertive / DOGMATIC, POSITIVE
assess / TAX; LEVY; VALUE
assessment / TAX; SCOT; STENT
assessor / RATER; LEVIER
asset / ESTATE; PROPERTY
assets / GOODS; ESTATE; EFFECTS
assiduous / BUSY; ACTIVE; CARE-FUL
assign / GIVE; ALLOT, GRANT
assign parts in a play / CAST
assign time / DATE
assign to / REFER
assignment / DUTY, POST, TASK
assimilate / ABSORB, DIGEST
assist / AID; ABET, HELP; SERVE
assistance / SUCCOR; SUPPORT
assistant / AIDE, ALLY; ASSOCIATE
assistant clergyman / CURATE
associate / PAL; MATE, PEER; FEL-LOW; COMRADE. MIX; JOIN, LINK
associated / ALLIED; CONJOINT
associated background / CONTEXT; AMBIENCE
association / CLUB, GILD; GUILD, LODGE, UNION; CLIQUE, LEAGUE
assort / ARRANGE; CLASSIFY
assorted / RANKED; DIVERSE
assortment / LOT; STOCK; VARIETY
assuage / CALM, EASE; ABATE, AL-LAY, SLAKE
assuaging / LENITIVE, SOOTHING
assume / ADOPT, FEIGN, USURP
assume a reverent posture / BOW; KNEEL
assumed character / PART, ROLE
assumed mannerism / AIR; POSE
assumed name / ALIAS; PENNAME; PSEUDONYM
assumption / PREMISE; PRETENSE
assurance / WORD; APLOMB, PLEDGE
assure / VOUCH; ADVISE, INFORM
assure dowry / ENDOW
assured / GUARANTEED
assuredly / DECIDEDLY
Assyrian capital / CALAH; KALAKH; NINEVEH
Assyrian conqueror / SARGON
Assyrian earth god / BEL
Assyrian queen / SEMIRAMIS
Assyrian sky god / ANAT
Assyrian war god / ASUR; ASSUR
aster / DAISY, OXEYE, TANSY
asterisk / STAR
astern / AFT; ABAFT; BEHIND
asteroid / EROS, HEBE, JUNO; CERES, VESTA; ICARUS, PALLAS; ASTRAEA
astir / AGOG; AFOOT; ACTIVE
astonish / AWE; DAZE, STUN; AMAZE
astonished / SURPRISED; DUM-FOUNDED
astonishing / WONDERFUL
astound / AMAZE, SHOCK
astray / LOST; AMISS
astringent / ALUM. STYPTIC
astrologer / CHALDEAN
astrologer of India / JOSHI
astrology / ASTROMANCY, STAR-GAZING
astronaut / GLENN; CONRAD, SHIRRA; GAGARIN; ARMSTRONG, COSMONAUT
astronaut's path / ORBIT
astronaut's word / AOK
astronomical / HUGE; URANIAN
astronomical instrument / ORRERY, SECTOR
astronomical measure / PARSEC; AZIMUTH
astute / SLY; KEEN; CLEAR, SHARP
asunder / APART
asylum / HAVEN; REFUGE; SHEL-TER
at / BY, IN; NEAR; ABOUT

at all / ANY; EVER
at all times / EER; EVER; ALWAYS
at any time / WHENEVER
at a distance / OFF, YON; AFAR
at ease / IDLE
at an end / OER; DONE, OVER
at a future time / ANON; LATER
at hand / HERE; NEARBY
at home / IN
at the home of / CHEZ
at large / ABROAD
at leisure / IDLE; LOAFING
at the masthead / ALOFT
at no time / NEER; NEVER
at odds / OUT
at once / NOW; PRONTO
at one time / ONCE
at the same time / YET
at that place / THERE; YONDER
at that time / THEN
at this place / HERE
at this time / NOW; HEREWITH
at the top / ATOP; ALOFT; APICAL
at what place / WHERE
at what time / WHEN
Atalanta's suitor / MELANION, ME-LEAGER, MILANION; HIPPO-MENES
ate / DINED; RUSTED, SUPPED
ate a small portion / NIBBLED
atelier / SHOP; STUDIO; WORK-SHOP
ates / SWEETSOP
Ate's father / ZEUS
Athamas' daughter / HELLE
Athamas' wife / INO; NEPHELE
Athapascan Indian / DENE, HUPA, TAKU; LIPAN; APACHE, NAVAJO
atheist / INFIDEL; UNBELIEVER
Athena / PALLAS; MINERVA
Athena's shield / EGIS; AEGIS
Athena's temple / PARTHENON
Athena's tree / OLIVE
Athenian / ATTIC
Athenian historian / XENOPHON
Athenian judge / ARCHON
Athenian statesman / SOLON; PERICLES
Athens' citadel / ACROPOLIS
Athens' district / DEME
Athens' last king / CODRUS
Athens' marketplace / AGORA
athlete / PLAYER; ACROBAT, GYMNAST
athlete's crown / LAUREL
athlete's prize / MEDAL
athlete's shoes / SPIKES; SNEAKERS
athletic / LUSTY; ROBUST, SINEWY
athletic contest / AGON; GAMES, SPORT
athletic field / ARENA; STADIUM

athletic game / SPORT
athletics / SPORTS; EXERCISES
athirst / EAGER
athwart / OVER; ASLANT; AGAINST
atilt / ASKEW; SLANTING
atip / TIPTOE
atis / SWEETSOP; MONKSHOOD
Atlantic cold wind / SORA
Atlantic flyer / BYRD; LINDBERGH
atlas / TABLE; PORTOLANO
Atli's wife / GUDRUN
atmosphere / AIR; AURA; MEDIUM
atmospheric disturbance / STORM
atmospheric illusion / MIRAGE
atom / BIT, DOT, JOT; IOTA, MITE, WHIT; GRAIN, MONAD, SCRAP, SPECK
atom part / ION; PROTON; NEUTRON; ELECTRON
atomic submarine / NAUTILUS
atomize / SPRAY
atomy / MOTE; PYGMY; SKELETON
atone / AMEND; REDEEM; EXPIATE
atoned / APPEASED, REDEEMED
atonement / AMENDS; EXPIATION
atony / DEBILITY, WEAKNESS
atop / ON; UPON; ABOVE
Atreus' father / PELOPS
Atreus' killer / AEGISTHUS
Atreus' son / MENELAUS; AGAMEMNON
atrocious / CRUEL; WICKED; HEINOUS; FLAGRANT
atrocity / OUTRAGE; ENORMITY
attach / ADD, FIX, TIE; LINK; ANNEX, HITCH, STICK; APPEND
attache / LEGATE
attached / FOND
attached by a stem / SESSILE
attachment / LOVE; SEIZURE
attack / RAID; BESET; ASSAIL. ASSAULT
attack violently / RAID; STORM
attain / GET, WIN; EARN; REACH
attain success / ARRIVE
attaint / CORRUPT. DISGRACE
attar / OTTO
attempt / TRY; DARE, STAB; ESSAY. GO; ETTLE, TRIAL; EFFORT
attend / HEED, MIND, WAIT; GUARD
attend to / HELP; NURSE; LISTEN
attendant / AID; AIDE; VALET; ESCORT, LACKEY
attending / AT
attending spirit / ANGEL
attent / HEEDFUL
attention / EAR; CARE, HEED; NOTICE, REGARD
attention getter / PST; AHEM
attentive / ALIVE, AWAKE; CAREFUL, HEEDFUL

attentive consideration / EAR
attentive to details / MINUTIOSE
attenuate / DILUTE, RAREFY
attenuated / THIN; REDUCED
attest / CERTIFY, WITNESS
attestation / DEPOSITION
attic / LOFT; GARRET. See also Athenian
Attic harvest goddess / CARPO
Attic hero / THESEUS
attic resident / POET; METIC
Attica, pert. to / ATTIC
Attila / ATIL; ETZEL
Attila's people / HUNS
attire / RIG; GARB; ARRAY, DRESS, HABIT; OUTFIT; APPAREL, COSTUME
attired / CLOTHED
attitude / MIEN, POSE; BEARING
attitudinize / POSE
attorn / TRANSFER
attorney / AGENT; LAWYER
attorney in India / MUKTAR
attract / DRAW, LURE; CHARM
attractive / LOVELY, TAKING
attractiveness / CHARM
attributable / REFERABLE; ASSIGNABLE
attribute / OWE; REFER; IMPUTE. MARK; TRAIT; QUALITY
attribution / REASON; QUALITY
attune / PITCH; ACCORD; HARMONIZE
auction / SALE; VENDUE
auction again / RESELL
auction call / BID
audacious / BOLD; BRAZEN, DARING
audacity / CHEEK, NERVE; SPIRIT
audible / LOUD; CLEAR
audibly / ALOUD
audience / EAR; HOUSE; HEARING; ASSEMBLY
audient / HEARING; LISTENING
audit / EXAMINE
audition / HEARING
auditor / EXAMINER, LISTENER
auger / BORE; BORER; GIMLET
augment / ADD, EKE; GROW; EXPAND, EXTEND
augmentation / ADDITION
augur / BODE; PORTEND, PRESAGE. SOOTHSAYER
augury / OMEN, SIGN; AUSPICY, PORTENT
august / GRAND, NOBLE, REGAL; KINGLY; IMPOSING
August birthstone / PERIDOT; CARNELIAN
auld / OLD
aura / HALO; BUZZARD; EMANATION
aural / OTIC; AURICULAR

aureate / GILDED, GOLDEN, YELLOW
aureole / AURA, HALO; GLORY
auricle / EAR; PINNA; ATRIUM
auricular / OTIC; AURAL, EARED
auriferous mineral / QUARTZ
aurochs / TUR; URUS; WISENT
aurora / EOS; DAWN; SUNRISE
auroral / EOAN, ROSY; ROSEATE
auspice / OMEN
auspices / EGIS; AEGIS; PATRONAGE
auspicious / HAPPY, LUCKY; BRIGHT
austere / HARD, SOUR; HARSH
austerities / RIGORS
austerity / SEVERITY
austerity of manners / ASPERITY
austral / SOUTHERN
Australasian hawk / KAHU
Australia capital / CANBERRA
Australian aborigine / MARA; ARANDA, ARUNTA, KURNAI; MURNGIN
Australian aborigine woman / GIN; LUBRA
Australian aborigines' hut / MIAMIA
Australian anteater / ECHIDNA
Australian beefwood / BELAH, BELAR
Australian bellbird / MAKO
Australian bird / EMU; KOEL; COOEE, COOEY, GALAH; BROLGA; DRONGO; LORIKEET, LYREBIRD; CURRAWONG; KOOKABURRA
Australian boomerang / KILEY, KYLIE
Australian bullroarer / CHURINGA
Australian cape / HOWE, YORK; OTWAY
Australian city / PERTH; DARWIN, HOBART, SYDNEY; BRISBANE
Australian cockatiel / QUARRIAN
Australian cockatoo / ARARA, GALAH; LOOKOUT
Australian crawfish / YABBI, YABBY
Australian eternal abode / UNGUD; WONGAR; ALCHERA, ALTJIRA
Australian fern / NARDOO
Australian fish / MADO; SNOOK; MORWONG; LUNGFISH, MULLOWAY, TERAGLIN; SWEETLIPS
Australian honey possum / AIT
Australian honeyeater / TUI; BLUEEYE
Australian hut / MIAM, MIMI; WURLY; GUNYAH, WURLEY
Australian immigrant / JACKAROO
Australian insect / LAAP, LERP; WITCHETTY
Australian lake / EYRE; COLAC; BARLEE

Australian lizard / GOANNA, MOLOCH; GOHANNA; PERENTIE

Australian mallow / KURRAJONG

Australian marsupial / EURO, TAIT; KOALA; CUSCUS, NUMBAT, QUOKKA, WOMBAT; DASYURE, WALLABY; KANGAROO; BANDICOOT, PHALANGER

Australian money / DOLLAR

Australian monotreme / PLATYPUS

Australian moth / ATLAS

Australian mother goddess / MUMINA; KADJERI; KUNAPIPI

Australian musical camp / CORROBOREE

Australian native drum / UBAR

Australian native trumpet / DIDJERIDU

Australian opossum / PHALANGER

Australian peninsula / EYRE

Australian phalanger / ARIEL; CUSCUS

Australian port / SYDNEY; BRISBANE

Australian river / SWAN; PAROO; MURRAY; DARLING

Australian soldier / ANZAC

Australian spear-thrower / WOOMERA

Australian tree / KARI; BELAH, BILLA, MULGA, PENDA, TUART; SHEOAK; WADDYWOOD

Australian weapon / LILLIL; NULLANULLA

Australian wild dog / DINGO

Austria capital / VIENNA

Austrian city / GRAZ, LINZ; SALZBURG

Austrian money / FLORIN; KREUZER; SCHILLING

Austrian mountain pass / LOIBL; BRENNER

Austrian river / ILL, INN, MUR; DONAU; DANUBE

Austro-Italian Alps / TIROL, TYROL

authentic / PURE, REAL, TRUE

authenticate / RATIFY; CONFIRM; AUTHORIZE

authenticity / VALIDITY

author / HACK; WRITER; CREATOR

author of Odyssey / HOMER

author of The Raven / POE

author unknown / ANON; ANONYMOUS

authoritative / OFFICIAL, POSITIVE

authoritative answer / ORACLE

authoritative command / FIAT; ORDER

authoritative decree / ARRET, EDICT

authoritative permit / LICENSE

authoritative prohibition / VETO

authoritative pronouncement / DICTUM; MANDATE

authority / RULE, SWAY; POWER, RIGHT; EMPIRE

authorize / ALLOW; DIRECT, ENABLE, PERMIT

authorized / LEGAL, LICIT; LAWFUL

authorized permit / LICENSE

authorized version / KINGJAMES

authorizing delayed payment / MORATORY

authorizing letter / BREVE, BRIEF

author's draft / MANUSCRIPT

authorship / ORIGIN, SOURCE

auto / CAR; JALOPY; AUTOMOBILE

auto accessory / TIRE; HEATER, HUBCAP; BATTERY

auto body style / COUPE, SEDAN, TUDOR, WAGON; HARDTOP; HATCHBACK

auto court / MOTEL

auto shelter / GARAGE

autocracy / TYRANNY; AUTONOMY; DESPOTISM

autocratic / ARBITRARY

autograph / SIGNATURE; MANUSCRIPT

Autoharp / ZITHER

automatic / REPEATER. REFLEX; SPONTANEOUS

automaton / GOLEM, ROBOT; ANDROID

automobile / CAR; AUTO

automobile adjunct / JACK; CRANK

automobile body / CHASSIS, TONNEAU

automobile device / PLUG; BRAKE, CHOKE; CLUTCH

automobile engine / MOTOR

automobile for hire / CAB; HACK, TAXI; JITNEY; TAXICAB

automobile need / GAS, OIL; FUEL; GREASE

automobile noise / HONK, PING, SLAP, TOOT; RATTLE

automobile operator / DRIVER

automobile part / HOOD; FENDER; MUFFLER

automobile speed / LOW; HIGH; SECOND; REVERSE

automobilist / DRIVER

automotive transportation / BUS

auto's shoes / TIRES

autumn pear / BOSC

autumn period / FALL

auxiliary / SUB; ALAR; AIDING; ANCILLARY. AID; ALLY

auxiliary verb / MAY; SHALL

ava / KAVA

avail / USE; BOOT, HELP; PROFIT; BENEFIT

available / OPEN; HANDY, READY

available money / CASH
avalanche / SLIDE; DISASTER
avarice / GREED; CUPIDITY, RAPA-CITY
avaricious / MEAN; CLOSE; GREEDY, STINGY; MISERLY
avast / HOLD, STOP; CEASE
ave / HAIL
avenaceous grass / OATS
avenge / REPAY; REQUITE; VINDI-CATE
avenging angel / DANITE
avenging deity / ATE; FURY; ERINYS
avenue / MALL; ARTERY, STREET; THOROFARE
aver / SAY; STATE, VOUCH; AFFIRM
average / SOSO; USUAL; MEDIUM, NORMAL. PAR; MEAN, NORM; MIDDLE
averager / ADJUSTER
averse / LOTH; LOATH; OPPOSED
aversion / HATE; HATRED; DIS-TASTE
avert / AVOID; PREVENT
Avesta division / GATHA, YASHT, YASNA; VENDIDAD
aviary / CAGE; BIRDHOUSE
aviate / FLY
aviation / FLIGHT; AERONAUTICS
aviator / ACE; FLIER, PILOT
avid / KEEN; EAGER; GREEDY
avifauna / AVES; BIRDS, ORNIS
aviso / HINT; ADVICE; WARNING
avitic / ANCESTRAL
avocado / COYO; CHININ; AGUA-CATE
avocado sauce / GUACAMOLE
avocation / HOBBY, TRADE; CALL-ING
avoid / SHUN; DODGE, EVADE
avoid slyly / ELUDE
avouch / SAY; AVER, AVOW, TELL; STATE, SWEAR
avow / OWN; AVER; CONFESS
await / BIDE, STAY; ATTEND
await decision / PEND
awake / STIR; ROUSE. ALERT
awaken / SPUR, STIR; EXCITE
awakening / REVIVAL
award / GIVE, METE; ALLOT; BE-STOW. PRIZE
award of honor / BAYS; MEDAL; LAUREL

aware / HIP; ALERT; KNOWING, MINDFUL
awareness / SENSE
away / FAR, FRO, OFF, OUT; GONE; ABSENT
away, pref. / DE; APO
away from mouth / ABORAD, ABORAL
away from windward / ALEE
awe / FEAR; DREAD; RESPECT. APPAL
awesome / DIRE; TERRIFIC
awful / DIRE; GRAND; SOLEMN; FEARFUL
awkward / GAWKY, INEPT; CLUMSY
awkward boat / ARK
awkward person / LOUT; CLOWN, KLUTZ
awkwardly / STIFFLY
awl / DART; BODKIN
awn / BEARD; BRISTLE
awned / ARISTATE
awry / AGREE, BENT; AGLEY, ASKEW; ASKANT; CROOKED, OBLIQUE, TWISTED
ax / AXE; HATCHET
ax handle / HELVE
axilla / ARMPIT
axillary / ALAR
axiom / SAW; ADAGE, MAXIM; TRU-ISM; APHORISM; PRINCIPLE
axis deer / CHITAL
axle / ARBOR, SHAFT; SPINDLE
axlike tool / ADZE
aye / YES; EVER; ALWAYS
aye aye / YEA; INDEED
aye-aye / LEMUR
Aymara Indian / COLLA
azazel / EBLIS, IBLIS; SCAPEGOAT
Azerbaijan capital / BAKU
Azores island / PICO; CORVO, FAYAL
Azores town / ANGRA, HORTA
Aztec god / XIPE; EECATL, TLALOC
Aztec hero / QUETZALCOATL
Aztec Noah / NATA
Aztec spear / ATLATL
Aztec temple / TEOCALLI
azure / SKY; BLUE; CERULEAN
azure stone / LAPISLAZULI
azurite blue / BICE
azygous / ODD; ONLY; SINGLE
azyme / WAFER; MATZOTH

B

Baal / MOLOCH; BEELZEBUB
Baalite / IDOLATOR
baba / BABY, CAKE
Babbitt / ALLOY; BOURGEOIS; MEDIOCRITY
Babbitt's author / LEWIS

babble / GAB; CHAT; PRATE; GAB-BLE
babbler / HAVEREL
babe / TOT; BABY; CHILD; INFANT
babel / DIN; RACKET
Babism / BAHAI

Babism's founder / BAB; MIRZA
baboon / DRILL; CHACMA; HAMA-
DRYAD
baboon-headed god / HAPI; THOTH
babul gum / AMRAD
babul pods / GARAD
baby / TOT; BABE, DOLL; CHILD.
HUMOR
baby ailment / COLIC, CROUP
baby animal / TOTO
baby bear / CUB
baby bed / CRIB; CRADLE
baby carriage / PRAM; STROLLER
baby clothes / ROMPERS
baby food / PAP; PABULUM
baby grand / PIANO
baby lion / CUB
babyhood / INFANCY
Babylonia predecessor / SUMER
Babylonian Adam / ADAPA
Babylonian air god / ENLIL
Babylonian chief god / EA; ANU,
BEL; ADAD, ENKI; MARDUK
Babylonian chief priest / EN
Babylonian creator goddess /
ARURU
Babylonian dragon goddess /
TIAMAT
Babylonian earth god / BEL; ENLIL,
KINGU
Babylonian earth goddess /
DAMKINA
Babylonian fire god / GIRRU
Babylonian god / EA, ZU; ANU,
BEL; ADAD, ADDA, ADDU,
NABU, NEBO, DAGAN
Babylonian god of heavens / ANU;
ANSHAR
Babylonian goddess / NINA; NANAI;
ISHTAR
Babylonian goddess of death /
GULA
Babylonian goddess of the deep /
NINA
Babylonian goddess of heavens /
ISHTAR
Babylonian governor / PATESI
Babylonian grain goddess / HINLIL
Babylonian hades / ARALU
Babylonian healing god / NINIB
Babylonian healing goddess /
GULA
Babylonian hero / ETANA
Babylonian hunting god / NINIB;
NERGAL
Babylonian king / HAMMURABI;
NEBUCHADNEZZAR
Babylonian love goddess / ISTAR;
ISHTAR
Babylonian messenger god /
MUMMU
Babylonian moon god / SIN; ENZU;
NANNA

Babylonian mother goddess / ISH-
TAR
Babylonian mythical monster /
HUMBABA
Babylonian numeral / SAR; SAROS
Babylonian queen of gods /
NINGAL
Babylonian sea goddess / TIAMAT
Babylonian sky god / ANU
Babylonian storm god / ZU; ADAD,
ADDA, ADDU; HADAD; RAMMAN
Babylonian sun god / BABBAR,
NERGAL; NINURTA, SHAMASH
Babylonian tower / BABEL; ZIGGU-
RAT
Babylonian underworld goddess /
ALLATU
Babylonian vegetation god / NEBO;
TAMMUZ
Babylonian war god / IRRA; AS-
SHUR, MARDUK, NERGAL
Babylonian water god / EA; HEA;
APSU
Babylonian water goddess / TIAMAT
Babylonian wind god / ZU; ADAD,
ADDA, ADDU
Babylonian wisdom god / EA; NA-
BU, NEBO; MARDUK
baby's napkin / BIB
baby's nurse / NANA
baby's outfit / LAYETTE
baby's powder / TALC
baby's toy / DOLL; RATTLE
bac / VAT; CISTERN
bacalao / CODFISH, GROUPER
bacalao bird / MURRE
bacca / BERRY
baccate / PULPY; SUCCULENT
Bacchae / MAENADS
bacchanal / FEAST; REVELRY
bacchanalian / DIONYSIAC
bacchante / MAENAD
bacchante's cry / EVOE
bacchantic / NOISY; JOVIAL
bacchic celebration / ORGY
Bacchus' attendant / SATYR
Bacchus' mother / SEMELE
bachelor / UNMARRIED. CELIBATE
bacis / PROPHET
back / AID; ABET, HELP; UPHOLD.
AFT. HIND, REAR
back, pert. to / DORSAL
back, pref. / UN; UNA; RETRO
back of animal / NOTUM; DORSUM
back before the judge / RETRIAL
back entrance / POSTERN
back out of / RENEG, RENIG;
RENEGE
back payment / ARREAR
back of skull / OCCIPUT
back tooth / MOLAR
backbencher / PARTISAN; SUPPOR-
TER

backbite / SASS; DISPARAGE
backbone / GRIT; CHINE, PLUCK, SPINE
backbone curvature / LORDOSIS
backchat / SLANG
backer / ANGEL; ABETTOR, SPONSOR
backgammon / TABLES
background / REAR; HISTORY
backless / WEAK; FEARFUL
backslide / LAPSE; RELAPSE
backtalk / SASS
backward / DULL, LATE, SLOW
backyard area / PATIO
bacon / PORK; RASHER, REWARD
bacteria / GERMS; BACILLI; POLLUTION
bacteria culture medium / AGAR
bacterial dissolve / LYSIN
bacteriologist's wire / OESE
bad / ILL; EVIL, MEAN, POOR, VILE
bad, c.f. / MAL; CACO
bad, pref. / DYS, MAL
bad blood / HOSTILITY
bad dream / INCUBUS; NIGHTMARE
bad habit / VICE
bad luck / AMESACE; MISFORTUNE
bad mark / SCAR; DEMERIT
bad trip / BUMMER; FREAKOUT
badge / PIN; TOKEN; EMBLEM
badge of honor / MEDAL; RIBBON
badger / BAIT; PERSECUTE. BROCK; TELEDU
badger state / WISCONSIN
badgerlike mammal / PAHMI, RATEL
badinage / CHAFF; BANTER
badly / ILL
badly adjusted person / MISFIT
badly dressed / DOWDY; UNKEMPT
baffle / MAR; BALK, FOIL, MOCK, POSE; CHECK, ELUDE
baffling / EVASIVE; PUZZLING
baffling problem / POSER
bag / SAC; SACK; POUCH; VALISE. STEAL; ENTRAP
bag floating in air / BALLOON
bag net / FYKE; TRAWL
bagasse / ABACA; LINAGA
bagatelle / TRIFLE; PINBALL; COCKAMAROO
baggage / HUSSY; LUGGAGE; IMPEDIMENTA
baggage carrier / PORTER, REDCAP
bagnio / BORDELLO
bagpipe / MUSETTE; DOODLESACK
bagpipe hole / LILL
bagpipe music / PIBROCH
bagpipe pipe / DRONE; CHANTER
bagpipe player / PIPER; SKIRLER
bagpiper's garb / KILT
bagpipes' shrill / SKIRL

bags / CAPTURES. SLACKS
bah / TUT; PFUI, POOH
Bahama island / CAT; ABACO, EXUMA; ANDROS, BIMINI, INAGUA; WATLINGS, ELEUTHERA
Bahaman aborigine / LUCAYAN
Bahamas capital / NASSAU
Bahamas city / FREEPORT
Bahrain capital / MANAMA; MANAMEH
Bahrain island / SITKA
Bahrain money / DINAR
bail / LADE. HOOP, RYND, WALL; COURT; HANDLE; BARRIER, REPLEVIN, SECURITY; CROSSPIECE
Baile's father / BUAN
bailie / MAGISTRATE
bailiff / REEVE
bairn / CHILD; INFANT
bait / LURE, TRAP; ANNOY, DECOY, TEMPT. WORM; MORSEL
bake / PARCH; HARDEN
baked clay piece / TILE
baked food / PIE; BREAD
baker / COOK, OVEN
baker bird / HORNERO
baker's dozen / THIRTEEN
baker's itch / PSORIASIS
baker's kneading trough / BRAKE
baker's mop / SCOVEL
baker's receptacle / BREADPAN
baker's shovel / PEEL
baker's specialty / PIE; CAKE; BREAD; COOKIE
baker's trough / HUTCH
baking chamber / KILN, OAST, OVEN
baking dish / RAMEKIN; CASSEROLE
baking pit / IMU
Balaam's steed / ASS
balance / PAR; REST; SCALE; EXCESS. EVEN; POISE; SQUARE
Balance / LIBRA
balance due / ARREARS
balance ship's cargo / TRIM
balanced / SANE; SOBER
Bala-Rama's brother / KRISHNA
balas ruby / SPINEL
balcony / GALLERY, TERRACE
bald / BARE; NAKED; HAIRLESS
bald cypress / SABINO
balderdash / BUNK; RUBBISH; NONSENSE
Balder's fatal plant / MISTLETOE
Balder's father / ODIN
Balder's killer / HOD; HOTH, LOKI; HODER, HOTHR
Balder's mother / FRIGG
Balder's son / FORSETI
Balder's wife / NANNA
baldness / FAVUS; ACOMIA; ALOPECIA

baldpate / WIDGEON
bale / HARM; BUNDLE, SORROW; PACKAGE
Balearic island / IBIZA, IVIZA; MAJORCA; MALLORCA
Balearics language / CATALAN
baleful / BAD; MALIGN
Balinese xylophone / GAMELAN
balk / JIB; STOP; CHECK; BAFFLE
balk as a horse / REEST
Balkan country / GREECE; ALBANIA; BULGARIA
Balkanize / FRAGMENT
balked / SHIED
ball / DANCE, GLOBE; BULLET, PELLET, SPHERE
ball club / TEAM
ball game / HOCKEY; LACROSSE
ball hit low / LINER
ball of thread / CLEW
ballad / LAY, ODE; SONG; DERRY
ballan / WRASSE
ballast / POISE; WEIGHT
ballast of railroad / BED
ballet dance / ADAGIO; PASDEDEUX
ballet leap / JETE
ballet performer / DANSEUSE; BALLERINA
ballet shoes / POINTS
ballet skirt / TUTU
ballet step / PAS
ballet turn / FOUETTE; PIROUETTE
balloon car / BASKET; GONDOLA, NACELLE
balloon sail / SPINNAKER
ballot / VOTE; FRANCHISE
ballpoint's lack / INK
ballroom dance / HOP; TANGO, WALTZ; FOXTROT
ballyhoo / NOISE; PUFFERY
ballyrag / SCOLD; BADGER
balm / BALSAM; UNGUENT; OINTMENT
balm in Gilead / HOPE; COMFORT
balm of Gilead / MYRRH; BALSAM
balmy / MAD; SOFT; BLAND, SILLY, SWEET; ODOROUS
balsa / RAFT; CORKWOOD
balsalike wood / BONGO
balsam / FIR; BALM, TOLU; RESIN
balsamic resin / BALM; STORAX
Baltic island / OSEL; OESEL, OSSEL; SAREMA; SAAREMAA
Baltic seaport / KIEL; TURKU; DANZIG
Baltimore baseball team / ORIOLES
Baluchistan capital / KELAT
Baluchistan millet / JOWAR
Baluchistan mountain / HALA
Baluchistan people / BRAHOES
Baluchistan river / GAJ; BOLAN
baluster / COLUMN; BANISTER

balustrade / PARAPET, RAILING
Bambi's author / SALTEN
bamboo / CANE, REED
bamboo-shoot pickle / ACHAR
bamboozle / HOAX; CHEAT; DECEIVE
ban / BAR; CURSE; FORBID; INTERDICT
banal / STALE, TRITE; COMMON
banana / FEI; PLANTAIN
banana bunch / HAND, STEM
banana dish / SPLIT
banana oil / BOSH; NONSENSE
banana plant / MUSA
banana spider / TARANTULA
banana-like fruit / PLANTAIN
Bana's conqueror / KRISHNA
Bana's daughter / USHA
band / BELT, CREW, TAPE; FACIA, GROUP, STRAP, TROOP; FASCIA, FILLET, RIBBON
band of brain matter / LIGULA
band on an escutcheon / BEND, FESS
band leader / CONDUCTOR
band of leather / BELT; STRAP
band of muscle / TAENIA
band of retainers / CONVOY; RETINUE
band wheel / RIGGER
band worn in hair / FILLET, TAENIA
bandage / LIGATE. TAENIA; DRESSING
bandage on nose / ACCIPITER
banded / ALLIED, UNITED; STRIPED
bandit / ROBBER; BRIGAND
bandmaster / LEADER; CONDUCTOR
bandy / CART. DISCUSS; EXCHANGE
bane / WOE; HARM, RUIN; POISON
baneful / BAD, ILL; DEADLY; NOXIOUS
bang / BEAT, SLAM; THUMP
bang up / FINE; EXCELLENT
banger / LIE; SAUSAGE
Bangladesh capital / DACCA
Bangladesh city / CHITTAGONG
Bangladesh money / TAKA
Bangladesh Moslem / BIHARI
Bangladesh river / PADMA, SURMA; GANGES, JAMUNA, MEGHNA
bangle / CIRCLET; ORNAMENT
banian / BANYA; SIRCAR, TRADER
Bani's son / UEL
banish / OUST; EXILE, EXPEL
banishment / EVICTION; OSTRACISM
banister / BALUSTER; BALUSTRADE
banjo player / STRUMMER

bank / RELY, SAVE; DEPEND; DEPOSIT. BAR; TIER; BRINK, MOUND, RIDGE
bank book / PASSBOOK
bank credit / LOAN; SECURITY
bank employee / TELLER
bank examiner / AUDITOR
bank note / BILL
bank of a river / BRAE, RIPA
bank of sea / BEACH
banker / LENDER, TELLER
banker of India / SETH; SERAFF, SHROFF
banking game / FARO; BACCARAT
bankroll / WAD; ANGEL; BACKER
bankrupt / FAILURE
bankruptcy / LOSS, RUIN; FAILURE
banner / FLAG; ENSIGN, PENNON; PENNANT; GONFALON, STREAMER
banquet / FEAST; DINNER; CAROUSAL
banqueted / REGALED
bant / DIET
bantam / SMALL; PUGNACIOUS. ROOSTER
banteng / OX; TSINE
banter / JEER, JOKE, MOCK, TWIT; CHAFF, RALLY, TEASE. FUN, WIT; BADINAGE
bantling / BRAT; CHILD
Bantu / KAFFIR
Bantu language / ILA; LUBA, ZULU; MONGO, RONGA, SOTHO; THONGA
Bantu people / DAMARA; BAGANDA
Bantu personal prefix / BA, MU, WA
Bantu prefix for language / KI
Bantu tribe / KUA, RUA; BAYA, GOMA, SOGA, SUKU, VIRA; TONGA
Bantu tribesman / ZULU; DUALA; KAFFIR
banzai charge / SUICIDE ATTACK
baobab fruit / MONKEYBREAD
baobab leaves / LALO
baptismal bowl / FONT
baptismal font / LAVER; PISCINA
baptize / NAME; CHRISTEN; CONSECRATE
bar / CAKE, RAIL; INGOT; STRIPE. BAN; ESTOP; HINDER
bar for balancing / BEAM
bar legally / ESTOP
bar to slacken thread / EASER
bar to transmit force / LEVER
bar between wheels / AXLE
bar of wood or metal / RAIL
barb / DART; ARROW; PIGEON
barb of a feather / HARL, HERL
Barbados booze / RUM
Barbados capital / BRIDGETOWN
barbarian / HUN; GOTH

barbarity / FERITY; CRUELTY; SAVAGERY
barbarous / RUDE, WILD; CRUEL, ROUGH; BRUTAL, SAVAGE
Barbary ape / MAGOT; MACAQUE
Barbary fig / CACTUS; OPUNTIA
Barbary horse / BARB
Barbary pirates' conqueror / DECATUR
Barbary state / TUNIS; ALGIERS, MOROCCO, TRIPOLI
barbecue stove / GRILL
barbed implement / GAFF; SPEAR; HARPOON
barber / TONSOR; HECKLER
barber of Seville / FIGARO
barber's call / NEXT
barber's specialty / TRIM; SHAVE
barbershop group / QUARTET
bard / POET; MINSTREL
bard of Avon / SHAKESPEARE
bardic order / DRUID, FILID
bare / BALD, MERE, NUDE, OPEN; NAKED, PLAIN, STARK. STRIP; EXPOSE
bared / UNCOVERED
bared wound / SCAR
barefaced / IMPUDENT; SHAME-LESS
barely / JUST, ONLY; HARDLY, MERELY
bargain / BUY; SALE; TREAT. DEAL, SELL; AGREE; BARTER, PALTER; CHAFFER
barge / HOY, TOW; BOAT, LUMP, SCOW
bark / BAY, YAP, YIP; YELP. RIND; PINNACE; SAILBOAT
bark cloth / TAPA
bark exterior / ROSS
bark fiber / BASS, TAPA; OLONA, TAPPA, TERAP
bark shrilly / YIP; YELP
barking / LATRANT; COUGHING
barking deer / KAKAR; MUNTJAC
barking iron / SPUD
barley beard / AWN
barley water / PTISAN, TISANE
Barlow knife / JACKKNIFE
barm / FOAM; YEAST; FERMENT
barmy / BALMY; FLIGHTY
barn / SHED, SILO; STABLE
barn dance / PLAYPARTY; SQUARE-DANCE
Barnaby Rudge's raven / GRIP
barnstormer / ITINERANT
barnyard boss / ROOSTER
baroco / FAKOFO
barometer / GLASS; ANEROID
baron / LORD, PEER; NOBLE
baron of beef / SADDLE
baronet / BART
baronet's title / SIR

baronet's wife / DAME, LADY
baron's title / SIR
barracks / CASERN; CANTONMENT
barracuda / SPET; SENNET
barrage / DAM; SALVO; CURTAIN
barred / CROSSED; STRIPED; EXCLUDED
barred lace / GRILLE; GRILLEE
barrel / KEG, TUN; CASK, DRUM
barrel of herring / CADE
barrel maker / COOPER
barrel slat / STAVE
barrel stave / LAG; SLAT
barrel stopper / BUNG
barrel-organ animal / MONKEY
barren / ARID; EMPTY; EFFETE, FALLOW
barren land / REG; USAR; DESERT
barrenland surface / REH; USAR; ALKALI
barricade / BAR; ABATIS; BARRIER
Barrie character / PETERPAN
barrier / DAM; WALL; FENCE, HEDGE
barrier to surmount / HURDLE
barrister / LAWYER; COUNSEL; ATTORNEY
barrow / CART, HILL; MOUND; KURGAN; TUMULUS
bartender / TAPSTER
barter / SELL, SWAP; TRADE; EXCHANGE
bartering / DEALING
basal / RADICAL; FUNDAMENTAL
base / LOW; EVIL, MEAN, VILE; LOWLY, SNIDE; ABJECT. CAMP, HOME; ALKALI; CAUSTIC, STATION; PEDESTAL
base on balls / PASS, WALK
base of a column / PLINTH
base of common logarithm / TEN
base hit / DOUBLE, SINGLE, TRIPLE
base of vase / PEDESTAL
baseball arbiter / UMPIRE
baseball diamond / FIELD; INFIELD
baseball game part / INNING
baseball glove / MITT
baseball hit / HOMER; DOUBLE, SINGLE, TRIPLE
baseball inning / FRAME
baseball lefthander / SOUTHPAW
baseball marker / BASE, LINE, POLE; PLATE
baseball pitch / DROP; CURVE; SLIDER
baseball play / HIT, OUT; CATCH, SLIDE, STEAL
baseball players / NINE, TEAM
baseball signal / SIGN
baseball term / OUT, RUN; BUNT, FOUL; CATCH, LINER, PITCH, SLIDE, STEAL

baseball triumph / PENNANT
baseboard ornament / DADO
based / STATIONED
based on a standard pattern / MODULAR
baseless / IDLE; ABSURD
basement / CELLAR
basest / HUMBLEST
Bashan's king / OG
Bashaw / PASHA; BIGWIG
bashful / COY, SHY; TIMID; MODEST
basic / PRIMARY; ALKALINE; FUNDAMENTAL
basic facts / ABCs; ESSENTIALS
basic life substance / PROTEIN
basic part / ELEMENT
basic pattern / DESIGN
basilica / CHURCH
basin / PAN; DEEP, TALA; LAVER, VESSEL; DRAINAGE; DEPRESSION
basis / BASE, ROOT; GROUND, SUPPORT
basis of argument / PREMISE
basis of perfume / MUSK
basis of poi / TARO
bask / SUN
bask in the sun / APRICATE
basket / KISH, SKEP; CABAS; HAMPER; PANNIER
basket of balloon / CAR; NACELLE
basket for carrying load / PANNIER
basket for fish / WEEL; CRAIL, CREEL
basketball inventor / NAISMITH
basketball player / CAGER; HOOPSTER
basketball team / FIVE
basketry center / SLATH
basketry rod / OSIER, STAKE
basketry strip / RAND
Basque cap / BERET
Basque game / PELOTA
bass / LOW; DEEP; GRAVE. BASSO, DRONE; BURDEN; VIOLONE
bass saxhorn / TUBA
bass viol / VIOLADAGAMBA
bass violin / CELLO
basswood / LINDEN
bast / FIBER, RAMIE; PHLOEM
bast fiber / HEMP; RAMIE; CATENA
baste / TACK; CUDGEL; MOISTEN
basted / SEWED
bastille / PRISON
Basutoland / LESOTHO
bat / CLUB; CUDGEL, RACKET; NOCTULE, VAMPIRE; SEROTINE; PIPISTREL
Bataan bay / SUBIC
Bataan capital / BALANGA
Bataan town / MARIVELES
Batavia / JAKARTA

bate / LOWER; LESSEN, REDUCE; MODERATE
batfish / DIABLO
bath / ABLUTION; IMMERSION
bath crystals / SALTS
bathe / LAVE, SWIM, WASH; SHOWER
bathhouse / SAUNA; CABANA, BAGNIO
bathing suit / BIKINI, TRUNKS; MAILLOT
bathos / ANTICLIMAX
bathroom fixture / TUB; WASH-BASIN
Bathsheba's husband / DAVID, URIAH
Bathsheba's son / SOLOMON
baton / ROD; WAND; STAFF
batrachian / FROG, TOAD
batten / BAR, RIB; STRIP. THRIVE
batter / RAM; MAUL; ABUSE; BRUISE; BOMBARD. DOUGH, PASTE; HITTER
batter cake / WAFFLE
battering device / RAM
battery / GUNS
battery plate / GRID
battery terminal / POST; ANODE
battle / FIGHT; ACTION, AFFAIR, COMBAT
battle area / WING; FRONT; SECTOR
battle array / ACIES, HERSE; PHALANX
battle cry / YELL; WHOOP; SLOGAN
battle fleet / ARMADA; SQUADRON
battle formation / ARRAY, HERSE; SQUARE; ECHELON, PHALANX
battle-ax / HAG; POLEAX, TWIBIL; HALBERD
battlefield / LONE; ARENA; THEATER
battlefront / SECTOR
battleground / TERRAIN
battlement / CRENEL, MERLON
battleship / WARSHIP; DREADNAUGHT
batule / SPRINGBOARD
bauble / GEWGAW, TRIFLE; TRINKET
Bau's husband / NINIB
Baucis' husband / PHILEMON
Bavarian river / EGER, ISAR, LECH, MAIN
Bavaria's mad king / LUDWIG
bawdy / LEWD; OBSCENE
bawl / CRY; ROAR, WEEP; SHOUT; BELLOW, HALLOO
bawl out / SCOLD; BERATE, STRAFE; UPBRAID; PROCLAIM
bay / COVE; BIGHT, INLET, SINUS; LAUREL, BARK
Bay State / MASSACHUSETTS

bay tree / LAUREL
bay window / ORIEL; PAUNCH; MIRADOR
bayberry extract / BAYRUM
bayberry oil / MYRCIA
bayed / BARKED
baylike inlet / COVE
bayou / CREEK; SLOUGH; ESTUARY
bayou state / MISSISSIPPI
bays / CORONA; GARLAND
bazaar / FAIR, MART; FEAST; MARKET
be / AM, IS; ARE, ART, WAS; BEEN, LIVE, WAST; EXIST
be abundant / TEEM
be abusive / REVILE
be affectionate / LOVE; ADORE; CARESS
be affective / SHOW; PROVE
be agitated / SEETHE
be anxious / DREAD
be of assistance / HELP; AVAIL
be attentive / HEED, MIND; SERVE
be conveyed / RIDE
be in debt / OWE
be deprived / LOSE
be dogmatic / PONTIFICATE
be due / MATURE
be due to / DERIVE, RESULT
be enough / DO; SUFFICE
be erect / STAND
be fearless / DARE
be fond / CARE, LIKE, LOVE
be foolish / FRIVOL; SPLURGE
be foremost / LEAD, STAR
be furious / FUME, RAGE, RAVE
be harmonious / AGREE; ACCORD
be inactive / IDLE; VEGETATE
be indebted / OWE
be indignant / RESENT
be indisposed / AIL; COMPLAIN
be informed / HEAR, KNOW
be located / LIE
be lodged / BILLET
be mistaken / ERR
be motionless / STIFFEN; STAGNATE
be obligated / OWE
be off / GO, VA; SCAT, SHOO
be off guard / NAP, NOD
be on guard / BEWARE
be of the opinion / DEEM, FEEL; GUESS
be overfond / DOAT, DOTE
be partial to / FAVOR
be permissive / TOLERATE
be present / ATTEND
be ready for / AWAIT
be related / INHERE; CONNECT
be repeated / RECUR; REOCCUR
be silent / SHH; HUSH
be situated / LIE

be skilled in / KNOW
be smarter than / OUTWIT
be sorry / RUE; REGRET
be sorry for sins / REPENT
be sufficient / DO; SERVE
be suitable / BEFIT
be suspended / HANG, PEND
be uneasy / TOSS; FIDGET
be unsettled / PEND
be useful / AVAIL
be victorious / WIN
be violent / RAGE, RIOT; RAMPAGE
be wanting / FAIL
be willing / FAVOR; INCLINE
be zealous / PRESS; HUSTLE
beach / SAND; COAST, MARGE, SHORE. STRAND
beach cabin / CABANA
beach grass / MARRAM
beach shelter / CABANA; UMBRELLA
beach surface / SAND; SHINGLE
beachcomber / DRIFTER
beached / AGROUND
beacon / GUIDE; SIGNAL
Beaconsfield / DISRAELI
bead / DROP; BUBBLE; GLOBULE
bead with moisture / BEDEW
beaded lizard / GILA
beaded moisture / DEW, FOG; DRIZZLE
beadroll / ROSARY
beads / ROSARY; CHAPLET; NECKLACE
beads used as money / PEAG
beadsman / PENSIONER
beady / BUBBLY; GLITTERING
beagle / HOUND, SHARK
beak / NEB, NIB; BILL; MAGISTRATE
beaked / ROSTRATE
beaker / CUP
beam / SHINE; RADIATE. RAY; RAFTER
beam over door / LINTEL
beam outward / RADIATE
beam pleasantly / SMILE
beam support / TEMPLET; TEMPLATE
beaming / JOYOUS; MIRTHFUL
bean / GOA, SOY, URD; LIMA, NAVY, SOYA; MUNGO, PINTO, ROMAN; LEGUME; HARICOT
bean curd / TOFU
bean fly / MIDAS
bean plant / SENNA
bean plant for fodder / VETCH
bean tree / CAROB; CATALPA
bean weevil / HARIA
bean's eye / HILUM
beanshooter / SLINGSHOT; PEASHOOTER
Beantown / BOSTON

bear / HAVE, HOLD; CARRY, STAND; CONVEY, ENDURE, SUBMIT, SUFFER, UPHOLD, URSA; BRUIN
bear cat / PANDA
bear grass / YUCCA; SOURGRASS
bear out / CONFIRM
bear witness / AVOW; ATTEST, DEPONE
beard / BARB; BEAVER, GOATEE; WHISKERS
beard of grain / AWN; ARISTA
beard lichen / USNEA
bearded / BARBATE, HIRSUTE
bearded seal / MAKLUK
bearer / CARRIER
bearing / AIM, AIR, BED; MIEN, PORT; COURSE
bearing no name / UNTITLED; ANONYMOUS
bearing the title / TITULAR
bearlike / URSIN
bear's ear / ARICULA
beast / BRUTE; ANIMAL; CRITTER; QUADRUPED
beast, c.f. / THER; THERI, THERO; THERIO
beast of burden / OX; ASS, YAK; MULE; BURRO, CAMEL, LLAMA; DONKEY, ONAGER
beastly / VILE, NASTY; BRUTAL, COARSE
beastly noise / SNARL
beast's mother / DAM
beat / HIT, LAM, WIN; BEST, CANE, DRUB, DRUM, FLAP, FLAY, FLOG, LASH, PELT; FLAIL, POUND, SMITE, THROB, THUMP
beat incessantly / PELT
beat it / GO; SCRAM
beat poet / CORSO; GINSBERG
beat severely / FLAY; BATTER, THRASH
beat up / DRUB, LICK; BUFFET
beaten / DEFEATED, TROUNCED
beaten path / TRAIL
beater / BATTEN
beater for mortar / RAB
beatific / BLISSFUL
beating / FLOGGING; ZIGZAGGING
beau / FOP; DANDY; ESCORT, SUITOR
Beau Brummel / DANDY
beauteous / LOVELY
beautiful / FAIR; LOVELY, PRETTY
beautiful lady / BELLE
beautiful nymph / HOURI
beautiful white bird / SWAN; EGRET
beautiful writing / CALLIGRAPHY
beautify / DECK; ADORN, ARRAY, GRACE
beautifying / COSMETIC

beauty / CHARM, GRACE
beauty of movement / GRACE
beauty parlor / SALON
beauty treatment / RUB; FACIAL; MASSAGE
beaver / BEARD, VISOR; CASTOR, TOPPER
beaver skin / PLEW
beaver state / OREGON
because / AS; FOR; SINCE
beche-de-mer / TREPANG
Bechuanaland / BOTSWANA
beck / NOD; BROOK; COMMAND
beckon / NOD; WAVE, WINK; SIGNAL
become / GET, WAX; GROW, SUIT; BEFIT
become active / WAKEN; AWAKEN
become aware / SENSE; PERCEIVE
become bankrupt / FAIL
become blunt / DULL, SLOW
become blurred / DIM; MIST
become bored / TIRE
become entangled / FOUL
become exhausted / TIRE
become ill / AIL; SICKEN
become impaired / WEAR
become indistinct / DIM; BLUR, FADE
become insipid / PALL; STALE
become known / EMERGE
become less severe / RELENT, SOFTEN
become part of / MERGE
become shiny / BRIGHTEN
become slender / THIN; REDUCE
become solid / JELL; FREEZE; CONGEAL
become sour / TURN
become spray / SPUME
become tan / BURN
becoming / FIT; MEET; RIGHT; COMELY, PROPER
becoming slower / LENTANDO
becoming young / JUVENESCENT
bed / COT, KIP; BASE, CRIB, DOSS; COUCH; MATRIX, PALLET; STRATUM
bed board / SLAT
bed canopy / TESTER
bed coverlet / QUILT, SHEET; SPREAD
bed headrest / PILLOW
bed linen / CASE; SHEET
bed rail / SLAT
bed of roses / EDEN; LUXURY
bedclothes / LINEN
bedeck / ADORN; ORNAMENT
bedew / WET; MOISTEN
bedlam / RIOT; MELEE
Bedouin / ARAB; NOMAD
bedraggled / MUDDY
bedridden / LECTUAL

bedstead support / SLAT
bedtick / MATTRESS
bee / DRONE; WORKER; SOCIABLE
bee, c.f. / API
bee, pert. to / APIAN
bee house / HIVE, SKEP; APIARY
bee party / SOCIAL; SOCIABLE
bee swarm / BIKE
bee tree / LINDEN
beebalm / OSWEGOTEA
beebread / POLLEN; AMBROSIA
beechnuts / MAST
beef / MEAT, BRAWN; CATTLE
beef animal / OX; COW; STEER
beef cut / BARON, STEAK
beef on the hoof / CATTLE
beefy / FLESHY
beehive / SKEP; ALVEARY
Beehive State / UTAH
beehouse / HIVE; APIARY
beemaster / BEEKEEPER
beer / ALE; BOCK, BREW, MALT, SUDS; LAGER
beer conditioner / KRAUSEN
beer ingredient / HOPS, MALT
beer and molasses / CALIBOGUS
beer mug / TOBY; STEIN; SEIDEL; TANKARD
bee's pollen brush / SCOPA
bees' home / HIVE, NEST
beet / BEETROOT
beet variety / CHARD; MANGEL; MANGELWURZEL
Beethoven opera / FIDELIO
Beethoven sonata / KREUTZER; MOONLIGHT; APPASSIONATA
Beethoven symphony / EROICA
Beethoven's birthplace / BONN
beetle / DOR; ELATER, SCARAB, WEEVIL. OVERHANG
beetle-shaped jewel / SCARAB
beetling / JUTTING, LOOMING
befall / HAP; BETIDE, HAPPEN
befitting / APT, DUE, FIT; MEET; RIGHT
befog / BAFFLE; CONFUSE
befool / TRICK; DELUDE
before / ERE; ERER; AFORE, PRIOR; EARLIER
before, pref. / AD; PRE, PRO; ANTE
before any / FIRST
before birth / PRENATAL
before noon / AM
before now / HERETOFORE
before this / ERENOW
befoul / SPOIL, STAIN, SULLY, TAINT; CORRUPT, POLLUTE
befriend / AID; HELP; FAVOR; ASSIST
befuddle / ADDLE; CONFUSE
beg / ASK, SUE; PRAY; PLEAD; BESEECH

beg the question / QUIBBLE
began / STARTED; COMMENCED
beget / SIRE; FATHER; ENGENDER
beggar / FAKIR, ROGUE; MUMPER; MENDICANT
beggared / IMPOVERISHED
beggarly / MEAN, POOR
Beggar's Opera author / GAY
Beggar's Opera hero / MACHEATH
beggary / WANT; PENURY
begged / CADGED
begin / LEAD, OPEN, RISE; START
begin again / RENEW; RESUME
begin to appear / DAWN, RISE
beginner / BOOT, TYRO; NOVICE, ROOKIE; NEOPHYTE; POSTULANT; APPRENTICE
beginning / DAWN, GERM, RISE; ONSET, START; ORIGIN, OUTSET; GENESIS; INCEPTION
beginning existence / NASCENT
begird / BIND
begone / GO; AWAY, SCAT; SCOOT, SCRAM; DEPART
begrime / SOIL; BEFOUL
begrudged / ENVIED
beguile / AMUSE, CHEAT, CHEER; BEFOOL
behalf / SAKE; FAVOR, STEAD; INTEREST
behave / ACT; COMPORT, CONDUCT
behave toward / USE; TREAT
behavior / MIEN, PORT; BEARING
beheld / SAW; REGARDED
behest / TRUST; COMMAND, PRECEPT
behind / PAST; ABAFT, AFTER; ASTERN
behind time / LATE, SLOW
behind the times / PASSE, ANTIQUATED
behindhand / LATE; BACKWARD
behold / EYE, SEE; GAZE, LOOK, VIEW. LO; ECCE, VOILA
beholden / INDEBTED; OBLIGATED
behoof / BEHALF; INTEREST; ADVANTAGE
behoove / BEFIT; DEVOLVE
beige / ECRU; GREGE; NATURAL
being / ENS; ESSE; ENTITY; CREATURE
being in suspension / ABEYANT
belabor / BEAT, DRUB, FLOG
Bela's son / IRI
belate / DELAY; RETARD
belated / TARDY
belay / STOP; CEASE; SECURE; SURROUND
belch / BURP; ERUCTATION
beldam / HAG; CRONE, WITCH
beleaguer / BESET; BESIEGE

beleaguerment / SIEGE
belem / PARA
belfry / TOWER; STEEPLE
Belgian / FLEMING, WALLOON
Belgian battle / BULGE; WATERLOO; RAMILLIES
Belgian city / GENT; GHENT, LIEGE, YPRES; BRUGES, BRUGGE
Belgian French / WALLOON
Belgian lowland / POLDER
Belgian marble / RANCE, RANSE
Belgian river / LYS; MAAS, YSER; RUPEL; SCHELDT
Belgian seaport / OSTEND; ANTWERP
Belgian spa / SPA; OSTEND
Belgian violinist / YSAYE
Belgium capital / BRUSSELS; BRUXELLES
Belgrade marshal / TITO
belial / DEVIL, SATAN
belie / DENY; DISTORT, SLANDER
belief / ISM; IDEA, VIEW; CREDO, CREED, DOGMA, FAITH, TENET, TRUST; CREDIT
believe / TROW; OPINE, THINK; SUPPOSE
believer in god / DEIST; THEIST
belike / PROBABLY
Beli's festival / BELTANE
belittle / DECRY, LOWER; DERIDE
belittled / MINIMIZED; DISPARAGED
belittling exclamation / POOH
bell / GONG; CHIME; TOCSIN; COROLLA
bell magpie / CURRAWONG
bell set / CHIME; CARILLON
bell signaling prayer / ANGELUS
bell tower / BELFRY; STEEPLE; CAMPANILE
belladonna / NIGHTSHADE
belladonna alkaloid / ATROPINE; HYOSCIAMINE
belle / BEAUTY
Bellerophon's father / GLAUCOS
Bellerophon's steed / PEGASUS
Bellerophon's victim / CHIMAERA
belles-lettres / LITERATURE
bellhop / PAGE; FRONT
bellicose / WARLIKE; CONTENTIOUS
belligerent / HOSTILE; BELLICOSE
Bellini opera / NORMA
bellman / CRIER; WATCHMAN
bellow / LOW, MOO; BAWL
bellowing rowdy / ROARER
bell-ringing series / PEAL; CHANGES
bell's clapper / TONGUE
belly / WOMB; ABDOMEN. SWELL
bellyache / COLIC. CRAB; GRIPE
bellyband / SASH; GIRTH

belong / INHERE; APPERTAIN
belonging to her / HERS
belonging to him / HIS
belonging to it / ITS
belonging to them / THEIRS
belonging to us / OUR; OURS
belongings / GEAR; TRAPS; BAGGAGE
beloved / DEAR; SWEETHEART
beloved physician / LUKE
below / LOWER, NEATH, UNDER; BENEATH
below, pref. / INFRA
below the belt / FOUL; DIRTY
below par / AILING
belt / BAND, CEST, SASH, ZONE; STRAP; GIRDLE
belt conveyor / APRON
belt material / LEATHER
belt for sword / BALDRIC
Belus' daughter / DIDO
Belus' son / DANAUS; AEGYPTUS
belvedere / GAZEBO; PAVILION
bemoan / BEWAIL, LAMENT; DEPLORE
bemuddle / DAZE; BEMUSE; CONFUSE
ben / SON; HILL, PEAK
bench / PEW; BANC, SEAT; EXEDRA, SETTLE
bench hook / CRAMP
bench of judge / BANC
bench warmer / SUBSTITUTE; SECONDSTRINGER
bencher / LOAFER; OARSMAN
bend / BOW, NOD, SAG; ARCH, DRAW, FLEX, MOLD, TURN; CROOK, CURVE. SNY
bend downward / SAG; DROOP; DEFLEX
bend forward / BOW; STOOP
bend head / BOW, NOD
bend in heraldry / SLANT
bend in timber / SNY
bend upward / SNY
bender / TEAR, TOOT
bendy / OKRA
beneath / BELOW, UNDER
benedict / GROOM
Benedictine title / DOM
benediction / BENISON; BLESSING
benefaction / ALMS, BOON, GIFT; GRANT; GRATUITY
benefactor / DONOR; PATRON
beneficent / GOOD, KIND; BENIGN; LIBERAL
beneficial / GOOD; SALUTARY
beneficiary / GRANTEE; RECIPIENT
benefit / USE; GOOD; FAVOR; BEHALF. AVAIL, SERVE; PROFIT
benevolence / ALMS; MERCY; BOUNTY; CHARITY
benevolent / GOOD, KIND; HUMANE

Bengal antelope / CHOUKA; CHIKARA; CHINKARA
Bengal author / TAGORE
Bengal bison / GAUR
Bengal boat / BATEL
Bengal city / DACCA, PATNA
Bengal cotton / ADATI
Bengal groom / SYCE; SAICE
Bengal hemp / SUNN
Bengal mendicant / BAUL
Bengal nation / BANGLADESH
Bengal native / KOL; BANIAN
Bengal quince / BEL; BAEL
Bengal singer / BAUL
benign / GOOD, KIND; BLAND; GENIAL
benignity / BENEVOLENCE
benison / BLESSING
benjamin / COAT; BALSAM; BENZOIN
Benjamin's son / EHI; BELA; ASHBEL
benny / HAT; UPPER; OVERCOAT; BENZEDRINE
bent / BIAS, TURN; TREND; LEANING. BOWED; CURVED, FLEXED
benumb / DEADEN; STUPEFY
Beowulf's host / HROTHGAR
Beowulf's victim / GRENDEL
bequeath / WILL; ENDOW; DEMISE, DEVISE
bequest / DOWER; LEGACY
berate / LASH, RAIL; CHIDE, SCOLD
berber / MOOR, RIFF; HAMITE, TUAREG
bereave / STRIP; DIVEST; DEPRIVE
bereaved woman / WIDOW
bereft / LORN; DESTITUTE
bereft of a sweetheart / LOVELORN
beret / TAM
beri-beri / DROPSY
Berlin wool / WORSTED
Bermuda arrowroot / ARARU; ARARAO
Bermuda capital / HAMILTON
Bermuda grass / DOOB, DOUB; COUCH, KWEEK
Bermuda petrel / CAHOW, COHOW
berry / BACCA, GRAPE, SALAL; ACINUS; CURRANT, OLALLIE; BLUEBERRY; BLACKBERRY, GOOSEBERRY, PEPPERCORN, STRAWBERRY
berserk / AMOK; AMUCK, CRAZY
berserker / WARRIOR
berth / BED; BUNK; LOWER, UPPER; MOORING
bertha / COLLAR
beseech / ASK, BEG, BID; PRAY
beseeched / BADE; PLEADED
beset / PRESS, SIEGE; ASSAIL, HARASS

beset annoyingly / HARRY; PESTER
beshrew / NAG; CURSE; EXECRATE
beside / BY
beside, pref. / PAR; PARA
besides / BY; AND, TOO, YET; ALSO, ELSE, THEN; EXCEPT; MOREOVER
besiege / BESET; HARASS; BELEAGUER
beslaver / SMEAR; SLOBBER
besmirch / MAR; SOIL; SMEAR, SULLY
besom / MOP; BROOM; STRIGIL
besot / STUPEFY; INFATUATE
besought / PLED; BEGGED
bespatter / SPOT; MUDDY; SPLASH
bespeak / BETOKEN, RESERVE
bespread / COVER; SPREAD; SCATTER
best / FINEST. DEFEAT, OUTWIT; SURPASS. TOPS; FIRST
best achievement / RECORD
best part / CREAM; MARROW
bested / OVERCAME
bestial / LOW; FERAL; BRUTAL; BRUTISH
bestir / STIR; ROUSE
bestow / PUT; GIVE; AWARD, GRANT
bestow approval / NOD; SMILE
bestow as due / AWARD; REWARD
bestow profusely / RAIN; SHOWER
bestow upon / ENDOW
bestower / DONOR
bestrew / STROW; SCATTER
bet / STAKE, WAGER. GAMBLE
bet in faro / SLEEPER
bet on horses / PUNT
bet in roulette / BAS; CARRE
betake oneself / GO; REPAIR
bete noire / BUGBEAR
betel / SIRI; ARECA, BONGA
betel extract / CUTCH; CATECHU
betel leaf / PAN; BUYO, PAUN
betel nut / SERI, SIRI; SIRIH; SUPARI
betel palm / ARECA; PINANG
betel pepper / IKMO, ITMO
bethink / REFLECT; CONSIDER
betide / OCCUR; HAPPEN
betimes / ANON, RATH, SOON; EARLY
betoken / BODE, SHOW; AUGUR, PROVE
betray / SELL; SPILL; DECEIVE
betray confidence / LEAK; REVEAL
betrayal of country / TREASON
betrayer / RAT; SEDUCER, TRAITOR
betrayer of Jesus / JUDAS
betroth / AFFY; AFFIANCE
betrothal / ENGAGEMENT
better / GROW, MEND; AMEND,

EMEND, EXCEL, OUTDO; ADVANCE, IMPROVE. SUPERIOR
better fitted / ABLER
better half / SPOUSE
betting / WAGERS
betting apparatus / PARIMUTUEL
betting broker / BOOKIE; BOOKMAKER
betting guide / ODDS
betting system / PARLAY
betting tipster / TOUT
bettor's concern / ODDS
bettor's premonition / HUNCH
between / AMID; AMONG; AMIDST; BETWIXT
between, pref. / DIA; META; INTER
between heaven and hell / LIMBO; PURGATORY
between in law / MESNE
between rampart and ditch / RELAIS
between us / CONFIDENTIALLY
between-meals snack / BEVER
bevel / BEZEL, SLANT, SLOPE, SNAPE; INCLINE
bevel to join / MITER
bevel out / REAM
beverage / ADE, ALE, POP, TEA; WINE; CIDER, COCOA, DRINK, JUICE; COFFEE, LIQUOR. See also drink
beverage flavored with juniper / GIN
beverage herb / TEA; MATE, MINT; CAMOMILE
beverage from molasses / RUM
beverage popular in South America / MATE
beverage variety / RUM; BEER, KAVA, RAKI, SODA, WINE; COCOA, LAGER, TOKAY; ARRACK; COCKTAIL
Bevis' horse / ARUNDEL
Bevis' sword / MORGLAY
Bevis' wife / JOSIAN
bevy / COVEY, FLOCK, GROUP
bewail / RUE; WEEP; BEMOAN, LAMENT
beware / SHUN; AVOID; CAUTION
beware of the dog / CAVECANEM
bewilder / FOG; DAZE, STUN; DAZZLE; CONFUSE
bewildered / ASEA, LOST
bewilderment / CONFUSION
bewitch / HEX; CHARM; RAVISH; ENCHANT
bewitchment / CHARM; WITCHERY
bewray / EXPOSE, REVEAL
beyond / PAST; ACROSS, YONDER; FURTHER
beyond, pref. / SUR; META, PARA; ULTRA; PRETER
beyond belief / INCREDIBLE

beyond help / KAPUT
beyond limits / OUT
beyond time / AGO; PAST; PASSE
bezel / RIM; FACE; FACET
bezoar / ANTIDOTE
bhang / HEMP; HASHISH
Bharat / INDIA
Bhutan / DRUKYUL
Bhutan assembly / TSONGDU
Bhutan capital / THIMPU;
  PUNAKHA
Bhutan pine / KAIL
bias / PLY; BENT, CANT; SLANT;
  INCLINE; DIAGONAL,
  TENDENCY; PREJUDICE,
  PREDISPOSE
biased / PARTIAL; ONESIDED
biased person / BIGOT
bib / APRON; NAPKIN
bibaceous / SOTTISH; BIBULOUS
bibelot / BAUBLE, GEWGAW
bible / BOOK; SCRIPTURE
Bible version / DOUAI; GENEVA;
  MAZARIN, VULGATE; GUTEN-
  BERG; AUTHORIZED
Biblical / SCRIPTURAL
Biblical battle / JERICHO
Biblical character (female) / EVE;
  ADAH, JAEL, LEAH, MARY, RUTH;
  DINAH, EGLAH, HAGAR, JULIA,
  JUNIA, LYDIA, MERAB, NAOMI,
  RAHAB, SARAH, SARAI, SHUAH,
  TAMAR
Biblical character (male) / ER, IR,
  OG, UZ; ARA, COZ, DAN, ELI,
  ERI, GOG, HAM, IRA, IRI, JOB,
  NUN, URI; ABEL, ADAM, ADER,
  AMOS, ANUB, ATER, BOAZ, CAIN,
  CUSH, DOEG, EBAL, EBED, EKER,
  ENAN, ENON, ENOS, ESAU,
  EZRA, IRAD, JADA, JEHU, JOAB,
  KISH, LEVI, MASH, MOAB, NERI,
  NOAH, OBAL, OBED; ABIAH,
  ABIEL, AMASA, ANNAS, CALEB,
  ELIAS, HAMAN, HIRAM, ISAAC,
  JACOB, JAMES, JONAH, LABAN,
  NABAL, PELEG, SACAR, TOBIT
Biblical charioteer / JEHU
Biblical city / DAN, NOB, ONO;
  ARBA, AVEN, GATH, GAZA, IVAH,
  NAIN, TYRE, ZOAR; BABEL,
  DERBE, EKRON, MAGOG, SIDON,
  SODOM; HEBRON; NINEVEH;
  BETHLEHEM
Biblical coin / MITE; SHEKEL
Biblical cony / DAMAN
Biblical country / EDOM, ELAM,
  MOAB, SEBA; OPHIR, SHEBA;
  CANAAN
Biblical desert / PARAN
Biblical fortress / DATHEMA
Biblical garden / EDEN

Biblical garment / CESUTH
Biblical giant / ANAK, EMIM; GO-
  LIATH
Biblical high priest / ELI
Biblical hill / ZION
Biblical hunter / NIMROD
Biblical judge / ELI; EHUD, ELON;
  GIDEON, SAMSON; DEBORAH,
  OTHNIEL
Biblical king / OG; ASA, EVI; AGAG,
  AHAB, ELON, OMRI, SAUL;
  DAVID, HEROD, NADAB;
  SOLOMON
Biblical kingdom / EDOM, ELAM,
  ENON, MOAB, SEBA; JUDAH,
  SHEBA; ISRAEL; SAMARIA
Biblical land of plenty / GOSHEN
Biblical language / HEBREW,
  ARAMAIC
Biblical measure / CAB, HIN, KOR,
  LOG; OMER, SPAN; CUBIT, EP-
  HAH, HOMER
Biblical monster / REEM; BEHE-
  MOTH; LEVIATHAN
Biblical mountain / HOR; NAIN,
  NEBO, PEOR, SEIR; HOREB,
  SINAI, TABOR; ARARAT,
  GILEAD, HERMON, PISGAH
Biblical ornament / URIM; THUM-
  MIM
Biblical outcast / LEPER
Biblical passage / TEXT
Biblical patriarch / NOAH; ISAAC,
  JACOB; ISRAEL; ABRAHAM;
  METHUSELAH
Biblical people / EDOMITE, ELA-
  MITE, MOABITE
Biblical place / AHAVA; JORDAN,
  SHILOH; LEBANON
Biblical plain / MAMRE; SHARON;
  JEZREEL
Biblical poem / PSALM
Biblical priest / ELI
Biblical pronoun / YE; THY; THEE;
  THINE
Biblical prophet / AMOS; ELIAS;
  BALAAM, ELISHA
Biblical punishment / STONING
Biblical queen / SHEBA; ESTHER,
  VASHTI; JEZEBEL
Biblical reading gloss / KRI; KERE,
  QERI; KETIB
Biblical river / NILE; ARNON; JOR-
  DAN, KISHON, PISHON
Biblical shepherd / ABEL; DAVID
Biblical spice / MYRRH; STACTE
Biblical strong man / SAMSON
Biblical town / CANA; ENDOR;
  BETHEL; NAZARETH
Biblical vessel / ARK
Biblical villain / HAMAN
Biblical weed / TARE

BIBLE, BOOKS OF
(with standard abbreviation and testament)

	Abbreviation	Testament
Acts	ACTS	New
Amos	—	Old
Chronicles	CHRON	Old
Colossians	COL	New
Corinthians	COR	New
Daniel	DAN	Old
Deuteronomy	DEUT	Old
Ecclesiastes	ECCLES	Old
Ephesians	EPH	New
Esther	—	Old
Exodus	EXOD	Old
Ezekiel	EZEK	Old
Ezra	—	Old
Galatians	GAL	New
Genesis	GEN	Old
Habakkuk	HAB	Old
Haggai	HAG	Old
Hebrews	HEB	New
Hosea	HOS	Old
Isaiah	ISA	Old
James	—	New
Jeremiah	JER	Old
Job	—	Old
Joel	—	Old
John, St.	JOHN	New
John	—	New
Jonah	JON	Old
Joshua	JOSH	Old
Jude	—	New
Judges	JUDG	Old
Kings	—	Old
Lamentations	LAM	Old
Leviticus	LEV	Old
Luke, St.	LUKE	New
Malachi	MAL	Old
Mark, St.	MARK	New
Matthew, St.	MATT	New
Micah	MIC	Old
Nahum	NAH	Old
Nehemiah	NEH	Old
Numbers	NUM	Old
Obadiah	OBAD	Old
Peter	PET	New
Philemon	PHILEM	New
Philippians	PHIL	New
Proverbs	PROV	Old
Psalms	PS (pl. PSS)	Old
Revelation	REV	New
Romans	ROM	New
Ruth	—	Old
Samuel	SAM	Old
Song of Solomon	SONG OF SOL	Old
Thessalonians	THESS	New
Timothy	TIM	New
Titus	—	New
Zechariah	ZECH	Old
Zephaniah	ZEPH	Old

Biblical well / AIN; ESEK
Biblical wilderness / SIN
Biblical witch's home / ENDOR
Biblical word / MENE; SELAH
Biblical word for armies / SABAOTH
bicker / CAVIL; WRANGLE
bickering / JANGLE, STRIFE; DISPUTE
bicycle / BIKE
bicycle seat / SADDLE
bicycle for two / TANDEM
bid / ASK; CALL, PRAY; OFFER; CHARGE
bid in bridge / CUE; PASS, SLAM; SHIFT; DOUBLE
bid fair / PROMISE
bid for twelve tricks / SLAM
bidder-upper / CAPPER
biddy / HEN; FOWL, MAID; CHICKEN
bide / STAY, WAIT; TARRY; REMAIN
Bidpui's forte / FABLE
bier / PYRE; CATAFALQUE
biff / BLOW; WHACK; STRIKE
bifold / DOUBLE
big / HUGE, GREAT, GROSS, LARGE
big bet / DOUBLEORNOTHING
Big Cassino / TEN
big deer / ELK
big game / FINALE
big game gun / ROER, ROHR
big house / PENITENTIARY
big man / HERO
big market / EMPORIUM
big military man / BRASSHAT
big school dance / SENIORPROM
big shot / VIP; BRASS, NABOB
big soup kettle / MARMITE
big talk / BRAG
big toe / HALLUX
big top / CIRCUS
big tree / SEQUOIA
biggest / LARGEST
biggest land animal / ELEPHANT
biggest mammal / WHALE
bight / BAY; COVE, LOOP; NOOSE
bigot / FANATIC; DOGMATIST
bigoted / NARROW; INTOLERANT, PREJUDICED
bilbo / RAPIER; SHACKLE
bile / GALL; CHOLER, SPLEEN
bilk / GYP; HOAX; CHEAT; SWINDLE
bill / NEB, TAB; BEAK, LIST; DRAFT, SCORE. DUN; KISS; CARESS
bill book / LEDGER
bill of fare / MENU; CARTE
bill in restaurant / TAB
bill stroke / PECK
billet doux / LOVELETTER
billfish / GAR; SAURY
billhook / SNAGGER

billiard stick / CUE; REST; BRIDGE
billiard stroke / BANK,\KISS; CAROM, MASSE; SCRATCH
billiard term / BALK; POOL, SPOT; ENGLISH
billingsgate / PROFANITY
billionaire / NABOB; PLUTOCRAT
billjim / AUSTRALIAN
billot / BULLION
billow / SEA; WAVE; SURGE
bill's base / CERE
billy / CAN; CLUB, GOAT
bin / CRIB; BUNKER
binary / DUAL; DOUBLE; TWOFOLD
bind / TIE; TAPE, WRAP; SWATH
bind in irons / GYVE; FETTER
bind the mouth / GAG
bind to secrecy / TILE, TYLE
bind up / LASH; TRUSS; BANDAGE
binder / COVER; DEPOSIT
binding / VALID; COSTIVE; STRINGENT. COVER; FILLET; BANDAGE
binding machine / BALER
bindlestiff / TRAMP
bine / STEM
binge / BAT, RIP; SPREE
bingo / KENO; BEANO, LOTTO
binnacle / COMPASS
biographical fragment / ANECDOTE
biography / LIFE; MEMOIR; HISTORY
biological / BIOTIC. VACCINE
biological category / GENUS, ORDER; PHYLUM
biological decadence / PARACME
biological factor / DNA; GENE
biological monster / TERAS; TERATISM
biologically defective / DYSEGENIC
biosis / LIFE; VITALITY
birch / FLOG, WHIP
birchbark craft / CANOE
bird / ARA, DAW, EMU, JAY, ROC; CLEE, COCK, CROW, DOVE, FINK, GIRL, GLED, HUIA, IIWA, JACU, KALA, KIWI, KOEL, KORA, KUKU, LARK, LOON, LORO, LORY, LOUN, LOWA, LULU, LUPE, MAKU, MAMO, MIRO, MOHO, MORO, MYNA, NENE, PAPE, PEHO, PISK, RAIL, RAYA, ROOK, RUFF, RUPE, RURU, SKUA, SMEE, SMEW, SORA, STIB, SWAN, TEAL, TERN, TOCK, TOCO, TODY, UTUM, WAEG, WREN, YATU, YENI, YUTU; ARTIN, DIVER, DRAKE, EAGLE, EGRET, GLEDE, MERLE, ROBIN, SERIN
bird of Aphrodite / DOVE; SPARROW
bird that carried Sinbad / ROC
bird dog / SETTER; POINTER

bird food / SEED; GRAIN; MILLET
bird house / CAGE, COTE, NEST; AVIARY
bird of Juno / PEACOCK
bird of Jupiter / EAGLE
bird killed for plumage / HERON
bird of legend / ROC; SIMURG
bird of myth / PHOENIX
bird that never alights / HUMA
bird note / CHIP; CHIRP, TWEET
bird originally called penguin / GREATAUK
bird of paradise / APUS; LYRE-BIRD, MANUCODE
bird of peace / DOVE
bird of prey / ERN, OWL; ERNE, HAWK, KITE; EAGLE; ELANET
bird wing part / ALULA; FEATHER, PRIMARY
birdmen / AVIATORS
birds / AVES
birds, pert. to / AVIAN, AVINE
bird's beak / NEB
bird's craw / MAW; CROP
bird's crest / TUFT
bird's cry / CAW, COO; CHIRP, TWEET
birds' eggs collector / OOLOGIST
bird's identifying tag / LEGBAND
birds' migration route / FLYWAY
birds of a region / ORNIS; AVI-FAUNA
bird's shelter / COTE, NEST
bird's tweet / CHEEP
birdseye view / PANORAMA
birth / RACE; BLOOD; ORIGIN
birth, pert. to / NATAL
birth rate / NATALITY
birthday poem / GENETHLIAC
birthday suit / BUFF, SKIN
birthmark / MOLE; NEVUS; NAEVUS
birthplace / NEST; ORIGIN
birthplace of Apollo / DELOS
birthplace of Constantine / NIS; NISH
birthplace of Diana / DELOS
birthplace of Henry the IV / PAU
birthplace of Mohammed / MECCA
birthplace of the Muses / PIERIA
birthplace of Orpheus / PIERIA
birthright / HERITAGE; PATRIMONY
birthwort / PIPEVINE; CLEMATITE
bis / AGAIN; ENCORE
biscuit / BUN; RUSK; COOKIE; CRACKER
bishop / PONTIFF, PRELATE, PRI-MATE
bishop in chess / ALFIL; LAUFER
bishop of Rome / POPE
bishopric / SEE; DIOCESE
bishop's cap / HURA; ZUCCHETTO

bishop's headdress / MITER, MITRE
bishop's move / DIAGONAL
bishop's office / SEE; LAWN
bishop's region / SEE; DIOCESE
bishop's robe / ALB; COPE; CHI-MAR, ROCHET; GREMIAL
bishop's staff / CROSIER
bishop's title / ABBA
bison / WISENT; AUROCHS, BUF-FALO
bit / ACE; DROP, MITE, WHIT; SCRAP; MORSEL; SNAFFLE
bite / CUT, EAT, NIP; CHOP, GRIP, SNAP. MORSEL
bite the dust / DIE; LOSE
bite gently / NIBBLE
biter / CHEAT
biting / ACID; ACRID, SHARP
bitingly ironic / ACERB; SARCASTIC
bito tree oil / ZACHUN
bits / ANA
bitt / BOLLARD
bitter / HARD, WILD; ACERB, ACRID, CRUEL
bitter bark / NIEPA, NIOTA
bitter drug / ALOES; QUASSIA
bitter feeling / HATRED
bitter herb / RUE; GENTIAN; CEN-TAURY
bitter vetch / ERS
bitter water / MARAH
bitterly scornful / SARDONIC
bittern / HERON; KAKKAK; STAKE-DRIVER
bitterness / ACOR; RANCOR; RE-MORSE
bittern's cry / BILL, BOOM
bittersweet / DULCAMARA
bitumen / TAR; PITCH; ASPHALT
bivalve / CLAM; MUSSEL, OYSTER, PECTEN; MOLLUSK, SCALLOP
bivouac / CAMP; ENCAMPMENT
bizarre / ODD; OUTRE; QUAINT
Bizet opera / CARMEN
black / JET; DARK, EBON, INKY; MURKY, RAVEN, SABLE, SOOTY. NEGRO
black, c.f. / ATRO; MELAN; MELANO
black alloy / NIELLO
black art / MAGIC; NECROMANCY
black astringent / KATH
black and blue / LIVID
black and blue area / BRUISE
black cat / FAMILIAR
black cuckoo / ANI
black diamond / COAL
black drink / YAUPON
black earth / CHERNOZEM
black eye / SHINER
black gang / STOKERS
black garnet/ MELANITE

black goldfish / MOOR
black grain / URD
black gum / TUPELO; PEPPERIDGE
black hand / CAMORRA
black haw / SLOE
black hematite / PSILOMELANE
black hole / DUNGEON
Black Jack / PERSHING
black magic / SORCERY; NECRO-
  MANCY
black marble / LUCULITE
black mark / GIG; DEMERIT
black mineral / JET; COAL
black nightshade / MOREL;
  DUSCLE
black ocher / WAD; WADD
black pine / MIRO; LOBLOLLY
Black Plague / BUBONIC
black rhinoceros / BORELE
black rock / BASALT, GALENA
Black Sea / EUXINE
Black Sea peninsula / CRIMEA
Black Sea port / VARNA; ADESSA
black shirt / FASCIST
black silver / STEPHANITE
black snake / RACER
black substance / TAR; COAL,
  SOOT; PITCH
black suit / CLUBS; SPADES
black tea / BOHEA, PEKOE
black tern / DARR
black vulture / URUBU
black wood / EBONY
black-backed gull / COB
blackball / REJECT
blackberry / BRAMBLE, OLALLIE
blackbird / ANI, DAW; CROW,
  MERL, ROOK; MERLE, OUZEL,
  RAVEN; JACKDAW, REDWING;
  STARLING. SLAVE; SHANGHAI
blackbirder / SLAVER
blackboard / SLATE
blackbreast / DUNLIN
blackbuck / SASIN
blackcap / CHICKADEE
blacken / LOWER; DARKEN, DE-
  FAME, MALIGN
black-eyed susan/ OXEYE
blackface performer / MINSTREL
black-fin snapper / SESI
blackfish / TAUTOG
blackguard / RASCAL; VILLAIN
blackjack / COSH; SANDBAG;
  TWENTYONE
blackleg / SCAB
blackmail / EXTORTION
blackout / SKIT; FAINT; ECLIPSE
blacksmith / FARRIER
blacksmith's shop / FORGE;
  SMITHY
blacksmith's tool / ANVIL, SWAGE
blacktail fish / DASSY, RUFFE

black-tailed gazelle / GOAL
blackthorn fruit / HAW; SLOE
black-white mixture / GRAY, GREY;
  MULATTO
blackwort / COMFREY
blade / OAR; BEAU, LEAF; SWORD
blade of grass / SPEAR; LAMINA
blah / BUNK; NONSENSE. ILL
blain / BLISTER, PUSTULE
blamable / CULPABLE; REPREHEN-
  SIBLE
blame / ACCUSE; CENSURE, CON-
  DEMN. REPROOF; DISAPPROVAL
blameless / PURE; SINLESS; INNO-
  CENT
blanch / SCALD; BLEACH, WHITEN
bland / MILD, OPEN, SOFT; SUAVE
blank / BARE, VOID; EMPTY
blanket / RUG; COVER, QUILT; AF-
  GHAN
blanket cloak / PONCHO, SERAPE
blankness / NEGATION
blare / BLAST; BELLOW, BLAZON
blare of trumpet / FANFARE, TAN-
  TARA
blarney / HUMBUG; FLATTERY
blase / BORED, SATED
blaspheme / CURSE, SWEAR; RE-
  VILE
blasphemy / CURSE; PROFANITY
blast / BLOW, KILL, RUIN, SEAR;
  BURST. GALE, GUST; STORM;
  TEMPEST
blast furnace / SMELTER
blast furnace part / BOSH; TUYERE
blast of horn / TOOT; BLARE
blasted / BARREN, DAMNED
blasting explosive / TNT; TONITE;
  DYNAMITE
blatant / NOISY; GARISH, VULGAR
blather / BLEAT; BABBLE
blatherskite / CHATTERER. WORTH-
  LESS
blaubok / ETAAC
blaze / FLAME, FLARE, GUIDE.
  MARK
blazer / JACKET
blazing / AFIRE; BURNING
blazon / DISPLAY; EMBELLISH
blazoned / BLARED; PROCLAIMED
bleach / WHITEN; ETOLIATE
bleach in light / SUN
bleaching ingredient / HYPO;
  CHLORIDE
bleaching vat / KEIR, KIER
bleak / RAW; BARE, COLD; DREAR
bleak plain / TUNDRA
blear / DIM; BLUR
bleariness / LIPPITUDE
bleat / BLAT; WHINE. BAA
bleb / BULLA; BUBBLE; BLISTER
bleed / HURT, OOZE, TRIM

bleeding / HEMORRHAGE, PHLE-BOTOMY

bleeding heart / WAHOO; DO-GOODER

blemish / DIM, MAR; BLOT, BLUR, SCAR, SOIL, SPOT; SPECK, STAIN, SULLY. FLAW; FAULT; MACULA

blemish in cloth / AMPER

blench / QUAIL; FLINCH

blend / MIX; FUSE; MERGE, UNITE; MINGLE

blend of light and shadow / PEN-UMBRA; CHIAROSCURO

blend thoroughly / MARRY

blennylike fish / EELPOUT

bless / SAIN; ANELE, EXTOL; BENTSH, HALLOW, PRAISE; PROTECT

blessed / HOLY; BLEST, HAPPY

blessed event / BABY; BIRTH

blessedness / JOY; BLISS; DE-LIGHT, ECSTASY

blessing / BOON; GRACE; BENISON

blight / NIP; WITHER. SMUT

blind / EYELESS, OBSCURE; HEED-LESS. SHADE; SCREEN; BLINKER, SHUTTER. SEEL

blind alley / IMPASSE; CULDESAC

blind cetacean / SUSU

blind the eyes / SEEL; HOODWINK

blind god / HODER, HODUR

blind impulse / ATE

blind street / DEADEND

blinded / SHADED; BENIGHTED

blindness / CECITY; IGNORANCE

blink / BAT; WINK; GLIMMER

bliss / JOY; GLEE; RAPTURE

blissful / HAPPY; EDENIC; ELYSIAN

blissful place / EDEN; PARADISE

blissful state / RAPTURE; FELICITY

blister / SCORCH. BLEB, BLOB, SORE; BULLA

blithe / GAY; MERRY, RIANT; JOC-UND

blithesome / JOYOUS; SPORTIVE

blitz / REDDOG; OVERPOWER

blizzard / BLAST, STORM

bloat / DISTEND, INFLATE

bloated / TUMID; TURGID; SWOL-LEN

blob / BUBBLE; BLISTER, GLOBULE

block / BAR, DAM; STOP. NOG; FATHEAD; SCAFFOLD

block by overcrowding / CONGEST

block to stop wheel / SKID, TRIG

block up / BAR, DAM

block of wood / BUST, LOON; CHOCK

blockade / BESIEGE; OBSTRUCT. PEN

blockage / DAM

blockbuster / BOMB

blockhead / ASS, OAF; DOLT, LOUT, MOME; BOOBY, DUNCE; DUL-LARD; NUMSKULL

blockhouse / FORT

bloke / CHAP, TOFF

blond / FAIRHEADED

blood / GORE, RAKE; BLADE; TEM-PER; LINEAGE

blood, c.f. / HEM; HAEM, HEMO; HAEMO

blood, pert. to / HEMAL, HEMIC; HAEMAL, HAEMIC

blood ailment / ANEMIA; HEMO-PHILIA

blood clot / THROMBUS

blood deficiency condition / ANEMIA

blood factor / RH

blood feud / VENDETTA

blood fluid / SERUM; PLASMA

blood of gods / ICHOR

blood horse / THOROUGHBRED

blood money / CRO; GALANAS

blood part / FIBRIN; PLATELET

blood poisoning / PYEMIA; SEP-TICEMIA

blood relative / KIN, SIB

blood vessel / VEIN; AORTA; AR-TERY

blood vessel, pert. to / VENOUS; ARTERIAL

blood-curdling / GHASTLY; TERRI-FYING

bloodhound / LYAM, LYME; HUN-TER, JAVERT

bloodhound's ancestor / TALBOT

bloodily / CRUELLY

bloodless / PALE; ANEMIC

bloodlessness / ANEMIA

blood-letting / PHLEBOTOMY

bloodlike / HEMATOID

bloodshed / CARNAGE; BUTCHERY

bloodsucker / LEECH; EXTORTION-IST

bloodsucking animal / LEECH

bloodsucking insect / BEDBUG; MOSQUITO

bloodsucking monster / LAMIA; VAMPIRE

bloodsucking parasite / TICK

bloodthirsty / GORY; CRUEL; SAV-AGE

bloody / GORY; SANGUINARY

bloom / BUD; FUZZ, GLOW; FLUSH, FLOWER; BLOSSOM

blooming / ROSY; RADIANT

Bloomsbury habitué / WOOLF; KEYNES

blossom / BLOW; BLOOM; FLOWER

blot / MAR; BLUR, FOUL, SPOT. BLEMISH

blot out / OBLITERATE

blotch / BLOB, MESS; STAIN. DAUB; MOTTLE

blouse / MIDDY, SMOCK, WAIST

blouse ruffle / JABOT

blow / BRAG, GUST, PANT, PUFF, WAFT; BLAST, IMPEL. RAP; COUP, CRIG, GALE, ONER, SLAP, SWAT; KNOCK, THUMP

blow air through nose / SNORE, SNORT

blow a horn / HONK, TOOT

blow intermittently / FLAW, GUST,

blow up / EXPLODE, INFLATE

blowfish / PUFFER

blowfly / BLUEBOTTLE

blowhard / WINDBAG; BRAGGART

blowhole / NOSTRIL; SPIRACLE

blowout / FLAT; PARTY, SPREE

blowpipe / BLOWGUN

blubber / WEEP. FAT; LARD

blubber strip / LIPPER

blubber stripper / FLENSER

bludgeon / BAT; CLUB; BILLY; CUDGEL; TRUNCHEON

blue / SAD; AZURE; UNHAPPY; DE-PRESSED

blue bird / JAY

blue blood / ARISTOCRAT

blue book / GUIDE; DIRECTORY

blue color / AQUA, BICE, NAVY; SMALT; COBALT; PEACOCK, PHTHALO; CERULEAN; ULTRA-MARINE

blue dye / WOAD; INDIGO

blue eagle / NRA

blue gas / OZONE

blue glass / SMALT

blue gray / MERLE, PEARL, SLATE

blue greenish / CYAN, SAXE, TEAL

Blue Grotto's site / CAPRI

blue ground / KIMBERLITE

blue gum / EUCALYPTUS

Blue Hen state / DELAWARE

blue jeans / LEVIS; DUNGAREES

blue jeans material / DENIM

blue john / FLUORITE; FLUORSPAR

blue moon / NEVER

Blue Nile source / TANA

blueback / TROUT; HERRING

Bluebeard's wife / FATIMA

blueberry dessert / PIE

bluebird as metaphor / HAPPINESS

bluebonnet / LUPINE

bluebottle / BLOWFLY; CORN-FLOWER

blue-chip / SECURE; QUALITY

bluecoat / SAILOR; POLICEMAN

bluefin / TUNA

bluefish / SAURY; TAILER

bluegill / SUNFISH

bluegrass / POA

Bluegrass state / KENTUCKY

bluejacket / SAILOR

blue-pencil / EDIT

blueprint / PLAN

blues / DUMPS, GLOOM

bluespar / LAZULITE

bluff / RUDE; BLUNT, GRUFF, ROUGH, STEEP, SURLY; ABRUPT, COARSE, CLIFF

bluing / RINSE; INDIGO

bluish semi-precious stone / LAZULI

blunder / ERR; BUNGLE. SLIP; BONER

blunderer / GAZOB

blunt / DULL, RUDE; BLUFF; ABRUPT, OBTUSE; BRUSQUE. DEADEN; STUPEFY

blunted lance head / MORNE

blur / DIM; BLOT; BLEAR, STAIN

blurred / FUZZY; SMUDGED

blurt out / BLAT

blush / BLOOM, FLUSH; REDDEN

blushing / SHY; ROSY

bluster / ROISTER, SWAGGER

blustering / BOLD; BLUFF; IMPO-LITE

blusterous / NOISY, ROUGH

bo tree / FIG; PIPAL

boa / ABOMA, SCART; ANACONDA

boa constrictor / ANACONDA

Boadicea's tribe / ICENI

Boann's lover / DAGDA

Boann's son / ANGUS; OENGUS

boar / HOG; SWINE; BARROW

board / PLANK. EMBARK

board for book cover / MILLBOARD

board game / GO; DRA, TAB; ALEA, DILI, LUDO, MILL, NARD, TAFL, WARI; CHESS, DAJAM, HALMA, SEEGA, SNAKE; MERELS, PA-CHIS, TABLES; MANCALA, PA-CHISI, PATOLLI; CHECKERS, DRAUGHTS, FIDCHELL; BACK-GAMMON

board a plane / ENPLANE

boarder / LODGER, ROOMER

boarding of horses / LIVERY

boardinghouse / LODGINGS

boarish / CRUEL; SWINISH

boast / BRAG; EXALT, VAUNT; GLORIFY

boasted / CROWED

boaster / WINDBAG; BRAGGART

boastful behavior / PARADO; BRA-VADO

boastful talk / GAS; RANT; BLUFF

boasting / BRAGGING, VAUNTING. VAINGLORY

boat / ARK, TUG; DORY, PUNT, SCOW; BARGE, CANOE, SKIFF; CORACLE

boat blade / OAR

boat body / HULL

boat canvas / SAIL
boat channel marker / BUOY
boat with decks cut / RAZEE
boat moorage / MARINA
boat part / AFT, BOW, RIB; DECK, HELM, HULL, KEEL, PROW; STERN; TILLER
boat propeller / OAR; SCREW, WHEEL
boat race / REGATTA
boat song / BARCAROLE
boatman / ROWER; GONDOLIER
boatman of Hades / CHARON
boat's deck / POOP; ORLOP
boat's forward part / BOW; PROW
boat's frame / HULL
boat's rear / STERN
boat's tiller / HELM
boat-shaped / NAVICULAR
boat-shaped clock / NEF
boatswain / BOSUM; JAEGER
boatswain's whistle / PIPE
Boaz' father / SALMON
Boaz' grandson / JESSE
Boas' son / OBED
Boaz' wife / RUTH
bob / SHAKE. FLOAT, PLUMB; PENDANT
bobbery / HUBBUB, TUMULT
bobbin / PIRN, REEL; SPOOL
bobbin's fram / CREEL
bobolink / ORTOLAN; RICEBIRD
bobtail / RABBLE
bobwhite / COLIN, QUAIL; PARTRIDGE
bocardo / DOKMAROK
Boccaccio's book / DECAMERON
boche / HUN; GERMAN
bode / OMEN; AUGUR; PORTEND
bodice / CHOLI, STAYS, WAIST
bodice posy / CORSAGE
bodily / SOMATIC; PHYSICAL
bodily manipulation / RUB; MASSAGE
bodily secretion / BILE; SWEAT
bodkin / AWL, PIN; NEEDLE
body / SOMA; TORSO; CORPSE, LICHAM; SUBSTANCE
body, c.f. / SOMA; SOMATO
body, pert. to / SOMATIC
body that attracts / MAGNET
body bone / RIB; SACRUM; STERNUM
body of cavalry / TROOP
body cavity / SINUS
body of investigators / COMMITTEE
body of Jewish law / TORAH; TALMUD
body joint / HIP
body of jurors / PANEL
body of laws / CODE
body of men / ARMY; FORCE, POSSE, SQUAD

body of Moslem scholars / ULEMA
body organ / LUNG; GLAND, HEART, LIVER
body of an organism / SOMA
body organs / VITALS
body preserved after death / MUMMY
body servant / MAID; VALET
body in solar system / SUN; MOON; COMET; PLANET; SATELLITE
body of soldiers / ARMY; CORPS, SQUAD, TROOP; COMPANY, MILITIA, PHALANX, PLATOON; REGIMENT; BATTALION
body of water / SEA; LAKE, POND, POOL; OCEAN
body as a whole, pert. to / SYSTEMIC
bodyguard / ESCORT; RETINUE
body's trunk / TORSO
Boeotian capital / THEBES
Boeotian region / IONIA
Boer camp / LAAGER
Boer language / TAAL; AFRIKAANS
bog / FEN, SOG; MIRE, QUAG, SINK, SYRT; MARSH, SWAMP; MORASS, MUSKEG
bog down / CONK, FAIL; STALL
bog peat / CESS, MOSS
bog plant / ABAMA
bog product / MOSS, PEAT; CRANBERRY
bogey / BOGIE; ONEOVER; STANDARD
boggart / SPOOK; BUGBEAR
boggle / JILT; BOTCH; HESITATE
boggy / SPONGY; SQUELCHY
bogie / BOGLE; SPECTER; SCARECROW
bogus / FAKE, SHAM; PHONEY
bohemian / GYPSY. UNCONVENTIONAL
Bohemian city / PILSEN
Bohemian dance / REDOWA
Bohemian river / EGER, LABE; MOLDAU
boil / STEW; SEETHE. PUSTULE
boil down / DECOCT, SIMMER
boil on eyelid / STYE
boil slowly / STEW; SIMMER
boiled fruit sirup / ROB
boiled meal / MUSH; CEREAL
boiled rice / CANIN
boiler / TANK; HEATER
boiler patch / SPUT
boiling / HOT; SIZZLING
boisterous / LOUD; NOISY; VIOLENT
boisterous cry / ROAR; OUTCRY
boisterous play / ROMP; HORSEPLAY
Bokhara tribesman / ERSAR
bolas / MISSILE

bold / PERT, RUDE; BRAVE, NERVY, STEEP; BRAZEN, DARING, HEROIC
boldface / HEAVY
bole / STEM; TRUNK
bolero / DANCE; JACKET
"Bolero" composer / RAVEL
Bolivar's birthplace / CARACAS
Bolivia capital / LAPAZ, SUCRE
Bolivian city / ORURO; POTOSI
Bolivian Indian / ITE, URO; ITEN, LECO, MOJO; CHOLO; AYMARA
Bolivian lake / POOPO; TITICACA
Bolivian mountain / ILLIMANI
Bolivian mountains / ANDES
Bolivian river / BENI; GUAPORE
boll / POD; CAPSULE
boll weevil / PICUDO
bolo / KNIFE; MACHETE
bolshevik / RED; LENIN
bolster / AID; SUPPORT. PAD; PROP; PILLOW; CUSHION
bolt / DART, SIFT; BLURT; DEPART, FASTEN, SCREEN. PIN, ROD; LOCK, ROLL; ARROW, RIVET
bolt fastener / NUT; TOGGLE
bomb / ATOM; SHELL; PETARD; GRENADE
bomb hole / PIT; CRATER
bomb thrower / TERRORIST
bombard / SHELL; BATTER, RAFALE, STRAFE
bombarded / ATTACKED
bombast / RANT, RAVE. FUSTIAN
bombastic / TURGID; POMPOUS; INFLATED; HIGHFLOWN
bombproof chamber / SHELTER; CASEMATE
Bona Dea / FAUNA
bona fide / GENUINE
bonanza / MINE; STRIKE, WEALTH
Bonaparte / NAPOLEON
bond / TIE; NEXUS; COVENANT, SECURITY
bondage / SERFDOM, SLAVERY; THRALDOM
bonded / MORTGAGED
bondman / SERF; VASSAL
bondsman / HELOT, SLAVE
bone / OS; RIB; SPINE
bone, c.f. / OSSI, OSTE; OSSEO, OSTEO
bone, pert. to / OSTEAL; OSSEOUS
bone cavity / SINUS; ANTRUM
bone covering / PERIOSTEUM
bone disease / RICKETS
bone doctor / OSTEOPATH
bone at end of spine / COCCYX, SACRUM
bone of finger / PHALANGE
bone of forearm / ULNA; RADIUS
bone of jaw / MANDIBLE

bone of leg / FEMUR, TIBIA
bone of palate / PALATINE
bone scraper / XYSTER
bone of skull / VOMER
bone tissue / MARROW, MEDULLA
bone of upper arm / HUMERUS
bone of upper jaw / MAXILLA
boned fish / FILET; FILLET
boner / FLUB, SLIP; ERROR
bones / DICE; DOMINOES
boneset / COMFREY; AGUEWEED
boneyard / CEMETERY; SCRAPHEAP
bonhomie / FELLOWSHIP
boniface / INNKEEPER
bonito / SKIPJACK
bonne / MAID; NURSE
bonnet / CAP, HAT; HOOD
bonnet monkey / ZATI; MUNGA
bonny / GAY; BLITHE, PRETTY
bonnyclabber / CURD, SKYR
bonus / PREMIUM; DIVIDEND
bony / THIN; OSTEAL; OSSEOUS
bony fish / CARP, SHAD; TELEOST
bony scaled / SCUTE
bonyfish / CHIRO; MENHADEN
bonzer / TOPS; EXCELLENT
boo / HISS, JEER
boob tube / TV; SCREEN
boobook / MOREPORK
booby / FOOL; DUNCE, NODDY; STUPID
booby prize / LOW
booby trap / AMBUSH; PITFALL
boodle / SWAG
boohoo / CRY, SOB; WEEP
book / MO; TOME; LIBER; LEDGER, PRIMER, VOLUME
Book / BIBLE
book of accounts / LEDGER
book collector / BIBLIOPHILE
book cover / CASE; FOREL; FORREL, JACKET
book of devotions / MISSAL
book of extracts / ANTHOLOGY
book with few sheets / BROCHURE, PAMPHLET
book of fiction / NOVEL
book of the gospel / JOHN, LUKE, MARK; MATTHEW
Book of Hours / HORA
book jacket description / BLURB
book of Jewish law / TORAH; TALMUD; MISHNAH
book of the largest size / FOLIO
book list / BIBLIOGRAPHY
book louse / PSOCID
book lover / BIBLIOPHILE
book in manuscript / CODEX; CODICES
book of maps / ATLAS
book of nobility / PEERAGE

book palm / TARA; TALIERA

book part / LEAF, PAGE; CHAPTER, PREFACE, SECTION; APPENDIX

book of personal comments / DIARY; COMMONPLACE

book used by priest / BREVIARY

book of psalms / PSALTER

book of rubrics / ORDO

book salesman / COLPORTER

book for school / TEXT; PRIMER

book section / CHAPTER

book slipcase / FOREL

book thief / BIBLIOKLEPT

bookbinder's fabric / SUPER; BUCKRAM

bookbinder's shop / BINDERY

bookbinding / BIBLIOPEGY

bookbinding style / YAPP; FOREL, TRADE

bookbinding tool / KEY, TIP; GAUGE

bookcase / SHELVING

bookkeeping entry / ITEM; DEBIT; CREDIT

bookkeeping summary / LEDGER

booklet / BROCHURE, PAMPHLET

bookmaker / BOOKIE

bookplate / EXLIBRIS

books of Moses / PENTATEUCH

book's physical makeup / FORMAT

bookseller / BIBLIOPOLE

boom / ROAR. SPAR; GROWTH

boom times / UPS; PROSPERITY

boomerang / KILEY. RECOIL

booming / AROAR

boon / GIFT; FAVOR; BLESSING. MERRY; JOVIAL

boon companions / PALS

boondocks / STICKS; HINTERLAND

boor / OAF; CLOD, KERN, LOUT; CHURL; RUSTIC; PEASANT

boorish / DULL, RUDE; ROUGH

boorish person / CLOWN; LUBBER

boost / LIFT, PUSH; HOIST, RAISE

boot / KICK; PROFIT. SHOE; BROGAN

boot hill / CEMETERY

bootes / HERDSMAN

booth / SUQ; LOGE, SOOK, SOUK; STALL, STAND

bootlace / LACET

bootleg liquor / HOOCH

bootlick / FAWN

boots / AVAILS

boots for fishing / WADERS

booty / LOOT, PELF; SPOILS

borax / TINCAL

borax element / BORON

bordeaux wine / MEDOC; CLARET, GRAVES

border / HEM, RIM; EDGE, RAND, SIDE. ABUT; SKIRT

border for a picture / MAT; FRAME

border of plants / PLATBAND

borderland / PALE; MARCH; FRONTIER

bore / IRK, VEX; PALL, TIRE. EAGRE; CALIBER

bore into / EAT; RUST; CORRODE

Boreas' father / ASTRAEUS

Boreas' mother / EOS; AURORA

Boreas' son / ZETES; CALAIS

bored / BLASE, TIRED, WEARY

boredom / ENNUI

borer / BIT; DRILL; PIDDOCK; SHIPWORM

boring / DULL; TEDIOUS

boring implement / AWL, BIT; AUGER, BRACE, DRILL; GIMLET, WIMBLE

born / NEE; NATE; INNATE

born again / RENASCENT

borne / RIDDEN; CARRIED

Borneo country / BRUNEI; SARAWAK

Borneo mountain / KINABULU

Borneo native / DYAK

Borneo pepper / ARA

Borneo primate / GIBBON, SIAMANG; ORANGUTAN

Borneo river / BARITO, RAJANG

Borneo squirrel shrew / PENTAIL

Borneo tribesman / DYAK, IBAN; DAYAK

borough / TOWN; BURGH; VILLAGE

borrow / LOAN; ADOPT; OBTAIN

boscage / SHAW; WOODS; THICKET

bosh / ROT; POOH; HUMBUG

bosom friend / PAL

boss / STUD; FOREMAN, MANAGER

boss of shield / UMBO

bossy / OVERBEARING. COW

Boston / HUB; BEANTOWN

Boston area / BACKBAY

Boston family / CABOT, ELIOT; LOWELL

Boston intellectual / BRAHMIN

Boston suburb / REVERE; BROOKLINE

botanical sac / ASCUS, THECA

botany / WOOL; FLORA

botch / MESS. BUNGLE

both / TWO; PAIR

both, pref. / AMBI; AMPHI

bother / AIL, VEX; BORE; ANNOY, WORRY. ADO; FUSS, TODO

bothersome / PLAGUY; TROUBLESOME

Botswana / BECHUANALAND

Botswana capital / GABORONE

Botswana desert / KALAHARI

Botswana money / RAND

bottle / JAR; VIAL; FLASK; CARAFE; DECANTER

bottle of glass / VIAL; CARAFE

bottle of leather / OLPE
bottle for liquids / CARBOY
bottle for oil / CRUET, FLASK
bottle stopper / CAT, TOP; CORK
bottle top / CAP
bottle tree / KURRAJONG
bottle for vinegar / CRUET
bottled drink / POP
bottle-nosed dolphin / PORPOISE
bottom / BASE, FOOT, ROOT; BASIS
bottom of foot / SOLE
bottom of ship / KEEL
bottomless gulf / ABYSS
bottomless pit / ABADDON
bouchal / BOY
bouffant / FULL; PUFFED
bough / LIMB; BRANCH
boughs of tree / RAMAGE
boulevard / DRIVE; AVENUE
bounce / LEAP; SPRING; REBOUND,
VIGOR; BLUSTER
bounced / FIRED
bound / JUMP, LEAP; SPRING; CON-
FINE, BASE; AMBIT, LIMIT; BOR-
DER, HELD, TIED
bound hand and foot / TIEDUP
bound to succeed / SUREFIRE
bound by a vow / VOTARY
boundary / METE, SIDE; LIMIT;
MARGIN
boundary, c.f. / OR; ORI
bounder / CAD; KNAVE
bounding area / FRINGE, MARGIN
bounding line / SIDE; LIMIT
bounding main / SEA; OCEAN
boundless / INFINITE; UNLIMITED
bounds / AMBIT; COMPASS
bounteous / LIBERAL; MUNIFICENT
bountiful / AMPLE; PROFUSE;
ABUNDANT
bounty / GIFT; BONUS; REWARD
bouquet / POSY; AROMA, SPRAY;
NOSEGAY
bourdon / WAND; BATON, STAFF;
CUDGEL
bourn / GOAL; BOUND, BROOK;
STREAM
bourock / HEAP; MOUND
bousy / DRUNKEN; BESOTTED
bout / ESSAY, SETTO, TRIAL; CON-
TEST
bout of pleasure / FLING
boutonniere / BOUQUET; BUTTON-
HOLE
bovine / DULL; STOLID
bovine animal / OX; COW, YAK;
ANOA, BULL, GAUR, ZEBU;
BISON, STEER
bovine quadrupeds / OXEN; CATTLE
bovine sound / MOO
bow / NOD; BEND; STOOP. PROW;
CURVE

bower / ARBOR, KNAVE; RECESS;
RETREAT
bowfin / MUDFISH
bowing / RAKA; OBEISANCE
bowl / BASIN; CRATER, TUREEN;
STADIUM
bowl in cricket / GOOGLY, SWERVE,
YORKER
bowler / DERBY
bowlike curve / ARC; ARCH
bowling game / BOCCIE; TENPINS;
SKITTLES
bowling green / RINK
bowling lane / ALLEY
bowling term / SPARE, SPLIT; GUT-
TER, STRIKE
bowman / ARCHER
box / SPAR. CASE, LOGE; CRATE,
CHEST
box for alms / ARCA
box elder / MAPLE
box opener / PRY; CHISEL; PAN-
DORA
box for packing / KIT; CASE;
CRATE
box sleigh / POD; PUNG; CARIOLE
box for tea / CANISTER
boxed / ENCASED
boxer / DOG; FIGHTER; PUGILIST
boxing / RING
boxing using the feet / SAVATE
boxing match / BOUT, MILL; FIGHT
boxing term / KO; JAB, TKO; BOLO
boxwood tree / SERON
boy / BUB, BUD, LAD, SON, TAD;
YOUTH
boy friend / BEAU; ESCORT
Boy Scout award / MERITBADGE
Boy Scout convention / JAMBOREE
Boy Scout past 18 / SCOUTER
Boy Scout unit / TROOP
boyhood / YOUTH
boyish / PUERILE
boys' author / ALGER, HENTY
boys in blue / ELIS; SAILORS
boy's toy / TOP; KITE, YOYO
B.P.O.E. member / ELK
brabble / BRAWL; DISPUTE,
WRANGLE
brace / PAIR, PROP; TRUSS; SUP-
PORT
brace with sticks / ROD
bracelet / ARMLET
bracer / TONIC; PICKMEUP
braces / SUSPENDERS
bracket candlestick / SCONCE
bract of grass flower / GLUME,
LEMMA, PALEA, PALET;
VALVULE
brad / NAIL
brae / CLEVE; HILLSIDE
brag / CROW; BOAST, VAUNT

braggadocio / BOASTER; BRAGGART

braggart / SNORTER, WINDBAG

Bragi's wife / IDUN; ITHUN

Brahma / ATMAN

Brahman precept / SUTRA

Brahman title / AYA

Brahmany bull / ZEBU

Brahma's son / DAKSHA

Brahma's wife / SARASVATI

braid / CUE; PLAT; LACET, PLAIT, QUEUE, TRESS. WEAVE

braided loop in clothing / FROG

braided thong / ROMAL

brain / MIND; INTELLECT; INTELLIGENCE. BASH

brain, pert. to / CEREBRAL

brain box / PAN; SKULL

brain canal / ITER

brain groove / SULCUS

brain layer / OBEX; CORTEX

brain matter / ALBA

brain membrane / TELA

brain neoplasm / GLIOMA

brain part / PIA; LOBE, PONS

brain wave / IDEA; THOUGHT

brainy / WISE; ACUTE, SHARP, SMART

brake / FERN; BRUSH; THICKET

brake part / DRUM, SHOE

braky / ROUGH; THORNY; BRAMBLY

brambly / THORNY; PRICKLY

bran / CHAFF, HUSKS

branch / ARM; LIMB, RAME, TWIG; BOUGH. DIVIDE, RAMIFY

branch, pert. to / RAMAL; RAMOSE; RAMULOSE

branch of antler / PRONG

branch of the sea / ARM

branch of track / SIDING

branched / RAMOSE, RAMOUS; RAMIFIED

branched candlestick / MENORAH; CANDELABRA; CANDELABRUM

branches / ARMS, RAMI

branchiae / GILLS

branching ornament / SPRAY; BOUQUET

brand / TAB; KIND, MARK; STAMP; STIGMA. SEAR; DENOUNCE

branded / NAMED; GRADED

brandish / WIELD; FLAUNT; FLOURISH

brand-new / UNUSED

brandy / COGNAC

brandy from grape pomace / MARC

brandy and soda / PEG

Bran's brother / MANAWYDDAN

Bran's father / LLYR

Bran's sister / BRANWEN

Bran's son / CARADOC

brash / BOLD; SAUCY; IMPUDENT

brass / WHEELS; BIGWIGS

brass hat / GENERAL, OFFICER

brass instrument / HORN, TUBA; BUGLE; CORNET; TROMBONE

brass man / TALOS, TALUS

brassbound / RIGID

brassie / TWOWOOD

brassy / BRAZEN; IMPUDENT

brat / IMP; CHILD

brattle / RATTLE; SCAMPER

bravado / BLUSTER; DEFIANCE

brave / BOLD; STOUT; DARING. DARE, DEFY. HERO; WARRIOR

brave man / HERO

bravo / OLE

bravura / BRILLIANCE

braw / FINE, GOOD; HANDSOME

brawl / ROW; FRAY, RIOT; MELEE; FRACAS

brawny / HARD; TOUGH; ROBUST, SINEWY

bray / HEEHAW

brayer / PESTLE; SPREADER

brazen / PERT; NERVY, SAUCY

Brazil capital / RIO; BRASILIA

Brazilian armadillo / TATU; TATOU

Brazilian bird / ARA; AGAMI; SERIEMA

Brazilian city / MANAUS, RECIFE; SANTAREM

Brazilian club moss / PILLIGAN

Brazilian composer / VILLALOBOS

Brazilian dance / SAMBA

Brazilian drink / ASSAI

Brazilian fish / PIABA

Brazilian flycatcher / YETAPA

Brazilian forest / SELVA

Brazilian grassland / CAMPO

Brazilian Indian / GE; YAO; ACRO, CAME, DIAU, MAKU, MURA, PURI, TUPI; ANDOA, ARAUA, CARIB, GUANA, SIUSI

Brazilian macaw / ARARA; MARACAN

Brazilian mammal / TAPIR

Brazilian money / REI; MILREIS; CRUZEIRO

Brazilian monkey / GUARIBA

Brazilian novelist / MACHADO

Brazilian palm / JUPATI

Brazilian parrot / ARA

Brazilian plant / CAROA

Brazilian plateau / MATOGROSSO

Brazilian product / COFFEE, RUBBER

Brazilian river / APA, ICA; PARA; AMAZON

Brazilian rubber tree / ULE; PARA

Brazilian seaport / RIO; PARA; BAHIA, BELEM, CEARA, NATAL; RECIFE, SANTOS

Brazilian snake / JARARACA
Brazilian tree / APA; ANDA; ARA-ROBA, GUARABU
Brazilian waterfall / IGUAZU; IGUASSU
Brazil's discoverer / CABRAL
breach / GAP; RENT; FRACTURE
breach of etiquette / SOLECISM
bread / BUN; LOAF, PONE, ROLL
bread of affliction / MATZOS
bread basket / STOMACH
bread and butter / LIVELIHOOD
bread end / HEEL
bread from heaven / MANNA
bread mixed with milk / PANADA
bread mold / ERGOT; PENICILLIUM
bread part / CRUST, SLICE
bread pudding / RANDA
bread shovel / PEEL
bread slicer / KNIFE
bread spread / JAM; OLEO; JELLY; BUTTER
bread steeped in broth / BREWIS
bread variety / RYE; CORN; BLACK, WHEAT; RAISIN
bread and wine / EUCHARIST
breadfruit / RIMA; AFFON; CASTANA; SCREWPINE
breadwinner / SUPPORTER
break / DAWN, OPEN, REND, SNAP, TAME, TEAR; BURST, CRACK, PAUSE, SEVER, SMASH. GAP; RIFT; CHASM
break apart / DISRUPT, SHATTER
break asunder / RIVE
break away / FLEE; ESCAPE
break in boy's voice / PONTICELLO
break contact / PART
break of day / DAWN
break even / TIE; DRAW
break a hole in / STAVE
break in / INURE, TRAIN
break in illegally / FORCE
break in upon / INTERRUPT
break off / END; SNAP; ADJOURN
break out / RASH. ERUPT
break phone connection / HANGUP
break suddenly / POP; SNAP
break up / LAUGH; DISBAND, SHATTER
break without warning / SNAP
break one's word / RENEGE
breakable / BRITTLE, FRAGILE
breakbone fever / DENGUE
breaker of images / ICONOCLAST
breakers / SURF
breakfast dish / EGG; BACON, TOAST; CEREAL; PANCAKES
breakfast roll / BUN
breaking forth / ERUPTIVE
breakstone / CALCULUS
breakwater / COB; MOLE, PIER; JETTY

bream / SCUP; SHINER; SUNFISH
breastbone / RIB; STERNUM
breastbone, pert. to / STERNAL
breast-feeding animal / MAMMAL
breastplate / URIM; ARMOR, EPHOD; THORAX
breastplate for lance rest / FAUCRE
breastwork / REDAN; PARAPET
breath / AIR; WIND
breath, c.f. / SPIRO
breath of life / SOUL; PRANA
breathe / LIVE; RESPIRE
breathe in / INHALE
breathe noisily in sleep / SNORE
breathe out / EXHALE
breathe quickly / GASP, PANT
breathed / SPIRATE; ASPIRATE, RESPIRED
breather / REST
breathing / RALE; STRIDOR; RESPIRING
breathing organ / LUNG
breathing orifice / SPIRACLE
breathing place / PAUSE
breathless / WINDED; PANTING
bred / RAISED, REARED
bred by hand / CADE
brede / EMBROIDERY
breechcloth / CLOUT, DIAPER
breeches / TREWS; BRITCHES, TROUSERS
breed / BEAR, REAR; BEGET, HATCH, RAISE. ILK; LINE, RACE; FAMILY
breed of cattle / ANGUS, DEVON; JERSEY
breed of chicken / BANTAM; DOMINICKER
breed of dog / POM, PUG; CHOW, DANE; COLLIE
breed of draft horse / SHIRE; PERCHERON
breed of sheep / MERINO
breed of swine / SPOT; DUROC; TAMWORTH
breeding / MANNERS, REARING; TRAINING
breeze / AURA, WIND; ZEPHYR
brehon / JUDGE; LAWYER
Brennus' dictum / VAEVICTIS
Bres' wife / BRIG
Breton poet / PROUX
breve / SHORT
brevet / PATENT; LICENSE, WARRANT
breviary / TOTUM; PORTAS
brevity / ECONOMY; TERSENESS
brew / ALE; BEER; LAGER. CON-COCT
brewer's grain / CORN, MALT; BARLEY
brewer's refuse / DRAFF
brewer's vat / TUN; KEEL

brewer's yeast / BARM
brewing / GAAL, GAIL, GYLE
brewing agent / HOPS, MALT; YEAST
Briareus' brother / GYES; COTTUS
bric-a-brac / CURIO; TRINKET
bric-a-brac stand / ETAGERE, WHATNOT
brick / TILE; ADOBE; EXEMPLAR
brick carrier / HOD
brick oven / KILN; FURNACE
brick refuse / SAMEL; SANDAL
brick of wood / NOG; DOOK
brickbat / DORNICK, MISSILE
brick-binding material / MORTAR
bricklayer / MASON
bricklayer's tool / TROWEL
bridal bed / MARRIAGE
bride / WIFE; NEWLYWED
bride of the sea / VENUS
bridegroom / BENEDICT
bridegroom's gift to the bride / HANDSEL
bridesman / GROOMSMAN
Bridewell / GAOL; PRISON
bridge / SPAN; CANTILEVER
bridge bid / PASS, SLAM; DOUBLE; REDOUBLE
bridge builder / PONTIST; ENGINEER
bridge convention / BLACKWOOD
bridge framework / TRESTLE
bridge over highway / OVERPASS
bridge holding / TENACE
bridge maneuver / FINESSE
bridge player's aim / LEG; GAME; RUBBER
bridge predecessor / WHIST
bridge over ravine / VIADUCT
bridge suit / TRUMPS
bridge type / BASCULE; CANTILEVER
bridge of violin / MAGAS
bridle / BIT; GUIDE. RESTRAIN
bridle without a bit / HACKAMORE
bridle strap / CAVESSON
bridoon / SNAFFLE
brie / CHEESE
brief / CURT; SHORT, TERSE; CONCISE. WRIT; EPITOME
brief comic sketch / SKIT
brief introduction / PROEM
brief news item / FLASH
brief quotation / SNIP; SNIPPET
brief story / CONTE
brief summary / PRECIS
brier / PIPE; BRIAR, THORN
brig / CELL, COOP, JAIL
brigand / BANDIT, PIRATE, ROBBER
bright / APT; KEEN, ROSY; ACUTE, ALERT, CLEAR, LUCID, NITID, RIANT, SMART, WITTY

bright colored / RED
bright glow / GLARE
bright star / SUN; NOVA, VEGA; RIGEL, SPICA; ALTAIR, SIRIUS; ANTARES, CANOPUS, CAPELLA, PROCYON; ACHERNAR, ARCTURUS; ALDEBARAN
bright unsteady light / FLARE
bright witty thought / MOT; EPIGRAM
brightened / LIT
brightest star in constellation / ALPHA
brightly / BRISKLY
brightly colored fish / OPAH
brightly colored monkey / MANDRILL
bright-topped bird / REDHEAD
Brigit's father / DAGDA
Brigit's husband / BRES
brilliancy / ECLAT; SPLENDOR
brilliant / BRIGHT, FAMOUS; SPLENDID
brilliant bird / ORIOLE, TROGON; TANAGER
brilliant fish / OPAH; WRASSE; CATALINA
brim / LIP; EDGE; BRINK
brimful / OVERFLOWING
brimless cap / FEZ, TAM; TOQUE
brimming / WATERY; TEARFUL
brimstone / SULFUR; SULPHUR
brindled / SPOTTED; STREAKED
brine / BRACK; PICKLE
brine pit / WYCH
bring / DRAW; CARRY, FETCH; CONVEY
bring about / CAUSE; OCCASION
bring from abroad / IMPORT
bring back / RETURN; RESTORE
bring bad luck / HEX; HOODOO
bring charges against / SUE; ACCUSE, DELATE
bring to a close / END; STOP; TERMINATE
bring to completion / FINISH
bring into conflict / ENGAGE
bring as a consequence / ENTAIL
bring into court / SUE; ARRAIGN
bring down / FELL; DEFEAT
bring into equilibrium / POISE; STEADY
bring into existence / CREATE; ORIGINATE
bring forth / EAN; BEAR
bring into harmony / TUNE; TUNEUP
bring to life again / REVIVE
bring to mind / RECALL, REMIND; REMEMBER
bring on / INCUR; INDUCE; CONDUCT
bring out / ELICIT; PUBLISH

bring into play / USE
bring into a row / TRUE; ALIGN, ALINE
bring to standstill / HALT, STOP; STALL
bring together / UNITE; COMPILE; ASSEMBLE
bring up / REAR; RAISE; FOSTER
brink / RIM; EDGE; VERGE; MARGIN
briny deep / SEA; OCEAN
brioche / ROLL; SAVARIN
Briseis' master / ACHILLES
brisk / LIVE, SPRY; AGILE, FRESH, QUICK
briskly / SNAPPILY; SPRIGHTLY
bristle / AWN; SETA; CHAETA
bristle, **pert. to** / SETAL
bristly / HISPID, SETOSE
Britain / UK; ALBION
Britain personified / BRITANNIA
British / See also English
British bailiff / REEVE
British bar / PUB; LOCAL
British composer / ARNE; ELGAR; COATES
British conservative / TORY
British Guiana / GUYANA
British Guiana hardwood / KAKARALI; MONKEYPOT
British Guiana river / POTARO; DEMERARA
British gun / STEN
British hereditary title / DUKE; BARON; PRINCE; BARONET
British herring measure / CRAN
British Honduras / BELIZE
British Honduras capital / BELMOPAN
British India / RAJ
British island / MAN; WIGHT; SHEPPEY
British Isles inhabitant / SCOT; COCKNEY; WELSHMAN
British king / LUD; BRAN, BRUT, CNUT, KNUT, LEAR; ARTHUR, BLADUD, CANUTE; ARTEGAL, BELINUS
British legislator / MP
British machine gun / BREN
British money / CROWN, PENCE, POUND; GUINEA, TANNER; HA-PENNY; SHILLING; HALFPENNY
British poet / GRAY; AUDEN, BY-RON, CAREW, DONNE, ELIOT; DAVIES
British princess / ANNE
British prison / GOAL
British queen / BESS, MARY; ANNE
British royal house / YORK; TUDOR
British sailor / LIMEY
British sculptor / EPSTEIN

British soldier / TOMMY
British Solomons island / SAVO; RENDOVA; CHOISEUL; GUADAL-CANAL; VELLALAVELLA
British spa / BATH; MARGATE
British spy / ANDRE
Britisher / BRETON
Britomartis' pursuer / MINOS
Brittany / ARMORICA
brittle / CRISP, FRAIL; FRAGILE
brittle cookie / SNAP
broach / AWL; SPIT; SPIKE; SKEWER
broad / OPEN, VAST, WIDE; AMPLE, LARGE
broad, c.f. / PLAT; PLATY
broad band / BAR; FESS; STRIPE
broad flat piece in back of chair / SPLAT
broad hill / LOMA; LOMITA
broad neck scarf / ASCOT, SHAWL
broad piece of cloth / SHEET
broad pronunciation / DRAWL; PLATEASM
broad smile / GRIN
broad thoroughfare / AVENUE; HIGHWAY; BOULEVARD
broadbill / DUCK; SCAUP
broadcast / SOW; SHOUT; TRANS-MIT
broadcasting / RADIO
broaden / WIDEN; SPREAD
broadly inclusive / GENERAL
broadminded / OPEN; FRANK
broadside / SALVO; VOLLEY; THROWAWAY
broadsword / GLAIVE; CLAYMORE
Broadway hit / SMASH; SUCCESS
Broadway sign / SRO
Brobdingnagian / GIGANTIC
brogue / ACCENT, BROGAN
broil / BRAWL, GRILL; QUARREL, FRAY
broke / BANKRUPT
broken / PATCHY; CRUSHED; IMPERFECT
broken marriage / DIVORCE
broken paper / CASSE
broken pottery / SHERD; POTS-HERD
brokenhearted / STRICKEN; INCON-SOLABLE
broker / AGENT; FACTOR; REALTOR
broker's fee / AGIO; COMMISSION
bromide / BANALITY; PLATITUDE
Bronx cheer / RAZZ; RASPBERRY
bronze / TAN; SCULPTURE
bronze coating / PATINA
bronze coin / AES, AVO, MIL, ORE, PIE, SEN; CENT, PICE; GROSZ
bronze variety / LATTEN

brooch / PIN; CLASP
brood / SIT; HATCH; PONDER. SET; NIDE, TEAM
brood of pheasants / NYE
brook / BEAR; ABIDE. RUN; BURN, RILL
broom / BRUSH; BARSOM
broom plant / SPART
broom of twigs / BESOM
broth / SOUP; BOUILLON
brothel keeper / MADAM
brother / FRA; FRIAR; FELLOW, FRATER
brother, c.f. / FRAT; ADELPHO
brother of husband / LEVIR
Brother Jonathan / UNCLESAM
brother of Moses / AARON
brother of Romulus / REMUS
brotherhood / CLAN; JUNTO; CLIQUE
brotherly / KIND; CORDIAL; FRATERNAL
brought about / CAUSED
brought up / BRED; REARED
brow / FOREHEAD
brow of hill / BRAE, SNAB
brow ridge / GLABELLA
brow of steep place / BRIM, EDGE
browbeat / BULLY; HECTOR
brown / TAN; SAUTE, TOAST
brown bat / NOCTULE
brown coal / LIGNITE
brown color / TAN; RUSK; SEPIA, TENNE, UMBER; BISTER, RUS-SET, SIENNA, SORREL
brown horse / BAY; ROAN; SORREL; CHESTNUT
brown off / IRE; ANGER, PEEVE
brown paper / KRAFT
brown photographic print / SEPIA
brown pigment / UMBER; BISTER
brown sauce / ROUX
brown shirt / SA; NAZI
brown study / REVERIE
brown in sun / TAN
brown and white / ROAN
brownie / NIS, NIX; NISSE; COOKIE, SPRITE
Browning character / PIPPA
brownish color / DUN, TAN
brownline / VANDYKE; SILVER-PRINT
browse / FEED; GRAZE
bruin / BEAR
bruise / HIT; BRAY; CRUSH, POUND; BATTER, INJURE. WALE; CONTUSION
bruit / RUMOR; REPORT
brunette / DARK
Brunhild's brother / ATLI
Brunhild's daughter / ASLAUG
Brunhild's husband / SIGURD

brunt / ONSET, SHOCK; ATTACK
brush / SKIM; SWEEP. THICKET; SKIRMISH
brush up / CRAM; REVIEW
brush wolf / COYOTE
brushing sound / SWISH
brushwood / BRAKE, COPSE, TINET; TINSEL
brusque / CURT; BLUNT; ABRUPT
brut / DRY, SEC
brutal / RUDE; CRUEL, HARSH, ROUGH
brutal fellow / BEAST
brute / BEAST. CRUDE; SAVAGE
brutish / DULL; GROSS; CARNAL, STOLID
bubble / FOAM. BEAD, BLEB
bubbler / CHEAT; DRUMFISH, SWINDLER
buccaneer / PIRATE, ROBBER; CORSAIR
Bucephalus' master / ALEXANDER
buck / MALE; COUNTER; ANTE-LOPE. CHARGE, PLUNGE
bucket / PAIL; SCUTTLE
buckeye / CORNY. OHIOAN
Buckeye state / OHIO
buckle / BEND, JOIN; TWIST, CLASP
buckled / BENT; WARPED
buckler / SHIELD
buckthorn / CASCARA
buckwheat tree / TITI
bucolic / RURAL; RUSTIC; PASTORAL
bud / BLOOM; SPROUT; BURGEON. CION; SHOOT; BLOSSOM
Buddha / FO; AMIDA
Buddha's birthplace / LUMBINI
Buddha's cousin / DEVADATTA
Buddha's early name / SIDDHARTHA
Buddha's family name / GAUTAMA
Buddha's horse / KANTAKA
Buddha's mother / MAYA
Buddha's son / RAHULA
Buddha's squire / ANANDA
Buddha's wife / YASODHARA
Buddhist angel / DEVA
Buddhist church in Japan / TERA
Buddhist city / HASA
Buddhist deity / DEV; DEVA
Buddhist delusion / MOHA
Buddhist demon / MARA
Buddhist fable / JATAKA
Buddhist fate / KARMA
Buddhist festival / BON
Buddhist final state / NIRVANA
Buddhist gateway / TORAN
Buddhist hell / NARAKA
Buddhist law of effect / KARMA

Buddhist literary language / PALI
Buddhist monk / BO; LAMA; ARHAT, BONZE; ARAHAT; TALAPOIN
Buddhist mound / STUPA
Buddhist novice / GOYIN
Buddhist paradise / JODO; GOKURAKU
Buddhist pillar / LAT
Buddhist religious painting / TANKA
Buddhist reliquary / STUPA
Buddhist sacred city / LHASA
Buddhist sacred language / PALI
Buddhist saint / ARHAT, LOHAN
Buddhist sect / ZEN; MAHA, YANA; HINAYANA
Buddhist shrine / DAGOBA
Buddhist temple / VIHARA
Buddhist temple tower / VIMANA
Buddhist title / MAHATMA
buddy / PAL; CHUM; CRONY
budge / STIR
budgie / PARAKEET
buff / POLISH. SKIN
buffalo / OX; ARNA; ARNEE, BISON; WISENT. COW; BULLDOZE
buffalo meat / BILTONG
buffed leather / SUEDE
buffet / BOX; SLAP, TOSS; SMITE. CUPBOARD
buffoon / DOR; MIME, ZANY; CLOWN; MUMMER
bug / MITE; BEDBUG, BEETLE, INSECT
bugaboo / BUGBEAR, SPECTER
bugbear / OGRE; GOBLIN; BUGABOO
buggy / SURREY. CRAZY; PECULIAR
bugle call / TAPS; CHARGE, TATTOO; RETREAT, TANTARA; ASSEMBLY, REVEILLE
bugle sound / MOT; BLARE
bugleweed / INDIGO
build / FORM, MAKE, REAR; ERECT, FRAME
builder / CONTRACTOR
building / HOUSE; EDIFICE
building addition / ELL; WING; ANNEX
building for arms / ARSENAL
building division / ROOM; FLOOR
building for grain / SILO; ELEVATOR
building for horses / STABLE
building lot / PLOT, SITE
building for manufacture / SHOP; FACTORY
building material / STEEL; MORTAR; CONCRETE
building for militia / ARMORY
building mud / ADOBE

building part / ROOF, WING; ATTIC; BASEMENT
built / SHAPED; CONSTRUCTED
built-out window / BAY; ORIEL
Bulgaria capital / SOFIA
Bulgarian city / VARNA; PLOVDIV
Bulgarian king's title / TSAR
Bulgarian money / LEV; STOTINKA
Bulgarian Moslem / POMAK
Bulgarian range / BALKAN; RHODOPE
Bulgarian river / STRUMA; MARITSA
Bulgarian sectary / BOGOMIL
Bulgarian weight / OKA, OKE
Bulgarian writer / VAZOV
bulge / BELLY. BUG
bulimia / HUNGER; VORACITY
bulk / BODY, MASS, SIZE; VOLUME
bulk sales / WHOLESALE
bulkiness / AMPLITUDE
bulky / BIG; LARGE, THICK
bull / COP; NARK; TAURUS
Bull Moose / PROGRESSIVE
bullet / SHOT, SLUG; DUMDUM
bullet size / CALIBER, CALIBRE
bullet sound / PFF, ZIP; SWISH
bulletin / REPORT; ANNOUNCEMENT
bulletproof shelter / ABRI
bullet's bounce / RICOCHET
bullfight / CORRIDA
bullfight cry / OLE
bullfighter / TORERO; MATADOR; TOREADOR
bullfighter on foot / TORERO
bullfighter's cape and rod / MULETA
bullfighter's maneuver / VERONICA
bullfighter's queue / COLETA
bullfinch / ALP, OLP
bullhead / CATFISH
bullheaded / STUPID; OBSTINATE
bull-headed god / MONT; MENTU
bull-like / TAURINE
bullpen / PRISON, RELIEF
bull's-eye / DAISY; TARGET
bully / HECTOR. BRAVO, TOUGH; SWAGGERER. FINE, GOOD
bully tree / BALATA
bullying / BLUSTERING; OVERBEARING
bulrush / TULE; SEDGE; CATTAIL, PAPYRUS
bulwark / BASTION, CITADEL, RAMPART
bum / IDLER; SPONGER
bumbershoot / UMBRELLA
bumble / ERR
bump / JOLT, OUST; THUMP; COLLIDE. SWELLING
bumper / BUFFER; GLASSFUL. SUCCESSFUL

bumpkin / YAP; HICK; CLOWN, YOKEL
bun / WIG; LOAD, ROLL
bunch / WAD; TUFT, WISP; CLUSTER
bunch of flowers / BOUQUET, NOSEGAY
bunch up for leap / CROUCH
bunco / SWINDLE
bundle / ROLL; PARCEL; PACKAGE. HURRY
bundle of grain / SHEAF
bundle of hay / BALE
bundle of sticks / FAGOT
bundled / BALED
bungle / BOTCH; MISMANAGE
bunk / BED, COT. BOSH; HUMBUG
bunt / PUSH; SHOVE
bunting / CIRL; FLAGS; TOWHEE; ORTOLAN
bunting fabric / ETAMINE
buoy / FLOAT; SUPPORT
buoy type / CAN, DAN, NUN, NUT; BELL, SPAR
buoyancy / CHEER; ANIMATION
buoyant / GAY; LIGHT; JOCUND
buoyed goods / LIGAN
buran / STORM; BLIZZARD
burbot / LING, LOTA; EELPOUT
Burchell's zebra / DAUW
burden / LOAD, ONUS; CARGO, DRIFT, TENOR. LADE; CUMBER, IMPEDE
burdensome / HEAVY; WEIGHTY; GRIEVOUS
bureau / AGENCY; DRESSER; DEPARTMENT
burfish / ATINGA
burg / CITY, TOWN; BOROUGH
burgee / FLAG; PENNANT
burgeon / BUD; SPROUT
burglar / YEGG; THIEF; ROBBER
burglar's tool / BAR; JEMMY, JIMMY; PICKLOCK
burial / FUNERAL; INTERMENT
burial case / COFFIN
burial chamber / AHU; VAULT
burial mound / BARROW; TUMULUS
burial pile / PYRE
burlap fiber / HEMP, JUTE
burlesque / FARCE; COMEDY, PARODY; MOCKERY. DROLL
burlesque comic / BANANA
burlesque dancer / STRIPPER
burly / BULKY, LARGE
Burma capital / AVA; RANGOON
Burmese chief / BO; BOH; WOON
Burmese city / MOULMEIN
Burmese dagger / DAH, DOW
Burmese demon / NAT
Burmese gate / TORAN
Burmese gem deposit / BYON

Burmese hills / NAGA
Burmese knife / DAB, DAH, DOW
Burmese language / WA; MON; PEGU
Burmese measure / DHA, LAN
Burmese money / KYAT
Burmese mountains / YOMA; DAWNA
Burmese native / WA; LAI, MON; CHIN, SHAN; KAREN; KACHIN
Burmese plateau / SHAN
Burmese river / CHINDWIN; IRRAWADDY
Burmese robber / DACOIT
Burmese seaport / RANGOON
Burmese shrimp / NAPEE
Burmese three-stringed violin / TURR
Burmese town / LASHIO; MANDALAY
Burmese travel shelter / ZAYAT
Burmese tribesman / SHAN
burn / CHAR, SEAR; SCALD, SINGE, SMART; SCORCH
burn to ashes / CREMATE; INCINERATE
burn brightly / FLAME, FLARE
burn partially / CHAR
burn slightly / SINGE
burn slowly / SMOLDER
burn with steam / SCALD
burn unsteadily / FLICKER
burned sugar / CARAMEL
burning / HOT; FIERY; ARDENT, TORRID
burning bush / WAHOO
burning particle / SPARK
burning pile / PYRE
burnish / RUB; GLOSS; POLISH
burnt offering / HOLOCAUST, SACRIFICE
burr in wood / KNAR
burro / DONKEY; JACKASS
burrow / DIG; MINE; EXCAVATE
burrowing animal / MOLE; RATEL; GOPHER, MARMOT; AARDVARK
burrowing insect / BORER; ANTLION
burrowing marsupial / WOMBAT
burrowing rodent / VISCACHA; CHINCHILLA
burrowing in sand / ARENICOLE
burst / POP; OPEN; BLAST, CRACK
burst, c.f. / RRHAGE; RRHAGIA
burst asunder / SPLIT; DISRUPT
burst of fireworks / SALVO
burst forth / ERUPT, SALLY
burst of temper / TANTRUM
Burundi capital / BUJUMBURA
Burundi deity / IMANA
Burundi language / KIRUNDI, SWAHILI
Burundi pygmy people / BATWA

Burundi tribe / HUTU; BATWA, TUTSI; BAHUTU; BATUTSI
bury / HIDE; CACHE, INTER; ENTOMB, INHUME; CONCEAL
burying / BURIAL
bus / AUTO, HEAP; JITNEY; OMNIBUS
bush / TOD; SHRUB; FOREST; COUNTRY
bush leagues / MINORS
bush telegraph / RUMOR
bushmen / SAAN
bushranger / MUGGER
bushwhack / AMBUSH
bushwhacker / GUERRILLA
bushy / DUMOSE, SHAGGY
bushy clump / TOD
bushy hair / SHAG; NATURAL
business / DEAL; CRAFT, TRADE; MATTER; CALLING; COMMERCE, VOCATION
business abbreviation / CO; INC, ULT; INRE, PROX
business advantage / PROFIT; INTEREST
business agreement / DEAL, SALE; CONTRACT
business connection / CONTACT
business customer / ACCOUNT
business decline / SLUMP
business getter / AD; TOUT; AGENT; SALESMAN
business girl / STENO
business house / FIRM, SHOP; COMPANY
business index / SALES
business organization / JCS, NAM; COFC; KIWANIS
business profit / NET
business reverse / LOSS
business transaction / SALE
business trust / CARTEL
buss / KISS; SMACK
bust / BOSOM, CHEST; BREAST; STATUETTE
bustard / GOOSE, PAAUW
busted / ARRESTED
bustle / ADO; TODO, FUSS, STIR
bustling / BUSY; AGITATED
bustling with activity / AHUM
busy / BRISK; NIMBLE; ENGAGED
busy commotion / BUSTLE
busy fellow / DOER
busy ghoul / GRAVEROBBER
busy insect / ANT, BEE
busy place / HIVE
busy with / AT
busybody / PRY; SNOOP; MEDDLER
but / IF; YET; ONLY, SAVE; STILL; EXCEPT, THOUGH, UNLESS
butcher bird / SHRIKE
butcher's hook / GAMBREL
butcher's pin / SKEWER

butcher's tool / KNIFE; CLEAVER
butchery / CARNAGE; BLOODSHED, SLAUGHTER
butt / RAM; THRUST. CASK, GOAL; TARGET
butt of joke / GOAT; VICTIM
butte / MESA; RIDGE
butter cask / TUB; FIRKIN
butter of India / GHI; GHEE
butter knife / SPREADER
butter substitute / OLEO; MARGARINE
butter tree / SHEA
butterbird / BOBOLINK
butterbur / CLEAT; OXWORT
butterfingers / BOTCHER. CLUMSY
butterfly / IO; CLEAT, DIANA, SATYR; IDALIA, URSULA; MONARCH, SKIPPER
butterfly fish / BLENNY; GURNARD
butterfly larva / CATERPILLAR
butterfly lily / SEGO
butting / BOUNDARY
button / STUD; WHISKERS
button part / SHANK
buttons / PAGE
buttress / PIER, PROP; SUPPORT
buxom / JOLLY, PLUMP; COMELY, ROBUST
buy / ACQUIRE; PURCHASE
buy back / REDEEM
buy groceries / SHOP; MARKET
buy or sell / DEAL
buyer / AGENT; EMPTOR, VENDEE
buzz / HUM; WHIR; DRONE. GOSSIP
buzzard / HAWK; VULTURE
buzzing beetle / DOR
buzzing insect / BEE
buzzing sound / WHIR
by / AT; PER, VIA; NEAR; CLOSE
by all means / ASSUREDLY, CERTAINLY
by birth / NEE; CONGENITAL
by and by / ANON
by chance / PERADVENTURE
by means of / PER
by nature / BORN; NATURAL
by oneself / ALONE
by reason of / FOR
by way of / VIA
by word of mouth / ORAL; PAROL; SPOKEN
bye / SECONDARY
bygone / AGO; PAST; ANCIENT
bypasses / DETOURS, TUNNELS
bypath / WAY; LANE
byre / BARN; STABLE
bystander / SPECTATOR
byword / PROVERB; NICKNAME
Byzantine capital / CONSTANTINOPLE

C

Caaba location / MECCA
caam / HEDDLES
caama / ASSE
cab / HACK, TAXI; ARABA; HANSOM
cab counter / TAXIMETER
cab driver / HACKIE
cabal / SET; GANG, PLOT; JUNTO
caballero / SENOR; KNIGHT
cabaret / FLOORSHOW; RESTAURANT
cabassou / TATOUAY; ARMADILLO
cabbage / CHOU, COLE, KAIL; KRAUT
cabbage salad / SLAW; COLESLAW
cabbage tree / TI; ANGELIN
cabbage type / SAVOY; COLLARDS
cabbagelike plant / COLE, KALE
cabbagelike vegetable / KOHLRABI
cabin / HUT; LODGE; SALOON
cabinet / FILE; BAHUT; ETAGERE; ADVISERS, CUPBOARD; EXECUTIVES
cabinet wood / TEAK; ROSEWOOD
cable / GUY; ROPE; CHAIN; HAWSER
cablegram / WIRE; MESSAGE
cabree / PRONGHORN
cabriolet / BUGGY; CARRIAGE
cabrit / ANTELOPE; PRONGHORN
cacao powder / BROMA
cache / HIDE; CONCEAL
cachet / SEAL; COVER, STAMP
cactus / CEREUS, MESCAL; OPUNTIA
cactus drink / CALINCHE, COLONCHE
cactus fruit / TUNA; SABRA
cad / HEEL; KNAVE; BOUNDER
cadaver / BODY; STIFF; CORPSE
cadaverous / PALE; HAGGARD
caddis fly / CADEW
Caddoan Indian / REE; ADAI
cadence / METER; RHYTHM
cadent / FALLING; DESCENDING
cadet / LAD; PLEBE; JUNIOR
cadger / HAWKER; MOOCHER, SPONGER
cadillo / COCKLEBUR
Cadiz' ancient name / GADES
cadmium yellow / NASTURTIUM
Cadmus' city / THEBES
Cadmus' daughter / INO; AGAVE
Cadmus' father / AGENOR
Cadmus' gift / ALPHABET
Cadmus' mother / AGRIOPE
Cadmus' sister / EUROPA
Cadmus' wife / HARMONIA
cadre / SKELETON; FRAMEWORK
caduceus wearers / AMA; DOCTORS
Caen's river / ORNE

Caesar's colleague / POMPEY; CRASSUS
Caesar's message / VENIVIDIVICI
Caesar's mother / AURELIA
Caesar's murderer / CASCA; BRUTUS; CASSIUS
Caesar's son / CAESARION
Caesar's son-in-law / POMPEY
Caesar's wife / POMPEIA; CALPURNIA
caesura / HALT, REST, STOP; PAUSE
cafe / BISTRO; SALOON; CABARET
caffein nut / COLA, KOLA
cage / MEW, PEN; COOP; CONFINE
cage for elevator / CAR
cage game / BASKETBALL
cage for hawks / MEW
cage for poultry / COOP
caged / PENT; IMPRISONED
cagy / SLY; SHREWD; CUNNING
cahoots / COLLUSION; PARTNERSHIP
caiman / JACARE, YACARE
Cain's brother / ABEL
Cain's crime / FRATRICIDE
Cain's father / ADAM
Cain's land / NOD
Cain's son / ENOCH
Cain's victim / ABEL
Cain's wife / ADAH
cairngorm / QUARTZ
caisson / BOX; CHEST, WAGON
caisson disease / BENDS
caitiff / KNAVE; COWARD, WRETCH
cajeput / LAUREL
cajole / COAX, FAWN; CHEAT, TEASE
cajolery / BLARNEY; FLATTERY
cajuput / PAPERBARK
cake / BAR, BUN; FARL; TORTE
cake of bread / LOAF
cake froster / ICER; DECORATOR
cake ingredient / EGG; FLOUR
cake mix / BATTER
cake in pipe bowl / DOTTLE
caked with carbon / COKY
cakewalk / STRUT
calabash / GOURD; DIPPER
calaboose / PEN; JAIL; LOCKUP
Calabria's ancient name / BRUTTIUM
calamitous / SAD; DIRE, EVIL
calamity / WOE; BLOW, EVIL
Calaveras amphibian / JUMPING-FROG
calcareous deposit / TUFA
calcareous earth / LIMESTONE
calcium oxide / LIME
calcium sulfate / GYPSUM; PLASTER

calculate / FIT, SUM; PLAN, RATE
calculated / FIGURED
calculation / OPINION; ESTIMATE
calculator / ABACUS; COUNTER; SOROBAN, SUANPAN, SWANPAN
calculous / STONY; GRITTY
Calcutta atrocity / BLACKHOLE
Calcutta weight / PANK, PAWA
Calcutta's river / HOOGHLY
Calder's specialty / MOBILE
caldron / POT; BOILER, KETTLE
Caledonian / SCOT; SCOTSMAN
calefacient / HEATING, WARMING
calendar / LIST, ORDO; ALMANAC
calender / ROLLER; SMOOTHER
calf / DOBY; DIGIE; MAVERICK
calf, pert. to the / SURAL
calf flesh / VEAL
calf leather / KIP
calf meat / VEAL
calf without mother / DOGIE
calf's cry / BLAT
Calgary's rodeo / STAMPEDE
caliber / BORE, SIZE; GAUGE
calico / SALLOO
calico horse / PAINT, PINTO
calid / WARM
caliduct / STEAMPIPE
California army post / ORD
California bay / SUISUN
California bulrush / TULE
California capital / SACRAMENTO
California city / NAPA; FRESNO
California college / USC; MILLS
California dam / OROVILLE
California desert / MOJAVE
California holly / TOYON
California Indian / ARA; HUPA, KATO, KOSO, MONO, NOZI, POMO, TATU, YANA, YUKI; HOOPA, KAWIA; MAIDU, MIWOK, WINTU
California lake / CLEAR, TAHOE
California live oak / ENCINA
California missionary / SERRA
California mountain / MUIR; LASSEN, SHASTA; PALOMAR, WHITNEY
California park / YOSEMITE
California plant / AMOLE
California range / SIERRAS
California river / EEL; TRINITY
California rockfish / RENA; REINA
California shrub / SALAL
California state flower / POPPY
California state tree / REDWOOD
California tree / REDWOOD
California valley / DEATH
California volcano / LASSEN
California white oak / ROBLE
California wine area / NAPA

Californian fault / SANANDREAS
California's motto / EUREKA
California's nickname / GOLDEN
caliph / ALI; IMAM, OMAR; HARUN
calk / COPY; TRACE; CHINSE
calk on football shoe / CLEAT
call / CRY, DUB; DIAL, NAME
call for aid / APPEAL
call for attention / HO; HEY; PST
call a baby / NAME
call back / RENEGE, REVOKE
call boy / PAGE
call at bridge / BID
call of cattle / LOW, MOO
call to cattle / SOOK; SOOKY
call forth / EVOKE; ELICIT
call for help / SOS; MAYDAY
call loudly / CRY; HAIL, YELL
call to mind / RECALL; REMEMBER
call by name / PAGE
call to prayer / ADAN, AZAN
call for repeat / BIS; ENCORE
call for review / SUMMON
call together / MUSTER, SUMMON
call upon / VISIT; SUMMON
call for urgently / DEMAND
calla / LILY
callant / BOY, LAD
called / NAMED; DUBBED, PHONED, STYLED, TERMED, TITLED, YCLEPT
caller / GUEST; SUITOR
calligrapher / PENMAN
calling / DUTY, NAME, WORK
callous / DULL, HARD; CRUEL
calloused / HORNY; HARDENED
callow / UNFLEDGED; INEXPERIENCED
callus / CLAVUS, TYLOMA
calm / COOL, EASY, MILD; QUIET
calmly / PATIENTLY
calmness / COOL; ATARAXY
caloric / THERMAL
calorie / THERM; CALORY, THERME
calotte / SKULLCAP; ZUCCHETTO
calumet / PIPE; PEACEPIPE
calumniate / SLUR; ABUSE; DEFAME
calumniator / DEFAMER; LIBELLER
calumnious / ABUSIVE; INSULTING
calumny / OBLOQUY, SLANDER
Calvary / GOLGOTHA
Calvinist / BEREAN; HUGUENOT
calvous / BALD; NAKED
calypter / ALULA; SQUAMA
calyx / CUP; PERIANTH
calyx section / SEPAL
cam / COG; TAPPET
camaraderie / LOYALTY; FELLOWSHIP
camarilla / CABAL; CLIQUE
camass / LOBELIA

camass bread / PASSHICO
Cambodia capital / PNOMPENH
Cambodian lake / TONLESAP
Cambodian language / KHMER
Cambodian money / RIEL
Cambodian people / KHMER
Cambodian river / MEKONG
Cambodian temple / ANGKORWAT
Cambria / WALES
cambric / JACONET
cambric grass / RAMIE
Cambridge college / PEMBROKE
Cambridge examination / TRIPOS
Cambridge river / CAM
Cambridge school / MIT; HARVARD
Cambridge servant / GYP
Cambridge student / SIZAR; OP-TIME; WRANGLER
came upon / MET
camel / OONT; DELOUL; BACTRIAN
camel driver / SARWAN
camellia / JAPONICA
camellike animal / LLAMA; ALPACA
camelopard / GIRAFFE
Camelot lady / ENID; ELAINE
Camelot queen / GUINEVERE
camel's hair cloth / ABA; CAMLET
camel's hair robe / ABA
cameo / ANAGLYPH
cameo cutting tool / SPADE
cameo stone / ONYX; SARDONYX
camera eye / LENS
camera moving platform / DOLLY
camera prop / TRIPOD
Cameroon capital / YAOUNDE
Cameroon river / SANAGA
Cameroon seaport / KRIBI; DOUALA
Cameroon tribe / ABO; GARA, SARA
camisole / TUNIC, WAIST; CAMISA
camouflage / HIDE; CONCEAL
camoufleur / DECEIVER

camp / ENCAMP; BIVOUAC. TABOR
camp, pert. to / CASTRAL
camp follower / SUTLER
camp out / HUT; TENT
camp shelter / TENT
Campanian town / CLMAE; SALERNO
campanile / BELLTOWER
campanula / HAREBELL; BELLFLOWER
camphor / ALANT; BORNEOL, CAMPHOL
campus / QUAD; COURT; GROUNDS
can / MAY, TIN; PRESERVE
Canaanite / BYBLOS, UGARIT
Canada goose / OUTARDE
Canadian / CANUCK
Canadian canal / SOO; WELLAND
Canadian city / BANFF; QUEBEC, OTTAWA; CALGARY, TORONTO; MONTREAL, WINNIPEG; VAN-COUVER
Canadian court decree / ARRET
Canadian emblem / MAPLELEAF
Canadian essayist / LEACOCK
Canadian Indian / AHT; CREE, DENE, TAKU, TATU; NISKA, TINNE
Canadian lake / CREE, SEUL; ABITIBI, NIPIGON
Canadian larch / EPINETTE
Canadian measure / PIED; ARPENT
Canadian mountain / LOGAN; ROB-SON
Canadian national park / YOHO
Canadian novelist / MCLENNAN
Canadian officer / MOUNTIE
Canadian peak / LOGAN; LUCANIA
Canadian peninsula / GASPE
Canadian physician / OSLER; BANTING
Canadian poet / SERVICE

CANADA

Province	Abbreviation	Capital
Alberta	ALTA	EDMONTON
British Columbia	BC	VICTORIA
Manitoba	MAN	WINNIPEG
New Brunswick	NB	FREDERICTON
Newfoundland	NEWF	STJOHNS
Nova Scotia	NS	HALIFAX
Ontario	ONT	TORONTO
Prince Edward Island	PEI	CHARLOTTETOWN
Quebec	QUE	QUEBEC
Saskatchewan	SASK	REGINA
Northwest Territories	NWT	—
Yukon Territory	YT	WHITEHORSE

The Capital of Canada is OTTAWA.

Canadian porcupine / URSON
Canadian range / CARIBOO, SEL-
KIRK
Canadian river / SEAL; KNIFE,
LIARD, PEACE, SLAVE, YUKON
Canadian squash / CUSHAW
canal / DUCT; MEATUS; CHANNEL
canal bank / BERM
canal in Canada / WELLAND
canal in Central America / PANAMA
canal in Egypt / SUEZ
canal in Germany / KIEL
canal in New York / ERIE
Canal Zone lake / GATUN
Canal Zone town / ANCON; BAL-
BOA
canape / APPETIZER
canape item / ROE; ANCHOVY
canard / TALE; HOAX; RUMOR,
STORY
canary / BIRD, WINE
Canary island / PALMA; GOMERA
canary yellow / MELINE
canasta play / MELD
cancel / DELE, VOID; ANNUL
canceled / NULLED
cancellation / ERASURE
cancer / CRAB; TUMOR; GROWTH
Cancer or Capricorn / TROPIC
candelabrum / LAMP; CANDLE-
STICK
Candia / CRETE
candid / FAIR, FREE, OPEN; FRANK
candidate / NOMINEE; CLAIMANT
candidates' list / LEET; SLATE
candiote / CRETAN
candle / LIGHT, TAPER; BOUGIE
candle cord / WICK
candle holder / SCONCE; PRICKET
candle material / WAX; TALLOW
candle snuff / SNAST; SNASTE
candlenut / AMA; KUKUI; BANKUL
candlenut bark fiber / AEA
candlewood / PINE
candor / OPENNESS; FRANKNESS
candy / MINTS; COMFIT, SWEETS
candy base / SUGAR; FONDANT
candytuft / IBERIS
cane / FLAY, FLOG, WHIP. STEM
canine / CUR, DOG, PET; FICE
canine breed / HOUND; SETTER
canine disease / MANGE; RABIES
canine tooth / CUSPID; EYETOOTH
canine variety / FOX; WOLF;
JACKAL
Canio's wife / NEDDA
canister / BOX; CASE; CALIN
cankerous / ULCEROUS; MALIG-
NANT
cannabis / HEMP; HASHISH; MARI-
HUANA, MARIJUANA
cannon / GUN; SAKER; MORTAR

cannon knob / CASCABEL
cannot / CANT
canny / ASTUTE, SHREWD; CAU-
TIOUS
canoe / DUGOUT; PIRAGUA,
PIROGUE
canoe of Africa / BONGO, BUNGO
canoe of Central America / PITPAN
canoe of Eskimos / BIDAR, KAYAK,
UMIAK; BIDARKA
canoe of Hawaii / WAAPA
canoe of Malabar / TONEE
canoe of Malaya / PAHI, PRAH,
PRAO, PRAU, PROA; PRAHO,
PRAHU
canoe of New Zealand / WAKA
canoe of Philippines / BANCA
canoe propeller / OAR; PADDLE
canon / LAW; RULE; BIBLE; DE-
CREE
canonic / REGULAR; ECCLESIAS-
TIC
canonical / ORTHODOX
canonical dress / ALB; COPE
canonical hour / SEXT; LAUDS,
NONES, PRIME; MATINS, TIERCE;
VESPERS; COMPLINE
canonical law of Islam / SHARIA
canonize / SAINT; SANCTIFY
canonized person / SAINT
canonry / BENEFICE
canopy / COVER, SHADE; TESTER
canopy of altar / BALDACHIN
cant / TIP; HEEL. ARGOT; JARGON
cant hook / PEAVY, PEEVY; PEA-
VEY
cant of thieves / ARGOT, SLANG
cantaloupe / CANTELOPE, MUSK-
MELON
cantankerous order / SCAT; SHUSH
cantata / ORATORIO, SERENATA
canted / ALIST
canteen / PX; FLASK, STORE
canter / LOPE
Canterbury archbishop / ANSELM,
BECKET; CRANMER
Canterbury Tales author /
CHAUCER
Canterbury Tales host / BAILLY
Canterbury Tales inn / TABARD
canticle / ODE; SONG
cantillate / CHANT; INTONE
canting / PIOUS; WHINING
canto / FIT; SONG; FYTTE
canton / DISTRICT
Canton / KWANGCHOW
Cantonese factory / HONG
cantor / PRECENTOR; CHOIR-
MASTER
canuck / CANADIAN
Canute's wife / EMMA
canvas / DUCK, SAIL, TUKE

canvas bed / COT
canvas holder / EASEL
canvas piece / TARPAULIN
canvas propeller / SAIL
canvas rain cover / TARP
canvas shelter / TENT
canvas shoes / KEDS
canvass / SIFT; STUDY; DEBATE
canvass politically / ELECTIONEER
canyon / GULCH; RAVINE, VALLEY
canyon opening / ABRA
canyon wall / DALLE
canzona / AIR; ARIA
caoutchouc / CAUCHO, RUBBER
cap / FEZ, TAM; COIF, ETON
capable / FIT; ABLE; ADAPTED
capable of being hammered / MAL-
  LEABLE
capable of enduring / WIRY;
  STRONG
capable of extension / ELASTIC
capable of movement / MOTILE
capacious / WIDE; AMPLE, LARGE
capacitate / ENABLE; QUALIFY
capacity / GIFT; ROOM; POWER
capacity measure / PINT; LITER,
  LITRE, QUART; BUSHEL, GALLON
capacity unit in electricity / FARAD
cape / RAS; NAZE, NESS, ROBE
cape in Africa / GOODHOPE
Cape Cod resort / TRURO; HYAN-
  NIS
cape of fur / PALATINE
Cape Horn land / PATAGONIA
cape jasmine / GARDENIA
cape in Massachusetts / ANN, COD
cape in North Carolina / HATTERAS
cape in Nova Scotia / SABLE
Cape Province capital / CAPETOWN
cape in South America / HORN
Cape Verde capital / PRAIA
Cape Verde island / SAL; FOGO
cape worn by Pope / FANON,
  ORALE
Capek character / ROBOT
Capek work / RUR
capelike garment / COPE; DOLMAN
capelin / SMELT
caper / DIDO, JUMP, LEAP, SKIP
capistrate / HOODED
capital / SEAT; FUNDS. MAJOR
capital of Bundesrepublik / BONN
capital of DDR / BERLIN
capital of EIRE / BAILEATHA-
  CLIATH
capital gain / PROFIT; INTEREST
capital of Hellas / ATHENAI
capital invested / SUM
capital of Italia / ROMA
capital of Polska / WARSZAWA
capital of U.S.S.R. MOSKVA
capitalist / NABOB; MAGNATE

capitation / TAX
Capitol Hill denizen / SENATOR;
  REPRESENTATIVE
capitulate / SURRENDER
Capri cavern / BLUEGROTTO
caprice / WHIM; FANCY, HUMOR
capricious / ODD; QUEER; FICKLE
capsize /UPEND, UPSET; OVER-
  TURN
capsule / POD, SAC; AMPULE
captain / MASTER; COMMANDER
caption / LEGEND; HEADING
captious / CROSS; TOUCHY; FRET-
  FUL
captivate / WIN; HOLD; CATCH
captivating / AMIABLE; ALLURING
captive / POW; PRISONER
captive as a pawn / HOSTAGE
captivity / BONDAGE, SLAVERY
capture / BAG, NAB, NET; TAKE
capture by device / BAG, NET; TRAP
capture fish / HOOK, LAND
capture fowl / BAG
captured / CAUGHT, SEIZED
Capuchin / FRANCISCAN
capuchin monkey / SAI
car / AUTO, TRAM; COACH; VEHI-
  CLE
car, as to capacity / SEATER
car in bad shape / HEAP
car under balloon / BASKET
car cylinder disk / PISTON
car driver / MOTORIST; CHAUF-
  FEUR
car gear / LOW; HIGH; REVERSE
carabao / BUFFALO
caracal / LYNX
caracul / SHEEP; KARAKUL
carafe / FLASK
carapace / SHELL
caravan / TRAIN, WAGON; CAFILA
caravan animal / CAMEL
caravanlike vehicle / CAMPER
caravansary / CHAN, KHAN; HOTEL
caravel of Columbus / NINA;
  PINTA; SANTAMARIA
carbohydrate / SUGAR; STARCH
carbolic acid / PHENOL
carbon / SOOT; CHARCOAL; LAMP-
  BLACK
carbon diamond / BORT
carbon powder / SOOT
carbuncle / RUBY; GARNET; BLEM-
  ISH
carcajou / WOLVERINE
carcinoma / TUMOR; CANCER;
  NEOPLASM
card / ACE; MENU; CARTE, TAROT;
  POSTAL. COMB; HETCHEL
card above the nine / HONOR
card combination / TENACE
card in euchre / BOWER

card in faro / SODA
card game / LOO, PAM, RUM;
BRAG, FARO, SKAT, VINT;
MONTE, NULLO, PEDRO, POKER,
RUMMY, STUSS, WHIST; BRIDGE,
ECARTE, FANTAN, FLINCH,
HEARTS; BEZIQUE CANASTA,
CASSINO; PINOCHLE
card game for one / SOLITAIRE
card game for two / ECARTE
card holding / TENACE
card manipulation / SLEIGHT
card play / FINESSE
card sequence / RUN; STRAIGHT
card sharper / CHEAT
card suit / CLUBS; HEARTS,
SPADES; DIAMONDS
card from a sweetheart / VALEN-
TINE
card wool / TUM; ROVE; TEASE
cardboard box / CARTON
Cardiff giant / HOAX
cardigan / JACKET
cardinal / CHIEF; PRINCIPAL. PRE-
LATE
cardinal point / EAST, WEST;
NORTH, SOUTH
cardinal virtue / JUSTICE; PRU-
DENCE; FORTITUDE; TEMPER-
ANCE
cardinal's hat / BIRETTA
cards / GAME
care / WORRY; DESIRE, REGARD;
CONCERN. HEED, MIND, TEND;
NURSE
care deeply / LOVE; ADORE
care for / NURSE; ATTEND, RE-
GARD
careen / TIP; CANT, LIST, TILT
career / COURSE; CALLING. RUN;
RUSH
carefree / GAY; BLITHE
careful / UNEASY; ANXIOUS, HEED-
FUL
careful watch / VIGILANCE
careless / SLACK; REMISS; HEED-
LESS
careless mistake / BONER
caress / PAT, PET; CODDLE, FON-
DLE
caretaker / GUARDIAN
cargo / LOAD; GOODS; BURDEN;
FREIGHT
cargo overboard / JETSAM
Carian city / CNIDUS; MILETUS
Carian king / MAUSOLUS
Carib Indian / YAO; TRIO
Caribbean islands / ANTILLES
caribou / REINDEER
caricature / PARODY; CARTOON;
TRAVESTY
caries / DECAY

cariole / CART
cark / CARE; TROUBLE
carking / WORRYING
carl / CHURL; RUSTIC
Carlisle students / INDIANS
Carmen composer / BIZET
carmine / RED; CRIMSON
Carnac sight / DOLMEN, MENHIR
carnage / HAVOC; BLOODSHED;
SLAUGHTER
carnal / ANIMAL, FLESHY, IMPURE
carnation / PINK
carnelian / SARD; CHALCEDONY
carnelian bead / ARANGO
carnival / FETE; FEAST, REVEL
carnival barker / SPIELER
carnival feature / RIDE; CLOWN;
SIDESHOW
carnivore / CAT; RATEL; MEAT-
EATER
carnivorous cat / LION, LYNX;
KODKOD, MARGAY
carnivorous mammal / WOLF; MAR-
TEN, WEASEL
carnivorous quadruped / HYENA;
JACKAL
carnose / FLESHY
carol / SING; WARBLE. NOEL,
SONG
caroler / WAIT
Carolina Indian / CATAWBA
Carolina rail / SORA
Caroline Islands group / PALAU,
PELEW
Carolines Island / YAP; TRUK
carom / REBOUND
carone / KETONE
carousal / BINGE, REVEL, SPREE
carouse / FEAST; DEBAUCH, WAS-
SAIL
carp / CAVIL. KOI; DACE; SHINER
Carpathian range / TATRA
carpenter / JOINER
carpenter's tool / SAW; PLANE;
HAMMER
carpentry joint / MORTISE
carpet / MAT, RUG; DRUGGET
carpet from Afghanistan / HERAT;
HERATI
carpet from the Caucasus / BAKU,
KUBA
carpet cleaner / VACUUM;
SWEEPER
carpet from India / AGRA
carpet with long pile / AFGHAN
carpet of Persia / KALI; SENNA;
ISFAHAN
carpet with thick pile / MOQUETTE
carpet variety / WILTON; AXMIN-
STER
carplike fish / IDE, RUD; CHUB,
DACE, ROUD, RUDD; ROACH

carpus / WRIST
carpus part / RADIALE; SCAPHOID
carriage / AIR, GIG, RIG; GAIT, MIEN, SHAY, WALK; POISE; CALASH, LANDAU
carriage of India / EKKA
carriage of Java / SADO
carried / BORNE
carried away / RAPT; DISTRAIT
carried on the wind / AIRBORNE
carrier / BUS, CAR, VAN; TRAM; TOTER
carrier of bad luck / JINX; JONAH; HOODOO
Carroll heroine / ALICE
carrotlike plant / DILL; ANISE; CARAWAY, CHERVIL, PARSNIP
carrousel / MERRYGOROUND
carry / LUG; BEAR, TOTE; IMPEL
carry across water / RAFT, SHIP; FERRY
carry away / ELOIN; BEWITCH
carry off / ABDUCT; SUCCEED
carry on / STORM; PERSIST; CONTINUE
carry on war / WAGE
carry out / DO; EXECUTE
carry out again / REDO; REENACT
carry over / TIDE
carry past a rough time / TIDE
carry weight / COUNT; MATTER
carryall / BUS; CASE; RUCKSACK
carrying case / ETUI
carrying charge / TOLL; CARTAGE
carrying off / DEFERENT
carrying weapons / ARMED
cart / HAUL. VAN; DRAY; WAGON
cartage / HAULAGE
carte / CARD, MENU; THRUST
carte blanche / AUTHORITY
Carthage, pert. to / PUNIC
Carthage's citadel / BYRSA
Carthage's enemy / CATO
Carthaginian general / HANNO; HIMILCO; HAMILCAR; HANNIBAL
Carthaginian moon goddess / TANIT; TANITH
Carthaginian queen / DIDO; ELISSA
cartilage / GRISTLE
cartilage, c.f. / CHONDR; CHONDRO
cartilage of eyelid / TARSUS
carting vehicle / VAN; TRUCK
cartography / MAPPING
carton / BOX; CASE
cartoon / EPURE; DESIGN, SKETCH
cartoonist / ARNO, CAPP, NAST; KIRBY
cartridge / SHELL; BULLET, CASING
carve / CUT; SLICE; INCISE
carved gem / CAMEO

carved image / BUST; RELIEF, STATUE
carving tool / BURIN, GOUGE; CHISEL
casaba / MELON
cascade / FALL; WATERFALL
Cascades mountain / RAINIER
case / BOX; CHEST, CRATE. STATE, TRIAL
case denoting place / LOCATIVE
case in grammar / DATIVE; GENITIVE
case for a light / LAMP
case for shipping / BOX; CRATE
case shot / SHRAPNEL
case for small toiletries / ETUI, ETWEE
caseous / CHEESY
caserne / BARRACKS
cash / COIN; MONEY; SPECIE
cash box / TILL; REGISTER
cash and carry / SELFSERVICE
cash refund / REBATE
cash register sign / NOSALE
cashew / CAJU
cashew oil / CARDOL
casing / FRAME, LINER
casino / PARLOR; CASSINO
cask / KEG, TUB, TUN, VAT; BUTT
casket / CHEST; COFFER, COFFIN
Caspian port / BAKU; RESHT
Caspian source / VOLGA
casque / HELMET
Cassandra's brother / HELENUS
Cassandra's father / PRIAM
cassation / ABROGATION
cassava / AIPI, AYPI, JUCA, YUCA; MANIOC
cassava drink / CASIRI; CASSAREEP
cassava starch granules / TAPIOCA
casserole / POT
cassette ribbon / TAPE
cassino point / ACE; SPADES
cassonade / SUGAR
cassowary / MURUP; MOORUP
cast / FORM, HURL, SHED, SEND, VOTE; DRIVE, FLING, HEAVE, IMPEL, PITCH, SLING, THROW. LOOK, MIEN; SHADE, TINGE, TOUCH
cast aside / DISCARD
cast away / HEAVE, THROW
cast bait lightly / DAP
cast a ballot / VOTE
cast down / ABASE; CONDEMN
cast feathers / MEW
cast glances / LEER, OGLE
cast metal / PIG, YET; INGOT
cast out / EGEST, EXPEL
castaway / WAIF; WRECK; OUTCAST

caste / JATI, SECT; CLASS, VARNA
caste of India / MEO; AHIR, BICE, GOLA, MALI
caste of Tamil merchants / CHETTY
caster / CRUET, WHEEL; ROLLER
castigate / CORRECT; CHASTISE
castigatory / PUNITIVE
Castile river / DUERO, TAGUS
Castilian queen / ISABELLA
casting mold / DIE; MATRIX
castle / FORT, ROOK; PALACE
castle ditch / MOAT
castle in France / CHATEAU
castor bean poison / RICIN
castor oil plant / KIKI; RICINUS
Castor and Pollux / GEMINI
Castor's brother / POLLUX
Castor's mother / LEDA
Castor's slayer / IDAS
castrated animal / SEG; SEGG
castrated bull / OX
castrated horse / GELDING
casual / ACCIDENTAL, OCCA-SIONAL
casual event / HAPPENING
casualty / DEATH; CHANCE; ACCI-DENT, FORTUITY
casuarina / BELAH; SHEOAK; BEEF-WOOD
cat / GIB; PUSS; FELID, TABBY; FELINE, MOUSER; GRIMALKIN
cat of Africa / CIVET, GENET; GENETTE
cat of America / PUMA; COUGAR, JAGUAR
cat with no tail / MANX
cat variety / MANX; ANGORA, MAR-GAY, OCELOT; MALTESE, PER-SIAN, SIAMESE
cataclysm / DELUGE; DEBACLE
catacomb / TOMB; CRYPT
Catalan poet / VERDAGUER
catalogue / LIST, ROLL; INDEX, TA-BLE
Catalonia river / EBRO
catamaran / BOAT, RAFT; FLOAT
cataphora / LETHARGY
cataplasm / POULTICE
catapult / ONAGER; SLINGSHOT
cataract / FLOOD; WATERFALL
catastrophe / CALAMITY, DISASTER
catcall / BOO
catch / COP, NET; GRAB, HAUL, HOOK, NAIL, SNAG, TRAP; GRASP, SEIZE, SNARE. HASP; CLASP
catch a breath / GASP, PANT
catch to fasten hatch / DOGBOLT
catch phrase / CRY; SLOGAN
catch sight of / SEE; ESPY
catch suddenly / NAB; SNATCH
catch a thief / NAB
catch unawares / TRAP; SNARE

catch up with / OVERTAKE
catchall word / ETC; ETAL; ETCET-ERA
catcher's glove / MITT
catching / WINSOME; CHARMING; CONTAGIOUS
catching device / NET; TRAP
catchword / CUE; SHIBBOLETH
catechu / CUTCH; ACACIA
catechulike resin / KINO
categorical / DIRECT; EMPHATIC, EXPLICIT, POSITIVE
categories / GENERA
category / CLASS, GENRE; HEAD-ING
catena / CHAIN
catenate / LINK; CONNECT
cater / SERVE; PURVEY, SUPPLY
cater to low taste / PANDER
caterer / VIVANDIER; VIVANDIERE
caterpillar / WERI, WORM; AWETO, ERUCA, LARVA; WOUBIT
caterpillar hair / SETA
caterpillar's web / TENT
caterwaul / MEOW, MIAU; MIAOW
catfish / POUT; DORAD; DOCMAC; BULLHEAD
catharize / PURIFY; CLEANSE
cathartic / LAXATIVE; PURGATIVE
Cathay / CHINA
cat-headed goddess / MUT; BAST
cathedral / SOBOR; MINSTER
cathode emanation / ELECTRON
cathode's opposite / ANODE
catholic / GENERAL, LIBERAL; UNI-VERSAL
Catholic tribunal / ROTA; SIGNA-TURA
Catholic's Holy Father / POPE
catkin / AMENT
catlike / FELINE, SILENT
catling / KITTEN
catnap / NOD; DOZE; DROWSE
catnip / NEP; CATMINT
cat's cry / MEW; MEOW, MIAU, PURR, WAUL; MIAUL
cat's foot / PAW
Catskills sleeper / RIP
catspaw / GULL, TOOL; STOOGE
cat's pet name / PUSS; PUSSY
cattail / TULE; CATKIN; MATREED; REEDMACE
cattail of India / REREE
cattail of New Zealand / RAUPO
cattle / COWS, HERD, KINE, OXEN
cattle breed / ANGUS, DEVON; JER-SEY; GUERNSEY, HEREFORD, HOLSTEIN, LONGHORN
cattle dealer / DROVER
cattle disease / ANTHRAX, MUR-RAIN
cattle enclosure / RUN; CORRAL
cattle farm / RANCH

cattle food / MASH
cattle land / RANGE; PASTURE
cattle stealing / ABIGEAT; RUS-
TLING
cattle tether / AWEBAND
cattle thief / RUSTLER
catty / SLY; SPITEFUL; MALICIOUS
caucasian / WHITE
caucasian goat / TUR, ZAC; TEHR
caucasian language / LAZ, UDI;
ANDI, AVAR
Caucasus mountain / ELBRUZ
Caucasus native / IMER, SVAN;
OSSET; CHECHEN
Caucasus pass / DARYAL
caucho tree / ULE
caucus / POWWOW; MEETING;
CONCLAVE
caudal appendage / TAIL
caught sight of / SPIED; SPOTTED
cauldron / POT; CALDRON
caulis / STEM
caulk / CALK; SHAPE, TRACE;
CHINSE
causal / BASIC; CAUSATIVE
causal science / ETIOLOGY
cause / AIM, END; SUIT; ACTION,
MOTIVE, ORIGIN. BEGET;
CREATE, EFFECT
cause for action / SUIT
cause to adhere / FUSE; STICK,
UNITE
cause to branch / DIVIDE, RAMIFY
cause to coalesce / MERGE
cause to disclose / ELICIT
cause emotion / EXCITE; AGITATE
cause exhaustion / WEAR; DRAIN;
WEAKEN
cause to flow / POUR
cause to go / SEND; PROPEL
cause of legal action / GRAVAMEN
cause pain / AFFLICT
cause panic / ALARM
cause to revolve / SPIN, TURN
cause of ruin / SIN; BANE, VICE
cause to shake / JOLT; SHOCK
cause to soar / FLY
cause to sound / BEAT, BLOW;
BLAST
cause sudden fear / STARTLE
causeway / DIKE, PATH
causing laughter / COMIC, FUNNY;
RISIBLE
causing repletion / SATING
causing strain / TENSIVE
caustic / HOT; TART; ACRID; BIT-
ING; ERODENT
caustic solution / LYE; LIME;
ALKALI
caustic substance / LYE; ACID;
PHENOL
cauterize / BURN, SEAR; BRAND
cautery plant / MOXA

caution / CARE; ADVICE; CONCERN.
WARN; ADMONISH
cautious / WARY; CHARY; CARE-
FUL
cavalier / SIR; KNIGHT; HORSE-
MAN. CURT; HAUGHTY; ARRO-
GANT, INSOLENT
cavalry flag / GUIDON
cavalry soldier / ULAN; UHLAN;
LANCER; DRAGOON
cavalry sword / SABER
cavalry weapon / LANCE, SABER
cavalryman / TROOPER
cavalryman of Algeria /SPAHI
cavalryman of Hungary / HUSSAR
cavalryman of India / SOWAR
cave / DEN; ABRI, GROT; ANTRE;
CAVERN, GROTTO
cave in / COLLAPSE
cave inhabitant / TROGLODYTE
cave man / NEANDERTHAL
cave prober / SPELUNKER
cave science / SPELEOLOGY
cave stone form / STALACTITE;
STALAGMITE
cavern / CAVE
cavernous / HOLLOW; CELLULAR
caviar / ROE; IKRA
caviar fish / STERLET; STURGEON
cavil / CARP; NITPICK, QUIBBLE
caviler / SOPHIST
cavity / GAP, PIT, SAC; HOLE, VOID;
CLEFT, SINUS; ANTRUM
cavity of the cheek / ANTRUM
cavity of the ear / ANTRUM
cavity of pollen sac / LOCULUS
cavity in a stone / VUG; VOOG,
VUGG, VUGH; GEODE
cavity for a tenon / MORTISE
cavort / CAPER; FROLIC, PRANCE
cavorting / PLAYING; GAMBOLING
cavy / MARA; AGOUTI, APEREA
Cawdor's thane / MACBETH
cay / KEY; ISLE; ISLET
cayenne / CHILI, WHIST; PEPPER
cayman / JACARE, YACARE
cayuse / PONY; BRONCO
cease / END; HALT, QUIT, STOP;
DESIST
cease opposing / YIELD; SURREN-
DER
cease work / QUIT, REST
ceaseless / ENDLESS, ETERNAL
ceaselessly / AYE, EER; EVER
cebine monkey / SAI; CAPUCHIN
cecity / BLINDNESS
Cecrops' city / ATHENS
Cecrops' daughter / HERSE
Cecrops' successor / THESEUS
cedar of India / DEODAR
cede / FORGO, GRANT, YIELD;
SURRENDER
cedrat / CITRON

ceil / COVER; OVERLAY
ceiling / TOP; LACUNAR
ceiling of room / DOME
Celebes city / MAKASSAR
Celebes ox / ANOA
celebrate / FETE, LAUD; EXTOL, HONOR; PRAISE
celebrated / FAMED, NOTED; FAMOUS; EMINENT
celebration / FETE, GALA; FEAST, REVEL
celebrity / FAME, HERO, LION, STAR; GLORY
celerity / HASTE, SPEED; RAPIDITY
celerylike plant / UDO
celestial / DIVINE; ANGELIC, ELYSIAN
celestial being / ANGEL; CHERUB, SERAPH
celestial body / STAR; COMET; SATELLITE
celestial phenomenon / NEBULA
celestial realm / SKY; HEAVENS
celestial sphere / ORB; PLANET
celibate / ASCETIC; UNMARRIED
cell / GERM, ROOM; CAVITY; BATTERY
cell, suffix / CYTE
cella / NAOS
cellaret / CABINET; TANTALUS
cello / VIOLONCELLO
cellular compartment / LOCULUS
cellulose, c.f. / CELLO, CELLU
celt / AX; HOE; CHISEL
Celt / ERSE, GAEL, KELT, MANX; BRETON
Celt of legend/ IR; ITH, MIL, NAR; EBER; MILEDH
Celtic / ERSE, MANX; IRISH, SCOTS, WELSH; BRETON, KELTIC; CORNISH
Celtic chief god / DAGDA
Celtic chieftain / TANIST
Celtic dart / COLP
Celtic fertility goddess / MACHA
Celtic hero / FINN; CUCHULAIN
Celtic language / ERSE; IRISH, WELSH; GAELIC
Celtic medical deity / DIANCECHT
Celtic mother of gods / ANA, ANU; DANA, DANU; BRIGIT
Celtic otherworld / TIRNANOG
Celtic paradise / AVALON
Celtic priest / DRUID
Celtic sea god / LER
Celtic smithy deity / GOBNIU
Celtic solar deity / LUG; LLEW, LUGH
Celtic thunder god / TANAROS
cement / GLUE, LIME, LUTE; PASTE; MASTIC
cemetery marker / TOMBSTONE
cenobite / MONK; CONVENTUAL

cenobium / CONVENT
cenosity / DIRT; FILTH
cense / INCENSE, PERFUME
censer / THURIBLE
censor / CRITIC; MAGISTRATE
censorial / CARPING; CRITICAL
censorious / SEVERE; CAPTIOUS
censorship symbol / MRSGRUNDY
censurable / REPREHENSIBLE
censure / FLAY; CAVIL, CHIDE, SCOLD, SLATE. BLAME; REPROOF
census / COUNTING; TABULATION
cent / RED; PENNY; COPPER
centaur / BIFORM, CHIRON; HORSEMAN
centaur of Hinduism / GANDHARVA
centennial / CENTENARY
center / HUB; CORE; FOCUS, HEART; MIDDLE; NUCLEUS
center, pert. to / FOCAL; CENTRAL
center of attention / TARGET; CYNOSURE
center wall in Roman circus / SPINA
centerpiece / EPERGNE
centesimal / HUNDREDTH
centesimal unit / GRAD
centipede / VERI; MYRIAPOD
central / MID; CHIEF, FOCAL
Central African Republic capital / BANGUI
Central African Republic trade language / SANGHO
Central American bird / COIN, GUAN, JACU; SYLPH, TURCO; CONDOR; SERIEMA
Central American gum tree / TUNO, TUNU
Central American Indian / KU; BOA, DUY, IKA, MAM, OSA, ZOE; CHOL, CORA, CUNA, MAYA, PAYA; AZTEC, LENKA
Central American tree / ULE; EBOE; AMATE
Central Asian fox / ADIVE; CORSAC
Central Asian mountains / ALTAI
Central Asian ox / YAK
central line / DIAMETER
central mosque / JAMI
central part / CORE, PITH; HEART
central part of root / STELE
central personage / HERO, LEAD, STAR; HEROINE
central point / FOCUS
centric / CENTRAL
century / AGE, EON, ERA; HUNDRED
century plant / PITA; AGAVE; MAGUEY
cepa / ONION
cephalalgia / HEADACHE

cephalopod / SQUID; OCTOPUS
ceramic square / TILE
ceramic worker / POTTER
cerate / WAXY. CERE
cere / WAX
cereal / GRAIN; FARINA
cereal bowl / PORRINGER
cereal chaff / BRAN
cereal fodder / SORGO
cereal grain / OAT, RYE; RICE; WHEAT
cereal grass / OAT, RYE; MAND, RAGI; MAIZE, RAGGI, WHEAT; MILLET, RAGGEE; SORGHUM
celebrate / THINK; PONDER
ceremonial / RITUAL. RITE
ceremonial chamber / KIVA
ceremonial dance / PAVAN; FORMAL
ceremonial display / POMP
ceremonial procession / PARADE; PAGEANT
ceremonially unclean / TREF
ceremonious / PRIM; STIFF; FORMAL
ceremony / FETE, FORM, POMP, RITE, SHOW; DISPLAY
Ceres / DEMETER
Ceres' daughter / PROSERPINE
Ceres' father / SATURN
Ceres' festival / CEREALIA
Ceres' sacred flower / POPPY
cerise / CHERRY
certain / REAL, SURE; FIXED; ACTUAL
certain gesture / SIGN
certain pitcher / CREAMER
certainly / YWIS; CERTES, SURELY
certainty / FACT
certes / ASSUREDLY, CERTAINLY
certificate / SCRIP; DOCUMENT
certificate in lieu of cash / CHECK, SCRIP
certify / VOUCH; ASSURE, ATTEST; DECLARE
certify a will / PROBATE
certitude / ASSURANCE, CERTAINTY
cerulean / BLUE; AZURE
cervine / DEERLIKE
cess / ASSESS. TAX
cessation / LULL, REST, STOP; PAUSE
cesspool / DRAIN; CISTERN
cestode / TAENIA; TAPEWORM
cestus / BELT; GIRDLE
cetacean / ORC; CETE; WHALE; DOLPHIN, NARWHAL; PORPOISE
cete / WHALE
Ceylon / SERENDIB, SRILANKA; TAPROBANE
Ceylon capital / COLOMBO
Ceylon governor / DISAWA

Ceylon moss /AGAR; JAFFNA
Ceylon sand-coral / PAAR
Ceylonese aborigine / VEDDA; VEDDAH
Ceylonese boat / DONI; DHONI
Ceylonese city / GALLE, KANDY
Ceylonese garment / SARONG
Ceylonese hill dweller / TODA
Ceylonese language / PALI; TAMIL
Ceylonese lizard / CHEECHA
Ceylonese lotus / NELUMBO
Ceylonese monkey / MAHA; TOQUE; LANGUR
Ceylonese people / TAMIL; SINHALESE
Ceylonese tree / DOON
cha / TEA
chabuk / WHIP
chachalaca / GUAN
chacma /BABOON
Chaco Indian / TOBA; PILAGA
Chad / TCHAD
Chad capital / FORTLAMY
Chad city / BOKORO
Chad mountains / TIBESTI
Chad river / CHARI
chafe / IRK, RUB, VEX; FRET, FROT, GALL
chaff / GUY; BANTER. HUSK
chaff of grain / BRAN
chaffer / HAGGLE; DISPUTE
chaffinch / CHINK, SPINK; ROBINET
chaffy bract / GLUME, PALEA, PALET
chagrin / VEX; ABASH, ANNOY. SHAME
Chahar capital / KALGAN
chain / BOND; RESTRAIN. TYE; CATENA, FETTER; SHACKLE
chain armor / MAIL
chain of hills / ASAR; SWEDISH; APPENNINES
chain part / LINK, RING
chain set with gems / SAUTOIR
chainlike / CATENARY, CATENATE
chainman's pole / BANDEROLLE
chair / SEAT; SEDAN; PROFESSORSHIP
chair carried on poles / SEDAN
chair for one with problem / HOTSEAT
chair part / RUNG, WING; STRETCHER
chair type / ROCKER; WINDSOR
chair-back piece / SPLAT
chairman's mallet / GAVEL
chaise / GIG; SHAY; CARRIAGE
chakar / CLERK; SERVANT
chalcedony / ONYX, SARD; AGATE, CHERT, PRASE
Chaldea / BABYLONIA
chaldean / SOOTHSAYER

Chaldean city / UR
Chaldean cycle / SAROS
chalet / CABIN, LODGE; COTTAGE
chalice / AMA, CUP; AMULA, GRAIL;
  GOBLET
chalice covering / AER; PALL
chalk / CRAYON, CREDIT. WHITEN
chalky / WHITISH
challenge / GAGE; CLAIM; DE-
  MAND. DARE, DEFY; BRAVE
chamber / ROOM; CAVITY
chamber, pert. to / CAMERAL
chamber of the heart / ATRIUM
chambered mollusk / NAUTILUS
chambers of judge / CAMERA
chameleonlike lizard / AGAMA
chamfer / BEVEL
champagne / AY; AVIZE
champagne rating / SEC; BRUT
champion / HERO; LEADER; PALA-
  DIN. DEFEND
champion of the people / TRIBUNE
chance / HAP, LOT; LUCK, RISK;
  HAZARD. OCCUR; BEFALL
chance at bat / LICK
chance discovery / SERENDIPITY
chancel / SANCTUARY
chancel area / BEMA
chances / ODDS
change / VARY; ALTER, AMEND,
  EMEND. FLUX; VARIETY; MUTA-
  TION
change the color of / DYE
change course / VEER; REVERSE
change direction / CANT, TACK,
  TURN, VEER
change to opposite / REVERSE
change place / MOVE; RELOCATE
change to suit / ADAPT
changeable / GIDDY; FICKLE; MU-
  TABLE
changeless / FIRM; STEADY; CON-
  STANT
changeling / OAF; OUPHE
changing lizard / CHAMELEON
channel / BAY, GAT, GUT, WAY;
  DUCT, NECK; CHUTE, FLUME;
  GROOVE
Channel Island / SARK; JERSEY
channel marker / NUN; BUOY,
  SPAR; FLOAT
Channel seaport / STMALO
channel on TV / STATION
chant / MELE, SING; INTONE
chanteuse / SINGER
chanticleer / COCK; ROOSTER
chantry / CHAPEL
chaos / DISORDER; CONFUSION
chaos of Babylonian myth / APSU
chaos of Egyptian myth / NU; NUN
chaos of Norse myth / GINNUNGA-
  GAP

chaos of Polynesian myth / PO
chap / LAD, MAN; FELLOW. CRACK
chapeau / HAT
chapeaux / MILLINERY
chapel / BETHEL, VESTRY; CHAN-
  TRY
chapel in Vatican / SISTINE
chaperon / HOOD; DUENNA,
  MATRON
chapfallen / DEJECTED
chaplain / PADRE; CLERGYMAN
chaplet / ANADEM, WREATH;
  CORONAL, GARLAND
chapman / HAWKER, TRADER
chapped / KIBED, SPLIT
chapter of the Koran / SURA
char / BURN, SEAR; SCORCH.
  CHORE
character / KIND, MARK, ROLE,
  SIGN, SORT, TONE; STAMP,
  STYLE, TRAIT
character of alphabet / RUNE; LET-
  TER
characteristic / MARK; TRAIT; FEA-
  TURE
characterize / MARK; DESCRIBE;
  DESIGNATE
characterized by dependence / AN-
  ACLITIC
characters in a play / CAST
charade / ENIGMA, PUZZLE
charcoal / CARBO; SKETCH
charge / FEE, TAX; CARE, COST,
  FARE, LOAD, RATE, RUSH; ON-
  SET, PRICE, TRUST; ATTACK; AS-
  SAULT. BID; DEBIT; INDICT, IM-
  PUTE
charge with crime / ACCUSE, IN-
  DICT
charge with a debt / DEBIT
charge with gas / AERATE
charge on property / TAX; LIEN
charge for transportation / FARE
charge for transporting mail /
  POSTAGE
charge for using a bridge / TOLL
chargeable / RATABLE; IMPUTABLE
charged / RAMMED, RUSHED
charged with electricity / LIVE
charged particle / ION
charger / STEED; PLATTER
chariness / FRUGALITY
chariot / ESSED; CARRIAGE
chariot carrying a god / RATH;
  RATHA
chariot with four wheels / QUAD-
  RIGA
chariot race arena / CIRCUS
chariot with two horses / BIGA
chariot with two wheels / ESSED
charioteer / JEHU; BENHUR
charisma / IT; GRACE, POWER

charitable / KIND, MILD; HUMANE, TENDER; LENIENT, LIBERAL; GENEROUS

charitable donation / ALMS; LARGESSE

charity / ALMS, LOVE; BOUNTY, GOWPEN; HUMANITY, KINDNESS

charivari / SERENADE, SHIVAREE

charlatan / CHEAT, QUACK; EMPIRIC; IMPOSTOR

Charlemagne's archbishop / TURPIN

Charlemagne's brother / CARLOMAN

Charlemagne's champion / ROLAND

Charlemagne's counselor / ALCUIN

Charlemagne's enemy / GANELON

Charlemagne's father / PEPIN

Charlemagne's horse / BAYARD

Charlemagne's knight / PALADIN

Charlemagne's paladin / NAMO; OGIER; HOLGER, MAUGIS; ROLAND; ORLANDO, RINALDO

Charlemagne's sword / JOYEUSE

Charlemagne's wife / HAMILTRUDE

Charleston fort / SUMTER

Charlotte Bronte book / EMMA; SHIRLEY

charm / JUJU; GRACE, OBEAH, SPELL; AMULET, FETISH, GRIGRI; TRINKET; TALISMAN. ALLURE, ENTICE, SUBDUE; ATTRACT

charming / LOVELY; WINNING; PLEASING

Charon's father / EREBUS

Charon's fee / OBOL; OBOLUS

Charon's mother / NOX

Charon's river / STYX; ACHERON

chart / MAP; PLAN, PLOT; GRAPH

charter / HIRE, RENT; LEASE

chary / SHY; WARY; FRUGAL; PRUDENT; CAUTIOUS

charybdis / WHIRLPOOL

Charybdis' confederate / SCYLLA

chase / TRACK; EMBOSS, PURSUE. HUNT

chaser / BRACER, CHASSE

chasers of badmen / POSSE

chasm / GAP, PIT; GULF; ABYSS, CLEFT

chassé / GLIDE

chassis / FRAME; FRAMEWORK

chaste / PURE; MODEST, VESTAL; ELEGANT; SPOTLESS

chasten / SMITE; PUNISH, PURIFY, REFORM

chastened / HUMBLED; DISCIPLINED

chasteness / CHASTITY; SIMPLICITY

chastise / SPANK; BERATE, PUNISH

chastity / PURITY

chasuble / MANTLE; PLANETA; VESTMENT

chat / GOSSIP; CHATTER, PRATTLE. COSE, COZE; CONFAB

Chateaubriand hero / RENE; CHACTAS

Chateaubriand heroine / ATALA

chateaubriant / STEAK

chatted / CHINNED

chattels / GOODS; EFFECTS; MOVABLES

chatter / GAB, GAS, YAP; CHIN, TALK; PRATE

chatter idly / GABBLE; PRATTLE

chatterbox / PIET; PRATER

chattering bird / PIE; MAGPIE

chawbacon / LOUT; BUMPKIN

cheap / LOW; MEAN, POOR; PALTRY; INEXPENSIVE

cheap ornament / BAUBLE, TINSEL

cheat / BAM, CON, FOB, FUB, GYP; BILK, DUPE, GULL, HOAX, MUMP; COZEN, MULCT, STICK, TRICK; FLEECE, SHAM; FRAUD; SWINDLER

cheat on a bet / WELCH, WELSH

cheaters / EYEGLASSES

chebec / XEBEC

check / BAR, NIP; CURB, HALT, MARK, REIN, STEM, STOP, TEST; BRAKE, STUNT. TAB; DRAFT; DAMPER; CONTROL

check for entertainment / PASS; TICKET

checkerboard / EXCHEQUER

checkers / DRAUGHTS

checkers opening / ALMA, DYKE, FIFE; CROSS, KELSO

checkers term / HUFF, SHOT; CROWN, STROKE

checkrein / BRIDLE

cheddar / CHEESE

cheek / GALL, GENA, JOWL; BRASS, SAUCE

cheek, pert. to / GENAL, MALAR

cheekbone / MALAR; ZYGOMA

cheekiness / NERVE

cheeky / BRAZEN; IMPUDENT

cheer / JOY, RAH; BRAVO, MIRTH; GAIETY. ELATE; ANIMATE, GLADDEN

cheer for matador / OLE

cheer up / LIVEN; ENLIVEN

cheerful / GAY; GLAD; JOLLY; BLITHE, GENIAL

cheerfulness / MIRTH; GAIETY; SUNSHINE

cheerless / SAD; DRAB; DREARY

cheery / CHEERFUL

cheery word / HI

cheese / CURD; CASEIN
cheese, pert. to / CASEIC; CASEOUS
cheese dish / FONDUE; RAREBIT
cheese variety / BLUE, BRIE, EDAM; CREAM, GOUDA, SWISS; ROMANO; CHEDDAR, GRUYERE, SAPSAGO, STILTON; BELPAESE; LIMBURGER
cheeseparing / MEAN; MISERLY
cheesy / WORTHLESS
cheetah / YOUSE, YOUZE
chef / COOK; CHIEF
cheia / CLAW; NOVICE
chemical accelerator / CATALYST
chemical compound / AMIDE, AMINE, ESTER, IMIDE, IMINE
chemical element (gas) / NEON; ARGON, XENON; HELIUM, OXYGEN; KRYPTON; CHLORINE, FLUORINE, HYDROGEN, NITROGEN
chemical element (metal) / TIN; GOLD, IRON, LEAD, ZINC; CERIUM, CESIUM, COBALT, COPPER, NICKEL, SILVER, SODIUM
chemical prefix / OX; ACI, OXA, OXY; AMIDO, AMINO
chemical salt / SAL; ESTER
chemical suffix / AL, OL, YL; ANE, ASI, ENE, ESE, IDE, INE, ITE, OLE, ONE, OSE; ENOL
chemical test / ASSAY
chemical vessel / ALUDE, UDELL; ALUDEL, BEAKER, RETORT
chemist / DRUGGIST; APOTHECARY
cherish / LOVE; NURSE; ESTEEM, FOSTER, HARBOR; COMFORT
cherished possession / MEMENTO; HEIRLOOM, KEEPSAKE
cheroot / CIGAR
cherry / GEAN; MAZZARD, MORELLO
cherry color / CERISE
cherry part / PIT; STONE
cherub / ANGEL
Chesapeake Bay peninsula / DELMARVA
chess defeat / MATE; CHECKMATE
chess move / FORK; CASTLE; FIANCHETTO
chess opening / PIRC; DEBUT; GAMBIT; RUYLOPEZ
chess piece / MAN; KING, PAWN, ROOK; QUEEN; BISHOP, CASTLE, KNIGHT
chess pieces / MEN
chess term / MATE; ISOLANI; EXCHANGE; ENPASSANT; OPPOSITION
chest / KIT; CASE, SAFE; COFFER, THORAX
chest of acacia wood / ARK

chest bone / RIB; COSTA; STERNUM
chest of drawers / HIGHBOY
chest sound / RALE
chesterfield / SOFA; OVERCOAT
chestnut / RATA; CALLUS, MARRON
chestnut, pert. to / CASTANEAN
chesty / VAIN; CONCEITED
chevalier / KNIGHT; GALLANT; HORSEMAN
chevrotain / NAPU; KANCHIL; MEMINNA
chevy / HUNT; CHASE, CHIVY, WORRY
chew / BITE, CHAM; CHAMP, MUNCH; CRUNCH; MASTICATE
chew audibly / CRUNCH
chewing tobacco / CHAW, QUID
chewing tooth / MOLAR
chewink / TOWHEE
chewy candy / GUM; CARAMEL
chewy fruit / FIG
Chianti bottle / FIASCO
chibouk / PIPE
chic / SMART; MODISH; STYLISH
Chicago district / LOOP
chicane / ARTIFICE
chicanery / DECEIT; TRICKERY
chickadee / TITMOUSE
chickaree / SQUIRREL
chicken / HEN; FOWL; POULTRY, TIMID; AFRAID
chicken breed / BANTAM; LEGHORN; DOMINIQUE, WYANDOTTE
chicken for skillet / FRYER
chickenhearted / COWARDLY
chickenhouse / COOP
chickenlike fowl / RASORES
chickenpox / VARICELLA
chickpea / BUB; GRAM; CHICH, CICER; GARBANZO; GARAVANCE
chicle tree / SAPOTA
chicory / ENDIVE
chicorylike herb / ENDIVE
chide / BLAME; REBUKE; REPROVE
chide severely / SCOLD
chide vehemently / BERATE
chief / ARCH, MAIN; FIRST, PRIME, HEAD; LEADER
chief, as a title in India / MIR
chief actor / HERO, STAR
chief actress / HEROINE
chief of the Apostles / PETER
chief city / CAPITAL; METROPOLIS
chief executive / PRESIDENT
chief of Janizaries / DEY
chief monk / ABBOT
chief official / PREMIER
chief stress / BRUNT
chief support / MAINSTAY
chief workman / BOSS; FOREMAN

chiefly / MAINLY; PRINCIPALLY
chiefs and braves / AMERICAN
    INDIANS
chieftain / LEADER; CAPTAIN
chigger / MITE
chilblain / KIBE; PERNIO
child / TAD, TOT; BABY, BATA,
    TYKE; BAIRN; INFANT
child, c.f. / PED; PEDO; PAEDO
child of streets / ARAB; GAMIN;
    URCHIN
childhood disease / MEASLES
childish handwriting / SCRAWL
childish walk / CRAWL; TODDLE
childlike / NAIVE; PUERILE; IN-
    FANTILE
children / KIDS
children of Uranus and Gaea /
    TITANS
child's ailment / CROUP
child's apron / BIB; PINAFORE
child's book / PRIMER, READER
child's carriage / GOCART; STROL-
    LER
child's game / TAG; LEAPFROG;
    HOPSCOTCH
child's playroom / NURSERY
child's primary class / KINDERGAR-
    TEN
child's toy bear / TEDDY
Chile capital / SANTIAGO
Chilean archipelago / TIERRADEL-
    FUEGO
Chilean area / PATAGONIA
Chilean city / TEMUCO; VALPA-
    RAISO
Chilean coin / PESO
Chilean desert / ATACAMA
Chilean Indian / AUCA
Chilean Island / EASTER; RAPANUI
Chilean money / ESCUDO
Chilean poet / NERUDA; MISTRAL
Chilean river / ITATA; BIOBIO
Chilean seaport / IZUIZUE
Chilean timber tree / PELU; RAULI;
    MUERMO
Chilean volcano / ANTUCO
Chilean workman / ROTO
chill / ICE; COOL. AGUE
chill by formality / FROST
chills and fever / FLU; AGUE; MA-
    LARIA
chilly / ICY, RAW; COLD; BLEAK
chime / PEAL, RING. HARMONY
chimerical / WILD; ABSURD; FAN-
    CIFUL
chimney / LUM; FLUE, VENT;
    STACK; PASSAGE
chimney compartment / FLUE
chimney deposit / SOOT
chimney passage / FLUE, PIPE
chimney recess / INGLENOOK

chimpanzee / BONOBO, NCHEGA
chin / MENTUM. CHATTER,
    PALAVER
chin, c.f. / GENIO
chin whiskers / GALWAYS
china / SPODE; DISHES; PORCE-
    LAIN, TABLEWARE
China / CATHAY. See also Chinese
China blue / NIKKO
China capital / PEKING, TAIPEI;
    NANKING, PEIPING; CHUNG-
    KING
china in China / TEACUP
China grass / BON
China tea / HYSON
china wax / PELA
Chinese / SERIC, SINIC; SINAIC.
    SERES
Chinese, c.f. / SINO
Chinese abacus / SUANPAN, SWAN-
    PAN
Chinese aborigine / YAO; MANS,
    MIAO
Chinese antelope / GORAL, SEROW;
    DZEREN, TSERIN
Chinese arch / PAILOU
Chinese aromatic root / GINSENG
Chinese association / TONG
Chinese boat / JUNK; SAMPAN
Chinese bronze coin / LI
Chinese cabbage / BOKCHOY, PAK-
    CHOI
Chinese Caucasian / LOLO, NOSU
Chinese chess / SIANGKI
Chinese chestnut / LING
Chinese city / AMOY; PEKIN; CAN-
    TON, HANKOW, MUKDEN, PE-
    KING; NANKING; TIENTSIN
Chinese civet / RASSE
Chinese cloth / MOXA, PULO
Chinese coin / LI, PU; TAEL, TIAO,
    YUAN; TSIEN
Chinese condiment / NAPEE
Chinese deer / ELAPHURE
Chinese desert / GOBI; SHAMO
Chinese dialect / WU; HAKKA; CAN-
    TONESE
Chinese dog / CHOW, PEKE
Chinese duck / MANDARIN
Chinese duck eggs / PIDAN
Chinese early race / KHITANS
Chinese factory / HONG
Chinese feudal state / WEI
Chinese fish / TREPANG
Chinese flute / TCHE
Chinese game / FANTAN;
    MAHJONGG
Chinese god / GHOS, JOSS, SHEN
Chinese grape / WAMPEE
Chinese grass / RAMIE
Chinese herb / CHA, TEA; GINSENG
Chinese idol / GHOS, JOSS

CHINESE DYNASTIES

In chronological order
"Early Period"
  HSIA (c. 2205–c. 1766 B.C.)
  SHANG (or YIN) (c. 1766–c. 1122 B.C.)
  CHOU (c. 1122–256 B.C.)
"Middle Period"
  CHIN (221–207 B.C.)
  HAN (202 B.C.–A.D. 221)
  "The six dynasties" (WU; CHI, SHA, SHU, WEI; CHEN; LIANG;
    others)
  SUI (598–618)
  TANG (618–906)
  "The five dynasties and ten states" (907–960)
"Early Modern Period"
  SUNG (960–1279)
  YUAN (MONGOL) (1280–1368)
  MING (1368–1644)
  CHING (MANCHU) (1644–1912)

Spelling variants
  WU;
  CHI, HAN, KIN, SHA, SHU, SIN, SUI, TSI, WEI, YIN;
    CHEN, CHIN, CHOU, CHOW, HSIA, LIAO,
    MING, SUNG, TANG, TSIN, YUAN;
  CHING, LIANG, SHANG;
  MANCHU, MONGOL

Chinese island / MATSU; QUEMOY
Chinese laborer / COOLY; COOLIE
Chinese lake / POYANG; KOKONOR
Chinese language / MANDARIN;
  CANTONESE
Chinese luck symbol / BAT
Chinese measure / HO, HU, LI,
  MU, RI, TU; TUA; CHIH, TAEL,
  TSUN; CHANG
Chinese measure of length / LI;
  TSUN
Chinese mile / LI
Chinese monetary unit / TAEL,
  YUAN
Chinese money / LI, PU; CASH,
  MACE, TAEL, TIAO, YUAN; LI-
  ANG, SYCEE
Chinese monkey / DOUC
Chinese mountains / KUNLUN;
  NANSHAN
Chinese musical instrument / KIN
Chinese mythical animal / DRAGON
Chinese negative principle / YIN
Chinese noodles / MEIN
Chinese nurse / AMAH
Chinese obeisance / COTOW; KOW-
  TOW
Chinese official / KUAN, KWAN;
  TAOYAN; MANDARIN
Chinese oil / TUNG
Chinese orange / MANDARIN
Chinese pagoda / TAA
Chinese peak / AMNEMACHIN
Chinese peninsula / LIAOTUNG

Chinese philosopher / MOTI; LAO-
  TZE; CONFUCIUS
Chinese plant / RAMIE; GINSENG
Chinese poet / LIPO
Chinese porcelain / JU, KO; CELA-
  DON
Chinese positive principle / YANG
Chinese pottery / CHUN, KUAN,
  MING, TING
Chinese pound / CATTY
Chinese province / SHANSI;
  KIANGSI
Chinese public official / MANDARIN
Chinese puzzle / TANGRAM
Chinese religion / TAOISM
Chinese rice gruel / CONGEE
Chinese river / SI; GAN, MIN, PEH;
  AMUR, TUNG; HWANG, PEARL;
  YELLOW; HWANGHO, SALWEEN,
  SIKIANG, YANGTZE
Chinese river boat / SAMPAN
Chinese ruler / YAO, YAU; YAOU
Chinese sauce / SOY
Chinese seaport / AMOY; DAIREN;
  SHANGHAI
Chinese secret society / TONG
Chinese sedge / KALI, MATI
Chinese ship / JUNK
Chinese shop / TOKO
Chinese shrub / CHA, REA, TEA
Chinese silk / PONGEE; SHANTUNG
Chinese silver ingot / SYCEE
Chinese skiff / SAMPAN
Chinese sky deity / TIEN

Chinese society / HUI; HOEY, TONG; BOXER

Chinese stringed instrument / KIN; SAMISEN

Chinese tax / LIKIN

Chinese tea / CHA; BOHEA; OOLONG

Chinese temple / TAA; PAGODA

Chinese treaty port / AMOY; ICHANG; FOOCHOW

Chinese tree / LICHEE, LITCHI

Chinese vegetable / UDO

Chinese wax insect / PELA

Chinese way / TAO

Chinese weight / HAO; CATTY, PICUL, TSIEN

Chinese wormwood / MOXA

chinin / COYO

chink / RIFT, RIMA, RIME; FISSURE

chinky / RIMAL; RIMOSE

chinook / JARGON; FLATHEAD

Chinook salmon / QUINNAT

Chinooks / TILLICUM

chip / FLAKE; FRAGMENT. NICK

chip of stone / FLAKE, SPALL; GALLET

chip stone / NIG

chipmunk / CHIPPY, HACKEE

chipper / PERT, SPRY; ACTIVE

Chippewa / See also OJIBWA

chippy / PICKUP; CHIPMUNK

chiro / ELOPS

chiropodist / PODIATRIST

chirp / PEEP; TWEET; TWITTER

chirps / CHIRRUPS

chirrup / PEEP, TWIT

chisel / CHEAT, GOUGE

chit / BILL, GIRL, NOTE

chivalrous / GALLANT; SPIRITED

chivalrous enterprise / QUEST

chocolate / CANDY

chocolate drink / COCOA

chocolate nut / CACAO

chocolate powder / COCOA; PINOLE

choice / FINE, RARE; COSTLY; NOTABLE. CREAM, ELITE; OPTION

choice food / CATES; VIANDS

choice morsel / TIDBIT

choice part / ELITE

choice playing marble / ALLEY

choicest / BEST; PRIME

choicest part / MARROW

choir singer / CHORISTER

choir vestment / COTTA; SURPLICE

choke / BAR, GAG; CLOG, STOP; BLOCK

choke up / DAM; FREEZE

chokedamp / BLACKDAMP

choker / TIE; COLLAR, CRAVAT

choler / IRE; BILE, FURY, RAGE; ANGER

choleric / IRATE; BILIOUS; IRACUND

cholla / CACTUS; OPUNTIA

choose / OPT; CULL, PICK; SELECT

choose for office / VOTE; ELECT, SLATE

chop / AXE, CUT, HEW, LOP; HACK

chop finely / MINCE

chop off / LOP; PRUNE

chop roughly / HACK

chophouse / INN; TAVERN

chopped cabbage / SLAW; SAUERKRAUT

chopped mixture / HASH

chopper / BLOCK, HEWER; BUTCHER

chopping tool / AX; AXE, SAX; HATCHET

choppy / PECKY; SPASMODIC

chopsticks / FOY, JEE; HASI

choral composition / MOTET; ANTHEM, CANTATA; ORATORIO

choral music / HYMN; MOTET; ANTHEM; CANTATA

choral singers / CHOIR; CHORUS

choral vestment / CAPE; COTTA

chorale / HYMN; MELODY

chord / SECANT; CONCORD, DISCORD, EMOTION, HARMONY

chord of three tones / TRIAD, TRINE

chore / JOB; TASK; STINT

choreography / BALLET; DANCING

chortle / LAUGH; CHUCKLE

chosen / ELECT; SELECTED

Chosen / KOREA

chough / JACKDAW

chouse / CHEAT; SWINDLE

chow / FOOD, GRUB

chowchow / OLIO

christen / NAME; BAPTIZE

Christian of Eastern Rite / UNIAT; UNIATE; MELKITE; MARONITE

Christian era / AD, CE

Christian feast / AGAPE

Christian Science founder / EDDY

Christian symbol / ROOD; CROSS; ICHTHOS

Christmas / NOEL, YULE, XMAS

Christmas berry / TOYON

Christmas crib / CRADLE, CRECHE

Christmas decoration / MISTLETOE

Christmas drink / NOG; NOGG

Christmas feast / NATIVITY

Christmas ornament / STAR; TINSEL

Christmas rose / HELLEBORE

Christmas singer / WAKE; CAROLER

Christmas song / NOEL; CAROL, NOWEL

Christmas visitor / KRISS, SANTA

Christmas wreath / HOLLY

Christ's thorn / NABK, NUBKX; JUJUBE

Christ's word on the cross / ELOI

chromosome / IDANT
chromosome division / MITOSIS
chronic / NONACUTE; RECURRENT
chronicle / ANNAL, DIARY;
  ANNALS, MEMOIR, RECORD
chronicler / DIARIST; ANNALIST;
  HISTORIAN
chronological discrepancy / EPACT
chrysalis / KELL, PUPA
chrysanthemum / MUM; KIKU
chrysanthemum crest / KIKUMON
chrysolite / OLIVINE, PERIDOT
chthonian / INFERNAL; UNDER-
  WORLD
chub / CHEVIN, TAUTOG; HERRING
chubby / FAT; PLUMP; ROTUND
chuck / TOSS; FLING. GRUB, FOOD
chuckle / LAUGH; CHORTLE
chucklehead / CLOD, DOLT, FOOL
chukker sport / POLO
chum / PAL; MATE; CRONY; PARD-
  NER
chump / SAP; BLOCK; NUMSKULL
chunk / GOB; LUMP; STUMP; GOB-
  BET
chunk of cast metal / INGOT
church / FANE; CHAPEL; BASILICA
church basin / STOUP
church calendar / ORDO
church ceremony / MASS
church chapel / ORATORY
church council / SYNOD
church creed / NICENE
church dignitary / BISHOP; PRE-
  LATE; CARDINAL
church dish / OSTIA, PATEN
church dissenter / SECTARY;
  SCHISMATIC
church doorkeeper / OSTIARY
Church of England, pert. to /
  ANGLICAN
church gallery / LOFT
church garment / ABA, ALB; COPE;
  AMICE, COTTA, STOLE
church ground / GLEBE
church law / CANON
church maintenance / PREBEND
church of monastery / CONVENT,
  MINSTER
church officer / BEADLE, DEACON,
  PASTOR, PRIEST, SEXTON, VER-
  GER; MINISTER
church official / DEAN, POPE;
  ELDER; CARDINAL
church part / PEW; APSE, BEMA,
  NAVE; AISLE, ALTAR, STALL;
  PARVIS; CHANCEL
church reader / LECTOR
church reading desk / LECTERN
church recess / APSE; RELIQUARY
church reliquary / PYX
church seat / PEW; BENCH
church section / APSE, NAVE

church service / MASS, RITE
church service book / MISSAL
church singers / CHOIR
church vault / CRYPT
churchman / DEACON, MEMBER;
  PRELATE
churchmen / CLERGY
church's tenth / TITHE
churchyard / CEMETERY
churl / BOOR; CARLE, CEORL,
  KNAVE; PEASANT, VILLEIN
churlish / MOROSE; ILLBRED
churn plunger / DASHER
chute / DUCT; FLUME; RAPIDS
cibol / ONION; SHALLOT
cicada / CIGALE, LOCUST
cicatrix / SCAR
cicerone / GUIDE
Cid's horse / BABIECA
Cid's name / BIVAR
Cid's sword / COLADA, TIZONA
Cid's wife / ISMENA, XIMENA
cierge / CANDLE
cigar / CLARO, SEGAR, STOGY;
  CORONA, STOGIE; CHEROOT,
  LONDRES; PANATELA
cigar tobacco / HAVANA
cigarette / FAG; DRAG; GASPER
cigarfish / SCAD
cilia / EYELASHES
cinch / GRIP, HOLD; GIRTH. EASY,
  PIPE, SURE
Cincinnati nine / REDS
cincture / BELT; GIRDLE
cinder / ASH; EMBER, GLEED
cinema / MOVIES
cinema pioneer / GRIFFITH
cinematic honor / OSCAR
cinnabar / VERMILION
cinnamon / CASSIA
cinque / FIVE
cion / BUD; TWIG; GRAFT; SPROUT
Cipango / JAPAN
cipher / CODE, NULL, ZERO;
  OUGHT; NAUGHT
cipher breaker / DECODER
Circe's brother / AEETES
Circe's home / AEAEA
Circe's niece / MEDEA
Circe's son / TELEGONUS
circle / CIRC, HOOP, LOOP, RING;
  GROUP, ROUND; CIRQUE;
  COTERIE
circle, c.f. / GYRO
circle around the moon / HALO
circle of friends / COTERIE
circle of light / HALO; NIMBUS
circle part / ARC; SECTOR; SEG-
  MENT
circlet / HOOP; FILLET; BRACELET
circuit/ LAP; TOUR; AMBIT, CYCLE,
  ORBIT; HOOKUP
circuit of judges / EYRE

circuitous / DEVIOUS, WINDING; INDIRECT
circular / ROUND. NOTICE
circular band / HOOP; FILLET
circular disk / WAFER; PLATTER
circular path / ORBIT
circular turn / LOOP
circulate / MOVE, PASS; SPREAD; DIFFUSE
circumference / PERIPHERY
circumscribe / BOUND, LIMIT; RESTRICT
circumscribed / NARROW
circumspect / CHARY; HEEDFUL, PRUDENT
circumstance / HAP; FACT; EVENT; INCIDENT
circumstantial / ACCIDENTAL, INCIDENTAL
circumstantially / EXACTLY; MINUTELY
circumvention / ARTIFICE; STRATAGEM
circus apparatus / TRAPEZE
circus entertainer / CLOWN; TRAPEZIST
circus tent / BIGTOP
cirque / CWM; CORRIE
cisco / HERRING; WHITEFISH
cistercian / MONK
cistern / BAC, VAT; TANK
cit / CITIZEN; TOWNSMAN
citadel / FORT; CASTLE; ACROPOLIS; STRONGHOLD
citadel of Moscow / KREMLIN
citation / SUMMONS; QUOTATION
cite / CALL, NAME; QUOTE, REFER
cited / MENTIONED
citified / URBAN
citizen / FREEMAN; TOWNSMAN
citizen, suffix / ITE
citizen soldier body / MILITIA
citron / ETROG; CEDRAT, ETHROG
citron yellow / MIMOSA
citrus disease / SCALE; CANKER
citrus drink / ADE; LEMONADE
citrus fruit / LIME; LEMON; ORANGE; KUMQUAT; SHADDOCK
citrus preserves / MARMALADE
city / METROPOLIS. URBAN. See also individual countries
city, pert. to / CIVIC, URBAN; MUNICIPAL
city of angels / LA; LOSANGELES
city of bells / STRASBOURG
city of brotherly love / PHILADELPHIA
city of churches / BROOKLYN
city conduits / SEWERS
city of conferences / GENEVA
city of David / JERUSALEM
city district / SLUM, WARD; BARRIO, GHETTO

city dweller / URBANITE
city of God / ZION; CHURCH, HEAVEN; PARADISE
city of hundred towers / PAVIA
city of Italia / GENOVA, MILANO, NAPOLI, TORINO; FIRENZE, LIVORNO, VENETIA
city of kings / LIMA
city of lights / PARIS
city of lilies / FLORENCE
city of luxury / SYBARIS
city of masts / LONDON
city of monuments / BALTIMORE
city newspaper / DAILY
city outskirts / SUBURBS
city of palaces / ROME; CALCUTTA
city pall / SMOG
city of the plains / SODOM; GOMORRAH
city political division / WARD; DISTRICT
city of the prophet / MEDINA
city of rams / CANTON
city of refuge / GOLAN; HEBRON, MEDINA
city of roses / PASADENA
city of saints / MONTREAL, SALTLAKE
city of seven hills / ROME
city square / PARK; BLOCK
city of the sun / RHODES; BAALBEK; HELIOPOLIS
city of three kings / COLOGNE
city tract / LOT
city of the tribes / GALWAY
city of victory / CAIRO
city of the violet crown / ATHENS
city of the west / GLASGOW
city's water supply / RESERVOIR
city-state / POLIS
civet / RASSE, TODDY; MUSANG; MAMPALON
civet of India / ZIBET; TANGALUNG
civet of Madagascar / FOUSSA
civetlike animal / GENET
civic / URBAN
civil / CIVIC, SUAVE; POLITE, URBANE
civil injury / TORT
civil officer / MAGISTRATE
Civil War admiral / FARRAGUT
Civil War battle / SHILOH; BULLRUN, MALVERN; ANTIETAM
Civil War bullets / MINIES
Civil War general / LEE; POPE; BRAGG, EWELL, GRANT, MEADE, SCOTT, SYKES, CUSTER, HOOKER; FORREST, JACKSON
civilian dress / MUFTI
civility / COURTESY; POLITENESS
civilization / CULTURE; REFINEMENT

civilize / POLISH, REFINE; EDU-CATE, IMPROVE
clad / ROBED; GARBED; DRESSED
claim / ASK; ASSERT, DEMAND. LIEN, TITLE; RIGHT
claim against property / LIEN
clam / CHAMA, RAZOR, SOLEN; QUAHOG; TRIDACNA
clamber / CLIMB; ASCEND
clammy / WET; DAMP, SOFT
clamor / ADO, DIN; NOISE; HUB-BUB
clamorous / LOUD; BLATANT; TURBULENT
clamp / NIP. VISE
clamping device / PIN; VISE
clan / GENS, SEPT; TRIBE
clan emblem / TOTEM
clan head / ALDER
clan quarrel / FEUD
clandestine / SLY; HIDDEN, SECRET; PRIVATE
clandestine meeting / TRYST
clang / DING; CLAMOR
clanged / RANG
clangor / DIN; CLANK; RATTLE
clap / APPLAUD
claptrap / BOSH; BUNK; NON-SENSE
claret / BLOOD
claret wine / MEDOC
clarify / CLEAR, PURGE; DEFINE
clarify by melting / RENDER
clarinet range / CHALUMEAU
clarinet socket / BIRN
clarity / PURITY; LUCIDITY; PRE-CISION
claro / CIGAR
clash / JAR; COLLIDE. CONFLICT
clasp / HOLD; GRASP, SEIZE, CLIP, HASP
clasp pin / BROOCH
clasping device / CLIP, LOCK
class / ILK; HEAD, KIND, RANK, SECT, SORT, TYPE; CASTE, GENRE, GENUS, GRADE, GROUP, ORDER
class, pert. to / GENERAL, GENERIC
class period / SESSION
class of society / CASTE
classic / PURE; STANDARD
classic Italian poet / TASSO
classical dance / BALLET
classical language / GREEK; LATIN
classification / TAXONOMY; ARRANGEMENT
classification method / SYSTEM
classified / SORTED; GROUPED
classify / RANK, RATE, SORT, TYPE; GRADE, LABEL
clatter / DIN; CLACK; RATTLE

clattering / GOSSIPING
clause / ARTICLE, PROVISO; SEN-TENCE; CONDITION, PROVISION
clavier / PIANO; KEYBOARD
claw / NAIL; TALON, UNCUS; UN-GUIS. SCRATCH
claw of crustacean / CHELA; CHELAE
claw ornament / SPUR; GRIFFE
clay / BOLE, LOAM, MARL; ARGIL, EARTH, LOESS; KAOLIN; LATERITE
clay box / SAGGER
clay composition / LUTE
clay eating / PICA; GEOPHAGIA
clay lump / PUG
clay manure / MALM, MARL
clay marble / KNICKER
clay pigeon / DUPE, GULL; VICTIM
clayey deposit / MARL
clay-pigeon shooting / SKEET
clay-pipe die / DOD
clean / FAIR, NEAT, PURE; CLEAR; CHASTE, KOSHER. WIPE; PUR-IFY
clean with a cloth / WIPE
clean clothes / SPOT, WASH; BRUSH
clean the deck / MOP; SWAB
clean fun / SPORT
clean house / DUST; SWEEP; VACUUM
clean up / GAIN; PROFIT
cleaning agent / SOAP; DETERGENT
cleaning house / DUSTING; SCRUB-BING
cleaning implement / MOP; BROOM BRUSH; DUSTER, VACUUM; CLEANER
cleaning rod / RAMROD
cleanse / BATHE, PURGE, SCOUR, SCRUB
cleanser / SOAP; POWDER; DETER-GENT
cleansing process / BATH; RINSE; SHOWER
clear / FAIR, FREE, OPEN, PURE; LUCID, PLAIN, SUNNY; BRIGHT, LIMPID, SERENE. NET, RID; SOLVE; ACQUIT
clear of blame / EXONERATE
clear of charges / FREE; ACQUIT
clear gain / NET; PROFIT
clear rope lead / WAPP
clear of suspicion / VINDICATE
clear things out / WEED
clearance / RELEASE REMOVAL; DISCHARGE
cleared / NETTED; CLARIFIED
clearing / GLADE, GROVE
clearly / PLAINLY; PALPABLY
cleat / SPIKE, WEDGE

cleavable / DIVISIBLE

cleave / CUT, HEW; HOLD, OPEN, PART, REND, RIVE, TEAR

cleavers / BEDSTRAW; CATCH-WEED

cleaving tool / FROE

cleek / HOOK; CROOK; FOURWOOD

cleft / CUT, GAP; RIFT, RIMA; CHASM

cleft in a rock / RIVA

clegg / HORSEFLY

clemency / MERCY; LENITY

clement / MILD; GENTLE; LENIENT

Clementine's father / MINER

clench / GRIP, HOLD

clenched hand / FIST

Cleopatra's attendant / IRAS

Cleopatra's lover / ANTONY

Cleopatra's needle / OBELISK

Cleopatra's pet / ASP

Cleopatra's son / CAESARION

clergyman / ABBE; CANON, VICAR; CLERIC, CURATE, DIVINE, PARSON, PASTOR, PRIEST, RECTOR; MINISTER

clergyman's assignment / PARISH; PASTORATE

clergyman's cap / BIRETTA

clergyman's salary / STIPEND

clergyman's stage / ALTAR; PULPIT

clergyman's title / PADRE; FATHER; REVEREND

clerical collar / RABAT

clerical dress / ALB; VESTMENT

clerical worker / TYPIST

clerihew's inventor / BENTLEY

clerk / SCRIBE; SALESMAN; ATTENDANT

clerk in bank / TELLER

clerk in store / CASHIER; SALESMAN; SALESLADY

Cleveland's river / CUYAHOGA

clever / APT; ABLE CUTE; HANDY, READY, SLICK, SMART

clever retort / REPARTEE

clever saying / MOT

cleverly stylish / CHIC

click beetle / DOR; ELATER; ELATERID

client / PATRON; CUSTOMER

clientele / FOLLOWING

cliff / BANK, CRAG, KLIP; ESCARP; PRECIPICE

climatic conditions / WEATHER

climax / END, TOP; ACME; APOGEE, SUMMIT

climb / RISE, SHIN, SOAR; MOUNT

climb crawlingly / CREEP; CLAMBER

climb the sky / SOAR

climber / SCALER

climbing / SCADENT, SCALING

climbing device / ROPE; PITON, STEPS; LADDER

climbing fern / NITO; AGSAM

climbing fish / ANABAS, SALMON

climbing palm / RATTAN

climbing pepper / ARA; BETEL

climbing plant / HOP, IVY, PEA; BINE, VINE; LIANA, LIANE; CREEPER

climbing plant organ / TENDRIL

clime / TRACT; REGION; CLIMATE

clinch / NAIL; RIVET; GRAPPLE

cling / CLASP, STICK, TWINE; ADHERE, CLEAVE, COHERE

cling with fondness / HUG; EMBRACE

clinging / HOLDING

clinic / DISPENSARY

clink / JAIL. JINGLE, TINKLE

clinker / ASH; SLAG

clip / MOW, NIP; COLL; SHEAR

clip off branches / PRUNE

clip suddenly / SNIP

clipped / SHORN

clique / BAND, RING; COTERIE

cloaca / PRIVY, SEWER; CESSPOOL

cloak / ABA; ROBE, WRAP; CAPOT, MANTA; CAPOTE, MANTLE; GARMENT, MANTEAU. HIDE, MASK, VEIL; COVER

cloak with hood / CAPOTE

cloak of India / CHOGA

cloaked / CAPED

clock / TIMER, WATCH

clock face / DIAL

clock part / DIAL; DETENT; PENDULUM

clock like a ship / NEF

clocked / TIMED

clodhopper / BOOR, LOUT; RUSTIC

clog / BURDEN, FETTER, HAMPER, HINDER, IMPEDE. GETA; SABOT; PATTEN

cloister / PRIORY; CONVENT; HERMITAGE

clone ancestor / ORTET

clone member / RAMET

close / FIRM, MEAN, NEAR, NIGH, SHUT; DENSE. END; SEAL; CEASE; FINISH. FINALE

close associate / PAL; CRONY; PARTNER

close by / NEAR, NIGH

close of day / EEN, EVE; NIGHT; SUNSET; EVENING

close the eyes of / SEEL

close firmly / BAR, DAM; SHUT

close loop / KINK

close relative / MA, PA; KIN, SIS, SON; FATHER, MOTHER, PARENT, SISTER; BROTHER; DAUGHTER

close tightly / SEAL
closed / SHUT
closed again / RESEALED
closed car / SEDAN
closed curve / CIRCLE; ELLIPSE
close-fitting coat / JACKET, REEFER
closely woven material / GAUZE
closer / NEARER
closing chord sequence / CADENCE,
    CADENZA
closing part / FINALE; STRETTO
closing sequence / CODA
closure / LIEN; CLOSING; SHUT-
    TING
clot / GEL; JELL; COAGULATE
cloth / REP; BRIN, FELT, LENO,
    MARL, SILK; BAIZE, DENIM,
    SATIN, SERGE, TAMMY, TWEED;
    CANVAS, FABRIC, MELTON; SAT-
    INET, WORSTED
cloth from bark / TAPA
cloth cover on shipboard / TARP;
    CAPOT; CANVAS
cloth for drying / TOWEL
cloth from flax / LINEN
cloth kerchief / BANDANA; BAN-
    DANNA
cloth measure / ELL; YARD
cloth plug / DOSSIL
cloth remnant / RAG; FENT
clothe / TOG; GIRD, ROBE, VEST;
    ARRAY, DRESS, ENDUE
clothed / CLAD; GARBED; ATTIRED
clothes / GARB, TOGS; DRESS, AT-
    TIRE; APPAREL, RAIMENT
clothes moth / TINEA
clothes stand / RACK, TREE
clothes tree / COSTUMER
clothespress / KAS; ARMOIRE
clothing / GARB; COSTUME; GAR-
    MENTS
cloud / BLUR, HAZE, MIST, SMUR;
    CIRRUS, NIMBUS; CUMULUS
cloud dragon / AHI
cloudberry / MOLKA
clouded mentally / HAZY; CON-
    FUSED
cloudless / CLEAR, SUNNY
cloudy / DIM; DARK, DULL, HAZY;
    DUSKY, MISTY
clout / HIT; SLAP, SWAT
clove / BUD; SPICE
clover / HUBAM; ALSIKE; MELILOT,
    TREFOIL; SAINFOIN
cloverlike plant / MEDIC, SULLA;
    MEDICK
clown / MIME, ZANY; JESTER; BUF-
    FOON, BUMPKIN
clownish / RUDE; CLUMSY,
    RUSTIC; BOORISH
cloy / GLUT, PALL, SATE; SURFEIT
club / BAT; MACE; GROUP; SO-
    CIETY; SODALITY

club fee / DUES
club member / BROTHER
club for women / ZONTA; SOROR-
    ITY
clubfoot / TALIPES
clubshaped / CLAVATE
clue / CUE, TIP; HINT, SIGN
clump / BUSH, TUFT; BUNCH;
    CLUSTER
clump of dirt / CLOD
clump of ivy / TOD
clumsily handled / PAWED;
    BOTCHED
clumsy / HEAVY, INEPT; GAUCHE;
    AWKWARD, UNCOUTH
clumsy cut / HACK
clumsy person / OX; KLUTZ
clumsy shoes / CLOGS; KLOMPEN
clumsy workman / BOTCHER,
    BUNGLER, BUTCHER
cluse / GORGE
cluster / NEP; CYME, TUFT;
    BUNCH, SORUS
cluster bean / GUAR
cluster of stars / CLOUD;
    PLEIADES
clutch / NAB; GRAB, GRIP, HOLD;
    CATCH, GRASP
clutter / LITTER; DISORDER
clysmic / CLEANSING
Clytemnestra's lover / AEGISTHUS
Clytemnestra's mother / LEDA
Clytemnestra's son / ORESTES
Clytemnestra's twin / CASTOR
cnemis / SHIN; TIBIA
coach / BUS; STAGE; CARRIER
coach dog / DALMATIAN
coach privately / TUTOR
coachman / JEHU; DRIVER
coagulate / GEL; CAKE, CLOT
coagulated milk / CURD
coal / FUEL; LIGNITE; ANTHRACITE
coal bed / SEAM
coal box / BIN, HOD; BUNKER
coal car / CORB, TRAM; TENDER
coal deposit / SOOT
coal measure / TON
coal miner / COLLIER
coal oil / KEROSENE; PETROLEUM
coal scuttle / HOD
coal size / EGG, NUT, PEA; STOVE
coal tar derivative / DYE; PITCH
coal after treatment / COKE
coal variety / CANNEL; LIGNITE
coaler / FREIGHTER
coalesce / JOIN; BLEND, UNITE
coalfish / SEY; CUDDY; SAITHE
coalition / MASS; UNION; FUSION
coal-mine gas / DAMP
coarse / MEAN, RUDE, VILE;
    CRASS
coarse basket / SKEP
coarse cinnamon bark / CASSIA

coarse cloth / BAIZE, CRASH; BURLAP
coarse cotton cloth / SCRIM, SURAT
coarse file / RASP
coarse grain / MEAL, SAMP
coarse grass / REED; SEDGE
coarse hair / KEMP
coarse nap / SHAG
coarse seaweed / DULCE
coarse toweling / TERRY
coarse wool / GARE
coarse wool fabric / TAMIN; KERSEY, TAMINE
coarse woolen blanket / COTTA
coarsely ground corn / SAMP
coast / BEACH, SHORE. GLIDE
coast bird / GULL, TERN
coastal / LITTORAL
coastal area / TIDELAND
coastal range of India / GHAT
coaster / BOB; SLED
coastline / SEASHORE
coat / ABA; COVER, LAYER
coat of an animal / FUR; PELAGE
coat of armor / HAUBERK
coat of arms / CREST
coat with gold / GILD
coat of hair / MELOTE
coat lining / SATEEN
coat of mail / BRINIE, BYRNIE
coat with metal / PLATE, TERNE
coat part / LAPEL, SKIRT; SLEEVE
coax / BEG; TEASE; CAJOLE
cob / GULL, LUMP, SWAN; SPIDER
cobber / PAL; COMPANION
cobble / MEND; BOTCH. STONE
cobbler / SUTOR; SHOEMAKER
cobbler's saint / CRISPIN
cobbler's tool / AWL; LAST
cobbler's wax / CODE
cobia / BONITO
cobra / HAJE, NAGA; MAMBA; RINGHALS
cocaine / COKE, DUST; SNOW
cocaine source / COCA
Cochin China capital / SAIGON
Cochin China monkey / DOUC
cock / TAP; VANE; ROOSTER
cockade / BADGE; ROSETTE
cock-a-hoop / AGEE; ELATED
cockateel / PARROT
cockatoo / ARARA, GALAH
cocked hat / SCRAPER, TRICORN
cocker / SPANIEL, PET; PAMPER
cockeye / SQUINT; CROSSEYE
cockeyed / AWRY; SKEWED
Cockney poet / HUNT; KEATS
cockpit of Europe / BELGIUM
cockscomb / CELOSIA, COXCOMB
cocksure / CERTAIN
cocktail / MARTINI, SIDECAR
cocktail room / LOUNGE

cocky / VAIN; POMPOUS; CONCEITED
cocky person / BANTAM
coco / HEAD, TARO
cocoa / BROMA, CACAO; CHOCOLATE
co-conspirators / CONFEDERATES
coconut fiber / COIR, KOIR, KYAR
coconut of India / NARGIL
coconut juice / MILK
coconut meat / COPRA
coconut palm / NIOG
cocoon / CLEW, CLUE
cocoon of silkworm / CLEW
cocoon thread / BAVE
cocotte / FLIRT; WANTON; STEWPAN
cod / HAKE, POOR; BURBOT; BACALAO
cod, pert. to / GADOID
coddle / COCKER, PAMPER
coddled boy / MILKSOP
code / LAW; CANON; CIPHER
code message / PLAINTEXT
code signal / ROGER
code system / MORSE
code of the west / RANGELAW
codicil / RIDER; APPENDIX
codify / DIGEST
codlike fish / CUSK, HAKE, LING
coefficient / MULTIPLIER
coerce / CURB; DRIVE, FORCE
coeval / COEXISTENT; CONTEMPORARY
coffee / RIO; BREW, JAVA; MOCHA
coffee alkaloid / CAFFEINE
coffee bean / NIB
coffee container / CUP
coffee cup / FINJAN; FEENJON
coffee cup stand / ZARF
coffee extender / CHICORY
coffee grind / DRIP, FINE; COARSE
coffee grinder / MILL
coffee house / CAFE; BISTRO
coffee maker / POT, URN; SILEX; PERCOLATOR
coffee roast / BLEND
coffee senna / CASSIA
coffer / ARK, PYX; CHEST; CAISSON
coffin / CASKET; SARCOPHAGUS
coffin cover / PALL
coffin stand / BIER; CATAFALQUE
coffinnail / BUTT; CIGARETTE
cog / GEAR, PAWL; TOOTH. LIE
cogent / VALID; POTENT, STRONG
cogitate / MULL, MUSE; THINK
cognate / AKIN; ALLIED; RELATED
cognizance / KEN; AWARENESS
cognizant / AWARE
cognomen / EPITHET, SURNAME
cogwheel / GEAR
cohere / BIND; CLING, STICK

coherence of ideas / LOGIC, SENSE
coherent / CONNECTED; CONSISTENT
coif / CAP; SKULLCAP
coiffeur / HAIRDRESSER
coiffure / HAIRDO; HEADDRESS
coign / ANGLE; CORNER
coil / CURL, WIND; TWIST; SPIRAL
coil, c.f. / SPIRO
coil of hair / CURL
coil of yarn / SKEIN
coin / ANGLE, MONEY; CORNER,
    SPECIE. MINT; INVENT. See also
    money under individual countries
coin of the Bible / MITE; BEKAH;
    SHEKEL, TALENT
coin blank / PLANCHET
coin collecting / NUMISMATICS
coin disk / FLAN
coin receptacle / SLOT; METER
coin substitute / SLUG
coin tester / SARAF; SHROFF
coinage / INVENTION
coincide / JIBE; AGREE; CONCUR
coincidence / CHANCE; FORTUITY
coined money / SPECIE
coiner / COUNTERFEITER
coiner of words / NEOLOGIST
coins / CASH; CHANGE
coin's edging / MILLING, REEDING
coin's face / HEADS; OBVERSE
coin's reverse side / TAILS, VERSO
col / PASS; SADDLE
colander / SIEVE; STRAINER
cold / ICY, RAW; ALGID. RHEUM;
    CORYZA; CATARRH; RHINITIS
cold, c.f. / CRYO
cold Adriatic wind / BORA
cold blood / SANGFROID; NONCHALANCE
cold crystals / SNOW
cold cuts / DELICATESSEN
cold and damp / RAW; DANK
cold drink / SODA; FRAPPE
cold feet / FEAR, FUNK
cold months / WINTER
cold shoulder / CUT; SNUB; REBUFF
cold steel / BAYONET
cold stone / SLAB
cold sufferer / SNEEZER
cold Texas wind / NORTHER
cold weather garment / MANTA,
    PARKA; OVERCOAT
cold wind / BISE, PUNA; MISTRAL
cold zone / ARCTIC; ANTARCTIC
cold-blooded / CALLOUS, STOICAL
cold-blooded animal / FISH;
    REPTILE
coldly / ICILY
coldly hard / GLASSY
cold-producing / ALGIFIC
cole / KALE; CABBAGE

coleopteran / BEETLE
Coleridge's "ancient" / MARINER
colicky / ILEAC
colin / BOBWHITE
collaborate / AGREE, UNITE
collapse / FAIL, FALL; SHRINK
collapsible / FRAIL; UNSTEADY
collapsible boat / FALTBOAT
collar / ETON, RING; FICHU
collar of chain / TORQUE
collar for criminal / CANGUE
collar of flowers / LEI
collar of frills / RUFF
collar of gems / CHOKER;
    CARCANET
collar worn by Pope / FANON,
    ORALE
collarbone / CLAVICLE
collaret / FICHU
collate / GATHER; COMPARE
collateral / KINSMAN; SECURITY
collateral security / PLEDGE
collation / TEA; REPAST
colleague / ALLY; HELPER; PARTNER
collect / LEVY, POOL; AMASS
collect into a book / ANTHOLOGIZE
collect together / COMPILE
collected / CALM, COOL; PLACID
collected outfit / LAYETTE; TROUSSEAU
collected systematically / CORRELATED
collection / ANA, SET; HEAP, MASS
collection of animals / ZOO;
    MENAGERIE
collection of clothes / WARDROBE
collection of facts / ANA
collection of implements / KIT
collection of people / CROWD
collection of poems / SYLVA
collection of reports / DOSSIER
collection of tents / CAMP
collector of bird's nests / OOLOGIST
collector's hobby / PHILATELY
collector's item / CURIO; RARITY
colleen / GIRL, LASS
college / NORMAL, SCHOOL;
    ACADEMY
college benefactor / ENDOWER
college building / GYM, LAB; DORM
college class / LECTURE, SEMINAR
college concentration / MAJOR
college dance / HOP; PROM
college degree / AB, AM, BA, BS,
    CE, DD, EE, MA; LLB, LLD, MFA,
    PHD
college freshman / FROSH
college girl / COED
college goal / DEGREE
college graduate / ALUMNA;
    ALUMNUS
college grounds / QUAD; CAMPUS

college official / DEAN; REGENT
college permit for absence / EXEAT
college session / SEMESTER
college society / FRAT; SORORITY
college song / ALMAMATER
college student / COED, SOPH;
   FROSH; JUNIOR, SENIOR;
   FRESHMAN; SOPHOMORE
college teacher / DON; TUTOR
college term / SEMESTER
college treasurer / BURSAR
collegian / STUDENT
collide / RAM; CLASH, CRASH
collide like billiard balls / CANNON
collide with / HIT, RAM; BUMP
collier / MINER
colliery / PIT; MINE
collision / CLASH, CRASH, SHOCK
collision sport / FOOTBALL
colloidal liquid / GEL
colloidal substance / GUM
colloidal suspension / SOL
colloquial / COMMON; INFORMAL
colloquialism / IDIOM
colloquy / CHAT, TALK; PALAVER
collusion / FRAUD; DECEIT
Colombia capital / BOGOTA
Colombian city / CALI; MEDELLIN
Colombian Indian / BORO, DUIT,
   MUSO, MUZO, TAMA, TAPA;
   CHOCO
Colombian money / PESO
Colombian peak / CHITA, HUILA
Colombian river / META; CAUCA
colonel's insignia / EAGLE
colonial descendants / DARS
colonist / PIONEER, SETTLER
colonist's greeting to Indian /
   NETOP
colonizer / OECIST; PLANTER
colonnade / STOA; ARCADE
colophon / LOGO; EMBLEM
colophony / ROSIN
color / HUE; TINT; GUISE, TINGE.
   DYE; BLUSH, PAINT, STAIN
color, c.f. / CHROM; CHROMO
color of animal / ROAN; BRINDLE
color blindness / DALTONISM
color changer / TONER
color gamut / PALETTE
color halo / RAINBOW
color lightly / TINT; TINGE
color of moleskin / TAUPE
color spectrum / ROYGBIV,
   VIBGYOR
color spot / FLECK
color spreader / PRISM
color stripe / PLAGA
color variety / SHADE; NUANCE
color vehicle / MEGILP
Colorado capital / DENVER
Colorado city / PUEBLO
Colorado Indian / UTE; ARAPAHO

Colorado mountain / OSO; LONGS
Colorado park / ESTES
Colorado peak / PIKES
Colorado river / PLATTE
Colorado ski center / ASPEN
Colorado state flower / COLUMBINE
Colorado's nickname / SILVER;
   CENTENNIAL
colored / NEGRO; TINTED; PAINTED
colored band / STRIPE
colored chalk / CRAYON, PASTEL
colored kerchief / BANDANA;
   BANDANNA
colored layer of iris / UVEA
colored mosaic glass / SMALTO
colorful / RICH; VIVID; GORGEOUS
colorful bird / ORIOLE; TANAGER
colorful fish / BOCE, OPAH;
   WRASSE
colorful and rewarding conclusion /
   RAINBOWSEND
colorful workman / DYER
coloring agent / DYE; PAINT
coloring board / PALETTE
coloring matter / DYE; PAINT
colorist / PAINTER
colorless / WAN; DRAB, PALE
colorless liquor / GIN
colossal / HUGE, VAST; IMMENSE
colt / FOAL; PISTOL; REVOLVER
colter / PLOWSHARE
coltish / FRISKY
colubrine / SNAKELIKE
Columbia / AMERICA
Columbia River dam / BONNEVILLE
columbine / AQUILEGIA.
   DOVELIKE
Columbine's lover / HARLEQUIN
Columbus / COLON
Columbus' birthplace / GENOA
Columbus' captain / PINZON
Columbus' patron / ISABELLA
Columbus' ship / NINA; PINTA;
   SANTAMARIA
Columbus' son / DIEGO
Columbus' starting port / PALOS
column / PILLAR
column, pert. to / STELAR
column base / PLINTH
column as human figure / TELA-
   MON; CARYATID
column shaft / FUST, TIGE; SCAPE
columnar / TERETE
columnar arrangement / TABLE
columnar row / COLONNADE
column's curve / ENTASIS
coma / STUPOR; LETHARGY
Comanche / SNAKE; PADUCAH
Comanches' nemesis / RANGER
comate / PAL; COMPANION. HAIRY
comatose / TORPID
comb / HIVE; CREST; HACKLE.
   CURRY

comb wool / CARD; TEASE
combat / WAR; DUEL; FIGHT; BATTLE. OPPOSE, OPPUGN, RESIST
combat between knights / JOUST
combat place / ARENA, FIELD, LISTS
combative / MILITANT; PUGNACIOUS
combination / CABAL, UNION
combination of cards / MELD, PAIR; TENACE; STRAIGHT
combination of tones / TUNE; CHORD
combine / MIX; BLEND, MERGE
combine smoothly / BLEND
combined / JOINT; MINGLED
combing instrument / CARD
combmaker's file / CARLET
combustible / FIERY; INFLAMMABLE
combustible mineral / COAL, COKE
combustion / FIRE; FLAME
combustion product / ASH; SOOT
come / ENSUE, REACH; ACCRUE
come about / TACK; OCCUR
come across / DELIVER; DISCOVER
come again / RECUR; REPEAT
come ashore / LAND
come back / RECUR; RETURN
come before / HERALD; PRECEDE
come between / INTRUDE; INTERVENE
come by / GET
come clean / CONFESS
come closer / NEAR; CONVERGE
come a cropper / FAIL, FALL
come down / ALIGHT, WORSEN
come to an end / DIE; FINISH
come into existence / ARISE
come forth / RUN; GUSH; ISSUE
come forward / VOLUNTEER
come to full bloom / RIPEN
come to grief / FAIL; FOUNDER
come to a head / CULMINATE
come in / ENTER
come to mind / OCCUR
come near / APPROACH
come off / HAPPEN; SUCCEED
come on / IMPROVE; APPROACH
come out / APPEAR, EMERGE
come out ahead / WIN
come out even / DRAW
come to pass / BEFALL, HAPPEN
come to perfection / BLOOM, RIPEN
come to rest / SIT; STOP; PAUSE
come round / ACCEPT, ASSENT
come on scene / APPEAR
come short / MISS
come into sight / LOOM; EMERGE
come like sunrise / DAWN
come to terms / AGREE
come through / PAYUP; SUCCEED

come to / TOTAL; REVIVE
come together / MEET; AGREE
come uninvited / CRASH
come up / ARISE, REACH
come upon / MEET; DISCOVER
comeback / ANSWER; RECOVERY
comedian / COMIC
comedian's delight / LAUGHTER
comedian's foil / STOOGE
comedy / FARCE, HUMOR; SATIRE
comeliness / GRACE; BEAUTY
comely / FAIR; PRETTY, SEEMLY
come-on / BAIT; DECOY, SHILL
comestible / EDIBLE; EATABLE
comet's appendage / TAIL; TRAIN
comet's head / COMA
comet's path / ORBIT
comfit / SWEET; CONSERVE
comfort / AID; HELP; CHEER; REVIVE; CONSOLE. EASE, REST; SOLACE
comfortable / COSH, COZY, EASY
comfortable trousers / SLACKS
comforter / QUILT, SCARF; SAVIOUR
comfortless / DREARY; FORLORN
comic / DROLL, FUNNY; HUMOROUS
comic actor / ZANY; CLOWN, MIMIC
comic sketch / SKIT
comic strip / CARTOON
comical / FUNNY; LUDICROUS
comicality / HUMOR; HILARITY
coming / FUTURE; ARRIVAL
coming from above / SUPERNAL
coming forth / BUDDING; EMERGENT
comity / CIVILITY; POLITENESS
command / BID; ORDER; CHARGE, DIRECT. BECK, FIAT, HEST, RULE
command to cows / SOH
command to horses / GEE, HAW; WHOA
commandant / COMMANDER
commanded / BADE; ORDERED
commandeer / SEIZE
commandeer illegally / HIJACK
commander / CHIEF, RULER; LEADER
commander in EGYPT / SIRDAR
commanding / IMPERIOUS
commandment / LAW; PRECEPT
Commandments / DECALOGUE
commando / RAIDER; GUERRILLA
commemorate / REMEMBER; CELEBRATE
commemoration / PRAYER; ENCAENIA
commemorative disk / MEDAL
commence / OPEN; ENTER, START
commenced / GAN; BEGAN
commencement / ORIGIN, OUTSET
commend / LAUD; EXTOL, ORDER

commendable / WORTHY; MERITORIOUS
commensurate / PROPORTIONATE
comment / NOTE; MEMOIR, POSTIL
commentary / GLOSS; SCHOLION
commentary of the Talmud / GEMARA
commentator / CRITIC; EXEGETE
commerce / TRADE; BARTER
commerce, pert. to / MERCANTILE
commercial / AD. MERCANTILE
commercial agreement / CONTRACT
commercial conveyance / VAN; TRAIN, TRUCK; TAXICAB; AIRPLANE
commercial dealing / SALE; TRADE
commercial organization / BANK, MART, SHOP; STORE
commercial traveler / SALESMAN
commercial vessel / OILER; TANKER; FREIGHTER
comminate / CURSE; THREATEN
commingle / MIX; BLEND
comminute / GRIND; PULVERIZE
comminuted / FINE; DUSTY; FLOURY
commiserate / CONDOLE; SYMPATHIZE
commiserating sound / TSK
commiseration / PITY, RUTH
commission / TRUST; BREVET
commissioner / OFFICER; OFFICIAL
commit / ENGAGE, PLEDGE, CONSIGN
commit to custody / DEPOSIT
commit to memory / LEARN
commit moral error / SIN
commitment / PLEDGE; PROMISE
committed theft / STOLE; ROBBED
committee / GROUP, JUNTA; COUNCIL
committee meeting / SESSION
commodious / ROOMY; SPACIOUS
commodity / WARE; GOODS; STAPLE
common / LOW; MEAN; USUAL; COARSE
common abbreviation / ETC; ETAL
common adder / VIPER
common antiseptic / IODINE
common to both sexes / EPICENE
common breakfast item / EGG
common European adder / ASP
common gull / MEW
common heath / ERICA
common language / VERNACULAR
common law / USAGE
common metal / IRON
common sense / HORSESENSE
common swift / CRAN
common talk / RUMOR; GOSSIP

common Tibetan gazelle / GOA
common value / PAR
commoner / PLEB; PROLE; CITIZEN
commonly / USUALLY; GENERALLY
commonplace / TAME; BANAL, STALE, TRITE, USUAL. TRUISM; BROMIDE
commons / MESS; MASSES
commonsense / PRACTICAL
commonwealth / DEMOS, STATE
commotion / ADO; FUSS, STIR, TODO; NOISE; BUSTLE
commune / TOWN; PEOPLE; KIBBUTZ
commune in Holland / EDE
communicate / TALK; PHONE, SPEAK
communicate by air / RADIO
communicate orally / TALK; SPEAK
communicate by wire / PHONE
communicating corridor / AISLE
communication / TV; NEWS, WORD
communications satellite / TELSTAR
communications satellite system / INTELSTAT
communicative / REVELATORY
communion / CONVERSE, VIATICUM; AGREEMENT, EUCHARIST; FELLOWSHIP
communion cup / AMA
communion elements / HOST
communion plate / PATEN
communion service / MASS
communion table / ALTAR
communist / RED; BOLSHEVIK
Communist newspaper / PRAVDA, WORKER; IZVESTIA
community / SOCIETY; SIMILARITY
commute / ALTER; TRAVEL; EXCHANGE, REGULATE
commuter / TRAVELER
Comoro island / MOHELI; MAYOTTE
compact / FIRM, HARD; CLOSE, DENSE, PITHY. PACT; TREATY
compact body / PHALANX
compact by pounding / PACK, TAMP
companion / PAL; ALLY, MATE
Companion of Jehu / CHOUAN
companion of Paul / SILAS
companionable / MATEY; FRIENDLY
companionship / SOCIETY
companionway / STAIRS
company / BAND, CREW, FIRM, GANG, GILD; GUILD, HOUSE, POSSE, TROOP; GUESTS; SOCIETY
company of females / BEE; BEVY
company of males / STAG; SMOKER
company of players / CAST, TEAM; TROUPE
company of sailors / CREW

comparable / LIKE; EQUAL; SIMILAR

comparative / RELATIVE

compare / LIKEN; CONTRAST

compare critically / COLLATE

compare with a standard / WEIGH; MEASURE

compared costs / PRICED; SHOPPED

comparison / SIMILE; ANALOGY

compartment / CELL; PANEL

compass / CARRY; ATTAIN, EFFECT. RANGE; NEEDLE; PELORUS

compass case / BINNACLE

compass point / AIRT; RHUMB. NE, NW, SE, SW; ENE, ESE, NNE, NNW, SSE, SSW, WNW, WSW

compassion / PITY; RUTH; MERCY

compassionate / KIND; BENIGN

compatible / CONGENIAL

compeer / MATE; EQUAL

compel / MAKE; DRIVE, FORCE

compel attention / ARREST

compel obedience / ENFORCE

compendious / BRIEF, SHORT

compendium / DIGEST, PRECIS

compensate / PAY; AMEND, ATONE

compensation / FEE, UTU; HOOT; AMENDS; DAMAGES, PAYMENT

compensation for loss / INDEMNITY

compete / VIE; COPE, RACE; STRIVE

competed without winning / ALSO-RAN

competent / FIT; ABLE; CAPABLE

competition / CONTEST, RIVALRY

competitive sailing / YACHTRACE

competitor / RIVAL; OPPONENT

compilation / ANA; DIGEST; CHRESTOMATHY

compile / EDIT; COLLECT

compiler of synonyms / ROGET

complacence / EASE; CONTENT

complacent / SMUG; AFFABLE

complain / SOB; BEEF, CRAB, FRET, FUSS, KICK, MOAN, SIGH, WAIL

complainant / RELATOR; PLAINTIFF

complaint / MALADY, MURMUR, PLAINT; AILMENT, DISEASE, PROTEST

complaisance / COURTESY

complaisant / EASY; AFFABLE

complected / TWINED; INTER-WOVEN

complement / COMPLETE. SET; UNIT; QUANTITY

complete / FULL; ENDED, TOTAL, UTTER, WHOLE; ENTIRE, INTACT; PLENARY. CAP, END; FINISH

complete disorder / CHAOS

complete failure / FIASCO

complete penetration / SATURATION

completed / OER; DONE, OVER

completely / ALL; FULLY, QUITE

completely developed / RIPE

completely nutty / BANANAS

completely occupied / FULL; ENGROSSED

completion / END; FINIS; ENDING

complex / TANGLED; COMPOUND

complexion / HUE; BLEE, LOOK

compliant / WEAK; DOCILE; SUPPLE

complicated / ELABORATE

complication / NODE; SNARL

complicity / CONCERT; COLLUSION

compliment / PRAISE; ADULATE

comply / MEET, OBEY; ADAPT

component / PART; ELEMENT

comport / AGREE; BEHAVE

comportment / BEARING; BEHAVIOR

compose / CALM, FORM; ALLAY

compose poetry / POETIZE, VERSIFY

composed / COOL; QUIET, SOBER

composite / MIXED; COMPOUND

composite picture / COLLAGE, MONTAGE

composition / OPUS, WORK; ESSAY

composition for eight / OCTET

composition for five / QUINTET

composition for four / QUARTET

composition for nine / NONET

composition for one / SOLO

composition for seven / SEPTET

composition for six / SEXTET

composition for three / TRIO

composition for two / DUO; DUET

composition in music / HYMN, SONG; ETUDE, MOTET, OPERA, RONDO, SUITE; ANTHEM, SONATA

composition of select pieces / CENTO

compositor / PRINTER; TYPESETTER

composure / COOL; POISE; CALMNESS

compound / MIX; BLEND; MINGLE; COMBINE. JUMBLE, MEDLEY

compound ether / ESTER

compound in vitamin B / THIAMINE

comprehend / SEE; KNOW; GRASP, SENSE; DIGEST, EMBODY

comprehensible / INTELLIGIBLE

comprehension / KEN; MIND; FIELD

comprehensive / WIDE; BROAD

compress / NIP; CROWD, WRING; SQUEEZE. PAD; STUPE; BANDAGE

compress into a bundle / BALE

comprise / EMBODY; CONTAIN

compromise / AGREE; ADJUST

comptroller / ACCOUNTANT, CON-
TROLLER
compulsion / FORCE; DURESS
compulsive stealing / KLEPTO-
MANIA
compulsory / OBLIGATORY
compunction / QUALMS, REGRET
compute / COUNT; NUMBER,
RECKON
computer / ENIAC; UNIVAC
computer language / ALGOL,
COBOL; FORTRAN
computer position / ADDRESS
computer type / ANALOG
comrade / MATE; CRONY; FELLOW
comrade in arms / ALLY; SHIP-
MATE
con / GULL, READ; CHEAT, STUDY;
PERUSE. ANTI; AGAINST. PRIS-
ONER
concatenation / LINK; SERIES
concave / DISHED, HOLLOW
concave molding / COVE; CONGE
conceal / MEW; BURY, HIDE, MASK
concealed / PERDU, PRIVY
concealed observation / ESPIAL
concealed obstruction / SNAG,
TRAP
concealment / COVER; AMBUSH
concede / ADMIT, AGREE, GRANT
conceit / EGO; IDEA, QUIP, WHIM;
FANCY, QUIRK
conceited / VAIN; EGOTISTIC
conceited person / PRIG, SNOB
conceive / PLAN; THINK; IDEATE
concent / AGREE
concentrate / AMASS, FOCUS; CEN-
TER; CONDENSE
concentrated / INTENSIVE
concentrated light beam / LASER
concentration / MEMORY; CENTER-
ING; CUMULATION
concept / IDEA; IMAGE; NOTION
conception / FANCY, START;
THOUGHT; INCEPTION; IMPREG-
NATION
concern / CARE, FIRM; HOUSE; AF-
FAIR, MATTER, MOMENT. RE-
GARD
concerned / INVOLVED; INTER-
ESTED
concerned person / CARER
concerning / OF, ON, RE; ASTO,
INRE; ABOUT, ANENT
concerning birth / NATAL
concert / PLAN, PLOT; DEVISE.
CONCORD, HARMONY, MUSICAL
concert grand / PIANO
concert hall / ODEON; LYCEUM
concert manager / IMPRESARIO
concerted gunfire / SALVO; BAR-
RAGE
concertina / ACCORDION

conch / EAR; CHANK, SHELL;
WINKLE; TRUMPET
Conchobar / CONOR
Conchobar's father / CATHBAD
Conchobar's mother / NESSA
Conchobar's nephew / CUCHULAIN
Conchobar's sister / DECHTIRE
conciliate / ENGAGE, PACIFY; AP-
PEASE, MOLLIFY
conciliatory / IRENIC; PACIFIC
concise / CURT; BRIEF, PITHY,
SHORT, TERSE; LACONIC
conciseness / BREVITY
conclave / MEETING; CARDINALATE
conclude / BAR, END; STOP;
CLOSE, INFER; DECIDE, DEDUCE,
GATHER, SETTLE; RESOLVE
concluded / OVER; FINIS
concluding / FINAL; TERMINAL
concluding passage / CODA
conclusion / END; CLOSE; FINALE
conclusion of speech / PERORA-
TION
conclusive / FINAL; COGENT
concoct / BREW, PLAN, PLOT;
FRAME
concoction / PLAN; SCHEME
concord / AMITY, PEACE, UNITY
concordant / FRIENDLY; HARMO-
NIOUS
concordat / TREATY; COMPACT
concourse / THRONG; MEETING
concrete / REAL; SPECIFIC. PAVE-
MENT
concreted sugar / CAKE, CUBE
concur / HELP, JIBE; AGREE
concurrent / COINCIDENTAL
concussion / SHOCK
condemn / DAMN, DOOM; BLAME
condense / REDUCE; ABRIDGE
condensed vapor / FOG; STEAM
condescend / DEIGN, STOOP
condign / DESERVED, SUITABLE
condiment / DILL, SALT; CURRY,
SPICE; CATSUP, PEPPER; KETCH-
UP, MUSTARD, VINEGAR; SEA-
SONING
condiment from flower part / CA-
PER, CLOVE; SAFFRON
condiment vessel / CRUET; CASTER
condition / IF; CASE, RANK, TERM;
CLASS, GRADE, STATE; ESTATE,
FETTLE, PLIGHT
condition, suff. / ANCE, ENCE
condition of agreement / PROVISO
condition of harmony / ATTUNE-
MENT
condition of payment / TERM
condition requiring action / EMER-
GENCY
conditional release / PAROLE
conditions / TERMS; PROVISIONS;
RESERVATIONS

condole / LAMENT; SYMPATHIZE
condolence / PITY; COMMISERA-
TION
condone / PARDON; FORGIVE
condor / VULTURE
conduce / AID; HELP, TEND; SUB-
SERVE; CONTRIBUTE
conducive / LEADING; AUXILIARY
PROMOTIVE
conduct / RUN; LEAD, WAGE;
CARRY, GUIDE. MORALS; BEAR-
ING, MANNERS
conduct festivities / MC
conduct a meeting / PRESIDE
conduct to seat / USHER
conducted / LED
conductor / GUIDE; LEADER;
MAESTRO; CICERONE
conductor of electricity / WIRE
conductor's opposite / INSULATOR
conductor's wand / BATON
conduit / DUCT, MAIN, PIPE, TUBE;
DRAIN, SEWER; CHANNEL
cone / VOLCANO; STROBILE
cone-bearing tree / FIR; PINE
conepatl / SKUNK
cone-shaped / CONIC; CONICAL
coney / HARE; DAMAN; RABBIT
confab / CHAT, TALK
confection / COMFIT; CARAMEL;
SWEETMEAT
confection made with nuts / PRA-
LINE
confectionery / CANDY; CANDY-
STORE
confectionery flavor / VANILLA;
CHOCOLATE
confederacy / UNION; LEAGUE
confederate / ALLY; REBEL; ASSO-
CIATE. UNITED; LEAGUED
Confederate currency / BLUEBACK
Confederate general / LEE; BRAGG;
JACKSON
Confederate president / DAVIS
Confederate soldier / REB; GRAY-
BACK
Confederate uniform / GRAY; BUT-
TERNUT
confederation / UNION; LEAGUE
confer / DUB; GIVE; ENDOW,
GRANT
confer upon / BESTOW
conference / PARLEY, POWWOW
conferred with / CONSULTED
confess / OWN; AVOW; ADMIT,
GRANT
confession / CREDO, CREED
confessional / BOOTH
confidant / CRONY; FRIEND
confide / RELY; TRUST; DEPEND
confidence / FAITH, TRUST; BELIEF
confident / BOLD, SURE; SECURE;
CERTAIN, RELIANT

confidential / SECRET; FAITHFUL
confine / PEN; BIND, SEAL; CRAMP;
IMMURE. BOX, HEM, MEW;
CAGE, COOP; LIMIT
confine and contract / CRAMP
confine with a rope / TETHER
confined / JAILED; INCARCERATED
confinement / LYINGIN
confirm / FIX; AVER, BIND, SEAL
confirmed / ARRANT; INVETERATE
confiscate / SEIZE; IMPOUND
conflagration / FIRE; HOLOCAUST
conflict / WAR; FIGHT; BATTLE,
COMBAT, STRIFE; DISCORD;
STRUGGLE. JAR; CLASH
conflicting / OPPOSING
conform / OBEY; ADAPT, AGREE;
COMPLY, SQUARE
conform to shape / FIT
conformity / HARMONY; AGREE-
MENT
confound / MIX; STAM; ABASH,
BLEND, SHAME
confounded / ASTRAY, DAMNED
confrere / ASSOCIATE
confront / FACE, MEET; ACCOST
Confucian classic / ICHING
confuse / ABASH, BEFOG; BEMUSE
confused / ASEA; CHAOTIC, COM-
PLEX
confused jumble / MESS; WELTER
confused murmur / BUZZ
confused noise / DIN; BABEL
confusion / ADO; MESS; BABEL,
CHAOS, PANIC; TUMULT; FER-
MENT; DISORDER
confute / REFUTE; DISPROVE
congeal / GEL, SET; CLOT; FREEZE
congenial / BOON; KINDRED
congenital / INBORN, INNATE; NA-
TIVE
conger / EEL; MORAY
congested / CROWDED
conglomerate / HOLDINGCOMPANY
conglomeration / MASS
Congo / See also Zaire
Congo Bantu / RUA; WARUA
Congo capital / BRAZZAVILLE
Congo fish / LULU
Congo Kinshasa / ZAIRE
Congo trade language / LUBA
congregate / MASS, MEET; GATHER
congregation / HERD; SYNAXIS
congress / ASSEMBLY; LEGISLA-
TURE
congruence / AGREEMENT
congruent / SUITABLE
congruity / ACCORD; CONSO-
NANCE
congruous / FIT; MEET
conic / TAPERING
conic section / CIRCLE; ELLIPSE;
PARABOLA; HYPERBOLA

conical coil of thread / COP
conical lodge / TEEPEE
conical medieval headdress / HEN-NIN
coniferous tree / FIR, YEW; PINE; CEDAR, LARCH; SPRUCE
conjectural / DOUBTFUL
conjecture / WEEN; FANCY, GUESS, OPINE. NOTION, THEORY
conjoint / UNITED; ASSOCIATED
conjugal / MARITAL; CONNUBIAL
conjunction / OR; AND, BUT, EKE, FOR, NOR, YET; THAN
conjuncture / CRISIS; EXIGENCY
conjuration / INCANTATION
conjure / BEG; PRAY; CHARM; JUGGLE; BEWITCH, ENCHANT
conjure up / EVOKE
conjurer / MAGICIAN; ENCHANTER
connate / INNATE, UNITED
connect / ADD, TIE; JOIN, LINK
connect again / RELINK
connected / TIED; LEGATO; COHERENT
connected series / NEXUS
connected thoughts / CONTEXT
Connecticut capital / HARTFORD
Connecticut city / BRIDGEPORT
Connecticut river / THAMES
Connecticut state bird / ROBIN
Connecticut state flower / LAUREL
Connecticut university / YALE
Connecticut's nickname / NUTMEG
connecting link / BOND
connecting pipe / TEE; COLLAR
connection / LINK; NEXUS, UNION; KINSMAN; AFFINITY
connective / AND
connective tissue / FASCIA, TENDON
connective word / CONJUNCTION
connive / ABET; DISREGARD
Connla's father / CUCHULAIN
Connla's mother / AIFE; AOIFE
connoisseur / JUDGE; EXPERT
connotation / INFERENCE
connote / IMPLY; PREDICATE
connubial / MARITAL, NUPTIAL
conquer / WIN; GAIN; CRUSH; DEFEAT, HUMBLE
conqueror / HERO; VICTOR, WINNER
Conqueror / WILLIAM
conqueror of Mexico / CORTES, CORTEZ
conquers / BESTS
conquest / TRIUMPH, VICTORY
consanguineous / AKIN; ANCESTRAL
conscience / INWIT; SCRUPLES
conscientious / FAIR, JUST; EXACT; HONEST

conscious / AWARE; RATIONAL, SENSIBLE, SENTIENT
consciousness / LIMEN; AWARENESS
conscript / DRAFT; ENROLL. DRAFTEE
conscription / DRAFT
consecrate / BLESS; ANOINT, DEVOTE, HALLOW, ORDAIN; CHRISTEN, DEDICATE, SANCTIFY
consecrated / OBLATE; DEVOTED
consecutive / SUCCESSIVE
consensus / ACCORD; AGREEMENT
consent / AGREE; ASSENT, CONCUR. APPROVAL; COMPLIANCE, PERMISSION
consequence / END; EVENT, ISSUE
consequently / SO; ERGO; HENCE; THEREFORE
conservative / TORY; RIGHTIST
conserve / SAVE; PRESERVE
conserve of grape / JELLY, UVATE
conserve of tomato / PASTE; CATSUP; KETCHUP
consider / DEEM, HEED, MUSE, RATE; JUDGE, OPINE, THINK; ESTEEM
consider the chances / WEIGH
considerable / IMPORTANT
considerable number / MANY, MUCH
considerable time / YEARS
considerate / KIND; SOBER, STAID
consideration / HEED; PRICE; MOTIVE, REASON
considering / SINCE. ALLOWING
consign / COMMIT, REMAND
consignment / CARGO
consistency / DENSITY; UNIFORMITY
consistent / SOLID; UNIFORM; ACCORDANT
consisting of alternating speeches / STICHOMYTHIC
consisting of large particles / COARSE
consolation / SOLACE
console / SOOTHE; COMFORT, CONDOLE. CABINET
consolidate / KNIT; UNIFY, UNITE
consolidated annuity / CONSOL
consonance / CONCORD, HARMONY
consonant / LENE, LENIS, SURD; FORTIS, DENTAL, SONANT; SPIRANT; GUTTURAL, SIBILANT
consort / MATE; PARTNER; COMPANION
conspicuous / CLEAR, PLAIN; FAMOUS; SALIENT
conspicuous constellation / ORION; DIPPER

conspicuous prominence / FAME
conspiracy / PLOT; CABAL; IN-
TRIGUE
conspire / SCHEME; COLLUDE
constancy / LOYALTY; DEVOTION,
FIDELITY, FIRMNESS
constant / EVEN, FIRM, TRUE;
FIXED; STABLE
constant desire / ITCH; MANIA
constantly / EER; EVER
consternation / ALARM, PANIC; DIS-
MAY, TERROR
constituent / PART; MEMBER; ELE-
MENT
constitute / FIX; FORM, MAKE
constitution / LAW; FORM; FRAME,

HUMOR; MAKEUP, SPIRIT, TEM-
PER
Constitution / IRONSIDES
constitutional / LEGAL; LAWFUL;
NATURAL; FUNDAMENTAL.
WALK
Constitution's opponent / GUERRI-
ERE
constitutive / ELEMENTAL, ESSEN-
TIAL
constrain / TIE; CURB, HOLD;
DRIVE, FORCE, IMPEL
constraint / DURESS; RESERVE
constrict / BIND; CRAMP
constriction / COMPRESSION CON-
TRACTION

CONSTELLATIONS AND THEIR PRINCIPAL STARS
(* indicates a zodiacal constellation)

	Meaning	Principal Stars
Andromeda	—	ALPHERATZ
Antlia	PUMP	—
Apus	BIRD OF PARA-DISE	—
*Aquarius	WATER CARRIER	ALBALI, SKAT
Aquila	EAGLE	ALTAIR
Ara	ALTAR	—
*Aries	RAM	HAMAL
Auriga	CHARIOTEER	CAPELLA
Bootes	HERDSMAN	ARCTURUS
Caelum	GRAVING TOOL	—
Camelopardalis	GIRAFFE	—
*Cancer	CRAB	ALTARF
Canes Venatici	HUNTING DOGS	CORCAROLI
Canis Major	LARGER DOG	SIRIUS
Canis Minor	LESSER DOG	PROCYON
*Capricornus	HORNED GOAT	ALGEDI
carina	KEEL	CANOPUS
Cassiopeia	—	SCHEDIR
Centaurus	CENTAUR	AGENA, RIGIL-KENTAURUS
Cepheus	—	ALDERAMIN
Cetus	WHALE	MIRA
Chamaeleon	CHAMELEON	—
Circinus	PAIR OF COM-PASSES	—
Columba	DOVE	PHAET
Coma Berenices	BERENICE'S HAIR	—
Corona Australis	SOUTHERN CROWN	—
Corona Borealis	NORTHERN CROWN	ALPHECCA
Corvus	CROW	ALGORAB
Crater	CUP	ALKES
Crux	SOUTHERN CROSS	ACRUX, BETA-CRUCIS
Cygnus	SWAN	DENEB
Delphinus	DOLPHIN	ROTANEV
Dorado	GOLDFISH	—
Draco	DRAGON	ETAMIN, THUBAN
Equuleus	COLT	—

	Meaning	Principal Stars
Eridanus	—	ACHERNAR
Fornax	FURNACE	—
*Gemini	TWINS	CASTOR, POLLUX
Grus	CRANE	ALNAIR
Hercules	—	RASALGETHI
Horologium	CLOCK	—
Hydra	WATER MONSTER	ALPHARD
Hydrus	WATER SNAKE	—
Indus	INDIAN	—
Lacerta	LIZARD	—
*Leo	LION	REGULUS, DENE-BOLA
Leo Minor	SMALLER LION	—
Lepus	HARE	ARNEB
*Libra	BALANCE	KIFFA
Lupus	WOLF	—
Lynx	—	—
Lyra	LYRE	VEGA
Mensa	TABLE	—
Microscopium	MICROSCOPE	—
Monoceros	UNICORN	—
Musca	FLY	—
Norma	THE LEVEL	—
Octans	OCTANT	—
Ophiuchus	SERPENT HOLDER	YED, SABIK
Orion	HUNTER	RIGEL, BELLATRIX, BETELGEUSE
Pavo	PEACOCK	—
Pegasus	WINGED HORSE	ENIF, MARKAT, SCHEAB
Perseus	—	ALGOL
Phoenix	—	—
Pictor	EASEL	—
*Pisces	FISHES	—
Piscis Austrinus	SOUTHERN FISH	FOMALHAUT
Puppis	ARGO'S STERN	NAOS
Pyxis	MARINER'S COMPASS	—
Reticuluum	NET	—
Sagitta	ARROW	—
*Sagittarius	ARCHER	NUNKI, KAUS
*Scorpius	SCORPION	ANTARES
Sculptor	SCULPTOR'S WORKSHOP	—
Scutum	SHIELD	—
Serpens	SERPENT	—
Sextans	SEXTANT	—
*Taurus	BULL	ALDEBARAN, ELNATH
Telescopium	TELESCOPE	—
Triangulum	TRIANGLE	—
Triangulum Australe	SOUTHERN TRIANGLE	—
Tucana	TOUCAN	—
Ursa Major	LARGER BEAR	MIZAR, ALIOTH, MERAK, DUBHE
Ursa Minor	SMALLER BEAR	POLARIS
Vela	SAILS	MARKEB
*Virgo	VIRGIN	SPICA
Volans	FLYING FISH	—
Vulpecula	LITTLE FOX	—

constrictor / BOA; ABOMA; CAMOODI

construct / REAR; BUILD, ERECT

construct anew / REDO; REORGANIZE

construction / FORM; SHAPE; FIGURE; BUILDING

construction worker / MASON; ROOFER; RIVETER

construction worker's helmet / HARDHAT

constructor / BUILDER, ERECTOR

construe / DECODE; INTERPRET

consult / CONFER, REGARD; COUNSEL

consultation / CONFERENCE

consultative / DELIBERATIVE

consume / EAT, SUP, USE; BURN

consumed / ATE; USED; EATEN

consummate / END; CLOSE; EFFECT; FINISH. FINAL, WHOLE; COMPLETE

consummately / PERFECTLY

consummation / END; COMPLETION

consumption / USE; DECAY, WASTE; ATROPHY; MARASMUS, PHTHISIS

contact / TOUCH; SYZYGY; TANGENCY. RUB; ABUT, FEEL, MEET

contagion / PEST; VIRUS; MIASMA; INFECTION

contagious / CATCHING, EPIDEMIC; INFECTIOUS

contain / HOLD; EMBODY; ENCLOSE

container / BIN, BOX, CAN, JUG, POT, TUB, URN, VAT; CASE, PAIL, SACK, VASE

container for letter / ENVELOPE

container for mixing / BOWL; SHAKER

container for papers / FOLDER; HANAPER

contaminate / SMEAR, STAIN, SULLY, TAINT

contamination / FOULING; POLLUTION

contaminator / DEFILER; VITIATOR

contemn / SCORN, SPURN; DESPISE

contemplate / BROOD, STUDY, THINK

contemplative / THOUGHTFUL

contemporary / COEVAL; COEXISTENT

contempt / SCORN; DISDAIN

contemptible / LOW; BASE, MEAN, VILE; CHEAP

contemptuous / SNOOTY; HAUGHTY; DISDAINFUL

contemptuous cry / BAH, FIE; PFUI, PISH; PHOOEY

contemptuous look / FLEER, SNEER

contemptuous sound / HISS, HOOT, RAZZ; CATCALL, SNIGGER

contend / VIE; COPE, DEAL; ARGUE; ASSERT, STRIVE

contend in rivalry / COMPETE

contended / RACED; FOUGHT

content / PLEASE; GRATIFY. MATTER

contented / CHEERFUL; SATISFIED

contention / FEUD; TRIAL; STRIFE

contention in words / LOGOMACHY

contents of an atlas / MAPS

conterminate / ADJOINING

contest / AGON, BOUT, GAME, RACE; BATTLE. ARGUE; DEBATE; CONTEND

contest between two / DUEL

contest judge / UMPIRE; REFEREE

contest at law / LITIGATION

contest of nations / WAR

context / SETTING; AMBIENCE; STRUCTURE

contiguity / CONTACT

contiguous / NEAR, NEXT; ADJACENT, TOUCHING

continence / CHASTITY; RESTRAINT

continent / CHASTE. MAINLAND

continent / NA, SA; AFR, EUR; AMER, ASIA; AFRICA; AUSTRAL, EURASIA; ANTARCTICA

continent of legend / ATLANTIS

continent of past ages / MU; LEMURIA, PANGAEA; CASCADIA; GONDWANALAND

Continent personified / EUROPA

contingency / CASE; EVENT; CHANCE; FORTUITY

contingent / DEPENDENT. PART

continual / ENDLESS; CONSTANT; INCESSANT

continually / AYE, EER; EVER; ALWAYS; CONSTANTLY

continuation / SEQUEL; DURATION

continue / LAST, STAY; ABIDE, TARRY; ENDURE

continued story / SERIAL, SERIES

continuing over time / CHRONIC

continuous / UNBROKEN; CONNECTED

continuous beating / TATTOO; RATAPLAN

continuous noise / DIN; CLAMOR

contort / WARP; GNARL, TWIST

contorted / WRY; GNARLED

contortion / WRITHING; DEFORMITY

contour / SHAPE; OUTLINE, PROFILE

contour feather / PENNA

contract / KNIT; AGREE, INCUR; ABSORB, LESSEN, NARROW, REDUCE, SHRINK. PACT; LEASE; BRIDGE, TREATY; COVENANT

contract for service / HIRE; INDENTURE

contraction / NT; EEN, EER, OER, TIS; SPASM; ELISION

contraction of heart / SYSTOLE

contradict / DENY; BELIE, REBUT; IMPUGN, NEGATE

contradiction / DENIAL; PARADOX; REFUTATION

contralto voice / ALTO

contraption / DEVICE, GADGET; GIMMICK

contrapuntal sacred song / MOTET

contrary / UNRULY; ADVERSE, FROWARD, OPPOSED, REVERSE

contrary to reasoning / ILLOGICAL

contrary to rules / FOUL

contrary to true / FALSE

contrast / COMPARE. DIFFERENCE

contravene / VIOLATE; OBSTRUCT

contribute / GIVE; AFFORD, ASSIST

contribute to / FEED

contribution / GIFT; SCOT; DONATION

contrite / SORRY; PENITENT

contrition / REGRET; REMORSE; COMPUNCTION

contrivance / PLAN, PLOT; DESIGN

contrivance to wash ore / PAN

contrive / MAKE, PLAN; ADAPT, WEAVE

contrived / AWKWARD, LABORED

contrived cleverly / DAEDAL

control / CURB, REIN, RULE, SWAY

controversial / ERISTIC, POLEMIC; ARGUMENTATIVE

controversy / DEBATE, STRIFE

controvert / REFUTE; DISPROVE

contumely / SCORN; RUDENESS; INSOLENCE

contuse / WOUND; BRUISE

contusion / LUMP; BRUISE

conundrum / ENIGMA, RIDDLE

conundrum in pictures / REBUS

convalescence / RECUPERATION

convene / SIT; MEET; MUSTER, SUMMON; CONVOKE; ASSEMBLE

convenient / HANDY; FITTED, PROPER, USEFUL

convent / NUNNERY; CLOISTER; MONASTERY

convention / MEETING; CONVOCATION

conventional / USUAL, NOMIC; COMMON, FORMAL

converge / MEET; FOCUS; ASSEMBLE

conversant / FAMILIAR; PROFICIENT

conversation / CHAT, TALK; SPEECH; COLLOQUY

conversation line / PHONE

conversationalist / TALKER

converse / CHAT; SPEAK; COMMUNE; DISCOURSE. REVERSE; CONTRARY

convert / TURN; ALTER, APPLY, RENEW; CHANGE

convert to another religion / PROSELYTE

convert to Judaism / GER

convex / BOWED; ARCHED; GIBBOUS

convex molding / REED; OVOLO, TORUS

convexity of column / ENTASIS

convey / BEAR, CEDE, MOVE, SELL; CARRY, GRANT; DEMISE, DEVISE

convey for consideration / SELL

convey property / DEED; LEASE

conveyance / CAR; VEHICLE; TRANSFER

conveyance for the dead / HEARSE

conveyance of estate / DEMISE, REMISE

conveyer / BELT; MOVER; CARRIER

conveyer belt / APRON

convict /CON, LAG; FELON; CRIMINAL. CONDEMN

conviction / BELIEF; ASSURANCE

convince / ASSURE; PERSUADE

convincing / COGENT, CRUCIAL

convivial / JOLLY; JOVIAL; FESTIVE

convocation / SYNOD; COUNCIL; ASSEMBLY

convoke / COLLECT, CONVENE

convolution / COIL; TWIST, WHORL

convoy / ESCORT

convulse / SHAKE; AGITATE

convulsion / FIT; SPASM, THROE

convulsive cry / SOB; SIGH, MOAN

cony / DAS; PIKA; CONEY, CONGA, GANAM, HUTIA

cony of scriptures / HYRAX; DASSIE

coof / DOLT

cook / CHEF. HEAT

cook in fat / FRY

cook in oven / BAKE; ROAST

cookbook offering / RECIPE

cooked with water / BOILED, STEWED

cookery / CUISINE, KITCHEN

cookery guide / RECIPE

cookie / SNAP; WAFER; BISCUIT

cooking apparatus / ETNA, OVEN; RANGE, STOVE; HIBACHI

cooking banana / PLANTAIN

cooking herb / BAY; SAGE; BASIL; GARLIC
cooking instructions / RECIPE
cooking pan / SPIDER; GRIDDLE, SKILLET
cooking place / ETNA; PATIO, RANGE, STOVE; GALLEY; KITCHEN
cooking pot / OLLA; TUREEN
cooking procedure / FRY; BAKE, BOIL, DICE, STEW; BROIL, BROWN, CREAM, GRILL, MINCE, ROAST, SAUTE, SCALD, SHIRR; BRAISE
cooking smell / NIDOR
cookout / ROAST; BARBECUE
cool / CALM; QUIET, SOBER; FRIGID, PLACID, SEDATE; COMPOSED, IMPUDENT
cooler / CELL, JAIL; PRISON
Coolidge / CAL
cooling device / FAN; FRIDGE; REFRIGERATOR
cooling drink / ADE
coolness / APLOMB
coom / SOOT; REFUSE
coomb / CWM; CIRQUE
coon/ MAPACH; RACCOON
coonskin / CAP
coop / PEN; CAGE, CELL, JAIL; CORRAL; ENCLOSURE
cooperate / AGREE, UNITE; CONCUR
Cooperstown's lake / OTSEGO
coordinate / HARMONIZE. POSITION; MAGNITUDE
coordinate conjunction / OR; AND, BUT
coot / SCOTER
cootie / LOUSE
cop / STOP; SEIZE, STEAL. HEAD; SPOOL; POLICEMAN
copal / LAC; ANIME, RESIN
coparcenary / HEIRSHIP
copartner / ASSOCIATE
cope / HANDLE; CONTEND. CLOAK
Copenhagen / KOBENHAVN
Copenhagen native / DANE
Copenhagen sculptor / THORVALDSEN
Copenhagen park / TIVOLI
copied / APED; MODELED; IMITATED
copier / XEROX; TRANSCRIBER
copious / FULL, RICH; AMPLE; PLENTY; LIBERAL, PROFUSE, UBEROUS
copper / CALDRON; POLICEMAN
copper, pert. to / CUPRIC
copper acetate / VERDIGRIS
copper alloy / BRASS; BRONZE
copper carbonate / BICE; PATINA
copper money / AES; CENT; PENNY

copper sulfate / VITRIOL
Copperfield's aunt / BETSY
Copperfield's stepfather / MURDSTONE
Copperfield's wife / DORA; AGNES
copperhead / SNAKE; PROREB
copper-tin alloy / BRONZE
copper-zinc alloy / BRASS
coppice / HOLT; COPSE; THICKET
copra / COCONUT
copse / COPPICE
copt / EGYPTIAN, JACOBITE
coptic bishop / AMBA, ANBA
copy / STAT; IMAGE, MODEL; ECTYPE; REPLICA; FACSIMILE. APE; MIMIC; IMITATE
copycat / MIMIC; IMITATOR
copyist / SCRIBE; IMITATOR
copyright / PATENT
copyright infringement / PIRACY; PLAGIARY; PLAGIARISM
coquette / FLIRT; TRIFLE
coracle / SKINBOAT
coral / POLYP; MADREPORE, MILLEPORE
coral island / CAY, KEY; REEF
coral island matrix / ATOLL
corbel / ANCON, STRUT
corbie / CROW; RAVEN
cord / LINE, PILE, ROPE, WELT; TWINE; STRING
cord for corset / STAYLACE
cord for shoe / LACE
cordage fiber / DA; BAST, COIR, ERUC, FERU, HEMP, IMBE, JUTE, PITA; ABACA, ISTLE, SISAL; AMBARY, LINAGA
corded fabric / REP; REPP; PIQUE
Cordelia's father / LEAR
Cordelia's sister / REGAN; GONERIL
cordial / WARM; ARDENT, HEARTY
cordial drink / LIQUEUR; ANISETTE
cordial greeting / WELCOME
core / GIST, PITH; HEART; CENTER
core of casting mold / NOWEL; MATRIX
core to fashion metal / AME
Corinth epithet / BIMARIS
Corinthian colony / SYRACUSE
Corinthian fountain / PIRENE
Corinthian general / PISANDER
Corinthian king / POLYBUS
cork / FLOAT, SPILE; STOPPER
cork extract / CERIN
cork helmet / TOPI; TOPEE
Cork port / COBH
cork tissue / SUBER
corkwood / BALSA
corm / BULB, ROOT
corn / MAIZE; CALLUS, WHISKY. PICKLE
corn bread / CAKE, PIKI, PONE

corn cake / PONE
corn crake / RAIL
corn ear / COB
corn flag / GLADIOLUS
corn knife / MACHETE
corn lily / IXIA
corn meal / MASA; AMBROSIA
corn meal mush / SAMP; ATOLE
corn spike / COB, EAR
corncob / EAR; PIPE
corncrib / BIN
corned / CURED; SALTED
corneous / HARD; HORNY
corner / BEND, NOOK; ANGLE, COIGN, NICHE; RECESS. TREE
corner of diamond / BASE
Cornhusker / NEBRASKAN
cornhusking / BEE
cornish, pref. / PEN, POL, TRE
cornucopia / HORN
Cornwall mine / BAL
corny / TRITE; SCHMALTZY
corolla section / PETAL
corona / CIGAR, CROWN, TIARA
coronach / DIRGE
coronation / CROWNING
coronation stone / SCONE
coronet / CROWN, TIARA; DIADEM
corporal / NCO; CLOTH
corporeal / HYLIC; BODILY; FLESHLY; MATERIAL
corpse / BODY; CADAVER
corpulent / FAT; BULKY, BURLY, GROSS, OBESE, STOUT
corpuscle / ELECTRON; BLOOD-CELL
corral / PEN; ATAJO; STOCKADE. CAPTURE
correct / AMEND, EMEND; MODIFY, PUNISH. OK; FIT; TRUE; EXACT, RIGHT
correct manuscript / EDIT
correction / DISCIPLINE; CHASTISEMENT
correlative conjunction / OR; NOR
correlative of diastolic / SYSTOLIC
correlative of either / OR
correlative of neither / NOR
correspond / FIT; JIBE, SUIT; AGREE, MATCH, TALLY, WRITE
correspondence / LETTERS, WRITING; CONGRUITY; COMMUNICATION
correspondent / FITTED; ADAPTED, SIMILAR. REPORTER; COUNTERPART
corridor / HALLWAY, PASSAGE, WALKWAY
corroborate / ATTEST, VERIFY; CONFIRM, FORTIFY, SUSTAIN
corrode / EAT; BITE, GNAW, RUST
corrosion / RUST; EROSION
corrosion in metal / PITTING

corrosive / ACID; CAUSTIC
corrupt / ROT; BRIBE, DECAY, SPOIL, TAINT; DEBASE, DEFILE, ENTICE, INFECT, POISON. EVIL; VENAL; PUTRID, ROTTEN; SPOILED
corruption / DECAY, GRAFT; LAXITY; BRIBERY; DEPRAVITY
corsage / WAIST; BODICE; BOUQUET
corsair / PIRATE; BUCCANEER, PRIVATEER
corset / STAYS
corset bone / BUSK, STAY
Corsican town / CALVI, AJACCIO
cortege / TRAIN; RETINUE
cortex / BARK, RIND
corundum / EMERY
coruscate / GLITTER, SPARKLE
corvine bird / CROW, ROOK; RAVEN; CHOUGH
cos / LETTUCE, ROMAINE
Cosa Nostra / MAFIA
Cosette's mother / FANTINE
cosh / SANDBAG; BLACKJACK
cosmetic / CREAM, PAINT, ROUGE; LOTION; MASCARA
cosmic cycle / EON
cosmic order / RITA
cosmos / WORLD; UNIVERSE
cossack / TATAR; HORSEMAN
Cossack captain / SOTNIK
Cossack chief / ATAMAN, HETMAN
Cossack regiment / POLK, PULK
Cossack whip / KNOUT
cosset / PET; FONDLE, PAMPER. LAMB
cost / LOSS, PAIN, RATE; PRICE, VALUE, WORTH; CHARGE, OUTLAY
costa / RIB; VEIN; MIDRIB
Costa Rica capital / SANJOSE
Costa Rica city / CARTAGO
Costa Rican Indian / BOTO, VOTO
Costa Rican money / COLON
Costa Rican peninsula / OSA
Costa Rican seaport / LIMON
Costa Rican volcano / POAS; IRAZU
costliness / EXPENSE
costly / DEAR; SUMPTUOUS
costume / RIG; GARB; GETUP, HABIT; ATTIRE; GARMENT
costume accessory / SHAWL; CORSAGE; EARRINGS, NECKLACE
cot / BED, HUT; CRIB; REFUGE; CHARPOY
cote / SHED; SHELTER
coterie / SET; CROWD; CIRCLE, CLIQUE
cottage / CABIN, VILLA
cottage cheese / POPCORN; POTCHEESE; SCHMIERKASE
cottage of India / BARI

cottager / COTTER; VACATIONER
cotter / CLOT; SHRINK; CONGEAL
Cotton Belt / SOUTH
cotton bundle / BALE
cotton cloth blemish / NIT
cotton drill / DENIM
cotton of Egypt / SAK; PIMA; SAKEL
cotton fabric / JEAN, LAWN, LENO, MULL, PIMA; DENIM, KHAKI, MANTA, SCRIM, SURAT, TERRY, VOILE; CALICO, CHINTZ, MADRAS, MUSLIN, NANKIN, PENANG; CAMBRIC, GINGHAM, JACONET, NANKEEN, PERCALE; CRETONNE, NAINSOOK
cotton fiber / LINT
cotton gauze / LENO
cotton gin attachment / MOTER
cotton lawn / BATISTE
cotton pest / WEEVIL; BOLLWEEVIL
cotton seed fragment / MOTE
cotton seed vessel / BOLL
cotton seeding machine / GIN
cotton thread / LISLE
cotton tree / SIMAL
cottontail / RABBIT
cottonwood / ALAMO
couch / BED; LAIR, SOFA; DIVAN
couch, pert. to / SOFANE
couch to convey wounded / LITTER; STRETCHER
couch grass / QUICK; QUITCH
couched / ABED; LYING; COUCHANT
cougar / PUMA; PANTHER
cough / HACK; TUSSIS
cough, pert. to / BECHIC; TUSSIVE
cough drop / TROCHE; LOZENGE
cough remedy / SYRUP

coulter / PLOUGHSHARE
council / DIET; BOARD; COMPANY, MEETING; ASSEMBLY, CONGRESS
counsel / PLAN; ADVICE, DESIGN, LAWYER. REDE; ADVISE
counselor / LAWYER, MENTOR; ATTORNEY
count / HOLD; JUDGE, THINK, VALUE
Count / NOBLE
count off / ENUMERATE
count on / RELY
countenance / AID; ABET, BACK; FAVOR. LOOK, MIEN; ASPECT
counter / BAR. ADVERSE
counteract / CHANGE, DEFEAT, HINDER; PREVENT
counteracting agent / ANTIDOTE
counteractive / REMEDY
counteragent / SPY
counterfeit / BASE, FAKE, MOCK, SHAM; BOGUS, FALSE, PHONY, QUEER. FORGE; IMITATE
counterfeiter / COINER
counterfoil / STUB
counterirritant / SETON
countermand / RECALL, REVOKE
counterpart / COPY, LIKE, MATE, TWIN; FELLOW
counterpoise / BALANCE
countersign / WATCHWORD
countertenor / ALTO; FALSETTO
countervail / COMPENSATE
counting / RECKONING
counting frame / ABACUS; SWANPAN
countless / MYRIAD; INNUMERABLE

COUNTRIES AND THEIR CAPITALS

Afghanistan	KABUL
Albania	TIRANA
Algeria	ALGIERS
Andorra	ANDORRALAVELLA
Angola	LUANDA
Antigua	STJOHNS
Argentina	BUENOSAIRES
Australia	CANBERRA
Austria	VIENNA
Bahamas	NASSAU
Bahrain	MANAMA
Bangladesh	DACCA
Barbados	BRIDGETOWN
Belgium	BRUSSELS
Belize	BELMOPAN
Benin	PORTONOVO, COTONOU
Bermuda	HAMILTON
Bhutan	THIMPHU
Bolivia	SUCRE, LAPAZ
Botswana	GABORONE
Brazil	BRASILIA

British Solomon Islands	HONIARA
British Virgin Islands	ROADTOWN
Brunei	BANDARSERIBEGAWAN
Bulgaria	SOFIA
Burma	RANGOON
Burundi	BUJUMBURA
Cambodia (see Khmer Republic)	
Cameroon	YAOUNDE
Canada	OTTAWA
Cape Verde Islands	PRAIA
Cayman Islands	GEORGETOWN, PINANG
Central African Republic	BANGUI
Ceylon (see Sri Lanka)	
Chad	NDJAMENA
Chile	SANTIAGO
China, People's Republic of	PEKING
China, Republic of (see Taiwan)	
Colombia	BOGOTA
Comoro Islands	MORONI
Congo, Democratic Republic of (see Zaire)	
Congo (People's Republic of)	BRAZZAVILLE
Costa Rica	SANJOSE
Cuba	HAVANA
Cyprus	LEVKOSIA, NICOPIA
Czechoslovakia	PRAGUE
Dahomey (see Benin)	
Denmark	COPENHAGEN
Dominica	ROSEAU
Dominican Republic	SANTODOMINGO
Dutch Guiana (see Surinam)	
Ecuador	QUITO
Egypt	CAIRO
El Salvador	SANSALVADOR
England (see United Kingdom)	
Equatorial Guinea	MALABO, SANTAISABEL
Ethiopia	ADDISABABA
Faeroe Islands	TORSHAVN
Falkland Islands	STANLEY
Fiji	SUVA
Finland	HELSINKI
France	PARIS
French Guiana	CAYENNE
French Polynesia	PAPEETE
French Territory of Afars and Issas	DJIBOUTI
Gabon	LIBREVILLE
Gambia	BANJUL
Germany, West (BRD)	BONN
Germany, East (DDR)	EASTBERLIN
Ghana	ACCRA
Gilbert and Ellice Islands	TARAWA
Greece	ATHENS
Greenland	GODTHAAB
Grenada	STGEORGES
Guadeloupe	BASSETERRE
Guatemala	GUATEMALA
Guernsey	STPETERPORT
Guinea	CONAKRY
Guinea-Bissau	BISSAU
Guyana	GEORGETOWN
Haiti	PORTAUPRINCE
Honduras	TEGUCIGALPA
Hong Kong	VICTORIA

Hungary	BUDAPEST
Iceland	REYKJAVIK
India	NEWDELHI
Indonesia	DJAKARTA
Iran	TEHRAN
Iraq	BAGHDAD
Ireland	DUBLIN
Isle of Man	DOUGLAS
Israel	JERUSALEM
Italy	ROME
Ivory Coast	ABIDJAN
Jamaica	KINGSTON
Japan	TOKYO
Jersey	STHELIER
Jordan	AMMAN
Kenya	NAIROBI
Khmer Republic	PHNOMPENH
Korea, North	PYONGYANG
Korea, South	SEOUL
Kuwait	KUWAIT
Laos	VIENTIANE, LUANGPRABANG
Lebanon	BEIRUT
Lesotho	MASERU
Liberia	MONROVIA
Libya	TRIPOLI, BENGHAZI
Liechtenstein	VADUZ
Luxembourg	LUXEMBOURG
Macao	MACAO
Malagasy Republic (Madagascar)	TANANARIVE
Malawi	ZOMBA
Malaysia	KUALALUMPUR
Maldives	MALE
Mali	BAMAKO
Malta	VALLETTA
Martinique	FORTDEFRANCE
Mauritania	NOUAKCHOTT
Mauritius	PORTLOUIS
Mexico	MEXICOCITY
Monaco	MONACO
Mongolia	ULANBATOR
Montserrat	PLYMOUTH
Morocco	RABAT
Mozambique	CANPHUMO, LOURENCOMARQUES
Namibia	WINDHOEK
Nauru	(no capital)
Nepal	KATMANDU
Netherlands	AMSTERDAM
Netherlands Antilles	WILLEMSTAD
New Caledonia	NOUMEA
New Hebrides	VILA
New Zealand	WELLINGTON
Nicaragua	MANAGUA
Niger	NIAMEY
Nigeria	LAGOS
Northern Ireland	BELFAST
Norway	OSLO
Oman	MUSCAT
Orkney Islands	KIRKWALL
Pakistan	ISLAMABAD
Panama	PANAMA
Papua-New Guinea	PORTMORESBY
Paraguay	ASUNCION
Peru	LIMA

Philippines	QUEZONCITY
Pitcairn Island	ADAMSTOWN
Poland	WARSAW
Portugal	LISBON
Portuguese Guinea (see Guinea-Bissau)	
Portuguese Timor	DILI
Qatar	DOHA
Reunion	SAINTDENIS
Rhodesia (see Zimbabwe)	
Romania	BUCHAREST
Russia (see Union of Soviet Socialist Republics)	
Rwanda	KIGALI
St. Helena	JAMESTOWN
St. Kitts-Nevis	BASSETERRE
St. Lucia	CASTRIES
St. Pierre et Miquelon	STPIERRE
St. Vincent	KINGSTOWN
San Marino	SANMARINO
São Tomé e Principe	SAOTOME
Saudi Arabia	RIYADH
Scotland	EDINBURGH
Senegal	DAKAR
Seychelles	VICTORIA
Siam (see Thailand)	
Sierra Leone	FREETOWN
Sikkim	GANGTOK
Singapore	SINGAPORE
Somalia	MOGADISHU
South Africa, Republic of	PRETORIA, CAPETOWN
South-West Africa (see Namibia)	
Spain	MADRID
Spanish Sahara	ELAAIUN
Sri Lanka	COLOMBO
Sudan	KHARTOUM
Surinam	PARAMARIBO
Swaziland	MBABANE
Sweden	STOCKHOLM
Switzerland	BERN
Syria	DAMASCUS
Taiwan	TAIPEI
Tanzania	DARESSALAAM
Thailand	KRUNGTHEP, BANGKOK
Tibet	LHASA
Togo	LOME
Tonga	NUKUALOFA
Trinidad and Tobago	PORTOFSPAIN
Tunisia	TUNIS
Turkey	ANKARA
Turks and Caicos Islands	GRANDTURK
Uganda	KAMPALA
Union of Soviet Socialist Republics	MOSCOW
United Arab Emirates	ABUDHABI
United Kingdom	LONDON
United States	WASHINGTON (D.C.)
Upper Volta	QUAGADOUGOU
Uruguay	MONTEVIDEO
Vatican City, State of	VATICANCITY
Venezuela	CARACAS
Vietnam	HANOI, HOCHIMINH (SAIGON)
Wallis and Futuna Islands	MATAUTU
Western Samoa	APIA

Yemen, People's Democratic Republic of	ADEN, MEDINA ASSHAAB
Yemen Arab Republic	SANA
Yugoslavia	BELGRADE
Zaire	KINSHASA
Zambia	LUSAKA
Zimbabwe	SALISBURY

countrified / RURAL
country / HOME, LAND, SOIL; STATE; NATION, PEOPLE, REGION; DISTRICT. RURAL; RUSTIC
country, pert. to / RURAL; RUSTIC
country dance / REEL
country home / MANOR, VILLA
country now in Ethiopia / ERITREA
country road / LANE, PATH
country on Yellow Sea / KOREA
countryman / BOOR; SWAIN; FARMER, RUSTIC
county / SHIRE; DISTRICT
county officer / SHERIFF
coup / BLOW, FEAT; STROKE
couple / WED; UNITE; CONJOIN. DUO, TWO; DYAD, PAIR, YOKE
coupled / GEMEL; LINKED
coupler / LINK; SHACKLE
courage / GRIT, SAND; HEART
courageous / BOLD, BRAVE; HEROIC
courageous man / LION
courier / ESTAFET; MESSENGER
course / WAY; LINE, MODE, PATH, RACE, ROAD; CLASS, ROUTE, TENOR
course of dinner / SOUP; SALAD; ENTREE; DESSERT
course of operation / RUN
course of running water / BED
course of travel / WAY; ROUTE
courser / STEED
court / WOO; SOLICIT. PATIO
court, pert. to / ROTAL; JUDICIAL
court action / SUIT; TRIAL
court adjournment / RECESS
court attendant / CLERK; BAILIFF; COURTIER
court business / TRIAL
court crier's call / OYES, OYEZ
court decision / VERDICT
court document / BRIEF; RECORD
court exhibit / EVIDENCE
court fool / JESTER
court officer in Scotland / MACER
court order / BOND, WRIT; ARRET; MANDAMUS, SUBPOENA
court sitting / ASSIZE; SESSION
court with song / SERENADE
courteous / KIND, WARM; CIVIL
courtesan of ancient Greece / HETAERA

courtliness / ELEGANCE
courtly / AULIC; POLITE; ELEGANT, REFINED
courtship / SUIT; WOOING; ROMANCE
courtship dance / LAK
courtway / AREA; PATIO
cove / BAY; CHAP; INLET; SHELTER
covenant / BOND, DEED, PACT; TREATY; PROMISE
cover / HIDE, MASK; CLOAK, DRAPE, GUARD; SHIELD; CONCEAL. CAP; COAT; SCREEN
cover with an alloy / BRAZE
cover with asphalt / TAR; PAVE
cover with excuses / PALLIATE; EXTENUATE
cover with first paint coat / PRIME
cover with hoarfrost / RIME
cover inside / LINE
cover with pigment / PAINT
cover for pot / LID
cover with water / FLOOD
cover with wax / CERE
covered / HIDDEN; DRESSED
covered cloister / STOA; PORTICO
covered market / HALLE
covered passage / ARCADE
covered with sandy hillocks / DUNED
covered seat on elephant / HOWDAH
covered up / BURIED
covered wagon / SCHOONER; CONESTOGA
covering / DRESS; CANOPY, TEGMEN
covering for ankle / SPAT; GAITER
covering of beaches / SAND
covering on corn / HUSK
covering for the face / MASK
covering in front / APRON. FACING
covering of head / CAP, HAT; SCARF
covering of teeth / DENTINE
covering of watch dial / CRYSTAL
coverlet / QUILT; AFGHAN
covert / SLY; HIDDEN, SECRET. THICKET
covert satire / IRONY
coverture / LID; SHELTER
covet / ENVY, LUST; CRAVE; DESIRE
covetous / JEALOUS

covetousness / GREED; AVARICE

covey / BEVY; BROOD, FLOCK

cow / DAUNT; OVERAWE. BOSSY; BOVINE, CATTLE, JERSEY

cow barn / BYRE, SHED

cow without horns / MULEY

coward / CRAVEN; POLTROON, RECREANT

cowardly / TIMID; CHICKEN

cowardly person / SNEAK

cowboy / RIDER; PUNCHER, VAQUERO

cowboy chore / HERDING

cowboy movie / WESTERN

cowboy of South America / GAUCHO

cowboy's contest / RODEO

cowboy's garment / CHAPS

cowboy's hat / STETSON

cowboy's quirt / ROMAL

cowboy's spade / LOY

cower / QUAIL; CRINGE, SHRINK

cowfish / TORO; GRAMPUS, MANATEE

cow-headed goddess / ISIS; HATHOR

cowhide / WHIP; LEATHER

cowl / HOOD

coworker / PARTNER

cowpuncher / COWBOY

cowrie / SHELL; WAMPUM

cows / KINE; CATTLE

cow's call / MOO

cowslip / PRIMROSE

coxa / HIP

coxcomb / FOP; DUPE; EXQUISITE

coy / SHY; DEMURE, MODEST; BASHFUL; COQUETTISH

coyness / RESERVE; ARCHNESS

coyote / WOLF

coypu fur / NUTRIA

coze / CHAT, CHIN; GOSSIP

cozen / DUPE; CHEAT, TRICK

cozy / EASY, HOMY, SNUG. COVER

cozy retreat / DEN; NEST

crab / CLAW; LOUSE; CANCER, GROUCH; SOURPUSS

crab plover / DROME

crabbed / SOUR; CRUSTY, MOROSE

crabbedness / ACRIMONY; GRUFFNESS

crab-eating macaque / KRA

crab-eating mongoose / URVA

crab's claw / CHELA

crab's front / METOPE

crack / CHAP, JOKE, KIBE; CHINK; CREVICE, FISSURE; FRACTURE. SNAP. EXCELLENT

cracked / SPLIT; BROKEN, INSANE

cracker / BISCUIT, REDNECK; FIREWORK

crackle / SNAP; SPUTTER

crackling / CREPITANT

cracksman / BURGLAR

cradle / BED; CRIB; ORIGIN; INFANCY, TRUNDLE

cradle song / LULLABY

craft / ART; SKILL, TRADE; VESSEL; CUNNING

craftsman / HAND; ARTISAN, WORKMAN; MECHANIC

craftsman in cloth / TAILOR, WEAVER

craftsman in metal / SMITH

craftsman in stone / MASON

craftsman in wood / JOINER

crafty / SLY; ARCH, FOXY, WILY; ARTFUL, SHREWD, SUBTLE, TRICKY

crafty animal / FOX

crag / TOR; ARETE, CLIFF, STEEP

craggy / ROUGH; RUGGED, UNEVEN

craggy hill / TOR

crake / CROW, RAIL, SORA

cram / RAM, WAD; STUDY, STUFF

cramp / HINDER; RESTRAIN. KINK, KNOT; CLAMP, SPASM

cranberry / BILBERRY

crane / DAVIT, HERON; DERRICK

Crane / GRUS

crane of East Indies / SARUS

cranelike bird / CHUNGA; SERIEMA

crane's arm / GIB, JIB

crane's cry / CLANG

Crane's rival / BROM

cranial point / INION; PTERION; GLABELLA

cranium / HEAD; SKULL

crank / NUT; BEND; TWIST, WINCH; CAPRICE, FANATIC; CRACKPOT

cranky / PEEVISH

cranny / NOOK; CHINK; FISSURE

craps / DICE; HAZARD

crash / CLASH, SMASH. DIN

crasher / INTRUDER; INTERLOPER

crass / CRUDE, GROSS; COARSE, STUPID, VULGAR

crate / BOX; HEAP; PLANE; HAMPER

crater / PIT; HOLE; CALDERA

cravat / TIE; ASCOT, STOCK

crave / ASK, BEG; LONG, PRAY, SEEK, WISH; COVET, YEARN; DESIRE

craven / CUR; COWARD; RECREANT. COWARDLY

craving / YEN; DESIRE, THIRST; BULIMIA; APPETITE

craw / MAW; CROP

crawfish / YABBY; CRAWDAD

crawl / CREEP; GROVEL; SLITHER

crawling / FAWNING; GROVELING

crawling animal / WORM; SNAKE; REPTILE

crayon / CHALK; PASTEL, PENCIL
craze / FAD; MANIA; CRACKLE. AD-DLE; MADDEN, OBSESS; DE-RANGE
crazy / MAD; AMOK, DAFT, LOCO, WILD; DAFFY, LOONY; INSANE
crazy work / PATCHWORK
creak / GRATE; SQUEAK, SQUEAL
cream / TOP; BEST; ELITE. BEAT
cream cheese / CARRE
cream pastry / PUFF; ECLAIR; NA-POLEON
creamery / DAIRY
cream-wine mixture / SILLABUB
creamy color / ECRU
creamy white / IVORY
crease / FOLD, RUCK, RUGA, TUCK
create / FORM, MAKE; BEGET, BUILD
created / COMPOSED; ORIGINATED
creation / COSMOS, NATURE; GENESIS; UNIVERSE
creative / ORIGINAL; PRODUCTIVE
creator / GOD; AUTHOR; DEMI-URGE
creature / MAN; BODY; BEING, HORSE, THING; ANIMAL, PER-SON, WHISKY; CRITTER
credence / FAITH, TRUST; BELIEF
credentials / DIPLOMA, VOUCHER, WARRANT; CERTIFICATE
credible / LIKELY, WORTHY
credit / FAITH, HONOR, MERIT, TRUST. RELY; BELIEVE, CONFIDE
credit transfer / GIRO
creditor / DEBTEE, LENDER
credo / CREED, TENET; BELIEF
credulity / GULLIBILITY
creed / CREDO, TENET; CONFES-SION
creek / RIA; COVE, KILL; BAYOU; ESTERO
creel / BASKET
creep / FAWN; CRAWL. BORE, JERK
creep away / SLINK
creeper / IVY; VINE
creeping / REPTANT
creeping plant / IVY; VINE; LIANA
creeps / WILLIES; GOOSEFLESH; FORMICATION
creepy / EERIE, WEIRD; FEARSOME
creese / KRIS; DAGGER
cremate / BURN
crematory blaze / PYRE
Cremona / AMATI, STRAD, VIOLIN; GUARNERI
crenate / NOTCHED; SCALLOPED
creole / PATOIS; MESTIZO
creole state / LOUISIANA
creosoted hemp / OAKUM
crepitate / SNAP; CRACKLE
crescent / HORNED; GROWING

crescent moon's point / CUSP, HORN
crescent-shaped / LUNAR; LUNATE
crescent-shaped figure / LUNE
crescent-shaped mark / LUNULA
cresset / TORCH; BASKET
crest / COP, TOP; ACME, APEX, EDGE, PEAK, TUFT; CROWN, PLUME
crest of a cock / COMB
crest on mountain / ARETE
crested bird / HOOPOE
crested like a bird / PILEATED
crestfallen / COWED; ABASHED
Cretan / CANDIOT; CANDIOTE
Cretan bay / SUDA; CANEA
Cretan city / KNOSSOS
Cretan king / MINOS
Cretan monster / MINOTAUR
Cretan mountain / IDA
Cretan princess / ARIADNE
Cretan spikenard / PHU
Crete / CANDIA
Crete capital / CANEA
Crete seaport / CANDIA
cretin / IDIOT
cretism / LYING; FALSEHOOD
crevice / GAP; CRACK; BREACH
crew / MOB, SET; BAND, GANG
crew cut / HAIRSTYLE
crew member / MAN
crib / BIN; RACK; CRADLE, CRECHE, MANGER. COPY; CHEAT
cribbage discards / CRIB
cribbage jack / NOBS; HEELS
cribbage marker / PEG
cribbage pass / GO
cribbage schneider / LURCH
cricket / GRIG; STOOL; INSECT
cricket ball / EDGER
cricket field / PITCH
cricket goal / WICKET
cricket line / CREASE
cricket position / LEG; SLIP; MIDON
cricket run scored / BYE
cricket team / ELEVEN
cricket term / OVER, TICE, YORK; GOOGLY
cricket thrower / BOWLER
cricket's sound / CHIRP; STRIDU-LATION
cried / WEPT; SOBBED
crier / HERALD
crime / SIN; WRONG; FELONY
crime file / DOSSIER
Crimea capital / SIMFEROPOL
Crimean city / KERCH, YALTA
Crimean isthmus / PEREKOP
Crimean peninsula / KERCH
Crimean river / ALMA
Crimean War battle / INKERMAN; BALAKLAVA

criminal / FELON; CONVICT, CULPRIT. CULPABLE

criminal act / FELONY, MURDER

criminal band / MOB; GANG

criminal fire / ARSON

criminality / VICE; GUILT; OFFENSE

criminate / ACCUSE, CHARGE; ARRAIGN, IMPEACH

crimp / CREASE, GOFFER; WRINKLE

crimpy / FRIZZY

crimson / RED; BLOOD; CARMINE, SCARLET. BLUSH

cringe / FAWN; COWER, WINCE

crinkle / CRUMPLE, WRINKLE; CORRUGATE

crinkled fabric / CREPE

crinoline / HOOPSKIRT; FARTHINGALE

cripple / LAME, MAIM; IMPAIR

crisis / RUB; ACME, HEAD, PASS

crisp / CURT; TERSE; BRITTLE

crisp outside / CRUST

crispate / CURLED

crispin / SHOEMAKER

criterion / NORM, TEST; CANON; MEASURE; STANDARD; TOUCHSTONE

critic / JUDGE; CAVILER

critical / NICE; ACUTE, EXACT; CRUCIAL, EXIGENT

critical pressure / STRAIN

criticism / REVIEW; CENSURE; STRICTURE

criticize / CARP, SCAN; CAVIL

criticize mercilessly / FLAY; ROAST; CENSURE

criticize playfully / KID

critique / REVIEW; ANALYSIS

croak / CAW, DIE; GRUMBLE

Croat / SLAV; SLOVENE

Croatia / HRVATSKA

Croatian city / ZAGREB

crochet / KNIT

crochet needles / HOOKS

crochet stich / LOOP; CHAIN, PIQUE; TRICOT

crock / JAR; SMUT, SOOT; DUFFER

crockery / WARE; EARTHENWARE

crocodile / GOA; MUGGER; HYPOCRITE

crocodile-headed god / SOBK; SEBEK

crocodile-like reptile / NAKOO; CAYMAN, GAVIAL

crocus bulb / CORM

Croesus' agent / AESOP

Croesus' father / ALYATTES

Croesus' land / LYDIA

croft / FARM; CRYPT, GARTH

cromlech / DYSS; DOLMEN

Cromwell's follower / ROUNDHEAD

Cromwell's nickname / NOLL

crone / HAG; BELDAME

crony / EME, PAL; CHUM, MATE; BUDDY; FRIEND

crook / BEND; CHEAT, CURVE, THIEF; SWINDLER

crooked / WRY; AGEE, AWRY, BENT; ASKEW; TWISTED; DISHONEST

crooked rebate / KICKBACK

crop / MAW; CRAW, LOOP. GRAZE, YIELD; PRODUCE

crop of India / RABI; RUBBEE

crop source / SEEDS

croquet / ROQUE

croquet arch / HOOP; WICKET

croquet hoop / ARCH; WICKET

crosier / STAFF; CROZIER

cross / SOUR; ANGRY, IRATE, SULKY, SURLY. SPAN; INTERSECT. ROOD; TRIAL; CRUCIFIX

cross of life / ANKH

cross oneself / SAIN

cross out / EX; CUT; DELE; CANCEL, DELETE; BLUEPENCIL

cross over / SPAN

cross rib / LIERNE

cross a river / FORD

cross section / SLICE

cross stroke on a letter / SERIF

cross timber / SPALE

crossbar pattern / GRID

crossbeam / TRAVE, TREVE

crossbow / RODD; ARBALEST

crosscut saw / BRIAR

crosse / RACKET

crossed over water / WADED

cross-examine / GRILL; QUESTION

crossing in a fence / STILE

crossly / PEEVISHLY

crosspatch / GROUCH

crossruff / SEESAW

crossthreads / WEFT, WOOF

crosstie / SLEEPER

crotch / FORK, HOOK

crotchety / ODD; QUEER; FITFUL; WAYWARD; WHIMSICAL

crotchety person / CRANK

crouch / COWER, SQUAT, STOOP

crow / DAW; ROOK; CRAKE, RAVEN. AGA; BRAG; EXULT

crow call / CAW

crowbar / PRY; LEVER

crowd / JAM; CRAM, FILL; PRESS, SERRY. MOB; GANG, HERD, PACK, RUCK; HORDE

crowd together / PACK; SERRY

crowfoot / CALTROP; BUTTERCUP, CELANDINE

crowl / DWARF

crowlike / CORVINE

crown / PATE; CREST, PRIZE, TIARA; DIADEM. CAP

crown, pert. to / CORONARY
Crown colony / HONGKONG
crown of ancient Egypt / ATEF;
PSCHENT
crown of hat / POLL
crown of head / PATE, POLL
crown of the Pope / TIARA
crowned with ivy / HEDERATED
crow's foot / WRINKLE
crucial / SEVERE; CRITICAL
crucial point / CRUX, KNOT, NODE;
PIVOT
crucial time / CRISIS
crucifix / ROOD; CROSS
crude / RAW; RUDE; CRASS,
HARSH
crude borax / TINCAL
crude comedy missile / PIE
crude dwelling / HUT; HOVEL
crude metal / ORE
crude metal casting / PIG
crude person / BOOR, SLOB;
BEAST, BRUTE; RUFFIAN
crude stone tool / EOLITH
crude tartar / ARGOL
crude turpentine / GALIPOT
cruel / MEAN; BRUTAL, FIERCE,
OGRISH, SAVAGE
cruel person / SADIST
cruelty / INHUMANITY, SAVAGE-
NESS
cruet / AMA; VIAL; CASTER
cruise / SAIL; COAST. VACATION
cruise ship / YACHT; STEAMER
cruising / ASEA
crumb / ORT; FRAGMENT
crumbled easily / CRISP; FRIABLE
crummy / SOFT; LOUSY; ODIOUS
crummy hotel / FLEABAG
crumple / MUSS; RUMPLE;
WRINKLE
crunch / CHEW, MASH; CRUSH,
GRIND
cruor / GORE; GRUME
crusader / ZEALOT; PILGRIM
crusaders' city / ACRE
crusader's foe / SALADIN,
SARACEN
cruse / POT; DISH
cruset / CRUCIBLE
crush / CHEW, MASH, RUIN;
GRIND
crush with retort / SQUELCH
crush with teeth / CHEW; CHAMP,
GRIND
crushing snake / BOA; ABOMA;
ANACONDA
crushing tooth / MOLAR
Crusoe / CASTAWAY
crust / BRASS; BOLDNESS
crustacean / CRAB; PRAWN;
SHRIMP; LOBSTER; BARNACLE

crustacean's claw / CHELA
crustacean's covering / SHELL;
CHITIN
crustacean's feeler / ANTENNA
crustacean's larva / ALIMA
crustaceous / SHELLY
crusted dish / PIE
crusty / ROUGH, SURLY
crutch / PONY; SUPPORT
crux / CROSS; CRISIS
crux ansata / ANKH
cry / SOB; CALL, HOWL, MOAN,
WAIL, WEEP; SHOUT; LAMENT
cry of approval / OLE; BRAVO; HUR-
RAH
cry of baby / MEWL, PULE
cry of bacchanals / EVOE
cry of "behold" / LO
cry of bittern / BOOM
cry of cat / MEW; MEOW; MIAOU
cry for court silence / OYEZ
cry of cranes / CLANG
cry of crow / CAW; CROAK
cry of delight / OH
cry of disapproval / BOO; HOOT;
CATCALL
cry of disbelief / NO; WHAT
cry of distress / MOAN, WAIL
cry of dog / BAY; BARK
cry of donkey / BRAY
cry of encouragement / YOICKS
cry of horse / WHINNY
cry loudly / ROAR; SHOUT
cry out / CALL; EXCLAIM
cry of owl / HOOT; ULULU
cry of pain / OW; OUCH, YELP
cry of raven / CRONK
cry of sorrow / AY; ALAS
cry of terror / SCREAM
cry of triumph / AHA
cry of turkey / GOBBLE
crying / TEARY; URGENT
crying for rain / ARID
crypt / TOMB; VAULT
cryptic / HIDDEN, OCCULT, SECRET
cryptogam / MOSS
cryptogam's seed / SPORE
cryptonymous / INEFFABLE
crystal / CLEAR; TRANSPARENT.
GLASS; QUARTZ
crystal gazer / SEER; MEDIUM,
SCRYER
crystalline lens shape / BICONVEX
crystalline mineral / SPAR; SPINEL
crystallized rain / SNOW; SLEET
crystic, pert. to / ICE
cub / FRY, PUP; COLT; REPORTER
cub shark / LAMIA
Cuba capital / HABANA, HAVANA
Cuban bay / BROA
Cuban bird / TROGON
Cuban castle / MORRO

Cuban cigar / HAVANA
Cuban city / BAYAMO
Cuban dance / CONGA, DANZA, RUMBA; DANZON
Cuban fish / DIABLO; ESCOLAR
Cuban gourd instrument / MARACAS
Cuban measure / TAREA
Cuban rodent / HUTIA; PILORI
Cuban seaport / SANTIAGO
Cuban tobacco / CAPA; VUELTA
Cuban tree / CUYA
Cuban wind squall / BAYAMO
cube / DIE; TESSERA
cube root of eight / TWO
cube of two / EIGHT
cubeb / CIGARETTE
cubed / DICED
cube's side / SQUARE
cubic capacity of ship / TONNAGE
cubic content / VOLUME; CAPACITY
cubic decimeter / LITER, LITRE
cubic measure / CORD; STERE; BARREL, GALLON
cubic meter / STERE
cubicle / CELL
cubitus / ULNA; FOREARM
Cuchulain's childhood name / SETANTA
Cuchulain's father / LUG; SUALTAM
Cuchulain's mother / DECHTIRE
Cuchulain's son / CONNLA
Cuchulain's wife / EMER
cuckolded / HORNED
cuckoo / ANI; COEL, KOEL. MAD; GAGA; CRAZY
cuckoopint / ARUM; WAKEROBIN
cuculate / COWLED, HOODED
cucumber / CUKE, PEPO; PICKLE; GHERKIN
cucumber tree / BILIMBI; MAGNOLIA
cud / CHAW, QUID; RUMEN
cud-chewing animal / RUMINANT
cuddle / HUG; NESTLE
cuddy / ASS; DONKEY, STUPID; BLOCKHEAD
cudgel / BAT; CLUB; STAFF. DRUB
cudgel for killing fish / MUCKLE
cue / TIP; HINT; BRAID, QUEUE; PIGTAIL. PROMPT
cue ball / SPOT; WHITE
cuff / SLAP; SMACK; BUFFET, POMMEL. MANACLE; GAUNTLET
cuff fastener / TAB; LINK, STUD; BUTTON
cuirass / ARMOR; LORICA; BREASTPLATE
cuisine / COOKERY, KITCHEN
culinary art / COOKERY
culinary delight / PASTRY
culinary directions / RECIPE

culinary dressing / SAUCE
cull / PICK, SIFT, SORT
culm / STEM; SLACK; REFUSE; COALDUST
culminate / END; FINISH
culminating point / CLIMAX, FINALE, ZENITH
culmination / ACME, APEX
culpability / GUILT; LIABILITY
culpable / WRONG; GUILTY; BLAMABLE, CRIMINAL
culprit / FELON; ACCUSED
cult / ISM; SECT; RITUAL
cultivable / ARABLE
cultivate / HOE; GROW; FOSTER, GARDEN; CHERISH, DEVELOP
cultivate land / FARM, PLOW, TILL; HARROW
cultivated cherry / MORELLO
cultivated grass area / LAWN
cultivated ground / ARADA
cultivated yard / GARDEN
cultivating tool / HOE; PICK, RAKE; SPADE; HARROW
cultivation / TILTH; CULTURE, TILLAGE
cultivation method / JUM; JOOM
cultivator / HOE; FARMER, TILLER
culture / REFINEMENT; CIVILIZATION. PROPAGATE
culture hound / ESTHETE
culture medium / AGAR; GELATIN; AGARAGAR
cultured half-pearl / MABE
cultured woman / BLUESTOCKING
culver / PIGEON
culvert / DRAIN, SEWER; CONDUIT
cumber / HINDER; EMBARRASS
cumbersome / UNWIELDY; BURDENSOME
cumbrous / HEAVY; VEXATIOUS
cummerbund / BAND, SASH
cumshaw / TIP; BONUS
cumulative / ADDING; ACCRETING
cumulative bet / PARLAY
cumulus / HEAP, MASS, PILE
cuneiform / CUNEAL; WEDGESHAPED
cuneiform script / ELAMITE, HITTITE; SUMERIAN
cuniculus / MINE; BURROW
cunner / WRASSE
cunning / SLY; CUTE, FOXY, WILY; ASTUTE, CALLID, CRAFTY, DAEDAL, SHREWD, SUBTLE. ART; CRAFT
cup / MUG; TASS; CALIX, CRUSE, HANAP; CHALICE
cup of assayer / CUPEL; BEAKER
cup of flower / CALYX
cup handle / EAR
cup stand of metal / ZARF

cup with two handles / TIG
cupbearer / HEBE, SAKI; GANYMEDE
cupboard / AMBRY; CLOSET; CABINET
cupel / TEST; REFINE
Cupid / AMOR, EROS; PUTTO
cupidity / GREED; AVARICE
Cupid's lover / PSYCHE
Cupid's mother / VENUS
Cupid's title / DAN
cupola / DOME; TURRET; LANTERN
cupreous / COPPERY
cup-shaped / PEZIZOID
cur / MUT; MUTT; FEIST; MONGREL; KIYOODLE
curable / REMEDIABLE
curare / URALI; CURARI, OORALI
curassow / MITU
curate / CLERGYMAN
curative / REMEDIAL; MEDICINAL
curator / WARDEN; CUSTODIAN
curb / REIN; CHECK; BRIDLE, SUBDUE; REPRESS
curd of fermenting milk / YOGURT
curdle / THICKEN; COAGULATE
curdled / SOUR
curdled milk / CLABBER
curdling agent / RENNET
cure / FREE, HEAL; REMEDY; PRESERVE. CHARGE; SPECIFIC
cure hides / TAN
cure-all / ELIXIR; PANACEA
curfew / BELL; SIREN; SIGNAL
curio / RARITY; BIBELOT
curiosity / MARVEL, ODDITY, RARITY, WONDER; INTEREST, NOSINESS
curious / ODD; NEAT, NICE; PRYING; UNUSUAL
curl / COIL, FEAK; TRESS; RINGLET; FORELOCK. WIND; FRIZZ
curl around / COIL; TWINE
curled ornament / SCROLL
curlew / WHAUP
curlicue / ESS; CURVE; SPIRAL
curling mark / TEE
curling stone / HOG; PATLID
curling target / PARISH
curly / WAVY
curly cabbage / SAVOY
curmudgeon / CHURL; NIGGARD
currency / MONEY; CHANGE
current / EDDY, TIDE; STREAM. RIFE; COMMON; PREVALENT
current, c.f. / RHEO
current of air / WIND; DRAFT
current of electricity / AC, DC
current mode / FAD; STYLE; FASHION
currently / NOW; PRESENTLY
Currier's partner / IVES
currish / MEAN; SNAPPISH

curry a horse / CLEAN, DRESS
curry powder / SPICE
currycomb / GROOMER
curse / BAN; BANE, DAMN, OATH; PLAGUE; SCOURGE
cursed / HATED; DAMNED; HATEFUL
cursive capital letters / UNCIALS
cursory / BRIEF, HASTY, RAPID
curt / BRIEF, CRISP, SHORT, TERSE
curtail / CUT, END, LOP; CLIP
curtain / VEIL, WALL; DRAPE; SCREEN
curtain fabric / NET; SCRIM
curtain of fire / BARRAGE
curtain holder / ROD
curtain material / NINON, SCRIM
curtain stretcher / FRAME
curtains / DEATH; FINISH
curtal / BRIEF, SHORT
curtsy / BOW; OBEISANCE
curvate / BENT; ESSED; CURVED
curve / BOW, ESS; ARCH, BEND, LOOP, WIND; SINUS
curve downward / DEFLEX
curve of ship's plank / SNY
curved handle / BOOL
curved in / ADUNC; CONCAVE
curved line / ARC
curved molding / CYMA, OGEE; OGIVE
curved out / CONVEX
curved street / CRESCENT
curved support / RIB
curved sword / SABER, SABRE
curve's section / ARC
curvet / LEAP; BOUND, FRISK
cushat / PIGEON; RINGDOVE
cushion / MAT, PAD; PILLOW; HASSOCK
cushioned seat / SOFA; COUCH, DIVAN
Cush's father / HAM
Cush's son / SEBA; NIMROD
cusp / HORN, PEAK; POINT; ENTRANCE
cuspid / TOOTH
cuss / CURSE; FELLOW
custard apple / ATES; PAPAW; ANNONA; SWEETSOP
custard cake / ECLAIR; NAPOLEON
custard pie / FLAN
custodian / WARDEN; CURATOR, JANITOR; CARETAKER
custodian of funds / TREASURER
custody / CARE; WATCH; CHARGE
custom / LAW, TAX, URE, USE; DUTY, FORM, RITE, RULE, TOLL, WONT; HABIT, USAGE
custom in India / DASTUR
customary / USUAL; WONTED; ROUTINE
customary mode / USAGE

customary procedure / ROUTINE

customer / CLIENT, PATRON; PURCHASER

customs / MORES; MANNERS; FASHIONS

cut / BOB, HEW, LOP, NIP; CLIP, GASH, HACK, SLIT, TRIM; CROSS, FLING, LANCE, MINCE, SHEAR, SLASH. TAUNT, WOUND. CLEFT

cut apart / SEPARATE

cut asunder / SEVER, SPLIT

cut bread / SLICE

cut closely / SHAVE

cut into cubes / DICE

cut a disk / RECORD

cut down / MOW; CHOP, FELL, REAP

cut down on food / DIET

cut expenses / SAVE; RETRENCH

cut face of gem / FACET

cut fine lines / ETCH

cut grass / MOW; SCYTHE

cut of hair / BOB; TRIM; BRUSH

cut with knife / GASH; CARVE, SLASH

cut from large piece / CARVE; SEPARATE

cut lumber / SAW; CHOP

cut meat / CARVE, SLICE

cut of meat / CHOP, LOIN, RIBS, RUMP; FLANK, SHANK, STEAK; CUTLET; BRISKET, SHOULDER

cut off / LOP; DOCK, SNIP

cut off close / SHAVE

cut off as mane / ROACH

cut off in pronouncing / ELIDE

cut out / EXCISE

cut pattern / STENCIL

cut in pieces / DICE, HASH; MINCE

cut roughly / HACK; SLASH

cut short / BOB, LOP; CLIP, SNIP

cut small faces upon / FACET

cut a small piece off / SNIP

cut socially / SNUB

cut the top / TRUNCATE

cut in two / SEVER, SPLIT; BISECT

cutaneous / DERMAL

cutaway / COAT

cutch / CULTCH; CATECHU

cute/ SHARP; CLEVER; CUNNING

cutlery / KNIVES

cutter / SLED; SLOOP

cutthroat / RUFFIAN; ASSASSIN

cutting / KEEN; SHARP; BITING, SEVERE. CION, SLIP

cutting implement / AX; ADZ, AXE, HOB, SAW, SAX; ADZE; KNIFE, MOWER, RAZOR; SHEARS, SICKLE

cutting side of a saw / TEETH

cuttlefish / SEPIA, SQUID; OCTOPUS

cuttlefish fluid / INK

Cybele's consort / ATYS; ATTIS

Cyclades island / IOS; KEOS; DELOS, MILOS, NAVOS, PAROS TENOS, THERA

cycle / CIRCLE; BICYCLE; REVOLUTION

cycle in astronomy / SAROS

cyclist / RIDER; MOTORCYCLIST

cyclone / LOW; STORM; TORNADO, TWISTER

cyclone cellar / REFUGE

cyclopean / HUGE, VAST; TERRIFIC

Cyclops' mother / GE

Cyclops' vanquisher / NOMAN; ODYSSEUS

cyesis / GESTATION, PREGNANCY

cygnet / SWANLET

cylinder / TUBE; SPOOL; PLATEN, ROLLER

cylinder of tobacco / CIGAR; CAROTTE

cylindrical / TERETE; CONICAL

cylindrical and hollow / TUBULAR

cyma / GOLA

cyma reversa / OGEE

cymbals / TAL, ZEL; PIATTI

Cymbeline's daughter / IMOGEN

Cymbeline's stepson / CLOTEN

Cymric / WELSH

Cymric sea god / LLYR

Cymric sun god / GWYN, LLEU, LLEW

Cymric underworld god / ARAWN, PWYLL

cynanche / QUINSY; INFLAMMATION

cynegetics / HUNTING

cynic / SURLY; MOROSE; ASCETIC; SARCASTIC

cynical / CROSS, TESTY; CRUSTY; DERISIVE, PETULANT

cynosure / CENTER; URSAMINOR

Cynthia / LUNA; DIANA; ARTEMIS

cypress / LAWN, SILK; CEDAR; JACKPINE

cyprian / WANTON; LASCIVIOUS

cyprinoid fish / ID; CHI, IDE; CARP, CHUB, ORFE; BREAM, TENCH

Cypriote mountain / TROODOS

Cypriote town / PAPHOS; LIMASSOL

Cypriote underground / EOKA

Cyprus capital / NICOSIA

Cyrenaic / HEDONIC

Cyrenaica's ancient name / PENTAPOLIS

Cyrus' daughter / ATOSSA

cyst / BAG, SAC, WEN; POUCH

cystic / VESICULAR

Cytherea / VENUS; ASTARTE

czar / TSAR; TYRANT; DICTATOR

czar's daughter / CZAREVNA, TSAREVNA
czar's wife / CZARINA, TSARINA; CZARITZA, TSARITZA
Czech / SLAV; SLOVAK; BOHEMIAN
Czech composer / DVORAK
Czech novelist / CAPEK
Czech poet / MACHA
Czech religious leader / HUSS
Czechoslovakia capital / PRAHA; PRAGUE
Czechoslovakian city / BRNO; PLZEN
Czechoslovakian money / HALER; KORUNA
Czechoslovakian range / TATRA
Czechoslovakian region / BOHEMIA, MORAVIA; SLOVAKIA
Czechoslovakian river / VAH; ELBE, HRON, LABE, ODER; NITRA; MOLDAU, VLTAVA
czigany / GYPSY

D

D.A. / PROSECUTOR
dab / DIE; DABBER, DIBBLE
dabble / DIP; MIX; MESS; MOISTEN
dabbler / AMATEUR; DILETTANTE
dabchick / GREBE
Dacian king / DECEBALUS
dacoit / BANDIT
dad / PA; PAPA; DADDY; FATHER
daddle / DAWDLE, WADDLE. FIST
Daedalus' son / ICARUS
daffodil / JONQUIL; NARCISSUS
daft / CRAZY, DAFFY, SILLY
dag / PISTOL
Dagda's cousin / BOANN
Dagda's daughter / BRIGIT
Dagda's son / BODB; ANGUS; OENGUS
Dagestan city / DERBENT
dagger / DHU; CRIS, DIRK, KRIS, SNEE; CREES, KREES, SKEAN, SKENE
dagger as reference mark / OBELUS; OBELISK
dagger wound / GASH, STAB
Dahomean Negro / FON, TEM; EGBA
Dahomey capital / COTONOU; PORTONOVO
Dahomey city / ABOMEY
Dai Nippon / JAPAN
daily / DIURNAL; NEWSPAPER
daily record / LOG; DIARY
daily traveler / COMMUTER
dainty / CUTE, FINE, NICE, RARE. NICETY, TIDBIT; DELICACY
dainty viands / CATES
dairy product / EGGS, MILK; CREAM; BUTTER, CHEESE
dairymaid / DEY
dais / STAGE; ESTRADE
daisy / GOWAN, OXEYE; SHASTA
daisy fleabane / ERIGERON
Dakota mountains / BLACKHILLS
Dakota Territory capital / YANKTON
Dakota tribe / TETON; MANDAN, SANTEE; ARIKARA
dale / GLEN, VALE
Dallas college / SMU

dally / LAG, TOY; PLAY; DELAY
Dalmatian city / DUBROVNIK
dam / WAER, WEIR; BARRIER
dam for catching fish / GARTH
dam in Egypt / SUDD; ASWAN
dam on river / WEIR
dam up / STEM, STOP; CONFINE
damage / MAR; HARM, HURT; IM-PAIR
damage the legs of / LAME
daman / CONY; WABBER
Damascus king / ARETAS
Damascus river / ABANA; BARADA
dame / LADY; MADAM; MATRON
damn / CURSE; CONDEMN; SEN-TENCE
damnable / ODIOUS; HATEFUL
Damon's friend / PYTHIAS
damp / ABATE, ALLAY, CHECK. WET; COOL, DANK; CHILL, HUMID
damp and close / MUGGY
dampen / MOISTEN
damsel / LASS; MAIDEN, VIRGIN
damselfish / PINTANO
Danae's father / ACRISIUS
Danae's lover / ZEUS
Danae's son / PERSEUS
Danakil inhabitant / AFAR
Danaus' father / BELUS
dance / HAY, HEY, HOP, JIG; BALL
dance of Greece / HORMOS; GERANOS
dance hall / BALLROOM
dance of Israel / HORA, SHER
dance for joy / CAPER
dance of the South Pacific / WAH-WAHLUNG
dance of Spain / JOTA, POLO; TANGO
dance step / PAS; SKIP; CHASSE
dancer / ALMA, ALME; ALMEH, MAIKO
dancer in Peer Gynt / ANITRA
dancer's instrument / CASTANET
dancing shoes / PUMPS; POINTS
dandelion seed / CYPSELA
dandle / DANCE; FONDLE

Dando / DEADBEAT
dandy / FOP; DUDE; COXCOMB
danger / HARM, RISK; PERIL
Danger Archipelago / TUAMOTUS
danger signal / SOS; ALARM
dangerous / RISKY; INSECURE
dangerous woman / SIREN; VAMPIRE
Daniel / BELTESHAZZAR
Daniel's companion / MESHACH; ABEDNEGO, SHADRACH
Danish / PASTRY. See also Denmark
Danish astronomer / TYCHO
Danish author / BOJER; ANDERSEN
Danish capital / KOBENHAVN; COPENHAGEN
Danish cheese / TYBO
Danish city / AARHUS
Danish coin / ORE; KRONE
Danish composer / GADE
Danish county / AMT
Danish critic / BRANDES
Danish fjord / ISE, LIM
Danish glottal stop / STOD
Danish headman / JARL, YARL
Danish hero / OGIER; HOLGER
Danish island / ALS; AERO, MOEN
Danish king / CNUT, KNUT; CANUTE
Danish measure / ALEN, ESER, RODE
Danish money / ORA, ORE; ORAS
Danish physicist / BOHR
Danish seaport / ODENSE
Danish weight / LOD; ESER
dank / WET; DAMP; HUMID, MOIST
Dannemora prison / CLINTON
Dante's inspiration / BEATRICE
Danube gorge / IRONGATE
Danube tributary / INN, OLT, VAHI
Danube's former name / ISTER
Danzig / GDANSK
dap / DIB, DIP; DIBBLE
daphne / LAUREL; MEZEREON
Daphne's father / LADON
Daphne's love / CHLOE
dapper / NEAT; NATTY, SMART
dapple / SPOT; MOTTLE
dappled / ROAN; SPOTTED
darbies / HANDCUFFS
Darby's spouse / JOAN
Dardanelles / HELLESPONT
Dardanus' brother / IASION
dare / TRY; DAST, DEFY, FACE
daredevil / RECKLESS
Darien's founder / BALBOA
daring / BOLD; BRAVE; DOUGHTY
Darius' great defeat / MARATHON
dark / DIM; DEEP, EBON, VILE
dark blue / COBALT

dark cherry / MORELLO
dark complexioned / SWART
Dark Continent / AFRICA
dark gray / TAUPE
dark horse / ZAIN; UNKNOWN
dark red / MAROON
dark rock / BASALT, RUTILE
dark soil / LOAM
dark syrup / MOLASSES
dark wood / EBONY
darken / DIM; BLACKEN, OBSCURE
darkened / CLOUDED
darkness / MURK; GLOOM, NIGHT
darling / PET; DEAR, LOVE; DEARY
Darling children's guardian / NANA
darling among the Irish / ROON; AROON; ACUSHLA, ASTHORE
darn / MEND; PATCH
Darnay's substitute / CARTON
Darnay's wife / LUCIE
darnel / TARE, WEED
dart / BARB, DARB, ROLE; ARROW. BOLT, DASH, FLIT; BOUND, SCOOT
D'Artagnan's friend / ATHOS; ARAMIS; PORTHOS
D'Artagnan's girl / CONSTANCE
Darwin's ship / BEAGLE
dash / FLY, MIX; CAST, DART. ELAN, MARK; SPIRIT
dash against / LASH
dash in telegraphy / DAH
dashboard / PANEL
dashing / GAY; BRAVE, SHOWY
dastard / CAD; COWARD, CRAVEN
data / BASIS; FACTS; GROUNDS
date / AGE, ERA; TIME; EPOCH
date of assault / DDAY
date line on coin / EXERGUE
date plum / SAPOTE
date of Roman calendar / IDES
date sugar / GHOOR
date tree / PALM
dated / OLD; PASSE; OLD-FASHIONED
datum / FACT
daub / BLOB; COVER, SMEAR
daughter of Cadmus / INO; SEMELE
daughter of David / TAMAR
daughter of Demeter / KORE; PERSEPHONE
daughter of Herodias / SALOME
daughter of Loki / HEL
daughter of Ops / CERES
daughter of Tantalus / NIOBE
daunt / COW; TAME; APPAL, CHECK
dauntless / DARING; GALLANT
davenport / SOFA; COUCH; SETTEE
David's daughter / TAMAR
David's father / JESSE
David's general / JOAB; ABNER

David's reprover / NATHAN
David's son / ABSALOM, SOLOMON
David's victim / URIAH; GOLIATH
David's wife / MICHAL;
  BATHSHEBA
David's writings / PSALMS
davit / CRANE
daw / GRACKLE, JACKDAW
dawdle / LAG; IDLE, POKE; DALLY
dawn / DEW, EOS; MORN; SUNUP
dawn, c.f. / EO
dawn, pert. to / EOAN
dawn goddess / EOS; AURORA
dawn's emblem / DEW
dawn's greeter / ROOSTER
Dawson's river / YUKON
day, c.f. / HEMER; HEMERO
day of atonement / YOMKIPPUR
day before / EVE
day blindness / HEMERALOPIA
day of Brahma / KALPA
day in court / SAY; CHANCE
day lily / NIOBE; NIOBES
day nursery / CRECHE
day performance / MATINEE
day of rest / SABBATH
day scholar / EXTERN
day star / SUN
daybook / DIARY; JOURNAL
daybreak / DAWN
daydream / FANCY; REVERIE
dayflower / SPIDERWORT
dayfly / MAYFLY
day's march / ETAPE
days of old / ELD; YORE
daysman / UMPIRE
dayspring / DAWN; SUNRISE
daze / STUN; BEMUSE, BENUMB
dazed / ASEA; STUNNED
dazzle / DAZE; FLARE, GLARE
dazzling light / GLARE
dead / COLD, DULL, FLAT, GONE
dead body / CORPSE; CADAVER
dead bomb / DUD
dead end / IMPASSE; CULDESAC
dead flesh / CARRION
dead heat / TIE
dead pan / POKERFACE
Dead Sea fortress / MASADA

Dead Sea land / MOAB
Dead Sea river / JORDAN
Dead Sea town / ENGEDI
dead tree / SNAG; RAMPIKE
dead trees / DRIKI, DRYKI
deaden / DAMP, KILL, MUTE,
  NUMB
deadfall / MANTRAP
deadhead / EMPTY
deadline / LIMIT
deadlock / IMPASSE; STALEMATE
deadly / FELL; FATAL; LETHAL
deadly sin / ENVY, LUST; ANGER,
  PRIDE, SLOTH; GLUTTONY;
  COVETOUSNESS
deadly snake / ASP; COBRA
deadness / TORPOR
deaf / SURD; HEEDLESS; INEXOR-
  ABLE
deal / DOLE; ALLOT; CHAFFER
deal with / COPE; TRADE; HANDLE
dealer / MONGER, TRADER
dealer in cloth / DRAPER, MERCER
dealer in drugs / PUSHER
dealer in foods / GROCER;
  CATERER
dealer in men's furnishings /
  HABERDASHER
dealer in securities / BROKER
dealer in skins / TANNER;
  FURRIER
dean / DELL, DENE; DOYEN;
  SENIOR
dean, pert. to / DECANAL
dear / LOVED; COSTLY, VALUED
dearth / LACK, NEED, WANT
death / EXIT, FALL, MORT; DECAY
death, c.f. / THANATO
death announcements / NECROL-
  OGY
death camass / LOBELIA
death note / MORT
death notice / OBIT; OBITUARY
Death Valley range / PANAMINTS
death watch / VIGIL
deathless / IMMORTAL, UNFADING
debacle / ROUT; STAMPEDE
debar / DENY, SHUT, STOP; DETER
debase / SINK; ALLOY, LOWER

DAYS OF THE WEEK

	Abbreviation	Derivation
Sunday	SUN	SUN
Monday	MON	MOON
Tuesday	TUES	TIW, TYR
Wednesday	WED	WODEN
Thursday	THURS	THOR
Friday	FRI	FRIA, FREYA
Saturday	SAT	SATURN

debatable / AGON, MOOT; DUBIOUS

debate / MOOT; ARGUE. CONTROVERSY

debauch / DEFILE, RAVISH, SEDUCE; CORRUPT. ORGY, RIOT; REVEL

debauchee / RAKE, ROUE; SATYR

debilitate / WEAKEN; ENERVATE

debility / ATONY; FRAILTY

debit's opposite / CREDIT

debonair / SUAVE; JAUNTY; ELEGANT

debris / RUINS, SCREE, TRASH

debt / DUE; CLAIM, DEBIT, SCORE

debut / OPENING; ENTRANCE

decade / TEN; DECAD; DECENNIUM

decadence / DECAY; RETROGRESSION

Decameron author / BOCCACCIO

decamp / FLY, RUN; BOLT, FLEE

decant / POUR

decanter / CARAFE

decapitate / BEHEAD

decay / EBB, ROT; SINK, WANE. CARIES, DRYROT; WASTING

decay in trees / ROT; CONK, KONK

decayed / PUTRID, ROTTEN; CORRUPT

Deccan state / HYDERABAD

deceit / SHAM, WILE, CHEAT

deceitful / SLY; WILY; ARTFUL

deceive / BILK, DUPE, FLAM, FOOL

deceived / MISLED

deceiver / LIAR; TRICKSTER

decelerate / SLOW

December birthstone / RUBY; TURQUOISE

decent / MODEST, PROPER, SEEMLY

decently polite / CIVIL

deception / LIE; HOAX, WILE

deceptive trick / RUSE

decide / FIX, OPT; CLOSE; SETTLE

decide judicially / ADJUDGE

decide upon / ADOPT, ELECT

decimal basis / TEN

decipher / READ; SOLVE, SPELL

decision / DOOM; NERVE; VERDICT

decisive moment / CRISIS

deck / TRIM; ADORN, ARRAY. POOP; FLOOR, ORLOP

deck of cards / PACK

deck room for cooking / GALLEY

decked out / BEDIGHT; BEDIZENED

deckle on paper / EDGE, TRIM

declaim / RANT, RAVE; ORATE

declamation / TIRADE; ORATION

declamatory / LOUD; NOISY

declaration / AVOWAL; JUDGMENT

declare / SAY; AVER; STATE, UTTER

declare innocent / ACQUIT

declare openly / AVOW; PROFESS

declare for score / MELD

declared hostilities / WAR

decline / DIE, DIP, EBB; FALL

declining / setting

declining period / EVE; EVENING

declivity / SIDE; SCARP, SLOPE

decoction / TEA; CREMOR, PTISAN

decompose / ROT; DECAY; ANALYZE

decor / SCENERY; ORNAMENT

decorate / DECK, TRIM; ADORN

decorate with knobs / STUD

decorated baseboard / DADO

decorated initial / FAC

decorated wall area / DADO

decoration for valor / BADGE, MEDAL

decorative ensemble / DECOR

decorative plant / FERN

decorative ribbon / BOW; BAND

decorative stoneware / GRES

decorative vessel / URN; VASE

decorous / FIT; STAID; DECENT

decorum / ORDER; DECENCY

decoy / BAIT, LURE; PLANT, TEMPT

decoy duck / FAKER; TRAPPER

decrease / EBB; EASE, FAIL, WANE

decree / ACT, LAW; BULL, FIAT

decrement / DIMINUTION

decrepit / SPENT; EFFETE, INFIRM

decry / BLAME; CONDEMN, DETRACT

decumbent / PROSTRATE, RECLINING

decussation / CHIASMA; CROSSING

Dedan's father / RAAMAH; JOKSHAN

Dedan's sons / LEUMMIM; ASSHURIM

dedicate / APPLY; DEVOTE

dedicated follower / DISCIPLE

deduce / INFER; DERIVE, EVOLVE

deduction / REBATE; REMOVAL

deed / ACT; FACT, FEAT, GEST

deem / HOLD; FANCY, JUDGE, OPINE

deep / LOW; DARK; THICK; HIDDEN

deep affection / LOVE

deep black or blue alloy / NIELLO

deep blue pigment / SMALT

deep blue sea / OCEAN

deep bow / SALAAM, SCRAPE

deep dish / TUREEN

deep gong tone / BONG

deep gorge / RAVINE

deep groove / RUT

deep longing / YEARNING

deep mud / MIRE

deep sleep / SOPOR

deep-dish dessert / COBBLER, CUSTARD

deepen / CLOUD; DARKEN, DREDGE
deepest meaning / CORE, GIST
deeply engrossed / RAPT
deep-sea / ABYSSAL
deep-toned horn / TUBA
deer / DOE, ELK, ROE; HART, HIND, OLEN, STAG; MOOSE; CERVID
deer, pert. to / DAMINE; CERVINE
deer of Africa / DAMA; CHEVROTAIN
deer of Asia / AHU; AXIS, NAPU, RUSA, SHOU; KAKAR; CHITAL
deer grass / RHEXIA
deer hog / PARA; ATLAS
deer horn / BEZ; DAG; BALCON
deer of Japan / SIKA; SHIKA
deer meat / VENISON
deer of North America / MOOSE; CARIBOU
deer of Persia / MARAL
deer of South America / PITA, PUDU; GEMUL; GUEMAL, GUEMUL, MAZAME
deerhound / STAGHOUND
deerlet / NAPU; CHEVROTAIN
deerlike mammal / OKAPI
deer's antlers / ATTIRE
deer's cry / SAW; BELL, ROAR
deer's horn / DAG; ANTLER, POINTS
deer's neck pouch / BELL
deer's resting place / LAIR
deer's tail / FLAG, SCUT; SINGLE
deer's track / SLOT, VIEW
Deerslayer / BUMPPO
deface / MAR; SOIL; SPOIL
defamation / LIBEL; SLANDER
defame / ABUSE, LIBEL; MALIGN
Defarge woman's hobby / KNITTING
default / LACK, LOSS, MORA, WANT
defeat / BEAT, BEST, FOIL, ROUT
defeat at chess / MATE; CHECKMATE
defecate / FREE; PURIFY; CLARIFY
defect / FLAW, LACK, WANT; ERROR
defect in fabric / YAW; SCOB
defective / BAD; FAULTY
defective, pref. / MAL
defective explosive / DUD
defend / WARD; GUARD; ASSERT
defendant / REUS
defender / LAWYER; TRIBUNE; ADVOCATE, ATTORNEY; OMBUDSMAN; VINDICATOR
defense / PLEA; ALIBI, GUARD
defense alliance / NATO; SEATO
defense mechanism / PROJECTION; SUBLIMATION
defensible / TENABLE
defensive angle / RAVELIN

defensive bastion / FORT; STOCKADE
defensive covering / ARMOR; HELMET, SHIELD
defensive dike / ESTACADE
defensive outpost / BARBICAN
defensive plating / ARMOR
defensive slope / GLACIS
defensive work / MOAT; BOURN; ABATIS, TRENCH
defer / DELAY; PUTOFF, RETARD; ADJOURN; POSTPONE
deference / HONOR; HOMAGE
deficiency / LACK, WANT; ERROR
deficiency disease / SCURVY; RICKETS; BERIBERI, PELLAGRA; GLOSSITIS; XEROPHTHALMIA
deficient / SHORT; FAULTY
defile / MOIL, SOIL; SPOIL
define / FIX; BOUND, LIMIT
definite / EXACT; CERTAIN
definite amount / QUANTUM
definite article / THE
deflate / COLLAPSE, CONTRACT
deflated / FLAT
deflect / TURN; DIVERT, SWERVE
Defoe's hero / CRUSOE
deform / MAR; DISTORT; DISFIGURE
defraud / GYP, ROB; BILK, DUPE
deft / APT, PAT; HANDY; ADROIT
defunct / DEAD, GONE; DONEFOR
defy / DARE, FACE; BEARD, BRAVE
degenerate / ROT; DECAY; DECLINE
degrade / ABASE, LOWER; DEBASE
degrading / MENIAL; INFRADIG
degree / RANK, RATE, STEP; CLASS
degree in art / AB, BA, MA; BFA, MFA; BLITT
degree aspirant / CANDIDATE
degree in business / MBA
degree in dental science / DDS
degree in divinity / DD
degree in engineering / CE, EE, ME
degree extreme / EST, NTH
degree in law / LLB, LLD
degree in medicine / DD, MD; DVM
degree of numerals / ND, ST, TH; NTH
degree of progression / PACE; STAGE
degree in science / BS; BAC, DSC
degree of standing / RANK
dehydrate / DRY; PARCH; DESSICATE
Deianira's husband / HERCULES
deign / GRANT, LOWER, STOOP
Deiphobus' father / PRIMA
Deiphobus' slayer / MENELAUS
Deirdre's abductor / NAISI
Deirdre's father / PHELIM

deity / GOD; DEVA; NUMEN; GOD-DESS, JEHOVAH; DEMIURGE, DIVINITY. **See also god, the name of the culture, e.g. Norse god, or the attribution of the god, e.g., wind god, sky god, etc.**

deity of woods and flocks / FAUN

dejected / LOW, SAD; GLUM

delate / ACCUSE

Delaware capital / DOVER

Delaware city / WILMINGTON

Delaware Indian / ABNAKI, LENAPE, MUNSEE, UNAMEE; ALGONQUIN

Delaware state nickname / BLUE-HEN, DIAMOND

Delaware town / LEWES

delay / LAG; STOP, WAIT; DALLY

dele / CANCEL, DELETE, REMOVE

delectable girl / DISH

delectation / DELIGHT; PLEASURE

delegate / DEPUTY, LEGATE; SUB-STITUTE; COMMISSIONER. DE-PUTE

delete / DELE; ERASE; CANCEL

deleterious / BAD; HARMFUL

deliberate / PAUSE, THINK, WEIGH

deliberate cruelty / TORTURE

deliberately ignore / SNUB

Delibes work / LAKME, NAILA

delicacy / CATE, TACT; CAVIAR

delicate / FINE, WEAK; FRAIL

delicate creature / BUTTERFLY

delicate fabric / LACE, SILK

delicate gradation / NUANCE

delicate openwork / FILIGREE

delicately / SFOGATO

delicately pretty / MIGNON

delicatessen meat / SALAMI

delicious / TASTY; PLEASING

delight / CHARM, ELATE, REVEL, JOY; GLEE; BLISS; RELISH

delighted / GLAD; HAPPY

delightful company / CHARMER

Delilah's lover / SAMSON

Delilah's people / PHILISTINES

delineate / DRAW, LIMN; PAINT

delinquency / FAULT; FAILURE

deliquesce / MELT; LIQUEFY

delirious / GYTE

delirium / FRENZY; MADNESS

delirium tremens / DTS; HORRORS, JIMJAMS

delitescent / LATENT; DORMANT

deliver / RID; CEDE, FREE, SAVE, SEND; GRANT, SPEAK, UTTER, YIELD

deliver orally / TALK; ORATE, SPEAK, UTTER; PREACH, RECITE

dell / DALE, DENE, GLEN, VALE; COOMB; DINGLE, RAVINE, VAL-LEY

Delphic deity / APOLLO; DIONYSUS

Delphic message / ORACLE

Delphic priestess / PYTHIA

Delphic stone / OMPHALOS

delude / DUPE, FLAM, GULL; CHEAT, TRICK; IMPOSE; BE-GUILE, DECEIVE

deluge / FLOOD; ENGULF; INUN-DATE, OVERFLOW

delusion / LIE; RUSE, WILE; CHEAT, FRAUD, SNARE, TRICK

delusion in Buddhism / MOHA

delve / DIG; MINE, TILL; PROBE

demand / ASK; CLAIM, EXACT

demand payment / DUN, SUE

demand for repetition / BIS; EN-CORE

demean / ABASE, LOWER; DEBASE

demeanor / AIR; MIEN, PORT; CON-DUCT; BEHAVIOR, CARRIAGE

demented / MAD; BATTY, CRAZY

demented person / MANIAC

dementia praecox / HEBEPHRENIA

demerit / GIG

Demeter / BRIMO, CERES

Demeter's daughter / CORA, KORE; PERSEPHONE

demi, **pref.** / HALF, SEMI

demigod / HERO; GODKIN, GODLET

demise / DEATH

demit / OUST; LOWER; RESIGN

demiurgic / FORMANT; CREATIVE

Democritus Jr. / BURTON

demolish / RASE, RAZE, RUIN

demon / IMP; EVIL, OGRE, RAHU; DEVIL, FIEND, GUIDE, LAMIA

demon of the Arabs / JIN; GHUL, JINN; AFRIT, EBLIS, GENIE

demon of the Hindus / RAHU; ASURA; DAITYA

demon of the Japanese / ONI; KIT-SUNE; BAKEMONO

demon of men's dreams / SUCCU-BUS

demon of nightmare / MARA; IN-CUBUS

demon who robs graves / GHOUL

demon of vanity / ASMODEUS

demon of the Zoroastrians / DEV, DIV; DEVA; DAEVA

demonstrate / SHOW; PROVE

demonstration / PROOF; PARADE; DISPLAY, OVATION, SHOWING

demonstration model / DEMO

demonstrative pronoun / ONE; THAT, THIS; THESE, THOSE

demoralize / CORRUPT; UNDER-MINE

demos / PEOPLE; POPULACE

demulcent / SALEP

demur / DOUBT, PAUSE, WAVER; OBJECT; PROTEST

demure/ COY; PRIM; GRAVE, SOBER

den / CAVE, DIVE, HUNT, LAIR, NEST; HAUNT, STUDY; CAVERN

denary / TEN; DECAD; DECADE

denature / ALTER; CHANGE, WEAKEN

dene / DELL, DOWN

denial / NO; NAY; REFUSAL

denizen / CITIZEN; INHABITANT

Denmark / See Danish

Denmark's first king / GORM

Denmark's former name / THULE

Denmark's peninsula / JUTLAND

denominate / CALL, NAME, TERM; TITLE; ENTITLE

denomination / KIND, SECT; CLASS

denote / MARK, MEAN, SHOW; IMPLY; TYPIFY; BETOKEN, PORTEND

denoting final purpose / TELIC

denoting more than one / PLURAL

denoting position / ORDINAL

denouement / OUTCOME; SOLUTION; UNRAVELING; CATASTROPHE

denounce / ACCUSE, EXPOSE, SCATHE; ARRAIGN, CENSURE

dense / CLOSE, CRASS, THICK

dense growth / BRAKE; FOREST, JUNGLE

dense smoke / SMUDGE

dense thicket / CHAPARRAL

dense throng / MOB; MASS; PRESS

density / DORD, MASS

dent / DINT; NOTCH; HOLLOW

dental decay / CARIES

dental filling / GOLD; ALLOY, INLAY; CEMENT

dental tool / BURR; DRILL; SCALER; FORCEPS; DENTAGRA

dentalgia / TOOTHACHE

dentate / NOTCHED, SERRATE

dentine / IVORY

denture / PLATE, BRIDGE

denude / BARE; NAKED, SCALP

Denver's original name / AURARIA

deny / ABJURE, DISOWN, NEGATE, REFUSE, REJECT, RENEGE; DISAVOW

depart / GO; DIE, FLY; FLEE, MOVE, QUIT; LEAVE; BEGONE

depart in a hurry / GIT; SCAT; SCOOT; VAMOSE; VAMOOSE

depart secretly / ELOPE; DECAMP; ABSCOND

departed / DEAD, GONE

department in China / FU

department store / MART; EMPORIUM

department store event / SALE; SPECIAL

department store in Moscow / GOUM

departure / EXIT; EXODUS

depend / LEAN, RELY; HINGE, TRUST

dependant / MINION

dependency / COLONY

dependent / CLIENT, MINION; RETAINER; CONSEQUENCE. HELPLESS

depict / DRAW, LIMN; PAINT; PICTURE, PORTRAY; DESCRIBE

deplete / DRAIN, EMPTY; LESSEN

deplorable / SAD; GRIEVOUS

deplore / RUE; MOAN; GRIEVE

deplume / PLUCK, STRIP

depone / TESTIFY

deportee / EXILE

depose / REMOVE; TESTIFY

deposit / LAY, PUT, SET; LEAVE, PLACE. BED; DELTA

deposit in blood vessels / PLAQUE

deposit box / PYX; METER; PUSHKA

deposit of clay / MARL

deposit in flood plain / ALLUVIUM

deposit in gall bladder / CALCULUS

deposit by geyser / SINTER

deposit of gold particles / PLACER

deposit of ice crystals / RIME, SNOW; FROST; HOARFROST

deposit of minerals / LEAD, LODE, REEF, VEIN; POCKET; BONANZA

deposit of ore / GULF, LODE

deposit of sediment / DUST, SILT, SOOT

deposit of stream / GULF, SILT; DELTA; SEDIMENT

deposit on teeth / TARTAR

deposit by wind / LOESS

deposit in wine cask / ARGOL; TARTAR

depot / BASE; STATION; WAREHOUSE

deprave / CORRUPT, VITIATE

depraved / BAD; LOST; WICKED

depreciate / LOWER; LESSEN

depress / CHILL, LOWER; DAMPEN, DEBASE, DEJECT, HUMBLE, SADDEN

depressed / SAD; BLUE; SADDENED

depressing / TRISTE

depression / DIP, PIT; DENT

Depression era agency / NRA, WPA

depression between mountain peaks / COL, DIP

deprive / ROB; DEBAR, MULCT

deprive of food / STARVE

deprive of rank / DEMOTE

deprive of reason / DEMENT

deprive of sight / BLIND

deprive of weapons / DISARM

deprived / REFT; SHORN; BEREFT
depth / DEEP, GULF, HOLE; ABYSS
deputation / MISSION
deputy / AGENT, ENVOY, PROXY,
VICAR; DELEGATE; SURROGATE
deputy viceroy / NAWAB
derange / DEMENT
deranged / CRAZY; CRAZED, IN-
SANE
derby / HAT; RACE; BOWLER
derelict / ADRIFT; ABANDONED,
NEGLECTED. WRECK; CAST-
AWAY
deride / RAG; GIBE, JEER, JIBE,
MOCK; SCOFF, SCORN, SCOUT,
SNEER
derision / IRONY, SCORN; MOCK-
ERY
derivation / ROOT; CAUSE; ORIGIN,
SOURCE; DESCENT; BEGINNING
derive / GET; DRAW; INFER, TRACE
derived from fat / ADIPIC
derived by inference / ILLATIVE
derived of / FROM
derived from oil / OLEIC
derived by reasoning / DEDUCED
dermal / CUTANEOUS
derogatory grimace / SNEER
derogatory remark / SLUR; ASPER-
SION
derrick / RIG; CRANE, DAVIT;
STEEVE; GALLOWS
derring-do / BRAVERY
dervish / FAKER, FAKIR, FAQIR;
FAKEER, HERMIT, SADITE;
ASCETIC
dervish's cap / TAJ
dervish's ride / DOSA
descendant / ISSUE; PROGENY;
OFFSPRING, POSTERITY
descendant of Ham / HAMITE
descendant of Shem / SEMITE
descendants in the male line /
GENS
descended to ground / ALIT
describe / DRAW; TRACE; DEPICT,
RELATE; EXPLAIN, NARRATE
describe as / TAG; LABEL
describe grammatically / PARSE
descried / SEEN; ESPIED
descriptive attribution / EPITHET
descriptive name / TITLE
descriptive painting / GENRE
Desdemona's companion / EMILIA
Desdemona's father / BRABANTIO
Desdemona's foe / IAGO
Desdemona's husband / OTHELLO
desecrate / ABUSE; POLLUTE
desert / QUIT; LEAVE. ERG; KAM,
QUM; VOID; DASHT, WASTE;
HAMMADA. WILD; BARREN

desert in Africa / KARROO, NU-
BIAN, SAHARA; KALAHARI
desert alkali / REH
desert animal / CAMEL
desert in Arabia / RUBALKHALI
desert in Asia / GOBI, THAR;
SHAMO
desert in Australia / STURT;
ARUNTA
desert in California / MOJAVE
desert cat / BAYLYNX
desert in Chile / ATACAMA
desert in China / TAKLAMAKAN
desert date / BITO
desert dweller / ARAB; BEDOUIN,
EREMITE
Desert Fox / ROMMEL
desert in Israel / NEGEV
desert phenomenon / MIRAGE
desert plant / ALOE, PALM; AGAVE,
YUCCA; CACTUS; SAGUARO
desert train / CARAVAN
desert vision / MIRAGE
desert watering place / OASIS
desert wind / SIMOOM, SIMOON;
SIROCCO
deserter / RAT; RENEGADE
deserved / MEET; CONDIGN
deserving blame / GUILTY
desiccated / DRY; ARID, SERE
desiderate / NEED, WANT; DESIRE
design / AIM; DRIFT, MODEL,
SCOPE; OBJECT. PLAN; DEVISE
designate / DUB; NAME, TERM; LA-
BEL; ASSIGN, SELECT; APPOINT
designated area / SITE; LOCATION
desirable part / FAT; BEST; CREAM
desire / ASK; CARE, HOPE, LUST,
WANT, WISH; COVET, YEN; URGE
desirous / FAIN; EAGER; COVET-
OUS
desirous of food / HUNGRY
desist / END; REST, STAY, STOP
desk / PULPIT; EDITORS, LECTERN,
ROLLTOP, SECTION; SECRETARY
desolate / BARE, LORN, WILD
desolate region / DESERT
despairing / HOPELESS
despatch / SEND; DISPATCH
desperado / BRAVO, TOUGH;
HOODLUM, RUFFIAN; CRIMINAL
desperate / RASH, WILD; FRANTIC
despicable / LOW; BASE, MEAN
despise / HATE; SCORN, SCOUT,
SPURN; DETEST, LOATHE,
SLIGHT
despite / SCORN; HATRED; CON-
TEMPT. NOTWITHSTANDING
despoil / ROB; RUIN; SPOIL, STRIP;
FLEECE, RAVAGE; DEPRIVE
despoiled / REFT

despondent / LOW, SAD; BLUE
despondent period / DOWN; BLUES; JITTERS
despot / CZAR, TSAR, TZAR; TYRANT; AUTOCRAT, DICTATOR
dessert / ICE, PIE; CAKE, TART; SWEET; MOUSSE, TRIFLE; SHERBET
destination / AIM, END, LOT; DOOM, FATE, GOAL, STAR; HAVEN
destined / FATED, FETED; CHOSEN
destiny / LOT; DOOM, FATE; KARMA, STARS; DECREE; FORTUNE
destitute / LORN, POOR; NEEDY
destitute of hair / BALD
destitute of teeth / EDENTATE
destitution / WANT; POVERTY
destroy / GUT, RID; KILL, RASE, RAZE, RUIN, SLAY, UNDO; WASTE
destroy bit by bit /ERODE
destroyer of images / ICONOCLAST
destroying angel / DANITE; AMANITA
destruction / LOSS, RUIN; DEATH, HAVOC; DEMOLITION, SUBVERSION
destructive / DEADLY; BALEFUL
destructive insect / MOTH; LOCUST, WEEVIL; TERMITE
destructive maggot / MORM
destructive sugar cane disease / ILIAU
destructive wheat smut / BUNT
desudation / SWEATING
desuetude / DISUSE
detachable button / STUD
detachment / UNIT; ISOLATION
detail / ITEM; PARTICULAR
detain / HALT, HOLD, STAY, STOP
detect / SPY; ESPY, NOSE, SPOT
detecting device / RADAR, SONAR
detective / DICK; SLEUTH; GUMSHOE; HAWKSHAW, SHERLOCK
detective of A. C. Doyle / HOLMES
detective of D. Hammett / SPADE
detective of E. A. Poe / DUPIN
detective of D. Sayers / WIMSEY
detector of the invisible / NOSE, XRAY
detent / PAWL; CATCH
deter / HOLD, WARN; DETAIN, HINDER, RETARD; PREVENT; DISSUADE
detergent / SOAP; CLEANSER
deteriorate / ROT; FAIL, WEAR; DECAY; IMPAIR, REDUCE, WORSEN
deterioration / DECADENCE
determinate / SPECIFIC
determinate portion / DOSE

determination / GRIT, WILL; FINDING, PURPOSE
determine / FIX; LEAD, WILL; DECIDE, SETTLE, VERIFY; CERTIFY
determined / PAT, SET; RESOLUTE
detest / HATE; LOATHE; DESPISE
detonator / CAP; FUSE, FUZE
detour / BYPASS
detract / DECRY; LESSEN; DEROGATE, WITHDRAW; DISPARAGE
detriment / EVIL, HARM; DAMAGE
detritus / SCREE, TALUS; DEBRIS
Detroit product / AUTOMOBILE
Deucalion's father / PROMETHEUS
Deucalion's mother /CLYMENE
Deucalion's son / HELLEN
Deucalion's wife / PYRRHA
deuce / TWO; DEVIL
deuced / DEVILISH; CONFOUNDED
deus / GOD
Devas' king / INDRA
devastate / RUIN, SACK; WASTE
devastation / RUIN; HAVOC, WASTE
develop / GROW; VOLVE; EVOLVE, EXPAND, MATURE, UNFOLD; DISCLOSE
develop into another form / EVOLVE
develop rapidly / BOOM; FULMINATE
Devi / UMA; KALI, SATI; DURGA
Devi's consort / SIVA
deviate / ERR, YAW; BACK, VARY; LAPSE, STRAY, WHEEL; CHANGE
deviate from course / YAW; VEER; SHEER, STRAY
deviate from vertical / HADE
deviation / ERROR, LAPSE; MUTATION; VARIATION
device / PLAN, RUSE, TYPE; MOTTO; DESIGN, EMBLEM, LEGEND, SCHEME
device for gripping / VISE; CLAMP; PLIERS
device for opening / KEY
device to stop turning wheel / BRAKE, SPRAG
devil / IMP; DEMON, DEUCE, EBLIS, FIEND, SATAN; AZAZEL, BELIAL
devil, pert. to / SATANIC
devil, pert. to the / DIABOLIC
devil of the bottomless pit / APOLLYON
devil among the Gypsies / BENG; BENGH; BENGUI; RABUINO
devil of the Moslems / EBLIS, IBLIS; SHAITAN, SHEITAN
devil worship / SATANISM; DIABOLISM
devil-dog / MARINE
devilfish / RAY; MANTA; ANGLER; BATFISH
devilkin / IMP

devil-may-care / MADCAP; RECK-LESS
deviliry / MAGIC; DIABLERIE
devil's apple / MANDRAKE
devil's bones / DICE
devil's godmother / BABA
devil's picture book / CARDS
devil's tree of India / DITA
deviltry / MISCHIEF
devious / MAZY; CROOKED, ERRA-TIC
devise / PLAN; FRAME; CREATE, IN-VENT, SCHEME; CONCOCT, IM-AGINE
devoid / EMPTY; VACANT; WITH-OUT
Devonshire cream / BONNYCLAB-BER
devote / APPLY; DEDICATE
devoted / FOND; LIEGE, LOYAL
devoted adherent / VOTARY
devotee / FAN, IST; VOTARY; PAR-TISAN; ENTHUSIAST
devotion / LOVE, ZEAL; ARDOR
devotion of nine days / NOVENA
devotional / DEVOUT
devour / EAT; BOLT, WOLF; GORGE, SPEND, WASTE; CONSUME, DE-STROY
devouring / EDACIOUS
devout / HOLY; GODLY, GRAVE, PIOUS; SOLEMN; DEVOTED, EARNEST
devoutness / PIETY; DEVOTION
dewberry / MAYES; LOGANBERRY
dewlap / WATTLE
dewy / WET; ADEW; MOIST, RORAL RORIC; MOISTURE
dexterity / ART; EASE, TACT; KNACK, SKILL; ABILITY; APTI-TUDE
dexterous / APT; DEFT; HANDY
dexterous trick / SLEIGHT
diabetics' dose / INSULIN, ORI-NASE
diabolic / WICKED; IMPIOUS
diacritical mark / BREVE, TILDE; ACCENT, MACRON; DIERESIS
diadem / CROWN, TIARA
diagonal / BIAS; CATERCORNER, CATTYCORNER
diagram / MAP; CHART, GRAPH; OUTLINE
dialect / ARGOT, IDIOM, LINGO; JARGON, PATOIC, PATOIS, SPEECH
dialect of Chinese / MANDARIN; CANTONESE
dialect of Ethiopian / TIGRE; AM-HARIC, TIGRINA
dialect of Greek / ATTIC, DORIC, IONIC

dialect in Hindu sacred writings / PALI; VEDIC
diameter / BORE; CALIBER, CALI-PER
diamond / MOGUL, SANCY; ORLOFF; ADAMANT, INFIELD; KOHINOOR
diamond crystal / GLASSIE
diamond in heraldry / LOZENGE
diamond holder / DOP; DOPP; BEZEL, PRONG; CHATON
diamond scraps used in industry / BORT
diamond surface / FACET
diamond wheel / SKIVE
diamond-hard / ADAMANT
diamond-patterned socks / ARGYLES
diamond-shaped figure / RHOMB; LOZENGE
Diana / LUNA; DELIA; ARTEMIS, CYNTHIA
Diana monkey / ROLOWAY
Diana's father / JUPITER
Diana's grove / NEMEAN
Diana's mother / LATONA
Diana's twin / APOLLO
diaper / NAPPIE; BREECHCLOTH
diaphanous / THIN; SHEER
diaphragm / MIDRIFF
diaphragm, pert. to / PHRENIC
diarist / PEPYS
Diarmuid's chief / FINN
Diarmuid's consort / GRAINNE
Diarmuid's grandfather / DUIBNE
diary / LOG; MEMO; RECORD
diaskeuast / EDITOR; REVISER
diatonic note / DO, FA, LA, MI, RE, SI, TI; SOL
diatonic scale / GAMUT, MAJOR, MINOR
diatribe / ABUSE; SCREED, TIRADE
dib / DAB, DAP; PEBBLE
dibble / DAB, DAP, DIB, DIP
Diblaim's daughter / GOMER
dice / CRAP; BONES, CUBES
dice seven / NATURAL
dice six / SICE; BOXCAR
dice two / SNAKEEYES
Dickens character / PIP, TIM; DORA, GAMP, HEEP, NELL
Dickens' pen name / BOZ
dictate / BID; ORDER, UTTER; DE-CREE, DIRECT, ENJOIN, ORDAIN
dictionary / LEXICON; GLOSSARY, WORDBOOK; THESAURUS
dictionary writer / LEXICOGRAPHER
dictum / ADAGE, MAXIM; SAYING; APHORISM; ASSERTION
didactic / TEACHING; PRECEPTIVE
dido / ANTIC, CAPER, PRANK, TRICK; GAMBOL

Dido / ELISSA
Dido's father / BELUS
Dido's kingdom / CARTHAGE
Dido's lover / AENEAS
Dido's sister / ANNA
die / FADE; CEASE, DECAY; DEMISE, DEPART, EXPIRE, PERISH, WITHER
die for gambling / TAT; CUBE; CHUKREE, TESSERA
die for molding pipe clay / DOD
die-hard / BITTERENDER
diehard / TORY; STANDPATTER
diet / FARE, FOOD; CHEER; VIANDS; ALIMENT, COUNCIL. BANT, FAST
dietetics / SITOLOGY
differ / VARY; CONTEND, DEVIATE
difference / BREACH, DEBATE, SCHISM; DISCORD, DISPUTE
different / OTHER, DIVERS; DIVERSE, VARIANT
differently / ELSE; OTHERWISE
difficult / HARD; RIGID, KNOTTY
difficult, pref. / DYS
difficult problem / NUT; POSER
difficulty / ADO, RUB; KNOT, SNAG; STRAIT; CONTROVERSY
diffident / COY, SHY; MODEST
diffuse / STREW, STROW; SPREAD. WORDY; PROLIX; COPIOUS
diffusion / OSMOSIS, SCATTER; DISPERSION
dig / GRUB, MINE, PION, WORK; DELVE, SPADE, STUDY; BURROW
digest / STUDY; CODIFY, PONDER; ARRANGE, DISPOSE, REFLECT. CODE
digestive health / EUPEPSIA
digestive juice / PEPSIN, RENNIN
digestive organ / LIVER; STOMACH
digestive upset / DYSPEPSIA
digger tree / SABINE
digging, pert. to / FODIENT
digging implement / LOY; PICK, SPUD; SCOOP, SPADE; DREDGE
digit / TOE; FIGURE, FINGER, NUMBER; INTEGER, NUMERAL
digit on dog's foot / DEWCLAW
digit guard / STALL; THIMBLE
dignified / GRAND, LOFTY, NOBLE
dignify / ADORN, EXALT, GRACE
digression / LOOP; EPISODE; FLASHBACK; DIVERGENCE
dike / LEVEE; CAUSEWAY; INTRUSION
dilapidation / RUIN; DECAY, HAVOC
dilatation / ECTASIA; DILATION; EXPANSION
dilate / SWELL, WIDEN; EXPAND; DISTEND, ENLARGE; EXPATIATE
dilatory / IDLE, LAZY, LONG

dilemma / FIX; TRAP; DOUBT; PLIGHT; QUANDARY
dilettante / AMATEUR, DABBLER, DEVOTEE; SCIOLIST
diligence / CARE, HEED; COACH
diligent / BUSY; ACTIVE; OPEROSE
dill / ANET
dilly / LULU; BEAUT
diluent / SOLVENT; DISSOLVING
dilute / THIN; WEAKEN. FAINT
dim / DARK, DULL, HAZY, PALE
dimension / BULK, MASS, SIZE; EXTENT, VOLUME; MEASURE; CAPACITY
diminish / EBB; BATE, FADE, SINK, WANE, WAVE; ABATE, DWARF, LOWER
diminish width / PLOY
diminuendo / SLOWING
diminutive / WEE; TINY; DWARF
diminutive equine / PONY
diminutive fowl / BANTAM
diminutive suffix / ET, IE, OT; ILE, OLE, ULE; ETTE
Dimmesdale's daughter / PEARL
dimness of sight / CALIGO
dim-sighted / PURBLIND
din in / REPEAT
Dinah's mother / LEAH
dingle / DALE, DELL
dingy / DULL; DIRTY, RUSTY
dining alcove / OECUS; DINETTE
dining room / GRILL; CENACLE
dinkum / FAIR; HONEST, SQUARE
dinner jacket / TUXEDO
dinosaur / LIZARD; REPTILE; SAUROPOD, THEROPOD
dint / DENT, MARK; FORCE; IMPRINT
diocese / SEE; BISHOPRIC
Diomedes' father / TYDEUS
Diomedes' wife / AEGIALEIA
Dione's daughter / APHRODITE
Dione's son / PELOPS
dionysiac / BACCHIC
Dionysus / BACCHUS, ZAGREUS
Dionysus' follower / MAENAD
Dioscuri / TWINS; ANACES, ANAKES; CASTORANDPOLLUX
dip / DAP, DIB, SOP; DIVE, DOPP, DUCK, DUNK, LADE, SINK; DOUSE. PITCH, SAUSE, SOUSE; PICKPOCKET
dip the colors / SALUTE
dip out / BAIL, LADE
diploma / PARCHMENT, SHEEPSKIN
diplomacy / TACT; ADDRESS
diplomat / AGENT, ENVOY; CONSUL, HERALD; ATTACHE; MINISTER
diplomatic / ASTUTE, CLEVER

diplomatic art / TACT
dipody / SYZYGY; DIMETER
dipper / URSA, WAIN; LADLE, SCOOP, SPOON
dipsomaniac / SOT; TOPER; BOOZER
diptera / FLIES
Dirce's husband / LYCUS
Dirce's victim / ANTIOPE
dire / FATAL; DISMAL, FUNEST
direct / AIM, CON; COND, CONN, HEAD, LEAD, SHOW, WEND; DRIVE
direct attention to / REFER
direct lines of descent / PHYLA
direction / TREND; ADDRESS
direction in chorus / SOLI
direction in psalm / SELAH
direction to typesetter / STET
directly / FLAT; OPENLY; STRAIGHT
directly opposite / CONTRARY; DIAMETRICAL
director / BOSS, HEAD; LEADER; MANAGER
directory / GUIDE; REGISTER
dirge / HYMN, KEEN; LINOS, LINUS; LAMENT, MONODY; EPICEDE, REQUIEM
dirigible / ZEPPELIN
dirigible's cabin / NACELLE
dirk / SNY; SNEE; DAGGER; PONIARD
dirt / SOD; LOAM, SOIL; EARTH, FILTH, GRIME, TRASH; REFUSE
dirt settling to bottom / SILT
dirty / BAD, LOW; BASE, FOUL, MEAN, VILE; DINGY, GRIMY, MUDDY
dirty piece of wool / FRIB
Dis / PLUTO
disable / HURT LAME, MAIM
disabled / HURT; HARMED

disadvantage / LOSS; INJURY; DRAWBACK; DETRIMENT, PREJUDICE
disagreeable / ILL; MEAN, SICK
disagreeable task / CHORE
disagreement/ FIGHT, SCRAP
disagreer with doctrine / HERETIC
disappear / GO; FADE, PASS
disapproving sound / BOO; HISS
disarray / MESS, MUSS
disaster /WOE; EVIL, LOSS
disaster from the sea / TSUNAMI; TIDALWAVE
disavow / DENY; ABJURE, RECANT
disband / DEMOBILIZE
disbeliever / ATHEIST, DOUBTER, HERETIC, INFIDEL, SKEPTIC
disburden / RID; EASE; UNLOAD
disburse / PAY; SPEND; EXPEND
discard / RID; CAST, DROP, SHED; SCRAP, SLUFF; REJECT, SLOUGH
discern / SEE, SPY; ESPY, LOOK
discerner of the future / SEER
discerning / KEEN, SAGE; ACUTE
discernment / TACT; FLAIR, SENSE
discharge / PAY; EMIT, FIRE, FREE, SACK; ANNUL, BREAK, CLEAR
disciple / CHELA; APOSTLE, SCHOLAR; ADHERENT, FOLLOWER
disciple of Socrates / PLATO
disciplinarian / MARTINET
discipline / DRILL, ORDER; CONTROL. TRAIN; FERULE; CHASTEN
disclaim / DENY; DISOWN, REJECT; CASTOFF, DISAVOW; RENOUNCE
disclose / BARE, OPEN, TELL; BETRAY, EXPOSE, REVEAL, UNFOLD
discolored /DOTY; FADED, FOXED
discomfit / ROUT; DEFEAT, THWART
discomfort / PAIN; UNEASE

DISCIPLES OF JESUS

	Symbol
Andrew	CROSS
Bartholomew	KNIFE
James	SCALLOPSHELL
James the Less	POLE
John	CUPANDSERPENT
Judas	BAG
Jude	CLUB
Matthew	HALBERD
Matthias	BATTLEAX
Paul	SWORD
Peter	KEYS
Philip	STAFF
Simon	SAW
Thomas	LANCE

discompose / VEX; UPSET; HARASS
disconcert / JAR; BALK, FAZE;
ABASH, UPSET; BAFFLE, DEFEAT
disconnect / CUT; UNDO; SEVER
disconsolate / SAD; WOEFUL; FOR-
LORN, UNHAPPY; DESOLATE
discontinue / END; DROP, QUIT,
STOP; CEASE; DESIST; SUSPEND
discord / STRIFE; VARIANCE;
CACOPHONY, WRANGLING. JAR;
JANGLE
discount / AGIO, TARE; REBATE
discourage / APPAL, DETER; DE-
JECT, LESSEN; DEPRESS, DE-
PRIVE
discourse / TALK; HOMILY,
SCREED, SPEECH; DESCANT,
LECTURE
discover / SEE, SPY; ESPY, FIND,
SHOW, SPOT, TELL; LEARN; BE-
HOLD
discoverer of America / ERIC,
LEIF; COLUMBUS
discoverer of Tahiti / WALLIS
discredit / ABASE, SHAME; DIS-
GRACE, DISHONOR. ODIUM;
OBLOQUY
discreet / WARY, WISE; DEMURE
discrepancy between solar and lunar calendars / EPACT
discrete / DISTINCT, SEPARATE
discretion / TACT; SKILL
discriminating / NICE; ASTUTE
discrimination / SENSE, TASTE;
ACUMEN; INSIGHT; JUDGMENT
discus / DISK; QUOIT
discus thrower / DISCOBOLUS
discuss / SIFT; ARGUE, TREAT
discussion meeting / FORUM
disdain / POOH; SCORN, SPURN;
DESPISE. CONTEMPT; ARRO-
GANCE
disease / TB; MAL, POX, TIC; GOUT,
PEST; HIVES; MALADY
disease, pert. to / CLINIC, LOIMIC
disease, suff. / ITIS
disease of animals / COE, GID;
BLOAT, HOOSE, HOOVE, MANGE,
NENTA
disease of the brain / MADNESS
disease carrier / VECTOR
disease cause / GERM; VIRUS; BAC-
TERIA
disease of cereals / RUST, SMUT;
ERGOT
disease of childhood / MUMPS;
MEASLES
disease of the eye / GLAUCOMA,
TRACHOMA
disease of fowl / PIP; ROUP
disease fungus / SMUT; ERGOT
disease of grape vine / ESCA; ERI-
NOSE; APOPLEXY

disease of hair / PLICA
disease of hair follicles / SYCOSIS
disease of heart / MYOCARDITIS
disease of liver / HEPATITIS
disease of lung / PHTHSIS; EMPHY-
SEMA, PNEUMONIA
disease of nerves / NEURITIS
disease of pancreas / DIABETES
disease of plants / SCAB, SMUT;
SCALD
disease of skin / ACNE; ECZEMA;
ERYTHEMA, IMPETIGO;
DERMATITIS
disease of tobacco / CALICO,
MOSAIC
disease vector / RAT; INSECT; CAR-
RIER
disease from vitamin deficiency /
SCURVY; BERIBERI, PELLAGRA
diseased / ILL; SICK; MORBID; UN-
HEALTHY
diseases transmitted from animals
to men / ZOONOSES
disembark / LAND; ALIGHT, UN-
LOAD
disencumber / RID
disengage / FREE; CLEAR, RAVEL
disentangle / CARD, FREE, UNDO
disfigure / MAR; SPOIL; DEFACE
disfigurement / SCAR; BLOTCH
disgrace / STAIN, SULLY; DEBASE,
HUMBLE; DEGRADE, TARNISH.
ODIUM
disgruntled person / SOREHEAD
disguise / HIDE, MASK, VEIL;
CLOAK; MUFFLE, SHROUD; CON-
CEAL
disguised / COVERT, MASKED
disgusting /ODIOUS; HATEFUL
dish / BOWL; PLATE; TUREEN, VES-
SEL; PLATTER
dish of greens / SALAD
dishabille / NEGLIGEE; HOUSE-
COAT
Dishan's son / UZ; ARAN
dishearten / PALL; DAUNT, DETER
dishevel / TOUSLE
dishonest / SNIDE; UNFAIR
dishonor / ABASE, SHAME, STAIN
dishonorable / BASE, MEAN
Dishon's father / ANAH
Dishon's son / AMRAM; ESHBAN
disillusion / DISENCHANT
disinclined / AVERSE; RENITENT
disinfectant / CRESOL, PHENOL
disingenuous / HOLLOW; DISHON-
EST
disintegrate / ROT; DECAY, ERODE
disinter / DIGUP; EXHUME
disinterested / FAIR; BORED
disk / ATEN, DISC; QUOIT, WAFER
disk, pert. to / DISCAL; DISCOID
disk in hockey / PUCK

disk of metal / COIN; PATEN; SEQUIN

dislike ornament / PATERA

dislike / HATRED; DISGUST

dislike intensely / HATE; ABHOR

dislocate / LUXATE; UNHINGE

dislodged turf / DIVOT

dismal / SAD; DARK, DULL, GRAY

dismay / ALARM, APPAL, DAUNT, SCARE; APPALL. FEAR; DREAD; FRIGHT

dismember / REND; SEVER; DIVIDE

dismiss / FIRE, OUST, SACK; CONGE, DEMIT; REMOVE; CASHIER

dismissal / CONGE

dismount / LAND; ALIGHT

disorder / ILL; MESS, RIOT; CHAOS, DERAY, SNARL; JUMBLE

disordered / CHAOTIC; LITTERED

disorderly / PIED; MESSY, MUSSY; UNRULY; LAWLESS, RIOTOUS

disorderly behavior / RIOT

disoriented / LOST

disown / DENY; REJECT; DISAVOW

disparage / SLUR; DECRY; DEFAME

disparaging / SNIDE; DEFAMA-TORY, DEROGATORY, PEJORA-TIVE

disparaging remark / SLUR; OBLOQUY, SLANDER; ASPER-SION

dispassionate / CALM, COOL

dispatch / KILL, SEND. HASTE

dispatch boat / AVISO

dispel / ROUT; SCATTER; DISPERSE

dispense / DOLE; ALLOT; EXCUSE, EXEMPT; EXECUTE, RELEASE

dispenser of alms / ALMONER

displaced person / DP; EXILE; REFUGEE

display / AIR; OPEN, SHOW, WEAR

display frame / EASEL

displease / VEX, FRET, MIFF; ANGER, ANNOY, CHAFE, PIQUE

displeasure / ANGER, PIQUE

disport / PLAY; AMUSE, DIVERT, FROLIC; INDULGE

disposal problem / TRASH

dispose / BIAS, LEAD, MOVE; GROUP, ORDER, PLACE; ADJUST

disposed / APT, PRONE

disposition / BENT, BIAS, MIEN, MOOD, TURN; HUMOR, ORDER; METHOD

dispossess / OUST; EJECT, EVICT

disprove / REBUT; REFUTE

disputable / MOOT; QUESTIONABLE

disputant / ARGUER; DEBATER

disputatious / ERISTIC

dispute / DENY, SPAR; ARGUE; BICKER, DEBATE, IMPUGN, JAN-GLE. FEUD, SPAT, TIFF; BRAWL

disputed territory / NOMANSLAND

disquiet / PAIN; UNEASE, UNREST

Disraeli / BEACONSFIELD

Disraeli novel / TANCRED

disregard / DEFY, DENY, OMIT; WAIVE; IGNORE, SLIGHT; CON-DEMN

disregard temporarily / SHELVE

disreputable / SEAMY, SHADY; IN-FAMOUS, SHAMEFUL; SCANDALOUS

disrespectful / PERT, RUDE

disrupt / PART, REND; BREAK

dissemble / HIDE, MASK

disseminate / SOW; STREW; SPREAD

dissension / BREACH, STRIFE; DIS-CORD, DISPUTE

dissenter / HERETIC, SECTARY

dissertation / ESSAY; THESIS

dissimulate / FEIGN

dissolute / WILD; LOOSE; WANTON

dissolute person / RAKE, ROUE

dissolve / MELT, RUIN; SEVER, WASTE; DIVIDE; DESTROY; DISPERSE

distance / SPACE; LENGTH; COLD-NESS, INTERVAL; FRIGIDITY

distance indicator / ODOMETER

distance through / DIAMETER

distant / FAR, YON; AFAR, COLD; ALOOF, FAINT; FORMAL, FRIGID

distant, pref. / TEL; TELE

distantly / AFAR

distend / SWELL; DILATE, EX-PAND; INFLATE, STRETCH

distilled beverage / ALE; BREW

distilling apparatus / STILL; RE-TORT; ALEMBIC, MATRASS

distinct / CLEAR, PLAIN; EVIDENT, OBVIOUS; DEFINITE, SEPARATE

distinct part / UNIT; SECTION

distinction / FAME; HONOR

distinctive air / AURA, MIEN, PORT; GUISE

distinctive quality / CACHET

distinguish / SEE; MARK; DISCERN; PERCEIVE, SEPARATE; DESIGNATE

distinguished / NOTED; FAMOUS; EMINENT, NOTABLE, SUPREME

distinguishing symbol / BADGE, BRAND, MEDAL

distort / WARP; GNARL, SCREW; TWIST; DEFORM; PERVERT

distorted / WRY

distract / DIVERT, HARASS, MAD-DEN; CONFUSE, DERANGE, DIS-TURB

distracted / MAD; FRANTIC
distraint of chattels / NAAM
distress / PAIN; AGONY, GRIEF;
MISERY, SORROW; ANGUISH,
POVERTY. TAKE; SEIZE; GRIEVE
distress signal / SOS; ALARM
distressing / SARE, SORE; PAINFUL
distribute / DEAL, DOLE, METE
distribute proportionally / PRO-
RATE
distributed cards / DEALT
district / AREA, DEME, PALE,
WARD, ZONE. See also region
District of Columbia / WASHING-
TON
district in English history / SOC;
SOKE, WARD; MANOR, SHIRE
district of London / SOHO; EAST-
END
distrust / DOUBT; SUSPICION
distrustful / SHY, SLY
disturb / AIL, VEX; RILE, RIOT,
ROIL, STIR; ANNOY, WORRY;
AROUSE
disturb a speaker / HECKLE
disturbance / ROW; RIOT; FRACAS,
RUMPUS, TUMULT, UPROAR;
DISORDER
disturbance on radio / STATIC
disunite / SEVER; DETACH
disuse / LAPSE; DESUETUDE
disyllabic foot in poetry / IAMB;
CHOREUS, TROCHEE
ditch / RUT, SAP; DIKE, FOSS,
MOAT, RINE; FOSSE, SEWER;
TRENCH
ditch before a rampart / RELAIS
ditch's slope / SCARP
dithyramb / ODE; HYMN
dithyrambic / RHAPSODIC
ditto / TOO; ALSO, SAME
diurnal / DAILY; JOURNAL;
QUOTIDIAN
divagate / STRAY; WANDER; DI-
GRESS
divan / SOFA; COUCH; SETTEE
diva's solo / ARIA
dive / DEN; SWAN; GAINER,
HEADER
diver / LOON
divers / SUNDRY; SEVERAL,
VARIOUS
diver's disease / BENDS
diver's equipment / SCUBA, TANKS;
AIRHOSE; FLIPPERS, LIFELINE
diverse / UNLIKE; SEVERAL;
SEPARATE; DIFFERENT, MULTI-
FORM
diversify / VARY; CHANGE
diversion / GAME, PLAY; SPORT;
PASTIME; AMUSEMENT; RECRE-
ATION

divert / AMUSE, AVERT, PARRY,
SPORT; PLEASE; BEGUILE, DE-
FLECT
divest / DOFF; STRIP; DEPRIVE
divide / METE, PART, REND; ALLOT,
HALVE, SEVER, SHARE, SPLIT
divide for close analysis / DISSECT
divide honors / TIE
divide into layers / LAMINATE
divide metrically / SCAN
divide proportionately / SHARE;
AVERAGE, PRORATE
divide into three / TRISECT
divided / REFT; CLEFT, SPLIT
dividend / BONUS, SHARE; POR-
TION
divider / BUNTON, MERIST; COM-
PASS
dividing edge / LINE; BORDER
dividing wall / SEPTUM; BRATTICE
divination by birds' flight / AUGURY
divination by dreams / ONEIRO-
MANCY
divination by evoked spirits /
NECROMANCY
divination by examining liver /
HEPATOSCOPY
divination using flour / ALEURO-
MANCY
divination by formation of hand /
PALMISTRY; CHIROMANCY
divination by lots / SORS, SORT;
SORTES; SORTILEGE, SORTI-
LEGY
divination from markings on
shoulder blade / SCAPULO-
MANCY
divination from marks in the dirt /
GEOMANCY
divination by oracles / THEOMANCY
divination by playing cards /
CARTOMANCY
divination from sacrificial entrails /
HARUSPICY
divination by the stars / ASTROL-
OGY
divine / HOLY; SACRED; ANGELIC,
EXALTED, GODLIKE, SUPREME
divine being / GOD; DEITY
Divine Comedy author / DANTE
divine comfort / BLESSING
divine communication / ORACLE
divine creative word / LOGOS
divine favor / GRACE; BLESSING
Divine Pagan / HYPATIA
divine spirit / NUMEN
divine statement / ORACLE
divine word / GRACE, LOGOS
divine work / THEURGY
diviner / DOWSER
diving apparatus / SNORKEL;
AQUALUNG

Divination, Methods of

AUGURY	EMPYROMANCY
SORTES	HEPATOSCOPY
OOSCOPY	LECANOMANCY
GEOMANCY	LIBANOMANCY
PROPHECY	METOPOMANCY
AEROMANCY	PSYCHOMANCY
ASTROLOGY	RHABDOMANCY
EXTISPICY	SIDEROMANCY
HARUSPICY	CLEDONOMANCY
PALMISTRY	COSCINOMANCY
PYROMANCY	CATOPTROMANCY
AXINOMANCY	MACHAIROMANCY
CHIROMANCY	OMOPLATOSCOPY
CLEROMANCY	RHAPSODOMANCY
ELAEOMANCY	ASTRAGALOMANCY
HYDROMANCY	SORTESBIBLICAE
IATROMANCY	SPHONDULOMANCY
NECROMANCY	ALECTRYONOMANCY
ALEUROMANCY	SORTESHOMERICAE
CAPUCOMANCY	SORTESVERGILIANAE

living bird / AUK; LOON, SMEW
living rod / WAND
divinity / DEITY; GODHEAD
division / GAME, PART; CLASS
division of administration / BUREAU; DEPARTMENT
division of ancient Greece / DEME; DEMES
division of army / CORPS, SQUAD; COMPANY; DIVISION, REGIMENT
division of book / CHAPTER
division of building / ROOM; SUITE; APARTMENT
division of a calyx / SEPAL
division of city / WARD; PRECINCT
division of corolla / PETAL
division of a drama / ACT; SCENE
division of the earth / ZONE
division of a fight / ROUND
division of game / HALF; INNING, PERIOD, CHUKKER, QUARTER
division of geological time / AGE, EON, ERA; EPOCH, GROUP; PERIOD, SYSTEM
division of the Koran / SURA
division of mankind / RACE
division of movie serial / EPISODE
division of music / BAR; MOVEMENT
division of play / ACT; SCENE
division of poem / CANTO, VERSE; STANZA
division of Roman legion / COHORT
division of time / AGE, DAY, EON, ERA; HOUR, WEEK, YEAR; EPOCH, MONTH; DECADE, MINUTE, SEASON, SECOND; CENTURY

divorce / AHSAN, HASAN, SPLIT, TALAK. UNMARRY
divorce allowance / ALIMONY
divorce document / GET
divulge / BARE, TELL; VOICE; IMPART, REVEAL, SPREAD; DISCLOSE
Dixieland / SOUTH
"Dixie's" composer / EMMETT
dizziness / VERTIGO; GIDDINESS
dizziness, pert. to / DINIC
Dnieper tributary / PSEL, SOZH
Dniester tributary / STRY
do / ACT, END; FARE, MAKE; CHEAT
do again / REPEAT; ITERATE
do alone / SOLO
do away with / ABOLISH
do the bidding of / OBEY
do for / KILL; FINISH
do up / WRAP
do well / PROSPER
docile / TAME; GENTLE; COMPLIANT
dock / CUT; DEDUCT. PIER; WHARF
dock worker / STEVEDORE; LONGSHOREMAN
docket / CALENDAR
doctor / MD; DOC, PHD; MEDIC; PHYSICIAN
doctor gaining experience / INTERN; INTERNE
doctor of holy scripture / DHS, DSS
Doctor Jekyll's "altered ego" / HYDE
doctored dice / COGS; FULLAMS
doctor's assistant / AIDE; NURSE
doctrinaire / ISMY; DOGMATIC; IDEALISTIC

doctrinal formula / CREED
doctrine / ISM; CREED, DOGMA, TENET; BELIEF, GOSPEL; OPINION
document / PAPER, SCRIP; SCRIPT; INDENTURE; CERTIFICATE
document container / FILE; HANAPER
document folder / DOSSIER
document signed in a circle / ROUNDROBIN
dodder / SHAKE; TREMBLE. AMIL
doddering / SENILE
Dodecanese island / COO, COS, KOS; LERO, RODI, SIMI
dodge / MISS; ASIDE, AVOID, ELUDE, EVADE, TRICK
Dodgers' field / EBBETTS
Dodgson, C.L. / CARROLL
dodo / FOGY; FOSSIL; MOSSBACK
Dodo's son / ELEAZAR, ELHANAN
doe / TAG, TEG; DEER, HIND
doff / STRIP; REMOVE
dog / CUR, PET, PUP; ALAN, CHOW, DANE; BORER, CANIS, FEIST, HOUND, POOCH, WHELP; BANDOG, CANINE, COLLIE, POODLE, TOWSER; MASTIFF, SAMOYED, SPANIEL, TERRIER, WHIPPET; MALEMUTE
dog, c.f. / CANI, CYNO
dog of Australia / DINGO
dog bark / YAP, YIP
dog disease / MANGE; DISTEMPER
dog of FDR / FALA
dog of great size / ALAN, DANE
dog house / KENNEL
dog of Hungary / PULI; KUVASZ
dog used in hunting / ALAN; HOUND; BASSET, BEAGLE, SETTER, TALBOT; COURSER, HARRIER, POINTER; RETRIEVER
dog of India / DHOLE
dog of Japan / TOSA; AKITA, SHIBA
dog of mixed breed / MONGREL
dog of movie adventures / RINTINTIN
dog in Odyssey / ARGOS
dog in "Punch and Judy" / TOBY
dog rose / CANKER
dog salmon / KETA; HOLIA
dog of small size / POM, PUG, TOY; ALCO, PEKE; CHIHUAHUA
dog snapper / JOCU
dog in Sputnik / LAIKA
dog star / SEPT, SOPT; SIRIUS; CANICULA
dog in The Thin Man / ASTA
dog tooth / FANG
dog of the underworld / GARM; CERBERUS
dog of Wales / CORGI

dogdays / CANICULE
dogear / FOLD; ACROTERIUM
Doge's office / DOGATE; DOGEATE
dog-faced ape / AANI; BABOON; CYNOCEPHALUS
dog-fennel / HOGWEED
dogfish / SEPT, TOPE; BOWFIN, BURBOT, ROSSET; SQUALUS
dogie / CALF; MAVERICK
doglike animal / COYOTE, JACKAL
dogma / ISM; CANT; TENET
dogmatic / FORMAL; ARROGANT, POSITIVE; DOCTRINAL; PEREMPTORY
dogmatic principle / DICTUM
dogrose fruit / HIP
dogs, pert. to / CANINE
dog's chops / FLEWS
dog's foot / PAW
dog's yelp / YIP; KIYI
dogwood / OSIER, SUMAC; CORNEL
doily / MAT; NAPKIN; ANTIMACASSAR
doing the circuit / ONTOUR
doit / WHIT
dole / ALMS, METE; GRIEF, SHARE
doleful / SAD; DISMAL, RUEFUL
doleful sound / KNELL
doll / TOY; EFFIGY, PUPPET; MANIKIN; PLAYTHING
dollar / BUCK
dolly / TRAY; TRUCK
dolphin / SUSU; DORADO; PORPOISE
dolphinlike fish / INIA
dolt / ASS, OAF; CLOD, FOOL, LOUT; DUNCE; SIMPLETON
domain / BOURN, FIELD, RANGE, REALM, SCOPE; BOURNE, DEMESNE
dome support / THOLOBATE
domestic / MAID; MENIAL; SERVANT, TWEENEY; HOUSEMAID
domestic animal / ASS, CAT, COW, DOG, HOG, PIG, RAM, SOW; GOAT, MULE; HORSE
domestic birds / GEESE; POULTRY; CHICKENS
domestic pigeon / NUN; BARB
domestic slave / ESNE, SERF
domesticate / TAME
domesticated ox / YAK
domicile / HOME; ABODE, HOUSE
dominant feature / MOTIF
dominant person / MOGUL
dominate / BOSS, RULE, SWAY; GOVERN; CONTROL
domineer / LORD, RULE; BLUSTER
domineering / BOSSY, LORDLY
Dominican friar / JACOBIN
Dominican Republic measure / ONA
Dominica's capital / ROSEAU

dominion / RULE, SWAY; POWER, REALM, REIGN; EMPERY, EMPIRE

domino / COWL, MASK, TILE

domino game / SNIFF; MATADOR

domino spot / PIP

Don Juan / ROUE; SEDUCER

Don Quixote's horse / ROCINANTE, ROSINANTE

Don Quixote's lady / DULCINEA

Don Quixote's squire / SANCHO

Don River's ancient name / TANAIS

Donar / THOR

donate / GIVE; BESTOW; PRESENT

donation / GIFT; GRANT; PRESENT; CONTRIBUTION

done alone / SOLO

done for / FINISHED

Donizetti opera / LUCIA

donkey / ASS; MOKE, MULE; BURRO

donkey engine / YARDER

donkey-headed god / SET

donkey's cry / BRAY; HEEHAW

donnybrook / SETTO; BEDLAM

donor / GIVER; DONATOR; BESTOWER

don't / STOP; DESIST

doodad / DODAD; BAUBLE, DINGUS, GADGET, GEWGAW, JIGGER; JIMCRACK

doodlesack / BAGPIPE

doom / LOT; FATE, RUIN; DESTINY, VERDICT; JUDGMENT. CONDEMN

doom palm / DUM; DOUM

doomsday of Norse myth / RAGNAROK

door beam / LINTEL

door curtains / PORTIERE

door fastener / HASP, LOCK; LATCH

door frame / CASING

door guard / TILE; TILER

door handle / KNOB, PULL

door part / JAMB, RAIL, SASH, SILL; PANEL, STILE; LINTEL; MULLION

door pivot / HINGE

door post / ALETTE

door signal / BELL, RISP; KNOCKER

doorkeeper / GUARD, TILER, TYLER; PORTER; OSTIARY; OSTIARIUS

doorsill / THRESHOLD

do-over in tennis / LET

dope / INFO; DRUGS, STUPE

dope addict / FIEND; HOPHEAD

dopey / DULL, LOGY

dorado / CUIR; DOLPHIN

Dorcas / TABITHA

Doris' daughters / NEREIDS

Doris' father / OCEANUS

Doris' husband / NEREUS

Doris' mother / TETHYS

dormant / INERT, QUIET; ASLEEP

dormitory sound / SNORE

dormouse / LOIR; LEROT

dorp / HAMLET; VILLAGE

dorsal / BACK; NOTAL, UPPER

Dorus' father / HELLEN

dosage / UNIT

dose / PILL, UNIT; AMOUNT, POTION; PORTION. TREAT

dosseret / ABACUS

dossier / FILE

dossil / TENT; DRAIN, STUPE; SPIGOT, SPONGE, TAMPON; PLEDGET

dot / JOT; IOTA; DOWRY, POINT, SPECK; PERIOD. SCATTER, STIPPLE

dot in telegraphy / DIT

dote / ADORE; BABBLE, DRIVEL

doting / FOND

dotted / PINTO; PIEBALD

dotted in heraldry / SEME

dotterel / DUPE, GULL

double / DUAL, TWIN; TWAIN, TWICE; BINARY, BINATE, DUPLEX

double, pref. / BI, DI; BIS, DIS

double curve / ESS

double dagger / DIESIS

double double-bonded / DIENE

double helix / DNA

double impression / MACKLE

double meaning / AMBIGUITY

double in mirror / IMAGE

double moldboard plow / LISTER

double ring / GEMEL

double whole note / BREVE

double-faced / ANCIPITAL

double-headed rail / IRAIL

double-reed instrument / OBOE

doubletree / EVENER

doubt / SUSPENSE; DISBELIEF; UNCERTAINTY. QUERY; SUSPECT

doubter / THOMAS; SKEPTIC

doubtful / VAGUE; DUBIOUS

doubtless / ASSUREDLY, CERTAINLY

doughboy / SOLDIER

doughnut / SINKER; CRULLER

doughty / BRAVE; STRONG; VALIANT

dour / SOUR; GLOOMY, MOROSE

dove / CULVER, CUSHAT, PIGEON; COLUMBA, TUMBLER

dovekie / AUK; ALLE; ROTCH, ROTGE; ROTCHE; GUILLEMOT

dove's home / COTE; COLUMBARY

dove's note / COO

dowager / WIDOW; MATRON

dowel / PIN

dower / DOS; GIFT; DOWRY
down / NAP; DENE, DUNE, FUZZ, HILL, PILE; EIDER; UPLAND. VERTICAL
down, c.f. / CAT; CATA
down, pref. / DE
down feather / PLUMULE
down at heels / SEEDY
down payment / BINDER; DEPOSIT
down quilt / DUVET
Down Under / ANTIPODES, AUSTRALIA
Down Under army man / ANZAC
down-and-out / BROKE
downcast / SAD; BLUE; DEJECTED
downfall / RUIN; DEFEAT
downright / BLUNT, SHEER, STARK
downward dip / SYNCLINE
downy / FLOCCULENT
downy surface / NAP
dowry / DOS, DOT; DOWER, SULKA
dowry, pert. to / DOTAL; DOWERAL
doyen / DEAN; SENIOR
doze / NAP, NOD; SLOOM; CAT-NAP
drab / DULL, GRAY
drab and dull / DREARY
Dracula / VAMPIRE
draft / POTION, SKETCH; OUTLINE. LEVY; INDUCT; CONSCRIPT
draft animal / OX
drag / LUG, TOW, TUG; DRAW, HAUL
drag deer / TOLL, TUMP
drag one's heels / DELAY
dragnet / TRAWL
dragon / FIREDRAKE
dragon of darkness / RAHAB
dragon slain by Beowulf / GRENDEL
dragon slain by Sigurd / FAFNIR
dragon tail / KETU
dragonfly / DARNINGNEEDLE
dragon's teeth soldiers / SPARTOI
drain / SAP; MILK; EMPTY, LEACH; DEPLETE, VITIATE. SINK, SUMP
drainpipe / LEADER
drake / DUCK; DRAGON, METEOR
dram / NIP, PEG; SHOT, SLUG
drama / see also play, stage, theater
drama, pert. to / THESPIAN
drama company / TROUPE
drama group / ANTA
dramatic / STAGY, VIVID; SCENIC
dramatic piece / SKIT
dramatis personae / CAST
draped garland/ FESTOON
drapery / DRAPES; CURTAIN
drastic / DIRE; SEVERE; EXTREME
draught / PLAN, WIND; POTION, SKETCH; VERSION
draughts / CHECKERS
Dravidian / HO; KOL, KUI; KOTA,

MALE, NAIR, TODA, TULU; KANDH
draw / TIE, TOW, TUG, WIN; DRAG, GAIN, HAUL, LIMN, LURE, PULL
draw away / DIVERT
draw back / RECEDE, RETIRE
draw in chess / STALEMATE
draw close / NEAR; APPROACH
draw forth / ELICIT
draw off / DRAIN, EMPTY
draw out / LADE; BLEED, EDUCE, EVOKE; ELICIT; EXTRACT; LENGTHEN
draw play / FAKE
draw tight / FRAP; TAUTEN
draw together / GATHER
drawback / FAULT; DEFECT
drawing back / RETRAHENT
drawing guide / SPLINE
drawing implement / CURVE; CRAYON, PASTEL, PENCIL; TSQUARE
drawing room / SALON; SALOON
drawl / DRUNT
drawn game / TIE
drawn tight / TAUT
dray / VAN; CART; WAGON
dread / AWE; FEAR; ALARM; DIS-MAY, HORROR, TERROR
dreadful / DARE, DIRE; AWFUL
dream / FANCY; VISION; REVERIE, ROMANCE. IMAGINE
dream time / ALCHERINGA
dreamer / IDEALIST, ROMANTIC; VISIONARY
dreary / DREE; BLEAK; DISMAL
dredge / SCOOP; DEEPEN. MOP
dregs / LEAS, LEES, SCUM, SILT, SLAG; DROSS; REFUSE, SLUDGE
drench / WET; HOSE, SOAK; DOUSE, SOUSE, STEEP, TOUSE; IMBRUE
drenched / WET; ASOP; SOAKED
dress / RIG; GOWN, SUIT; FROCK, GUISE, HABIT, TOG; DECK, GARB; ADORN. See also garment
dress leather / DUB, TAN, TAW, TEW; CURRY
dress material / LENO, SILK; LINEN, SATIN, VOILE; COTTON, DIMITY
dress ornament / PIN; CLIP, SASH
dress ostentatiously / RIG; PRIMP, PRINK; BEDIZEN
dress of south seas / SARONG
dress as stone / DAB, NIG; NIDGE
dress suit / TAILS
dress trimming / GIMP, LACE; RUCHE; PIPING; RUCHING
dress up / ARRAY, PRINK; EMBEL-LISH
dress a wound / PANSE

dressed in rags / TATTERED
dresser / BUREAU
dressing / SAUCE; BANDAGE
dressing gown / ROBE; KIMONO; WRAPPER; PEIGNOIR
dressmaker / MODISTE; SEAMSTRESS, SEMPSTRESS
dried / SERE
dried acorns / CAMATA; CAMATINA
dried brick / ADOBE
dried coconut meat / COPRA
dried grape / RAISIN
dried grass / HAY
dried meat / JERKY; BILTONG, CHARQUI; PEMMICAN
dried orchid root / SALEP
dried plum / PRUNE
drift / AIM; HEAP, MARK; SCOPE, SWEEP, TENOR, TREND; COURSE
drift to leeward / SAG; CRAB
drill / BORE; TEACH, TRAIN; PIERCE; EXERCISE. BIT, RIG; AUGER
drink / GULP; QUAFF; IMBIBE. SWIG; DRAFT, SNORT; NECTAR, POTION. See also beverage
drink another's health / TOAST; PLEDGE
drink at Christmas / ALE, NOG, NOGG; WASSAIL; LAMBSWOOL
drink of the gods / NECTAR
drink heavily / TOPE
drink made of honey / MEAD; MORAT
drink in honor of / TOAST
drink lightly / SIP
drink of liquor / NIP, PEG, SIP; DRAM, SLUG; TASTE; BRACER, TIPPLE
drink from molasses / RUM
drink from palm tree / NIPA
drink of rum or gin / GROG; BUMBO
drink too much / TOPE; BOUSE; TIPPLE
drinking bout / SPREE; POTATION
drinking horn / RHYTON
drinking place / BAR, PUB, SPA; SALOON; FOUNTAIN, GROGGERY
drinking vessel / AMA, CUP, MUG, TIG, TYG; TASS; CYLIX, GOURD
drip / DROP; TRICKLE
dripping / ASOP
drive / GUIDE, IMPEL, PRESS
drive crazy / MADDEN; DERANGE
drive nail at angle / TOE; SLANT
drive off / ROUT; REPEL; REPULSE
drivel / DOTE; DROOL; SLAVER
driver / JEHU; CABBY, RIDER; HACKMAN; COACHMAN, ENGINEER

driving lines / REINS
drizzle / MIST, SMUR; SMURR; SPRINKLE
droll / ODD; COMIC, FUNNY, QUEER
droll fellow / WAG; ZANY; ROGUE
drollery / MOT; QUIP
dromedary / DELUL, CAMEL; MEHARI
drone / BEE, DOR, HUM; IDLER, SNAIL; BAGPIPE, HUMMING, LOUNGER
drool / DRIVEL, SLAVER; SLOBBER
droop / BOW, LOP, SAG; BEND, FLAG, HANG, LOLL, WILT; SLOUCH
drop / DRIP, FALL, OMIT, SINK; PLUMMET. BEAD, DRIB; GUTTA
drop bait gently / DAP
drop by drop / GUTTATIM
drop in / CALL; VISIT
drop of sorrow / TEAR
dropout / QUITTER; NONPARTICIPANT
dropsy / EDEMA; ASCITES; ANASARCA
dross / SCUM, SLAG; SPRUE, WASTE
drought / ARIDITY, DRYNESS
drove / HERD; FLOCK, HORDE. RODE
drove of horses / HERD; ATAJO, REMUDA
drown / DELUGE, ENGULF; IMMERSE
drowse / NAP, NOD; DOZE
drowsy / DOZY, DULL; SLEEPY, TORPID; OSCITANT, SLUGGISH
drub / BEAT, BENT; CUDGEL, THRASH; BELABOR, TROUNCE
drudge / FAG; MOIL, PLOD, TOIL; LABOR. HACK; SLAVE
drug / DOPE; OPIUM; HEROIN, OPIATE; NARCOTIC. STUPEFY
drug addict / FIEND; JUNKIE
drug dependency / HABIT; MONKEY
drug experience / TRIP
drug paraphernalia / OUTFIT
drug plant / ALOE
drug reaction / TRIP
drug seller / DEALER, PUSHER
drugget / MAT, RUG; CARPET
drug-induced languor / KEF; KAIF, KIFF
drum / TOPH; GUMBY, SNARE, TABOR; TABRET, TOMTOM; TAMBOUR, TIMBREL
drum call / DUB; DIAN, FLAM, ROLL, RUFF; TATOO; RAPPEL, RUFFLE, TATTOO; RATAPLAN

drum to haul cable / CAPSTAN
drumstick / LEG; TAMPON
drunkard / SOT; SOAK; DRUNK, SOUSE, TOPER; BIBBER
drunken spree / ORGY; BINGE
drupaceous fruit / PLUM
dry / SEC; ARID, DULL, SERE
dry, c.f. / XERO
dry, as wine / SEC; BRUT
dry biscuit / CRACKER; HARDTACK
dry desert wind / SIMOOM
dry fruit / FIG; CONE, PASA; PRUNE, REGMA; ACHENE, RAISIN
dry goods / TEXTILES
dry lake basin / PLAYA
dry measure / PECK; BUSHEL
dry riverbed / WADI
dry scale of fern stem / PALEA
dry spell / DROUTH; DROUGHT
dry by spreading / TED
drying cloth / RAG; TOWEL
drying oven / OAST
dry-stone diker / COWAN
duad / DYAD, PAIR; COUPLE
dub / CALL, NAME; TITLE; KNIGHT; ENTITLE. SILLY; STUPID; IGNORANT
dub in chess / PATZER
dubious apostle / THOMAS
Dublin / BAILEATHACLIATH
Dublin's dean / SWIFT
duchy, pert. to / DUCAL
duck / ANAS, DOGY, SMEE, SMEW, TARP, TEAL, TERN; EIDER, PEKIN
duck, pert. to / ANATINE
duck eggs / PIDAN
duck fit / PET; CONNIPTION
duck flock / KNOB, SORD, TEAM; FLUSH; FLIGHT; PADDLING
duck hunter's aid / BLIND, DECOY
duck hunter's boat / SKAG
Duck Soup stars / MARXES
duckbill / PLATYPUS; MONOTREME
ducklike bird / COOT
duck's call / QUACK
duck's egg / ZERO; GOOSEEGG
duckweed / LEMNA
duct / VAS; TUBE; CANAL; PASSAGE
ductile / TENSILE; TRACTABLE
ductless gland / PINEAL, THYMUS; THYROID; PANCREAS; PITUITARY
dude / FOP; DANDY; COXCOMB
dudgeon / PIQUE
due / FIT; OWED; OWING; PROPER; PAYABLE; BECOMING, SUITABLE
due statement / BILL; VOUCHER
duel / TILT; FENCE, FIGHT; COMBAT
duenna / GUARDIAN; CHAPERONE

dugout canoe / BANCA; PIRAGUA, PIROGUE
dukedom / DUCHY
dulcet / SWEET; PLEASANT
dulcimer / CANUN, CROWD, SITAR; CITOLE, SANTIR, ZITHER; CEMBALO
dull / DIM, DRY, DUN, SAD; DEAD, DRAB, LOGY, SLOW, TAME; BLUNT
dull color / DUN; DRAB, GRAY
dull finish / MAT; MATTE
dull by inaction / RUST, RUSTY
dull pain / ACHE
dull saying / PLATITUDE
dull sound / THUD
dullard / LOG, OAF; BOOR, BORE
dulled / OBTUNDED
dullness / PHLEGM; HEBETUDE
dulse / DILSE; DELISK; SEAWEED
duly / FITLY; REGULARLY
dumb / MUTE; STILL; SILENT
dumb performance / PANTOMIME
dumfound / STUN
dummy whist / MORT
dumose / BUSHY
dumpy / PUDGY, SHORT, SULKY
dun / MOUND; MAYFLY. ASK; IMPORTUNE. TAN; DULL, GRAY; SWARTHY
dunce / ASS, OAF; DOLT, FOOL
dune area / ERG; AREG
dunfly / CLEG; STOUT
dung beetle / DOR; SCARAB
dungaree material / DENIM
dunlin / STIB; SANDPIPER
duo / TWO; DUET, PAIR
dupe / USE; FOOL; CHEAT, CULLY, TRICK; CAJOLE, DELUDE, IMPOSE. GULL, TOOL; PIGEON
duplicate / DYAD; MODEL, TWAIN; DOUBLE. TWIN; BIFOLD, BINARY. COPY; DITTO; REPEAT; IMITATE. BIS; ENCORE
duplicate copy / STAT
duplicity / FRAUD; DECEIT; HYPOCRISY
durable / TOUGH; STABLE; ABIDING
durable fiber / SISAL
duramen / HEARTWOOD
durance / DURESS; IMPRISONMENT
duration / SPAN, TERM, TIME; SPACE; LENGTH, PERIOD; ETERNITY
duress / DURANCE; RESTRAINT
during / AT, IN; WHILE; WITHIN
durra / DARI, DURR; SORGHUM
durum / WHEAT
dusk / EVE; GLOOM; TWILIGHT
dusky / DIM; DARK; SWART; SWARTHY

dust / ASH; FLESH; POWDER
dustlike / POWDERY
Dutch / GERMAN. See also Holland, Netherlands
Dutch Antilles / ARUBA
Dutch badger / DAS
Dutch cheese / EDAM; DELFT, GOUDA; POTCHEESE; SCHMIERKASE
Dutch coin / DOIT; FLORIN
Dutch colonist / BOER
Dutch commune / EDE, EPE, OSS
Dutch dialect / TAAL
Dutch fishing boat / KOFF; DOGGER
Dutch Guiana / SURINAM
Dutch island / ARU; TEXEL
Dutch measure / EL; AAM, KAN, KOP, VAT; LEAN; ROEDE; STREEP
Dutch merchant ship / GALLIOT
Dutch news agency / ANETA
Dutch painter / CUYP, DOUW, HALS; STEEN; HOBBEMA; REM-BRANDT
Dutch philosopher / SPINOZA
Dutch poet / DACOSTA
Dutch printer / ELZEVIR, PLANTIN
Dutch Protestant / WALLOON
Dutch reclaimed land / POLDER
Dutch scholar / ERASMUS
Dutch South African / BOER
Dutch title of address / MEVROUW; MIJNHEER
Dutch uncle / EME, OOM
duty / JOB, TAX; TASK, TOLL; CHORE; CUSTOM, DEVOIR, DHARMA
dwarf / GRIG, RUNT; GNOME, PIGMY, PYGMY, TROLL; MANI-KIN
dwarf animal / RUNT
dwarf avatar of Vishnu / VAMANA
dwarf cattle / NATA; NIATA
dwarf king / ALBERICH
dwarf in Snow White / DOC; DOPEY, HAPPY; GRUMPY, SLEEPY, SNEEZY; BASHFUL
dwarfish / SMALL; NANOID
dwarfishness / NANISM
dwell / BIDE, LIVE, STAY, STOP
dwell tediously / HARP
dwell upon / BROOD
dweller / TENANT; RESIDENT

dwelling / HOME; ABODE, HOUSE, HOVEL; MANSION; DOMICILE
dwelling in caves / SPELAEAN
dwelling on a crag / EYRIE
dwelling on water / HOUSEBOAT
dwelt / RESIDED
dwindle / FADE, PINE, SINK
dyak knife / PARANG
dye / COLOR, IMBUE, STAIN. AAL, LIT; ANIL, WELD, WOAD, WOLD
dye again / RECOLOR
dye base / ANILINE
dye component / AZO; DIAZO
dye for hair / HENNA
dye plant / CHAY, WOAD; SUMAC
dye for silk / LUTEOLIN
dyeing process / BATIK
dyeing substance / CHAY, KATH, KINO; KUTCH, MUREX
dyer / STAINER
dyer's grape / POKEWEED
dyer's rocket / RESEDA; MIGNONETTE
dyer's vat / AGER
dyestuff / MADDER; ORPIMENT
dyewood / TUI; FUSTET, FUSTIC
dying fire / EMBERS
dynamic / ENERGETIC
dynamite / DUALIN
dynamite's inventor / NOBEL
dynamo / GENERATOR
dynamo part / ARMATURE
dynast / RULER; GOVERNOR
dynasty / REALM; KINGDOM; DOMINION; SOVEREIGNTY
dynasty of China / HAN, TSI, WEI; CHIN, HSIA, MING, SUNG, TANG, YUAN; MANCHU, MON-GOL
dynasty in Egypt / HYKSOS; PTOLEMIES
dynasty of Europe / HABSBURG, HAPSBURG
dynasty of France / SAVOY; BOURBON
dynasty of Russia / RURIKS; ROMANOVS
dynasty of Sweden / VASA; BERNADOTTE
dyspepsia / PYROSIS; GASTRITIS, HEARTBURN; ERUCTATION
Dzhugashvili / STALIN

E

each / ONE, PER; EVERY; APIECE
eager / HOT; AGOG, AVID, KEEN; ARDENT, INTENT; ANXIOUS
eagerness / ELAN, ZEAL
eagle / ERN; ERNE, GIER; BERGUT
eagle owl / BUBO; KATOGLE
eagle's nest / EYRY; AERIE, EYRIE
eaglestone / ETITE

eagre / BORE
ear / LUG; HEED; PINNA, SPIKE
ear, pert. to / OTIC; AURAL
ear bone / AMBOS, ANVIL, INCUS; STAPES; OSSICLE, OTOLITH
ear cavity / SACCULE, UTRICLE
ear of corn / COB; SPIKE; MEALIE
ear covering / EARLAP

ear doctor / AURIST; OTOLOGIST
ear of grain / SPICA, SPIKE
ear inflammation / OTITIS
ear prominence / LOBE; TRAGUS
ear on saddle / LUG
ear shell / ORMER; ABALONE
ear wax / CERUMEN
ear of wheat / SPICA, SPIKE
earache / OTALGY; OTALGIA
eared / AURICULATE
earl / JARL; NOBLEMAN
earlier / PRIOR; PREVIOUS
earlike part / LUG; EARLAP
early / ANON, SOON; BETIMES
early alphabet / OGAM, OGUM; OGHAM, RUNES; FUTHORC
early Bible version / ITALA; TARGUM; PESHITTA; DIATESSARON
early bloodhound / TALBOT
early British / CELTS, CYMRY, ICENI, JUTES, PICTS
early Chinese money / PU
early Christian love feast / AGAPE
early church desk / AMBO
early Egyptian Christian / COPT
early English money / ORA
early Irish freeman / AIRE
early leader / EPONYM; PIONEER
early musical symbol / NEUME, VIRGA; CLIVIS
early Norse gods / AESIR, VANIR
early Persian / MEDE
early silk makers / SERES
early Spanish kingdom / LEON
early spring flower / CROCUS
early Venetian coin / BEZZO
earn / EKE, WIN; GAIN; MERIT
earnest / WARM; EAGER, GRAVE; ARDENT, INTENT, INTENSE. PLEDGE
earnest money / ARRHA; HANDSEL
earnings / WAGES; PROFITS
earring / EARDROP, PENDANT
earth / SOD; CLAY, DIRT, LAND, LOAM, MARL, SOIL; GLOBE, WORLD
earth / c.f. / GE; GEA, GEO
earth, pert. to / GEAL; TERRENE
earth deposit in rocks / GUHR
earth god / GEB, KEB, SEB; DAGDA
earth goddess / GE; DANA, ERDA, GAEA; CERES; TERRA; DEMETER
earth mound / TELL, TEPE; RAMPART
earth pigment / OCHER; SIENNA
earth sediment / SILT
earthenware / JAR, JUG, MUG, POT; ECHEA; JASPER; CROCKERY
earthenware maker / POTTER
earthenware pot / OLLA
earthkin / TERRELLA
earthly / VILE; VENAL; SORDID

earthnut / ARNUT, CHUFA; PEANUT
earthquake / SEISM; TREMOR; TEMBLOR
earthquake, pert. to / SEISMIC
earth's crust / LITHOSPHERE
Earth's satellite / MOON
earthwork / AGGER, REDAN
earthworm / ESS
earthy / DULL; COARSE
earthy material / LOAM, MARL, SOIL
ease / RID; ALLAY, RELAX; PACIFY. CALM, REST; QUIET; RELIEF, REPOSE
eased / RELIEVED
easily / FACILELY, SMOOTHLY
easily affected / IRRITABLE
easily angered / IRASCIBLE
easily bent / LIMP; FLEXIBLE
easily broken / FRAIL; FRAGILE
easily carried / PORTABLE
easily convinced / WEAK; PLIABLE
easily frightened / SCARY, TIMID
easily moved / PORTABLE
East / ASIA; LEVANT, ORIENT
East African antelope / GERENUK
East African coin / PESA; GIRSH
East African country / KENYA
East African hartebeest / TORA
East African mountain / BATU, KIBO, MERU
East African native / SAB; HEHE
East African sky god / NGAI
East African tree / MOLI; BAOBAB
East African weight / OKA; KASM
East Asian crocodile / MUGGER
East Asian fiber / RAMIE
East Asian weight / KIN; TAEL
East Asian wild sheep / ARGALI
east end of church / APSE
East European / SLAV
East Indian antelope / CHIRU, SASIN, SEROW; NILGAI
East Indian ape / GIBBON
East Indian ascetic / YOGI; FAKIR
East Indian bird / MALEO, SARUS, SHARMA; LEIPOA, MALLEE; MEGAPODE
East Indian boat / OOLAK; LANCHA
East Indian cart / TONGA
East Indian cattle / GAYAL
East Indian cereal grass / RAGI
East Indian civet / RASSE
East Indian coasting vessel / PATAMAR
East Indian coin / ANNA, PICE, PAISA, RUPEE
East Indian cola tree / OADAL
East Indian cuckoo / KOEL
East Indian dodder / AMIL
East Indian dye tree / DHAK
East Indian fabric / TASH, TASS
East Indian fiber plant / DA; OADAL

East Indian fiber ropes / MALOO
East Indian fish / DORAB
East Indian food staple / RAGI, RICE; RAGEE
East Indian fruit / DURIAN
East Indian goat-antelope / GORAL, SEROW, TAKIN
East Indian groom's talisman / TALI
East Indian hemp / KEF
East Indian herb / PIA, REA; SOLA; SESAME
East Indian jackal / KOLA
East Indian knife / KUKRI
East Indian lady's maid / AYAH
East Indian land owner / ZAMINDAR
East Indian language / DYAK; TAMIL
East Indian law / ADAT
East Indian macaque / KRA
East Indian monkey / WANDEROO
East Indian musical instrument / BINA, VINA; SITAR
East Indian ox / GAUR, ZEBU
East Indian palm / NIPA
East Indian palm civet / MUSANG
East Indian peasant / RYOT
East Indian pheasant / MONAL
East Indian plant / DAL; AMIL, JUTE, SOLA; BENNE, MUDAR, RAMIE
East Indian pleasure garden / VIHARA
East Indian primate / LORIS; TUPAIA; TARSIER
East Indian purified butter / GHI; GHEE
East Indian rosewood / BITI
East Indian sailor / LASCAR
East Indian snake / COBRA, KRAIT
East Indian soldier / SEPOY
East Indian sun helmet / TOPI
East Indian tamarind / AMLI
East Indian temple / PAGODA
East Indian title / MIR; KHAN, MIAN; MALIK, NAWAB, RAJAH
East Indian tree / BO; AOH, DAR, ENG, MEE, SAL; ALUS, AMLI, POON, TEAK; AMPAC, KHAIR, NIEPA, PALAY, SALAI, SIRIS; BANYAN, SISSOO
East Indian vine / GILO, ODAL
East Indian water vessel / LOTA
East Indian weapon / PATA
East Indian weight / SER; TOLA; BAHAR, CATTY
East Indian wild cattle / ANOA, GAUR; BANTENG, CARABAO, TAMAROU
East Indian wild dog / DHOLE
East Indian wild goat / MARKHOR
East Indian wild sheep / URIAL
East Indies / MALAYA; INDONESIA

east Mediterranean country / EGYPT, SYRIA; ISRAEL, TURKEY
east Mediterranean island / CRETE; CYPRUS
east wind / EURUS
Easter / PAAS, PACE; PASCH
Easter, pert. to / PASCHAL
Easter flower / LILY
eastern / ORTIVE; ORIENTAL
eastern Asiatic people / SERES
eastern bishop's title / ABBA
eastern Catholic / UNIAT; MARONITE
Eastern church doxology / DOXA; KAINYN
eastern folk dance / KOLO
eastern garment / SARI; HAORI, HAPPI; KIMONO, SARONG; CHEONGSAM
eastern inhabitant / YANKEE; CHINESE, MALAYAN
eastern Mediterranean lands / LEVANT
eastern mendicant / FAKIR
eastern potentate / EMIR, RAJA; AMEER, RAJAH; SHOGUN
eastern salutation / SALAAM
eastern title / AGA, ALI, RAS
eastern university / NYU; YALE
eastern vessel / JUNK; LORCHA
eastern water vessel / LOTA; LOTAH; AFTABA
easy / QUIET; FACILE, SIMPLE
easy chair / ROCKER; RECLINER
easy to do / FACILE, SIMPLE
easy gait / LOPE, TROT; AMBLE; CANTER
easy to manage / DOCILE, WIELDY
easy mark / DUPE; SIMPLETON
easy position / SINECURE
easy work / SNAP; CINCH; PICNIC
easy-paced horse / PAD; AMBLER
eat / SUP; CHEW, DINE, FEED, GNAW
eat away / GNAW; ERODE; CORRODE
eat evening meal / SUP
eat greedily / GORGE, RAVEN
eat little by little / NIBBLE
eat main meal / DINE
eat meagerly / DIET
eat noisily / SLURP
eat a small portion / TRY; TASTE
eat voraciously / GORGE, RAVEN
eatable / FIT; EDIBLE; ESCULENT
eaten away / EROSE
eater, c.f. / PHAGA, PHAGE
eating, pert. to / DIETARY
eating away / CAUSTIC; CORROSIVE
eating place / INN; CAFE; DINER, GRILL; TAVERN; RESTAURANT
eating regimen / DIET

ebb / SINK, WANE; RECEDE. NEAP
ebb and flow / TIDE
Eber's son / PELÉG; JOKTAN
ebon / CHAR, DARK; BLACK
ebriate / DRUNK
ebullience / BUBBLING
ebullient / BOILING; AGITATED
eccentric / ODD; ERRATIC, STRANGE
eccentric moving part / CAM
eccentric person / NUT
eccentricity / TWIST; CROTCHET
ecclesiastic / CLERIC, PRIEST
ecclesiastical / SACRED; PRIESTLY
ecclesiastical cape / CAPPA
ecclesiastical cloth / FANON
ecclesiastical council / SYNOD
ecclesiastical court / ROTA
ecclesiastical decree / CANON
ecclesiastical district / SEE; PARISH
ecclesiastical headdress / MITER
ecclesiastical hour / NONE, SEXT; LAUDS, PRIME; MATINS, TIERCE; ORTHROS, VESPERS; COMPLINE
ecclesiastical law / CANON
ecclesiastical metropolitan / EPARCH
ecclesiastical plate / PATEN
ecclesiastical ritual book / ORDO
ecclesiastical scarf / ORALE
ecclesiastical vestment / ALB; CAPE; AMICE, ORALE, STOLE
echinate / PRICKLY; BRISTLING
echo / IMITATE, RESOUND
éclat / GLORY; RENOWN; SPLENDOR
eclipse / DIM; CLOUD, OUTDO
eclogue / IDYL; PASTORAL
economic / FRUGAL; THRIFTY
economical / SPARING; PROVIDENT
economize / SAVE; SCRIMP
economize severely / SCRIMP
economy / THRIFT; FRUGALITY
ecru / TAN; BEIGE
ecstasy / JOY; BLISS; RAPTURE
ecstatic / GLAD; ENRAPT
ecstatic utterance / RHAPSODY
ectal / EXTERIOR
Ecuador capital / QUITO
Ecuador islands / GALAPAGOS
Ecuador money / SUCRE
Ecuador river / NAPO; DAULE
Ecuador volcano / SANGAY
Ecuadorian Indian / ANDOA, COFAN
edacious / GREEDY
edacity / GLUTTONY
edam / CHEESE
eddy / SWIRL, WHIRL; VORTEX
edematous / PUFFY, TUMID; SWOLLEN
Eden / PARADISE

edenic / ARCADIAN, BLISSFUL
Eden's river / GIHON, PISON
edentate / TOOTHLESS
edge / HEM, LIP, RIM; BRIM. TAT; SIDLE; SHARPEN
edge of cup / LIP
edge of fleece / ABB
edge of hat / BRIM
edge of highway / SHOULDER
edge of hill / BROW
edge of page / MARGIN
edge of pitcher / LIP
edge of road / BERM
edge of roof / EAVE
edge of skirt / HEM
edge of street / CURB, KERB
edged / KEEN; SHARP
edged implement / KNIFE, RAZOR
edged tool / AX; ADZE; CHISEL
edged unevenly / EROSE
edging / RIM; PICOT
edgy / SHARP, TENSE; NERVOUS
edible / ESCULENT
edible agaric / BLEWITS
edible bird / CAPON, SQUAB
edible bulb / ONION; SHALLOT
edible fish / COD, EEL; BASS, CUSK, SOLE, TUNA; GRUNT, PERCH, PORGY; SALMON; HALIBUT, SARDINE
edible fruit meat / PULP
edible fungus / CEPE; MOREL; AGARIC; BLEWITS, TRUFFLE; MUSHROOM
edible gland / NOIX
edible grain / OAT; CORN; WHEAT; CEREAL
edible mollusk / CLAM; OYSTER
edible mudworm / IPO
edible nut / CASHEW; FILBERT
edible part / MEAT
edible part of nut / MEAT
edible plant /FRUIT; VEGETABLE
edible root / OCA, YAM; BEET, TARO; CARROT, DAIKON, GINGER, MANIOC, POTATO, RADISH
edible rootstock / ROI; TARO
edible seaweed / AGAR; DULSE
edible seed / OAT, PEA; BEAN, CORN; LENTIL
edible shoot / UDO; SPROUT
edible tuber / OCA, YAM; TARO
edible turtle / TERRAPIN
edict / ACT, LAW; FIAT; UKASE
edifice / PILE; HOUSE; BUILDING
edify / GROW; ERECT; INFORM
edit / REDACT, REVISE
edition / ISSUE; PRINTING
edition of paper / EXTRA; BULLDOG
editor / REDACTOR; DIASKEUAST
editor's concern / NEWS; FACTS
Edom / ESAU

Edom mountain / SEIR
Edomite / OMAR; IDUMEAN
Edomite city / PAU
Edomite duke / UZ; IRAM; TEMAN
Edomite king / BELA
Edomite queen / MEHETABEL
educate / TEACH, TRAIN; INSTRUCT
educated / BRED; TRAINED
educated persons / SAVANTS; LITERATI
educational institution / SCHOOL; ACADEMY, COLLEGE
educational society / NEA
educator / TUTOR; TEACHER
educe / DRAW; EVOKE; ELICIT
educt / EXTRACT
Edward's nickname / ED; NED, TED
eel / ELE; ELVER, MORAY; CONGER; LAMPREY; ANGUILLA
eel-like salamander / SIREN
eelpout / BLENNY, BURBOT
eel-shaped amphibian / OLM; SIREN
eelworm / NEMA
eely / WRIGGLY
eerie / SCARY, WEIRD; UNCANNY
efface / RASE; ERASE; CANCEL
effect / DO; ACHIEVE. ISSUE
effective / CAUSAL, COGENT, POTENT, USEFUL; TELLING
effective as of prior time / RETROACTIVE
effectiveness / LEVERAGE
effects / GOODS; PROPERTY
effeminate / EPICENE, UNMANLY
effeminate boy / SISSY; MILKSOP
effeminate dandy / FOP; EXQUISITE
effervesce / HISS; BUBBLE
effete / JADED, WEARY; BARREN
efficacious / VALID; POTENT
efficacy / FORCE, POWER, VIGOR
efficient / APT; ABLE; CAPABLE
effigy / GUY; DOLL, IDOL; IMAGE
efflorescent / BLOSSOMING
effluence / EMANATION
effluvium / MIASMA
effort / DINT; ESSAY, NISUS
effortless / EASY; GRACEFUL
effrontery / BOLDNESS; IMPUDENCE
effulgence / LUSTER; RADIANCE
effulgent / LUMINOUS, SPLENDID
effuse / LOOSE; DIFFUSE
effusive / GUSHING
eft / EVET, NEWT; TRITON
egest / VOID; EXCRETE
egg / OVUM. URGE; INCITE
egg, c.f. / OO; OVI, OVO
egg dish / OMELET; SOUFFLE
egg drink / NOG
egg of insect / NIT

egg and milk dish / CUSTARD
egg white / GLAIR; ALBUMEN
egg yolk / YELK; YELLOW; VITELLUS
eggs / OVA, ROE; SPAWN
eggs of sturgeon / CAVIAR
egg-shaped / OOID; OVATE, OVOID
egg-shaped ornament / OVA
egis / SHIELD; AUSPICES
eglantine / DOGROSE; SWEETBRIER
ego / SELF; VANITY; PERSONALITY
egoism / PRIDE; VANITY
egotism / CONCEIT
egotistic / SELFISH
egregious / GROSS; FLAGRANT
egress / EXIT; DEPARTURE
egret / HERON, PLUME; AIGRETTE
egret monkey / MACAQUE
Egypt canal / SUEZ
Egypt capital / CAIRO
Egypt city / CAIRO
Egypt river / NILE
Egyptian / BEJA, COPT; GYPSY
Egyptian air god / SHU
Egyptian alloy / ASEM
Egyptian beer / BOSA; BOUZA
Egyptian bird / IBIS
Egyptian boat / BARIS
Egyptian cadaver / MUMMY
Egyptian cat-headed goddess / BAST; BÁSTET, UBASTI
Egyptian celestial goddess / NUT
Egyptian Christian / COPT
Egyptian city / SAIS; THEBES
Egyptian cobra / HAJE
Egyptian cobra goddess / UDOT
Egyptian cotton / MACO, PIMA
Egyptian cow goddess / HATHOR
Egyptian creator / NU; PTAH
Egyptian cross / ANKH
Egyptian crown / ATEF
Egyptian dancing girls / ALMES
Egyptian deity / BES, TEM; AMON
Egyptian depression / QATTARA
Egyptian dog-headed ape / AANI
Egyptian dog-headed god / ANUBIS
Egyptian dry measure / ARDEB
Egyptian earth god / GEB, KEB
Egyptian falcon god / HORUS
Egyptian fish / SAIDE
Egyptian funeral effigy / USHABTI
Egyptian god of evil / SET; SETH
Egyptian god of healing / SERAPIS
Egyptian god of the lower world / OSIRIS
Egyptian god of magic / THOTH
Egyptian god of pleasure / BES
Egyptian god of procreation / MIN
Egyptian god of waters / NUN
Egyptian god of wisdom / THOTH
Egyptian goddess / MUT; ISIS
Egyptian goddess of heaven / NUT

Egyptian hawk-headed god / HORUS
Egyptian heaven / AALU, AARU
Egyptian ibis-headed god / THOTH
Egyptian immortal heart / AB; HATI
Egyptian judge of dead / OSIRIS
Egyptian king / TUT; PHARAOH, PTOLEMY, RAMESES
Egyptian king of gods / AMEN, AMON, AMUN; AMMON
Egyptian language / COPTIC
Egyptian leaping mouse / JERBOA
Egyptian liquid measure / HEN
Egyptian lizard / ADDA; WORRAL
Egyptian love goddess / MUT; SATI; HATHOR
Egyptian lute / NABLA
Egyptian maternity goddess / APET
Egyptian measure / KET, PIK
Egyptian money / ASPER
Egyptian month / AHET, APAP
Egyptian moon god / YAH
Egyptian moon goddess / ISIS
Egyptian peasant / FELLAH
Egyptian phoenix / BENU
Egyptian political group / WAFD
Egyptian primeval chaos / NU
Egyptian queen of the gods / SATI
Egyptian ram-headed god / BA; AMEN, AMON, AMUN; AMMON, KHNUM
Egyptian sacred beetle / SCARAB
Egyptian sacred bull / APIS
Egyptian sentinel / GHAFFIR
Egyptian singing girl / ALME
Egyptian skink / ADDA
Egyptian sky goddess / NUT
Egyptian snake / ASP
Egyptian solar deity / RA, SU
Egyptian solar disk / ATEN, ATON
Egyptian soul / BA, KA; SAHU
Egyptian star god / SOTHIS
Egyptian sun god / RA; TEM, TUM; AMEN, AMON, AMUN, ATMU, ATUM; AMMON, HORUS
Egyptian symbol of eternal life / SCARAB
Egyptian symbol of life / ANKH
Egyptian tambourine / RIKK
Egyptian thorn / BABUL, KIKAR
Egyptian tomb / MASTABA, PYRAMID
Egyptian truth goddess / MA; MAAT
Egyptian underworld god / OSIRIS; SERAPIS
Egyptian unit of capacity / ARDEB
Egyptian viceroy / KHEDIVE
Egyptian war goddess / NIT
Egyptian wolf god / UPWAWET
Egyptian writing material / PAPYRUS
eh? / HAH; ANAN
eider / DOWN, DUCK

eidolon / ICON; IMAGE; PHANTOM
eight / OCTAD; OCTAVE
eight, c.f. / OCTA, OCTI, OCTO
eight days after feast / UTAS; OCTAVE
eighth of circle / OCTANT
eighth of gallon / PINT
eighth of mile / FURLONG
eighth note / QUAVER
eighth of Orkney mark / URE
eight-sided figure / OCTAGON
Einstein theory / RELATIVITY
Eire / ERIN; IRELAND
Eire capital / DUBLIN
Eire city / CORK; SLIGO; TRALEE
Eire lake / REE; CONN, DERG
Eire legislature / DAIL; SEANAD
Eire river / ERNE, NORE, SUIR; BOYNE, LAGAN; LIFFEY; SHANNON
Eisenhower / IKE
either / OR; ANY, ONE, TOO
either end of yard / YARDARM
ejaculation / EXCLAMATION
eject / EMIT, OMIT, OUST, SPEW
eject in jet / SPOUT, SPURT
eject violently / SPEW; VOMIT
ejecta / REFUSE
ejection / EXPULSION
eke / ADD, IMP, YMP; AUGMENT
elaborate / ORNATE. IMPROVE
elaborate speech / ORATION
elaborate style / ROCOCO; BAROQUE
Elam capital / SUSA
Elam's father / SHEM
elan / DASH; ARDOR, VERVE
eland / IMPOFO; ANTELOPE
elanet / KITE
elapse / PASS; EXPIRE
elasmobranch / RAY; SHARK, SKATE
elastic / SPRINGY; RESILIENT
elastic fluid / GAS
elastic knitted cloth / JERSEY
elastic porous mass / SPONGE
elate / EXALT; GLADDEN
elating / EXULTING; INSPIRING
elation / JOY; EUPHORIA
elative / SUPERLATIVE
Elbe tributary / EGER, ISER; VLTAVA
elbow / ANCON. NUDGE; JOSTLE
elbow in pipe / ELL
elbow room / EASE; FREEDOM
elbow-shaped shaft / CRANK
elder / OLDER; FORMER, SENIOR
elderly / OLD; AGED; SENILE
elderly man / GRAYBEARD
elderly woman / CRONE; DOWAGER
eldest / AINE; EIGNE; OLDEST
eldest son / INHERITOR
elect / VOTE; CHOOSE, PREFER

elected official / VEEP; MAYOR;
  GOVERNOR; PRESIDENT;
  CONGRESSMAN
election / POLL; BALLOT
election report / RETURNS
electioneering / CANVASSING
elector / VOTER
electric catfish / RAAD
electric current / AC, DC
electric current measure / VOLT,
  WATT; AMPERE
electric fire / HEATER
electric force / OD; ELOD
electric light / ARC
electric resistance unit / OHM
electrical atmosphere / AURA
electrical coil / TESLA; SOLENOID
electrical device / FILTER; RESIS-
  TOR; CAPACITOR, CONDENSER
electrical generator / DYNAMO
electrical measuring instrument /
  AMMETER; VOLTMETER
electrical od / ELOD
electrical particle / ION
electrical phenomenon / ARC;
  SPARK

electrical rectifier / DIODE
electrical reluctance unit / REL;
  OERSTED
electricity unit / ES; AMP, MHO,
  MIL, OHM; VOLT, WATT; FARAD,
  HENRY, WEBER; AMPERE; ELEC-
  TRON
electricity in atmosphere / STATIC
electrified particle / ION
electrode / ANODE; CATHODE
elegance / GRACE; POLISH
elegant / FINE, NEAT; GENTEEL
elegant expression / PERIOD;
  ATTICISM
elegy / ODE; DIRGE; LAMENT
element / PART; FACTOR;
  COMPONENT
element in organic matter /
  CARBON
element of same atomic number /
  ISOTOPE
elemental / PRIMARY;
  FUNDAMENTAL
elementary / PLAIN; SIMPLE
elementary substance / GAS;
  METAL

Elements (Chemical) and Symbols

	Symbol
actinium	AC
aluminum	AL
americium	AM
antimony	SB
argon	AR
arsenic	AS
astatine	AT
barium	BA
berkelium	BK
beryllium	BE
bismuth	BI
boron	B
bromine	BR
cadmium	CD
calcium	CA
californium	CF
carbon	C
cerium	CE
cesium	CS
chlorine	CL
chromium	CR
cobalt	CO
copper	CU
curium	CM
dysprosium	DY
einsteinium	ES
erbium	ER
europium	EU
fermium	FM
fluorine	F
francium	FR
gadolinium	GD
gallium	GA

	Symbol
germanium	GE
gold	AU
hafnium	HF
hahnium	HA
helium	HE
holmium	HO
hydrogen	H
indium	IN
iodine	I
iridium	IR
iron	FE
krypton	KR
lanthanium	LA
lawrencium	LR
lead	PB
lithium	LI
lutetium	LU
magnesium	MG
manganese	MN
mendelevium	MD
mercury	HG
molybdenum	MO
neodymium	ND
neon	NE
neptunium	NP
nickel	NI
niobium (ex columbium)	NB
nitrogen	N
nobelium	NO
osmium	OS
oxygen	O
palladium	PD
phosphorus	P
platinum	PT
plutonium	PU
polonium	PO
potassium	K
praseodymium	PR
promethium	PM
protactinium	PA
radium	RA
radon	RN
rhenium	RE
rhodium	RH
rubidium	RB
ruthenium	RU
rutherfordium	RF
samarium	SM
scandium	SC
selenium	SE
silicon	SI
silver	AG
sodium	NA
strontium	SR
sulfur	S
tantalum	TA
technetium	TC
tellurium	TE
terbium	TB
thallium	TL
thorium	TH
thulium	TM

	Symbol
tin	SN
titanium	TI
tungsten (or wolfram)	W
uranium	U
vanadium	V
xenon	XE
ytterbium	YB
yttrium	Y
zinc	ZN
zirconium	ZR

---

elemi/ ANIME, RESIN; CONIMA

elephant / HATHI; PACHYDERM

elephant attendant / MAHOUT

elephant goad / ANKUS

elephant seat / HOUDAH, HOWDAH

elephant-carrying bird / ROC

elephant's cry / TRUMPET

elephant's ear / TARO; BEGONIA; CALADIUM

elephant's tooth / TUSK; IVORY

elephant's tusk / TUSH; IVORY

elevate / LIFT, REAR, RISE; HOIST

elevated / HIGH; RAISED

elevated railway / EL

elevated in rank / PROMOTED

elevated roadway / VIADUCT

elevation of land / HILL, MESA, RISE; BUTTE; RIDEAU; MOUNTAIN

elevator / LIFT; WAREHOUSE

elevator car / CAGE

elevator well / SHAFT

elf / FAY, IMP, NIX; OUPH, PERI; FAIRY, GNOME, PIXIE; SPRITE

elf king / ERLKING

elfin / FEY; ELDRITCH

elfish / MISCHIEVOUS

elicit / DRAW; EDUCE, EVOKE

elide / OMIT, SKIP, SLUR

Elijah / ELIAS

eligible / FIT; ABLE; SUITABLE

eliminate / OMIT, OUST; EJECT, EXPEL; BANISH; DELETE, REMOVE

elision / SYNCOPE; OMISSION

elite / BEST, PICK; CREAM

elixir / AMRITA; PANACEA

Elizabeth I / ORIANA; GLORIANA

elk / ALCE, STAG; MOOSE; WAPITI

ell / WING; CUBIT

ellipse / OVAL

ellipsis / SYNCOPE; OMISSION

elliptical / OVAL; OVATE, TERSE; CONCISE, CRYPTIC, LACONIC

elm / ULME

elm fruit / KEY; SAMARA

elocution / ORATORY

elocutionist / ORATOR; SPEAKER

eloign / HIDE

elongate / EXTEND; STRETCH

elongated / OBLONG; PROLATE

elongated fish / EEL, GAR; PIKE

elope / ESCAPE; ABSCOND

eloquence / ORATORY; RHETORIC

eloquent / SUBLIME; EXPRESSIVE

eloquent speaker / ORATOR

else / BESIDES; OTHERWISE

elucidate / CLEAR; EXPLAIN

elucidation / SOLUTION

elude / BALK, FOIL, SHUN; DODGE

elusion / ARTIFICE

elusive / DECEPTIVE; FALLACIOUS

elver / CONGER

elysian / HAPPY; BLISSFUL

Elysium / EDEN; PARADISE

emaciated / TABID; MARCID, SKINNY

emanate / FLOW, RISE; ISSUE

emanation / RAY; AURA; EFFLUX

emancipate / FREE; LIBERATE

emancipation / FREEDOM

emancipator / ABE; LINCOLN

embalm / CERE; PRESERVE

embalmed body / MUMMY

embankment / DAM; BUND, DIKE, MOLE; DIGUE, LEVEE; TERRACE

embark / SHIP; BOARD

embarrass / VEX; ABASH, ANNOY

embarrassed / RED; BLUSHING

embarrassing mistake / BLOOPER

embassy / MISSION; LEGATION

embassy member / AIDE; ATTACHE

embed / SET; PLANT

embedded dirt / GRIME

embellish / DECK, GILD, TRIM; ADORN; BEDECK; EMBLAZE

embellished / FINE; SHOWY; ORNATE

ember / COAL; CINDER

embezzle / ROB; PECULATE

embezzler / CHEAT, THIEF

emblaze / ADORN; DECORATE

emblem / MARK, SIGN; BADGE; DEVICE, SYMBOL; INSIGNIA

emblem of authority / MACE, STAR; BADGE, BATON; FASCES; CHEVRON

emblem of morning / DEW

emblem of U.S. / EAGLE
emblem of Wales / LEEK
emblematic / TYPICAL; SYM-
  BOLICAL
embodiment / AVATAR, MAKEUP
embody / INCORPORATE
embolden / ABET; CHEER; INCITE
emboss / RAISE, STAMP
embrace / HUG; FOLD, HOLD;
  ADOPT
embrocation / LINIMENT
embroider / ADORN; EMBELLISH
embroidery frame / TABORET
embroidery thread / CREWEL
embroil / CONFUSE, INVOLVE
embrown / TAN; DARKEN
emend / EDIT; ALTER; REVISE
emendator / EDITOR
emerald / BERYL, GREEN;
  SMARAGD
Emerald Isle / ERIN; IRELAND
emerge / RISE; ISSUE; APPEAR
emerged / AROSE
emergency / PASS; PINCH; CRISIS,
  STRAIT; URGENCY; EXIGENCY
emeritus / RETIRED; HONORARY
emery / ABRASIVE, CORUNDUM
emetic / IPECAC
emeute / RIOT
emigrant settlement / COLONY
emigre / EMIGRANT
eminence / FAME, HILL, RANK
eminent / HIGH; GREAT, LOFTY
eminent person / VIP; GRANDEE
emirate / DUBAI, QATAR; KUWAIT,
  SHARJA; BAHRAIN
emissary / SPY; AGENT, ENVOY
emit / SHED, VENT; EJECT;
  ERUPT, EXUDE, ISSUE, VOICE;
  EXHALE
emit air / BLOW
emit heat / BURN, GLOW
emit light / GLOW; SHINE
emit liquid / SPOUT, SPURT
emit odor / REEK, SMELL
emit ray / BEAM; RADIATE
emit smoke / FUME
emit sound / SIGH; GROAN, SNORT
emit vapor / SPRAY, STEAM
Emmentaler / SWISS; GRUYERE
emmet / ANT
emolument / GAIN; INCOME,
  SALARY
emote / HAM; OVERACT
emotion / FEELING, PASSION
emotional / DRAMATIC
emotional strain / ANXIETY
emperor / CZAR; KAISER, MIKADO
emperor of Japan / MIKADO
emperor of Russia / CZAR, TSAR
emperor's wife / CZARINA,
  EMPRESS

emphasis / ICTUS; ACCENT,
  STRESS
emphasize / UNDERSCORE
emphatic / LOUD; POTENT;
  DECIDED
empire / RULE, SWAY; REALM;
  NATION; COMMAND, CONTROL,
  KINGDOM
Empire State / NY
employ / USE; HIRE; ENGAGE
employ diligently / PLY
employ for money / HIRE; ENGAGE
employee / MAN; HAND; WORKER
employees / STAFF; PERSONNEL
employer / BOSS, USER; HIRER
employment / JOB; WORK; CRAFT,
  PLACE, TRADE; AGENCY, OFFICE
emporium / MART, SHOP; STORE
empower / ENABLE; AUTHORIZE
emptiness / INANITY, VACANCY
empty / BARE, IDLE, VAIN, VOID;
  INANE; DEVOID, HOLLOW,
  VACANT
empty by lading / BAIL; SCOOP
empty of liquid / DRAIN
empty shell / DUD; BLANK;
  CASING
empty-headed person / BOOB,
  FOOL; NODDY; NITWIT;
  SIMPLETON
emu / RHEA; CASSOWARY
emu apple / COLANE
emulate / VIE; MATCH, RIVAL
emulator / COMPETITOR
emyd / TURTLE
enable / EMPOWER
enact / PASS; PERFORM;
  LEGISLATE
enactment / LAW; STATUTE
enamel / FLOSS, GLAZE; POLISH
enameled metalware / TOLE
enamelware / LIMOGES;
  CLOISONNE
enamor / CHARM; CAPTIVATE
enamored / FOND; SMITTEN
encamp / TENT; BIVOUAC
encampment / CAMP; LEAGUER
encase / WRAP; ENSHEATH
enchant / CHARM; BEWITCH
enchanted / RAPT; ENTRANCED
enchanter / MAGICIAN, SORCERER
enchanting / PLEASING;
  DELIGHTFUL
enchantment / MAGIC, SPELL;
  RAPTURE, SORCERY
enchantress / VAMP; CIRCE, SIREN
encircle / HEM, PEN; GIRD, RING;
  BESET; ENCLASP, ENVIRON;
  SURROUND
encircling band / ZONE; GIRDLE
enclose / MEW, PEN; CONFINE
enclose within walls / MURE

enclosed / WITHIN; INTERNAL
enclosed area / SEPT, YARD
enclosed bottle / CARBOY
enclosed car / SEDAN
enclosed field / AGER; STADIUM
enclosed ravine / CWM; COOM;
    COOMB; CIRQUE, CORRIE
enclosed space / QUAD, YARD;
    GARTH; COMPASS
enclosure / MEW, PEN, REE, STY;
    BAWN, CAGE, COOP, YARD;
    CORRAL; PADDOCK; STOCKADE
enclosure for cattle / ATAJO,
    KRAAL; CORRAL
enclosure of piling / PALISADE
enclosure for sheep / PEN; FOLD
enclosure for storage / BIN;
    CHEST; LOCKER
encomium / ELOGE; PRAISE
encompass / RING; BEGIRD
encompassed / AMID; SUR-
    ROUNDED
encore / BIS; AGAIN; REPEAT
encounter / FIGHT, ONSET;
    BATTLE, COMBAT. COPE, MEET;
    ENGAGE
encounter boldly / BEARD, FRONT
encourage / EGG; ABET, URGE;
    FOSTER, INCITE, SECOND; AD-
    VANCE
encroach / INFRINGE, TRESPASS
encroachment / INROAD;
    INVASION
encumber / LOAD; IMPEDE,
    SADDLE
encurl / TWINE, TWIST
encyclopedia / PANDECT;
    THESAURUS
encyst / ENCAPSULATE
end / AIM, TIP; GOAL; FINIS,
    LIMIT, OMEGA; CLIMAX, FINALE,
    OBJECT. KILL, STOP; CEASE,
    CLOSE; FINISH
end, c.f. / TELO; TELEO
end of bread / HEEL, RIND; CRUST
end car of freight train / CA-
    BOOSE
end of a hammer / CLAW, PEEN
end man / BONES, TAMBO
end of ship's yard / ARM
endanger / RISK; PERIL; EXPOSE
endearing / LOVABLE
endeavor / AIM, TRY; SEEK; STRIVE
ended / DONE, OVER; FINISHED
endemic / PECULIAR; INDIGENOUS
ending / CLOSE, FINIS; FINALE
ending of adjective / ER; EST
ending of adverb / LY
ending of noun / EN, ES
ending of verb / ISE, IZE
endive / WITLOOF; ESCAROLE

endless / ETERNAL; INFINITE
endless sameness / RUT; TREAD-
    MILL
endorse / OK; BACK, SIGN;
    VOUCH; RATIFY; APPROVE,
    CONFIRM
endorsed / SIGNED
endorsement / BACKING
endorsing / RECOMMENDING
endow / VEST; ENDUE; FURNISH
endowment / FUND, GIFT; DOWER
endue / ENDOW; ASSUME, CLOTHE
endurable / BEARABLE
endurance / STAMINA; PATIENCE
endurance contest / MARATHON
endure / BEAR, LAST; ABIDE,
    STAND
enduring / PERMANENT;
    PERSISTENT
endways / LENGTHWISE
enemy / FOE; RIVAL; ADVERSARY
enemy scout / SPY
energetic / DYNAMIC; FORCIBLE
energetic person / DOER
energumen / NUT; FANATIC
energy / PEP, VIM, ZIP; FORCE,
    MIGHT, POWER, VIGOR; SPIRIT
energy unit / BTU, ERG, RAD
enervate / SAP; WEAKEN;
    ENFEEBLE
enfold / LAP; WRAP; SURROUND
enforce / COMPEL; CONSTRAIN
enforcement / COMPULSION
enfranchise / FREE; LIBERATE
engage / HIRE, WAGE; AGREE;
    ASSUME, ATTACK, EMPLOY,
    ENLIST
engage attention / INTEREST
engage in / WAGE; PARTICIPATE
engage a lawyer / RETAIN
engage for pay / HIRE; EMPLOY
engage in play / DALLY, SPORT
engage with / MESH; UNITE
engaged / BUSY; CHOSEN,
    INTENT; AFFIANCED
engagement / DATE; ACTION,
    BATTLE, PLEDGE; BETROTHAL
engaging / PLEDGING. ATTRAC-
    TIVE
engender / BEGET, BREED;
    PRODUCE
engendered / BRED; EXCITED
engine / MOTOR; DIESEL;
    MACHINE
engine part / PISTON, STATOR
engine of war / RAM; ONAGER
engineer / STEER; MANAGE
engineering degree / CE, EE, ME
engineer's booth / CAB
engineless plane / GLIDER
England / ALBION

England's air force / RAF
English / SAXON; BRITISH
English admiral / NELSON
English architect / WREN
English astronomer / HALLEY
English author / MORE, OPIE,
WEST; AMORY, ARLEN, BACON,
DEFOE, ELIOT, HARDY, MILNE,
READE, SHUTE, WAUGH, WELLS
English baby carriage / PRAM
English billiards game / SNOOKER
English car / MG; ROVER; JAGUAR
English cathedral / CANTERBURY
English cathedral city / ELY; YORK;
TRURO
English cheese / NESSEL; STILTON
English city / YORK; LEEDS; LON-
DON; CHESTER
English clown / GRIMALDI
English coin / BOB, MAG; PENNY;
GUINEA, TANNER; FARTHING
English college / ETON; BALIOL
English composer / ARNE; ELGAR
English conservative / TORY
English county / SHIRE
English dance / HAY; MORRIS
English diarist / PEPYS; EVELYN
English divine / INGE; DONNE
English draft horse / SHIRE
English dramatist / KYD; LYLY,
SHAW; UDALL; PINERO;
MARLOWE
English dynasty / TUDOR; STUART
English emblem / LION, ROSE
English essayist / ELIA, LAMB
English explorer / ROSS; CABOT,
SCOTT; RALEIGH
English forest / ARDEN; SHER-
WOOD
English-French battle / CRECY;
CRESSY; POITIERS
English gun / STEN
English halfpenny / MAG
English humorist / LEAR; STERNE
English king / BRAN, CNUT, KNUT,
ALFRED, CANUTE; STEPHEN
English law court / SOC; EYRE,
LEET; GEMOT
English lexicographer / MURRAY
English monk / BEDE; CAEDMON
English muffin / SCONE
English murderer / ARAM
English note / POUND
English painter / ORPEN;
ROMNEY
English philosopher / HUME, JOAD;
BACON; RUSSELL, SPENCER
English playwright / SHAW
English poet / GRAY; AUDEN,
BLAKE, BYRON, CAREW, DONNE,
ELIOT, KEATS, NOYES, PERCY,
WATTS

English poet laureate / KAY, PYE;
ROWE, TATE; LEWIS; AUSTIN,
EUSDEN, WARTON; BRIDGES;
BETJEMAN
English policeman / BOBBY
English political party / TORY,
WHIG
English porcelain / SPODE
English port / DEAL; DOVER
English prime minister / DISRAELI
English princess / ANNE, MARY
English prison / GAOL
English queen / ANNE, MARY,
MAUD; MATILDA; VICTORIA;
ELIZABETH
English race course / ASCOT,
EPSOM
English rebel leader / CADE
English river / DEE, EXE, TEE, URE,
USK, WYE; AVON, OUSE, TEES,
TYNE; TRENT
English royal house / YORK;
TUDOR; STUART; HANOVER,
WINDSOR
English sailor / LIMEY
English school / ETON; RUGBY;
HARROW
English sculptor / MOORE;
EPSTEIN
English singing group / BEATLES
English spy / ANDRE
English statesman / EDEN, PITT
English streetcar / TRAM
English tavern / PUB
English theatre manager / TREE
English title / DUKE; BARON;
PRINCE; BARONET, DUCHESS
English victory / CRECY; CRESSY;
AGINCOURT
English watering place / BATH;
MARGATE
English weight / TOD; STONE
English woman politician / LEE;
ASTOR
English writer on games / HOYLE
engorge / EAT; CRAM; DEVOUR
engrail / VARIEGATE
engrave / CUT; CARVE; INCISE
engrave with acid / ETCH
engrave by dots / STIPPLE
engraver / CHASER, ETCHER
engraver's tool / BURIN; MATTOIR
engraving / CUT; RELIEF
engross / ABSORB, ENGAGE;
THICKEN
engrossed / RAPT
engulf / WHELM; ABSORB;
SWALLOW
enhance / RAISE; HEIGHTEN
enigma / PUZZLE, RIDDLE,
SECRET; CHARADE, MYSTERY
enigmatic / MYSTIC; OBSCURE

enigmatical person / SPHINX
enisle / ISOLATE
enjoin / BID; ORDER; DIRECT,
FORBID, ORDAIN; APPOINT,
COMMAND
enjoy / LIKE; SAVOR; RELISH
enjoy together / SHARE
enjoyment / FUN; GAIETY;
PLEASURE
enkindle / FIRE; ROUSE
enlace / ENMESH
enlarge / GROW; SWELL; DILATE,
EXPAND, EXTEND, SPREAD
enlarge an opening / REAM; FLARE
enlarged nasal tissue / ADENOIDS
enlarged thyroid / GOITER
enlighten / EDIFY, TEACH; INFORM
enlist / JOIN; ENTER; ENROLL
enlist as seaman / SAIL; SHIP
enlisted man / GI; PRIVATE,
RECRUIT
enliven / ELATE, ROUSE; VIVIFY
enmesh / ENLACE, TANGLE
enmity / ANIMUS, HATRED;
RANCOR
ennead / NINE
ennoble / EXALT; DIGNIFY
ennui / TEDIUM; BOREDOM
Enoch's father / CAIN; JARED
Enoch's son / IRAD; METHUSELAH
enormity / OUTRAGE; ATROCITY
enormous / HUGE, VAST;
IMMENSE
Enos' father / SETH
enough / ENOW; PLENTY. STOP
enounce / STATE, UTTER
enrage / ANGER; MADDEN;
INCENSE
enraged / MAD; IRATE; INCENSED
enrapt / GLAD; ECSTATIC
enrapture / CHARM; BEWITCH
enrich / LARD; ADORN, ENDOW
enrobe / CLOTHE, INVEST
enroll / JOIN; ENTER; REGISTER
enrollment / LIST; REGISTRY
ensconce / HIDE; SETTLE
ensemble / SUITE, WHOLE;
COSTUME
ensheathe / ENCASE
enshroud / COVER; CONCEAL
ensign / FLAG; BADGE; BANNER
ensign bearer / ANCIENT;
GONFALON
ensile / SILO
enslave / ENTHRALL; SUBJUGATE
ensnare / NET; TRAP; ENTRAP
ensnarl / INVOLVE; ENTANGLE
ensue / ISSUE; FOLLOW, RESULT
entail / INVOLVE; WITHHOLD
entangle / MAT; WEB; KNOT, MESH
entanglement / COIL, KNOT
entente / TREATY; CONCORD

enter / JOIN; ENROLL, PIERCE
enter in hostile manner / INVADE
enterprise / EFFORT; ATTEMPT,
VENTURE; ACTIVITY;
ENDEAVOR
enterprising / BOLD; DARING
entertain / AMUSE; DIVERT,
REGALE
entertain sumptuously / REGALE
entertainer / HOST; ACTOR, COMIC
entertainment / FEAST; BANQUET,
PASTIME; FESTIVAL; AMUSE-
MENT
enthrall / ENSLAVE; CAPTIVATE
enthrone / SEAT; INVEST; ELEVATE
enthusiasm / PEP; ZEAL; VERVE;
ENERGY, FERVOR, SPIRIT,
WARMTH
enthusiast / FAN; ZEALOT;
BOOSTER, FANATIC
enthusiastic / KEEN; EAGER
enthusiastic acclaim / OVATION
entice / BAIT, COAX, LURE;
CHARM, DECOY, TEMPT;
ALLURE
enticement / BAIT, DRAW, LURE
enticing / EXOTIC
enticing woman / VAMP; SIREN;
LORELEI
entire / PURE; SOLID, TOTAL,
WHOLE; PERFECT; COMPLETE
entire range / GAMUT
entirely / FULLY, QUITE; TOTALLY
entirety / WHOLE; COMPLETENESS
entitle / NAME; QUALIFY
entity / ENS; UNIT; BEING
entomb / BURY; INTER, INURN
entourage / MILIEU; ATTENDANTS
entrails / GUTS; BOWELS;
VISCERA
entrain / BOARD
entrance / ADIT, DOOR, GATE;
ENTRY, INLET, MOUTH, PORCH;
AVENUE, PORTAL, DOORWAY,
INGRESS. CHARM; BEWITCH,
ENCHANT
entrance hall / FOYER, LOBBY
entranced / RAPT
entranceway / GATE; PORTAL
entrancing / WONDERFUL
entrant / NOVICE; CONTESTANT
entrap / BAG; CATCH; TREPAN
entreat / ASK, BEG, WOO; PRAY
entreat again / REURGE
entreaty / PLEA; APPEAL, PRAYER
entrepot / DEPOT; GODOWN
entrust / CONFIDE, CONSIGN,
DEPOSIT, INTRUST; DELEGATE
entry / ITEM; ACCESS; PAIRING,
PASSAGE; CONTESTANT
entry in an account / DEBIT;
CREDIT

entwine / WEAVE; ENLACE; WREATHE
entwined / WOVE. LACED, WOVEN
enumerate / TELL; COUNT; NUMBER
enumeration / LIST, TALE; CATALOG
enunciate / SPEAK, UTTER; DECLARE
enure / HARDEN; ACCUSTOM
envelop / HIDE, WRAP; ENFOLD
envelope / CASE; WRAPPER
envious / GREEN; JEALOUS
environ / SURROUND; ENCOMPASS
environment / MEDIUM, MILIEU
environs / NEIGHBORHOOD
envisage / FACE; IMAGINE
envoy / LEGATE; AMBASSADOR
envy / HATE, SPITE; MALICE; ILLWILL. COVET; GRUDGE
enzyme / ASE; PEPSIN, RENNIN
enzyme in olive oil / OLEASE
eon / AGE; OLAM; ETERNITY
Eos / DAWN; AURORA
ephah fraction / OMER
ephebe / YOUTH
ephemeral / FLEETING, TEMPORAL
epic / POEM, SAGA. GRAND, NOBLE
epic poem / EPOS; ILIAD; AENEID, EPOPEE; BEOWULF; KALEVALA
epicene / NEUTER; SEXLESS
epicure / GOURMET; GASTRONOME
epidemic / WIDESPREAD. FLU; PEST
epidermic growth / WART; RAMENTUM
epidermis / BARK, SKIN
epigram / MOT; ADAGE, GNOME
Epimetheus' wife / PANDORA
Epirus inhabitant / EPIROTE
episcopacy / PRELACY
episcopal charge / SEE; DIOCESE
episode / EVENT, SCENE; INCIDENT
episperm / TESTA
epistle / NOTE; LETTER; MISSIVE
epithesis / PARAGOGE
epithet / NAME; APPELLATION
epitome / BRIEF; SUMMARY; SYNOPSIS; COMPENDIUM
epoch / AGE, ERA; DATE
epochal / ERAL
epode / AFTERSONG
eponym / ANCESTOR
epopee / EPIC, EPOS
equable / EVEN; UNIFORM; MODERATE
equal / EVEN; ALIKE; UNIFORM. ARE, TIE. PEER; RIVAL; FELLOW

equal, c.f. / ISO; PARI
equal chance / TOSSUP
equal-angled / ISOGONAL
equality / PAR; PARITY
equalize / DRAW, EVEN
equally / AS; SAME; ALIKE
equally advanced / ABREAST
equanimity / POISE; CALMNESS
equatorial constellation / CETUS, HYDRA, ORION, VIRGO; AQUILA
equestrian / RIDER; HORSEMAN
equiangular figure / ISOGON
equidistant lines / PARALLELS
equilibrium / POISE; BALANCE
equine / ASS; MARE; HORSE, ZEBRA; DONKEY; STALLION
equip / FIT, RIG; ACCOUTER
equip with crew / MAN
equipage / ATTIRE, OUTFIT
equipment / RIG; GEAR; TACKLE
equipoise / BALANCE; EQUILIBRIUM
equitable / EVEN, FAIR, JUST; VALID; HONEST, PROPER
equitably / JUSTLY; IMPARTIALLY
equity / RIGHT; FAIRNESS
equivalence / PAR
equivalent / TANTAMOUNT
equivocal / EVASIVE; AMBIGUOUS
equivocate / PALTER, QUIBBLE
equivocation / LIE; EVASION; DECEPTION
era / AGE; TIME; EPOCH; PERIOD
era, pert. to / ERAL
eradicate / RID; ROUT; ERASE; UPROOT; DESTROY; ELIMINATE
eradication / DESTRUCTION
eral / EPOCHAL
erase / DELE; EFFACE; OBLITERATE
eraser / RUBBER
erasure / BLOT; DELETION
ere / BEFORE, SOONER
ere now / HERETOFORE
erebus / HADES, LIMBO
erect / REAR; BUILD, RAISE; ELEVATE. TALL; UPRIGHT; VERTICAL
eremite / HERMIT; RECLUSE
erewhile / FORMERLY
ergo / HENCE
eri / ERIA; SILKWORM
erica / HEATH
Eries / INDIANS; IROQUOIANS
Erin / EIRE; IRELAND
Erinyes / FURIES
Eri's father / GAD
Eris / DISCORD
Eris' brother / ARES
Eris' companion / BELLONA
Eris' sister / NEMESIS

Eritrea capital / ASMARA
Eritrean measure / DERAH
ermine / PEAN; STOAT; ERMELIN
erode / EAT; WEAR; CORRODE
eroded / EATEN, RUSTY
Eros / AMOR, LOVE; CUPID
erose / EATEN; UNEVEN;
   NOTCHED
erosive / CAUSTIC
erostrate / BEAKLESS
erotic / BAWDY; LOVING;
   AMATORY
err / SIN; FAIL, FALL, SLIP;
   LAPSE, STRAY; OFFEND
errand / MANDATE; MISSION
errand boy / PAGE; RUNNER
errant / ROVING; WANDERING
errata / TYPOS; MISTAKES
erratic / ODD; QUEER; ECCENTRIC
erring / SINFUL; FALLIBLE
erroneous / FALSE, WRONG;
   FAULTY, UNTRUE; MISTAKEN;
   INCORRECT
erroneous statement / FALLACY
error / SIN; SLIP; FAULT;
   BLUNDER, MISDEED, MISSTEP,
   MISTAKE
error in printing / TYPO; ERRATUM
Er's father / JUDAH
Er's wife / TAMAR
erse / IRISH, SCOTS; GAELIC
erst / QUONDAM; FORMERLY
erubescent / REDDISH; BLUSHING
erudite / WISE; LEARNED;
   INFORMED
erudite judge / PUNDIT
erudite person / PEDANT, SAVANT
erudition / LORE; WISDOM
erupt / EMIT; BURST; EXPLODE
erupting mountain / VOLCANO
erupting spring / GEYSER
Esau / EDOM
Esau's brother / JACOB
Esau's father / ISAAC
Esau's home / SEIR
Esau's wife / ADAH
escapade / PRANK; MISDEED
escape / FLY, RUN; FLEE; AVOID
escape as gas / LEAK; BLEED
escarole / ENDIVE
escarpment / BANK; CLIFF, SLOPE
escheat / REVERSION
eschew / SHUN; AVOID
escort / USHER; CONVOY, SQUIRE.
   ATTEND; CONDUCT; ACCOM-
   PANY
escritoire / DESK; TABLE; BUREAU
escrow / BOND, DEED; DEPOSIT
esculent / EDIBLE; EATABLE
escutcheon band / BAR; FESS
Esdras' angel / URIEL
esker / AS, OS; KAME; RIDGE

eskers / OSAR
Eskimo / ITA; ATKA, YUIT; ALEUT,
   HUSKY, INUIT; INNUIN, INNUIT;
   ESQUIMAU, MALEMUIT,
   UNALASKA
Eskimo boat / KIAK, KYAK; BIDAR,
   BIDER, KAIAK, KAYAK, UMIAK;
   OOMIAK; BIDARKA
Eskimo boot / KAMIK; MUKLUK
Eskimo dog / HUSKY
Eskimo dwelling / IGLU; IGDLU,
   IGLOO, TOPEK, TUPEK, TUPIK
Eskimo house of assembly /
   KASHGA
Eskimo outer garment / PARKA;
   NETCHA, TEMIAK
Eskimo woman's boat / UMIAK
Eskimo woman's knife / ULU
esne / SERF; THRALL
esoteric / INNER; SECRET
especially / MAINLY; CHIEFLY
espionage agent / SPY
espouse / WED; ADOPT, MARRY
esprit de corps / MORALE
espy / SEE, SPY; SPOT; DETECT
esquire / SQUIRE; ARMIGER
essay / AIM, TRY; ATTEMPT.
   PAPER, THEME, TRIAL; EFFORT
essence / ODOR, PITH, SOUL;
   ATTAR
essence of roses / ATTAR
essence of something / PITH, SELF;
   PRINCIPLE
essential / PURE; VITAL;
   NECESSARY, REQUISITE
essential being / ESSE
essential to life / VITAL
essential matter / MATERIA
essential part / CORE; FACTOR,
   MARROW; ELEMENT
essentially / PERSE; INNATELY
establish / FIX, SET; BASE, FORM,
   REAR; ENACT, FOUND, PLACE
established / SET
established quantity / UNIT;
   MEASURE
established rule / STANDARD
established value / PAR
establishment / MENAGE;
   BUSINESS
estate / LAND, RANK; ACRES;
   DOMAIN
estate manager / STEWARD
estate owned / ALOD; ALODIUM
estate of widow / DOWER
esteem / DEEM, HOLD; HONOR,
   PRIZE, VALUE. RESPECT;
   REVERENCE
esteem of many persons / POPU-
   LARITY
Esther's uncle / MORDECAI
esthetics / TASTE; BEAUTY

Esthonian / ESTH; ESTONIAN
estimable / WORTHY; DESERVING
estimate / RANK, RATE; COUNT, JUDGE, PRIZE, VALUE; ASSESS
estimated / VALUED; AVERAGED
estimation / HONOR; ESTEEM, RE-PUTE; RESPECT
Estonia capital / REVAL; TALLIN
Estonian city / NARVA, TARTU
Estonian island / MUHU; VORMSI
Estonian lake / VIRTS; PEIPUS
Estonian measure / LIIN
Estonian money / KROON
estop / BAR; HINDER, IMPEDE
estrange / PART; SPLIT; ALIENATE
estuary / ARM, RIA; FIRTH
esurient / GREEDY, HUNGRY
etagere / SHELVES, WHATNOT
etape / DEPOT; STOCKADE
etch / BITE; SCORE; ENGRAVE
eternal / ABIDING, AGELESS, END-LESS, UNDYING; IMMORTAL
Eternal City / ROMA, ROME
eternally / EVER; FOREVER
eternity / AYE; OLAM; ALWAYS
etesian / ANNUAL; PERIODIC
ether / SKY; ESTER, SPACE
ether compound / ESTER
ethereal / AERY, AIRY; CELESTIAL
ethereal salt / ESTER
ethical / MORAL; HONEST; UPRIGHT
ethical address / SERMON
ethically neutral / AMORAL
ethics / MORALS
Ethiopia / CUSH; ABYSSINIA
Ethiopia capital / ADDISABABA
Ethiopian city / HARAR
Ethiopian lake / TANA
Ethiopian language / GEEZ; TIGRE
Ethiopian river / DAWA, NILE
Ethiopian title / RAS; NEGUS
Ethiopian tribesman / BEJA, ITTU
Ethiopic / GEEZ
ethnic / PAGAN; RACIAL
ethnological group / TRIBE
etiolate / BLANCH, BLEACH, WHITEN
etiolated / PALE; SPINDLING
etiquette / USAGE; MANNERS
etna / HEATER; VOLCANO
eton / CAP; COLLAR, JACKET
Eton game / WALL; FIVES
Etruscan god / USIL; TINIA, TURAN
Etruscan goddess / CUPRA, LOSNA
Etruscan Minerva / MENRFA, MENRVA
eucalyptus / GUM; MALLEE
eucalyptus eater / KOALA
eucalyptus secretion / KINO, LAAP, LARP, LERP

eucalyptus tree / YATE; JARRAH
eucharistic case / PIX, PYX; CIBORIUM
eucharistic cloth / FANON, FANUM
eucharistic plate / PATEN; PATINA
eucharistic spoon / LABIS
eucharistic wafer / HOST
eulogy / ELOGE; PRAISE; ENCOMIUM
Eumenides / FURIES
euphemism / DISGUISE; PERIPHRASIS
euphonious / MELLOW; MUSICAL
euphorbia / SPURGE
euphoria / WELLBEING
Eurasian plant / LENTIL, MADDER
Eurasian range / URALS
Euripides heroine / ELECTRA
European / DANE, FINN, LAPP, LETT, POLE, SERB, SLAV; CROAT, GREEK, SWEDE, SWISS; SLOVAK
European bass / BRASSE
European bay / BISCAY
European bird / MEW, PIE, QUA; FINCH, MAVIS, MERLE, OUSEL, SERIN; CUCKOO, HOOPOE, LORIOT
European bison / AUROCHS
European blackbird / MERL; AMSEL, MERLE, OUSEL
European canal / KIEL
European cavalryman / UHLAN; HUSSAR; COSSACK
European city / BRNO, CLUJ, LODZ, ESSEN, LYONS, MILAN, TURIN
European clover / ALSIKE
European deer / ROE
European dormouse / LOIR; LEROT
European fish / DAB, IDE; BOCE, DACE, DORY, RUFF, TOPE; BREAM, TENCH, TONNO; PLAICE, SENNET, WRASSE
European forage plant / ERS
European grand duchy / LUXEM-BOURG
European grape / MUSCAT
European gulf / RIGA; BOTHNIA
European hawk / FALLER
European herb / BALM, DILL, MINT; ANISE, CLARY; BENNET, FENNEL, HYSSOP, SAVORY; DIT-TANY; TARRAGON
European industrial basin / RUHR, SAAR
European ivy / HEDERA
European kite / GLEAD, GLEDE
European lake / COMO; LADOGA
European linden / LIME, TEIL
European mountains / ALPS; URALS

European peninsula / ITALY; CRIMEA, IBERIA
European plover / DOTTEREL
European porgy / PARGO
European principality / MONACO; LIECHTENSTEIN
European rabbit / CONY; LEPORID
European republic / EIRE; FRANCE
European resort / NICE; CANNES
European river / PO; BUG; EDER, EGER, ELBE, EURE, ISAR, ISER, MAAS, ODER, OISE, SAAR, YSER; ISERE, DRAVA, LOIRE, MEUSE, RHINE, RHONE, TIBER, VOLGA; DANUBE
European rodent / LEMMING
European sea / BLACK; AEGEAN, BALTIC; ADRIATIC
European shad / ALOSE, ALLIS; ALLICE
European snake / ADDER, VIPER
European strait / DOVER; KATTE-GAT; BOSPOROUS, SKAGERRAK
European subway / METRO
European throstle / MAVIS
European toy dog / GRIFFON
European tree / CADE, SORB; MEDLAR; LENTISK
European weed / KECK; GORSE; FATHEN; CATSEAR; CLEAVERS, KNOTWEED
evacuate / VOID; EMPTY; PULLOUT
evade / SHUN; AVOID, DODGE, ELUDE
evaluate / RATE; APPRAISE
evanescent / FLEETING; TRANSITORY
evangel / GOSPEL
evangelist / JOHN, LUKE, MARK, MATTHEW; REVIVALIST
evanish / DISAPPEAR
Eva's friend / TOPSY
evasion / SHIFT; EXCUSE
evasive / SHY, SLY; SHIFTY
eve / DUSK; SUNDOWN; TWILIGHT
even / EEN; FAIR, JUST; EQUAL, FLUSH, LEVEL, PLAIN; SMOOTH
even if / THO; ALTHOUGH, GRANT-ING
even now / YET; ALREADY
even score / TIE; DRAW; STAND-OFF
evening / EEN, EVE; DUSK; NIGHT
evening coat / WRAP
evening party / SOIREE
evening prayer / VESPER; EVEN-SONG
evening song / EVENSONG, SERENADE
evening star / VENUS; HESPER, VESPER; HESPERUS
evening wrap / CAPE; CLOAK
evenly / SMOOTHLY; UNIFORMLY

evenness / EQUALITY; REGULARITY
evenness of mind / POISE; EQUANIMITY; NONCHALANCE
event / DEED, FACT; ISSUE; RESULT
event in history / AFFAIR; EPISODE; INCIDENT
eventful / NOTABLE; MOMENTOUS
events / OCCASIONS
eventual / ULTIMATE; CONTINGENT
eventual destiny / DOOM, FATE
eventually / ATLAST; FINALLY
eventuate / HAPPEN, RESULT
ever / AYE, EER; ONCE; ALWAYS; FOREVER; ETERNALLY
everglade state / FLORIDA
evergreen / ETERNAL; IMMORTAL
evergreen bean / CAROB
evergreen oak / HOLM
evergreen shrub / BOX; FURZE, HOLLY; MYRTLE; JUNIPER; OLEANDER
evergreen tree / FIR, YEW; PINE; CAROB, CEDAR, OLIVE, SAVIN; BALSAM, LAUREL, SPRUCE
everlasting / ENDLESS, ETERNAL; TIMELESS, UNENDING
evermore / ALWAYS; ETERNALLY
evert / OVERTHROW
every / ALL; EACH; WHOLE; ENTIRE
every day / DAILY; QUOTIDIAN
every item / ALL
everybody's uncle / SAM
everyday / PLAIN; ORDINARY
everyone / ALL; EVERYBODY
everything / ALL
Eve's husband / ADAM
Eve's son / ABEL, CAIN, SETH
Eve's temptation / APPLE
Eve's tempter / SATAN; SERPENT
evict / EJECT, EXPEL; BANISH
evicted / OUSTED
eviction notice / OUSTER
evidence / PROOF; TESTIMONY. SHOW; PROVE; EVINCE; MANI-FEST
evident / OPEN; CLEAR, PLAIN; PATENT; OBVIOUS, VISIBLE
evil / BAD, ILL; BASE, VILE. WOE; BANE, HARM, PAIN, VICE
evil act / SIN; CRIME; MISDEED
evil eye / JETTATURA
evil habit / VICE
evil intent / DOLUS; MALICE
evil spirit / OKI; BAKA, BOKO; ASURA, DEMON, DEVIL, FIEND, GHOUL
evildoer / SINNER; MISCREANT
evince / SHOW; EVOKE; DISPLAY
evoke / EDUCE; ELICIT, SUMMON

evoking laughter / RISIBLE
evolve / EXPAND, UNFOLD; DEVELOP
ewe / YOW; CRONE
ewer / JUG; PITCHER
ex / OUT; FROM; WITHOUT
exacerbate / EXASPERATE
exact / NICE; CLOSE, RIGID; STRICT; CAREFUL, PRECISE, ACCURATE, BLEED, WREAK; EXTORT
exact copy / IMAGE; REPLICA; DUPLICATE, FACSIMILE
exact counterpart / SAME; MATCH
exact illegally / EXTORT
exact point / X; TEE
exact retaliation / AVENGE
exacting / SEVERE; ARDUOUS
exaction / TAX; EXTORTION
exactly / PRECISELY; ACCURATELY
exactly suitable / PAT
exactness / RIGOR; PRECISION
exaggerate / OVERDO; ENLARGE
exaggerated comedy / FARCE
exaggeration / LIE; HYPERBOLE
exalt / LAUD; BLESS, ELATE, EXTOL, HONOR, RAISE; DIGNIFY
exaltation JOY; ELATION
exalted / EMINENT, SUBLIME
exalted in character / BIG; GREAT; HEROIC
exalted in rank / NOBLE; PRINCELY
examination / TEST; SEARCH
examination of accounts / AUDIT
examination to amend / EDITING
examination of cadaver / AUTOPSY
examination in depth / STUDY
examination of records / REVIEW; RESEARCH
examine / PRY, SPY; LOOK, SCAN, TEST; SEARCH; EXPLORE, INQUIRE
examine again / RETEST
examine in court / TRY; QUESTION
examine by touch / FEEL; PALPATE
examine and verify / AUDIT
example / CASE, COPY; MODEL
exasperate / VEX; ANGER; NETTLE
exasperated / MAD; IRED; CHAFED
exasperation / HEAT; ANGER
excavate / DIG; MINE; DREDGE
excavation / CUT, PIT, SAP; MINE, WELL; SHAFT; BURROW, TUNNEL
excavation for ore / MINE; STOPE
excavator / MINER; DIGGER
exceed / CAP, TOP; BEST, PASS; EXCEL, OUTDO; BETTER, OUTRUN
exceedingly / VERY; HIGHLY
exceedingly changeable / PROTEAN
excel / BEST, STAR; EXCEED

excellence / MERIT, WORTH; VIRTUE
excellent / AONE, FINE, GOOD, RARE; PRIME; CHOICE
excelling / BEST
except / BUT; SAVE; UNLESS; BESIDES, BAR; OMIT; OBJECT
exceptional / SPECIAL, UNUSUAL
excerpt / QUOTE; EXTRACT
excess / NIMIETY, SURPLUS; OVERPLUS; REMAINDER; DEBAUCHERY
excess of chances / ODDS
excess of solar over lunar year / EPACT
excessive / EXTREME; VEHEMENT; IMMODERATE, INORDINATE
excessive eating / GLUTTONY
excessive exaggeration / ELA
excessive interest rate / USURY
excessively / TOO; OVER, VERY
excessively fond / DOTING
exchange / SWAP; BANDY, TRADE; BARTER, RAP; BOURSE, CHANGE
exchange allowance / AGIO
exchange for cash / SALE
exchange medium in East / SHOE; SYCEE
exchequer / FISC; PURSE; TREASURY
excide / CUT; EXCISE
excitable / HASTY; IRRITABLE
excite / STIR; ELATE, ROUSE; AWAKEN, ELICIT, FOMENT; AGITATE
excite animosity / NETTLE
excite fondness / INFATUATE
excite sympathy / TOUCH; DISARM
excited / AGOG; ARDENT; NERVOUS
excitement / ADO; STIR; FUROR
exclaim / CRY; SHOUT; VOCIFERATE
exclamation / AH, HA, HI, HO, LA, MY, OW, UM; ACH, AHA, BAH, BOO, FIE, HAW, HEY, OHO, TUT, VOW, WOW; AHEM, ALAK, ALAS, OUCH
exclamation of annoyance / DARN, DRAT
exclamation of contempt / BAH, FOH, PAH
exclamation of disgust / AW; BAH, FIE, RAH, UGH, YAH; RATS, TUSH
exclamation of displeasure / BAH, BOO; HISS
exclamation of exaltation / EVOE
exclamation to frighten / BOO
exclamation to gain attention / HEY, PST; AHEM, HIST, HOLA, YOHO

exclamation of hesitation / ER
exclamation of pity / AY; MY; AYE
exclamation of regret / ALAS
exclamation of relief / PHEW
exclamation of surprise / EH, OH
exclamation of triumph / HA; RAY
exclamation of wonder / HA
exclude / BAN; BAR; DEBAR, EXPEL
exclusive / SOLE; NARROW, SELECT
exclusive group / ELITE; CLIQUE
exclusively / ONLY; ALONE; SOLELY
excommunicate / BAN; PROSCRIBE
excoriate / RUB; GALL; ABRADE
excrescence / CORN, WART; GROWTH
excrete / EMIT, VENT; EGEST
excruciate / AGONIZE, TORTURE
exculpate / EXONERATE, VINDICATE
excursion / TOUR, TRIP; JAUNT
excursionist / TOURIST; SIGHT-SEER
excusable / VENIAL; PARDONABLE
excuse / REMIT; ACQUIT, EXEMPT, PARDON; ABSOLVE, CONDONE, FORGIVE; PLEA; ALIBI; APOLOGY
excuse for not appearing in court / ESSOIN
execrable / VILE; CURSED; DAMNABLE, DIABOLIC, NAUSEOUS
execrate / ABHOR; DETEST
execrated / SWORE; CURSED
execration / CURSE; ANATHEMA
execute / DO; ACT; SIGN; EFFECT, FINISH; ACHIEVE, PERFORM
execute by hanging / LYNCH, SCRAG; STRINGUP
execution by mob / LYNCHING
executioner / HANGMAN; HEADSMAN
executor / AGENT; ADMINISTRATOR
exemplar / MODEL; PATTERN
exemplary / WORTHY; CORRECT; VIRTUOUS; ESTIMABLE
exempt / FREE; CLEAR; RELEASE
exemption / IMMUNITY; PRIVILEGE
exercise / USE; APPLY, DRILL, EXERT. TASK; ACTION, LESSON
exercise control / DOMINATE
exercise sovereign power / RULE; REIGN
exercising foresight / PROVIDENT
exert / STRAIN; PRACTICE
exert pressure / PUSH; PRESS; SQUEEZE
exertion / ACT, ADO; EFFORT
ex-GI / VET; VETERAN

exhalation / ODOR; STEAM; BREATH
exhale / EMIT; EXUDE
exhaust / FAG, SAP; TIRE; DRAIN
exhausted / WORN; FAINT, SPENT, TIRED; EFFETE; DEPLETED
exhaustion / LOSS; DEPLETION
exhaustive / TIRING
exhibit / SHOW, WEAR; DISPLAY
exhibit emotion / ACT; EMOTE
exhibit spite / GLOAT
exhibiting movement / MOBILE
exhibition / SCENE, SIGHT; PARADE; PAGEANT; SPECTACLE
exhibition room / GALLERY
exhilarate / ELATE; ENLIVEN
exhort / URGE; ADVISE, INCITE
exhortation / WARNING; ADMONITION
exhortation to duty / SERMON
exigency / NEED; DEMAND
exigent / URGENT; PRESSING
exiguous / SMALL; SLENDER
exile / BANISH, DEPORT. EXPULSION
exist / AM, BE, IS; ARE; LIVE; ABIDE; ENDURE; BREATHE
existence / ENS; ESSE; BEING
existent / ALIVE; EXTANT
existentialist / CAMUS; SARTRE
exit / LEAVE; DEPART. EGRESS, OUTLET
exodus / FLIGHT; DEPARTURE
exonerate / FREE; CLEAR; ACQUIT, EXCUSE, EXEMPT; ABSOLVE
exorbitance / EXCESS
exorbitant / UNDUE; INORDINATE
exorbitant interest / USURY
exoteric / OBVIOUS; EXTERNAL
exotic / ODD; GARISH; FOREIGN, STRANGE; OUTLANDISH
expand / GROW, OPEN; SWELL; DI-LATE, SPREAD, UNFOLD; AMPLIFY
expanse / SEA; AREA, ROOM; TRACT
expanse of heaven / COPE; PLENUM
expanse of land / PLAIN, REACH
expansive / WIDE; AMPLE; SPACIOUS
expatriate / EXILE; BANISH
expect / HOPE; ANTICIPATE
expectation / PROSPECT, RELIANCE
expectorate / SPIT
expediency / SHIFT; FITNESS; PROPRIETY
expedient / FIT; PROPER, USEFUL. MEANS; RESORT; RESOURCE
expedite / URGE; HURRY, PRESS; HASTEN; ADVANCE

expedition / TREK; HASTE; SAFARI
expeditious / QUICK, RAPID
expel / OUST; EJECT, EVICT; DEPORT, REMOVE
expel air / BLOW
expel air from lungs / COUGH; EXHALE
expend / PAY, USE; SPEND, WASTE
expend uselessly / WASTE
expenditure / COST; PAYMENT
expense / COST; PRICE; OUTLAY
expense schedule / BUDGET
expensive / DEAR, HIGH; COSTLY
experience / FEEL, LIVE, TEST; LEARN; UNDERGO. TRIAL; KNOWLEDGE
experience again / RELIVE
experience regret / RUE; REPENT
experienced / MET; LIVED, TRIED; UNDERWENT. EXPERT; PRACTICAL
experiencing feelings / SENTIENT
experiment / TEST; TRIAL. TRY
experimental / TENTATIVE
experimental workshop / LAB; LABORATORY
expert / APT; ABLE; ADEPT; ADROIT, VERSED. SPECIALIST
expert aviator / ACE
expert in cutting gems / LAPIDARY
expert in precious stones / GEMMOLOGIST
expertly / DEFTLY
expertness / SKILL; EXPERTISE
expiate / ATONE
expiration / END; CLOSE
expire / DIE, END; CEASE; PERISH
explain / CLEAR, SOLVE; DEFINE
explanation / KEY; SENSE; ACCOUNT
explanatory / EXEGETIC
explanatory postscript / ENVOI; AFTERWORD
expletive / OATH; REDUNDANCY
explicate / EXPLAIN; INTERPRET
explicit / PLAIN; DEFINITE
explode / BURST; DETONATE
exploding meteor / BOLIDE
exploding star / NOVA
exploit / ACT; DEED, FEAT, GEST
explore / SCOUT; SEARCH; INQUIRE
explorer / BYRD, COOK, ERIC, GAMA, KINO, PIKE, SOTO; BOONE, CABOT, CLARK, DRAKE, LEWIS, PEARY, SCOTT; BALBOA, BERING, HUDSON
explosion / BLAST; DETONATION
explosive / TNT; NITRO; TONITE; CORDITE, LYDDITE; DYNAMITE, MELINITE; FULMINATE, GELIGNITE

explosive detonator / CAP; FUZE
explosive device / BOMB; SHELL; PETARD; GRENADE, TORPEDO
explosive sound / POP; BANG, BOOM
export / SHIP
expose / AIR; BARE, OPEN; REVEAL, UNMASK; DISPLAY, EXHIBIT
expose to ridicule / RAG; LAMPOON, PILLORY
expose sham / DEBUNK
exposed / UNGUARDED
exposition / FAIR; DISPLAY
expositor / EXEGETE; INTERPRETER
expostulate / REMONSTRATE
exposure / SHOT; REVELATION
exposure to air / AERATION
expound / REVEAL; EXPLAIN
express / STATE, UTTER; ASSERT
express by action / GESTURE
express approval / CLAP; CHEER, SMILE; APPLAUD
express disapproval / BOO; HISS; SNEER, DEPRECATE
express discontent / BEEF; GRIPE
express gratitude / THANK
express indirectly / IMPLY
express in order / ENUMERATE
express pleasure / SMILE; CHUCKLE
express verbally / SPEAK, UTTER
expressing homage / REVERENT
expression / MIEN; TERM; ASPECT, PHRASE, SPEECH; UTTERANCE
expression of disgust / RATS
expression of gratitude / THANKS
expression of sorrow / ALAS, EHEU
expression of witness / OATH
expressionless / DEAD; BLANK
expressive / VIVID; ELOQUENT
expressive movement / NOD; MUDRA; GESTURE
expressly / SPECIALLY
expropriate / TAKE; DEPRIVE
expulsion / REMOVAL; EJECTION
expulsion of demons / EXORCISM
expunge / ERASE, DELETE, EFFACE
exquisite / FINE, KEEN, NICE, RARE; ACUTE, EXACT; CHOICE, SUPERB; INTENSE, PERFECT
ex-ruler / CZAR, TSAR; KAISER
ex-serviceman / VET; VETERAN
extant / EXISTING
extend / JUT, LIE, RUN; OFFER, REACH, WIDEN; DILATE, EXPAND, SPREAD; AMPLIFY, AUGMENT
extend across / LAP; SPAN; COVER
extend depth / DEEPEN
extend a formation / DEPLOY

extend a loan / RENEW
extend to / REACH
extend toward / RANGE; STRETCH
extended / RAN; SPREAD.
LENGTHY
extended journey / TOUR; VOYAGE
extended trade / COMMERCE
extended view / VISTA; PANORAMA
extended written contract / PACT;
TREATISE
extension / TAIL; BRANCH;
RENEWAL
extension of building / WING;
ANNEX
extensive / LONG, WIDE; AMPLE,
LARGE; SPACIOUS
extensive plain / LLANO, PAMPA,
STEPPE, TUNDRA; PRAIRIE,
SAVANNA
extensively / WIDELY; LARGELY
extent / AREA, SIZE, SPAN; AMBIT
extent of canvas / SAIL
extenuate / EXCUSE; PALLIATE
exterior / OUT; ECTAL, OUTER;
FOREIGN, OUTSIDE, OUTWARD,
SURFACE; EXTERNAL;
EXTRINSIC
exterminate / DESTROY; ANNIHI-
LATE
extermination / EXTIRPATION
external / OUTER; FOREIGN, OUT-
SIDE
external, c.f. / ECTO
external aspect / AIR; MIEN;
GUISE; DEMEANOR
external covering / BARK, COAT,
HUSK, PELT, RIND, SKIN;
JACKET
external part / OUTSIDE
external world / NONEGO
externally / OUTWARDLY
extinct / DEAD; EXTINGUISHED
extinct bird / MOA; DODO, MAMO
extinct elephant / MAMMOTH;
MASTODON, STEGODON
extinct "penguin" / GREATAUK
extinct reptile / DINOSAUR
extinct wild ox / URUS
extinct zebra / QUAGGA
extinction / DEATH; ABOLISHMENT
extinguish / VOID; QUENCH;
SUFFOCATE; EXTERMINATE
extirpate / UPROOT; DESTROY
extol / LAUD; BOAST, EXALT;
PRAISE; APPLAUD, COMMEND
extort / BLEED, EXACT, FORCE
extra / OVER, PLUS; ADDED,
SPARE
extra card in deck / JOKER
extra hours of work / OVERTIME
extra leaf / TIPIN; INSERT
extra payment / BONUS; PREMIUM

extra supply / RESERVE;
RESERVOIR
extra in theater / SUPE; SUPER
extract / DRAW; EDUCT, QUOTE;
ELICIT. ESSENCE, EXCERPT
extract with difficulty / PRY
extraneous / EXOTIC, FOREIGN
extraordinary / ODD; RARE;
SIGNAL
extraordinary person / ONER;
ORIGINAL; CHARACTER
extraordinary in size / HUGE;
GIANT
extraordinary thing / MARVEL;
PRODIGY
extravagance / WASTE; EXCESS
extravagant / OUTRE; LAVISH;
PROFUSE; PRODIGAL;
EXCESSIVE
extravagant admirer / IDOLATOR
extravagant person / WASTREL
extreme / LAST; FINAL, ULTRA;
UTMOST; DRASTIC, HIGHEST
extreme conservative / BOURBON
extreme degree / NTH
extreme degree, suffix / EST
extreme emotion / LOVE, RAGE
extreme unction / SACRAMENT
extremely / VERY; EXCEEDINGLY
extremely wicked / NEFARIOUS
extremist / DIEHARD, RADICAL
extremity / END, TIP, TOE; EDGE,
FOOT, HAND, TAIL
extremity of an axis / POLE
extricate / FREE; LIBERATE
extrovert / LOUDMOUTH.
OUTGOING
extrude / FORM; EJECT, SHAPE
exuberant / LAVISH; COPIOUS,
PROFUSE; PROLIFIC
exuberate / TEEM; ABOUND
exudation of trees / GUM, LAC,
SAP; RESIN; RUBBER
exude / OOZE, SEEP; BLEED
exult / CROW; REJOICE;
CELEBRATE
exultant / ELATED; JUBILANT
exultation / JOY; ECSTACY
exuviate / CAST, MOLT, SHED
eye / EE; EEN, ORB; OPTIC. SEE;
OGLE, VIEW; WATCH; OBSERVE
eye, pert. to / OPTIC
eye askance / LEER, OGLE
eye coat / SCLERA; CONJUNCTIVA
eye cosmetic / KOHL; MASCARA
eye globe / EYEBALL
eye inflammation / IRITIS;
PINKEYE; CONJUNCTIVITIS
eye inner coat / RETINA
eye layer / UVEA; CHORIOID
eye part / IRIS, LENS, UVEA;
FOVEA, PUPIL; CORNEA, RETINA

eye of seed / HILUM
eye shield / PATCH; GOGGLES
eye socket / ORBIT
eye worm / LOA
eyeball coat / CORNEA
eyeglass / LENS; SPECS; OCULAR; MONOCLE
eyeglass frame / RIM
eyeglasses / SPECTACLES
eyeglasses on handle / LOR-GNETTE
eyelash / LEBREE, CILIUM
eyelash makeup / MASCARA
eyelashes / CILIA
eyelet / GROMMET; LOOPHOLE

eyelid, pert. to / PALPEBRAL
eyelid droop / PTOSIS
eyelid infection / STY; STYE; HORDEOLUM
eyers / OGLERS; WATCHERS
eyes / EEN. EXAMINES
eyeshade / VISOR; BLINDER
eyesight / VISION
eyesore / DUMP; FRIGHT, PIGSTY
eyestalk / STIPE; PEDUNCLE
eyewash / BALONEY; APPLESAUCE
eyot / AIT; ISLE; ISLET
eyrie / NEST; AERIE
Ezra / ESDRAS

F

F in school / FAILING, FAILURE
fabaceous / BEANLIKE
fabian / SHAW; CAUTIOUS
fable / TALE; STORY; APOLOG
fable writer / AESOP; BIDPAI, PILPAY; PHAEDRUS
fabled animal / DRAGON; UNI-CORN; BASILISK
fabled being / OGRE; GIANT, GNOME
fabled bird / ROC; RUKH; SIMURG
fabled dwarf / GNOME, TROLL
fabled giant / OGRE; TITAN
fabled herb / MOLY; PANACE
fabled Hindu mountain / MERU
fabled horned horse / UNICORN
fabric / REP, WEB; ACCA, BAFT, DRAB, DUCK, IKAT, LAWN, LENO, MOFF, PILE, REPP, SILK, SUSI, TAPA, TUKE; CRAPE, CREPE; LINEN
fabric crossthreads / WEFT
fabric edge / WELT; SELVAGE
fabric merchant / DRAPER, MERCER
fabric of metal threads / LAME
fabric from remnants / MUNGO
fabricant / MAKER; MANUFAC-TURER
fabricate / COIN, MAKE; FORGE
fabrication / LIE; FABLE, FRAME; FICTION, FORGERY, UNTRUTH
fabricator / LIAR; COINER
fabulist / LIAR; TALETELLER
fabulous / UNREAL; EXTREME; MYTHICAL
fabulous animal / DRAGON
fabulous bird / ROC
fabulous tale / LEGEND; PARABLE; APOLOGUE
facade / FRONT
face / MUG; LOOK, MOUE; FRONT; ASPECT, FACADE, VISAGE. MEET; BRAVE; CONFRONT

face brazenly / STARE; OUTFACE
face card / JACK, KING; HONOR, KNAVE, QUEEN; PICTURE
face of clock / DIAL
face of compass / DIAL
face of diamond / FACET
face down / PRONE. COW
face to face / VISAVIS
face of glacier / SNOUT
face guard / MASK; BEAVER
face hair / BEARD; MUSTACHE
face having hands / DIAL
face with masonry / REVET
face reddener / SHAME
face of tool BASIL, BEZEL; SURFACE
face up / SUPINE
face value / PAR
face veil / YASHMAK
facet of gem / BEZEL, BEZIL, BIZEL, CROWN, CULET, TABLE; COLLET
facetious / GAY; FUNNY; JOCOSE; WAGGISH; HUMOROUS
facetious person / WAG, WIT; COMIC
facetiousness / HUMOR
facial / BEAUTY TREATMENT
facial bone / JAW; VOMER; MAXILLA
facial expression / POUT; SMILE
facial feature / CHIN, EYES, NOSE; DIMPLE; LINEAMENT
facial ornament / BEARD, PATCH
facial part / JAW; CHIN; CHEEK
facial shape / MOON, OVAL
facient / DOER; AGENT
facile / EASY, MILD; PLIANT
facilitate / AID; EASE; EXPEDITE
facility / ART; EASE; KNACK, MEANS; ABILITY, PLIANCY
facing / ORNAMENT. TOWARD
facing a glacier / STOSS
facinorous / WICKED

facsimile / REPLICA; LIKENESS
fact / DEED; DATUM, EVENT, TRUTH
fact presented / DATUM
faction / SECT, SIDE; CABAL, JUNTO, PARTY; CLIQUE; COTERIE
factious / CRUSTY; LITIGIOUS
factitious / SHAM; ARTIFICIAL
factor / AGENT; ELEMENT
factor in heredity / GENE
factory / MILL, SHOP; PLANT
factoryhand / WORKER; OPERATOR
facts / DATA; TRUTHS
factual / REAL, TRUE; ACTUAL
facultative / OPTIONAL; PERMISSIVE
faculty / ART; EASE, GIFT; POWER, SKILL; TALENT; ABILITY
faculty of perception / SENSE
facundity / ELOQUENCE
fad / RAGE, WHIM; CRAZE, HOBBY
fade / DIE, DIM; FAIL, PALE, WANE
faded / FAINT, PASSE; WILTED
fading / DECAY; FLUCTUATION
faerie / FAIRYLAND
faerie queen / GLORIANA
Faerie Queen author / SPENSER
Faerie Queen character / ATE, UNA; ALMA; TALUS; AMORET, DUESSA; ACRASIA
Faeroe island / STROMO; STREY-MOY
Faeroes' bird net / FLEYG
Faeroes' capital / TORSHAVN
Faeroes' colonizer / KAMBAN
Faeroes' gale / OE
Faeroes' sheep / FAAR
Fafnir's brother / REGIN
Fafnir's slayer / SIGURD; SIEG-FRIED
fag / TIRE; WEARY; EXHAUST
fag end / BUTT, HEEL, RUMP
fagot / TWIGS; BUNDLE; FASCINE
fail / ERR; FALL, MISS, OMIT, SINK, WANE; CEASE, FLUNK, LAPSE, PETER; DECLINE, DEFAULT
fail to declare fully / UNDERSTATE
fail to develop / STAGNATE
fail to follow suit / RENEG; RENEGE
fail to hit / MISS
fail to move freely / BIND
fail to pay a debt / WELCH, WELSH
fail to reach / MISS
failing / DEFECT, FOIBLE; BLEMISH
failing in duty / DELINQUENT
failure / DUD; FLOP, LOSS; DECAY; FIASCO; DECLINE, DEFAULT

failure of attention / LAPSE
fain / GLAD; EAGER; CONTENT
faineance / SLOTH; IDLENESS
faineant / LAZY; INACTIVE. LOAFER
faint / DIM; PALE, WEAK; TIMID; FEEBLE, SLIGHT. SWOON; SYN-COPE
faint of hue / PALE
faint remnant / TRACE
faint shine / SPARK; FLICKER, GLIMMER
faint trace / TINGE
fainthearted / AFRAID
fainting spell / SYNCOPE
faintly / WEAKLY
faintness / WEAKNESS
fair / EVEN, JUST, OPEN; BLOND, CLEAR. MART; BAZAAR, KERMIS
fair-complexioned / BLOND; BLONDE
fair-haired / BLOND; BLONDE; TOWHEADED
fairly / OPENLY; HONORABLY
fairness / BEAUTY, CANDOR, EQUITY
fair-spoken / SLICK; SMOOTH
fairway call / FORE
fairway injury / DIVOT
fairy / ELF, FAY; PERI, PIXY, PUCK, VILA, VILY; BONGA, SYLPH, WILLY; SPRITE; BROWNIE
fairy chief / PUCK
fairy child / CHANGELING
fairy cobbler / LEPRECHAUN
fairy finger / FOXGLOVE
fairy fort / LIS; SHEE; SIDHE
fairy ghost / SPRITE
fairy godmother / GUARDIAN; PATRONESS
fairy king / OBERON
fairy queen / MAB; TITANIA
fairy shoemaker / LEPRECHAUN
fairy spirit of death / BANSHEE
fairy story / LIE; HOAX; TALLTALE
fairy tale / FANTASY
fairy tale writer / PERRAULT
fairyland / AVALON; WONDER-LAND
faith / CREED, DOGMA, TROTH, TRUST; BELIEF, CREDIT
faith, pert. to / PISTIC
faithful / LEAL, TRUE; EXACT, LIEGE, LOYAL; HONEST, STANCH
faithful friend / DOG; ACHATES
faithless / FALSE; DISLOYAL
fake / DODGE; FALSIFY. HOAX; CHEAT, FRAUD, TRICK. SHAM; SPURIOUS; COUNTERFEIT
fake hair / WIG; PERUKE, TOUPEE
fake jewelry / PASTE

fakement / DECEPTION
faker / FRAUD; HUMBUG; SWINDLER
fakir / YOGI; ASCETIC
falbala / FURBELOW
falcate / HOOKED
falcon / GYR; HAWK; HOBBY, SACER, SAKER; LANNER, LUGGAR, MERLIN, TERCEL; KESTREL, SAKERET; LANNERET; PEREGRINE
falcon-headed god / RA; MONT; HORUS, KHONS, MENTU; SOKARI
falconry bait / LURE
falconry ribbon / JESS
falderol / TRIFLE; FOLDEROL, NONSENSE
fall / DIE, ERR, SIN; DROP, PLOP, SINK, SLIP; DROOP, SPILL. AUTUMN; CADENCE
fall abundantly / PELT, POUR, TEEM
fall back / RECEDE; RETREAT
fall back on / RESORT
fall behind / LAG
fall to bottom / SINK
fall clumsily / FLOP
fall into disuse / LAPSE
fall in drops / DRIB, DRIP; PATTER
fall flower / MUM; ASTER; COSMOS
fall to former state / REVERT; RELAPSE
fall forward / PITCH; TOPPLE
fall fruit / PEAR
fall guy / DUPE; PATSY; PIGEON
fall ill / SICKEN
fall month / OCT, NOV; SEPT
fall to one's knees / KNEEL
fall season / AUTUMN; HARVESTTIME
fall short / FAIL, LACK, MISS
fall suddenly / DROP, FLOP, PLOP
fall as the tide / EBB
fall upon / POUNCE; ASSAULT
fallacious / ILLUSIVE; DECEPTIVE
fallacy / IDOLUM; MISTAKE, SOPHISM
fallen / SUNK; RUINED; DEGRADED
fallfish / CHUB
fallible / FAULTY; ERRABLE
falling / CADENT; DECLINING
falling and rising cyclically / TIDAL
falling sickness / EPILEPSY, GRANDMAL
falling star / METEOR
fallow / IDLE; UNTILLED
falls / CATARACT
false / FAKE, SHAM; BOGUS, WRONG; FORGED, UNTRUE; DISLOYAL, SPURIOUS; DISHONEST, ERRONEOUS

false, pref. / PSEUDO
false alarm / PHONY
false friend / JUDAS; TURNCOAT
false front / FACADE
false god / BAAL, IDOL
false hair / RAT, WIG; TOUPEE
false idol / GOLDENCALF
false move / SLIP; LAPSE; MISSTEP
false name / ALIAS; ANONYM; PSEUDONYM
false oath / PERJURY
false pretense / SHAM
false report / LIBEL; CANARD
false show / FAKERY, TINSEL
false teeth / DENTURE; DENTURES
false thought / ERROR; IDOLUM; FALLACY
false wing / ALULA
falsehearted / FICKLE; PERFIDIOUS
falsehood / FIB, LIE; TALE; CHEAT, FRAUD
falsification / FORGERY; PERVERSION
falsifier / LIAR; FAKER; FORGER
falsify / PERVERT; COUNTERFEIT; MISREPRESENT
Falstaffian / COARSE, JOVIAL; BOASTFUL
Falstaff's aide / NYM; PETO; PISTOL
Falstaff's friend / HAL
falter / LAG; REEL; WAVER; TOTTER
fame / ECLAT, GLORY, HONOR, KUDOS; LAUREL, RENOWN
famed / NOTED; RENOWNED
famed athlete / OWENS; THORPE
famed auto racer / MOSS; OLDFIELD
famed bandmaster / PRYOR, SOUSA
famed baseball player / OTT; COBB, MAYS; RUTH; AARON; WADDELL
famed beach near Venice / LIDO
famed bridge player / GOREN; STAYMAN; BLACKWOOD
famed cardinal / NEWMAN; RICHELIEU
famed cartoonist / NAST
famed chess player / EUWE; EVANS; LASKER; FISCHER; CAPABLANCA
famed composer / BACH; BIZET; VERDI; HANDEL, MOZART, WAGNER; STRAUSS
famed conductor / BULOW; TOSCANINI
famed detective of fiction / CHAN, FELL, MOTO; DUPIN, MASON, QUEEN, SPADE, VANCE, WOLFE; HAMMER, HOLMES, POIROT, WIMSEY; MAIGRET
famed Fall River murdered family / BORDENS

famed falls / NIAGARA
famed fiddler / NERO
famed Florentine family / MEDICI
famed football player / GIPP;
BAUGH; GRANGE, THORPE
famed footballers / FOUR-
HORSEMEN
famed friend / DAMON; PYTHIAS
famed general / IKE, LEE;
PERSHING
famed golfer / HOGAN, JONES,
SNEAD; PALMER
famed horse / ZEV; KELSO;
MANOWAR; CITATION
famed horse race / DERBY;
PREAKNESS
famed institute / MIT; STEVENS
famed jockey / LONG; SANDE;
ARCARO
famed loch / NESS
famed mail service / PONY-
EXPRESS
famed mountains / ALPS; ANDES;
SIERRA
famed for multiplication / RABBITS
famed murderer / ARAM, CAIN;
CRIPPEN
famed New York waterway / ERIE-
CANAL
famed opera / AIDA; FAUST;
CARMEN
famed opera house / MET; LASCALA
famed painting / MONALISA
famed penologist / LAWES
famed performing horse /
LIPPIZANER
famed philanthropist / RIIS; NOBEL
famed prizefighter / GREB; LOUIS;
DEMPSEY; SULLIVAN
famed Quaker / FOX; PENN
famed runner / NURMI, OWENS
famed Saxon lady / GODIVA
famed see-through shoe / GLASS-
SLIPPER
famed ship / NINA
famed singing family / KING;
TRAPP
famed tennis player / BUDGE;
TILDEN
famed tennis trophy / DAVISCUP
famed tenor / CARUSO
famed tower city / PISA
famed Tunisian pass / KASSERINE
famed uncle / SAM, TOM
famed Venetian bridge / RIALTO
famed violin / AMATI, STRAD
famed volcano / ETNA
familiar / OLD; FREE; CLOSE; COR-
DIAL. SPIRIT
familiar saying / SAW, TAG;
PROVERB
familiar spirit/ DAEMON

familiarity / FREEDOM; INTIMACY
family / ILK; CLAN, HOME, LINE;
HOUSE, TRIBE; KINDRED
family abode / HOME; HEARTH
family descent / BLOODLINE
family emblem / CREST, TOTEM
family member / MA, PA; DAD,
MAW, MOM, POP, SIS, SON;
SONNY; GRAMPS, GRANNY
family name / SURNAME;
COGNOMEN
family partiality / NEPOTISM
family slogan / MOTTO
family tree / LINE; LINEAGE;
PEDIGREE
famine / DEARTH; SCARCITY
famish / STARVE
famous / NOTED; EMINENT;
RENOWNED
famously / WELL; ADMIRABLY
fan / BUG; VANE; ROOTER,
ZEALOT; DEVOTEE. COOL;
WINNOW
fan dancer / RAND
fan form / PLICATE
fan palm / TALIPOT; PALMETTO
fan slat / BRIN
fan that swings / OGI; PUNKAH
fanatic / BIGOT; ZEALOT. MAD;
LUNATIC
fanatical / CRAZY, RABID
fanatical enthusiast / DEMON
fanatical partisan / ZEALOT
fanaticism / FRENZY
fancied / DREAMT; IMAGINED.
IDEAL
fanciful / WILD; UNREAL; WHIMSI-
CAL; CAPRICIOUS
fanciful notion / IMAGE
fanciful story / YARN; TALLTALE
fancy / FAD; IDEA, WHIM; DREAM,
HUMOR, TASTE; NOTION, VAG-
ARY. LIKE; SUPPOSE. FANCIFUL;
ELABORATE
fancy button / STUD
fancy clothes / FINERY
fancy enameled metalware / TOLE
fancy goldfish / COMET; CALICO
fancy man / PIMP; GIGOLO
fancy pants / SISSY; EFFEMINATE
fancy trimming / FRILL
fancywork / LACE; TATTING;
EMBROIDERY
fandango / BALL; DANCE
fane / BANNER, CHURCH, TEMPLE
fanfare / TANTARA; FLOURISH;
TRUMPETS; TANTARARA
fang / TUSK; TALON, TOOTH
fanleaf palm / BURI; TALIPOT; PAL-
METTO
fanlight / TRANSOM
fanlike / PLICATE

fanner / KESTREL

fanning device / PUNKA; PUNKAH; FLABELLUM

fanon / ORALE; MANIPLE

fantail / PIGEON

fantastic / ODD; QUEER; UNREAL; STRANGE; FANCIFUL; GROTESQUE

fantastic creature / WYVERN; CHIMERA

fantasy / DREAM; FIGMENT; PHANTASM

fantasy in sleep / NIGHTMARE

fantod / FUSS; FIDGET

far / REMOTE. WIDELY

far, c.f. / TEL; TELE

far away / DREAMY; DISTANT

far below / LOW; DEEP

far from dead / ALIVEANDKICKING

far from generous / MEAN

far northern European / LAPP

far off / AFAR; REMOTE; DISTANT

far from subtle / CRUDE

faraway country / THULE; ANTIPODES

farce / MIME, SHAM, SHOW; EXODE

farcical / ABSURD; LUDICROUS

fare / DO; DIET; PROSPER. TOLL; VICTUAL; PASSENGER

farewell / AVE; BYBY, TATA, VALE; ADDIO, ADIEU, ADIOS, ALOHA; GOODBY; GOODBYE

farfetched / QUEER; FORCED; ROUNDABOUT

far-gone / WORN; SMITTEN; ADVANCED

farina / MEAL; FLOUR; STARCH

farinaceous drink / PTISAN, TISANE

farinaceous food / SAGO; SALEP; TAPIOCA

farm / PLOW, TILL. CROFT, DAIRY, RANCH

farm animal / COW, EWE; MULE; HORSE

farm building / BARN, BYRE, SILO; STABLE

farm machine / PLOW; REAPER; TRACTOR

farm produce / OATS; GRAIN, WHEAT

farm as a whole / GRANGE

farm worker / HAND

farm yield / CROP

farmer / KULAK; COTTER; CROFTER, GRANGER, PLANTER

farmer of India / MEO; RYOT

farmer of South Africa / BOER

farmer's seeding tool / HOEDRILL

farmers' lodge / GRANGE

farmhouse / ONSTEAD

farming / HUSBANDRY; AGRICULTURE

farmland / ARADA, ARADO

farmstead / BYRE

farmyard / WERF; BARTON

farness / DISTANCE

faro card / CASE, HOCK, SODA

farolike game / STUSS

Farragut's victory / MOBILEBAY

farrow / PIG; LITTER

farseeing / WISE; SAGACIOUS

far-shooting / LONGRANGE

farsightedness / PRESBYOPIA

farther than / BEYOND

farthest in / INMOST; INNERMOST

farthest limit / UTTERMOST

farthest point / APOGEE

fascia / BAND, BELT, SASH; TAENIA

fascicle / FEUILLETON

fascinate / CHARM; BEWITCH, ENCHANT, IMPRESS

fascinating woman / SIREN; VAMPIRE

fascination / GLAMOUR

fash / VEX; ANNOY

fashion / FORM, MOLD; ADAPT. FAD; MODE, SORT; SHAPE; CUSTOM, MANNER

fashion center / PARIS

fashion designer / DIOR; CHANEL

fashion plate / BEAU; DANDY

fashionable / CHIC; SMART

fashionable dressmaker / MODISTE

fashionable reception / SALON; SOIREE

fashioned / CREATED

fashioned again / REMADE

fast / FIRM, WILD; APACE, FIXED, FLEET, RAPID, SWIFT; PRESTO, SPEEDY, STEADY; PERMANENT. DIET

fast, c.f. / TACHY

fast ballroom dance / ONESTEP

fast days / LENT; RAMADAN

fast driver / RACER; SPEEDER; DRAGSTER

fast galley / DROMON; DROMOND

fast plane / JET

fast runner / SPRINTER

fast train / EXPRESS, LIMITED

fasten / PEG, PIN, TIE; BIND, GIRD, LACE, LINK, SNIB, TACK, WELD; AFFIX, PASTE, RIVET

fasten a boat / MOOR

fasten firmly / GLUE; CLAMP

fasten with metal / WELD; RIVET; SOLDER

fasten securely / BOLT, LOCK, NAIL, SEAL; BRACE

fasten with staples / PIN; BOLT

fastened / JOINED, UNITED

fastener / NUT; BITT. BRAD, CLIP, HASP, HOOK, SNAP, STUD; CLEAT, DOWEL, STRAP; BUTTON, CLEVIS, COTTER

fastening / CLASP, LATCH
fastening rod / BOLT; RIVET
faster / SPEEDIER
fastidious / NICE; DAINTY; FINI-
CAL, REFINED
fastidious diner / EPICURE
fasting / ABSTINENCE
fasting period / LENT; RAMADAN
fastness / CITADEL; STRONGHOLD
fastuous / PROUD; HAUGHTY
fat / FOZY, OILY, RICH; BROAD,
HEAVY, OBESE, PLUMP, STOUT;
FLESHY, GREASY, PORTLY; ADI-
POSE. LARD, LIPA, SUET; ESTER
fat, c.f. / LIP; ADIP, STEAT
fat, pert. to / ADIPIC; ADIPOSE
fat for candles / TALLOW
fat solid / STEARIN
Fata Morgana / MIRAGE
fatal / FEY; DEADLY, FUNEST,
LETHAL, MORTAL
fatal epidemic / PEST
fatality / DOOM; DEATH; DESTINY
fatbird / OILBIRD; SANDPIPER
Fate / CLOTHO; ATROPOS;
LACHESIS
fate / LOT; DOOM; FORTUNE
fate in Buddhism / KARMA
fate in Islam / KISMET
fated / DESTINED; INEVITABLE
fateful / DIRE; FATAL
Fates / MOIRAI, PARCAE
fathead / IDIOT
fatheaded / STUPID
father / PA; DAD, POP; ABBA,
ABBE, PAPA, SIRE; DADDY,
PADRE, PATER; PARENT. BEGET;
GENERATE
father of Abner / NER
Father Abraham / LINCOLN
father of Agamemnon / ATREUS
father of Ajax / TELAMON
father of all / ADAM
father of Canaanite giants / ANAK
Father Christmas / SANTACLAUS
father of David / JESSE
father of drama / THESPIS
father of gods / AMON, ZEUS;
JUPITER
father of his country / CICERO;
WASHINGTON
father of history / HERODOTUS
father of Jacob / ISAAC
father of Joshua / NUN
father of lies / SUT; SATAN

father of medicine / HIPPOCRATES
father of Menelaus / ATREUS
father of music / JUBAL
father of navigation / HENRY
father of Peleg / EBER
father of poetry / HOMER;
ORPHEUS
father of psychiatry / FREUD
father of rivers / APIDANUS
Father Superior / ABBOT
father of surgery / PARE
father of the symphony / HAYDN
Father Time's clock / HOURGLASS
Father Time's implement / SCYTHE
father of waters / MISSISSIPPI
fathered / SIRED
fatherhood / PATERNITY
father's brother / EME; UNCLE
father's side kin / AGNAT; AGNATE
father's sister / AUNT
fathom / TRY; TEST; DELVE,
PLUMB, PROBE, SOUND
fathomless / ABYSSAL
fatidic / PROPHETIC
fatigue / FAG; TIRE; WEARY. TOIL;
LASSITUDE, WEARINESS
fatigued / BORED, JADED, SPENT
fatiguing / BORING; TEDIOUS
Fatima's descendant / SEID; SAYID;
FATIMID
Fatima's father / MOHAMMED
Fatima's husband / ALI; BLUE-
BEARD
Fatima's sister / ANNE
Fatima's step-brother / ALI
fatten / BATTEN, ENRICH
fatter / STOUTER
fatty / OILY; GREASY; ADIPOSE
fatty fruit / OLIVE; AVOCADO
fatty secretion / SEBUM
fatty tissue / SUET
fatty tumor / LIPOMA
fatuity / WEAKNESS; SILLINESS
fatuous / INANE; FOOLISH;
ILLUSORY
faubourg / SUBURB; BANLIEU
faucet / TAP; COCK; SPIGOT;
ROBINET
fault / FLAW, SLIP, VICE; DEFECT
fault angle / HADE
faultfinder / CRAB; CRANK; CRITIC
faultfinding / CARPING; CAPTIOUS
faultless / PURE; CLEAN; PERFECT
faultless creature / VIRGIN;
PARAGON

Fates, Three	
determined fate	LACHESIS
spun life thread	CLOTHO
cut life thread	ATROPOS

faulty / BAD; UNFIT, WRONG; FLAWED
faun / SATYR; PANISC, PANISK; SILENUS
Fauna's father / PICUS
Faunus' son / ACIS
Faunus' wife / FAUNA
Faust author / GOETHE
Faust composer / GOUNOD
Faust's mistress / HELEN; GRETCHEN, MARGARET
Faust's servant / WAGNER
Faustulus' wife / ACCALARENTIA
faux pas / SLIP; ERROR, GAFFE
favonian / MILD; AUSPICIOUS
favor / BOON, GIFT; GRACE, TOKEN; LETTER, REGARD. AID; HELP; OBLIGE
favor to relatives / NEPOTISM
favorable / GOOD; SUITABLE; CONDUCIVE; BENEFICIAL
favorable attention / EAR; STUDY
favorable outcome of illness / LYSIS
favorable vote / AY; AYE, YEA, YES
favored / EXEMPT; FEATURED; PROTECTED
favored one / PET
favoring / PRO
favoring nephews / NEPOTIC
favoring one side / PARTISAN
favorite / PET; DEAR, IDOL; MINION
favorite dessert / APPLEPIE
favorite son / NOMINEE
favoritism / NEPOTISM
favors with a ballot / VOTESFOR
favus / BALDNESS
fawn / CRINGE; FLATTER. DEER, FAON
fawning / FLATTERY. SERVILE
fawning adherent / TOADY
fawning for favors / PARASITIC
fawnskin costume / NEBRIS
fay / ELF; FAIRY; SPRITE. FIT; CLEAN
faze / ANNOY, DAUNT; DISTURB
fealty / HOMAGE; LOYALTY
fear / AWE; DREAD; DISMAY, FRIGHT, PHOBIA, TERROR; CONCERN
fear of cats / AILUROPHOBIA
fear of closed areas / CLAUSTROPHOBIA
fear of darkness / NYCTOPHOBIA
fear of dying / THANATOPHOBIA
fear greatly / DREAD
fear of heights / ACROPHOBIA; HYPSOPHOBIA
fear of men / ANDROPHOBIA
fear of mice / MUSOPHOBIA
fear of novelty / NEOPHOBIA
fear of open areas / AGORAPHOBIA
fear of pain / ALGOPHOBIA

fear of strangers / XENOPHOBIA
fear of thirteen / TRISKAIDEKAPHOBIA
fear of thunder / BRONTOPHOBIA
fear of women / GYNOPHOBIA
fear and wonder / AWE
fearful / DIRE; AWFUL, TIMID; AFRAID, TREPID; NERVOUS; COWARDLY
fearful, c.f. / DIN; DINO
fearless / BRAVE; GALLANT, VALIANT; INTREPID, VALOROUS
fearlessness / INTREPIDITY
fearsome / TERRIBLE
fearsome creature / MONSTER
feasible / POSSIBLE
feast / FETE; FIESTA, REPAST; BANQUET, DELIGHT. TREAT; REGALE
Feast of Lanterns / OBON
Feast of Lights / HANUKKA; CHANUKAH
Feast of Lots / PURIM
Feast of the Nativity / CHRISTMAS
feast upon / DINE
Feast of Weeks / SHABUOT, SHEVUOS
feat / ACT; DEED; STUNT, TRICK
feather / PENNA, PINNA, PLUMA, PLUME; PINION
feather an arrow / IMP, YMP; FLEDGE, FLETCH
feather barb / HARL, HERL
feather cloak / MAMO
feather grass / STIPA
feather hook / HAMULUS
feather key / FIN
feather palm / EJOO, IROK; GOMUTI
feather part / BARB; QUILL, SCAPE
feather quill / CALAMUS
feather scarf / BOA
feather shaft / SCAPE
featherbrained / GIDDY
feathered animal / BIRD
feathered shaft / ARROW
featherer / FLETCHER
featherless / CALLOW
feathers / DOWN; PLUMAGE
featly / ADROITLY, CLEVERLY
feature / STAR; DISPLAY. TRAIT; ASPECT; LINEAMENT; CHARACTERISTIC
featured / SHOWN; DISPLAYED
featured performer / HEADLINER
feaze / DISTURB, UNRAVEL; DISCONCERT
febrile disease / TYPHUS; MALARIA; BRUCELLOSIS
February birthstone / AMETHYST
feckless / SHIFTLESS
feculent / MUDDY; TURBID
fecund / PROLIFIC

fed / ATE; EATEN; NOURISHED
federal / CENTRAL; FEDERATIVE
Federalist author / JAY; MADISON; HAMILTON
federate / UNITE
federation / UNION; LEAGUE; ALLIANCE
fee / DUES, FIEF; PRICE; CHARGE; PAYMENT; GRATUITY, RETAINER
fee farm / MANOR
fee for grazing / AGIST
fee paid to a lawyer / RETAINER
feeble / DULL, PUNY, WEAK; ANILE, FAINT, FRAIL; DEBILE, INFIRM
feebleminded / SIMPLE; IMBECILE
feebleminded person / OAF; FOOL; MORON; DOTARD; DULLARD; BONEHEAD
feed / DINE; GRAZE; BROWSE, SUPPLY; NOURISH, NURTURE. FODDER
feed to the full / SATE
feed the kitty / ANTE
feeder / NURSE; TRIBUTARY
feeding bin / MANGER
feedstuff / FODDER
feel / TEST; SENSE, TOUCH
feel aversion / UG
feel displeased / REPINE
feel elated / GLOW
feel indignant / RESENT
feel one's way / GROPE
feel poorly / AIL
feel remorse / RUE; REPENT
feel sorry about / REGRET
feel sympathy / PITY; YEARN
feel thrilled / TINGLE
feel want of / MISS; YEARN
feeler / PALP; ANTENNA; TENTACLE
feeling / TOUCH; EMOTION, PASSION
feeling of anger / IRE
feeling dismal / BLAH
feeling at fault / RUEFUL
feeling of hostility / IRE; ANIMUS
feelings / SENSIBILITIES
feet, pert. to / PEDAL
feeze / WORRY
feign / ACT; FAKE, SHAM; ASSUME; PRETEND; SIMULATE
feign illness / MALINGER
feint / MOCK; TRICK; PRETENSE
feint in fencing / APPEL
feldspar / ALBITE; FELSPAR; ANDESINE
Félibrige writer / MISTRAL
felicitate / CONGRATULATE
felicitous / HAPPY; TIMELY
felicity / BLISS; APTNESS, DELIGHT, FITNESS
felid / CAT; LION, LYNX, PUMA; KITTY, TIGER; BOBCAT, JAGUAR,

KODKOD, MARGAY, OCELOT, SERVAL; CHEETAH, LEOPARD
feline / CAT; FELID. CATLIKE; STEALTHY
feline treat / CATNIP
fell / CUT, HEW. MOOR, PELT, SKIN. CRUEL; FIERCE, SAVAGE; PITILESS
fellah / PEASANT
felled tree barrier / ABATIS; ABATTIS
fellow / GUY, LAD; CHAP, MATE; EQUAL; GEEZER; COMRADE; COLLEAGUE
fellow feeling / PITY
fellow traveler / PINKO
fellowship / SOCIETY; BONHOMIE, INTIMACY, SODALITY; COMMUNION
felon / OUTLAW; CULPRIT, CONVICT, PANARIS, WHITLOW; CRIMINAL; PARONYCHIA
felonious burning / ARSON
felony / CRIME
felt / GROPED, SENSED
felt compunction / RUED; SMARTED
felt contrition / REPENTED
felt fabric / BAIZE
felt hat / FEDORA
feltlike / PANNOSE
feltwort / MULLEIN
felwort / GENTIAN
female / GIRL, LADY; WOMAN. DISTAFF; FEMININE
female, c.f. / GYNE, GYNO; GYNECO
female, suffix / ENNE, ETTE, TRIX
female ant / GYNE
female antelope / DOE
female bear / URSA
female bird / HEN
female buck / DOE
female chicken / HEN; BIDDY
female college student / COED
female deer / DOE, ROE, TEG; HIND
female demon / SUCCUBUS
female disciple / DORCAS; TABITHA
female elephant / COW; KOOMKIE
female ferret / JILL
female fowl less showy than the male / PEAHEN
female fox / VIXEN
female hog / SOW; GILT
female hormone / ESTROGEN
female horse / MARE
female Indian buffalo / ARNEE
female inheritor / HEIRESS
female institutional officer / MATRON
female kangaroo / GIN
female lobster / HEN
female mime / MIMA
female monster / GORGON
female performer / ARTISTE

female pig / SOW
female praying figure / ORANT
female prophet / SEERESS
female rabbit / DOE
female rat / DOE
female relative / MA; MOM, SIS; AUNT; MATER, NIECE; MOTHER, SISTER; DAUGHTER
female ruff / REE; REEVE
female salmon / HEN; RAUN
female seal / MATKA
female servant / HANDMAID
female sheep / EWE; EWES
female singer / ALTO, DIVA; SOPRANO; CONTRALTO
female sovereign / QUEEN; CZARINA, EMPRESS, TSARINA; MAHARANI, PRINCESS
female sponsor / GODMOTHER
female swan / PEN
female title / MS; MRS; DAME, MISS; MADAM; SENORA
female warrior / AMAZON
female wild buffalo / ARNEE
female yak / DRI, NAK
females / SHES
feminine / TENDER; WOMANLY
feminine garment / GOWN; DRESS, FROCK, SKIRT
feminine name / EVA, EVE; ALDA, AVIS, ENID, RITA; ADELA, AGNES, BETTY, EMILY, GRACE, LAURA, NORMA
feminine possessive / HERS
feminine pronoun / HER, SHE
feminine suffix / ESS, INA; ETTE
feminist / LIBBER
femme de chambre / CHAMBERMAID
femme fatale / VAMP; SIREN
femur / THIGHBONE
fen / BOG; MOSS; MARSH, SWAMP; MORASS
fence / GUARD; DEFEND; PROTECT, RAIL; BULWARK; BOUNDARY, RECEIVER
fence part / PALE, POST, RAIL; PALING, PICKET
fence post / STAKE
fence of shrubs / HEDGE
fence steps / STILE
fence of upright stakes / PALISADE
fencer / DUELIST; SWORDSMAN
fencer's cry / HAI, HAY; SASA; TOUCHE
fencer's dummy / PEL
fencer's movement / VOLT; LUNGE, VOLTE
fencer's shield / PLASTRON
fencing contest / DUEL
fencing hit / PUNTO
fencing position / CARTE; QUARTE, TIERCE; SECONDE, SEPTIME

fencing term / FORTE; FOIBLE, TOUCHE; RIPOSTE; TACAUTAC
fencing thrust / HAY; BUTT; APPEL, LUNGE, PUNTO; REMISE; REPRISE, RIPOSTE
fencing weapon / EPEE, FOIL, TUCK; SABER, SABRE, SWORD; RAPIER
fend / WARD; GUARD, PARRY; PROTECT
fender / CURB; COWCATCHER
fender bump / DENT
fenestra / HOLE; WINDOW; OPENING
fennel / HEMP, HERB; ANISE
fenny / MARSHY
Fenris' father / LOKI
Fenris' fetters / GLEIPNIR
Fenris' slayer / VIDAR
feracious / FERTILE
feral / WILD; DEADLY, FERINE, FIERCE, SAVAGE; UNTAMED
Ferber novel / SOBIG; SHOWBOAT
fere / MATE, PEER. STRONG
feria / HOLIDAYS
ferine / WILD; FERAL
ferity / BRUTALITY
ferment / BARM, ZYME; YEAST; HUBBUB, TUMULT. EXCITE; EFFERVESCE
fermentation vat / GYLE
fermented drink / ALE; BEER, MEAD, NIPA, WINE; CIDER, KVASS, PERRY; KUMISS
fermented palm juice / SURA
fern / HEII, NITO, PALA, PULU; BRAKE, NARDU; NARDOO; BRACKEN, ELKHORN; POLYPODY; MAIDENHAIR
fern leaf / FROND; CROSIER
fern root / ROI
fern seed / SORUS, SPORE
fern spore cluster / SORUS
ferntickle / FRECKLE
ferny underbrush / BRACKEN
ferocious / FELL, GRIM, WILD; CRUEL; BRUTAL, FIERCE, SAVAGE
ferocity / RAGE; VIOLENCE
Ferrara noble family / ESTE
ferret / PRY; SEARCH. HOB; POLECAT
ferrule / TIP
ferry / BOAT, FORD
ferry slip / DOCK
ferryboat / BAC; PONT
ferryman of Hades / CHARON
fertile / RICH; FECUND; FRUITFUL
Fertile Crescent lands / MESOPOTAMIA
fertile loam / LOESS
fertile spot / OASES, OASIS
fertilize / DRESS; IMPREGNATE
fertilize flowers / POLLINATE

fertilizer / MARL; GUANO; MANURE; NITRATE

fertilizer for the garden / COMPOST

ferule / ROD; RULER, STICK

fervency / ARDOR; VEHEMENCE

fervent / WARM; EAGER; ARDENT

fervid / HOT; FIERY; INTENSE

fervor / ZEAL, ZEST; ARDOR, FLAME

festal / GAY; JOYOUS; MIRTHFUL

festal paper discs / CONFETTI

fester / ROT; RANKLE; SUPPURATE

festination / HASTE, HURRY

festival / ALE, BEE; FAIR, FEIS, FETE, GALA; FEAST, FERIA, REVEL, TREAT; FIESTA, KERMES, KERMIS; BANQUET, HOLIDAY, KERMESS, KERMISS; CARNIVAL, JAMBOREE

festive / GAY; MERRY; CONVIVIAL

festive gathering / FETE; FEAST

festive spread / GALA

festive stepping / MASQUE; MASQUERADE

festivity / MIRTH; GAIETY; JOLLITY; FESTIVAL, HILARITY

festoon / LEI; SWAG; WREATH; GARLAND. DECORATE

fetch / GET; BRING, REACH. WRAITH

fete / HOLIDAY; FESTIVAL

feted / REGALED

fetid / OLID, RANK; STINKING

fetish / OBI; IDOL, JUJU, ZEME, ZEMI; CHARM, IMAGE, OBEAH; GRIGRI

fetor / FUST; STINK; MIASMA, STENCH

fetter / GYVE; CHAIN; SHACKLE. BIND; HINDER

fettle / BEAT, LINE, MULL. CONDITION

feud / FIEF, FRAY; BROIL

feud to the death / VENDETTA

feudal benefice / FEU

feudal estate / FEOD, FEUD, FIEF; CLASS

feudal jurisdiction / SOC; SOKE; FEOFF

feudal laborer / SERF; THEOW

feudal lord / LIEGE

feudal payment / TAC

feudal service / AVERA

feudal service, pert. to / BANAL

feudal tax / TAILAGE, TALLAGE

feudal tenant / VASSAL; SOCAGER

feudal tribute / HERIOT

fever / AGUE; PYREXIA

fever sore / HERPES

fever spot / PETECHIA

fever tree / BLUEGUM

fever type / AGUE; QUARTAN, TERTIAN

feverish / FEBRILE, FRANTIC

few / SOME; SCANT

few, c.f. / OLIG; OLIGO

fey / ELFIN; DOOMED

fez / TARBOOSH

fiasco / FLASK; FAILURE

fiat / EDICT, ORDER; DECREE

fib / LIE; FALSEHOOD; TARA-DIDDLE

fiber / BAST, HEMP, JUTE, PITA; DATIL, ISTLE, RAMIE, SISAL; RAFFIA, STAPLE, THREAD

fiber of century plant / PITA

fiber clusters in wool / NEP

fiber for cordage / DA; COIR, ERUC, FERU, HEMP, IMBE, JUTE, RHEA; ABACA, SISAL; AMBARY

fiber for hats / DATIL

fiber knot / NEP

fiber of peacock feathers / MARL

fiber plant / ALOE, FLAX, HEMP, IXLE, SANA, SUNN; CAROA, ISTLE, IXTLE, RAMIE, SISAL; COTTON

fiber refuse / KEMP

fiber wood / BAST

fiber of wool / PILE

fiberboard / MASONITE

fiberboard ingredient / BAGASSE

fibers to be made into thread / SLIVER

fibrillate / TWITCH

fibula / CLASP; LEGBONE

fickle / UNSTABLE, VARIABLE, VOLATILE, WAVERING

fickle lover / JILT

fickle month / APRIL

fiction / LIE; FANCY, NOVEL; FIGMENT, FORGERY

fictional / FABULOUS; LEGENDARY

fictional dog / BOB, JIP, LAD; ASTA; LASSIE

fictional name / DOE; ALIAS

fictional sailor / SINBAD

fictional story / TALE; FABLE; PARABLE, ROMANCE

fictitious / FALSE; UNREAL; FANCIFUL, INVENTED

fid / KEY; MARLINSPIKE

fiddle / VIOLIN. POTTER

fiddledeedee / NONSENSE

fidelity / TRUTH; HONESTY; DEVOTION, RELIANCE; CONSTANCY

fidgety / RESTIVE; RESTLESS

Fido / DOG; WATCHDOG

fiduciary / TRUSTEE

fie / SHAME

field / LEA; ACRE, AGER, WANG, WONG; CROFT, GLEBE; MEADOW

field of activity / METIER, OFFICE, SPHERE; DEPARTMENT

field bird / PLOVER

Field of Blood / ACELDAMA
field of combat / RINK; ARENA;
  TERRAIN; TILTYARD
field deity / PAN; FAUN; SILVANUS
field dog / HUNTER, SETTER
field duck / BUSTARD
field event / JUMP; THROW
field flower / DAISY, GOWAN
field glass / TELESCOPE;
  BINOCULARS
field of honor / DUEL
field of knowledge / KEN
field mouse / VOLE
field officer / MAJOR; COLONEL
field rat / KUSU; METAD
field of snow / FIRN, NEVE
field sport / JUMP; HUNTING;
  POLEVAULT
fieldfare / ROBIN
fieldwork / INTERVIEW
fiend / DEMON, DEVIL, SATAN;
  ADDICT
fiendish / CRUEL; MALIGN; DIA-
  BOLIC
fierce / GRIM, WILD; SAVAGE; VIO-
  LENT; RAVENOUS
fiery / HOT; ARDENT, FERVID;
  FERVENT, INTENSE; VEHEMENT
fiery cross / CRANTARA;
  CROSTARIE
fiery horse / STEED
fiesta / FETE; HOLIDAY; FESTIVAL
fifth finger / PINKY; PINKIE;
  MINIMUS
fig / SNAP; TRIFLE
fig leaf / MODESTY
fig marigold / SAMH; SEAFIG; ICE-
  PLANT
fig variety / BURMA, ELEME,
  ELEMI; SMYRNA
fight / ROW; CLEM, FRAY; MELEE,
  SCRAP, BOX; SPAR; STRIVE
fight against / REPEL; RESIST
fight back / RESIST
fight for / DEFEND
fight off / REPEL; REPULSE
fight official / REFEREE
fight for reform / CRUSADE
fight with swords / DUEL
fighter / BOXER; WARRIOR
fighter plane / SPAD, ZERO
fighting fish / BETTA
figurative / FLORID, ORNATE;
  FLOWERY, TYPICAL; ALLE-
  GORIC
figurative language / TROPE
figure / FORM, IDEA; DIGIT, IMAGE,
  PRICE, SHAPE, SOLID, TROPE;
  EFFIGY, EMBLEM, NUMBER,
  SYMBOL. COMPUTE; CALCULATE
figure of equal sides / ISAGON,
  ISOGON
figure of a god / IDOL

figure as pilaster / TELAMON;
  CARYATID
figure roughly / ESTIMATE
figure of speech / TROPE; SIMILE;
  ALLEGORY, METAPHOR
figured fabric / BATIK, PRINT; BAT-
  TIK, CALICO, DAMASK; PAISLEY
figurehead / FRONT
figurine / STATUE; STATUETTE
figwort / MULLEIN; TOADFLAX
Fiji capital / SUVA
Fiji discoverer / TASMAN
Fiji island / KORO, NGAU; VITILEVU
Fijian chestnut / RATA
Fijian fish / ONGU
Fijian tree / BURI
filament / FIBER; ELATER, THREAD
filament of a feather / DOWL
filament in the skin / HAIR
filbert / HAZELNUT
filbertlike fruit / COBNUT
filch / ROB; CRIB, HOOK; PINCH,
  STEAL, SWIPE; PILFER
file / ROW; RASP. ENTER; SCRAPE
file alphabetically / INDEX
file of documents / DOSSIER
filefish / TRIGGERFISH
filibeg / KILT
filibuster / BUCCANEER.
  HARANGUE
filigree / BASKETRY; ARABESQUE
filing envelope / FOLDER
filing folder projection / TAB
Filipino / see also Philippine
Filipino chief / DATTO; ILOCANO
Filipino food / BAHA, TARO
Filipino guerrilla / HUK
Filipino knife / BOLO
Filipino native / ATA; MORO; IGO-
  ROT; TAGALOG
Filipino peasant / TAO
Filipino servant / BATA
fill / CROWD, GORGE, STORE,
  STUFF
fill with air / BLOW; INFLATE
fill with cargo / LOADUP
fill to excess / GLUT, SATE;
  SATURATE
fill with fear / AWE; SCARE; DIS-
  MAY; TERRIFY; FRIGHTEN
fill a hole by sewing / DARN; PATCH
fill out / PAD; STUFF
fill with pride / SWELL
filled / FULL; REPLETE
filled with fissures / RIMOSE;
  AREOLAR
filled with reverence / AWED
filled space / SOLID; PLENUM
filler / ITEM; SPOUT; FUNNEL
fillet / BAND, ORLE; LISTEL
fillet under frieze / TAENIA,
  REGULA
fillet for hair / SNOOD

fillip / FLIP, SNAP; BRACER
filly / GAL; MARE
film / MIST; LAYER; CINEMA; NEGATIVE
film excerpt / CLIP
film fan / CINEAST
film-editing apparatus / MOVIOLA
filmy / GAUZY; CLOUDY
filose / THREADLIKE
filter / SIEVE. OOZE, SEEP; PURIFY
filth / DIRT, SMUT; GRIME, OFFAL
filthiness / SQUALOR; IMPURITY
filthy / FOUL, VILE; DIRTY, GROSS
filthy lucre / PELF; MAMMON
filthy place / STY
fimbriated / FRINGED
Fimbul winter's sequel / RAGNAROK
fin / FIVER; FLIPPER; BARNDOOR
final / LAST; ULTIMATE; CONCLUSIVE
final bit / LASTSTRAW
final desperation / LASTGASP
final discharge / QUIETUS
final examination / GREATGO
final goal / END; TERMINUS
final judgment / DOOM, FATE
final moves in chess / ENDGAME
final outcome / RESULT, UPSHOT
finale / BOW, END; CLOSE; FINISH
finale of symphony / CODA
finality / COMPLETENESS
finally / COMLPETELY, EVENTUALLY
financial / FISCAL; NUMMARY; MONETARY
financial disaster / CRASH
financial institution / BANK
financial instrument / DEED; MORTGAGE
finback / RORQUAL
finch / MORO; JUNCO, SERIN, TARIN; LINNET, SISKIN, TOWHEE; BUNTING
find / GAIN; CATCH; ATTAIN, DETECT, LOCATE, NOTICE
find the answer / SOLVE
find fault / NAG; CARP; CAVIL
find a new place / RELOCATE
find out / LEARN; DETECT, SEARCH
find position of / DISCOVER
find things out / PROBE
finder / LOCATOR
fine / KEEN, NICE, PURE, THIN; CLEAR, SHARP; DAINTY, MINUTE, PRETTY. MULCT; CLARIFY
fine china / SPODE
fine clothes / REGALIA
fine cotton fabric / MADRAS
fine cretonne / TOILE
fine dinnerware / CHINA
fine edging for fabric / GIMP; GALLOON

fine fabric / LAWN, SILK; SATIN
fine feathers / PLUMAGE
fine feeling / TASTE
fine-grained rock / SHALE
fine line in lettering / SERIF
fine linen / LAWN; DAMASK; CAMBRIC
fine for murder / CRO
fine feeling / TASTE
fine net / TULLE
fine parchment / VELLUM
fine performer / ARTIST; ARTISTE
fine powder / DUST
fine rain / DEW; MIST; SEREIN
fine sheer fabric / SWISS
fine silk netting / TULLE
fine stone / GEM
fine stone particles / SAND; GRAVEL
fine white clay / KAOLIN
fine wool / MERINO
fined / AMERCED
fine-feathered bird / EGRET; PEACOCK
finely ground fiber / FLOC; FLOCK
finely ground matter / MEAL; FLOUR
finer / NICER; SHARPER, THINNER
finery / FRILLS; REGALIA
finesse / RUSE; SKILL; ARTIFICE
finest / BEST
Fingal's bard / ULLIN
Fingal's dog / BRAN
Fingal's father / COMHAL
Fingal's kingdom / MORVEN
Fingal's mother / MORNA
Fingal's people / FENIANS
Fingal's realm / MORVEN
Fingal's son / FERGUS, OSSIAN
Fingal's sword / LUNO
fingent / FORMING, MOLDING
finger / DIGIT; POINTER. PAW; FEEL
finger bone / PHALANX
finger cymbal / CASTANET
finger game / MORA; MORRA
finger inflammation / FELON; AGNAIL
finger spelling / DACTYLOGRAPHY
fingerless glove / MITT; MITTEN
fingerling / PARR; MIDGET
fingernail / UNGUAL, UNGUIS
fingernail's crescent / LUNULE
fingerprint / LOOP; WHORL
fingerprint science / DACTYLOLOGY
finial / EPI; ORNAMENT
finial on pagoda / TEE
finical / NICE; FUSSY; DAINTY
finish / END; ENDING, FINALE
finish / DO; END; CLOSE; POLISH. FINALE
finish for cake / ICING
finish first / WIN

finish second / PLACE
finish third / SHOW
finished / OER; DONE, OVER; ENDED
finished edge / HEM; WELT; SELVAGE
finisher / EDGER, ENDER; PERFECTER
finishing line / GOAL, TAPE
finishing stroke of letter / SERIF
finite / BOUNDED, LIMITED
finjan holder / ZARF
Finland / SUOMI
Finland capital / HELSINKI; HELSINGFORS
Finland city / OULU; TAMPERE
Finland islands / ALAND
Finland Isthmus / KARELIA
Finland lake / INARI; SAIMAA
Finland port / ABO; PORI; TURKU; PORVOO
Finnish author / KIVI; CANTH
Finnish bath / SAUNA
Finnish composer / SIBELIUS
Finnish dialect / KAREL
Finnish epic poem / KALEVALA
Finnish god / JUMALA
Finnish money / MARKKA
Finnish musical instrument / KANTELE
Finnish poem / RUNE
Finnish underworld / TUONELA
Finno-Ugric language / VOT; LAPP; MAGYAR, OSTYAK
Finn's warriors / FENIANS
fiord / FJORD, INLET
fir genus / ABIES
fire / SHOOT; IGNITE, KINDLE. HEAT; ARDOR, FLAME; SPIRIT
fire, c.f. / PYR; IGNI
fire, pert. to / IGNEOUS
fire basket / CRESSET
fire bed / GRATE
fire bullet / TRACER
fire damp / METHANE
fire drill / CHARK
fire dweller / SALAMANDER
fire god / AGNI, ATAR, LOKI; VESTA; VULCAN
fire opal / GIRASOL
fire particle / EMBER, FLAME, SPARK
fire of passion / RAGA
fire warden / RANGER
fire whistle / ALARM, SIREN
fire worshipper / PARSI; PARSEE
firearm / GUN; RIFLE; MAUSER, PISTOL; CARBINE, SHOTGUN
firearm capsule / CARTRIDGE
firebrand / AGITATOR, MILITANT
firebug / PYROMANIAC
firecracker / SQUIB; PETARD
fired clay / TILE

firedog / ANDIRON
firedrake / DRAGON
fireman / STOKER
Firenze / FLORENCE
fireplace / HOB; GRATE, INGLE; HEARTH
fireplace part / HOB; SPIT; GRATE; HEARTH, MANTEL
fireplace shelf / HOB
fireplug / HYDRANT
fireside / HOME; INGLE; HEARTH
firewood / LOGS; BAVIN, FAGOT; CORDWOOD
firewood bundle / FAGOT
firework / CAP; GERB; SQUIB; ROCKET
firing pin / TIGE
firm / FAST, HARD; FIXED, SOLID; SECURE, STABLE. HOUSE; COMPANY, CONCERN
firm clasp / GRIP
firm as toast / CRISPEN
firmament / SKY; HEAVEN, WELKIN
firmly / FAST; SECURELY
firmly embedded / ROOTED
firmly established / INSOLID
firmly united / SOLID; WELDED
firmness / CERTAINTY, STABILITY
firmness of mind / CONSTANCY
firn / NEVE
first / CHIEF, PRIME; MAIDEN; CAPITAL, INITIAL; ORIGINAL, PRIMEVAL, PRISTINE
first, pref. / PROTO
first aid box / KIT
first American-born / DARE
first appearance / BOW; DEBUT; VERNISSAGE
first choice / PICK; ELITE; REFUSAL
first class / AONE; EXCELLENT
first classman / PLEBE; FRESHMAN
first finger / INDEX
first five books of Bible / TORAH; PENTATEUCH
first fruits / ANNATES
first game in a series / OPENER
first gift / HANDSEL
first high priest / AARON
first king of Israel / SAUL
first letter / ALPHA; INITIAL
first man / ADAM, ASKE, YAMA
first man in space / GAGARIN
first metric pattern in longer piece / STROPHE
first murderer / CAIN
first part in chorus / PRIMO
first performance / DEBUT; PREMIERE
first pope / PETER
first principle / ABC; SEED; ARCHE; RUDIMENT
first rate / ACE; PRIME, SUPER
first showing / PREMIERE

first team / VARSITY; REGULARS
first wife of Adam / LILITH
first wife of Jude the Obscure / ARABELLA
first year cadet / PLEBE
first year midshipman / MIDDIE
first year's revenue / ANNATS; ANNATES
first-born / HEIR; EIGNE; ELDEST
first-grade subject / ABCS
firsthand / NEW; AUTHENTIC, DIRECTLY
firth / KYLE; FRITH; ESTUARY
fiscal / BURSAL; FINANCIAL
fish / ANGLE, TRAWL, TROLL; SEARCH
fish, pert. to / PISCINE; ICHTHYAL, ICHTHYIC; PISCATORY
fish of Atlantic / CUSK, HAKE, SCUP, SHAD; TAUTOG; ESCOLAR, HERRING; MENHADEN
fish basket / WEEL; CREEL
fish from boat / HARL; TRAWL, TROLL
fish cleaner / SCALER
fish condiment / PASTE
fish delicacy / ROE; CAVIAR
fish eggs / ROE; SPAWN
fish hawk / OSPREY
fish horde / SHOAL; SCHOOL
fish measure / MEASE; BARREL
fish with a moving lure / TROLL
fish net / SEINE; SAGENE
fish with net / SEINE, TRAWL
fish part / FIN; BONE; SCALE
fish pickle / ALEC
fish poison / CUBE
fish poisoning / CIGUATERA
fish portion / FILET, STEAK; FILLET
fish prong / PEW; GAFF, PUGH
fish propeller / FIN; TAIL
fish relish / GARUM; CAVIAR; BOTARGO
fish and rice dish / KEDGEREE
fish sauce / ALEC
fish scraper / SCALER
fish spear / GIG; GAFF; HARPOON
fish stew / BOUILLABAISSE
fish that sticks on another / RE-MORA; PEGADOT
fish trap / WEEL, WEIR; EELPOT
fish variety / ID; COD, DAB, EEL, GAR, IDE, RAY; BASS, CARP, CHUB, DACE, HAKE, HIKU, LIJA, LING, MADO, MASU, OPAH, ORFE, PARR, PETO, PIKE, POGY, RUDD, SHAD, SOLE, TUNA, ULUA; PERCH, SCROD, SHARK, SKATE, SPRAT, TROUT, TUNNY; CONGER, DARTER, MULLET, SAL-MON, SENNET, TARPON, TOM-COD, WRASSE; HADDOCK, SAR-DINE; MACKEREL, STURGEON

fish whisker / BARBEL
fish of zodiac / PISCES
fish-eating bird / AUK; HERON; PELICAN
fish-eating mammal / OTTER
fisher / PEKAN; ANGLER, MARTEN, SEINER, WEJACK; PISCATOR
fisher for congers / EELER
fisherman / ANGLER, SEINER
fisherman's aid / BAIT, LINE, WORM
fisherman's basket / WEEL; CREEL
fishhook / GIG; BARB, GAFF, GAPE; ANGLE, DRAIL, KIRBY
fishhook array / GIG; TROTLINE
fishhook money / LARI; LARIN
fishhook part / BARB
fishing bait / WORM; HELL-GRAMITE
fishing bait resting on bottom / LEGER; LEDGER
fishing basket / CREEL
fishing boat / DORY, TROW; SMACK; DOGGER; TRAWLER
fishing device / NET, ROD; LINE, POLE, REEL, WEIR; FLOAT
fishing gear / TEW; TACKLE
fishing grounds / HAAF; BANKS
fishing line / TROT
fishing line cork / BOB; FLOAT, QUILL
fishing line leader / SNELL
fishing net / FYKE; SEINE, TRAWL; SAGENE; SPILLER
fishing pole / ROD
fishing sloop / SMACK
fishing worm / CRAWLER, TAGTAIL
fishlike mammal / ORC; WHALE; DOLPHIN; PORPOISE
fishline / TROT; SNELL, TRAWL, TROLL
fish-poison tree / BITO, CUBE, HURA, KUMU, NEKA; CUSPA; ASSACA
fish's breathing organ / GILL
fishy / DULL; VACANT; QUESTION-ABLE
fissile rock / SHALE, SLATE; SCHIST
fission element / PLUTONIUM
fissure / GAP; ABRA, RENT, RIFT, SEAM; CHASM, CHINK, CLEFT, CRACK
fissure in pipe / LEAK
fist / HAND, NEAF, NEIF; INDEX, NIEVE
fist fight / MILL
fit / APT; ABLE, MEET, RIPE, WELL; DECENT, PROPER. MESH, SUIT; ADAPT, EQUIP. SPASM; CAPRICE
fit of anger / PET; TANTRUM
fit an arrow / NOCK
fit of chills / AGUE
fit clothing to / TAILOR

fit to eat / EDIBLE; EATABLE
fit for farming / ARABLE
fit for food / EDIBLE; ESCULENT
fit of fury / RAGE
fit for human consumption / ED-
IBLE; POTABLE
fit inside / NEST
fit to a mortise / TENON
fit out / EQUIP; OUTFIT; PREPARE
fit of peevishness / PET; HUFF
fit to sail / SEAWORTHY
fit with tackling / RIG
fit time / OCCASION; OPPOR-
TUNITY
fit together / MESH; MITER, PIECE
fit well / SUIT
fit to work / ABLE
fitchew / FITCH; POLECAT
fitful / FICKLE; MUTABLE
fitted / SUITED; ADAPTED
fitted garment / REEFER
fitting / APT, PAT; PROPER; APPRO-
PRIATE
fitting in behavior / GOOD, NICE;
DECENT
fitting tightly / SNUG
Fiume / RIEKA; RIJEKA
five in card game / PEDRO
five dollar bill / CEE, FIN, VEE;
FIVER
five franc coin / ECU
five as a group / PENTAD; QUINTET
five iron / MASHIE
Five Nations / IROQUOIS
Five Towns / POTTERIES
five working days / WEEK
five-faced solid / WEDGE; PYRAMID
five-sided plane figure / PENTAGON
five-year period / LUSTER;
LUSTRUM
five-year-old red deer / STAG
fix / SET, TIE; MEND; ADJUST, RE-
PAIR, SETTLE. PREDICAMENT
fix firmly / ROOT; ANCHOR;
ESTABLISH
fix in the ground / SET; EMBED,
PLANT
fix worth of / RATE; ASSESS
fixation / MANIA; OBSESSION,
STABILITY
fixed / SET; FIRM; STABLE, STEADY
fixed charge / FEE; RATE; PRICE
fixed income / RENTE; ANNUITY,
PENSION
fixed measure / RATE
fixed pay / WAGE; SALARY;
STIPEND
fixed regard / ATTENTION
fixed routine / RUT; ROTE
fixed salary / STIPEND
fixed time / ERA; DATE, KIST, TERM;
EPOCH; APPOINTMENT
fixed value on / ASSESSED

fixing / OUTFIT; ORNAMENT;
APPARATUS
fixings / MAKINGS; TRIMMINGS
fizzle / FIASCO; CONFUSION. FAIL
fjord / FIORD
Fjorgynn's son / THOR
flabbergast / AMAZE; ASTOUND;
ASTONISH
flabby / WEAK; FLESHY; FLACCID
flaccid / LAX; LIMP, SOFT; FLABBY
flag / IRIS, JACK; BANNER, COL-
ORS, ENSIGN, GUIDON, PEN-
NON, PENNANT. SAG; PINE,
SINK; SIGNAL
flag in mourning / HALFMAST;
HALFSTAFF
flag as symbol / EMBLEM
flagellant / PENITENTE
flagellate / FLOG, LASH, WHIP
flageolet / FLUTE; LARIGOT
flagitious / WICKED
flagon / EWER; CARAFE
flagpole / MAST; STAFF
flag-raising's island / IWO
flagrant / RANK; GROSS; CRYING
flag's free end / FLY
flag's upper corner / UNION;
CANTON
flagstaff / MAST, POLE
flagstone / SHALE, SLATE; PAVING
flail / BEAT; THRESH
flair / SENSE; TALENT; DISCERN-
MENT
flake / CHIP, PEEL; SCALE
flaky / CRAZY, SCALY; LAMINAR;
SQUAMOUS
flaky mineral / MICA; ISINGLASS,
MUSCOVITE
flam / CHEAT, TRICK. FALSE. LIE
flambeau / LIGHT, TORCH
flamboyant / SHOWY; ORNATE
flame / ARDOR; BLAZE, FERVOR.
HEAT; EXCITE
flame flower / AZALEA
flame up brightly / FLARE
flamen / PRIEST
flamenco / GYPSY
flaming / AFIRE, AGLOW, FLAMY;
BLAZING
flaming light / TORCH
flan / CAKE; CUSTARD
Flanders city / LILLE
flange / RIM
flank / LEER, LOIN, SIDE. SKIRT
flannel / NOG; LANA; WASHRAG
flannelmouth / CATFISH
flap / TAB; FOLD, LOMA, SLAT,
WING. SLAP
flapjack / PANCAKE; WHEATCAKE
flapper / DUCK; CUTIE; CHICKEN,
FLIPPER
flare / BLAZE, GLARE. FUSEE,
FUZEE

flare out / RING
flared edge / LIP; FLANGE
flaring / BRIGHT, FLASHY
flaring tenons / DOVETAILS
flash / BLAZE, GLINT. GLEAM, SPARK. SHAM
flash of lightning / BOLT; LEVIN
flashlight / TORCH
flashy / GAUDY, SHOWY; SPORTY, TAWDRY
flashy set of wheels / SPORTSCAR
flask / JUG; OLPE, VIAL; CANTEEN
flat / LOW, DULL, EVEN, TAME; LEVEL, PLAIN, PLANE, VAPID; SMOOTH; INSIPID, PROSAIC, SHALLOW. SHOAL; APARTMENT
flat on one's back / SUPINE
flat breastboned / RATITE
flat cap / TAM; BERET
flat disc / RECORD; PLATTER
flat molding / FILLET
flat in music / MOL; MOLLE
flat part of step / TREAD
flat piece of floating ice / FLOE
flat projection / LEDGE, SHELF
flat for rent / ROOMS
flat round piece / DISC, DISK, PUCK; PLATE
flat surface / AREA; PLANE
flat and unmusical / TONELESS
flatboat sailor / BARGEE
flat-bottomed boat / ARK; DORY, KEEL, PUNT, SCOW; BARGE; BATEAU; PONTOON
flatfish / DAB, RAY; SOLE; BRILL, FLUKE, SKATE; PLAICE, TURBOT; HALIBUT, PETRALE; FLOUNDER
flatiron / SADIRON
flatten glass / PANE; PLATTEN
flatten out / AVERAGE, DEPRESS
flattened / OBLATE; PLANATE
flattener for roadway / ROLLER
flatter / PALP; PLEASE; BLANDISH, PERSUADE
flatter servilely / ADULATE
flatterer / TOADY; PARASITE; SYCOPHANT
flattery / BLARNEY; CAJOLERY
flat-topped hill / MESA, MOOR; PLATEAU
flat-topped ridge / LOMA
flaunt / BRAG; BOAST; BRANDISH
flavor / GUST, SALT, TANG, ZEST; AROMA, SAPOR, SMACK. LACE; SEASON
flavor enhancer / MSG; CONDIMENT
flavored with mint / SAGY
flavorer / SPICE; CONDIMENT
flavorful / SAPID
flavoring / ORGEAT; EXTRACT
flavoring plant / HERB, LEEK, MACE, MINT, SAGE; ANISE, BASIL; LICORICE

flavorless / FLAT; VAPID
flavorsome / TASTY; SAPOROUS
flaw / RIFT, SPOT; BREAK, CLEFT, CRACK, FAULT, SPECK; DEFECT
flawless / IDEAL; PERFECT
flax / LIN
flax cleaner / HATCHEL
flax fabric / TOW; LINEN
flax fiber / TOW
flax filament / HARL; HARLE
flaxen fabric / LINEN; DAMASK
flaxseed / LINSEED
flay / BEAT, CANE, SKIN; REPROVE
flayed god / XIPE
flea / CHIGOE, INSECT, JIGGER; DAPHNIA
Fleance's father / BANQUO
fleche / POINT, SPIRE
fleck / SPOT; STREAK. VARIEGATE
fled / ESCAPED
fledgling / FRY; NESTLING; STRIPLING
flee / LAM, RUN; AVOID; HASTEN, VANISH; SCATTER
flee instantly / BOLT
flee to wed / ELOPE
fleece / ABB; FELL, WOOL. ROB; CHEAT
fleeced / SHORN; SWINDLED
fleecy / WOOLLY
fleer / MOCK; SCOFF, SNEER
fleet / RAPID, SWIFT. NAVY
fleet animal / DEER, HARE; CHEETAH
fleet Greek girl / ATALANTA
fleet horse / RACER; COURSER
fleet of small ships / FLOTILLA
fleeting / PASSING; TRANSIENT
fleetness / SPEED; CELERITY
flemish / COIL
Flemish geographer / MERCATOR
Flemish painter / MASSYS, RUBENS; TENIERS
flense / CUT; STRIP
flesh / BODY, MEAT, PULP
flesh, pert. to / CARNOSE
flesh of cattle / BEEF, VEAL
flesh of deer / VENISON
flesh food / STEAK; HAMBURGER
flesh hides / SLATE
flesh of hog / HAM; PORK; BACON
flesh kneader / MASSEUR
flesh of sheep / LAMB; MUTTON
flesh-eating mammal / CARNIVORE
flesher / BUTCHER, SCRAPER
fleshiness / CORPULENCE
fleshly / CARNAL; SENSUAL
fleshy / FAT; GROSS, OBESE, PLUMP
fleshy fruit / POME; BACCA, DRUPE
fleshy projection of palate / UVULA
fleshy underground stem / ROOT; TUBER; RHIZOME

Fletcher's partner / BEAUMONT
fleur de lis / LIS, LYS; IRIS, LISS
flew / SOARED, WINGED
flex / BEND. CABLE
flexibility / EASE
flexible / LITHE; DOCILE, PLIANT, SUPPLE; AFFABLE
flexible leather strip / BELT; STRAP
flexible link / TIE
flexible pipe / HOSE
flexible twig / OSIER, WITHE; RATTAN, WICKER
flexuous / ZIGZAG; SINUOUS
flick / FLIP, WHIP; STREAK
flicker / FLARE, WAVER; FLUTTER
flickering / ERRATIC, LAMBENT
flier / PILOT; PLUNGE, AVIATOR
flight / FLOCK; EXODUS, HEGIRA
flight, c.f. / AERO
flight essential / WING
flight of steps / STAIRCASE
flight of wild fowl / SKEIN
flightless bird / EMU, MOA; KIWI, RHEA, WEKA; OSTRICH, PENGUIN
flight's start / TAKEOFF
flighty / WILD; GIDDY; VOLATILE
flimflam / TRICK; DECEPTION. SHIFTY
flimsiest / SCANTIEST
flimsy / THIN, WEAK; FRAIL; SLIGHT; FOOLISH, SHALLOW
flinch / SHY; COWER, QUAIL
fling / SHY; CAST, DART, HURL
flint / CHERT; QUARTZ; IMPLEMENT
flint scraper / RACLOIR; GRATTOIR
flintlock / FUSIL; MUSKET; HARQUEBUS
flinty / HARD; OBDURATE
flip / SNAP, TOSS; FLICK. FILLIP
flippant / BOLD, GLIB, PERT; FORWARD
flirt / OGLE, WINK. JILT; COQUETTE
flirtatious / COY
flit / GAD; DART, SKIM; HOVER; FLUTTER
float / WAFT; DRIFT, GLIDE. BUOY, CORK, RAFT
float upward / FLY; RISE, SOAR
float in water / SAIL, SWIM
floating / AWASH; NATANT; DRIFTING
floating bridge / PONTOON
floating ice / BERG, FLOE; GROWLER
floating lily leaf / PAD
floating matter / FLOTSAM
floating Nile vegetation / SUDD
floating ocean organisms / PLANKTON
floating platform / RAFT

floating vessel / BOAT, SHIP; BARGE, CANOE
floating zoo / ARK
floccillation / CARPHOLOGY
flocculent / WOOLY
flock / HERD, PACK; CROWD, TROOP
flock, pert. to / GREGAL; GREGARIOUS
flock of flying geese / SKEIN
flock of herons / SEDGE, SIEGE
flock of quail / BEVY
flock of swimming geese / GAGGLE
flock of wild fowl / TRIP
flog / BEAT, CANE, LASH, WHIP
flood / SEA; EAGRE, SPATE; DELUGE; FRESHET. INUNDATE, SUBMERGE
flood hero / MANU, NOAH; COXCOX; DEUCALION
floodgate / CLOW; SLUICE; PENSTOCK
floor / LEVEL, STORY
floor cloth / MOP
floor covering / MAT, RUG; CARPET; LINOLEUM
floor mat / DRUGGET
floor show / CABARET
flooring material / TILE
flora / PLANTS; FLOWERS; VEGETATION
flora and fauna / LIFE; BIOTA
Florence / FIRENZE
Florentine cathedral / DUOMO
Florentine family / MEDICI
Florentine gallery / UFFIZI
Florentine iris / IREOS, ORRIS
Florentine museum / BARGELLO
Florentine palace / PITTI
florid / RUDDY; ORNATE; FLOWERY
florid style / ROCOCO
Florida cape / KENNEDY; CANAVERAL
Florida capital / TALLAHASSEE
Florida city / MIAMI, OCALA, TAMPA
Florida discoverer / PONCEDELEON
Florida fish / SALENA, TARPON; SNAPPER, MACKEREL
Florida Indian / CALUSA; SEMINOLE
Florida islands / KEYS
Florida lake / OKEECHOBEE
Florida national park / EVERGLADES
Florida river / STJOHNS
Florida state nickname / SUNSHINE; EVERGLADE
flory / VAIN; POMPOUS
floss / SILK; THREAD
flotilla / FLEET; ARMADA
flotsam / DRIFTER; WRECKAGE
flounce / TRIM; FURBELOW

flounder / DAB; PLAICE; FLATFISH.
ROLL
flour / ATA; ATTA; MEAL; FARINA
flour beetle / WEEVIL
flour container / BIN
flour sifter / BOLTER
flourish / GROW; WAVE; BOAST,
WIELD; THRIVE; BLOSSOM. FAN-
FARE, ROULADE
flourish boldly / BRANDISH
flourish of trumpets / BLARE; FAN-
FARE, TANTARA
flourishing / FRIM; THRIVING,
VIGOROUS
flout / DEFY, JEER, MOCK, SNEER;
INSULT
flow / RUN; SPREAD. FLUX;
ABUNDANCE
flow, c.f. / RRHEA
flow back / EBB; RECEDE
flow in cadence / LILT
flow copiously / POUR
flow forth / ERUPT; EMANATE
flow from / ISSUE
flow noisily / BABBLE, GURGLE
flow out / DRAIN, SPILL
flow of rhythm / CADENCE
flow steadily / RUN; STREAM
flow of water / FLOOD, RIVER;
STREAM
flower / BLOOM, ELITE, PRIME;
BLOSSOM
flower, pert. to / FLORAL
flower of bean family / WISTARIA
flower beetle / CHAFER
flower bud / KNOT
flower bunch / POSY; BOUQUET,
NOSEGAY
flower cluster / CYME; UMBEL;
CORYMB, RACEME
flower container / POT, URN; VASE
flower dust / POLLEN
flower in early spring / BUD
flower emanation / AROMA, SMELL;
FRAGRANCE
flower envelope / PERIANTH
flower extract / ATAR, OTTO; AT-
TAR, OTTAR
flower of forgetfulness / LOTUS
flower garland / ANADEM; CHAPLET
flower goddess / FLORA
flower head / CAPITULUM
flower holder / URN; VASE
flower leaf / BRACT
flower organ / PISTIL, STAMEN
flower part / BRACT, PETAL, SEPAL;
ANTHER, CARPEL, PISTIL, STA-
MEN; COROLLA; PERICARP
flower pistil / CARPEL
flower plot / BED; GARDEN
flower pot / JARDINIERE
flower spike / AMENT; SPADIX

flower stalk / PETIOLE
flower stand / EPERGNE
flower turning to sun / HELIOTROPE
flower variety / LILY, ROSE; DAISY,
LILAC, PEONY, PHLOX, POPPY;
DAHLIA
flower-eating / ANTHOPHAGOUS
flowering evergreen / OLEANDER
flowerless plant / IVY; FERN, MOSS;
FUNGUS, LICHEN
flowerlike / ANTHOID
flowers' visitor / BEE
flower-shaped ornament / LIS;
FLEURON, ROSETTE
flowery / ORNATE; EMBELLISHED
flowery kingdom / CHINA
flowing / FLUENT; COPIOUS
flowing alongside / PRETERLABENT
flowing and ebbing / TIDAL
flowing forth / EMANENT
flowing garment / CAPE, ROBE
flu / INFLUENZA
fluctuate / VARY; WAVER; UNDU-
LATE
flue / DUCT, LINT, PIPE; CHIMNEY
fluent / GLIB; LIQUID; COPIOUS
fluff / NAP; LINT. SPREAD
fluffy / downy; feathery
fluid / SAP; WHEY; JUICE, SERUM;
LIQUID
fluid rock / LAVA, SLAG
fluidity unit / RHE
fluke / BARB; ACCIDENT; TREMA-
TODE
flume / CHUTE; SLUICE; CHANNEL
flummery / TRASH; EMPTINESS
flunk / FAIL; SHIRK
flunky / SNOB; LACKEY, MENIAL;
HIRELING
flurried / EXCITED; AGITATED
flurry / WORRY; RUFFLE; FLUSTER,
ADO; TODO; HURRY
flush / GLOW; BLOOM, BLUSH;
REDDEN. EVEN; ABUNDANT
flushed / RED
Flushing Meadow event / WORLDS-
FAIR
fluster / FUDDLE; AGITATE,
CONFUSE
flute / BIN, NAY; FIFE; PUNGI;
GROOVE; MATALAN
flute, c.f. / AULO
flute player / FLUTIST; FLAUTIST
flute stop / VENTAGE
fluted / CORRUGATED
flutelike instrument / QUILL;
SYRINX; PANPIPE; FLAGEOLET
flutelike overtone / HARMONIC
fluting / PIPING; CHAMFER,
GADROON
flutter / FLAP, FLIT; VIBRATE
fluttering / PITAPAT

flux / FLOW, FUSE, MELT. DYSEN-
TERY
fly / FLEE, FLIT, SOAR, WAVE,
WING; AVIATE, DECAMP. FLAP,
GNAT; MIDGE; BOTFLY, TSETSE
fly agaric / AMANITA
fly alone / SOLO
fly ball / POPUP
fly block / PULLEY
fly for fishing / DUN; HERL; ALDER;
CAHILL, CLARET, HACKLE
fly high / SOAR
fly larva / BOT; BOTT; MAGGOT
fly in the ointment / CATCH
fly before the wind / SCUD; SPANK
flyaway / GIDDY; UNSTEADY.
MIRAGE
flycatcher / TODY; POWEE;
PHOEBE, SUNDEW; KISKADEE
flyer / PILOT; AVIATOR; HANDBILL
flying / AVIATION. VOLANT; VOLI-
TANT
flying boat / SEAPLANE
flying colors / SUCCESS, VICTORY
flying device / KITE; GLIDER; BAL-
LOON
Flying Dutchman composer /
WAGNER
flying expert / ACE
flying fettle / YARAK
flying field / AIRDROME
flying fish / GURNARD
flying fox / KALONG
flying island / LAPUTA
flying lemur / COLUGO
flying limb / WING
flying machine / JET; PLANE; AIR-
PLANE; HELICOPTER
flying mammal / BAT
flying saucer / UFO
flying spray / SPINDRIFT
flyspeck / IOTA, MOTE
foam / SUDS; FROTH, SPRAY,
SPUME; LATHER
foamy yeast on liquor / BARM
fob / CHEAT. PENDANT
focus / ADJUST; CONVERGE.
CENTER
fodder / FEED; GRASS; FORAGE,
SILAGE
fodder pit / SILO
fodder plant / ERS; VETCH;
ALFALFA
fodder stored in a silo / HAY;
SILAGE
fodder tower / SILO, TANK
fodder trough / BIN; CRIB;
MANGER
foe / ENEMY; OPPONENT
fog / HAR, RAG; HAAR, HAZE,
MIST; BRUME, VAPOR; PEASOUP
foggy / HAZY; OBTUSE; OBSCURE

foggy rain / MIST; DRIZZLE
foghorn / SIREN, SYREN; SIRENE
foible / FAULT; DEFECT; WEAK-
NESS
foil / BALK; CHECK; BAFFLE. EPEE
foil for comic / BANANA, STOOGE
foison / VIGOR; HARVEST;
STRENGTH
foist / FOB; PALM; MISPLACE.
BARGE
fold / LOOP, SEAM, WRAP; CREASE,
RIMPLE; ENVELOP. LAP; FLAP,
RUGA
fold of cloth / PLY; PLAIT, PLEAT
fold of neck skin / DEWLAP
fold over / HEM, LAP
fold on ruminant's throat / DEWLAP
folded / PLIED; PLICATE
folded once / FOLIO
folded twice / QUARTO
folderol / FALDEROL
folding bed / COT
folding money / DOLLAR; DOLLARS
folding seat / XCHAIR
folding stand / EASEL
foliage / LEAVES; VERDURE
foliage plant / IVY; FERN; COLEUS;
ASPIDISTRA; PHILODENDRON
folio / LEAF, PAGE; NUMBER
foliole / LEAFLET
folk / RACE; MASSES; SERVANTS
folk tale / MARCHEN
folklore / BELIEF, CUSTOM;
TRADITION
folks / PEOPLE; PERSONS
folkways / MORES
follow / DOG, TAG; COPY, OBEY,
TAIL; CHASE, ENSUE, TRACE
follow after / TRAIL; PURSUE
follow close behind / HEEL;
SHADOW
follow game / STALK
follow orders / OBEY; COMPLY
follow tenaciously / DOG
followed a clue / SLEUTHED
follower / FAN, IST, ITE; DISCIPLE,
HENCHMAN, IMITATOR
follower, suff. / IST, ITE
follower of Arius / ARIAN
follower of Attila / HUN
follower of Christ / DISCIPLE;
CHRISTIAN
follower of fashion / MODIST
follower of Garibaldi / REDSHIRT
follower of Zeno / STOIC
following / SECT; METIER. NEXT;
AFTER
follow-up / SEQUEL
folly / SIN; NONSENSE, RASHNESS
foment / ABET, STIR; INSTIGATE
Fomorian defeat / MOYTURA
Fomorian deity / BALOR

fond / DOTING, LOVING; DEVOTED

fond stroke / PAT

fond of women / UXORIOUS; PHILOGYNOUS

fondle / PET; CARESS, COCKER, CUDDLE

fondness / LOVE; TASTE; LIKING, RELISH; APPETITE; AFFECTION

font / LAVER, STOUP; ORIGIN, SOURCE

font of Muses / HIPPOCRENE

Fontenoy victor / SAXE

food / CHOW, DIET, FARE, GRUB, MEAT, RICE; BREAD; FORAGE, VIANDS; ALIMENT; VICTUALS

food, c.f. / SITO

food for all / WHEAT

food for birds / SEED, SUET, WORM

food for colt / MARESMILK

food element / PROTEIN, VITAMIN

food fish / COD, EEL; BASS, CARP, CERO, HAKE, LING, PIKE, SCUP, SHAD, SOLE, SPOT, TUNA; HILSA, SCROD, SMELT, TROUT, TUNNY; MULLET, PLAICE, RO-BALO, SALEMA, SALMON, TURBOT; ALEWIFE, HALIBUT, POMPANO, SARDINE, SNAPPER; MACKEREL

food of the gods / AMRITA; AMBROSIA

food for growing culture / AGAR

food of Hawaii / POI

food from heaven / MANNA

food of the indolent / LOTUS

food list / MENU; CARTE

food material / PEA; BEAN, CORN, OATS, RICE; WHEAT; TAPIOCA

food meat / BEEF, FOWL, LAMB, PORK, VEAL

food merchant / GROCER; BUTCHER; VICTUALER

food morsel / ORT; BITE

food in New Zealand / KAIKAI

food plant / taro; vegetable

food poisoning / ptomaine

food in Polynesia / KAI

food portion / RATION

food queue of '30s / BREADLINE

food regimen / DIET

food room / PANTRY, SPENCE

food for soldiers / RATION

food staple / RICE; BREAD, WHEAT

food starch / SAGO; TAPIOCA; ARROWROOT

fool / ASS, OAF; DOLT, GABY, RACA, SIMP, ZANY; CLOWN, DUNCE; JESTER; BUFFOON. DUPE; DECEIVE

foolery / FOLLY; NONSENSE; HORSEPLAY

foolhardy / RASH; HEADLONG, RECKLESS

fooling / BANTER; MUMMERY

foolish / MAD; DAFT, IDLE, SELY, VAIN, ZANY; BATTY, DAFFY, IN-ANE, INEPT, SEELY, SILLY; ABSURD

foolish fellow / SAP; SIMP; DUMMY; NOODLE

foolish person / ASS, SAP; DOTARD; SIMPLETON

foolish talk / DRIVEL; BLATHER, PRATTLE

foolishness / FOLLY; FATUITY; NONSENSE, TOMMYROT

fool's bauble / MAROTTE

fool's gold / PYRITE

fool's headdress / CAPANDBELLS

fool's paradise / DELUSION, ILLUSION

foot / PAW; BASE, IAMB

foot, c.f. / POD; PEDE, PODO

foot, pert. to / PEDAL

foot ailment / CORN, WART; BUN-ION, CALLUS

foot of animal / PAD, PAW; HOOF

foot of a column / PEDESTAL

foot covering / BOOT, SHOE, SOCK

foot extremity / TOE; HEEL

foot of insect / TARSUS

foot lever / PEDAL; TREADLE

foot part / ARCH; INSTEP

foot in poetry / IAMB; PAEON; DACTYL, IAMBUS; ANAPEST, SPONDEE, TROCHEE

foot soldier / KERN, PEON; INFANTRYMAN

foot soldiers / INFANTRY

foot specialist / PODIATRIST; CHIROPODIST

foot of three syllables / DACTYL; ANAPEST

foot traveler / HIKER; PEDESTRIAN

foot of two syllables / IAMB; PYRRHIC, SPONDEE, TROCHEE

football / BLADDER, PIGSKIN

football field / OVAL, ARENA; STADIUM; GRIDIRON

football kick / DROP, PUNT; PLACEMENT

football pass / FORWARD, LATERAL

football play / KICK, PASS; REVERSE

football player / END; GUARD; CENTER, TACKLE; HALFBACK; LINEBACKER; QUARTERBACK

football team / ELEVEN

football term / DOWN; SAFETY

footboy / PAGE; LACKEY; ATTENDANT

footed vase / URN

footfall / STEP; TREAD

footing / BASIS; STATUS; FOUNDATION

footless / FREE; APODAL

footless animal / APOD; APODE
footlights / STAGE
footlike part / PES
footling / SILLY; TRIVIAL
footloose / FREE; ROVING
footnote / GLOSS; COMMENT
footpad / GOON, THUG; MUGGER; HIGHWAYMAN
footpath of canal / TOWPATH
footprint / TRACK; FOOTFALL
foots / DREGS; SEDIMENT
footstalk of leaf / STRIG; PETIOLE
footstep / MARK; TRACE, TREAD
footstool / HASSOCK, OTTOMAN, TABORET
footway / PATH, WALK; TRAIL
footwear / BOOTS, SHOES, SOCKS
footwear insert for shaping / SHOETREE
footwiper / MAT
foozle / BUNGLE
fop / BEAU, DUDE; DANDY, SWELL
foppish / COXCOMBICAL
for / BY, TO; PRO; SINCE; BECAUSE
for each / PER; APIECE
for example / AS, EC, EG, SO
for fear that / LEST
for instance / AS, EG
for men only / STAG
for the most part / GENERALLY
for a reason / SO; THEREFORE
for shame / FIE
for what reason / WHY
For Whom The Bell Tolls character / PILAR
forage / FODDER
forage plant / ERS; GUAR; GRASS, SULLA; ALSIKE, LUCERN; ALFALFA
foramen / PORE; FENESTRA
foray / RAVAGE; PILLAGE. RAID
forbear / HOLD; AVOID, CEASE, PAUSE; DESIST, ENDURE
forbearance / MERCY; ABSTI- NENCE, TOLERATION
forbearing / PATIENT; TOLERANT
forbid / BAN; TABU, VETO; TABOO; ENJOIN, OPPOSE
forbiddance of atomic explosion / TESTBAN
forbidden / TABU, TREF; TABOO; TEREFA; ILLICIT
forbidden city / LHASA, MECCA; PEKING
forbidden fruit / FIG; APPLE
forbidden land / TIBET
forbidding / GRIM; STERN; UNPLEASANT
force / VIM, VIS; ARMY, DINT, HOST; DRIVE, MIGHT, POWER, VIGOR; ENERGY. PUSH, URGE;
IMPEL, PRESS, WREST; COERCE, COMPEL
force to action / IMPEL
force air through nose / SNORE, SNORT
force of attack / BRUNT
force down / RAM; DETRUDE, OPPRESS
force of evil / YIN
force forward / IMPEL
force of goodness / YANG
force with legal authority / LAW; POSSE
force of men / ARMY; CORPS, POSSE
force of nature / ELEMENT, WEATHER
force onward / URGE; DRIVE
force that twists / TORQUE; TORSION
force unit / DYNE
forced / AFFECTED, STRAINED
forced route change / DETOUR
forced silence / GAG
force-feeding / GASTROGAVAGE
forceful / DYNAMIC; ENERGETIC
forcefully / AMAIN
forcemeat / FARCE; MINCEMEAT
forcene in heraldry / REARING
forcible / COGENT, MIGHTY, STRONG
forcibly / VIOLENTLY
ford / WADE; CROSS. PASS
"Ford's Folly" / EDSEL
fore / VAN; FRONT; BEFORE. FORWARD
fore part of airplane / NOSE
fore part of ship / BOW; PROW, STEM
fore-and-aft rigged vessel / SLOOP; SCHOONER
forearm, pert. to / CUBITAL
forearm bone / ULNA; RADIUS
forebear / PARENT; ANCESTOR
forebode / AUGUR; BETOKEN, POR- TEND, PRESAGE; FORESHADOW
foreboding / OMEN; PORTENT
forecast / FORESEE, PREDICT. REPORT
forecaster / SEER
forefather / SIRE; ANCESTOR; PROGENITOR
forefinger / INDEX
forefoot / PAW, PUD
forefront / VAN; FACADE
foregoing / PRIOR; FORMER; PRE- CEDING
forehanded / TIMELY; THRIFTY
forehead / BROW; SINCIPUT
forehead, pert. to / METOPIC
forehead ornamental spot / TILAKA
forehead strap / TUMPLINE

foreign / ALIEN; EXOTIC, REMOTE

foreign, c.f. / XENO

foreigner / ALIEN, HAOLE; PAKEHA; STRANGER

foreigners' quarter in Istanbul / PERA; BEYOGLU

foreignness / IRRELEVANCY

foreknowledge / FORESIGHT; PRESCIENCE

foreland / HEADLAND

forelimb / ARM; WING

foreman / BOSS; OVERSEER

foremost / MAIN; CHIEF, FIRST

foremost part / BOW, VAN; HEAD, NOSE; FRONT

foremost segment / ACRON

forenamed / AFORESAID

forenoon / AM; MORN; MORNING

foreordain / DOOM; DESTINE

forepart / FACE; FRONT

forerun / USHER; PRECEDE

forerunner / HERALD; HARBINGER

forerunner of OGPU / CHEKA

foresail / FORECOURSE

foresee / DIVINE; PREDICT; FORECAST

foreshadow / BODE; FORETELL

foresight / VISION; PRUDENCE

foreskin / PREPUCE

forest / BOIS, WALD, WOLD; MATTA, TREES, WOODS; WOODLAND. RUSTIC, SYLVAN

forest, pert. to / SILVAN, SYLVAN; NEMORAL

forest clearing / GLADE; CAMASS

forest divinity / DRYAD; SILVANUS

forest often flooded / GAPO

forest ox / ANOA

forest path / TRAIL

forest path marking / BLAZE

forest warden / RANGER; FORESTER

forestall / AVERT; ANTICIPATE

forestry / TIMBER; TREEFARMING

foretell / SPAE; AUGUR, INSEE

foreteller / SEER; PROPHET

forethought / CARE; PRECAUTION

foretoken / BODE, OMEN: PRESAGE

forever / AY, AYE; ETERNITY. ETERN; ENDLESS, ETERNAL. AKE, EER; ETERNALLY

forewarning / OMEN; PORTENT

foreword / NOTICE; PREFACE

forfeit / FAIL, LOSE. FINE; PENALTY

forfeiture / LOSS; AMERCEMENT

forfend / FORBID; PREVENT

forgather / ASSEMBLE

forge / BEAT, FORM; FEIGN, FRAME, SHAPE; COUNTERFEIT. ANVIL; SMITHY; FURNACE

forge tongs / TU; TEU, TEW; TUARN

forger / PENMAN; COUNTERFEITER

forgery / FAKE; FABRICATION

forget / SLIGHT; NEGLECT; OVERLOOK

forgetful / CARELESS; NEGLIGENT

forgetfulness / LETHE; OBLIVION

forgive / REMIT; EXCUSE, PARDON

forgiveness / AMNESTY; ABSOLUTION

forgiving / CLEMENT; MERCIFUL

forgo / CEDE; REMIT, WAIVE, YIELD

forgotten / NEGLECTED; UNREMEMBERED

fork / DIG, PAY; DIVIDE. PRONG; BRANCH, CROTCH; JUNCTION

fork tine / PRONG

forked / BIFID; ZIGZAG; FURCATE

fork-tailed gull / XEMA

forlorn / LONE, LOST; BEREFT; DESERTED, DESOLATE, FORSAKEN

form / MOLD, RANK, RITE; BLANK, CLASS, GUISE, IMAGE, SHAPE, STYLE. MAKE; FRAME; CREATE

form, pert. to / MODAL

form of cocoa / BROMA

form a curve / ARCH

form of diversion / GAME; CARDS, SPORT

form of expression / DICTION

form into fabric / KNIT; WEAVE

form of false thinking / IDOLA

form froth / LATHER

form of government / BALLOT, POLITY

form in grains / PEARL

form of greeting / BOW, NOD; WAVE; HANDCLASP

form of iron / PIG; STEEL

form into jelly / GEL, SET; JELL

form of John / IAN; IVAN, SEAN

form in layers / LAMINATE, STRATIFY

form in line / EVEN; ALIGN, ARRAY

form of lottery / KENO; TONTINE

form in the mind / SHAPE; IDEATE

form from model / COPY; IMITATE

form of oxygen / OZONE

form in philosophy / EIDOS; ASPECT; SPECIES

form of polite address / SIR; MADAM

form of prayer / GRACE; LITANY

form of riddle / REBUS; CHARADE

form of type / ROMAN; ITALIC; CURSIVE; BOLDFACE

form of "until" / TIL; TILL

form of verse / ODE; RONDEL, SONNET; BALLADE; LIMERICK

form words from letters / SPELL

form of worship / RITE; RITUAL; LITURGY, SERVICE

form of writing / POEM; PROSE

formal / SET; PRIM; EXACT, FIXED, STIFF; DISTANT, PRECISE

formal address / LECTURE, ORATION

formal agreement / CONTRACT, COVENANT

formal argument / DEBATE

formal assembly / DIET; SYNOD; CONCLAVE, CONGRESS

formal choice / VOTE; ELECTION

formal coat / TUXEDO; CUTAWAY

formal dance / BALL, PROM; COTILLION

formal document / CHARTER; INDENTURE

formal essay / TREATISE; MONOGRAPH

formal eulogy / CITATION

formal fight / DUEL; MATCH

formal international agreement / PACT; TREATY

formal leavetaking / CONGE

formal permission / PERMIT; LICENSE; IMPRIMATUR

formal procession / MARCH; PARADE

formal reproof / CENSURE; REPRIMAND

formal social presentation / DEBUT

formalism / RIGIDITY; PUNCTILIO

formalist in teaching / PEDANT

formality / FORMULA; CEREMONY, PROTOCOL

format / SHAPE, STYLE; ARRANGEMENT

formation / SHAPE; STRUCTURE

formation of troops / PARADE; ECHELON

formative / PLASTIC; GERMINAL

formed into bundles / BALED

former / ERER, ERST; FIRST, PRIOR; WHILOM; QUONDAM; PREVIOUS. EX

former autocrat / CZAR, TSAR; KAISER, SULTAN

former Brazilian coin / REIS

former days / ELD; PAST, YORE

former English coin / RYAL; CROWN, GROAT; FARTHING

former English prime minister / EDEN, GREY, PEEL, PITT; ATTLEE; DISRAELI; CHURCHILL

former French coin / SOU

former gang lord / CAPONE

former Hungarian district / BANAT

former Japanese capital / KYOTO

former operatic star / ALDA; EAMES, HOMER; CARUSO, SCOTTI

former Ottoman court / PORTE

former Persian kingly title / SOPHY

former Portuguese India / GOA

former public conveyance / STAGE

former Russian ruler / CZAR, TSAR; LENIN; STALIN

former Russian state council / DUMA

former Spanish coin / REAL; PISTOLA, PISTOLE

former Spanish kingdom / LEON; ARAGON; CASTILE

former Tunisian governor / BEY

former Turkish title / DEY; SULTAN

former Venetian ruler / DOGE

formerly / AGO; ERST, ONCE. NEE

formerly, pref. / EX

formicid / ANT

formidable / FEARFUL; POWERFUL

forming / FINGENT

Formosa / TAIWAN

Formosa capital / TAIPEH, TAIPEI

Formosa seaport / CHILUNG

formula / RULE; MODEL; RECIPE

formula of faith / CREED; DOCTRINE

formula for solution / KEY; HYPOTHESIS

formulate / DRAFT, ENACT; INDITE

fornicate / ARCHED; VAULTED

forsake / QUIT; LEAVE; DESERT

forsaken / LORN; FORLORN; ABANDONED

forsaker of the faith / APOSTATE

Forseti's father / BALDER

Forseti's palace / GLITNIR

forswear / ABJURE

Forsyte family founder / JOLYON

Forsytes' defender / SOAMES

fort / PA; REDAN; CASTLE; BULWARK, RAVELIN, REDOUBT; FORTRESS

fort wall / PARAPET, RAMPART

forte / STRONGPOINT. LOUD

fortean phenomenon / PORTENT

forth / OUT; AWAY; ABROAD, ONWARD

forthwith / NOW; ANON; INSTANTLY

fortification / ABATIS, GLACIS; CITADEL

fortification ditch / MOAT; FOSSE, SCARP; TRENCH

fortification of felled trees / ABATIS

fortified / ARMED; STRENGTHENED

fortified place / LIS; LISS; LINES; GARRISON, STOCKADE

fortified residence / CASTLE

fortify / ARM, MAN; BRACE; STRENGTHEN

fortitude / COURAGE; ENDURANCE

fortress / KEEP; CITADEL; STRONGHOLD

fortuitous / CASUAL; ACCIDENTAL

Fortuna's father / OCEANUS

fortunate / HAPPY, LUCKY; FAVORED

Four Horsemen of the Apocalypse

	Color of Horse
CONQUEST (war)	WHITE
FAMINE	BLACK
PESTILENCE (slaughter)	RED
DEATH	PALE

Fortunate Isles / CANARIES
fortune / HAP, LOT; FATE, LUCK, STAR; RICHES, WEALTH
fortune hunter / ADVENTURER, GOLDDIGGER
fortune teller / SEER; SIBYL; ORACLE; PALMIST
forty days' fast / LENT; CAREME
forty days' isolation / QUARANTINE
forty winks / NAP
forty-five / PISTOL
forty-five degree angle / OCTANT
forty-niner / ARGONAUT
forward / BOLD; EAGER, EARLY, READY; BRAZEN, PROMPT; EARNEST, WILLING. SEND, SHIP; DIRECT. ON, TO; AHEAD
forward part / FORE, HEAD; FRONT
forward part of ship / BOW; PROW, STEM
forwardness / PERTNESS; IMPUDENCE
foss / MOAT; CANAL
fossa / PIT; CAVITY
fosse / MOAT; DITCH
fossil / BONES; CALAMITE, DINOSAUR. ANTIQUATED
fossil footprint / ICHNITE
fossil fuel / OIL; COAL, PEAT; SHALEOIL
fossil plant / CALAMITE
fossil resin / AMBER, COPAL, KAURI; GLESSITE
fossil worm track / CAST; NEREITE
fossilize / PETRIFY
fossorial / DIGGING; BURROWING
foster / FEED, HELP, REAR; NURSE
foster child / DALT; NURRY
Foster song / OHSUSANNAH
fought / BATTLED, STRIVEN
foughten field / BATTLEFIELD
foul / LOW; RANK, VILE; DIRTY, NASTY; CLOUDY, COARSE, FILTHY
foul ball / PHONY

foul fiend / DEVIL, SATAN
foul play / MURDER
foul-mouthed / PROFANE; SCURRILOUS
foul-smelling / OLID; FETID, REEKY
foul-weather gear / OILSKINS
foumart / POLECAT
found / FIX, SET; BASE, CAST, MOLD; ENDOW
found object / TROVE
found in a pod / PEA; BEAN
found at some dances / STAGLINE; WALLFLOWER
foundation / BED; BASE, ROOT; BOTTOM, GROUND
foundation timber / SILL
founded in experience / EMPIRICAL
founded in truth / VALID
founder / SINK; FALTER. CASTER; ORIGINATOR
founder of French dynasty / CAPET
foundling / WAIF; STRAY
fountain / JET; FONS, FONT; SOURCE, SPRING
fountain drink / POP; MALT, SODA
fountain nymph / EGERIA
fountain of youth / BIMINI
fountain of youth seeker / DELEON
four, c.f. / TETRA; QUADRI
four bagger / HOMER; HOMERUN
four gills / PINT
four hundred / ELITE; SOCIETY
four inches / HAND
Four Million author / OHENRY
four pecks / BUSHEL
four quarts / GALLON
fourflusher / PHONEY; BLUFFER
four-footed / TETRAPOD
four-footed animal / BEAST; QUADRUPED
four-in-hand / TIE; ASCOT
four-legged reptile / CAIMAN, LIZARD, TURTLE; DINOSAUR
fourpence / GROAT
four-poster / BED

Four Horsemen of Notre Dame

	Position
STUHLDREHER	QUARTERBACK
MILLER	HALFBACK
CROWLEY	HALFBACK
LAYDEN	FULLBACK

fourscore / EIGHTY
four-sided figure / TETRAGON
four-sided stele / OBELISK
foursome / QUARTET
foursquare / BOLD; DIRECT
fourteen line poem / SONNET
fourteen pounds / STONE
fourth / QUARTER
fourth of a bushel / PECK
fourth caliph / ALI
fourth estate / PRESS
four-wheeled vehicle / AUTO, TRAP; WAGON; BERLIN, LANDAU, SURREY; PHAETON; BROUGHAM, VICTORIA; AUTOMOBILE
fowl / HEN; BIRD, COCK; CAPON; CHICKEN, POULTRY
fowl-like chickens / RASORES
fowl's enclosure / COOP
fowl's organ / GIBLET
fox / TOD; ASSE; CAAMA; CORSAC, FENNEC, RENARD; KARAGAN
fox, pert. to / VULPINE
fox of fable / REYNARD
fox fire / WILLOWTHEWISP
fox hunter's coat / PINK
foxbane / ACONITE
foxglove / MULLEIN; DIGITALIS; FINGERROOT
foxiness / CUNNING; SHREWDNESS
foxlike / ALOPECOID
fox's cry / BARK
fox's face / MASK
fox's foot / PAD
fox's lair / DEN; EARTH
fox's tail / BRUSH
foxtail's tip / TAG; CHAFE
foxy / SLY; WILY; CRAFTY; VULPINE
foxy move / RUSE
foyer / ENTRY, LOBBY
fra / MONK; FRIAR
frab / NAG; SCOLD
fracas / BRAWL, MELEE; UPROAR
fraction / PART; PIECE; DECIMAL
fraction term / ALIQUOT; NUMERATOR; DENOMINATOR
fractional currency / SCRIP
fractious / CROSS, TESTY; UNRULY; FRETFUL, PEEVISH
fracture / RENT, RIFT; BREACH. BREAK, CRACK
fragile / WEAK; FRAIL; BRITTLE
fragment / BIT, END, ORT, RAG; CHIP, SNIP; CRUMB, PIECE, SCARP
fragment of cloth / RAG; SCRAP; TATTER
fragment of food / ORT
fragment of pottery / SHARD, SHERD

fragments of literary material / ANA; MISCELLANY
fragrance / ODOR; AROMA, SCENT
fragrant / OLID; OLENT, SPICY; ODOROUS; AROMATIC
fragrant extract / ATTAR; CLOVES
fragrant flower / ROSE; LILAC; CHAMPAC, JASMINE
fragrant herb / MINT; ANISE, BASIL; ROSEMARY
fragrant leaf / MINT
fragrant ointment / NARD; BALSAM; SPIKENARD
fragrant resin / ELEME, ELEMI; BALSAM; BENZOIN
fragrant shrub / TIARA
fragrant unguent / POMADE
fragrant wood / ALOES, CEDAR; AGALLOCH
frail / PUNY, WEAK; DELICATE
frailty / FAULT; FOIBLE; INFIRMITY
frambesia / PIAN, YAWS
frame / FORM, MAKE, MOLD, PLAN. BORDER, CASING; CHASSIS
frame of bars / GRATE
frame for calculating / ABACUS
frame for drying skins / HERSE
frame for fire / CRESSET
frame in glass annealing / DROSSER
frame of horseman's seat / SADDLETREE
frame of mind / MOOD; HUMOR; TEMPER
frame in soap-making / SESS
frame to stretch cloth / TENTER
frame up / PLOT; CONSPIRACY
frame for winding fishline / CADER
frame of a window / CASING
frame for windowpanes / SASH
framed fight / SETUP
framework / RACK; CADRE; SCAFFOLD
framework of crossed slats / LATTICE, TRELLIS
framework of rods / GRATE
France / GAUL. See also French
France capital / PARIS
France's patron saint / DENIS
France's symbol / COCK; MARIANNE
franchise / VOTE; RIGHT; PRIVILEGE
Franciscan / CAPUCHIN, MINORITE
Franciscan nun / CLARE
Franco-Prussian war battle / SEDAN
frangible / WEAK; FRAIL; FEEBLE
frank / EASY, FREE, OPEN; CANDID

France, Old Provinces of

	English Name	Capital
Alsace	—	STRASBOURG
Angoumois	—	ANGOULEME
Anjou	—	ANGERS
Aunis	—	LAROCHELLE
Auvergne	—	CLERMONTFERRAND
Bearn	—	PAU
Berry	—	BOURGES
Bourbonnais	—	MOULINS
Bourgogne	BURGUNDY	DIJON
Bretagne	BRITTANY	RENNES
Champagne	—	TROYES
Comte de Foix	—	FOIX
Dauphine	—	GRENOBLE
Flandre	FLANDERS	LILLE
Franche-Comte	—	BESANCON
Gascogne	GASCONY	AUCH
Guyenne	—	BORDEAUX
Ile-de-France	—	PARIS
Languedoc	—	TOULOUSE
Limousin	—	LIMOGES
Lorraine	—	NANCY
Lyonnais	LYONS	LYON
Maine	—	LEMANS
Marche	—	GUERET
Nivernais	—	NEVERS
Normandie	NORMANDY	ROUEN
Orleanais	—	ORLEANS
Picardie	PICARDY	AMIENS
Poitou	—	POITIERS
Provence	—	AIX
Roussillon	—	PERPIGNAN
Saintonge	—	SAINTES
Touraine	—	TOURS

Frankenstein author / MARY-SHELLEY

frankfurter / FRANK; HOTDOG, WIENER

Frankie's boyfriend / JOHNNY

frankincense / THUS; OLIBANUM

Frankish division / SALIAN; RIPUARIAN

Frankish dynasty / MEROVINGIAN

Frankish king / PEPIN; CLOVIS

Frankish kingdom / BURGUNDY, NEUSTRIA

Frankish peasant / LEUD; LITUS

Frankish victory / TOURS

Franklin's birthplace / BOSTON

Franklin's city / PHILADELPHIA

Franklin's pen name / POOR-RICHARD

Franks, pert. to / SALIC; SALIAN

frantic / MAD; WILD; RAGING, RAVING; FURIOUS; FRENZIED

fraternal / AKIN; BROTHERLY

fraternity / ORDER; CIRCLE; SOCIETY

fraternize / CONSORT; ASSOCIATE; SYMPATHIZE

fraud / FAKE, HOAX, JAPE, RUSE, SHAM, WILE; TRICK; DECEIT, FAKERY, HUMBUG

fraudulent / FALSE; DECEPTIVE; COUNTERFEIT

fraught / LADEN; CHARGED

fray / RIOT; FIGHT, MELEE, SETTO. RUB; BROIL, CHAFE, RAVEL

freak / WHIM; ANTIC, FANCY, QUIRK; VAGARY; CAPRICE

freakish / FRISKY; ERRATIC

freckle / DAPPLE. LENTIGO

free / EASY, OPEN;. CLEAR, FRANK, LOOSE; EXEMPT, GRATIS. RID; LOOSEN; RELEASE

free from anxiety / REASSURE

free from danger / SAVE; RESCUE; DELIVER

free from dirt / CLEAN, CLEAR

free from disorder / ARRANGE

free at the gas station / AIR, MAP

free of germs / ASEPTIC, STERILE
free from impurity / PURGE; REFINE; CLEANSE
free lance / MERCENARY
free meal / TREAT
free of moisture / DRY; ARID, SERE
free by payment / BAIL; RANSOM, REDEEM
free from punishment / EXEMPT; AMNESTY
free from restraint / UNTIE; LOOSEN
free of risk / SAFE; SECURE
free from slavery / MANUMIT; LIBERATE; EMANCIPATE
free ticket / PASS; ANNIEOAKLEY
free verse / VERSLIBRE
freebooter / PIRATE; BUCCANEER
freedman / LAET; EXSLAVE
freedom / PLAY; RANGE, SCOPE; LIBERTY, LICENSE
freedom from constraint / EASE
freedom of entry / ENTREE
freedom from liability / IMMUNITY; EXEMPTION
free-for-all / FIGHT, MELEE
freehand / UNGUIDED
freehanded / LIBERAL; GENEROUS
freehold / ALOD, MULK, ODAL, UDAL
freeholder / YEOMAN
freeing / RELEASING; DISCHARGING
freeloader / SCHNORRER
freely / FRANKLY; LIBERALLY
freeman / CEORL, CHURL, THANE; CITIZEN
free-spoken / OPEN; FRANK
freethinker / AGNOSTIC
freewill / VOLUNTARY
freeze / ICE; NUMB; CHILL; GELATE, HARDEN; CONGEAL; REFRIGERATE
freezing up / ICINGOVER
freight / LADE, LOAD. CARGO
freight boat / ARK; SCOW; BARGE, OILER; TANKER; FLATBOAT
freight car / BOXCAR, REEFER; GONDOLA
freighted / SHIPPED
freighter / SHIP; VESSEL; SHIPPER
Frémont's father-in-law / BENTON
Frémont's wife / JESSIE
French / GALLIC; ROMANCE. See also France
French, c.f. / FRANCO
French actor / RAIMU, TALMA
French actress / RACHEL
French airplane / AVION
French annuity / RENTE

French anthem / MARSEILLAISE
French art group / FAUVES; BARBIZON
French article / LA, LE, UN; DES, LES, UNE
French artist / DORE, DUFY; COROT, DEGAS, MANET, MONET; BRAQUE, DERAIN, MILLET, RENOIR; MATISSE, ROUAULT, UTRILLO
French astrologer / NOSTRA-DAMUS
French attendant / CONCIERGE
French author / SUE; GIDE, HUGO, LOTI, SAND, ZOLA; CAMUS, DUMAS, RENAN, STAEL, TAINE, VERNE; BALZAC, MUSSET, RACINE, SARTRE; COCTEAU, MOLIERE, VALERY; VOLTAIRE; MONTHERLANT
French aviator / BLERIOT
French baked pastry / QUICHE
French bean / FEVE; HARICOT
French blue / ULTRAMARINE
French bookbinding style / GROLIER
French boxing / SAVATE
French brandy / FINE, MARC; COGNAC; ARMAGNAC, EAUDEVIE
French cafe / BISTRO; ESTAMINET
French Canadian / CANUCK
French cap / BERET
French cardinal / MAZARIN; RICHELIEU
French caricaturist / DAUMIER
French carriage / FIACRE
French castle / CHATEAU
French cathedral city / AMIENS
French chalk / TALC
French champagne / AY; AVIZE, BOUZY
French cheese / GEX; BRIE, ERVY; CANTAL
French chemist / PASTEUR
French china / LIMOGES
French chocolate / MOUSSE
French city / AIX; CAEN, LYON, NICE, SENS; ARLES, BLOIS, LILLE, NANCY, PARIS, REIMS; AMIENS, CANNES, NANTES, RENNES, SEVRES; ALENCON, LIMOGES
French clergyman / ABBE, PERE
French coin / ECU, SOU; BLANC, FRANC; DENIER; CENTIME
French collection of tales / HEPTAMERON
French composer / LALO; AUBER, BIZET, IBERT, LULLY, RAVEL; GOUNOD; DEBUSSY; MASSENET
French criminal / APACHE

French critic / TAINE
French department officer / PREFECT
French detective force / SURETE
French district / ARRONDISSEMENT
French doughboy / POILU
French dramatist / HUGO; GUITRY, RACINE, SARDOU, SCRIBE; CLAUDEL, MOLIERE, ROSTAND; MARIVAUX
French dynasty / CAPET; VALOIS; BOURBON
French ecclesiastical title / ABBE
French emblem / FLEURDELIS
French emperor / NAPOLEON
French empress / EUGENIE
French enamelware / LIMOGES
French engraver / DORE; CALLOT
French essayist / GIDE; MONTAIGNE
French exclamation / ZUT; HEIN
French existentialist / CAMUS; SARTRE; BEAUVOIR
French explorer / CARTIER, JOLLIET, LASALLE; RADISSON
French faddist / GALLOMANIAC
French farewell / ADIEU
French fighter plane / MYSTERE

French fries / CHIPS
French general / FOCH; HOCHE; GAMELIN, LECLERC
French girl's name / RENEE
French governess / MADEMOISELLE
French guerrillas / MAQUIS
French Guiana area / ININI
French Guiana capital / CAYENNE
French heroine / JOANOFARC
French high fashion / COUTURE
French historian / RENAN, TAINE; GUIZOT
French illustrator / DORE; MANET, MORIN, OUDRY; GILLOT; GAVARNI, LAUTREC
French impressionist / MONET
French India city / MAHE; PONDICHERY
French Indochina capital / HANOI
French Island / IF, RE; YEU
French lace / VAL; CLUNY; ALENCON
French land measure / ARPENT; QUARTERON
French landscape painter / COROT, MONET; CLAUDE
French language / LANGUEDOC, PROVENCAL

French Departments

	Capital
Ain	BOURG
Aisne	LAON
Allier	MOULINS
Alpes-Maritimes	NICE
Ardèche	PRIVAS
Ardennes	MEZIERES
Ariège	FOIX
Aube	TROYES
Aude	CARCASSONNE
Aveyron	RODEZ
Bas-Rhin	STRASBOURG
Basses-Alpes	DIGNE
Basses-Pyrénées	PAU
Belfort, Territoire de	BELFORT
Bouches-du-Rhône	MARSEILLES
Calvados	CAEN
Cantal	AURILLAC
Charente	ANGOULEME
Charente-Maritime	LAROCHELLE
Cher	BOURGES
Corrèze	TULLE
Corse	AJACCIO
Côte-d'Or	DIJON
Côtes-du-Nord	SAINTBRIEUC
Creuse	GUERET
Deux-Sèvres	NIORT
Dordogne	PERIGUEUX
Doubs	BESANCON
Drôme	VALENCE

	Capital
Eure	EVREUX
Eure-et-Loir	CHARTRES
Finistère	QUIMPER
Gard	NIMES
Gers	AUCH
Gironde	BORDEAUX
Haute-Garonne	TOULOUSE
Haute-Loire	LEPUY
Haute-Marne	CHAUMONT
Hautes-Alpes	GAP
Haute-Saône	VESOUL
Haute-Savoie	ANNECY
Hautes-Pyrénées	TARBES
Haute-Vienne	LIMOGES
Haut-Rhin	COLMAR
Hérault	MONTPELLIER
Ille-et-Vilaine	RENNES
Indre	CHATEAUROUX
Indre-et-Loire	TOURS
Isère	GRENOBLE
Jura	LONSLESAUNIER
Landes	MONTDEMARSAN
Loire	SAINTETIENNE
Loire-Inférieure	NANTES
Loiret	ORLEANS
Loir-et-Cher	BLOIS
Lot	CAHORS
Lot-et-Garonne	AGEN
Lozère	MENDE
Maine-et-Loire	ANGERS
Manche	SAINTLO
Marne	CHALONSSURMARNE
Mayenne	LAVAL
Meurthe-et-Moselle	NANCY
Meuse	BARLEDUC
Morbihan	VANNES
Moselle	METZ
Nièvre	NEVERS
Nord	LILLE
Oise	BEAUVAIS
Orne	ALENCON
Pas-de-Calais	ARRAS
Puy-de-Dôme	CLERMONTFERRAND
Pyrénées-Orientales	PERPIGNAN
Rhône	LYON
Saône-et-Loire	MACON
Sarthe	LEMANS
Savoie	CHAMBERY
Seine	PARIS
Seine-et-Marne	MELUN
Seine-et-Oise	VERSAILLES
Seine-Inférieure	ROUEN
Somme	AMIENS
Tarn	ALBI
Tarn-et-Garonne	MONTAUBAN
Var	DRAGUIGNAN
Vaucluse	AVIGNON
Vendée	LAROCHESURYON
Vienne	POITIERS
Vosges	EPINAL
Yonne	AUXERRE

French leave / AWOL; HOOKY
French legal cap / MORTIER
French legal decree / ARRET
French linguist / BREAL; MASPERO
French liqueur / ANISETTE
French literary prize / GONCOURT
French marshal / NEY; SAXE; MURAT
French mathematician / BOREL; CAUCHY, FERMAT, GALOIS, PASCAL
French measure of length / LIEUE, TOISE
French meat dish / PATE; SALMI; ENTRECOTE
French metaphysician / DESCARTES
French middle school / LYCEE
French money / SOU; FRANC, LIVRE; CENTIME; LOUISDOR
French mountain / BLANC, CENIS
French mountain range / JURA; VOSGES; CEVENNES
French native / BRETON, GASCON, NORMAN
French naturalist / BUFFON
French naval station / BREST; TOULON
French needlepoint lace / ALENCON
French novelist / SUE; HUGO, LOTI, SAND, ZOLA; CAMUS, DUMAS; BALZAC, LESAGE, PROUST; COLETTE
French nursemaid / BONNE
French opera / FAUST, LAKME, MANON; CARMEN
French opera pioneer / LULLY
French painter / DORE; COROT, DAVID, DEGAS, GELEE, MANET, MONET; BRAQUE, CLOUET, INGRES, MILLET, RENOIR, TISSOT; BOUCHER, CEZANNE, CHARDIN, ROUAULT
French pancake / CREPE
French parliament / HOUSE, SENAT
French pastry / ECLAIR; NAPOLEON
French patron saint / DENIS
French perfume / CHANELV
French philosopher / COMTE; ABELARD; ROUSSEAU
French physicist / CURIE; AMPERE; BROGLIE
French physiologist / RICHET
French poet / CHAR, HUGO, LABE; MAROT; ARAGON, ELUARD, MUSSET, VALERY, VILLON; CHENIER, RIMBAUD, RONSARD; MALLARME, VERLAINE
French pointillist / SEURAT

French policeman / FLIC; GENDARME
French political club / JACOBIN
French porcelain / SEVRES; LIMOGES
French priest / ABBE, CURE, PERE
French prison / BASTILLE
French pronoun / TE; CES, ILS, MES, TOI, UNE; ELLE
French protestant / CAMISARD, HUGUENOT
French psychologist / BINET, RIBOT; CHARCOT
French quisling / LAVAL
French racecourse / AUTEUIL
French refugee / EMIGRE
French resort / PAU; NICE; CANNES
French resort area / RIVIERA
French restaurant / BISTRO
French Revolution leader / MARAT; CLOOTS, DANTON, HEBERT; ROBESPIERRE
French Revolution month / NIVOSE; FLOREAL, PRAIRAL, VENTOSE; BRUMAIRE, FERVIDOR, FRIMAIRE, GERMINAL, MESSIDOR, PLUVIOSE; FRUCTIDOR, THERMIDOR; VENDEMAIRE
French Revolution party / JACOBIN; MOUNTAIN; GIRONDIST
French revolutionary song / CAIRA
French river / AIN, LYS; AIRE, EURE, OISE, ORNE, SAAR, YSER; ISERE, LOIRE, MARNE, MEUSE, RHONE, SAONE, SARRE, SEINE, SOMME, VESLE, YONNE; SCARPE; GARONNE
French royal edict / ARRET
French royal family / CAPET; VALOIS; BOURBON
French saint / JOAN; MARTIN
French satirist / MAROT; CHENIER; RABELAIS
French school / ECOLE, LYCEE; INSTITUT
French scientist / CURIE; BUFFON, PERRIN; PASTEUR
French sculptor / RODIN; HOUDON; BARTHOLDI
French seaport / BREST; CALAIS, NANTES; BORDEAUX; CHERBOURG, MARSEILLE
French season / ETE; HIVER; PRINTEMPS
French sect / ALBIGENSES
French security / RENTE
French servant / BONNE, VALET
French shop / BOUTIQUE
French shrine / LOURDES

French singer / PIAF; SABLON; CHANTEUSE
French sleeping car / WAGONLIT
French soldier / POILU; ZOUAVE; CHASSEUR
French soprano / PONS; CALVE
French southland / MIDI
French stock market / BOURSE
French stoneware / GRES
French subway / METRO
French symbol / LIS; LILY
French tapestry / GOBELIN
French verse form / RONDEL; VIRELAI
French vineyard / CRU
French wine / VIN; SEVE; MEDOC; PONTAC; PONTACQ
French wine plant / CEP
French writer / SUE; GIDE, HUGO, LOTI, ZOLA; CAMUS, DUMAS, RENAN, STAEL, VERNE; PROUST, RACINE, SARTRE; COCTEAU, GAUTIER; ROUSSEAU
French-Belgian river / YSER
Frenchman / FROG, GAUL
Frenchman's name / RENE
frenetic / FURIOUS; FRENZIED
frenzied RABID; FRANTIC; DELIRIOUS
frenzied manner / AMOK, FURY; AMUCK; BERSERK
frenzied woman / MAENAD; BACCHANTE
frenzy / RAGE; FUROR, MANIA
frequency of tone / PITCH
frequent / HAUNT. OFT; OFTEN. COMMON
frequent use / HABIT; PRACTICE
frequenter / HABITUE
frequently / OFT; OFTEN
fresh / NEW, RAW; BOLD, COOL, FAIR, PURE, ROSY; BRISK, NOVEL
fresh air / OZONE
fresh horses / RELAY
fresh information / NEWS
fresh talk / SASS
freshen / RENEW; REVIVE
freshen masonry appearance / REGRATE, REPOINT
freshet / FLOOD, SPATE
fresh-water catfish / POUT; MUDCAT; BULLHEAD
fresh-water dolphin / INIA
fresh-water duck / TEAL; WIDGEON
fresh-water fish / ID; IDE; BASS, DACE, ESOX, POUT; ROACH; BURBOT, DARTER
fresh-water mussel / UNIO
fresh-water tortoise / EMYD
fret / NAG; FUSS, GALL, STEW; ANNOY, CHAFE, WORRY; HARASS

fret with annoyance / FUME
fretful / TESTY; PEEVISH; PETULANT
fretted / WORN; EROSE
fretwork / FILIGREE, ORNAMENT
Freya's brother / FREY
Freya's father / NJORD
Freya's husband / ODIN
Freya's necklace / BRISINGAMEN
Frey's home / ALFHEIM
Frey's magic ship / SKIDBLADNIR
Frey's wife / GERDA
friar / FRA; MONK
friar's hood / COWL; CAPUCHE
friary / MONASTERY
fribble / TRIFLE
friction / DISCORD, FACTION; ABRASION
friction match / LUCIFER
frictional / EROSIVE
Friday's master / CRUSOE
fried cake / CRULLER; DOUGHNUT
fried food / SCRAPPLE
fried rolled meat / RISSOLE
fried-egg dish / OMELET
friend / PAL; ALLY, CHUM; AMIGO, CRONY
friend of King David / REI
friend of the people / DEMOPHIL; DEMOPHILE
friend of Pythias / DAMON
friend of St. Paul / PHILEMON
friendless / LONELY; ABANDONED
friendliness / AMITY; AFFECTION
friendly / KIND, WARM; GENIAL, SOCIAL; AFFABLE, CORDIAL
friendly dwarf / PUCK; BROWNIE; LEPRECHAUN
friendly greeting to Indian / HOW; NETOP
friendly hint / TIP; POINTER
Friendly Islands / TONGA
friendly relations / INTIMACY
friendly talk / CHAT
friends and neighbors / KITH
Friends' pronoun / THY; THEE
friendship / AMITY
frigate bird / IWA
Frigg's assistant / GNA; HLIN
Frigg's brother-in-law / VE
Frigg's day / FRIDAY
Frigg's home / FENSALIR
Frigg's husband / ODIN
Frigg's sister / FULLA
Frigg's son / BALDER
fright / AWE; FEAR, FUNK; DREAD, PANIC; DISMAY, TERROR
frighten / FLEY; ALARM, DAUNT, SCARE; APPALL
frighten away / SHOO; CHASE
frighten off / DETER
frightened / TIMID; SCARED

frightened feeling / FEAR
frightening / SCARY; SPOOKY
frightening sound / BOO
frightful / GRIM; AWFUL, SCARY;
    HORRID; FEARFUL, GHASTLY
frightful giant / OGRE
frightful object / BOGY; BOGEY
frigid / ICY; COLD, DULL; STIFF;
    GLACIAL
frigidly / ICILY; COLDLY
frill / RUCHE; RUFFLE; FLOUNCE
frill at the neck / RUFF; JABOT
fringe / EDGE; BORDER, MARGIN
fringed / FIMBRIATE, LACINATE
frippery / TRASH; TRUMPERY
frisk / PLAY, ROMP; CAPER,
    SPORT; SEARCH
frisky / PEART; LIVELY
frit / FUSE, MELT
frith / FIRTH; ESTUARY
fritter / WASTE; DISSIPATE
frivolity / LEVITY
frivolous / GAY; INANE, LIGHT,
    SILLY
fro / AWAY, FROM; BACKWARD
frock / GOWN; DRESS, HABIT
frog / LOOP; ANURAN;
    AMPHIBIAN, FRENCHMAN
frog genus / RANA; ANURA
frog-headed goddess / HEKET
froglike amphibian / TOAD
frogmouth / MOREPORK
frogs, pert. to / RANINE
Froissart subject / CHIVALRY
frolic / FUN; LARK, ROMP; SPREE;
    GAIETY. CAPER; CAVORT
frolic merrily / FRISK
frolicsome / GAY; SPORTIVE
from / OF; AWAY; SINCE
from, pref. / AB, DE
from dusk to dawn / OVERNIGHT
from here / HENCE
from now / HENCEFORTH
from there / SINCE; THENCE,
    WHENCE
from when / SINCE
from where / WHENCE
frond / LEAF; THALLUS; PALMLEAF
frondescence / FOLIAGE
frondose / LEAFY; THALLOID
front / FACE, FORE; FACADE
front of an army / VAN; LINES
front page box / EAR
front part of helmet / NASAL,
    VISOR
front of ship / BOW; BEAK, PROW,
    STEM
front view / FACADE
frontier / BOUND, LIMIT; BORDER
frontier historian / TURNER
frontier post / FORT; FACTORY

frontiersman / SCOUT; TRADER;
    TRAPPER
frontlet / TIARA; FRONTAL
frost / ICE; COLD, HOAR, RIME.
    CLOUD; WHITEN; GRIZZLE
frost giants' father / YMIR
frost-covered / RIMED
frosted / ETCHED; CHILLED
frostfish / SMELT; TOMCOD
frosting / ICING
frostlike covering / RIME
frosty / COLD; CHILL, GELID
froth / FOAM, HEAD; SPUME.
    BUBBLE
froth from soap / SUDS; LATHER
frothlike / SPUMY; YEASTY
frothy / EMPTY; YEASTY;
    FRIVOLOUS
frothy wave / COMBER
frow / FRUMP, WOMAN
froward / WAYWARD; PERVERSE
frown / LOUR, POUT; SCOWL;
    GLOWER
frowning / GLUM; DREARY
frowzy / MOLDY, MUSTY; UNTIDY
frowzy woman / DOWD; FRUMP;
    SLATTERN
froze / ICED; CHOKEDUP
frozen / ICY; FRORE, GELID
frozen delicacy / ICE; FRAPPE,
    MOUSSE, SERBET; SHERBET,
    SPUMONI; NESSELRODE
frozen dew / RIME
frozen rain / HAIL, SNOW; SLEET
frozen spike / ICICLE
frozen water / ICE
fructuous / FRUITFUL
frugal / CHARY, SAVING;
    PRUDENT, THRIFTY
frugality / ECONOMY; PARSIMONY
fruit / FIG; DATE, LIME, PEAR,
    PLUM, SLOE; APPLE, BERRY,
    CATES, GRAPE, LEMON, MELON,
    OLIVE; BANANA, CHERRY,
    ORANGE, PAPAYA, TOMATO;
    APRICOT, DESSERT, KUMQUAT,
    PRODUCT; OFFSPRING. BEAR;
    YIELD
fruit, c.f. / CARP; CARPO
fruit box / LUG
fruit for cake / RAISIN
fruit of cereal / EAR; CARYOPSIS
fruit cooked in sirup / COMPOTE
fruit decay / BLET, MOLD;
    MILDEW
fruit dessert / GRUNT, SLUMP
fruit dot on fern / SORUS
fruit drink / ADE; CIDER, PERRY,
    PUNCH; RATAFIA
fruit of elm / SAMARA
fruit of evergreen / CONE

fruit flesh / PULP
fruit of fungi / AECIUM, TELIUM
fruit for gin / SLOE
fruit of gourd vine / PEPO; MELON, SETON
fruit with hard shell / NUT; SEED; GOURD; COCONUT
fruit of Indian pepper / CUBEB
fruit jar seal / LUTE
fruit jelly / JAM, ROB; RHOB; MARMALADE
fruit juice / ADE; CIDER
fruit kernel / PIT; CORE, SEED; STONE
fruit of maple / SAMARA
fruit for marmalade / ORANGE, QUINCE
fruit of nut / MEAT; KERNEL
fruit of oak / ACORN
fruit of oblivion / LOTUS
fruit often accompanying prunes / APRICOTS
fruit of palm / DATE; COCONUT
fruit of papaya / PAPAW; PAWPAW
fruit peel / RIND, SKIN
fruit pit / PIP; SEED; STONE
fruit preserve / JAM; COMPOTE
fruit pulp / PAP; POMACE
fruit refuse / MARC
fruit of rose / HIP
fruit seed / PIP
fruit seller / COSTER
fruit solids / MASH; POMACE
fruit spike / EAR
fruit squeezer / JUICER, REAMER
fruit stone / PIT
fruit sugar / FRUCTOSE, LEVULOSE
fruit used in jelly / PLUM; BERRY, GRAPE, GUAVA; CHERRY
fruit vine / GRAPE, MELON
fruit-eating beetle / BORER
fruitful / RICH; FECUND; PROLIFIC
fruitfulness / UBERTY; FERTILITY
fruiting spike / EAR
fruition / USE; ATTAINMENT
fruitless / IDLE, VAIN; FUTILE
fruitless hunt / WILDGOOSECHASE
fruity / RICH
frump / VEX; SULK; FLOUT, SLOVEN
frustrate / BALK, FOIL; BAFFLE, DEFEAT, SCOTCH, THWART
frustration / FIASCO; BAFFLEMENT
fry / COOK; FRIZZLE. YOUNG; PICNIC
fry quickly / SAUTE
frying pan / FRYER; SPIDER; SKILLET
fub / CHEAT; DECEIVE
fuddle / STUPEFY; INTOXICATE

fuddled / DRUNK, TIPSY; MUDDLED
Fuegan Indian / ONA; YAHGAN
fuel / GAS, OIL; COAL, COKE, PEAT; CHARCOAL. STOKE
fuel ship / OILER; COALER, TANKER
fugacious / FLEETING, VOLATILE
fugitive / RUNAWAY. UNSTABLE
fugitive alien / EMIGRE
fugitive slave / MAROON
fugue master composer / BACH
fugue part / DUX; COMES, PEDAL; STRETTO
fulcrum of oar / LOCK; THOLE
fulfill / MEET; ANSWER, COMPLY; EXECUTE
fulfillment / DISCHARGE; OBSERVANCE
fulgent / BRIGHT; RADIANT
fulgurous / FLASHING
fuliginous / DUSKY, SOOTY
full / AMPLE, LADEN; FILLED; PLENARY
full apology / AMENDE
full of bloodshed / GORY
full cargo / BOATLOAD
full of depressions / PITTED, POCKED
full of dignity / SEDATE
full dress / TAILS; FORMAL
full of excitement / AGOG
full of fear / SCARED; TIMOROUS
full of fight / SCRAPPY
full of fissures / RIMOSE
full of flavor / TASTY, ZESTY
full grown / RIPE; ADULT; MATURE
full of holes like a sponge / POROSE
full house / JAM, SRO
full of ideas / INVENTIVE
full of marsh grass / REEDY
full moon / PLENILUNE
full of, suffix / OSE
full of seaweed / KELPY
full of small spaces POROUS; AREOLAR
full supply / PLENTY
full of trees / TIMBERED
fullness / SATIETY; REPLETION
fully / WHOLLY; PERFECTLY; COMPLETELY
fully attended meeting / PLENUM
fully constituted / PLENARY
fully developed animal form / ZOON
fulminate / EXPLODE, THUNDER; DETONATE
fulsome / COARSE; FAWNING; OFFENSIVE
Fulton's folly / CLERMONT

Fulton's submarine / NAUTILUS
fumble / DROP, FLUB; GROPE
fume / RAGE, REEK. GAS;
    SMOKE, VAPOR
fumigate / AIR; SMOKE;
    DISINFECT
fumigator / AERATOR
fun / GAME, PLAY; MIRTH, SPORT
function / ACT, USE; DUTY, RITE;
    PARTY, POWER; ACTION,
    OFFICE. DO, GO; RUN; WORK;
    SERVE
function in trigonometry / SINE;
    COSINE; TANGENT
functional part / ORGAN
functionary / OFFICIAL
fund / VEIN; STOCK; CAPITAL,
    RESERVE; ENDOWMENT
fundament / BASE; BUTTOCKS;
    FOUNDATION
fundamental / BASIC; PRIMARY;
    ESSENTIAL
fundamental document / CHARTER
fundamental law / CONSTITUTION
fundamental measurement / UNIT
fundamental reason / RATIONALE
fundamental tone / KEY
fundamentalist / CONSERVATIVE
funeral / RITES; BURIAL;
    EXEQUIES
funeral bell / KNELL
funeral car / HEARSE
funeral director / UNDERTAKER
funeral hymn / DIRGE, NENIA;
    THRENODY
funeral notice / OBIT; OBITUARY
funeral oration / ELOGE; EULOGY
funeral pile / PYRE
funeral song / DIRGE
funeral vigil / WAKE
funereal / SAD; GLOOMY,
    SOLEMN, SOMBER; MOURNFUL
fungus / MOLD, RUST, SMUT;
    MILDEW
fungus cells / ASCI
fungus disease / TINEA; THRUSH;
    MYCOSIS; RINGWORM;
    MONILIASIS
fungus disease of plant / SCAB;
    ERGOT
fungus dots, pert. to / TELIAL
fungus growth / MOLD, WART;
    MILDEW

fungus sac / ASCUS
fungus tissue / TRAMA
funk / FRIGHT; COWARDICE
funk hole / DUGOUT
funny / ODD; COMIC, DROLL;
    AMUSING
funny business / SHAM; TRICKERY
funny and risque / RIBALD
funny but vulgar / BROAD
fur / MINK, PELT, SEAL, VAIR;
    CIVET, COYPU, GENET, SABLE;
    BEAVER, MARTEN, NUTRIA,
    PELAGE, PELTRY; MINIVER
fur animal / FOX; MINK, SEAL;
    GENET, OTTER, SABLE; BEAVER,
    ERMINE, MARTEN; MUSKRAT
fur in heraldry / PEAN, VAIR;
    ERMINE
fur hunter / TRAPPER
fur neckpiece / BOA; STOLE;
    TIPPET
fur skin / PELT
fur skin of beaver / PLEW
furbelow / FRILL; RUFFLE;
    FLOUNCE
furbish / POLISH; DECORATE
furibund / EXCITED; FRENZIED
Furies / DIRAE; ERINYES
Furies euphemistically /
    EUMENIDES
furious / MAD; WILD; IRATE;
    FIERCE, RAGING, RAVING
furious driver / JEHU
furious storm / TEMPEST,
    TYPHOON; HURRICANE
furious woman / MAENAD
furl / FOLD, ROLL
fur-lined cloak / PELISSE
furlough / LEAVE; ABSENCE
furnace / KILN, OAST, OVEN;
    FORGE; HEATER
furnace mouth / BOCCA
furnace process / SMELTING
furnace tender / STOKER
furnish / RIG; GIVE; CATER, EQUIP
furnish an analog / PARALLEL
furnish with authority / VEST;
    ENDOW
furnish with battlements /
    CRENELLATE
furnish a crew / MAN
furnish with feathers / IMP;
    FLEDGE

Furies, Three

ALECTO (the unresting)
MEGAERA (the jealous)
TISIPHONE (the avenger)

furnish with food / FEED; CATER
furnish money / ENDOW; DONATE; CONTRIBUTE
furnish with new weapons / REARM
furnish with notes / ANNOTATE
furnish with rugs / CARPET
furnish for service / FIT; EQUIP; SUPPLY
furnish with weapons / ARM
furnishings / DECOR; TRAPPINGS
furniture / GEAR; GOODS; OUTFIT; CHATTELS, EQUIPAGE
furniture connection / MORTISE
furniture decoration / BUHL
furniture designer / ADAM; EAMES
furniture wheels / CASTERS
furor / ADO; RAGE; FRENZY; EXCITEMENT
furrow / RUT; LINE; STRIA; GROOVE, TRENCH; WRINKLE. PLOW
furrowed / RIVOSE
furs / PELTRY
further / AID; ABET; ASSIST. AND, TOO, YET; AGAIN. REMOTE; GREATER
further disavowal / REDENIAL
furtherance / ADVANCEMENT
furthermore / TOO; ALSO; BESIDES; MOREOVER

furthermost / FURTHEST, GREATEST
furtive / SLY; SECRET; STEALTHY
furtive look / PEEP
furtive type / SNEAK
furuncle / BOIL
Fury / ALECTO; MEGAERA; TISIPHONE
fury / IRE; RAGE; ANGER, SHREW
furze / WHIN; GORSE
fuse / WELD; BLEND; ANNEAL
fuse incompletely / FRIT
fused glass / FRIT
fused metal / SLAG
fuselage / BODY
fusible substance / METAL; SOLDER
fusion / BLEND, UNION; COALITION
fuss / ADO; FRET, TODO; BUSTLE
fussock / FAT; AWKWARD
fussy / BUSY; FIDGETY, FINICAL
fustian / RANT; BOMBAST; BALDERDASH
fusty / MOLDY; OFFICIOUS
futile / IDLE, VAIN; USELESS
future / TOMORROW. COMING
fuzz / NAP; LINT; POLICE
fylfot / SWASTIKA

G

gab / TALK; MOUTH, PRATE; CHATTER
gabardine / TWILL; GABERDINE
gabble / BABBLE, JABBER; CHATTER
gabby / GOSSIPY
gaberdine / CLOAK, SMOCK
gaberlunzie / BEGGAR; WANDERER
gabi / TARO
Gabon capital / LIBREVILLE
Gabon resident / SCHWEITZER
Gabon town / LAMBARENE
Gabon's first president / MBA
Gabriel's horn / TRUMP; TRUMPET
gaby / FOOL; DUNCE
gad / ROAM; RAMBLE. ROD; GOAD
gadabout / IDLER
gadfly / PEST; SCOURGE; HORSE-FLY
gadget / GISMO, GIZMO; NOVELTY
Gadhelic / MANX, GAELIC
Gad's father / JACOB
Gad's full brother / ASHER
Gad's mother / ZILPAH
Gad's son / ERI; ARELI, HAGGI
Gad's tribe / ERITES
Gadshill resident / DICKENS
gadwall / DUCK
Gaea / GE

Gaea's husband / URANUS
Gaea's parent / CHAOS
Gael / CELT; SCOT; HIGHLANDER
Gaelic / ERSE; CELTIC; GADHELIC
Gaelic exclamation of surprise / OCH
Gaelic hero / FINN; OSSIAN
Gaelic order of poets / BARDS, FILID
Gaelic poem / AISLING
Gaelic sea god / LER
gaff / BOOM, HOOK, SPAR, SPUR
gag / CHOKE, HEAVE. JOKE; TRICK
gag line / CAPTION
gage / PAWN, PLUM; GAUGE, GLOVE
gaggle / CACKLE
gaiety / GLEE, SHOW; CHEER; FINERY, GAYETY; DELIGHT
gaily mischievous / ARCH
gain / GET, NET, WIN; EARN, REAP; REACH. PROFIT; EARNINGS
gain advantage over / BEAT; WORST
gain by labor / EARN
gain momentum / SPEED; AC-CELERATE
gain as profit / NET
gain the upper hand / MASTER
gainly / SHAPELY; GRACEFUL

gainsay / DENY; OPPOSE; DISPUTE
gait / LOPE, PACE, RACK, STEP, TROT, WALK; AMBLE; CANTER, GALLOP
gaited horse / PACER; TROTTER
gaiters / SPATS; LEGGINGS
gala / FETE, SHOW; FESTIVAL. GAY; FESTIVE
gala day / HOLIDAY
Galahad's father / LANCELOT
Galahad's kingdom / SARRAS
Galahad's mother / ELAINE
Galapagos naturalist / DARWIN
Galapagos reptile / TORTOISE
Galatea / FLIRT, NYMPH
Galatea's lover / ACIS; PYGMALION
galaxy / BEVY; UNIVERSE
Galba's successor / OTHO
gale / GUST, WIND; BLAST, STORM
Galen's forte / MEDICINE
Galician city / CRACOW; CORUNNA
Galilee capital / TIBERIAS
Galilee Sea / KINNERET, TIBERIAS
Galilee town / CANA; NAZARETH
Galilee tribe / NAPHTALI
gall / VEX; FRET; CHAFE; IRRITATE. BILE; RANCOR; IMPUDENCE
gall on an oak / OAKAPPLE
galla ox / ZEBU; SANGA
Gallagher's pal / SHEAN
gallant / GAY; BOLD; BRAVE
gallantry / VALOR; COURAGE
gallery / LOFT; ALURE, SALON; BALCONY; CORRIDOR
galley / AESC; BARGE, PROOF; BIREME, DROMON; KITCHEN, TRIREME
gallic / FRENCH; GAULISH
galliman fry / HASH, OLIO, STEW
gallinaceous / HENLIKE; RASORIAL
gallinaceous tropical bird / GUAN; CURASSOW
gallinipper / MOSQUITO
gallinule / RAIL; MOORHEN
Gallipoli battle / SUVLABAY
gallivant / GAD; IDLE; FLIRT
galliwasp / LIZARD
gallop / RUN; LEAP, PELT; HASTEN
gallop recklessly / TANTIVY
gallop slowly / LOPE
galloping dominoes / DICE
gallows / DROP; NOOSE; GIBBET
gallows bird / ROGUE; CRIMINAL
galluses / BRACES; SUSPENDERS
Galofalo / CHARYBDIS
galop / DANCE; TWOSTEP
galore / LOTS; PLENTY
galosh / ARCTIC; OVERSHOE
galvanic / VOLTAIC; STIMULATING
galvanize / ZINC; EXCITE
Galveston Plan official / COM- MISSIONER

Galway Bay islands / ARAN
galways / WHISKERS
gam / LEG, POD; HERD. CALL; VISIT
gambado / BOUND, CAPER
Gambia capital / BATHURST
Gambian money / DALASI
Gambier island / MANGAREVA
gamble / BET; GAME. RISK
gambler / DICER, SHARK, SHARP
gambler's wager / LAY; ANTE; STAKE
gambling, pert. to / ALEATORY
gambling assistant / TOUT; CROUPIER
gambling capital / RENO; LAS-VEGAS; MONTECARLO
gambling cubes / DICE
gambling game / DICE, FARO, KENO, PICO; MONTE, POKER, STUSS
gambling game for large group / BINGO
gambling house / CASINO
gambol / HOP; LEAP, PLAY, ROMP, SKIP; CAPER, FRISK; FROLIC
Gambrinus' invention / ALE; BEER
game / TAG; PLAN, PREY; SPORT; QUARRY, SCHEME; PASTIME. PLAY; GAMBLE. READY. See also sport
game from Africa / WARI; MANCALA
game like bagatelle / TIVOLI
game bird / GUAN; SNIPE; GROUSE; PHEASANT
game of cards / LU; LOO, NAP, PAM, PAN, PUT, RUM; FARO, SKAT, SOLO; CINCH, MACAO, MONTE, OMBER, OMBRE, PITCH, POKER, RUMMY, STUSS, WHIST; BASSET, BRIDGE, EUCHRE, HEARTS, PINOCH, ROUNCE
game at carnival / PITCHPENNY
game of chance / LOO; KENO; BINGO; ROULETTE
game for children / TAG; DIBS; JACKS; LEAPFROG
game like croquet / MALL; PALL-MALL
game with dice / PIG; CRAPS; HAZARD
game expert / HOYLE
game of feigning death / POSSUM
game of fingers / MORA; MORRA
game fish / BASS, CERO, SCAD, TUNA; SARGO, TROUT; MARLIN, SALMON
game for hotrodders / CHICKEN
game for loggers / BIRLING
game of marbles / COB, TAW; HOGO

game for no tricks / NULLO
game of oriental origin / CHESS
game piece / MAN; COUNTER
game played on a board / GO;
   CHESS, HALMA; PACHISI;
   CHECKERS, DRAUGHTS
game in pub / DARTS
game of skill / POOL; CHESS
game with special pieces / MA-
   JONG; MAHJONG; DOMINOES
gamecock / STAG
gamekeeper / RANGER, WARDEN
gamely / PLUCKILY
gamete / GERM; ZYGOTE
gamin / BOY, TAD; ARAB
gaming cube / DIE
gaming piece / MAN; DOMINO
gammer / WIFE; WOMAN
gammon / HAM; HUMBUG. HOAX
gamp / UMBRELLA
gamut / RANGE; EXTENT
gamy / PLUCKY
gander / STEG; GOOSE
Gandhi's system / SATYAGRAHA
Gandhi's title / MAHATMA
Ganelon / GAN; TRAITOR
Ganesha's father / SHIVA
Ganesha's mother / PARVATI
gang / BAND, CREW; CABAL,
   SQUAD
ganger / BOSS; LEADER; FOREMAN
Ganges barge / PUTELI; PUTELEE
Ganges crocodilian / GAVIAL
Ganges dolphin / SOOSOO
gangling / LANKY; AWKWARD
gangplank / RAMP; GANGWAY
gangrel / STUPID; AWKWARD
gangrene / NECROSIS
gangster / THUG; MAFIOSO;
   RACKETEER
gangue / VEIN
gangway / PLANK; PASSAGE
gannet / GOOSE, SOLAN;
   WOODIBIS
ganoid fish / GAR; BELUGA,
   BICHIR, BOWFIN; STURGEON
gantry / RACK; FRAME; SUPPORT
ganymede / WAITER; CUPBEARER
Ganymede's abductor / ZEUS
Ganymede's bird / EAGLE
Ganymede's brother / ILUS
Ganymede's father / TROS
gaol / JAIL
gap / PASS, RIFT; CHASM, CHINK,
   CLEFT; BREACH
gap in hedge / MUSE; MEUSE
gap in mountains / COL; PASS
gape / GAZE, YAWN; STARE
gapeseed / SPECTACLE
gar / PIKE; SNOOK; NEEDLEFISH
garab / BAHAN
garage / SHOP; HANGAR; SHELTER

garb / HABIT, ROBES; RAIMENT
garb of a highlander / KILT
garb of prisoner / STRIPES
garbage / OFFAL; REFUSE
garbage heap / MIDDEN
garbed / CLAD; DRESSED
garble / DISTORT, PERVERT; MIS-
   QUOTE
garden / GROW; CULTIVATE. PLOT
garden of the Bible / EDEN; PARA-
   DISE; GETHSEMANE
garden bower / NOOK; ARBOR
Garden City / CHICAGO
garden of eden / PARADISE
garden flower / LILY, ROSE; ASTER,
   PANSY, PEONY; ALYSSUM
garden fruit / MELON; TOMATO
garden party / FETE
garden sage / SALVIA
garden shrub / AZALEA
garden soil / DIRT, LOAM
Garden State / NEW JERSEY
garden tending / WEEDING
garden tool / HOE; HOSE, RAKE;
   SPADE; TROWEL
gardening / HORTICULTURE
Gareth's nickname / BEAUMAINS
gargantuan / HUGE; MIGHTY
Gargantua's author / RABELAIS
Gargantua's son / PANTAGRUEL
garish / GAUDY; DAZZLING
garland / LEI; BAYS; ANADEM,
   WREATH; CHAPLET, FESTOON
garlic / RAMSONS
garlic root / MOLY
garment / ABA; CAPE, COAT, GARB,
   GOWN, JAMA, ROBE, SARI, SLIP,
   VEST; DHOTI, DRESS, FROCK,
   HABIT, SIMAR, SKIRT, STOLE,
   TUNIC; DHOOTI, JACKET,
   MANTLE, RAGLAN, ULSTER,
   APPAREL, CHEMISE, CLOTHES,
   COSTUME. See also dress
garment for bishop / CHIMAR;
   CHIMERE
garment edge / HEM
garment fastener / PIN; FROG;
   CLASP; ZIPPER
garment insert / GORE; GUSSET
garment maker / TAILOR
garment of Malaysia / SARONG
garment part / LAPEL; COLLAR
garment for priest / ALB; AMICE,
   COTTA, EPHOD; CASSOCK; SUR-
   PLICE
garment for rain / PONCHO;
   SLICKER
garments / GARB; UNIFORM
garner / REAP; STOCK; GATHER
garnet / PYROPE; ALMANDITE,
   CARBUNCLE
garnish / ADORN; DECORATE

garnish of toast / SIPPET; CROUTON
garnishment / LIEN; SUMMONS
garret / LOFT; ATTIC
garrison / FORT; TROOPS; BARRACKS
garron / NAG
garrot / SEADUCK; GOLDENEYE
garrote / STRANGLE, THROTTLE
garrulous / TALKATIVE
garter / BADGE, ORDER; ELASTIC
Garuda's father / KASYAPA
Garuda's foe / INDRA; SERPENT
Garuda's mother / VINATA
gas / FUEL; ETHER, VAPOR; GASOLINE; ASPHYXIANT
gas bag / BALLOON
gas for dirigible / HELIUM; HYDROGEN
gasconade / BOAST; BLUSTER
gaseous / TENUOUS; SERIFORM
gaseous, c.f. / AER; AERI
gaseous, compound / BUTANE, ETHANE; METHANE
gaseous element / NEON; ARGON, RADON, XENON; HELIUM, OXYGEN; KRYPTON; CHLORINE, FLUORINE, HYDROGEN, NITROGEN
gaseous mixture / AIR
gash / CUT; SLIT; WOUND
gasket / WASHER; LASHING, PACKING
gasoline / PETROL
gasoline additive / OCTANE
Gasoline Alley character / SKEEZIX
gasoline engine part / VALVE; INJECTOR; CARBURETOR
gasoline jelly / NAPALM
gasoline rating / OCTANE
gasp / PANT; LABOR; SWELTER
Gaspar's companion / MELCHIOR; BALTHAZAR
gasper / CIGARETTE
gassy / INFLATED; TALKATIVE
gastronome / EPICURE, GOURMET
gastrophile / GLUTTON; GOURMAND
gastropod / SLUG; MUREX, SNAIL, WHELK; LIMPET, WINKLE; ABALONE
gastropod shell / COWRIE
gat / PISTOL; CHANNEL
gate / BAB, GIT, YAT; DOOR; STILE; PORTAL
gatehouse / LODGE
gateway / CHANNEL; ENTRANCE
gateway to Shinto temple / TORII
gather / CROP, CULL, FOLD, GAIN, MEET, PICK, REAP; AMASS, GLEAN
gather and bind / SHEAVE

gather facts / STUDY; EXAMINE; RESEARCH
gather by reasoning / INFER; DEDUCE, DERIVE
gather scattered grain / GLEAN
gather together / COLLECT
gatherer / COLLATOR; COLLECTOR
gathering / BEE; CROWD; MEETING
gathering of grouse / LEK
gathering implement / RAKE; BROOM; VACUUM
Gath's hero / GOLIATH
Gath's king / ACHISH
gatling gun / REPEATER
gauche / CLUMSY; AWKWARD
gaucho tree / USE
gaucho weapon / BOLA; BOLAS
gaud / FINERY; TRINKET
gaudy / GAY; SHOWY; GARISH
gaudy ornament / BAUBLE, TINSEL
gaudy spectacle / GALA; PARADE; PAGEANT
Gaugamela victor / ALEXANDER
gauge / GAGE, RATE; METER
gauge indicator / HAND; NEEDLE
Gaulish people / REMI; CELTS, AEDUI; BELGAE; SEQUANI
Gaulish priest / DRUID
gaum / TAR; PAVE; SMEAR
gaunt / LANK, LEAN; SPARE; MEAGER; DESOLATE, RAWBONED
gauntlet / GLOVE; CHALLENGE
Gautama / BUDDHA
gauzy fabric / LENO; LISSE, MARLI, TULLE; TISSUE; CHIFFON
gave an account / REPORTED
gave apple to Aphrodite / PARIS
gave back / RETURNED
gave birth / BORE; BEGOT
gave heed to / ATTENDED, LISTENED
gave in / RELENTED
gave visual attention / LOOKED
gavel / RENT; SHEAF; MALLET
gavial / NAKOO
gavotte / DANCE
Gawain's brother / GARETH; GAHERIS; AGRAVAIN
Gawain's father / LOT
Gawain's half-brother / MORDRED
Gawain's opponent / GREENKNIGHT
gawk / OAF; CUCKOO; SIMPLETON
gawky / RAW; AWKWARD, UNCOUTH
gay / AIRY; GAUDY, HAPPY, JOLLY, MERRY, RIANT; BLITHE, JOVIAL
gay blade / LOTHARIO
gay science / POETRY
gaysome / GLAD; MERRY; JOYOUS
Gaza victor / ALLENBY

gaze / GAWK, LOOK, OGLE; STARE
gaze attentively / PORE
gaze fiercely / GLARE; GLOWER
gaze rudely / STARE
gazebo / CUPOLA; GALLERY;
  BELVEDERE
gazelle / AHU, GOA; ADMI, CORA,
  MOHR; ADDRA, KORIN, MHORR
gazette / JOURNAL; NEWSPAPER
gazob / BLUNDERER
gear / CAM, RIG; DRESS; OUTFIT,
  TACKLE; HARNESS
gear for diving / FINS; SNORKEL
gear with teeth / COG
gear wheel / PINION
Geats' prince / BEOWULF
Geb's consort / NUT
Geb's daughter / ISIS
Geb's son / SET; OSIRIS
gee / MOVE, TURN. RIGHT
geezer / CODGER, GALOOT
gel / JELL; CONGEAL
gelatinous / VISCOUS; MALACOID
gelatinous matter / AGAR; COLLIN
Gelderland city / EDE; ARNHEM
gelid / ICY; COLD; FROSTY
gem / JADE, ONYX, OPAL, RUBY,
  SARD; AGATE, BERYL, JEWEL,
  PEARL, STONE, TOPAZ; GARNET,
  IOLITE, JASPER, SPINEL; DIA-
  MOND, EMERALD, PERIDOT;
  SAPPHIRE
gem cut with design / INTAGLIO
gem cut in relief / CAMEO
gem cutter / LAPIDARY
gem facet / BEZEL, CULET, TABLE
Gem State / IDAHO
gem surface / FACET
gem weight / CARAT, KARAT
Gemara part / HAGGADA,
  HALAKAH
gematria / NUMEROLOGY
gemel / TWIN; DOUBLE
Gemini / TWINS
Gemini partner / CASTOR, POLLUX
gemmy / BRILLIANT;
  GLITTERING
gender / BEGET. SEX
genealogical record / TREE; DE-
  SCENT; PEDIGREE
genealogy / LINEAGE; PEDIGREE
genera / KINDS, SORTS
general / USUAL, VAGUE; COM-
  MON; INEXACT; ORDINARY.
  CHIEF
general aspect / MIEN; SCENE
general assembly / PLENUM;
  LEGISLATURE
general assistant / AIDE
general direction / TENOR, TREND
general fight / MELEE; FREE-
  FORALL
general pardon / AMNESTY

general summary / SYNOPSIS
general type / MEAN; AVERAGE
generality / MAJORITY, POPULACE
generalize / INFER; EXTEND
generally / OFTEN; USUALLY
generalship / MANAGEMENT
generate / FORM; BEGET, BREED;
  DEVELOP, PRODUCE; ENGENDER
generating cell / GAMETE
generation / AGE, ERA; BREED;
  PERIOD; PROGENY
generosity / LIBERALITY
generous / NOBLE; STRONG;
  LIBERAL
genesis / ORIGIN; BEGINNING
genethliac / NATIVITY
Geneva in German / GENF
Geneva's lake / LEMAN; SENECA
Geneva's river / RHONE
genial / WARM; MERRY; JOVIAL
geniality / GAIETY; VIVACITY
genic / GENETIC
genie / JINNI; SPIRIT
genip tree / GENIPAX
genipa wood / LANA
genius / BENT, GIFT; DEITY
genius's work / ART
Genoese family / DORIA
genre / KIND, TYPE; STYLE
gens / CLAN
Genseric's subjects / VANDALS
genteel / NICE; REFINED
gentile / PAGAN; ETHNIC
gentiles / GOYIM
gentility / POLISH; SUAVITY;
  CIVILITY, COURTESY
gentle / KIND, MILD, MEEK;
  BLAND, QUIET; DOCILE, PLACID,
  TENDER
gentle blow / PAT; CHUCK
gentle heat / TEPOR
gentle reminder / HINT
gentle slope / GLACIS
gentle touch / CARESS
gentle wind / AURA; BREEZE
gentleman / MAN, SIR; AMATEUR
gentleman's gentleman / VALET
gentleness / LENITY; MILDNESS
gentlewoman / LADY; ATTENDANT
genuflect / KNEEL; WORSHIP
genuine / OPEN, PURE, REAL, TRUE
genus / KIND, RACE, SORT; CLASS,
  GROUP, LOGIC, ORDER
genus, pert. to / GENERIC
genus of African rhinos / DICEROS
genus of African trees / COLA
genus of alpacas / LAMA
genus of ants / ATTA; ANOMMA
genus of apes / PAN; PONGO
genus of aquatic plants / TRAPA
genus of baboons / PAPIO
genus of bass / ROCCUS
genus of bears / URSUS

genus of bedbugs / CIMEX
genus of beeches / FAGUS
genus of bees / APIS; OSMIA; BOMBUS
genus of beetles / AMARA, HISPA
genus of birches / BETULA
genus of bivalve mollusks / MYA; LEDA
genus of bowfins / AMIA
genus of burbots / LOTA
genus of bustards / OTIS
genus of butterflies / DANAUS, EN-CLOE, MORPHO, PIERIS; SATYRUS
genus of camels / CAMELUS
genus of cats / FELIS
genus of cattle / BOS
genus of cetaceans / INIA; PHY-SETER; DELPHINUS
genus of cherries / PRUNUS
genus of codfish / GADUS
genus of corn / ZEA
genus of cottonwoods / POPULUS
genus of crickets / ACHETA; GRYLLUS
genus of damselfish / ABUDEFDUF
genus of deer / DAMA; CERVUS
genus of dogs / CANIS
genus of dragonflies / ANAX
genus of dung flies / SCATOPHAGA
genus of earwigs / FORFICULA
genus of eels / MURAENA; AN-GUILLA
genus of elephants / ELEPHAS; LOXODONTA
genus of evergreens / ABIES, PI-CEA, PINUS, THUJA, TSUGA
genus of fireflies / LUCIOLA
genus of flax / LINUM
genus of foxes / VULPES
genus of frogs / HYLA, RANA; ANURA
genus of fruit flies / DROSOPHILA
genus of geese / ANSER
genus of goats / CAPRA
genus of grasses / POA; AVENA; BROMUS; FESTUCA, HORDEUM
genus of grasshoppers / LOCUSTA
genus of hawks / BUTEO, FALCO
genus of heather / ERICA
genus of herbs / RUTA; SALVIA; MELISSA, MONARDA; POTERIUM
genus of herrings / CLUPEA
genus of holly / ILEX
genus of hoopoes / UPUPA
genus of horse flies / TABANUS
genus of horses / EQUUS
genus of house flies / MUSCA
genus of ivies / HEDERA
genus of larch / LARIX
genus of latrine flies / FANNIA
genus of lice / PEDICULUS
genus of lions / PANTHERA

genus of lizards / UTA; SEPS; AGAMA; IGUANA
genus of mackerels / SCOMBER
genus of magpies / PICA
genus of maples / ACER
genus of march flies / BIBIO
genus of men / HOMO
genus of mice / MUS
genus of minks / MUSTELA
genus of mints / MENTHA; KOELLIA
genus of mistletoes / VISCUM
genus of mockingbirds / MIMUS
genus of mole rats / SPALAX
genus of moles / TALPA
genus of monkeys / CEBUS; ATELES, MACACA; ALOUATTA
genus of moose / ALCES
genus of mosquitoes / AEDES, CULEX; ANOPHELES
genus of moths / TINEA; BOMBYX
genus of mullet / MUGIL
genus of musk ox / OVIBOS
genus of nettles / URTICA
genus of nuthatches / SITTA
genus of oaks / QUERCUS
genus of oats / AVENA
genus of oil-pool flies / PSILOPA
genus of olives / OLEA
genus of onions / ALLIUM
genus of opossums / MARMOSA; DIDELPHIS
genus of orioles / ICTERUS
genus of otters / LUTRA
genus of owls / BUBO, OTUS; STRIX
genus of pandas / AILURUS
genus of pigeons / COLUMBA
genus of pikes / ESOX
genus of ragweed / AMBROSIA
genus of ravens / CORVUS
genus of reindeer / RANGIFER
genus of roaches / BLATTA
genus of robins / TURDUS
genus of salmon / SALMO
genus of seahorses / HIPPO-CAMPUS
genus of sealions / ZALOPHUS
genus of seals / PHOCA
genus of seaweeds / LAMINARIA
genus of skates / RAJA
genus of Spanish fly / LYTTA
genus of sparrows / PASSER
genus of sturgeons / HUSO
genus of swallows / HIRUNDO
genus of swine / SUS
genus of termites / TERMES
genus of tsetse flies / GLOSSINA
genus of tupelos / NYSSA
genus of wasp flies / CONOPS
genus of wasps / SIREX, SPHEX
genus of water scorpions / NEPA
genus of water striders / GERRIS
genus of waterbucks / KOBUS

genus of willows / SALIX
genus of wolverines / GULO
genus of worms / FILARIA
genus of zebras / EQUUS
geode / VUG; DRUSE
geognost / GEOLOGIST
geographical cyclopedia / GAZET-TEER
geographical diagram / MAP; CHART; PORTOLAN
geological age / ERA; EPOCH; PE-RIOD, SYSTEM
geological division / BALA, LIAS
geological era / AZOIC; CENOZOIC, MESOZOIC
geological find / OIL; FOSSIL
geological formation / IONE; BENCH; TERRACE, TERRANE
geological period / ECOCENE; MIO-CENE, PERMIAN; CAMBRIAN, JURASSIC, PLIOCENE, TRIASSIC
geological prefix / EO; MIO; OLIGO
geological stage / GUNZ, RISS, WURM
geological suffix / IAN; CENE
geometric axis / ABSCISSA, ORDI-NATE
geometric curve / HELIX; FOLIUM, SPIRAL; CYCLOID; PARABOLA
geometric figure / CONE, CUBE, LUNE; PRISM, RHOMB; CIRCLE, SQUARE; ELLIPSE, POLYGON
geometric line / CHORD, LOCUS; SECANT; TANGENT
geometric proportion / RATIO
geometric ratio / PI; SINE
geometric rule / THEOREM
geometric solid / CONE, CUBE; PRISM; CYLINDER; ELLIPSOID
geometrician / EUCLID; GEOMETER
geophagy / PICA
geoponics / FARMING; HUS-BANDRY
Georgia capital / ATLANTA
Georgia city / MACON; AUGUSTA
Georgia mountain / STONE
Georgia Peach / COBB
Georgia river / COOSA, FLINT
Georgia state nickname / PEACH; CRACKER
Georgia state tree / LIVEOAK
Georgia swamp / OKEFINOKEE
Georgian capital / TIFLIS
Georgian city / BATUM
Georgian mountain / ELBRUS
Georgian mountains / CAUCASUS
Georgian native / IMER
georgic / RURAL; RUSTIC
Geraint's wife / ENID
geratic / GERONTIC
Gerda's husband / FREY
gerent / MANAGER

germ / BUD, BUG; SEED; OVARY, SPORE; EMBRYO
germ cell / EGG; OVUM; SPERM
germ free / ASEPTIC, STERILE
German / HUN; BOCHE, FRITZ; COUSIN, TEUTON
German admiral / SPEE
German apple cake / STRUDEL
German area / HARZ, RUHR, SAAR
German army camp / STALAG
German article / DAS, DER, DIE, EIN; EINE
German author / AUE; BOLL, MANN; HEINE, HESSE, RILKE; GOETHE
German beer / MUM; BIER, BOCK
German bomber / STUKA
German canal / KIEL
German cannon / BERTHA
German capital / BONN; BERLIN
German cavalryman / UHLAN
German chancellor / ADENAUER, BISMARCK
German city / EMS, ULM; ESSEN; BERLIN
German coffee cake / STOLLEN
German coin / MARK; THALER; PFENNIG
German colonial coin / PESA
German composer / BACH; WAGNER
German dictator / HITLER
German Egyptologist / EBERS
German emperor's title / KAISER
German empire / REICH
German engraver / DURER, STOSS
German exclamation / ACH; HEIL, HOCH
German forest guardian / WALD-GRAVE
German highway / AUTOBAHN
German inventor / BENZ, OTTO
German knight / RITTER
German lancer / ULAN; UHLAN
German league / BUND; VEREIN
German linguist / BOPP; GRIMM
German mathematician / KLEIN
German measles / RUBELLA
German militia / LANDWEHR
German money / MARK; PFENNIG
German name prefix / VON
German naval commander / SPEE; DOENITZ
German painter / MARC, ROOS; DURER, ERNST; CRANACH, HOLBEIN
German parliament / REICHSTAG
German philosopher / KANT, MARX; HEGEL; FICHTE; NIETZSCHE
German poet / HEINE; GOETHE
German port / HAMBURG, STETTIN
German president / EBERT

German printer / GUTENBERG
German pronoun / DU; ICH, SIE
German reformer / LUTHER
German rifle / MAUSER
German river / EMS; EDER, ELBE, ESER, ISAR, ODER, RUHR, SAAR; RHINE, WESER
German scientist / OHM; KOCH, MACH; HABER, HERTZ; BUNSEN
German socialist / MARX; ENGELS; LUXEMBURG
German soldier / KRAUT, UHLAN; HEINIE
German state / BADEN, HESSE, LIPPE; SAXONY
German steel city / ESSEN
German title / VON; GRAF, HERR
German toast / PROSIT
German traditionally military / PRUSSIAN
German tribal region / GAU
German warplane / STUKA; FOKKER
German watering place / EMS; BADEN
German wine / HOCK; MOSELLE
German-Czech region / SUDETEN
germander / VERONICA
germane / APT; AKIN; FITTING; PERTINENT; APPROPRIATE
Germanic deity / DONAR, TIWAZ, WODAN, WODEN
Germanic letter / RUNE; FRAKTUR
Germanic tribesman / GOTH, JUTE; FRANK, SAXON; TEUTON
Germany / ALLEMAGNE; DEUTSCH-LAND. See also German
germicide / ANTISEPTIC
germinate / BUD; SHOOT; SPROUT
germinated barley / MALT
germs / VIRUSES; BACTERIA
gest / GESTE; GESTURE; AD-VENTURE
gesticulate / WAVE; GESTURE
gesture / MIME; ACTION, MOTION
gesture of affection / PAT; CARESS
gesture of contempt / CUT, FIG; SNOOK
gesture dance of Fiji / SIVA
gesture in dances of India / MUDRA
gesture of indifference / SHRUG
gesundheit / PROSIT; BLESSYOU
get / WIN; EARN, GAIN; ATTAIN, OBTAIN, SECURE; ACHIEVE
get along / FARE; AGREE; PROSPER
get away / SCAT; SCRAM; DEPART
get away from / SLIP; ELUDE, EVADE; ESCAPE
get back / REDEEM, REGAIN, RE-TURN
get the benefit of / USE
get estate / INHERIT

get from / DERIVE
get going / BEGIN
get hold of / ACQUIRE
get information / LEARN
get lost / SCAT, SHOO; SCRAM; BEATIT
get lucky / HIT
get metal from ore / SMELT
get money for / SELL
get money by intimidation / EXTORT
get one's bearings / ORIENTATE
get out / GO; LEAVE, SCRAM, SPLIT
get out of sight / HIDE
get ragged / FRAY
get a rash / BREAKOUT
get ready / PREPARE; REHEARSE
get rid of / SHED
get there / ARRIVE
get together / MEET; UNITE
get up / ARISE; AROUSE
get well / RECOVER
get-together / REUNION
Gettysburg loser / LEE
Gettysburg orator / EVERETT
Gettysburg victor / MEADE
getup / DRESS, HABIT; FINERY; COSTUME
get-up-and-go / ENERGY
gewgaw / TOY; GAUD; TRIFLE
geyser deposit / SINTER; TERRACE; GEYSERITE; TRAVERTINE
Ghana, pert. to / GHANAIAN
Ghana capital / ACCRA
Ghana lake / VOLTA
Ghana money / CEDI
Ghana people / EWE; FANTI; ASHANTI
Ghana river / OFIN, TANO; VOLTA
ghastly / GRIM, PALE; LURID; PAL-LID; HAGGARD, HIDEOUS
ghetto tenement owner / SLUM-LORD
ghost / BHUT, HANT, SOUL; IMAGE, LARVA, LEMUR, SHADE, SPOOK; SHADOW, SPIRIT, WRAITH; PHANTOM
Ghost Dance founder / WOVOKA
ghost fish / CHIRO
ghostly / SPIRITUAL; SUPER-NATURAL
ghostly being / GHOUL; VAMPIRE
ghoul / NECROPHAGE; GRAVE-ROBBER
ghoulish / DEMONIAC, FIENDISH
GI / DRAFTEE, SOLDIER
GI meal / MESS; KRATION
GI's address / APO
giant / ETEN, OGRE; TITAN; MON-STER. HUGE; BULKY
giant armadillo / TATU; TATOU
giant bulrush / TULE
giant cactus / SAGUARO

giant clam / TRIDACNA
giant grass / OTATE
giant killed by David / GOLIATH
giant killer / JACK; DAVID; APOLLO
giant Mexican grass / OTATE
giant perch / BEKTI; COCKUP
giant squid / KRAKEN
Giants' burial place / ETNA
Giant's Causeway rock / BASALT
Giant's Dance / STONEHENGE
Giants' mother / GE
gib / JIB; SALMON, TOMCAT
gibberish / GAMMON, JABBER, JARGON; TWADDLE
gibbet / NOOSE; GALLOWS; SCAFFOLD
gibbon / LAR; HOOLOCK, SIAMANG
gibbous / CONVEX; HUNCHED
gibe / JAPE, JEER, MOCK, TWIT
giblets / GEWGAWS, GIZZARD
Gibraltar bay / ALGECIRAS
Gibraltar founder / TARIQ
Gibraltar's opposite / CEUTA
Gibson cocktail garnish / ONION
giddy / DIZZY; FICKLE; FLIGHTY
gift / TIP; ALMS, BOON; DOWER, POWER; BOUNTY, GENIUS; HANDSEL
gift to develop / TALENT
gift-giver / SANTA
gig / BOAT; DEMERIT; CARRIAGE
gigantic / HUGE, VAST; GIANT, TITAN; IMMENSE
gigantic person / TITAN; MOUNTAIN
giggle / TITTER; SNIGGER
gila monster / LIZARD
Gilbert Island / BETIO, MAKIN; TARAWA
Gilbert and Sullivan opera / MIKADO; PINAFORE
gild / ADORN, PAINT, PLATE
gilded / COATED, PLATED
gilded brass / ORMOLU
Gilead's father / MACHIR
Gilgamesh's companion / EABANI
Gilgamesh's foe / HUMBABA
Gilgamesh's land / ERECH
gill / GUT; BROOK; WATTLE
gillie / ATTENDANT
gilt / SOW; DORE; GILDING
gimcrack / SHOWY; TRUMPERY
gimp / LIMP; BRAID; ENERGY
gin / TRAP; RUMMY, TRICK; SEEDER; MACHINE; HOLLANDS. IF
gin mill / BAR
ginger / PEP; SPUNK; FLAVOR
ginger cookie / SNAP
gingerbread / FANCY; TAWDRY
gingerbread palm / DUM; DOOM
gingerly / DAINTILY; CAUTIOUSLY
ginkgo tree / MAIDENHAIR

gipsy / GYPSY, NOMAD; GITANO, ROMANY; TSIGANE; WANDERER
giraffe / CAMELOPARD
giraffelike mammal / OKAPI
girasol / OPAL; HELIOTROPE
gird / BELT, BIND; BRACE
girder / BEAM; HBEAM, IBEAM, TRUSS
girdle / OBI; BAND, BELT, CEST, SASH, ZONE; BRACE, GIRTH; CINCTURE; SURCINGLE. ENCIRCLE
girdle fillers / HIPS
girl / GAL, SIS; BIRD, LASS, MAID, MISS; CHICK; DAMSEL
girl Friday / SECRETARY
girl graduate / ALUMNA
girl hunter / WOLF
girl at mirror / PRIMPER
girl relative / NIECE; SISTER
girl from Russia / OLGA
girl student / COED
girlfriend / STEADY; SWEETIE; SWEETHEART
girl's name / ADA, EVA, INA, MAE; ALMA, DORA, ETTA, LISA, MARY, NORA, VERA; ANITA, CELIA, ELENA
girl's plaything / DOLL; JACKS; JUMPROPE
girn / GRIN; SNARL
Girondist of 1790s / ISNARD; BRISSOT
girt / MOORED; ENCIRCLED; SURROUNDED
girth / CINCH; CIRCUMFERENCE
gist / NUB; CORE, PITH; POINT; KERNEL; ESSENCE
give / PAY, EMIT, HAND; ALLOW, GRANT, YIELD
give aid / HELP; ASSIST
give back / RETURN; RESTORE
give character to / ENDUE
give emphasis / STRESS
give the eye / OGLE
give forth / EMIT; SPEAK
give fresh strength / RENEW
give holy orders / ORDAIN
give in to / YIELD; SUBMIT
give legal assent / SANCTION
give life to / BIRTH
give lip to / SASS
give a meal to / FEED
give off / EMIT
give pause / DETER
give a prize / AWARD
give a rank to / RATE
give a tenth part / TITHE
give for a time / LEND, LOAN
give too much medicine / OVERDOSE
give up / CEDE, QUIT; YIELD; SURRENDER

give up the ghost / DIE
give voice to / UTTER
given condition / DATA; PREMISE
giver / DONOR; BENEFACTOR
giver of weapons / ARMER
Giza sight / SPHINX; PYRAMID
gizzard / CRAW; THROAT
glabrous / SMOOTH; HAIRLESS
glace / ICED; SHINY; FROZEN
glacial / ICY; FRIGID; FROSTED
glacial crack / CREVAS; CREVASSE
glacial crag / NUNATAK
glacial deposit / TAIL; MORAINE
glacial era / ICEAGE
glacial hill / DRUMLIN
glacial hollow / CIRQUE, CORRIE
glacial period / GUNZ, RISS, WURM;
   MINDEL
glacial pinnacle / SERAC
glacial ridge / OS; KAME, OSAR,
   PAHA; ESKAR, ESKER
glacial snow / FIRN, NEVE
glacial space / CREVASSE; BERG-
   SCHRUND
glaciated area / ICECAP
glacier fragment / BERG
glacis / SLOPE
glad / HAPPY; ELATED, JOYOUS;
   PLEASED; CHEERFUL
glad tidings / GOSPEL; EVANGEL
gladden / CHEER; DELIGHT, RE-
   JOICE
glade / DELL, GLEN, PARK; GLEAM
gladiate / ENSATE; XIPHOID
gladiator / FIGHTER, MIRMILLO;
   RETIARIUS, SWORDSMAN
gladiator's trainer / LANISTA
gladly / FAIN, LIEF; WILLINGLY
gladness / BLISS
gladsome / GAY; JOYOUS
gladstone / PORTMANTEAU
glaik / MOCKERY
glaikit / DAFT; GIDDY; FOOLISH
Glamorgan city / CARDIFF
Glamorgan river / TAFF, TAWE
glamorous / ALLURING;
   ENTRANCING
glamour / CHARM, MAGIC;
   WITCHERY
glance / SEE; LOOK, PEEP; FLASH
glance through / SCAN, SKIM
glancing rebound / RICOCHET
gland / ACORN, ORGAN
gland, c.f. / ADEN; ADENO
gland-shaped / ADENOID
glandular disorder / ADENIA;
   ADENITIS
glandular inflammation / ADENITIS
glandular secretion / HORMONE
glare / GLOW; FLARE, GLEAM,
   SHINE, STARE
glaring light / BLAZE, FLARE
glary / ICY; SLICK; SMOOTH

Glasgow's river / CLYDE
glass / LENS, PANE; GOBLET, MIR-
   ROR; TUMBLER; BAROMETER
glass artisan / GLAZIER
glass colored with cobalt / SMALT
glass cover for food / BELL;
   CLOCHE
glass flask / MATRASS
glass fragments / CULLET
glass handling rod / PUNTY
glass ingredient / SILICA
glass jar / BOCAL; TALLBOY
glass with marbled effect /
   SCHMELZ
glass for mosaic / TESSERA
glass panel / PANE
glass only partly fused / FRIT; FRITT
glass for paste jewels / STRASS
glass rod / CANE
glass showcase / VITRINE
glass tempering / ANNEALING
glass tube / PIPETTE
glass used in lab / BEAKER, RE-
   TORT; TESTTUBE
glass vessel / VIAL; FLASK, PHIAL;
   AMPULE, BOTTLE, CARBOY
glasses / SPECS; SHADES;
   GOGGLES; SPECTACLES
glasslike / VITRIC
glassmaker's oven / LEER, LEHR
glassmaker's rod / PONTY; PONTIL
glasswort / KALI; SALTWORT
glassy / GLAZED, SMOOTH; HY-
   ALINE; VITREOUS
glassy paint / ENAMEL
glassy rock / QUARTZ; OBSIDIAN
Glauce's father / CREON
Glaucus' father / MINOS
Glaucus' slayer / AJAX
Glaucus' son / BELLEROPHON
glaze / FILM; GLOSS; ENAMEL
glaze on Chinese porcelain / EEL-
   SKIN
glazed / DULL; GLASSY
glazed pottery / STONEWARE
glazier's tack / BRAD; POINT
gleam / GLINT; FLICKER, GLIM-
   MER. RAY; DART; FLASH
gleamed / SHONE
glean / INFER; GARNER; COLLECT
glebe / SOD; CLOD; CHURCHLAND
glede / HAWK, KITE
glee / SONG; CHEER; GAIETY
gleeful / MERRY
gleeman / TROUBADOUR
gleg / GAY; KEEN; HAPPY, SHARP;
   BRIGHT, CHEERFUL
gleit / MUCUS, SLIME
glen / DELL; DINGLE, VALLEY
glib / FLUENT, SMOOTH; VOLUBLE
glib speech / PATTER; RIGMAROLE
glide / SLIP, SLUR; SLIDE
glide as an airplane / VOLPLANE

glide away / ELAPSE
glide over ice / SKI; SKATE
glide over water / SAIL, SKIM
glimmer / GLEAM; FLICKER. GLIMPSE
glimpse / SEE; ESPY, PEEK
glint / FLASH, GLEAM
glisten / GLITTER, SPARKLE
glistened / SHONE; SHIMMERED
glister / GLITTER, SPARKLE
glitter / FLASH, GLEAM, GLINT; CORUSCATE. BRILLIANCE
glittering ornament / SPANGLE
gloaming / TWILIGHT
gloat / EXULT
global / ROUND; WORLDWIDE
globe / ORB; BALL; EARTH; BREAST, SPHERE, EYEBALL
globe-trotter / TRAVELER
globose / ROTUND
globule / BEAD, DROP
glonoin / NITROGLYCERIN
gloom / DUSK, MURK; SADNESS; DARKNESS; DEJECTION
gloomy / SAD; DARK; ADUST, DREAR, DUSKY, LURID; DISMAL, DREARY
Gloomy Dean / INGE
gloomy mood / DUMPS
glorify / LAUD; BLESS, EXALT, EXTOL; PRAISE
glorious / GRAND, NOBLE; FAMOUS
glory / FAME, HALO, POMP; ECLAT
gloss / SHEEN; LUSTER, LUSTRE, POLISH, VENEER
glossary / LEXICON; VOCABULARY
glossoid / TONGUELIKE
glossy / NITID, SHINY, SLEEK; LUSTROUS
glossy cloth / SILK; SATIN; ALPACA
glossy paint / ENAMEL; LACQUER, VARNISH
glottal stop / STOD; CATCH
Gloucester city / BRISTOL
Gloucester river / WYE; AVON
Gloucester's cape / ANN
glove / MIT; GANT, MITT; COVER; MITTEN; GAUNTLET
glove blank / TRANK
glove leather / KID, KIP; NAPA; SUEDE
glow / SHINE; RADIATE. WARMTH
glower / FROWN, GLARE, SCOWL
glowing / HOT, RED; FIERY; ARDENT
glowing coal / EMBER
glowworm / FIREFLY
glucose / SUGAR; DEXTROSE
glucoside / GEIN, RUTIN
glue / STICK; CEMENT, FASTEN
glum / GLOOMY, MOROSE, SULLEN
glut / CRAM, SATE, STUFF; SATIATE
glutinous / GLUEY; VISCID

glutition / SWALLOWING
glutton / GOURMAND; WOLVERENE
gluttonize / OVEREAT
gluttonous person / PIG
gluttony / GREED; INEBRIETY; CRAPULENCE
G-men / NIS; FBI; FEDS
gnar / GROWL, SNARL
gnarl / KNOT; GROWL, TWIST
gnarled / CRAGGY, RUGGED; DISTORTED
gnash teeth / CHAMP, GRIND
gnat / MIDGE; BLACKFLY
gnathion / BUTTON
gnaw / BITE, CHEW, FRET; NIBBLE
gnaw away / RUST; ERODE; CORRODE
gnawer inside / ULCER
gnawing animal / RAT; BEAVER, GOPHER, RODENT
gnome / NIS, SAW; DWARF; GOBLIN, KOBOLD; LEPRECHAUN
gnomic / PITHY; SENTENTIOUS
gnomon / PIN; STYLE
gnosis / INSIGHT; KNOWLEDGE
Gnostic / HERETIC
Gnostic sectarian / MANI; SIMON
gnu / KOKOON; WILDEBEEST
go / FIT, GAE; MOVE, PASS, STIR, SUIT, WEND; LEAVE; DEPART
go abroad / MIGRATE
go around / BYPASS, DETOUR
go ashore / LAND; DISEMBARK
go back / EBB; REVERT
go bankrupt / FAIL
go to bed / RETIRE
go before / LEAD; PRECEDE
go by / PASS
go by car / DRIVE, MOTOR
go edgeways / SIDLE
go in / ENTER
go mounted / RIDE
go by plane / FLY, JET
go by ship / SAIL
go toward the sunrise / EAST
go west / DIE
go toward the west / WESTER
go with / ACCOMPANY
goad / GAD; PROD, SPUR; INCITE
go-ahead signal / NOW; GREEN
goal / AIM, END, NET; OBJECT, TARGET
goal of pilgrimage / MECCA
goat / TUR, ZAC; IBEX, TAHR; ANGORA, BHARAL; MARKHOR
goat antelope / GORAL, SEROW; CHAMOIS
goat call / BLEAT
goat god / PAN
goat hair cloth / CAMLET, MOHAIR
goatee / BEARD
goatish / RUTTY; CAPRINE, LUSTFUL

goatlike / CAPRIC; HIRCINE
goatsucker / POTOO; NIGHTJAR; WHIPPOORWILL
gob / TAR; LUMP, MASS; CHUNK; SAILOR
gobbet / CLOT; PIECE
gobble / BOLT, GULP, WOLF; RAVEN
gobbler / TURKEY
gobelin / TAPESTRY
Gobi Desert / SHAMO; HANHAI
Gobi Desert area / ALASHAN
Gobi Desert lake / HARA
gobloid southern fish / TETARD
goblet / CUP; TASS; HANAP
goblin / ELF; NIS; POOK, PUCK; GNOME, NISSE, OUPHE; KOBOLD, SPRITE
goby / MAPO
gobylike fish / DRAGONET
god / IDOL; DEITY; CREATOR; DEMIURGE, DIVINITY. See also such specific headings as Greek, Norse, Roman, etc.
god of agriculture / TAMU; OGMIOS
god of Arcadia / PAN
god of arts / SIVA; APOLLO
god of chaos / NU; NUN
god of childbirth / BES
god of craftsmen / LUG; PTAH; KOSHAR, VULCAN, WELAND; GOIBNIU, GWYDION; TVASHTRI; HEPHAESTUS
god of creation / IO; PTAH, TANE, TIRI, YETL; BRAHMA, MARDUK
god of dance / BES; SIVA
god of darkness / SET; LOKI; DYLAN
god of dawn / BOCHICA
god of the dead / MOT; ODIN, YAMA; ORCUS
god of destruction / SIVA
god of discord / LOKI
god of drink / SIRIS; KVASTR
god of earth / GEB, SEB; JORD; ENLIL
god of evening star / HESPERUS
god of evil / BES, SET; AHRIMAN
god of evil eye / BALOR
god of fertility / FREY; NINIB, RONGO
god of fields / PAN; FAUN; TELIPINU
god of fire / AGNI, LOKI; DAGDA; VULCAN
god of flocks / PAN; VELES; TAMMUZ
god of fortune / GANESHA
god of Hades / DIS; PLUTO
god of harvests / MIN; CRONUS; AKAKANET
god of healing / KU; RUDRA; DIANCECHT
god of herds / FAUN

god of honesty / EBISU
god of hunt / ULLR; GWYNN
god of justice / PTAH; FORSETI
god of kitchen / KOJIN
god of light / AMIDA; APOLLO, BALDER
god of love / AMOR, EROS, KAMA; ANGUS, BHAGA, CUPID, FREYR; FRIKKO
god with many arms / SIVA; BRIAREUS
god of Memphis / APIS, PTAH
god of metal working / KOSHAR, VULCAN, WELAND; HEPHAESTUS
god of mirth / MOMUS, UZUME
god of mischief / LOK; LOKE, LOKI
god of moon / SIN; SOMA; THOTH
god of morning star / ASVIN; PHOSPHORUS
god of music / BES; BRAN; APOLLO
god of nature / MIN; MAMTOU
god of north wind / BOREAS
god of Panopolis / MIN; KHEM
god of pastures / PAN
god of peace / FORSETI
god of pleasure / BES
god of poetry / BRAN; BRAGI
god of procreation / MIN; KANE, TANE
god of prosperity / JESSIS
god of rain / BAAL, CHAC; INDRA, RONGO; TLALOC; SUSANOO; PARJANYA
god of revelry / COMUS
god of ridicule / MOMUS
god of rivers / HAPI
god of roads / DOSOJIN
god of sea / EA; LER, YAM; HLER; AEGIR, DYLAN; TRITON; NEPTUNE, SUSANOO; MANANNAN, POSEIDON
god of skiing / ULL; ULLR
god of the sky / ANU, TIU, TIW, TYR, ZIO, ZIU; TIEN, ZEUS; INDRA, TINIA; URANUS
god of sleep / MORPHEUS
god of the solar disk / RA
god of southeast wind / EURUS
god of springs / BORVO; GRANNOS
god of storm / ZU; ADAD, INTI, THOR; MARUT
god of sun / RA; SOL, TEM; AMEN, AMON, LUGH, USIL; NUADA; APOLLO, HELIOS, VISHNU; SHAMASH, SUSANOO
god of thunder / DIS; ADAD, THOR, ZEUS; DONAR, PERUN
god of truth / VARUNA
god of underworld / DIS; BILE, BRAN, MATH, NYJA; EMMAO, HADES, PLUTO, PWYLL; OSIRIS; SERAPIS

god of war / ER, TU; NET, TYR; ARES, MARS, ODIN; ASHUR, INDRA, WODEN; ZABABA

god of watchfulness / ANPU; ARGUS, JANUS; HEIMDALL

god of wealth / KUVERA, PLUTOS; DAIKOKU

god of wind / ADAD, ODIN, VAYU; AEOLUS, TYPHON; HURACAN

god of wine / BACCHUS; DIONYSUS

god of wisdom / EA; NEBO, ODIN; THOTH; MARDUK; GANESHA; DAINICHI

god of youth / APOLLO

goddess of agriculture / OPS; CERES; DEMETER

goddess of the altar fire / VESTA; BRIGIT

goddess of the arts / MUSE; ATHENA

goddess of beauty / FREYA; LAKSHMI

goddess of the chase / DIANA; ARTEMIS

goddess of childbirth / ILITHYIA

goddess of crops / ANENA, ANONA; ANNONA

goddess of dawn / EOS; ETAIN, USHAS; AURORA, THESAN

goddess of the dead / HEL, NUT; FREYJA

goddess of destiny / URD; NONA, NORN

goddess of destruction / ARA; KALI; DURGA

goddess of discord / ATE; ERIS; DISCORDIA

goddess of earth / GE; OPS; DANA, ERDA, GAEA, PAPA; CERES, TERRA; DEMETER; PRITHIVI

goddess of faithfulness / FIDES

goddess of fertility / MA; DON, OPS; DANU; FRIGG, FRIJA; ISHTAR; ASTARTE, DEMETER, NERTHUS

goddess of fire / BRIGIT, HESTIA

goddess of flowers / FLORA, NANNA; CHLORIS

goddess of fortune / TYCHE; LAKSHMI

goddess of fruit / POMONA

goddess of harvest / OPS; CARPO, CERES

goddess of healing / EIR; GULA, HINA; BRIGIT

goddess of hearth / FRIGG, VESTA

goddess of hope / SPES

goddess of horses / EPONA

goddess of the hunt / DIANA; ARTEMIS

goddess of infatuation / ATE

goddess of justice / MA; MAAT; THEMIS; ASTRAEA

goddess of light / CUPRA

goddess of love / DWYN, ISIS; FREYA, VENUS; FREYJA, ISHTAR; ASTARTE; KAMADEVA; APHRODITE

goddess of magic / HECATE

goddess of marriage / HERA; FRIGG

goddess of maternity / MUT; APET

goddess of mercy / KWANNON

goddess of mischief / ATE; ERIS

goddess of moon / AAH; CHIA, ISIS, LUNA; DIANA, LOSNA, NANNA; HECATE, SELENA, SELENE; ARTEMIS, ASTARTE, SUSANOO

goddess of morning / USHAS; AURORA

goddess of music / BENTEN

goddess of nature / ISIS; CYBELE; ARTEMIS

goddess of night / NOX, NYX; RATRI

goddess of peace / IRENE; EIRENE

goddess of plenty / OPS; NEHALENNIA

goddess of poetry / BRIGIT; SARASVATI

goddess of prosperity / SALUS

goddess of the rainbow / IRIS; IXCHEL

goddess of retribution / ARA, ATE

goddess of revenge / NEMESIS

goddess of rice / INARI

goddess of rivers / ANQET, BOANN

goddess of the sea / RAN; NINA; THETIS

goddess of skiing / SKADI

goddess of sky / NUT; JUNO

goddess of sorrow / MARA

goddess of speech / VACH

goddess of splendor / UMA

goddess of storms / RAN

goddess of sun / SHAPASH; AMATERASU

goddess of truth / MAAT

goddess of underworld / HEL; GERD; ALLATU

goddess of vegetation / KORE; CERES

goddess of vengeance / NEMESIS

goddess of victory / NIKE

goddess of volcanoes / PELE

goddess of war / ALEA, ENYO; BELLONA; MORRIGAN

goddess of wealth / FORTUNA, LAKSHMI

goddess of wisdom / USHAS; ATHENA, PALLAS; MINERVA

goddess of the woods / DIANA; ARTEMIS

goddess of youth / HEBE; IDUNN

goddesses of destiny / FATES, NORNS

goddesses with one eye among them / GRAIAE

godfather / PADRINO, SPONSOR

godhood / DIVINITY
Godiva's husband / LEOFRIC
godlike / divine; heavenly
godliness / PIETY; DEVOTION
godly / DEVOUT; SAINTLY
godly person / ANGEL, SAINT
God's acre / CHURCHYARD
gods' messenger / HERMES
gods of Teutonic pantheon / AESIR, VANIR
godsend / BOON; WINDFALL
godspeed / SUCCESS
Goethe drama / FAUST
goffer / CRIMP, FLUTE
goffered / TOOLED; EMBOSSED
goggle / BULGE, STARE
goggler / SCAD; AKULE
goggles / GLASSES; SUNGLASSES
going / LEAVING
golconda / MINE; ELDORADO
Golconda's riches / DIAMONDS
gold / COIN; AURUM, MONEY; WEALTH
gold, c.f. / AURI, AURO
gold, pert. to / AURIC
gold in alchemy / SOL
gold braid / ORRIS
Gold Bug author / POE
gold carp / GOLDFISH
gold cloth / LAME
Gold Coast city / ACCRA
Gold Coast inhabitant / GA; EWE; FANTI
gold coin / DUCAT, LOUIS; GUINEA
gold covered / GILT; GILDED
gold deposit / LODE; PLACER
gold digger / VAMP; MINER
gold discoverer / SUTTER; MARSHALL
gold district / RAND; OPHIR; KLONDIKE
gold embroidery / ORPHREY
gold field / RAND; OPHIR
gold in heraldry / OR
gold mass / INGOT; NUGGET
gold mosaic / ORMOLU
gold paint / GILT
gold seeker / ARGONAUT
gold sheet / FOIL, LEAF; LATTEN
gold unit / CARAT
gold vessel / CUPEL
gold washing pan / BATEA
goldbrick / SHIRKER, SWINDLE
golden / YELLOW; AUREATE, HALCYON
golden age / MILLENNIUM
golden-apple guardian /IDUN; ITHUNN
golden-apple judge / PARIS
golden-apple recipient / APHRO-DITE
golden-apples guard / LADON
golden-apples land / HESPERIA

golden-apples stealer / ATLAS
golden bough / MISTLETOE
golden bug / LADYBIRD
golden-calf maker / AARON
golden cup / BUTTERCUP
Golden Fleece country / COLCHIS
Golden Fleece guardian / AEETES
Golden Fleece seeker / JASON; ARGONAUT
Golden Hind captain / DRAKE
golden hoard / RHEINGOLD
Golden Horde capital / SARAI
Golden Horde founder / BATU
Golden Horde member / KIPCHAK
Golden Horn / HALIC
golden metal / ORMOLU
golden oriole / PIROL; LORIOT
golden shiner / DACE
Golden State / CALIFORNIA
golden-touch king / MIDAS
Golden Treasury editor / PALGRAVE
goldenrod / SOLIDAGO
goldenseal / ICEROOT
goldfinch / REDCAP
goldfish / CARP
gold-silver alloy / ASEM
goldsmith's crucible / CREVET, CRUSET
goldstone / AVENTURINE
golem / BOOBY; AUTOMATON
golf attendant / CADDY
golf club / IRON, WOOD; CLEEK, SPOON; DRIVER, MASHIE, PUT-TER; BRASSIE, MIDIRON, NIBLICK
golf club end / TOE; NOSE
golf club socket / HOSEL
golf course / LINKS
golf error / PULL; SLICE
golf hazard / TRAP; ROUGH
golf hole / CUP
golf instructor / PRO
golf match / FOURSOME
golf mound / TEE
golf peg / TEE
golf position / STANCE
golf pro / BOROS, HOGAN, SNEAD; PALMER; NICKLAUS
golf score / PAR; BOGEY, EAGLE; BIRDIE, STROKE
golf starting place / TEE
golf stroke / BAFF, CHIP, LOFT, PUTT, SHOT; DRIVE; SCLAFF
golf turf / DIVOT
golfer's warning / FORE
Golgotha / CALVARY; CEMETERY
Goliath / GIANT
Goliath's home / GATH
Goliath's slayer / DAVID
gombeen man / USURER
gomeral / FOOL
Gomer's husband / HOSEA
gomuti / ARENG

gondola / CAR; BOAT
gondola cabin / FELZE
gondoliers' city / VENICE
gondolier's song / BARCAROLLE
gone / AGO, OUT; AWAY, LOST,
PAST
gone from the board / TAKEN
gone by / AGO; PAST
gone from the table / EATEN
gonef / THIEF
goneness / WEAKNESS
Goneril's husband / ALBANY
Goneril's father / LEAR
Goneril's sister / REGAN; CORDELIA
gonfalon / FLAG; BANNER;
STANDARD
gong / BELL; ALARM; TAMTAM
gony / ALBATROSS
goober / PEANUT
good / OK; FIT; FULL, KIND, OKAY,
TRUE; PIOUS; PROPER, USEFUL
good, pref. / EU
Good Book / BIBLE
good deal / LOT
good digestion / EUPEPSIA
good fortune / HAP, HIT; BREAK
good friend / PAL
good guy / HERO; PALADIN
good health / SOUNDNESS, WELL-
BEING
good judgment / COMMONSENSE
Good Knight / BAYARD
good luck / FORTUNE
good manners / CIVILITY,
COURTESY
good meal / REPAST
good name / HONOR
good natured / AMIABLE;
PLEASANT
good order / EUTAXY, KILTER
good quality / VIRTUE
good quoits throw / RINGER
good ship's wood / TEAK
good swimmer / FISH
good tidings / GOSPEL; EVANGEL
good times / UPS
good turn / HAND; FAVOR;
BENEFIT
good will / AMITY, FAVOR
goodbye / AVE; TATA; ADIEU,
ALOHA; FAREWELL
goodliness / GRACE
good-looking / PRETTY; HAND-
SOME; BEAUTIFUL
good-luck charm / MASCOT;
TALISMAN
good-luck gift / HANDSEL
goodly / FINE; COMELY; PLEASANT
goodman / HUSBAND
goodness / WORTH; VIRTUE,
PROBITY
goods / PROOF, WARES; EFFECTS

goods cast adrift / LAGAN, LIGAN
goods for disposal / STOCK, WARES
goods floating after shipwreck /
JETSAM; WAVESON
goods shipped / FREIGHT
goods sunk at sea / LAGAN, LIGAN
goods thrown into sea / JETSAM
goody / SWEETMEAT
goof / ERROR; SIMPLETON
googul / GUM; BDELLIUM
goon / THUG; HOODLUM
goony bird / ALBATROSS
goose / BRANT, SOLAN; GANDER
goose cry / HONK, YANG; WHISTLE
goose egg / ZERO; BLANK
goose flesh / PIMPLES
goose grease / AXUNGE
goose of Hawaii / NENE
Gopher State / MINNESOTA
Gordian Knot opener / ALEXANDER
Gordium's problem / KNOT
gore / STAB; PIERCE. BLOOD;
GUSSET
gorge / CRAM, GLUT; STUFF.
ABYSS, CHASM; NULLAH,
RAVINE
gorgeous / RICH; GRAND, SHOWY;
SPLENDID
Gorge's sister / DEIANIRA
gorget / BREASTPLATE
Gorgon / MEDUSA, STHENO;
EURYALE
Gorgon's father / PHORCYS
Gorgon's hair / SERPENTS
Gorgon's mother / CETO
gorilla / APE; THUG; BRUTE
gormand / GLUTTON
gormandizer / GLUTTON;
GOURMAND
gorse / WHIN; FURZE; JUNIPER
gory / BLOODY; SANGUINARY
gosling / GOOSE; CATKIN
gospel / TRUTH; EVANGEL;
DOCTRINE
gospel book / JOHN, LUKE, MARK;
MATTHEW
gospel side / LEFT
gospeler / PASTOR; EVANGELIST
gossamer / SOFT, THIN; FLIMSY.
WEB
gossip / CHAT; NORATE, TATTLE;
CHATTER. EME, GUP; RUMOR
gossoon / BOY, LAD; PAGE
got off / LIT; SENT
Gotham inhabitant / FOOL
gothic / BAROQUE
Gothic bard / RUNER
Gothic chief / ALARIC
Gothic type / SANSERIF
Goths' branch / VISIGOTHS;
OSTROGOTHS
gouda / CHEESE

gouge / CHEAT; CHISEL; SWINDLE

goulash / STEW; RAGOUT; MULLIGAN

Gounod opera / FAUST

gourd / HEAD, PEPO; DIPPER, SQUASH; PUMPKIN; CALABASH, CUCURBIT

gourd fruit / PEPO; MELON; SQUASH

gourd rattle / MARACA

gourmand / GLUTTON

gourmet / EPICURE; GOURMAND

gout / DITCH; PODAGRA

Govannon's brother / AMAETHON

govern / RUN; CURB, RULE; REIGN; BRIDLE, DIRECT, MANAGE

governance / CONTROL; GOVERNMENT

governess / DUENNA; TEACHER

governing principle / LAW; RULE; CRITERION

government / RULE; STATE; REGIME; DOMINION

government agency / VA; AEC, CAB, CIA, FBI, FCC, FTC, GSA, ICC, SBA, SEC, TVA; NASA, NLRB, USIA

government agents / FBI; GMEN, TMEN

government by bishops / EPISCOPATE

government department / BUREAU

government duty / TAX; LEVY; TARIFF

government by a few / OLIGARCHY

government representative / CONSUL; SENATOR; DIPLOMAT, MINISTER

government by the rich / PLUTOCRACY

government by women / GYNARCHY

government's share / TAX

governor / POP, SIR; PILOT, RULER; GERENT, REGENT; REGULATOR

governor in Persia / SATRAP

gowan / DAISY

gowk / FOOL; CUCKOO

gowl / CRY; HOWL, YELL

gown / ROBE; DRESS, FROCK

gowned / ATTIRED

gowpen / CHARITY, HANDFUL

goyim / GENTILES

gra / LOVE; SWEETHEART

grab / NAB; SEIZE; CLUTCH, COLLAR

grabble / GRAB; GROPE; SPRAWL

Gracchi's mater / CORNELIA

grace / EASE; CHARM, FAVOR, MERCY. ADORN, HONOR; DIGNIFY

graceful / EASY, FEAT; GAINLY; ELEGANT, FLOWING

graceful animal / DEER; GAZELLE

graceful bird / SWAN

graceful dance / TANGO, WALTZ

graceful rhythm / LILT

graceful woman / SYLPH

gracefulness / ELEGANCE

graceless / UNGODLY; DEPRAVED

Graces / AGLAIA, THALIA; CHARITES; EUPHROSYNE

Graces' mother / AEGLE

gracile / SLENDER

gracious / FAIR, KIND; CIVIL; POLITE; TENDER; AFFABLE

gracious woman / LADY

grackle / DAW; JACKDAW; BLACKBIRD

gradation / TINGE; NUANCE

grade / RANK, STEP; CLASS, STAGE; RATING. MARK, RATE, SORT

graded / CLASSIFIED

gradient / RAMP; SLOPE; INCLINE

gradual / EASY, SLOW; MODULATED. ANTIPHON

gradually weaken / SAP; EXHAUST

graduate / ALUMNA; ALUMNUS. PASS

graduated tube / BURET; BURETTE

graduation document / DIPLOMA; TESTAMUR; SHEEPSKIN

graft / IMP, YMP; CION; BRIBE, SCION, SHOOT

gratfed in heraldry / ENTE

grafting / TOIL; JOINING; INSERTING

Graia / ENYO; DEINO

Graiae mother / CETO

grail / AMA, CUP; CHALICE, PLATTER; SANGRAAL

Grail knight / BORS; GALAHAD; PARSIFAL; LOHENGRIN, PERCIVALE

grain / JOT, OAT, RYE; CORN, RICE, SEED, WALE, WHIT; SPELT, WHEAT, BARLEY, CEREAL, KERNEL

grain, c.f. / CHONDR; CHONDRO

grain, pert. to / OATEN

grain beard / AWN; ARISTA

grain beetle / WEEVIL; CADELLE

grain bristles / AWN; ARISTA

grain bundle / COP; SHEAF, SHOCK, STOOK

grain food / OATS

grain fungus / SMUT; ERGOT

grain grinder / QUERN; MILLER; MILLSTONE

grain to be ground / GRIST

grain husk / BRAN; GLUME

grain market / PIT

grain measure / MOY; PECK; GRIST; BUSHEL

grain shell / BRAN, HUSK; CHAFF

grain sorghum / DURR, MILO;
  CHEHA, DARRA, DURRA;
  DOURAH, HEGARI
grain for sowing / OATSEED
grain stalk / HAULM, STRAW
grain thresher / FLAIL
grain warehouse / SILO; GRANARY;
  ELEVATOR
grain of wood / BATE
grain-cleaning machine / AWNER
grainy limestone / OOLITE
gramary / MAGIC
gramercy / THANKS
grammarian / PHILOLOGIST
grammatical case / DATIVE; ABLA-
  TIVE, GENITIVE
grammatical class / GENDER
grammatical fault / SOLECISM
grammatical relationship / SYNTAX
gram-molecular weight / MOLE
gramophone / PHONOGRAPH
grampus / ORC; ORCA; KILLER
Granada building / ALHAMBRA
granary / GOLA, GUNJ, SILO;
  GUNGE; ELEVATOR
grand / EPIC, HIGH; CHIEF, GREAT,
  NOBLE; AUGUST, LORDLY, SU-
  PERB; STATELY, SUBLIME
Grand Banks peril / ICEBERG
Grand Banks product / COD
Grand Canal bridge / RIALTO
Grand Canyon river / COLORADO
grand division of time / EON;
  EPOCH
Grand Lama's city / LHASA
grand slam / VOLE
Grand Teton peak / MORAN
grandam / GRANDMA; GRAND-
  MOTHER
grandchild / OE, OY; OYE
grandee / NOBLE; NOBLEMAN
grandeur / POMP; ECLAT;
  SPLENDOR
grandfather / AIEL; GRANDPA
grandiloquent / BOMBASTIC
grandiose / EPIC; COSMIC
grandmother / GRANNY; GRAN-
  DAM, GRANDMA
grandparents, pert. to / AVAL
grandsire / ANCESTOR
grange / FARM; LODGE
granite porphyry / ELVAN
granitic / RIGID, STERN
granny / KNOT; GRANDMOTHER.
  OLD; DULL; STUPID
grant / CEDE, GIVE, LEAD; ADMIT,
  ALLOT, ALLOW, YIELD; CONFER,
  CONVEY, IMPART; CONCEDE;
  TRANSFER. BOON, GIFT, MISE;
  STIPEND
grant absolution / SHRIVE
grant of rights / ENAM; JAGIR;
  PATENT; CHARTER

granted / YES
granular / GRAINY
granular material / SAND; SUGAR
granular snowfield / FIRN, NEVE
granulate / KERN; GRAIN;
  ROUGHEN
grape / UVA; RASP; GAMAY, PINOT,
  SYRAH, VITIS; ACINUS, MALAGA,
  MUSCAT, SIRRAH; CATAWBA,
  CONCORD; GRENACHE,
  RIESLING
grape, pert. to / ACINIC
grape bunch / BOB
grape conserve / JAM; UVATE
grape disease / ESCA; COLEUR
grape drink / WINE; JUICE
grape fermentation stimulant /
  STUM
grape juice / DIBS, MUST, STUM
grape for malmsey / MALVASIA
grape parasite / PROCRIS
grape pest / PHYLLOXERA
grape plant / VINE
grape pomace / RAPE
grape refuse / MARC, MASH;
  BAGASSE
grape seed / ACINUS
grape sugar / MALTOSE; DEXTROSE
grape syrup / SAPA
grapeflower / HYACINTH
grapefruit / POMELO, PUMELO;
  SHADDOCK
Grapes of Wrath author / STEIN-
  BECK
Grapes of Wrath family / JOAD
graph / MAP; CHART; DIAGRAM
graphic / VIVID; STRIKING;
  PICTORIAL
graphic symbol / LOGO; LOGOTYPE,
  THERBLIG; CHARACTER
graphite / KISH; LEAD; PLUMBAGO
grapnel / ANCHOR
grapple / SEIZE; CLINCH, TACKLE;
  WRESTLE
grapple for oysters / TONG
grappling iron / TONGS; CRAMPON,
  GRAPNEL
Grasmere resident / WORDSWORTH
grasp / NAB; GRAB, GRIP, HOLD;
  CATCH, CLASP. REACH, SCOPE
grasping / AVID; GREEDY, STINGY;
  MISERLY; COVETOUS
grass / POA; HERB, ICHU, LAWN,
  REED; BAMBOO, DARNEL;
  PASTURE
grass, pert. to / GRAMINACEOUS
grass for basketry / OTATE;
  ESPARTO
grass dried for fodder / HAY
grass flower bract / LEMMA, PALEA
grass genus / POA; AVENA; BRO-
  MUS, HOLCUS; FESTUCA
grass for hay / FESCUE; TIMOTHY

grass husk / GLUME

grass leaf / BLADE

grass for making rope / MUNG, MUNJ

grass for paper-making / ALFA; ESPARTO

grass roots / PROVINCES; ELECTORATE; CONSTITUENCY

grass rope / SOGA

grass rug / MAT

grass stem / CULM; HAULM, STALK

grass for thatching / ALANG, COGON; ALANGALANG

grass tree / TI; YUCCA; BLACKBOY; LANCEWOOD

grass tuft / CLUMP; TUSSOCK

grass variety / RIE; REED; BROME; FESCUE

grass widow / DIVORCEE

grass-cloth plant / RAMIE

grass-covered earth / SOD; LAWN; SWARD

grasshopper / GRIG; LOCUST

grasshopperlike insect / CRICKET, KATYDID

grassland / LEA; VELD; RANGE; MEADOW; SAVANNA

grasslike herb / RUSH; SEDGE

grassy clearing / GLADE

grassy expanse / HEATH

grassy field / LEA

grassy ground / SWARD

grassy yard / LAWN

grate / RUB; RASP, WEAR; GRIDE, GRIND; ABRADE

grateful / OBLIGED; BEHOLDEN

gratification / DELIGHT

gratified / GLAD; PLEASED

gratify / SATE; ARRIDE, PLEASE; CONTENT

grating / GRID; GRILL; GRILLE, HARSH; RASPING

gratis / FREE; NOCHARGE

gratitude / THANKS; GRATEFULNESS

gratuitous / FREE; UNSOUGHT; VOLUNTARY

gratuitous aid / BOON; LARGESS

gratuity / FEE, TIP; DOLE, GIFT; BONUS, PILON; PREMIUM, PRESENT; LAGNIAPPE

gravamen / CAUSE; GRIEVANCE

grave / DEEP; QUIET, SOBER; SEDATE, SOLEMN. PIT; TOMB, VAULT

grave cloth / PALL

grave digger / SEXTON

grave marker / CAIRN, STELA, STELE; TOMBSTONE

grave mound / BARROW; TUMULUS

grave robber / GHOUL

grave wax / ADIPOCERE

graveclothes / SHROUD; CEREMENT

gravel / GRIT, SAND; STONE

gravel desert / GIBBER

graven image / IDOL

gravestone / SLAB; STELA; TOMBSTONE

graveyard / CEMETERY; NECROPOLIS

graveyard inscription / EPITAPH

graving implement / BURIN; STYLET

gravitate / FALL, TEND

gravity / MOMENT, WEIGHT

gravure / INTAGLIO; ENGRAVING

gravy / PIE; GRAFT, JUICE

gravy dish / BOAT

gray / OLD; DRAB; ASHEN, SLATE; DISMAL, LEADEN

gray, c.f. / POLIO

gray with age / HOARY

gray duck / GADWALL

gray goose / GREYLAG

gray matter / BRAINS

gray parrot / JAKO

gray rock / SLATE

gray sea trout / WEAKFISH

gray whale / BALEEN

grayback / REB; LOUSE, SCAUP

grayback herring / CISCO

graybeard / ELDER; PATRIARCH

gray-headed / HOAR; HOARY

grayish brown / DUN; TAUPE

grayish green / RESEDA

grayish tan / BEIGE

graywacke / SANDSTONE

graze / RUB; AGIST, TOUCH; BROWSE

grazing land / RANGE; PASTURE

grease / FAT, OIL; LARD, SAIM; AXUNGE. BRIBE

grease a palm / BRIBE

grease wheels / AID; EXPEDITE

greasepaint / STAGE; MAKEUP

greasewood / CHICO; CHAMISO

greasy / OILY; SMOOTH; UNCTUOUS

greasy material / LARD; POMADE; FATBACK

greasy slope / SHOOT

great / BIG; HUGE, VAST; BULKY, CHIEF, GRAND, LARGE, NOBLE, PROUD; AUGUST; IMMENSE, SUBLIME

great, c.f. / MEGA

great, pref. / ARCH

great abundance / SCADS

great amount / LOT; LOTS

great barracuda / PICUDA

Great Barrier island / OTEA

Great Basin river / SEVIER

Great Basin state / NEVADA

Great Bear / DIPPER; URSAMAJOR

Great Britain / ALBION; BRITANNIA
great calamity / DISASTER; CATASTROPHE
Great Cham / JOHNSON
great coat / PALETOT
Great Commoner / PITT
great crowd / HORDE
great desert / GOBI; HANHAI, SAHARA
great distance / FAR
great divide / DEATH
Great Duke / WELLINGTON
Great Emancipator / ABE; LINCOLN
great enthusiasm / ZEAL
great extinct beast / MAMMOTH; MASTODON
great go / FINALS
Great Goddess / DEMETER
great grandfather / BESAIEL
great haste / SPEED
Great Horde division / DULAT; KANGLI
Great Indian Desert / THAR
great joy / ELATION
Great Lake / ERIE; HURON; ONTARIO; MICHIGAN, SUPERIOR
Great Lakes explorer / CHAMPLAIN
Great Lakes Indian / ERIE; HURON
great lie / WHOPPER
great liking / LOVE
great lover / ROMEO
Great Meadows fort / NECESSITY
Great Mother / CYBELE
great number / LAC; LAKH, LOTS, MANY, MUCH; CRORE; MYRIAD; MULTITUDE
great outpouring / GUSH; FLOOD
great personage / VIP; MOGUL, NABOB
great poem / EPIC
great quantity / SEA; MASS, SLEW
great realm / EMPIRE
great relish / ZEST; GUSTO, VERVE
Great Sea / MEDITERRANEAN
great sufferer / MARTYR
Great Trail terminus / DETROIT
great unknown / DEATH
great unwashed / MASSES; WORKERS
great violin / STRAD
great volcano / ETNA
Great White Father / PRESIDENT
Great White Way / BROADWAY
Great White Whale / MOBYDICK
greatcoat / OVERCOAT
greater part / BULK
greatly, pref. / ANA
grebe / DABCHICK
Grecian / GREEK; HELLENE
Greece / ELLAS; HELLAS. See also Greek
Greece, pert. to / GRECO

Greece capital / ATHENS
greed / LUST; AVARICE; CUPIDITY, VORACITY
greediness / GLUTTONY, RAPACITY
greedy / AVID; COVETOUS, ESURIENT
greedy person / HOG, PIG; CORMORANT
Greek / ATTIC; ARGIVE; GRECIAN; HELLENIC. HELLENE
Greek A / ALPHA
Greek abbess / AMMA
Greek amphitheatre / ODEUM
Greek architectural order / DORIC, IONIC; CORINTHIAN
Greek assembly / PNYX; AGORA; APELLA; ECCLESIA
Greek author / ZENO; AESOP, HOMER, PLATO, TIMON; HESIOD, PINDAR, SAPPHO, STRABO, THALES; PLUTARCH
Greek avenging spirit / KER; ERINYS
Greek banishment / OSTRACISM
Greek beauty / LAIS; HELEN; PHRYNE
Greek calends / NEVER
Greek Catholic / UNIAT; UNIATE
Greek cheese / FETA, VIZE; TELEME
Greek chief goddess / HERA
Greek church / UNIATE; ORTHODOX
Greek church father / ORIGEN; CLEMENT
Greek citadel / ACROPOLIS
Greek city / ARTA, ELIS; PATRAS, SPARTA, THEBES; CORINTH; SALONIKA
Greek city-state / THEBES; CORINTH
Greek clan subdivision / OBE
Greek coin / OBOL; LEPTON, STATER; DRACHMA
Greek colony / SYRACUSE; BYZANTIUM
Greek column / DORIC, IONIC
Greek commonalty / DEMOS
Greek commune / DEME
Greek counselor /NESTOR
Greek courtesan / PHRYNE; ASPASIA
Greek dance / CHOROS, KORDAX, SYRTOS; GERANOS; BOUZOUKI
Greek dialect / IONIC; AEOLIC
Greek district / ATTICA; ARGOLIS
Greek drama / MIME; TRAGEDY
Greek dramatist / PYTHON; THESPIS; CRATINUS; EURIPIDES, SOPHOCLES
Greek earth goddess / DEMETER
Greek earthenware jar / AMPHORA
Greek enchantress / CIRCE, MEDEA
Greek epic / ILIAD; ODYSSEY

Greek epic poet / HOMER
Greek fabulist / AESOP; BABRIUS
Greek festival / AGON; DELIA, HALOA
Greek festival city / NEMEA; OLYMPIA
Greek flask / OLPE
Greek flier / ICARUS
Greek fortified hill / ACROPOLIS
Greek fury / ALECTO, ERINYS, MEGARA; TISIPHONE
Greek galley / TRIREME
Greek garment / TUNIC; CHITON, PEPLOS; CHLAMYS
Greek geographer / HANNO; PTOLEMY
Greek ghost / KER
Greek god of commerce / HERMES
Greek god of dreams / MORPHEUS
Greek god of love / EROS
Greek god of marriage / HYMEN
Greek god of metal-working / HEPHAESTUS, HEPHAISTOS
Greek god of revelry / COMUS
Greek god of the sea / NEREUS, TRITON; POSEIDON
Greek god of the sun / APOLLO, HELIOS; PHOEBUS
Greek god of war / ARES
Greek god of wind / AEOLUS
Greek goddess of agriculture / DEMETER
Greek goddess of amorality / ATE
Greek goddess of dawn / EOS
Greek goddess of earth / DEMETER
Greek goddess of flowers / CHLORIS
Greek goddess of health / HYGEIA
Greek goddess of justice / THEMIS
Greek goddess of love / APHRODITE
Greek goddess of moon / SELENE; ARTEMIS
Greek goddess of retribution / ARA
Greek goddess of war / ENYO
Greek goddess of wisdom / ATHENA, ATHENE, PALLAS
Greek goddess of youth / HEBE
Greek goddesses of fate / MOIRAI
Greek harp / LYRE
Greek hero / AJAX; JASON; CADMUS, HECTOR; ACHILLES, HERACLES, HERCULES
Greek historian / CTESIAS; XENOPHON; HERODOTUS; THUCYDIDES
Greek initiate / MYSTES
Greek inventor / DAEDALUS
Greek island / CORFU, CRETE, DELOS, MELOS, SAMOS; LESBOS, RHODES
Greek islands / SPORADES
Greek lawgiver / DRACO, MINOS, SOLON

Greek leather flask / OLPE
Greek letter / MU, NU, PI, XI; CHI, ETA, PHI, PSI, RHO, TAU; BETA, IOTA, ZETA; ALPHA, DELTA, GAMMA, KAPPA, OMEGA, SIGMA, THETA; LAMBDA; EPSILON, OMICRON, UPSILON
Greek love god / EROS
Greek magistrate / ARCHON
Greek marketplace / AGORA
Greek mathematician / EUCLID; ARCHIMEDES
Greek measure of length / HEMA; STADIUM
Greek military discharge / DIPLOMA
Greek military formation / PHALANX
Greek monk / CALOYER
Greek monks' settlement / SCETE, SKETE
Greek monster / SPHINX; CHIMERA
Greek month / GAMELION
Greek moon goddess / HECATE, SELENE; ARTEMIS
Greek mountain / IDA; OSSA; PELION; HELICON, OLYMPUS
Greek musical instrument / LYRE; AULOS; SYRINX; CITHARA; BARBITOS
Greek musical note / MESE, NETE; HYPATON
Greek musical scale / MODE; LYDIAN; PHRYGIAN
Greek musician / SACADAS; TERPANDER
Greek obsolete letter / SAN; KOPDA; DIGAMMA
Greek oracle / DELPHI, DODONA
Greek orthodox abbot / HEGUMEN
Greek orthodox monk / CALOYER
Greek painter / AETION, ZEUXIS; APELLES
Greek peninsula / MOREA; CHALCIDICE; PELOPONNESUS
Greek philosopher / ZENO; PLATO, STOIC; THALES, SOCRATES; ARISTOTLE
Greek philosophical school / STOA; PORCH; ELEATIC; MILESIAN
Greek physician / GALEN; DIOCLES
Greek pillar / STELA, STELE
Greek poem / ODE; EPIC; PAEAN
Greek poet / ARION, HOMER; HESIOD, PINDAR, SAPPHO; TERPANDER
Greek political division / DEME
Greek port / ENOS; CORINTH, PIRAEUS
Greek portico / STOA; XYSTUS
Greek priest / MYST, PAPA
Greek province / NOME
Greek queen of gods / HERA, HERE

Greek resident alien / METIC
Greek resistance force / EDES,
  ELAS
Greek river / PENEUS
Greek sculptor / MYRON; CALLON;
  PHIDIAS; PRAXITELES
Greek sea / AEGEAN, EUXINE,
  IONIAN
Greek seer / CALCHAS; TIRESIAS
Greek serf / HELOT; PENEST
Greek shield / PELTA
Greek slave / DOULOS
Greek slave woman / IAMBE
Greek soldier / HOPLITE
Greek sorceress / CIRCE, MEDEA
Greek spirit of fate / KER
Greek sports contest / AGON
Greek statesman / LYSANDER,
  PERICLES; ARISTIDES
Greek sylvan deity / PAN; SATYR;
  SILENUS
Greek temple / NAOS
Greek tetrachord part / NETE;
  HYPATON
Greek theater / ODEON, ODEUM
Greek theaters / ODEA
Greek town / SERES; SPARTA
Greek township / DEME
Greek urn for ashes / DINOS;
  DEINOS
Greek vase / PELIKE; AMPHORA;
  LECYTHUS
Greek verb tense / AORIST
Greek visionary / SIBYL; CAS-
  SANDRA
Greek voyage report / PERIPLUS
Greek war cry / ALALA
Greek warrior / AJAX
Greek warship / CATAPHRACT
Greek weight / MINA, OBOL;
  TALENT
Greek wine / RETSINA
Greek witch goddess / HECATE
green / RAW; PALE; FRESH; CAL-
  LOW, SICKLY, UNRIPE; VER-
  DANT. VERD, VERT; OLIVE;
  RESEDA
green, c.f. / VERD; PRASEO
green algae / SCUM; DESMID
green arrow / YARROW
Green Bay eleven / PACKERS
green bean / HARICOT
green cheese / SAPSAGO
green dragon / JACKINTHEPULPIT
green drake / MAYFLY
green fly / APHID
green with foliage / VERDANT
green gem / JADE; EMERALD,
  OLIVINE, PERIDOT
green goods / COUNTERFEIT
green grape / NIAGARA; RIESLING;
  CHARDONNAY
green in heraldry / VERT

green land / ERIN; IRELAND
Green Mansions heroine / RIMA
green mineral / JADE; ERINITE
green monkey / GUENON
green moth / LUNA
Green Mountain Boys' chief / ALLEN
Green Mountain State / VERMONT
green oxide on bronze / PATINA
green plum / GAGE
green porcelain / CELADON
green stone / JADE; JASPER;
  PERIDOT
green tea / CHANG, HYSON; GYO-
  KURO, HIKICHA
green vegetable / PEA; KALE; CAB-
  BAGE, LETTUCE, SPINACH
greenback / BILL; MONEY
greenbark / PALOVERDE
green-eyed / ENVIOUS, JEALOUS
greenfinch / GROSBEAK
greenfly / APHID; PLANTLOUSE
greengage / PLUM
greenhead / SCAUP; MALLARD;
  HORSEFLY
greenheart / BEBEERU
greenhorn / JAY; NOVICE; IMMI-
  GRANT; TENDERFOOT
greenhouse / HOTHOUSE; CON-
  SERVATORY
Greenland capital / GODHAVN;
  GODTHAAB
Greenland discoverer / ERIC
Greenland eskimo / ITA; AGTO;
  NUGSUAK; KALADLIT
Greenland polar base / ETAB
greenling / CULTUS; LINGCOD,
  POLLOCK
greenroom / LOUNGE; ANTEROOM
greensand / MARL
greensickness / CHLOROSIS
greensward / LEA, SOD
Greenwich time / GMT
Greenwich Village / BOHEMIA
greenwood / FOREST
greeny / NOVICE; GREENHORN
greet / HAIL; ACCOST; ADDRESS
greet cordially / WELCOME
greeting / HI; AVE, BOW, HOW;
  HAIL; HELLO; SALUTE; WEL-
  COME
gregarious / SOCIAL; SOCIABLE;
  CONVIVIAL
gremlin / IMP; SPRITE
grenade / BOMB; SHELL; PINE-
  APPLE
grew older / AGED; RIPENED
grey / GRAY
greyhound / COURSER
grid / SCREEN; GRATING,
  NETWORK
griddle / PAN; GRILL
griddle cake / OATCAKE, PANCAKE;
  FLAPJACK

gride / RASP

gridiron / FIELD, GRILL; FOOTBALL

grief / WO; WOE; DOLE, PAIN; DOLOR; MISERY

grievance / BURDEN, INJURY

grieve / CRY; PINE, WEEP; MOURN; LAMENT

grievous / SAD; SORE; HEAVY; HURTFUL, NOXIOUS, PAINFUL

grievously afflicted / SMITTEN

Griffin's animal enemy / HORSE

Griffin's trust / GOLD

grifter / CONMAN; PITCHMAN

grig / EEL; CRICKET; GRASSHOPPER. IRK

grill / GRATE; GRIDIRON. QUIZ; SWEAT

grim / DIRE, UGLY; CRUEL, GAUNT, STARK, STERN

grimace / MOP, MOW; MOUE; SMIRK

grimalkin / SHECAT

grime / DIRT, SMUT, SOOT

griminess / SOIL

grimy / DIRTY; FILTHY

grin / SMILE

grin with disdain / SNEER

grind / RUB; BRAY; GRATE. TEETH; TROUBLE

grind to powder / PULVERIZE, TRITURATE

grinders / TEETH; MOLARS

grinding machine / MILL; LATHE

grinding stone / MANO; QUERN; METATE

grinding tooth / MOLAR

grinding vessel / MORTAR

grindstone / HONE, MANO

gringo / AMERICAN

grip / GRASP; CLUTCH. FLU; VALISE

gripe / SEIZE; CLUTCH. COMPLAINT

grippe / FLU

gripping device / DOG; VISE; CLAMP; FINGER

grisly / GHASTLY, HIDEOUS

grist / CORN; GRAIN

gristle / CARTILAGE

grit / SAND; SPUNK; GRAVEL; BACKBONE

gritty / SANDY; PLUCKY

grivet / TOTA, WAAG; GUENON

grizzly / GRAY

groan / MOAN; LAMENT

groceries / FOOD; VICTUALS; VEGETABLES

grog / RUM

groggery / BAR; GROGSHOP

groggy / DAZED, TIPSY; UNSTEADY

gromatics / SURVEYING

grommet / BECKET, EYELET, WASHER

groom / BRUSH, CURRY, PREEN. SAIS, SICE, SYCE; HOSTLER; BRIDEGROOM

groom and bride / COUPLE

groom hair / COMB; BRUSH, CURRY

groom's companion / BRIDE

groove / RUT; SLOT; HABIT; FURROW. SWING

groove in gun barrel / RIFLING

groove in pilaster / STRIA

grooved part of joint / RABBET

grooved wheel / SHEAVE

groovy / HIP; WITHIT

grope / FEEL; PROBE; FUMBLE, TICKLE

grosbeak / FINCH; WARBLER; CARDINAL

gross / BIG; DULL, RUDE; BULKY, CRASS. TOTAL

gross amount / SUM; TOTAL; AGGREGATE

grotesque / ODD; ANTIC; GOTHIC; BIZARRE; WHIMSICAL; EXTRAVAGANT. CARICATURE

grotesque figure / GUY; MONSTER

grotto / CAVE; CAVERN

grouch / BEAR, CRAB

grouchy / SULKY; BEARISH

ground / BASE, LAND, SOIL; EARTH; BELIEF; TERRAIN, SET; REST; FOUND

ground beetle / CARABID

ground grain / MEAL; FLOUR, GRIST

ground for grazing / PASTURE

ground hog / MARMOT; AARDVARK; WOODCHUCK

Ground Hog Day / CANDLEMAS

ground ivy / CREEPER

ground raised and sloped / TERRACE

ground slightly elevated / RIDEAU

ground squirrel / GOPHER; CHIPMUNK

ground traveled / MILEAGE, YARDAGE; DISTANCE

groundless / FALSE; UNFOUNDED

groundnut / GOOBER, PEANUT

grounds / LEES; DREGS; SEDIMENT

ground-water source / AQUIFER

ground-water surface / TABLE

groundwork / BASIS; PREPARATION

group / SET; BAND, TEAM, UNIT; COTERIE

group of animals / HERD; DROVE, FLOCK

group of bees / HIVE; SWARM

group of birds / COVEY, FLOCK; FLIGHT

group of cattle / MOB; HERD; DROVE

group of eight / OCTAD, OCTET; OCTAVE, OGDOAD

group of fish / SCHOOL
group of five / PENTAD; QUINTET
group of four / TETRAD; QUARTET; QUARTETTE
group of genera / FAMILY
group of graduate students / SEMINAR
group of graduates / ALUMNI; ALUMNAE
group of hounds / PACK
group with like outlook / SECT; PARTY
group of lions / PRIDE
group of Moslem scholars / ULEMA
group of nine / ENNEAD
group of plants / PLOT; GARDEN
group of players / TEAM; COMPANY
group of puppies / LITTER
group of racehorses / STABLE, STRING
group of seals / POD
group of seven / HEPTAD, SEPTET
group of sheep / FLOCK
group of six / SEXTET
group of species / GENUS
group of students / CLASS
group of ten / DECAD; DECADE
group of tents / CAMP
group of three / TRIO
group together / GATHER; COL-LATE, COLLECT; ASSEMBLE
group of trees / GROVE; FOREST
group of wolves / PACK
grouper / GAG; MERO; CABRILLA, ROCKFISH
grouse / MUIRFOWL; PARTRIDGE, PTARMIGAN
grout / MORTAR; FILLING
grouty / CROSS, SULKY; GROUCHY
grove / DELL, TOPE, WOOD; COPSE
grove, c.f. / NEMO
grove of small trees / COPSE
grovel / FAWN, WORM; COWER; WELTER
groveling / MEAN; CRAWLING
grow / WAX; GAIN; RAISE, SWELL; EXTEND, MATURE, SPROUT
grow calm / QUIESCE
grow cordial / THAW
grow dim / BLUR, FADE, PALE
grow drowsy / NOD; TIRE
grow dull / PALL; TARNISH
grow faint / WEAKEN
grow larger / WAX; SWELL; EXPAND
grow less / EBB; WANE; ABATE; SHRINK
grow old / AGE
grow older / MATURE, MELLOW
grow smaller / SHRINK
grow to be / BECOME
grower / FARMER, RAISER

growing along the ground / DE-CUMBENT
growing in empty lots / RUDERAL
growing in marshes / ULIGINOSE
growing in meadows / CAM-PESTRAL
growing out / ENATE
growing plant life / VERDURE
growing for several years / PEREN-NIAL
growing together / ADNATE
growing for two years / BIENNIAL
growing under snow / NIVAL
growl / GIRN, GNAR, YARR; GRUMBLE
growler / CAN; BASS, FLOE, PAIL, WAVE
grown-up / ADULT; MATURE, NUBILE
growth / CROP, SPUR; TUMOR; PRODUCT; INCREASE
growth on skin / WEN; WART; KELOID
grub / FOOD; LARVA. DIG; ROOT, TOIL
grubby / DIRTY; UNKEMPT
grudge / PIQUE, SPITE; MALICE, RANCOR
grudge nurse / SOREHEAD
grudging / ENVIOUS
grue / FEAR; SHIVER. BIT
gruel / ATOLE; LOBLOLLY, POR-RIDGE
gruel of maize meal / SAMP; ATOLE
gruesome / GRISLY, MORBID; MACABRE
gruff / RUDE; BLUNT, HARSH; GRUMPY; BRUSQUE, UNCIVIL
grum / SURLY, THICK
grumble / HONE; CROAK, DRUNT, GROWL; MUTTER, REPINE
grumpy / CROSS, SURLY
grunt / SNORT; COMPLAIN. DRUM; RONCO
grunter / HOG
grunting ox / YAK
guacharo / OILBIRD
Guadalcanal river / LUNGA; TENARU
Guadeloupe capital / BASSETERRE
Guam capital / AGANA
Guam discoverer / MAGELLAN
Guam harbor / APRA
Guam native / CHAMORRO
Guam port / PITI
Guam tree / IPIL
Guam's island group / MARIANAS
guanaco / LLAMA
guano / BALSA; IGUANA, MANURE
guarantee / ENSURE, PLEDGE. SURETY; WARRANTY

guarantee payment / ENDORSE
guaranty / WARRANTY
guard / CARE, FEND, TEND; WATCH; CONVOY, DEFEND. TILE; TILER; KEEPER, SENTRY; BULWARK; WATCHMAN
guard on foil's end / BUTTON
guarded / CAREFUL; CAUTIOUS
guardhouse / BRIG; LOCKUP; STOCKADE
guardian / ARGUS; KEEPER, PATRON; CERBERUS, DEFENDER; CUSTODIAN. TUTELARY
guardian spirit / ANGEL; GENIUS
guardianship / CARE; PROTECTION
Guatemala city /COBAN
Guatemala fruit / ANAY
Guatemala Indian / MAM; CHOL, ITZA, IXIL, MAYA; PIPIL, XINCA
Guatemala lake / PETEN
Guatemala money / QUETZAL
Guatemala mountain / ATITLAN
Guatemala river / POLOCHIC
guava / ARACA; GUAYABA
guavina / GOBY
gudgeon / PIN; DUPE; SOCKET; KILLIFISH
Gudrun's husband / ATLI; HELGI; HERWIG, SIGURD
guenon monkey / MONA; GRIVET, NISNAS
guepard / CHEETAH
guerdon / MEED; PRIZE; REWARD
guerrilla / PARTISAN; IRREGULAR; BUSHWHACKER
guess / THINK; BELIEVE, SURMISE
guessing game / BUFF; MORRA; HULGUL; CHARADE; COFFEE-POT
guest / LODGER; VISITOR
guest book / ALBUM
guest house / INN; HOTEL; HOSTEL
guff / SASS; BALONEY
guffaw / HEEHAW; HORSELAUGH
guffer / EELPOUT
gugal / RESIN; BDELLIUM
guggle / WINDPIPE
Guiana ebony tree / WAMARA
Guiana tree / MORA

guide / LEAD; PILOT, STEER; MANAGE. KEY; RULE; RUDDER; CHANNEL, MONITOR
guide book / CHART; BAEDEKER, BRADSHAW, HANDBOOK; VADEMECUM
guide to navigation / BUOY; BEACON; COMPASS
guided / LED; STEERED
guided missile / NIKE, THOR; ATLAS, TITAN; BOMARC; JUPITER; REDSTONE; MINUTEMAN
guiding / POLAR
guiding statement / MOTTO, PLANK; SLOGAN; EPIGRAPH
guiding thread / CLUE
guidon / FLAG; BANNER
Guienne capital / BORDEAUX
guild / GILD; HANSE; COMPANY, SOCIETY; ASSOCIATION
guilder / FLORIN, GULDEN
guile / CRAFT; DECEIT; CUNNING
guileful / SLY; ARTFUL; INSIDIOUS
guileless / NAIVE; CANDID; ARTLESS
guillemets / QUOTES
guillemot / AUK; LOOM; MURRE; DOVEKIE
guillotine cart / TUMBREL
guilt / SIN; CRIME; INIQUITY
guiltless / INNOCENT
guilty / EVIL; NOCENT; CULPABLE
guilty person / CULPRIT
guimpe / TUCKER; CHEMISETTE
Guinea bight / BENIN
Guinea capital / CONAKRY
guinea corn / DURRA; MILLET
guinea fowl / KEET; PINTADO
Guinea money / SILY
guinea pig / CAVY; APEREA; SUBJECT
Guinea tree / AKEE, MORA
Guinea tribe / SUSU; FULANI
Guinevere's husband / ARTHUR
Guinevere's lover / LANCELOT
guipure / GIMP, LACE
guise / FORM, GARB, MIEN; DRESS, SHAPE; ASPECT; SEMBLANCE
guitar fiddle / VIELLE

Guido's Scale

ALT
ELA
ELAMI
FA
LA
RE
MI
SOL
UT

guitar finger strip / FRET
guitar fish / RAY
guitar string tuner / KEY
guitarlike instrument / LUTE; SITAR; CITHER; BANDORE
Gujarati race / YADAVA
gula / OGEE; GULLET, THROAT
Gula's husband / NINIB
gulch / GULLY; ARROYO, CANYON, RAVINE
gulden / FLORIN
gules / RED; BLAZON
gulf / ABYSS, CHASM, DEPTH
gulf in Africa / ADEN; GUINEA
gulf in Asia / OMAN; PERSIAN
gulf in Baltic Sea / RIGA; BOTHNIA
gulf in Caribbean / DARIEN
gulf in Central America / DULCE; NICOYA
gulf in Chile / PENAS
gulf in India / CUTCH; MANNAR
gulf in Mediterranean / TARANTO
gulf in New Guinea / HUON
gulf in North America / ALASKA, MEXICO
gulf in Siberia / OB
gulfweed / SARGASSO
gull / DUPE; CHEAT, COZEN. MEW; SKUA; KITTIWAKE
gullet / GAP, MAW; CRAW
gullible / EASY; GREEN, NAIVE; CREDULOUS
gullible person / DUPE, GULL; GULPIN
Gulliver's debased men / YAHOOS
Gulliver's land of dwarfs / LILLIPUT
gull-like / LARINE
gull-like bird / TERN; NODDY; FULMAR, JAEGER
gully / WADI; DONGA, DUNGA; RAVINE; CHANNEL
gulosity / GREED
gulp / BOLT, SWIG; GOBBLE
gum / PASTE, RESIN; ADHESIVE
gum, c.f. / ULE
gum arabic / ACACIA, ACACIN
gum astringent / MOUTHWASH
gum inflammation / ULITIS
gum resin / ULA; DAMAR, ELEMI, LOBAN, MYRRH
gum shoes / RUBBERS; SNEAKERS; OVERSHOES
gum tree / ICICA, KIKAR; BALATA, CHICLE, TUPELO, TURARA; GAMBOGE; EUCALYPT
gum variety / KINO; XYLAN; CHICLE; CAMPHOR; TRAGACANTH
gumbo / MUD; OCRA, OKRA, OKRO, OOZE; CREOLE
gumbo limbo tree / GOMART
gumbo vegetable / OKRA

gummed paper / STAMP; STICKER
gummed part / FLAP
gumption / DRIVE, SKILL, SPUNK; SAGACITY
gumptious / SMART; SHREWD
gums / ULA
gums, c.f. / ULO
gums, pert. to / ULETIC
gun / GAT, ROD; BREN, STEN; PIECE, RIFLE; CANNON, HEATER, MORTAR, PISTOL, POMPOM, ROSCOE; SYRINGE; HOWITZER, REVOLVER
gun cleaner / RAMROD
gun dog / BEAGLE, SETTER; BIRDDOG, POINTER
gun emplacement / BATTERY
gun for game / CAPPISTOL
gunboat / SKIP; WARSHIP; CATAMARAN
guncotton / PYROXYLIN
gunfire / SALVO, SHOTS; VOLLEY; BARRAGE; BROADSIDE, FUSILLADE
gunk / CHEAT. GOO
gunlock catch / SEAR
gunman / THUG; ASSASSIN, GANGSTER
gunnel / GUNWALE
gunner / RIFLEMAN; ARTILLERYMAN
gunner's mate / ARMORER
gunny cloth / TAT; HEMP, JUTE; BURLAP
guns / ARMS; TROOPS
guns on a warship / TURRET; BATTERY; BROADSIDE
Gunther's brother / HAGEN
Gunther's mother / GRIMHILDE
Gunther's sister / GUTRUNE
Gunther's subjects / GIBICHUNGS
Gunther's wife / BRYNHILDE
gunwale / GUNNEL
gunwale pin / THOLE
guppy / TOPMINNOW
gurgle / PURL; BUBBLE
Gurkha knife / KUKRI
gush / FLOW, POUR, RUSH; SPOUT, SPURT
gush out / SPEW
gusset / GORE
gust / FIT; ZEST; BLAST; SQUALL
gust of wind / FLAW; SQUALL
gusto / ZEST; RELISH; DELIGHT
gusty / BLOWY, WINDY; BLUSTERY
gut / PLUNDER; EVISCERATE. STRING; CHANNEL; INTESTINE
guts / WILL; DARING
gutta mixture / SOH
gutter / SEWER; CHANNEL
guttler / GLUTTON
guttural / GRUM; HUSKY, VELAR

guttural sound / BURR; GRUNT
guy / GAG; ROPE, WIRE; EFFIGY, FELLOW. RIDICULE
guy rope / STAY, VANG
Guyana capital / GEORGETOWN
Guyana falls / KAIETEUR
Guyana Indian / BONI, TRIO; ACURIA, ARAWAK
Guyana mountain / RORAIMA
Guyana river / DEMERARA
Guyana town / SUDDIE
Guyana waterfall / KAIETEUR
Guyenne / AQUITAINE
guzzler / SOT; DRUNK, TOPER
Gwydion's art / PROPHECY
Gwynn's companion / OWL
Gwynn's father / NUDD
Gyges' kingdom / LYDIA
gym shoes / SNEAKERS
gymkhana / MEET

gymnast / TURNER; ATHLETE
gymnastic bar / TRAPEZE
gymnastic feat / KIP; CARTWHEEL
gyp / CHEAT; SWINDLE
gypsum / LIME, YESO; GESSO; PLASTER
gypsy / ROM; CALO. See also gipsy
gypsy gentleman / RYE
gypsy jazz great / REINHARDT
gypsy tongue / ROMANY
gypsy trade / TINSMITHING
gyral / WHIRLING
gyrate / SPIN, WIND; SHIRL; REVOLVE
gyration / ROTATION
gyre / EDDY; VORTEX
gyrose / WAVY; UNDULATE
gyves / IRONS; FETTERS; SHACKLES

H

habile / SKILLFUL
habiliment / GARB, ROBE; DRESS
habit / RUT, WAY; DRESS, USAGE
habitant / DWELLER; RESIDENT
habitat plant form / ECAD
habitation / DEN; HOME, LAIR, NEST; ABODE, HOUSE; LODGING
habitual / USUAL; COMMON, WONTED
habitual drunkard / SOT; TOPER
habitually complaining / QUERULOUS; DISCONTENTED
habitually silent / TACITURN
habituate / ENURE, INURE
habituate to locale / ACCLIMATE
habitué / REGULAR
habitué of track / HORSEPLAYER
hacienda / FARM; RANCH; ESTATE
hack / CAB; COACH, COUGH, HORSE; DRUDGE. CUT
hack weeds / HOE
hackle / FLY; COMB, TEAR; FEATHER
hackmatack / TAMARACK
hackneyed / WORN; BANAL, STALE, TRITE; COMMON
hackneyed wording / CLICHE
had been / WAS; WERE
had debts / OWED
had on / WORE
Hades / DIS; ADES, HELL; ORCUS, PLUTO, SHEOL; EREBUS; TARTARUS
Hades' brother / ZEUS; POSEIDON
Hades' daughters / FURIES
Hades' father / CRONUS
Hades's mother / RHEA

Hades river / STYX; LETHE; ACHERON
Hades' wife / PERSEPHONE
Haemon's father / CREON
haft / HILT; HELVE
hag / CRONE, WITCH; BELDAM
hagfish / BORER
haggard / WAN; LEAN, WILD, WORN
Haggard's novel / SHE
haggle / CUT; HACK; BARGAIN
hail / AVE; GREET; ACCOST, SALUTE
Haile Selassie title / RAS; NEGUS
hair / TRESS
hair, c.f. / PIL; PILO; TRICH; TRICHO
hair ailment / MANGE; XERASIA; TRICHOSIS
hair braid / PLAIT; PIGTAIL
hair covering / NET; SNOOD
hair dressing / SPRAY; POMADE
hair dressing aid / NET, PIN; COMB; BRUSH; CURLER
hair dye / TINT; HENNA, RINSE
hair on end / HORRIPILATION
hair fastener / CLIP; SLIDE; HAIRPIN; BARRETTE, BOBBYPIN
hair line of letter / SERIF
hair ornament / BOW, PIN; RIBBON
hair piece / RAT, WIG; FALL, ROLL; TOUPEE, WIGLET
hair ringlet / LOCK
hair wave / PERM; PERMANENT
hair worn in knot / BUN; CHIGNON
haircloth / CILICE
hair-color restorer / RINSE
hairdresser / BARBER; COIFFEUR

hairless / BALD; GLABROUS
hairlike projection / CILIUM
hairy / COMATE, PILOSE; HIRSUTE
hairy biped / APE; PRIMATE
hairy ox / YAK
Haiti capital / PORTAUPRINCE
Haiti money / GOURDE
Haiti outlaw / CACO
Haiti town / CAYES
Haitian evil spirit / BAKA
Haitian island / HISPANIOLA
Haitian ruler / TOUSSAINT;
    DESSALINES
halcyon / CALM; PEACEFUL
Halcyone's spouse / CEYX
hale / SOUND; HEARTY, ROBUST,
    STRONG; HEALTHY; VIGOROUS
half / MOIETY
half, pref. / DEMI, HEMI, SEMI;
    DICHO
half asleep / DROWSY
half baked / ABSURD; FOOLISH
half diameter / RADIUS
half dozen / SIX
half em / EN
half farthing / MITE
half gable / AILERON
half lawful / SEMILEGAL
half moon / LUNETTE
half note / MINIM
half pint / CUP
half quart / PINT
half semibreve / MINIM
half-breed / METIS; MUSTEE;
    MESTIZO, MULATTO
half-mask / DOMINO
halfpenny / MAG
half-suppressed laugh / SNICKER
halfway / MID; MIDWAY; BETWEEN
halfway house / INN; TAVERN
half-wit / FOOL; IMBECILE;
    BLOCKHEAD
halitus / BREATH
hall / AULA, ROOM; SALON;
    BUILDING, CORRIDOR
hall for athletics / GYM; XYST;
    ARENA; GYMNASIUM
hallow / BLESS, HONOR;
    DEDICATE
hallowed / HOLY; SACRED
Halloween / TRICKORTREAT
Hallowmass / ALLHALLOWS
hallucination / ERROR; BELIEF,
    VISION; CHIMERA, FANTASY,
    PHANTOM; DELIRIUM
halo / AURA, NIMB; GLORY;
    AREOLA, NIMBUS; AUREOLA,
    AUREOLE
halogen / IODINE; BROMINE;
    ASTATINE, CHLORINE,
    FLUORINE
halt / HOLD, LIMP, STEM, STOP;
    CEASE, PAUSE. LAME; CRIPPLED

halter / ROPE; NOOSE
halting / LAME
halting place / STAGE
halve / CUT; BISECT
Hamburg's river / ELBE
hamfatter / HAM; ACTOR
Hamite / FELAH, GALLA; BERBER,
    TUAREG
Hamitic language / AGAO, BEJA;
    GALLA; COPTIC, KABYLE;
    EGYPTIAN
hamlet / DORP, TOWN; VILLAGE
Hamlet's friend / HORATIO
Hamlet's girl / OPHELIA
Hamlet's home / DENMARK;
    ELSINORE
Hamlet's mother / GERTRUDE
Hamlet's slayer / LAERTES
Hamlet's uncle / CLAUDIUS
hammer / MAUL; MADGE; MALLET,
    OLIVER, SLEDGE. BEAT; POUND
hammer end / CLAW, PEEN, POLL
hammer in medicine / PLEXOR;
    PLESSOR
hammer and tongs / FORCE,
    NOISE; VIOLENCE
hammerwort / PELLITORY
hammock / COUCH, SWING
hamper / CLOG; HINDER, IMPEDE.
    PED; BASKET, WICKER;
    HANAPER
Ham's son / CUSH, PHUT;
    CANAAN
hamstring / CRIPPLE, DISABLE
hanap / CUP
hand / FIN, PAW; NEAF, WORK;
    INDEX, SKILL, TOUCH; WORK-
    MAN; HANDWRITING. GIVE
hand, pert. to / CHIRAL
hand in glove / CLOSE; INTIMATE
hand gun / PISTOL
hand on hip / AKIMBO
hand out / DOLE
hand over / DELIVER
hand part / PALM; FINGER;
    KNUCKLE
hand pump / SYRINGE; ATOMIZER
hand reaper / SCYTHE, SICKLE
handbag / CABAS, PURSE;
    CLUTCH; RETICULE
handbill / FLYER; DODGER;
    LEAFLET
handbook / MANUAL
handclasp / GRIP
handful of hay / WISP
handicraft / ART; SKILL
handle / ACT, BUY, USE; FEEL,
    SELL, WORK; GRASP, TOUCH.
    EAR, LUG; ANSA, HAFT, HILT,
    KNOB; HELVE
handle bar / MUSTACHE
handle certain goods / DEALIN
handle of jack plane / TOTE

handle of pail / BAIL
handle of printing press / ROUNCE
handle of rudder / TILLER
handle of scythe / SNATH, SNEAD
handle violently / PAW; MAUL
handled container / PAIL
handler / AGENT, COACH
hands on hips / AKIMBO
handsel / GIFT; EARNEST
handshake / GRIP
handsome / BRAW; AMPLE;
  COMELY; ELEGANT, LIBERAL,
  STATELY
handsome man / ADONIS, APOLLO
handstone / MANO; HANDAX
handwriting / SCRIPT; PENMAN-
  SHIP
handwritten arabesque on signature / PARAPH
handwritten document / MANU-
  SCRIPT
handwritten and signed letter /
  ALS
handy / DEFT, NEAR; READY;
  ADROIT
hang / PEND, REST; CLING,
  DRAPE, DROOP, GROUP, HOVER;
  IMPEND; EXECUTE, INCLINE,
  SUSPEND
hang about / LOITER
hang down / LOP, SAG; DANGLE
hang over / LOOM; IMPEND
hangar / DOCK, SHED
hangdog / LOW; MEAN; SNEAKING
hanger / HOOK; STRAP, SWORD
hanging / ARRAS, NOOSE; GIBBET;
  CURTAIN, VALANCE. PENDENT
hanging behind altar / DORSAL,
  DOSSAL, DOSSER
hanging decoration / TASSEL;
  PENDANT
hanging down / ALOP
hanging loosely / BAGGY
hangman / EXECUTIONER
hangnail / AGNAIL; WHITLOW
hangover / HEAD; CRAPULENCE
hank / RAN; COIL, RING; SKEIN
hanker / LONG; CRAVE, YEARN
hankering / YEN; ITCH
hanky-panky / TRICKERY;
  CONJURING
Hannibal's conqueror / SCIPIO
Hannibal's father / BARCA;
  HAMILCAR
Hannibal's great victory / CANNAE
Hanoi's port / HAIPHONG
Hanse town / RIGA; BREMEN,
  LUBECK
hap / LOT; LUCK; CHANCE;
  FORTUNE
haphazard / CHANCE, RANDOM
hapless / UNLUCKY; WRETCHED
haply / PERHAPS; PERCHANCE

happen / OCCUR; BEFALL, BETIDE
happen again / RECUR; RETURN
happening / HAP, LOT; EVENT;
  INCIDENT
happiness / JOY; BLISS; GAIETY
happy / APT, GAY; GLAD; LUCKY;
  JOYOUS; CHARMED, CONTENT
happy festivity / GALA
happy-go-lucky / CARELESS;
  EASYGOING
harangue / TIRADE; ADDRESS,
  ORATION; DIATRIBE. NAG;
  RANT; BERATE
Haran's father / TERAH
Haran's son / LOT
harass / IRK, NAG, VEX; BAIT,
  FRET, GALL; BESET, WORRY;
  BOTHER
harbinger / USHER; HERALD;
  FORERUNNER
harbor / HOLD; COVER, LODGE;
  SHELTER. BAY; COVE, PORT;
  HAVEN; REFUGE; RETREAT
harbor city / PORT
harbor marker / BUOY
harbor vessel / TUG; TOWBOAT
hard / SET; FIRM, IRON; CRUEL,
  HARSH, ROUGH, SOLID, STIFF,
  STONY; SEVERE, UNKIND,
  WICKED; ADAMANT, COMPACT,
  COMPLEX
hard, pref. / DYS
hard to approach / DISTANT
hard body tissue / BONE
hard brittle biscuit / CRACKNEL
hard cash / MONEY; SPECIE
hard cheese / JACK; SWISS;
  ROMANO, SBRINZ; CHEDDAR;
  PARMESAN
hard to climb / STEEP
hard coal / ANTHRACITE
hard drawn / TAUT; TENSE
hard drinker / SOT
hard fat / LARD, SUET
hard feelings / ANIMUS
hard glossy finish / ENAMEL;
  LACQUER
hard green cheese / SAPSAGO
hard metal / IRON; STEEL
hard mineral / EMERY; SPINEL
hard money / CASH; SPECIE
hard outer cover / CRUST, SHELL
hard question / POSER; PUZZLER
hard resin / COPAL
hard shell / BARK; CRUST; CHITIN
hard up / POOR; BROKE; PINCHED
hard work / TOIL; LABOR; INDUS-
  TRY
hard-baked bread / RUSK
hard-boiled / CRUEL, HARSH,
  ROUGH, TOUGH
harden / JEL, SET; CAKE; ENURE,
  INURE; OSSIFY

harden sails / TAN
hardened / CALLOUS; CONFIRMED
hardened dry mass / CAKE
hardened place / CALLUS
hardhat in tunnel / SANDHOG
hard-hearted / PITILESS; UNFEELING
hardihood / BRASS, PLUCK; COURAGE
hardiness / TOUGHNESS
hardly / BARELY, MERELY; CRUELLY
hard-shelled fruit / NUT
hardship / TOIL, WANT; RIGOR
hard-twisted thread / LISLE
hardware / TOOLS; MACHINES
hardwood / ASH, ELM, OAK; IPIL, LANA, TEAK; BEECH, BIRCH, EBONY, MAPLE; HICKORY
hardy / BOLD, HALE, WELL; BRAVE
hardy tamarisk / ATHEL, ATLEE
hare / WAT; CONEY; LEVERET
harebrained / WILD; GIDDY
harehound / HARRIER
harelike / LEPORINE
harem / ZENANA; SERAGLIO
harem dweller / KADEIN; ODALISQUE
harem room / ODA
hare's tail / SCUT; BULRUSH
Hari / VISHNU; KRISHNA
hark / HEAR, HEED, LIST; ATTEND, HARKEN, LISTEN; HEARKEN
harlequin / CLOWN, COMIC; BUFFOON
harlot of Jericho / RAHAB
harm / ILL; BALE, BANE, EVIL; WRONG, DERE, HURT; DAMAGE, INJURE
harmful / BAD, ILL; FOUL; NOCENT
harmful influence / BANE
harmless / MILD; INNOCUOUS
Harmonia's father / ARES
Harmonia's husband / CADMUS
Harmonia's mother / APHRODITE
harmonious / DULCET; AMIABLE, CORDIAL, MUSICAL, TUNEFUL
harmonize / GEE; TONE, TUNE; AGREE, BLEND, CHIME; ACCORD
harmonizer / ATTUNER
harmony / AMITY, PEACE; ACCORD; CONCERT, CONCORD, ONENESS
harness / GEAR; ARMOR; TACKLE
harness horse / PACER; TROTTER
harness part / BIT; HAME, REIN; TRACE; BLINDS, BRIDLE, COLLAR, HALTER, SADDLE; CRUPPER
harness together / PAIR, TEAM

harp / KOTO, LYRE; TRIGON; CITHARA
harp constellation / LYRA
harper / MINSTREL
harplike chord / ARPEGGIO
harpoon / GAFF; SPEAR
harpy / AELLO; CELAENO, MONSTER, OCYPETE, PODARGE
harquebus part / CROC
harridan / HAG; VIRAGO
harried / BESET
harrier / HAWK; HOUND
harrow / TEAR; BREAK; DISTURB; LACERATE
harry / ANNOY; HARASS, RAVAGE; TORMENT
harsh / RUDE, SOUR; ACERB, BLUNT, GRUFF, ROUGH, STERN; BRUTAL, SEVERE; AUSTERE, RASPING, RAUCOUS
harsh alkali / LYE
harsh loud cry / BRAY
harsh overseer / SLAVEDRIVER
harsh sound / STRIDOR
harsh sounding / GRATING; STRIDENT
harsh tasting / ACERB; BITTER
harshness / RIGOR; ASPERITY
hart / DEER, STAG
hartebeest / ASSE, TORA; CAAMA, KAAMA, LECAMA; BUBALIS, KONGONI
hartshorn / ANTLER; SALVOLATILE
harum-scarum / BOLD, WILD; GIDDY
harvest / REAP, TAKE; GLEAN, CROP
harvest goddess / OPS
harvest in India / RABI; RABBI; RUBBEE
harvesting implement / FORK, RAKE; SCYTHE, SICKLE; HAYFORK
harvesting machine / MOWER; BINDER, REAPER, TEDDER
harvestman / DADDYLONGLEGS
Harz mountain peak / BROCKEN
has / OWNS; POSSESSES
has being / IS; EXISTS
has permission / MAY
hash / MESS; MINCE; JUMBLE
hashish / HEMP; BHANG
hashish plant / HEMP
Haslemere resident / TENNYSON
hasp / CATCH, CLASP
hassock / TUFT; STOOL; TABORET, TUSSOCK
haste / HURRY, SPEED; URGENCY
hasten / FLY, HIE, RUN; MOVE, RACE; HASTE, HURRY, SPEED
hasten away / FLEE, SCAT; SCOOT
hastened / SPED
hastily / PELLMELL

Hastings victor / WILLIAM

hasty / RASH; BRASH, EAGER, FIERY, QUICK, SWIFT; ABRUPT

hasty pudding / MUSH; SEPON; SUPAWN

hat / CAP, TAM; BERET, MILAN, TOPEE, TOQUE; BONNET, CLOCHE, FEDORA, PANAMA; CAUBEEN, CHAPEAU

hat material / FELT

hat ornament / PIN; CLIP; FEATHER

hat plant / SOLA

hat rim / BRIM

hat of soldier / KEPI; BUSBY, SHAKO; HELMET

hatch / BROOD; CONCOCT. LID; DOOR

hatchel / TEASE; TORMENT. COMB; HACKLE

hatchet / AX; AXE; MOGO; HACHE; CHOPPER; TOMAHAWK

hatching apparatus / INCUBATOR

hate / ABHOR; DETEST, LOATHE; DESPISE

hateful / CURSED, ODIOUS

hateful person / CUR, RAT; TOAD

Hathor's son / RA; SHU

hatred / ODIUM; ENMITY, RANCOR

hatred in Buddhism / DOSA

hatter / MILLINER; ECCENTRIC

hatter's mallet / BEATER

haughtiness / AIRS; PRIDE; VANITY; DISDAIN; ARROGANCE

haughty / LOFTY, PROUD; IMPERIOUS

haul / LUG, TOW, TUG; CART, DRAG, DRAW, HALE, PULL, TOTE; SHIFT

haulage / CARTAGE, FREIGHT

hauled by truck / TRAILERED

haunch / HIP; BUTTOCK

haunt / DEN; DIVE, LAIR, NEST; GHOST. VISIT; OBSESS; INHABIT; FREQUENT

Hausaland town / KANO

hautboy / OBOE

hauteur / PRIDE

Havana / CIGAR

Havana castle / MORRO

Havana drive / MALECON

have / HAE, OWN; BEAR, FEEL, HOLD, KEEP, TAKE; CHEAT, ENJOY, OPINE; OBTAIN

have ambition / ASPIRE, STRIVE

have being / AM; ARE

have confidence / HOPE; TRUST; BELIEVE

have debts / OWE

have effect / TELL; COUNT, WEIGH

have excess flow of saliva / DROOL; SLAVER

have mercy / SPARE; FORGIVE

have a night out / PAINTTHETOWN

have not / LACK, NEED

have on / WEAR

have power to / CAN

have recourse to / RESORT

have same opinion / AGREE

have strong wish for / COVET; DESIRE

have to / MUST

haven / PORT; REFUGE, SAFETY; SHELTER

have-not / POOR; UNDER-DEVELOPED

haversack / BAG; KNAPSACK

having ability / ABLE; COMPETENT

having arisen / UP

having billing / FEATURED

having branched antennae / RAMICORN

having broad meaning / GENERAL, GENERIC

having broad views / CATHOLIC, ECLECTIC; BROADMINDED

having a caudal appendage / TAILED

having a certain madness / MANIC

having a certain sound / TONAL

having claws / TALONED

having a comb / CRESTED

having digits / TOED

having an end / FINITE

having feathers / PENNATE

having feeling / SENSATE; SENTIENT; SENSITIVE

having feet / PEDATE

having good judgment / WISE

having a good memory / RETENTIVE

having left / OFF

having little depth / SHALLOW

having lobes / LOBAR

having made a will / TESTATE

having natural luster / NAIF

having no feet / APODAL

having no interest / SUPINE; INDIFFERENT

having no owner / FREE

having no troubles / CAREFREE

having obligations / OWING

having offensive odor / OLID; FETID; SMELLY

having painful feet / FOOTSORE

having a pointed end / CUSPED; CUSPATE

having potentiality / LATENT

having purpose / TELIC

having recourse / RESORTING

having rhythm / CADENT

having scalloped margin / CRENATE

having a spire / STEEPLED

having three cusps / TRICORN

having three sides / TRIANGULAR

having two feet / BIPEDAL
having uniform teeth / ISODENT
having a voice / VOCAL
having weapons / ARMED
havoc / RUIN; CARNAGE;
　SLAUGHTER
Hawaii capital / HONOLULU
Hawaii state bird / NENE
Hawaii state flower / HIBISCUS
Hawaii state tree / KUKUI
Hawaiian / KANAKA
Hawaiian acacia / KOA
Hawaiian antonym of tabu / NOA
Hawaiian arrowroot / PIA
Hawaiian baking pit / IMU
Hawaiian ballad / MELE
Hawaiian bark fiber / OLONA
Hawaiian bird / IO, OO, OU; OMU;
　IIWI, KOAE, MAMO, MANA,
　OMAO, OOAA, PUEO; ALALA;
　PALILA
Hawaiian berry / OHELO
Hawaiian cairn / AHU
Hawaiian cliffs / PALI
Hawaiian cloak of feathers / MAMO
Hawaiian coffee / KONA
Hawaiian dance / HULA
Hawaiian fabric / KAPA, TAPA
Hawaiian family totem /
　AUMAKUA
Hawaiian farewell / ALOHA
Hawaiian feast / LUAU
Hawaiian fern / HELI, PULU;
　IWAIWA
Hawaiian fish / AHI, AKU, AWA;
　ULUA; AKULE
Hawaiian flower / LEHUA
Hawaiian flycatcher / ELEPAIO
Hawaiian food / POI
Hawaiian garland / LEI
Hawaiian god / KANE
Hawaiian goddess of fire / PELE
Hawaiian goose / NENE
Hawaiian gooseberry / POHA
Hawaiian grass / HILO; KIAWE
Hawaiian greeting / ALOHA
Hawaiian hawk / IO
Hawaiian herb / HOLA; AUHUHU
Hawaiian honey eater / OOAA;
　KIOEA
Hawaiian honeycreeper / OU;
　AKEPA
Hawaiian island / MAUI, OAHU;
　KAUAI, LANAI; NIIHAU;
　MOLOKAI
Hawaiian loincloth / MALO
Hawaiian medicine man / KAHUNA
Hawaiian musical instrument /
　UKE; UKULELE
Hawaiian necklace / LEI
Hawaiian nobility / ALII
Hawaiian plover / KOLEA
Hawaiian seaport / HILO

Hawaiian shrub / AKIA; AALII,
　AKALA, HAPUU, OHELO;
　PUKEAWE
Hawaiian stormy wind / KONA
Hawaiian string figures / HEI
Hawaiian temple / HEIAU
Hawaiian thrush / OMAO
Hawaiian timber tree / KOA;
　OHIA; ILIAHI
Hawaiian tree fern / PULU;
　HAPUU; AMAUMAU, HAPUIII
Hawaiian veranda / LANAI
Hawaiian volcano / KILAUEA;
　MAUNALOA
Hawaiian volcano goddess / PELE
Hawaiian war god / KU
hawbuck / LOUT
hawk / IO; KITE; ELANET, FALCON;
　GOSHAWK, HARRIER, KESTREL;
　CARACARA
hawk moth / SPHINX
hawk parrot / HIA
hawker / PEDDLER
hawkeye state / IOWA
hawk's cage / MEW
hawk's leash / LOYN, LUNE
hawser / ROPE; CABLE; MOORING
hawser bean / BITT
hawthorn flower / MAY
hawthorn fruit / HAW
hay / GRASS; FODDER
hay storage area / MOW; LOFT,
　SILO
haycock / PILE, RICK; STACK
haying implement / BINDER,
　TEDDER
hayseed / HICK; FARMER, RUSTIC
hazard / DARE, RISK; STAKE;
　CHANCE. PERIL; DANGER;
　CASUALTY, JEOPARDY
hazardous / RUM; RISKY; UNSAFE
haze / FOG; MIST, SMOG;
　OBSCURITY. ABUSE; HARASS,
　PURSUE
hazelnut / FILBERT
hazy / DIM; VAGUE
head / COP, NOB, TOP; ACME;
　FORE, NOLL, PATE, TETE;
　CAPUT, CHIEF; LEADER,
　NODDLE, NOGGIN, NOODLE.
　LEAD, MOVE; GUIDE
head of convent / ABBESS
head cook / CHEF
head cooler / ICEBAG
head covering / HOOD, VEIL;
　NUBIA, SCARF, SHAWL;
　WIMPLE. See also hat
head of ecclesiastical province /
　BISHOP, EPARCH
head gesture / NOD
head of hair / MANE; CRINE
head over heels / TOPSYTURVY
head of moving group / VAN

head organ / EAR, EYE; NOSE; BRAIN, MOUTH
head part / FACE; SCALP
head of wolf or boar / HURE
headache / CEPHALALGIA
headband RIBBON, TAENIA
headdress BOW; TIARA; HENNIN, RIBBON; COIFFURE, MANTILLA
headdress of widow / BANDORE
headed / LED
headed bolt / RIVET
headgear of ecclesiastic / MITER, MITRE; BIRETTA, CALOTTA; ZUCCHETTO
heading / TITLE, TOPIC; CAPTION
headland / RAS; CAPE, NAZE, NESS
headless / STUPID; WITLESS
headliner / ACE; HERO, STAR
headlong / RASH; HURRIED
headman / CHIEF; LEADER
headstrong RASH; VIOLENT; STUBBORN; OBSTINATE; SELFWILLED
headway / INTERVAL, PROGRESS
headwear / HAT
heal / CURE; PURIFY; RESTORE; RECONCILE
healer / MEDIC; DOCTOR
healing / MEDICINAL
healing art / MEDICINE
healing unguent / BALM; SALVE; OINTMENT
health / TOAST, VIGOR; SANITY
health, c.f. / SANI
health resort / SPA; BATHS; SPRINGS
healthy / HALE, SANE, WELL; SOUND
heap / MASS, PILE, RAFT; HOARD, STACK. AMASS; ACCUMULATE
heap of hay / MOW; TASS; STACK
heap of stones / CAIRN, SCREE, TALUS
hear / HEED; ATTEND, HARKEN, LISTEN
hear accidentally / OVERHEAR
hear as judge / SIT, TRY
hear ye / OYES, OYEZ
hearer / AUDITOR
hearing / OYER; TRIAL; EARSHOT; AUDITION
hearken / SEE HARK
hearsay / RUMOR; GOSSIP, REPORT
heart / COR; CORE; KERNEL, SPIRIT; COURAGE, EMOTION; AFFECTION
heart, pert. to / CARDIAC
heart beat / SYSTOLE; DIASTOLE
heart chamber / ATRIUM; AURICLE; VENTRICLE
heart cherry / GEAN

heart disease / ANGINA; MYOCARDITIS
heart weighed before Osiris / AB
heartache / GRIEF; SORROW; ANGUISH
heartbeat / PULSATION
heartbroken / INCONSOLABLE
heartburn / PYROSIS; CARDIALGIA; INDIGESTION
hearten / CHEER; INSPIRIT
heartfelt / TRUE; EARNEST, SINCERE
hearth / HOME; INGLE; FIRESIDE
heartily / WARMLY; ARDENTLY
heartless / CRUEL; PITILESS
heart-rending / DISTRESSING
heartsease / PANSY; VIOLET; SELFHEAL; PERSICARY
heart-shaped / CORDATE; CARDIOID
heartsore / GRIEVED
heartwhole / SINCERE; FANCYFREE
heartwood / DURAMEN
hearty / DEEP, FULL, HALE, OPEN, RICH, TRUE, WARM, WELL; HEAVY, SOUND; ROBUST; CORDIAL, EARNEST
heat / LAP, SUN; FIRE, RAYS; ARDOR, CALOR. WARM; TOAST; EXCITE
heat, c.f. / THERM; THERMO
heat, pert. to / CALORIC, THERMAL, THERMIC
heat conductor / STEAMPIPE
heat excessively / BURN, MELT; ROAST; SCORCH
heat producer / FUEL
heat spreader / RADIATOR
heat, sweeten, and spice / MULL
heat unit / THERM
heated / HOT; WARM; WARMED
heated drink / NEGUS, TODDY
heater / STOVE; FURNACE; RADIATOR
heath / MOOR; ERICA; HEATHER
heathen / PAGAN; INFIDEL
heathen image / IDOL
heather / LING; HEATH
heating vessel / STILL; BOILER, RETORT
heave / CAST, HAUL, HURL, LIFT, TOSS; FLING, HOIST, SCEND, SURGE, VOMIT
heaven / SKY; PARADISE; FIRMAMENT
heavenly / BLEST; DIVINE, EDENIC; SAINTLY; CELESTIAL
heavenly being / GOD; ANGEL, SAINT; CHERUB, SERAPH
heavenly body / SUN; MOON, STAR; COMET; METEOR, PLANET; LUMINARY; SATELLITE
heavenly food / MANNA

heavenly place / PARADISE
heavens, pert. to / URANIC; CELESTIAL
heaven-storming tower / BABEL
heaver / LIFTER, LOADER
heavily polluted air / SMOG; SMAZE
heaviness / GLOOM; WEIGHT; LANGUOR, SADNESS; DULLNESS
heavy / SAD; DARK, DEEP, DULL, HARD, LOUD, MIRY, SLOW; DENSE, INERT, LADEN, MUDDY, SOGGY; CLAMMY, CLAYEY, TORPID; WEIGHTY
heavy blow / ONER; SMASH
heavy book / TOME
heavy boot / STOGY; BROGAN, BROGUE
heavy brown paper / KRAFT
heavy curtains / DRAPES
heavy gas / RADON, XENON; KRYPTON, TRITIUM; DEUTERIUM
heavy hammer / MAUL; SLEDGE
heavy harrow / DRAG
heavy mooring line / CABLE
heavy nail / SPIKE; TENPENNY
heavy spar / BARITE
heavy and sweet / SIRUPY, SUGARY
heavy wagon / VAN; DRAY; TRUCK
heavy weight / TON
heavy wood / BEECH, EBONY, LARCH; HICKORY
heavy woolen material / WORSTED
heavy-faced type / BOLD; BOLD-FACE
heavy-hearted / SAD; GLOOMY; SORROWFUL
heavyweight / BIGWIG
hebdomad / WEEK
Hebe / JUVENTAS
Heber's wife / JAEL
Hebe's father / ZEUS
Hebe's husband / HERCULES
hebetate / DULL; BLUNT
hebetude / LETHARGY; STUPIDITY
Hebrew / JEW; ISRAELITE
Hebrew, pert. to / HEBRAIC
Hebrew acrostic word / AGLA
Hebrew avenger of blood / GOEL
Hebrew dirge / KINNAH
Hebrew god / EL; ADONAI, YAHWEH
Hebrew judge / ELON
Hebrew king / SAUL; DAVID; SOLOMON
Hebrew kingdom / JUDAH; ISRAEL
Hebrew lawgiver / MOSES
Hebrew letter / HE, PE; AIN, MEM, NUN, SIN, TAV, TAW, VAU, WAW; ALEF, AYIN, BETH, CAPH, KOPH, RESH, SHIN, TETH, YODH; ALEPH, CHETH, GIMEL, LAMED, SADHE, ZAYIN; DALETH, LAMEDH, SAMEKH
Hebrew marginal reading / KRI, QRI; KERE
Hebrew measure / HEN, HIN, KAB, KER, KOR, LOG; OMER; EPHAH
Hebrew musical instrument / ASOR, TOPH
Hebrew name for God / EL; ADONAI, ELOHIM, JAHVEH
Hebrew name for Syria / ARAM
Hebrew patriarch / ISAAC, JACOB; ABRAHAM
Hebrew plural ending / IM
Hebrew prophet / AMOS, JOEL; ELIAS, HOSEA, MICAH, NAHUM; DANIEL, ELISHA, HAGBAI, ISAIAH; MALACHI; HABAKKUK, JEREMIAH
Hebrew proselyte / GER
Hebrew teacher / RAB, REB; RABBI
Hebrew vowel / TSERE; KAMETS
Hebrews' eponym / EBER
Hebrides island / EIGG, IONA, MULL, SKYE; BARRA, ISLAY, TIREE
Hecate's companions / DOGS
Hecate's milieu / CROSSROADS
hecatomb / SACRIFICE
heck / RACK
heckle / RAZZ; BADGER, HINDER
hectic EXCITED; FEVERISH; BREAKNECK
hector / ANNOY, WORRY; HARASS; IRRITATE; INTIMIDATE
Hector's father / PRAM
Hector's mother / HECUBA
Hector's slayer / ACHILLES
Hector's son / ASTYANAX
Hector's victim / PATROCLUS
Hector's wife / ANDROMACHE
Hecuba's husband / PRIAM
Hecuba's son / PARIS; HECTOR
heddles of loom / CAAM
hedge / BET; SELL; ENCLOSE. FENCE; PRIVET; THICKET
hedge plant / PRIVET; HAWTHORN
hedge sparrow / DONEY
hedgehog / GYMNURE
hedgehoglike mammal / TENREC
hedgerow / REW; QUICKSET
hedge-trimming / TOPIARY
heed / CARE, HEAR, LOOK, MARK, MIND, NOTE, OBEY. EAR; ATTENTION
heedless / RASH; IMPRUDENT, NEGLIGENT
heedlessness / TEMERITY; INATTENTION
heehaw / BRAY; GUFFAW; LAUGHTER

heel / CANT, LEAN, TILT. CAD; CALX; BOUNDER
heel, c.f. / TALO
heel over / TIP; LIST; CAREEN
heeler / COBBLER; HANGERON
heeling over / ALIST
heft / LIFT; WEIGH. BULK; WEIGHT
hegemony / PREDOMINANCE
hegira / HAJ; HADJ; EXODUS, FLIGHT
heifer / QUEY
heifer loved by Zeus / IO
height / TOP; ACME, APEX; SUMMIT; ELEVATION
heighten / PRAISE; AMPLIFY, AUGMENT, ELEVATE, ENHANCE, IMPROVE
heighten appetite / WHET
Heimdall's horse / GULLTOPP
Heimdall's sword / HOFUD
Heimdall's trust / RAINBOW
heinous / ODIOUS, WICKED; ATROCIOUS
heir / SON; HERITOR, LEGATEE
heirloom / CHATTEL; HERITAGE
Hejaz capital / MECCA
Hejaz town / TAIF; MEDINA
Hejaz seaport / JIDDA
held / KEPT; CONTAINED
held in common / JOINT; SHARED
held in esteem / POPULAR; RESPECTED
held session / MET, SAT
Helen of Troy's abductor / PARIS
Helen of Troy's daughter / HERMIONE
Helen of Troy's evoker / FAUSTUS
Helen of Troy's husband / MENE-LAUS
Helen of Troy's mother / LEDA
helianthus / SUNFLOWER
helical / SPIRAL
Helicon spring / AGANIPPE; HIPPOCRENE
Heliopolis / ON; BAALBEK
Heliopolitan black bull / MNEVIS
Helios / SOL
Helios' daughter / CIRCE
helix / SPIRAL
hell / See Hades
hell on earth / MISERY
hell for leather / FAST; SPEEDY
Hellas / GREECE
hellbender / SPREE; SALAMANDER
hellcat / HAG; WITCH; VIRAGO; HELLHAG
Hellene / GREEK
Hellenic / GREEK; GRECIAN
Helle's brother / PHRIXUS
Helle's mother / NEPHELE
Helle's mount / RAM

Hellespont / DARDANELLES
Hellespont swimmer / BYRON; LEANDER
hellhag / HELLCAT
hellhound / DEMON, FIEND
hellish / CRUEL; WICKED; INFERNAL
hello / HI; HAIL; HULLO
helm / WHEEL; HELMET, TILLER
helmet / MORION
helmet's faceguard / VISOR; BEAVER
helmet's front / VENTAIL; AVENTAIL
helmet's plume / PANACHE
helmet-shaped / GALEATE; GALEIFORM
helmet-shaped flower part / GALEA
helmsman / PILOT; STEERSMAN
Heloise's lover / ABELARD
helot / SERF; SLAVE; BONDSMAN
help / AID, ABET, BACK, CURE, HEAL, LEND, TIDE, SERVE, STEAD; ASSIST. HIRE; RELIEF; ASSISTANCE
help over difficulty / TIDEOVER
help for the needy / ALMS; CHARITY
helper / AIDE, ALLY; ASSISTANT
helpful / USEFUL; BENEFICIAL
helpless / WEAK; INFIRM; IMPOTENT
helpmate / WIFE; HUSBAND; HELPMEET
Hel's canine guardian / GARM
helter-skelter / ADO; DISORDER; CONFUSION
Helvetic / SWISS; HELVETIAN
hem / EDGE; BORDER, MARGIN
hem in / BESET; SURROUND
hemophiliac / BLEEDER
hemorrhage / BLEED. BLEEDING
hemp / POT; RINE; BHANG, GANJA, GRASS, NOOSE, RAMIE, SISAL; CHARAS; MARIHUANA, MARIJUANA
hemp cloth / BURLAP; HESSIAN
hemp fiber / TOW; SUNN; ABACA
hen fruit / EGG
hen roost / PERCH
henbill / COOT; DABCHICK
hence / SO; ERGO; THEREFORE. AWAY; BEGONE, DEPART
henchman / HELPER; FOLLOWER
Hengist's brother / HORSA
henhussy / COTQUEAN
henpeck / NAG; DOMINEER
Henry VIII family / TUDOR
Henry VIII's wife / ANNE, JANE; CATHERINE
Henry nickname / HAL; HARRY
hen's call / CACKLE

hep / HIP; ONTO; AWARE
Hephaestus / VULCAN
Hephaestus' mother / HERA
Hephaestus' wife / CHARIS;
  APHRODITE
herald / CRIER; MESSENGER.
  ANNOUNCE, PROCLAIM
heraldic / FETIAL
heraldic chaplet / ORLE
heraldic charge / BAR; BEND,
  FESS, PALE, PILE; CHIEF;
  SALTIRE
heraldic color / OR; VERT; AZURE,
  GULES, SABLE, TENNE;
  ARGENT; TINCTURE
heraldic cross / PATEE; MOLINE,
  POMMEE; AVELLAN
heraldic fur / VAIR; ERMINE,
  POTENT
heraldic iris / LIS
heraldic metal / OR; ARGENT
herald's coat / TABARD
heralds, pert. to / FETIAL
Hera's husband / ZEUS
Hera's mother / RHEA
Hera's rival / IO; LETO; SEMELE
Hera's son / ARES; HEPHAESTUS
herb / IVA, RUE; ALOE, DILL, LEEK,
  MACE, MINT, MOLY, SAGE,
  WORT; ANISE, BASIL, MEDIC,
  SEDUM, TANSY, THYME;
  CATNIP, FENNEL, YARROW;
  CARAWAY, DITTANY, OREGANO,
  PARSLEY; ROSEMARY,
  TARRAGON; CORIANDER
herb of carrot family / ANISE
herb of goosefoot family / BLITE;
  QUINOA
herb of grace / RUE
herb medicine / ALOES
herb of rose family / AVENS
herbage / GREENERY; PASTURAGE
herculean HUGE; STRONG;
  DIFFICULT
Hercules' cloak / LIONSKIN
Hercules' mother / ALCMENE
Hercules' poisoner / IOLE
herd / LEAD, TEND; DRIVE, UNITE;
  ASSEMBLE. CROWD, DROVE,
  FLOCK; HERDSMAN
herd of horses / BAND; CAVVY;
  CAVIYA, MANADA, REMUDA
herd of whales / GAM, POD
nerd of wild boars / SOUNDER
herdsman / HERD; COWBOY,
  HERDER
here / NOW; PRESENT
hereafter / FUTURE
hereditary / LINEAL; ANCESTRAL,
  INHERITED
hereditary class / CASTE
hereditary factor / GENE

hereditary land / ODAL, UDAL
hereditary rulers / DYNASTY
hereinafter / AFTER; SUBSE-
  QUENTLY
hereon / HEREUPON
heretic / DISSENTER. ARIAN;
  SCHISMATIC
heretical doctrine / HERESY
heretical sect's leader / HERESI-
  ARCH
heretofore / BEFORE; FORMERLY,
  HITHERTO
heritage / BIRTHRIGHT;
  INHERITANCE
Hermes / MERCURY
Hermes' father / ZEUS
Hermes' hat / PETASUS
Hermes' invention / LYRE; THEFT
Hermes' mother / MAIA
Hermes' sandals / TALARIA
Hermes' son / PAN; AUTOLYCUS
Hermes' staff / CADUCEUS
hermetic / OCCULT; AIRTIGHT
Hermione's father / MENELAUS
Hermione's husband / ORESTES
Hermione's mother / HELEN
hermit / EREMITE, RECLUSE,
  ANCHORITE
hermit saint / GILES; DANIEL,
  SIMEON
hermitage / CLOISTER
hermitlike / EREMITIC
hern / HERON
hero / LEAD; DEMIGOD, PALADIN;
  PROTAGONIST
hero of "in" crowd / LION
hero in opera / TENOR
Herodias' daughter / SALOME
Herod's wife / HERODIAS
heroic / EPIC; BRAVE; DRASTIC,
  VALIANT, VIOLENT; FEARLESS
heroic poem / EPIC, EPOS
heroic tale / EPIC, GEST, SAGA
heroically brave and enduring /
  SPARTAN
heroism / VALOR; PROWESS;
  GALLANTRY
heron / HERN; CRANE, EGRET,
  HERLE; BITTERN
heron flock / SEDGE
Hero's beloved / LEANDER
herring / ALEC, BRIT, RAUN, SILE;
  CISCO, SPRAT
herring, pert. to / CLUPEOID
herring measure / CADE
herringbone / CROSSSTITCH
herringlike fish / SHAD; CISCO;
  ALEWIFE, ANCHOVY
herself / SHE
Hesione's father / LAOMEDON
Hesione's husband / TELAMON
hesitant noise / ER

hesitate / HAW, HEM; HALT, STOP; DELAY, DEMUR, PAUSE, WAVER; FALTER, TEETER; SCRUPLE, STAMMER

hesitate in speech / STAMMER, STUTTER

hesitation syllable / ER, UH, UM

hesperian / WESTERN; OCCIDENTAL

Hesperides' treasure / APPLES

Hesperus' mother / EOS

Hesse city / MAINZ; DARMSTADT

Hesse river / LAHN, FULDA

hest / BEHEST; COMMAND

Hestia's mother / RHEA

Hestia's province / HEARTH

heterdoxy / HERESY

hew / CUT; CHOP, HACK; CLEAVE

hewing tool / AX; ADZE; CLEAVER

hex / JINX; SPELL, WITCH. BEWITCH

hey to a sailor / AHOY

heyday / BLOOM, PRIME

Hezekiah's father / AHAZ

Hezekiah's mother / ABI

hiatus / GAP; BREAK, CLEFT; LACUNA; FISSURE, OPENING; INTERRUPTION

Hibbing's range / MESABI

hibernal / WINTRY

hibernating animal / BEAR; SLEEPER

Hibernia / ERIN; IRELAND

hiccup / YEX

hick / RUBE; YOKEL; HAYSEED

hickory / CANE; PECAN; SHAGBARK

hickory nut / PIGNUT

hidden / DEEP; INNER; ARCANE, COVERT, MASKED, OCCULT, SECRET

hidden language / CODE

hidden marksman / SNIPER

hide / MASK, STOW, WHIP; CACHE, CLOAK, COVER; CONCEAL. BARK, HULL, PEEL, PELT, RIND, SKIN

hide of beast / KIP; FELL, PELT, SKIN

hide by interposing / ECLIPSE

hide the loot / STASH

hide strap / RIEM

hidebound / NARROW; BIGOTED

hideous / GRIM, UGLY; GRISLY

hideous giant / OGRE

hiding place / CACHE, COVER; HIDEOUT

hie / RUN; HURRY, SPEED; HASTEN

hierarchy / SERIES; RANKING

hi-fi speaker / WOOFER; MONITOR, TWEETER

higgle / HAGGLE; BARGAIN, CHAFFER

higgledy-piggledy / JUMBLED; TOPSYTURVY

high / ALT; TALL; ACUTE, CHIEF, GREAT, LOFTY, NOBLE, PROUD; COSTLY, SHRILL; CAPITAL, EXALTED. UP; ABOVE, ALOFT

high, c.f. / ALTI; HYPSI

high card / HONOR

high church / CEREMONIAL, LITURGICAL

high concept / DREAM, IDEAL; VISION

high crag / TOR

high in esteem / HONORED; RESPECTED

high expectancy / HOPE

high explosive / TNT; LYDDITE; DYNAMITE

high falutin / POMPOUS; PRETENTIOUS

high flyer / KITE

high life / JETSET; SOCIETY

high mountains / ALPS; ANDES; ROCKIES, SIERRAS; HIMALAYAS

high muckymuck / BOSS, HEAD; SUPERIOR

high nest / EYRY; AERIE, EYRIE

high note / ALT, ELA

high position / EMINENCE

high priest / PONTIFF; HIERARCH, PONTIFEX

high railway / EL; ELEVATED; FUNICULAR

high rank / DIGNITY, PRIMACY; EMINENCE

high regard / HONOR; ESTEEM

high in scale / ALT

high silk hat / SNOB, TILE; TOPHAT, TOPPER

high spirits / GLEE; CHEER; GAIETY

high tableland / MESA; MESETA; PLATEAU

high temperature / HEAT

high tennis shot / LOB

high thin cloud / CIRRUS

high vocal part / CANTO

high volley / LOB

high water / FLOOD; DELUGE; INUNDATION

high wind / GALE; TORNADO, TYPHOON; HURRICANE

highbinder / ROWDY; RUFFIAN; CUTTHROAT

highbrow / BOOKISH; BLUESTOCKING

high-card pool game / REDDOG

high-colored / RED; FLORID

higher / TALLER

higher in place / OVER; ABOVE
higher in rank / SENIOR; SUPERIOR
higher than / ABOVE
highest / SUPREME, TALLEST; UPPERMOST
highest card / ACE; JOKER
highest card in loo / PAM
highest degree / UTMOST
highest in gamut / ELA
highest mountain / PEAK; EVEREST
highest point / ACME, APEX, NOON, PEAK; APOGEE, SUMMIT, ZENITH; PINNACLE
highest ranking prelate / POPE; ARCHBISHOP
high-handed / ARBITRARY; OVERBEARING
high-hat / SNUB. SNOBBISH
highlander / SCOT
highlander's costume / KILT; KILTS; TARTAN
highlander's pouch / SPORRAN
Highlands dance / FLING
Highlands liquor / SCOTCH
Highlands mountains / GRAMPIANS
highly / VERY; GREATLY
highly decorated / ORNATE, ROCOCO; BAROQUE
highly efficient / EXPERT
highly malignant / VIRULENT
highly respected / HONORED; ESTEEMED
highly seasoned / SPICY; SPICED; DEVILED
highly wrought / OVERDONE; ELABORATE
highly seasoned dish / CURRY
high-minded / PROUD; ARROGANT
high-pitched noise / TING; TINKLE
high-strung / TENSE; NERVOUS
high-toned / DIGNIFIED; FASHIONABLE
high-trajectory cannon / MORTAR; HOWITZER
highway / ITER, PIKE, ROAD; AVENUE, STREET
highway charge / TOLL
highway division / LANE
highway hazard / DRUNK; SPEEDER; TAILGATER
highway marker / SIGN; MILESTONE
highwayman / PAD; BANDIT
hijack / STICKUP; COMMANDEER
hijacker / PIRATE
hike / MARCH, TRAMP
hilarious / GAY; JOLLY, MERRY; JOCOSE, JOVIAL, JOYOUS; FESTIVE, GLEEFUL, JOCULAR

hilarious show / FARCE
hilarity / GLEE; MIRTH; GAIETY
hill / TOR; BRAE, HEAP, LOMA; MOUND
hill dweller of India / BHIL, GOND, TODA; DOGRA
hill in Rome / CAELIAN, VIMINAL; AVENTINE, PALATINE, QUIRINAL; ESQUILINE; CAPITOLINE
hill in San Francisco / NOB; RUSSIAN; TELEGRAPH
hillock / TELL, TUMP; KOPJE; BARROW
hillside dugout / ABRI, CAVE; GROTTO
hillside rubble / SCREE
hilum / PORTA
Himalayan animal / PANDA
Himalayan antelope / GORAL, SEROW
Himalayan broadbill / RAYS
Himalayan country / NEPAL, TIBET; BHUTAN, SIKKIM
Himalayan herb / ATIS
Himalayan monkey / LANGUR
Himalayan peak / EVEREST
Himalayan pheasant / MONAL
Himalayan river / INDUS; GANGES, MEKONG; BRAHMAPUTRA
Himalayan wild goat / KYL; KAIL, KRAS, TAHR, TAIR, THAR; MARKHOR
Himalayan wild sheep / SNA; BHARAL, NAHOOR
hind / BACK, DEER, REAR; RUSTIC; PEASANT
hind part of saddle / CANTLE
hinder / BAR, LET; STOP; CHECK
hindermost / LAST; REARMOST
hindrance / BAR; BALK; CHECK
Hindu adept / MAHATMA
Hindu age / YUGA; KALPA
Hindu army man / SIKH; SEPOY; GHURKA
Hindu ascetic / YOGI; FAKIR
Hindu asceticism / YOGA
Hindu atheist / NASTIKA
Hindu beggar / NAGA
Hindu caste / TELI; SUDRA; VAISYA; BRAHMAN; KSHATRIYA
Hindu celestial bard / GANDHARVA
Hindu charitable grant / ENAM
Hindu clerk / BABU
Hindu cloister / MATH
Hindu cymbals / TAL
Hindu demigod / YAKSHA
Hindu demon / RAHU; ASURA; RAKSHA, VRITRA
Hindu dress / SARI

Hindu eclipse demon / KETU
Hindu elixir of life / AMRITA
Hindu epic / RAMAYANA;
  MAHABHARATA
Hindu female slave / DASI
Hindu festival / HOLI, PUJA;
  DEWALI, DIWALI
Hindu game / PASA; RAFAYA;
  CHAUPUR, GANJIFA, PACHISI;
  ASHTAPADA
Hindu garment / SARI; DHOTI,
  SAREE; BANIAN, BANYAN
Hindu giant / BANA
Hindu god / KA; RAMA; VISHNU
Hindu god of creation / BRAHMA;
  PRAJAPATI
Hindu god of death / KALI, YAMA
Hindu god of desire / KAMA
Hindu god of destruction / SIVA;
  RUDRA, SHIVA
Hindu god of earth / KRISHNA
Hindu god of fire / AGNI
Hindu god of good fortune /
  GANESHA
Hindu god of nature / PARJANYA
Hindu god of preservation /
  VISHNU
Hindu god of sky / DYAUS,
  INDRA; VARUNA
Hindu god of storm / RUDRA
Hindu god of sun / SURYA
Hindu god of time / KALA
Hindu god of vegetation / KRISHNA
Hindu god of wealth / AGNI;
  BAGHA, BHAGA; VARUNA
Hindu god of wind / VATA, VAYU
Hindu god of wrath / MANYU
Hindu goddess / DEVI; DURGA,
  GAURI; PARVATI
Hindu goddess of beauty / SRI;
  LAKSHMI
Hindu goddess of dawn / USAS;
  USHAS
Hindu goddess of destruction /
  KALI
Hindu goddess of nature / UMA
Hindu goddess of plenty /
  PURANDI
Hindu goddess of prosperity / SRI;
  LAKSHMI
Hindu goddess of rivers /
  SARASVATI
Hindu goddess of splendor / UMA
Hindu gods' dwelling place / MERU
Hindu goldsmith / SONAR
Hindu heavenly nymph / APSARA
Hindu hereditary class / CASTE
Hindu hero / RAMA; ARJUNA
Hindu home of gods / MERU
Hindu honorific suffix / JI
Hindu lawgiver / MANU
Hindu life force / JIVA

Hindu life principle / JIVA;
  ATMAN, PRANA
Hindu love god / RAMA
Hindu meal / ATA; ATTA
Hindu mendicant / FAKIR; FAKEER
Hindu merchant / BANYA; BANIAN
Hindu midwife / DHAI
Hindu military caste / KSHATRIYA
Hindu monkey god / HANUMAN
Hindu month / PUS; ASIN, JETH,
  KUAR, MAGH; AGHAN, ASARH,
  CHAIT, KATIK, SAWAN;
  BHADON, PHAGUN; BAISAKH
Hindu mother goddess / KALI;
  SHAKTA, SHAKTI
Hindu mother goddesses / MATRIS
Hindu mountain of fable / MERU
Hindu musical instrument / TAL;
  BINA, VINA; SAROD, SITAR
Hindu mystic word / OM
Hindu peasant / RYOT
Hindu philosophy / YOGA;
  VEDANTA
Hindu prince / RAJA, RANA;
  RAJAH; MAHARAJAH
Hindu princess / RANI; RANEE;
  MAHARANI; MAHARANEE
Hindu religious books, pert. to /
  VEDIC
Hindu religious chant / OM
Hindu religious teacher / GURU;
  ACHARYA
Hindu sacred city / BENARES
Hindu scripture / GITA, VEDA;
  AGAMA, SUTRA; PURANAS,
  TANTRAS; BRAHMANAS;
  BHAGAVADGITA
Hindu serpent king / SESHA
Hindu supreme deity / BRAHMA,
  VARUNA
Hindu tax grant / ENAM; JAGIR;
  JAGHIR
Hindu term of respect / SAHIB;
  SAHIBA
Hindu title / AYA, SRI; SWAMI;
  PANDIT, PUNDIT; ACHARYA,
  MAHATMA, SRIMATI
Hindu trinity / TRIMURTI
Hindu unknown god / KA
Hindu upper caste / BRAHMIN
Hindu weight / SER; KONA, TOLA;
  MASHA
Hindu widow's suicide / SATTEE,
  SUTTEE
Hindu winged being / GARUDA
Hindu woman's dress / SARI;
  SAREE
Hindu world soul / ATMAN
Hindustan / IND; INDIA
Hindustani / URDU; DAKHINI
hinge / JOINT, PIVOT
hinged cover / LID

hint / CUE; IMPLY, REFER; ALLUDE. TIP; CLUE; TRACE; POINTER
hip / ILIA; HAUNCH. HEP
hip bone / ILIUM
hip joint / COXA
hip and with it / GROOVY
hippodrome / ARENA; CIRCUS; AUDITORIUM, RACECOURSE
hippo-headed goddess / TAUERET
Hippolyta's husband / THESEUS
Hippolytus' father / THESEUS
Hippolytus' stepmother / PHAEDRA
hippopotamus / HIPPO; ZEEKOE
hire / LET; RENT; BRIBE, LEASE; EMPLOY. FEE, PAY; WAGES; SALARY; STIPEND; ALLOWANCE; COMPENSATION
hired car / CAB; HACK, TAXI; RENTER; TAXICAB
hired carriage / HACK; FIACRE; HACKNEY
hired thugs / GOONS
hireling / FREELANCE, MERCENARY
hirer and firer / BOSS
hirsute / HAIRY; HISPID, SHAGGY; UNSHAVED
hirsute adornment / BEARD, BRUSH; MUSTACHE, WHISKERS; MOUSTACHE
hirsute growth / HAIR
Hispaniola ruler / BOYER
hiss / BOO; SISS
hissing sound / SIBILANCE
historic Dutch town / BREDA
historic Italian town / ATRI
historic remnant / RELIC
historical period / AGE, ERA; EPOCH, TIME
history / ANNALS, RECORD; ARCHIVE, DOSSIER; CHRONICLE
history of a life / MEMOIR; BIOGRAPHY
history's muse / CLIO
histrionic art / DRAMA
hit / BAT, BOP, WIN; BUMP, GAIN, SLUG; CLASH, SMITE, TOUCH; LARRUP
hit aloft / LOB
hit with a car / RUNOVER
hit gently / TAP
hit the ground / LAND
hit ground before golf ball / SCLAFF
hit hard / LAM; SWAT
hit lightly / BUNT
hit with open hand / SLAP
hit with pitched ball / BEAN
hit the silk / PARACHUTE
hit of a sort / BUNT; SCRATCH
hit vigorously / LAMBASTE

hitch / CATCH; OBSTACLE; IMPEDIMENT. TIE
hither / HERE; NEARER
hitherto / YET; HERE
Hittites / KHATTI
Hittites' eponym / HETH
hive / SKEP; SWARM; BEEHIVE
hives / ITCH, RASH; UREDO; URTICARIA
hoar / OLD; GRAY; WHITE; FROSTY
hoard / SAVE; AMASS, LAYUP, STORE; COLLECT, HUSBAND
hoarder / MISER
hoarfrost / RAG; RIME; FROST
hoarse / GRUFF, HARSH, HUSKY
hoax / BILK; CHEAT; DELUDE; DECEIVE. JOKE, RUSE; FRAUD, SPOOF, TRICK; CANARD
hob / ELF, HUB, PEG, PIN; SEAT; PUNCH, SHELF
Hobart's mountain / WELLINGTON
hobble / LIMP; STRAP; IMPEDE; SHACKLE
hobbly / ROUGH
hobby / FAD; HORSE; AVOCATION
hobgoblin / ELF, IMP; PUCK; SPRITE; BUGBEAR; APPARITION
hobnob / CHAT; CONSORT
hobo / BUM; TRAMP; VAGRANT; VAGABOND
hock / PAWN. KNEE, WINE; ANKLE; GAMBREL
hockey / HURLEY; HURLING
hockey disk / PUCK
hockey player / ICEMAN
hockey team / SIX; SEXTET
hocus / DRUG, HOAX; CHEAT
hocus-pocus / TRICK; SLEIGHT; LEGERDEMAIN
hod / JOG, TUB; TROUGH; SCUTTLE
hodge / HICK; RUSTIC
hodgepodge / MESS, OLIO; JUMBLE
hoe / TILL, WEED; SCRAPE; CULTIVATE
hog / CUT; GRASP; CORNER; MONOPOLIZE. PIG, SOW; BOAR; SWINE; GLUTTON
hog deer / AXIS
hog fat / LARD; BACON
hog plum / AMRA, JOBO
hog thigh / HAM
hoggish / RUDE; ROUGH; SELFISH, UNCLEAN; GLUTTONOUS
hog's food / MAST
hog's innards / HASLET
hogshead / CASK; BARREL
hogwash / SWILL; REFUSE
hoi polloi / MASSES; POPULACE
hoiden / ROMP; HOYDEN, TOMBOY

hoist / LIFT; HEAVE, RAISE; ELEVATE

hoisted / HOVE

hoisting apparatus / GIN; CRANE, WINCH; DERRICK; ELEVATOR

hoity-toity / GIDDY; FLIGHTY, HAUGHTY

Hokkaido city / OTARU; SAPPORO

Hokkaido river / ISHIKARI

hokum / BUNK, CORN; NONSENSE

hold / OWN, USE; BIND, HAVE, KEEP, STAY; CLING, GRASP, JUDGE; DETAIN, HARBOR. STOP; AVAST

hold aloof / REFRAIN

hold back / DAM; STEM; DELAY, DETER; DETAIN; RESTRAIN

hold in common / SHARE

hold a conference / MEET

hold in custody / JAIL; CONFINE

hold dear / LOVE; CHERISH; TREASURE

hold fast / PIN; HOOK; CLING; SUPPORT

hold in favor / PREFER

hold firmly / GRIP

hold one's ground / STAND, STICK; RESIST

hold out / LAST; STAND; ENDURE, RESIST

hold for ransom / KIDNAP

hold in regard / ESTEEM; RESPECT

hold by right / OWN; POSSESS

hold same view / AGREE; CONCUR

hold a session / SIT; MEET; GATHER

hold under spell / CHARM; BEWITCH, ENCHANT

hold together / CLAMP; COHERE, FASTEN

hold up / ROB; BEAR; STAND; SUPPORT

hold in war / INTERN; CAPTURE

holder / OWNER; HANDLE, TENANT; CHAMPION; CONTAINER

holder of lease / LESSEE

holding / ESTATE, TENURE; PROPERTY

holding at bridge / HONORS, TENACE

holding device / PIN; CLIP, VICE; CLAMP, TONGS

holdup / ROBBERY

hole / PIT; SLOT; CAVITY, CRATER, EYELET; OPENING, ORIFICE

hole in ground / PIT; BURROW

hole mender / DARNER, TINKER

hole for molten metal / GATE; SPRUE

hole in one / ACE

hole for sleeve / SCYE; ARMSEYE

holiday / FERIA; FIESTA; VACATION

holiday song / CAROL; WASSAIL

holiness / PIETY; PURITY; SANCTITY

Holland / See Dutch, Netherlands

hollands / GIN

hollow / EMPTY, FALSE; SUNKEN, VACANT; CAVERNOUS. PIT; DENT, HOLE, VOID; GROOVE; DEPRESSION

hollow cylinder / DRUM, PIPE, TUBE

hollow dish / CUP; BOWL; BASIN

hollow glass vessel / JAR; BOTTLE

hollow grass / CANE, REED

hollow metal vessel / POT; BELL

hollow out / DIG; MINE

hollow rock nodule / GEODE

hollow-horned ruminant / GOAT

holly / HOLM, ILEX; DAHOON, YAUPON; CASSINE

Hollywood award / OSCAR

Holmes' word / ELEMENTARY

holocryptic / ENIGMATIC

holy / GOOD, PURE; BLEST, GODLY, PIOUS; DEVOUT, DIVINE, SACRED; BLESSED, SAINTLY, SINLESS

Holy City / KIEV, ROME, ZION; LHASA, MECCA; MEDINA; BENARES; JERUSALEM

holy city of Shiites / KARBALA

holy communion / EUCHARIST

holy emetic / YAUPON

holy hay / ALFALFA, LUCERNE; SAINFOIN

Holy Island / LINDISFARNE

Holy Land / PALESTINE

Holy Land city / DAN; BEERSHEBA, JERUSALEM

holy person / SAINT; MARTYR; VENERABLE

holy picture / ICON, IKON

Holy Roman Empire dynasty / HAPSBURG

holy rood / CROSS; CRUCIFIX

holy spirit / GOD; HOLYGHOST

holy war / JIHAD; CRUSADE

holy week services / TENEBRAE

holy writ / BIBLE; SCRIPTURE

holy-water font / CRUET, STOUP

homage / DUTY; HONOR; FEALTY; LOYALTY, RESPECT, SERVICE; DEFERENCE, REVERENCE; ALLEGIANCE, SUBMISSION, VENERATION

home / ABODE, HOUSE; FAMILY, HEARTH; COUNTRY, HABITAT; DOMICILE. NEAR; CLOSE; DOMESTIC

home of Abraham / UR

home of bees / HIVE
home of the free / AMERICA
home of Irish kings / TARA
home reserve / MILITIA;
  LANDWEHR; TERRITORIALS
home run / HOMER
home of Saul's witch / ENDOR
home for traveler / HOTEL, MOTEL
home workshop tool / POWERSAW
home of Zeno / ELEA
homeless animal / STRAY;
  MAVERICK
homeless child / WAIF; GAMIN;
  STREETARAB
homelike / COZY; FAMILIAR
homely / UGLY; PLAIN; SIMPLE;
  DOMESTIC, UNCOMELY;
  UNPRETENTIOUS
homer / PIGEON; HOMERUN
Homer epic / ILIAD; ODYSSEY
homeric / EPIC
homespun / RUSSET, RUSTIC
homesteader / NESTER; SETTLER
homicide / MURDER; KILLING
homicide compensation / CRO;
  GALANAS
homily / SERMON
hominy / SAMP; GRITS
hominy dish / POSOLE
homo / MAN
homo sapiens / MAN
homogeneity / SIMILARITY,
  UNIFORMITY
homologate / RATIFY; APPROVE,
  CONFIRM
homologous / SAME; SIMILAR;
  CORRESPONDING
homologous segment / ISOMERE
homonym / NAMESAKE, NICK-
  NAME; HOMOPHONE
homunculus / DWARF; MANIKIN
Honduras capital / TEGUCIGALPA
Honduras Indian / PAYA, SUMO
Honduras money / LEMPIRA
Honduras river / ULUA; AGUAN
hone / STROP; SHARPEN.
  WHETSTONE
honest / FAIR, JUST, OPEN, REAL,
  TRUE; FRANK, RIGHT; CHASTE;
  SINCERE, UPRIGHT; FAITHFUL,
  RELIABLE
honest Abe / LINCOLN
honest John / SQUARE
honesty / HONOR; CANDOR,
  VIRTUE
honey / MEL; NECTAR, DARLING
honey badger / RATEL
honey beverage / MEAD; CYSER,
  MORAT; PYMENT; KRUPNIK,
  PIGMENT; BRACKETS;
  HIPPOCRAS, METHEGLIN
honey buzzard / PERN
honey eater / IAO; MOHO; MANUAO

honey store / COMB
honeybee / DINGAR; DESERET
honeycomb division / CELL
honeycomblike / FAVOSE;
  FAVIFORM
honeyed / SUGARY
honeysuckle / WOODBINE;
  EGLANTINE
Hong Kong peninsula / KOWLOON
Hong Kong river / PEARL; CANTON
Honolulu suburb / WAIKIKI
Honolulu's island / OAHU
honor / ADORE, EXALT; CREDIT,
  ESTEEM, REVERE; ENNOBLE.
  FAME; GLORY; HOMAGE,
  RENOWN, REPUTE; DIGNITY;
  CHASTITY, GRANDEUR
honor card / ACE, TEN; JACK,
  KING; QUEEN; FACECARD
honor with festivities / FETE
honorable / NOBLE; HONEST,
  WORTHY
honorable mention / CITATION
honorably retired / EMERITUS
honorarium / TIP; GRATUITY
honorary commission / BREVET
Honshu bay / ISE; MUTSU
Honshu seaport / KOBE; OSAKA;
  YOKOHAMA
hooch / ALKY; BOOZE; LIQUOR
hood / COWL; HOODLUM
hooded garment / COWL; PARKA
hooded merganser / SMEW
hoodlum / GOON; BULLY, ROWDY
hoodoo / JINX; JONAH
hood-shaped cap / COIF
hoodwink / DUPE, FOOL; CHEAT,
  COVER
hoof / WALK; TRAMP. FOOT;
  UNGUIS
hoofed / UNGULATE
hook / BEND, GORE, HOLD, TRAP;
  CLASP, CURVE. CAPE; PUNCH;
  SICKLE
hook money / LARI; LARIN;
  LARREE
hook for a pot / CLEEK
hookah / NARGILE; NARGHILE,
  NARGILEH
hooked / CURVED, HAMATE;
  FALCATE; AQUILINE
hooked nail / TENTER
hook's point / BARB
hooky player / TRUANT
hooligan / ROWDY, TOUGH;
  HOODLUM
hoop / BAIL, BAND, RING;
  WHOOP; CRINOLINE
hooper / COOPER
hoopoe genus / UPUPA
hoopskirt / CRINOLINE
hoosegow / JAIL; POKEY; LOCKUP
Hoosier poet / RILEY

Hoosier State / IND; INDIANA
hooter / OWL; WHISTLE
Hoover Dam's lake / MEAD
hop / LEAP; DANCE; FLIGHT, SPRING
hop harvester's basket / BIN
hop kiln / OST; OAST, OSTE
hop mold / FEN
hop plant / LUPULUS; MARJORAM
hope / FAITH, TRUST; RELIANCE. WISH; DESIRE
Hopei city / PEKING; TIENTSIN
hopelessness / DESPAIR
Hophni's father / ELI
hoplites' formation / PHALANX
hop-o'-my-thumb / DWARF, PYGMY
hopper / FUNNEL, TROUGH
hopple / HOBBLE, TETHER
hopscotch stone / TAW, TOR; DUMP, PUCK; POTSY; PEEVER, SCOTCH; POTSHERD; PALLY-ULLY
hora / DANCE
Hora / AUXO, DIKE; KARPO; EIRENE, THALLO; EUNOMIA
horde / ARMY, HOST, PACK; CROWD, DROVE, SWARM, TRIBE; THRONG
hordeolum / STY; STYE
Horeb / SINAI
horizontal / FLAT; LEVEL; ACROSS
horizontal beam over opening / LINTEL
horizontal coping stone / TABLET
horizontal rack in fireplace / ANDIRON
horn / DAG; TUBA; BUGLE; ANTLER, CORNET, KLAXON, SHOFAR; TROMBONE
horn, c.f. / KERA; KERAS
horn on auto / KLAXON
horn call in hunting / MORT
horn of crescent moon / CUSP
horn of plenty / CORNUCOPIA
horn quicksilver / CALOMEL
horn signal / SENNET
horn sound / TOOT; BLARE, BLAST; FANFARE
horn tissue / SCUR
hornbill / TOCK
horned horse / UNICORN
horned owl / BUBO
horned viper / ASP
hornet / WASP; YELLOWJACKET
hornless animal / POLLARD
hornlike / CERATOID
hornswoggle / HOAX; CHEAT; HUMBUG
horny / HARD; CALLOUS; CERATOID
horny tissue substance / KERATIN

horrible / DIRE, GRIM; AWFUL; HORRID; DIREFUL; DREADFUL
horrid / GLOOMY; HIDEOUS
horripilation / GOOSEFLESH
horror / AWE; FEAR; DREAD, PANIC; FRIGHT, TERROR; DELIRIUM
horror tale author / POE
hors de combat / BEAT; BROKEN; DISABLED
hors d'oeuvre / CANAPE, RELISH; ANTIPASTO
horse / BAY, COB, GEE, NAG; ARAB, BARB, COLT, MARE, MERE, ROAN; FILLY, FRAME, MILER, MOUNT, PACER, PINTO, STAND, STEED, WALER; EQUINE, FENCER, HUNTER, JENNET, PADNAG; CABALLO, COURSER, GELDING, SUPPORT, TROTTER; STALLION, YARRAMAN
horse, pert. to / EQUINE
horse blanket / MANTA
horse breed / MORGAN, ORLOFF; ARABIAN; LIPIZZAN; APPALOOSA
horse in chess / KNIGHT
horse chestnut / BUCKEYE
horse color / BAY, DUN; ROAN; PINTO; SORREL; CHESTNUT, PALOMINO
horse dealer / COPER; DAVID-HARUM
horse disease / SOOR; FARCY, SURRA; CANKER, LAMPAS; SPAVIN; GLANDERS; STRING-HALT
horse doctor / VET; HIPPIATER; VETERINARIAN
horse eyeshades / BLINDERS
horse fodder / HAY; OATS
horse genus / EQUUS
horse goddess of Gaul / EPONA
horse guide / BIT; REIN
horse harness part / BIT; CURB, HAME, REIN; SNAFFLE
horse herd / CAVVY; CAVIYA, REMUDA
horse leg part / HOCK; CANNON; FETLOCK, PASTERN
horse mackerel / SCAD; JUREL, TUNNY
horse with one-sided gait / PACER
horse player / BETTOR
horse player's paper / TIPSHEET
horse in race / ENTRY, PACER; MAIDEN, PLATER; TROTTER
horse rising on hind legs / REARER
horse saddle part / TREE; CANTLE, POMMEL
horse sense / COMMONSENSE
horse tender / GROOM; OSTLER; HOSTLER

horseback game / POLO
horse-drawn cab / HANSOM
horsefly / BOT; GADFLY
horsehair / MANE, TAIL
horseleach / VAMPIRE
horseman / RIDER; COWBOY,
JOCKEY, KNIGHT; COSSACK;
CAVALIER; EQUESTRIAN
horseman of South America /
GAUCHO; LLANERO
horseman's turn / CARACOL;
CARACOLE
horsemanship / MANEGE
horsepox / VARIOLA
horse's gait / RUN; LOPE, PACE,
RACE, RACK, STEP, TROT;
GALLOP
horse's hock / GAMBREL
horse's sidewise movement / VOLT
horse's upper foot / PASTERN
horseshoe spike / CALK
horseshoeing frame / TRAVE
horseshoer / SMITH; FARRIER;
BLACKSMITH
horseweed / RAGWEED; FLEABANE
horticulture / GARDENING;
CULTIVATION
Horus among the Greeks /
HARPOCRATES
Horus's father / OSIRIS
Horus's mother / ISIS
hose / SOCKS; STOCKINGS.
WATER; DRENCH
Hosea's wife / GOMER
hospice / ASYLUM; SHELTER
hospital attendant / AIDE; NURSE;
INTERN; INTERNE, ORDERLY;
THERAPIST
hospital section / WARD
hospitality / WELCOME
host / ARMY; CROWD, HORDE;
THRONG; BONIFACE, LAND-
LORD; SACRIFICE
host in mass / BREAD, WAFER
hostage / PAWN; PLEDGE
hostelry / INN; HOTEL; HOSTEL,
TAVERN
hostess / STEWARDESS;
ENTERTAINER
hostile / ANTI; ADVERSE,
WARLIKE
hostile ceremony / WARDANCE
hostile longing / ENVY
hostility / WAR; ANIMUS,
ENMITY; BELLIGERENCE
hot / ACRID, EAGER, FIERY,
SHARP; ARDENT, BITING,
HEATED, TORRID
hot dog / FRANK; WIENER;
FRANKFURTER
hot drink / TEA; COCOA, NEGUS,
TODDY; COFFEE, POSSET

hot dry wind / KAMSIN, SIMOOM,
SIMOON, SOLANO; KHAMSIN,
SIROCCO
hot and humid / STEAMY, SWEATY
hot iron for searing / CAUTER
hot place / OVEN
hot spirits and lemon / GROG
hot spring / GEYSER
hot temper / IRISH
hot wine beverage / NEGUS
hot-blooded / ARDENT;
PASSIONATE
hotchpotch / STEW; JUMBLE;
HODGEPODGE
hotel / INN; LODGE; HOSTEL
hotel for boaters / BOATEL
hotel for motorists / MOTEL
hot-headed / RASH; FIERY;
IMPETUOUS
hot-tempered / PEPPERY;
IRASCIBLE
Hottentot / NAMA; GRIQUA;
KHOISAN
hough / HOCK. HAWK
hound / HUNT; CHASE, TRACK.
ADDICT, BASSET, BEAGLE;
HARRIER
houndfish / SHARK; DOGFISH
hour of the day / TIME
hourglass / SANDGLASS
hourly / HORAL
house / INN, PAD; CASA, FIRM,
HOME, IZBA, RACE, ROOF;
ABODE, HOTEL, LODGE, TRIBE,
VILLA; FAMILY, PALACE,
TAVERN; COMPANY, CONCERN,
COTTAGE, EDIFICE, KINDRED,
LINEAGE, MANSION; DOMICILE;
RESIDENCE; LEGISLATURE.
SHELTER
house, pert. to / DOMAL
house on an estate / MANOR
house pet / CAT, DOG; CANARY
house plant / FERN; CACTUS;
ASPIDISTRA
house of religious retirement /
CONVENT, NUNNERY;
MONASTERY
house on wheels / CAMPER;
CARAVAN
house wing / ELL; ANNEX
house of worship / BETHEL,
CHURCH, TEMPLE
housebreaker / BURGLAR
housefly larva / MAGGOT
household / FAMILY, MENAGE
household god / DI; LAR; PENATE
household gods / LARES
household implement / MOP;
IRON; BROOM; DUSTER,
HANGER, VACUUM; SWEEPER;
STEAMIRON

housekeeper / JANITOR; DOMESTIC
housekeeping / OIKOLOGY
housemaid's knee / BURSITIS
housetop / ROOF; ATTIC
housewarming / INFARE
housing / LODGING, SHELTER
housing companion / ROOMMATE
housing of a turbine wheel / STATOR
hove / CAST; HOISTED
hovel / HUT; SHED; SHANTY
hover / FLIT; LINGER; FLUTTER
howbeit / NEVERTHELESS
howdah / AMBARI
however / BUT, YET; NEVERTHE-LESS
howitzer / CANNON
howl / BAY, CRY; BAWL, ROAR, WAIL; LAUGH; ULULATE
howler monkey / ARABA
howling / KEEN, WILD; DREARY, SAVAGE; EXTREME, ULULANT
howling monkey / MONO; ARABA; HOWLER
how-to book / MANUAL
hoyden / ROMP; HOIDEN, TOMBOY
hub / CORE, NAVE; CENTER
hub of the universe / BOSTON
hubble-bubble / HOOKAH; CHATTER
hubbub / ADO, DIN; STIR; BUSTLE
hubby / HUSBAND
huckaback / TOWELING
hucklebone / ANKLE; HIPBONE
huckster / HAWKER; PEDDLER
huddle / MEET; GATHER, NESTLE; COLLECT
Hudson River cliffs / PALISADES
Hudson seal / MUSKRAT
Hudson town / NYACK
Hudsonian curlew / WHIMBREL
hue / TINT; COLOR, SHADE, TINGE; CLAMOR
hue and cry / CHASE; OUTCRY
huff / BLOW, PUFF; HECTOR
hug / GRIP; EMBRACE
huge / BIG; VAST; BULKY, GIANT, GREAT, LARGE; IMMENSE, MASSIVE
huge amount / SCADS
huge lizard / IGUANA; MONITOR, TUATARA
huge person / GIANT; MONSTER
huge thing / MONSTER, PRODIGY
huge toad / AGUA
hugger-mugger / JUMBLE, MUDDLE; CONFUSION
hulking / BULKY; CLUMSY
hull / POD; HUSK; SHELL
hullabaloo / DIN; UPROAR

hulled grain / GROATS
hum / BUZZ; CROON, DRONE
human / MAN; HOMO. MORTAL; FALLIBLE
human being / MAN; WOMAN; PERSON
human frailty / OLDADAM
human race / MAN; MANKIND
human trunk / TORSO
humane / KIND; TENDER; MERCIFUL
humanity / MAN; NATURE, REASON; CHARITY, CULTURE, MANKIND
humanlike anthropoid / APEMAN
humble / ABASE, CRUSH, LOWER, SHAME. LOW; MEEK, MEAN; LOWLY
humble worker / MENIAL
humblebee / BUMBLEBEE
humbug / SHAM; FRAUD. HOAX; CHEAT; DECEIVE
humdinger / PIP; LULU; DAISY, JEWEL
humdrum 7 DULL; TEDIOUS; MONOTONOUS
humid / DAMP, DANK; MOIST
humiliate / ABASE, SHAME; DEBASE; MORTIFY
humility / MODESTY; MEEKNESS
hummeling machine / AWNER
humming / BIG; GREAT; ACTIVE; BUZZING
hummingbird / COLIBRI
hummock / KNOLL; HILLOCK
humor / FUN, WIT; MOOD, VEIN, WHIM; TEMPER; CAPRICE, CONCEIT. BABY, BEND; DIVERT; INDULGE
humorist / WAG, WIT; COMEDIAN
humorous / DROLL, FUNNY, WITTY
humorous play / FARCE; COMEDY
humorously odd / DROLL
humpback / HUNCHBACK
humpback salmon / PINK; HADDO, HOLIA, HUMPY
hun / TATAR; GERMAN, VANDAL
hunch / HUMP; THRUST; INTUITION
Hunchback of Notre Dame / QUASIMODO
hundred square meters / ARE
hundred years / CENTURY
hundred-handed giant / GYES; COTTUS; BRIAREUS
hundredth of a dollar / CENT
hundredth of a franc / CENTIME
hundredth of a mark / PFENNIG
hundredth of a pound / NEWPENNY
hundredweight / CWT; CENTAL; CENTNER, QUINTAL

hundredweight of nails / KEG
Hungarian / MAGYAR
Hungarian cheese / DAMEN
Hungarian city / PECS; SZEGED
Hungarian dish / GOULASH
Hungarian dog / PULI
Hungarian gipsy / CZIGANY,
   TZIGANE
Hungarian lake / BALATON
Hungarian measure / MAROK
Hungarian money / PENGO;
   FORINT
Hungarian musical instrument /
   CEMBALO
Hungarian national dance /
   CZARDAS
Hungarian patriot / KOSSUTH
Hungarian region / BANAT
Hungarian river / TISZA
Hungarian stew / GOULASH
Hungarian turnip / KOHLRABI
Hungarian wine / TOKAY
Hungary capital / BUDAPEST
hunger / DESIRE, THIRST;
   APPETITE; STARVATION
hungry / AVID; RAVENOUS;
   VORACIOUS
hunk / GOB; LUMP, MASS; CHUNK
hunks / MISER
hunky dory / OK; EVEN, GOOD,
   OKAY
Huns' king / ATLI; ETZEL;
   ATTILA
hunt / SEEK; TRAIL; FOLLOW,
   PURSUE. CHASE, QUEST;
   SAFARI, SHIKAR; PURSUIT
hunt illegally / POACH
hunted beasts / DEER, GAME
hunter / HOUND, JAGER, ORION;
   JAEGER, NIMROD; SHIKARI,
   TRAPPER; HUNTSMAN
hunter constellation / ORION
hunter's attendant / GILLY;
   GILLIE
hunter's horn / BUGLE
hunting bird / FALCON
hunting birds' nests / NESTING
hunting box / CABIN, LODGE
hunting cry / HO; SOHO, YOOI;
   HALLOO, YOICKS; TALLYHO
hunting dog / ALAN; ALAND,
   HOUND; BASSET, BEAGLE,
   BORZOI, SETTER; POINTER,
   SPANIEL
hunting goddess / DIANA, SKADI;
   ARTEMIS
hunting hat / TERAI; MONTERO
hunting platform / MACHAN
huntsman's cap / MONTERO
Hupeh city / HANKOW
Hupeh river / HAN
hurdle / FENCE; BARRIER. LEAP;
   MASTER

hurdy-gurdy / LIRA, ROTA;
   BARRELORGAN
hurl / CAST, TOSS; FLING, PITCH
hurley stick / CAMAN; CAMMOCK
hurly-burly / TUMULT;
   COMMOTION
hurricane / GALE; STORM;
   CYCLONE, TYPHOON
hurricane center / EYE
hurried / RAN; SPED
hurry / HIE, RUN; RUSH; URGE;
   SPEED; HASTEN; QUICKEN
hurry-scurry / CONFUSION
hurt / CUT, MAR; ACHE, HARM,
   MAIM; SLASH, WOUND; IMPAIR,
   INJURE, GRIEVE. DERE, LOSS,
   PAIN; DAMAGE, INJURY.
   PAINED; DAMAGED
hurtful / SORE; BALEFUL,
   BANEFUL, MALEFIC, NOXIOUS;
   INJURIOUS
hurtle / DASH; FLING; COLLIDE
husband / HUBBY; SPOUSE.
   MANAGE; CULTIVATE,
   ECONOMIZE
husband of Helen of Troy /
   MENELAUS
husband of Titania / OBERON
husbandman / FARMER, TILLER
husbandry / THRIFT; FARMING
hush / CALM, LULL; ALLAY,
   QUIET. SH; TUT
hush money / BRIBE
hush-hush / SECRET
husk / HULL; SHELL, SHUCK
husk of fruit / GLUME, LEMMA
husks of grain / BRAN; CHAFF
husky / BURLY; HOARSE, STRONG.
   ESKIMO
hustle / PUSH; SHOVE; JOSTLE.
   FORCE; ENERGY
hut / BARI; CABIN, HOVEL,
   HUTCH, JACAL, SHACK; NISSEN,
   SHANTY
hut of Navajo / HOGAN
hutch / BOX, PEN; COOP; CHEST
huzzah / HURRAH
hyacinth / JACINTH
hybrid / MIXED; CROSSED,
   MONGREL; HALFBREED
hybrid animal / MULE; HINNY
hybrid bison and cow / CATTALO
hydrate lime / SLAKE
hydraulic pump / RAM
hydrocarbon / TOLAN; BUTANE,
   CETANE, ETHANE, MELENE,
   OCTANE, PYRENE, RETENE;
   BENZENE, TERPENE
hydrocarbon radical / AMYL;
   ETHYL; METHYL
hydrogen isotope / TRITIUM;
   DEUTERIUM
hydrophobia / RABIES

hydrophobia, pert. to / LYSSIC
hydroplane / SEAPLANE
hygiene / HEALTH; SANITATION
Hymen's father / APOLLO
Hymettus product / HONEY
hymn / ODE; SONG; PSALM
hymn, for choir / CHORALE
hymn of praise / PAEAN; ANTHEM
hymn tune / CHORAL; CHORALE
hyperborean / ARCTIC, FRIGID;
    NORTHERN
Hyperion's daughter / EOS;
    SELENE
Hyperion's father / URANUS
Hyperion's mother / GE

Hyperion's son / HELIOS
hypnotic state / TRANCE
hypnotism / HYPNOSIS;
    MESMERISM
hypocrisy / CANT; DECEIT
hypocrite / TARTUFE; PHARISEE,
    TARTUFFE
hypocritical statement / CANT
hypodermic / NEEDLE
hypothetical force / OD; BIOD,
    ELOD, ODYL; PANTOD
hysteria / FURY; FRENZY, MOTHER
hysteria in men / TARASSIS
hysterics / FIT

I

I do / YES
I have found it / EUREKA
iambic foot / IAMB; IAMBUS
Iapetus' son / PROMETHEUS
Iapetus' wife / ASIA; CLYMENE
ibex / KYL, TUR, ZAC; KAIL
ibis-headed god / THOTH
Ibsen character / ASE; NORA,
    PEER; EKDAL, HEDDA; ROSMER
icarian / RISKY; INFIRM, UNSAFE
ice / SISH, SNOW; FROST,
    SHERBET, CHILL
ice, pert. to / CRYSTIC
ice box / FREEZER; REFRIGERATOR
ice a cake / FROST; FRAPPE
ice cleat / CRAMPON
ice cream dish / SPLIT; SUNDAE
ice cream wafer cup / CONE
ice crystals / SNOW; SLEET
ice game / CURLING
ice house / IGLOO
ice mass / PAN; BERG, CALF,
    FLOE, PACK, RAFT; GROWLER,
    ICEBERG
ice pinnacle / SERAC
ice river / GLACIER
ice runner / SKI; SLED; SKATE
ice sport / HOCKEY
iced / GLACE; GLACED, GLAZED
Iceland capital / REYKJAVIK
Iceland money / KRONA
Iceland parliament / ALTHING
Iceland phenomenon / HECLA,
    HEKLA; GEYSIR; SURTSEY
Icelandic bard / SCALD, SKALD
Icelandic epic / EDDA, SAGA
Icelandic measure / FET; ALIN
ichneumon / MONGOOSE
ichthyic / PISCINE; ICHTHYAL
icing / FROSTING
icon / IMAGE; FIGURE
icterus / JAUNDICE
ictus / FIT; STRESS

icy / COLD; GELID; FRIGID,
    WINTRY
id est / IE
Idaho capital / BOISE
Idaho mountains / LEMHI
Idaho river / SNAKE; SALMON
Idaho state flower / SYRINGA
Idaho state nickname / GEM
idea / PLAN; FANCY, IMAGE
ideal / MENTAL, UNREAL;
    PERFECT
ideal land / EDEN; DIXIE, THULE;
    BEULAH, CANAAN, OCEANA,
    UTOPIA
ideal score in golf / PAR
idealist / DREAMER; VISIONARY
ideally / MENTALLY
ideally rural / ARCADIAN
ideate / FANCY; CREATE;
    CONCEIVE
identical / ONE; SAME; SELFSAME
identification mark / TAG; BRAND,
    LABEL, NOTCH; MARKER
ideology / ISM; CREED; DOCTRINE
idiocy / FOLLY; AMENTIA,
    FATUITY
idiom / DIALECT; LANGUAGE
idiosyncrasy / ODDITY;
    IDIOCRASY
idiot / OAF; FOOL; MORON;
    CRETIN
idiotic / DAFT; ABSURD;
    FATUOUS
idle / LAZY, VAIN; EMPTY, INERT
idle talk / GAB, GAS; GOSSIP
idleness / SLOTH; ACEDIA,
    APATHY
idler / DRONE, LAZER; LOAFER
idol / PET; BAAL, JOSS, LION
idolatrous / PAGAN; HEATHEN
idolatry / BAALISM; FETISHISM
idolize / LOVE; ADORE, EXALT
Idumaea / EDOM

idyl / ECLOGUE; PASTORAL
igneous / FIRELIKE, PLUTONIC
Igneous rock / LAVA; MAGMA;
BASALT, GABBRO; DIABASE,
GRANITE
Ignis fatuus / DELUSION
Ignite / BURN, FIRE, GLOW, HEAT
ignited / LIT; LIVE; ALIVE, FIRED
ignoble / LOW; BASE, MEAN
ignominious / SHAMEFUL
ignominy / INFAMY; OBLOQUY
ignoramus / DOLT; DUNCE
ignorance / DARKNESS;
NESCIENCE
ignorant / DARK; BLIND; STUPID
ignore / CUT; OMIT, PASS, SNUB
iguana / GOANA; GOANNA;
TUATARA
ilex / OAK; HOLM; HOLLY
Iliad's author / HOMER
ilk / KIND, NAME, SORT; BREED
ill / BAD; SICK, UGLY; CROSS,
SURLY; ACHING, AILING,
UNKIND
ill, pref. / MAL
ill behaved / RUDE; UNCOUTH
ill humor / CHOLER, DANDER
ill humored / SAD; DOWN; CROSS
ill mannered / IMPOLITE
ill natured / SOUR; BILED, CROSS
ill tempered / CRUSTY; CRABBED
ill use / ABUSE; INJURY, MISUSE
ill will / SPITE; ANIMUS, GRUDGE
illation / INFERENCE
illegal / ILLICIT; UNLAWFUL
illegal act / FOUL; CRIME; FELONY
illegal whisky / POTEEN;
POTHEEN; MOONSHINE
illimitable / INFINITE; BOUNDLESS
Illinois capital / SPRINGFIELD
Illinois city / ALTON; JOLIET
Illinois river / FOX; OHIO
Illinois state bird / CARDINAL
Illinois state flower / VIOLET
Illinois state nickname / SUCKER;
PRAIRIE
Illinois state tree / BUROAK
illiterate / UNLEARNED
illness / MALADY; AILMENT,
DISEASE; DISORDER, SICKNESS
ill-tempered woman / FURY;
SCOLD, SHREW, VIXEN;
BELDAM, VIRAGO
illuminate / LIGHT; INSPIRE
illuminated / ORNATE
illumination unit / LUX; PHOT;
LUMEN
illusion / MYTH, SHOW; ERROR
illusionist / CONJUROR,
MAGICIAN
illusive / DELUSIVE; DECEPTIVE
illustrate / ADORN; DEPICT

illustration / DRAWING, ETCHING,
EXAMPLE, PICTURE; INSTANCE
illustrative motion / NOD; MIME
illustrious / GREAT, NOBLE
image / BUST, COPY, ICON, IDEA,
IDOL, IKON; TROPE; EFFIGY
image of a god / IDOL
image of a saint / ICON, IKON
imaginably true / POSSIBLE
imaginary / WILD; DREAMY,
UNREAL
imaginary beast / NAGA; HARPY,
HODAG, LAMIA; DRAGON,
GARUDA, KRAKEN, SPHINX,
SQUONK; CENTAUR
Imaginary zone in heavens /
ZODIAC
imagination / IDEA, PLOT; FANCY
imaginative writing / POETRY;
FICTION, ROMANCE
imagine / FORM; DREAM, FANCY
imagined threat / BUGABOO
imbecile / AMENT, IDIOT; CRETIN
imbecility / DOTAGE; AMENTIA,
FATUITY; DEBILITY, SENILITY
imbibe / GET, SIP; GAIN, GULP;
DRINK; GATHER, RECEIVE;
ACQUIRE
imbroglio / INTRIGUE;
CONFUSION
imbrue / WET; SOAK; FLOOD,
STAIN
imbue / DYE; STEEP, TINGE
imitate / APE; COPY, ECHO, MIME
imitation / COPY, SHAM; PARODY
imitation gold leaf / ORMOLU
imitation morocco / ROAN
imitation pearl / PASTE; OLIVET
imitation satin / SATEEN
imitation velvet / VELVETEEN
imitative / MOCK, SHAM; APISH
imitator / APE; ECHO; MIMIC
immaculate / PURE; INNOCENT
immaterial / SMALL; TRIVIAL
immature / RAW; CRUDE, GREEN
immature blossom / BUD
immature insect / IMAGO
immediate / NEAR; CLOSE;
DIRECT
immediately / NOW; ANON, STAT;
PRESTO, PRONTO; CLOSELY;
DIRECTLY
immediately following / NEXT
immense / HUGE, VAST; GREAT,
LARGE, VASTY; TITANIC;
COLOSSAL
immerse / DIP; DUCK, DUNK, SINK
imminence / PERIL; THREAT
imminent / NEAR, NIGH; CLOSE
immobile / STILL; UNMOVABLE
immoderate / UNDUE; EXCESSIVE
immodest / BOLD, LEWD; GROSS

immoral / BAD; LEWD; LOOSE
immortal / ABIDING, ETERNAL
immortalize / DEIFY, EXALT
immortally / ETERNALLY
immovable / SET; FIRM; FIXED
immunity / CHARTER, FREEDOM,
LIBERTY, RELEASE; EXEMPTION
immunizing substance / HAPTEN;
HAPTENE; ANTIBODY
immure / ENTOMB, WALLUP;
CONFINE
immutable / FIRM; PERMANENT
imp / ELF; BRAT; DEMON, DEVIL
impact / BRUNT; COLLISION
impair / MAR, SAP; HARM, RUIN
impair by inaction / RUST; ERODE
impale / FIX; GORE, SPIT; SPEAR
impalpable / INTANGIBLE
impart / GIVE, LEND, TELL; GRANT
impart knowledge / TEACH;
INFORM
impart new vigor / REANIMATE
impartial / EVEN, FAIR, FREE
impassable / BARRED, CLOSED
impassioned / FIERY; ARDENT
impassive / STOIC; STOLID
impassive countenance / DEADPAN
impatient / HOT, HASTY, EAGER
impeach / ACCUSE, CHARGE,
INDICT
impede / BAR; CLOG, STOP;
BLOCK
impediment / BAR; DRAG; CHECK
impel / MOVE, PUSH, SEND, SPUR
impend / OVERHANG, THREATEN
impenitent / SINFUL, WICKED
imperative / URGENT; BINDING
imperfect / WEAK; FRAIL; ERRING
imperfect, c.f. / ATEL; ATELO
imperfect, pref. / MAL, MIS
imperfect bomb / DUD
imperfection / FLAW, LACK, VICE
imperial / REGAL, ROYAL;
QUEENLY
imperial domain / EMPIRE
imperil / RISK; MENACE;
ENDANGER
imperious / LORDLY, URGENT,
WILFUL; HAUGHTY; ARROGANT,
DESPOTIC
impersonate / ACT; REPRESENT
impertinence / SASS
impertinent / BOLD, PERT, RUDE;
SASSY, SAUCY; FORWARD, UN-
CIVIL
impertinent girl / MINX; HUSSY
imperturbable / CALM, COOL
impetrate / ENTREAT; PETITION
impetuosity / DASH, ELAN; FORCE
impetuous / HOT, RASH; EAGER
impetus / IMPULSE; MOMENTUM
impinge / DASH; CLASH; STRIKE

impious / SINFUL, WICKED
impish / ELFIN, ELVAN; ELFISH
implacable / PITILESS; MERCILESS
implant firmly / ENROOT
implanted / LODGED, ROOTED
implement / GEAR, TOOL; UTENSIL
implement for digging / SPADE;
SHOVEL, TROWEL
implement for hand-grinding /
MANO; METATE, MORTAR,
PESTLE
implement set / KIT; GEAR, TRAPS;
OUTFIT, TACKLE; APPARATUS
implement to skid logs / TODE
implicate / CONNECT, EMBROIL
implied / TACIT; CONNECTED
implore / ASK, BEG, PRAY; CRAVE
imply / HINT, MEAN; CONNOTE
impolite / CURT, RUDE; COARSE
imporous / DENSE, SOLID;
COMPACT
importance / IMPORT, MOMENT
important / GRAVE, GREAT, VITAL
important personage / VIP; BRASS,
MOGUL; BIGWIG; TOPDOG;
BIGSHOT
importer / AGENT; SHIPPER
importunate / URGENT
importune / BEG, DUN; PRAY;
URGE
impose / ASK, FIX, LAY, SET, TAX
impose a fine / AMERCE, SCONCE
impose as taxes / LEVY; ASSESS
imposed work / TASK; CHORE
imposing / EPIC; GRAND, NOBLE
imposing building / EDIFICE
imposition / TAX; LEVY; CHEAT
impossible / ABSURD, FUTILE
impossible playing position /
BIND; STIMIE, STYMIE;
ZUGZWANG
impost / TAX; DUTY, LEVY, RATE
imposter / CHEAT, KNAVE, QUACK
imposture / SHAM; FRAUD; DECEIT
impotent / WEAK; FRAIL; FEEBLE
imprecation / OATH; CURSE
impregnate / IMBUE; INFUSE
impregnate with salt / CORN
impresario / AGENT; MANAGER
impress / AWE, FIX; MARK, MOVE;
PRINT, STAMP; AFFECT,
COMPEL
impress deeply / ETCH; ENGRAVE
impress by repetition / DIN
impression / DENT, IDEA; FANCY
impressionable / PLASTIC
impressionist painter / DEGAS,
MANET, MONET; RENOIR,
SISLEY
impressive / MOVING, SOLEMN
imprimatur / LICENSE; APPROVAL
imprint / DINT, MARK; STAMP

imprison / CAGE, JAIL; COMMIT
imprisonment / DURESS; DURANCE
improbable / UNLIKELY; UNEXPECTED
improbable story / YARN; FABLE
impromptu / OFFHAND; EXTEMPORE
improper / AMISS, UNFIT, WRONG
impropriety / LAPSE, WRONG
improve / GAIN, GROW, MEND
improvement / PROGRESS
improvident / CARELESS, PRODIGAL
improvise / VAMP; ADLIB
imprudent / LACK, RASH; HEEDLESS
impudence / LIP; BRASS, CHEEK
impudent / BOLD, FLIP, PERT
impugn / ASSAIL, ATTACK, OPPOSE
impulse / ELAN; FORCE; MOTIVE
impulsive / RASH; HASTY; WAYWARD
impunity / FREEDOM; IMMUNITY
impure / FOUL; DIRTY, MIXED
impure opal / MENILITE
imputation / BLAME; CHARGE
impute / FAULT; CHARGE; ASCRIBE
imshee / GO; BEGONE
in / AT; INTO, WITH; AMONG
in abundance / ENOUGH, GALORE
in addition / AND, TOO, YET; ALSO, PLUS; BESIDES, FURTHER
in advance / VAN; LEAD; AHEAD
in the capacity of / AS; QUA
in the case of / INRE
in case that / IF, SO; LEST
in circumference / AROUND
in the direction of / TO; TOWARD
in a dither / AGOG; EAGER
in earnest / FIRM; EAGER; WILLING
in error / WRONG
in excess / TOO; OVER; EXTRA
in fact / TRUE; TRULY; INDEED
in front / AHEAD; BEFORE; LEADING
in gear / READY; MESHED
in good season / EARLY; BETIMES
in good spirit / HIGH; ELATED
in harmony / AGREED; ATTUNED
in honor of / FOR; AFTER
in the know / HIP; AWARE
in lieu of / FOR
in like manner / AS, SO; EVEN
in line / AROW; ALINE; SERIAL
in matter of / AS; ALA; INRE
in the middle / MID; AMID; AMONG
in name only / NOMINAL, TITULAR
in the near future / ANON, SOON
in no manner / NEVER, NOWAY

in one's dotage / ANILE; SENILE
in operation / AFOOT, GOING
in order that / SO
in and out / FITFUL; IRREGULAR
in passing / ENPASSANT
in person / LIVE
in pigtails / BRAIDED
in place of / FOR; INSTEAD
in position / SET; FIXED, READY
in quick time / FAST; PRESTO
in the rear / AREAR; ASTERN
in regard to / ANENT; APROPOS; TOUCHING
in respect to / OF; ASTO; ABOUT
in a row / AROW; ALINE
in the same place / IBID
in sequence / SERIATIM
in some place / SOMEWHERE
in spite of / MAUGRE; DESPITE
in store for / AWAITING
in the style of / ALA; LIKE
in that place / THERE; THEREIN
in this place / HERE; HEREIN
in this way / SO; THUS
in toto / ENTIRELY; COMPLETELY
in a trice / ANON; PRESTO
in truth / AMEN; VERILY
in want / POOR; NEEDY; DESTITUTE
in what manner / HOW
in what place / WHERE; WHEREIN
in what way / HOW
inability / IMPOTENCE; INCAPACITY
inability to concentrate / APROSEXIA
inability to construct sentences / ACATAPHASIA
inability to differentiate tones / AMUSIA
inability to feel / ANAPHIA; ANESTHESIA
inability to identify objects / AGNOSIA
inability to pronounce words / ALEXIA; APHEMIA, APHONIA
inability to stand up / ASTASIA
inability to take action / ABULIA; ABOULIA
inability to taste / AGEUSIS
inability to vocalize / ALALIA
inability to write / AGRAPHIA
inaccessible / SHUT; CLOSED
inaccuracy / SLIP; ERROR; MISTAKE
inaccurate / WRONG; INEXACT
inaction / TORPOR; IDLENESS
inactive / IDLE, LAZY; INERT
inadequate / SHORT; DEFICIENT
inadvertency / ERROR; BLUNDER
inamorata / LOVER; MISTRESS
inane / EMPTY, SILLY; OBTUSE

inanimate / DEAD; INERT
inappropriate / INAPT, UNFIT
inarticulate / DUMB; APHONIC
inasmuch as / AS; SINCE; SEEING
inaugurate / OPEN; INDUCT
inauspicious / MALIGN; HOSTILE
inbeing / ESSENCE; EXISTENCE
inborn / INBRED, INNATE, NATIVE
Inca / QUECHUAN
Inca capital / CUZCO
Inca conqueror / PIZARRO
Inca death god / SUPAI
Inca earth goddess / PACHAMAMA
Inca founder / MANCO
Inca king / ATAHUALPA
Inca sky city / MACHUPICCHU
Inca string record / QUIPU
Inca sun god / INTI; CHOUN
Inca vestals / ACLLA
incandescence / GLOW; GLEAM
incandescent bit / EMBER, SPARK
incantation / CHARM, CURSE,
    SPELL; PRAYER; CANTRAP,
    CANTRIP
incapable / WEAK; INAPT, UNAPT,
    UNFIT; FEEBLE, UNABLE; WANT-
    ING
incapacitate / DISABLE
incarcerate / PEN; CONFINE
incarnation / AVATAR; EPIPHANY
incarnation of Vishnu / RAMA;
    KALKI, KURMA, AVATAR,
    BUDDHA, MATSYA, VAMANA,
    VARAHA; KRISHNA; BALARMA;
    NARASINGHA; RAMACHANDRA
incase / CASE; ENCHASE;
    SURROUND
incautious / RASH; UNWARY
incense / BURN, FUME; INFLAME.
    MYRRH; BALSAM, STACTE;
    TACAMAHAC
incense burner / THURIBLE
incensed / MAD; ANGRY, IRATE
incentive / BROD, GOAD, PROD
incessant / STEADY; CONSTANT
incessantly / EVER; ALWAYS
incident / ACT; EVENT; AFFAIR
incidental / BYE; STRAY; CASUAL
incidentally / OBITER; CASUALLY
incinerator / RETORT; FURNACE
incipient / INITIAL; INCHOATE
incipient laugh / GRIN; SMILE
incised / CUT; NOTCHED;
    ENGRAVED
incision / CUT; GASH; NOTCH
incite / EGG; ABET, EDGE, GOAD
inclement / RAW; HARSH; SEVERE
inclination / BOB, BOW, NOD
inclination of the head / NOD
incline / DIP; BEND, LEAN, TEND
incline from vertical / HADE

inclined / APT; FAIN; PRONE
inclined trough / CHUTE, FLUME
inclined way / RAMP
inclose / PEN; SHUT, WRAP;
    COVER
include / HOLD; CONTAIN,
    EMBRACE
including / AND, TOO; ALSO, WITH
including everything / OVERALL
incognito / UNKNOWN; DISGUISED
incognizant / UNAWARE
incoherent / WILD; LOOSE
income / GAIN, RENT, TAKE
income by labor / PAY; WAGE;
    WAGES; SALARY; STIPEND
income from wealth / RENT;
    PROFIT, USANCE; INTEREST
incommode / VEX; ANNOY;
    MOLEST
incomparable / RARE; PEERLESS
incompetent / WEAK; UNFIT
incomplete / PARTIAL; DEFECTIVE
incongruous / ALIEN; ABSURD
inconsiderate / RASH; GIDDY
inconsistent / UNSTABLE;
    CHANGEABLE, DISCREPANT
inconstant / FICKLE; MUTABLE
inconvenience / VEX; ANNOY
incorporate / MIX; BLEND, UNITE
incorrect / AMISS, FALSE, WRONG
incorrect term / MISNOMER
incrassate / THICKEN;
    INSPISSATE
increase / ADD, EKE, WAX; GROW,
    RISE; ISSUE, RAISE; DEEPEN
increase in size / WAX; GROW
increase suddenly / ZOOM
increase three times / TRIPLE
increase twice / DOUBLE
increasing / ANABATIC, CRESCENT
incredible / FABULOUS;
    MARVELOUS
increment / ACCRUAL; INCREASE
incriminate / ACCUSE, CHARGE
incrustation / SCAB, SCAR
incrustation on teeth / PLAQUE
    TARTAR
incubus / ONUS; DEMON, FIEND;
    NIGHTMARE
incult / RUDE, WILD; CRUDE
incumbent / BINDING, LEANING
incursion / RAID; FORAY; INROAD
incus / ANVIL
Ind / INDIA
indebted / DUE; OWING; OBLIGED
indecent / GROSS, NASTY; COARSE
indecisive / UNSTEADY; FALTER-
    ING
indeed / ARU, YEA, YES; ARRO;
    TRULY; REALLY, VERILY
indefatigable / SEDULOUS

indefinite / DIM; LOOSE, VAGUE
indefinite amount / ANY, FEW; MANY, SOME; UMPTY
indefinite article / A; AN
indefinite occasion / ANYTIME
indefinite pronoun / ANY, ONE
indehiscent fruit / UVA; PEPO; MELON; LOMENT, SAMARA, SQUASH
indelicate / COARSE; IMMODEST
indent / CUT; BIND, DENT; BEGIN
indentation / DENT, DINT; CHOIL
indented / EROSE; ZIGZAG
indented cake / WAFFLE
independent / FREE; LIBERAL
independent Ireland / EIRE
indeterminate / VAGUE; UNSETTLED
indeterminate quantity / ANY, FEW; MANY, SOME
index / LIST; TABLE; EXPONENT
index mark / FIST
India / IND; BHARAT; HINDUSTAN
India capital / NEWDELHI
India city / AGRA; DELHI; BOMBAY
India city noted for gem cutting / GOLCONDA
India language / PALI, URDU; HINDI, TAMIL; MARATHI; SANSKRIT
India money / ANNA, PICE; PAISA, RUPEE
India river / BEAS, RAVI; INDUS
Indian / See India, East Indian, American Indian, and names of states, countries, etc.
Indian, c.f. / INDO
Indian corn / SAMP; KANGA, MAIZE
Indian fig / BANYAN
Indian hemp / KEF; SUNN; GANJA
Indian madder / MUNJEET
Indian mahogany / TOON; ROHAN
Indian meal / CORNMEAL
Indian millet / DURRA; SORGHUM
Indian mulberry / AL; AAL, ACH
Indian ocean vessel / DHOW
Indian peace pipe / CALUMET
Indian pony / CAYUSE
Indian potato / YAMP; SUNFLOWER
Indian yellow / PURI; PIURI
Indiana capital / INDIANAPOLIS
Indiana city / GARY; MUNCIE
Indiana lake region / DUNES
Indiana river / EEL; OHIO; WHITE
Indiana settlement / VINCENNES
Indiana state flower / PEONY; ZINNIA
Indiana state nickname / HOOSIER
Indiana tribe / WEA; MIAMI
indicate / BODE, MARK, READ
indicating succession / ORDINAL
indication / HINT, MARK, SIGN
indicator / CLUE, DIAL, VANE

indict / ACCUSE, CHARGE, PUNISH
indifference / APATHY; UNCONCERN
indifferent / COOL; BLASE
indigence / NEED, WANT; PENURY
indigene / NATIVE; ABORIGINE
indigenous / LOCAL; INNATE
indigent / POOR; NEEDY; DESTITUTE
indigestion / APEPSY; ANOREXIA
indignant / ANGRY, IRATE, WROTH
indignation / IRE; FURY, RAGE
indignity / INSULT, SLIGHT
indigo / ANIL, BLUE, WOAD
indigo bird / FINCH
indigo plant / ANIL
indigo snake / GOPHERSNAKE
indirect reference / HINT
indiscreet / RASH; UNWISE
indiscretion / SLIP; FOLLY
indiscriminate / MIXED; MINGLED
indisposition / MALADY; AILMENT
indisputable / SURE; CERTAIN
indistinct / DIM; VAGUE; BLURRED
indite / PEN; WRITE; COMPOSE
individual / SOLE; SINGLE
individual, c.f. / AUTO, IDIO
individual performance / SOLO
individuality / EGO; SELF; SEITY
indivisible particle / MONAD
Indochina city / HUE; HANOI
Indochina region / LAOS, SIAM; ANNAM; COCHIN; VIETNAM; CAMBODIA
Indochinese language / AO, WA; AKA, ANU, LAI, LAO, MRO, MRU, PWO, SAK, TAI
Indochinese outrigger / GAYYOU
Indochinese tribe / ITO, KHA, LAO, MEO, MRU, TAI; SHAN
indoctrinate / COACH, IMBUE
Indo-European / ARYA; ARYAN
indolence / SLOTH; LAZINESS
indolent / IDLE, LAZY, SLOW
Indo-Malayan animal / NAPU; LORIS; GYMNURE, KANCHIL; CHEVROTAIN
Indonesia / NUSANTARA
Indonesia capital / BATAVIA, JAKARTA; DJAKARTA
Indonesia city / BANDUNG, MAKASAR
Indonesia island / BALI, JAVA; CERAM, TIMOR; BORNEO, MADURA
Indonesian / ATA; BATAK, DAYAK
indoor game / POOL; BINGO, CARDS, CHESS, HALMA; BILLIARDS
indorsement / OK; APPROVAL
indubitable / SURE; EVIDENT
induce / ACT, EGG; LEAD, MAKE

inductance unit / HENRY
inductive argument / EPAGOGE
inductive reasoning / INDUCTION
indue / ENDOW; CLOTHE, INVEST
indulge / ALLOW, FAVOR, HUMOR
indulgence / FAVOR; EXCESS
indulgent / EASY, KIND, MILD
indurate / HARDEN
industrial diamond / BORT
industrial labor union / CIO, IWW
industrialist / TYCOON; MAGNATE
industrious / BUSY; BRISK
industrious insect / ANT, BEE
inebriate / INTOXICATE. SOT
ineffectual / IDLE, VAIN, WEAK
inept / UNFIT; ABSURD, CLUMSY
inequality / ODDS; DEVIATION
inequitable / UNJUST
inert / DEAD, DULL, LAZY; SUPINE
inert gas / NEON; ARGON, NITON,
   RADON, XENON; HELIUM;
   KRYPTON
inevitable result / NEMESIS
inexact / WRONG; ERRONEOUS
inexorable / FIRM, HARD; CRUEL
inexpensive / CHEAP; BARGAIN
inexpensive cigar / STOGY; STOGIE
inexperienced / LAY, RAW;
   CALLOW
inexperienced person / TYRO;
   NOVICE, ROOKIE; FLEDGLING
inextricable / MAZY; INVOLVED
infallible / CERTAIN; UNERRING
infamous / BAD; BASE, EVIL, VILE
infamy / ODIUM, SHAME;
   OBLOQUY
infancy / CRADLE; BABYHOOD
infant / BABE, BABY; CHILD
infant's bed / CRIB
infant's complaint / COLIC
infant's enclosure / PLAYPEN
infant's food / PAP; MILK; GRUEL
infant's whimper / MEWL
infatuation / ATE; FOLLY
infect / TAINT; DEFILE, POISON
infectious / CATCHING, DEFILING
infelicitous / UNLUCKY; ILLTIMED
infer / ACCEPT, DEDUCE, DEDUCT
inference / COROLLARY, DEDUC-
   TION
inferential / ILLATIVE
inferior / BAD, LOW, SUB; POOR
inferior, pref. / SUB; HYPO
inferior anthracite / CULM
inferior cloth / RAG; SHODDY
inferior diamond / BORT
inferior dwelling / HUT; DUMP
inferior horse / NAG, TIT; JADE
inferior ware / PLUG; HURTS
infernal / DARK; HELLISH
infernal regions / PIT; HELL;
   ABYSS, HADES, SHEOL; NARAKA
Inferno author / DANTE

infertile / ARID; BARREN, OTIOSE
infest / VEX; ANNOY, BESET
infidel / PAGAN; GIAOUR, KAFFIR;
   ATHEIST, HEATHEN, HERETIC,
   SKEPTIC; AGNOSTIC; UN-
   BELIEVER
infidelity / ADULTERY, UNBELIEF
infinite / ENDLESS, ETERNAL
infinitesimal / ATOMIC, MINUTE
infinitive indicator / TO
infinity / AYE; OLAM; ETERNITY
infirm / LAME, WEAK; ANILE
infirmity / FOIBLE, MALADY
inflame / FIRE; ANGER; AROSE
inflame with love / ENAMOR
inflamed / RED; SORE; HEATED
inflammable / EXCITABLE
inflammable substance / PUNK;
   AMADOU, TINDER
inflammation of eyes /IRITIS;
   PINKEYE; TRACHOMA;
   KLIEGEYES
inflammation of the gum / ULITIS
inflammation of the shoulder /
   OMITIS
inflate / ELATE, SWELL; EXPAND
inflated / GASSY, TUMID; PUFFED
inflated toy / BALLOON
inflect / BOW; BEND, VARY
inflect a verb / CONJUGATE
inflexible / IRON; RIGID, STEEL
inflict / DEAL; WREAK; IMPOSE
inflorescence / BUD; CYME;
   AMENT, BLOOM, SPIKE, UMBEL;
   CATKIN
influence / WIN; LEAD, MOVE
influence dishonestly / BRIBE
influential / POTENT; POWERFUL
influential person / HEAVYWEIGHT
influenza / GRIP; GRIPPE
influx / FLOW, TIDE; ONSET
infold / LAP; FOLD, WRAP; COVER
inform / TELL, WARN; ADVISE
informal conversation / CHAT
information / DATA, LORE, NEWS
information seeker / SPY; PROBER
informed / HEP, HIP; AWARE.
   TOLD
informer / SPY; BLAB, NARK
infra / BELOW; BENEATH
infraction / SIN; BREACH
infrequent / RARE; SELDOM
infringement / VIOLATION
infuriate / IRE; ANGER; ENRAGE
infuse / IMBUE, STEEP; IMPART
infusion / TEA; TINCTURE
infusoria / PROTOZOA; PARA-
   MECIUM
ingenious / ABLE, KEEN; ACUTE
ingenuous / ABLE, OPEN; FRANK
ingest / EAT, SUP; DEVOUR
ingle / FIRE; BLAZE
ingot / BAR, PIG; SHOE; SYCEE

ingredient / PART; FACTOR
ingredient in brewing / MALT, MASH; YEAST
ingredient of varnish / LAC; RESIN
ingress / ENTRY, INLET
Ingrian Finn / VOT
inhabit / ABIDE, DWELL; OCCUPY
inhabitant / CIT, ITE; INMATE
inhabitant of, suffix / AN, ER, OT; IAN, ITE, OTE
inhabitant of Liverpool / LIVERPOLITAN, LIVERPUDLIAN
inhabitant of Los Angeles / ANGELENO
inhabitant of the moon / SELENITE
inhale / SNIFF; BREATHE, INSPIRE
inherent / INBORN, INBRED
inheritance / ENTAIL; HEREDITY
inheritance factor / DNA; GENE
inheritor / HEIR; DEVISEE
inhibit / CHECK; PROHIBIT
inhuman / FELL; CRUEL; BRUTAL
inhume / BURY; INTER; ENTOMB
inimical / ADVERSE, HOSTILE
iniquitous / EVIL; SINFUL
iniquity / SIN; EVIL, VICE
initial / FIRST; CAPITAL
initial appearance / DEBUT
initiate / OPEN; BEGIN, START
injection / HYPO, SHOT; ENEMA
injudicious / RASH; HASTY
injunction / WRIT; ORDER
injure / MAR; HARM, HURT, MAIM
injurious / EVIL; FATAL, NOISY
injury / DERE, EVIL, HARM, HURT
inking implement / PAD; BRAYER
inkling / HINT
inky / EBON; BLACK
inlaid decoration / BUHL; MOSAIC, NIELLO, TARSIA; INTARSIA
inlaid work / MARQUETRY
inland body of water / LAKE, POND; BROOK, CANAL, RIVER
inlet / ARM, BAY, GEO, GIO, RIA, VOE; COVE, SLEW; CREEK, FIORD, FIRTH, FJORD, FRITH; SLOUGH
inmost section / CORE, PITH; HEART; KERNEL, MARROW; NUCLEUS
inn / KHAN; CABAC, FONDA, HAVEN
inn of Canterbury Tales / TABARD
innate / INBORN, NATIVE; INSIDE
inner, c.f. / ENTO
inner bark / CORTEX
inner part of eye / UVEA; RETINA
inner room / DEN
inner surface covering / LINING
inner tissue of plant / BAST; PHLOEM
inner wall of ditch / SCARP
innermost part / CORE, PITH

Innisfail / ERIN; IRELAND
innkeeper / HOST; PADRONE
innocent / FREE, PURE; LAWFUL
innominate bone / PELVIS; HIPBONE
innovation / CHANGE; NOVELTY
innuendo / HINT, SLUR
innuit / ESKIMO
innumerable / MANY; UMPTY
inoperative / IDLE, VOID
inordinate / UNDUE; EXCESSIVE
inorganic substance / MINERAL
inquire / ASK, PRY; SEEK; SNOOP
inquiry / QUERY; SEARCH
inquiry for lost article / TRACER
inquisitive / NOSY; PRYING
inquisitive meddler / SNOOP
inre / REGARDING
insane / MAD; LUNY; BATTY, CRAZY
insane asylum / BEDLAM; MAD-HOUSE
insanity / MANIA; MADNESS
insatiable / GREEDY; RAVENOUS
inscribe / PEN; DRAW; ENTER
inscription / ENTRY; COLOPHON
inscrutable / HIDDEN; MYSTERIOUS
inscrutable person / SPHINX
insect / ANT, BEE, BUG, DOR, ERI
insect in adult stage / IMAGO
insect bite / STING
insect body / THORAX
insect body air sac / AGROSTAT
insect eater / BIRD, TOAD
insect feeler / PALP; ANTENNA
insect in immature stage / GRUB, PUPA; LARVA; MAGGOT
insect killer / DDT; PYRETHRUM
insect leg segment / COXA; FEMUR
insect secretion / LAC, WAX; LAAP, LERP; HONEYDEW
insect sound / HUM; BUZZ; CHIRP
insect-eating bird / TODY
insect's metamorphic stage / MOLT, PUPA; IMAGO, LARVA; INSTAR
insecure / RISKY, SHAKY; CHANCY
insecure knot / GRANNY
inseminate / SOW; PLANT; IMPLANT
insensate / BRUTISH; SOULLESS
insensible / NUM; DULL, NUMB
insert / PUT; ENTER, INLAY
insertion / INSET, PANEL
insertion mark / CARET
insertion of one word in another / TMESIS
inset / INLAY, PANEL; INFLUX
inside / INNER; PRIVATE; INTERNAL
inside influence / DRAG, PULL
insidious / SLY; WILY; ARTFUL

insight / KEN; INTUITION
insignia / BAR; BADGE, MEDAL; EMBLEM; REGALIA
insignificant / NULL, TINY
insignificant part / ATOM, IOTA
insignificant person / MITE, RUNT, SNIP; PINHEAD; MEDIOCRITY
insignificant thing / BIT, FIG
insincere speech / BUNK, CANT
insinuate / HINT, WORM; IMPLY
insipid / FLAT, TAME; HEAVY
insist / URGE, PRESS; DEMAND
insofar as / QUA
insolent / PERT, RUDE; SAUCY
insouciant / CARELESS
inspect / PRY; LOOK, TEST
inspiration / FLASH; ANIMUS
inspire / STIR; CHEER, ELATE
inspissate / DENSIFY, THICKEN
instability / MUTABILITY
install / SEAT; PLACE; INDUCT
instance / CASE; POINT; EXAMPLE
instant / MO; FLASH, JIFFY
instar / GRUB, PUPA; IMAGO, LARVA
instauration / REPAIR; RENEWAL
instate / INDUCT; INSTALL
instead / OR; ELSE
instigate / EGG; ABET, GOAD
instinctive / INNATE; NATURAL
institute / FIX; FORM; BEGIN
institute suit / SUE; FILE
institution / FIRM
institution of learning / LYCEE; SCHOOL; ACADEMY, COLLEGE; SEMINARY; GYMNASIUM; UNIVERSITY; CONSERVATORY
instruct / BRIEF, EDIFY, ORDER
instructed privately / TUTORED
instruction / RULE; ORDER; ADVICE, LESSON; COMMAND, COUNSEL
instruction book / MANUAL
instructive / DIDACTIC
instructive discourse / SERMON, SPEECH; LECTURE
instrument / DEED, TOOL; AGENT
instrument board / DASH; PANEL
instrument of discipline / WHIP; FERULE
instrument to measure electrical strength / AMMETER; VOLT-METER
instrument to measure height / SEXTANT; OROMETER, QUAD-RANT; ALTIMETER
instrument to mow grass / MOWER; SCYTHE
instrument for spraying water / HOSE; NOZZLE
instrument of torture / BOOT, RACK, WHIP; THUMBSCREW
instrumental / HELPFUL

instrumentalist / PLAYER
instrumentality / MEANS; AGENCY
insubordinate / BAD; UNRULY
insufferable / UNBEARABLE
insufficient / UNFIT; SCANTY
insular / NARROW; ISOLATED
insulate / DETACH, ENISLE
insulation / MICA, TAPE; CAULK-ING, ROCKWOOL; ISOLATION
insulin discoverer / BEST; BANT-ING
insult / CAG; SLAP; ABUSE
insulting / RUDE; SAUCY; ABUSIVE
insulting language / AFFRONT
insurance / POLICY; CONTRACT
insurance contract / POLICY
insurance type / FIRE, LIFE; THEFT; HEALTH; ANNUITY, FLOATER, TONTINE; ACCIDENT, BURGLARY, HOSPITAL, PROPERTY; COLLISION, LIABILITY; AUTOMOBILE
insure / COVER; ASSURE
insurgent / REBEL; RIOTER; UPSTART; MUTINEER
insurrection / MUTINY, REVOLT
intact / WHOLE; ENTIRE; UNINJURED
integer / ZERO; DIGIT; FIGURE
integral / ONE, SUM; TOTAL
integrity / HONOR; PURITY
integument / ARIL, DERM, PELT
intellect / MIND, NOUS; BRAIN
intellect, pert. to / NOETIC
intellectual / IDEAL; MENTAL
intellectually / IDEALLY
intelligence / WIT; MIND, NEWS
intelligent / APT; KEEN; ACUTE
intelligible / CLEAR, PLAIN
intemperate / DRUNKEN, EXTREME
intend / AIM; MEAN; DESIGN
intended / LOVER; AFFIANCED
intended for discussion / MOOT
intenerate / SOFTEN
intense / DEEP, KEEN; ACUTE
intensify / DEEPEN; HEIGHTEN
intension / WILL, ZEAL
intensity / DEPTH, MIGHT
intent / AIM; MARK, VIEW, WILL
intention / AIM, END; IDEA
intentional / DELIBERATE
inter / BURY; ENTOMB
intercalary LEAP; INSERTED
intercede / PLEAD; MEDIATE
intercept / STOP; SEIZE; CUTOFF
interconnection / NEXUS; LINKAGE
intercourse / COITION; COM-MERCE, DEALINGS; CONNEC-TION, FELLOWSHIP
interdict / BAN, BAR; VETO; DEBAR; FORBID; PROHIBIT, RESTRAIN

Interdiction / BAN; TABU, VETO
interest / CARE, PART, ZEAL; SHARE, USURY; BEHALF, PROFIT
interfere / CLASH; MEDDLE, MOLEST, OPPOSE; INTRUDE; CONFLICT
Interferer / MARPLOT
interim / PAUSE; INTERVAL. MEANTIME; MEANWHILE
Interior / HOME; INNER; INLAND, INSIDE; DOMESTIC, INTERNAL
interior, c.f. / ENT; ENTO
interior of ancient temple / CELLA
interjection / AH, AW, EH, HA, HM, HO, OH, OW; HUH, OOF, PST, SHH, TSK, TST, ULP, WOW, YAY, YUK; AHEM, GLUB, GOSH, OUCH
interlace / KNIT; BRAID, WEAVE
interlacement / NET; KNOT, MESH
interlock / KNIT, KNOT, LINK
interloper / INTRUDER
interlude / JIG; BREAK, FARCE, PAUSE; RECESS; INTERIM; ENTRACTE
Intermediary / AGENT; MEDIATOR
intermediate / MESNE; MIDDLE; BETWEEN; INTERJACENT. INTERPOSE
Intermediate point / MEAN; MEDIAN
interment / BURIAL; INHUMATION
intermezzo / INTERLUDE
intermingle / MIX; BLEND
intermission / REST, STOP; DELAY, PAUSE; RECESS; INTERIM; INTERVAL
intermit / REST; ABATE, CEASE; FORBEAR, SUBSIDE, SUSPEND
intermix / MIX; MINGLE; SHUFFLE
internal / INNER; INSIDE, IN-WARD; DOMESTIC, ENCLOSED, INTERIOR
internal decay / BLET
internal organs / GUTS; VITALS; IN-NARDS, VISCERA
internally / INLY; INWARDLY
international agreement / PACT; CARTEL, TREATY; ENTENTE
International language / RO; IDO; LATIN; VOLAPUK; ESPERANTO
interpret / READ, REDE; SOLVE; DECODE, DEFINE, UNFOLD, RENDER
interpretation / SENSE; MEANING, VERSION; EXEGESIS, SOLUTION
Interpretation of dreams / ONEIROMANCY
interpreter / GUIDE; DRAGOMAN; EXPOSITOR; METAPHRAST
interrogate / ASK; QUERY
interrogation / EXAM, QUIZ

interrogative / HOW, WHO, WHY; WHAT, WHEN; WHERE
interrupt / END; STOP; BREAK, DELAY; DIVIDE, HINDER; DISTURB
interruption / GAP; BREAK; HIATUS; CESSATION
intersect / CUT; JOIN, MEET
intersecting line / SECANT
intersperse / STREW; SCATTER
interstice / CHINK, CLEFT
intertwine / KNIT, LACE; WEAVE
interval / GAP; REST, SPAN, STOP
intervening / BETWEEN; MEDIATING
interview / VISIT; MEETING
interweave / MAT; LACE, PLAT; BRAID, PLAIT, TWINE, WEAVE
intestinal / ALVINE
intestine / GUT; BOWEL, COLON; BOWELS; ENTRAILS
intimacy / NEARNESS; CLOSE-NESS
intimate / NEAR; CLOSE, HOMEY
intimation / CUE; HINT; SUG-GESTION; ANNOUNCEMENT
intimidate / AWE, COW; DAMP; ALARM, DAUNT, DETER, SCARE
into / IN, TO; AMONG; INSIDE
intolerant / SET; BIASED, LITTLE, NARROW; BIGOTED; DOGMATIC
intolerant person / BIGOT
intone / SING; CHANT, SPEAK
intoxicated / LIT; HIGH, LUSH, SOSH; DRUNK, MUZZY, TIGHT, TIPSY
intoxicating / HEADY, LIGHT
intoxicating drink / GIN, RUM; GROG, SOMA; BOOZE, HOOCH; LIQUOR, WHISKY; ALCOHOL, SPIRITS, WHISKEY
intractable / UNRULY
intrepid / BOLD; BRAVE; DARING, HEROIC; DOUGHTY, GALLANT
intrepidity / NERVE, VALOR
intricate / DEDAL; DAEDAL; COMPLEX, GORDIAN; INVOLVED
intricate organ of human body / EAR, EYE; LUNG, NOSE, SKIN; BRAIN
intrigue / PLOT, RUSE; CABAL; AFFAIR, BRIGUE; LIAISON; ARTIFICE
intrinsic / REAL, TRUE; INBORN, INBRED, INWARD, NATIVE; GENUINE
introduce / ADMIT, BEGIN, BRING, IMMIT, USHER; BROACH, HERALD
introduction / DEBUT, PROEM; ENTREE; ISAGOGE, PREFACE, PRELUDE; EXORDIUM, FORE-WORD, PREAMBLE

introductory / EXORDIAL;
PREFATORY; PRECURSORY;
PRELIMINARY

intrude / MEDDLE; OBTRUDE

intrust / ENTRUST

intuition / HUNCH

inundate / DROWN; OVERFLOW,
SUBMERGE; OVERWHELM

inundation / FLOOD, SPATE;
DELUGE; CATACLYSM

inure / SET, USE; TRAIN; HARDEN,
SEASON; TOUGHEN

inutile / USELESS; UNPROFITABLE

invade / RAID; ENTER; ASSAIL,
ATTACK

invalid / NULL, SICK, VOID, WEAK;
FRAIL; FEEBLE, INFIRM, SICKLY

invalidate / ANNUL, QUASH;
CANCEL, VACATE, WEAKEN

invariable / STEADY; CONSTANT

invasion / RAID; FORAY; INROAD

invective / ABUSE; CURSE; SATIRE;
CENSURE, SARCASM; DIATRIBE

inveigh / RAIL; ASSAIL; CENSURE

inveigle / LURE; DECOY, TEMPT

invent / COIN; FEIGN, FORGE

invention / FIGMENT; CREATION;
DISCOVERY; FABRICATION

inventor / AUTHOR; CREATOR

inventor of AC motor / TESLA

inventor of airplane simulator /
LINK

inventor of battery / VOLTA

inventor of cotton gin / WHITNEY

inventor of dynamite / NOBEL

inventor of elevator / OTIS

inventor of frosted bulb / PIPKIN

inventor of harp / JUBAL

inventor of lock / YALE

inventor of mine safety lamp /
DAVY

inventor of movable type /
GUTENBERG

inventor of pneumatic tire /
DUNLOP

inventor of printing for blind /
BRAILLE

inventor of punch card /
HOLLERITH

inventor of radio / MARCONI

inventor of rotary press / HOE

inventor of safety pin / HUNT

inventor of safety razor / GILLETTE

inventor of sewing machine /
HOWE

inventor of steam engine / WATT

inventor of telegraph code / MORSE

inventor of telephone / BELL

inventor of telescope / GALILEO

inventor of television / BAIRD

inventor of zipper / JUDSON

inventor's claim of rights /
PATENT

inventory / LIST; STOCK; RECORD

invert / TURN; UPSET; CHANGE

invertebrate animal / WORM;
INSECT, MEDUSA, SPIDER,
SPONGE; MOLLUSC, MOLLUSK;
PROTOZOAN

invest / LAY; VEST; ARRAY, DRESS,
ENDOW, ENDUE, INDUE, PLACE

investigate / SIFT; PROBE, STUDY

investigation / SEARCH; INQUIRY

inveterate / CHRONIC; HABITUAL,
HARDENED, SPITEFUL

invigorate / BRACE, NERVE;
ANIMATE, REFRESH;
STRENGTHEN

invisible emanation / AURA;
AROMA

invite / ASK, BID; CALL, LEAD;
ALLURE, ENTICE, SUMMON;
ATTRACT

invited / BADE

inviting / TEMPTING; SEDUCTIVE

invocation / PRAYER; ENTREATY

invoice / BILL; MANIFEST

invoke / CALL, PRAY; ADJURE,
APPEAL; ADDRESS, BESEECH

involucre / WHORL; ROSETTE

involuntary / AUTOMATIC,
UNWILLING; COMPULSORY;
INSTINCTIVE

involuntary movement / REFLEX

involve / WRAP; BLEND, COVER,
IMPLY, RAISE, UNITE; ENGAGE

inward / INNER; SECRET, WITHIN

inwardly / INLY; SECRETLY

inwards / INNARDS, INSIDES;
ENTRAILS. ENTAD

iodine / HALOGEN; GERMICIDE

iodine, pert. to / IODIC

iodine source / KELP

ion / ANION; CATION; MOLECULE

Ionian city / MYUS, TEOS; CHIOS,
SAMOS; PRIENE; EPHESUS,
MILETUS

Ionian island / CORFU, PAXOS,
ZANTE; ITHACA

iota / BIT, DOT, JOT; ATOM, MITE,
WHIT; GRAIN, SCRAP, SPARK,
TRACE

Iowa capital / DESMOINES

Iowa city / WATERLOO

Iowa college / COE; GRINNELL

Iowa college town / AMES

Iowa Indian / FOX, SAC; SAUK

Iowa state flower / WILDROSE

Iowa state nickname / HAWKEYE

Iowa state tree / OAK

ipse dixit / DOGMA; DICTUM

Iran / ELAM; PERSIA

Iran capital / TEHRAN; TEHERAN
Iranian / TAT; KURD; PERSIAN
Iranian city / KUM, QUM; YEZD; ABADAN, SHIRAZ, TABRIZ; BUSHIRE, ISFAHAN
Iranian language / FARSI
Iranian money / RIAL; DINAR
Iranian mountains / ELBURZ, ZAGROS
Iranian people / MEDES
Iranian ruined city / PERSEPOLIS
Iranian ruler / SHAH
Iranian Turk / SART
Iraq / IRAK; MESOPOTAMIA
Iraq capital / BAGDAD; BAGHDAD
Iraqi city / BASRA, HILLA, MOSUL
Iraqi money / DINAR
Iraqi river / TIGRIS; EUPHRATES
irascibility / IRE; ANGER, WRATH; CHOLER; PASSION
irascible / HOT; ANGRY, FIERY, HASTY, TESTY; TOUCHY; IRACUND
irate / MAD; ANGRY, WRATH, WROTH
ire / FURY, RAGE; ANGER, WRATH
Ireland / EIRE, ERIN; INNISFAIL See Eire, Irish
Ireland, pert. to / IRISH; CELTIC; HIBERNIAN
Ireland capital / DUBLIN
Ireland's ancient name / IERNE; HIBERNIA
Irene / PAX
irenic / SERENE; HENOTIC, PACIFIC; PEACEFUL; CONCILIATORY
iridescent / IRISED; OPALINE; NACREOUS
iridescent gem / OPAL; GIRASOL
iris / FLAG; ORRIS; RAINBOW
iris in heraldry / LIS
Irish / ERSE; CELTIC, TEMPER
Irish accent / BLAS; BROGUE
Irish assembly / FEIS
Irish battle cry / ABU; ABOO
Irish board game / FIDCHELL
Irish cattle / KERRY
Irish church / KIL; KILL
Irish clan / SEPT
Irish coronation stone / LIA; LIAFAIL
Irish cudgel / ALPEEN; SHILLALA; SHILLELAGH
Irish death omen / BANSHEE
Irish dirge / ULLAGONE
Irish elf / LEPRECHAUN
Irish emblem / HARP; SHAMROCK
Irish exclamation / ARU; AROO, ARRA; WHIST, WURRA
Irish fair / AONACH
Irish fairies / SHEE; SIDHE
Irish festival / SAMHAIN

Irish fort / DUN
Irish Free State / EIRE
Irish goddess of battle / BADB, BODB
Irish gods' mother / ANA, ANU; DANA, DANU
Irish hero / FINN; OSSIAN
Irish heroine / DEIRDRE
Irish hill fort / RATH
Irish hockey / HURLEY
Irish island / ARAN
Irish kingdom / MEATH; ULSTER; MUNSTER; CONNACHT, LEINSTER; CONNAUGHT
Irish kings' home / TARA
Irish knife / KHU; SKEAN, SKENE
Irish lake / LOUGH
Irish language / ERSE; CELTIC, GAELIC, KELTIC
Irish lassie / COLLEEN
Irish legalist / BREHON
Irish legislature / DAIL; SEANAD
Irish metalworker / CAIRD
Irish monk's cell / KIL; KILL
Irish peasant / KERN
Irish poet / AE; COLUM, MOORE, WILDE, YEATS
Irish rebel force / IRA
Irish saint / PATRICK
Irish sea god / LER
Irish societal estate / AIRE
Irish songfest / FEIS
Irish storyteller / SHANACHIE
Irish taboo / GEIS
Irish tribe / SIOL; CINEL
Irish variant of John / IAN; SEAN
Irish verse / RANN
Irish written characters / OGAM, OGUM; OGHAM
Irishman / PAT; AIRE, CELT; PADDY; TEAGUE; MILESIAN; HIBERNIAN
irk / IRE, VEX; TIRE; ANNOY CHAFE, WEARY; NETTLE; IRRITATE
irksome / DREARY, PLAGUY; TEDIOUS
iron / FERRUM, FETTER; MANACLE. PRESS; MANGLE, SMOOTH. FIRM, HARD; INFLEXIBLE
iron, pert. to / FERRIC; FERROUS
iron alloy / STEEL
iron casting / PIG
iron disulfide / PYRITE
iron hammer block / ANVIL
iron handed / CRUEL, HARSH
iron hearted / BRAVE; DOUGHTY
iron hook / GAFF
iron in meteorite / SIDERITE
iron ore / HEMATITE; MAGNETITE
iron oxide / RUST; HEMATITE
iron symbol / FE
ironbound / RIGID; UNYIELDING

ironclad / SAFE; UNBREAKABLE. MONITOR
ironer / MANGLE; MANGLER, PRESSER
ironic / SATIRIC; PARADOXIC
ironic composition / SATIRE
ironmongery / HARDWARE
irons / GYVES; CHAINS; FETTERS; MANACLES
ironwood / ACLE, TITI; COLIMA, MOPANE, PURIRI; BREAKAX; MESQUITE
irony / SATIRE; SARCASM
Iroquoian Indian / ERIE; HURON
Iroquois tribe / CAYUGA, MOHAWK, ONEIDA, SENECA; ONONDAGA
irrational / SURD; CRAZY, SILLY; ABSURD, UNWISE, FOOLISH, LUNATIC; DEMENTED; EXTRAVAGANT
irrational number / E; PI; SURD
irregular / WILD; EROSE, LOOSE, ATYPIC, FITFUL, UNEVEN; ERRATIC
irregular triangle / SCALENE
irregularity / JOG; ANOMALY; ROUGHNESS; ABERRATION, INFRACTION
irregularly notched / EROSE
irrelevant / FOREIGN; UNRELATED; EXTRANEOUS; IMPERTINENT
irreligious / PAGAN; WICKED; GODLESS, IMPIOUS, OPPOSED, PROFANE
irremovable / FIRM; FIXED; STABLE; LASTING, SETTLED; PERMANENT
irrespective / HEEDLESS; REGARDLESS
irreverent / AWELESS, IMPIOUS, PROFANE; UNDEVOUT; BLASPHEMOUS
irrevocable / FINAL; DECISIVE, ULTIMATE
irrigate / WATER; MOISTEN
irrigation ditch / DRAIN, FLUME; SLUICE; LATERAL
irritability / CHOLER, DANDER, TEMPER; PETULANCE
irritable / HOT; EDGY; FIERY, HASTY, TESTY; TETCHY, TOUCHY
irritable person / WASP; TARTAR
irritant / TOXIN; POISON; ALLERGEN; HISTAMINE
irritate / IRE, VEX; FRET, GALL, RILE; ANGER, ANNOY, CHAFE, GRATE, PEEVE, PIQUE, TEASE, WORRY
irritation / ITCH; PIQUE
irruption / INROAD; RUSHING
Irving character / RIP
is able / CAN
is composed / CONSISTS

is concerned / CARES
is of consequence / MATTERS
is conveyed / RIDES
is at fault / ERRS; WANDERS
is fond of / CARES, LIKES, LOVES
is not / NIS; AINT, ISNT
is suitable / FITS
is unable / CANNOT
is victorious / WINS
Isaac's son / EDOM, ESAU; JACOB
Isaac's wife / REBECCA, REBEKAH
Ishmael / EXILE; PARIAH; OUTCAST
Ishmael's mother / HAGAR
isinglass / MICA; KANTEN; GELATIN
Isis' husband / OSIRIS
Isis' realm / MOON; AMENTI
Isis' son / HORUS
Islamic / MOSLEM; MOHAMMEDAN
Islamic scripture / KORAN, QURAN; ALCORAN, ALKORAN
Islamic teacher / ALIM; MULLAH
island / OE; AIT, ALT, CAY, ILE, KAY, KEY; EYOT, HOLM, ILOT, ISLE; ATOLL, ISLET
island, pert. to / INSULAR
island in Carolines / YAP; TRUK; PONAPE
island at center of Earth / MERU
island off China / QUEMOY
island off France / IF, RE; YEU; SARK; CORSICA
island in Galway Bay / ARAN
island group / ARCHIPELAGO
island in the Hebrides / IONA, SKYE, UIST
island inhabitant / NESIOTE
island in Ionian group / CORFU, PAXOS, ZANTE; CERIGO, ITHACA
island off Ireland / ARAN, TORY; RATHLIN
island off Italy / ELBA; CAPRI; ISCHIA, LIPARI, SICILY
island off Jutland / LAESO, SAMSO
island in Micronesia / SUK; GUAM, MAUG; NAURU; BIKINI, JULUIT
island belonging to Netherlands / ARUBA
island in North Sea / TEXEL
island in Persian Gulf / KISHM, QUISHM
island in Riga Gulf / OESEL; SAREMA
island in a river / AIT, BAR; EYOT, HOLM
island source of marble / PAROS
island in the South Seas / ATOLL
island off Sumatra / NIAS, RIAU; RIOUW; BANGKA
island off Timor / MOA; LETI, ROTI
island off Tuscany / ELBA
islands in Baltic Sea / ALAND
Isle of Man / MONA

Isle of Man, pert. to / MANX
Isle of Man capital / DOUGLAS
Isle of Man judge / DEEMSTER
Isle of Man native / MANXMAN
Isle of Wight resort / RYDE; COWES
Islet / AIT, ALT, CAY; CALF, EYOT, HOLM
Ism / DOGMA; BELIEF; DOCTRINE
Ismaelian / SHIITE
Isogonic / EQUIANGULAR
Isolate / DETACH, ENSILE, ISLAND, SINGLE; INSULATE, SEPARATE
Isolated / ALONE, APART; INSULAR; DETACHED, SECLUDED, SEPARATE
Isolated hill / BUTTE
Isolated pawn / ISOLANI
Isolated steepsided hill / COMB; BUTTE, ESKER; HOGBACK
Isolation / SOLITUDE; SECLUSION
Isolde / ISOLT; YSEULT
Isolde's love / TRISTAN
Isonomy / EQUALITY
Israel / ZION; JACOB; CANAAN; PALESTINE
Israel judges' rule / KRITARCHY
Israel seaport / ACRE
Israeli city / EILAT, HAIFA; ASHDOD; TELAVIV
Israeli desert / NEGEV
Israeli legislature / KNESSET
Israeli money / AGOROT, PRUTAH
Israeli port / ELATH, HAIFA
Israelite / JEW; HEBREW
Israelite king / AHAB, ELAH, JEHU, OMRI, SAUL; DAVID, JOASH, JORAM, NADAB; BAASHA; SOLOMON
Israelite tribe / DAN, GAD; LEVI; ASHER, JUDAH; JOSEPH, REUBEN, SIMEON, ZEBULUN; BENJAMIN, ISSACHAR, NAPHTALI
Issue / EMIT, EXIT, FLOW, GUSH, POUR, RISE; ARISE, ENSUE, PRINT; EMERGE, FOLLOW, RESULT, SPRING; EMANATE, PUBLISH. END; COPY, FLUX; EVENT; EFFECT, EGRESS, OUTLET, UPSHOT; CONTEST, PROGENY
Issued in instalments / SERIAL
Issuing forth / EMANANT
Ist / ITE; FOLLOWER
Istanbul / BYZANTIUM; CONSTANTINOPLE
Istanbul section / PERA; FANAR; BEYOGLU
Isthmus / NECK
It hung in the well / BUCKET
Italian, c.f. / ITALO
Italian adventurer / CASANOVA
Italian astronomer / GALILEO

Italian atelier / BOTTEGA
Italian author / CROCE, DANTE, VERGA; CELLINI, MANZONI
Italian capital / ROMA, ROME
Italian cathedral city / PISA; MILAN
Italian cheese / BRA; ASIN; BITTO; ROMANO; RICOTTA; PECORINO; FORMAGGIO, MOZARELLA
Italian city / ALBA, ASTI, BARI, ESTE, NOLA, PISA; GENOA, MILAN, PADUA, SIENA, TRENT, TURIN; GENOVA, MILANO, MODENA, NAPLES, NAPOLI, TORINO, TRENTO, VENICE, VERONA; BOLOGNA, FERRARA, FIRENZE, LEGHORN, LIVORNO, SASSARI, SULMONA, TARANTO, TRIESTE, VENEZIA; FLORENCE
Italian coin / LIRA, LIRE; SOLDO
Italian composer / BOITO, GUIDO, VERDI; PUCCINI, ROSSINI
Italian custom house / DOGANA
Italian dance / VOLTA; TARANTELLA
Italian dictator / MUSSOLINI
Italian dish / PASTA, PIZZA; LASAGNE, RAVIOLI, RISOTTO; SPAGHETTI
Italian family / ESTE; CENCI, DORIA; BORGIA, MEDICI; COLONNA
Italian finger game / MORA
Italian game / MORA; BOCCIE
Italian inventor / MARCONI
Italian island / ELBA, LIDO; CAPRI; SICILY; SICILIA; SARDINIA
Italian judge / GIUDICE, PODESTA
Italian lake / COMO; GARDA; MAGGIORE; TRASIMENO
Italian language / OSCAN; SABINE, TUSCAN; MARSIAN
Italian marble / CARRARA
Italian money / LIRA, LIRE
Italian mountain ridge / APPENNINES
Italian noble family / ESTE
Italian painter / RENI; LIPPI, VINCI; ANDREA, CRESPI, GIOTTO, TITIAN; RAPHAEL; RAFFAELE
Italian physicist / FERMI, VOLTA; GALVANI
Italian poet / DANTE, TASSO; ARIOSTO, MONTALE; LEOPARDI; ALIGHIERI, DANNUNZIO
Italian pottery / MAJOLICA
Italian printer / ALDUS; BODONI; ARRIGHI, SONCINO
Italian red-shirt leader / GARIBALDI

Italian resort / LIDO; CAPRI; LOCARNO
Italian river / PO; ARNO, RENE; ADIGE, FIUME, PIAVE, TIBER
Italian royal family / ESTE; SAVOY
Italian sculptor / LEONI; CELLINI; DONATELLO; MICHELANGELO
Italian seaport / POLA; GENOA, GENOVA, NAPLES, NAPOLI; TRIESTE
Italian secret society / MAFIA; MAFFIA; CAMORRA
Italian singer / AMATI, BONCI, PATTI, PINZA; CARUSO, SCHIPA
Italian title / DON, SER; CONDE, DONNA; BARONE; SIGNORA, SIGNORE; CONTESSA; CAVALIERO
Italian university town / BARI, PISA; PADUA; BOLOGNA
Italian violin / AMATI, STRAD; CREMONA; GUARNIERI; STRADIVARI
Italian violin maker / AMATI; GUARNIERI; STRADIVARI
Italian volcano / ETNA; VESUVIO; VESUVIUS; STROMBOLI
Italian wine / BAROLO; CHIANTI, FALERNO, MARSALA, ORVIETO
Italian wine center / ASTI
Italic dialect / OSCAN; UMBRIAN

Italy / ITALIA; AUSONIA. See Italian
itch / PSORA; SCABIES; PRURITUS; IRRITATION
item / ENTRY; DETAIL; ARTICLE
item of business / AGENDA; AGENDUM
item of property / ASSET
item taking precedence / PRIORITY
iterate / ECHO; REPEAT; RESTATE
itinerant / ROVING; NOMADIC; WANDERING, HOBO; TRAVELER
itinerant merchant / PEDLAR; CHAPMAN, PEDDLER
itinerary / PLAN; ROUTE
itineration / EYRE, TOUR; JOURNEY
ivory / TUSK; DENTINE
Ivory Coast capital / ABIDJAN
Ivory Coast people / DAN; ANYI; BAULE; SENUFO
ivy / VINE; CLIMBER, CREEPER
ivy, pert. to / HEDERIC
Ivy League college / ELI; PENN, YALE; BROWN; COLGATE, HARVARD; COLUMBIA; DARTMOUTH, PRINCETON
ivy tree / LAUREL
Izmir / SMYRNA
Iznik / NICAEA

J

jaal / IBEX
jab / DIG; POKE; PUNCH; THRUST
Jabal's brother / JUBAL
Jabal's descendants / TENT-DWELLERS
Jabal's father / LAMECH
Jabal's mother / ADAH
jabber / GAB, YAK, YAP; TALK; PRATE; BABBLE, GABBLE, MUMBLE
Jabberwocky / RIGMAROLE
Jabberwocky word / MIMSY; BRILLIG
jabot / FRILL; RUFFLE; CASCADE
jacinth / ZIRCON; HYACINTH
jack / JUG; NOB; FLAG, HOOK, LIFT, NIBS, SPIT; HOIST, KNAVE
jack of all trades / TINKER; HANDYMAN
jack of clubs / PAM
jack in euchre / BOWER
Jack Horner's find / PLUM
Jack Ketch / HANGMAN; EXECUTIONER
jack pine / LODGEPOLE
jack pot / POT; POOL; STAKE
jack rabbit / HARE

Jack Sprat's diet / LEAN
jack up / LIFT; RAISE
jackal god / APUAT
jackal-headed god / ANUBIS
jackanapes / PRIG; COXCOMB
jackass / ASS; DOLT, FOOL; DONKEY
jackdaw / DAW; CROW; GRACKLE
jacket / COAT, ETON, JUPE, VEST; COVER; BOLERO, CASING, COATEE, JERKIN, REEFER; SPENCER; ENVELOPE
jack-in-the-pulpit / ARAD, ARUM; AROID
jackknife game / MUMBLETYPEG
Jack-o'-lantern / WILLOTHEWISP
Jack's climbing companion / JILL
Jack's giant victim / CORMORAN
Jack's ladder to the sky / BEANSTALK
jacksnipe / SNIPE; SANDPIPER
jackstone / DIB
jacobin / FRIAR; PIGEON; RADICAL
Jacob's brother / EDOM, ESAU
Jacob's daughter / DINAH
Jacob's father / ISAAC
Jacob's father-in-law / LABAN

Jacob's ladder / PHLOX; BITTER-
SWEET
Jacob's later name / ISRAEL
Jacob's mother / REBECCA
Jacob's son / DAN, GAD; LEVI;
ASHER, JUDAH; JOSEPH,
REUBEN, SIMEON; ZEBULUN;
BENJAMIN, ISSACHAR,
NAPHTALI
Jacob's twin / ESAU
Jacob's wife / LEAH; RACHEL
jade / FAG; TIRE, WEARY, WORRY;
HARASS; EXHAUST, FATIGUE
jaded / SATED; EFFETE
jaeger / SKUA; HUNTER
Jael's victim / SISERA
Jaffa / YAFO; JOPPA
jab / BARB; NOTCH
jagged / CLEFT, EROSE; UNEVEN
Jaggers' client / MAGWITCH
Jaggers' ward / PIP
jaguar / TIGER, TIGRE; LEOPARD
jai alai / PELOTA
jai alai court / FRONTON
jai alai racquet / CESTA
jail / PEN; POKEY; COOLER,
LOCKUP, PRISON; BRIDEWELL
jail sentence / RAP
jailbird / CRIMINAL, PRISONER
Jaipur's former capital / AMBER
jake / OK; GOOD; RIGHT; PROPER
Jalisco Indian / CORA; NAYARIT
Jaina residents / WHITEOAKS
jam / HOST, MASS; CROWD;
THRONG; CONSERVE, CROWD-
ING; MULTITUDE
Jamaica bitter wood / QUASSIA
Jamaica capital / KINGSTON
Jamaica cobnut / QUABE
Jamaica drink / RUM
Jamaica tourist town /
MONTEGOBAY
jamboree / SPREE; REVELRY
Jamestown's captain / SMITH
jamlike / MARMALADY
Jane Eyre hero / ROCHESTER
jangle / JAR; SPAR, SPAT; CLANG,
CLASH; BICKER; CHATTER,
DISPUTE
janitor / PORTER, SEXTON;
CARETAKER
Janizary chief / DEY
January birthstone / GARNET
Janus's month / JANUARY
Japan / NIPPON; CIPANGO
Japan work / LACQUER, VARNISH
Japanese abacus / SOROBAN
Japanese aborigine / AINO, AINU
Japanese admiral / ITO
Japanese airplane / ZERO
Japanese alphabet / KATAKANA

Japanese American / ISSEI, KIBEI,
NISEI; SANSEI
Japanese ancient capital / NARA
Japanese apricot / UME
Japanese army reserve / HOJU
Japanese art of self-defense /
JUDO; KENDO; AIKIDO, KARATE;
JUJITSU, JUJUTSU; JIUJITSU
Japanese badge / MON; KIRIMON
Japanese baron / HAN; DAIMIO
Japanese battle shout / BANZAI
Japanese bay / ISE; YEDO; TOKYO
Japanese bean paste / MISO
Japanese beetle / CHAFER
Japanese box for seal / INRO
Japanese bream / TAI
Japanese buddhist sect / ZEN
Japanese cape / YA; IRO, OKI,
OMA, TOI; DAIO, JIZO, MELA,
MINO, NOMO, SADA, SAWA,
SUZU
Japanese capital / TOKIO, TOKYO
Japanese carp / KOI
Japanese carriage / SADO;
RICKSHA; RICKSHAW;
JINRIKISHA
Japanese cedar / SUGI
Japanese celery / UDO
Japanese chess / SHOGI
Japanese city / KOBE; KYOTO,
OSAKA
Japanese clay figure / HANIWA
Japanese clogs / GETA
Japanese cooking batter /
TEMPURA
Japanese dancer / GEISHA
Japanese deity / AMIDA, AMITA
Japanese drama / NO; KABUKI,
NOGAKU
Japanese elder statesman / GENRO
Japanese emperor / MIKADO
Japanese entertainer / GEISHA
Japanese family crest / MON
Japanese fan / OGI
Japanese festival / BON
Japanese footwear / CLOG, GETA,
ZORI; HAKIMONO
Japanese game / GO; SHOGI
Japanese garment / OBI; MINO;
HAORI, HAPPI; KIMONO
Japanese gateway / TORII
Japanese hair style / MAGE;
CHOCHO
Japanese happiness god / EBISU
Japanese helmet / JINGASA
Japanese imperial city / FU
Japanese island / HONSHU,
KYUSHU; SHIKOKU; HOKKAIDO
Japanese lake / BIWA
Japanese land measure / RI, SE;
CHOBU

Japanese legislature / DIET
Japanese mackerel / SABA
Japanese mat / TATAMI
Japanese measure / MO, RI, SE, TO; CHO, KAN, RIN, SHO, TAN; KOKU
Japanese military ruler / SHOGUN
Japanese money / BU, MO; RIN, SEN, YEN; OBAN; TEMPO
Japanese mountain / FUJI, YARI
Japanese musical instrument / FUE, SHO; BIWA, KOTO; SAMISEN
Japanese national park / ASO; AKAN; NIKKO, UNZEN; DAISEN
Japanese naval victory / TSUSHIMA
Japanese news service / DOMEI
Japanese noodles / SOBA
Japanese ornament / NETSUKE
Japanese outcast / ETA; YETA
Japanese pagoda / TAA
Japanese palanquin / NORIMON
Japanese paper art / ORIGAMI
Japanese port / OSAKA; SASEBO
Japanese portable boxes / INRO
Japanese pottery / AWATA
Japanese radish / DAIKON
Japanese raw fish / SASHIMI
Japanese religion / SHINTO; BUDDHISM
Japanese rice paste / AME
Japanese rice wine / SAKE
Japanese robe / KIMONO
Japanese sash / OBI
Japanese school of painting / KANO; UKIYOE
Japanese script / KANA; KATA-KANA
Japanese scroll / KAKEMONO
Japanese seal / HAN; INGYO
Japanese seaport / OSAKA
Japanese seaweed / NORI
Japanese sect / ZEN
Japanese Shinto deity / KAMI
Japanese ship / MARU
Japanese ship title / MARU
Japanese shogunate family / TOKUGAWA
Japanese sliding door / FUSUMA
Japanese sock / TABI, TABO
Japanese sole / HIRAME
Japanese statue of Buddha / DAIBUTSU
Japanese suicide / SEPPUKU; HARAKIRI, HARIKIRI
Japanese suicide pilot / KAMIKAZE
Japanese sword / CATAN, TACHI
Japanese tidal wave / TSUNAMI
Japanese tuna / MAGURO
Japanese tunnel / KANMON

Japanese verse / UTA; HAIKU, HOKKU, TAUKA; SENRYU
Japanese vine / KUDZU
Japanese warrior class / SAMURAI
Japanese weight / MO; FUN, RIN
Japanese wine / SAKE, SAKI
Japanese woman diver / AMA
Japanese wrestling / JUDO, SUMO
Japanese writing / KANA
Japanese zodiac sign / MI; INU; TORA
Japan's first emperor / JIMMU
Japan's first shogun / YORITOMO
jape / GIBE, JEST; TRICK
Japheth's father / NOAH
Japheth's son / GOMER
Jaques' humor / MELANCHOLY
jar / JOLT; CLASH, GRATE, SHAKE, SHOCK; JANGLE, JOGGLE, JOUNCE, URN; EWER, OLLA; CRUSE
jar ring / LUTE
jardiniere / POT, URN; VASE
jargon / CANT; ARGOT, IDIOM, LINGO, SLANG, STUFF, TRASH
jasmine / BELA; PAPAW; JESSAMY
Jason's father / AESON
Jason's follower / ARGONAUT
Jason's ship / ARGO
Jason's teacher / CHIRON
Jason's wife / MEDEA
jaundiced / SOUR; YELLOW
jaunt / ROAM, TOUR, TRIP; SALLY
jaunty / GAY; AIRY; DEBONAIR
java / COFFEE
Java seaport / BATAVIA, JAKARTA; CHERIBON, SURABAYA
Java tea / MINT
Javanese city / BANDUNG
Javanese civet / RASSE
Javanese conveyance / SADO
Javanese language / KAVI, KAWI; SASSAK
Javanese pepper / CUBEB
Javanese tree / UPAS
Javanese volcano / GEDE; MERAPI, SEMERU, SLAMET
Javanese weight / AMAT, TALI
javelin / DART; ARROW, JERID, SPEAR; ASSEGAI
Javert's prey / VALJEAN
jaw / TALK; PALAVER, CHAP, CHOP; MAXILLA; MANDIBLE
jaw, c.f. / GNATHO
jaw muscle / MASSETER
jawless / AGNATHIC
jay / HAM; BUMPKIN; GREEN-HORN
jayhawker / KANSAN; GUERRILLA
Jayhawker state / KANSAS

jazz / BEAT; SYNCOPATION
jazz fiend / CAT
jealous / ENVIOUS; VIGILANT
jealousy / SUSPICION
jeans / LEVIS, PANTS; TROUSERS
jeans material / DENIM
jeer / BOO; GIBE, MOCK; FLOUT,
   SCOFF, SPURN, TAUNT, DERIDE
Jeeves's work / VALET
Jefferson document /
   DECLARATION
Jefferson home / MONTICELLO
Jehoshaphat's son / JEHU
Jehoshaphat's wife / ATHALIAH
Jehovah / GOD, JAH; YAHWEH
jehu / COACHMAN
Jehu's rival / JORAM
jejune / DRY; ARID, VOID; EMPTY
Jekyll's alter ego / HYDE
jelly basis / PECTIN
jelly fruit / BERRY, GRAPE,
   GUAVA
jelly of fruit juice and flour /
   KISSEL
jelly of meat / ASPIC
jellyfish / QUARL; MEDUSA
jellyfish's umbrella / PILEUS
jellylike stuff / GEL, GOO, JAM
jennet / ASS; HORSE; DONKEY
jeopardize / IMPERIL; ENDANGER
jeopardy / RISK; PERIL; DANGER
jeremiad / LAMENT
Jeremiah's friend / BARUCH
Jerez's famous product / SHERRY
Jericho's conqueror / JOSHUA
Jericho's failed defense / WALLS
jerk / BOB; PULL, YANK. SPASM
jerked beef / JERKY; CHARQUI
jerkwater / PETTY; BACKWARD
jerky / SUDDEN; SPASMODIC
jerky motion / BOB; HITCH
Jeroboam's father / NEBAT
jerry / HAT, POT
jerrybuilt / FLIMSY
Jersey's capital / STHELIER
Jerusalem / ZION; SALEM
Jerusalem artichoke / GIRASOL
Jerusalem hill / SION, ZION
Jerusalem mosque / OMAR
Jerusalem oak / AMBROSE
Jerusalem thorn / RETAMA;
   CATECHU
Jerusalem's destroyer /
   NEBUCHADNEZZAR
Jess / LEASH, STRAP; RIBBON
jessamine / JASMINE, JESSAMY
Jesse's daughter / ABIGAIL
Jesse's father / OBED
Jesse's son / DAVID, ELIAB
Jessica's lover / LORENZO
jessur / DABOIA, DABOYA;
   SERPENT

jest / FUN; GAME, JAPE, JOKE,
   QUIP; CRANK, HUMOR, QUIRK,
   SALLY
jester / WAG; FOOL, MIME;
   CLOWN
jester's garment / MOTLEY
Jesuits' founder / LOYOLA
Jesus / LAMB; CHRIST, SAVIOR;
   SAVIOUR; REDEEMER
Jesus' home / NAZARETH
jet / JUT; GUSH; SHOOT, SPOUT,
   SPRAY, SPURT; STREAM
jet vapor / CONTRAIL
jetty / MOLE, PIER, QUAY; WHARF
Jew / HEBREW, SEMITE;
   ISRAELITE
jewel / GEM; BIJOU, PEARL, STONE
jewel mounting / PAVE; BEZEL
jewel set / PARURE
jeweled headdress / TIARA;
   DIADEM
jeweler's weight / CARAT, KARAT
Jewish / JUDAIC. See also Hebrew
Jewish ascetic / ESSENE
Jewish benediction / SHEMA
Jewish dispersion / DIASPORA
Jewish doxology / KADDISH
Jewish festival / PURIM, SEDER;
   SUCCOTH
Jewish high priest / ELI
Jewish language / LADINO;
   YIDDISH
Jewish Law / TORAH
Jewish lawgiver / MOSES
Jewish legendary automaton /
   GOLEM
Jewish month / AB; ADAR, ELUL,
   IYAR; NISAN, SIVAN; KISLEV,
   SHEBAT, TAMMUZ, TEBETH,
   TISHRI; HESHVAN
Jewish mystical doctrine / CABALA,
   KABALA
Jewish prayer book / MAHZOR,
   SIDDUR
Jewish quarter / GHETTO
Jewish skullcap / YARMULKE
Jewish teacher / RABBI
Jewish title of honor / RAB; GAON
Jewish weight / BATH, OMER;
   JERAH
Jews, pert. to / JUDAIC; HEBRAIC,
   SEMITIC
Jezebel's husband / AHAB
Jezebel's victim / NABOTH
jib / GIB; BALK, BOOM, SAIL
jibe / GIBE; AGREE, TAUNT
jiffy / TRICE; MOMENT, SECOND
jig / DANCE, GUIDE; FISHHOOK
jiggle / JERK, MOVE, ROCK;
   SHAKE
"Jiggs" creator / MCMANUS
jigsaw / PUZZLE; SCROLLSAW

Jilt / BETRAY, DESERT
Jim's friend / HUCK
jimson weed / DATURA; THORN-
APPLE
Jind's capital / SANGRUR
jingle / RING; CLINK. DOGGEREL
jingoism / BOBADILISM
Jingo's son / OJIN; HACHIMAN
jinn's abode / KAF
jinrikisha / RICKSHAW
jinx / HEX; JONAH; HOODOO
jipijapa hat / PANAMA
jitney / BUS; NICKEL
jiujitsu / JUDO; JUJITSU
Jizo's office / SAVIOUR
Joan of Arc / PUCELLE
Joan of Arc's birthplace /
DOMREMY
Joan's spouse / DARBY
job / HIRE, TASK, WORK; CHORE
jobber / AGENT; MIDDLEMAN
Job's comforter / BOIL; ELIHU;
BILDAD; ELIPHAZ
Job's daughter / JEMIMA
Job's friend / BILDAD, ZOPHAR;
ELIPHAZ
Job's tears / COIX; ADLAI
Jocasta's husband / LAIUS
Jocasta's son / OEDIPUS
jockey / RIDER; EQUESTRIAN
jocko / CHIMPANZEE
jocose / GAY; DROLL, FUNNY,
JOLLY, MERRY; JOCUND;
JOCULAR
jocularity / WIT; MERRIMENT
jocund / GAY; MERRY; JOVIAL,
JOYFUL, JOYOUS, LIVELY;
MIRTHFUL
jog / JOLT, PROD, PUSH, TROT
Johannesburg's region / RAND
John Bull / BRITON; ENGLISHMAN
John from Russia / IVAN
John-a-dreams / SLUGGARD
johnnycake / PONE; HOECAKE
Johnson's biographer / BOSWELL
join / ADD, PIN; ALLY, LINK, MEET,
MELD, PAIR, SEAM, TEAM,
WELD, YOKE; ANNEX, ENTER,
MERGE, UNION, UNITE;
ADHERE, ADJOIN, APPEND,
ATTACH, ENGAGE, ENLINK,
LEAGUE, SOLDER; COMBINE,
CONNECT, CONTACT, MORTISE;
COALESCE; ACCOMPANY,
ASSOCIATE, INTERSECT;
CONFEDERATE
join army / ENLIST
join wood / BUTT; RABBET
joint / DEN; SEAM; HINGE, TENON
joint of arm / ELBOW, WRIST;
SHOULDER
joint cavity / BURSA

joint component / TENON;
MORTISE
joint of finger / KNUCKLE
joint of leg / HIP; KNEE; ANKLE
joint at right angle / ELL; KNEE
jointed stem / CULM
joist / BEAM, STUD; TIMBER
joke / GAG, PUN, WIT; JAPE, JEST,
QUIP
joke with / KID, RIB; JOSH, RALLY
joker / WAG
jollification / REVEL, SPREE
jollity / MIRTH; MERRIMENT
jolly / GAY; FUNNY, MERRY,
PLUMP; BLITHE, CHEERY,
GENIAL, JOCUND
jolly boat / YAWL
Jolly Roger's color / BLACK
jolt / JAR; BUMP, JERK; SHAKE
Jonah / JINX
Jonathan's friend / DAVID
jonquil / DAFFODIL
Jordan capital / AMMAN
Jordanian dynasty / HASHEMITE
Jordanian money / DINAR
Jordanian mountain / NEBO
Jordanian river / YARMUK
Jordanian seaport / AQABA
Jordan's outlet / DEADSEA
Jordan's source / HERMON
Jo's sister / AMY, MEG; BETH
Josaphat's friend / BARLAAM
Joseph's coat / COLEUS;
OPUNTIA; AMARANTH
Joseph's father / JACOB
Joseph's master / POTIPHAR
Joseph's mother / RACHEL
josh / GUY, KID, RIB; HOAX, JOKE
Joshua tree / YUCCA; LILYTREE
Joshua's father / NUN
Josiah's father / AMON
joss / GOD; IDOL
joss house / TEMPLE
jostle / JOG; JOLT, PUSH; ELBOW,
NUDGE; HUSTLE, THRUST;
INCOMMODE
jot / ACE, BIT; ATOM, IOTA, MITE,
WHIT; GRAIN, SPECK; TITTLE
jot down / NOTE
Jotunn / GIANTS
jounce / BUMP, JOLT; SHAKE
journal / LOG; DIARY, PAPER
journalist / EDITOR; REPORTER
journey / HIKE, ITER, TOUR, TREK,
TRIP, JAUNT; VOYAGE
journey on circuit / EYRE
journey on foot / HIKE; TRAMP
joust / JUST, TILT; CLASH;
COMBAT
jousting arena / LISTS
Jove / JUPITER
jovial / GAY; GLAD; JOLLY, MERRY

joviality / GLEE; BLISS, CHARM, MIRTH; GAIETY
joy / GAIETY; DELIGHT, ECSTACY, ELATION, RAPTURE
joyful / GAY; GALA, GLAD; ALIVE, HAPPY, MERRY, RIANT; BLITHE
joyful hymn / CAROL, PAEAN; ANTHEM, TEDEUM
joyless / DEAD, DULL; UNHAPPY
Juan Fernandez inhabitant / SELKIRK
Juba's wife / SELENE
Jubate / MANED
jubilance / ELATION, TRIUMPH
jubilant / JOYOUS; EXULTANT
jubilee / FESTIVAL; CELEBRATION
Judah's capital / JERUSALEM
Judah's father / JACOB
Judah's king / ASA; JOSIAH
Judah's mother / LEAH
Judah's son / ER; ONON; SHELAH
Judas / APOSTLE, TRAITOR; INFORMER, ISCARIOT
Judas elephant / KOOMRIE
Judas tree / GALLOWS
Judean king / HEROD
Judean procurator / PILATE
judge / TRY; DEEM, DOOM, RATE; OPINE, THINK. JURAT, TRIER; CRITIC, UMPIRE; ARBITER
judge in Hades / MINOS; AEACUS; TRIPTOLEMOS; RHADA-MANTHUS
judge's chamber / CAMERA
judge's circuit / EYRE, ITER
judge's robe / GOWN, TOGA
judgment / DOOM, VIEW; AWARD, SENSE; WISDOM
judicial order / WRIT
judicious / COOL, SAGE, WISE; SOBER, SOLID, SOUND, STAID
Judith's husband / MANASSES
Judith's victim / HOLOPHERNES
judo / JIUJITSU
Judy's husband / PUNCH
jug / EWER, JAIL, TOBY; CRUSE
Juggernaut location / PURI
juggler / FAKIR; MOUNTEBANK
jugglery / DECEIT; CHEATING
Jugoslavian / See Yugoslavian
Jugurtha's conqueror / MARIUS
Jugurtha's stepfather / MICIPSA
juice / SAP; FLUID; LIQUID
juicy / MOIST, SAPPY; LUSCIOUS
juicy part of fruit / PULP
jujitsu / JUDO
jujube / ELB, BER; LOZENGE
Jules Verne character / NEMO; ROBUR
Julian's epithet / APOSTATE
Juliet's father / CAPULET
Juliet's fiance / PARIS
Juliet's lover / ROMEO

Julius Caesar's eulogist / ANTONY
Julius Caesar's last words / ETTUBRUTE
Julius Caesar's slayer / BRUTUS
July birthstone / ONYX, RUBY; TURQUOISE
July flower / GILLY; GILLIFLOWER
jumble / PI; MIX, PIE; CAKE, HASH, MESS, OLIO
jumbled type / PI; PIE
jumbo / BIG; HUGE, VAST
Jumna tributary / KEN; SIND; BETWA
jump / HOP; LEAP, SKIP; BOUND, CAPER, START, VAULT. BODICE
jumper / WIRE; BLOUSE, JACKET
jumping amphibian / FROG, TOAD
jumping frog county / CALAVERAS
jumping frog's owner / SMILEY
jumping stick / POGO
junco / FINCH; SNOWBIRD
junction / UNION; LINKING
junction line / SEAM; JOINT
junction of rivers / CONFLUENCE
juncture / UNION; CRISIS
June birthstone / AGATE, PEARL; MOONSTONE
June bug / DOR
Juneberry / SERVICEBERRY
jungle / BRUSH, TREES; FOREST
jungle beast / CARNIVORE
Jungle Book author / KIPLING
Jungle Book hero / MOWGLI
Jungle Book python / KAA
Jungle Book tiger / SHEREKHAN
jungle cat / LION; TIGER, TIGRE; JAGUAR; LEOPARD
Jungle of Sinclair / STOCKYARDS
jungle trek / SAFARI
junior / CADET; YOUNGER; BEGINNER
juniper / CADE, EZEL, PINE; GORSE, LARCH, RETEM, SAVIN
junk / ROPE; CABLE; SCRAPS
junket / CURD; FEAST; PICNIC
Juno / UNI; HERA
Juno's bird / PEACOCK
Juno's husband / JUPITER
Juno's messenger / IRIS
Juno's tears / VERVAIN
junta / COUNCIL; ASSEMBLY
junto / CABAL; CLIQUE; FACTION
Jupiter / JOVE, ZEUS; AMMON
Jupiter's consort / JUNO
Jupiter's daughter / VENUS; MINERVA
Jupiter's father / SATURN
Jupiter's moon / IO; EUROPA; CALLISTO, GANYMEDE
Jupiter's mother / OPS
Jupiter's son / ARCAS; CASTOR
Jupiter's temple / CAPITOL
Jurassic animal / DINOSAUR

Jurgen's trade / PAWNBROKER
juridical / LEGAL; JUDICIAL
jurisdiction / LAW, SOC; SOKE;
    VENUE; DISTRICT; AUTHORITY
jurisprudence / LAW; CODE
juror / ASSIZER; TALESMAN
jury list / PANEL
just / DUE, FIT; FAIR, TRUE;
    EXACT, MORAL, RIGHT. BARELY,
    EXACTLY
justice / LAW; JUDGE; EQUITY;
    FAIRNESS; RECTITUDE
justice of the peace / JP; SQUIRE;
    MAGISTRATE
justifiable / DEFENSIBLE

justify / EXCUSE; WARRANT
Justinian's book / PANDECTS
justly / RIGHTLY
justness / LAW; ORDER, RIGHT
jut / BULGE; PROJECT; PROTRUDE
jute / DESI, HEMP; BURLAP
jute fabric / TAT; MATS; GUNNY
Jutland island / FIN; MOEN
jutty / JETTY
Juvenal's forte / SATIRE
juvenile / YOUNG; JUNIOR,
    YOUTHY
juvenile murder / TEENICIDE
juxtaposition / CONTACT
jynx / WRYNECK

K

K in baseball / STRIKEOUT
K in chess / KING
kaaba location / MECCA
kaama / HARTEBEEST
kabob / CABOB
Kaffir corn / MILLET
Kaffir language / XOSA; XHOSA
Kaffir tribe / ZULU; BANTU
kafta / KAT
kalak / CANOE
kaikai / FOOD, GRUB; TUCKER
kale / BILLS; MONEY; CABBAGE
kali / POTASH; GLASSWORT
Kaliningrad's former name /
    KONIGSBERG
kalmuck / ELEUT
Kalymnos' capital / POTHEA
Kama's mount / SPARROW
Kama's wife / RATI
kanaka / HAWAIIAN; POLYNESIAN
Kandahar's rescuer / ROBERTS
kangaroo / JOEY; BOOMER
kangaroo bear / KOALA
Kansas capital / TOPEKA
Kansas city / IOLA; TOPEKA;
    ABILENE, WICHITA
Kansas City settlement / WEST-
    PORT
Kansas explorer / CORONADO
Kansas river / SALINE;
    REPUBLICAN
Kansas state animal / BUFFALO
Kansas state flower / SUNFLOWER
Kansas State football team /
    WILDCATS
Kansas state nickname / JAYHAWK
Kansu's capital / LANCHOW
kaolin / CLAY
kaput / DOOMED, RUINED
karagan / FOX; CORSAC
Karakorum's founder / GENGHIS-
    KHAN
Karel Capek opus / RUR
Karelian lake / ONEGA

Karelian town / KEM
Karnak's neighbor / LUXOR
Kashgar / SHUFU
Kashmiri alphabet / SARADA
Kashmiri language / DARD;
    KHOWA, SHINA; PISACA
Kashmiri town / LEH; SRINAGAR
kat / KAFTA
Kate's tamer / PETRUCHIO
Katrina's suitor / BROM; ICHABOD
Kauai town / LIHUE; HANALEI
Kaunas / KOVNO, KOWNO
kauri tree / PINE; KAWAKA
kava / AVA; DRINK; PEPPER
kayak / CANOE
Kay's father / ECTOR
Kazakhstan capital / ALMAATA
Kazan inhabitants / TATARS
Keats poem / LAMIA
keck / HEAVE, RETCH, VOMIT
kedge / WARP; ANCHOR
keek / SPY; PEEP
keeker / SPY; PEEPER
keel / FIN; CAREEN; CAPSIZE
keel part / SKEG
keel-billed cuckoo / ANI
keelboat / BARGE
keelless / RATITE
keel-shaped structure / CARINA
keen / FINE, NICE; ACUTE, EAGER,
    QUICK, SHARP; ARDENT,
    BITING. DIRGE
keenly / POIGNANTLY
keenness / ACUMEN
keep / HOLD; GUARD, HONOR,
    LODGE
keep from action / HOLD; DETER
keep apart / DIVIDE; SEPARATE
keep away from / HIDE; AVOID
keep back / HOLD; DETER; DETAIN
keep clear / SHUN; AVOID;
    ESCHEW
keep close / HUG; HOLD
keep control / HOLD

keep custody / DETAIN
keep going / CONTINUE
keep from occurring / PREVENT
keep order / GUARD; POLICE
keep out / BAR; EXCEPT; EXCLUDE
keep from proceeding / DETER
keep from progressing / DELAY
keep quiet / REST; SHUTUP
keep in repair / SERVICE
keep from shaking / STEADY
keep in store / RESERVE
keep tally / COUNT, SCORE
keep waiting / DETAIN
keep watch / SPY; GUARD
keeper / GUARD; JAILER, WARDEN
keeper of marches / MARGRAVE
keeper of park / RANGER
keeping / CARE; CHARGE;
  CUSTODY
keepsake / RELIC, TOKEN;
  MEMENTO
keeve / TUB, VAT; KIVER
kef / DRUG; LANGUOR; NARCOTIC
keg / CASK; BARREL, FIRKIN
kegler / BOWLER
Keijo / SEOUL
kelep / ANT
kelp / WRACK; SEAWEED
kelp ashes / VAREC
keltic / MANX; IRISH, SCOTS,
  WELSH; BRETON, CELTIC;
  CORNISH
ken / DEN; RESORT; KNOWLEDGE
Kenilworth's lord / DUDLEY;
  LEICESTER
kennel / LAIR; GUTTER;
  DOGHOUSE
Kent city / CANTERBURY
Kentish fire / APPLAUSE
Kentish king / ETHELBERT
Kent's county seat / MAIDSTONE
Kentucky bluegrass / POA
Kentucky capital / FRANKFORT
Kentucky city / PARIS; LEXINGTON
Kentucky college / BEREA
Kentucky football team / WILD-
  CATS
Kentucky horse race / DERBY
Kentucky native / CORNCRACKER
Kentucky state flower / GOLDEN-
  ROD
Kentucky state nickname / BLUE-
  GRASS
Kenya capital / NAIROBI
Kenya city / KISUMU
Kenya lake / RUDOLF
Kenya language / SWAHILI
Kenya river / TANA
Kenya seaport / MOMBASA
Kenya tribesman / LUO; MASAI;
  KIKUYU, MAUMAU
kerb / CURB

kerchief / MADRAS; BANDANA;
  BABUSHKA, BANDANNA,
  KAFFIYEH; HEADCLOTH
Keres indian / SIA, ZIA; ACOMA
kermess / FESTIVAL;
  ENTERTAINMENT
kern / BOOR; PEASANT
kernel / NUT; CORE, SEED; GRAIN
kerosene / COALOIL, LAMBOIL
kestrel / HAWK
keta / OOGSALMON
ketch / YACHT; VESSEL
ketchup / SAUCE; CATSUP
ketone / CARONE; ACETONE
kettle / POT; VESSEL; CALDRON
kettle of fish / MESS; PICKLE
kettledrum / NAKER; ATABAL,
  TIMBAL; TIMPANI
kevel / BOLLARD
key / CAY; CLEF, CLUE, ISLE;
  CLAMP GUIDE, ISLET, PITCH
key fruit / SAMARA
Key of the Mediterranean /
  GIBRALTAR
key notch / WARD
key to raise pitch / DITAL
keyboard / MANUAL
keyed up / AGOG
keyhole guard / TAPPET
keynote / PITCH. FUNDAMENTAL
key-shaped / URDE, URDY;
  CLECHE
Keystone State / PA; PENNA;
  PENNSYLVANIA
khaki / ORAB; CLOTH; UNIFORM
khan / AGA, ALI, INN; CHIEF;
  PRINCE; GOVERNOR;
  CARAVANSARY
khanjee / OVERSEER
Khartoum's conqueror / MAHDI
khatti / HITTITE
Khond earth goddess / TARI
Khond language / KUI
kiang / ASS; ONAGER
Kiangsi capital / NANCHANG
kibe / CHILBLAIN; INFLAMMATION
kibosh / HUMBUG; NONSENSE
kick / BOOT, PUNT; RECOIL
kick the bucket / DIE
kicker / REBEL; PUNTER;
  OBJECTOR
kid / BOY, KIP; GOAT; CHILD
kidnap / STEAL; ABDUCT, DETAIN
kidney bean / BON
kidney stone / JADEITE; NEPHRITE
kidneys, pert. to / RENAL
Kikuyu deity / MOGAI
Kilauea's goddess / PELE
Kilauea's mountain / MAUNALOA
kill / SLAY; DEADEN, DEFEAT,
  MURDER. PREY; CREEK
kill with stones / LAPIDATE

killed / SLEW; SLAIN

killer / ASSASSIN, MURDERER

killer of Achilles / PARIS

killer whale / ORC; ORCA; GRAMPUS

killing of close relative / PARRICIDE

killing of father / PATRICIDE

killing of king / REGICIDE

killing of mother / MATRICIDE

killing of wolf / LUPICIDE

Kilmer's famous poem / TREES

kiln / OST; OAST, OVEN; HEATER

kilt / PLAID; FILIBEG; PHILIBEG

Kimberley mine / DEBEERS

kimono sash / OBI

kin / AFFINITY, RELATION, RELATIVE

kind / ILK, SET; TYPE, SORT. GOOD; BENIGN, GENTLE, TENDER

kind of — / See principal noun

kind act / FAVOR

kindergarten / SCHOOL; NURSERY

kindle / BURN, FIRE, FUME, GLOW

kindly / BENIGN; AMIABLE

kindred / KIN, SIB; FAMILY

kine / COWS; CATTLE

king / REX, REY, ROI; CARD

king, pert. to / REGAL, ROYAL; REGNAL

King Arthur's abode / CAMELOT

King Arthur's death place / CAMLAN

King Arthur's father / UTHER; PENDRAGON

King Arthur's father-in-law / LEODOGRANCE

King Arthur's fool / DAGONET

King Arthur's half-sister / MORGAUSE, MORGAWSE

King Arthur's lance / RON

King Arthur's last home / AVALON

King Arthur's mother / IGERNE, IGRAIN, YGERNE, IGRAINE, IGRAYNE

King Arthur's nephew / GAWAIN, MODRED, MORDRED

King Arthur's seneschal / KAY

King Arthur's shield / PRIDWIN

King Arthur's sister / MORGAN; MORGANA

King Arthur's sword / EXCALIBUR

King Arthur's wife / GUINEVER; GUINEVERE

King of Bath / NASH

king of beasts / LION

king of birds / EAGLE

king cobra / SNAKE

king crab / LIMULUS; HORSESHOE

King Ethelred / UNREADY

King of fairies / OBERON

king of the forest / OAK

king of fresh-water fish / SALMON

king of golden touch / MIDAS

King Gradlon's capital / IS, YS

King of Huns / ATLI; ETZEL; ATTILA

king of the jungle / LION

King of Kings / GOD; CHRIST

King Lear's daughter / REGAN; GONERIL; CORDELIA

King Lear's dog / TRAY

king of metals / GOLD

King of Midian / EVI, HUR, ZUR

king of Pylos / NESTOR

king topper / ACE

king of the underworld / DEVIL, HADES, PLUTO, SATAN

king of waters / AMAZON

kingdom / RULE; REALM; EMPIRE

kingdom of Alexander / MACEDONIA

kingfish / CERO, HAKE, OPAH; CERRO; SIERRA; MACKEREL

kingly / GRAND, REGAL, ROYAL

kingmaker / WARWICK

kings of Cologne / MAGI

king's evil / SCROFULA

king's fruit / MANGOSTEEN

kings of Orient / MAGI

king's steward / DAPIFER

kink / WHIM; TWIST; CROCHET

kink in thread / BURL, KNOT

kinkajou / POTTO; HONEYBEAR

kinky / QUEER; TWISTED; ECCENTRIC

kinsfolk / SIB; KINDRED; RELATIONS

kinship / NASAB

kinsman / SIB; RELATION, RELATIVE

kiosk / BANDSTAND, NEWSSTAND

kip / SKIN; BROTHEL, LEATHER

kippeen / CANE; STICK; CUDGEL

kipper / SALMON; HERRING. CURE

Kirghiz capital / FRUNZE; PISHPEK

kiri / CLUB; STICK; KNOCKERRIE

kirn / HARVESTHOME

kirtle / PETTICOAT

kismet / FATE; DESTINY

kiss / BUSS; SMACK, TOUCH; CARESS, SALUTE; OSCULATE

Kiss sculptor / RODIN

kist / BOX; CHEST

kit / SET, TUB; BROOD, TOOLS; FAMILY, OUTFIT, VIOLIN

Kit-Cat portrait painter / KNELLER

kitchen / BUT; GALLEY; SCULLERY

kitchen duty / KP

kitchen fixture / OVEN, SINK; RANGE; ICEBOX; REFRIGERATOR

kitchen linen / APRON, TOWEL

kitchen midden / JOMON

kitchen of ship / GALLEY

kitchen stove / RANGE
kitchen utensils / PAN, POT;
   CORER, DICER, FRIER, LADLE,
   MIXER, RICER, SCOOP; BEATER,
   FUNNEL, GRATER, JUICER, KET-
   TLE, OPENER, PEELER;
   ROASTER, SPATULA, TOASTER;
   COLANDER
kitchener / COOK; RANGE;
   SERVANT
kite / GLED, SAIL, SOAR; GLEDE.
   ELANET
kite part / RIB; TAIL
kith / KIN; FRIENDS, KINDRED
kittenish / GAY; GIDDY; PLAYFUL
kittiwake / GULL, WAEG
kitty / CAT, PET; POOL; KITTEN
kivu / TETSE; TEETSE, TZETZE
kiwi / APTERYX
kiyoodle / CUR, DOG; MONGREL
Klamath sucker / YEN
Klan / KKK
klaxon / HORN. HONK
klieg eyes / EDEMA; INFLAMMA-
   TION
knack / ART; HANG; SKILL, TRICK
knaggy / KNOTTY
knap / BITE, KNOB, SNAP, TALK
knapsack / BAG; SACK
knarl / KNAG, NODE; GNARL,
   KNURL
knave / CAD; JACK; CHEAT,
   ROGUE, SCAMP; RASCAL,
   VARLET; VILLAIN
knave of clubs / PAM
knave in cribbage / NOB
knavish / TRICK; ROGUISH
knead / ELT; MOLD; MASSAGE
knee / BEND, GENU; KNEEL,
   JOINT
knee bone / DIB; PATELLA
knee joint in fowl / HOCK
kneecap / ROTULA; KNEEPAN,
   PATELLA
kneel / BEND; GENUFLECT
knee-length garment / TUNIC
kneeler / WORSHIPER
kneeling bench / PRIEDIEU
knell / BELL, OMEN, RING, TOLL
knickerbockers / BREECHES
knickknack / PRETTY, TRIFLE;
   TRINKET; GIMCRACK,
   KICKSHAW
knife / BOLO, CHIV, DIRK, SHIV,
   SNEE; BLADE, BOWIE; BARLOW,
   BODKIN, CARVER, CUTTER,
   DAGGER; MACHETE, MACHETTE,
   STILETTO. STAB
knife case / SHEATH; SCABBARD
knife to cut loops in pile /
   TREVAT, TREVET, TRIVAT,
   TRIVET

knife dealer / CUTLER
knife sharpener / HONE
knight / EQUES; GALLANT,
   PALADIN
Knight of La Mancha / QUIXOTE
knight of the road / HOBO;
   TRAMP
Knight of the Swan / LOHENGRIN
knighthood / RANK; DIGNITY
knight's cloak / MANTLE, TABARD
knight's fight / JOUST
knight's title / SIR; CAVALIER
knight's wife / DAME, LADY
knit / DRAW, JOIN, MEND;
   WEAVE
knitted blanket / AFGHAN
knitted fabric / TRICOT
knitted garment / SWEATER
knitting instrument / NEEDLE
knitting machine guide / SLEY
knitting stitch / PURL; BACKSTITCH
knitting yarn / WORSTED
knob / BOSS, HILL, LUMP, NODE
knob in medicine / TUBERCLE
knobbed / KNOBBY, NODOSE,
   TOROUS
knobkerrie / CLUB, KIRI; STICK
knock / HIT, RAP; BEAT; DRIVE
knock lightly / RAP, TAP
knockabout / YACHT. BOISTEROUS
knockdown / IRRESISTIBLE
knocked down / SOLD; FLOORED
knocker / KNOB; HINGE; RAPPER
knock-knee / XLEG; INKNEE,
   VALGUS
knockout / KO; PIP; KAYO
knoll / HILL; MOUND; HILLOCK
knop / BOSS, KNOB, STUD;
   BUTTON
knot / LUMP, MILE, NODE, SNAG;
   GNARL, GROUP, KNURL, NODUS
knot in fiber / NEP; NOIL, NURL
knot of hair / BUN, RAT; CHIGNON
knot lace / TAT, TIE; TATT
knot in wood / BURL, GNAR, KNAR
knotless / ENODAL
knotted / NODED; ENTANGLED
knotted lace / MACRAME,
   TATTING; KNOTTING
knotted rope / NOOSE
knotty / NODAL; GNARLY, NODOSE
knout / WHIP; SCOURGE
know / KEN, WIS, WOT; DISCERN
knowing / HIP; WISE; AWARE;
   SHREWD; CUNNING; INFORMED
know-it-all / ORACLE; QUIDNUNC,
   WISEACRE
knowledge / KEN; LORE; OLOGY,
   SKILL; WISDOM; SCIENCE;
   LEARNING
knowledge, pert. to / GNOSTIC
known / ACCEPTED; RECOGNIZED

knuckle / YIELD; SUBMIT. JOINT
knucklebone / DIB, DIE; TALUS; COCKAL; ASTRAGALUS, HUCKLEBONE
knucklebones / DOLOS
knur / KNOT; DWARF
Knut / CANUTE
koala's diet / EUCALYPTUS
kobold / NIS; DWARF, KNURL, NISSE; GOBLIN, SPRITE; HOBGOBLIN
Koch's lymph / TUBERCULIN
kodak / CAMERA
Kohinoor / DIAMOND
kohlrabi / CABBAGE
kokoon / GNU
Kol dialect / HO
Komodo dragon / VARANUS
kopeck / COIN; COPEK, KOPEK
kopje / KOP; HILLOCK
Koran chapter / SURA
Koran scholars / ULAMA, ULEMA
Koran teacher / MUFTI; MULLAH
Korea / CHOSEN
Korean alphabet / HANGUL
Korean apricot / ANSU
Korean capital / KEIJO, SEOUL; PYONGYANG

Korean city / PUSAN
Korean county / KUN
Korean ex-president / RHEE
Korean money / WON; CHON
Korean mountain / PAEKTU
Korean port / PUSAN
Korean river / YALU
kosher / PURE; CLEAN; KASHER
kosher opposite / TREF
Kra tribal group / GI; KRUMAN
kraken / MONSTER, OCTOPUS
Krazy Kat's creator / HERRIMAN
Krishna's people / YADAVA
Kriss Kringle / SANTACLAUS
Kruman tribal group / GI; KRA
Krupp gun / CANNON
Krupp works location / ESSEN
K-2 / GODWINAUSTEN
Kublai's capital / CAMBALUC
Kublai's grandfather / GENGHIS
Kui / KANDH
Kuomintang department / YUAN
Kurile inhabitant / AINU
kurrajong / CALOOL
kurume / AZALEA
Kusan Indian / COOS
Kuwaiti lamb dish / QUZI
Kyushu volcano / ASO; ASOSAN

L

L.A. phenomenon / SMOG
La Boheme heroine / MIMI
La Brea fossil / SABRETOOTH
La Fontaine's forte / FABLE
La Mancha's knight / QUIXOTE
La Paz's mountain / ILLIMANI
lab / LABORATORY
Laban's daughter / LEAH; RACHEL
labarum / BANNER
labba / PACA
label / TAG; MARK; BRAND, STAMP; DOCKET. TAB; PASTER; CODICIL
labial / LIPLIKE
labial malformation / HARELIP
labile / UNSTABLE
labor / MOIL, MOVE, ROLL, TOIL, WORK; EXERT, PITCH; SUFFER; TRAVAIL. PAIN, TASK; DUTIES, EFFORT; DRUDGERY, EXERTION; CHILDBIRTH, DIFFICULTY
labor duty / FATIGUE
labor group / GUILD, UNION; BROTHERHOOD
labor hard / STRIVE
labor union / AFL, CIO, ELA, ILA, ITA; ILGWU; AFLCIO
labor union branch / LOCAL
labor union symbol / BUG; BUTTON
labor weapon / STRIKE
laboratory culture medium / AGAR

laboratory vessel / RETORT; ALEMBIC; CRUCIBLE, TEST-TUBE
labored / HEAVY, STIFF; STUDIED; ELABORATE; OVERWROUGHT
labored breath / GASP, PANT
laborer / MAN; HAND, PEON, SERF; NAVVY; TOILER, WORKER; WORKMAN; EMPLOYEE, OPERATOR; OPERATIVE; WORKINGMAN
laborious / ACTIVE, TRYING; ARDUOUS, ONEROUS, TEDIOUS; DILIGENT, SEDULOUS, TIRE-SOME, TOILSOME; DIFFICULT, FATIGUING, WEARISOME
Labrador harbor / NAIN; HOPE-DALE
Labrador lake / DYKE; LOBSTICK
Labrador tea / LEDUM
labyrinth / MAZE; DAEDAL; INTRICACY
labyrinth inventor / DAEDALUS
lac / RESIN; VARNISH
laccolith / INTRUSION
lace / TIE; BEAT, BIND, LASH, TRIM; FASTEN, THREAD; INTERWEAVE. NET, VAL; CLUNY, FILET; ALENCON, BINDING, MALINES, MECHLIN, POTLACE; TRIMMING

lace edging / FRILL, PICOT
lace opening / EYELET
lace pattern / TOILE
lace ruffle / JABOT
lace scarf / MANTILLA
lace of square holes / FILET
lacerate / CUT, RIP, REND, TEAR;
SEVER, WOUND; CLEAVE,
MANGLE, HARROW
lace's tip / AGLET
lacet / BRAID
laches / NEGLIGENCE
Lachesis' chore / SPINNING
Lachish conqueror / JOSHUA
lachrymose / SAD; TEARFUL
lacing / THRASHING; SHOE-
STRING
lacing string / THONG
lack / NEED, WANT; DEARTH,
FAMINE; DEFICIT, FAILURE;
SCARCITY
lack of activity / INERTIA
lack of appetite / ASITIA
lack of difficulty / EASE
lack of discipline / LAXITY
lack of energy / FLATNESS
lack of good qualities / EVIL;
BADNESS; OFFENSIVENESS
lack of harmony / DISCORD
lack of money / IMPECUNIOUS-
NESS
lack of muscular coordination /
ATAXIA
lack of sophistication / NAIVETE
lack of tone / ATONY
lackadaisical / BLAH; PENSIVE
lackey / FLUNKY, WAITER;
FOOTMAN; ATTENDANT
lacking / SHY; ABSENT, DEVOID;
NEEDFUL; DESTITUTE
lacking money / BROKE
lacking spirit / LAZY, POKY;
LISTLESS
lacking stiffness / LIMP; FLACCID;
FLEXIBLE
lacking strength / SOFT, WEAK;
FEEBLE, PLIANT
lacking tonic key / ATONAL
Laconian cape / MATAPAN
Laconian clan subdivision / OBE
Laconian range / TAYGETUS
Laconian river / EUROTAS
Laconia's capital / SPARTA
laconic / CURT; BRIEF, PITHY,
SHORT, TERSE; COMPACT,
CONCISE; SUCCINCT, VIGOROUS
laconism / EPIGRAM
lacquer / LAC; JAPAN
lacquered metalware / TOLE
lactescent / MILKY
lacuna / GAP, PIT; SPACE, HIATUS,
HOLLOW

lad / BOY; YOUTH; STRIPLING
Ladakh capital / LEH
Ladakh mountains / KARAKORAM
ladder / STEPS; STEPLADDER
ladder in hosiery / RUN
ladder part / RUNG
ladder for scaling wall / SCALADE,
SCALADO; ESCALADE,
ESCALDDO
ladderlike / SCALAR
lade / DIP; BAIL, LOAD, STOW;
HEAVE, THROW; BURDEN;
FREIGHT
la-di-da / FOP; DANDY, SWELL;
COXCOMB
ladle / CUP, DIP; SCOOP, SPOON;
DIPPER
Ladon's charge / APPLES
Ladon's slayer / HERCULES
ladrone / THIEF; BANDIT, PIRATE,
ROBBER; BRIGAND; GUERRILLA
Ladrones / MARIANAS
Ladrones island / GUAM; SAIPAN
Ladrones native / CHAMORRO
lady / BIBI, DAME, MARY; WOMAN;
FEMALE; MISTRESS, SHRIMATI
Lady of Christ's / MILTON
Lady Day / ASSUMPTION;
ANNUNCIATION
Lady of the Lake / ELLEN, NIMUE;
VIVIAN
ladybird / BEETLE, INSECT;
LADYBUG
ladyfish / WRASSE; TENPOUNDER
ladykiller / DANDY, FLIRT;
COXCOMB; CASANOVA
ladylike / GENTEEL, REFINED
ladylove / SWEETHEART
lady's bower / CLEMATIS
lady's handbag / CABAS, PURSE
lady's headdress / COIF; CROWN,
TIARA; DIADEM, WIMPLE;
CHAPEAU; MANTILLA
lady's maid / ABIGAIL
lady's outer garment / ROBE;
SIMAR
lady's slipper / ORCHID
lady's sunshade / PARASOL
lady's thumb / PEACHWORT
Laelaps' master / CEPHALUS
Laertes' father / POLONIUS
Laertes' sister / OPHELIA
Laertes' son / ULYSSES;
ODYSSEUS
lag / IDLE, SLOW; DELAY, TARRY,
TRAIL; DAWDLE, FALTER,
LINGER, LOITER. FELON;
JAILBIRD, LOITERER
Lagash king / GUDEA
lager / BEER
laggard / IDLER; LOITERER.
SLOW; REMISS; BACKWARD

lagniappe / TIP; BONUS
lagoon / LAKE, POND, POOL;
LIMAN
lagostoma / HARELIP
Lahore garden / SHALIMAR
laic / CIVIL; AMATEUR, SECULAR;
NONPROFESSIONAL
laid / LINED
laid out flat / PORRECT
lair / DEN, ROW; CAVE; HAUNT;
COVERT, GROTTO; SHELTER
lair of badger / EARTH
lair of deer / LIGGING
lair of fox / EARTH
lair of hare / FORM
laissez faire / FREEDOM; FREE-
REIN; NONINTERFERENCE
laissez faire proponent /
PHYSIOCRAT
laity / LAYMEN, PEOPLE
Laius' son / OEDIPUS
Laius' wife / JOCASTA
lake / LOCH, MERE, POND;
LAGOON
lake, pert. to / LACUSTRINE
lake city / CHICAGO
lake fish / BASS, CHUB, PIKE;
PERCH, SMELT, TROUT;
BURBOT, POLLAN, SAUGER;
CRAPPIE; BLUEGILL, GRAYLING,
STURGEON; NAMAYCUSH;
MUSKELLUNGE
Lake George / HORICON
Lake poet / SOUTHEY; COLE-
RIDGE; WORDSWORTH
Lake State / MICHIGAN
Lake Success organization / UN
lake tributary / INLET
lake trout / TOGUE; MACKINAW
lake of volcanic origin / MAAR
lake whitefish / CISCO, POWAN
Lakshmi's consort / VISHNU
Lakshmi's son / KAMA
Lalage / COURTESAN
lam / FLEE; WHACK
lamaist / TIBETAN
lamb / EAN, EWE, TAG; YEAN;
EANLING
lamb of God / AGNUSDEI
lamb roast / LEG; GIGOT
Lambaréné resident / SCHWEITZER
lambaste / BEAT; THRASH
lambent / GLOWING, PLAYING;
TOUCHING; FLICKERING
lambkin / LAMB; CHILD; YOUNG-
STER
lamblike / MEEK; GENTLE
Lamb's pen name / ELIA
lame / HALT, POOR, WEAK;
FEEBLE, INFIRM; HOBBLING,
UNSOUND; CRIPPLED, DIS-
ABLED; DEFECTIVE, IMPERFECT.
CRIPPLE, DISABLE

lame duck / CARRYOVER
lame walk / LIMP
lamebrain / OAF; DOLT; IDIOT
Lamech's ancestor / CAIN
Lamech's father / METHUSELAH
Lamech's son / NOAH; JABAL,
JUBAL
Lamech's wife / ADA; ZILLAH
lamellate / PLATED, SCALED
lament / CRY, RUE; MOAN, PINE,
SIGH, WAIL, WEEP; MOURN; BE-
MOAN, BEWAIL, BEWEEP;
GRIEVE, REGRET; DEPLORE.
ELEGY, LINOS; OUTCRY, PLAINT
lament for the dead / KEEN.
DIRGE, LINOS
lamia / WITCH
lamina / COAT, LEAF; BLADE,
LAYER, PLATE, SCALE; TISSUE
laminated rock / SHALE; GNEISS,
SCHIST; SANDSTONE
laminose / PLATELIKE
lamp / ETNA, GLIM; CRUSE, LIGHT,
TORCH; BURNER, LUCERN;
LANTERN
lamp black / SOOT
lamp chamber in lighthouse /
LIGHTROOM
lamp frame / STAND; CRESSET
lamp fuel / GAS, OIL; KEROSENE
lamp part / WICK; BURNER;
CHIMNEY
lamplighter / BASS, WICK; SPILL;
CALICO
lampoon / SKIT; SQUIB; SATIRE.
RIDICULE, SATIRIZE
lamprey / EEL
Lanark city / GLASGOW
Lanark river / CLYDE
lanate / HAIRY, WOOLY; LANOSE
Lancashire city / LIVERPOOL;
MANCHESTER
Lancashire group / BEATLES
Lancashire resort / BLACKPOOL
Lancashire river / MERSEY
lance / CUT; OPEN, STAB; SLASH;
PIERCE, THRUST. DART; SPEAR;
JAVELIN
lance snake / FERDELANCE
lance support / REST
lancelet / AMPHIOXUS
Lancelot's beloved / ELAINE;
GUINEVER; GUINEVERE
Lancelot's father / BAN
Lancelot's son / GALAHAD
lancer / UHLAN; HUSSAR;
LANCIER; QUADRILLE;
CAVALRYMAN
lancet / KNIFE; STYLET, TROCAR
lancewood / CIGUA
lanoinate / CUT; STAB, TEAR;
SLASH; INCISE, PIERCE;
LACERATE

land / SOIL; EARTH, SHORE, TERRA; ESTATE, GROUND; ACREAGE, COUNTRY, SURFACE. ALIGHT, ARRIVE, DEBARK; CAPTURE; DISEMBARK
land area / ACREAGE
land of bondage / EGYPT
land breeze / TERRAL
Land of Cakes / SCOTLAND
land connection / NECK
land conveyance / DEED, LIEN
land destruction / EROSION
land east of Eden / NOD
land of the erl / ASSAM
land held absolutely / ALOD, UDAL
Land of Lakes / MICHIGAN
Land League founder / PARNELL
Land of Lincoln / ILLINOIS
land lying fallow / LEA; ARDER
land mass / CONTINENT
land measure / AB; ARE, ROD; ACRE, ROOD, YOKE; METER; DECARE; SECTION
Land of the Midnight Sun / NORWAY
Land of Milk and Honey / ISRAEL
land of nod / SLEEP
land point / CAPE, SPIT
land of promise / EDEN; CANAAN, HEAVEN; PARADISE; PALESTINE
land in return for services / FEOFF
land rise / HILL
Land of the Rising Sun / JAPAN
land settler / NESTER, SOONER; COLONIST, SQUATTER
Land of the Shamrock / EIRE, ERIN; IRELAND
land spring / LAVANT
land tax register / CADASTRE
land tenure / FEU; SOCAGE; BURGAGE; GAVELKIND, LEASEHOLD
Land of the Thistle / SCOTLAND
land turtle / TORTOISE
land amid water / ISLE; ATOLL, ISLET; ISLAND; ARCHIPELAGO
land weathering / EROSION
land west of Eden / NOD
Land of the White Elephant / SIAM
landed estate / MANOR; DEMESNE
landgrabber / NESTER, SOONER; SQUATTER
landholder / LAIRD, MESNE, THANE; ZAMINDAR
landing hook / GAFF
landing place / KEY; DUMP, GHAT, PIER, PORT, QUAI, QUAY; LEVEE, WHARF; AIRPORT, STATION; PLATFORM
landing place of the Ark / ARARAT
landing slip / PIER
landloper / BEGGAR; VAGRANT; VAGABOND

landlord / HOST; LAIRD, OWNER; LEASER; BONIFACE; INN-KEEPER
landmark / COPA, MERE, TREE; CAUSE, GUIDE, HOUSE, SENAL, VILLA; ESTATE; FEATURE; BOUNDARY; WATERSHED
landmark of stones / CAIRN
landrail / CORNCRAKE
landscape / VIEW; SCENE, VISTA; SURVEY; PAYSAGE, PICTURE, SCENERY
landscape gardener / TOPIARIST
landslide / MANDATE; LANDSLIP
lane / PATH, ROAD, WYND; ALLEY; STREET; PASSAGE
lang syne / AGO; PAST, YORE
Langobard king / ALBOIN; AISTULF
language / ARGOT, VOICE; SPEECH, TONGUE; DIALECT, DICTION; UTTERANCE; EXPRESSION, VERNACULAR
language of Biblical times / ARAMAIC
language form / IDIOM
language of India / URDU; HINDI, HINDU, TAMIL; BENGALI, MARATHI; GUJARATI; HINDUSTANI
language of thieves / ARGOT
language of a trade / JARGON
langue d'oc / PROVENCAL
languid / WAN; DULL, SLOW, WEAK; FAINT, SLACK; DREAMY, TORPID; WANTING; LISTLESS, SLUGGISH; SPIRITLESS
languish / FADE, FLAG, PINE; DROOP; WEAKEN
languor / KEF; KAIF, KIFF; LASSITUDE
langur / MAHA
laniary / CANINE
lank / LEAN, SLIM, THIN; GAUNT; MEAGER, SKINNY; SCRAGGY, SLENDER
lanky / LEAN, TALL, THIN
lanose / WOOLY
lantern feast / BON; OBON
lanuginous / DOWNY
lanyard / CORD, ROPE, WAPP; THONG; LANIARD
Lao Tse's doctrine / TAO, WAY
Laocoon's father / PRIAM
Laodamia's father / ACASTUS
Laodamia's husband / PROTESILAUS
laodicean / INDIFFERENT
Laomedon's father / ILUS
Laomedon's son / PRIAM; TITHONUS
Laos battlefield / PLAINOFJARS
Laos capital / VIENTIANE; LUANGPRABANG

Laos money / KIP
Laos native / LAO, MEO; LOLO, THAI
Laos river / NGUM; MEKONG
Laotian Buddha / PRABANG
Laotian rebels / PATHETLAO
Lao-tze doctrine / TAO
lap / BEND, FOLD, LICK, ROLL; ENFOLD, UNFOLD; TRUNCATE. CIRCUIT; POLISHER; EXTENSION
lap dog / PET, POM; POODLE; PEKINESE; POMERANIAN
lapactic / LAXATIVE
lapel / FACING, REVERE, REVERS
lapidary / GEMCUTTER
lapidate / KILL; STONE
lapin / RABBIT
Lapiths' foes / CENTAURS
Lapiths' king / IXION
Lapland animal / REINDEER
Lapland lake / INARI, TORNE
Lapland peninsula / KOLA
Lapland sled / PULKA
Lapp / LAPLANDER
lapped joint / SCARF
lappet / PAN; FLAP, LOBE; LAPEL; WATTLE
Lapp's sledge / PULK; PULKA
lapse / ERR, SIN; FAIL, FALL, PASS, SINK, SLIP, VOID; GLIDE; ELAPSE; DEFAULT. COMA; ERROR; MISSTEP, MISTAKE
Laputa's residents / QUACKS
lapwing / PEWIT; HOOPOE, PLOVER, TIRWIT; TREUTARO
larboard / LEFT, PORT; LEFTHAND
larceny / THEFT; ROBBERY; STEALING
larch / TAMARAC; TAMARACK
lard / FAT; ADEPS; GREASE
larder / PANTRY; BUTTERY; PROVISIONS
large / BIG; FULL, HUGE, LONG, VAST, WIDE; AMPLE, BROAD, BULKY, GREAT; COPIOUS, IMMENSE, LIBERAL; GENEROUS, SPACIOUS; EXTENSIVE
large, c.f. / MACRO
large amount / MASS, RAFT, SCAD, SLEW; SCADS; PLENTY
large animal / COW, ELK; MULE; BISON, CAMEL, HORSE, LLAMA, MOOSE, STEER, WHALE; BEHEMOTH, ELEPHANT
large antelope / ADDAX, ELAND; IMPALA
large armadillo / TATOUAY
large artery / AORTA
large basket / HAMPER
large bell / GONG

large bird / EMU; EAGLE, HERON, STORK; OSTRICH, PELICAN
large body of land / CONTINENT
large body of water / SEA; OCEAN, RIVER
large book / TOME; FOLIO
large bottle / JAR, JUG; CARBOY
large bundle / BALE
large cask / TUN
large coffee maker / URN
large container / VAT
large deer / ELK
large dish / TUREEN; PLATTER
large dog / MASTIFF; GREATDANE
large extinct bird / MOA
large family / TRIBE
large knife / SNEE
large letter UNCIAL; CAPITAL
large lizard / IGUANA; MONITOR
large lowlands mound / TERP
large melon / CASABA
large merchant ship / ARGOSY
large mosquito / GALLINIPPER
large nail / SPIKE
large number / HOST; SCORE; GOOGOL, MYRIAD; BILLION, MILLION, ZILLION
large ornate cupboard / ARMOIRE
large parrot / KEA; MACAW
large pear / BOSC
large pill / BOLUS
large quantity / SEA; MASS
large receptacle / URN
large reptile / SAURIAN
large scale / SCUTE
large showy flower / PEONY; DAHLIA
large snake / BOA; PYTHON
large stream / RIVER
large turtle / ARRAU
large umbrella / GAMP
large wine bottle / MAGNUM
large-billed cuckoo / ANI
largely / VASTLY; GREATLY; EXTENSIVELY
larger than life-size / HEROIC
large-scale / EXTENSIVE
largess / GIFT; BOUNTY; LARGESSE
largest continent / ASIA
largest size book / FOLIO
larghetto / SLOW; SLOWLY
largo / SLOW; SLOWLY
lariat / LAZO, ROPE; LASSO, NOOSE, REATA, RIATA
larine / GULLLIKE
Larissa's river / PENEUS
lark / PRANK; FROLIC; LAVROCK, SKYLARK; ALOUETTE, SONGBIRD
larklike bird / PIPIT; TITLARK

larrikin / HOODLUM
larrup / BEAT, FLOG
larva / BOT, LOA; BOTT, GRUB, PUPA; GHOST, LEMUR, NYMPH; INSECT, MAGGOT; SPECTER, WIGGLER; NAUPLIUS; CHRYSALIS
larval frog / TADPOLE
Las Bela river / HAB
Las Vegas feature / STRIP
lascivious / LEWD; LOOSE; WANTON; LUSTFUL; LECHEROUS; LIBIDINOUS
laser / BEAM; LIGHT, PURGE
laserwort / FRANKINCENSE
lash / TIE; BEAT, BIND, FLOG, ROPE, WHIP; ABUSE, BASTE; BERATE, FASTEN, STRIKE; CENSURE, LAMPOON, SCOURGE; SATIRIZE; CASTIGATE, QUIRT, THONG; EYELASH, SARCASM
lashed / BOUND; TRICED
lasher / WEIR
lass / GIRL, MAID; MAIDEN; COLLEEN
lassitude / FATIGUE, INERTIA, LANGUOR; WEAKNESS
lasso / LINE, ROPE; MCGAY, NOOSE, REATA, RIATA; LARIAT, MECATE; CABESTRO, PASSROPE
last / FINAL; LATEST, LOWEST, UTMOST; EXTREME; HINDMOST, ULTIMATE DURE; ENDURE; CONTINUE. OMEGA; ULTIMA
Last of the Barons / WARWICK
last but one / PENULT; PENULTIMATE
last car on freight train / CABOOSE
last ditch / DESPERATION
Last of the Goths / RODERICK
last grain cut / MAG; KIRN, MARE, MELL; CLIACK; CARLINE
last honors / BURIAL
last judgment / DOOMSDAY
last letter / ZED; OMEGA
last mentioned / LATTER
last minute / CRISIS
last Mohican / UNCAS
last month / ULT; ULTIMO
last musical passage / CODA
last name / SURNAME
last part / TAILEND
last passes of matador's muleta / FAENA
Last Post / TAPS
last remnant / END
last rites / FUNERAL
Last of the Saxons / HAROLD
last section / FINIS; FINALE
last sheaf / NECK

last state of insect / IMAGO
Last Supper representation / CENA
last thing one loses / SHIRT
Last of the Tribunes / RIENZI
last to yield / DIEHARD
lasting / DURABLE, ENDURING; PERMANENT, PERPETUAL
latch / BAR; BOLT, HASP, HOOK, LOCK; CATCH, CLASP, SNECK; SECURE
latch on to / GLOM
latchet / LACE; SHOESTRING
Latchfords / SPURS
late / NEW; SLOW; TARDY; RECENT; DELAYED, OVERDUE; DECEASED
late, c.f. / NEO
late information / EXTRA; BULLETIN
lateen-rigged boat / DOW; DHOW; SETEE; MISTIC
lately / OFLATE; LATTERLY, RECENTLY
lately acquired / NEW
latent / HIDDEN, OCCULT, SECRET, UNSEEN, VEILED; DORMANT; CONCEALED INVISIBLE, LATESCENT POTENTIAL, QUIESCENT
lateral / SIDEWISE
lateral boundary / SIDE
lateral point of nose / ALARE
lateritious / BRICKRED
latex product / BALATA, CHICLE, RUBBER
lath / SLAT; STRIP
lather / FOAM, SOAP, SUDS; FROTH
latifundia workman / COLONUS
Latin / ROMAN; ROMANCE
Latin American country / CUBA, PERU; CHILE, BRAZIL, GUYANA, MEXICO, PANAMA; BOLIVIA, ECUADOR, URUGUAY; COLOMBIA, HONDURAS, PARAGUAY, SALVADOR; ARGENTINA COSTARICA, GUATEMALA, NICARAGUA, VENEZUELA; ELSALVADOR, PUERTORICO
Latin American dance / CONGA, RUMBA, SAMBA, TANGO
Latin American knife / MACHETE
Latin American money / PESO; MEDIE, MEDIO
Latin dramatist / SENECA; PLAUTUS
Latin epic / AENEID
Latin poet / OVID; HORACE; CATULLUS
Latin Quarter resident / STUDENT
Latin scholar / LATINIST

Latinus' father / FAUNUS
Latinus' mother / MARICA
latitude / RANGE, SCOPE; EXTENT, LAXITY; BREADTH
latitudinarian / LIBERAL
Latona / LETO
Latona's daughter / DIANA
Latona's son / APOLLO
latria / WORSHIP
latter / NEW; LATE; MODERN, RECENT
Latter-Day Saint / MORMON
lattice / BOWER; GRILLE; TRELLIS; CANCELLI; CROSSWORK
latticework bower / ARBOR
Latvia capital / RIGA
Latvian / LETT. LETTIC
Latvian money / LAT; SANTIM
Latvian river / AA; DVINA
Latvian town / TSESIS
laud / ADORE, EXALT, EXTOL; PRAISE; APPLAUD, COMMEND, GLORIFY, MAGNIFY, WORSHIP; EULOGIZE; CELEBRATE
laugh / CROW, JEER, MOCK, ROAR; FLEER, SNEER, SNORT, SPLIT; CACKLE, DERIDE, GUFFAW; CHORTLE, CHUCKLE
laughable / COMIC, DROLL, FUNNY, MERRY; AMUSING, COMICAL; HUMOROUS, MIRTH-FUL; LUDICROUS; RIDICULOUS
laughing / MERRY, RIANT; RIDENT
laughing animal / HYENA
laughing bird / LOON
laughing gull / PEWIT
laughing jackass / KOOKABURRA
laughingstock / BUTT
laugh-provoking / RISIBLE
laughter / HEEHAW
laughter, pert. to / GELASTIC
launch / DART, HURL, SEND; FLOAT, LANCE; PLUNGE, PROPEL. BOAT; PINNACE
launching site / PAD; STOCKS
launder / IRON, WASH
laundry aid / IRON, LINE, PINS, SOAP; DRIER; BLEACH, IRONER, MANGLE, WASHER; DETERGENT
Laura's lover / PETRARCH
laureate / EXCELLENT; PREEMINENT
laurel / BAY, IVY; FAME; CROWN, HONIR, SHRUB; DAPHNE, WREATH
lava / AA; ASH; CINDER, COULEE, LATITE, PUMICE, SCORIA; PAHOEHOE
lavage / WASHING
lavaliere / LOCKET; PENDANT; ORNAMENT
Lavater's science / PHYSIOGNOMY

lavatory / LOO; TOILET; REST-ROOM, WASHROOM
lave / LADE, WASH; BATHE, RINSE; SHOWER; CLEANSE
lavender / ASPIC
Lavengro's author / BORROW
laver / FONT
Lavinia's father / TITUS
Lavinium's founder / AENEAS
lavish / FREE; LIBERAL, PROFUSE; PRODIGAL, WASTEFUL; EXTRAV-GANT. WASTE; BESTOW, EX-PEND; SQUANDER
law / LEX, ACT; CODE, JURE, RULE, SUIT; AXIOM, CANON, EDICT, ORDER; CUSTOM, DECREE; FORMULA, JUSTICE, MANDATE, PROCESS, STATUTE; ENACT-MENT, ORDINANCE. See also legal
law, pert. to / JURAL; FORENSIC
law book / CODEX
law case / SUIT; TRIAL; ACTION; LITIGATION
law of conduct / CODE; CANON
law degree / LLB
law of male royal inheritance / SALIC
law of Moses / TORA; TORAH; PENTATEUCH
law officer / JUDGE; BAILIFF; AT-TORNEY; POLICEMAN, SOLICI-TOR
law principle / JUS
law profession / BAR
law-abiding / MEEK, MILD; GEN-TLE, HONEST; STRAIGHT; OB-SERVANT, REPUTABLE
lawbreaker / FELON; CRIMINAL
lawful / JUST; LEGAL, LEGIT, LICIT, VALID; PROPER; ABIDING; RIGHTFUL; LEGITIMATE; CON-FORMABLE, PERMISSIBLE
lawless / UNRULY; UNGOVERNED; DISOBEDIENT
lawless demonstration / RIOT
lawmaker / MP; SOLON; DEPUTY; SENATOR; LEGISLATOR
lawmaking body / DIET; SENATE; ASSEMBLY, CONGRESS; REICHSTAG; PARLIAMENT; LEGISLATURE
lawman / RANGER; SHERIFF
lawn / GLADE, GRASS, SWARD; BATISTE, CAMBRIC
Lawrence's stamping grounds / ARABIA
laws of Manu / SUTRA
lawyer / LEGIST; COUNSEL; ADVO-CATE, ATTORNEY, LEGALIST; BARRISTER, COUNSELOR, SOLI-CITOR

lawyers' fee / RETAINER
lawyers' patron saint / IVES
lax / FLAT, WEAK; LOOSE, SLACK, VAGUE; FLABBY, REMISS; RELAXED; BACKWARD, CARELESS, DILATORY, DROOPING, HEEDLESS
laxative / SALTS; PHYSIC; APERIENT; CATHARTIC, PURGATIVE
laxity / LOOSENESS
lay / BET, PUT, SET; CALM, SINK; PLACE, QUIET, STAKE, STILL, WAGER; ASSESS, CHARGE, DEVISE, IMPOSE, IMPUTE, SCHEME, SETTLE; APPEASE, ASCRIBE, CONCOCT, DEPOSIT, DEPRESS, PREPARE; CONTRIVE. SONG; DITTY; BALLAD. LAIC; NONPROFESSIONAL
lay aside / TABLE
lay away / BURY; STORE; DEPOSIT
lay bare / DENUDE, EXPOSE
lay burden upon / SADDLE; ENTRUST
lay an egg / FLOP; MISCARRY
lay figure / DOLL; IMAGE, MODEL; PUPPET
lay hidden / HIDE, LURK
lay low / HIDE
lay off / FIRE
lay up / HEAP; STORE
Layard's dig / NINEVEH
layer / BED, COT, HEN, PLY, ROW; COAT, TIER; LEVEL; LAMINA, REGION, SITTER; STRATUM. PROVINE
layer of the iris / UVEA
layer of mineral / LODE, MINE, SEAM, VEIN; STREAK; FISSURE
layer in rock / LAMMA
layer of skin / DERMA
layer of wood / PLY; VENEER
layered rock / SHALE
layman / LAIC; AMATEUR
layout / RIG; DESIGN, MAKEUP, OUTFIT; TABLEAU; EQUIPMENT, TRAPPINGS
lazar / LEPER
lazaretto / HOSPITAL; PESTHOUSE
Lazarus / BEGGAR
lazy / IDLE; INERT; AVERSE, OTIOSE, SUPINE, TORPID; DORMANT; INACTIVE, INDOLENT
lazy fellow / BUM; DRONE, IDLER; LOAFER; SLIVING; LAZZARONE
lazy Susan / TURNTABLE
Le Sage hero / GILBLAS
lea / MEAD; SWARD; MEADOW; PASTURE; GRASSLAND
leach / WASH; DRAIN; DISSOLVE; LIXIVIATE, PERCOLATE

lead / GO; HEAD, PASS; EXCEL, GUIDE, SPEND, START; ALLURE, DIRECT, ENTICE, ESCORT, INDUCE; CONDUCT, PROCEED, SURPASS; OUTSTRIP. VAN; CLUE, SHOT; METAL; BULLET; PLUMMET
lead astray / LURE; SEDUCE
lead monoxide / LITHARGE
lead ore / GALENA; CERUSSITE
lead in pencil / GRAPHITE
lead poisoning / PLUMBISM
lead runner / PACER
lead strap / REIN
lead sulphide / GALENA
lead-colored / LIVID
leaden / HEAVY; SLUGGISH
leader / COCK, HEAD; CHIEF, GUIDE, SNELL; TENDON, WINNER; PIONEER; DIRECTOR, ETHNARCH, SUPERIOR; COMMANDER, CONDUCTOR
leader of Argonauts / JASON
leader of chorus / CANTOR; PRECENTOR
leader of flock / PASTOR; SHEPHERD; BELLWETHER
leader of regiment / COLONEL
leading / CHIEF; RULING; CAPITAL, GUIDING; DIRECTING, GOVERNING, PRINCIPAL. AHEAD
leading edge / FRONT
leading group / VAN
leading lady / DIVA, STAR; HEROINE
leading man / HERO, STAR
leading part / ROLE
lead-tin alloy / CALIN, TERNE
leaf / FOIL, PAGE; BRACT, FROND, SHEET; LAMINA; FOLIAGE
leaf appendage / STIPEL; STIPULE, TENDRIL
leaf of a book / PAGE; SHEET
leaf bud / GEMMA
leaf of calyx / SEPAL
leaf of corolla / PETAL
leaf of grass / BLADE
leaf of palmyra palm / OLE; OLLA
leaf part / BLADE, STALK; PETIOLE, STIPULE
leaf pore / STOMA
leaf scale / RAMENTUM
leaf secretion / LERP
leaf vein / RIB
leaf of water lily / PAD
leaf-cutting ant / ATTA
leaflet / FLYER, FOLIO, PINNA, TRACT; FOLDER; CIRCULAR, HANDBILL
leaf-miner beetle / HISPA
leaf's curve / EPINASTY

leafstalk / PETIOLE
leafy shelter / ARBOR, BOWER, SHADE
leafy vegetable / COS; KALE; ENDIVE; CABBAGE, LETTUCE, ROMAINE, SPINACH
league / BUND, PACT; UNION; COMBINE, ENTENTE; ALLIANCE; COALITION; FEDERATION; ASSOCIATION, COMBINATION, CONFEDERACY; CONFEDERATION
league of nations / UN; BUND; ENTENTE; ALLIANCE; COALITION
League of Nations, abbr. / LOFN
Leah's father / LABAN
Leah's sister / RACHEL
Leah's son / LEVI; JUDAH; REUBEN, SIMEON; ZEBULUN; ISSACHAR
leak / DRIP, OOZE, SEEP; TATTLE
Leakey's site / OLDUVAI
lean / TIP; BEND, BEAR, CANT, HEEL, LIST, RELY, REST, TEND, TILT; SLANT, SLOPE, TRUST; CAREEN, DEPEND, REPOSE; CONFIDE, DEVIATE, INCLINE. BARE, LANK, TAME, THIN; GAUNT, SPARE; BARREN, MEAGER, SCANTY, SKINNY; PITIFUL, SCRAGGY, SLENDER, STERILE; INADEQUATE
lean to one side / CAREEN
lean pork chop / GRISKIN
Leander's sweetheart / HERO
leaning tower city / PISA
leanness / SLIMNESS; DEVIATION; INCLINATION
lean-to / SHED; SHACK; LINTER; PENTHOUSE
leap / HOP, LEP; DIVE, JUMP, SKIP; BOUND, CAPER, FRISK, LUNGE, VAULT; BOUNCE, GAMBOL, SPRING. SALTO, SAULT; CURVET; CAPRIOLE
leap a gap / SPAN
leap upon / POUNCE
leaping amphibian / FROG, TOAD
leaping marsupial / KANGAROO
learn / CON; GAIN; STUDY; MASTER; MEMORIZE; ASCERTAIN
learned / WISE; EXPERT, VERSED; ERUDITE, KNOWING, SKILLED; INFORMED, LETTERED; SCHOLARLY
learned brahmin / PUNDIT
learned person / SAGE; DOCTOR, PANDIT, PUNDIT, SAVANT; SCHOLAR; SCIENTIST

learner / PUPIL; SCHOLAR, STUDENT; BEGINNER; APPRENTICE
learning / ART; LORE; CULTURE; EDUCATION, ERUDITION, KNOWLEDGE; ATTAINMENTS, SCHOLARSHIP
Learoyd's companion / MULVANEY, ORTHERIS
Lear's daughter / REGAN; GONERIL; CORDELIA
Lear's favorite stanza / LIMERICK
lease / LET; HIRE, RENT; DEMISE; CHARTER. TENURE
lease grantor / LESSOR
leaseholder / TENANT
leash / CORD, ROPE; STRAP, THONG; TETHER
least / FEWEST, LOWEST; SMALLEST
least agreeable / WORST
least amount / MINIMUM
least costly /-CHEAPEST
least difficult / EASIEST
least original / TRITEST
least relaxed / TENSEST
leather / ELK, KID, KIP; BOCK, CALF, HIDE, NAPA, ROAN, SKIN; ALUTA, MOCHA, STRAP, SUEDE; LEVANT, OXHIDE, SKIVER, VELLUM; CANEPIN, COWHIDE. HONE, WHIP
leather, c.f. / SCYTO
leather bottle / OLPE; MATARA, MUSSUK
leather calk / CLEAT
leather cuirass / LORICA
leather footwear / PAC; BOOT, SHOE; SANDAL; JACKBOOT
leather hamper / BUFFALO
leather for heel / RAND
leather purse of Highlander / SPORRAN
leather strip / WELT; THONG
leatherback / TURTLE
leatherfish / LIJA
leatherneck / MARINE
Leatherstocking's name / BUMPPO; HAWKEYE
leather-working tool / GOUGE, PUNCH; POMMEL, SKIVER
leave / GO; EXIT, QUIT; SCRAM; DEMISE, DEPART, RETIRE, TRAVEL, VACATE; ABANDON, FORSAKE; BEQUEATH, WITHDRAW. LIBERTY, LICENSE; FAREWELL; DEPARTURE; PERMISSION
leave of absence / EXEAT
leave employment / QUIT; RESIGN
leave the flock / STRAY

leave helpless / MAROON;
STRAND; ABANDON
leave off / QUIT, STOP; CEASE,
BELAY; DESIST
leave out / CUT; OMIT, SLUR;
ELIDE
leaven / BARM; YEAST; ENZYME;
FERMENT
leaves / PAGES; FOLIAGE
Leaves of Grass author / WHITMAN
leave-talking / ADIEU, CONGE
leaving / ORT; CULL; DREGS,
RELIC, SCRAP; REFUSE;
REMAINS, REMNANT, RESIDUE;
FRAGMENT
leaving a will / TESTATE
Lebanon capital / BEIRUT
Lebanon river / LITANI; ORONTES
Lebanon town / ZAHLE; BAALBEK,
TRIPOLI
lebbek / COCO; SIRIS
lecherous / LUSTFUL
lecherous look / LEER
lectern / AMBO, DESK; PULPIT;
BOOKSTAND; ESCRITOIRE
lecture / SERMON, SPEECH;
ADDRESS; DISCOURSE,
REPRIMAND. RATE; SCOLD
lecturer / DOCENT, LECTOR;
SPEAKER, TEACHER
Leda's daughter / HELEN;
CLYTEMNESTRA
Leda's husband / TYNDAREUS
Leda's lover / SWAN, ZEUS
Leda's son / CASTOR, POLLUX;
POLYDEUCES
ledge / RIM; BERM, EDGE, REEF;
LAYER, RIDGE, SHELF
ledge behind an altar / RETABLE
ledger entry / ITEM; DEBIT;
CREDIT
Ledo Road terminus / BHAMO;
MYITKYINA
lee / SHELTER
leech / GILL; BARNACLE,
PARASITE; BLOODSUCKER
leech, pert. to / BDELLOID
leer / EYE; GAZE, LOOK, OGLE;
GLANCE
leery / WARY; SUSPICIOUS
lees / DREGS; MOTHER; SEDIMENT
lee's opposite / STOSS; WEATHER
Leeward island / SABA; NEVIS,
NIHOA, TATAA; LAYSAN;
ANTIGUA, BARBUDA; ANGUILLA,
DOMINICA; GUADELOUPE,
MONTSERRAT
left / GONE, WENT; DEPARTED.
PORT; LARBOARD
left, c.f. / LEVO; LAEVO
left after expenses / NET; PROFIT;
CLEARED
left hand / SINISTER

left-hand page / VERSO
left-handed / AWKWARD; SOUTH-
PAW; MALICIOUS
left-handed pitcher / SOUTHPAW
leftist / RED; PINKO
leftover / END, ORT; SCRAP;
REMNANT
left-winger / RED; SOUTHPAW
leg / ARM, GAM, PIN; CRUS,
GAME, HEAT, LIMB, PROP;
SUPPORT. GET, RUN; LEAVE;
VANISH
leg armor / JAMB; GREAVE;
CHAUSSES
leg bone / SHIN; TIBIA; FIBULA
leg covering / HOSE; PANTS;
PEDULE, PUTTEE, SLACKS;
STOCKING, TROUSERS;
PANTALOONS
leg joint / HIP; KNEE, ANKLE
leg joint of animal / HOCK
leg of lamb / GIGOT
leg part / CALF, KNEE, SHIN;
ANKLE, SHANK, THIGH
legacy / GIFT, WILL; BEQUEST;
TESTAMENT
legal / LICIT; LAWFUL;
LEGITIMATE. See also law
legal action / RES; ACTA, CASE,
SUIT; APPEAL; HEARING;
JUDGMENT, REPLEVIN;
LITIGATION
legal attachment / LIEN
legal bar to action / ESTOPPEL
legal charge / DUE, FEE; FINE
legal claim / LIEN
legal contest / TRIAL
legal deed / ACT; EDICT; ACTION;
MANDATE, PROCESS;
JUDGMENT; ENACTMENT;
PROCEEDING
legal defense / PLEA; ALIBI;
DEMURRER, REBUTTAL;
OBJECTION
legal delay / MORA; CONTINUANCE
legal document / DEED, LIEN,
NOTE, WRIT; LEASE, ORDER;
EXHIBIT, MANDATE; MORTGAGE,
SUBPOENA
legal example / PRECEDENT
legal offense / TORT; CRIME,
DELIT, MALUM; DELICT,
FELONY; VIOLATION;
MISDEMEANOR
legal official / JUDGE; LAWYER,
NOTARY; BAILIFF; DEFENDER;
PROSECUTOR
legal possession / SEISIN, SEIZIN;
DEMESNE
legal profession / BAR, LAW
legal suit for many / CLASSACTION
legal thing / RES
legal warning / CAVEAT

legally binding / VALID
legally permitted / LICIT
legatee / HEIR; HEIRESS; RECIPIENT
legation / EMBASSY
legend / MYTH, SAGA, TALE; FABLE, STORY; CAPTION, FICTION; INSCRIPTION
legend on the cross / INRI
legendary bird / ROC; SIMURGH
legendary founder of Rome / REMUS; ROMULUS
legerdemain / MAGIC; SLEIGHTOFHAND
leggings / GAITERS, PUTTEES
Leghorn / LIVORNO
legible / CLEAR; DISTINCT, READABLE
legion / ARMY; GROUP; SOCIETY; MULTITUDE
legion's division / COHORT; MANIPLE
legislate / ENACT; EFFECT
legislation / ACT, LAW; CODE; CANON, EDICT; ASSIZE; STATUTE
legislator / SOLON; SENATOR; LAWMAKER; CONGRESSMAN
legislature / DIET; HOUSE; SENATE; CONGRESS; PARLIAMENT
legitimate / FAIR, REAL, TRUE; LEGAL, LICIT, VALID; LAWFUL; CORRECT, DEDUCED, GENUINE; BEGOTTEN; WARRANTED
legitimate theater / DRAMA
leg-like part / CRUS
legman / REPORTER
leg-of-mutton sleeve / GIGOT
Legree / SLAVEDRIVER
legume / PEA, POD, UVA; BEAN; PULSE; LENTIL, LOMENT; LIMA-BEAN
Leibniz' invention / CALCULUS
Leicester's family name / DUDLEY
Leicester's wife / AMYROBSART
Leiden's printing family / ELZEVIR
Leif's father / ERIC
leister / SPEAR; TRIDENT
leisure / EASE, REST; OTIUM; REPOSE; FREEDOM. SPARE-TIME
leitmotif / MOTIF, THEME
Leix river / NORE
lemma / THEME; PREMISE
lemon grass / RUSA, SIRI
lemon yellow / CHLOR; ORPIMENT
lemonlike fruit / LIME, CITRON
lemur / LORI, MAKI, VARI; AVAHI, INDRI, LORIS, POTTO; AYEAYE, COLUGO, GALAGO, MONKEY, SIFAKA, SPIRIT

Lena city / YAKUTSK
Lena tributary / ALDAN, VITIM
lend / LOAN; GRANT; FURNISH
lend a hand / AID; ASSIST
lene / MUTE; SMOOTH; UNASPIRATED
length / REACH; EXTENT; DURATION; LONGITUDE
length, c.f. / LONGI
length of life /AGE; YEARS
length measure / PIK; FOOT, INCH, MILE, SPAN, YARD; METER, METRE, VERST; ARSHIN, MICRON, PARSEC; KILOMETER, LIGHTYEAR
lengthen / EKE; EXTEND; PROLONG, STRETCH
lengthwise thread / WARP
lengthy / LONG; PROLIX; TEDIOUS, VERBOSE; TIRESOME; WEARISOME
lenient / MILD, SOFT; GENTLE, PLACID, TENDER; CLEMENT; SOOTHING
Leningrad museum / HERMITAGE
Leningrad's bay / KRONSHTADT
Leningrad's former name / PETROGRAD
Leningrad's river / NEVA
lenitive / MILD; EMOLLIENT
lenity / MERCY; MILDNESS
lens / GLASS; MENISCUS
lens-shaped seed / LENTIL
lent / FAST; CAREME; QUADRAGESIMA. AFFORDED
lentigo / EPHELIS; FRECKLE
Leon river / DUERO
Leonardo's teacher / VERROCCHIO
Leonidas defended it / THERMOPYLAE
Leonora's husband / FLORESTAN
Leonora's pseudonym / FIDELIO
leopard / PARD; PANTHER
Leopoldville / KINSHASA
Lepanto's victor / DONJOHN
leper / LAZAR; OUTCAST
Leper King / BALDWIN
lepers' hospital / LAZARETTO
lepers' island / MOLOKAI
Leporello's master / GIOVANNI
leporine / HARELIKE
leprechaun's secret / TREASURE
leprechaun's trade / COBBLING
leprous / LEPROSE; LEPROTIC
lerot / DORMOUSE
Lesbia's poet / CATULLUS
Lesbos poet / SAPPHO; ALCAEUS
Lesbos town / MYTILENE
lesion / SORE; INJURY
Lesotho / BASUTOLAND
Lesotho capital / MASERU
Lesotho chieftain / MOSHESH

Lesotho money / RAND
less / MENO, POCO; FEWER, MINOR, MINUS; SMALLER
less, pref. / MIS
less adulterated / PURER
less convincing / LAMER
less than deadly / NONFATAL
less than elegant / SEEDY
less hazardous / SAFER
less jaded / FRESHER
less populous / SPARSER
less undignified / SOBERER
less well off / POORER
lessee / RENTER, TENANT
lessen / BATE, EASE, WANE; ABATE, LOWER, TAPER; REDUCE, SHRINK; ABRIDGE, DEPLETE, DWINDLE; DECREASE, DIMINISH, MITIGATE, PALLIATE
lessening of pace / SLOWUP; SLOWDOWN
Lessing character / NATHAN
lesson / LECTURE; EXERCISE
lesson of fable / MORAL
lest / EXCEPT, UNLESS
let / HIRE, OMIT, RENT; ALLOW, GRANT, LEASE; ENABLE, HINDER, PERMIT, SUFFER; ABANDON; DISCHARGE; RELINQUISH. OBSTACLE; IMPEDIMENT
let bait bob / DIB, DAP
let down / LOWER, RELAX
let fall / DROP
let go / FIRE, FREE; UNHAND; RELEASE
let go to pot / NEGLECT
let in / ADMIT
let it stand / STA; STET
let out / EMIT

let up / REST, STOP; ABATE, CEASE
lethal / FATAL; DEADLY
lethargic / DULL; INERT; DROWSY, SLEEPY, TORPID; COMATOSE, SLUGGISH
lethargy / COMA, SOPOR; APATHY, STUPOR, TORPOR; INERTIA; DULLNESS, INACTION, LAZINESS; INDOLENCE, INERTNESS, STUPIDITY, TORPIDITY
lethe / DEATH; OBLIVION
Leto's daughter / ARTEMIS
Leto's father / COEUS
Leto's mother / PHOEBE
Leto's son / APOLLO
letter / MAIL, NOTE; SYMBOL; EPISTLE, MESSAGE, MISSIVE; CHARACTER
letter carrier / MAILMAN, POSTMAN
letter of challenge / DEFI, DEFY; CARTEL
letter by letter / LITERATIM
letter from pope / BULL; BRIEF; ENCYCLICAL
letterhead / STATIONERY
letter's cross stroke / SERIF
letters of marque recipient / PRIVATEER
letters patent / LICENSE
lettuce / COS; ENDIVE; ICEBERG, ROMAINE
Levant / EAST
Levantine garment / CAFTAN, KAFTAN
Levantine headdress / FEZ; TURBAN
Levantine lute / OUD
Levantine madder / ALIZARI

LETTERS, ENGLISH

	Plural
CEE	CEES
DEE	DEES
EFF	EFFS
GEE	GEES
AITCH	AITCHES
EYE	EYES
JAY	JAYS
KAY	KAYS
ELL	ELLS
PEE	PEES
CUE	CUES
ESS	ESSES
TEE	TEES
VEE	VEES
WYE	WYES
ZEE	ZEES

Levantine measure / DRA, PIK
Levantine vessel / BUM; DHOW, SAIC; XEBEC; SETTEE
Levantine wind / SHAMAL; KHAMSIN
levee / DIKE, DYKE, PIER, QUAY; DURBAR; RECEPTION
level / CALM, EVEN, FLAT; EQUAL, FLUSH, PLAIN; SMOOTH; HORIZONTAL. AIM; RASE, RAZE; GRADE, PLANE. LINE; EQUALITY, STANDARD
level cut on hillside / TERRACE
level forestless tract / STEPPE
level surface / PLANE
level-headed / CALM, COOL, SANE
leveling piece / SHIM
lever / BAR, PRY; PEVY; CRANK, PEAVY, PEEVY; HANDLE, PEAVEY, PEEVEY, TAPPET; CROWBAR
lever in a loom / LAM
leviathan / WHALE
Leviathan's author / HOBBES
levigate / POLISH, SMOOTH; PULVERIZE
Levi's father / JACOB
levi's manufacturer / STRAUSS
Levi's son / KOHATH, MERARI; GERSHON
levitate / RISE; FLOAT
levite / DEACON
levity / GAIETY, VANITY; CONDUCT; FRIVOLITY, GIDDINESS, LIGHTNESS; VOLATILITY
levulose / SUGAR; FRUCTOSE
levy / TAX; SEIZE; ASSESS, CHARGE; COLLECT. CESS; IMPOST
Lewis Carroll / DODGSON
Lewis Carroll character / ALICE
lexicographer / DRUDGE, EDITOR; COMPILER; ONOMASTIC
lexicon / WORDBOOK; DICTIONARY, VOCABULARY
lexiphanic / SESQUIPEDALIAN
Leyte capital / TACLOBAN
Lhasa palace / POTALA
Lhasa's country / TIBET
liability / DEBT; OBLIGATION
liable / APT; BOUND; EXPOSED, OBLIGED, SUBJECT; ANSWERABLE; ACCOUNTABLE, RESPONSIBLE
liable to punishment / GUILTY
liable to taxation / RATABLE
liaison / CONTACT; INTIMACY
liana / CIPO, VINE
liang / TAEL
liar / FIBBER; ANANIAS; PREVARICATOR
libation / POTION; SACRIFICE

libel / ACCUSE, CHARGE, DEFAME, INJURE, MALIGN; ASPERSE, LAMPOON, SLANDER. CALUMNY; ROORBACK
liber / BOOK
liberal / FREE, LEFT; BROAD; REFINED; ABUNDANT, CATHOLIC, ECLECTIC, GENEROUS, TOLERANT; BOUNTEOUS, BOUNTIFUL, PLENTIFUL; CHARITABLE, MUNIFICENT
liberal gift / BOUNTY; LARGESS; LARGESSE
liberate / FREE; RANSOM, REDEEM; DELIVER, MANUMIT, RELEASE; EMANCIPATE
Liberator / BOLIVAR
liberators / FREERS
Liberia capital / MONROVIA
Liberian city / SINO; HARPER
Liberian river / CESS, MANO
Liberian tribe / GI; KRA, KRU, VAI; GOLA; BASSA
libertine / RAKE, ROUE; DEBAUCHEE
liberty / LEAVE; FREEDOM, LICENSE; IMMUNITY; FRANCHISE
libido / ID
Libra / SCALES; BALANCE
librate / VIBRATE, OSCILLATE
libretto / BOOK, TEXT; SCORE, WORDS; SCRIPT
Libya capital / TRIPOLI; BENGHAZI
Libyan area / FEZZAN
Libyan desert / HAMRA
Libyan gulf / SIDRA
Libyan measure / DRA, PIK; DRAA
Libyan oasis / SEBHA
Libyan town / HOMS; DERNA; GADAMES
Libyan tribesman / SENUSSI
lice-infested / LOUSY
license / ABUSE, GRANT, LEAVE, RIGHT; EXCESS, PERMIT; AUTHORITY; PERMISSION
licentious / LAX; LOOSE; IMMORAL, LUSTFUL; UNCHASTE, UNCURBED; DEBAUCHED, DISSOLUTE, LECHEROUS; LASCIVIOUS, PROFLIGATE
lichen / MOSS, RASH; ECZEMA, FUNGUS; PARELLA, PARELLE; EPIPHYTE
licit / LEGAL; LAWFUL
lick / LAP; BEAT, FLOG; CHASTISE, VANQUISH
lickerish / LECHEROUS
lickspittle / TOADY; BOOTLICKER
licorice bean of India / JEQUIRITY
licorice pastille / CACHOU

licorice seed / GOONCH
licorice stick / CLARINET
lictor's emblem / FASCES
lid / CAP, HAT, TOP; FLAP; COVER;
  OPERCULUM
lie / FIB; FICTION, UNTRUTH;
  DELUSION, ILLUSION; FALSE-
  HOOD. LEAN, REST; PLACE;
  RECLINE; PREVARICATE
lie about / BASK, LOLL
lie in ambush / HIDE, LURK
lie face down / PRONATE
lie face up / SUPINATE
Liechtenstein capital / VADUZ
Liechtenstein money / FRANC;
  RAPPEN
lief / FAIN; FREELY, GLADLY
liege / LORD; VASSAL; OVERLORD;
  SOVEREIGN
lien / CLAIM
lieu / PLACE, STEAD
lieutenant / AIDE
life / BIOS; BIOTA; CAREER,
  MEMOIR, SPIRIT; CONDUCT,
  HISTORY, SOCIETY; ACTIVITY,
  VITALITY, VIVACITY; ANIMA-
  TION, BIOGRAPHY, BRISKNESS,
  EXISTENCE
life, c.f. / BIO
life, pert. to / VITAL; BIOTIC
life chain / DNA
life essence / ATMAN, OUSIA
life of the party / ANIMATOR
life preserver / SAP; COSH, VEST;
  MAEWEST; LIFEBUOY; BLACK-
  JACK
life raft / BALSA
life of Reilly / LUXURY
life science / BIOLOGY
life story / BIO; VITA; BIOGRAPHY
lifebelt filling / KAPOK
lifeboat crane / DAVIT
lifeless / DEAD, DULL, TAME;
  AMORT, AZOIC, INERT; TORPID;
  DEFUNCT, EXTINCT, INSIPID,
  PASSIVE; LISTLESS, SLUGGISH
lifelike / TRUE; REALISTIC
lifesaver / LIFEGUARD
lifetime / AGE; YEARS
lift / AID, PRY; BOOST, ELATE,
  ERECT, EXALT, HEAVE, HOIST,
  RAISE, STEAL; ELEVATE.
  ELEVATOR
lift high / EXALT
lift with lever / PRY
lift price / UP; RAISE
lifting implement / JACK; CRANE,
  HOIST, LEVER, TONGS;
  ELEVATOR
ligature / TIE; BAND, BOND;
  TAENIA; BANDAGE, DIGRAPH;
  LOGOTYPE

light / GAY; AIRY, EASY, PALE;
  CLEAR, DIZZY, LEGER, LOOSE;
  BRIGHT, FICKLE, NIMBLE, POR-
  OUS, SLIGHT, SPONGY; BUOY-
  ANT, WHITISH; GRACEFUL,
  TRIFLING, UNCHASTE;
  UNSUBSTANTIAL. GUIDE;
  IGNITE, ILLUME, KINDLE;
  INFLAME; BRIGHTEN;
  IRRADIATE. ARC, DAY; LAMP,
  PANE; GLEAM, FLASH, KLEIG,
  KLIEG, TAPER, TORCH; ASPECT,
  WINDOW; LANTERN; ILLUMINA-
  TION
light, c.f. / LUCI, PHOT; PHOTO
light and airy / ETHEREAL
light anchor / KEDGE
light beam / LASER
light boat / YAWL; CANOE, SKIFF;
  WHERRY; SHALLOP
light brown / TAN
light carriage / GIG; SHAY; BUGGY,
  SULKY; CALASH, CHAISE,
  SURREY; PHAETON
light cigar / CLARO
light circle / HALO, NIMB;
  CORONA, NIMBUS; AUREOLA,
  AUREOLE
light coat / ALPACA, DUSTER
light gray / ASH
light hammer / MALLET
light helmet / POT; MORION,
  SALLET; BASINET
light hit / BUNT
light machine gun / STEN
light material / GAUZE; COTTON;
  BATISTE, ETAMINE; PARAMATTA
light meal / TEA; BITE; SNACK;
  COLLATION
light medieval cannon / ROBINET
light missile / PELLET
light opera / OPERETTA
light overcoat / TOPCOAT
light racing boat / SCULL, SHELL
light rain / HAZE, MIST; SHOWER;
  DRIZZLE
light reflector / MIRROR
light science / OPTICS
light shade / PASTEL
light shoes / SANDALS; SLIPPERS
light signal / GO; STOP; FLARE,
  FLASH; LANTERN
light style / AIRINESS
light tan / ECRU; BEIGE; ALMOND
light touch / DAB, PAT, PET
light unit / LUX, PYR, RAD; PHOT;
  LUMEN; CANDLE, CARCEL,
  HEFNER; LAMBERT
light weight / OUNCE
light wood / BALSA
light wool fabric / ALPACA
light yellow / BUFF

lighter / BOAT, SCOW; BARGE, SPILL
lightest / AIRIEST
lightface's opposite / BOLDFACE
lightheaded / DIZZY, GIDDY; DELIRIOUS, FRIVOLOUS
lighthearted / GAY; LIVELY; VOLATILE; SPRIGHTLY
light-heavyweight / CRUISER-WEIGHT
lighthouse / FANAL, PHARE; BEACON, PHAROS
lighting implement / BULB; TORCH; CRESSET
lightless / UNLIT
lightly colored / TINTED
lightly cooked / RARE
lightning / BOLT, LAIT; FLASH, LEVIN
lightning bug / FIREFLY
lightning chess / BLITZ
lightning rod / GROUND; ARRESTER; CONDUCTOR
lightning rod inventor / FRANKLIN
light-refracting lens / PRISM
lights / LUNGS
lights out signal / TAPS
light-tube gas / NEON; ARGON
lightweight rider / JOCKEY
ligneous / WOODY; WOODEN, XYLOID; LIGNOSE; LIGNESCENT
lignite / WOODCOAL
lignose / LIGNIN; CELLULOSE
likable / PLEASING
like / ENJOY; ADMIRE, PREFER, RELISH. SORT; COUNTERPART. AKIN; EQUAL; SIMILAR; DISPOSED; RESEMBLING. AS; PROBABLY
like, suffix / IC; INE, ISH, OID
like better / PREFER
like a flash / SPEEDY
like a modest girl / DEMURE
like a sponge / POROUS
like the sun's satellites / PLANETARY
like tiles / TEGULAR
likelihood / CHANCE; PROBABILITY
likely / APT; COMELY; CREDIBLE, PROBABLE, SUITABLE; SEEMINGLY. PROBABLY
liken / COMPARE
likeness / COPY, ICON; IMAGE; EFFIGY; PICTURE; PORTRAIT; FACSIMILE
likewise / SO; EKE, TOO; ALSO; DITTO; BESIDES; MOREOVER
likewise not / NOR
liking / BENT, BIAS, WISH; DESIRE; LEANING; FONDNESS, TENDENCY

lilac color / MAUVE; LAVENDER
lilies of France / FLEURDELIS
Liliom's girl friend / JULIE
Lilith's man / ADAM
Lilith's successor / EVE
lilliputian / TINY; PIGMY
lilt / SWING; CADENCE
lily / LIS, LYS; ALOE, ARUM, IXIA; CALLA, LOTUS, NIOBE, ONION, TULIP, WOKAS, YUCCA
lily maid of Astolat / ELAINE
lily of Utah / SEGO
lily-livered / COWARDLY
limaciform / SLUGLIKE
Lima's port city / CALLAO
limb / ARM, LEG; EDGE, HAND; BOUGH; BORDER, BRANCH
limb appendage / ENDITE
limber / LITHE; PLIANT; PLIABLE
limbless / ACOLOUS
limbo / OBLIVION; PURGATORY
lime / CLAY; SNARE; CITRUS; BIRDLIME; LIMESTONE
lime hound / LYAM; BLOODHOUND
lime tree / BASS, TEIL, TEYL; LINDEN
lime tree bark / BAST
limelight / GLARE; SPOTLIGHT
limen / THRESHOLD
limestone mineral / CALCITE
limestone variety / CHALK; MARBLE
limicoline bird / SNIPE; AVOCET, CURLEW, PLOVER; SANDPIPER
limit / END, FIX; BOUND, CHECK, STENT, STINT; CONFINE, ISOLATE; INSULATE, RESTRAIN, RESTRICT; CIRCUMSCRIBE. POLE, TERM; BOURN; BORDER, BOURNE, EXTENT; BOUNDARY, SOLSTICE; HINDRANCE, RESTRAINT; OBSTRUCTION, RESTRICTION
limit of tree growth / TIMBERLINE
limited / FINITE
limited amount / ALLOWANCE
limited by time / TEMPORAL; TEMPORARY
limivorous / MUDEATING
limn / DRAW; PAINT; DEPICT, SKETCH; ILLUSTRATE
Limoges product / PORCELAIN
limp / LAX; SOFT; FLABBY, LIMBER; FLACCID, HALTING; FLEXIBLE. CLOP; FALTER, HOBBLE
limpid / PURE; CLEAR, LUCID; BRIGHT; CRYSTAL; PELLUCID; TRANSLUCENT, TRANSPARENT
limulus / KINGCRAB
lin / FLAX, LINN; LINDEN; WATERFALL

Lincoln assassin / BOOTH
Lincoln's biographer / SANDBURG
Lincoln's first vice president / HAMLIN
Lincoln's general / GRANT
Lincoln's law partner / HERNDON
Lincoln's mother / NANCY
Lincoln's opponent in debate / DOUGLAS
Lincoln's photographer / BRADY
Lincoln's private secretary / HAY
Lincoln's Secretary of State / SEWARD
Lincoln's Secretary of War / STANTON
Lincoln's wife / MARYTODD
linden / LIN; BASS, LIME, LINN, TEIL, TEYL; BASSWOOD
line / ROW; CORD, MARK, RANK, REIN, TIER; CLASS, ROUTE, STRIA, VERSE; COURSE, EXTENT, LENGTH, LETTER, STRING; EQUATOR, LINEAGE; BOUNDARY; PEDIGREE; DIRECTION; OCCUPATION. RULE; STREAK; OUTLINE
line, pert. to / LINEAR
line of battle / FRONT
line with brick / REVET
line at bus stop / QUEUE
line in circle / RADIUS; DIAMETER
line of descent / LINEAGE
line to fasten sail / EARING
line in geometry / CHORD
line of hills / RIDGE
line to hydrant / HOSE
line the inside / CEIL
line of junction / HEM; SEAM
line of light / BEAM
line made by folding / CREASE
line of mowed grain / SWATH
line of persons / CUE; RANK; QUEUE
line of poem / STICH
line of poetry / VERSE
line of revolution / AXIS
line with soft material / PAD
line of soldiers / FILE, RANK; COLUMN
line with stone / STEEN
line of succession / DYNASTY
line in trigonometry / SECANT; TANGENT
line on weather map / ISOBAR
line where compass points true north / AGONE
lineage / LINE, RACE; BIRTH, BLOOD, BREED, HOUSE, STOCK; FAMILY, STRAIN; PROGENY; ANCESTOR, ANCESTRY, PEDIGREE; GENEALOGY; EXTRACTION, PROGENITOR; DESCENDANTS

lineament / FEATURE, OUTLINE
lined up / AROW
lineman / END; GUARD; CENTER, TACKLE; BLOCKER, WIREMAN; SURVEYOR; INSPECTOR, REPAIRMAN
linen / CREA, FLAX, LAWN; CLOTH, CRASH, SCRIM, TOILE; DAMASK, DOWLAS, NAPERY, SHEETS; CAMBRIC, HOLLAND, NAPKINS; LINGERIE; UNDERWEAR; TABLECLOTH
linen fuzz / LINT
linen plant / FLAX
linen scraps / LINT
linen tape / INKLE
linen vestment / ALB; AMICE
linens closet / EWERY
linen-wool cloth / LINSEYWOOLSEY
liner / SHIP; LINING; STEAMSHIP
lines of different colors / STRIPES
lines on lens / GRATING, RETICLE; RETICULE; CROSSHAIRS
lines like spokes / RADII
lineup / TEAM; MUSTER; FORMATION
ling / COD; HAKE; BURBOT; HEATHER
linger / LAG; STAY, WAIT; DALLY, DELAY, HOVER, TARRY; DAWDLE, LOITER; SAUNTER
linger too long / OVERSTAY
lingerie / LINEN; UNDERWEAR; UNDERCLOTHING
lingering, as illness / CHRONIC
lingo / CANT; ARGOT; JARGON; DIALECT; LANGUAGE
lingua / GLOSSA; PROBOSCIS
lingua franca / PIDGIN
linguist / POLYGLOT; PHILOLOGIST
liniment / BALM; ARNICA, LOTION
lining material / SILK; PAPER; SATEEN
lining of a well / STEAN, STEEN
link / TIE; BIND, JOIN, LOCK, YOKE; CHAIN, UNITE; ATTACH, COUPLE, FASTEN; CONJOIN, CONNECT; CATENATE; INTERLOCK. BOND, LOOP, RING; NEXUS, TORCH; CONNECTION
linos / DIRGE
Linotype inventor / MERGANTHALER
linseed / FLAXSEED
lint / FUZZ; FLUFF; DRESSING
lion / LEO; SIMBA; CARNIVORE
lion cub / LIONET
Lion of God / ALI
lion group / PRIDE
lion monkey / TAMARIN; MARMOSET

lion of zodiac / LEO
lioness-headed goddess / SEKHMET
lion-headed consort of Ra / MUT; MAUT
lion-headed god / NEFERTUM
lion-hearted / BRAVE; COURAGEOUS
lion-like / LEONINE
lion's companion / UNICORN
lion's foot / EDELWEISS
lion's hair / MANE
lion's share / BEST, MOST
lion's tooth / DANDELION
lion-tailed macaque / WANDEROO
lip / RIM; BRIM, EDGE; BORDER, LABIUM, SPEECH, KISS; UTTER
lip, pert. to / LABIAL
lip ornament / LABRET
liparous / FATTY, OBESE; LIPOID
lipped / LABIATE
liquefied by heat / FUSIL; FUSILE
liquefy / RUN; HEAT, MELT, THAW; RENDER
liqueur / ANIS, MARC; AURUM, CREME, NOYAU; GENEPI, KIRSCH, KUMMEL, STREGA; CORDIAL, CURACAO, QUETSCH, RATAFIA; ABSINTHE, ALKERMES, ANISETTE; COINTREAU; CHARTREUSE; BENEDICTINE
liquid / SOFT; CLEAR, FLUID; DULCET, SMOOTH; FLOWING
liquid container / CAN, KEG, SEA; LAKE, PAIL, POND, POOL, TANK, VIAL; GLASS; BARREL, BOTTLE, BUCKET; TUMBLER
liquid dose / POTION
liquid explosive / NITRO
liquid fat / OIL; ELAIN, OLEIN; ELAINE; FURFURAL
liquid ketone / ACETONE
liquid loss / LEAK
liquid measure / OZ, PT, QT; GAL; PINT; MINIM, OUNCE, QUART; GALLON
liquid pitch / TAR
liquid preparation / LOTION
liquidate / PAY; KILL; CLEAR; ADJUST, SETTLE; AMORTIZE; DISCHARGE; EXTINGUISH
liquidless / ANEROID
liquids, pert. to / HYDRAULIC
liquor / ALE, GIN, RUM, RYE; ARAK, GROG, RAKI; DRINK, VODKA; ARRACK, MESCAL, SCOTCH, SPIRIT, WHISKY; AKVAVIT, AQUAVIT, BOURBON, CORDIAL, LIQUEUR, MASTIKA, TEQUILA, WHISKEY; HYDROMEL; SLIVOVITSA; AGUARDIENTE

liquor manufacturer / DISTILLER
liquor-bottle holder / CELLARET
liripoop / TIPPET
Lisbon's river / TAGUS
lissome / LITHE; NIMBLE, SUPPLE, SVELTE; FLEXIBLE
lissome woman / SYLPH
list / SEW, TIP; EDGE, HEEL, TILT; BOUND, ENROL, LIMIT; CAREEN, CHOOSE, ENLIST, ENROLL; HEARKEN, INVOICE, ITEMIZE; TABULATE. CAST, LEET, ROLL, ROTA; SLATE, STRIP; BORDER, FILLET, LISTREL, ROSTER; AGENDUM, CATALOG, SELVAGE; REGISTER, SCHEDULE; CATALOGUE
list of actors / CAST
list of candidates / SLATE; BALLOT
list of dishes / MENU
list each / ENUMERATE
list of errors / ERRATA
list of players / ROSTER
listed / ITEMIZED
listen / HARK, HEAR, HEED; ATTEND, HARKEN; HEARKEN
listen secretly / BUG, SPY; EAVESDROP
listener / AUDITOR
listening device / BUG; TRUMPET
Lister's forte / ANTISEPSIS
listless / MOPISH; LANGUID; CARELESS, HEEDLESS; INDIFFERENT
listlessness / ENNUI, SLOTH; APATHY, TORPOR; LASSITUDE
lists / ARENA; TILTYARD
lit / DYE; STAIN, IGNITED, LIGHTED; ILLUMINATED
litany / PRAYER; PETITION, RESPONSE
literal / REAL, TRUE; EXACT, PLAIN; ACTUAL, FORMAL, STRICT, VERBAL; CORRECT, GENUINE, NOMINAL, PRECISE, PRIMARY; ACCURATE, DEFINITE, EXPLICIT
literally thus / SIC
literary composition / DRAMA, ESSAY, NOVEL, PAPER, STORY; THESIS; ARTICLE, NOVELLA, TRAGEDY; DOCUMENT; NOVEL-ETTE
literary extracts / ANA; NOTES; ANALECTS
literary hack / GRUB; GARRETEER
literary master / STYLIST
literary patchwork / CENTO
literary scraps / ANA
literary shrine / STRATFORD
literary worker / EDITOR
literati / AVANTGARDE

literature / LETTERS; LEARNING
lithe / AGILE; PLIANT, SUPPLE, SVELTE; LISSOME; FLEXIBLE
lithe as an eel / LIMBER
lithium oxide / LITHIA
lithograph / PRINT; CHROMO
lithometeor / DUSTSTORM
lithosphere / CRUST
Lithuania / LIETUVA
Lithuania capital / KOVNO, VILNA, WILNO; KAUNAS; VILNIUS, VILNYUS
Lithuanian / BALT, LETT; AESTII
Lithuanian money / LIT; LITAS; SKATIKU
Lithuanian river / NEMAN; NEMUNAS
Lithuanian seaport / MEMEL
litigant / SUER
litigate / CONTEND
litigation / CASE; CONTEST, LAWSUIT
litotes / UNDERSTATEMENT
litter / BED, HAY, PAD; BIER, MESS; DOOLI, STRAW, TRASH, YOUNG; DOOLIE; CLUTTER; CONFUSION, FRAMEWORK; UNTIDINESS. BIRTH, STREW; SCATTER
litter of pigs / FARROW
little / SMA, WEE; MEAN, POCO, PUNY, TINY; BRIEF, DWARF, PETIT, PETTY, SHORT, SMALL; FEEBLE, NARROW, PALTRY, SLIGHT; SELFISH, SLENDER, TRIVIAL; DIMINUTIVE; UN-IMPORTANT. BIT; MITE
little, c.f. / MICRO
little auk / ROTCHE; DOVEKIE
little ball / PELLET
Little Bear / URSAMINOR
little bird / TIT; WREN
little boy / LAD, TAD; TYKE; SHAVER; YOUNGSTER
little carpet / MAT
little cassino / TWO
little child / TOT
Little Corporal / NAPOLEON
little cycle / SCOOTER
Little Dorrit swindler / MERDLE
little Dorrit's name / AMY
little drink / NIP, SIP
little egg / OVULE
little fastener / PIN
little Father / CZAR, TSAR
little finger / PINKIE; MINIMUS
little flower / FLORET
Little Giant / DOUGLAS
little girl / SIS; LASS; MISSY
little island / AIT; EYOT, ISLE; ISLET
Little Minister's town / THRUMS
Little Nell's surname / TRENT

little piece / BIT; MORSEL
little pitcher / CREAMER
little pleasantness / AMENITY
little ring / ANNULET
Little Russia / UKRAINE
little toe / MINIMUS
littlest antelope / DIKDIK
littlest dog / CHIHUAHUA
littlest fish / GOBY
littlest flowering plant / DUCK-WEED
littlest human bone / STAPES
littlest living organism / PPLO
littlest mammal / SHREW
littoral / COAST, SHORE
Littré's major opus / DICTIONARY
liturgical headdress / MITER, MITRE
liturgy / MASS, RITE; RITUAL; WORSHIP; EUCHARIST
Lityerses' father / MIDAS
Lityerses' slayer / HERCULES
live / ARE; FEED, LAST; ABIDE, DWELL, EXIST; ENDURE, REMAIN, RESIDE; BREATHE, COHABIT, SUBSIST, SURVIVE; CONTINUE, SURVIVED. BRISK, QUICK, CHARGED, IGNITED, TEEMING; SWARMING; EFFEC-TIVE, ENERGETIC; UNEX-PLODED; INTERESTING
live coal / EMBER
live in the country / RUSTICATE
live down / OUTGROW
live in a tent / CAMP
live wire / GOGETTER
livelihood / MEANS; LIVING; SUPPORT; SUBSTANCE; SUSTENANCE; MAINTENANCE
liveliness / LILT; SPIRIT; VIVACITY; ANIMATION, BRISKNESS, SWIFTNESS
lively / GAY; AIRY, PERT, RACY, SPRY, YARE; AGILE, ALERT, BRISK, JOLLY, PEART, QUICK, VIVID; ACTIVE, BLITHE, JOCUND, JOYOUS, NIMBLE, SUPPLE; BUOYANT, GLEEFUL, GLOWING, NERVOUS, PIQUANT, ANIMATED, RATTLING, SPIRITED, VIGOROUS, VOLATILE; SPARKLING, SPRIGHTLY, VIVACIOUS
lively dance / HOP, JIG; REEL; GALOP
lively Italian dance / TARANTELLA
lively person / GRIG
liven / CHEER, ROUSE; ANIMATE; INSPIRIT
liver / HEPAR
liver, pert. to / HEPATIC
liver disease / CIRRHOSIS, HEPATITIS

liver secretion / BILE, GALL
liver spot / CHLOASMA
liverish / GRUMPY; BILIOUS
Liverpool group / BEATLES
liverwort / AGRIMONY, HEPATICA
livery / UNIFORM
livid / WAN; ASHY, PALE; ASHEN; DISCOLORED
living / BENEFICE; LIVELIHOOD. ALIVE, QUICK; EXTANT
living off another / PARASITIC
living being / ANIMA; ORGANISM
living dead / ZOMBI; ZOMBIE
living on land or water / AMPHIBIAN
living room / PARLOR
living room display piece / HUTCH
living in the woods / NEMORAL
Livingstone's greeter / STANLEY
Livonian / LIV; ESTH, LETT
Livorno / LEGHORN
lixiviation / LEACHING; EXTRACTION, SEPARATION
lixivium / LYE; ALKALI
lizard / ADDA, DABB, GILA, IBID, NERT, SEPS, URAN; AGAMA, ANOLI, GECKO, GUANA, SKINK, VARAN; HARDIM, IGUANA, MOLOCH; LACERTA, MONITOR, REPTILE, SAURIAN, TARENTE; CHAMELEON; LACERTIDAE
lizard, c.f. / SAUR; SAURO
lizardlike amphibian / EFT; NEWT; SALAMANDER
llamalike animal / ALPACA, VICUNA; GUANACO
llano / PLAIN
Lloyd's business / INSURANCE
lo / SEE; ECCE, LOOK; BEHOLD
load / ONUS; CARGO; BURDEN, CHARGE, WEIGHT; FREIGHT; PRESSURE; ENCUMBRANCE. WEIGH; SADDLE
load with burden / SADDLE; PRESSURE
load cargo / LADE
loaded / DRUNK, LADEN; INTOXICATED
loads / HEAPS, SCADS
loads of dough / PILES
loadstar / LODESTAR, POLESTAR
loadstone / MAGNET; LODESTONE
loaf / IDLE, LAZE; LOITER, LOUNGE. CAKE; BREAD
loafer / SHOE, WAFF; IDLER; CADGER; SLIPPER; LARRIKIN
loam / DIRT, SOIL; EARTH, LOESS
loan / LEND; GRANT
loath / LOTH; AVERSE; BACKWARD, HESITANT; RELUCTANT, UNWILLING; INDISPOSED; DISINCLINED

loathe / HATE; ABHOR; DETEST; DESPISE; ABOMINATE
loathing / NAUSEA; DISGUST; AVERSION
loathsome / FOUL, VILE; ODIOUS; HATEFUL; APPALLING, OFFENSIVE; DETESTABLE, DISGUSTING
lob / BOWL, LUMP, TOSS; THROW; RETURN
lobbing cannon / MORTAR
lobby / HALL; FOYER; ACCESS; HALLWAY, PASSAGE; VESTIBULE
lobo / TIMBERWOLF
lobster claw / CHELA; NIPPER, PINCER; GLORYPEA
lobster roe / CORAL
lobster trap / POT; CAGE
local / EDAPHIC, TOPICAL; REGIONAL; SECTIONAL
local expression / IDIOM
locale / SITE; PLACE, SCENE; LOCALITY
locality / AREA, SITE, SPOT; LOCUS, PLACE, VENUE
locate / FIND, LIVE, MARK, SPOT; PLACE, STAND; SETTLE; SITUATE; LOCALIZE; DETERMINE, ESTABLISH
locate elsewhere / RESITE
location / SITE, SPOT; PLACE; POSITION
loch of the monster / NESS
lock / HUG; BOLT, SHUT; FASTEN, SECURE; CONFINE. DAG; CURL, TUFT; TRESS; RINGLET
lock clasp / HASP
lock opener / KEY; CODE
locker / CASE, SAFE; CHEST, TRUNK; CABINET
Locke's "blank mind" / TABULARASA
locket / PENDANT
lockjaw / TETANUS, TRISMUS
lockout / EXCLUSION
lockup / JUG; JAIL; PRISON; HOOSEGOW; CALABOOSE
loco / MAD; INSANE
locomotive / ENGINE
Locrine's daughter / SABRINA
Locrine's father / BRUTUS
loculus / SAC; CAVITY; CHAMBER
locum tenens / DEPUTY; SUBSTITUTE
locus / LINE; CURVE, PLACE
locust / WETA; ACACIA, CICADA, CICALA; GRASSHOPPER
locust sound / STRIDULATION
locust tree / CAROB; ACACIA
locution / PHRASE; EXPRESSION
lode / REEF, VEIN; BONANZA

lodestar / GUIDE; POLARIS; POLESTAR
lodestone / MAGNET
lodge / LIE; PLACE; RESIDE; DEPOSIT, IMPLANT. DEN, HUT; ROOM; ABODE, CABIN, HOUSE; WIGWAM; COTTAGE; DWELLING
lodger / GUEST; ROOMER
loft / ATTIC; GALLERY. SLANT
lofted tennis shot / LOB
lofty / AERY, EPIC, HIGH, TALL; AERIE, PROUD; AERIAL; EMINENT, EXALTED, HAUGHTY, STATELY, SUBLIME; ELEVATED, IMPOSING, MAJESTIC; DIGNIFIED
lofty dwelling / AERIE
lofty peak / CIMA, CRAG; HEIGHT; PINNACLE
log / DIARY; RECORD, TIMBER; LOGBOOK; LOGARITHM
log estimate / SCALAGE
log float / RAFT
log roller / BIRLER
log sled / TODE
log splitter / WEDGE; LOGGER
loge / BOX; BOOTH, STALL
loggerhead / TURTLE; BLOCKHEAD
loggerheads / CROSSPURPOSES
logger's boot / PAC
logger's implement / CALK; PEAVY; PEAVEY
loggia / ARCADE; GALLERY
logging pole / KILHIG
logical analysis / SYLLOGISM
logical comparison / ANALOGY
logical deduction / CONCLUSION
logical fallacy / IDOL; IDOLUM
logical mode / BAROCO; CELARENT
logical opposite / CONTRARY
logical series / SORITES
logical statement / LEMMA; PREMISE
logion / SAYING; PROVERB
logograph / ANAGRAM
logotype / EMBLEM; LIGATURE
logrolling contest / ROLEO
logy / DOPY
Lohengrin's father / PARZIVAL
Lohengrin's wife / ELSA
loincloth / MALO, MARO, PANE; DHOTI, PAGNE; DHOOTI; GSTRING
loincloth of hajji / IZAR
loir / DORMOUSE
loiter / LAG; LURK, WAIT; DALLY, DELAY, TARRY; LINGER; SAUNTER
Loki's daughter / HEL; HELA
Loki's son / VALI; NERVE; FENRIS
Loki's victim / BALDER

Loki's wife / SIGYN
loll / LAZE; DROOP; LOUNGE, SPRAWL; RECLINE
Lollards' leader / WYCLIF
lombard / BANKER; MONEY-LENDER
Lombardy capital / MILAN
Lombardy river / PO
London airport / GATWICK; HEATHROW
London art gallery / TATE
London bar / PUB
London Bridge's relocation / ARIZONA
London Bridge's river / THAMES
London character / BUCK; LARSEN
London club / UNION; KITCAT; SAVAGE; CARLTON, GARRICK
London district / SOHO; LAMBETH, PIMLICO; BELGRAVIA; BLOOMS-BURY, SHOREDITCH
London hawker / COSTER
London market / BILLINGSGATE
London native / COCKNEY
London park / HYDE
London prison / CLINK; NEWGATE; MARSHALSEA
London statue / GOG; EROS; LIONS, MAGOG; NELSON; ACHILLES, PETERPAN
London street / BOND; BAKER
London street entertainer / PEARLIE
London subway / TUBE
lone / SOLE, SOLO; LONELY, SINGLE; WIDOWED; DESERTED, LONESOME, SECLUDED, SOLITARY; UNMARRIED
lone performance / SOLO
Lone Ranger's aide / TONTO
Lone Star State / TEXAS
lonely / LORN; FORLORN; DESERTED, LONESOME, SECLUDED, SOLITARY; UNFREQUENTED
loner / HERMIT; SOLITARY
long / YEN; PINE; COVET, CRAVE, YEARN; ASPIRE, DESIRE, HANKER, LINGER. FAR; SLOW, TALL; WORDY; PROLIX; LENGTHY, TEDIOUS; EXTENDED
long, c.f. / LONGI
long ago / ELD; PAST, YORE
long blouse / TUNIC
long bushing / SLEEVE
long cylinder / PIPE
long distance race / MARATHON
long dozen / THIRTEEN
long drink / SWIG
long fish / EEL
long furred cloak / PELISSE

long glove / GAUNTLET
long golf shot / DRIVE
long hill / RIDGE
Long Island bay / JAMAICA, PECONIC
Long John Silver's pet / PARROT
long journey / TOUR; VOYAGE; ODYSSEY
long life / LONGEVITY
long life to / VIVA, VIVE
long limbed / RANGY
long line of people / CROCODILE
long live / VIVA, VIVE; VIVAT
long look / STARE
long measure / ELL
long metal pin / SKEWER
long narrative / EPIC, SAGA; NOVEL
long narrow bit / STRIP
long narrow spade / LOY
long nose / SNOUT; PROBOSCIS
long overblouse / TUNIC
long period / EON
long run / MILE
long seat / PEW; BENCH; SETTEE
long short story / NOVELET
long shot / RISK
long speech / SCREED; DESCANT
long step / STRIDE
long story / SERIAL
long suit / FORTE
long time / EON
Long Tom / CANNON
long tooth / FANG, TUSK
long in the tooth / OLD; AGING; ELDERLY; MOTHEATEN
long walk / HIKE, TREK
long way off / FAR; AFAR; DISTANT
long-armed ape / GIBBON, WOUWOU; SIAMANG
long-billed bird / SNIPE, STORK
long-distance race / MARATHON
long-drawn / TEDIOUS; PROTRACTED
long-eared animal / HARE
longer than broad / OBLONG
longhair / INTELLECTUAL
long-haired ox / YAK
longhand / HANDWRITING
long-handled implement / HOE; BILL, RAKE; SPEAR; POLEAX, SCYTHE, SHOVEL; GISARME, HALBERD, HAYFORK
long-handled spoon / LADLE; DIPPER
longheaded / WISE
longing / YEN; DESIRE; CRAVING; YEARNING
longitude index / MERIDIAN
long-lasting / CHRONIC; ENDURING

long-legged bird / RAIL; AGAMI, CRANE, EGRET, HERON, STEVE, STILT, STORK, WADER; AVOCET, CURLEW
long-legged monkey / LANGUR
long-lived patriarch / METHUSELAH
long-necked bird / SWAN; HERON
long-nosed fish / GAR; PIKE
long-range gun / RIFLE
longshoreman / DOCKER; STEVEDORE
longsome / BORING; TEDIOUS
long-suffering / MEEK; PATIENT
long-tailed primate / KRA, SAI; KAHA; LANGUR
longwinded / PROLIX; TEDIOUS, VERBOSE
look / LO; CON, EYE, SEE; GAZE, LEER, PEEK, PEEP, PEER, PORE, SCAN, SEEK, SEEM, VIEW; SIGHT, WATCH; APPEAR, BEHOLD, GLANCE, REGARD, SEARCH, DISCERN, EXAMINE. CAST, MIEN; ASPECT, MANNER; FEATURE; APPEARANCE, COMPLEXION
look after / MIND, TEND; NURSE; ATTEND
look angrily / GLARE
look as if / SEEM
look askance / LEER, OGLE
look at / EYE; SCAN
look for / SEEK
look forward to / AWAIT; ANTICIPATE
look here / HIST
look intently / CON; PORE; STARE; SEARCH
look into / PRY; PEEK, PEEP, SEEK
look like / RESEMBLE
look out / BEWARE
look over / SCAN; EXAMINE
look slyly / PEEK, PEEP
look steadily / CON; GAZE, SCAN; STARE
look sullen / POUT; GLOWER
look up to / ADMIRE
looking for danger / WARY
looking glass / MIRROR
looking as if gnawed / EROSE
looking like gold / GILT
lookout / GUARD, TOWER, VISTA, WATCH; SENTRY; CONCERN, OUTLOOK; SENTINEL
looks / APPEARANCE
loom / AUK; LOON; MURRE; HANDLE, PUFFIN; JACQUARD. EMERGE, IMPEND; MATERIALIZE
loom heddles / CAAM
loom part / LAM; REED, SLEY

loon / GREBE; MADMAN
loony / MAD; NUTS; CRAZY, NUTTY
loop / ANSA; BIGHT, NOOSE, PICOT; CIRCLE
Loop city / CHICAGO
loop in lariat / HONDA, HONDO
loop for lifting / TAB; CROP
Loop railroad / EL
loophole / MUSE; MEUSE; EYELET, OILLET; OPENING; PEEPHOLE
loose / LAX; EASY, FREE; SLACK, VAGUE; WANTON; UNBOUND; RAMBLING; DESULTORY, DISSOLUTE; INDEFINITE, UNFASTENED. OPEN, UNDO; RELAX, UNTIE; UNBIND; RELEASE; UNTETHER
loose coat / SIMAR; RAGLAN; PALETOT; MANTEVIL
loose dress / ROBE; MUUMUU; PEIGNOIR; MOTHERHUBBARD
loose garment / CAMIS, CAMUS, CYMAR, SIMAR; CAMISE
loosely woven fabric / GAUZE; ETAMINE
loosen / UNTIE
loot / ROB; SACK; PLUNDER, BOOTY; SPOILS; PILLAGE
lop / CUT; CHOP, HANG, SNAG, SNED, SNIP, TRIM; DROOP, PRUNE; SNATHE; TRUNCATE
lopsided / AGEE, ALOP; ALIST; UNEVEN
loquacious / GLIB; FLUENT, SMOOTH; FLOWING, VOLUBLE; AFFLUENT; GARRULOUS, TALKATIVE; CHATTERING; MULTILOQUOUS
loquacity / GAB; GARRULITY
loquat / BIWA
lord / DUKE, EARL, PEER; BARON, COUNT, JESUS, LIEGE, RULER; MASTER; JEHOVAH, MARQUIS; GOVERNOR, NOBLEMAN
Lord High Executioner / KOKO
lordliness / DIGNITY
lordly / NOBLE, PROUD; HAUGHTY; DESPOTIC; IMPERIOUS; ARISTOCRATIC
Lord's Day / SABBATH
lord's demesne / MANOR; PALACE; MANSION
Lord's prayer / PATERNOSTER
Lord's supper / CENA, MASS; COMMUNION, EUCHARIST
lord's wife / LADY
lore / WISDOM; LEARNING; ERUDITION, KNOWLEDGE; INSTRUCTION
lorelei / SIREN
Lorelei's river / RHINE

lorgnon / LORGNETTE
lorica / SHELL; CUIRASS
lorn / BEREFT; FORSAKEN
Lorna Doone's sweetheart / RIDD
Lorraine's companion / ALSACE
lorry / TRUCK, WAGON; HANDCART
Los Angeles / LA
Los Angeles eleven / RAMS
Los Angeles nine / ANGELS; DODGERS
lose / AMIT, FAIL, MISS; SPILL, STRAY, WASTE, YIELD; MISLAY; FORFEIT; MISPLACE, SQUANDER
lose blood / BLEED; HEMORRHAGE
lose color / FADE, PALE; DROOP, FAINT
lose from container / SPILL
lose footing / SLIP, TRIP; STUMBLE
lose force / EBB
lose freshness / FADE, WILT; STALE
lose health / AIL
lose heat / COOL
lose hope / GIVEUP; DESPAIR, DESPOND
lose luster / TARNISH
lose moisture / DRY, SET; HARDEN, WITHER
lose value / DEPRECIATE
lose vigor / LAG; FLAG, IDLE, LAZE; WEAKEN
lose zest / JADE
losing dice throw / CRAP
loss / WASTE; DAMAGE, DEFEAT, INJURY; FAILURE; DETRIMENT, PRIVATION; FORFEITURE; DEPRIVATION
loss of appetite / ANOREXIA
loss of eyebrows / MADAROSIS
loss of fetus / ABORTION; MISCARRIAGE
loss of hair / ALOPECIA, BALDNESS
loss of hope / DESPAIR
loss of memory / AMNESIA
loss of speech / APHASIA
loss of vision / AMAUROSIS, BLINDNESS
loss of will power / ABULIA
lost / GONE; ASTRAY, RUINED; MISLAID, MISSING; DESTROYED, FORFEITED, PERPLEXED
lost animal / STRAY; ESTRAY
lost wax / CIREPERDU
lot / DOOM, FATE, MUCH, PLOT, SCAD; SHARE; CHANCE, HAZARD, PARCEL; DESTINY, FORTUNE, PORTION; DIVISION, QUANTITY

lothario / RAKE; LIBERTINE
lotion / BALM, WASH
Lot's birthplace / UR
Lot's father / HARAN
Lot's residence / SODOM
Lot's sister / MILCAH
Lot's son / MOAB; GARETH, GAWAIN; GAHERIS; AGRAVAIN, BENAMINI
Lot's uncle / ABRAHAM
Lot's wife / WAHELA
lots of hair / MANE
lottery / CHANCE, RAFFLE; DRAWING
lotus / LOTE; MELILOT, TREFOIL; WATERLILY
lotus eater / DREAMER
lotus tree / SADR
lotus-headed god / NEFERTUM
loud / NOISY, SHOWY; FLASHY; EMPHATIC, POSITIVE, VEHEMENT; CLAMOROUS; BOISTEROUS, STENTORIAN
loud / FORTE; FORTISSIMO
loud bang / REPORT
loud call / CRY, YAP; BARK, HOWL, YAWP, YELL; SCREAM
loud hum / ZOOM
loud noise / DIN; BANG, ROAR, SHOT, WAIL; CLANG; CLAMOR
loud whinny / NEIGH
loudest insect / CICADA
loudly complaining / CLAMOROUS
loud-mouthed / NOISY; VULGAR; BLATANT; OFFENSIVE
loudness measure / PHON, SONE
loudness unit / DECIBEL
loudspeaker / CONE; WOOFER, SPEAKER, TWEETER; AMPLIFIER, MEGAPHONE; TRANSDUCER
loud-voiced person / STENTOR
Louis XVI's nickname / VETO
Louisbourg's captor / AMHERST
Louise's composer / CHARPENTIER
Louisiana capital / BATONROUGE
Louisiana city / MONROE; SHREVEPORT
Louisiana county / PARISH
Louisiana immigrant / CAJUN; ISLENO; ACADIAN
Louisiana native / CREOLE
Louisiana purchaser / JEFFERSON
Louisiana river / RED; SABINE; OUACHITA; MISSISSIPPI
Louisiana state flower / MAGNOLIA
Louisiana state nickname / CREOLE; PELICAN
Louisiana swampland / BAYOU
Louisiana university / TULANE
lounge / IDLE, LAZE, LOAF, LOLL; LOITER. SOFA; COUCH, LOBBY; PARLOR

loup-garou / WEREWOLF
Lourdes saint / BERNADETTE
louse egg / NIT
lout / OAF; BOOR; LOOBY, YAHOO; BUMPKIN; BLOCKHEAD. CLUMSY; AWKWARD; UNGAINLY; UNSKILLED; UNGRACEFUL, UNSKILLFUL
louver / SLIT, VENT; TURRET; LANTERN; ABATVENT
Louvre treasure / MONALISA
lovable / AMIABLE; EXCELLENT; ATTRACTIVE
love / JO; GRA; ZERO; AGRAH, AMOUR; LIKING, REGARD; CHARITY; DEVOTION, FONDNESS; AFFECTION; ATTACHMENT. CARE; ADORE; CHERISH
love, c.f. / AMAT; PHILO
love, pert. to / EROTIC; AMATORY
love affair / AMOUR; INTRIGUE
love apple / TOMATO
love to excess / DOAT, DOTE; ADORE
love feast / AGAPE
love god / AMOR, EROS, KAMA; ANGUS, BHAGD, CUPID; AIZENMYOO
love goddess / ISIS; ATHOR, FREYA, TURAN, VENUS; FRIGGA, HATHOR, ISHTAR; ASTARTE; APHRODITE, ASHTORETH
love knot / AMORET
love missive / VALENTINE; BILLETDOUX
love potion / PHILTER, PHILTRE; APHRODISIAC
love story / ROMANCE
love token / RING; AMORET
love uncritically / DOTE; ADORE
love writings / EROTICA
lovebird / PARROT
loved by John Ridd / LORNADOONE
love-lies-bleeding / AMARANTH
lovelorn / JILTED; FORSAKEN
lovely / SWEET; AMIABLE; CHARMING, EXCITING, PLEASING; ADMIRABLE, BEAUTIFUL, BEAUTEOUS
lovely complexion / PEACHESANDCREAM
love-making / SUIT; WOOING; SPOONING; COURTSHIP
loveman / CLEAVERS; GOOSEGRASS
lover / AMI; BEAU; LEMAN, ROMEO, SWAIN, WOOER; SUITOR; PARAMOUR; INAMORATA; SWEETHEART
lover of books / READER; BIBLIOPHILE

lover of cruelty / SADIST; MASOCHIST
lover of one's country / PATRIOT
lovers' meeting / TRYST; RENDEZVOUS
love's archer / CUPID
loving / FOND; AMATIVE, AMATORY, AMOROUS, DEVOTED; AFFECTIONATE
loving, c.f. / PHIL; PHILE, PHILO
loving admirer / ADORER
loving dedication / DEVOTION
loving murmur / COO
low / BASE, MEAN, POOR, SOFT, VILE, WEAK; CHEAP, GRAVE, LOWLY, PLAIN; ABJECT, FEEBLE, HUMBLE, MENIAL, SIMPLE, VULGAR; IGNOBLE, SERVILE, SHALLOW, SLAVISH, SUBDUED. MOO; BELLOW. BELOW, UNDER
low bed / COT; CRIB
low bow / KOWTOW, SALAAM; OBEISANCE
low countries / BELGIUM; LUXEMBOURG; NETHERLANDS
low deck of ship / ORLOP
low flat-bottom boat / BARGE; KEELBOAT
low gaiter / SPAT
low hand in poker / PAIR
low haunt / DEN; DIVE
low island / KEY; ATOLL
low land / CARSE; POLDER; BOTTOMS
low place in meadow / SWALE
low point in orbit / PERIGEE
low priced / SALE
low score on a hole / EAGLE; BIRDIE
low section of a city / SLUM
low shoes / PUMPS
low slipper / MULE
low sound / HUM; MOAN; DRONE; MURMUR, RUMBLE
low spirits / BLUES, DUMPS
low tide / EBB; NEAP
low voice / ALTO, BASS; CONTRALTO
low-bred dog / CUR; MUTT, TYKE; MONGREL
lowbrow / CLOD; HARDHAT
low-caste laborer / TOTY
low-down / DOPE, INFO; SCOOP
lower / DIM; BATE, DROP, FALL, SINK, VAIL; ABASE, DEMIT, FROWN; DEBASE, DEMEAN, DEMOTE, HUMBLE, LESSEN, REDUCE, WEAKEN; DEGRADE, DEPRESS, LETDOWN; DECREASE, DIMINISH; DISCREDIT, HUMILIATE. NETHER
Lower California / BAJA
Lower California city / MEXICALI

Lower California resort / TIJUANA; ENSENADA
lower case / MINUSCULE
lower the colors / DIP
lower corner of a sail / CLEW
Lower Depths author / GORKY
lower end of mast / HEEL; BOTTOM
lower one's self / DEIGN; CONDESCEND
lower part of crankcase / OILPAN
lower part of wall / WAINSCOT
lower in rank / DEMOTE, REDUCE; DEGRADE. JUNIOR
lower region / HELL; UNDERWORLD
lower in social status / DECLASS
lowering / DARK; MURKY; CLOUDY, GLOOMY; OVERCAST
lowest / LEAST; NETHERMOST
lowest deck / ORLOP
lowest high tide / NEAP
lowest point / BASE, ROOT, ZERO; NADIR; BOTTOM; PERIGEE
lowest quarter on ship / STEERAGE
lowest voice / BASS
low-grade tea / BOHEA
lowing sound / MOO
lowland near river / HOLM
low-spirited / DOWN, DULL; DEPRESSED; MELANCHOLY; DOWNHEARTED
loxia / WRYNECK; TORTICOLLIS
loyal / LEAL, REAL, TRUE; STANCH; DEVOTED, STAUNCH; FAITHFUL; TRUEHEARTED
loyalist / TORY; PATRIOT
loyalty / FEALTY; DEVOTION, FIDELITY; ALLEGIANCE
Loyalty island / LIFE, MARE, UVEA
lozenge / RHOMB; PASTIL; ROTULA, TROCHE; DIAMOND, PASTILE; PASTILLE
LSD / ACID
luau / FEAST
lubricant / OIL; GREASE; GRAPHITE
lubricate / OIL; GREASE
lubricator / OILER; OILCAN
lubricity / LEWDNESS; SENSUALITY, SHIFTINESS; SLIPPERINESS
lucarne / DORMER
Lucasta's poet / LOVELACE
luce / PIKE; FLEURDELYS
lucent / CLEAR; SHINING
lucerne / LYNX; FODDER, MEDICK; ALFALFA
lucid / SANE; CLEAR, SOBER, SOUND; BRIGHT, LIMPID; BEAMING, RADIANT, SHINING
lucidity / SANITY; CLARITY; RADIANCE
lucifer / DEMON, DEVIL, MATCH, SATAN, VENUS

Lucina's province / CHILDBIRTH
luck / HAP, LOT; CESS, FATE;
    CHANCE, HAZARD; FORTUNE,
    SUCCESS; ACCIDENT,
    CASUALTY
luck, pert. to / ALEATORY
luckless / HAPLESS;
    UNFORTUNATE
luckless player / LOSER
lucky / FAVORABLE, FORTUNATE;
    AUSPICIOUS, SUCCESSFUL
lucky charm / FETISH, MASCOT;
    TALISMAN; ALECTORIA
lucky stroke / HIT; KILLING
lucrative / PAYING; GAINFUL;
    PROFITABLE
lucre / GAIN, PELF; MONEY;
    PROFIT, RICHES; EMOLUMENT
Lucretia's attacker / SEXTUS
luculent / LUCID
Lucullan / LAVISH; ABUNDANT
ludicrous / COMIC, DROLL,
    FUNNY; ABSURD; COMICAL,
    RISIBLE; FARCICAL;
    BURLESQUE, LAUGHABLE;
    RIDICULOUS
Ludolph's number / PI
Lud's father / HELI
Lud's town / LONDON
lues / SYPHILIS
lug / DRAG, DRAW, HAUL, PULL,
    EAR; LOOP; HANDLE
luggage / BAGS; TRUNKS;
    BAGGAGE
luggar / FALCON
Luggnagg inhabitant /
    STRULDBRUG
lugubrious / SAD; DOLEFUL;
    MOURNFUL
lugworm / LOB; SANDWORM
lukewarm / COOL; TEPID
lukewarmth / TEPOR
lull / CALM, HUSH, ROCK; ABATE,
    CEASE, QUIET, STILL; SOOTHE;
    COMPOSE, SUBSIDE; TRANQUIL-
    IZE, PAUSE; RESPITE
lumber / LOGS, WOOD; SHAMBLE;
    FLOUNDER
Lumber State / MAINE
lumberjack / LOGGER
lumberman's tool / AX; ADZE;
    PEAVEY
luminary / SUN; MOON, STAR
luminous / CLEAR, LIGHT, LUCID;
    BRIGHT; RADIANT, SHINING;
    BRILLIANT
luminous body / SUN; STAR;
    METEOR
luminous heavenly cloud / NEBULA
luminous mass of light / NIMBUS
luminous radiation / AURA
luminous solar envelope / CORONA

lummox / LOUT; KLUTZ; LUBBER;
    FUMBLER
lump / GOB, LOB, NUB, WAD;
    CLOD, CLOT, HEAP, HUNK,
    KNOB, MASS, NODE, SWAD;
    PIECE, SLICE, WHOLE; NODULE;
    SWELLING
lump of clay / BAT; CLOD
lump in fibers / SLUB
lump sum / TALE; GROSS, TOTAL,
    WHOLE, WORKS; AGGREGATE
lumpish / DULL; HEAVY; STOLID;
    SPIRITLESS
Luna / MOON; SELENE
lunacy / MANIA; MADNESS;
    INSANITY; DERANGEMENT
lunar months / MOONS;
    LUNATIONS
lunar "sea" / MARE
lunar vista / MOONSCAPE
lunatic / MAD; CRAZY, LOONY;
    INSANE; MONTHLY; DEMENTED,
    MANIAC; MADMAN; BEDLAMITE
lunch / TIFFIN; LUNCHEON
luncheon / TIFFIN
lunchroom / CAFE; DINER, GRILL;
    EATERY; COUNTER
lunchwagon / DINER
lung, c.f. / PULMO
lung sound / RALE; BRUIT;
    RATTLE; FREMITUS
lunge / LURCH; THRUST
lungfish / CERATODUS
lungi / SCARF; TURBAN
lungs / LIGHTS
lupine / SAVAGE; WOLFISH
lurch / ROLL; CAREEN
lure / BAIT, DRAW; DECOY,
    TEMPT; ALLURE, ENTICE;
    ATTRACT
lure to destruction / ENTRAP
lurid / WAN; PALE, WILD;
    GHASTLY; SENSATIONAL
lurk / HIDE; PROWL, SKULK,
    SLINK, STEAL
luscious / RICH; SWEET; SAVORY;
    HONEYED; TOOTHSOME
luscious fruit / PEACH; NECTARINE
lush / RANK, RICH, RIPE; JUICY;
    PROFUSE; OVERRIPE;
    LUXURIANT, DRUNK, TOPER;
    DRUNKARD
Lusiad's author / CAMOENS
Lusitania / PORTUGAL
lusory / MERRY; LIVELY;
    PLAYFUL; SPORTIVE
lust / DESIRE; VORACITY;
    CONCUPISCENCE
luster / GLOSS, SHEEN, SHINE;
    LUSTRE, RENOWN, REPUTE;
    GLITTER; EMINENCE, RADI-
    ANCE, SPLENDOR

lusterless / DIM, MAT; DULL; MATTE
lustful / CARNAL, ROBUST; PRURIENT; LECHEROUS; LASCIVIOUS
lustrate / PURIFY
lustration / CLEANSING
lustrous / NAIF; BEAMY, NITID; BRIGHT, GLOSSY, LUCENT, ORIENT, SHEENY; RADIANT; LUMINOUS; BRILLIANT, EFFULGENT
lustrous fabric / SILK; SATIN; POPLIN, SATEEN
lustrous mineral / SPAR
lustrum / QUINQUENNIUM
lusty / BURLY; BRAWNY, ROBUST, STRONG, STURDY; HEALTHY; LUSTROUS, MUSCULAR, STAL-WART, VIGOROUS; CORPULENT
lute / TAR; CLAY; CAULK; CEMENT; MANDORE, THEORBO; MANDO-LIN; CHITARRONE
Lutetia / PARIS
lutianoid fish / SESI; SNAPPER
lutin / PIXY; SPRITE
luting / SEAL; PACKING
lutose / MUDDY
luxate / DISJOINT; DISLOCATE
Luxembourg city / ESCH
Luxembourg river / OUR; SAUER
luxuriance / RICHNESS; ABUNDANCE, PROFUSION
luxuriant / LUSH, RANK, RICH; PROFUSE; PRODIGAL
luxuriate / BASK; REVEL; INDULGE
luxurious / LUSH, RICH; PLUSH; EXTRAVAGANT
luxury boat / LINER, YACHT
luxury lover / SYBARITE
Luzon city / BAGUIO, MANILA
Luzon inhabitant / TAGALOG
Luzon river / AGNO; PASIG
lycanthrope / WEREWOLF
Lycaon's daughter / CALLISTO
lycée / HIGHSCHOOL

lyceum / SCHOOL; ACADEMY; SEMINARY
Lyceum teacher / ARISTOTLE
Lycidas' original / KING
Lycomedes' daughter / DEIDAMIA
Lycomedes' guest / ACHILLES
Lycophron's father / PERIANDER
Lycurgus / LAWGIVER
Lycurgus' city / SPARTA
Lycus' wife / DIRCE
Lydia capital / SARDIS
Lydian dynasty / MERMNAD
Lydian invention / COINAGE
Lydian king / ARDYS, GYGES; CROESUS; ALYATTES
Lydian queen / OMPHALE
Lydian river / HERMUS; CAYSTER
lying / FALSE; UNTRUE; RECUMBENT; MENDACIOUS, UNTRUTHFUL
lying down / ABED; RECLINING
lying face down / PRONE
lying on one's back / SUPINE
lying tale / FUDGE
Lyly's style / EUPHUISM
lymphatic / PUFFY; SLUGGISH
Lynceus' brother / IDAS
Lynceus' forte / FARSIGHT
Lynette's champion / GARETH
lynx / BOBCAT; CARACAL, WILDCAT
Lyons' river / RHONE, SAONE
lypothymia / MELANCHOLY; DESPONDENCY
lyre / HARP
lyric / POEM, SONG; WORDS
lyric muse / ERATO
lyric poem / ODE; SONG; MELIC
lyric poem division / STANZA
lyrical / ODIC; MELIC
lyrics / WORDS
lyrist / POET; ODIST
Lysander's love / HERMIA
lysis / DISSOLUTION
Lysistrata author / ARISTOPHANES
Lytton's pen name / MEREDITH

M

ma / MOM; MAMA; MAMMA, MATER; MOTHER
ma'am / MADAM
Mabinogion hero / PRYDERI
Mabinogion prince / PWYLL
macabre / EERIE, WEIRD; GHASTLY
macaco / MACAQUE
macadamize / TAR; PAVE
Macao inhabitant / MACANESE
Macao money / AVO; PATACA
Macao's principal business / GAMBLING

macaque / BRUH; MACACO, RHESUS
macarize / LAUD; BLESS
macaroni / FOP; DANDY
macaroni variety / ZITI; DITALI, FORATI, STELLE; FUSILLI, GNOCCHI
macaronic / MIXED; JUMBLED
macaw / ARA; ARAR; ARARA; MARACAN
Macbeth's slayer / MACDUFF
Macbeth's victim / BANQUO, DUNCAN

Macbeth's wife / GRUACH
Maccabees / HASMONEANS
Maccabees' patriarch / MAT-
    TATHIAS
mace / CUE; CLUB; MACER, STAFF
macebearer / BEDEL, MACER
Macedonian capital / PELLA
Macedonian city / PYDNA; EDESSA
Macedonian king / ALEXANDER
Macedonia's last king / PERSEUS
macerate / RET; SOAK; STEEP
macerater / PULPER
Macheath's father-in-law /
    PEACHUM
Macheath's profession / HIGH-
    WAYMAN
Macheath's wife / POLLY
machete / BOLO
machiavellian / WILY; ASTUTE
machin / MACAQUE
machination / PLOT; SCHEME
machine / RIG; MOTOR; ENGINE
machine to calender paper /
    PLATER
machine to cut grass / MOWER
machine for finishing / EDGER
machine to grind grain / MILL
machine gun / BREN, STEN; MAXIM
machine to lift weights / GIN; JACK;
    DERRICK
machine to make machine parts /
    MACHINETOOL
machine to mature cloth / AGER
machine part / CAM, COG, GIB,
    HUB; AXLE, GEAR, PAWL; ROTOR
machine pin / COTTER
machine to separate cotton from
    seeds / GIN
machine to separate grain from
    hay / THRESHER
machine to shape wood / LATHE
machine to spread hay / TEDDER
machine tool / DRILL, LATHE
machinery, pert. to / MECHANICAL
machinist's helper / OILER
machree / DEAR; BELOVED
Machu Picchu discoverer /
    BINGHAM
Mackenzie River town / AKLAVIK
mackerel-like fish / CERO, SCAD
mackintosh / WATERPROOF
macled / SPOTTED
macrobiosis / LONGEVITY
macrocosm / UNIVERSE
macrology / REDUNDANCY
macroseism / TEMBLOR
macula / MARK, SPOT; SUNSPOT
maculate / BLOTCHED;
    BLEMISHED
mad / WILD; ANGRY, CRAZY, IRATE
Mad Cavalier / RUPERT
Madagascar capital / TANANARIVE
Madagascar civet / FOSSA

Madagascar insectivore / TENREC
Madagascar lemur / AYEAYE
Madagascar native / BARA; MERINA
Madagascar primate / LEMUR
Madagascar seaport / TAMATAVE
madam / MAM, MUM; LADY, MAAM
Madame Butterfly author /
    BELASCO
Madame Butterfly composer /
    PUCCINI
Madame Butterfly heroine /
    CHOCHOSAN, CIOCIOSAN
madcap / RASH, WILD; ECCENTRIC
madden / CRAZE; ENRAGE;
    INFURIATE
madder / RUBIA; GARANCE,
    MUNJEET
madding / RAGING; FURIOUS
made / BUILT; FORMED; PRO-
    DUCED
made of distinct parts / COMPOSITE
made fast / SECURED
made first bid / OPENED
made of flowers / FLORAL
made of grain / CEREAL
made into leather / TAWED;
    TANNED
made noise / BANGED; WHOOPED
made of oak / OAKEN
made reparation / ATONED
made sleep noises / SNORED
made smooth / PLANED, RUBBED
made of thin strips / SLATTED
made threefold / TRIPLED
made a thrust / LUNGED
made of tile / TEGULAR
Madeira capital / FUNCHAL
madhouse / ASYLUM, BEDLAM
Madison's wife / DOLLY; DOLLEY
madman / MANIAC; LUNATIC
madness / FURY, RAGE; MANIA;
    FRENZY, LUNACY; DELIRIUM
Madoc's reputed discovery /
    AMERICA
madonna / MARY; VIRGIN
Madras coast / MALABAR;
    COROMANDEL
Madras mountains / GHATS
Madrid museum / PRADO
madrigal / FALA, SONG
Maecenas' protege / HORACE,
    VIRGIL
maelstrom / WHIRLPOOL
maenad / SHREW; BACCHANTE
maestro / MASTER; TEACHER
Maeterlinck play / BLUEBIRD
Maeterlinck's insects / BEES
mafeesh / DEAD; KAPUT
maffick / EXULT
mafura tree / ROKA
magazine / ARSENAL; PERIODICAL
mage / WIZARD
magenta / FUCHSIN; FUCHSINE

maggot / MAWK; FANCY, LARVA
Magi / CASPAR; GASPAR; WISE-
  MEN; MELCHIOR; BALTHASAR
magian / MAGUS; ZORCASTRIAN
magic / OBI; OBIA; GOETY, OBEAH
magic, pert. to / THAUMATURGIC
magical stone / AGATE; AMULET
magician / MAGE; MAGUS; MERLIN
magician's rod / WAND
magician's word / PRESTO
magisterial / LOFTY; IMPERIOUS
magma / PASTE
Magna Carta signer / JOHN
Magna Carta site / RUNNYMEDE
Magna Mater / RHEA
magnanimous / BRAVE, LOFTY
magnate / MOGUL, NABOB;
  TYCOON
magnet / LOADSTONE, LODE-
  STONE
magnet, c.f. / MAGNETO
magnetic extremity / POLE
magnetic strip / TAPE
magnetism / IT; MESMERISM
magneto / GENERATOR
magnificence / POMP; STATE
magnificent / GRAND, NOBLE,
  SHOWY
magnify / LAUD; EXTOL; AMPLIFY
magnifying glass / LENS; LOUPE
magniloquent / POMPOUS;
  BOMBASTIC
magnitude / SIZE; EXTENT,
  VOLUME
Magnolia State / MISSISSIPPI
magpie / PIE; CROW, MAGG, PICA
magsman / CHEAT; SWINDLER
maguey / ALOE; AGAVE
Magyar / HUNGARIAN
Mahabharata holy mountain /
  MERU
Mahabharata princes / PANDAVAS
Mahabharata princess / DRAUPADI
Mahan's dictum / SEAPOWER
Mahdi's victory / KHARTOUM
mah-jongg piece / TILE
mahogany / CAOBA
mahogany pine / TOTARA
mahogany-like wood / TOON
Mahomet / MAHOUND; MO-
  HAMMED
Mahori / POLYNESIAN
Maia / BONADEA
Maia's father / ATLAS
Maia's mother / PLEIONE
Maia's son / HERMES
maid / GIRL, LASS; BONNE,
  NYMPH; DAMSEL, MAIDEN,
  VIRGIN; MAIDEN
maid of all work / SLAVEY
Maid Marian's companion /
  ROBINHOOD

Maid of Orleans / JOANOFARC
maiden / GIRL. NEW; PURE; FIRST
maiden name / NEE
maidenhair tree / GINKGO
maidenhead / HYMEN; VIRGINITY
mail / POST; ARMOR; LETTERS
mail boat / JACKET; PAQUEBOT
maim / MAR; LAME; INJURE;
  CRIPPLE
main / CHIEF, FIRST, SHEER;
  DIRECT. OCEAN; PRINCIPLE
main blood vessel / VEIN; AORTA
main cabin / SALOON
main dish / ROAST; ENTREE
main facade /PEDIMENT
main force of attack / BRUNT
main idea / GIST; THEME; SUB-
  JECT
main point / NUB; GIST, PITH
main road / ARTERY; FREEWAY
Maine capital / AUGUSTA
Maine city / BATH; RUMFORD
Maine lake / SEBAGO
Maine mountain / KATAHDIN
Maine national park / ACADIA
Maine river / SACO
Maine state bird / CHICKADEE
Maine state motto / DIRIGO
Maine state nickname / PINETREE
mainland / CONTINENT
mainland Japan / HONSHU
mainprise / BAIL
maintain / AVER, HOLD, KEEP
maintain order / POLICE; REGU-
  LATE
maintenance / UPKEEP; DEFENSE
Maintenon's husband / SCARRON
Mainz river / MAIN; RHINE
maize / CORN
maize bread / PIKI, PONE; DODGER
maize genus / ZEA
maize meal / MASA
maize and pepper dish / TAMALE
majestic / GRAND, LOFTY, NOBLE
majesty / DIGNITY; GRANDEUR
major / SENIOR; GREATER
Major Barbara author / SHAW
major key / DUR
Majorca capital / PALMA
major-domo / STEWARD; OVER-
  SEER
make / DO; GET; FIND, FORM, GAIN,
  MOLD; FORCE, FRAME, INCUR,
  RAISE
make additions / ADD, EKE; EX-
  TEND; ENLARGE
make allegations against / ACCUSE,
  CHARGE
make allusion to / HINT
make amends / ATONE; EXPIATE
make angry / IRE; RILE; INCENSE
make arrangements / PLAN

make believe / FEIGN; PRETEND
make a botch of / BLUR, FLUB
make broader / OPEN; WIDEN
make certain / ASSURE, INSURE
make changes / ALTER, AMEND
make chess move / MATE, PUSH
make choice / OPT; PREFER,
   SELECT
make clear / CLEAN; CLARIFY
make cloth / WEAVE
make a cocoon / SPIN
make comfortable / EASE; QUIET
make of commodity / BRAND
make common fund / POOL
make complicated / SNARL
make corrections / EDIT; AMEND
make crackling sound / CRINK
make damp / WET; MOISTEN
make destitute / STRIP; BEREAVE
make docile / TAME
make edging / TAT
make effort / TRY; EXERT
make empty / VACATE
make an end of / KILL; WASTE
make equal / EVEN; EQUATE
make even and flat / LEVEL
make excuses / EVADE, STALL
make eyes / LEER, OGLE; FLIRT
make into fabric / KNIT; WEAVE
make fast / BELAY; SECURE
make feathers smooth / PREEN
make finer / TUNE; FILTER, STRAIN
make firm / FIX, TIE; SECURE
make first move / LEAD, OPEN
make a foray / RAID; RANSACK
make fun of / GUY, RIB; TEASE
make glad / AMUSE, CHEER;
   PLEASE
make glossy / SHINE, SLEEK
make good / REDEEM
make harmonious / TUNE
make harsh noise / BRAY
make haste / HURRY, SPEED
make hazy / DIM; BEDIM
make hedge / PLASH; PLEACH
make a hole / BORE; DRILL
make imitation of / APE; COPY
make infirm / HURT, LAME; INJURE
make irate / IRK, VEX; ANGER
make knight / DUB
make known /TELL; RELATE,
   REPORT
make laborious research / DIG;
   SEEK; DELVE; SEARCH
make lace / TAT
make late / SLOW; DELAY
make into law / ENACT; DECREE
make lean / DIET; EMACIATE
make leather / TAN, TAW
make less bright / DIM; OBSCURE
make less dense / THIN; WATER

make less flexible / HARDEN
make less tight / LOOSEN
make lighter / LEAVEN
make a list / ITEMIZE
make lively / PERK
make a long deep incision / GASH
make a loud noise / BANG
make lustrous / SHINE; POLISH
make mention / HINT; REFER
make merry / REVEL
make misstep / TRIP; STUMBLE
make a mistake / ERR; BLUNDER
make a motion / MOVE; GESTURE
make muddy / ROIL
make neat / REDD; GROOM
make nest / NIDIFY; NIDULATE
make note of / JOT
make obeisance / BOW
make objection / DEMUR; OPPOSE
make as one / UNE; UNITE
make one's way / WEND
make over / REDO; REVAMP;
   REMODEL
make play on words / PUN
make plump / FATTEN; INFLATE
make poetry / VERSIFY
make possible / ENABLE
make pretext / PRETEND
make public / AIR; BRUIT, NOISE
make quiet / CALM, HUSH; SOOTHE
make ready / PREPARE
make reparation / ATONE; EXPIATE
make request / ASK, BEG, SUE
make requittal for / REPAY
make resolute / STEEL; HARDEN
make rigid / TENSE
make safe / GAR; FASTEN, SECURE
make scornful noise / SNORT
make a showy display / SPLURGE
make sleek / TRIM; PREEN
make slower / IMPEDE, RETARD
make smooth / SLICK
make sorrowful / SADDEN
make speech / ORATE; LECTURE
make suds / LATHER
make supremely happy / BEATIFY
make sure / ASSURE, SETTLE
make a sweater / KNIT
make thread / SPIN
make tight / CALK, KNOT; BATTEN
make turbid / ROIL; CONFUSE
make untidy / LITTER
make up / AGREE, ATONE, PAINT
make use of / AVAIL
make vigorous / LIVEN, ROUSE
make void / ANNUL; CANCEL
make a web / SPIN
make well / CURE, HEAL
make words / SPELL
make wrinkles / FOLD; CREASE
make-believe / SHAM; FANTASY

maker / DOER; AUTHOR; BUILDER
maker of fermented liquor / BREWER
maker of wills / TESTATOR
makeshift / TEMPORARY
make-up / ROUGE; FORMAT, LAY-OUT, POWDER; MASCARA; LIP-STICK
Malabar capital / CALICUT
Malabar native / NAIR
Malaccan measure / ASTA
malacia / SOFTENING
maladroit CLUMSY; AWKWARD
malady / DISEASE, ILLNESS
Malagasy / MADAGASCAR
malaise / DISCOMFORT
malapert / BOLD, PERT; SAUCY
malapropos / INAPT; IRRELEVANT
malaria / MIASMA; PALUDISM
malarial fever / AGUE; QUARTAN, TERTIAN
malathion / INSECTICIDE
Malawi capital / ZOMBA
Malawi lake / NYASA
Malawi money / KWACHA
Malay berry / DUKU; LANSA; LANSEH
Malay canoe / PRAO, PRAU, PROA
Malay common law / ADAT
Malay dagger / KRIS; CREES
Malay dementia / AMOK; AMUCK
Malay garment / BAJU; KABAYA, SARONG
Malay gibbon / LAR
Malay headman / DATO, DATU; DATTO
Malay island / ALOR, BALI, JAVA; TIMOR; BORNEO; CELEBES, SUMATRA
Malay isthmus / KRA
Malay jumping disease / LATA
Malay knife / KRIS; PARANG
Malay money / ORA, TRA; TAM-PANG
Malay negrito / ATA, ITA; AETA
Malay palm / GEBANG
Malay title of respect / TUAN
Malay verse form / PANTUN
Malaysia capital / KUALALUMPUR
Malaysian language / MALAY
Malaysian states / KEDAH, PERAK, SABAH; JOHORE, PAHANG, PENANG
malcontent / UNEASY; UNHAPPY
Maldives capital / MALE
Maldives product / COIR
male / BOY, HIM, MAN. MANLY
male antelope / BUCK
male bee / DRONE
male caryatid / ATLAS; TELAMON
male cat / GIB, TOM
male chicken / COCK; ROOSTER

male child / SON
male deer / BUCK, HART, STAG
male duck / DRAKE
male falcon / TERCEL
male ferret / HOB
male forebears / SIRES; FATHERS
male fox / STAG
male goat / RAM, TUP; BUCK, BILLY
male goose/ GANDER
male hare / BUCK
male hawk / TERCEL; TERCELET
male hog / BOAR
male horse / STUD; STALLION
male parties / STAGS
male rabbit / BUCK
male ruminant / OX; BUCK, BULL; STEER
male salmon / GIB; COCK
male servant / BOY, MAN; PAGE; VALET; BUTLER
male sheep / RAM; TUP; WETHER
male swan / COB
male swine / BOAR; BARROW
male turkey / TOM
male voice / BASS; BASSO, TENOR
malediction / CURSE; IMPRE-CATION
malefactor / FELON; CULPRIT
malefic / EVIL; MALIGN; HURTFUL
malevolence SPITE; MALICE
malfeasance / MISDEED
Mali capital / BAMAKO
Mali city / GOA; TIMBUKTU
Mali people / FULANI, TUAREG; SONGHAI
Mali river / NIGER; SENEGAL
malice / ENVY, HATE; PIQUE
malicious / ILL; EVIL; CATTY
malicious burning / ARSON
malicious damage /SABOTAGE
malicious glance / LEER
malicious person / FURY; BEAST
malicious woman / CAT, HAG; VIXEN; VIRAGO
malign / DECRY, LIBEL; DEFAME, REVILE, VILIFY. EVIL; BANEFUL
malign influence / EVILEYE
malignant / EVIL; DEADLY
malignant spirit / KER; HARPY
maligner / REVILER
malignity / HATE; HATRED, RANCOR
malingerer / FAKER; SHIRKER
malison / CURSE; EXECRATION
mall / WALK; AVENUE, MALLET
malleable / SOFT; DUCTILE
malleable metal / TIN; GOLD, LEAD; COPPER
mallet / MALL, MAUL; GAVEL
malodorous / FETID; SMELLY
Malory's subject / ARTHUR

malpractice / MISCONDUCT
malt drink / ALE; BEER; STOUT; PORTER
Malta capital / VALLETTA
Malta island / GOZO; COMINO
Malthus' bugaboo / POPULATION
Malthusian doctrine today / ZPG
maltreat / ABUSE; ILLUSE
malversation / FRAUD
Malwa capital / UJJAIN
mama / MA; MOM; MAMMA, MAMMY
mamma / UDDER; BREAST
mammon / RICHES, WEALTH
mammoth / HUGE, VAST; GIANT
man / VIR, WER; ALE; HUMAN
man of all trades / FACTOTUM
man and apes / PRIMATES
man of brass / TALOS
man in charge / LEADER; MANAGER
Man of Destiny / NAPOLEON
man dressed as woman / QUEEN
man Friday / SERVANT
man of great beauty / ADONIS
man of great riches / NABOB
man of great strength / SAMSON; HERCULES
man of learning / PUNDIT, SAVANT
man of letters / AUTHOR, WRITER
Man Without a Country / NOLAN
man of the world / SOPHISTICATE
manacle / TIE; BIND; CHAIN
manage / RUN; RULE; GUIDE, STEER
manageable / EASY, YARE; DOCILE
manager / BOSS; FACTOR, GERENT
manana / TOMORROW
Manassas battle / BULLRUN
Manasseh's brother / EPHRAIM
Manasseh's city / ANER
Manasseh's father / JOSEPH
Manchukuo emperor / PUYI; KANGTE
Manchuria, pert. to / MANCHU
Manchurian city / HARBIN, MUKDEN
Manchurian river / YALU; SUNGARI
Manchurian seaport / ANTUNG
manciple / STEWARD; PURVEYOR
mandarin orange / TANGERINE
mandarin's home / YAMEN, YAMUN
mandate / LAW; EDICT, ORDER
mandatory / OBLIGATORY
mandible / JAW; JAWBONE
mandragora / MANDRAKE
manducate / EAT; CHEW
man-eater / LION; SHARK, TIGER
Manette's daughter / LUCIE
maneuver / TRICK; ARTIFICE
manful / BRAVE; RESOLUTE
manger / BIN, BOX; CRIB; CRECHE
mangle / EAT, MAR; HACK, MAIM

mango / AMINI
mangy / MEAN; FILTHY, SCURVY
manhattan cocktail garnish / CHERRY
Manhattan district / CHELSEA
Manhattan District chief / GROVES
Manhattan District scientist / RABI, UREY; OPPENHEIMER
Manhattan street / WALL; BOWERY
Manhattan's purchaser / MINUIT
mania / CRAZE; FRENZY; EXCITEMENT
maniac / NUT; MADMAN, PSYCHO
maniacal / MAD
manicurist's aid / FILE
manifest / SHOW; PROVE; ATTEST
manifestation / DISPLAY
manifesto / EDICT; DECLARATION
manifold / DIVERS, SUNDRY
manikin / DWARF; FIGURE
manila / HEMP; ABACA
Manila Bay island / CORREGIDOR
Manila boat / BILALO
manila braid / TAGAL
Manila victor / DEWEY
Manila's founder / LEGASPI
Manila's river / PASIG
manioc / CASSAVA, TAPIOCA
maniple / FANO; FANON, FANUM
manipulate / USE; ADAPT, WIELD
Manipur capital / IMPHAL
Manitoba capital / WINNIPEG
Manitoba rebel / RIEL
Manitoba river / NELSON
Manitoba town / FLINFLON
mankeeper / NEWT
mankind / MEN; HUMANITY
manly / BOLD, FIRM; BRAVE, HARDY
manna / LAAP, LERP
mannequin / MODEL
manner / AIR, WAY; LOOK, MIEN
mannerism / AFFECTATION
mannerly / CIVIL; POLITE; URBANE
manners / DEPORTMENT
mannish / MASCULINE
manor / ESTATE; DEMESNE, MANSION
manorial court / LEET
man's hat / BERET, DERBY; BOWLER, FEDORA, TOPPER; STETSON; SOMBRERO
man's name / ELI, GUY, IAN, IRA; ADAM, ALAN, AMOS, CARL, DANA, DION, EMIL, ENOS, ERIC, EVAN, EZRA, HANS, JOEL, JOHN, JOSE, JUAN, JUDE, KARL, LEON, LUKE, MARC, MARK, NEIL, NOEL, OTTO, OWEN, PAUL; BASIL, HIRAM, HOMER, ALBERT, DONALD, GEORGE, OLIVER, SAMSON, STEVEN, WARREN; ANTHONY, ANTONIO, CHARLES

man's nickname / AL; ABE, ALF, BEN, BOB, DON, JOE, MAC, MAX, MOE, NED, TED, TOM; ALGY, ANDY, BART, BERT, BILL, BONY, DAVE, DAVY, DICK, DODE, FRED, GENE, JACK, JAKE, JOCK, JOEY, MART, MIKE, MOSE, NOLL, PETE, PHIL, RUBE, TOBY, TONY, WALT, ZACK, ZEKE; CHUCK

mansion / HOUSE, MANOR, VILLA

manslaughter / MURDER; HOMICIDE

mansuetude / CIVILITY, MILDNESS

mantic / DIVINATORY

mantilla / CAPE, VEIL; SCARF

mantis shrimp / SQUILLA

mantle / CAPE, ROBE; CLOAK; BURNER, MANTUA, SHEATH; PALLIUM

Manto's parent / TIRESIAS

Manto's son / OCNUS; MOPSUS

Mantuan ruling family / GONZAGA

manual / TEXT; HANDBOOK, KEYBOARD

manual digit / THUMB; FINGER

manual training system / SLOID, SLOJD, SLOYD

manual vocation / CRAFT, TRADE

manual worker / LABORER

manufacture / MAKE; PRODUCE

manufacturing plant / MILL, SHOP

manumission / FREEDOM; EMANCIPATION

manure / DUNG; FERTILIZER

manuscript / MS; CODEX; SCRIPT

Manx capital / DOUGLAS

Manx judge / DEEMSTER

Manxman author / CAINE

many / DIVERS, SUNDRY; SEVERAL, VARIOUS

many-colored / PIED; MOTLEY; RAINBOW; IRIDESCENT, POLYCHROME

many-colored stone / OPAL; AGATE

many-eyed guardian / ARGUS

many-sided / VERSATILE

Manzoni novel / BETROTHED

Maori canoe / WAKA

Maori chief / RANGATIRA

Maori compensation / UTU

Maori demon / TAIPO

Maori hut / WHARE

Maori knife / PATU

Maori pine / TOTARA

Maori rootstock food / ROI

Maori tattoo / MOKO

Maori tattooing implement / UHI

Maori village / KAIK

Maori war club / MERE, RATA

Maori woman / WAHINE

map / PLAN, PLAT; CHART; SKETCH

map book / ATLAS

maple genus / ACER

maple seed / SAMARA

maple tree spigot / SPILE

mapmaker / CARTOGRAPHER

maquillage / MAKEUP

mar / HARM, HURT, RUIN, SCAR

marabou / STORK; ARGALA; ADJUTANT

marantic / WASTING

marathon / RACE; ORDEAL; CONTEST

Marathon's victor / MILTIADES

maraud / LOOT; PILLAGE, PLUNDER

marble / MIB, MIG, TAW; BALL, MIGG; AGATE, AGGIE, ALLEY, RANCE

marble-like / MARMOREAL

marbles game / COB, LAG, TAW; RINGERS

Marceau's mimed character / BIP

march / MONTH; BORDER, PARADE; FRONTIER, PROGRESS, ADVANCE

March birthstone / JASPER; BLOODSTONE

March date / IDES

March girl / JO; AMY, MEG; BETH

march king / SOUSA

marching call / HEP, HUP; FORWARD

marchpane / MARZIPAN

marcid / WEAK; TABID; EMACIATED

Mardi Gras monarch / REX

Marduk's father / EA

Marduk's son / NEBO

Marduk's victim / TIAMAT

mare / HAG; JADE; YAUD

Mare Nostrum of Italy / MEDITERRANEAN

Margaret / MAG, MEG, PEG; GRETA, PEGGY

margarine / OLEO; BUTTERINE

margin / HEM, LIP, RIM; BRIM, EDGE; BRINK, LIMIT

marginal note / GLOSS; POSTIL

margosa / NIM; NEEM; NEEMBA

Marianas discoverer / MAGELLAN

Marianas island / ROTA; SAIPAN, TINIAN

marihuana / POT; HEMP; MARYJANE

marihuana cigarette / POT; JOINT; REEFER

marihuana cigarette end / ROACH

marinade / BRINE

marinate / PICKLE

marine / NAVAL; OCEANIC, PELAGIC

marine crustacean / CRAB; SHRIMP

marine gastropod / WHELK; COWRIE, LIMPET, TRITON; ABALONE; NERITOID

marine mollusk / CLAM; MUSSEL, OYSTER; SCALLOP

marine people / MERMEN; MERMAIDS

marine plant / AGAR, KELP, MOSS

marine shell / CONCH

marine skeleton / CORAL; SPONGE

marine snail / WELK, WILK; WHELK; TRITON

marine wood borer / GRIBBLE

marine worm / LURG; SYLLID

mariner / GOB, TAR; SALT; SAILOR

marionette / PUPPET

maritime / MARINE; OCEANIC

marjoram / DITTANY; ORIGANUM

mark / RUT, TAB; LANE, NOTE, SIGN, SPOT; BADGE, BRAND, LABEL, STAMP, TOKEN, TRACE. SHOW; INDEX; NOTICE, OBJECT, REMARK; ENGRAVE

mark aimed at / TEE; TARGET; BULLSEYE

mark of a blow / DENT; MOUSE; BRUISE

mark under c / CEDILLA

mark by cutting / NOTCH, SCORE; ENGRAVE

mark of infamy / BRAND; STIGMA

mark of injury / SCAR

mark for insertion / CARET

mark to let stand / STET

mark the limits / DEFINE; OUTLINE

mark with lines / LINE; STREAK

mark of omission / DELE; CARET

mark of pronunciation / TILDE; AC-CENT; CEDILLA

mark with red / RUBRICATE

mark to shoot at / BUTT, WAND

mark the skin / TATTOO

mark with spots / DOT; FLECK; DAPPLE, MOTTLE, SPECKLE, STIPPLE

mark over a vowel / BREVE; ACCENT, MACRON, UMLAUT; DIERESIS

marked with bars / STRIPED

marked by distinction / FAMOUS; EMINENT; SUPERIOR

marked by repetition / ECHOING, ITERANT; RECURRENT

marked by time / AGED; DATED

marked by wounds / SCARRED

marker / PEG; SIGN; STELE, STONE

market / MART, SHOP; PASAR, STORE; BAZAAR. SELL, VEND

market place / MART; AGORA, BAZAR, FORUM, PASAR; BAZAAR

marketable / SALABLE; VENDIBLE

Mark's wife / ISOUD; ISOLDE

marl / CLAY, LOAM; EARTH; MANURE

Marley's partner / SCROOGE

Marlowe's masterpiece / FAUSTUS

marmalade tree / MAMEY, MAMIE; MAMMEE, SAPOTE

marmoset / MICO; PINCHE, SAGOIN; TAMARIN, WISTITI

marmot / BOBAC; GOPHER; WOODCHUCK; PRAIRIEDOG

marooned / DESERTED, STRANDED

Marpessa's father / EVENUS

Marpessa's lover / IDAS

Marquand's Japanese detective / MOTO

marquee / TENT

Marquesas island / HIVAOA; NUKUHIVA

marquetry / INLAY

Marquis's cockroach / ARCHY

marriage / WEDLOCK; NUPTIALS

marriage, c.f. / GAMO

marriage, pert. to / BRIDAL; MARITAL, NUPTIAL; CONJUGAL

marriage announcement / BANS; BANNS

marriage hater / MISOGAMIST

marriage partner / MATE; SPOUSE

marriage settlement / DOS, DOT; DOTE; DOWER, DOWRY; PORTION

marriage vow / IDO; TROTH

marriageable / NUBILE

married / WED; WEDDED

married man / BENEDICT

married woman / MATRON

marrow / PITH; SPOUSE, SQUASH

marry / WED; MATE, WIVE; ESPOUSE

marry again / REWED

Mars / ARES

Mars, pert. to / MARTIAN

Mars' Hill / AREOPAGUS

Mars markings / CANALS

Mars' sacred animal / WOLF

Mars' satellite / DEIMOS, PHOBOS

Marseillaise composer / DELISLE

marsh / BOG, FEN; SLEU; LIMAN, SWALE, SWAMP; MORASS, SLOUGH

marsh bird / RAIL, SORA; SNIPE, STILT; BITTERN

marsh crocodile / GOA; MUGGER

marsh gas / METHANE

marsh grass / REED; SEDGE; FESCUE

marsh hen / COOT, RAIL; BITTERN

marsh marigold / COWSLIP

marsh plant / REED, TULE; SEDGE; BULRUSH, CATTAIL

marsh tea / LEDUM

marshal / LEAD; ARRAY, GUIDE
Marshalls island / MILI; BIKINI, JALUIT; ENIWETOK
marshwort / CRANBERRY
marshy / WET; BOGGY; PALUDAL, PALUDIC; PALUDINE; PALUDINAL
marshy inlet / SLEW; SLOUGH
marshy land / BOG; SWALE; MORASS
marsupial / KOALA; CUSCUS, POSSUM, WOMBAT; DASYURE, OPPOSSUM; KANGAROO; BANDI-COOT
mart / STORE; MARKET; EMPORIUM
marten / SABLE; FISHER
martial / WARLIKE; MILITARY
Martial's forte / EPIGRAM
Martian priests / SALII
martinet / PRECISIAN
martini decoration / OLIVE
Martinique capital / FORTDE-FRANCE
Martinique volcano / PELEE
martyr / TORMENT, TORTURE
marvel / WONDER; MIRACLE, PRODIGY
marvelous / AMAZING; WONDER-FUL
Marx brothers / CHICO, HARPO, ZEPPO; GROUCHO
Marx magnum opus / CAPITAL; DASKAPITAL
Maryland bay / CHESAPEAKE
Maryland capital / ANNAPOLIS
Maryland city / BALTIMORE
Maryland patron / CALVERT
Maryland river / POTOMAC
Maryland state nickname / COCKADE, OLDLINE; FREE-STATE
Maryland town / BOWIE
mascot / PET; CHARM; TALISMAN
masculine / BOLD, MALE; MANLY
masculine or feminine name / LEE; MARION
masculine name / See man's name
masculine pronoun / HE; HIM, HIS
mash / MESS, PULP; CRUSH
masjid / MESJID, MOSQUE, MUSJID
mask / PLEA, RUSE, VEIL; CLOAK, TRICK, VISOR; DOMINO, MASQUE, SCREEN, PRETEXT. HIDE; COVER
masker / MUMMER; MASQUERADER
mason / WASP; BUILDER; BRICKLAYER
Masonic doorkeeper / TILER
masque designer / INIGOJONES

masque interpreter / TRUCHMAN
masque by Jonson / CHLORIDIA
masque by Milton / COMUS
mass / GOB, PAT, WAD; BODY, BULK, HEAP, LUMP, SIZE; GROSS, WHOLE
mass, suffix / MAS
mass of bread / LOAF
mass of cast iron / INGOT
mass of fibers / TOW
mass flight / EXODUS
mass of floating ice / BERG, FLOE
mass of floating logs / JAM; RAFT; DRIVE
mass of hay / MOW; STACK
mass meeting / RALLY; MUSTER
mass prayer book / MISSAL
mass of spores / SORUS
mass of untidy hair / MOP
mass of vapor / CLOUD; NEBULE
mass of water / GUSH; FLOOD; DE-LUGE; NIAGARA
mass of yarn / COP
Massachusetts cape / ANN, COD
Massachusetts capital / BOSTON
Massachusetts city / LYNN; SALEM
Massachusetts mountain / TOM
Massachusetts school / MIT; TUFTS; AMHERST; BRANDEIS
Massachusetts settler / PILGRIM
Massachusetts state bird / CHICK-ADEE
Massachusetts state flower / MAYFLOWER
Massachusetts state nickname / BAYSTATE; OLDCOLONY
Massachusetts state tree / ELM
massacre / POGROM; BUTCHERY
massage / RUB; KNEAD
Massenet opera / MANON, THAIS
masses / MOBS; CROWDS, PEOPLE
massive / HUGE; BULKY, HEAVY, LARGE, MASSY, SOLID; IMMENSE
mast / NUTS, POLE, SPAR, SPIR
mast support / BIBB; CHEEK, HOUND
mast tree / CORKOAK
master / DAN; BAAS, BOSS, HEAD, LORD, MIAN; CHIEF, OWNER, RULER. LEARN; SUBDUE; CONQUER
master stroke / COUP; KNOCKOUT
mastered / GOT, WON
masterful / SKILLFUL; IMPERIOUS
masterly / CLEVER, EXPERT
masterpiece / CHEFDOEUVRE
Masters' "anthology" / SPOONRIVER

mastery / RULE, SWAY; SKILL
mastic tree / ACOMA; GUMBO-LIMBO
masticate / GUM; CHAW, CHEW
mastiff / ALAN
mastigosis / WHIPPING
mastology / MAMMALOGY
mastwood / POON
mat / DOILY; CARPET; CUSHION. SNARL, TWIST; ENTANGLE. DULL
match / MATE, PAIR, SUIT, TEAM; COMPARE. PEER, TWIN; EQUAL
matched group / SET
matchless / PEERLESS; UNEQUALED
matchlock / MUSKET; GUNLOCK
matchmaker / BROKER; SHADKAN; SCHADCHEN, SCHATCHEN
mate / CHUM; EQUAL, MATCH; FELLOW, SPOUSE. PAIR; MARRY
mated / PAIRED; MATCHED; DEFEATED
material / STUFF; FABRIC, GROUND
material for dressing wounds / LINT; GAUZE
material for gas mantles / CERIA; THORIA
material for musical strings / GUT; CATGUT
material wealth / RICHES
maternal / MOTHERLY
matgrass / NARD; FOGFRUIT
math / CROP; MOWING
mathematical angle / RADIAN
mathematical function / SINE; COSINE; TANGENT; LOGARITHM
mathematical line / VECTOR
mathematical quantity / SCALAR, VECTOR; OPERAND; MAGNITUDE
mathematical ratio / PI; SINE
mathematical term / PI; COSH, SECH, SINE, SINH, TANH; COSINE
mathematics branch / TRIG; CONICS; ALGEBRA; CALCULUS
Mato Grosso river / ARINOS, CUIABA
matriculate / ENTER; ENROLL
matrimonial / NUPTIAL; CONNUBIAL
matrimony / WEDLOCK; MARRIAGE
matrix / BED, MAT; MOLD, WOMB
matron's title / MAAM; MADAM; MADAME, SENORA; SIGNORA
matted hair / SHAG
matter / BODY; EVENT, SENSE
matter of fact / DRY; LITERAL

matter under inquiry / CASE
matter in law / RES
Matterhorn / MONTCERVIN
matting / MATS
mattress / TICK; PAILLASSE, PALLIASSE
mature / AGE; GROW; MELLOW, SEASON. DUE, FIT; RIPE; ADULT
mature insect / IMAGO
mature reproductive cell / EGG; GERM; SPERM; GAMETE
matutinal / EARLY; MATINAL
maudlin / DRUNK, SILLY; STUPID
Maugham's master spy / ASHENDEN
Maui mountain / EKE; HALEAKALA
maul / ABUSE; MISTREAT. HAMMER
Maumau country / KENYA
Mauna Loa crater / KILAUEA
maunder / RAMBLE
Maupassant story / BELAMI
Mauritania capital / NOUAKCHOTT
Mauritania inhabitant / MOOR
Mauritius capital / PORTLOUIS
mausoleum / TOMB
mausoleum at Agra / TAJMAHAL
Mausolus' tomb in Caria / MAUSOLEUM
mauve / LILAC
maverick / DOGIE; DISSENTER
mavourneen / DARLING
maw / MA; MOM; CRAW, CROP
mawkish / FLAT; VAPID; SICKLY; INSIPID; NAUSEOUS
maxilla / JAW; JAWBONE
maxim / SAW; ITEM, RULE; ADAGE, AXIOM, MORAL, MOTTO; APHORISM
Maximilian's empress / CARLOTTA
maximum / MOST; HIGHEST; GREATEST
May birthstone / AGATE; EMERALD
May Day in Europe / LABORDAY
May first / MAYDAY; BELTANE; BELTAINE; WALPURGIS
may fly / DUN; EPHEMERID
Mayan Indian / MAM; CHOL, ITZA
maybe / HAPLY; LIKELY; PERHAPS
mayday / SOS
mayflower / ANEMONE, ARBUTUS, COWSLIP; HAWTHORN, HEPATICA
Mayflower document / COMPACT
mayor in Latin America / ALCALDE
Mazarin's predecessor / RICHELIEU
maze / DAZE; PUZZLE; LABYRINTH
mazeltov / GOODLUCK
Mazeppa's author / BYRON
mazuma / MONEY; WEALTH
McGuffey book / READER

me / MYSELF
mead / HYDROMEL; METHEGLIN
mead constituent / HONEY
Meade's victory / GETTYSBURG
meadow / LEA; MEAD; PASTURE
meadow barley / RIE
meadow hen / COOT; BITTERN
meadow lark / MEDLAR
meadow mouse / VOLE
meadow saxifrage / SESELI
meadowsweet / SPIREA
meager / DRY; BARE, DULL, LEAN, MEAN, POOR, THIN, WEAK; GAUNT
meal / MESS; LUNCH, SNACK, CEREAL, DINNER, FARINA, REPAST
meal for the mill / GRIST
meal of parched corn / NOCAKE
meal ticket / SUCKER; EASYMARK
mean / LOW; BASE, VILE, CRUEL, DIRTY, PETTY, SNIDE; ABJECT, BRUTAL, IMPLY; DENOTE
mean dwelling / HUT; SHED; SHANTY
mean hoarder / MISER
mean values / AVERAGES
meander / WIND; TWINE; WANDER
meaning / AIM; SENSE; DESIGN
meaning, pert. to / SEMANTIC
meaningless refrain / FALA; DERRY; DERRYDOWN
means / WAY; MODE; INCOME, MANNER, METHOD, RICHES, WEALTH
means of access / DOOR, GATE
means of communication / TV; SIGN, WIRE; MEDIA, RADIO; LETTER
means of conveyance / BUS, CAR; AUTO; PLANE, TRAIN
means of defense / ARMS, FORT; WEAPONS; FORTRESS, MUNI-MENT
means of exerting force / LEVER
means of livelihood / JOB; WORK; CRAFT, TRADE; BUSINESS
mean-spirited / LOW; BASE
meantime / INTERIM; MEANWHILE
measles / RUBEOLA
measly / MEAN, POOR
measure / EM, EN; ARE, LAW, TON; ACRE, AREA, RULE; DANCE, METER; EXTENT. METE, . SCAN; ALLOT, GAUGE
measure, pert. to / METRIC
measure of capacity / CUP, TON; DRAM, GILL, PECK, PINT; LITER, LITRE, QUART, STERE; BARREL, BUSHEL, GALLON
measure of cloth / ELL; YARD
measure of distance / LI, RI; DRA, ELL, PIK, ROD; COSS, FOOT,

HATH, HAUT, MILE, YARD; CUBIT, METER, METRE, VERST
measure of duration / TIME
measure of extent / ARE; ACRE
measure of medicine / DOSE
measure out / METE
measure of paper / REAM; QUIRE
measure of sound / BEL; DECIBEL
measure of spirits / PEG; FIFTH; JIGGER
measure of thickness / CALIPER
measure of weight / TON; DRAM, GRAM; CARAT, GRAIN, OUNCE, POUND
measure of wire diameter / MIL
measure of wood / CORD
measure of yarn / LEA; SKEIN
measurement downward / DEPTH
measuring instrument / LOG; DIAL, RULE, TAPE; CHAIN, CLOCK, GAUGE
measuring stick / ROD; POLE, RULE; RULER; DIPSTICK
meat / HAM; BEEF, FOOD, LAMB, PORK, VEAL; FLESH, TRIPE; KID-NEY
meat cake / PATTY; RISSOLE; HAMBURGER
meat cut / HAM, RIB; CHOP, LOIN, RUMP; FILET, STEAK, TBONE; FILLET; BRISKET
meat in dough shells / WONTON; PELMENY, RAVIOLI; KREPLACH
meat jelly / ASPIC
meat paste / PATE; SPREAD
meat on skewer / CABOB, KABOB, KEBAB; SHASLIK; SHASHLIK
meatless / LENTEN, MAIGRE; FRUITARIAN, VEGETARIAN
meat-vegetable dish / HASH, STEW; RAGOUT; GOULASH; CHOPSUEY
meaty / RICH; JUICY, PITHY
mecca / AIM; GOAL
Mecca pilgrimage / HADJ, HAJJ
Mecca pilgrimage costume / IHRAM
Mecca shrine / CAABA, KAABA
Mecca's port / JIDDA
mechanic / HAND; ARTISAN, WORKMAN; ARTIFICER, MACHINIST
mechanical / AUTOMATIC; SPIRIT-LESS; INVOLUNTARY
mechanical advantage / LEVERAGE
mechanical arrangement / DEVICE
mechanical bar / LEVER; CROW-BAR
mechanical contrivance / MOTOR; ENGINE; MACHINE
mechanical man / ROBOT; ANDROID
mechanical part / CAM, COG; GEAR

mechanical repetition / ROTE; TRACING

mechanics branch / STATICS; DYNAMICS, KINETICS

mechanism / MACHINE; APPARATUS

Mechlin lace / MALINE; MALINES

medal / BADGE; MEDALLION

medallion / MEDAL; TABLET

meddle / PRY; TAMPER; INTRUDE

meddler / BUSYBODY

meddlesome / INTRUSIVE, OFFICIOUS

mede / MEDIAN

Medea's father / AEETES

Medea's husband / JASON

Medea's native land / COLCHIS

media / TV; FILM; MOVIE, RADIO; MAGAZINE; NEWSPAPER; TELEVISION

medial / MEAN; MEDIAN, MIDDLE; AVERAGE

median ridge / RAPHE

mediate / ARBITRATE, RECONCILE

mediator / INTERCESSOR

medic / DOCTOR, MEDICK; ALFALFA, LUCERNE

medical / IATRIC; CURATIVE, IATRICAL

medical examiner / CORONER

medical man / DOC; LEECH; DOCTOR; PHYSICIAN

medical nitroglycerin / GLONOIN

medical society / AMA

medical specialist / OCULIST; INTERNIST; GYNECOLOGIST

medicated lozenge / TABELLA

Medicean library founder / LORENZO

medicinal / CURATIVE, REMEDIAL

medicinal application / SALVE; UNGUENT; OINTMENT; EMBROCATION

medicinal bark / COTO

medicinal cigarette / CUBEB

medicinal gum / KINO

medicinal herb / ALOE; SENNA

medicinal pellet / PILL; CACHET

medicinal plant / AGAR, ALOE, HERB; ANISE, JALAP, ORRIS, SENNA, TANSY; ARNICA, CROTON, IPECAC

medicinal portion / DOSE; DOSAGE

medicinal shrub / ALEM; SENNA

medicine / DRUG, PILL; TONIC

medicine, pert. to / IATRIC; MEDICINAL

medicine to allay pain / ANODYNE

medicine distributor / DOCTOR; DRUGGIST; PHARMACIST

medicine man / PRIEST, SHAMAN

Medicis' city / FLORENCE

medieval China / SERES; CATHAY

medieval dagger / ANLACE; MISERICORD

medieval fiddle / GIGA

medieval fortress / CASTLE

medieval helmet / ARMET; HEAUME

medieval military machine / ASS; BOAR, MULE; DONKEY, ONAGER

medieval minstrel / TROUBADOUR

medieval money / ORA; OBOLE

medieval narrative / SAGA

medieval organization / GILD

medieval playing card / TAROT

medieval poetic tale / LAI, LAY; ROMANCE, ROMAUNT

medieval satirist / GOLIARD

medieval science / ALCHEMY

medieval ship / NEF; AESC; XEBEC

medieval sport / ARCHERY, TILTING; FALCONRY

medieval weapon / MACE, PIKE; ESTOC, LANCE, ONCIN, SPEAR

Medina's port / YENBO

mediocre / SOSO; MEDIUM; AVERAGE

meditate / MULL, MUSE, PLAN; BROOD, STUDY, THINK

meditate upon / WEIGH

meditative / MUSING; THOUGHT-FUL

Mediterranean / ITALIAN; ALBANIAN, CORSICAN, SICILIAN

Mediterranean East / LEVANT

Mediterranean fish / TONNO

Mediterranean grass / DISS

Mediterranean Island / ELBA, GOZO; CAPRI, CRETE, MALTA; LIPARI

Mediterranean port / ORAN

Mediterranean resort / LIDO, NICE; MONTECARLO

Mediterranean resort area / RIVIERA

Mediterranean sea / AEGEAN, IONIAN; ADRIATIC

Mediterranean tree / CAROB, OLIVE

Mediterranean vessel / SAIC; SETEE, XEBEC, ZEBEC; MISTIC, TARTAN; FELUCCA, POLACRE

Mediterranean wind / SOLANO; MISTRAL, SIROCCO; LEVANTER

medium / MEAN; MEANS; PSYCHIC

medium of communication / WORD; RADIO, VOICE, WORDS; LETTER; MISSIVE

medium of exchange / MONEY

medium's effluvium / ECTOPLASM

medium's session / SEANCE

medlar / LOQUAT, MESPIL

medley / OLIO, OLLA; JUMBLE; FARRAGO, MELANGE, MIXTURE; POTPOURRI
medley of familiar airs / FANTASY; FANTASIA
medusa / JELLYFISH
Medusa's killer / PERSEUS
meed / REWARD; RECOMPENSE
meek / MILD, TAME; GENTLE, HUMBLE, MODEST; YIELDING; SUBMISSIVE
meer / MEAR; BOUNDARY
meet / SIT; JOIN; UNITE; CONFER
meeting / UNION; PARLEY; COMPANY, CONFLUX, SESSION; ASSEMBLY
meeting by appointment / DATE
meeting for discussion / INTERVIEW
meeting place for students / CLASSROOM
meeting of students / CLASS; SEMINAR
megacycle today / MEGAHERTZ
Megiddo battle / ARMAGEDDON
megillah / CATALOGUE
megrims / BLUES; DEPRESSION
Mehitabel's motto / TOUJOURSGAI
meiosis / UNDERSTATEMENT
meistersinger / SACHS
meistersingers' founder / FRAUENLOB
Mekong city / PHNOMPENH, VIENTIANE
Mekong source / TIBET
mel / HONEY
melancholy / SAD; BLUE, GLUM; DREAR; DISMAL, GLOOMY, RUEFUL
melancholy song / BLUES; THRENODY
Melanesian / FIJIAN; TARAPON
Melanesian islands / FIJI; SOLOMONS
melange / MEDLEY; MIXTURE
Melbourne's river / YARRAYARRA
meld / BLEND, SCORE
Meleager's father / OENEUS
Meleager's mother / ALTHEA
Meleager's prey / BOAR
melee / FRAY; BRAWL; FIGHT; AFFRAY, BATTLE; SCUFFLE
melic / LYRIC
melilot / CLEVER
meliorate / BETTER, REFINE; IMPROVE
mellifluent / SWEET; SMOOTH
mellow / AGED, RICH, RIPE, SOFT. AGE; RIPEN; SOFTEN
melodic theme / LEITMOTIF
melodious / LYRIC; ARIOSO

melodrama classic / BELLS; EASTLYNNE
melodramatic / SENSATIONAL
melody / AIR; ARIA, SONG, TUNE
melon / PEPO; CASABA; HONEYDEW, MUSKMELON; CANTALOUP; CANTALOUPE
melonlike fruit / PAPAYA
melt / FUSE, PASS, THAW; BLEND
melt down / RENDER; CLARIFY
Melville novel / OMOO; TYPEE; MOBYDICK
member / LIMB, PART; ORGAN
member of diplomatic staff / CHARGE; ATTACHE
member of down under forces / ANZAC
member of electorate / VOTER
member of gang / HOOD; MOHOCK; HOODLUM, MOBSTER
member of governing board / REGENT; DIRECTOR
member of laity / LAIC; LAYMAN
member of religious community / CENOBITE; CONVENTUAL
member of religious order / FRA; MONK; FRIAR
member of vitamin B complex / BIOTIN, NIACIN; THIAMINE
membership / SEAT, VOTE
membership fee / DUES
membrane / PIA, WEB; CAUL, TELA, VELA
Memel / KLAIPEDA
memento / RELIC, TOKEN; KEEPSAKE
Memnon's father / TITHONUS
Memnon's kingdom / ETHIOPA
Memnon's mother / EOS
Memnon's slayer / ACHILLES
memo / MEMORANDUM
memoir / LIFE; ELOGE; RECORD
memoirs / AUTOBIOGRAPHY
memorabilia / ANA; MISCELLANEA
memorable / FAMED, GREAT, NOTED
memorandum / CHIT, MEMO, NOTE
memorial / PETITION; TOMBSTONE
memorial column / LAT, XAT
memorial heap of stones / CAIRN
memorial inscription / RIP; EPITAPH; HICJACET
memory / FAME; REPUTATION; REMEMBRANCE
memory, pert. to / MNEMONIC
memory loss / AMNESIA
Memphis street / BEALE
Memphis god / PTAH
men / MALES; ADULTS, PIECES
men and apes / PRIMATES
men and boys / MALES

men among the Houyhnhnms / YAHOOS
men of learning / SAVANTS
men of letters / LITERATI
men working on a boat / CREW
men working together / CREW, GANG, TEAM; SHIFT
menace / THREAT. IMPERIL
menage / HOUSEHOLD
menagerie / ZOO
Mencken's magazine / MERCURY
mend / FIX, SEW; DARN, HEAL, HELP
mend as bone / KNIT
mend shoes / COBBLE
mend socks / DARN
mend temporarily / PATCH
mendacious / LYING; UNTRUE
mendacious person / LIAR; FIBBER; ANANIAS
mender / FIXER; DOCTOR, TINKER
Menderes river / MEANDER; SCAMANDER
mendicant / MONK; FAKIR; BEGGAR
mendicant friar / SERVITE
mendicity / BEGGING
Menelaus' brother / AGAMEMNON
Menelaus' daughter / HERMIONE
Menelaus' father / ATREUS
Menelaus' kingdom / SPARTA
Menelaus' wife / HELEN
menhir / MONOLITH
menial / DRUDGE, FLUNKY, LACKEY, SLAVEY, VARLET; SERVANT
Menlo Park inventor / EDISON
Mennonite / AMISH; HERRITE
men's social gathering / STAG
men's underwear / SHORTS; TSHIRTS; SKIVVIES
mensa / TABLE
menstruum / SOLVENT
mentagra / SYCOSIS
mental / PHRENIC; INTERNAL
mental alertness / WIT; AGILITY
mental bent / BIAS; SLANT
mental conception / IDEA; CONCEPT
mental condition / MOOD; MORALE
mental confusion / FOG; HAZE
mental deficiency / IDIOCY; AMENTIA; IMBECILITY
mental deficient / IDIOT, MORON; IMBECILE
mental derangement / MANIA
mental sharpness / ACUMEN
mental shock / TRAUMA
mental specter / IDOLUM; EIDOLON
mental strain / TENSION

mental training / STUDY; EDUCATION
mentally deranged / INSANE; MANIACAL; PSYCHOTIC
mentally dull / SLOW
mentally feeble / DOTTY; MORONIC
mentally sound / SANE; RATIONAL
mention / CITE, HINT, NAME, TELL
mention officially / CITE
mentor / TUTOR; TEACHER
Mentor's friend / ODYSSEUS
Mentor's pupil / TELEMACHUS
mentum / CHIN
menu / CARTE; BILLOFFARE
Mephistopheles / DEVIL; MEPHISTO
mephitic / FOUL; NOXIOUS; STINKING
mephitis / MIASMA, STENCH
mercantile establishment / STORE; MARKET
Merced River valley / YOSEMITE
mercenary / VENAL; SORDID; GRASPING. HIRELING
mercenary of American Revolution / HESSIAN
mercenary of India / SEPOY
merchandise / WARE; GOODS, STOCK, WARES. SELL; TRADE
merchant / BUYER; DEALER, SELLER, TRADER, VENDER; PEDDLER
merchant of Bagdad / SINBAD
merchant fleet / ARGOSY
merchant in India / SETH
merchant mariner / SAILOR, SEAMAN
merchant ship / OILER; ARGOSY, COALER, PACKET, TRADER; COLLIER, STEAMER; INDIAMAN; FREIGHTER
Merchant of Venice / ANTONIO
Merchant of Venice heroine / PORTIA
Merchant of Venice villain / SHYLOCK
merchants' group / GILD; HANSE
merciful / KIND; HUMANE, TENDER; CLEMENT, LENIENT
merciless / HARD; CRUEL; SAVAGE
mercurial / FICKLE, FLIGHTY; VOLATILE
mercurous chloride / CALOMEL
mercury / QUICKSILVER
Mercury / HERMES
mercury ore / CINNABAR
mercy / PITY; BLESSING, CLEMENCY
mercy killing / EUTHANASIA

mere / LAKE, PART, POND, POOL;
MARSH. BARE, ONLY, SOLE;
SIMPLE
mere taste / NIP, SIP; BITE
mere youth / LAD; STRIPLING
merely / BUT; JUST, ONLY;
BARELY
meretricious / CHEAP; TAWDRY
merganser duck / NUN; SMEE,
SMEW; HERALD, WEASER;
GARBILL
merge / FUSE, JOIN; UNITE
Mergenthaler invention /
LINOTYPE
merger / UNION; FUSION;
COMBINE
meridian / NOON; MIDDAY, ZENITH
Merimée story / CARMEN
merit / CLAIM, RIGHT, VALUE,
WORTH. EARN, RATE; DESERVE
merited / PROPER; CONDIGN
merl / MERLE; BLACKBIRD
Merlin's craft / BARD
Merlin's seducer / NIMUE; VIVIAN
Merlin's talent / MAGIC
mermaid / SIREN; NERCID,
UNDINE
Mermaid habitué / JONSON;
RALEIGH; SHAKESPEARE
Merodach / MARDUK
Merovingian king / CLOVIS
Merrimack vacationer / THOREAU
merriment / JOY, FUN; GLEE;
MIRTH, SPORT; FROLIC,
GAIETY, GAYETY; JOLLITY;
HILARITY
merry / GAY; BRISK, DROLL,
FUNNY, JOLLY, SUNNY; BLITHE,
JOCOSE
merry king / COLE; WENZEL;
WENCESLAUS
Merry Wives' catspaw / FALSTAFF
Merry Wives' residence / WINDSOR
merry-andrew / CLOWN, JOKER
merry-go-round / CAROUSEL;
CARROUSEL, WHIRLIGIG;
ROUNDABOUT
merrymaker / REVELER;
CAROUSER; CELEBRANT
merrymaking / REVEL; JOLLITY
Mersey River city / LIVERPOOL
mesa / PLATEAU; TABLELAND
mescal / AGAVE; MAGUEY
mescaline / PEYOTE
mesh / NET, WEB; NETTING.
ENSNARE
mesh instrument / SIEVE; SIFTER
meshed fabric / NET, WEB; LACE;
TULLE; NETTING
meshlike cap / SNOOD; HAIRNET
mesial / MIDDLE; MEDIAL
mesmeric force / OD; ODYL
mesmerism / HYPNOTISM

Mesopotamia / IRAK, IRAQ;
BABYLONIA
Mesopotamian boat / GUFA, KUFA
Mesopotamian city / UR; URFA;
CTESIPHON
Mesopotamian river / TIGRIS;
EUPHRATES
Mesopotamians / IRAQIS;
ASSYRIANS; BABYLONIANS
mesotron / MESON
Mesozoic period / JURASSIC,
TRIASSIC
mesquite / PACAY; ALGARROBA
mess / SOIL; DIRTY; JUMBLE
mess in / MEDDLE
message / NOTE, WORD; NOTICE
Messalina's husband / CLAUDIUS
messan / CUR, DOG; MONGREL
messenger / PAGE; ANGEL,
ENVOY; HERALD; COURIER;
EMISSARY
messenger of the gods / IRIS;
ANGEL; HERMES; MERCURY
Messiah / JESUS; LIBERATOR
Messiah's composer / HANDEL
messy / DIRTY; SLOPPY, UNTIDY
mestizo / METIS; HALFCASTE
met / SAT; CONVENED;
SATISFIED
met secretly / TRYSTED
metal / ORE; GOLD, IRON, LEAD;
ALLOY, STEEL; COPPER, SILVER
metal alloy / BRASS, MONEL;
BRONZE, SOLDER; AMALGAM
metal bar / ROD; RAIL, INGOT
metal box / CANISTER
metal casting / PIG; INGOT
metal circlet / RING; ARMLET
metal container / CAN, POT, TIN;
DRUM, PAIL
metal disk / COIN; MEDAL,
PATEN; SEQUIN
metal dross / SLAG
metal eye of lariat / HONDA,
HONDO; HONDOO
metal eyelet / GROMMET,
GRUMMET
metal fastener / NUT, PIN; HASP,
NAIL; RIVET, SCREW
metal filings / LEMEL, SCOBS
metal framework for fire / GRATE
metal goods / CUTLERY; HARD-
WARE
metal leaf / FOIL
metal missile / BOMB, SHELL;
GRENADE, TORPEDO
metal molding / PIG
metal money / COIN; SPECIE
metal nugget / PRILL
metal pin / RIVET
metal refuse / SLAG; SCORIA
metal spacer in printing / LEAD,
SLUG

metal suit / MAIL; ARMOR
metal sulfides / MATTE
metal thread / WIRE; CABLE
metal tip of lace / AGLET; AIGLET
metal worker / SMITH; FORGER
metal-bearing deposit / LEAD, LODE, VEIN
metal-bearing material / ORE
metallic / TINNY; CLINKING
metallic article / HARDWARE
metallic cement / SOLDER, SOWDER
metallic cloth / LAME; TINSEL
metallic element / TIN; GOLD, IRON, LEAD, ZINC; COPPER, SILVER
metallic mixture / ALLOY; BRONZE
metallic sound / DING, DONG, PING, RING; CHIME, CLANK, CLINK
metalliferous rock / ORE; MINERAL
metalworking god / VULCAN; MULCIBER, VOLCANUS; HAPHAESTUS, HEPHAISTOS
metalworking tool / DIE; ANVIL, DRILL, LATHE, SWAGE, TONGS
metamere / SOMITE; SEGMENT
metamorphic rock / SLATE; GNEISS, MARBLE, SCHIST
metamorphosis / TRANSFORMA-TION
metaphore / TROPE; SIMILE
metaphorical / FIGURATIVE
metaphrast / TRANSLATOR
metaphysical English poet / CAREW, DONNE; MARVELL
metathesis / TRANSPOSITION
mete / DOLE; ALLOT; ASSIGN
metempsychosis / TRANS-MIGRATION
meteor / BOLIS; ANTLID, BOLIDE, LEONID; ORIONID, PERSEID
meteorological instrument / BAROMETER; ANEMOMETER, HYETOMETER; THERMOMETER
meteorologist / FORECASTER
meter / METRE; RHYTHM; INSTRUMENT
metheglin / MEAD; HYDROMEL
method / WAY; MODE; ORDER; SYSTEM
method actors' mentor / STRAS-BERG
method of cooking / FRY; BAKE, BOIL, STEW; ROAST, SAUTE; BRAISE
method of dyeing / BATIK; TIEDYE
methodical / ORDERLY; SYSTEMATIC
Methodist founder / WESLEY; WHITEFIELD
methodize / ARRANGE; REGULATE
metic in Athens / ALIEN

meticulous / CAREFUL, FINICKY
métier / WORK; TRADE; PROFESSION
Metis' husband / ZEUS
Metis' mother / TETHYS
metric measure / AR; ARE; GRAM, KILO; LITER, LITRE, METER, STERE, TONNE; DECARE; CENTARE, HECTARE
metric quart / LITER, LITRE
metrical composition / POEM
metrical foot / IAMB; DACTYL; ANAPEST, TROCHEE
metrical foot part / ARSIS; THESIS
metrical short syllable / MORA
metrical stress / ICTUS
metrical unit of verse / FOOT
metropolis / CITY
metropolitan / URBAN
mettle / ARDOR; SPIRIT, TEMPER
mettlesome / SPUNKY; SPIRITED
Meuse River city / NAMUR, SEDAN
mew / GULL; STABLE. MEOW; IMMURE; CONFINE
Mexican / AZTEC; CHICANO
Mexican alcoholic drink / SOTOL; MESCAL, PULQUE; TEQUILA
Mexican avocado / COYO; CHININ
Mexican beverage / MESCAL
Mexican city / OAXACA, TAMPICO; ACAPULCO; GUADALAJARA
Mexican corn cake / TORTILLA
Mexican corn mush / ATOLE
Mexican dish / TACO; TAMAL; TAMALE; ENCHILADA
Mexican epithet for American / GRINGO
Mexican fiber / PITA; DATIL, ISTLE, IXTLE, SISAL
Mexican god of sowing / XIPE
Mexican grass / TEOSINTE
Mexican guardian spirit / NAGUAL
Mexican hut / JACAL
Mexican Indian / MAM, NIO, ZOE; CHOL, CORA, IXIL, MAYA, MIXE, PIMA, SERI, SUMA, URES; AZ-TEC, OTOMI, ZOQUE; TOLTEC; HUICHOL
Mexican laborer / PEON
Mexican lake / PATZCUARO
Mexican mountain / COLIMA; POPOCATEPETL
Mexican painter / OROZCO, RIVERA, TAMAYO; SIQUEIROS
Mexican peasant / PEON
Mexican pine / OCOTE, PINON
Mexican plant / JALAP; CHAPOTE
Mexican ranch / RANCHO; HA-CIENDA
Mexican river / BALSAS, PANUCO
Mexican rubber tree / ULE
Mexican salamander / AXOLOTL

Mexican seed tea / CHIA
Mexican shawl / SERAPE
Mexican soap plant / AMOLE
Mexican tree / ULE; ABETO, ALAMO
Mexican weight / ARROBA, TERCIO
Mexican yucca / DATIL
Mexico money / PESO, TLAC, TLACO
Mexico mountain range / SIERRA-MADRE
Mexico peninsula / YUCATAN
Mexico port / TAMPICO; VERACRUZ
Mexico volcano / PARICUTIN
Mexico's conqueror / CORTES, CORTEZ
mezzaine / ENTRESOL
miasmic / NOXIOUS; POISONOUS
mica / TALC; GLIST; ISINGLASS
mice, pert. to / MURINE
Michaelmas daisy / ASTER
Michaelmas fowl / GOOSE
Michael's wards / ISRAEL
Michelangelo fresco location / SISTINE
Michelangelo sculpture / DAVID, PIETA
Michigan capital / LANSING
Michigan city / FLINT, NILES
Michigan peninsula / KEWEENAW
Michigan state bird / ROBIN
Michigan state flower / APPLE-BLOSSOM
Michigan state nickname / AUTO, LAKE; WOLVERINE
mico / MARMOSET
microbe / GERM; BACILLUS
Micronesian island group / BONIN, PALAU, PELEW; MARIANA
microorganism / GERM; VIRUS; MICROBE
microscopic / WEE; TINY; MINUTE
microscopic animal / AMOEBA; ROTIFER; ANIMALCULE, IN-FUSORIAN
microspore / POLLEN
mid / CENTER, MIDDLE; HALFWAY
Midas' kingdom / PHRYGIA
Midas' unwanted gift / GOLDEN-TOUCH
midday / NOON; NOONDAY; MERIDIAN
midden / DUNGHILL, JUNKPILE
middle / MID; MEAN; MESNE; CEN-TER, MEDIAL, MEDIAN; CEN-TRAL
middle, c.f. / MESO
Middle Ages, pert. to / MEDIEVAL
middle of body / WAIST
Middle East land / IRAK, IRAN, IRAQ; EGYPT, SYRIA; ISRAEL, JORDAN, PERSIA; LEBANON
middle finger / MEDIUS
middling / FAIR, SOSO; AVERAGE

middlings of wheat / DUNST
middy / PLEBE; REEFER; MIDSHIP-MAN
Midgard / EARTH
midge / GNAT; PUNKIE; NOSCEUM
midget / RUNT; DWARF, PIGMY, PYGMY
midland / INLAND; CENTRAL
midshipman / MIDDY; TOADFISH
midst of / AMONG; AMIDST
mien / AIR; LOOK; ASPECT, MAN-NER
miff / SPAT, TIFF
miffy / TOUCHY; OFFENDED
might / FORCE, POWER; POTENCY; STRENGTH; PUISSANCE
mighty / ABLE, BOLD, HUGE, VAST; GREAT; POTENT, ROBUST, STRONG
mignon / SMALL; SLIGHT
mignonette / LACE; GREEN; RESEDA
migraine / HEADACHE
migrant / ROVING. EMIGRANT
migrate / TREK; TRAVEL
migration / TREK; EXODUS
migratory / ROVING; NOMADIC
migratory worker / HOBO, OKIE
Mikado's court / DAIRI
Mikado's factotum / POOHBAH
Mikado's hero / NANKIPOO
Mikado's heroine / YUMYUM
Mikado's land / JAPAN; NIPPON
Milanese family / SFORZA; VISCONTI
Milan's opera house / LASCALA
mild / SHY; KIND, MEEK, SOFT, TAME; BLAND; GENTLE, PLACID
mild cigar / CLARO
mild expletive / GEE; DARN, DRAT, EGAD, GOSH, HECK; GOLLY; SHUCKS
mild rebuke / TSK, TUT
mildew / MOLD, MUST, RUST; BLIGHT
mildness / LENITY
mileage recorder / ODOMETER
Miled's son / IR; ITH; EBER
Milesian / IRISH
milestone / STELE; MARKER
Miletian philosopher / THALES
milfoil / YARROW
miliaria / RASH; PRICKLYHEAT
milieu / MEDIUM; SETTING
militant / WARLIKE; COMBATIVE; AGGRESSIVE
military / MARTIAL, WARLIKE
military art / TACTICS; STRATEGY
military assistant / AIDE; ATTACHE
military boat / LSM, LST; PONTON
military chaplain / PADRE
military combat area / FRONT; SECTOR

military command / FIRE; ATEASE

military commission / RANK; BREVET

military decoration / DSO; MEDAL

military encounter / BATTLE; SKIRMISH; FIREFIGHT; ENGAGEMENT

military examination / REVIEW

military excavation / TRENCH; FOXHOLE

military force / ARMY; TROOP

military formation / ECHELON

military gesture / SALUTE

military group / UNIT; CADRE, CORPS; LEGION

military headwear / CAP; KEPI; BERET, BUSBY, SHAKO; HELMET

military installation / CAMP, FORT, POST; FORTRESS

military landing place / BEACH-HEAD

military maneuver / DRILL

military obstacle / WIRE; ABATIS

military officer / AIDE; MAJOR; CAPTAIN, COLONEL, GENERAL

military organization / ARMY; MARINES

military police officer / PROVOST

military policeman / MP

military post / BASE; COMMAND, STATION; GARRISON

military prisoner / POW

military projectile / BALL, BOMB; ARROW, GRAPE, SHELL, SPEAR

military retail store / PX

military shelter / TENT; BARRACKS

military signal / TAPS; CHARGE

military spectacle / MARCH; PARADE

military student / CADET

military sword / SABER

military training in school / ROTC

military unit / SQUAD; COMPANY, PLATOON; REGIMENT, BATTALION; DETACHMENT

military vehicle / JEEP, TANK

military warehouse / ETAPE; ARMORY; ARSENAL

military watchword / PAROLE; PASSWORD; COUNTERSIGN

militate / EFFECT; OPERATE; INFLUENCE

militia / RESERVE; SOLDIERY

milk, c.f. / LAC; LACT; LACTO

milk, pert. to / LACTIC

milk coagulator / RENNET, RENNIN

milk component / WHEY; CREAM

milk depot / DAIRY

milk glass / OPALINE

milk in pharmacy / LAC

milk protein / CASEIN

milk serum / WHEY

milk sugar / LACTOSE

milkfish / AWA; SABALO

milksop / SISSY; WEAKLING

Milky Way / GALAXY

Milky Way, pert. to / GALACTIC

mill / SHOP; QUERN, WORKS; FACTORY. GRIND, FIGHT; STRIKE

mill, pert. to / MOLINARY

Millay poem / RENASCENCE

milled / GROUND; KNURLED

millenarian / CHILIAST

millennium / GOLDENAGE

millet grass / JOAR; CHENA, DURRA, JOWAR; MILIUM

milliard / BILLION

milliner / HATTER

millinery / HATS; BONNETS

millionaire / NABOB; PLUTOCRAT

millpond / DAM; RESERVOIR

millstone / QUERN; BURSTONE

millstone support / RIND, RYND

millwheel board / AWE

Milne character / POOH; POOHBEAR

milo / SORGHUM

Milo's sport / WRESTLING

milt / SPERM; SPLEEN

Milton poem / LALLEGRO

Milton tract against censors / AREOPAGITICA

Milton's masque / COMUS

mime / APE; APER; CLOWN, MIMIC

mime's performance / DUMBSHOW

Mime's ward / SIEGFRIED

mimic / APE; COPY, MOCK; IMITATE

Mimir's horn / GIALLAR

Mimi's lover / RODOLFO, RUDOLPH

mimosa / ACACIA, WATTLE, YELLOW

minacious / MENACING, MINATORY

mince / CHOP, CLIP, HASH; PRINK

minced dish / HASH; FARCE; HAMBURGER

minced oath / GAD, GED, GEE, LUD; DARN, DERN, DRAT, DURN, ECOD, EGAD, HECK, OONS, SWOW

mind / IDEA, NOUS, SOUL; BRAIN

mind, pert. to / MENTAL

mind function / THOUGHT; IDEATION

Mindanao inhabitant / ATA; AETA, MORO

Mindanao volcano / APO

mindful / CAREFUL; ATTENTIVE

Mindoro city / CALAPAN

Mindoro inhabitant / TAGALOG

mine / PIT; BANK; STOPE; BURROW, QUARRY; BONANZA; COLLIERY. SAP

mine / MY

mine car / TRAM

mine drain pit / SUMP
mine entrance / ADIT
mine manager / OPERATOR
mine a narrow vein / RESUE
mine passage / ADIT; STULM
mine roof support / NOG; PILE
mine section / PANEL
mine step / LOB
mine sweeper / PARAVANE
mine vein / LODE
mineral / ORE; MARL, SALT, SPAR; METAL STONE; SILICA
mineral deposit / LODE, SEAM
mineral pitch / ASPHALT
mineral source / ORE
mineral spring / SPA
mineral tar / BREA
mineral washer / JIG
miner's bird / CANARY
miner's chisel / GAD
miner's compass / DIAL
miner's lamp / DAVY
miner's nail / SPAD
miner's pick / MANDREL, MANDRIL
miners' tool / TREPAN
Minerva / ATHENA
Minerva's bird / OWL
Minerva's province / WISDOM
Ming pottery / PORCELAIN
mingle / MIX; JOIN; ADMIX, BLEND
Mingo / IROQUOIS
Mingrelian / GEORGIAN
mingy / STINGY
miniature / MINIM, SMALL; MINUTE
miniature representation / MODEL
minify / LESSEN; MINIMIZE
minim / DROP; MINIMUM; HALFNOTE
minimize / REDUCE; BELITTLE
minimum / LEAST; TRIFLE
minimus / PINKY
mining excavation / STOPE
mining hazard / GAS; CAVEIN; METHANE
mining passage / BORD
mining prop / STEIL
mining refuse / GOB; GOAF
minion / DAINTY, PRETTY; ELEGANT
minish / LESSEN; DIMINISH
minister / AGENT, ENVOY; CLERIC, CURIE, DIVINE, PARSON, PASTOR, PRIEST, RECTOR; DOMINIE, HELPTEND; NURSE, SERVE
minister of a chapel / VICAR
ministerial / CLERICAL
minister's dwelling / MANSE; PARSONAGE
minister's title / REVEREND
minister / PARSON
Minnie's husband / HIAWATHA

minnesinger / TROUBADOUR
minnesinger's hero / TANNHAUSER
Minnesota capital / STPAUL
Minnesota city / DULUTH
Minnesota native / GOPHER
Minnesota ore area / MESABI
Minnesota river / RED
Minnesota state bird / LOON
Minnesota state nickname / GOPHER; NORTHSTAR
Minoan center / KNOSSOS
minor / LESSER; SMALLER, YOUNGER
minor devil / IMP
minor items / TRIFLES; MINUTIAE
minor planet / ASTEROID; PLANETOID, SATELLITE
minor prophet / AMOS, JOEL; HOSEA, JONAH, MICAH, NAHUM; HAGGAI
Minorca city / MAHON
minority / YOUTH; NONAGE
minority dwelling area / GHETTO
Minos' daughter / ARIADNE, PHAEDRA
Minos' kingdom / CRETE
Minos' wife / PASIPHAE
minotaur's destroyer / THESEUS
minstrel / BARD, BHAT, POET; SCALD, SKALD; HARPER, SINGER
minstrel show feature / OLIO; ENDMEN; BLACKFACE; INTERLOCUTOR
minstrel song / LAI, LAY; BALLAD
mint / COIN; MARJORAM. UNUSED
mint drink / TEA; JULEP
mintage / COINAGE
mintlike herb / MONARDA
minus / LESS; LACKING; NEGATIVE
minute / WEE; TINY; EXACT, SMALL; LITTLE, SLIGHT. NOTE; SUMMARY
minute difference / SHADE; NUANCE; GRADATION
minute distinction / NICETY; SUBTLETY
minute groove / STRIA
minute ice crystals / RIME; FROST; HOARFROST
minute mark / DOT, JOT; IOTA
Minute Men / MILITIA
minute opening / PORE; STOMA; PINHOLE
minute organism / MONAD, SPORE
minute parasite / MITE
minute particle / ATOM, MOTE; GRAIN; MOLECULE
minute reproductive body / SPORE
minutely / EXACTLY; METICULOUSLY
minutiae / DETAILS
miracle / MARVEL, WONDER

miracle play / MYSTERY
mirage / SERAB; VISION; LOOMING
Miranda's father / PROSPERO
mire / MUD; MUCK; OOZE
Miriam's brother / AARON, MOSES
Miriam's father / AMRAM
mirror / GLASS; CRYSTAL; SPECULUM. REFLECT
mirth / FUN, JOY; GLEE; GAIETY
mirthful / GAY; HAPPY; JOVIAL
misadventure / MISHAP; ACCIDENT
misanthrope / CYNIC, TIMON
misanthropy / MISANDRY
misapply / MISUSE; PERVERT
misapprehend / MISTAKE
misbehavior / RUDENESS
miscalculate / ERR
miscellaneous / MIXED; VARIOUS
miscellany / ANA; OLIO; MIXTURE
mischance / MISHAP; MIS-FORTUNE
mischief / HOB, ILL; BANE, EVIL, HARM, HURT; INJURY; DEVILTRY
mischievous / BAD, SLY; ARCH, EVIL, PUCK; ELFIN
mischievous child / IMP; BRAT
mischievous doing / PRANK, TRICK; CANTRIP
mischievous spirit / ELF, IMP; PUCK; PIXIE; GOBLIN
misconceive / MISTAKE
misconduct / MISBEHAVIOR
misconduct mark / GIG; DEMERIT
misconstrue / MISINTERPRET
miscreant / KNAVE, ROGUE, SCAMP; RASCAL; VILLAIN. BASE; DEPRAVED
misdeed / SIN; CRIME; OFFENSE
misdemeanor / MISDEED, OFFENSE
misdirect / DECEIVE, MISLEAD
miser / HOARDER, NIGGARD; SKIN-FLINT
miserable / LOW; MEAN; ABJECT
miserly / CLOSE, TIGHT; STINGY
misery / WOE; EVIL, PAIN; GRIEF; SORROW; CALAMITY
misfortune / ILL, WOE; BLOW, EVIL
misgiving / FEAR; DOUBT, QUALM
misgovern / MISRULE
mishap / ACCIDENT; MISFORTUNE
Mishnah tractate / YOMA; ABOTH
misinterpret / ERR; MISJUDGE
mislay / LOSE; MISPLACE
mislead / DELUDE; DECEIVE
misleading / FALSE; FALLACIOUS
misplace / LOSE
misplay / MUFF; ERROR; BOBBLE, FUMBLE
misprints / TYPOS; ERRATA
misrepresent / FALSIFY

miss / ERR; FAIL, FALL, LOSE, OMIT, SKIP. GIRL, LASS
missel thrush / MAVIS
misshapen / DEFORMED
missile / BOMB, DART; ARROW, BOLAS, LANCE, SNARK, SPEAR; BULLET
missile that comes back / BOOMERANG
missile launching site / PAD
missile shelter / SILO
missing / LOST; ABSENT; LACKING
missing link / MANAPE
mission / DUTY; TRUST; CHARGE, ERRAND; EMBASSY, MESSAGE, PURPOSE
Mississippi Bubble promoter / LAW
Mississippi capital / JACKSON
Mississippi city / BILOXI, LAUREL, OXFORD; NATCHEZ
Mississippi Indian / TIOU; HOUMA, YAZOO; BILOXI, GRIGRA; NATCHEZ
Mississippi river / PEARL, YAZOO
Mississippi River mouth / PASS
Mississippi River source / ITASCA
Mississippi state bird / MOCKING-BIRD
Mississippi state nickname / MAGNOLIA
missive / NOTE; LETTER; EPISTLE
Missouri capital / JEFFERSONCITY
Missouri city / JOPLIN; SEDALIA
Missouri mountains / OZARKS
Missouri river / SALT; GRAND, OSAGE; MERAMEC
Missouri state bird / BLUEBIRD
Missouri state flower / HAWTHORN
Missouri state nickname / OZARK; SHOWME
Missouri state tree / DOGWOOD
Missouri town / HANNIBAL
misspend / WASTE; SQUANDER
misstep / SLIP, TRIP; STUMBLE
mist / FOG, RAG; SMUR; SPRAY, STEAM, VAPOR; MIZZLE; DRIZZLE
mistake / BONER, ERROR; BLUNDER
mistake in printing / TYPO; ERRATUM
mistaken / OFF; WRONG; ERRONEOUS
mister / MR; SIR
mistily / DIMLY; OBSCURELY
mistranslate / MISRENDER
mistreat / MAUL; ABUSE; MAL-TREAT
mistress / MRS; DAME, WIFE
mistress of the world / ROME
mistrust / DOUBT; SUSPICION
misty / DIM; HAZY; FOGGY; OBSCURE

misunderstand / MISTAKE
misunderstanding / IMBROGLIO; DISAGREEMENT
misuse / ABUSE, WASTE; RAVISH
mite / ATOM, TICK; ACARI, ATOMY
mitigate / EASE; ABATE, ALLAY
mix / JOIN, STIR; ADDLE, BLEND, KNEAD, UNITE; ASSORT, MINGLE
mix as eggs / BEAT; SCRAMBLE
mix by hand / KNEAD; MANIPULATE
mix together / COMPOUND
mixed bag / OLLA; MEDLEY
mixed drink / NOG; NEGUS, TODDY; COCKTAIL
mixed type / PI
mixed up / MUDDLED; CONFUSED
mixing implement / MIXER; AGITATOR
mixture / HASH, OLIO, STEW; BLEND; MEDLEY; AMALGAM, MELANGE
mixture of minerals / MAGMA
mixture of pork and meal / SCRAPPLE
mixture of spirits and water / GROG; HIGHBALL
mix-up / FIGHT, MELEE; MUDDLE
mo / BOOK
Moab king / EGLON, MESHA
Moabite / EMIM
Moabite king / MESHA
moan / GROAN; LAMENT; COMPLAIN
moat / FOSS; DITCH, FOSSE; GRAFFE
mob / GANG; CROWD; RABBLE, THRONG
mobile / FACILE; MOVABLE
Mobile Bay victor / FARRAGUT
mobster's girl / MOLL
Moby Dick author / MELVILLE
Moby Dick ship / PEQUOD
Moby Dick's hunter / AHAB
Moby Dick's narrator / ISHMAEL
moccasin / PAC; VIPER; LARRIGAN
mock / APE; DEFY, DUPE, GIBE, JEER, JIBE, LEER; CHAFF, CHEAT
mock attack / FEINT
mock orange / SYRINGA
mock pennyroyal / HEDEOMA
mockery / GAME, SHAM; FARCE, IRONY; SARCASM; DELUSION
mocking / DERISIVE
mode / WAY; RULE; MEANS, STYLE
mode, **pert. to** / MODAL
mode of action / PLAN; PROCESS
mode of expression / STYLE
mode of procedure / METHOD
mode of transportation / BUS, CAB, CAR; AUTO, SHIP, TAXI; PLANE

mode of walking / GAIT
model / COPY, NORM, TYPE; IMAGE; DESIGN; EXAMPLE, MANIKIN; PARADIGM, SPECIMEN; FACSIMILE
model to follow / EXAMPLE, PATTERN; TEMPLATE
model of perfection / IDEAL; PARAGON; STANDARD
Modenese ruling family / ESTE
moderate / COOL; ABATE, QUIET; LESSEN, SEASON, SOFTEN, TEMPER. MILD; SOBER; FRUGAL, STEADY
moderately good / FAIR; AVERAGE
moderately moist / MESIC
moderately slow / ANDANTE
moderating / ABATING; RELAXING
moderation / SOBRIETY; RESTRAINT
modern / NEW; NOVEL; RECENT
modern African dance / HIGHLIFE
modern apprentice / TRAINEE
modern detecting device / BUG; RADAR, SONAR
modern light invention / LASER
Modernismo pioneer / DARIO
modernize / ADAPT; REMODEL
modest / SHY; MEEK, PRIM; CHASTE, DECENT, DEMURE, PROPER; BASHFUL
modesty / DECORUM, RESERVE; TIMIDITY
modicum / SCRAP; TINCTURE; SMATTERING
modified species / ECAD; MUTATION
modify / VARY; ALTER, EMEND
modify quicklime / SLAKE
modish / CHIC; SMART; STYLISH
modiste / DRESSMAKER
Modoc Indian leader / CAPTAINJACK
Modred's father / LÔT
Modred's slayer / ARTHUR
modus / MODE; MANNER, METHOD
modus operandi /MO
mogul / VIP; MONGOL, TYCOON
Mogul emperor / AKBAR, BABER
Mohacs victors / TURKS
Mohammedan / ARAB, MORO, TURK; MOSLEM. ISLAMIC. See also Islamic, Moslem
Mohammedan Bulgarian / POMAK
Mohammedan charitable gift / WAKF, WAQF
Mohammedan chief / EMIR; DATTO
Mohammedan commander / AGA; AGHA
Mohammedan conqueror of Jerusalem / OMAR
Mohammedan councilor/ VIZIER

Mohammedan demon / EBLIS, JINNI
Mohammedan emblem / CRESCENT
Mohammedan enemy of Crusaders / SARACEN
Mohammedan fairy / PERI
Mohammedan headware / FEZ; TURBAN
Mohammedan hospice / IMARET
Mohammedan javelin / JERID; JEREED
Mohammedan judge / CADI, KADI, KAZI, RAZI; HAKIM, MULLA; MULLAH
Mohammedan leader / AGA; AGHA
Mohammedan legal advisor / MUFTI
Mohammedan marriage settlement / MAHR
Mohammedan minister of state / VIZIR, WAZIR; VIZIER
Mohammedan month / RABRA, RAJAB, SAFAR; JUMADA, SHABAN; RAMADAN, SHAWWAL; DULKAADA, MUHARRAM, ZULKADAH
Mohammedan noble / AMIR, EMIR
Mohammedan physician / HAKIM
Mohammedan prayer orientation / KIBLAH
Mohammedan prince / AMIR, EMIR; AMEER, EMEER
Mohammedan queen / BEGUM
Mohammedan religion / ISLAM
Mohammedan ruler / AGA; AGHA; CALIF, KALIF, RAJAH; CALIPH, SULTAN
Mohammedan ruler's decree / IRADE
Mohammedan saber / YATAGHAN
Mohammedan school / MADRASA
Mohammedan schoolmaster / KHOJA
Mohammedan title / AGA, ALI, SID; RAIS, SIDI; SAYID; CALIPH
Mohammedan tunic / JAMA; JAMAH
Mohammedan woman's veil / YASHMAK
Mohammedan woman's wrap / IZAR
Mohammedan women's quarters / HAREM; ZENANA; SERAGLIO
Mohammed's adopted son / ALI
Mohammed's associate / ASHAB
Mohammed's birthplace / MECCA
Mohammed's burial place / MEDINA
Mohammed's companions / ASHAB
Mohammed's daughter / FATIMA, ZAYNAB; RUQAYYA

Mohammed's father / ABDULLAH
Mohammed's father-in-law / ABUBAKR
Mohammed's flight / HIJRA; HEGIRA
Mohammed's followers / MOSLEMS, MUSLIMS
Mohammed's horse / ALBORAK
Mohammed's mother / AMINA
Mohammed's rule / FADDA
Mohammed's son-in-law / ALI
Mohammed's title / NABI; RASUL
Mohammed's tribe / KOREISH, QURAYSH
Mohammed's uncle / ABBAS; ABUTALIB
Mohammed's wife / AISHA, SAUDA; AYESHA, KADIJA
Mohawk chief / BRANT; HIAWATHA
Mohegan chief / UNCAS; PHILIP
Mohican / MOHEGAN
moider / WORRY; BOTHER; PERPLEX
moiety / HALF, PART
moil / TOIL; DRUDGE
Moirae / FATES; PARCAE
moiré / WATERED
moist / DAMP, DANK, DEWY, UVID
moist spot / SIPE
moisten / WET; LICK; ANOINT, DAMPEN, IMBRUE; SPRINKLE
moisten by dipping / SOP; DUNK
moistened clay / LOAM
moisture / DAMPNESS, HUMIDITY
moisture in drops / DEW; RAIN
mojarra / PATAO
Moki / HOPI; MOQUI
molar / GRINDER; WISDOMTOOTH
molar tooth / WANG
molasses / SIRUP; TREACLE
mold / DIE, GIT; GEAT, LOAM, MUST, RUST, SMUT; MOULD; BLIGHT, MATRIX. CAST, FORM; MODEL, SHAPE
mold for casting / MATRIX
Moldavian city / KISHINEV
molder / ROT; DECAY; CRUMBLE
molding / AME; BEAD, CYMA, GULA, LIST, OGEE, REED; CONGE, OVOLO
molding corner / ARIS; ARRIS
molding tool / DIE; GOUGE; SHAPER
moldy / MUCID, MUSTY; MILDEWED
mole / PIER; JETTY, TALPA, TAUPE
mole cricket / CHANGA
mole gray / TAUPE
molecule / PARTICLE
molecule part / ION; ATOM
molehill / TRIFLE; HILLOCK

molelike animal / DESMAN
moleskin / TAUPE
molest / VEX; FRET; ANNOY,
    CHAFE
Molière character / TARTUFE;
    TARTUFFE
Molière's surname / POQUELIN
mollify / CALM, EASE; ALLAY
mollusk / CLAM, WELK, WILK;
    CHAMA, MUREX, SNAIL, WHELK;
    CHITON, LIMPET, MUSSEL,
    OYSTER; ABALONE
mollusk shell / ABALONE, SCAL-
    LOP; TRIDACNA
mollusk used for bait / LIMPET
mollusk's rasp / RADULA
mollycoddle / PAMPER. MILKSOP
Molnar play / LILIOM
Molokai colonist / LEPER
Molotov cocktail / GRENADE
molt / MEW; SHED; MOULT
molten / MELTED
molten glass / METAL; PARISON
molten rock / LAVA; MAGMA
Moluccas island / CERAM; AM-
    BOINA; HALMAHERA
Moluccas island group / KAI, OBI;
    AROE; BABAR, BANDA
mom / MA; MAMA; MOTHER
moment / MO; JIFF; FLASH, TRICE
momentary / BRIEF; FLEETING
momentary sensation / GLISK
momentary stop / REST; PAUSE
momentous / GRAVE; SERIOUS,
    WEIGHTY; IMPORTANT
momentum / IMPETUS
Mommur's ruler / OBERON
Momus's art / CRITICISM
Mona Lisa / GIOCONDA
Mona Lisa painter / VINCI;
    LEONARDO
Monaco, pert. to / MONACAN;
    MONEGASQUE
Monaco's ruling family / GRIMALDI
monadic / ATOMIC
monarch / CZAR, KING, TSAR;
    QUEEN, RULER; CALIPH,
    KAISER, SULTAN; CZARINA,
    EMPEROR
monarch's son / PRINCE
monarchy / KINGDOM
monarda / BERGAMOT; HORSE-
    MINT
monastery / ABBEY; MANDRA
monastery church / MINSTER
monastery room / CELL
monastery superior / ABBOT,
    PRIOR; ABBESS; PRIORESS
monastic / MONK. MONKISH
monastic house / ABBEY; PRIORY;
    MONASTERY
monetary / FISCAL; NUMMARY;
    FINANCIAL, PECUNIARY

monetary affairs / FINANCE;
    ECONOMICS
monetary penalty / FINE; MULCT
monetary settlement / FEE; SCOT;
    PAYMENT
monetary unit / BILL, COIN, NOTE
money / CASH, COIN, CUSH, GELT,
    GOLD, KALE, PELF; BREAD,
    DOUGH; MAZUMA, SPECIE;
    CURRENCY
money, pert. to / PECUNIARY
money on account / INSTALLMENT
money back / REBATE, REFUND
money box / SAFE, TILL; COFFER,
    DRAWER; REGISTER
money certificate / BILL, BOND;
    CHECK, SCRIP; CHEQUE;
    WARRANT
money exchange premium / AGIO
money hoarder / MISER; NIGGARD
money management / FINANCE
money market / BOURSE; EX-
    CHANGE
money overdue / ARREARS
money owed / DEBT; DEBIT;
    LIABILITY; OBLIGATION
money paid / SCOT; ADVANCE,
    PAYMENT, STIPEND
money placed in bank / DEPOSIT
money reserve / FUND; NESTEGG
money risked / BET; STAKE,
    WAGER
moneylender / BROKER, USURER;
    MAHAJAN; FINANCER
monger / DEALER, HAWKER,
    PEDLAR
Mongol / TATAR; BURIAT, TARTAR;
    KALMUCK, KHALKHA
Mongol conqueror of India /
    MOGUL
Mongolia capital / URGA;
    ULANBATOR
Mongolian desert / GOBI; SHAMO
Mongolian language / KHALKA
Mongolian legislature / HURAL
Mongolian money / TUGHRIK
Mongolian province / AIMAK
Mongolian river / ORKHON
Mongolian tent / YURT
Mongolian warrior / TATAR;
    TARTAR
Mongoloid Burmese / SHAN
mongoose / URVA; ICHNEUMON
mongrel / CUR, MUT; MUTT;
    HYBRID
moniker / MARK, NAME; NICK-
    NAME
monitor lizard / URAN; VARAN
Monitor's inventor / ERICSSON
monitory / WARNING
monk / FRIAR; MONASTIC; RELI-
    GIOUS
monk parrot / LORO

monkey / APE, LAR, SAI; DOUC, MONA, MONO, SIME, TITI, TOTA, WAAG; ARABA, PATAS, PATES, VITOE; BABOON, GRIVET, GUENON, LANGUR

monkey business / PRANK; ANTICS; TRICKERY; TOMFOOLERY

monkey puzzle / PINON

monkeylike animal / APE; LEMUR, LORIS, POTTO; AYEAYE, SIFAKA; TARSIER

monkish / MONASTIC

monk's hood / COWL

monk's room / CELL

monk's shaven crown / TONSURE

monk's title / FRA; ABBOT; BROTHER

monkshood / ATIS; ACONITE

Monmouth river / USK, WYE; EBBW

monoceros / UNICORN; SWORDFISH

monocot / LILY, PALM; GRASS

monocrat / AUTOCRAT

monody / DIRGE; LAMENT

monograph / PAPER; THESIS

monolith / CRAG; MENHIR, PILLAR

monologue / SPEECH; HARANGUE; SOLILOQUY

monomania / CRAZE; OBSESSION

monopoly / POOL; TRUST; CARTEL

monosaccharide / RIBOSE; GLUCOSE; FRUCTOSE; ARABINOSE

monotheist / DEIST; THEIST; UNITARIAN

monotonous / DULL; HUMDRUM, TEDIOUS, UNIFORM; TIRESOME, UNVARIED

monotony / SAMENESS; UNIFORMITY

monotreme / ECHIDNA; PLATYPUS

Monsieur / SIR; MISTER

monster / GHUL, NAGA, OGRE; BRUTE, DEMON, FIEND, GHOUL, GIANT, LAMIA; DRAGON KRAKEN, MARVEL, SPHINX; ANOMALY, CHIMERA

monster, c.f. / TERATO

monster Beowulf slew / GRENDEL

monster Hercules killed / HYDRA

monster, part man, part bull / MINOTAUR

monster with woman's head, bird's body / HARPY

monstrosity / FREAK; MONSTER

monstrous / BIG; HUGE, VAST; HIDEOUS, IMMENSE; COLOSSAL, DREADFUL

monstrous lizard / DRAGON

Montagues' enemies / CAPULETS

Montagues' scion / ROMEO

Montana capital / HELENA

Montana city / BUTTE; BILLINGS

Montana Indian / CREE, CROW, HOHE; BLOOD; ATSINA, PIEGAN, SALISH; SIKSIKA; FLATHEAD

Montana mountains / LEWIS; ABSAROKA

Montana national park / GLACIER

Montana river / SUN; TETON; POWDER; BIGHORN; GALLATIN

Montana state flower / BITTERROOT

Montana state nickname / MOUNTAIN, TREASURE

Monte Carlo's principality / MONACO

Monte Cristo's name / DANTES

Montenegro capital / CETINJE; TITOGRAD

Monterey author / STEINBECK

Montezuma's captor / CORTES, CORTEZ

montgolfier / BALLOON

Montgomery's victory / ALAMEIN

month current / INST; INSTANT

month preceding / ULT; ULTIMO

MONTHS

	Abbreviation	Derivation
January	JAN	JANUS
February	FEB	FEBRUA
March	MAR	MARS
April	APR	APHRODITE
May	—	MAIA
June	JE	JUNO
July	JY	JULIUS (CAESAR)
August	AUG	AUGUSTUS (CAESAR)
September	SEPT	SEPTEM (SEVEN)*
October	OCT	OCTO (EIGHT)*
November	NOV	NOVEM (NINE)*
December	DEC	DECEM (TEN)*

* The year used to begin in March; the old numbers survive in the names of these months.

monthly payment / DUES, RENT
Montmartre church / SACRECOEUR
Montmartre denizen / ARTIST
Montreal canal / LACHINE
Montserrat peak / SOUFRIERE
monument / GRAVE, DOLMEN, PILLAR, STATUE; CENOTAPH, MEGALITH
Monument Valley inhabitant / NAVAJO
Monument Valley phenomenon / MITTENS
monumental / GREAT, GROSS; MASSIVE; IMPOSING
moo / LOW; LOWING
mooch / SKULK, SNEAK, STEAL; PANHANDLE
mood / HUMOR; TEMPER; INCLINATION
moody / GLUM, SOUR, SULKY; MOROSE
Moody and Sankey compositions / HYMNS
moon / LUNA; MONTH; CRESCENT
moon, pert. to / LUNAR
moon age at beginning of year / EPACT
moon god / SIN
moon goddess / ISIS, LUNA; DIANA, LASNA, NANNA; HECATE, PHOEBE, SELENE; ARTEMIS, ASTARTE, CYNTHIA
moon inhabitant / SELENITE
moon valley / RILL; RILLE
moonbeam / RAY
mooncalf / DOLT; IDIOT
moonfaced / ROUND
moonflower / ACHETE
moon's first quarter / CRESCENT
moonshine / BOOZE; NONSENSE
Moonstone detective / CUFF
moonstruck / CRAZED; LUNATIC
moonwort / HONESTY, LUNARIA
moony / WEAK; DREAMY; MOONLIT
moor / FEN; HEATH, MORISCO; MOROCCAN. ANCHOR, FASTEN, SECURE
moor fowl / GROUSE
moor grass / BENT; SUNDEW
moor hen / COOT; GORHEN
moorage / MOORING
moorberry / BILBERRY; CRANBERRY
mooring post / DOLPHIN
Moorish / MORISCO; MORESQUE
Moorish drum / ATABAL
Moorish palace / ALCAZAR; ALHAMBRA
Moors, pert. to / MOORISH
moory / DARK; BOGGY; MARSHY
moose / ELK; ALCE
moose's dewlap / BELL
moot / ARGUE, PLEAD; PROPOSE

mop / DUST, SWAB, SWOB, WIPE
mope / PINE, SULK
moppet / BABY, DOLL; CHILD
moquette / SHAG; CARPET
Moqui / HOPI
moral / GOOD, JUST; RIGHT; HONEST, STRICT; ETHICAL. MAXIM
moral attitude / ETHOS
moral excellence / MERIT; VIRTUE
moral fault / VICE; DEPRAVITY, TURPITUDE
moral maxim / PRECEPT
moral offense / SIN; EVIL
moral philosophy / ETHICS; ETHOLOGY
moral slip / LAPSE
morality play classic / EVERYMAN
morally healthy / CLEAN; DECENT
morals / ETHICS; MORALITY
morass / BOG, FEN; QUAG; SWAMP
Moravian capital / BRNO
moray / EEL; CONGER, HAMLET
morbid / SICKLY; TAINTED
morbid appetite / LIMOSIS
morbid breathing sound / RALE
morbid desire / CACOETHES
morbid emotion / HYSTERIA
morbid secretion / PUS
morbific exhalation / MIASMA; MALARIA
mordacious / ACRID, SHARP
mordant / KEEN; BITING; CAUSTIC
Mordecai's niece / ESTHER
more / BIS; PLUS; AGAIN, EXTRA; ENCORE, LONGER; BESIDES, FURTHER
more acute / WORSE; KEENER
more ancient / OLDER; HOARIER
more blooming / ROSIER; FRESHER
more briny / SALTIER
more comely / FAIRER; CLASSIER
more compact / DENSER
more crippled / LAMER
more delicate / FINER; SOFTER
more distant / FARTHER, REMOTER
more docile / TAMER
more evil / WORSE; WICKEDER
more fashionable CHICQUER
more ignoble / BASER
more intimate / CLOSER, NEARER
more lucid / SANER; CLEARER
more mature RIPER
more needy / POORER
more pallid / PALER; WANNER
more profound / DEEPER
more sagacious / WISER; SMARTER
more sallow / YELLOWER
more secure / SAFER
more than / OVER; ABOVE
more than a few / MANY
more than one / FEW; MANY, SOME
more turbulent / ROUGHER

more unsightly / UGLIER
more unusual / ODDER, RARER
more vaporous / STEAMIER
more verdant / GREENER
more willing / RATHER
more worldly EARTHIER
moreover / AND, BUT, TOO; ALSO
More's ideal island / UTOPIA
mores / CUSTOMS
moresque / MOORISH, MORISCO
Morgan's stamping ground /
    SPANISHMAIN
Morgiana's boss / ALIBABA
Moriah edifice / TEMPLE
moribund / DYING
morindin dye / AAL
moringa seed / BEN; BEHEN
morisco / MOOR; MORESQUE
mormon / MANDRILL
Mormon defense group / DANITES
Mormon leader / SMITH, YOUNG
Mormon State / UTAH
morn / MORNING
morning / AM; DAWN; MATIN
morning, pert. to / MATINAL;
    MATUTINAL
morning moisture / DEW
morning music / MATIN; AUBADE
morning reception / LEVEE
morning service / MATIN; MATINS
morning star / DAYSTAR, LUCIFER
morning-glory / NIL
Moro / SULU; ILANO, LANAO,
    SAMAL
Moro chief / DATO; DATTO
Moro cloak / JABUL
Moro knife / BARONG
Moro priest / SARIP
Moroccan berber / RIFF
Moroccan cape / NUN; NOUN
Moroccan city / CEUTA; TANGIER
Moroccan hilly region / RIF; RIFF
Moroccan money / OKIA, RIAL
Moroccan mountain range / ATLAS
Moroccan native / MOOR
Moroccan public land / GISH
Moroccan ruler / SULTAN
Moroccan tree / SANDARAC
Moroccan tribal chief / KAID
Morocco capital / RABAT
moronic / STUPID

morose / SAD; BLUE, GLUM,
    GRUM, SOUR; MOODY, SURLY;
    GLOOMY
morosis / DULLNESS; STUPIDITY
Morpheus' province / SLEEP
morphine / MORPHIA; NARCOTIC
Morrigu's bird / RAVEN
morsel / BIT, ORT, SOP; BITE
mortal / MAN; HUMAN; ADAMITE.
    FATAL; DEADLY, LETHAL; EX-
    TREME
mortal remains / BODY, CLAY,
    LICH; BONES; RELICS; CARCASS
mortality / DEATH; HUMANITY
mortar / METATE, PETARD,
    STUCCO
mortar beater / RAB
mortar carrier / HOD
mortar ingredient / LIME, SAND
mortar utensil / PESTLE
mortarboard decoration / TASSEL
mortician / UNDERTAKER
mortification of tissue /
    GANGRENE, NECROSIS
mortify / VEX; ABASH, ANNOY,
    SHAME, SPITE, WORRY; HARASS
mortise fitting / TENON
mortuary vehicle / HEARSE
Mosaic law / TORAH
mosaic piece / TILE; TESSERA
Moscow castle / KREMLIN
Moses' brother / AARON
Moses' father-in-law / JETHRO
Moses' sister / MIRIAM
Moses' spy / IGAL; CALEB, NAHBI,
    PALTI; JOSHUA
Moses' wife / ZIPPORAH
Moslem / MUSLIM; SARACEN;
    MOHAMMEDAN
Moslem apostle / RASUL
Moslem ascetic / SUFI; FAKIR;
    DERVISH
Moslem bible / KORAN; ALCORAN
Moslem blessing / BISMILLAH
Moslem call to prayer / ADAN,
    AZAN
Moslem caller to prayer / MUEZZIN
Moslem canon lawyer / MUFTI
Moslem charity / WAKF, WAQF
Moslem converts / ANSAR
Moslem creed / KELIMA; KALIMAH

MORTAL SINS, SEVEN

ENVY
LUST
PRIDE
SLOTH
WRATH
AVARICE
GLUTTONY

Moslem festival / BAIRAM
Moslem garment / IZAR
Moslem god / ALLAH
Moslem hermit / MARABOUT
Moslem hero / GHAZI
Moslem holy book / KORAN,
  QURAN; ALKORAN
Moslem holy city / MECCA;
  MEDINA
Moslem holy war / JIHAD
Moslem law institute / ULEMA
Moslem marriage / MOTA, MUTA
Moslem mendicant / FAKIR;
  FAKEER
Moslem messiah / MAHDI
Moslem monastery / KHANKAH
Moslem month of fasting /
  RAMADAN
Moslem mystic / SUFI
Moslem nymph / HOURI
Moslem orthodox / HANIF;
  HANIFITE
Moslem pilgrim / HADJI, HAJJI
Moslem pilgrimage to Mecca /
  HAJ; HADJ, HAJJ
Moslem pilgrim's garment /
  IHRAM
Moslem potentate / AGA; AGHA
Moslem prayer / ZIKR; DHIKR,
  NAMAZ, RAKAT, SALAT
Moslem prayer locale / IDGAH
Moslem prayer orientation /
  QIBLA; KIBLAH
Moslem pre-prayer ablution /
  WUDU, WUZU
Moslem priest / IMAM; KHATIB
Moslem prophet / NABI;
  MOHAMMED
Moslem pulpit / MIMBAR, MINBAR
Moslem purist / WAHABI;
  WAHHABI
Moslem religion / ISLAM;
  MOHAMMEDANISM
Moslem religious leader / IMAM
Moslem religious meeting / MAJLIS
Moslem religious teacher / ALIM;
  MULLA; MULLAH
Moslem revelation / WAHJ
Moslem saint / PIR; SANTON
Moslem saint's tomb / PIR
Moslem savant / HAKIM
Moslem sect / SUFI; ISAWA
Moslem sermon / KHUTBAH
Moslem shrine / CAABA, KAABA
Moslem teacher / ALIM, COJA;
  KHOJA, MULLA; MULLAH
Moslem temple / MOSK; MASJID,
  MOSQUE, MUSJID
Moslem tenet / IJMA; SUNNA;
  HADITH, SUNNAH
Moslem theological group / ULEMA

Moslem tradition / SUNNA;
  HADITH
Moslem witnesses to truth / ISNAD
mosque / JAMI; MASJID
mosque turret / MINARET
mosque warden / NAZIR
moss / LICHEN; BRYOPHYTE
moss leaf part / ALA
mossback / FOGY, TORY
mossbunker / POGY; MENHADEN
Mossgiel resident / BURNS
Mossi language / MO; MOLE
mosslike herb / LICHEN;
  STONECROP
most / MAXIMUM; GREATEST
most acid / SOUREST
most beautiful / FAIREST
most certain / SUREST
most courageous / GAMEST
most dreadful / WORST; DIREST
most excellent / BEST
most fashionable / LATEST
most favorable / OPTIMAL,
  OPTIMUM
most fertile / RANKEST
most glutinous / SLIMIEST
most hazardous / RISKIEST
Most Holy Lord / SSD
most humid / DAMPEST, WETTEST
most humorous / FUNNIEST
most indigent / POOREST
most indolent / LAZIEST
most inferior / WORST
most insane / MADDEST
most irascible / TESTIEST
most loathsome / FOULEST
most painful / SOREST
most pert / SAUCIEST
most precipitous / STEEPEST
most rational / SANEST
most recent / LATEST, NEWEST
most subdued / TAMEST
most tractable / EASIEST
most uncanny / EERIEST
most unimportant / LEAST
most unresponsive / COLDEST
most wan / PALEST
mostly / MAINLY; CHIEFLY
mot / SAYING
mote / SPECK; PARTICLE
moth / IO; LUNA; EGGER, REGAL
mother / MA; DAM, INA, MOM;
  AMMA, MAMA, MERE; MADRE,
  MAMMA, MATER
mother of all men / EVE
mother of Apollo / LETO
mother of Arthur / YGERNE
Mother of Believers / AYESHA
Mother Carey's chicken / PETREL
Mother of Cities / KIEV
mother country / HOMELAND

mother or father / PARENT
mother of gods / ANA; FRIG, RHEA;
   CYBELE, FRIGGA
Mother Hubbard's companion /
   DOG
mother of Ishmael / HAGAR
Mother of Presidents / VIRGINIA
mother turned to stone / NIOBE
motherhood / MATERNITY
motherless calf / DOGY; DOGIE
motherly / MATERNAL
mother-of-pearl / NACRE
mother-of-pearl shell / OYSTER;
   ABALONE
motif / THEME; SUBJECT
motion / ACT, AIR; GAIT; ACTION
motion picture / FILM; FLICK,
   MOVIE; CINEMA
motion picture award / OSCAR
motion picture floodlight / KLEIG,
   KLIEG
motion of rearing / PESADE
motion of the sea / SEND, TIDE
motionless / INERT, STILL
motivate / IMPEL; INCITE, INDUCE
motivating / CAUSAL;
   STIMULATING
motive / IDEA, SPUR; CAUSE
motley / VARIEGATED;
   PARTICOLORED
motor / ENGINE. DRIVE
motor aphasia / ALALIA
motor coach / BUS; OMNIBUS
motor part / CAM; GEAR; ROTOR
motor truck / RIG, VAN; LORRY
motor vehicle / BUS; AUTO, JEEP,
   TAXI; CYCLE, TRUCK
motorcar / AUTO; AUTOMOBILE
motorcycle passenger's place /
   SIDECAR
motorist's lodging / MOTEL
motorless aircraft / BALLOON
motorless plane / GLIDER
mottle / SPOT; BLOTCH, DAPPLE
mottled / PIED, ROEY; DAPPLED
mottled appearance in mahogany /
   ROE
motto / SAW; ADAGE, MAXIM
moue / GRIMACE
moul / PATTERN
mould / MOLD
moult / MOLT, SHED
mound / TEE; DUNE, HEAP, HILL
mound of sand / DUNE
mount / RISE, SOAR; ARISE,
   CLIMB
mount where ark landed / ARARAT
Mount of Olives / OLIVET
Mount Vernon's river / POTOMAC
Mount Vesuvius city / POMPEII
mountain / ALP, BEN; BERG

mountain, c.f. / ORO
mountain ash / SORB; ROWAN
mountain cat / PUMA; BOBCAT,
   COUGAR
mountain chain / RANGE; DIVIDE
mountain crest / ARETE
mountain defile / COL, GAP; GATE
mountain dew / WHISKEY;
   MOONSHINE
mountain goat / IBEX; MARKHOR
mountain gorge / CLOUGH,
   RAVINE
mountain kangaroo / WALLAROO
mountain lake / TARN
mountain man / TRAPPER
mountain nymph / OREAD
mountain peak / ALP; CRAG;
   CREST
mountain range / ALPS; ANDES
mountain recess / CWM; CORRIE
mountain ridge / SPUR; ARETE,
   RANGE; HOGBACK
mountain science / OROGRAPHY
mountain sheep / BIGHORN
mountain sickness / PUNA, VETA;
   SOROCHE
mountain spinach / ORACH;
   ORACHE
mountain top / PEAK; CREST
mountain-building / OROGENY
mountain-climbing spike / PITON
mountain-growing / MONTANE
Mountain's leader / MARAT;
   DANTON
mountebank / QUACK; CHARLATAN
mounted sentinel / VEDETTE
mounting device / STEPS, STILE;
   LADDER
mourn / WEEP; BEMOAN, GRIEVE
mournful / SAD; DIRE; DISMAL,
   WOEFUL; DOLEFUL, PITEOUS
mournful cry / KEEN, WAIL
mournful song / DIRGE;
   THRENODY
mourning / DOLOR, GRIEF;
   SORROW
mourning band / CRAPE, CREPE
mourning dress / WEEDS
mourning fabric / ALMA; CRAPE
mourning poem / ELEGY; MONODY
mourning sound / KEEN, WAIL
mouse / VOLE
mousebird / COLY; SHRIKE
mouselike animal / SHREW;
   JERBOA
mousseline / CHANTILLY
Mousterian man / NEANDERTHAL
mouth / OS; GRIMACE, OPENING
mouth, c.f. / ORO
mouth, pert. to / ORAL
mouth open / AGAPE

mouth organ / HARMONICA
mouth part / GUM, LIP; TOOTH; PALATE, TONGUE
mouth of river / LADE; FRITH
mouth of volcano / VENT; CRATER; CALDERA; FUMAROLE
mouthful / BITE
mouthlike opening / PORE; STOMA
mouthpiece / REED; BOCAL; LAWYER
mouthpiece of bagpipe / MUSE
mouthy / OROTUND; BOMBASTIC
movable / MOBILE; PORTABLE
movable frame of loom / LAY; SLEY; BATTEN
movable portal / DOOR, GATE
move / GO; LEAD, PUSH, STIR, WALK; BUDGE, IMPEL, MARCH; AFFECT, AWAKEN, CHANGE, INCITE
move across / TRAVERSE
move ahead steadily / FORGE; PRESSON; PROGRESS
move to another place / SWITCH
move away from / EBB; RECEDE
move awkwardly / LUMBER
move back and forth / WAG; FLAP, SWAY, WAVE; SWING, WAVER; SEESAW
move a camera / PAN; TRACK
move in a circle / EDDY; SWIRL
move confusedly / MILL
move downward / DESCEND
move at an easy pace / AMBLE; STROLL
move forward / ADVANCE; PROGRESS
move furtively / PROWL, SKULK
move helically / TWIRL; SPIRAL
move lightly / FLIT, SKIP
move merrily / TRIP; DANCE
move noisily / TRAMP; CLATTER
move out / LEAVE; VACATE
move quickly / RUN; SCAT, SCUD
move rapidly / FLY, RIP, RUN; DART, JUMP, RACE; CAREEN, HURTLE
move in reverse / BACK; BACKUP
move rhythmically / DANCE, MARCH; WAGGLE, OSCILLATE
move round and round / EDDY
move sideways / EDGE, SKID, SLUE; SIDLE
move silently / TIPTOE
move slowly / LAG; DRAG, INCH; CREEP
move smoothly / FLOW, SAIL
move over snow / SKI; MUSH, SLED
move stealthily / PROWL, SLINK, SNEAK, STEAL
move suddenly / DART, FLIT; START

move upward / FLY; RISE, SOAR
move vigorously / STIR
move through water / SAIL, SWIM
move on wheels / ROLL
movement / CAUSE, TAXIS, TREND; ACTION, MOTION; TROPISM; PROGRESS
movement of the feet / GAIT
movement in gymnastics / KIP; PIKE, TUCK
movement of panicky group / STAMPEDE
movement of the sea / TIDE, WAVE
mover of scenery / STAGEHAND
movie / FILM; CINEMA
movie dog / ASTA; LASSIE
movie eats / CANDY; POPCORN
movie process / TODDAO, THREED; CINERAMA; TECHNICOLOR
movie synopsis / SCENARIO
moving / ASTIR; MOTILE; STIRRING, TOUCHING; AFFECTING, IMPELLING
moving about / ASTIR; STIRRING
moving force / AGENT; SPIRIT
moving part / AXLE; ROTOR, SCREW
moving picture / FILM; MOVIE; CINEMA
moving stairs / ESCALATOR
moving truck / VAN
mow / CUT; CLIP, MOCK. LOFT
mow of hay / DRESS, GOAF, RICK
mowed grass / HAY
mowed strip / SWATH; WINDROW
Mowgli's teacher / BAGHEERA
moxie / GUTS; NERVE
Mozambique native / YAO; NDAU
Mozambique river / SAVE; LIMPOPO
Mozambique town / BEIRA
Mozart cataloguer / KOCHEL
much / AMPLE; PLENTY; ABUNDANT. ABOUT; NEARLY
mucilage / GUM; GLUE
muck / DIRT, DUNG, MIRE; SLIME
muck about / IDLE; PUTTER
muckle / MUCH; PLENTY
muckworm / GRUB; MISER
mucky / DIRTY; FILTHY
mucous membrane / MUCOSA
muculent / SLIMY; VISCOUS
mud / MIRE, OOZE, SLIME; MURGEON
mud, c.f. / LIMI
mud deposit / SILT; ALLUVIUM
mud eel / SIREN
mud volcano / SALSE
muddle / MIX; STIR; ADDLE
muddled / ASEA; MUZZY; CONFUSED
muddy / ROIL. MIRY; SLUDGY

muddy ground / BOG; MIRE, MUCK
mud-ingesting / LIMIVOROUS
mud-inhabiting / LIMICOLOUS
mudlark / GAMIN, PIPIT; URCHIN
muffin / COB, GEM; DUMPLING
muffle / MUTE, WRAP; DEADEN
muffler / VEIL; SCARF; TIPPET
mug / CUP, NOG, POT; FACE, TOBY
mugger / GOA; TINKER; FOOTPAD;
    GARROTER; CROCODILE
Mugwump / INDEPENDENT
mulberry / AL; AAL, ACH, AWL
mulberry bark cloth / TAPA; TAPPA
mulberry drink / MORAT
Mulciber / VULCAN
mulct / BILK, FINE. PENALTY
mule / ASS; FOOL; HYBRID
mule driver / MULETEER,
    MULETRESS
mule's call / BRAY
muley / HORNLESS, STUBBORN
Mulford cowboy / HOPALONG
muliebrous / EFFEMINATE
mulier / WIFE; WOMAN; MOTHER
mulish / STUBBORN; OBSTINATE
mull / PONDER; MEDITATE
mullet / BOBO; SUCKER; GOAT-
    FISH
mulligatawney flavoring / CURRY
multifarious / MANIFOLD
multiform / DIVERSE
multiple / MANY; COLLECTIVE.
    PRODUCT
multiplicand / FACIEND
multiplication result / TOTAL
multiplied by / TIMES
multiplier / FACIENT; OPERATOR
multiply / INCREASE
multipotent / POWERFUL
multitude / MOB; ARMY, HOST;
    CROWD, HORDE, SWARM;
    LEGION
multitudinous / MYRIAD;
    NUMEROUS
mum / MOTHER; SILENCE;
    CHRYSANTHEMUM. SILENT
mumble / GUM; MUMP; MUTTER
mummer / ACTOR
mummery / MASKING;
    BUFFOONERY
mummified / DRIED; SHRUNKEN
mummify / EMBALM; PRESERVE
mump / BEG; SULK; CHEAT,
    WHINE
mumps / PAROTITIS
munch / CHEW; CHAMP, CHOMP
mundane / EARTHLY, WORLDLY;
    TEMPORAL
mundify / WASH; DEBRIDE
Mundy character / JIMGRIM
Munich museum / PINAKOTHEK
Munich's river / ISAR

municipal corporation / CITY,
    TOWN
municipal officer / MAYOR;
    MANAGER; MAGISTRATE
municipality / CITY, TOWN
munificence / BOUNTY;
    LIBERALITY
munificent / FREE; LAVISH;
    LIBERAL; GENEROUS
muniment / DEFENSE;
    PROTECTION
munitions repository / ARMORY;
    ARSENAL
Munro pen name / SAKI
murder / KILL, SLAY; BURKE;
    MANGLE; BUTCHER, DESTROY.
    HOMICIDE
murder fine / CRO; MURDRUM
murder by mob action / LYNCHING
murder by suffocation / BURKE,
    CHOKE, GARROTE, SMOTHER;
    STRANGLE, THROTTLE
murderer / KILLER, SLAYER
murderous / DEADLY;
    INTERNECINE
mure / IMMURE
murk / DARK; GLOOM; DARKNESS
murky / DIM; DARK; DUSKY,
    FOGGY
murky condition / FOG; SMOG
murmur / COO, HUM; PURL,
    PURR
murrain / PLAGUE; ANTHRAX
murre / AUK; GUILLEMOT
muscle / BEEF, THEW; BRAWN
muscle, c.f. / INO
muscle of abdomen / CREMASTER,
    DIAPHRAGM
muscle of arm / BICEPS; TRICEPS
muscle cord / SINEW; TENDON
muscle of leg / POPLITEUS,
    SARTORIUS
muscle of mouth / LIP.
    BUCCINATOR
muscle of neck / TRAPEZIUS
muscle of shoulder / DELTOID
muscle for stretching / TENSOR
musclelike / MYOID
muscovite / MICA
Muscovite / RUSS; RUSSIAN
Muscovy / RUSSIA
muscovy duck / PATO
muscovy glass / MICA
muscular / BRAWNY, SINEWY
muscular inability in walking /
    ABASIA
muscular incoordination / ATAXY;
    ATAXIA
muscular spasm / TIC; TETANY
muse / GAZE, REVE; DREAM,
    THINK
muse of astronomy / URANIA

MUSES, NINE

astronomy	URANIA
comedy	THALIA
flutes	EUTERPE
heroic epic	CALLIOPE
history	CLIO
lyric poetry (dance)	TERPSICHORE
lyric poetry (hymns)	ERATO
mime	POLYHYMNIA
tragedy	MELPOMENE

muse of choral song / TERPSICHORE
muse of comedy / THALIA
muse of dancing / TERPSICHORE
muse of epic / CALLIOPE
muse of heroic poetry / CALLIOPE
muse of history / CLIO
muse of hymns / ERATO
muse of idyllic poetry / THALIA
muse of lyric poetry / EUTERPE
muse of mime / POLYMNIA; POLYHYMNIA
muse moodily / BROOD
muse of music / EUTERPE
muse of oratory / POLYMNIA; POLYHYMNIA
muse of tragedy / MELPOMENE
Muses (collectively) / PIERIDES
Muses, pert. to / PIERIAN
Muses' leader / APOLLO; CALLIOPE
Muses' region / AONIA; HELICON
musette / BAGPIPE
museum official / CURATOR
mush / PAP; ATOLE, SEPON; SUPAWN
mushroom / MOREL; AGARIC, FUNGUS; AMANITA, BOLETUS; TOADSTOOL
mushroom cap / PILEUS
mushy / PULPY; SENTIMENTAL
music / MELODY; HARMONY
music clef / BASS; TENOR; TREBLE
music for eight / OCTET
music for five / QUINTET
music for four / QUARTET
music for a group / CHORAL, CHORUS; CHORALE; SYMPHONY
music hall / GAFF; ODEON, ODEUM
music hall star / ROBEY; LAUDER
music for nine / NONET
music for one / SOLO
music for six / SEXTET; SEXTETTE
music for three / TRIO
music for two / DUO; DUET
musical / LYRIC, MELIC; DULCET
musical air / LILT, SONG, TUNE
musical beat / TAKT; SWING
musical bell / CHIME; TAMTAM

musical character / DOT; CLEF, FLAT, NOTE, REST; BREVE, MINIM
musical close / CODA; FINALE
musical comedy / REVUE; OPERETTA
musical composition / RAG; DUET, GLEE, HYMN, OPUS, RAGA, SONG, TRIO; FUGUE, OPERA, RONDO, SCORE; ANTHEM, ARIOSO, BALLAD, SEXTET, SONATA; BALLADE, CANTATA
musical congress / MOD; FEIS; EISTEDDFOD
musical direction / RIT, STA; RALL; FORTE, LARGO, LENTO; DACAPO; ALLEGRO, ANDANTE; CRESCENDO
musical drama / OPERA; OPERETTA
musical drama, pert. to / OPERATIC
musical flourish / TRILL; CADENZA
musical group / BAND; COMBO; CHORUS; ORCHESTRA
musical instrument / SAX, UKE; ASOR, BINA, DRUM, FIFE, GIGA, GORA, HARP, HORN, LUTE, LYRE, OBOE, PIPE, REED, TUBA, VINA, VIOL; BANJO, BUGLE, CELLO, FLUTE, ORGAN, PIANO, REBEC, SITAR, SNARE, VIOLA; CORNET, GUITAR, LAVIER; SPINET, TUMTUM, VIOLIN; HELICON, MARIMBA, OCARINA, SAXHORN
musical instrument part / KEY; REED; PEDAL; BRIDGE, PISTON
musical interval / REST; OCTAVE
musical jump / SALTO
musical key / MAJOR, MINOR
musical note in scale of Guido / UT; ALT, ELA
musical passage / CADENZA
musical pause / REST
musical performance / REVUE; CONCERT, RECITAL
musical pipe / OAT; REED; DRONE
musical pipes / BAGPIPE, MUSETTE; CORNEMUSE

musical program / RECITAL
musical sacred composition /
HYMN; MOTET; ANTHEM,
TEDEUM; CANTATA; ORATORIO
musical salute / TAPS; AUBADE
musical shake / TRILL; TREMOLO
musical show / REVUE; BALLET;
MUSICAL; OPERETTA
musical solo / ARIA; ARIOSO;
CADENZA
musical sound / NOTE, TONE
musical sound, pert. to / TONAL
musical study / ETUDE
musical sweet potato / OCARINA
musical syllable / DO, FA, LA, MI,
RE, SI, SO, TI; ELA, SOL
musical symbol / See musical
character
musical theme / TEMA; MOTIF
musical upbeat / ARSIS;
ANACRUSIS
musical work / OP; OPUS; OPERA,
REVUE; SONATA; CONCERTO
musician / BUGLER; CELLIST,
DRUMMER, PIANIST;
COMPOSER, ORGANIST
musician's wand / BATON
musing / REVERIE; MEDITATION
musk cat / CIVET
muskeg / SWAMP; BOGLAND
musket / FUSIL; FLINTLOCK,
MATCHLOCK
musketeer / ATHOS; ARAMIS;
PORTHOS; DARTAGNAN
Muskhogean Indian / CREEK;
YAMASI; CHOCTAW; FLATHEAD,
SEMINOLE
muskmelon / CASABA; HONEY-
DEW; CANTALOUP;
CANTALOUPE
muslin / BAN; MULL; ADATI,
MOSAL, SHELA; NAINSOOK,
TARLATAN
muss / MESS; MUDDLE, RUMPLE
mussel / UNIO; NAIAD; BIVALVE
Musset's traveling companion /
GEORGESAND
Mussolini / DUCE
Mussulman / MOSLEM; SARACEN;
MOHAMMEDAN
mussy / DISORDERLY
must / MOLD, SAPA, STUM;
MILDEW
mustache monkey / MOUSTOC
mustang / BRONCO; BRONCHO
mustard / SENVY; SINAPIS
mustard plant / CRESS;
CHARLOCK
musteline animal / MINK; OTTER,
RATEL, SKUNK; BADGER,
MARTEN
muster / GATHER, SUMMON;

CONVENE, MARSHAL;
ASSEMBLE
musty / OLD; FOUL, FUSTY, SOUR;
FETID, MOLDY, STALE;
MILDEWED
mut / CUR, DOG; MUTT;
MONGREL
mutable / FICKLE, FITFUL
mutate / ALTER; CHANGE
mutation / SPORT; CHANGE
mute / MUM; DUMB, LENE;
SILENT; SPEECHLESS.
DEADEN, MUFFLE
mute consonant / LENE, STOP
muted / SILENT; MUFFLED
mutilate / GELD, MAIM; GARBLE,
MANGLE; CRIPPLE
mutilated god / XIPE; CRONUS,
OSIRIS
mutilation / MAYHEM
mutinous / UNRULY; RIOTOUS;
INSURGENT, SEDITIOUS
mutiny / REVOLT; INSURRECTION
Mut's husband / AMEN, AMON
mutter / GROWL; RUMBLE;
GRUMBLE
muttonfish / PAUA, SAMA; PORGY
Mutt's little friend / JEFF
mutual / JOINT; COMMON;
RECIPROCAL
mutual discourse / DIALOG;
COLLOQUY
mutually planned / AGREED
muzhik / PEASANT
muzzle / SNOUT. GAG
muzzy / DAZED; INDISTINCT
my / MINE
my lady / MADAM; MADAME,
MILADY
Mycenean king / AGAMEMNON
mycosis / TINEA; RINGWORM
myopic / NEARSIGHTED
myriad / MANY; COUNTLESS
myriapod / MILLIPEDE
myrmidon / FOLLOWER
Myron's great statue /
DISCOBOLUS
Myrrha's son / ADONIS
mysteries / RITES; ARCANA
mysterious / DIM; DARK, DEEP;
RUNIC; HIDDEN, MYSTIC,
OCCULT
mystery / RUNE; CABALA, ENIGMA
mystery novel / WHODUNIT
mystic / DARK; OCCULT
mystic ejaculation / OM
mystic word / ABRACADABRA
mystify / PUZZLE; CONFUSE
myth / LIE; SAGA, TALE; FABLE;
LEGEND; FICTION, PARABLE
myth, pert. to / MYTHIC;
MYTHICAL

mythical / UNREAL; FANCIFUL
mythical Assyrian queen / SEMIRAMIS
mythical bird / ROC; GARUDA; SIMURGH
mythical continent / ATLANTIS
mythical drink of the gods / SOMA; NECTAR
mythical ferryman / CHARON
mythical giant / YMIR; TITAN
mythical horse / PEGASUS
mythical hunter / ORION; MELEAGER

mythical king / ATLI, BRAN, LEAR; CREON, MIDAS, MINOS; ARTHUR
mythical monster / OGRE; GIANT; DRAGON
mythical mountains / KAF, QAF
mythical river / STYX; PHLEGETHON
mythical submerged island / MU, YS; LEMURIA; ATLANTIS
mythology, pert. to / MYTHIC; MYTHICAL; MYTHOLOGICAL
Mytilene / LESBOS
Mytyl's companion / TYLTYL

N

nab / GRAB, TRAP; CATCH; SNATCH
nabal / MISER
Nabal's wife / ABIGAIL
nabob / MOGUL; BIGWIG; PLUTO-CRAT
nacre / PEARL
naevus / MOLE; BIRTHMARK
nag / FRET; ANNOY, TEASE. HORSE
Naga tribe / AO; LHOTA
nahoor / SNA
naiad / NYMPH
nail / HOB; BRAD, STUD, TACK
nail angled in / TOED
nail with open head / SPAD
nailing / CLINCHING
naive / CANDID; ARTLESS, SINCERE
naked / BARE, NUDE; PLAIN
nakoo / GAVIAL
namayoush / TOGUE
nambypamby / SHALLOW; AFFECTED
name / DUB; CALL; CLEPE. FAME, TERM; HONOR, TITLE; CREDIT
name for Athena / ALEA
name as authority / CITE; QUOTE
name in grammar / NOUN
name for a monkey / NED; NEDDY
name for office / NOMINATE
name plate / FACIA
named / TAGGED, TITLED, YCLEPT
nameless / UNMARKED; ANON-YMOUS
namely / VIZ; TOWIT; SCILICET
names / CHRISTENS
names, pert. to / NOMINAL
namesake / HOMONYM
nana / NURSE; PINEAPPLE. DWARF
Nanna's husband / BALDER
nanoid / DWARFISH
Naomi's chosen name / MARA
Naomi's daughter-in-law / RUTH
naos / CELLA; TEMPLE
nap / NOD; DOZE. PILE; SIESTA
naps / LEATHER
nape / NUCHA; SCRUFF; NIDDICK

nape, pert. to / NUCHAL
napery / LINEN
naphtha / PETROLEUM
napkin / BIB; DIDY; DIDIE; DIAPER
Naples / NAPOLI
Naples, pert. to / NEAPOLITAN
Naples insurgent / MASANIELLO
napoleon / NAP; PAM; PASTRY
Napoleonic marshal / NEY; SOULT
Napoleonic victory / ULM; JENA, LODI; WAGRAM; MARENGO; AUSTERLITZ
Napoleon's brother-in-law / MURAT
Napoleon's downfall / WATERLOO
Napoleon's island / ELBA; CORSICA
Napoleon's nickname / COR-PORAL, CORSICAN
napoo / DONE, GONE; KAPUT
napped cloth / PLUSH
napped leather / SUEDE
nappy / PILY; DROWSY, SHAGGY
nap-raising device / GIG; TEASEL
narcism / EGO
narcissus / JONQUIL; DAFFODIL
Narcissus' admirer / ECHO
narcosis / COMA; STUPOR
narcotic / DOPE, DRUG; OPIATE
narcotic drug / POT; HEMP; BHANG
narcotic languor / KEF
narcotic plant / KAT; COCA; DUTRA
nard / VALERIAN; SPIKENARD
nares / NOSTRILS
nark / SPY; STOOLIE; INFORMER
narrate / TELL; RECITE, RELATE
narration / STORY; ACCOUNT
narrative / TALE; STORY; ACCOUNT
narrative poem / LAY; BALLAD
narrator / TELLER
narrow / NEAR; CLOSE, EXACT
narrow, c.f. / STEN; STENO
narrow band / ORLE; TAPE; STRIA
narrow board / LATH, SLAT; BATTEN
narrow body of water / BAB; CANAL; STRAIT; CHANNEL
narrow channel / GAT; RACE

narrow fabric / TAPE; FILLET
narrow glass container / TUBE
narrow inlet / GAT, RIA; FIRTH
narrow opening / GASH, RIMA, SLIT, SLOT; CLEFT
narrow pass / ABRA; DEFILE
narrow path / LANE; ALLEY
narrow piece / STRIP; RIBBON
narrow ridge / ESKER
narrow strait / GORGE
narrow stretch of land / NECK
narrow strip / BELT
narrow trimming / EDGING; HEMMING
narrow valley / COMBE; STRATH
narrow-minded / SMALL; BIGOTED
narthex / LOBBY; VESTIBULE
nary / NO; NONE; NEVER
nasal / NARINE, RHINAL
nasal cavity / SINUS; ANTRUM
nasal tone / TWANG
nascent / APPEARING, INCIPIENT
nasty / FOUL, VILE; GROSS, FILTHY
nasua / COATI
natal / BIRTH; NATIVE
nation / RACE; REALM, STATE
national / GENERAL; PATRIOTIC
national bird / EAGLE
national emblem / FLAG; CREST
national emblem of U.S. / EAGLE
national guard / MILITIA
national song / ANTHEM
native / RAW; INBORN. ITE, SON
native ability / TALENT
native American / INDIAN; AMERIND
native of ancient Persia / MEDE
native of Athens / GREEK
native of Attu / ALEUT; ALASKAN
native of Brittany / BRETON
native chief of India / SIRDAR
native country / HOME
native garment / SARONG
native Indian soldier / SEPOY
native intelligence / COMMONSENSE
native of Khatti / HITTITE
native lead sulphite / GALENA
native metal / ORE
native of, suffix / ER; ESE, IAN, ITE, IVE
native of Rio / CARIOCA
native of Thailand / SIAMESE
nativity / CHRISTMAS
NATO / ALLIANCE
natrium / SODIUM
nattily / NEATLY, TIDILY
natty / NICE, PRIM, TRIM; DANDY
natural / RAW; BORN, REAL; INNATE, NATIVE, SIMPLE; ARTLESS
natural ability / GIFT; TALENT
natural abode / PATRIA; HABITAT

natural aptitude / FLAIR; TALENT
natural in craps / SEVEN; ELEVEN
natural drift / TIDE; SWING
natural elevation / HILL; MOUNT
natural essence / GUNA
natural fat / ESTER
natural force / ELEMENT
natural luster / NAIF
natural metal / ORE
natural power / OD
natural result / CONSEQUENCE
natural state / ROUGH; UNREFINED
natural sweet / MEL; HONEY
natural talent / DOWER; ABILITY
naturalization / CITIZENSHIP
naturalness / EASE
nature / KIND, MIND, SORT, TYPE
nature spirit / NAT
naught / NIL; ZERO; CIPHER
naughty / BAD; WICKED; PERVERSE
nauseous / LOATHSOME, SICKENING
nautical / NAVAL; MARINE
nautical call / AHOY
nautical command / AVAST, BELAY
nautical hazard / FOG; GALE, BERG
nautical instrument / SEXTANT
nautical map / CHART
nautical measure / KNOT
nautical rope / TYE; VANG; HAWSER, NETTLE; MARLINE
"Nautilus" captain / NEMO
Navaho / DINE; NAVAJO
Navaho hut / HOGAN
naval / MARITIME, NAUTICAL
naval chief / ADMIRAL
naval clerk / YEOMAN
naval force / FLEET; ARMADA
naval insubordinate / MUTINEER
naval jail / BRIG
naval officer / ENSIGN; ADMIRAL
naval weapon / POMPOM; TORPEDO
nave / HUB; ARCADE, CENTER
navigable part of stream / CHANNEL, PASSAGE
navigate / MOVE, SAIL; STEER
navigate in air / FLY; AVIATE
navigation aid / BUOY; LORAN, RADAR, SONAR
navigator / SAILOR; MARINER
Navy servicewoman / WAVE
Navy warrant officer / BOSUN
nawab / MOGUL, NABOB
Nazarene / JESUS; CHRIST
Nazi camp / DACHAU
Nazi symbol / SWASTIKA
Nazi trooper / SA, SS
nchega / CHIMP
Neanderthal / CAVEMAN
neap / LOW

neaped / BEACHED; GROUNDED
Neapolitan opera house / SAN-CARLO
Neapolitan outlaws / CAMORRA
near / DEAR; CLOSE, SHORT; NARROW. AT, BY; NIGH; ABOUT
near, pref. / PARA; JUXTA
near by / AT; GIN; CLOSE; BESIDE
near the ear / OTIC; PAROTIC
Near East native / ARAB, TURK
Near Eastern coach / ARABA
Near Eastern dry valley / WADI
near the eye / OCULAR
near at hand / NIGH; CLOSE
near the stern / AFT
near to / AT, BY, ON
nearest / NEXT; CLOSEST
nearest star / SUN
nearly / ALMOST; CLOSELY
nearly alike / SIMILAR
nearly corresponding / TWIN
nearsighted / MYOPIC; SANDBLIND
neat / NET; NICE, PRIM, PURE, TIDY, TRIG, TRIM; CLEAN. CATTLE
neatherd / COWBOY, DROVER
neb / TIP; BEAK, BILL, NOSE
Nebraska boosters / AKSARBEN
Nebraska capital / LINCOLN
Nebraska city / OMAHA, WAHOO
Nebraska Indian / OTO; OTOE; KIOWA; PAWNEE
Nebraska river / LOUP; PLATTE
Nebraska state flower / GOLDEN-ROD
Nebraska state nickname / BLACK-WATER, CORNHUSKER
nebris / FAWNSKIN
nebula / CLOUD; GALAXY; UNIVERSE
nebulous / HAZY; VAGUE; CLOUDY
nebulous part of comet / COMA
nebulous visitor / COMET
necessary / NEEDFUL; ESSENTIAL
necessary to life / VITAL
necessitate / FORCE; COMPEL
necessity / NEED, WANT; POVERTY
necessity of life / AIR; FOOD
neck / CAPE, NAPE, PLUG. SPOON
neck artery / CAROTID
neck decoration / FICHU, JABOT
neck of garment / COLLAR
neck hair / MANE
neck ornament / GORGET, TORQUE
neckcloth / TIE; ASCOT; CRAVAT
necklace / LEI; BEADS; RIVIERE
neckpiece / BOA; ASCOT, SCARF
necktie / BOW; ASCOT; CRAVAT
necromancer / HEX; WIZARD
necromancy / GOETY, MAGIC
necropolis / CEMETERY
necropsy / AUTOPSY; POST-MORTEM

nectar / HONEY; HYDROMEL
neddy / ASS; DONKEY; SIMPLETON
nee / BORN
need / LACK, MISS, WANT, PENURY
needful / NECESSARY, REQUISITE
neediness / POVERTY; INDIGENCE
needle / HECKLE. BODKIN; COMPASS
needle bug / NEPA
needle bush / HAKEA
needle case / ETUI; ETWEE
needlefish / GAR; BILLFISH
needlelike bristle / SPICULE
needle-shaped / ACUATE; ACERATE
needless / USELESS; UNNECESSARY
needlework / SEWING; SAMPLER; EMBROIDERY, PETITPOINT
needy / POOR; INDIGENT; DESTITUTE
ne'er-do-well / LOSEL; SCALAWAG
nef / CLOCK
nefarious / EVIL, VILE; WICKED
negate / DENY, VETO; REJECT
negation / NO; NOT; DENIAL
negative / NE, NO; NAY, NON, NOT
negative, pref. / IR, UN; DIS
negative particle / ANION
negative pole / CATHODE
negative vote / NAY
neglect / OMIT; FORGET. LACHES
neglected / UNDONE; UNTENDED
negligent / LAX; REMISS; CARELESS
negotiable / LIQUID; TRANSFERABLE
negotiable instrument / DEED
negotiate / DEAL, SELL; TREAT
Negrillo / PYGMY; BUSHMAN
negrito / ATA, ITA; AETA, AKKA
Negro / BLACK. COLORED
Negro of Africa / GA, HA; AJA, EWE, FON, IBO, KRU, MUM, SAB, SUK, TEM, THO, TIV, YAO
negro dance / JUBA
neigh / NICKER, WHINNY
neighbor / INTIMATE
neighborhood / VICINITY
neighboring / VICINAL; ADJACENT
neighborly / HOSPITABLE
neighborly gathering / BEE; KLATCH, SOCIAL
neither animal nor vegetable / MINERAL
neither here nor there / NOWHERE
neither milk nor meat / PAREVE
Nelson's victory / TRAFALGAR
nemesis / BANE; AVENGER
nene / GOOSE
neon / GAS; SIGN; LIGHT
neophyte / TYRO; NOVICE
neoplasm / TUMOR; GROWTH
neoteric / MODERN, RECENT

nep / KNOT; CATMINT
Nepal capital / KATMANDU
Nepal mountain / AWI; EVEREST
Nepal native / KHA; SHERPA
Nepalese hat / TERAI
Nepalese kingdom / MUSTANG
Nepalese warrior / GURKHA
nephew / NEVE; NEPOTE
nephew, pert. to / NEPOTAL
nephrite / JADE
Neptune / LER; POSEIDON
Neptune's satellite / NEREID
Neptune's spear / TRIDENT
Nero / TYRANT; FIDDLER
Nero's instrument / LYRE; FIDDLE
Nero's mother / AGRIPPINA
nerve / FORCE, PLUCK, VIGOR
nerve, c.f. / NEUR; NEURO
nerve cell / NEURON
nerve cell process / AXON
nerve center / GANGLION
nerve network / RETE; PLEXUS
nerve white matter / ALBA
nerveless / WEAK; FEEBLE
nervous / EDGY; TENSE; UNEASY
nervous disorder / TIC; CHOREA
nervous frenzy / AMOK
nervous reaction / SHAKES
nervous system, pert. to / NEURAL
nervous twitch / TIC
nervy / CHEEKY; SPIRITED
nescient / UNAWARE; AGNOSTIC
ness / CAPE; HEADLAND
nest / DEN, NID; AERIE, NIDUS
nest on a crag / AERIE, EYRIE
nest of eagle / AERY; AERIE
nest egg / RESERVE
nest of pheasant / NIDE
nest-building fish / ACARA, ACARE
nestle / CUDDLE; SNUGGLE
nestling / EYAS; CHICK
Nestor / SAGE; ADVISER
net / GET; YIELD, GIN, WEB; GAIN,
  MESH, TRAP, WEIR; CLEAR
net fabric / TULLE; MALINE
net for fishing / SEINE, TRAWL
net of hairs / RETICLE
net worth / VALUE; ASSETS
nether / LOWER, UNDER
Netherlands / See Dutch
Netherlands capital / AMSTERDAM
Netherlands measure / EL; ROEDE
Netherlands money / FLORIN, GUL-
  DEN; GUILDER
Netherlands port / ROTTERDAM
Netherlands reclaimed land /
  POLDER
Netherlands river / LEK; MAAS
Netherlands royal city / HAGUE
netlike / RETICULAR
netting / MESH; GAUZE
nettle / IRK, VEX; FRET. BUR
nettle rash / UREDO; URTICARIA

network / WEB; MESH, RETE;
  PLEXUS
network of strips / LATTICE
network of threads / FABRIC
neuroglia / GLIA
neurotic stealing / KLEPTOMANIA
neuter / NEUTRAL, SEXLESS
neuter pronoun / IT
neutral / UNBIASED; INDIFFERENT
neutral color / ECRU, GRAY; BEIGE
neutralize / NULLIFY; COUNTER-
  ACT
Nevada capital / CARSONCITY
Nevada city / ELY; ELKO, RENO
Nevada Indian / WASHO; DIGGER
Nevada lake / MEAD; TAHOE
Nevada river / TRUCKEE
Nevada state flower / SAGEBRUSH
Nevada state nickname / SILVER;
  SAGEBRUSH
Nevada state tree / PINON
neve /FIRN, SNOW
never / NAR; NARY, NEER
never-ending / CEASELESS
nevertheless / YET; STILL
nevus / MOLE; BIRTHMARK
new / LATE; FRESH, NOVEL;
  MODERN
new, c.f. / NEA, NEO
New Caledonia bird / KAGU
New Caledonia capital / NOUMEA
New Deal agency / NRA, TVA, WPA
New England mountain / CADILLAC
New England river / WINOOSKI
New Englander / YANKEE
New Guinea nerve disease / KURU
New Guinea river / SEPIK
New Guinea territory / PAPUA
New Guinea town / LAE; WEWAK
New Hampshire capital / CONCORD
New Hampshire city / NASHUA
New Hampshire college / DART-
  MOUTH
New Hampshire lake / SUNAPEE
New Hampshire range / PRESI-
  DENTIAL
New Hampshire state flower /
  LILAC
New Hampshire state nickname /
  GRANITE
New Hampshire tree / BIRCH
New Haven university / YALE
New Hebrides capital / VILA
New Hebrides island / EPI; TANA
new horses / RELAY
New Jersey capital / TRENTON
New Jersey city / NEWARK
New Jersey nickname / GARDEN
New Jersey river / TOMS; RARITAN
New Jersey state flower / VIOLET
New Mexico bird / ROADRUNNER
New Mexico capital / SANTAFE
New Mexico city / HOBBS, RATON

New Mexico Indian / SIA; PIRO, TANO, TAOS, TEWA, TIWA, ZUNI; ACOMA, JEMEZ, KERES, MANSO, PECOS
New Mexico river / GILA; PECOS
New Mexico state flower / YUCCA
New Mexico tree / PINON
New Mexico's former name / CIBOLA
new star / NOVA
New Testament part / GOSPEL
new wine / MUST
new word / NEOLOGISM
New York airport / KENNEDY
New York capital / ALBANY
New York city / TROY; OLEAN
New York City / GOTHAM
New York City borough / BRONX, QUEENS; BROOKLYN, RICHMOND; MANHATTAN
New York City county / BRONX, KINGS; QUEENS; NEWYORK; RICHMOND
New York eleven / JETS; GIANTS
New York five / NETS; KNICKS
New York harbor island / ELLIS
New York Indian / ONEIDA, SENECA
New York lake / GEORGE, PLACID
New York lakes / FINGER
New York nine / METS; YANKS
New York prison / ATTICA; SINGSING
New York river / HUDSON, MOHAWK
New York stadium / SHEA; YANKEE
New York state canal / ERIE
New York state flower / ROSE
New York state motto / EXCELSIOR
New York state nickname / EMPIRE
New York subway / BMT, IND, IRT
New York summer time / EDT
New Zealand aborigine / MAORI
New Zealand bird / KEA, MOA, TUI; HUIA, KAKI, KIWI; APTERYX
New Zealand Christmas tree / RATA
New Zealand clan / ATI
New Zealand district / OTAGO
New Zealand fish / IHI; HIKU
New Zealand flightless bird / KIWI, WEKA; TAKAHE
New Zealand fruit pigeon / KUKU
New Zealand hedge / KARO; KOHUHU
New Zealand hill fort / PA; PAH
New Zealand laburnum / KOWHAI
New Zealand lake / TAUPO; TEANAU
New Zealand mollusk / PIPI
New Zealand morepork / PEHO, RURU
New Zealand mountain / COOK

New Zealand national flower / KOWHIA
New Zealand night imp / TAIPO
New Zealand palm / NIKAU
New Zealand parrot / KEA; KAKA
New Zealand parson bird / POE; KOKO
New Zealand pine / KAURI; KAWAKA
New Zealand plant / AKA; RATA
New Zealand reptile / TUATARA
New Zealand river / CLUTHA
New Zealand shrub / TUTU; KOWHIA
New Zealand smelt / INANGA
New Zealand soldier / ANZAC
New Zealand spider / KATIPO
New Zealand timber tree / MIRO, RIMU; KAURI; TOTARA
New Zealand tree / KOPI, NAIO, PUKA, TAWA, TORU, WHAU; KARAKA
New Zealand tucker / KAIKAI
New Zealand volcano / RUAPEHU
newborn lamb / EAN; YEAN
newcomer / TYRO; NOVICE; ENTRANT
Newfoundland cape / RACE
Newfoundland peninsula / AVALON
newly hatched salmon / ALEVIN
newly married man / GROOM; BENEDICT; BRIDEGROOM
newly married woman / BRIDE
newly picked / FRESH
newness / RECENT; RECENCY
news / ADVICE; TIDINGS
news agency / AP, AT, UP; INS, UPI; TASS; ANETA. DOMEI; REUTERS
news article / DISPATCH
news editors / DESK
news gatherer / LEGMAN; REPORTER
news publication / DAILY, PAPER
news report / EXTRA; BULLETIN
news stand / KIOSK
news story / ITEM; SCOOP
newsboy / NEWSY; CARRIER
newsman / REPORTER
newspaper article / FEATURE
newspaper edition / EXTRA; BULLDOG
newspaper man / EDITOR; REPORTER
newspaper writer / COLUMNIST
newspaperdom / PRESS
newt / EFT; TRITON; SALAMANDER
next / ENSUING, NEAREST
next to the last / PENULT
nexus / TIE; BOND, LINK
niagara / FLOOD; WATERFALL
nib / END; BEAK; POINT
nibble / BITE, GNAW, KNAB, PECK

niblick / CLUB, IRON
Nicaragua capital / MANAGUA
Nicaragua Indian / MIXE, RAMA
Nicaragua money / CORDOBA
nice / FINE, GOOD, NEAT, TIDY
nice discernment / TACT; ACUMEN
nicety / ACCURACY; PRECISION
niche / NOOK; ALCOVE, CORNER
Nichols' hero / ABIE
nick / DENT; NOTCH
nickel alloy / INVAR, MONEL
nickel coin / JITNEY
nickelodeon / MOVIE
nickname / AGNOMEN, EPITHET
nicotinic acid / NIACIN
nictitate / WINK
nictitating membrane / HAW
nide / NEST
nidor / ODOR, REEK; SCENT
niello / INLAY
nieve / FIST, HAND
nifty / SMART; CLASSY, CLEVER
Niger capital / NIAMEY
Niger delta native / IBO; IJAW
Niger river / JOLIBA
Niger river mouth / NUN; BONNY
Niger tributary / BENUE
Nigeria capital / LAGOS
Nigerian city / EDE; KANO; IBADAN
Nigerian secessionists / BIAFRANS
Nigerian tribe / IBO, TIV; EKOI;
    HAUSA; YORUBA
niggard / MISER, PIKER; TIGHT-
    WAD
niggardly / GREEDY, STINGY
niggle / FUSS; TRIFLE
nigh / NEAR; CLOSE, HANDY.
    ABOUT
nighness / PROXIMITY
night / EVENING; DARKNESS
night before / EVE
night club / CABARET
night owl / PROWLER
night song / SERENADE
night stand / TABORET
nightfall / EEN, EVE; SUNSET
nighthawk / BULLBAT; MOREPORK
nightingale / BULBUL; PHILOMEL
nightjar / POTOO
nightmare / DREAM; INCUBUS
nightmare demon / MARA;
    EPHIALTES
nightshade / HENBANE; BELLA-
    DONNA
nighty / NIGHTGOWN; NIGHTSHIRT
nil / NONE; NIHIL; NOTHING
Nile beauty / CLEO
Nile boat / CANGIA, SANDAL
Nile dam / ASWAN; MAKWAR
Nile falls / RIPON; MURCHISON
Nile god / HAPI
Nile island / RODA

Nile lake / NO; TANA
Nile monkey / GRIVET
Nile mouth / ROSETTA; DAMIETTA
Nile river plants / SUDD
Nile tributary / ATBARA, KAGERA
Nilotic Negro / JUR; NUER; DINKA;
    SHILLUK
nim / STEAL
nimble / LISH, SPRY; AGILE
nimbus / AURA, HALO; AUREOLE
nimiety / SURPLUS
nimrod / HUNTER
nimshi / FOOL
nincompoop / SAP; BOOB, FOOL
nine / TEAM; MUSES, NONET;
    ENNEAD
nine, c.f. / ENNEA
nine day devotion / NOVENA
nine goddesses / MUSES
nine inches / SPAN
nine-angled polygon / NONAGON
ninefold / NONUPLE
nine-foot minnow of India / MAH-
    SIR, MAHSUR; MAHSEER
nine-headed monster / HYDRA
ninekiller / SHRIKE
nineteenth hole / BAR; SHOWER
nineteenth-century dance / GALOP
ninny / ASS; FOOL; DUNCE
Niobe's husband / AMPHION
nip / BITE, PECK; DRINK, PINCH
nipa palm / ATAP; ATTAP
nipping / KEEN; SHARP
nipple / PAP; TEAT; COUPLING
Nippon / JAPAN
nis / NIX; NIXIE; GOBLIN
nisus / DRIVE; EFFORT
niter / NITRATE; SALTPETER
nitid / SHINY; BRIGHT, GLOSSY
niton / RADON
nitrate / NITER, NITRE
nitric acid / AQUAFORTIS
nitric acid salt / NITRATE
nitrogen / AZOTE
nitrous acid salt / NITRITE
nitwit / FOOL; IDIOT; PINHEAD
nix / NO; NOTHING
no / NAY, NIX, NOE; NONE
no bid / PASS
no longer living / DEAD; EXTINCT
no longer used / OBSOLETE
no matter which / ANY; EITHER
no more than / BUT; ONLY
no objection / OK; YES; ACCEPT
no points / LOVE
no value / NULL
Noah / NOE
Noah, pert. to / NOAIC; NOETIC
Noah's boat / ARK
Noah's flood / DELUGE
Noah's landing place / ARARAT
Noah's messenger / DOVE; RAVEN

Noah's son / HAM; SHEM; JAPHETH

nob / HEAD, KNOB; NABOB, SWELL

nobby / STYLISH

Nobel's invention / DYNAMITE

nobility / RANK; PEERAGE

noble / EPIC; GRAND, LOFTY

nobleman / SIR; DUKE, EARL, LORD, PEER; BARON, COUNT, THANE

noblewoman / PEERESS; COUNTESS

nobody / NOONE; NONENTITY

nocent / GUILTY; HARMFUL

nocturnal animal / BAT; COON

nocturnal bird / OWL

nocturnal spirit / LEMUR

nocturne / LULLABY; SERENADE

nocuous / HARMFUL; POISONOUS

nod / BECK, BEND; DROWSE. BOW

nodal / KNOBBY, KNOTTY, NODOSE

nodding / NUTANT; CERNUOUS

noddy / FOOL, NOIO, TERN; FULMAR

node / KNOB, KNOT, KNUR, LUMP

nodose antenna / NODICORN

nodule / KNOT, LUMP, NODE

nodule of stone / GEODE

noe / NOAH

noel / CAROL, NOWEL; CHRISTMAS

noetic / INTELLECTUAL

nog / PEG, PIN; DRINK

noise / CRY, DIN; ROAR; SOUND

noise of surf / ROAR, ROTE

noised abroad / AIRED; BRUITED

noiseless / SILENT

noisome / NOXIOUS; DISGUSTING

noisy / LOUD; BLATANT; CLAMOROUS

noisy bird / PIE; CROW; MAGPIE

noisy disturbance / AFFRAY

noisy frolic / SPREE

noisy ghost / POLTERGEIST

nom de plume / ALIAS; PENNAME

nomad / ARAB; ROVER, STRAY

nomadic / PASTORAL

nomen / NAME

nomenclature / ONYMY; TERMINOLOGY

nomic / USUAL; ORDINARY

nominal / PAR; TITULAR

nominate / NAME; APPOINT

nominee / CHOICE; CANDIDATE

nonage / MINORITY

nonchalant / COOL; INDIFFERENT

noncircular machine piece / CAM

noncommissioned officer / CORPORAL, SERGEANT

noncommittal / NEUTRAL

nonconducting insulator / GLASS

nonconformist / ODDBALL, SECTARY

nondescript / ODD; ABNORMAL

nonentity / NOBODY

nonesuch / ONER; PARAGON

nonexistent / NULL

nonfeasance / NEGLECT

nonferrous alloy / TULA

non-Jew / GOY; GENTILE

nonmetrical language / PROSE

nonmigratory / RESIDENT

non-Moslem / RAYA; RAYAH

nonpareil / UNEQUALED. PARAGON

nonplus / STUMP; PUZZLE

nonprofessional / LAYMAN; AMATEUR. LAY; LAIC; LAICAL

nonseagoing ship / HULK

nonsense / BAH, ROT; BOSH, PISH, POOH; FOLLY, FUDGE, HOOEY, STUFF

nonsensical / INANE, SILLY

nonsensical talk / HOGWASH

noodle / DUD; NINNY; SIMPLETON

noodle course / LASAGNA, RAVIOLI

noodles / MEIN; FARFEL; LOKSHEN

nook / DEN; CORNER, CRANNY

noon / MIDDAY; NOONDAY; MERIDIAN

noose / NET; LOOP; SNARE; HALTER

nopal / CACTUS

nordic / NORSE; SCANDINAVIAN

noria / WATERWHEEL

norm / MODEL; STANDARD

norma / SQUARE; TEMPLATE

normal / SANE; USUAL; REGULAR

normal value / PAR

Normandy, pert. to / NORMAN

Normandy capital / ROUEN

Normandy city / CAEN, STLO

Normandy horse / PERCHERON

Normandy peninsula / COTENTIN

Normandy river / EURE, ORNE

norn / URTH, WYRD

Norse / NORDIC. See also Norwegian

Norse Adam / ASK; ASKR

Norse afterworld / VALHALLA

Norse bard/ SCALD

Norse chieftain / JARL

Norse epic / EDDA

Norse explorer / ERIC, LEIF

Norse fates / NORNS

Norse giant / SURT, YMIR; BAUGI, HYMIR, JOTUN, MIMIR, THRYM

Norse god of evil / LOKI

Norse god of fertility / FREY

Norse god of light / BALDER

Norse god of mischief / LOKI

Norse god of poetry / BRAGI

Norse god of sea / HLER; AEGIR

Norse god of skis / ULL

Norse god of sky / TIU, TIW, TYR

Norse god of thunder / THOR

Norse god of war / TY; TYR; ODIN
Norse god of wind / VAYU
Norse god of wisdom / ODIN
Norse goddess of beauty / FREYA
Norse goddess of betrothal / VOR
Norse goddess of death / HEL
Norse goddess of destiny / URD
Norse goddess of drowning / RAN
Norse goddess of flowers / NANNA
Norse goddess of healing / EIR
Norse goddess of love / FREYA
Norse goddess of lower world / HEL;
　GERD
Norse goddess of maidens /
　GEFION
Norse goddess of sea / RAN
Norse goddesses of fate / NORNS
Norse gods / AESIR, VANIR
Norse hero / EGIL; EGILL
Norse home of gods / ASGARD
Norse legend / EDDA, SAGA
Norse letter / RUNE
Norse minstrel / SCALD, SKALD
Norse mythological wolf / FENRIS
Norse poet / SCALD, SKALD
Norse poetry / RUNE
Norse saint / OLAF
Norse sea monster / KRAKEN
Norse serpent of myth / MIDGARD
Norse settlement / VINLAND
Norse tree of myth / YGGDRASIL
Norse underworld dog / GARM
Norse warrior / BERSERKER
Norseman / NORMAN, VIKING
North African / BERBER, TUAREG;
　BEDOUIN. See also African
North African country / EGYPT,
　LIBYA; ALGERIA, MOROCCO,
　TUNISIA
North African garment / HAIK
North African grass / ALFA
North African jackal / DIEB
North African language / BERBER
North African native / RIF; HAMITE,
　SENUSI
North African seaport / ORAN
North African tribesman / BERBER
North Albanian / GHEG
North American / See American
North American evergreen /
　MADRONA
North American Indian / MOHAVE,
　MOJAVE; MAHICAN, MOHEGAN,
　MOHICAN
North American larch / TAMARACK;
　HACKMATACK
North American mink / VISON
North American scoter / COOT
North Atlantic fish / COD; SALMON
North Atlantic islands / AZORES;
　FAEROES; ANTILLES, CANARIES
North Atlantic sea / LABRADOR,
　SARGASSO

North Borneo weight / PARA
North Carolina cape / FEAR;
　HATTERAS
North Carolina capital / RALEIGH
North Carolina city / DURHAM
North Carolina colony / ROANOKE
North Carolina river / TAR
North Carolina sound / PAMLICO
North Carolina state flower /
　DOGWOOD
North Carolina state nickname /
　TARHEEL; OLDNORTH
North Carolinian / TARHEEL
North Caucasian language / UDI;
　AVAR; CHECHEN
North Dakota capital / BISMARCK
North Dakota city / FARGO, MINOT
North Dakota river / RED; MOUSE
North Dakota state nickname /
　SIOUX; FLICKERTAIL
North European / FINN, LAPP,
　LETT, SLAV; SCANDINAVIAN
North Pole discoverer / PEARY;
　HENSON
North Star / POLARIS; POLESTAR
North Syrian deity / EL
north wind / BOREAS
northeast wind / BORA
northern / BOREAL; SEPTEN-
　TRIONAL
northern constellation / BEAR
northern road / ALCAN
northern sea / KARA; BERING
northernmost country / THULE
Norway / NORGE
Norway capital / OSLO
Norway land division / AMT; FYLKE
Norway money / ORE; KRONE
Norway parliament / STORTING
Norway river / OI; KLAR, OTRA
Norway whirlpool / MAELSTROM
Norwegian / NORSE. NORSEMAN
Norwegian city / VARDO; BERGEN
Norwegian composer / BULL;
　GRIEG
Norwegian estuary / FIORD, FJORD
Norwegian explorer / AMUNDSEN
Norwegian islands / LOFOTEN
Norwegian language / NORSE
Norwegian measure / FOT, POT
Norwegian parliament / STORTING
Norwegian saint / OLAF
Norwegian statesman / LIE; LANGE
Norwegian writer / IBSEN;
　HAMSUN
nose / SNOOP. CONK; NASUS,
　SNOOT
nose, c.f. / NAS; RHIN; RRHINE
nose, pert. to / NASAL; RHINAL
nose bone / VOMER
nose cartilage / SEPTUM
nose illness / COLD; CORYZA
nose opening / NARIS; NOSTRIL

nosegay / POSY
nostalgia / HOMESICKNESS
nostril / NARIS; THRILL
nostrils, pert. to / NARIC; NARIAL; NARINE
nostril-shaped / NARIFORM
nostrum / MEDICINE
nosy / INQUISITIVE
not / NO; NARY
not, pref. / IM, IN, UN; DIS, MIS, NON
not abstract / SOLID; CONCRETE
not abundant / RARE; SCANT
not accompanied / SOLO; ACAPPELLA
not acquired / NATIVE; INTRINSIC
not active / STATIC; RESTING
not all / FEW; SOME
not amateurish / PROFESSIONAL
not any / NO; NARY, NONE
not attractive / UGLY; HOMELY
not awake / ABED; ASLEEP
not bound / FREE
not bright / DIM; DULL
not concerned / CAREFREE
not confined / FREE; LOOSE
not covered / BARE; NAKED
not definite / VAGUE
not difficult / EASY; SIMPLE
not dumb / SMART; BRIGHT
not even / ODD; ROUGH
not ever / NEER; NEVER
not excited / CALM; RELAXED
not exciting / PALE, TAME
not extreme / CONSERVATIVE
not firm / LOOSE, SHAKY; UNSTEADY
not forbidden / PERMITTED
not foreign / DOMESTIC, HOMESPUN
not general / LOCAL; PARTICULAR
not genuine / FAKE; IMITATION
not guilty / INNOCENT
not harsh / KIND; LENIENT
not healthful / TOXIC; MORBID
not here / THERE; ABSENT
not home / OUT
not inhabited / EMPTY; VACANT
not leaving a will / INTESTATE
not liable / EXEMPT
not local / EXPRESS, GENERAL
not long ago / LATELY; RECENTLY
not long in use / NEWISH
not many / FEW; SOME
not moving / FIRM, INERT; STATIC
not native / EXOTIC; ACQUIRED
not now / LATER; EVENTUALLY
not obtuse / ACUTE, ALERT, SHARP
not obvious / SUBTLE; SUBTILE
not particular / GENERAL
not partitioned / UNDIVIDED

not pessimistic / OPTIMISTIC
not positive / NEGATIVE
not precise / FAULTY; INEXACT
not professional / LAIC; AMATEUR
not real / IDEAL; ILLUSORY
not relaxed / TAUT; UPTIGHT
not ripe / RAW; GREEN; IMMATURE
not a service man / CIVILIAN
not settled / MOOT; DESERT
not shut / OPEN
not sound / WEAK; AILING
not specific / VAGUE; GENERAL
not stationary / MOBILE; PORTABLE
not straight / BENT; CROOKED
not in style / PASSE; OUTMODED
not sure / DOUBTFUL
not sweet / SOUR; ACRID; PUNGENT
not tame / FERAL
not there / MAD, OUT; HERE
not these / THOSE
not this / THAT
not tight / LAX
not transferable / INALIENABLE
not transparent / OPAQUE
not understood / UNCLEAR
not wild / TAME
not working / OFF; IDLE
notable / EMINENT; EVENTFUL
notable period / AGE, ERA; EPOCH
notable personage / LION; MOGUL
notch / COG, GAB, GAP; DENT, KERF, NICK, NOCK; CRENA, HILUM
notched / EROSE; CRENATE, SERRATE
notched bar / RATCH
notched wheel / COG; GEAR
notching on coin / MILLING, REEDING
note / HEED, MARK; REGARD; COMMENT. CHIT, MEMO, NETE; BREVE
note of excuse / AEGER
note during hunt / MORT; TANTIVY
note in margin / GLOSS; POSTIL
note in music / DO, FA, LA, MI, RE, SI, SO, TI, UT; ALT, ELA, SOL
note the speed / TIME
note the time / DATE
noted / FAMED; FAMOUS; EMINENT
notes / MINUTES; MEMORANDA
note's stem / FILUM
noteworthy / SPECIAL; REMARKABLE
nothing / NIL, NIX; NULL, ZERO
nothing more than / MERE
nothingness / VOID; VACUITY
notice / SEE; HEED, MARK, NOTE

notice in orders / CITE
notice of proposed marriage / BANNS
noticeable / SIGNAL; REMARKABLE
notification / ADVICE
notify / TELL, WARN; INFORM
notion / BEE, FAD; IDEA, WHIM
notional / IDEAL; IMAGINARY
notoriety / FAME; ECLAT
notorious / KNOWN, NOTED; ARRANT
notwithstanding / BUT, YET; MAUGRE; DESPITE, HOWEVER; ALTHOUGH
nougat / FONDANT
nought / NULL, ZERO; NAUGHT
noughts and crosses / TICKTACK-TOE
noumenon / IMAGE; PERCEPTION
noun / NAME; SUBJECT; SUBSTAN-TIVE
noun, suffix / AC, ER; ATE, ENT, ICS, ION, IST, ITE; ENCE, ETTE
noun form / CASE
noun with two cases / DIPTOTE
noun without case ending / APTOTE
nourish / FEED; FOSTER; CHERISH
nourished / PROMOTED; SUP-PORTED
nourishing / ALIBLE; HEALTHFUL
nourishing substance / FOOD; MANNA; PABULUM; NUTRIMENT
nourishment / DIET, FOOD
nous / MIND; REASON; INTELLECT
nova / STAR
Nova Scotia / ACADIA
Nova Scotia bay / FUNDY; MAHONE
Nova Scotia cape / CANSO, SABLE
Nova Scotia capital / HALIFAX
Nova Scotia inhabitant / BLUE-NOSE
Nova Scotia seaport / TRURO
Nova Scotia strait / CANSO
novation / SUBSTITUTION
novel / NEW; RARE; MODERN, RECENT. STORY; FICTION, ROMANCE
novelist / AUTHOR, WRITER
novella / TALE
novelty / FAD; TRINKET
November birthstone / TOPAZ
novice / TYRO; ROOKIE; ACOLYTE, AMATEUR; BEGINNER, DEBUTANT
novitiate / NOVICE
now / TODAY; PRONTO; FORTH-WITH
now and then / SOMETIME
nowel / HYMN, NOEL; CAROL
nowise / NOT; NOWAY
nowt / OX; NODDY

noxious / DEADLY; BANEFUL
noxious air / MALARIA
noxious emanation / EFFLUVIA
noxious material / BANE; POISON
noxious plant / WEED
nozzle / ROSE
nozzle in furnace / TUYERE
nuance / SHADE, TINGE
nub / KNOT, LUMP, PITH; KERNEL
nubia / CLOUD; MANTLE
nucha / NAPE
nuclear / INNER; CENTRAL
nuclear bomb / ABOMB
nuclear particle / PROTON
nuclear reactor / PILE
nuclear submarine / NAUTILUS
nucleus / CORE; GERM; CADRE
nude / BARE; NAKED; UNCLOTHED
nudes / PINUPS
nudge / DIG, JAB; POKE, PROD
nudibranch / SLUG
nugacious / TRIVIAL; TRIFLING
nugatory / NULL, VOID; FUTILE
nugget / LUMP; CHUNK
nuisance / BANE, BORE, PEST
null / VOID; EMPTY; NUGATORY
nullah / GULLY
nullify / UNDO, VOID; ANNUL
numb / TORPID; INSENSITIVE
number / COUNT; RECKON; COM-PUTE. HOST, UNIT; CROWD, DIGIT; FIGURE
number four wood / CLEEK
number three wood / SPOON
number two wood / BRASSIE
numbered / MENE
numbered disc / DIAL
numbers / POETRY; ARITHMETIC
numbers lottery / TERN
numbers one can play / REPER-TOIRE
numerical suffix / RD, ST, TH; TEEN
numerous / MANY; PLENTY; VARIOUS
Numidian king / JUGURTHA
numskull / ASS; BLOCKHEAD
nun / SMEW; PIGEON, SISTER
nuncheon / BRUNCH
nuncio / LEGATE
nuncupative / ORAL; UNWRITTEN
nunnery / CONVENT
nun's dress / HABIT
Nun's son / JOSHUA
nuptial / BRIDAL; MARITAL
nuque / NAPE; NUCHA
nurse / IYA; AMAH, AYAH, BABA, NANA. FOSTER; CHERISH, NUR-TURE
nurse shark / GATA
nursery / CRECHE
nursery school / KINDERGARTEN
nursling / INFANT

nurture / FEED; NURSE; NOURISH
nut / FAN; COLA, KOLA; BETEL,
 LICHI, PECAN; ALMOND, BRAZIL,
 CASHEW, LICHEE, WALNUT
nut, ·pert. to / NUCAL
nut confection / NOUGAT; PRA-
 LINE; MARZIPAN; MARCHPANE
nutation / LIBRATION; OSCILLA-
 TION
nutmeg coating / MACE
Nutmeg State / CONNECTICUT
nutria / COYPU
nutriment / FOOD; SUSTENANCE
nutritious / NOURISHING
nutritive / ALIBLE
nuts / MAST. BATTY, WACKY
nutty / NUTS; CRAZY
nuzzle / NOSE; NESTLE
Nyasaland / MALAWI
nymph / PUPA, LARVA; MAIDEN

nymph of air / SYLPH
nymph changed into a bear /
 CALLISTO
nymph changed to a rock / ECHO
nymph of fountains / NAIAD
nymph of hills / OREAD
nymph who became laurel /
 DAPHNE
nymph of Moslem paradise /
 HOURI
nymph of mountains / OREAD
nymph of the ocean / OCEANID
nymph of trees / DRYAD; HAMA-
 DRYAD
nymph of waters / NAIAD; NEREID,
 UNDINE
nymph of woods / DRYAD
nymphs / HESPERIDES
Nyx's daughter / ERIS

O

oaf / DOLT, LOUT; IDIOT; BUMPKIN
oafish / SILLY; SIMPLE; BOORISH
Oahu city / HONOLULU
Oahu cliff / PALI
Oahu mountain / KAALA
Oahu token / LEI
oak apple / GALL
oak fruit / MAST; ACORN
oak gall / NUTGALL
oak genus / QUERCUS
oak lichen / EVERNIA
oak nut / GALL; ACORN
oak tree / ROBLE; ENCINA
oakwood / MESA; DURANGO
oar / BLADE, SCULL; PADDLE. ROW
oar blade / PALM, PEEL, WASH
oar fulcrum / THOLE; ROWLOCK
oar shaft / LOOM
oar at transom / SCULL
oarlock / PIN; THOLE; RESTER
oar-propelled ship / GALLEY
oarsman / ROWER; SCULLER
oasis / BAR; WADI; SALOON
oast / KILN, OVEN; HOPKILN
oat genus / AVENA
oater / WESTERN
oath / VOW; WORD; CURSE;
 PLEDGE
oatmeal / PORRIDGE
oats / GRAIN; CEREAL
oats for horse / FARE, FEED
oats paid for rent / AVENAGE
obdurate / HARD; CALLOUS
obeah / CHARM
obedient / DUTIFUL; AMENABLE
obeisance / BOW; CURTSY,
 SALAAM
obelisk / PYLON; DAGGER, NEEDLE
Oberon's messenger / PUCK

Oberon's wife / TITANIA
obese / FAT; PORTLY; CORPULENT
obey / HEED, MIND; COMPLY,
 SUBMIT
obfuscate / CONFUSE; BEWILDER
obi / SASH; GIRDLE
obit / OBITUARY; OBSEQUIES
obiter / INCIDENTALLY
obituary notice / OBIT;
 NECROLOGY
object / CAVIL, DEMUR. AIM, END
object of affection / IDOL; LOVER
object of aim / BUTT, GOAL, MARK;
 TARGET
object glass / LENS
object of worship / ICON, IDOL
objection / CAVIL; PROTEST
objective / AIM, END; BUTT, GOAL
objective case / DATIVE;
 ACCUSATIVE
objector / DISSENTER;
 PROTESTANT
objet d'art / CURIO
objurgate / CHIDE, SCOLD; RE-
 PROVE
oblate / DEVOTED; FLATTENED
obligate / BIND
obligation / TIE; BOND, DEBT
obligatory / BOUNDEN
oblige / SERVE; COMPEL, PLEASE
obliged / DUTYBOUND; CON-
 STRAINED
obliging / KIND; CIVIL; AFFABLE
oblique / AWRY, SKEW; SLANT
oblique, c.f. / LOX; LOXO
oblique position / CANT
obliquely / AWRY; ASKEW
obliterate / ERASE; EFFACE;
 EXPUNGE

obliteration / BLOT; RASURE
oblivion / LETHE, LIMBO; AMNESTY
oblivious / FORGETFUL
oblong / ELLIPTICAL; RECTANGULAR
oblong casting / PIG; INGOT
obloquy / ABUSE, ODIUM, SHAME
obnoxious / VILE; ODIOUS
oboe / SHAWM; CHANTER, HAUTBOY
obol / COIN
obscene / FOUL, LEWD; COARSE
obscure / DIM, FOG; BLUR; BEDIM. DARK, DEEP; MISTY, VAGUE; HUMBLE
obscurity / HAZE; CALIGO; OPACITY
obsequies / WAKE; RITES; FUNERAL
obsequious / SERVILE; COMPLIANT
obsequious person / TOADY; FAWNER
observance / RITE; USAGE; CUSTOM
observant / MINDFUL; OBEDIENT
observation / NOTE; REMARK
observe / LO; EYE, SEE; HEED, LOOK, MARK, NOTE, VIEW; WATCH
observe duly / KEEP; FOLLOW
observed / SAW; EYED; REMARKED
observer / BYSTANDER, SPECTATOR
obsessed / HAUNTED; INFATUATED
obsidian / GLASS
obsolete / DEAD, PAST; PASSE
obstacle / BAR, DAM, LET, RUB
obstinacy / TENACITY; STUBBORNNESS
obstinate / SET; DOGGED, MULISH
obstruct / BAR, DAM; CLOG, STOP
obstruction / BAR; BARRIER
obtain / GET, WIN; EARN, GAIN
obtain control of / TAKE; MASTER
obtain laboriously / EKE; EARN
obtained / GOT, WON; NETTED
obtrude / INTRUDE; ENCROACH
obtuse / DULL, SLOW; BLUNT, DENSE
obverse / FRONT, HEADS
obviate / PREVENT; PRECLUDE
obvious / OPEN; OVERT, PLAIN
obvious fact / AXIOM, MAXIM; TRUISM
occasion / NEED, SELE, TIME; NONCE; GROUND, MOTIVE
occasional / ODD; IRREGULAR
occident / WEST; EUROPE
occipital bump / INION
occlude / SHUT; CLOSE; OBSTRUCT

occult / DARK; HIDDEN, MYSTIC, SECRET; CRYPTIC, OBSCURE; ABSTRUSE
occultism / CABALA; ESOTERICS
occupant / TENANT; INCUMBENT
occupation / JOB; WORK; CRAFT, TRADE; METIER
occupied / BUSY, RAPT; TAKEN
occupied in / AT
occupy / USE; FILL, HOLD; COVER
occupying the whole / FILLING
occur / APPEAR, BETIDE, HAPPEN
occurrence / EVENT; AFFAIR
occurring every day / DIURNAL
occurring every third day / TERTIAN
occurring every year / ANNUAL, YEARLY; ETESIAN
occurring irregularly / SPORADIC
occurring regularly / USUAL; HABITUAL; CUSTOMARY
occurring in the spring / VERNAL
ocean / SEA; DEEP, MAIN; BRINE
ocean, pert. to / MARINE; PELAGIC
ocean route / LANE; PASSAGE
ocean vessel / SHIP; LINER
oceanic tunicate / ASCIDIAN
Oceanus / TITAN
Oceanus' wife / TETHYS
ocellus / EYELET
och / OH; SORROW
ocher / GOLD; OCHRE; YELLOW
octave / UTAS; EIGHTH
Octavia's husband / NERO; ANTONY
October birthstone / OPAL; AQUAMARINE
October brew / ALE
octopus / POLYP, POULP, SQUID
octopus' arm / TENTACLE
octuple / EIGHTFOLD
ocular / OPTIC; VISUAL. EYEPIECE
odd / ORRA, RARE; DROLL, QUEER; UNEVEN, QUAINT, UNIQUE; BIZARRE
oddity / QUIRK; ECCENTRICITY
odds / CHANCES; DISSENSION
ode / POEM; LYRIC
odeon / HALL; THEATER
odic force of electricty / ELOD
odic type / HORATIAN, PINDARIC
Odin / WODEN, WOTAN
Odin's brother / VE; VILI
Odin's dwelling / VALHALLA
Odin's horse / SLEIPNIR
Odin's son / SIGI, THOR; BALDER
Odin's spear / GUNGNIR
Odin's wife / GRID; FRIGG
Odin's wolf / GERE, GERI; FREKI
odious / HATEFUL; OFFENSIVE
odium / HATRED; OFFENSIVE
odium / HATRED, STIGMA; DISGRACE

odor / AROMA, SCENT, SMELL; PERFUME
odor of game / FUMET; FEWMET
odoriferous root / IRONE
odorless / AOSMIC
odorous / BALMY; FRAGRANT
Odysseus / ULIXES; ULYSSES
Odysseus' dog / ARGOS
Odysseus' friend / MENTOR
Odysseus' kingdom / ITHACA
Odysseus' son / TELEMACHUS
Odysseus' wife / PENELOPE
Odyssey author / HOMER
Oedipus' daughter / ISMENE; ANTIGONE
Oedipus' father / LAIUS
Oedipus' mother / JOCASTA
Oedipus' son / ETEOCLES; POLYNICES
Oenone's husband / PARIS
of / FROM; ABOUT; ACCORDING
of age / ADULT
of an age / AET, ETA; ERAL
of the backbone / SPINAL
of bees / APIAN
of the birds / AVIAN
of birth / NATAL
of body structure / ANATOMIC
of branches / RAMAL
of bristles / SETAL
of central government / FEDERAL
of a central point / FOCAL, FOCUS
of the cheek / GENAL, MALAR
of the chest / PECTORAL
of the dawn / EOAN; MATINAL
of a dukedom / DUCAL
of each /ANA
of the ear / OTIC; AURAL
of greatest age / OLDEST
of greatest extent / WIDEST; LONGEST
of the hip / SCIATIC
of last month / ULTIMO
of low rank / PLEBEIAN
of me / MY; MINE
of the memory / MNESIS; MNESTIC
of the mind / MENTAL
of the moon / LUNAR
of the mouth / ORAL
of necessity / PERFORCE
of Norway / NORSE
of the nose / NASAL
of old age / ANILE; SENILE
of one mind / AGREED
of the palm / VOLAR
of punishment / PENAL
of a sail / VELIC
of the sole / VOLAR; PLANTAR
of the subject / RE; INRE
of the sun / SOLAR
of the teeth / DENTAL
off / AWAY; BEGONE, SKEWED
off guard / UNAWARES

offal / WASTE; REFUSE; GARBAGE
offend / CAG, ERR, SIN, VEX
offender / CULPRIT; CRIMINAL
offense / SIN; HARM; CRIME, FAULT
offense at law / TORT; MALUM
offense less than felony / DELICT
offensive / RUDE; OBNOXIOUS
offensive action / ENTRY; ATTACK
offensive odor / FETOR, STINK
offensively glaring / GARISH
offer / BID; SHOW; OCCUR; ADDUCE
offer made at auction / BID
offer solemnly / VOW; AVER
offering / ALMS; TRIBUTE; OBLATION
offering of wares / SALE; VENDUE
offhand / CASUAL; IMPROMPTU
office / DUTY; POST; BUREAU
office cabinet / FILE
office of the Curia / DATARY; CHANCERY
office for the dead / DIRGE
office furniture / DESK, FILE, TRAY; CHAIR; BASKET; BOOKCASE
office head / BOSS; MANAGER
office item / PEN; CLIP, DESK
office machine / ADDER; CALCULATOR, TYPEWRITER
office note / MEMO; MEMORANDUM
office utility / PHONE; TELEPHONE
officeholders / INS
officer / COP; MANAGER, SHERIFF
officer of ancient Rome / LICTOR
officer in charge / COMMISSIONER
officer of foreign affairs / AMBASSADOR
officer of the King's stables / AVENER
officer at race track / STEWARD
officer's assistant / AIDE
officer's honorary commission / BREVET
official / MAGNATE; FUNCTIONARY
official advisers / CABINET
official command / EDICT, UKASE; DECREE; MANDATE
official declaration / MANIFESTO
official document / DEED
official endorsement / SEAL, VISA, VISE
official examiner / CENSOR
official garment / ROBE; VESTMENT
official interdiction / VETO
official list in election / SLATE
official note / PAPER; MEMOIR
official proof of a will / PROBATE
official record / CENSUS; PROTOCOL, REGISTER
official representative / ENVOY

official seal / STAMP; SIGNET
official session / SITTING
official sign of approval / SEAL
official of weights / SEALER
officiate / PRESIDE; MINISTER
officious / FORWARD; MEDDLING
offish / ALOOF
offscour / SCOUR; CLEANSE
offscouring / DIRT; DREGS; REFUSE
offset / SPOIL; BALANCE
offshoot / CION, SLIP, SPUR
offspring / HEIR; CHILD, ISSUE
offspring of stallion and she-donkey / HINNY
offtake / DEDUCTION
often / OFT; FREQUENTLY
ogdoad / OCTAD
ogee / CYMA; MOLDING
ogive / ARCH
ogle / EYE; LEER; STARE
ogre / GIANT; MONSTER
ogrish / CRUEL; MONSTROUS
ogygian / ANCIENT
Ohio capital / COLUMBUS
Ohio city / LIMA; XENIA; CANTON
Ohio river / BLACK, MIAMI
Ohio state nickname / BUCKEYE
Ohio state tree / BUCKEYE
oho / SURPRISE
oikology / ECOLOGY
oil / FAT; BALM, FUEL. ANOINT
oil, c.f. / OLEO
oil, pert. to / OLEIC
oil, suffix / OL
oil bottle / CRUET, CRUSE; AMPULLA
oil container / DRUM, TANK
oil for lamps / KEROSENE
oil of orange flower / NEROLI
oil of roses / ATAR, OTTO; ATTAR
oil ship / OILER; TANKER
oil tree / EBO; EBOE, PALM; MAHUA, MOHWA; ILLIPI; CANDLENUT
oil well / SHAFT; BORING, GUSHER
oilbird / GUACHARO
oil-color medium / DAMAR, COPAL; MEGILP; MEGUILP, VARNISH
oiler / CAN; SHIP; TANKER
oilfish / ESCOLAR
oillet / EYELET; LOOPHOLE
oils / PAINT
oilskin / SLICKER; WATERPROOF
oilstone / HONE; WHETSTONE
oily / FAT; GLIB; FATTY; GREASY
oily fruit / OLIVE
oily hydrocarbon / OCTANE
oily ketone / IRONE; CARONE
oily substance / FAT; GREASE
oil-yielding seed / FLAXSEED
oil-yielding tree / EBO; EBOE, TUNG; CAJUPUT

ointment / BALM; SALVE; LOTION
Ojibwa / OJIBWAY; CHIPPEWA
Ojibwa secret order / MIDE
OK / OKEH; RIGHT, ROGER; CORRECT
Okie / MIGRANT
Okinawa capital / NAHA
Okinawa chain / RYUKYUS
Okinawa neighbor / IE; KUME
Oklahoma city / ADA; ALVA, ENID
Oklahoma Indian / KAW, OTO; LOUP, OTOE; CADDO, CREEK, KANSA, KIOWA, OSAGE, PONCA; PAWNEE
Oklahoma lake / TEXOMA
Oklahoma mountains / WICHITAS
Oklahoma river / RED; CIMARRON
Oklahoma state flower / MISTLETOE
Oklahoma state nickname / SOONER
Oklahoma state tree / REDBUD
okra / GOMBO, GUMBO
old / ELD; AGED, USED; ANILE
old Abe / LINCOLN
old Adam / SIN
old age, pert. to / ANILE; SENILE
old alphabet letter / RUNE
old alphabetical symbol / RUNE; OGHAM
old auto / JALOPY; JALOPPY
old ballad / DERRY
old boy / DEVIL
old cannon / CULVERIN
old card game / LOO, PAM; ECARTE
old cards / TAROT
old cat / GRIMALKIN
old cloth measure / ELL; NAIL
old clothes / RAGS
old coin / ECU; RAP; DUCAT
old crone / HAG
old dagger / SNEE
old dance / PAVAN; GAVOTTE
old dog / ROVER; TOWSER
old dominion / VIRGINIA
old drink / POSSET
old English coin / ORA; GROAT
old English jurisdiction / SOC
old English leasehold / TAC; TAKE
old English legal court / LEET, MOOT
old English letter / EDH, ETH, WEN; YOGH; THORN
old English militia / FYRD
old French coin / ECU, SOU
old French measure / PIED; MINOT
old French poem / DIT, LAI
old French verse form / RONDEAU
old glory / FLAG; BALLADE
old Greek coin / OBOL; TETRADRACHM
old hand / STAGER
old horse / NAG; GARRAN, PADNAG

old horse dealer / KNACKER
old iron / SCRAP
old Italian house / ESTE
old joke / CHESTNUT; JOEMILLER
old maid / SPINSTER; FUSS-
BUDGET
old man / POP; CODGER, GAFFER
old musical instrument / LYRE,
ROTA; REBEC; SISTRUM
old musical symbol / NEUME
old name of Tokyo / EDO
Old Nick / DEVIL
old person / FOGY; DOTARD
old pistol / DAG; DAGG..
old Roman jar / OLLA
old sailor / TAR; SALT; SEADOG
old saw / ADAGE, MAXIM;
PROVERB
old saying / SAW; ADAGE
Old Scratch / DEVIL, SATAN
old Siamese coin / AT; ATT
old Siamese measure / SESTI
Old Sod / ERIN; IRELAND
old ship / NAU, NEF; CARAVEL
old string instrument / VIOL
Old Testament animal / DAMAN;
BEHEMOTH
Old Testament book / ESTHER;
GENESIS. See also Bible, Books
of the
Old Testament object / URIM;
THUMMIN
Old Testament people / EMIM
Old Testament word / SELAH
old thrusting sword / ESTOC
old times / ELD; YORE
old violin / STRAD
old warship / FRIGATE; MANOF-
WAR
old woman / HAG; CRONE;
BELDAM
old womanish / ANILE
old wool weight / TOD
olden / ANCIENT, ANTIQUE
older / ELDER; SENIOR, STALER
oldest city in the world /
DAMASCUS
oldest member / DEAN; DOYEN
old-fashioned / PASSE; FOGRAM
old-fashioned rifle pin / TIGE
old-time / ARCHAIC, QUONDAM
old-timer / VET; PIONEER
oldwife / SPOT; BREAM;
MENHADEN
oleaginous / OILY; UNCTUOUS
olent / BALMY; FRAGRANT,
REDOLENT
oleoresin / ANIME, COPAL, ELEMI
olfactory organ / NOSE
olibanum / FRANKINCENSE
olio / STEW; MEDLEY; HODGE-
PODGE
olive genus / OLEA

olive tree / OLEA; OLEASTER
Oliver Twist character / FAGIN,
NANCY, SYKES
Oliver's nickname / NOLL
olla / JUG, POT; OLIO; PALMLEAF
olla podrida / STEW; MEDLEY
Oman capital / MUSCAT
Omar's home / PERSIA
omega / END; LAST; DEATH
omen / SIGN; AUGURY; PORTENT
ominous / FATEFUL; SINISTER
omission / LACK; LACHES; DE-
FAULT
omission mark / CARET
omission of syllable / HAPLOLOGY
omission of vowel / ELISION,
SYNCOPE
omit / CUT; DELE, SKIP; DELETE
omit part of word / ELIDE
omitting part / ELLIPTICAL
omnipotent / GOD; ALMIGHTY
omniscient one / POLYMATH
on / AT; NEAR, UPON; ABOUT,
ABOVE. AHEAD
on behalf of / FOR
on the contrary / NO; BUT
on the go / BUSY
on guard / ALERT, AWAKE
on land / ASHORE
on the line of / AROW; ALONG
on the ocean / ASEA
on the sheltered side / ALEE
on the summit / ATOP
on that account / THEREFOR
on this side / HERE
on vacation / OFF; AWAY
on the wall / MURAL
on the way / ENROUTE
onager / ASS; KIANG; CATAPULT
Onan's brother / ER; SHELAH
Onan's father / JUDAH
once / FORMER; FORMERLY
once again / OER; ANEW, MORE
once around / LAP
once more / BIS; AGAIN; ENCORE
on-dit / RUMOR; GOSSIP
one / AN; ACE, AIN, ANY; SAME,
UNIT; PERSON; ANYBODY,
INTEGER
one, c.f. / UNI; MONO
one, pref. / UNI; MONO
one who acts for a sheriff /
DEPUTY, ELISOR
one addressed / YOU; THOU
one after / NEXT
one against / CON; ANTI
one in Army count / HUP
one avoiding life / ESCAPIST
one who blows horn / BUGLER
one who breaks laws / FELON
one who brings bad luck / JINX;
JONAH
one casting a ballot / VOTER

one in charge / BOSS; MANAGER
one of Charlemagne's peers / OLIVER, ROLAND
one of children of same parents / SIBLING
one who competes / CONTESTANT
one excavating ore / MINER
one who excels / ACE; WINNER
one in favor / PRO
one who fights / COMBATANT
one following another / TANDEM; SERIATIM
one who follows / SHADOW
one who is for / PRO
one who furnishes tips / TOUT
one who gives / DONOR; DONATOR
one who gives evidence / DEPONENT
one who glazes / ENAMELER
one of the Gorgons / MEDUSA
one of the holy family / MARY; JOSEPH
one hundred lakhs / CRORE
one hundred sixty square rods / ACRE
one hundred square meters / AR; ARE
one hundred thousand rupees / LAC; LAKH
one of the Hungarian people / MAGYAR
one of a Japanese race / AINU
one of the Jinn / GENIE
one lavishing affection / DOTER
one leaving school / DROPOUT
one of the Little Women / JO; AMY, MEG; BETH
one who lives on others / SPONGER; PARASITE
one who makes barrels / COOPER
one who makes clothes / TAILOR
one making a gift / DONOR
one making a will / TESTATOR
one millionth of a meter / MICRON
one who mimics / MIME; IMITATOR
one of mixed breed / MONGREL
one in music / SOLO
one of natural kingdoms / ANIMAL; MINERAL; VEGETABLE
one not a sailor / LANDLUBBER
one who is opposed / ANTI
one of a pair / MATE, TWIN
one of pleasant countenance / SMILER
one who presides / CHAIRMAN; CHAIRPERSON
one who receives / RECIPIENT
one who rules by fear / TYRANT; TERRORIST
one seeing the bright side / OPTIMIST
one who sells / VENDER; MERCHANT

one shooting at men / SNIPER
one skilled in language / LINGUIST; TRANSLATOR
one tending flowers / FLORIST
one who testifies / WITNESS; DEPONENT
one of three equal parts / THIRD
one who transgresses / SINNER
one treated with partiality / PET; FAVORITE
one twelfth of a foot / INCH
one of two / EITHER
one under par / BIRDIE
one versed in languages / LINGUIST, POLYGLOT
one who is with another / BUDDY; CONSORT; COMPANION
one working dough / KNEADER
one-bagger / SINGLE
one-eyed giant / CYCLOPS
one-horse carriage / GIG, RIG
one-horse town / BURG
oneness / UNITY; HARMONY
one-night stand / BARNSTORM
onerous / HARD; HEAVY; WEIGHTY
one-seeded winged fruit / SAMARA
onesided / BIASED, UNFAIR, UNJUST
onion / CEPA, LEEK; CHIVE, CIBOL; SHALLOT; ESCHALOT
only / MERE, SOLE; ALONE; SINGLE
onomatopoeic / ECHOIC; IMITATIVE
onrush / ONSET; ATTACK
onset / START; OUTSET; BEGINNING
onslaught / ATTACK, CHARGE
onto / AWARE
onus / DUTY; BURDEN, WEIGHT
onward / AHEAD, ALONG; FORWARD
onyx / SARD; CAMEO; NICOLO
oodles / LOTS, MANY
oolong / TEA
oom / UNCLE
oorial / SHA
ooze / LEAK, SEEP. MUD; MIRE
oozy / MUDDY
opah / CRAVO; KINGFISH
opal / GIRASOL, HYALITE
opaque / DARK; MURKY; OBSCURE
open / AJAR, FREE, MILD; AGAPE, BLAND, CLEAR. OPE; DAWN, UNDO
open auto / COUPE; CONVERTIBLE
open cabinet / ETAGERE
open court / QUAD; PATIO; AREAWAY
open door / WELCOME
open gallery / LOGGIA; BALCONY
open hostility / WAR; CONFLICT
open land / MOOR; FIELD, HEATH
open meadow / VEGA

open place in a wood / GLADE
open shoes / SANDALS
open to debate / MOOT
open to view / BARE, SHOW;
DISPLAY
open vessel / PAN, POT, TUB
open wide / GAPE, YAWN; AGAPE
opener / KEY
opener in poker / JACKS
open-faced / FRANK; HONEST
open-handed / LIBERAL;
GENEROUS
open-hearted / FRANK; CANDID
opening / GAP; DAWN, HOLE, PORE
opening in helmet / VUE; VISOR
opening in metal mold / GIT
opening in nose / NARIS; NOSTRIL
opening in pack ice / GLADE
opening to underground conduit /
MANHOLE
openwork fabric / NET; LACE
opera / BORIS, MANON, ORFEO,
THAIS; MARTHA, MIGNON,
SALOME
opera by Beethoven / FIDELIO
opera by Bellini / NORMA
opera by Bizet / CARMEN
opera by Donizetti / LUCIA
opera by Gounod / FAUST
opera by Mascagni / PAGLIACCI
opera by Massenet / MANON,
THAIS
opera by Puccini / TOSCA;
BOHEME
opera by Verdi / AIDA; ERNANI,
OTELLO; RIGOLETTO, TROVA-
TORE
opera by Wagner / RIENZI;
LOHENGRIN, SIEGFRIED;
TANNHAUSER
opera composer / BOITO; BRITTEN,
MENOTTI
opera extra / SUPER
opera glass / BINOCULAR,
LORGNETTE
opera hat / GIBUS; TOPPER
opera house / MET; LASCALA
opera solo / ARIA
opera star / DIVA
opera text / LIBRETTO
operate / ACT, RUN; WORK; GUIDE
operate on skull / TREPAN
operation / FORCE; ACTION,
AGENCY
operative / SPY; AGENT; ARTISAN,
WORKMAN. ACTING; BINDING
operator / WORKER; MACHINIST
operculum / LID
operetta composer / FRIML,
LEHAR; HERBERT, ROMBERG
Ophelia's brother / LAERTES
Ophelia's father / POLONIUS
ophidian / SNAKE; SERPENT

opiate / DOPE, DRUG; ANODYNE
opine / JUDGE, THINK; PONDER
opinion / IDEA, VIEW; CREDO
opinionated / FIRM; DOGMATIC
opinionated person / BIGOT
opium / DRUG; NARCOTIC
opium derivative / MORPHINE
opium seed / MAW; MOHN
opium source / POPPY
opossum / MARSUPIAL
opponent / FOE; ANTI; ENEMY
opportune / FIT, PAT; MEET
opportunity / CHANCE; OPENING
oppose / DENY, FACE; CHECK,
REPEL; COMBAT, IMPUGN,
THWART
opposed / AVERSE; AGAINST
opposed, pref. / ANTI
opposed to apathetic / EMOTIONAL
opposed to cathode / ANODE
opposed to express / LOCAL, TACIT
opposed to solo / TUTTI
opposed to specific / GENERAL
opposed to vacuum / PLENUM
opposing / HOSTILE, JARRING
opposite / FACING; COUNTER
opposite of alee / AWEATHER
opposite of apogee / PERIGEE
opposite of credit / DEBIT
opposite extremities / POLES
opposite of hither / YON; YONDER
opposie midship / ABEAM
opposite of right / LEFT; WRONG
opposite of slice / HOOK
opposite of stoss / LEE
opposite of taboo / NOA
opposite to us / THEM; OTHERS
opposite of van / REAR
opposite of windward / LEEWARD
opposition / HOSTILITY
oppress / LOAD; CRUSH, WRONG
oppression / TYRANNY; HARDSHIP
oppressive / HARD; CRUEL, HEAVY
opprobrious / ABUSIVE; INSULT-
ING
opprobrium / ODIUM; INFAMY;
OBLOQUY, SCANDAL; CON-
TEMPT, DISGRACE
Ops / RHEA; CYBELE, TELLUS
Ops' daughter / CERES
Ops' festival / OPALIA
Ops' husband / SATURN
opt / PICK; CHOOSE, SELECT
optic / EYE
optical glass / LENS
optical illusion / MIRAGE
optical instrument / PRISM;
BINOCULAR, PERISCOPE, TELE-
SCOPE; MICROSCOPE
optical instrument grid / RETICLE
optical instrument part / LENS
optical maser / LASER
optimistic / HOPEFUL; SANGUINE

optimum / BEST, PEAK; PRIME
option / CHOICE; SELECTION
opulence / PLENTY, RICHES
opulent / RICH; PROFUSE, WEALTHY
opuntia / TUNA; SABRA; CACTUS
opus / WORK; COMPOSITION
oracle of Apollo / CLAROS, DELPHI, DIDYMA
oracle of Asclepius / EPIDAURUS
oracle of Zeus / DODONA
oracular / VATIC; AMBIGUOUS
orage / GALE; STORM; TEMPEST
oral / ALOUD, PAROL, VOCAL; SPOKEN, VERBAL; UNWRITTEN
oral utterance / PAROL; SPEECH
orale / CAPE; FANON
orange bird / ORIOLE
orange drink / ADE
orange dye / HENNA; MANDARIN
orange flower oil / NEROLI
orange in heraldry / TENNE
orange mineral / REALGAR
orange peel / RIND
orange pekoe / TEA
orange seed / PIP
orange segment / LITH
orange squeezer / REAMER
orange type / NAVEL; MANDARIN, VALENCIA; TANGERINE
Orangeman / ULSTERMAN
orange-red stone / SARD
orangery / GROVE
orangutan / APE; MIAS; ORANG, PONGO, SATYR
orarion / STOLE
orate / TALK; SPEAK; PREACH
oration / ADDRESS; HARANGUE
orator / RHETOR; ELOCUTIONIST
oratorical / DECLAMATORY
oratorio / PASSION
oratory / CHAPEL; ELOCUTION
orb / EYE; BALL, STAR; GLOBE
orb of day / SUN
orb of vision / EYE
orbed / LUNAR, ROUND; SPHERICAL
orbit / PATH; SOCKET; CIRCUIT
orbit point / AUGE; APSIS; APOGEE; PERIGEE
orbit point nearest Earth / PERIGEE
orbital / ROUND; SPHERIC
orc / ORCA; WHALE; GRAMPUS
orchestra / BAND
orchestra director / LEADER; MAESTRO; CONDUCTOR
orchestra section / WIND; BRASS; STRING; PERCUSSION
orchestral instrument / BASS, DRUM, OBOE; CELLO, FLUTE; CORNET, VIOLIN; CLARINET, TROMBONE
orchestrate / ADAPT, SCORE

orchid with fragrant leaves / FAAM; FAHAM
orchid root or tuber / SALEP
orcus / HADES, PLUTO
ordain / ORDER; DECREE, DIRECT
ordeal / TEST; TRIAL; STRUGGLE
order / LAW; FIAT, RANK, RULE; CANON, EDICT, GRADE. BID; TIDY; ARRAY; ARRANGE
order of animals, suffix / INI; ACEA
order of architecture / DORIC, IONIC
order back / REMAND
order of business / AGENDA, DOCKET; SCHEDULE
order of Catholic Church / JESUITS, MARISTS; SERVITES
order of preference / PRIORITY
ordered / BADE; SERRIED
orderliness / SYSTEM
orderly / NEAT, TIDY, TRIM
orderly arrangement / ARRAY; SYSTEM; SEQUENCE
orderly list / CALENDAR
ordinal number / NTH; FIRST, THIRD; FOURTH, SECOND
ordinal number suffix / ND, ST, TH; ETH
ordinance / ACT, LAW; RITE, RULE
ordinary / PLAIN, USUAL; COMMON
ordnance / GUNS; ARMOR; ARTILLERY
ordnance piece / CANNON, MORTAR; BOMBARD; HOWITZER
ore / METAL; MINERAL
ore of aluminum / BAUXITE
ore of copper / AZURITE, CUPRITE
ore deposit / BED; LODE, MINE, REEF; BONANZA
ore excavation / MINE; STOPE
ore extraction / MINING
ore of gold / TELLURIDE
ore of iron / GOETHITE, HEMATITE
ore of lead / GALENA; ANGLESITE
ore of mercury / CINNABAR
ore receptacle / MORTAR
ore refiner / SMELTER
ore of silver / ARGENTITE
ore of sulfur / PYRITES
oread / NYMPH
ore-bearing rock / GANGUE
ore-dressing machine / VANNER
Oregon capital / SALEM
Oregon city / EUGENE
Oregon Indian / ALSEA, KUSAN, MODOC; CAYUSE; CHINOOK, KLAMATH
Oregon mountain / HOOD
Oregon river / SNAKE; OWYHEE
Oregon state nickname / BEAVER
orexis / DESIRE; APPETITE
organ / EAR, EYE; NOSE; MEMBER

organ bass note / PEDAL
organ of the body / HEART, LIVER
organ cactus / SAGUARO
organ desk / CONSOLE
organ handle / STOP
organ of insect / PALP; ANTENNA
organ part / STOP; KEYBOARD
organ pedal / SWELL
organ pipe / FLUE, REED; MONTRE
organ of secretion / GLAND
organ of speech / LIP; MOUTH;
   LARYNX, THROAT, TONGUE
organ stop / REED, SEXT. GAMBA
organic / VITAL; LIVING; RADICAL
organic portion of soil / HUMUS
organism / PLANT; ANIMAL
organism living on a host /
   BARNACLE, PARASITE
organist / TANAGER; PERFORMER
organization / CLUB, FORM; SO-
   CIETY; STRUCTURE
organize / ADJUST; ARRANGE
organized group / CORPS, POSSE
organized official body / BOARD;
   COUNCIL
orgy / REVEL; EXCESS; DEBAUCH
Oriana / ELIZABETH
oriel / WINDOW
orient / EAST; PEARL
oriental / ASIAN; ASIATIC, EAST-
   ERN; LEVANTINE. See also
   - eastern
oriental bird / MINA
oriental bow / SALAAM
oriental city / DELHI, HANOI,
   TOKYO; CANTON, PEKING;
   NANKING
oriental country / SIAM; CHINA,
   INDIA, JAPAN, NEPAL, TIBET
oriental cymbal / ZEL
oriental dish / PILAU, PILAW
oriental flower / LOTUS
oriental greeting / SALAM; SALAAM
oriental grocer / BAKAL
oriental inn / SERAI
oriental interpreter / DRAGOMAN
oriental lady / HANUM; KHANUM
oriental liquor / ARRACK
oriental lord / KHAN
oriental maid / AMA; AMAH, AYAH
oriental market / SUQ; SOOK,
   SOUK; BAZAR; BAZAAR
oriental musical instrument / TAR;
   SITAR; SAMISEN
oriental nurse / AMA, IYA; AMAH
oriental porter / HAMAL
oriental prince / AMIR, EMIR
oriental sailor / LASCAR
oriental sauce / SOY
oriental sword / SCIMITAR
oriental temple / TAA; PAGODA
oriental weight / MO; SER; ROTL

oriental wild horse / TARPAN
oriental women's quarters /
   HAREM; SERAIL, ZENANA;
   SERAGLIO
orifice / HOLE, PORE, VENT
orifice of sponge / OSTIUM
origin / FONT, RISE, ROOT, SEED
origin, pert. to / GENETIC
origin, suffix / OTE
original / NEW; FIRST; PRIMARY
original inhabitant / NATIVE;
   ABORIGINE
original sin / ADAM
originate / COIN, FORM; ARISE
originator / MAKER; AUTHOR
Orinoco tributary / ARO; META
oriole / PIROL; CORIOT
Orion star / RIGEL; BETELGEUSE
orison / PRAYER; SUPPLICATION
orlop / DECK
ormer / ABALONE; EARSHELL
ornament / ADORN, GRACE;
   EMBOSS. BOW, PIN; BEAD,
   OUCH; BROOCH
ornament of Indian temple turret /
   AMALAKA
ornament on spire / EPI
ornamental / FANCY; DECORATIVE
ornamental ball / BEAD; POMPON
ornamental button / STUD
ornamental capital leter / FAC;
   SWASH; VERSAL
ornamenal circlet / BANGLE
ornamental device / ARABESQUE
ornamental edge / PICOT; FRINGE
ornamental grass / NETI; EULALIA
ornamental knob / STUD
ornamental knot / BOW
ornamental mat / DOILY
ornamental plant / FERN, PALM
ornamental scheme / DECOR
ornamentation / TOOLING
ornate / SHOWY; FLORID;
   ELABORATE
ornery / CONTRARY, ORDINARY
ornis / BIRDS; AVIFAUNA
orography / OROLOGY
orphaned / BEREFT
Orpheus' instrument / LYRE
Orpheus' slayers / MAENADS
Orpheus' wife / EURYDICE
orphic / MYSTIC; ESOTERIC
orris / IRIS
ort / BIT; CRUMB, SCRAP; MORSEL
orthodox / STANDARD; CANONICAL
orthodox Moslem / SUNNITE
orthography / SPELLING
ortolan / SORA; BUNTING; WHEAT-
   EAR
os / BONE; ESKER, MOUTH
oscillate / WAG; ROCK, SWAY
oscillation / NUTATION; LIBRATION

oscine bird / CHAT; ORIOLE
oscitant / DROWSY, GAPING
osculate / BUSS, KISS; SMACK
osier / ROD; WAND; WITHE; WILLOW
Osiris' brother / SET
Osiris' crown / ATEF
Osiris' realm / AMENTI
Osiris' son / HORUS
Osiris' wife / ISIS
osprey / AIGRETTE, FISHHAWK
osseous / BONY
ossuary / URN; CHARNELL; CATACOMB
ost / KILN, OAST, OVEN
ostensible / AVOWED; NOMINAL
ostentation / POMP, SHOW; PARADE
ostentatious / ARTY, VAIN; GAUDY
ostiary / DOORKEEPER
ostiole / PORE; STOMA; ORIFICE
ostracism / TABU; TABOO
ostracize / EXILE; BANISH
ostrich / RHEA
ostrich-like bird / EMU; EMEU; MURUP; MOORUP; CASSOWARY
otaheite arrowroot / PIA
otalgia / EARACHE
Otello composer / VERDI
Othello / MOOR
Othello's ensign / IAGO
Othello's wife / DESDEMONA
other / ELSE; ALTERNATE, DIFFERENT
other, c.f. / ALLO
otherness / ALTERITY
otherwise / ELSE; ALIAS; ALITER
otherwise named / OR; AKA; ALIAS
otic / AURAL; AUDITORY; AURICULAR
otiose / IDLE; USELESS; INACTIVE
otiosity / FUTILITY; UNEMPLOYMENT
oto / SIOUX; CHIWERE
otter / MUSTELID
otter brown / LOUTRE; PERIQUE
ottoman / SEAT, TURK; TURKISH
ottoman court / PORTE
ottoman official / PASHA; BASHAW
ottoman standard / ALEM
ouch / CLASP; BROOCH. AI; OW
ought / ZERO; AUGHT; CIPHER, NOUGHT. SHOULD
ounce / LEOPARD
our country / USA; AMERICA
our homeland / AMERICA
our mutual friend / HARMON; ROKESMITH
our national emblem / EAGLE
ourselves / US, WE
oust / EJECT, EVICT, EXPEL
out / EX; AWAY; FORTH; OUTSIDE

out of bed / UP; ASTIR
out of breath / BLOWN; WINDED
out of date / OLD; STALE
out of / FROM. SHY; SHORT
out of, pref. / DE, EC, EX
out of order / INOPERATIVE
out of the ordinary / RARE; UNUSUAL
out of the right way / ASTRAY
out of style / OLD; PASSE
out of town / AWAY
out of the way / REMOTE
out of the wind / ALEE
out-and-out / STARK, UTTER
outback / BUSH
outbreak / RASH, RIOT; MELEE; EMEUTE; EPIDEMIC, ERUPTION
outbuilding / BARN, SHED; STABLE
outburst / SPATE, STORM
outcast / EXILE, LEPER; PARIAH
outcome / END; FATE; ISSUE
outcrop / BASSET
outcry / CLAMOR, TUMULT; HULLABALOO
outdo / CAP; EXCEL; EXCEED
outdoor game / GOLF, POLO; BOCCE; TENNIS; CRICKET, CURLING; BASEBALL, FOOTBALL
outdoor party / FRY; FETE; PICNIC; BARBECUE
outdoor presentation / PARADE
outdoor sport / FISHING, HUNTING
outdoor staircase / PERRON
outer / ECTAL; EXTERIOR, EXTERNAL
outer angle / CANT
outer bounds / MARGIN; PERIMETER
outer covering / COAT, HULL, HUSK, RIND, SKIN, WRAP; CRUST
outer garment / CAPE, COAT, ROBE; PARKA; CAPOTE; PALETOT
outer portion of Earth / SIAL; CRUST
outer room / BUT
outer seed coating / TESTA
outfit / KIT, RIG; GEAR, SUIT
outfit for an infant / LAYETTE
outgo / EXPENSE
outgoing / WARM; EXTROVERTED
outhouse / PRIVY
outing / JAUNT; AIRING
outlander / ALIEN; FOREIGNER
outlandish / RUDE; ALIEN, OUTRE; QUEER; EXOTIC, RUSTIC, VULGAR
outlaw / BAN; EXCLUDE. FELON; BANDIT; BRIGAND; HIGHWAYMAN
outlay / COST; PRICE; EXPENSE

outlet / EXIT, VENT; EGRESS, MEDIUM; RECEPTACLE

outline / PLAN; DRAFT, TRACE; SKETCH. SYNOPSIS

outline of screen play / SCENARIO; TREATMENT

outlive / SURVIVE

outlook / VIEW; RANGE, SCOPE

outlying settlement / COLONY; OUTPOST

outmoded / PASSE, STALE; ARCHAIC

outmoded padding / BUSTLE

outpatient dispensary / CLINIC

outpouring / FLOOD; EFFLUX, TIRADE; TORRENT

outrage / ABUSE; AFFRONT. INJURY, INSULT; OFFENSE; VIOLENCE

outrageous / FURIOUS, VIOLENT; FLAGRANT; ATROCIOUS

outrigger / PRAU, PROA; CANOE

outright / POSITIVE. COMPLETELY

outset / START; OPENING

outside / EXTERIOR; SUPERFICIES. EXTERNAL

outside, c.f. / ECT; ECTO

outside bark / ROSS

outside covering / CAPE, COAT, ROBE, WRAP; MANTA; MANTLE; WRAPPER; OVERCOAT

outsider / ALIEN; VISITOR

outskirts / BORDER; ENVIRONS

outskirts of city / SUBURB

outspoken / BLUNT, FRANK; CANDID

outstanding / UNPAID; NOTABLE

outstanding account / DEBT

outstanding endowment / GIFT; SKILL; TALENT; ABILITY

outstanding event / OCCASION

outstrip / BEST; DISTANCE

outward / ECTAD, OUTER; PUBLIC

outward appearance / AIR; MIEN

outward sign / EVIDENCE

outward-going person / EXTROVERT

outwit / BALK, FOIL; DEFEAT

outwork / RAMPART, RAVELIN

ova / EGGS, SEED

oval / ELLIPSE. OVATE; ELLIPTIC

ovate / EGGSHAPED

ovation / TRIUMPH; APPLAUSE

oven / KILN, LEHR, OAST; BAKER

oven-cooked / BAKED

over / DONE, MORE, PAST; ENDED, EXTRA; FINISHED. OER; ATOP, UPON; ABOVE, AGAIN; ACROSS, BEYOND

over, pref. / SUPER, TRANS

over again / BIS; ANEW; ENCORE

over there / YON; YONDER

over with / DONE; ENDED

overage / SURPLUS; SUPER-ANNUATED

overawe / COW; DAUNT; INTIMIDATE

overbearing / BOSSY, PROUD; HAUGHTY; ARROGANT

overblouse / TUNIC

overbusy / FUSSY

overcast / LAP, LAY; COVER. DARK; MISTY; CLOUDY

overcoat / RAGLAN, ULSTER; PALETOT, TOPCOAT; RAINCOAT

overcome / BEAT, BEST, ROUT; QUELL; DEFEAT, MASTER, SUBDUE;

overcome with horror / APPAL

overdecorated / ORNATE

overdue / LATE

overdue bill / ARREAR

overfeed / CRAM, SATE; GORGE

overflow / FLOOD; DEBORD; INUNDATE

overflowing / COPIOUS; ABUNDANT

overfond / DOTING

overhang / JUT; BEETLE; PROJECT

overhasty / RASH; DARING

overhaul / FIX; REDO; RENEW

overhead / COST; EXPENSES. ABOVE, ALOFT

overhead railway / EL

overjoyed / GLAD; ELATED

overlay / LAP; COVER; ENCRUST

overlook / ERR; MISS, OMIT, SKIP; IGNORE, PARDON, REVIEW, SURVEY

overlord / LIEGE; AUTOCRAT

overly / TOO; EXTRA; TOOTOO

overmuch / TOO

overnice / FINICAL, FINIKEN

overnice person / PRIG

overpass / TRANSCEND. SPAN; CULVERT, VIADUCT

overplus / EXCESS; RESIDUE

overpower / AWE; MASTER, SUBDUE; OVERCOME, VANQUISH

overreach / DUPE, GULL; CHEAT, COZEN; DEFRAUD, SWINDLE

override / ANNUL; DISREGARD

overripe / STALE; ROTTED, ROTTEN

overripen / BRIT; BRITE

overrun / RAVAGE; DESPOIL

oversea post office / APO

overseas message / CABLE

oversee / INSPECT; SUPERVISE

overseer / BOSS; REEVE; CURATOR, MANAGER; SUPERVISOR, TASKMASTER

overseer of conduct / CENSOR; CHAPERON

overshadow / ECLIPSE; DOMINATE
overshoe / ARCTIC, GALOSH,
  RUBBER
oversight / SLIP; ERROR, LAPSE
overspread / COVER; BLANKET
overstate / EXAGGERATE
overt / OPEN; PATENT, PUBLIC
overtake / CATCH, REACH
overtax / OVERDO, STRAIN
overthrow / BEAT, FOIL, ROUT,
  RUIN; UPSET; DEFEAT
overture / OFFER; PRELUDE
overturn / TIP; UPSET; REVERSE,
  SUBVERT
overvalue / OVERRATE; OVER-
  PRIZE
overwhelm / AWE; STUN; CRUSH,
  SWAMP; DELUGE
overwhelming amount / SEA
overwrought / TIRED, WEARY;
  OVERDONE, OVERWORN;
  OVERWORKED
ovine / SHEEPLIKE
ovoid / EGGSHAPED
ovule / EGG; GERM, OVUM, SEED
ovum / EGG; GERM, SEED; SPORE
owala tree / BOBO
owing / DUE; IMPUTABLE
owl / HOOTER
owlish / NOCTURNAL
owl-like / STRIGINE
owl's cry / HOOT, WHOO
own / AVOW, HAVE, HOLD;
  ADMIT; POSSESS. AIN
own up to / ADMIT; CONFESS
owner / HOLDER; PROPRIETOR
ownership / TITLE; POSSESSION

owns / HAS
ox / BOS, YAK; NEAT, ZEBU;
  STEER
ox of Caesar's time / URUS
ox of Celebes / ANOA
ox of India / GAUR, ZEBU; GAYAL
ox of Tibet / YAK
oxalis / OCA
oxen / KINE
oxen's harness / YOKE
oxeye daisy / SHASTA
oxford / SHOE
Oxford graduate / OXONIAN
oxhead / OAF; DOLT
oxhide strap / REIM, RIEM;
  THONG
oxide of iron / RUST
oxidize / RUST; DISCOLOR
oxlike / BOVINE
oxlike antelope / KUDU; ELAND;
  NILGAI
oxlike quadruped / YAK; GAUR,
  ZEBU; BISON, GAYAL; BUFFALO
oxter / ARMPIT
oxygen compound / OXIDE
oxygen form / OZONE
oxygenate / AERATE; OXIDIZE
oyster / REEFER
oyster bed material / CULCH,
  CUTCH; CULTCH
oyster tree / MANGROVE
oysterbird / SANDERLING
oysterfish / TAUTOG; TAUTAUG
Oz author / BAUM
Ozark town / AVA
ozone / ATMOSPHERE

P

pa / DAD, POP; PAPA
pabulum / FOOD; NOURISHMENT
pac / MOCCASIN
paca / CAVY
pacate / CALM; SERENE
pace / GAIT, RATE, STEP; AMBLE
pacemaker / LEADER
pacha / PASHA
Pachacamac's people / YUNCAN
pachyderm / ELEPHANT
pacific / CALM, MILD; IRENIC
Pacific aroid / TARO
Pacific discoverer / BALBOA
Pacific Grove denizen / MONARCH
Pacific island / BALI, GUAM, NIUE
Pacific island cloth / TAPA
Pacific island group / SAMOA
Pacific Ocean deep / MINDANAO
Pacific peninsula / BAJA; KOREA
Pacific pine / IE; HALA
Pacific shrub / SALAL

Pacific tree / HALA, IPIL
pacificate / PACIFY
pacificator / APPEASER
pacifier / SOP; NIPPLE
pacifist / CO
pacify / CALM, EASE, HUSH, LULL
pack / WAD; BALE, CRAM, LADE,
  LOAD, STOW, TAMP. BAND,
  GANG
pack animal / ASS; MULE; BURRO,
  LLAMA; DONKEY; JACKASS
pack of cards / DECK
pack cargo / LADE, LOAD, STOW
pack with clay / TAMP
pack down / TAMP
pack fully / CRAM
pack horse / SUMPTER
pack of hounds / HUNT
package / BALE; CARTON, PARCEL
package box / CRATE; CARTON
package of pepper / ROBBIN

packed / STEEVED
packing / OAKUM; GASKET,
    SPONGE
packman / PEDDLER
paco / FRANK; ALPACA
pact / TREATY; COMPACT
paction / CONTRACT
pad / BED; ROOM; PALLET, TABLET
padded jacket / ACTON
padding / FILLING; STUFFING
paddle / OAR; SCULL. ROW
paddock / FROG, TOAD; CORRAL
paddy / IRISHMAN
padmelon / QUOKKA
padnag / AMBLE
padre / PRIEST
padrone / INNKEEPER
Paduan ruling family / CARRARA
paean / HYMN, SONG
pagan / HEATHEN. ETHNIC;
    GENTILE
pagan god / BAAL
pagan image / ICON, IDOL; FETISH
paganism / IDOLATRY
page / BOY; LEAF; FOLIO, RECTO,
    SHEET, VERSO; BELLHOP;
    MESSENGER
page number / FOLIO
pageant / POMP, SHOW; PARADE
pageantry / FLOURISH
Pagliacci character / NEDDA
Pagliacci composer / LEON-
    CAVALLO
Pagliacci hero / CANIO
pagoda / TA; TAA; TOWER;
    TEMPLE
pagoda finial / EPI, TEE
paid public announcement / AD
pail / COG; COGUE, SKEEL;
    BUCKET
Paimpol's publicist / LOTI
pain / WOE; ACHE, PANG; AGONY,
    GRIEF, THROE. VEX; FRET
pain, c.f. / AGRA
pain killer / OPIATE; ANODYNE
Paine's religion / DEISM
painful / SORE; ANNOYING
painful toe disease / GOUT
painstaking / CAREFUL;
    SEDULOUS
paint / DYE; DECK; ADORN,
    COLOR; DEPICT; PORTRAY.
    ROUGE; PIGMENT
paint brush / PENCIL;
    HAWKWEED
paint coarsely / DAUB
paint with cosmetic / ROUGE
paint with dots / STIPPLE
paint for face / FARD; COSMETIC
painted bunting / PAPE
painter / ARTIST
painter's aid / BRUSH, EASEL;
    MAHLSTICK, MAULSTICK

painter's tripod / EASEL
painting / MURAL; CANVAS,
    CHROMO; PICTURE, PORTRAIT
painting of dead Christ / PIETA
painting medium / OIL;
    ENCAUSTIC; WATERCOLOR
painting on plaster / SECCO;
    FRESCO
painting style / GENRE; IMPASTO
painting of Virgin / MADONNA
painting on wall / MURAL
pair / DUO, TWO; DYAD, SPAN,
    TEAM; BRACE, TWAIN
paired / MATED
paired in heraldry / GEMEL
paired horses / SPAN, TEAM
paired oxen / YOKE
Paisley / SHAWL; CASHMERE
pakeha / FOREIGNER
Pakistan area / SIND;
    BALUCHISTAN
Pakistan capital / ISLAMABAD
Pakistan city / KARACHI;
    RAWALPINDI
Pakistan money / RUPEE
Pakistan statesman / JINNAH
pal / CHUM, MATE, PARD; CRONY
palace / COURT; MANSION
paladin / HERO; KNIGHT;
    CHAMPION
Palamedes' brother / OEAX
Palamedes' mother / CLYMENE
palanquin / JAUN, KAGO; DOOLI
palanquin porter / HAMAL;
    SIRDAR
palatable / SAPID, TASTY
palate / TASTE; RELISH
palate area / UVULA, VELUM
palatial / PALATINE;
    MAGNIFICENT
palatine / ROYAL; SOVEREIGN
Palau island / ANGAUR;
    PELELIU
palaver / TALK; GIBBERISH;
    CONFERENCE
pale / DIM, WAN; ASHY; ASHEN,
    FAINT, PASTY, WHITE; PALLID,
    SALLOW. FADE; BLANCH.
    STAKE; PICKET
pale brown / TAN
pale green / BOA; NILE
pale red / PINK
pale tinge / TINT
pale violet / LAVENDER
pale yellow / CANARY
palea / BRACT, PALET; VALVULE
palebuck / ORIBI
paleness / PALLOR
Palestine / CANAAN. See also
    Israel
Palestine capital / JERUSALEM
Palestine city / DAN; HAIFA
Palestine money / MIL; PIASTRE

Palestine mountain / NEBO;
  SINAI; CARMEL, GILEAD,
  PISGAH
Palestine plain / ESDRAELON
Palestine river / JORDAN, QISHON
Palestinian well / EN; AIN
Palestrina composition /
  MAGNIFICAT
paletot / OVERCOAT
palette / BOARD; COLORS, TABLET
palfrey / HORSE
pali / CLIFF; PRECIPICE
palindromic word / ERE, EVE, TAT;
  BOOB, NOON; KAYAK, MADAM,
  REFER
palingenesis / REBIRTH
palinode / RETRACTION
Palinurus / PILOT
palisade / CLIFF, FENCE
pall / CLOY; CLOAK
Pallas / ATHENA; MINERVA
Pallas' wife / STYX
palliate / EASE; ALLAY, COVER
pallid / WAN; PALE; ASHEN
pallor / WANNESS
palm / TI; COCO, NIOG, SAGO;
  ARECA, ASSAI; GEBANG;
  TALIPOT
palm of Africa / DUM; DOOM
palm of Asia / ARECA, ARENG,
  BETEL; GOMUTI
palm of Brazil / ASSAI
palm cockatoo / ARARA
palm drink / NIPA; ASSAI
palm of East Indies / ATAP, NIPA
palm fiber / TAL; BURI; DATIL;
  RAFFIA
palm of hand / LOOF, VOLA;
  THENAR
palm leaf / OLA; OLLA; FROND
palm leaf mat / YAPA
palm lily / TI
palm liquor / GUR; BENO, BINO,
  TUBA; TODDY; JAGGERY
palm off / COG, FOB; FOIST
palm sago / GOMUTI
palm of South America / DATIL
palm starch / SAGO
palm of West Indies / GRIGRI
palmate / BROAD; WEBFOOTED
palmer / PILGRIM
palmetto fruit / SABAL
Palmetto State / SOUTHCAROLINA
palmistry / CHIROMANCY
palmy / HAPPY; GOLDEN;
  HALCYON
palmyra leaf / OLA, OLE; OLLA
palmyra palm / BRAB
palmyra palm fiber / TAL
Palmyra's queen / ZENOBIA
Palo Alto school / STANFORD
Palo Alto victor / TAYLOR
Palomar spectacle / TELESCOPE

palp / FEELER
palpable / CLEAR; EVIDENT
palpitate / BEAT, PANT; THROB
palpitation / PALMUS;
  TACHYCARDIA
palsied / SHAKING; PARALYZED
palter / TRIFLE; CHAFFER
paltry / MEAN, POOR; CHEAP,
  PETTY, SMALL
paludal / SWAMPY
paludine / BOGGY; MARSHY
paludism / MALARIA
pam / NAP
pampas / PLAINS
pampas cat / KODKOD
pamper / PET; HUMOR, SPOIL;
  CODDLE, COSHER, COSSET
pampered / LUXURIANT
pamphlet / TRACT; BOOKLET
pan / BASIN; SPIDER; SKILLET
Pan / GOATGOD
pan for incense / CENSER
panacea / CURE; ELIXIR; CUREALL
panache / VERVE; SWAGGER
panada / BREADPULP
Panama Canal lock / GATUN
Panama gum tree / COPA, YAYA
Panama Indian / CUNA; CUEVA
Panama money / BALBOA
Panama mountain / CHIRIQUI
Panama river / TUIRA
Panama seaport / COLON
Panama's former name / DARIEN
Panamint Indian / KOSO
panatela / CIGAR
Panay city / ILOILO
Panay negrito / ATI
pancake / HOTCAKE; FLAPJACK
pancreas / SWEETBREAD
pancreas secretion / INSULIN
panda / WAH; BEARCAT
pandect / CODE; DIGEST
pandemonium / HELL, RIOT, VICE
pander / BAWD, PIMP. PROCURE
pandiculate / YAWN; STRETCH
Pandora's husband / EPIMETHEUS
panegyric / ELOGE; EULOGY
panel / JURY, LIST, PANE
panel in frieze / METOPE;
  TRIGLYPH
panel of jurors / VENIRE
panel member / JUROR
pang / ACHE, PAIN; GRIPE, THROE
Pangloss's pupil / CANDIDE
pangolin / MANIS; ANTEATER
Panhandle city / AMARILLO
Panhandle State / WESTVIRGINIA
panhandler / BEGGAR
panic / FEAR, FUNK; FRIGHT
panic grass / MILLET
pannage / MAST
pannier / BASKET, DOSSER
panoply / ARMOR, COVER

panorama / VIEW; SCAPE, VISTA
panoramic / SCENIC
panpipe / REED; SYRINX
Pan's father / HERMES
Pan's lover / ECHO; SYRINX
pant / GASP, LONG, PUFF; THROB
pantheon / TEMPLE
panther / PARD, PUMA; COUGAR
panther's cry / SAW
pantile / HARDTACK
panting / POLYPNEA
pantomime / DUMBSHOW
pantomimist / MARCEAU
pantry / AMBRY; LARDER, SPENCE
pants / TROUSERS
pap / PULP, TEAT; DRIVEL
papa / PA; DAD; POPE; BABOON,
    FATHER; VULTURE
Papal church / ROMAN; LATERAN;
    CATHOLIC
Papal court / CURIA
Papal decree / DECRETAL
Papal letter / BULL; ENCYCLICAL
Papal palace / LATERAN, VATICAN
Papal vestment / FANO; FANON,
    FANUM, ORALE, PHAND;
    FANNEL
papaya / PAPAW; PAWPAW
paper / ESSAY; JOURNAL;
    DOCUMENT
paper cabinet / FILE
paper edge / DECKLE
paper fastener / CLIP; STAPLE
paper folded once / FOLIO
paper holding drug dose /
    CHARTULA
paper identifying mark / WATER-
    MARK
paper for lighting / SPILL
paper measure / REAM; QUIRE
paper money / NOTE; CHECK,
    DRAFT
paper mulberry / KOZO
paper mulberry bark / TAPA
paper nautilus / ARGONAUT
paper scrap / CASSE; RETREE
paper size / CAP; DEMY, POTT
paper tube for tobacco / SPILL
paper-making machine / FOUR-
    DRINIER
papers / DOCUMENTS
papilloma / CORN, WART; TUMOR
papoose / BABY; CHILD
pappy / SOFT; MARSHY. DADDY
Papua river / FLY
Papua town / BUNA, DARU
par / PARITY; EQUALITY
para / RUBBER
parable / FABLE; ALLEGORY
parachute body / CANOPY
parachutist's cry / GERONIMO
paraclete / INTERCESSOR
parade / ARRAY, MARCH, STRUT;

FLAUNT. POMP; PAGEANT;
    SPECTACLE
paradigm / MODEL; PATTERN
paradise / EDEN; BLISS; HEAVEN
paradise inhabitant / HOURI
Paradise Lost author / MILTON
paradise ruled by Amita / JODO
paradisiac / EDENIC
paradox / CONTRADICTION
paragon / TYPE; JEWEL, MODEL;
    PALADIN, PATTERN; EXEMPLAR
paragram / PUN
paragraph / ITEM; PASSAGE
Paraguay capital / ASUNCION
Paraguay lake / YPOA
Paraguay money / GUARANI
Paraguay river / PILCOMAYO
Paraguay tea / MATE; YERBAMATE
Paraguayan city / ITA; VILLARRICA
Paraguayan disputed area / CHACO
parakeet / BUDGIE; BUDGERIGAR
parallel / EVEN; EQUAL;
    CORRESPONDING
parallel of latitude / TROPIC
parallelogram / RHOMB
paralysis / PALSY; PARESIS
paralytic / PALSIED, PARETIC
paralyze / BENUMB, DEADEN
parameter / GAUGE; MEASURE
paramount / CHIEF; EMINENT,
    SUPREME
paramour / LEMAN, LOVER,
    SWAIN; INAMORATO
paranoid's bete noire / PARANEE
parapet / WALL; REDAN; RAMPART
parapet opening / CRENEL;
    EMBRASURE
parapet's intercrenellation /
    MERLON
paraph / FLOURISH
paraphrase / REWORD
parapsychology study / ESP, PSI
Para's present name / BELEM
parasite / DRONE, LEECH,
    LOUSE, TOADY; FLUNKY,
    SPONGE, SUCKER
parasite in blood / TRYP
parasite causing malaria /
    PLASMODIUM
parasitic disease / SURRA;
    NAGANA
parasitic fish / PEGA; REMORA
parasitic insect / FLEA, MITE
parasitic plant / FUNGUS
parasol / SUNSHADE, UMBRELLA
paravane / OTTER
parbuckle / HOIST, SLING
parcae / NONA; FATES, MORTA;
    CLOTHO, DECUMA; ATROPOS;
    LACHESIS
parcel / LOT; PART, PLAT, PLOT;
    TRACT; BUNDLE. LET; METE;
    ALLOT

parcener / COHEIR
parch / DRY; BURN, SEAR;
    SCORCH
parched / ARID, SERE; THIRSTY
parchment / DEED, SKIN; FOREL
parchment roll / PELL; SCROLL
parchment used again / PALIMP-
    SEST
pard / FRIEND; LEOPARD,
    PANTHER
pardon / CLEAR, REMIT; ACQUIT,
    EXCUSE, SHRIVE. AMNESTY
pardonable / VENIAL; EXPIABLE
pare / PEEL, SKIN; SHAVE; LESSEN
parent / MOM, POP; SIRE; FATHER,
    MOTHER
Parent Teacher Association / PTA
parentage / BIRTH, STOCK;
    FAMILY, ORIGIN; DESCENT,
    LINEAGE
parental / PRIMARY
parental love / STORGE
parenthetical remark / ASIDE
parents / ANCESTORS, FORE-
    BEARS
paresis / PARALYSIS
paretic / PARALYTIC
parget / COAT; PLASTER;
    WHITEWASH
pargo / PORGY; SNAPPER
pariah / OUTCAST
parietary / PELLITORY
Paris / PAREE; LUTETIA. See also
    Parisian
Paris' father / PRIAM
Paris' mother / HECUBA
Paris river / SEINE
Paris ruffian / APACHE
Paris suburb / MEUDON; STCLOUD
Paris subway / METRO
Paris' wife / OENONE
parish / COUNTY;
    CONGREGATION
parish, pert. to / PAROCHIAL
parish deputy / CURATE
parish land / GLEBE
parish officer / RECTOR
parish priest / VICAR
Parisian airport / ORLY
Parisian artists' quarter /
    MONTMARTRE
Parisian cathedral / NOTREDAME
Parisian college / SORBONNE
Parisian food market / LESHALLES
Parisian museum / LOUVRE
Parisian park / LUXEMBOURG
Parisian section / BOIS, CITE;
    PASSY
Parisian shopgirl / GRISETTE
Parisian stockmarket / BOURSE
Parisian tower / EIFFEL
Parisian wine district / BERCY

parity / PAR; EQUALITY, SAME-
    NESS
park in Rockies / ESTES; GLACIER
parking bugaboo / METER
parking place / LOT; CURB;
    GARAGE
parlance / IDIOM; DICTION
parlay / BET; WAGER; DOUBLING
parley / PALAVER; CONFERENCE.
    TREAT; DISCUSS
parliament / DIET; KNESSET
Parliament report / HANSARD
parlor / SALON; CHAMBER;
    POOLROOM
parlous / RISKY; DANGEROUS
Parnassian poet / HEREDIA
Parnassian spring / CASTALIAN
parochial / NARROW; LIMITED
parodist / CLOWN, MIMIC
parody / SATIRE; TRAVESTY;
    BURLESQUE; CARICATURE
parol / ORAL; UNWRITTEN
parole / PROMISE, RELEASE;
    WATCHWORD
paronomasia / PUN
paroxysm / FIT; SPASM, THROE
parrakeet / BUDGIE
parrot / ARA, KEA; KAKA, LORY;
    ARARA, CAGIT, MACAW
parrot of Brazil / ARA
parrot fish / LORO, SCAR; LAUIA;
    COTORO, SCARID
parrot hawk / HIA
parrotlike / ARINE
parry / FEND; AVERT, EVADE
Parsi / GABAR; GHEBER, PARSEE;
    ZOROASTRIAN
Parsi priest / MOBED
Parsi scripture / AVESTA
Parsifal's quest / GRAIL
Parsifal's uncle / AMFORTAS
parsimonious / CLOSE; FRUGAL
parsley camphor / APIOLE
parsley fern / STONEBRAKE
parsley-like plant / DILL; ANISE
parson / PASTOR, RECTOR;
    MINISTER, PREACHER
parson bird / POE, TUE, TUI; KOKO
parsonage / MANSE; RECTORY
part / BREAK, SEVER; CLEAVE,
    SUNDER. BIT; ROLE, SIDE,
    SOME
part above ground / TOP
part of barn / MOW; SILO
part of Bible / PROPHETS;
    TESTAMENT
part of book / LEAF, PAGE;
    CHAPTER
part of car / HOOD; WIPER;
    BUMPER, FENDER
part of church / APSE, NAVE;
    AISLE, ALTAR

part of circle / ARC; SECTOR
part of clarinet / REED
part of coat / LAPEL; SLEEVE
part of dynamo / ROTOR
part of egg / YOLK; WHITE
part of eye / UVEA; CORNEA
part of fish line / SNELL
part of flower / PETAL, SEPAL;
PISTIL, STAMEN
part of foot / TOE; ARCH, HEEL
part of funeral cortege / HEARSE
part of furniture joint / MORTISE
part of Great Britain / DOWNS,
WALES
part of Greek drama / CHORUS,
EXODOS
part of Greek tetrachord / NETE
part of hammer / CLAW, PEEN
part of hand / PALM; THUMB;
FINGER
part of harness / HAME
part of head / SCALP; CRANIUM
part of horse's foot / HOOF;
PASTERN
part of horse's leg / HOCK;
CANNON
part of infinitive / TO
part of leg / KNEE, SHIN
part of locomotive / CAB
part of meal / SALAD; COURSE
part of pedestal / BASE, DADO
part in play / LEAD, ROLE
part of play / ACT; SCENE
part of shoe / HEEL, RAND, SOLE,
VAMP, WELT; INSOLE
part of skull / INION
part song / ROUND
part of speech / NOUN, VERB;
ADVERB; PRONOUN;
ADJECTIVE; CONJUNCTION,
PREPOSITION; INTERJECTION
part of staircase / RISER, TREAD
part of verb paradigm /
PARTICIPLE
part of wheel / RIM; NAVE; FELLY,
SPOKE
part of whole / PIECE; MEMBER
part of window frame / SASH, SILL
part with / LEAVE; ABANDON
partake / USE; SHARE; INDULGE
parted / GONE; CLEFT
Parthenon's hill / ACROPOLIS
Parthian city / CTESIPHON
Partholan's wife / DALNY
partial / PRO; BIASED
partial, pref. / HEMI, SEMI
partial darkness / SHADE;
SHADOW
partial to / FAVORABLE
partial word list / GLOSSARY
partially / PARTLY; SOMEWHAT
participant / MEMBER, PLAYER

participate / SHARE; PARTAKE
participation / CONCURRENCE
participator / PARTNER
participial ending / ED; ING
particle / BIT, ION, JOT; ATOM,
IOTA, MITE, MOTE, WHIT
particle denoting negative / UN;
NON
particle with electrical charge / ION
particle of fire / SPARK
particle of matter / ATOM
particle with negative charge /
ELECTRON
particle in nucleus / MESON;
PROTON; NEUTRON
particle with positive charge /
PROTON
particle of water / DROP
particolored / PIED; MOTLEY;
PIEBALD
particolored horse / ROAN;
PINTO; CALICO
particular / ODD; EXACT, FUSSY;
MINUTE. ITEM; DETAIL
particular class / MODE, TYPE
particular instance / CASE
particular printing / EDITION
particularly / ESPECIALLY
parting / FAREWELL
partisan / DEVOTEE; CHAMPION,
HENCHMAN
partisan feeling / ANIMUS
partition / CELL, WALL; SEPTUM
partlet / HEN; BIDDY; COLLAR
partly fused glass / FRIT
partly open / AJAR
partly parasitic shrub / MISTLETOE
partner / ALLY, MATE; SHARER,
SPOUSE; CONSORT
partnership / FIRM; HOUSE,
UNION
partridge / YUTU; QUAIL; CHUKAR,
GROUSE, SEESEE; TINAMOU
partridge's call / JUCK
parts essential to life / VITALS
parturition / CHILDBIRTH
party / BEE; FETE, GALA, RING,
SECT, SIDE; CABAL, JUNTO;
CIRCLE, CLIQUE, LEAGUE;
BLOWOUT, COTERIE
party accessory / COASTER
party celebrating new home /
HOUSEWARMING
party favors / SNAPPERS
party goody / CANAPE
party line / POLICY
party member / CARDCARRIER
parula / WARBLER
parvenu / UPSTART; ARRIVISTE
pas in ballet / STEP
pas de deux / DUET
Pasadena site / ROSEBOWL

pasha / BASHAW
Pasiphae's daughter / PHAEDRA
Pasiphae's husband / MINOS
Pasiphae's mother / PERSEIS
Pasiphae's offspring / MINOTAUR
pasquinade / LAMPOON
pass / GO; DIE; FADE, MOVE, OMIT,
 VOID; ADOPT. COL, GAP; ABRA,
 PATH; BYWAY, NOTCH; TICKET
pass away / DIE; ELAPSE, PERISH
pass the buck / BLAME
pass by / ELAPSE
pass imperceptibly / SHADE, SLIDE
pass into law / ENACT
pass off as genuine / FAKE; FOIST
pass on / DIE
pass on information / RELAY
pass over / SKIP; CROSS, ELIDE
pass over quickly / SKIM
pass pompously / SWEEP
pass in review / PARADE
pass a rope through / REEVE
pass slowly / DRAG
pass swiftly / FLY, RUN
pass through / CROSS; PENETRATE
pass through carefully / REEVE;
 THREAD
pass through hills / GAP
pass through mountains / NOTCH;
 DEFILE
pass through sieve / SIFT; SCREEN
pass through skin / SWEAT;
 TRANSUDE
pass time idly / LOAF
pass as vapor / EVAPORATE
passable / FAIR, SOSO; MIDDLING
passage / GUT, WAY; EXIT, ITER,
 ROAD; AISLE, ALLEY, ALURE;
 PHRASE
passage in anatomy / ITER
passage through banks / GAT
passage of Bible / TEXT
passage through canal lock /
 LOCKAGE
passage covered over / ARCADE
passage for fluid / DUCT; CANAL
passage into fort / POSTERN
passage into / ADIT; ENTRY,
 INLET
passage money / FARE
passage in music / CADENZA,
 STRETTO
passage out / EXIT; EGRESS
passage through / TRANSIT
passage between walls / SLYPE
passageway / HALL; AISLE;
 WALKWAY
passe / DATED; OUTDATED,
 OUTMODED
passe person / HASBEEN
passed / EX; FORMER
passementerie / BRAIDING

passenger / FARE; RIDER;
 WAYFARER
passenger plane / JET
passenger train / LOCAL; EXPRESS
passenger vessel / LINER;
 STEAMER
passerine bird / CROW; FINCH
passim / THROUGHOUT
passing / GOING; LEAVING
passing fancy / WHIM; CAPRICE
passing fashions / FADS
passion / IRE; FURY, GLOW, LOVE,
 LUST, RAGE, ZEAL; ARDOR;
 FERVOR
passion in Buddhism / RAGA
passionate / HOT; ANGRY;
 EXCITABLE
passive / INERT, QUIET; PATIENT
Passover / PASCH; PASCHA,
 PESACH
Passover, pert. to / PASCHAL
Passover bread / AZYM; AZYME;
 MATZOTH
Passover festival meal / SEDER
passport / VISA, VISE; PERMIT
password / SIGN; WATCHWORD
past / AGO; GONE, OVER; SPENT
past, pref. / PRETER
past all aid / GONE
past participle ending / ED, EN
past tense / AORIST; IMPERFECT,
 PRETERITE
pasta / ZITI; DITALI; GNOCCHI,
 RAVIOLI; MACARONI;
 SPAGHETTI
paste / GLUE; CREAM, DOUGH;
 CEMENT, STRASS. IMITATION
pasteboard / CARD; TICKET
pasteboard container / CARTON
pasted art work / COLLAGE,
 MONTAGE
pastel / TINT; CRAYON
pastime / PLAY; SPORT;
 DIVERSION
pastor / PARSON, PRIEST,
 RECTOR; MINISTER, SHEPHERD
pastoral / RURAL; RUSTIC;
 IDYLLIC. IDYL
pastoral instrument / OAT; PIPE
pastoral place / ARCADIA
pastoral poem / IDYL; IDYLL;
 BUCOLIC, ECLOGUE
pastoral poet / BION; THEOCRITUS
pastoral staff / PEDA; CROOK,
 PEDUM; CROSIER
pastor's assistant / CURATE
pastose / IMPASTED
pastry / PIE; FLAN, TART; COOKIE
pastry shop / BAKERY
pasture / ING, LEA; GRASS, GRAZE,
 RANGE. AGIST
pasture grass / GRAMA

pasty / MEATPIE
pasul / UNFIT
pat / DAB, TAP; CARESS, STROKE.
APT, FIT; EXACT; TIMELY;
SUITABLE
pata / TURBAN
pataca / DOLLAR
Patagonian deity / SETEBOS
Patagonian hare / MARA
Patagonian native / ONA
Patagonian river / CHICO; CHUBUT
patch / MEND. PLOT, VAMP;
PIECE
patchwork poem / CENTO
pate / HEAD; CROWN
pate de foie gras / GOOSELIVERS
patella / ROTULA; KNEECAP,
KNEEPAN
paten / ARCA, DISC; PLATE
patent / GRANT. OBVIOUS
patent medicine / ELIXIR, REMEDY;
NOSTRUM
pater / DAD
patera / DISH; SAUCER
paterfamilias / FATHER
paternal / CAREFUL; FATHERLY
paternal heritage / PATRIMONY
paternalism / REGULATION
paternity / PARENTAGE;
AUTHORSHIP
path / WAY; BEAT, BERM, LANE,
ROAD; SPOOR, TRACE, TRACK;
CASAUN
path of comet / ORBIT
path in mathematics / LOCUS
path of truth / TAO
pathema / DISEASE
pathetic / SAD; MOVING;
TOUCHING
pathetic insincerity / BATHOS
pathfinder / BLAZER; PIONEER
pathless / UNEXPLORED
pathogen / GERM; VIRUS
pathologist / DIAGNOSTICIAN
pathology / ABNORMALITY
pathos / SYMPATHY;
TRANSIENCE
pathosis / DISEASE
patience / CALM; FORTITUDE
patient / CASE; INVALID.
ENDURING, RESIGNED;
PERSEVERING
patient man / JOB
patient woman / GRISELDA
patio / YARD; COURTYARD
patois / CANT; ARGOT; JARGON;
DIALECT
patriarch / ELDER; FATHER
patriarch of the church / BISHOP
patriarch of Scripture / ISAAC,
JACOB; ABRAHAM
patrician / NOBLE; ARISTOCRAT
patrilocal / VIRILOCAL

patrimonial / PATERNAL;
HEREDITARY
patrimony / HERITAGE
patriot / IRREDENTIST
patriotic group / DAR
Patroclus' friend / ACHILLES
Patroclus' slayer / HECTOR
patrol / SCOUT, WATCH
patroiman / CONSTABLE,
POLICEMAN
patrolman's path / BEAT
patron / GUEST, SAINT; CLIENT;
GUARDIAN; BENEFACTOR
patron saint of cobblers /
CRISPIN
patron saint of cripples / GILES
patron saint of England / GEORGE
patron saint of fishermen / PETER
patron saint of France / DENIS
patron saint of goldsmiths / ELOY
patron saint of Ireland / PATRICK
patron saint of lawyers / IVES
patron saint of Norway / OLAF
patron saint of painters / LUKE
patron saint of sailors / ELMO
patron saint of Scotland / ANDREW
patron saint of Spain / JAMES;
SANTIAGO
patron saint of thieves / DISMAS
patron saint of Wales / DAVID
patronage / AEGIS; SUPPORT
patronize / AID; HELP; FAVOR;
ASSIST, DEFEND
patsy / BUTT; SCAPEGOAT
patter / JARGON, MUMBLE;
CHATTER
pattern / MOLD, NORM, TYPE;
IDEAL, MODEL; DESIGN
pattern of large squares / DAMIER
pattern of squares / CHECKER-
WORK
patulous / OPEN; DISTENDED
paucity / LACK; SCARCITY
Paul / SAUL
Paul Pry / SNOOPER
paulownia tree / KIRI
Paul's birthplace / TARSUS
Paul's companion / SILAS;
SOPATER
paunch / POT; BELLY;
CORPORATION
pauperism / NEED, WANT;
PENURY
pause / HALT, REST, STOP, WAIT;
DELAY, TARRY, WAVER. BREAK,
SELAH; CESURA; CAESURA,
RESPITE
pave / TAR; COVER; SURFACE
paver's mallet / TUP; PAVIOR
pavilion / TENT; MARQUEE
pavilion in garden / GAZEBO;
BELVEDERE
paving block / SETT

paving material / TAR; FLAG; SLATE; CEMENT
pavis / SHIELD
Pavlova's dance / SWAN; CYGNE
paw / PUD; FOOT, HAND; PATTE
pawl / CATCH, CLICK; DETENT
pawn / HOCK. MAN; INSTRUMENT
Pawnee Indian / LOUP; CHADI, SKIDI, SKIRI; TAPAGE
Pawnee ritual / HAKO
pawnshop / HOCKSHOP
pax / PEACE
pay / REMIT; DEFRAY, EXPEND. WAGES; SALARY; STIPEND
pay attention / HARK, HEED
pay back / REFUND; RETALIATE
pay beforehand / PREPAY
pay dirt / ORE; METAL; FORTUNE
pay for everyone / TREAT
pay homage to / HONOR; PRAISE
pay the kitty / ANTE
pay out / SPEND; SLACKEN
pay a visit / CALL
payable / DUE
paying client / CUSTOMER
paymaster / BUXY; BAKSHI, BUKSHI, PURSER; CASHIER
payment / FEE; COST; RECOMPENSE
payment back / REBATE
payment for death / CRO; ERIC
payment for learning / TUITION
pea / PILL; LEGUME
pea tree / AGATI; KATURAI
peace / PAX; CALM; AMITY, QUIET; CONCORD, NIRVANA
peace goddess / IRENE
peace of mind / SERENITY
peace officer / MARSHAL; CONSTABLE; POLICEMAN
peace pipe / CALUMET
peace tribunal / HAGUE
peaceable / GENTLE, SERENE
peaceful / CALM; IRENIC
peach / PAVY; CLING; BABCOCK, ELBERTA; FREESTONE, NECTARINE
peach pit / STONE; PUTAMEN
Peach State / GEORGIA
peacock / MAO; PAON, PAVO, PAWN
peacock, pert. to / PAVONINE
peacock blue / PAON
peacock butterfly / IO
peacock fish / WRASSE
peak / ALP, TIP, TOP; ACME, APEX, CRAG, CUSP; CREST; CLIMAX
peaked / WAN; PALE; SHRUNKEN
peal / RING, TOLL; CHIME
peanut / MANI, WART; GOOBER, MANILA, SHRIMP; EARTHNUT, EARTHPEA; GROUNDNUT

pear / BOSC, POME; ANJOU; SECKEL; BARTLETT
pear cider / PERRY
pearl / GEM; RING; NACRE, ONION, UNION; ORIENT
Pearl of the Antilles / CUBA
Pearl Buck heroine / OLAN
pearl diver / DISHWASHER
pearl fisher / DIVER
pearl imitation / OLIVET
pearl millet / BAJRA; BAJREE
Pearl of the Orient / CEYLON
pearl plant / GROMEL; GROMWELL
pearly / CLEAR; PELLUCID
pear-shaped / PYRIFORM
pear-shaped pot / ALUDEL
peart / BRISK, SAUCY; FRISKY
peas as in porridge / PEASE
peasant / CARL, PEON, RYOT, SERF; CEORL, CHURL, RURAL; FELLAH, RUSTIC; LABORER
peasant in India / RYOT
peat / BOG; MOSS, TURF
peat spade / SLADE
peavey / CANTHOOK
peba / ARMADILLO
pebble / STONE; JACKSTONE
pebbles / SCREE; GRAVEL
pecan / NOGAL; HICKORY
peccant / BAD; WRONG; ERRING
peccary / JAVALI; KAIRUNI
peck / DAB, DOT, EAT, NIP; KNIP
peckish / HUNGRY
Pecksniffian / HYPOCRITICAL
pectinate / COMBLIKE
pectize / CONGEAL
peculate / EMBEZZLE
peculator / THIEF; ROBBER
peculiar / ODD; RARE; QUEER; SPECIAL, STRANGE, UNUSUAL; SINGULAR
peculiar, c.f. / IDIO
peculiar institution / SLAVERY
peculiar to a language / IDIOMATIC
peculiarity / QUIRK, TRAIT
pecuniary penalty / FINE; MULCT
padagogic / STILTED; PEDANTIC
pedagogue / TUTOR; TEACHER
pedal / LEVER; TREADLE
pedal digit / TOE
pedaled / BIKED
pedant / SCHOLAR, TEACHER; PRECISION
pedantic / FORMAL; STILTED
peddle / HAWK, SELL, VEND
peddler / HAWKER, PEDLAR
pedestal / ANTA, BASE; GAINE; SUPPORT
pedestal part / DADO; PLINTH
pedestal's dado / SOLIDUM
pedestrian / WALKER. DULL
pedicel / RAY; FOOTSTALK

pedicure / CHIROPODIST
pedigree / LINE, RACE; BREED,
STOCK; FAMILY, STRAIN
peduncle / STEM; STALK, STIPE
peduncle of plant / SCAPE
peek / LOOK, PEEP, PEER;
GLANCE
peel / HUSK, PARE, SKIN; STRIP.
BARK, HULL, RIND
peeler / BOBBY; POLICEMAN
peep / CRY; PEEK; CHEEP, CHIRP
peepers / EYES
peepshow / RAREE
peer / PRY; GAZE, LOOK. LORD,
MATE; NOBLE; COMPEER,
COMRADE
peer of Charlemagne / OLIVER
Peer Gynt composer / GRIEG
Peer Gynt's author / IBSEN
Peer Gynt's mother / ASE
Peer Gynt's sweetheart / SOLVEIG
peer of the realm / DUKE, EARL;
BARON; MARQUESS, VISCOUNT
peerage / NOBILITY
peeress / LADY; DUCHESS
peerless / UNIQUE; MATCHLESS,
NONPAREIL
peeve / IRE, IRK, VEX; FRET
peevish / SOUR; CROSS, MOODY,
TECHY, TESTY; PETTISH
peewee / LARK; LAPWING. SMALL
peg / HOB, NOB, PIN, TEE; KNAG,
PLUG; DOWEL; MARKER
peg of wood / NOG; DOWEL;
TRENAIL; TREENAIL
pega / REMORA
Pegasus' captor / BELLEROPHON
Pegasus' mother / MEDUSA
pegu ironwood / AOLE
pejorative / DISPARAGING;
DEPRECIATIVE
Peke / LAPDOG
pelage / FUR
pelagic / MARINE; ABYSSAL,
OCEANIC
Peleg's son / REU
Peleus' brother / TELAMON
Peleus' father / AEACUS
Peleus' son / ACHILLES
Peleus' subjects / MYRMIDONS
Peleus' wife / ANTIGONE
pelf / MONEY; WEALTH
Pelican State / LOUISIANA
Pelion inhabitant / CENTAUR
pelite / SHALE
pellet / PILL; BULLET; MISSILE
pellicle / FILM, SCUM, SKIN
pellitory / BERTRAM; PARIETARY
pellmell / HASTILY; DISORDERED
pellucid / CLEAR, SHEER; LIMPID
pelma / SOLE
Peloponnesian city / SPARTA
Peloponnesus / MOREA

Pelops' father / TANTALUS
Pelops' son / ATREUS; THYESTES
pelota court / FRONTON
pelota implement / CESTA
pelt / FUR; FELL, HIDE, SKIN.
HURL; THROW; PEPPER
pelt of Siberian squirrel /
CALABAR, CALABER
peltast / INFANTRYMAN
peltate / SCUTIFORM
pelted with rocks / STONED
peltry / FURS; SKINS
pelu / KOWHAI
pelvic bone / ILIUM; SACRUM
pelvic bone, pert. to / ILIAC
pen / MEW; WRITE; INDITE. STY;
COOP, COTE; QUILL; CORRAL
penciling / OUTLINING
pend / HANG; AWAIT
pendant / BOB, FOB, LOP; LOCKET
pendent / HANGING;
SUSPENDED
pending / COMING; UNDECIDED.
DURING
pendulous / PENDENT; DROOPING
pendulum weight / BOB
Penelope's father / ICARIUS
Penelope's husband / ULYSSES;
ODYSSEUS
Penelope's occupation / WEAVING
Penelope's son / TELEMACHUS
penetralia / CORE; SANCTUARY
penetrant / ACUTE; SUBTLE
penetrate / BORE, GORE; ENTER,
REACH; FATHOM, PIERCE;
DISCERN
penetrating / KEEN; ACUTE, SHARP
penetrating flavor / TANG
penetration / INSIGHT;
PERFORATION
penfish / SQUID
penguin / GENTOO, JOHNNY
peninsula / NECK; CHERSONESE
peninsula in Black Sea / CRIMEA
pen name / PSEUDONYM
pen point / NEB, NIB
penal / PUNITIVE
penalize / FINE; MULCT; AMERCE
penalty / FINE; FORFEIT
penance / DECREE, SORROW;
ABSTINENCE, CONFESSION,
CONTRITION
pence / PENNIES
penchant / GENIUS; INCLINATION
pencil / LEAD, RAYS; BRUSH
penciled / DRAWN; WRITTEN
peninsula on Mediterranean /
ITALY; IBERIA
penitence / REGRET, SORROW
penitent / CONTRITE;
REPENTANT
penitential chant / MISERERE
penitential season / LENT

PEN NAMES (PSEUDONYMS)

	Pen Name
François Marie Arouet	VOLTAIRE
Henri Beyle	STENDHAL
Anne Brontë	ACTONBELL
Charlotte Brontë	CURRERBELL
Emily Brontë	ELLISBELL
John Dickson Carr	CARTERDICKSON
Samuel Langhorne Clemens	MARKTWAIN
Anthony Berkeley Cox	FRANCISILES
John Creasey	JJMARRIC
Frederic Dannay and Manfred Lee	ELLERYQUEEN
Charles Dickens	BOZ
Charles Lutwidge Dodgson	LEWISCARROLL
Amandine Aurore Dupin, Baroness Dudevant	GEORGESAND
Mary Anne Evans	GEORGEELIOT
Frederick Faust	MAXBRAND
Erle Stanley Gardner	AAFAIR
Frederick Glidd	LUKESHORT
Evan Hunter	EDMCBAIN
Charles Lamb	ELIA
C. Day Lewis	NICHOLASBLAKE
Elizabeth Mackintosh	JOSEPHINETEY
Herman Cyril McNeile	SAPPER
F. de Montcorbier	VILLON
Hector Hugh Munro	SAKI
William Sydney Porter	OHENRY
Louise de la Ramée	OUIDA
George Russell	AE
J. I. M. Stewart	MICHAELINNES
Julien Viaud	PIERRELOTI
Arthur Sarsfield Ward	SAXROHMER

penitentiary / GAOL, JAIL; PRISON; BRIDEWELL
penman / AUTHOR, WRITER
penmanship / HAND; STYLE
pennant / BANNER, PENNON
pennate / WINGED
pennies, c.f. / PENCE
penniless / POOR; BROKE, NEEDY
pennon / BANNER; PENNANT
Pennsylvania battlefield / GETTYSBURG
Pennsylvania capital / HARRIS-BURG
Pennsylvania city / ERIE, YORK
Pennsylvania Dutch county / LANCASTER
Pennsylvania port / ERIE

Pennsylvania river / GENESEE
Pennsylvania sect / AMISH; QUAKER; FRIENDS
Pennsylvania state nickname / KEYSTONE
penny / CENT; COPPER, DENIER, STIVER
penologist / KEEPER, WARDEN
pensile / HANGING, PENDENT
pensive / SAD; GRAVE, SOBER
pent / PENNED; CONFINED
pentacle / STAR; PENTAGRAM
Pentateuch / LAW; TORAH
Pentecost / WHITSUNDAY
penthouse / DEN; SHED; LEANTO
penuche / FUDGE
penumbra / HALFSHADOW

PENTATEUCH (TORAH), BOOKS OF THE

GENESIS
EXODUS
LEVITICUS
NUMBERS
DEUTERONOMY

penurious / POOR; NEEDY; SORDID
penury / WANT; POVERTY;
INDIGENCE
peon / PAWN, SERF
people / MEN; CLAN, ONES, RACE;
CROWD, DEMOS, FOLKS, LAITY,
TRIBE; BEINGS, FAMILY,
HUMANS, NATION, PUBLIC.
INHABIT; POPULATE
people of ancient Asia / SERES
people described by Othello /
ANTHROPOPHAGI
people of ancient Europe / GAULS
people of ancient Italy / SABINES
people living today / MODERNS
people long dead / ANCIENTS
people of Nigeria / BENI
people Odysseus visited /
LOTOPHAGI
people Gulliver visited /
LILLIPUTIANS
pep / VIM; VERVE, VIGOR;
GINGER
pep up / STIR; EXCITE; ENLIVEN
pepo / GOURD, MELON; SQUASH;
PUMPKIN; CUCUMBER
pepper / PELT; SPRINKLE. AVA;
KAVA; BETEL, CHILI; CAYENNE
pepperwort / CRESS
peppery / HOT; FIERY
peppery sauce / TABASCO
Pepys' preoccupation / DIARY
Pequod's captain / AHAB
Pequod's harpooner / QUEEQUEG
Pequod's mate / STUBB
Pequod's owner / PELEG; BILDAD
per / BY; FOR; THROUGH
per annum / YEARLY
per capita / EACH
per diem / DAILY
per se / INTRINSICALLY
peradventure / HAP. POSSIBLY
Perak town / IPOH
perambulate / WALK; TRAVERSE
perambulator / PRAM; CARRIAGE
perceivable / DISCERNIBLE
perceive / SEE; FEEL, KNOW;
SENSE
perceive through senses / FEEL
percentage / FRACTION;
PROPORTION
perceptible by feeling / TACTILE
perceptible by hearing / AUDIBLE
perceptible by seeing / VISIBLE
perception / SENSE; ACUMEN
perceptive / SENSITIVE
perch / SIT; ROOST. FISH, POLE,
SEAT, SLAT
perchance / PERHAPS
perchlike fish / BASS; DARTER
percolate / OOZE, SEEP; LEACH;
FILTER
percussion / IMPACT; STRIKING

percussion cutter / GAD; DRILL;
CHISEL
percussion instrument / BELL,
DRUM, GONG, TRAP; PIATTI;
CYMBALS; TRIANGLE
perdition / LOSS, RUIN
perdu / HIDDEN; FORLORN
perdurable / ETERNAL
peregrine / FALCON. ALIEN;
EXOTIC; FOREIGN
peremptory / FINAL; ABSOLUTE,
DECISIVE
perennial / LASTING, UNDYING;
CONSTANT, ENDURING
perennial plant / PIA; MADDER;
RHUBARB; DIANTHUS,
HESPERIS; COLUMBINE,
COREOPSIS
perfect / PURE; IDEAL, MODEL,
WHOLE; ENTIRE; COMPLETE,
FINISHED, FLAWLESS
perfect, c.f. / TELEO
perfection / EXCELLENCE
perfectionist / PURIST;
PRECISIAN
perfectly / FULLY; EXACTLY
perfecto / CIGAR
perfervid / EAGER; ARDENT
perfidious / FALSE; DISLOYAL
perfidious person / TRAITOR;
RECREANT
perfidy / TREASON; DUPLICITY
perforate / BORE; DRILL; PIERCE,
RIDDLE; PUNCTURE;
TEREBRATE
perforated disk / WASHER
perforated globe / BEAD
perforated implement / SIEVE;
COLANDER, STRAINER
perforated template / STENCIL
perforation / HOLE; EYELET
perform / DO; ACT; PLAY; ENACT;
FULFIL
perform again / BIS; REDO; REACT
perform alone / SOLO
perform formally / SOLEMNIZE
perform offhand / ADLIB;
IMPROVISE
perform poorly / FAIL, FLUB
performance / ACT; DEED;
EXPLOIT; EXECUTION
performer / DOER; ACTOR; ARTIST
performing artist / ARTISTE
perfume / ATAR, ODOR, OTTO;
AROMA, ATTAR, CENSE, SCENT,
SMALL
perfume base / MUSK
perfume of roses / ATTAR
perfumed pad / SACHET
perfunctory / HASTY; AIMLESS;
CARELESS
perfuse / POUR; SPREAD;
SPRINKLE

Pergamene dynasty / ATTALID
pergola / ARBOR; TRELLIS
perhaps / HAPLY, MAYBE; MAYHAP
peri / FAIRY, SYLPH
periapt / CHARM; ANADEM, AMULET
pericarp / HUSK
Pericles' mistress / ASPASIA
pericope / TEXT
perigee's opposite / APOGEE
peril / RISK; DANGER, MENACE
period / AGE, DOT, END, EON, ERA; DATE, TIME; CYCLE, EPOCH, LIMIT
period at beginning / DAWN
period between day and night / TWILIGHT
period of fasting / LENT
period of history / ERA; TIME; EPOCH
period of a hundred years / CENTURY
period preceding / EVE
period of prosperity / UP; BOOM
period of a thousand years / CHILIAD
period of time / DAY, EON, ERA; HOUR, TERM, WEEK, YEAR; EPOCH, MONTH; DECADE, MINUTE, SECOND
period of two hundred years / BICENTENARY
period when it is dark / NIGHT
period when it is light / DAY
period of year / MONTH; SEASON
periodic / ETESIAN, REGULAR
periodical / MAGAZINE. RECURRENT
peripatetic / MOVING; ITINERANT
periphery / RIM; EDGES; PERIMETER
perique / TOBACCO
perish / DIE; FADE; CEASE, DECAY
perish with hunger / STARVE
perishable / MORTAL; TRANSIENT
perishing / DAMNED; FREEZING
perissodactyl / HORSE, RHINO
periwinkle / SNAIL; MYRTLE
perjury / FORSWEARING
perky / JAUNTY
permanent / FIXED; STABLE; ABIDING, DURABLE, LASTING
permeable / POROUS
permeate / IMBUE
permeating / PERVASIVE
permission / LEAVE; CONSENT
permission to enter / VISA
permission to leave / CONGE
permission to use / LOAN
permit / LET; ALLOW; ENDURE
permit for absence / VISA; EXEAT
permitted / LICIT; KOSHER

permutation / REARRANGEMENT
permute / ALTER; CHANGE
pernicious / BAD; EVIL; FATAL; DEADLY; BANEFUL, NOISOME
pernickety / FUSSY; OVERNICE
perorate / BOMBAST, DECLAIM
peroration / SUMMATION
peroxide / BLEACHED
perpendicular / SHEER; UPRIGHT. SINE; APOTHEM
perpetrate / DO; COMMIT
perpetration / OFFENSE
perpetual / CHRONIC, ENDLESS, ETERNAL; CONSTANT
perpetually / EVER
perplex / VEX; POSE; ANNOY, BESET, WORRY; BAFFLE
perplexing question / KNOT; PUZZLER; CONUNDRUM
perplexity / DOUBT; MYSTERY
perquisite / FEE; GIFT; BONUS
persecute / ANNOY, HARRY, TEASE; BADGER, HARASS
Persephone / CORA, KORE; DESPOINA
Persephone's child / ZAGREUS
Persephone's husband / HADES
Persephone's mother / DEMETER
Persepolis' founder / DARIUS
Perseus' city / MYCENAE
Perseus' mother / DANAE
Perseus' victim / MEDUSA
Perseus' wife / ANDROMEDA
perseverance / GRIT; PERSISTENCE
persevere / CONTINUE
Persia / IRAN. See also Iran
Persian / MEDE. IRANI
Persian angel of moon / MAH
Persian bird / BULBUL
Persian coin / KRAN, RIAL; DARIC
Persian demigod / YIMA
Persian dynasty / SASSANID
Persian epic poet / FIRDAUSI
Persian fairy / PERI
Persian gateway / DAR
Persian gazelle / CORA
Persian governor / SATRAP
Persian hymns / GATHAS
Persian king / CYRUS; DARIUS, XERXES; AHASUERUS; ARTAXERXES
Persian lyric poem / GHAZAL
Persian measure of distance / FARSAKH; PARASANG
Persian mystic / SUFI
Persian poet / OMAR; HAFIZ
Persian porcelain / GOMBROON
Persian priest / MAGUS
Persian race / LUR; KURD
Persian religion / BABISM
Persian rug / SENNA; NAMMAD
Persian ruler / SHAH

Persian sacred books / AVESTA
Persian title / MIR; AZAM, KHAN, SHAH; MIRZA
Persian water wheel / NORIA
Persian weight / SER; ABAS, SANG; ABBAS; GANDUM, MISKAL. NAKHOD
persiflage / BANTER; CHATTER
persimmon / GAB; GAUB; CHAPOTE
persist / LAST; ENDURE, REMAIN
persistence / OBSTINACY
persistent / CONSTANT
persistent assault / SIEGE
persistent transgression / SIN
person / ONE; SELF, SOUL; BEING
person acting as sheriff / ELISOR
person addressed / YE; YOU; THOU
person of consequence / SOMEONE
person doing servile work / MENIAL
person enamored of self / NARCISSIST
person with experience / VETERAN
person of foresight / SAGE, SEER
person holding office / IN
person with loud voice / STENTOR
person owing money / DEBTOR
person running for office / CANDIDATE
person who serves / MENIAL
person with too many scruples / PRIG
personable / COMELY
personage / DON, MAN; NIBS
personal / PRIVATE
personal belongings / GEAR; TRAPS
personal interest / SELF
personal journal / DIARY
personal pronoun / HE, IT, WE; SHE, YOU; THEY
personality / IT; EGO; SELF
personalized ring / SIGNET
personification / EMBODIMENT
personification of Britain / JOHNBULL
personification of France / MARIANNE
personification of U.S. / UNCLESAM
personified / INCARNATE
personnel / CREW; STAFF
persons collectively / FOLKS
perspective / VIEW; SLANT, VISTA
perspicacious / ABLE; ASTUTE
perspicacity / ACUMEN
perspicuity / CLARITY
perspicuous / CLEAR, LUCID, PLAIN; OBVIOUS
perspiration / SUDOR, SWEAT
perspire / EXUDE, SWEAT

persuade / COAX, LEAD, MOVE, URGE; IMPEL
persuade by reason / CONVINCE
persuasion / CREED; BELIEF
persuasive / SOUND; COGENT; INDUCING
pert / BOLD, FREE; BRISK, SASSY, SAUCY, SMART; LIVELY; FORWARD
pert child / URCHIN
pert girl / CHIT, MINX; HUSSY
pertain / BELONG, RELATE
pertaining to / ANENT
pertaining to branches / RAMAL
pertaining to a city / URBAN
pertaining to fields / AGRARIAN
pertaining to mice / MURINE
pertaining to the palm / VOLAR
pertaining to strong feeling / EMOTIONAL
pertaining to what is taught / DOCTRINAL
Perth river / TAY; FORTH
pertinacious / FIRM; DOGGED, MULISH, STANCH
pertinence / SUITABILITY
pertinent / APT, FIT, PAT; PROPER; ADAPTED, FITTING, GERMANE
pertness / SAUCE
perturb / VEX; UPSET; AGITATE, DERANGE, DISTURB
Peru capital / LIMA
Peru-Chile disputed area / TACNA; TACNAARICA
peruke / WIG; PERIWIG
peruse / CON; READ, SCAN
Peruvian bird / YUTA, YUTU
Peruvian chieftain / INCA
Peruvian city / ICA; LIMA; CALLAO
Peruvian coin / SOL; DINERO
Peruvian dance / CUECA
Peruvian deity / CON; VIRACOCHA
Peruvian desert region / TACNA
Peruvian goddess / MAMA
Peruvian Indian / ANDE, ANTI, BORO, CANA, INCA, INKA, LAMA, PEBA, PIBA, PIRO, YNCA; CAMPA, CHIMU, CHOLO, COLAN, COLLA, COLLO, YUNCA; CHANCA, QUICHU; QUECHUA
Peruvian lake / TITICACA
Peruvian money / SOL
Peruvian mountain / HUASCARAN
Peruvian mountains / ANDES
Peruvian native language / AYMARA; QUECHUA
Peruvian plant / OCA
Peruvian river / NAPO; MARANON
Peruvian ruminant / PACO; LLAMA; ALPACA, VICUNA
Peruvian tinamou / YUTA, YUTU
Peruvian volcano / MISTI
pervade / FILL; IMBUE; PERMEATE

pervasive / SUFFUSIVE
perverse / BAD; CROSS, SURLY
pervert / TWIST; CORRUPT, DISTORT
perverted / WRY
pervicacious / WILLFUL; STUBBORN
pervious / OPEN; PERMEABLE
pesky / TROUBLESOME
peso / DURO; DOLLAR
pessimist / CYNIC
pessimistic / GLOOMY; DOUBTFUL
pest / BANE, BORE; CURSE; BLIGHT, PLAGUE; SCOURGE; NUISANCE
pester / NAG, VEX; FRET, GALL; ANNOY, CHAFE, HARRY, TEASE; BADGER, BOTHER, HARASS
pestiferous child / BRAT
pestilence / PEST; PLAGUE; SCOURGE
pestilent / NOXIOUS
pestilential / FATAL; DEADLY; BANEFUL, NOXIOUS
pestle / PILUM; MULLER
pestle's receptacle / METATE, MORTAR
pet / CADE, NECK; COSSET, FONDLE, HUFF; DARLING; FAVORITE
pet lamb / CADE; COSSET
pet name / DIMINUTIVE
petals / COROLLA
petard / FIRECRACKER
Peter the Great's coruler / IVAN
peter out / FAIL, TIRE; WEARY
Peter Pan's dog / NANA
Peter Pan's invisible friend / TINKERBELL
Peter Pan's pirate / HOOK, SMEE
peterman / BURGLAR; SAFECRACKER
petiole / STEM; STALK, STIPE
petit / SMALL; LITTLE
petite / NEAT, TRIM
petition / ASK, BEG, SUE; APPEAL; REQUEST, PLEA, SUIT; PRAYER
petitioner / APPLICANT
Petrarch's love / LAURA
petrified animal / FOSSIL
petrified plants / COAL
petrify / STUPEFY; ASTONISH
petrol / GAS; GASOLINE
petroleum derivative / BENZINE, NAPHTHA; GASOLINE
petrous / HARD; STONY
petticoat / SLIP; JUPON; KIRTLE, FEMININE, WOMANISH
petticoat trimming / FALBALA; FURBELOW
pettifogger / SHYSTER

pettiness / UNIMPORTANCE
petting / SPARKING
pettish / SULKY; FRETFUL
petty / MEAN; SMALL; LITTLE; INFERIOR, TRIFLING
petty bribe / SOP
petty objection / CAVIL
petty officer / NONCOM
petty prince / SATRAP
petty quarrel / MIFF, SPAT, TIFF
petty thief / PILFERER
petulant / CROSS, SHORT; FRETFUL
pew / SEAT; BENCH
pewee / PHOEBE
pewit / GULL; LAPWING
pewter coin / TRA
peyote / CACTUS, MESCAL
peyote drug / MESCALINE
pezizold / CUPSHAPED
Phaedra's husband / THESEUS
Phaedra's stepson / HIPPOLYTUS
phalanger / AIT; CUSCUS, POSSUM
phalanx / BODY; ARRAY, FORCE
phantasm / GHOST; DELUSION, ILLUSION
phantasy / IMAGINATION
phantom / GHOST, UMBRA; SHADOW, SPIRIT; EIDOLON, SPECTER
pharaoh / TUT; PEPI, SETI; MENES
pharaoh's chicken / VULTURE
pharaoh's crown / PSCHENT
pharisee / HYPOCRITE
pharmacist / DRUGGIST; APOTHECARY
pharmacy / DRUGSTORE
pharos / LIGHT; BEACON; LIGHTHOUSE
phase / SIDE; FACET, STAGE
pheasant / CHIR, GUAN; CHEER, MONAL; LEIPOA; TRAGOPAN; FRANCOLIN
pheasant brood / NID, NYE; NIDE
phial / VIAL; BOTTLE
Phidias' statue / ATHENA
Philadelphia school / DREXEL, TEMPLE
philander / FLIRT; TRIFLE
philanderer / ROUE; COQUETTE
philanthropic / KIND; LOVING; CHARITABLE
Philemon's wife / BAUCIS
Philippi victor / ANTONY
philippic / SCREED, TIRADE
Philippine aborigine / ATA, ITA
Philippine bay / ILLANA
Philippine boat / BANCA, CASCO
Philippine buffalo / CARABAO, TIMARAU
Philippine capital / MANILA, QUEZON

Philippine cedar / KALANTAS
Philippine chief / DATO, DATU; DATTO
Philippine dwarf race / AETA; NEGRITO
Philippine fennel / ANISE
Philippine fetish / ANITO
Philippine foodstuff / POI; SABA
Philippine hemp / ABACA; LINAGA
Philippine hemp textile / SABA
Philippine island / CEBU; LEYTE, PANAY, SAMAR; MINDANAO
Philippine knife / BOLO
Philippine language / ATA; MORO, TINO; BIKOL, ILOCO, TAGAL; IGOROT; ILOCANO, ILOKANO, TAGALOG
Philippine liquid measure / CHUPA, GANTA; APATAN
Philippine lizard / IBID, IBIT
Philippine mahogany / ASANA, NARRA
Philippine monkey / MACHIN
Philippine Moslem / MORO
Philippine mountain / APO, IBA
Philippine native / ATA, ITA; AETA, MORO, SULU, TINO; IGOROT; ILOCANO, ILOKANO, TAGALOG, VISAYAN
Philippine negrito / ATA, ITA; AETA
Philippine palm / NIPA
Philippine palm wine / BENO, BINO
Philippine parrot / ABACAY; CALANGAY
Philippine peasant / TAO
Philippine poisonous tree / LIGAS
Philippine rice / PAGA; MACAN
Philippine rice beer / PANGASI
Philippine sash / TAPIS
Philippine silk fabric / HUSI
Philippine skirt / SAYA
Philippine tree / DAO, IBA, IYO, TAO, TUA, TUI; ACLE, BOGO, DITA, IFIL, IPIL, TUWI, YPIL; AMAGA, CAHUY, LAUAN; CALANTAS
Philippine tribe / ATA; MORO
Philippine volcano / APO; TAAL
Philippine weapon / BOLO
philistine / PROSAIC; UNCULTURED
Philistine champion / GOLIATH
Philistine city / GATH, GAZA; EKRON; ASHDOD
Philistine deity / BAAL; DAGON
Philistine foe / DAVID; SAMSON
philodox / DOGMATIST
philomel / NIGHTINGALE
philosopher / SAGE
philosopher's disciples / SECT

philosopher's stone / ELIXIR
philosophical / CALM, COOL; SOUND; SEDATE; STOICAL; PLATONIC
philosophical doctrine / BELIEF
philosophical element / RECT
philosophical theory / MONISM
philosophize / REASON
philosophy / WISDOM; GENERALISM
Phineus' tormentors / HARPIES
phlegm / MUCUS; PITUITE
phlegmatic / COLD, DULL, TAME; HEAVY; FRIGID; SLUGGISH
phloem / BAST; TISSUE
phobia / FEAR; DREAD; AVERSION
phoca / SEAL
Phocian city / DELPHI
phoebe / MOON; PEWEE, PEWIT
phoebus / SOL, SUN; APOLLO
Phoenician capital / TYRE
Phoenician colony / CARTHAGE
Phoenician deity / BAAL; BALTIS; ASTARTE
Phoenician invention / ALPHABET
Phoenician port / TYRE; SIDON
phoned / CALLED, DIALED
phonetic notation system / IPA
phonetic sign / LETTER, SYMBOL
phonetic sound / CLICK; LABIAL; PALATAL
phonograph record / DISC; PLATTER
phony / FAKE; CROOKED
phosphate / SODA; APATITE
photo / STAT; PICTURE, TINTYPE; SNAPSHOT
photograph / MUG; FILM, SNAP; PRINT
photograph bath / FIXER, TONER; REDUCER; DEVELOPER
photograph book / ALBUM
photographer / CAMERAMAN
photography solution / HYPO
photogravure inventor / KLIETSCH
photoplay / MOVIE; CINEMA
photostat / PRINT
phrase / TERM; IDIOM, MOTTO; CLAUSE, SLOGAN
phraseology / STYLE; MANNER; DICTION
phratry / CLAN
Phrixus' father / ATHAMAS
Phrixus' gift to Aeetes / GOLDENFLEECE
Phrixus' mother / NEPHELE
Phrixus' sister / HELLE
Phrixus' stepmother / INO
Phrixus' wife / CHALCIOPE
Phrygian cap / LIBERTYCAP
Phrygian cap wearer / MARIANNE
Phrygian deity / MEN; ATYS; ATTIS

Phrygian king / MIDAS
phthisis / TB; CONSUMPTION
physical / SOMAL; SOMATIC; MATERIAL, SENSIBLE, TANGIBLE
physical constitution / FRAME
physical pain / ACHE, KINK; DOLOR
physician / DOC; LEECH, MEDIC; DOCTOR, HEALER, MEDICO; INTERNIST
physician, pert. to / IATRIC
physician's association / AMA
physician's symbol / CADUCEUS
physiognomy / PAN; FACE, PHIZ
physiological person / BION
pi / MESS; JUMBLE
piacevole / PLEASANTLY
piacular / EXPIATORY
pian / YAWS; FRAMBESIA
pianissimo / PP
piano / SPINET; PIANOFORTE
piano keys / IVORIES; EIGHTY-EIGHT
piano repairman / TUNER
piano studies / ETUDES
pianolike instrument / ORGAN; CELESTE
piaster / DOLLAR
piazza / SQUARE; PORTICO, VERANDA
pibroch / PIPETUNE
pica / MAGPIE; GEOPHAGY
Picardy river / SOMME
picaresque / ROGUISH; RASCALLY
picaroon / ROGUE; PIRATE, ROBBER
picayune / SMALL; TRIFLING
piccolo / FLUTE
pick / GET, ROB; CULL; CLEAN, PLUCK; CHOOSE, GATHER, NIBBLE
pick at / CARP; CAVIL
pick out / CULL; GLEAN; SELECT
pick up / PECK; GLEAN
pickaxlike tool / MATTOCK
picket / PALE; STAKE, SENTRY; OUTPOST
pickle / CORN; SOUSE; MARINATE, PRESERVE. ALEC, DILL; BRINE
pickled / DRUNK
pickled bamboo shoots / ACHAR
pickled meat / SOUSE
pickling herb / DILL; TURMERIC
pickling liquid / BRINE; MARINADE
picklock / WOOL; THIEF
pickpocket / DIP; WIRE; BOOSTER
picnic / JUNKET, OUTING
picnic basket / HAMPER
pictorial / GRAPHIC; ILLUSTRATED
pictorial caricature / CARTOON

picture / ICON; IMAGE, PHOTO, PRINT; PASTEL; DRAWING; LIKENESS, PAINTING, PORTRAIT. DRAW; PAINT
picture made with crayons / PASTEL
picture made with fragments / MOSAIC; COLLAGE
picture mounting / MAT; MATTE
picture puzzle / REBUS; JIGSAW
picture support / EASEL, STAND
picture tube / KINESCOPE
picture within camera / IMAGE
pictures / MOVIES
picturesque / SCENIC; ROMANTIC
Picus' son / FAUNUS
piddling / PETTY; TRIFLING
pie / MAGPIE, PASTRY
piebald horse / PINTO
piece / BIT, GUN; CHIP, COIN, LUMP, PART, PLAY; DRAMA, PATCH
piece broken off / CHIP; SLIVER; SPLINTER
piece of butter / PAT
piece of cloth / RAG; REMNANT
piece of eight / REAL
piece of furniture / SOFA; CHAIR, DIVAN, TABLE
piece of gossip / RUMOR
piece of ground / LOT; PLAT
piece of ice / CUBE, FLOE
piece inserted / SHIM; INSET
piece of log / SLAB
piece of lumber / PLANK
piece of money / CASH, COIN
piece of mosaic tile / TESSERA
piece of ordnance / CANNON
piece out / EKE; FILL
piece of paper / SLIP; SHEET
piece put in / INSET; GUSSET
piece of real property / LOT; PLAT, PLOT
piece of sculpture / STATUE
piece of soap / CAKE, FLAKE
piece of turf / SOD; PEAT; DIVOT
piece of wood / SLAT; SPRAG
pied / SPOTTED; VARIEGATED
pied horse / PINTO
Piedmontese ruling house / SAVOY
pie-eyed / DRUNK
pieplant / RHUBARB
pier / KEY; ANTA, DOCK, MOLE, QUAI, QUAY; JETTY, WHARF
pier glass / MIRROR
pier supports / PILINGS
pierce / GORE, STAB; DRILL, ENTER
pierce for cooking / SPIT
pierce many times / RIDDLE
pierce with a needle / PRICK
pierce with a spear / IMPALE
piercing / KEEN; SHARP

piercing tool / AWL
pierhead / DOCK; WHARF
Pierides / MUSES
Pierrot's gal / PIERRETTE
piety / GRACE; DEVOTION,
 SANCTITY
piffle / TWADDLE; NONSENSE
pig / HOG, SOW; INGOT, SHOAT,
 SHOTE, SWINE
pig brood / FARROW
pig pen / STY; FRANK
pigeon / NUN; BARB, DOVE;
 SQUAB
pigeon berry / POKE; SCOKE
pigeon grass / FOXTAIL
pigeon hawk / MERLIN
pigeon house / COTE; DOVECOT
pigeon pea / DAL, TUR
pigfish / GRUNT, PORGY;
 WRASSE
piggish / GREEDY; GLUTTONOUS
piglike animal / PECCARY
pigment / COLOR, PAINT
pigment for paint / OCHER
pigmy / DWARF, GNOME
pignorate / PAWN; PLEDGE
pignut / HICKORY
pigs / SWINE
pigs' feet / TROTTERS;
 PETTITOES
pigtail / CUE; BRAID, QUEUE
pigweed / KNOTWEED, PURSLANE
pike / GED; DORE, HOOK, ROAD;
 LUCET; HIGHWAY
pike genus / ESOX
pikelike fish / GAR; LUCE;
 MUSKIE, ROBALO
piker / WELCHER; TIGHTWAD
pilaster / ANTA, PIER; COLUMN
pilchard / SARDINE
pilcrow / FIST
pile / AMASS; COLLECT. NAP;
 HEAP; SPILE, STACK
pile for burning / PYRE
pile driver / RAM; HAMMER
pile of earth / HILL; MOUNT
pile of hay / MOW; RICK
pile of lumber / STACK
pileated / CRESTED
pile-driver weight / TUP
pileous / HAIRY
pilfer / ROB; FILCH, STEAL
pilferer / THIEF
pilgarlic / BALDHEAD
pilgrim / PALMER; TRAVELER
Pilgrim leader / STANDISH
pilgrimage city / KUM; MECCA;
 JERUSALEM
pilgrimage to Mecca / HADJ, HAJJ
piliferous / HAIRY
pill / BOLUS; PELLET
pill bug / SLATER, SOWBUG

pillage / LOOT, SACK; RIFLE,
 SPOIL. BOOTY; RAPINE
pillager / RAIDER; MARAUDER
pillar / LAT; PIER, POST, PROP;
 SHAFT, STELA, STELE; COLUMN
pillar coming to a point / OBELISK
pillar in mine / JAMB
pillarlike / STELAR
pillory / CANGUE, STOCKS
pillow / BOLSTER, CUSHION
pillow case / SHAM, SLIP, TICK
pilose / HAIRY
pilot / LEAD; GUIDE, STEER;
 CONVOY, DIRECT, ESCORT;
 CONDUCT
pilot fish / AMBERFISH
pilus / HAIR
Piman Indian / CORA, JOVA, MAYO,
 PIMA, XOVA, YAKI; YAQUI
pimento / ALLSPICE
pimiento / PEPPER
pimping / PUNY; PETTY
pimple / BLOTCH, PAPULE;
 PUSTULE
pin / FASTEN. NOG, PEG; BOLT;
 BADGE; BROOCH; SKITTLE
pin for bowling / SKITTLE
pin for broiling meat / SKEWER
pin in carpentry / DOWEL
pin in clavichord / TANGENT
pin in golf / FLAG
pin in gunwale / THOLE
pin for machinery / COTTER
pin in rifle / TIGE
pin for splicing rope / FID
pin of wood / PEG; COAK; DOWEL
pinafore / TIER; APRON
pincer / CHELA
pincers / TONGS; NIPPERS
pinch / NAB, NIP; SQUEEZE
pinch and twist / TWEAK
pinchbeck / SHAM; PHONY
pinched by frost / URLED
Pindaric poem / ODE
pindling / PUNY; SICKLY;
 WASTING
pine / FADE, FLAG, MOPE, SINK
pine cone / STROBILE
pine extract / AMBER, RESIN
pine for / YEARN
pine nut / PINON
pine tree / CONIFER
pine tree exudation / AMBER,
 RESIN
Pine Tree State / MAINE
pineapple / NANA, PINA; ANANA
pinecone shaped / PINEAL
pingpong racket / BAT; PADDLE
pinguid / FAT; GREASY
pinhead / NITWIT
pining / LANGUISHING
pinion / WING; SHACKLE. BIND

pink / PUNCH; PIERCE; SCALLOP.
ROSE; SCARLET; CARNATION.
ROSY
pinna / EAR, FIN; FEATHER
pinnacle / TOP, TOR; ACME, APEX;
CREST; TURRET
pinnacle of ice / SERAC
pinnacle ornament / EPI; FINIAL
pinner / POUNDKEEPER
pinning / DIRT; GRAVEL; PEBBLES
pinniped / SEAL; WALRUS
pinochle score / MELD
pinochle term / DIX; MARRIAGE
pintado / CERO, SIER; SIERRA
pintail / SMEE
pioneer / SETTLER; COLONIST
pious / DEVOUT; RELIGIOUS
pipe / FLUE, HOSE, TUBE; BRIAR,
BRIER; DUDEEN, HOOKAH;
CALUMET
pipe die / DOD
pipe fitting / ELL, TEE; NIPPLE
pipe with flared ends / HUB; HUBB
pipe guiding liquid / SPOUT;
GUTTER
pipelike / TUBULAR
piper / GURNARD
piper's son / TOM
pipette / TUBE; STRAW
pipit / MUDLARK, TITLARK
piquant / KEEN, RACY, TART;
SALTY
piquant sauce / REMOLADE
pique / DUDGEON, UMBRAGE
piquet term / PIC; CAPOT, REPIC
pirate / ROVER; CORSAIR
pirate flag / ROGER
Pirithous' best friend / THESEUS
Pirithous' father / IXION
Pirithous' mother / DIA
Pirithous' subjects / LAPITHS
Pirithous' wife / HIPPODAMIA
piroshki-like food / TURNOVER
pis aller / SHIFT; STOPGAP
Pisa spectacle / TOWER
piscator / ANGLER
piscine / ICHTHYIC
pisgah / NEBO
pismire / ANT; EMMET
pistil / OVARY
pistol / DAG, GUN; DAGG; HEATER;
SIDEARM; REVOLVER
pistol sheath / HOLSTER
piston / VALVE; CYLINDER
pit / GULF, HOLE, MINE, TRAP;
ABYSS, FOSSA, GRAVE, HADES,
STONE
pit a pat / BEAT; PALPITATION
Pitcairn settlers / MUTINEERS
pitch / FIX, SET; CAST, FALL,
HURL, TOSS; FLING. KEY, TAR
pitch tents / ENCAMP

pitcher / JUG; EWER, OLLA, TOBY;
CRUSE; TOSSER
pitcher and catcher / BATTERY
pitcher room / EWERY
pitcher's area / BOX; SLAB;
MOUND; RUBBER
pitcher's edge / LIP
pitcher's handle / EAR; ANSA
pitcher's illegal move / BALK
piteous / SAD; WOEFUL; DOLEFUL
pitfall / TRAP; SNARE; DANGER
pith / NUB; CORE, GIST, SOUL;
KERNEL, MARROW
pith helmet / TOPI; TOPEE
pithiest / MEATIEST
pithy / BRIEF, TERSE; COGENT
pithy saying / MOT; ADAGE
pitiable / FORLORN
pitiful / SORRY; PALTRY
pitiless / HARD; CRUEL; RUTHLESS
pittance / ALMS, DOLE;
ALLOWANCE
pitted / DENTED; FOVEATE
Pittsburgh baseball team /
PIRATES
Pittsburgh football team /
STEELERS
pituitary gland / HYPOPHYSIS
pituite / PHLEGM
pity / RUTH; MERCY; SYMPATHY
pityriasis / DANDRUFF
pityroid / SCALY
pity-rousing / PATHETIC
pivot / SLUE, TURN; HINGE. PIN
pivot bearing / JEWEL
pivot pin / PINTLE
pivotal point / AXIS; FULCRUM
pivoted catch / RATCHET
pixie / ELF; PIXY; SPRITE
pixilated / MAD, ODD; CRAZY
pizzeria specialty / PIZZA
placable / EASY; TRACTABLE
placard / BILL, SIGN; POSTER
placate / SOOTHE; APPEASE
place / AREA, LIEU, POST, RANK,
SEAT, SITE, SPOT; ABODE,
ESTRE, LOCUS, STEAD; LOCALE,
OFFICE; POSITION. FIX, LAY,
PUT, SET
place, pert. to / TOPICAL
place of activity / HUB; HIVE
place of amusement / CONEY-
ISLAND
place to anchor / PORT; HARBOR
place apart / ENISLE; ISOLATE
place of bliss / EDEN; HEAVEN;
PARADISE
place of business / OFFICE
place burden on / LADE, LOAD
place to carry boats / PORTAGE
place case is tried / COURT,
VENUE

place of Christ's first miracle / CANA
place of concealment / LAIR; CACHE
place of confinement / PEN; CELL
place of conflict / ARENA
place of darkness / EREBUS
place of delight / EDEN; PARADISE
place down / LAY, SET
place to eat / INN; CAFE, MESS; DINER, GRILL
place of education / SCHOOL; ACADEMY, COLLEGE; SEMINARY
place elsewhere / RELOCATE
place of entry / DOOR, PORT
place firmly / FASTEN
place of great noise / BEDLAM
place in ground / PLANT
place to grow plants / GARDEN; HOTHOUSE
place of honor / HEAD
place of justice / BAR; COURT
place in juxtaposition / APPOSE
place under legal obligation / RESTRAIN
place of legal trial / VENUE
place levy on / TAX; ASSESS
place mat / DOILY
place where metal is worked / MILL; FORGE
place names / TOPONYMY
place in new order / REARRANGE
place with no exit / CULDESAC
place of occurrence / SCENE
place in office / SEAT; ELECT
place in order / FILE; ARRANGE
place in pairs / GEMINATE
place of perdition / HELL
place of perfect harmony / UTOPIA
place under a promise / BIND
place of refuge / GITE, HOME, PORT; ASYLUM, HARBOR
place in restraint / JAIL; ARREST
place in retirement / WITHDRAW
place of retirement / RETREAT
place in rows / ALIGN, ALINE
place of sacrifice / ALTAR
place for safe keeping / VAULT
place of safety / HAVEN
place to store things / RACK; SHELF
place for storing grain / BIN; CRIB, SILO
place to swim / POOL; BEACH
place of trade / MART; STORE
place to warm up / BULLPEN
place of worship / ALTAR; CHAPEL, CHURCH, TEMPLE
placed at intervals / SPACED
placed in juxtaposition / APPOSED
places / PUTS. LOCI

placid / CALM, MILD; QUIET, SUANT; SERENE; PACIFIC; COMPOSED
plaga / STREAK, STRIPE
plagiarize / COPY, CRIB; PIRATE
plague / VEX; FRET, GALL, PEST; ANNOY, CHAFE, TAUNT
plaguy / ANNOYING
plaice / FLUKE; FLATFISH, FLOUNDER
plaid / MAUD; TARTAN
plain / BARE, EASY, EVEN, FLAT, OPEN, UGLY; CLEAR, FRANK, LEVEL; CANDID. CHOL, WOLD; LLANO, PAMPA, VELDT, WEALD; STEPPE, TUNDRA; SAVANNA
plain in Arctic / TUNDRA
plain in Argentina / PAMPA
plain in Asia / CHOL
plain clothes / MUFTI
plain in India / MAIDAN
plain in Japan / HARA
plain in North America / PRAIRIE
plain in Palestine / JEZREEL
plain in Russia / STEPPE
plain in South Africa / VELD
plain in South America / CAMPO, LLANO
plainly woven / UNI
Plains Indian / CREE, CROW, HOHE; KIOWA, OSAGE, PONCA, TETON
plaint / LAMENT
plaintiff / COMPLAINANT
plaintive / SAD; WOEFUL; DOLEFUL
plaintive melody / DIRGE
plaintively / PITEOUSLY
plait / PLY; BRAID; INTERWEAVE
plaited / PLICATE
plan / DESIGN, DEVISE; ARRANGE. PLAT; DRAFT; METHOD, SCHEME
plan of action / SCHEME
plan of procedure / PROGRAM; SCHEDULE
planate / FLAT
planche / TRAY
planchet / BLANK
planchette / POINTER
plane / EVEN, FLAT; LEVEL. JET
plane curve / ELLIPSE; PARABOLA
plane figure / CIRCLE; TRIANGLE
plane of gem / FACET
plane handle / TOTE
plane tree / CHINAR; SYCAMORE
planetarium / ORRERY
planetoid / ASTEROID
planet's path / ORBIT
plangent / BEATING; RESOUNDING

PLANETS AND THEIR SATELLITES

	Satellites
Mercury	—
Venus	—
Earth	MOON
Mars	PHOBOS, DEIMOS
Jupiter	IO, EUROPA, GANYMEDE, CALLISTO, 8 others numbered
Saturn	JANUS, MIMAS, ENCELADUS, TETHYS, DIONE, RHEA, TITAN, HYPERION, IAPETUS, PHOEBE
Uranus	MIRANDA, ARIEL, UMBRIEL, TITANIA, OBERON
Neptune	TRITON, NEREID
Pluto	—

Related word: ASTEROID

---

plangorous / WAILING
plank / SLAB; BOARD. PAY
plank's curve / SNY
plank's width / STRAKE
plankton / PLANKTER
planner / DESIGNER, PROVIDER
plant / SOW; SEED. FACTORY
plant apoplexy / ESCA
plant axis / STALK
plant breathing pore / STOMA
plant bud / CION
plant bulb / CAMASS
plant cell / SPORE
plant change of form / ECAD
plant cutting / SLIP; PHYTON
plant disease / ROT; RUST, SCAB, SMUT; MILDEW
plant embryo / GERM, SEED
plant exudation / GUM, LAC; RESIN, ROSIN; RUBBER
plant feeder / ROOT
plant insect / MITE; APHID
plant joined to another / GRAFT
plant life / FLORA
plant like lily / ALOE; CAMAS
plant louse / APHID
plant used in medicine / ALOE; SENNA
plant organ / STOMA; PISTIL
plant part / LEAF, ROOT, STEM; STALK; TENDRIL
plant of pink family / CAMPION
plant of the sea / ALGA; ENALID
plant of sedge family / BULRUSH
plant shoot / CION; GRAFT
plant used for soap / AMOLE
plant stem / CAULIS
plant substance / SAP; AMBER
plant used for ropes, bags, mats / JUTE
plantain / BANANA; SITFAST; SNAKEWEED
plantain lily / HOSTA

plantation / GROVE; COLONY; LATIFUNDIUM
planter / FARMER
plantigrade mammal / BEAR
planting device / DRILL; SEEDER
plants of an area / FLORA
plant-sucking insect / APHID
plaque / BROOCH, TABLET, TARTAR; ATHEROMA
plash / DASH; PLEACH, SPLASH. POOL; PUDDLE
plasma / FLUID
Plassey victor / CLIVE
plaster / GROUT; PARGET, STUCCO
plaster used by artists / GESSO
plaster of Paris / GYPSUM
plastic / PLIABLE; SYNTHETIC. POLYMER; ELASTOMER
plastic earth / PUG; CLAY
plastic paper substitute / PLAPER
plat / PLAN, PLOT; CHART
plate / CUT; DISH, GRID; ARMOR, PATEN; LAMINA, PATERA, SAUCER; ILLUSTRATION
plate bone / SCAPULA
plate for Eucharist / PATEN
plate to hurl / DISCUS
plate of reptile / SCUTE
plateau / MESA, PUNA; TABLELAND
plated / OVERLAID
plated with metal / COATED
platform / BEMA, DAIS; STAGE; PODIUM; ESTRADE
platform in mine / SOLLAR, SOLLER
platitude / TRUISM
Platonic / MENTAL; INCORPOREAL
Platonic idea / EIDOS
Platonic solid / POLYHEDRON
Plato's father / ARISTON
Plato's mentor / SOCRATES
Platte town / COZAD; KEARNEY

platter / DISH; PLATE
platy / FLAKY
platypus / DUCKBILL; MONOTREME
plaudit / APPLAUSE; ACCLAMATION
plausible / APPARENT, SPECIOUS
play / ROMP; ENACT; CAVORT, FROLIC, GAMBOL, DRAMA, SPORT
play area / GYM; PARK, YARD; FIELD; GYMNASIUM
play the banjo / STRUM
play in baseball / SQUEEZE
play in basketball / PICK
play in bridge / SLUFF, TRUMP; FINESSE
play clothes / JEANS
play division / ACT; SCENE
play in error / RENEGE
play first / LEAD
play in football / BUCK, PASS
play lightly with / TOY
play loosely / STRUM
play for money / GAMBLE
play for movie script / SCENARIO
play noisily / ROMP
play a part / ACT; PERFORM
play principal role / STAR
play segment / ACT; SCENE
play on stage / ACT; PERFORM
play on words / PUN
played before curtain / JIG; SKIT
player / ACTOR; GAMBLER
player on baseball team / INFIELDER
player on basketball team / GUARD
player who cuts cards / PONE
player on football team / END; BACK
player on hockey team / GOALIE
player in orchestra / MUSICIAN
playful / GAY; ARCH; MERRY; FRISKY, JOCUND, LUSORY
playground / OVAL, PARK, YARD
playhouse / THEATRE
playing card / ACE, TEN; JACK, KING, TREY; DEUCE, QUEEN, TAROT
playing card spot / PIP
playing card suit / CLUBS; HEARTS, SPADES; DIAMONDS

playing field / OVAL; ARENA
playing hooky / TRUANCY. TRUANT
playing marble / MIB, TAW; AGATE; SHOOTER
plaything / TOY; DOLL; BAUBLE
plaza / PIAZZA, SQUARE
plea / EXCUSE, PRAYER; APOLOGY
plea at law / ANSWER; ALLEGATION
pleach / PLAIT; INTERWEAVE
plead / BEG, SUE; PRAY; ARGUE
pleading at law / PAROLE
pleadings outline / BRIEF
pleasant / NICE; LEPID, SWEET; GENIAL; AMIABLE, AMUSING, LIKABLE; CHEERFUL; AGREE-ABLE
pleasant expression / GRIN; SMILE
pleasant period / GOODTIMES
pleasant smell / AROMA, SCENT
pleasant sound / LAUGH, MUSIC
pleasantly plump / ZAFTIG
pleasantry / BANTER, GAIETY
please / SUIT; ARRIDE; DELIGHT
pleased / GLAD
pleased as Punch / DELIGHTED
pleasing / NICE; WELCOME; PLEASANT
pleasing to the taste / SWEET; SAVORY
pleasing tones / MUSIC; HARMONY
pleasurable / GENIAL; DELECTABLE
pleasurable activity / GAME, PLAY
pleasure / FUN, JOY; ESTE, WILL, WISH; FAVOR; CHOICE, DESIRE
pleasure carriage / SURREY
pleasure craft / BOAT; BARGE, CANOE, YACHT
pleasure trip / JAUNT; VACATION
pleat / FOLD; PLAIT; GATHER
plebeian / MEAN; COMMON, VULGAR
plebescite / POLL, VOTE
pledge / VAS, VOW; BIND, GAGE, PAWN, SEAL; TOAST; COMMIT, ENGAGE; DEPOSIT. OATH; TOKEN, TROTH, TRUCE; SURETY; EARNEST
pledged faith / TROTH
pledged word / PAROLE
pledget / WAD; COMPRESS

PLEIADES, SEVEN
MAIA
CELENO
MEROPE
ALCYONE
ELECTRA
STEROPE
TAYGETA

plenary / FULL; COMPLETE
plenipotentiary / ENVOY
plenish / STOCK; FURNISH
plenitude / FULLNESS;
    EXUBERANCE
plenteous / AMPLE; ABUNDANT
plentiful / COPIOUS, PROFUSE
plantifully / GALORE
plenty / ABUNDANCE. AMPLE;
    ENOUGH
pleonastic / REDUNDANT
plessor test / REFLEX
plethora / EXCESS; SURPLUS
plexus / KNOT, RETE; NETWORK
pliable / SOFT; LITHE, DOCILE,
    LIMBER, SUPPLE
pliable substance / WAX; CLAY
pliant / PLASTIC; FLEXIBLE
plicate / FOLDED; PLAITED
pliers / PINCERS
plight / VOW; GAGE; PAWN;
    PLEDGE. SCRAPE; DILEMMA;
    PREDICAMENT
plinth / BASE, ORLE; SOCLE;
    BOTTOM
plod / SLOG; TRUDGE
plodding / SLOW; PAINSTAKING
plop / DROP, FALL
plot / PLAN; CABAL, DRAFT,
    FRAME; DEVISE. BED, LOT;
    PLAT; SCHEME; INTRIGUE
plot of land / LOT; ACRE, AREA,
    PLAT; PATCH; PARCEL
plot secretly / SCHEME; CONSPIRE
plotter / PLANNER; MAPMAKER
plough / PLOW
plouter / DABBLE, SPLASH
plover / LAPWING; DOTTEREL,
    KILLDEER
ploverlike bird / SANDPIPER
plow / TILL; FURROW
plow part / SHARE, SHETH,
    SLADE; COLTER, SHEATH;
    COULTER
plowed field / ERD; ARADA, GLEBE
plowland / HIDE; SULUNG;
    CARUCATE
plowman / FARMER, RUSTIC
ploy / JOKE; TRICK; FROLIC
pluck / GRIT, SAND; NERVE,
    SPUNK. PICK, PULL; SNATCH
pluck a guitar / STRUM
pluck up / SUMMON; ERADICATE
plucky / GAME; DOUGHTY
plug / BOTT, BUNG, CORK; ESTOP,
    SPILE; TAMPON; STOPPLE,
    TAMPION
plug of hemp / WAD
plug-ugly / TOUGH; HOODLUM
plum / GAGE, SLOE, DAMSON;
    ORLEANS
plum as a fruit / DRUPE

plumage / MAIL; MANTLE;
    FEATHERS
plumate / FEATHERED
plumb / VERTICAL;
    PERPENDICULAR
plumb bob / PLUMMET
plumbago / LEAD; GRAPHITE
plumcot's creator / BURBANK
plume / PREEN. CREST, EGRET;
    AIGRET; FEATHER
plumlike fruit / SLOE
plummet / DROP, FALL
plump / FAT; FULL; ROUND
    STOUT
plump child / FUB
plumpest / RIPEST; FULLEST
plumulaceous / SOFT; DOWNY
plunder / GUT, ROB; RAID, SACK;
    RAVEN; MARAUD, RAVAGE.
    LOOT, SWAG; BOOTY, RAVIN;
    RAPINE
plundered / REFT; PREYED
plundering / PREDATORY
plunge / DIP, DIVE, RUSH;
    DOUSE
plunge into water / DIP; DIVE
plunger / RAM; DIVER
plunger of churn / DASHER
plural ending / EN, ES
plurality / MOST; EXCESS
plurisy / EXCESS
plus / AND. ADDITION. POSITIVE
Pluto / DIS; ADES; AIDES, HADES,
    ORCUS
Pluto's brother / JUPITER,
    NEPTUNE
Pluto's color / BLACK
Pluto's dog / CERBERUS
Pluto's father / SATURN
Pluto's mother / OPS
Pluto's mother-in-law / CERES
Pluto's realm / UNDERWORLD
Pluto's wife / PROSERPINA
plutocrat / BOSS; RULER; LEADER
plutonic / IGNEOUS
pluvial / RAINY
ply / URGE, WORK; WIELD. FOLD
Plymouth settler / PILGRIM
plywood / VENEER
pneuma / SOUL; BREATH, SPIRIT
pneumatosis / GAS; FLATULENCE
pneumogastric nerve / VAGUS
pneumonia / PNEUMONITIS
pneumonic / PULMONIC
Po tributary / ADDA; OGLIO
poach / SHIRR; TRESPASS
poachy / MARSHY, SODDEN
Pocahontas' father / POWHATAN
Pocahontas' husband / ROLFE
pochard / SMEE
pocket / BAG; CAVITY
pocket billiards / POOL

pocket knife / BARLOW; JACKKNIFE
pocketbook / BAG; POUCH, PURSE; WALLET
pocosin / SWAMP
pod / BAG, SAC; BOLL; SCHOOL; CAPSULE, SILIQUE; CONTAINER
pod vegetables / PEAS; PEASE
pod-bearing tree / CAROB; ALGARROBA
pod-bearing vine / PEA; STRING-BEAN
podex / RUMP
podgy / PLUMP, PUDGY
podium / DAIS; PLATFORM
pods for tanning / PIPI; DIVIDIVI
Poe bird / RAVEN
Poe heroine / LENORE; ULALUME
Poe tale / LIGEIA; GOLDBUG
poem / LAY, ODE; EPIC, EPOS; ELEGY, EPODE, LYRIC, VERSE; BALLAD
poem, pert. to / ODIC
poem division / CANTO; PASSUS, SESTET, STANZA
poem with eight lines / TRIOLET
poem with fourteen lines / SONNET
poem with six stanzas / SESTINA
Poe's adopted family / ALLAN
Poe's wife / VIRGINIA
poesy / POEM; POETRY
poet / BARD; ODIST, RIMER; LYRIST
poet in early German / MINNESINGER
poet of the Finns / RUNER
poet of the Goths / RUNER
poet of Middle Ages / TROUVERE
poet in Norse / SKALD
poet in Old English / SCOP
poetaster / POETICULE, RHYMESTER
poetic contraction / EEN, EER, TIS; NEER
poetic foot / IAMB; DACTYL; TROCHEE
poetic inspiration / MUSE
poetic muse / ERATO; CALLIOPE
poetic pronoun / THY; THINE
poetic rhythm / METER
poetic spring / HELICON
poetic verb / DOST; SHALT
poetry / POESY, RHYME, VERSE
poetry, pert. to / ODIC; BARDIC; ELEGIAC
poetry without rhyme / BLANK-VERSE
pogrom / MASSACRE
pogue / KISS
poi / TARO
poignant / KEEN; ACRID, ACUTE, SHARP; BITING
poikilothermic / COLDBLOODED

point / AIM; SHOW; SHARPEN; PUNCTUATE, DOT, END, NEB, NIB, TIP, TOP; APEX, BARB, CAPE, CUSP, GIST, PEAK, SPOT; FOCUS
point aimed at / GOAL
point of antler / SNAG
point of arrow / HEAD
point where branch leaves limb / AXIL
point of chin / BUTTON
Point of compass / AIRT, EAST, WEST; AIRTH, NORTH, RHUMB, SOUTH
point of concentration / FOCUS
point of crescent moon / CUSP, HORN
point of crisis / APEX, PEAK
point of crossing / INTERSECT
point on curve / NODE
point in game / ACE
point a gun / AIM
point of intersection / VERTEX
point of land / SPIT
point of law / RES
point of leverage / FULCRUM
point in middle / MEAN; MEDIAN
point of missile / BARB
point in moon's orbit / APOGEE, SYZYGY; PERIGEE
point of potato's sprouting / EYE
point of rotation / PIVOT
point of spear / BLADE
point of story / NUB; CRUX
point straight down / NADIR
point straight up / ZENITH
point at top / APEX, PEAK
point of view / ANGLE, SLANT
pointed / KEEN; ACUTE, SHARP; DIRECT, GOTHIC, MARKED; ANGULAR
pointed arch / OGEE; OGIVE
pointed end / CUSP
pointed instrument / AWL, PIN; GOAD, PROD; NEEDLE
pointed mass of ice / SERAC; ICICLE
pointed metal piece / PIN; BRAD, NAIL; SPIKE; NEEDLE
pointed missile / DART; ARROW
pointed part on plant / BARB; THORN
pointed sewing implement / NEEDLE
pointed stake / PALE; PALISADE
pointed tip of growth / AWN
pointed tool / AWL, BIT; PUNCH
pointed weapon / PIKE; SPEAR
pointed wheel / TRACER
pointed wooden piece / PEG; STAKE
pointer / TIP; HAND, WAND; HOUND
pointer of sun dial / GNOMON

pointer used in synagogue / YAD
pointillist painter / SEURAT
pointing / PUNCTUATION
pointless / INANE, INEPT, STUPID
point-to-point race / STEEPLE-
CHASE
poise / BALANCE; CARRIAGE
poison / BANE; TOXIN, VENOM,
TAINT, VIRUS; CORRUPT
poison in hemlock / CONINE
poison ivy / PICRY
poison from snake / VENOM
poisonous / TOXIC; DEADLY;
VENOMOUS; INJURIOUS
poisonous alkaloid / NICOTINE
poisonous bean / CALABAR
poisonous chemical / STRYCHNINE
poisonous dye / AURIA; AURINE
poisonous element / ARSENIC
poisonous fish / FUGU
poisonous gas / ZYKLON;
CHLORINE
poisonous insect / ANT, BEE;
WASP; HORNET; CONENOSE
poisonous lizard / GILA
poisonous mushroom / AMANITA
poisonous plant / LOCO, POKE;
SUMAC; CASTOR; LOBELIA;
OLEANDER
poisonous snake / COBRA, KRAIT,
MAMBA; RATTLER
poisonous spider / BLACKWIDOW
poisonous substance / BIKH, BISH;
VENIN; IODINE; ARSENIC
poisonous tree / UPAS
poke / JAB; GOAD, PROD, PUSH,
URGE; NUDGE. BAG; BONNET,
POCKET
poke around / GROPE, PROBE
poke with the elbow / NUDGE
poke fun at / KID; JOSH
poker ancestor / BLUFF
poker hand / PAT; FULL; FLUSH
poker openers / JACKS
poker stake / POT; ANTE
poker token / CHIP
poker variety / STUD; TABLE-
STAKES
pokerfaced / INSCRUTABLE
pokeweed / POCAN, SCOKE;
GARGET
pokey / JAIL
poky / SLOW; STUFFY
Poland / See Polish
Poland capital / WARSAW
polar body / POLOCYTE
polar discoverer / PEARY;
AMUNDSEN
pole / ROD; PIKE, SLAV; CABER,
STAFF, STAKE, STICK
pole in Gaelic games / CABER
pole to handle fish / PEW; GAFF
pole on ship / MAST; SPRIT

pole of vehicle / NEAP; SHAFT
polecat / SKUNK, ZORIL; FITCHEW
polemarch / GENERAL
polemic / ARGUMENTATIVE
polemics / CONTROVERSY
pole-propelled boat / PUNT
polestar / POLARIS
police / GUARD; CONSTABULARY
police barrier / CORDON
police dog / SHEPHERD
police officer / AGENT; DETECTIVE
police official / INSPECTOR
police station record / BLOTTER
police sweep / DRAGNET
policeman / COP; FUZZ; BOBBY;
PEELER; OFFICER; GENDARME
policeman's club / MACE;
TRUNCHEON; NIGHTSTICK
policewoman / MATRON
policy / WIT; PLAN, RULE; SYSTEM
polio researcher / SALK; SABIN
polish / RUB, WAX; GLOSS, SCOUR,
SHINE; BURNISH, FURBISH.
SHEEN
Polish / POLE; POLACK
Polish assembly / SEIM, SEJM
Polish author / REJ
Polish cake / BABA
Polish cheese / RINNEN
Polish chemist / CURIE
Polish city / LODZ; CRACOW
Polish composer / CHOPIN
Polish courtesy title / PAN; PANI
Polish dramatist / KRASINSKI
Polish money / ZLOTY
Polish patriot / PULASKI
Polish pianist / PADEREWSKI
Polish poet / KRASICKI
Polish port / DANZIG, GDANSK
Polish river / BUG, SAN; BZURA,
NAREW, SERET, WISLA; VISTULA
polish vigorously / BUFF
Polish writer / MICKIEWICZ
polished / SLEEK; URBANE
polished manner / POISE;
URBANITY
polisher / BUFFER
polishing material / WAX; EMERY,
RABAT, ROUGE
polite / CIVIL; URBANE; AFFABLE,
ELEGANT, GENTEEL, REFINED
politeness / COMITY; AMENITY
politic / SLY; FOXY, WARY; CIVIL
political base / GRASSROOTS
political boodle / GRAFT
political faction / BLOC; PARTY
political meeting / CAUCUS
politico / POLITICIAN
poll / CLIP, HEAD, VOTE; BALLOT;
ELECTION
poll taker / ROPER; GALLUP
pollack / SEY; SAITHE
polled / SHORN; HORNLESS

pollen / MICROSPORE
pollen brush / SCOPA
pollen-bearing organ / STAMEN
pollex / THUMB
polliwog / TADPOLE
pollock / POLLACK
pollute / SOIL; ABUSE, STAIN,
  TAINT; DEBASE, DEFILE
polluted air / SMOG
Pollux's mother / LEDA
Pollux's twin / CASTOR
Pollyanna / OPTIMIST
Pollyanna's pastime / GLADGAME
polo horse / PONY
polo period / CHUKKER
polo stick / MALLET
Polonius' daughter / OPHELIA
Polonius' son / LAERTES
Polo's importation / SPAGHETTI
poltergeist / GHOST, SPOOK
poltroon / ARRANT, COWARD
polverine / POTASH
polychaete / ANNELID; TUBEWORM
polyglot / MULTILINGUAL
polygon of eight sides / OCTAGON
polygon of five sides / PENTAGON
polygon of four sides / TETRAGON;
  QUADRILATERAL
polygon of seven sides /
  HEPTAGON
polygon of six sides / HEXAGON
polygon of ten sides / DECAGON
polygon of three sides / TRIANGLE
polygon of twelve sides /
  DODECAGON
polymorphonuclear leucocyte /
  PHAGOCYTE
Polynesian / MAORI; KANAKA.
  See also Hawaiian
Polynesian arrowroot / PIA
Polynesian assembly / HUI
Polynesian banana / FEI
Polynesian beefwood / TOA; TOOA
Polynesian beverage / KAVA,
  KAWA
Polynesian chestnut / RATA
Polynesian cloth / TAPA
Polynesian dance / HULA, SIVA
Polynesian deity / KANE, TANE
Polynesian demigod / MAUI
Polynesian drink / AVA; KAVA
Polynesian fern / TARA
Polynesian first man / TIKI
Polynesian garment / PAREU
Polynesian island group / SAMOA
Polynesian language / MAORI;
  MAHORI, SAMOAN; HAWAIIAN,
  TAHITIAN
Polynesian oven / UMU
Polynesian palm lily / TI
Polynesian pepper / AVA; KAVA
Polynesian plant / PIA; TARO
polyp / CORAL, HYDRA, TUMOR

Polyphemus' blinder / ODYSSEUS
Polyphemus' father / POSEIDON
polyphonic / CONTRAPUNTAL
pomace / PULP
pome / PEAR; APPLE
pomegranate / BLOODAPPLE
pomegranate melon / DUDAIM
pomegranate syrup / GRENADINE
pomelo / GRAPEFRUIT
pomfret cake / LICORICE
pomp / SHOW; PARADE, DISPLAY
pompano / SCAD; SAUREL
Pompeia's husband / CAESAR
Pompeii's nemesis / VESUVIUS
pompous / GRAND; TURGID;
  STILTED
pompous show / PARADE;
  PAGEANT
pompous speech / HARANGUE
ponce / PIMP
poncho / CAPE, COAT; CLOAK
pond / LAKE, MERE, POOL;
  LAGOON
ponder / MUSE, PORE; BROOD,
  THINK, WEIGH; REFLECT
ponderous / DULL; HEAVY;
  MASSIVE
pone / CORNCAKE
poniard / DIRK; DAGGER, STYLET
pontiff / POPE; BISHOP; PONTIFEX
pontificate / DOGMATIZE
pontlevis / DRAWBRIDGE
pony / NAG; FELL; SHELTY
pony for a student / CRIB
pooch / DOG
pooh / PFUI, PISH; PSHAW
pooka / PUCK; FAIRY; SPRITE
pool / LIN, POT; ANTE, CARR,
  LINN; LAGOON; COMBINE;
  BILLIARDS
pool room / BILLIARDPARLOR
poon / DOMBA, KEENA;
  MASTWOOD
poop / DECK, FOOL; DICKEY
poor / BAD; LEAN, MEAN, THIN,
  WEAK; FRAIL, GAUNT, NEEDY;
  BARREN
poor actor / HAM
poor boy sandwich / HERO;
  SUBMARINE
poor cottage / HOVEL, SHACK
poor golf shot / DUB; HOOK;
  SLICE
poor joe / HERON
poor john / SALTFISH
poor player / DUB
poor writer's abode / GARRET
poorhouse / HOME; ALMSHOUSE
poorly / ILL; BADLY
poorly lit / DIM
pop / FIZZ, SODA; FATHER
pop artist / WARHOL
pop the question / PROPOSE

pope / PAPA, RUFF; BISHOP, SHRIKE
pope, pert. to / PAPAL
popeline / REP
popelote / DOLL; POPPER
pope's cape / FANO; FANON, ORALE
pope's court / CURIA
pope's crown / TIARA
pope's name / PAUL, PIUS; ADRIAN; CLEMENT, GREGORY, PACELLI
pope's palace / VATICAN
Popeye's girl friend / OLIVE
Popeye's rival / BLUTO
popinjay / FOP; PARROT; COXCOMB
poplar / ABELE, ALAMO, ASPEN
Poppaea's husband / NERO, OTHO
poppy / OPIUM; FOXGLOVE
poppy seed / MAW; MOHNSEED
poppycock / ROT; BALONEY
Pops conductor / FIEDLER
populace / MOB; DEMOS; MASSES
popular / COMMON; DEMOTIC; FAMILIAR, PLEBEIAN
popular ascription / CREDIT, REPUTE; ESTIMATE
popular girl / BELLE
popular singer / CROONER
popular success / HIT
popular talk / SLANG
populate / PEOPLE
porbeagle / SHARK
porcelain / CHINA; LIMOGES
porcelain from China / JU, KO
porcelain from Egypt / FAIENCE
porcelain from England / SPODE
porcelain from France / SEVRES
porcelain from Germany / MEISSEN
porcelain ingredient / KAOLIN; PETUNTSE
porcelain from Japan / IMARI
porcelain from the Orient / CELADON
porch / ANTA, STOA; LANAI, STOOP; PORTICO, VERANDA
porch swing / GLIDER
porcine / HOGGISH, PIGLIKE
porcine animal / HOG, PIG; SWINE
porcupine / URSON; TENREC
porcupine anteater / ECHIDNA
porcupine quill / SPINE
pore / STUDY; PONDER. STOMA
pore in plant stem / LENTICEL
porgy / TAI; SCUP; BREAM, PARGO
porker / HOG, PIG
porkfish / SISI
porky / GREASY; PORCUPINE
pornographic / EROTIC
porosis / CALLUS
porous / SPONGY; PERMEABLE

porous mass / SPONGE
porous material / FILTER
porous rock / TUFA, TUFF
porpoise / DOLPHIN
porrect / EXTEND; PRESENT
porridge / POB; SAMP; ATOLE, BROSE, GRUEL; OATMEAL
port / AIR; MIEN, WINE; HAVEN; HARBOR; LARBOARD
port of Athens / PIRAEUS
port of Rome / OSTIA
port wine city / OPORTO
portable bed / COT; CRIB
portable canopy / PARASOL
portable chair / SEDAN
portable fortification / MANTA; TESTUDO
portable hoist / CRANE
portable lamp / LANTERN
portable shelter / TENT
portable stove / ETNA
portable tub / TOSH
portal / DOOR, GATE; ENTRANCE
porte cochere / GATEWAY
portend / BODE; AUGUR; BETOKEN
portent / OMEN, SIGN
portentous / DIRE; OMINOUS
porter / ALE; HAMAL; REDCAP; CARRIER, OSTIARY
Portia's husband / BASSANIO
Portia's maid / NERISSA
Portia's servant / BALTHAZAR
Portia's suitor / ARAGON; MOROCCO
portico / STOA; PORCH
portiere / CURTAIN
portion / BIT, DAB; FATE, PART, SOME, WHIT; DOWRY, SHARE. DOLE
portion of medicine / DOSE
portion out / METE
portion of time / SPAN
Portland sago / CUCKOOPINT
portly / BURLY, OBESE; STATELY
portmanteau / TRUNK; VALISE; GLADSTONE
portmanteau word / BRILLIG
portrait / ICON; PICTURE
portray / ACT; DRAW, LIMN; DEPICT
portray without speaking / MIME
portrayal / DESCRIPTION
Portugal / LUSITANIA. See also Portuguese
Portuguese author / CAMOENS
Portuguese capital / LISBOA, LISBON
Portuguese city / ELVAS, EVORA
Portuguese coin / REI; ESCUDO
Portuguese colony / MACAO, TIMOR; ANGOLA; CABINDA
Portuguese explorer / DIAZ, GAMA

Portuguese Guinea capital / BISSAU
Portuguese imperialist / HENRY
Portuguese India towns / DIU, GOA; DAMAO
Portuguese islands / AZORES; MADEIRA
Portuguese river / SOA; SADO, TEJO; MINHO, TAGUS
Portuguese song / FADO
Portuguese Timor capital / DILI
Portuguese Timor money / AVO; PATACA
Portuguese title / DOM; DONA
Portuguese West Africa capital / LUANDA
pose / SIT; AFFECT, PUZZLE
pose for painting / SIT
Poseidon / NEPTUNE
Poseidon's brother / ZEUS; HADES
Poseidon's consort / AMPHITRITE
Poseidon's father / CRONUS
Poseidon's offspring / PEGASUS
Poseidon's son / TRITON; ANTAEUS
poser / STUMPER
poseur / PHONY
posit / POSTULATE
position / JOB; POST, RANK, SPOT
position in chess / STALEMATE
position in golf / STANCE
position with no work / SINECURE
positive / PLUS, REAL, SURE, TRUE
positive declaration / ASSERTION
positive electrode / ANODE
positive ion / CATION
positively / ABSOLUTELY
positivism / MECHANISM; CONFIDENCE
possess / OWN; HAVE, HOLD; OCCUPY
possess ambition / ASPIRE
possessed / HAD; OWNED. MAD
possesses ability / CAN
possessing being / EXTANT
possessing branches / RAMOSE
possessing courage / BRAVE
possessing feeling / SENTIENT
possessing feet / PEDATE
possessing a flat breastbone / RATITE
possessing hair / HIRSUTE
possessing hooves / UNGULATE
possessing knowledge / AWARE; KNOWING
possessing landed property / ACRED
possessing leaflets / FOLIOLATE
possessing leaves / LEAFY; FOLIATE

possessing a narrow orifice / ATENOPAIC
possessing no heat / COLD
possessing no limits / INFINITE
possessing a pile / RICH; NAPPED
possessing ribs / COSTATE
possessing rows / TIERED
possessing taste / SAPID; SAVORY
possessing tendons / SINEWED
possessing an untrimmed edge / DECKLED
possessing wings / ALAR; ALATE
possession / ASSET; TENURE
possession in law / SEISIN
possessions / RICHES, WEALTH
possessive pronoun / MY; HER, HIS, ITS, OUR; HERS, MINE, OURS, YOUR; THEIR, YOURS
possibility / CONTINGENCY
possible / FEASIBLE; POTENTIAL
possibly / HAPLY, MAYBE; PERHAPS; PERCHANCE; PERADVENTURE
possum / COON; OPOSSUM
post / BITT, MAIL, MALL; BERTH, PLACE, STAKE; OFFICE, PILLAR
post exchange / CANTEEN
post for hawser / BITT
post in India / DAK; DAUK, DAWK
postage stamp collecting / PHILATELY
postal aide / MAILMAN
postal seal / STAMP
postal zone number / ZIP
postcard collector / DELTIOLOGIST
poster / AD; BILL, CARD, SIGN
poster color / GOUACHE; DISTEMPER
posterior / REAR; HINDER
posterity / DESCENDANTS
postfix / SUFFIX
posthaste / APACE; INSTANTLY
posthole spade / LOY
postiche / TOUPEE
post-impressionist painter / MATISSE
postmark / CANCELLATION
postpone / DEFER, DELAY, TABLE
postprandial / AFTERDINNER
postulant / CANDIDATE
postulate / CLAIM, POSIT; DEMAND
posture / POSE; STANCE; ATTITUDE
posture in ballet / ARABESQUE
posture on horseback / SEAT
posy / BOUQUET, NOSEGAY
pot / OLLA; KETTLE; CALDRON
pot in India / LOTA; LOTAH
pot liquor / BROTH; BREWIS
potable / DRINKABLE

potamic / RIVERINE
potash / KALI; GLASSWORT
potassium / KALIUM
potassium nitrate / NITER, NITRE
potation / DRINK
potato / YAM; SPUD; PRATY,
   TATER, TUBER
potato bud / EYE
potato masher / RICER; GRENADE
pot-au-feu / STEW
potbelly / PAUNCH
poteen / MOONSHINE
potency / VIS, ZIP; JIVA; POWER
potent / COGENT, MIGHTY,
   STRONG
potentate / MONARCH;
   SOVEREIGN
potential / LATENT
potential energy / ERGAL
potential metal / ORE
pother / ADO; FUSS; BUSTLE
potherb / WORT; GREENS
potion / DOSE; DRAFT
Potiphar's wife / RAHIL; ZULEIKA
potliquor / STOCK
potpourri / OLIO; MEDLEY;
   MISCELLANY
potsherd / SHARD
potsy / BADGE; HOPSCOTCH
pottage / OATMEAL; PORRIDGE
potter / MESS; TRIFLE
potter's clay / ARGIL
potter's tool / PALLET
potter's wheel / KICK; LATHE,
   THROW
pottery / EARTHENWARE
pottery, pert. to / CERAMIC
pottery fragment / SHARD, SHERD
pottery glaze / SLIP
pottery oven / KILN
pouch / BAG, SAC; PURSE;
   POCKET
pouch-like / SACCATE
poulp / OCTOPUS
poult / PULLET, TURKEY
poultry / FOWL, HENS; BIRDS
poultry disease / PIP; ROUP
poultry farm / HENNERY
pounce / SEIZE, SWOOP
pound / BEAT, TAMP, TUND;
   THUMP
pound in / RAM
pounder / RAM; MORTAR, PESTLE
pour / FLOW, RAIN, TEEM;
   DECANT
pour off wine / DECANT
pour oil upon / ANELE; ANOINT
pour out / GUSH; STREAM
pour a sacrifice / LIBATE
pourboire / TIP
pout / FRET, MOPE, SULK
poverty / NEED, WANT; PENURY

poverty plant / HEATHER
pow / HEAD, POLL
powan / WHITEFISH
powder / DUST, TALC. PULVERIZE
powder holder / HORN
powdered aloes / PICRA
powdered baobab leaves / LALO
powdered lava / ASH
powdered mineral / TALCUM
powdered quartz / SILICA
powdered stone / SAND
powdery / DUSTY; FRIABLE
powdery carbon / SOOT
powdery residue / ASH; ASHES
power / VIM, VIS; DINT, GIFT,
   MANA, RULE, SWAY; FORCE,
   MIGHT
powerful / GREAT; POTENT,
   ROBUST
powerful blast / EXPLOSION
powerful dog / MASTIFF
powerless / DULL, WEAK; FRAIL
powwow / PARLEY; COUNCIL,
   MEETING; CONFERENCE
practicable / FEASIBLE, POSSIBLE
practical / ABLE; HANDY, UTILE
practical joke / HOAX, CAPER,
   PRANK; HUMBUG
practically / ALMOST, REALLY
practice / DO; PLY, USE; DRILL;
   REHEARSE. WONT; HABIT,
   USAGE
practice exercise / ETUDE
practice husbandry / FARM
practice magic / CONJURE
practiced / ABLE; VERSED;
   SKILLED
practitioner / HEALER
praetor / MAGISTRATE
pragmatic / PRACTICAL
Prague means of execution /
   DEFENESTRATION
prairie / PLAIN; MEADOW,
   STEPPE
prairie chicken / GROUSE
prairie dog / MARMOT
Prairie State / ILLINOIS
prairie wolf / COYOTE
praise / LAUD, PUFF; ADORE,
   EXALT, EXTOL. KUDOS;
   EULOGY, HOMAGE; TRIBUTE
praise God / HOSANNA;
   HALLELUJAH
praiseworthy / COMMENDABLE
praline / MARZIPAN; CONFECTION
prance / CAPER, CAVORT, SPRING
prank / DIDO, JOKE; ANTIC, TRICK
prase / CHALCEDONY
prate / GAB; BUCK, CHAT;
   PRATTLE
prattle / BABBLE; CHATTER
praxis / USAGE; CUSTOM

pray / BEG, SUE; CRAVE, DAVEN; INVOKE; BESEECH
prayer / AVE; BEAD, PLEA, SUIT; CREDO, MATIN; LITANY, ORISON
prayer bead / AVE; ROSARY
prayer bow of Moslem / RAKA
prayer for the dead / REQUIEM
prayer leader / IMAM; CANTOR
prayer shawl / TALLIT; TALLITH
prayer stick / PAHO
prayer of thanks / GRACE
prayerbook / ORDO; MISSAL, PORTAS; BREVIARY
prayerful / DEVOUT
prayer's end / AMEN
praying figure / ORANT
preach / EXHORT; DISCOURSE
preacher / MINISTER
preaching / HOMILY, SERMON
preamble / PREFACE, PRELUDE
prearrange / PLAN; CONCERT
prearranged list / SLATE; AGENDA
precarious / RISKY; DUBIOUS
precaution / FORESIGHT
precautious / CAREFUL
precede / LEAD; HERALD
precede in time / ANTEDATE
preceded / FORERAN
precedence / PRIORITY
precedent / GUIDE; EXAMPLE
preceding / PRIOR; FORMER; EARLIER; ANTERIOR
preceding night / EVE
precept / LAW; RULE; EDICT, MAXIM
preceptor / TUTOR; TEACHER
precepts / DICTA; PRINCIPLES
precinct / WARD; BOUND, LIMIT
precious / DEAR, RARE; COSTLY
precious metal / GOLD; SILVER
precious stone / GEM; OPAL, RUBY, SARD; BERYL; GARNET, ZIRCON; DIAMOND, EMERALD
precipice / CRAG, PALI; CLIFF
precipitate / RASH; STEEP; SUDDEN
precipitately / HEADLONG; HURRIEDLY
precipitation / RAIN; HASTE
precipitous / ABRUPT; BEETLING
precis / SUMMARY; ABSTRACT
precise / NEAT, NICE, PRIM, TIDY; EXACT, RIGID; STRICT; CORRECT
precise reasoning / LOGIC
precisely / ACCURATELY
precisian / STICKLER
precision / RIGOR; NICETY
preclude / BAR; AVERT, DEBAR
precocious / GIFTED; PREMATURE
preconceive / PRESUME
preconize / SUMMON; PUBLICIZE

precursor / OMEN; HERALD
precursory / PRIOR; ANTERIOR
predator / CARNIVORE
predatory / GREEDY; RAPACIOUS
predatory bird / OWL; HAWK
predatory insect / MANTIS
predestinate / FOREORDAIN
predestine / DOOM; ORDAIN
predetermine / PLAN; CONCOCT
predicament / FIX, JAM; PICKLE
predicant / PREACHING
predicate / SAY; AVER, BASE; AFFIRM
predicative / AFFIRMATORY
predict / BODE; AUGUR; PORTEND
prediction / PROPHECY
predictive / PORTENTOUS
predilection / BENT, BIAS; DESIRE
predisposed / PRONE; INCLINED
predominance / PREVALENCE
predominant / CHIEF, NOBLE; RULING; REGNANT, SUPREME; DOMINANT
predominate / PREVAIL; PREPONDERATE
preeminent / STAR; FIRST; CAPITAL
preeminently / SUPERLATIVELY
preemptory bid / SHUTOUT
preen / PLUME; PRIMP
preface / PROEM; FOREWORD
prefect / GOVERNOR; MAGISTRATE
prefecture / DISTRICT; JURISDICTION
prefer / LIKE, PICK; ELECT, FANCY
preferable / BETTER
preferably / RATHER, SOONER
preference / TASTE; CHOICE; ELECTION, PRIORITY
prefigure / FORESHADOW
prefix / AFFIX. PREFACE
pregnant / FERTILE, FRAUGHT; ENCEINTE
prehensile / GRASPING
prehistoric animal / AMMONITE, DINOSAUR; TRILOBITE
prehistoric mound / TELL, TEPE
prehistoric tool / CELT; EOLITH
prejudice / BIAS; INJURY, POISON
prejudiced / PARTIAL, TWISTED
prejudicial / HOSTILE, HURTFUL; INIMICAL
prelate / ABBOT; BISHOP; ARCHBISHOP
prelate's cap / BIRETTA
preliminary / PRIOR; INTRODUCTORY
preliminary vote / PRIMARY
prelims / FRONTMATTER
prelude / PROEM; OVERTURE
premature / EARLY; UNTIMELY
premeditate / PLAN; INTEND

premeditation / FORETHOUGHT
premier / CHIEF, FIRST;
  PRINCIPAL
premiere / DEBUT; OPENING
premise / PROPOUND. LEMMA;
  POSTULATE
premium / AGIO; BONUS; BOUNTY
premonish / WARN; ADVISE
premonition / OMEN; HUNCH
preparatory / PREFATORY;
  ANTECEDENT
preparatory meeting / CAUCUS
prepare / FIT, SET; GIRD, MAKE;
  EQUIP, PRIME
prepare for action / READY
prepare copy / EDIT
prepare for exam / CRAM
prepare flax / RET
prepare leather / TAN, TAW
prepare to resist / ARM
prepare for roasting / STUFF,
  TRUSS
prepared / FIT; ALERT, ARMED
prepense / PREMEDITATED
preponderate / PREVAIL;
  OUTWEIGH
preposition / AT, BY, IN, OF, ON,
  RE, TO, UP; ERE, FOR, MID, PER,
  VIA; ATOP, FROM, INTO, NEAR,
  ONTO, OVER, TILL, UNTO, WITH;
  AFTER, UNDER, UNTIL
prepossess / PREJUDICE
prepossessing / WINNING;
  ALLURING
preposterous / ABSURD; FOOLISH
preprandial drink / APERITIF
prerogative / RIGHT; PRIVILEGE
presage / BODE, OMEN; AUGUR;
  HERALD
presaged / FORETOLD
presbyopic / FARSIGHTED
preschool class / KINDERGARTEN
prescience / ANTICIPATION
prescribe / SET; ORDER, TREAT
prescribed / THETIC; ABSOLUTE
prescribed amount / DOSE
prescribed penalty / FINE;
  SENTENCE
presence / ATTENDANCE
presence of mind / WIT
present / GIVE; OFFER, POINT;
  BESTOW, CONFER, DONATE.
  BOON; GRANT; DONATION.
  NOW; HERE
present in brief / SUM; DIGEST;
  EPITOMIZE
present occasion / NOW; NONCE,
  TODAY
present oneself / REPORT
present a problem / POSE
presentable / FIT; READY
present-day / MODERN
presentiment / FOREBODING

presently / ANON, ENOW, SOON
presentment / NOTICE
preserve / CAN; CURE, KEEP,
  SAVE; SPARE; RESCUE, SHIELD;
  PROTECT
preserve in brine / CORN, SALT;
  PICKLE
preserve from decay / MUMMIFY
preserve by freezing / LYOPHILIZE
preserver / DEFENDER
preserves / JAM
preside / DIRECT, MANAGE
presidential nickname / ABE, CAL,
  FDR, IKE, JFK, LBJ; TEDDY
presidio / POST; GARRISON
press / JAM; CRAM, IRON, PUSH
press agent / FLACK
press agentry / PUBLICITY
press closely / OBLIGE
press clothes / IRON
press down / PIN; TAMP
press forward / HURRY
press hard / DRIVE
press on / ADVANCE
press for payment / DUN
press release / HANDOUT
pressed woolen fabric / FELT
pressing / URGENT
pressing implement / IRON
pressman / PRINTER; JOURNALIST
pressure / FORCE, HURRY;
  DURESS
pressure unit / BAR; BARAD,
  BARYE
prestidigitation / LEGERDEMAIN
prestidigitator / MAGICIAN
prestige / FACE; IZZAT, KUDOS
presto / QUICKLY; SUDDENLY
presume / DARE, DEEM; INFER
presumptuous / BOLD, RASH
pretend / FAKE, SHAM; FEIGN;
  COUNTERFEIT
pretend to be ill / MALINGER
pretend to have good cards / BLUFF
pretended / OSTENSIBLE
pretended courage / BRAVADO
pretender / SNOB; CLAIMANT
pretender to learning / CHARLATAN
pretender to piety / HYPOCRITE
pretender to scholarship /
  SCIOLIST
pretense / SHAM; FEINT; PRETEXT
pretension / AIRS, SHOW
pretentious / SHOWY; ROCOCO;
  ELABORATE
pretentious building / VILLA;
  CASTLE, PALACE
pretermit / MISS; ABANDON,
  NEGLECT
preternatural / SUPERNATURAL
pretext / PEG; ALIBI; EXCUSE
prettily / ELEGANTLY;
  PLEASINGLY

PRESIDENTS OF THE UNITED STATES AND THEIR WIVES

	Wife's Name
John Adams	ABIGAIL SMITH
John Quincy Adams	LOUISA CATHERINE JOHNSON
Chester Alan Arthur	ELLEN LEWIS HERNDON
James Buchanan	
Jimmy Carter	ROSALYNN SMITH
Grover Cleveland	FRANCES FOLSOM
Calvin Coolidge	GRACE ANNE GOODHUE
Dwight David Eisenhower	MAMIE GENEVA DOUD
Millard Fillmore	ABIGAIL POWERS
	CAROLINE CARMICHAEL MCINTOSH
Gerald Rudolph Ford	ELIZABETH BLOOMER WARREN
James Abram Garfield	LUCRETIA RUDOLPH
Ulysses Simpson Grant	JULIA DENT
Warren Gamaliel Harding	FLORENCE KLING DE WOLFE
Benjamin Harrison	CAROLINE LAVINIA SCOTT
	MARY SCOTT LORD DIMMICK
William Henry Harrison	ANNA SYMMES
Rutherford Birchard Hayes	LUCY WARE WEBB
Herbert Clark Hoover	LOU HENRY
Andrew Jackson	RACHEL DONELSON ROBARDS
Thomas Jefferson	MARTHA WAYLES SKELTON
Andrew Johnson	ELIZA MCCARDLE
Lyndon Baines Johnson	CLAUDIA ALTA TAYLOR
John Fitzgerald Kennedy	JACQUELINE LEE BOUVIER
Abraham Lincoln	MARY TODD
James Madison	DOROTHEA PAYNE TODD
William McKinley	IDA SAXTON
James Monroe	ELIZA KORTRIGHT
Richard Milhous Nixon	THEMIA CATHERINE PATRICIA RYAN
Franklin Pierce	JANE MEANS APPLETON
James Knox Polk	SARAH CHILDRESS
Franklin Delano Roosevelt	ANNA ELEANOR ROOSEVELT
Theodore Roosevelt	ALICE HATHAWAY LEE
	EDITH KERMIT CAROW
William Howard Taft	HELEN HERRON
Zachary Taylor	MARGARET SMITH
Harry S Truman	ELIZABETH VIRGINIA WALLACE
John Tyler	LETITIA CHRISTIAN
	JULIA GARDINER
Martin Van Buren	HANNAH HOES
George Washington	MARTHA DANDRIDGE CUSTIS
Woodrow Wilson	ELLEN LOUISE AXSON
	EDITH BOLLING GALT

---

pretty / FAIR, TRIM; BONNY; COMELY
pretty girl / DOLL; BEAUTY
prevail / WIN; SUCCEED, TRIUMPH
prevail on / INDUCE
prevailing / RIFE; DOMINANT
prevailing character / AIR; MOOD
prevalent / SPREAD, STRONG; WIDESPREAD
prevaricate / LIE; CAVIL, DODGE
prevarication / FALSEHOOD
prevaricator / LIAR; FIBBER

prevent / BAR; STOP, VETO; AVERT, BLOCK, CHECK, DEBAR, DETER, ESTOP; THWART
prevent in law / ESTOP
prevent from publishing / GAG; CENSOR
prevention / HINDRANCE
preventive / ANTIDOTE
preventive injection / SHOT; VACCINATION
previous / PRIOR; FORMER
previous night / EVE
previously / ERST; BEFORE

prevision / FORESIGHT
prey / LOOT; BOOTY, SPOIL; QUARRY
prey upon / RAVEN, RAVIN
Priam's daughter / CASSANDRA
Priam's father / LAOMEDON
Priam's kingdom / TROY
Priam's son / PARIS; HECTOR
Priam's wife / HECUBA
Pribilof resident / FURSEAL
price / COST, RATE; VALUE, WORTH
price of transportation / FARE
priceless / PRECIOUS, VALUABLE
prick / GOAD, HURT, PAIN, SPUR, URGE; DRIVE, STING. DOT, GAD
prickle / SETA; SPINE, THORN
prickling sensation / TINGLE
prickly / SETOSE; BRAMBLY; DIFFICULT
prickly heat / ITCH, RASH
prickly pear / TUNA; NOPAL; CACTUS; OPUNTIA
prickly plant / BRIAR, BRIER; NETTLE, TEASEL; THISTLE; ACANTHUS
prickly seed covering / BUR; BURR
prickly shrub / ROSE; BRIAR, GORSE
pride / POMP, SHOW; VANITY; CONCEIT, DIGNITY
pried / LEVERED, SNOOPED
priedieu / DESK
priest / FRA; ABBE, CURE; PADRE
priest of ancient Greece / MYSTAGOGUE
priest of ancient Rome / FLAMEN
priest of Celts / DRUID
priest's book / BREVIARY
priest's cap / BIRETTA
priest's vestment / ALB; COPE; AMICE, EPHOD, STOLE; CASSOCK, MANIPLE; CHASUBLE
prig / PRUDE
priggish / PRIM; AFFECTED
prill / NUGGET
prim / MIM; NEAT, NICE; STIFF
prima donna / DIVA
prima facie / APRIORI; APPARENT
primacy / SUPREMACY
primal / CHIEF, FIRST; ELEMENTAL
primarily / FIRST; PRINCIPALLY
primary / LEADING; ORIGINAL
primary, pref. / PROTO
primary color / RED; BLUE; GREEN; VIOLET, YELLOW
primate / APE; BISHOP; DIGNITARY
prime / CHIEF, FIRST; FOREMOST
prime minister / PREMIER
prime mover / MOTOR; ENGINE
primer / DONET
primeval / OLD; EARLY; ORIGINAL

primigenial / PRIMAL
primitive / EARLY; ANCIENT
primitive instrument / TABOR
primitive tool / CELT
primitively / ORIGINALLY
primness / STIFFNESS
primp / PREEN
primrose / SPINK; OXSLIP; COWSLIP. GAY
prince / RULER; SOVEREIGN
prince in Abyssinia / RAS
prince in Afghanistan / AMIR, EMIR
Prince Albert / FROCKCOAT
Prince Charming's token / SLIPPER
prince of the church / CARDINAL
Prince of Darkness / SATAN; AHRIMAN
prince in India / RAJA, RANA; RAJAH
Prince of Peace / CHRIST
Prince of Quacks / CAGLIOSTRO
prince in Slavic countries / KNEZ
Prince's author / MACHIAVELLI
princess in India / RANI; RANEE
princess in Moslem India / BEGUM
principal / TOP; ARCH, MAIN; CHIEF, FIRST
principal actor / HERO, STAR
principal college study / MAJOR
principal commodity / STAPLE
principal female character / HEROINE
principal male character / HERO
principal meal / CENA; DINNER
principality / ANGEL; PRINCEDOM
principally / MOSTLY; ESPECIALLY
principle / LAW; RULE; AXIOM, DOGMA, MAXIM, PRANA, TENET; ORIGIN, REASON
prink / PRIMP
print / DIE; STAMP; IMPRESS
printed fabric / BATIK; CALICO, CHINTZ, DAMASK; PAISLEY, PERCALE
printed journal / DAILY; NEWSPAPER
printed slur / LIBEL
printer / PRESSMAN; COMPOSITOR
printer's assistant / DEVIL
printer's error / TYPO; ERRATUM
printer's inker / BRAYER
printer's inscription / COLOPHON
printer's mark / DELE, STET; CARET
printer's measure / EM, EN; PICA, THIN; POINT
printer's proof / GALLEY
printer's space / EM, EN; QUAD, THIN; POINT
printer's term / RESET
printer's tray / CASE; STICK
printing / EDITION; TYPOGRAPHY

printing form / MAT; SIGNATURE
printing frame / CHASE; FRISKET
printing need / INK; PAPER
printing plate / CUT; STEREOTYPE
printing press part / BED; INKER, LEVER; PLATEN, ROLLER
prior / FORMER; EARLIER; ANTERIOR
prior to / ERE; BEFORE
priority / PREFERENCE
priory / CLOISTER
Priscian / GRAMMAR
prison / JUG, PEN; GAOL, JAIL, QUOD; CLINK; BASTILLE
prison chief / WARDEN
prison guard / SCREW; JAILER, KEEPER; TURNKEY
prison room / CELL
prison term / RAP; SENTENCE
prisoner / CON, LAG; CAPTIVE
prisoner's place during trial / DOCK
prisoner's surety / BAIL
pristine / ORIGINAL; UNTOUCHED
prittle-prattle / CHATTER
privacy / SOLITUDE; SECLUSION
private / HIDDEN, SECRET; RETIRED, SPECIAL; PERSONAL
private concert / MUSICALE
private detective / EYE
private entrance / POSTERN; BACKDOOR
private room / DEN; STUDY
private school / ACADEMY
private teacher / TUTOR
private wrong / TORT
privateer / RAIDER; CORSAIR
privately / APART; UNOFFICIALLY
privateness / PRIVACY
privation / LOSS, NEED, WANT
privative / NEGATIVE
privet / HEDGE
privilege / FAVOR, RIGHT; BENEFIT
privileged / EXEMPT, IMMUNE
privily / SECRETLY; PERSONALLY
privity / SECRECY; KNOWLEDGE
privy / SECRET; PRIVATE. OUTHOUSE
prize / PRY; VALUE; ESTEEM; ESTIMATE. GREE, MEED; AWARD, BOOTY, SPOIL; REWARD, TROPHY; GUERDON
prize for excellence / DESIRE
prize in numbers lottery / TERN
pro / TEACHER; PROFESSIONAL
pro rata / PROPORTIONALLY
pro tem / TEMPORARILY
proa / OUTRIGGER
probability / ODDS; CHANCE
probable / BELIKE, LIKELY; REASONABLE
probably / APPARENTLY

probation / TEST; TRIAL; PAROLE
probe / TEST; SEARCH; SCRUTINIZE. STYLET, TROCAR
probity / HONOR; VIRTUE; GOODNESS
problem / NUT; TASK; POSER; ENIGMA, RIDDLE; STUMPER
problem in arithmetic / SUM; EXAMPLE
problematical / DOUBTFUL
proboscid / ELEPHANT
proboscis / NOSE; SNOUT, TRUNK
proboscis monkey / KAHA
procedure / STEPS; PROCESS
proceed / GO; COME, FLOW, MOVE, PASS, WEND
proceed with difficulty / MOIL, WADE
proceedings / ACTA
proceeds / YIELD; INCOME; PRODUCE
process / SUMMONS; PROCEDURE
procession / FILE; MARCH, TRAIN; PARADE
proclaim / CRY; UTTER, VOICE
proclaim noisily / BLARE; BELLOW
proclaim openly / HERALD
proclamation / EDICT, DECREE; MANIFESTO
proclivity / BENT, BIAS; DRIFT
Procne's sister / PHILOMELA
procrastinate / DALLY, DELAY
procrastination / FABIANISM
procreate / BEAR; BEGET; FATHER
procreator / FATHER
Procris' husband / CEPHALUS
Procrustean measure / BED
proctor / PROXY; ADVISOR, MONITOR
procurator of Judea / PILATE
procure / GET, WIN; EARN, GAIN, REAP; EFFECT, OBTAIN
prod / GOAD, POKE, PUSH, STIR
prodigal / LAVISH; PROFUSE; WASTEFUL
prodigious / HUGE, VAST; ENORMOUS, MARVELOUS, MONSTROUS
prodigy / MARVEL; MIRACLE, PORTENT
prodrome / OMEN; WARNING
produce / BEAR, GIVE, MAKE, SHOW; BREED, CAUSE, YIELD. CROPS, FRUIT; EFFECT, RESULT; HARVEST
produce children / PROCREATE
produce design with acid / ETCH
produce fruit / BEAR
produced abroad / FOREIGN
produced by capital / INTEREST
produced here / DOMESTIC

producing cold / ALGIFIC
producing heat / CALORIC; CALORIFIC
producing motion / MOBILE, MOTILE
producing pus / PURULENT
product / CROP; FRUIT; RESULT
product of oxidation / RUST; ASHES
production / WORK; OUTPUT
production for stage / SHOW
productive / RICH; FERTILE
productive source / MINE; PLANT
proem / PREFACE, PRELUDE; PREAMBLE
profane / NOA; IMPURE, UNHOLY; IMPIOUS, WORLDLY. ABUSE; DEBASE
profanity / OATH; CURSE; INVECTIVE
profess / AVOW; SWEAR; DECLARE
professed / ACKNOWLEDGED
profession / ART; TRADE; CAREER
professional / PRO; SKILLED
professional beggar / MENDICANT
professional entertainer / ACTOR, COMIC; ARTIST
professional mourner / KEENER, WAILER
professional reader / ELOCUTIONIST
professional soldier / MERCENARY
professionally correct / ETHICAL
proffer / BID; OFFER; TENDER
proficiency / SKILL; DEXTERITY
proficient / ABLE; ADEPT; VERSED
profile / CONTOUR. OUTLINE
profit / USE; GAIN, VAIL; AVAIL. NET; ADVANTAGE
profitable / FAT; USEFUL; GAINFUL; LUCRATIVE
profitless / FUTILE; USELESS
profligate / CORRUPT, IMMORAL, VICIOUS
profound / DEEP; VIVID; SOLEMN, STRONG; INTENSE; ABSTRUSE; RECONDITE
profound dread / AWE
profound insensibility / COMA
profound knowledge / ERUDITION
profound wisdom / SAGACITY
profoundly earnest / INTENSE
profundity / DEPTH
profuse / LAVISH; COPIOUS
profusion / ABUNDANCE
prog / FOOD; PRICK
progenitor / SIRE; FATHER, PARENT; ANCESTOR
progeny / RACE, SEED; BREED, ISSUE, STOCK
prognosticate / AUGUR; PREDICT, PRESAGE

prognostication / OMEN
prognosticator / SEER; ORACLE; PROPHET
program / OUTLINE; SCHEDULE
program for meeting / AGENDA
progress / GO; GAIN; MARCH; ADVANCE. GROWTH
progressing by tens / DECIMAL
progressively / TEMPORALLY
prohibit / BAN, BAR; VETO; CHECK, DEBAR, ESTOP, TABOO; FORBID
prohibited / TABU; TABOO; ILLICIT
prohibition / BAN; EMBARGO
prohibitionist / DRY; TEETOTALER
prohibitionist organization / WCTU
prohibitory / RESTRICTIVE
project / JUT; ABUT, DRAW, HURL; BULGE, THROW; CONCOCT. IDEA, PLAN; DESIGN, SCHEME
projectile / SHELL; BULLET, ROCKET; GRENADE, MISSILE, TORPEDO
projecting edge / RIM; EAVE
projecting jaw / GIB
projecting part / KNOB
projecting part of wood joint / TENON
projecting peak of cap / VISOR
projecting piece / ARM, FIN; SHELF
projecting rim / FLANGE
projecting rock / TOR; CRAG
projecting tooth / FANG, SNAG
projecting window / BAY; ORIEL; DORMER
projection / LEG, LUG; BARB, BUMP, TAIL, WING; PRONG; SCHEME
projection at ankle / MALLEOLUS
projection on cog / TOOTH
projection on index card / TAB
prolapse / PTOSIS
proletariat / POOR; WORKERS
prolific / FERTILE. TEEMING
prolix / TEDIOUS, VERBOSE
prologue / PREFACE
prolong / DEFER, DELAY; EXTEND
prolongation / CUNCTATION
prolonged sound / HOWL
prolonged speech / TIRADE
promenade / MALL, WALK; PARADE
Promethean fire / INSPIRATION
Prometheus' father / IAPETUS
Prometheus' gift to man / FIRE
prominence / PEAK; PRESTIGE
prominent / CHIEF; MARKED; EMINENT, SALIENT; IMPORTANT

prominent person / LION, STAR
promiscuous / COMMON; CONFUSED
promise / VOW; AGREE, SWEAR; PLEDGE. WORD; COVENANT
promise to pay / IOU
Promised Land / CANAAN
promising / AUSPICIOUS
promissory note / IOU; PLEDGE
promontory / TOR; CAPE, NAZE, NESS; POINT; HEADLAND
promote / AID; ABET, HELP, STIR; RAISE; FOSTER, PREFER; ADVANCE
promoter / ENTREPRENEUR
promotion / CAMPAIGN; PREFERMENT
prompt / CUE; HINT, URGE; IMPEL. APT; YARE; ALERT, BRISK, QUICK
promptitude / QUICKNESS
promptly / ANON, SOON
promulgate / BLAZE, BRUIT
pronate / BENT; BOWED
prone / APT; FLAT; EAGER
proneness / PROPENSITY
prong / NIB; HOOK, NAIL, TINE; LANCE, TOOTH; BAYONET
pronged implement / FORK
pronghorn / CABREE, CABRET, CABRIE, CABRIT; ANTELOPE
pronoun / HE, IT, ME, US, WE, YE; HIM, ONE, SHE; THAT, THEE, THEM, THEY, THIS, THOU; THESE, THOSE. See also possessive pronoun
pronounce / SPEAK, UTTER; DECLARE
pronounce with emphasis / ACCENT, STRESS
pronounce imperfectly / LISP, SLUR; MUMBLE; LALLATE
pronouncement / DICTUM; DECLARATION
pronto / NOW; QUICKLY
pronunciation mark / BREVE, TILDE; CEDILLA; DIERESIS; DIACRITIC
proof / TEST; ASSAY, TRIAL
proof from typesetter / GALLEY
proofreader's aide / COPYHOLDER
proofreader's mark / DELE, STET; CARET
prop / HOLD; SHORE; BOLSTER, SUPPORT; BUTTRESS. LEG; STAY; BRACE
propaganda / PRESSAGENTRY
propagate / BEGET, BREED; SPREAD
propagated / PUBLISHED
propel / PEG, SHY; FLIP, MOVE, URGE; DRIVE, IMPEL; LAUNCH
propel a boat / OAR, ROW

propeller / FAN, OAR; BLADE, SCREW; DRIVER
propensity / BENT, BIAS; TENDENCY
proper / DUE, FIT; FAIR, JUST, MEET, PRIM; EXACT, RIGHT; DECENT
property / GEAR; ASSET, GOODS; ESTATE, REALTY, WEALTH; EFFECTS
property charge / TAX; LIEN
property independently owned / ALOD; ALLOD; ALODIUM; ALLODIUM
property in India / DHAN
property instrument / DEED; LEASE
property of matter / FORM, MASS; INERTIA; SUBSTANCE
property part / ASSET
property receiver / ALIENEE
property seller / ALIENOR
prophasis / OUTLOOK; PROGNOSIS
prophecy, pert. to / PYTHONIC
prophesy / AUGUR; DIVINE, PREACH; PREDICT; FORETELL
prophet / SAGE, SEER; AUGUR
prophet of the Bible / AMOS, ESAU, EZRA, JOEL; HOSEA, JONAH, MICAH, NAHUM; DANIEL, ELISHA, HAGGAI, ISAIAH; EZEKIEL; JEREMIAH
prophet of Islam / MAHOMET; MOHAMMED, MUHAMMAD
prophetess / SIBYL; SEERESS
prophetic / VATIC; VATICAL; ORACULAR; VATICINAL
prophets / VATES; NEBIIM
propinquity / KINSHIP; NEARNESS; PROXIMITY
propitiate / PACIFY; APPEASE
propitious / HAPPY, LUCKY; BENIGN
propone / ARGUE, OFFER
proponent / ADVOCATE
proportion / PART, RATE; RATIO
proportional / MODULAR
proportionate / COMMENSURATE
proportionately / PRORATA
proposal / BID; OFFER; DESIGN, SCHEME, TENDER; OVERTURE
propose / PRESENT, PROFFER
propose for office / NOMINATE
proposed international language / OD, RO; IDO; LATINO; VOLAPUK; ESPERANTO
proposed law / BILL
proposition / PLAN; LEMMA; THESIS; PREMISE, THEOREM
propound / SUBMIT; PROPOSE
propounding / STATING
proprietor / OWNER; HOLDER
propriety / DECENCY, DECORUM, MODESTY

proptosis / PROTRUSION
propulsive / IMPELLING
prorate / SHARE; DIVIDE
prorogate / DEFER, DELAY
prorogue / ADJOURN
prosaic / WORKADAY;
COMMONPLACE
proscribe / BAN; DOOM; BANISH,
FORBID, OUTLAW
prose / DULL; PLAIN; ORDINARY
prosecute / ACCUSE, FOLLOW
prosecute in court / SUE; ACCUSE;
LITIGATE
prosecutor / DA; SUER
proselyte / CONVERT
proselyte to Judaism / GER
Proserpina / PERSEPHONE
Proserpina's husband / PLUTO
prosit / SALUD, SKOAL, TOAST,
YASAS; CHEERS; SLAINTE
prosody / VERSIFICATION
prospect / HOPE, SHOW, VIEW;
SCENE, SIGHT
prospector / ARGONAUT
prosper / FARE; THRIVE; SUCCEED
prosperity / HAP; WEAL; WELFARE
Prospero's servant / ARIEL
prosperous / PALMY; THRIVING
prosperous times / UPS; BOOM
prostrate / BOW; RUIN; ABASE.
FLAT; PRONE; FALLEN
prosy / DRY; DULL; HEAVY;
JEJUNE; TEDIOUS; UNAFFECTED
protagonist / HERO; SPOKESMAN
protean / VERSATILE;
MULTIVARIOUS
protect / SAVE; BLESS, COVER
protected / SHIELDED
protecting / TUTELARY
protecting against, c.f. / PARA
protecting power / EGIS; AEGIS
protecting shelter / LEE
protection / ARMOR; REFUGE,
SAFETY, SHIELD; SHELTER
protection of inventor's rights /
PATENT
protection against loss /
INSURANCE
protection against plagiarism /
COPYRIGHT
protection rights / MUND; GRITH
protection for traveler / PASSPORT
protective / GUARDIAN
protective angle / REDAN
protective backing / PATRONAGE
protective covering / ARMOR,
PAINT
protective clothing / APRON;
COVERALL
protective exudation / INK
protective gear / MASK; GLOVES
protective headgear / HELMET,
MORION

protective sponsorship / AEGIS
protective trench / MOAT
protector / DEFENDER. See also
patron
protege / WARD; CLIENT;
DISCIPLE
protein food / EGG; MEAT, MILK
protest / AVER, AVOW; DEMUR;
AFFIRM, ASSERT, OBJECT;
DISSENT
protestant nonconformist /
SECTARY
prototype / IDEAL; PATTERN
prototype of book / MANUSCRIPT
protozoan / AMEBA; AMOEBA;
STENTOR; FORAMINIFER
protract / EKE; DELAY; EXTEND
protracted / DRAWNOUT
protractor / THEODOLITE
protrude / JUT; BULGE; PROJECT
protrude the lips / POUT
protruding / EXTENDING
protruding tooth / FANG, TUSH,
TUSK
protuberance / JAG, NUB, WEN;
BUMP, HUMP, KNOB, KNOT,
LOBE
protuberance of skull / INION
protuberant / TOROSE; BULGING
proud / VAIN; GRAND; HAUGHTY
prove / TRY; SHOW, TEST; EVINCE,
VERIFY; CONFIRM, EXAMINE
proved / QED. DEMONSTRATED
proved proposition / THEOREM
proven / SHOWN, TRIED; PROVED
provenance / ORIGIN
Provençal / LANGUEDOC
Provençal capital / AIX
Provençal poet / MISTRAL
Provençal poets group / FELIBRIGE
Provençal verse form / ALBA;
TENSON; SERENA; PARTIMEN
provender / HAY
proverb / SAW; ADAGE, AXIOM,
GNOME, MAXIM; BYWORD,
DICTUM, SAYING; APHORISM,
APOTHEGM
proverbial / FAMED; FAMOUS
provide / CATER, ENDOW, ENDUE
provide food / CATER
provide footwear / SHOE
provide funds / ENDOW
provide gear / EQUIP
provide for needs / SUPPLY
provide weapons / ARM
provided / IF
provided that / SO
provident / FRUGAL; PRUDENT,
THRIFTY; CAUTIOUS
province / COLONY, DOMAIN,
OFFICE, REGION, SPHERE
provincial speech / PATOIS
provision / GRIST; SUPPLY

provision merchant / GROCER
provisional / TENTATIVE
provisional stipulation / PROVISO
provisional word / WHEREAS
provisions / FARE; VIANDS
proviso / CLAUSE; STIPULATION
provoke / VEX; FRET, RILE, STIR
provoke to anger / IRE; ENRAGE
provoked / INCITED, NETTLED
provost / HEAD; CHIEF
prow / BOW; NOSE, STEM
prowess / VALOR; DARING;
  BRAVERY
prowl / LURK; SNEAK, STEAL
proximate / NEXT; DIRECT;
  NEAREST
proximity / PRESENCE, VICINITY;
  ADJACENCY; CONTIGUITY
proxy / AGENT; DEPUTY;
  ATTORNEY, DELEGATE
prude / PRIG
prudence / CAUTION; DISCRETION
prudent / SAGE, WARY, WISE;
  CHARY; FRUGAL, SAVING;
  CAREFUL
prudish / COY; NICE; DEMURE
prune / LOP; CLIP, SNED, TRIM;
  RAZEE. PLUM
prurient / LEWD; ITCHING
Prussian aristocrat / JUNKER
Prussian city / KIEL; POTSDAM
Prussian emperor / KAISER;
  WILHELM
Prussian river / ELBE, ODER
Prussian ruling house /
  HOHENZOLLERN
Prussian soldier / ULAN; UHLAN
Prussian spa / EMS
pry / NOSE, PEEP; SNOOP. LEVER
prying / CURIOUS
psalm / ODE; HYMN, SONG
psalm group / HALLEL
psalmist / DAVID
psalms word / SELAH
psalter / BOOK
pseudonym / NOM; ALIAS;
  ANANYM, ANONYM, PENNAME;
  NOMDEPLUME; NOMDEGUERRE.
  See also alias, pen name
PSI study / PARAPSYCHOLOGY
psyche / SOUL
Psyche's lover / CUPID
psychiatrist / JUNG; ADLER, BRILL,
  FREUD; SHRINK; ALIENIST
psychopathic / CRAZED
psychrometer / HYGROMETER
ptarmigan / RYPE
pteric / WINGLIKE
ptisan / TEA; BREW; TISANE
ptosis / PROLAPSE
ptyalism / DROOLING
pubertal psychosis /
  HEBEPHRENIA

public / OPEN; OVERT; COMMON;
  GENERAL. PEOPLE
public accusation / DENOUNCE-
  MENT
public announcer / CRIER;
  HERALD
public car / BUS, CAB; TAXI
public clerk / SCRIBE
public coach / BUS
public declaration / BULLETIN
public excitement / FUROR;
  FURORE
public gathering / FORUM;
  MEETING
public grounds / PARK
public house / INN; HOTEL, LODGE
public investigator / OMBUDSMAN
public land / PARK
public life / POLITICS
public lodging / INN; HOTEL,
  MOTEL
public notice / AD; EDICT
public officer / NOTARY;
  POLICEMAN
public opinion tester / GALLUP,
  HARRIS
public regard / REPUTE
public report / RUMOR
public sale / AUCTION
public speaking / ORATORY
public transport / BUS, CAB; TAXI;
  TRAIN
public walk / MALL; ALAMEDA
public warehouse / ETAPE
public way / ROAD; STREET;
  HIGHWAY
publication / ISSUE, PAPER;
  EDITION; MAGAZINE,
  PAMPHLET; NEWSPAPER
publicity / ADVERTISING
publicize / AIR; ANNOUNCE
publish / AIR; EDIT, EMIT; ISSUE,
  UTTER
publish illegally / PIRATE
published / OUT; ISSUED; PRINTED
published copy / EDITION
published price / LIST
publisher's description / BLURB
Puccini heroine / MIMI;
  CIOCIOSAN
Puccini opera / MANON, TOSCA
puck / RUBBER
pucker / CRIMP, PURSE. WRINKLE
pudding / PAP; DUFF, SAGO
pudding stone / CONGLOMERATE
puddinghead / DIMWIT; FATHEAD
puddle / POND, POOL; PLASH
puddock / KITE, TOAD; BUZZARD
pudency / MODESTY;
  DEMURENESS
pudgy / FAT; DUMPY, SHORT
pueblo ceremonial room / KIVA
pueblo dweller / HOPI; INDIAN

Pueblo Indian / HANO, HOPI, MOKI, PIRO, TANO, TAOS, TEWA, TIWA, ZUNI; JEMEZ, KERES, MOQUI, NAMBE
puerile / IDLE, WEAK; SILLY; CHILDISH, JUVENILE
Puerto Rican government / COMMONWEALTH
Puerto Rican island / MONA; CULEBRA, VIEQUES
Puerto Rican town / PONCE, YAUCO
Puerto Rico / BORINQUEN
Puerto Rico capital / SANJUAN
puff / BLOW, PANT, WAFT
puff up / BLOAT, ELATE; DISTEND
puffbird / BARBET; DREAMER
puffer / TAMBOR; PORPOISE
puffy muffin / POPOVER
Puget Sound city / TACOMA; SEATTLE
pugilism / BOXING; FIGHTING
pugilism, pert. to / FISTIC
pugilist / BOXER; FIGHTER
pugilist's aide / SECOND; HANDLER
pugnacious / BELLICOSE
pugnosed / CAMUS
puisne / JUNIOR; INFERIOR
puissant / POTENT, STRONG
pulchritude / GRACE; BEAUTY
pule / WHINE; WHIMPER
pull / LUG, TUG; DRAG, HALE, HAUL, HOLD, TEAR
pull after / TOW
pull along / DRAW
pull back / BLENCH, RECOIL
pull down / RAZE
pull forcibly / HAUL
pull off / AVULSE
pull out / EXTRACT
pull to pieces / REND
pull sharply / YANK
pull strings / PRESSURE
pull with tackle / BOUSE
pull through / SURVIVE
pull tight / BOUSE, TRICE
pull up / PLUCK; UPROOT
pull up sharply / BRAKE
pulled candy / TAFFY
pullet / HEN; CHICK
pulley frame / BLOCK
pulleywheel / SHEAVE
pullover / SWEATER
pullulate / TEEM; SPROUT
pulp / PITH; CHYME, FLESH
pulpit / AMBO, BEMA; CLERGY; ROSTRUM
pulpy / SOFT; SUCCULENT
pulpy fruit / UVA; BERRY, DRUPE, GRAPE
pulpy mass / POMACE
pulsate / BEAT; THROB; LIBRATE
pulse / BEAT; THROB; PULSIFIC

pulverize / MULL; GRIND, STAMP
pulverized tobacco / SNUFF
pulverizing machine / MILL; PESTLE
pulverous / DUSTY; POWDERY
puma / COUGAR; PANTHER
pummel / BEAT
pump handle / SWIPE
pun / PARONOMASIA
punch / ADE, JAB; PROD; NEGUS
Punch's dog / TOBY
Punch's wife / JUDY
punctate / POINTED, SPOTTED
punctilious / NICE; PRECISE
punctilious person / PRIG; PRECISIAN
punctual / EXACT; PROMPT
punctuate / STRESS; INTERRUPT
punctuation mark / DOT, DASH; COLON; COMMA, POINT; HYPHEN, PERIOD; GUILLEMET, SEMICOLON
puncture / STAB; PIERCE
punctured / PINKED
pundit / EXPERT; HORSEMOUTH
pung / SLED
pungency / POIGNANCY
pungent / HOT, TEZ; KEEN, RACY; ACRID, SHARP, SPICY, TANGY
pungent buds / CLOVES
pungent bulb / ONION; GARLIC
pungent seasoning / SPICE; CONDIMENT
pungent taste / TANG
pungi / BIN
pungle / SHRIVEL
Punic hero / HAMILCAR, HANNIBAL
punish / LASH; CHASTEN, CORRECT, SCOURGE; CHASTISE
punish by fine / MULCT; AMERCE
punishing rod / FERULE; BASTINADO
punishment / PENALTY
punishment, pert. to / PUNITIVE
punitive / PENAL
Punjab city / SIMLA; LAHORE
Punjab native / JAT
Punjab river / BEAS; SUTLEJ
Punjab warrior / SIKH
punk / BAD. BUNK; AMADOU
punkah / FAN
punt / KICK. BOAT
punting pole / QUANT
puny / MEAN, TINY, WEAK; FRAIL
pup / WHELP
pupa / INSTAR; CHRYSALIS
pupil / TYRO; NOVICE; LEARNER, STUDENT; DISCIPLE
puppet / DOLL; JUDY; PUNCH; MARIONETTE
puppet government / SATRAPY

puppet master / PUPPETEER
puppy / DOGLET
purchasable / VENAL; CORRUPT
purchase / BUY, GET; GAIN; ACATE
purdah / SECLUSION
pure / REAL; CLEAN, CLEAR, SHEER; CHASTE, HONEST
pure thought / NOESIS
pure trona / URAO
puree / SOUP
purely / ONLY; EASILY, SIMPLY
purely intellectual knowledge / NOESIS
purgative / PHYSIC; CATHARTIC
purgative drug / JALAP, SALTS, SENNA; CATHARTIC
purgative oil / CASTOR, CROTON
purgatory / LIMBO
purge / CLEAN, CLEAR, SCOUR
purification / LUSTRUM
purify / CLEAN, PURGE; FILTER, REFINE; CLEANSE; LUSTRATE
purl / RIB; EDDY, FLOW; RIPPLE
purloin / CRIB; FILCH, STEAL
purloined / PILFERED
purple / LIVID, REGAL; ORNATE, TYRIAN; CRIMSON
purple brown / PUCE
purple dye shell / MUREX
purple medic / LUCERNE
purple melic / MOORGRASS
purple ragwort / JACOBY
purple red / MAGENTA
purple seaweed / NORI, SION
purple shade / PUCE; LILAC, MAUVE; MODENA; MAGENTA
purple-flowered shrub / LILAC
purport / GIST; DRIFT, SCOPE, SENSE, TENOR
purpose / AIM, END; GOAL, PLAN, SAKE, VIEW; DRIFT
purposed / MEANT; INTENDED
purposeful / TELIC
purse / PUCKER; WRINKLE, BAG
purse net / SEINE
purser / BURSAR; CASHIER
pursue / PLY; HUNT, SEEK; CHASE
pursue covertly / STALK; SHADOW
pursuit / HUNT; CHASE
pursy / FAT; STOUT, THICK
purvey / SUPPLY; PROVIDE
purvey food / CATER
purveyor to army / SUTLER
purview / RANGE; EXTENT; CONTENT
push / URGE; BOOST, DRIVE, FORCE, IMPEL, PRESS
push away / SPURN
push down / DEPRESS
push forward / PROD; NUDGE
push on / ADVANCE, PROCEED

push up / LIFT; BOOST
pusher / FAN; DEALER
pusillanimous / WEAK; FAINT
pussy / CAT
pussycat / KITTY
pustule / PIMPLE; BLISTER
put / LAY, SET; APPLY, PLACE
put into action / START; ACTUATE; ACTIVATE
put aside / FOB; DAFF; TABLE
put away / EAT; STORE
put back / DEMOTE; RESTORE
put ball into play / SERVE; KICKOFF
put in bank / DEPOSIT
put before / APPOSE, PREFIX
put on desert island / MAROON
put in dossier / FILE
put down / LAY. DENIGRATE
put to flight / ROUT
put forth / MOOT; EXERT, ISSUE
put forth effort / TRY; EXERT
put on guard / WARN
put in / ENTER; INSERT
put load on / LADE; BURDEN
put money into / INVEST
put new shoes on / RETIRE
put new surface on / RETREAD
put off / DELAY
put on / DON
put in order / FILE, TIDY; ASSORT, POLICE, SETTLE; ARRANGE
put out / OUST; EJECT, EVICT
put out of mind / FORGET
put out of place / MISLAY
put into practice / USE
put in reciprocal relation / ADJUST; CORRELATE
put to rest / ALLAY
put into rhyme / VERSIFY
put right / AMEND
put to shame / ABASH
put together / COMPILE
put into type / SET
put up / CAN; ERECT; PRESERVE
put up with / TOLERATE
put to use / APPLY; UTILIZE
put in vessel / CAN, POT; LADE
putative / REPUTED; SUPPOSED
putrefaction / ROT; DECAY
putrefy / DECOMPOSE
putrescent / ROTTING
putrid / FOUL; ROTTEN; CORRUPT
Putsch / COUPDETAT
puttock / HAWK, KITE; BUZZARD
puzzle / POSE; BESET; BAFFLE. POSER, REBUS; RIDDLE; CHARADE; ACROSTIC
puzzling / CRYPTIC; ENIGMATIC
puzzling problem / SNAG; TEASER
Pwyll's realm / ANNWFN
Pwyll's wife / RHIANNON
Pygmalion's statue / GALATEA

pygmean / WEE; SMALL; DWARFISH

pygmy / ATOMY, DWARF; MANIKIN

pygmy chimpanzee / BONOBO

Pylades' friend / ORESTES

Pylades' wife / ELECTRA

pylon / TOWER; MARKER

pyramid builder / KHUFU; CHEOPS

Pyramus' lover / THISBE

Pyrenees chamois / IZARD

Pyrenees principality / ANDORRA

pyrexia / FEVER

pyriform / PEARSHAPED

pyromaniac / FIREBUG; ARSONIST

pyrosis / HEARTBURN

Pythagoras' isle / SAMOS

python / SERPENT; CONSTRICTOR

pythonic / ORACULAR; PROPHETIC

pyx / COFFER; CIBORIUM

pyxis / ARGO; JEWELCASE

Q

Q in chess / QUEEN

Q.E.D. word / ERAT, QUOD

Qatar capital / DOHA

quas / AS

quab / EELPOUT, GUDGEON

quack / HUMBUG; IMPOSTOR; CHARLATAN

quack medicine / CUREALL, NOSTRUM

quackery / IMPOSTURE; EMPIRICISM

quad / SPACE; CAMPUS

quadra / LISTEL, PLINTH

quadragenarian / FORTY

quadragesima / LENT

quadrangle / QUAD; SQUARE; QUADRILATERAL

quadrant / ARC; QUARTER

quadrat / EM, EN; SPACE

quadrate / ADAPT, AGREE

quadriga / CHARIOT

quadrille / DANCE

quadrille paper / GRAPH

quadruped / OX; ASS; DEER, MULE; BEAST, HORSE; ANIMAL, MAMMAL

quadruped's mother / DAM

quadruplicate / FOURFOLD

quaere / ASK; QUERY

quaff / SWIG; DRINK

quaggy / OOZY; BOGGY; SQUELCHY

quagmire / BOG, FEN; MORASS, SLOUGH

quahog / CLAM

quai / QUAY; EMBANKMENT

quail / COWER, QUAKE; FLINCH, COLIN; BOBWHITE; PARTRIDGE

quail flock / BEVY

quaint / ODD; DROLL; ANTIQUE, ARCHAIC, CURIOUS, STRANGE; FANCIFUL

quake / SHAKE; QUIVER; SHUDDER, TREMBLE, TREMOR; TEMBLOR

quaker / ASPEN

Quaker / FRIEND

Quaker City / PHILADELPHIA

Quaker poet / BARTON; WHITTIER

quaking / TREPID; SHAKING

quaking tree / ASPEN

qualification / ABILITY, FITNESS, SHADING

qualified / APT, FIT; ABLE; ADEQUATE

qualify / VARY; ABATE, ADAPT, LIMIT

quality / RANK, SORT; CLASS, TRAIT; NATURE, STATUS, TEMPER; CALIBER; NOBILITY, STANDING

quality, suffix / ANCE

quality of being poisonous / TOXICITY

quality of sound / TONE; PITCH; TIMBRE

quality of the unwanted / UNDESIRABILITY

qualm / DEMUR; NAUSEA; SCRUPLE

quandary / FIX; DOUBT; PLIGHT; DILEMMA

quantify / EXPRESS, MEASURE; INDICATE

quantity / SUM; MASS, PART, SIZE; SHARE; AMOUNT, EXTENT, ANY; SOME

quantity buying / WHOLESALE

quantity of matter / BULK, LUMP, MASS

quantity of medicine / DOSE; DOSAGE; DRAUGHT

quantity not expressible in whole numbers / SURD

quantity of paper / REAM; QUIRE; BUNDLE

quantity of yarn / LEA; HANK, REEL; SKEIN

quantity of years / AGE, ERA; PERIOD

quantum / BULK; AMOUNT; PORTION; INCREMENT

Quapaw Indian / ARKANSAS

quarantine / ISOLATION, RESTRAIN; INTERDICT

quarantine building / LAZARET

quarantine flag color / YELLOW

quarantine ship / LAZARETTO

quarrel / ROW; FEUD, SPAT, TIFF; BRAWL, BROIL, FIGHT; AFFRAY, DUSTUP, FRACAS, TUMULT; DISPUTE

quarrelsome / CROSS; BRAWLING, CHOLERIC; IRASCIBLE

quarry / PIT; GAME, PREY; EXCAVATION

quarryman / HEWER; GETTER; QUARRIER

quart / CARTE; FOURTH

quartan / AGUE; FEVER

quarter / COIN; MERCY; FOURTH, REGION; DISTRICT. LODGE; BILLET

quarter circle / QUADRANT

quarter note / CROTCHET

quarter pint / GILL

quarter year / RAITH

quarterbacks' replay day / MONDAY

quarter-round molding / OVOLO

quartet / TETRAD; FOURSOME

quartz / CACO, ONYX, SARD; AGATE, CHERT, FLINT, PRASE, SILEX; JASPER, SILICA; CRYSTAL

quash / ABATE, ANNUL; CANCEL, VACATE

quasi / ASIF; SEEMINGLY

quat / PIMPLE

quatch / FLAT

quatern / FOURFOLD

quaternion / FACTOR, TETRAD

quaver / SHAKE, TRILL; TREMBLE

quavering tone / VIBRATO

quavering voice / TREMOLO

quay / DOCK; JETTY, LEVEE, WHARF

quayside / DOCKS

quean / WENCH; HARLOT

queasy / DELICATE; SQUEAMISH

Quebec capital / QUEBEC

Quebec city / HULL; SHERBROOKE

Quebec explorer / CARTIER; CHAMPLAIN

Quebec peninsula / GASPE

Quebec waterfall / SHAWINIGAN; MONTMORENCY

Quebec's largest city / MONTREAL

Quebec's patron saint / ANNE

Quechua / INCA, PUNO; KESHWA

queen / REGINA; CZARINA; EMPRESS, TSARINA

Queen of the Adriatic / VENICE

Queen of the Antilles / CUBA

queen of Carthage / DIDO

Queen Charlotte's island Indian / HAIDA

Queen City / CINCINNATI

Queen Elizabeth I / ORIANA

queen of fairies / MAB, UNA; TITANIA

queen of the gods / HERA, JUNO, SATI

queen of heaven / HERA, MARY

queen of Ithaca / PENELOPE

queen of King Arthur / GUINEVERE

queen of Navarre / MARGARET

queen of night / MOON

queen of the Nile / CLEO; CLEOPATRA

Queen of the North / EDINBURGH

Queen of Scots / MARY

Queen of the Sea / TYRE

queen of Sheba / BALKIS

queen in solo / BASTA; SPADILLA

Queen Victoria's husband / ALBERT

queenly / ROYAL

queen's attendants / LADIES-INWAITING

Queens County area / JAMAICA; FLUSHING

Queensland bush nut / BOPPLE

Queensland cape / YORK

Queensland capital / BRISBANE

Queensland city / CAIRNS, GYMPIE

Queensland coral reef / BARRIER

Queensland hemp / SIDA; JELLYLEAF

Queensland river / BURDEKIN

Queensland tribe / GOA; KABI, WAKA

Queenstown / COBH

queer / ODD; DROLL; QUAINT; CURIOUS, ERRATIC, STRANGE, UNUSUAL; PECULIAR

queest / RINGDOVE

Queets Indians / QUAITSO

quell / CALM, CURB, HUSH, LULL; ALLAY, CHECK

Quelpart / CHEJU

Quemoy's neighbor / AMOY

quench / ALLAY; EXTINGUISH

quench thirst / SLAKE

querimonious / GROUCHY; MALCONTENT; COMPLAINING

quern / MILL; HANDMILL; MILLSTONE

querulous / CROSS; PEEVISH; PETULANT

query / ASK; QUESTION. INQUIRY

quest / HUNT; SEARCH; PURSUIT

quest for / SEEK

Questing Beast's hunter / PELLINORE

question / ASK; DOUBT, GRILL, QUERY; DEBATE; DISPUTE, INQUIRE. POINT, TOPIC; SUBJECT

question on the floor / MOTION

questionable / MOOT; SHADY; DOUBTFUL; EQUIVOCAL, UNCERTAIN

questioner / QUIZZER

quetzal / TROGON
Quetzalcoatl among Mayans / KUKULCAN
queue / CUE; LINE, TAIL; PIGTAIL
quibble / CAVIL, EVADE, PUN; TRIFLE
quick / FAST, KEEN; AGILE, ALERT, ALIVE, FLEET, HASTY, RAPID, READY, SHARP, SWIFT
quick blow / RAP, TAP; FILLIP
quick bread / MUFFIN; BISCUIT
quick drink / NIP
quick glance / PEEP; GLIMPSE
quick jerk / YANK; TWITCH
quick to learn / APT; SMART
quick look / GLANCE; GLIMPSE
quick in music / TOSTO; PRESTO; ALLEGRO
quick punch / JAB; CLIP
quick sketcher / OUTLINER
quick witted / APT; KEEN; ACUTE, ALERT
quicken / CHEER, HURRY; EXCITE, HASTEN
quickly / SOON; PRONTO; SWIFTLY
quickly attached without buttons / SNAPON
quickly donned / SLIPON
quickness / HASTE, SPEED; CELERITY
quicksand / SYRT; MORASS
quicksilver / MERCURY; HEAUTARIT; HYDRARGYRUM
quickstep / DANCE, MARCH
quid / CUD; PLUG; POUND; TOBACCO
quid pro quo / REJOINDER, TITFORTAT
quiddity / QUIBBLE
quiddle / DELAY; DAWDLE
quidnunc / SNOOP; GOSSIP
quiescence / REST; PEACE, QUIET; REPOSE
quiescent / LATENT, STATIC; DORMANT
quiet / CALM, EASE, HUSH, LULL; ALLAY; SOOTHE. MILD; INERT, STILL; GENTLE, PLACID, SERENE. REST; PEACE
quiet whisper / SH; PST, TST
quieting pain / ANALGESIC
quietist / MOLINIST
quietly humble / MEEK
quietude / PEACE; REPOSE; CALMNESS
quietus / REST; DEATH, PEACE
quilkin / FROG, TOAD
quill / PEN; STALK; WRITER; FEATHER; PLECTRUM
quill feather / REMEX
quill for winding silk / COP

quillai / SOAPBARK
quilled / PLAITED
quills / CALAMI
Quilp's wife / BETSY
quilt / COVER, DUVET, EIDER; COUNTERPANE
quilting / PADDING; STITCHING
quilting party / BEE
quinia / QUININE
quinine / TONIC; FEBRIFUGE
quinsy / ANGINA
quintessence / PITH; CREAM; ELIXIR; ESSENCE
quintet / FIVE
quintuple / FIVEFOLD
quip / GIBE, JEER, JEST, JOKE
quirk / KINK, WHIM; CRANK, TWIST
quirt / WHIP; ROMAL
quisling / TRAITOR
quit / FREE, STOP; CEASE, CLEAR, LEAVE; DEPART, RESIGN, RETIRE
quit office / RESIGN
quit the premises / VACATE
quitclaim / RELEASE; CONVEYANCE
quite / ALL; VERY; WHOLLY; TOTALLY
quite an amount / LOT
quite clear / LUCID
quite extended / LONG
quite involved / INTRICATE
quite a knack / TALENT
quite masculine / VIRILE
quite salable / COMMERCIAL
quite a storm / TEMPEST
quite a tease / BAITER
quite a twinge / STAB
quite worked up / IRATE
quittance / DISCHARGE
quitter / COWARD; SHIRKER
quitter of bed / RISER
quiver / SHAKE; SHIVER; SHUDDER, TREMBLE
Quivira / WICHITA
Quixote's author / CERVANTES
Quixote's horse / ROSINANTE
Quixote's squire / SANCHO
quixotic / WILD; FANCIFUL, ROMANTIC; VISIONARY
quiz / BANTER, PUZZLE; QUESTION
quizzical / COMICAL; QUERULOUS
quod / JAIL; COURT; PRISON
quodlibet / QUIBBLE; FANTASIA
quoin / WEDGE
quoit / RING; DISCUS
quoits peg / HOB
quokka / WALLABY; PADMELON
quondam / FORMER; ERSTWHILE

quorum / PLENUM; MAJORITY
quota / PART, RATE; SHARE; RATION
quotable witticism / MOT
quotation / EXTRACT, PASSAGE; CITATION
quotation mark / GUILLEMET

quote / CITE; ADDUCE, ALLEGE
quoth / SAID; SPAKE, SPOKE
quotha / INDEED
quotidian / DAILY, USUAL
quotient / ANSWER, RESULT
quotum / RATIO, SHARE
Quran / KORAN; ALKORAN

R

Ra / GOD; DEITY
raad / CATFISH
rabbet / GROOVE, RECESS
rabbi / MASTER; TEACHER; MINISTER
rabbish / RASH; BOISTEROUS
rabbit / CONY, HARE; BUNNY, CONEY, LAPIN, LEPRE
rabbit foot / CHARM; TALISMAN
rabbit fur / LAPIN
rabbit pen / HUTCH
rabbit root / SARSAPARILLA
rabbit's burrow / WARREN
rabbit's tail / SCUT
rabbity / OVERRUN
rabble / MOB; RAFF, ROUT; CROWD
rabble-rouser / FIREBRAND
Rabelaisian / GROSS; SATIRICAL
rabid / MAD; RAGING, RAVING; FURIOUS
rabid zeal / FANATICISM
rabies / LYSSA; HYDROPHOBIA
raca / WORTHLESS
raccoon / COON
raccoon-like mammal / COATI
race / ROOT; BREED, HOUSE, ISSUE, STOCK, TRIBE; COURSE; LINEAGE
race, pert. to / ETHNIC
race of animals / BREED
race for boats / REGATTA
race horse / MANTIS, PLATER; ARABIAN; THOROUGHBRED
race for a team / RELAY
race of wheat / SPELT
racecourse / RING, TURF; TRACK; CIRCUS
racecourse area / STRETCH
raced / RAN; SPED
raceme / SPIKE
racemose / BRANCHING
racer / RUNNER
race's end / TAPE; FINISH
racetrack circuit / LAP
racetrack prophet / TOUT; TIPSTER
Rachel's father / LABAN
Rachel's husband / JACOB
Rachel's sister / LEAH
Rachel's son / JOSEPH; BENJAMIN
rachis / AXIS; SPINE, STALK
rachitis / RICKETS

racial / ETHNIC
racial extermination / GENOCIDE
racial segregation / APARTHEID
Racine play / PHEDRE; ATHALIE
raciness / VIGOR; SPIRIT
racing / TURF
racing boat / GIG; SCULL, SHELL
racist / PREJUDICED
rack / WREST, WRING; DECANT, STRAIN. CRIB, PANG; FRAME
rack railway driver / CLIMBER
racket / BAT, DIN; NOISE, FROLIC, PATTEN, SCHEME; HULLA-BALOO, PROCEEDING; MERRYMAKING. HILARIOUS
racket game / PELOTA; LACROSSE
rackety / NOISY, ROWDY
raconteur / ANECDOTIST
racy / RICH, SMART, SPICY; LIVELY; PIQUANT, PUNGENT; SPIRITED
radar / DETECTOR
radar covering / RADOME
radar image / BLIP
radar screen / SCOPE
Radcliffe castle / UDOLPHO
Radcliffe locale / CAMBRIDGE
raddle / INTERWEAVE
raddlings / CHAFF, TWIGS; BRUSHWOOD
radial / RAYED; DIVERGING
radiale / NAVICULAR
radian / ARC; ANGLE
radiance / SHINE; LUSTER; GLISTER, GLITTER
radiant / BEAMING, GLOWING; GLORIOUS, LUMINOUS
radiate / EMIT, GLOW, SEND; EMANATE
radiation / WAVES; DIFFUSION
radiation marker / ALIDADE; THEODOLITE
radiator / COIL, DRUM; COOLER, HEATER
radical / RED; BASAL; EXTREME, ORGANIC. SURD
radicate / ROOT; PLANT
radicle / ROOTLET
Radigund's slayer / BRITOMART
radio / SET; WIRELESS; TRANSISTOR
radio advertiser / SPONSOR

radio amateur / HAM
radio antenna / AERIAL
radio award / EMMY
radio bulletin / FLASH
radio detection device / RADAR
radio external wire / AERIAL;
  ANTENNA
radio frequency group / BAND
radio interference / STATIC
radio man / ANNOUNCER
radio network / CHAIN
radio OK / ROGER
radio operator / SPARKS
radio organization / NETWORK
radio receiver / TUNER
radio tube / VALVE
radio tube part / GRID; PRONG
radio tuner / DIAL, KNOB
radioactive element / RADON;
  RADIUM; THORIUM, URANIUM
radioactive gas / NITON, RADON
radioactivity counter / GEIGER
radioactivity detector /
  ELECTROSCOPE
radioactivity ray / BETA; ALPHA,
  GAMMA
radiosonde / BALLOON
radium discoverer / CURIE
radium emanation / NITON,
  RADON
radius / AREA, RING; THROW
radius, pert. to / RADIAL
radix / ROOT, UNIT;
  FUNDAMENTAL
radon / NITON
raff / JUMBLE, REFUSE. LOW;
  MEAN
raffia fabric / RABANNA
raffish / FLASHY, VULGAR
raffle / DRAW; LOTTERY
raft / MOKI; BALSA, FLOAT;
  CATAMARAN
raft duck / SCAUP; REDHEAD
rafter / BEAM; SUPPORTER
rag / MOCK; TEASE. SHRED;
  TATTER
ragabash / RAGTAG; CANAILLE
ragamuffin / GAMIN; BEGGAR
rage / IRE; FURY; ANGER, FUROR,
  MANIA. FRET, FUME, RAMP,
  RANT
ragged / WORN; FRAYED
raging / ANGRY; FURIOUS
raging dragon / RAHAB
raging weather / STORM; TEMPEST
ragman / TRAMP
Ragnarok survivor / VALI; VIDAR
ragout / STEW; SALMI; GOULASH,
  HARICOT; MULLIGAN
rags / GARB; CLOTHES
ragtag / RABBLE
ragtime / SYNCOPATION
ragweed dust / POLLEN

rah / CHEER; HURRAH
Rahab's city / JERICHO
raid / FORAY; ATTACK, SORTIE;
  COMMANDO
raid for plunder / MARAUD
raider / PRIVATEER
rail / RANT; ABUSE, CHIDE. BAR;
  COOT, SORA, WEKA; CRAKE
rail at / BERATE
railbird / TIMER
railing / FENCE
railing on viaduct / PARAPET
raillery / HUMOR, IRONY; BANTER;
  BADINAGE
rail-like crane / LIMPKIN
railroad / RUSH; FRAME
railroad car / CABOOSE, PULLMAN
railroad charge / FARE
railroad coach / CAR
railroad engine / LOCOMOTIVE
railroad light / FLARE, FUSEE
railroad signal / SEMAPHORE
railroad station / DEPOT;
  TERMINAL
railroad tie / SLEEPER
railroad train / LOCAL; EXPRESS,
  FREIGHT, LIMITED
railroad viaduct / TRESTLE
Rail-Splitter / ABE; LINCOLN
railway / LINE; RAILROAD
raiment / GARB; ARRAY, DRESS
rain / MIST; MISLE; SEREIN,
  SHOWER
rain, pert. to / HYETAL
rain forest plant / LIANA;
  EPIPHYTE
rain gauge / UDOMETER;
  PLUVIOMETER
rain hard / POUR, TEEM; STORM
rain spout / DUCT, RONE;
  GARGOYLE
rain tree / SAMAN; ZAMANG
rainbird / KOEL; CUCKOO
rainbow / ARC; IRIS
rainbow, pert. to / IRIDAL
rainbow fish / MAORI, TROUT;
  WRASSE
rainbow flower / IRIS
raincoat / MACK; PONCHO;
  SLICKER
rainmaker / MAGICIAN
rain-snow mixture / SLEET
rainstorm / DOWNPOUR;
  CLOUDBURST
rainwash / CREEP
rainy / WET
rainy month / APRIL
rainy season / MONSOON
raise / GROW, LEVY, LIFT, REAR;
  BOOST, BREED, ERECT, EXALT,
  HOIST; AROUSE, EMBOSS. HIKE,
  RISE; INCREMENT
raise Cain / RANT; STORM

raise to second power / SQUARE
raise to third power / CUBE
raise up / HEFT; EXALT
raise vegetables / FARM
raised band / RIB; WELT
raised platform / DAIS; STAGE
raising device / JACK; HOIST;
  DERRICK
rajah's consort / RANI; RANEE
Rajputana desert / THAR
rake / ROUE; LOTHARIO;
  LIBERTINE. COLLECT
rake with gunfire / ENFILADE
rake off / REBATE; COMMISSION
rakehell / DEBAUCHEE
rakish / LOOSE; SPORTY, WANTON
rally / JEST, JOKE, MOCK; CHAFF,
  TAUNT. CROWD; MEETING
rallying cry / SLOGAN
ram / BUTT, CRAM, PUSH;
  POUND. TUP; ARIES; WETHER
ram in / TAMP
Ramadan / FAST
Rama's aide / SUGRIVA
Rama's father / DASARATHA
Rama's wife / SITA
ramate / BRANCHED
Ramayana's author / VALMIKI
ramble / GAD; ROAM, ROVE;
  RANGE. TRIP; JAUNT; STROLL
rambling / ROVING; DISCURSIVE,
  INCOHERENT
rambling trip / EXCURSION
rambunctious / WILD; UNRULY
rame / WAIL; BRANCH
Ramee penname / OUIDA
ram-headed god / AMON; KHNUM
rami / BRANCHES
ramie / CHINAGRASS
ramie product / FABRIC, MANTLE
ramified / RAMOSE
ramify / BRANCH, SPREAD
rammed clay / PISE
ramp / LEAP; CLIMB. INCLINE
rampage / RAGE; ANGER;
  VIOLENCE
rampageous / UNRULY
rampant / WANTON; FURIOUS;
  STANDING
rampart / BRAY, WALL; AGGER,
  GUARD, REDAN; VALLUM;
  BULWARK, PARAPET, RAVELIN
rampler / GYPSY, ROVER; RANGER
ram's horn trumpet / SHOFAR;
  SHOPHAR
ramshackle auto / JALOPY
ramson / GARLIC
ramstam / RECKLESS
ramus / BRANCH
ran / SPED; BOSSED; OPERATED
ran off to wed / ELOPED
rana / FROG
rance / PROP

ranch / FARM; ESTANCIA
ranch animal / HORSE, STEER
ranchero / HERDSMAN
rancid / RANK, SOUR; FETID,
  MUSTY; SMELLY
rancor / HATE; VENOM; MALICE
rancorous / SPITEFUL; MALIGNANT
rand / EDGE; STRIP; BORDER
random / STRAY; CASUAL,
  CHANCE
randy / LEWD, WILD; COARSE,
  VULGAR. VIRAGO
rang / CHIMED; CLANGED
range / ROW; AREA, KIND, LINE,
  RANK, SORT, TIER; CLASS,
  GAMUT, ORDER, SCOPE, STOVE;
  SIERRA. ROAM, ROVE
range of activity / ORBIT
range animal / HORSE, SHEEP,
  STEER
range finder / MEKOMETER,
  TELEMETER
range of hills / RIDGE
range of mountains / CHAIN
range of occurrence / INCIDENCE
range rider / COWBOY
range in the Rockies / LEMHI,
  TETON, UINTA; WASATCH
range in rows / ALIGN, ALINE
range of sight / KEN; SCOPE
range of South American
  mountains / ANDES
ranger / ROVER; WARDEN;
  BEDOUIN
Rangoon pagoda / SHWEDAGON
rangy / OPEN; LANKY, SPARE
ranine / FROGGY
rani's husband / RAJAH
rank / ROW; TIER; CASTE, CLASS,
  GRADE, ORDER, RANGE;
  DEGREE, STATUS. RATE. FOUL;
  GROSS, MUSTY; COARSE,
  RANCID
rank and file / COMMON. MOB;
  HERD
rank of nobility / DUKE, EARL
rankle / GALL; FESTER
rann / SONG; MARSH, VERSE
Ran's husband / AEGIR
ransack / RAKE, SACK; RIFLE
ransom / FREE; REDEEM,
  RESCUE. FORFEIT
rant / RAGE, RAIL, RAVE; BLUSTER
rap / BIT, BOP, DAB, PAT; BLOW,
  CHAT, SLAP; KNOCK; STRIKE,
  THWACK
rapacious / GREEDY; RAVENOUS
rapacious bird / SHRIKE
rapacious monster / HARPY
rapacity / AVARICE, EDACITY
rape / RAVISH; VIOLATE. POMACE
rapeseed / COLZA
raphe / SEAM; RIDGE; SUTURE

rapid / FAST; FLEET, QUICK
rapid musical passage / STRETTA, STRETTO
rapid speech / PATTER
rapide / EXPRESS
rapidity / HASTE; CELERITY, VELOCITY
rapids / WHITEWATER
rapier / TUCK; BILBO, SWORD
rapine / PILLAGE, PLUNDER
rapport / HARMONY; AFFINITY
rapprochement / DETENTE
rapscallion / ROGUE; RASCAL
rapt / INTENT; CHARMED; ECSTATIC
raptatorial / PREDACIOUS
raptor / OWL; EAGLE
raptorial / HAWKLIKE
rapture / JOY; BLISS; ECSTASY
rapturous / DIVINE; TRANSPORTED
rare / ODD; FINE; CHOICE, SCARCE; TENUOUS
rare earth / METAL
rare piece / CURIO
rarebit / WELSHRABBIT
raree / PEEPSHOW
rarefy / THIN; ATTENUATE
rarely / WELL; HARDLY, SELDOM
rarity / SCARCITY, THINNESS
Ra's antagonist / APEPI
Ra's consort / MUT
Ra's son / SHO
rascal / IMP; KNAVE, SCAMP; VARLET
rash / HASTY; UNWISE; CARELESS; AUDACIOUS. POX; HIVES; SCABIES; ERUPTION
rashness / FOLLY; TEMERITY
rasorial / SCRATCHING
rasp / FILE; GRATE; ABRADE, SCRAPE
rasping / HARSH
raspy / IRRITABLE
rat / BUN; SCAB; RODENT; DESERTER
rat hare / PIKA
rat of India / BANDICOOT
ratal / ASSESSMENT
rataplan / DRUMBEAT
rat-a-tat / RATTAT; DRUMMING
ratchet / HOLD, PAWL; DETENT
rate / ABUSE, BLAME, CHIDE, GRADE. TAX; DUTY, PACE; RATIO, SPEED
rate of exchange / BATTA; DISCOUNT
rate highly / VALUE
rate of speed / TEMPO
rath / FORT, HILL
rather / GEY; SOONER; INSTEAD
ratification / ENDORSEMENT
ratify / BIND, SEAL; APPROVE
rating / RANK; GRADE; SEAMAN

ratio / PROPORTION
ratiocinate / REASON
ration / DOLE; SHARE; ALLOWANCE
rational / FAIR, JUST, SANE, WISE; SOUND
rational integer / NORM
rational number / INTEGER
rationalize / THOB; REASON
rationing agency / OPA
ratite / UNKEELED
ratite bird / EMU, MOA; OSTRICH
rats, pert. to / MURINE
rattail / FILE
rattan / CANE, REED
rat-tat / KNOCK
ratter / TERRIER
rattle / RALE; SHAKE; CLATTER, CONFUSE
rattlebrain / FOOL
rattlesnake / BELLTAIL; SIDEWINDER
rattletraps / TRIFLES; KNICKKNACKS
rattling / NOISY; LIVELY
ratty / MEAN; NASTY; SHABBY
raucous / HOARSE; STRIDENT
ravage / EAT; RUIN, SACK; HAVOC, SPOIL, STRIP
rave / CRY; RAGE, RANT, YELL
ravel / FRAY, UNDO; UNWIND
raveled / SNARLED; UNSNARLED
ravelin / OUTWORK, REDOUBT, SALIENT
Raven author / POE
raven / BLACK
ravenous / HUNGRY, LUPINE; VORACIOUS
ravine / DALE, DELL, WADI, WADY; CLOVE, GORGE, GULCH, GULLY, KLOOF; CANYON, CLOUGH, HOLLOW
raving / FURIOUS, VIOLENT
ravioli-like food / WONTON; KREPLACH
ravish / CHARM, FORCE, SEIZE
raw / SORE; BLEAK, CRUDE; CHILLY
raw mineral / ORE
raw vegetable plate / SALAD
rawboned / LEAN, THIN; GAUNT; SKINNY
rawhide / CAT; WHIP; QUIRT, THONG; KURBASH. SJAMBOK
rax / STRETCH
ray / BEAM, IDEA; RADIUS. MANTA, SKATE; MOBULA; COWNOSE
ray, pert. to / RADIAL
rayless / DARK
rayon / VISCOSE
raze / CUT; RUIN; LEVEL; EFFACE
razee / PRUNE; SHORTEN

razor / BLADE; SHAVER. SHAVE
razor clam / SOLEN
hazor sharpener / HONE; STROP
razorback / HOG; FINBACK
razorbill / AUK
razor-billed auk / MURRE
razz / JEER; HECKLE
razzia / RAID; FORAY
razzle-dazzle / FLURRY;
    CONFUSION
re / ABOUT, ANENT
rea / RHEA; TURMERIC
reach / GAIN; TOUCH; ARRIVE,
    ATTAIN, OBTAIN. LIMIT;
    EXTENT
reach across / SPAN
reach a peak / CLIMAX
reach out / EXTEND
reach toward / ASPIRE
react / BEHAVE; RESPOND
reactance measure / OHM
reactionary / TORY; BOURBON
read / STUDY; PERUSE
read closely / SCAN
read a message into / UNRAVEL
read for pleasure / BROWSE
read publicly / PRELECT
read steadily / PORE
readable / LEGIBLE
reader / LECTOR, PRIMER
readership / AUDIENCE
readily / APTLY; EASILY
readiness / KNACK; ALACRITY;
    EXPEDITION
reading / PERUSAL, VARIANT
reading desk / AMBO; LECTERN
reading glass / MAGNIFIER
reading inability / ALEXIA
readjust / MODIFY
ready / FIT; NEAR, RIPE, YARE;
    ALERT, HANDY, PRONE;
    PROMPT
ready to eat / RIPE; COOKED
ready money / CASH
ready to wear / READYMADE
ready-made / TRITE; PRECUT
ready-made tie / TECK
reaffirm / REPEAT; REASSERT
real / TRUE; ACTUAL; FACTUAL,
    GENUINE
real estate / LAND; PROPERTY
real estate broker / AGENT;
    REALTOR
real estate contract / DEED;
    LEASE
real estate map / PLAT
real existence, pert. to / ONTAL;
    NOUMENAL
real McCoy / GENUINE
realgar / SANDARAC
realine / STRAIGHTEN
realistic art style / POP; GENRE

realistic novelist / BALZAC;
    FLAUBERT
reality / FACT; TRUTH; ACTUALITY
realize / GET, SEE; EARN, GAIN;
    SENSE
really / TRULY; INDEED
realm / STATE; DOMAIN, SPHERE;
    COUNTRY
realty / REALESTATE
ream / WIDEN; ENLARGE
reanimate / REVIVE
reap / CUT; GARNER, GATHER,
    SICKLE
reappear / BOBUP, POPUP, RECUR
rear / RISE; BREED, ERECT,
    RAISE. AFT; BACK, HIND;
    BEHIND
rear rampart / PARADOS
rear of vessel / AFT; STERN
rearhorse / MANTIS
rearward / AFT; ASTERN
reason / AIM, END, HOW; MIND,
    NOUS; LOGIC, SENSE
reasonable / FAIR, JUST, WISE;
    RIGHT
reasoning / LOGIC; PILPUL;
    ARGUMENT
reasoning faculty / WIT; MIND
reassure / COMFORT
reata / LAZO; LASSO, RIATA;
    LARIAT
rebate / REFUND; DISCOUNT
rebec of India / LUTE, VIOL;
    SAROD
Rebecca's brother / LABAN
Rebecca's father / BETHUEL
Rebecca's son / ESAU; JACOB
rebel / RISE; REVOLT. INSURGENT
rebellion / RIOT; FRONDE,
    MUTINY, REVOLT; SEDITION
rebirth / REVIVAL
rebirth in new body / REINCAR-
    NATION
reborn / REGENERATE
rebound / DAP; CAROM; REECHO;
    RICOCHET
rebozo / SHAWL; MANTILLA
rebs / CONFEDERATES
rebuff / SLAP, SNUB; CHECK,
    SCORN
rebuild / REMODEL;
    RECONSTRUCT
rebuke / BLAME, CHIDE, SCOLD
rebus / ENIGMA, PUZZLE;
    CHARADE
rebut / REFUTE
recalcitrant / DEFIANT, RESTIVE;
    RENITENT
recall / ANNUL; CANCEL, RECANT,
    REVOKE
recant / ANNUL, UNSAY; ABJURE
recap tires / RESURFACE

recapitulate / SUMUP; REPEAT, RESUME
recapitulation / REPRISE
recaption / REPRISAL; RECAPTURE
recapture / RESCUE; RETAKING
recast / REFORM; REMODEL
recede / EBB; WANE; ABATE
recedence / RECESSION
receding / REGRANTING
receipt / STUB; VOUCHER
receive / GET; HOLD, TAKE; GREET
receive testimony / HEAR
receive by will / INHERIT
receiver / FENCE; CATCHER; CUSTODIAN
recension / VERSION; REVISION
recent / NEW, NOW; LATE; FRESH, NOVEL; MODERN; NEOTERIC
recent, c.f. / NEO; CENE
recent events / NEWS
recept / IMAGE; PERCEPT
receptacle / BIN, BOX; TANK; TRAY
receptacle for holy water / STOUP
reception / TEA; LEVEE; PARTY; SOIREE
reception room / HALL; SALON; PARLOR
recess / APSE, NOOK; NICHE
recess in door / EMBRASURE
recess in room / ALCOVE
recess in wall / NICHE
recessional / DEPARTING
recessive / RECEDING; SUBORDINATE
recherche / CHOICE; UNCOMMON
rechristen / RENAME; RETITLE
recidivist / REPEATER
recipe / FORMULA, PATTERN
recipient / LEGATEE; RECEIVER
recipient of transfusion / DONEE
reciprocal / MUTUAL; ALTERNATE
reciprocal pronoun / EACHOTHER
reciprocate / RETURN; ALTERNATE
reciprocity / INTERCHANGE
recital / STORY; ACCOUNT, CONCERT
recitation / DISCOURSE
recitation to music / RECITATIVE
recite / TELL; COUNT; RELATE
recite metrically / SCAN; CHANT
recite repetitively / CHANT
reck / CARE, HEED
reckless / MAD; BOLD, RASH, WILD; RAMSTAM; CARELESS, HEEDLESS
reckless driver / JEHU
reckon / ARET, RATE; COUNT, TALLY, VALUE; ESTEEM; COMPUTE
reckoning / TAB; BILL; SCORE, TALLY

reckoning machine / ABACUS; SOROBAN, SUANPAN, SWANPAN
reclaim / TAME; RECALL, REDEEM
reclaimed area / POLDER
reclaimed wool / MUNGO
recline / LEAN, LOLL; REPOSE
recluse / MONK; HERMIT; ASCETIC, EREMITE; ANCHORET, SOLITARY
recognize / OWN; AVOW, KNOW; GRANT, GREET
recoil / SHY; QUAIL; BLENCH, FALTER, FLINCH
recollect / RECALL; REMEMBER
recollection / MEMORY
recommence / REPEAT, RESUME
recommend / ADVISE; SUGGEST
recommit / REMAND
recompense / REPAY; REWARD, PAY; MEED
reconcilable / COMPATIBLE, CONSISTENT
reconcile / HEAL; ATONE; PACIFY, SETTLE
recondite / HIDDEN, SECRET; ABTRUSE
reconnaissance / RECCO; SURVEY
reconnoiter / SCOUT; PICKET
reconstruct / REMAKE; REMODEL
record / NOTE; ENROL, ENTER. LP; LOG; DISC; MEMOIR, MINUTE; HISTORY, PLATTER
record book / LOG; LEDGER
record of dealings / ACTA
record of family background / GENEALOGY
record of investigation / FILE; DOSSIER
record of meeting / MINUTES
record of one year / ANNAL
record of patient / CHART
record speed / TIME
record of voyage / LOG
recorded / NOTED, TAPED
recorded proceedings / ACTA
recorder / FLUTE; REGISTRAR
recording device / TAPE; CASSETTE
records / ARCHIVES; CHRONICLES
recount / TELL; RELATE; NARRATE
recoup / REGAIN; RECOVER
recourse / RESORT
recover / SAVE; RALLY; RECOUP, REGAIN, RESCUE; RECLAIM
recover furniture / REUPHOLSTER
recover strength / RECUPERATE
recovered / WELL; BETTER
recreancy / DEFECTION
recreant / BASE, MEAN; FALSE; CRAVEN, UNTRUE. COWARD; APOSTATE, RENEGADE
re-create / REANIMATE

recreation / GAME, PLAY; SPORT; PASTIME
recreation place / PARK; GARDENS
recreational activity / GAME; SPORT
recreative / LUSORY
recrement / DREGS, DROSS; SCORIA
recriminate / CHARGE
recrimination / ACCUSATION
recrudescence / VIGOR; RENEWAL
recruit / ENLIST. BOOT; ROOKIE
rectangle / QUADRILATERAL
rectangular / OBLONG
rectangular column / PILASTER
rectifier / DETECTOR
rectify / MEND; AMEND, EMEND; ADJUST
rectilineal / STRAIGHT
rectitude / VIRTUE; HONESTY, PROBITY
rector / CHIEF; PASTOR; CLERGYMAN
rector's home / PARSONAGE
rectory / MANSE; PARSONAGE
recumbent / IDLE; LEANING; PROSTRATE
recuperate / RECOVER
recur / REPEAT, RETURN; INTERMIT
recurrent decimal / REPETEND
recurrent pattern / CYCLE
recurring theme / MOTIF
recusant / DISSENTER
recushion / REPAD
recycle / REUSE
red / CENT, ROSE; CERISE; CARMINE, CRIMSON, MAGENTA, NACARAT, SCARLET; ANARCHIST, COMMUNIST, VERMILION. ROSY; RUDDY
red arsenic / REALGAR
red bird / ROBIN; TANAGER; CARDINAL
red bream / SNAPPER
red cedar / TOON; SAVIN; JUNIPER
red corpuscle / ERYTHROCYTE
red deer / ROE; HART; ELAPHINE
red dye / LAKE; ANATO, AURIN, EOSIN, HENNA; ANATTO, AURINE, EOSINE; ALIZARIN
red dye root / CHAY, CHOY
red flannel garment / LONGJOHNS
Red Friar / TEMPLAR
red grape / CATAWBA
red grosbeak / CARDINAL
red grouper / MERO
red gurnard / ELLECK
red in heraldry / GULES
red horse / BAY; ROAN; CHESTNUT; STRAWBERRY

red kowhia / PARROTBILL
red man / INDIAN; REDSKIN
red mullet / GOATFISH; SURMULLET
red ocher / KEEL; RADDLE, RUDDLE
red pepper / CAYENNE, PAPRIKA
red perch / ROSEFISH
red pine / RIMU
red planet / MARS
red roundel in heraldry / GUZE
red sage / LANTANA
red seaweed / DULCE, DULSE
Red Sox city / BOSTON
red squirrel / BOOMER; CHICKAREE
red star / MARS; SPICA; BETELGEUSE
red swine / DUROC; TAMWORTH
red water sheep disease / RESP
red wine / PORT; CLARET; MALMSEY
red winter apple / WINESAP
red zircon / JACINTH
redact / EDIT; REVISE
redactor / EDITOR; REVISER
redan / FORTIFICATION
redargue / CONFUTE; DISPROVE
red-backed sandpiper / DUNLIN
red-bellied terrapin / SLIDER
red-bellied woodpecker / CHAB
red-berried evergreen / YEW
redbird / TANAGER; CARDINAL
redbreast / ROBIN
redcap / PORTER
redcoat / BRITISHER
redden / BLUSH, ROUGE
reddish / ROSY; ROSEATE
reddish brown / BAY; HENNA; AUBURN, SORREL; CHESTNUT, MAHOGANY
reddish purple / MAGENTA
reddish yellow / AMBER, HENNA, SUDAN; ORANGE, TITIAN
reddish-brown dye / HENNA
reddish-brown horse / BAY; ROAN; SORREL
redecorate / REDO
redecorate a room / REPAINT, REPAPER
rededicate / RECONSECRATE
redeem / SAVE; AMEND, RANSOM
Redeemer / SAVIOUR
redeeming feature / COMPENSA-TION
redemption / RELEASE; SALVATION
redeye / BASS, DRUM, RUDD
red-eyed carp / RUD; RUDD
redfish / DRUM; PERCH
red-letter / LUCKY
redolence / ODOR; AROMA; PERFUME

redolent / BALMY; SCENTED; FRAGRANT
redolent wood / CEDAR
redoubt / FORTIFICATION. DREAD
redoubtable / VALIANT
redound / ADD; CONTRIBUTE
redress / AMEND; REMEDY; COMPENSATE
redshank / CLEE; SANDPIPER
redshirt / ANARCHIST; GARIBALDIAN
redskin / INDIAN
reduce / BATE, DIET, PARE; DEMOTE
reduce to ash / BURN
reduce to ashes / CREMATE
reduce to bondage / ENSLAVE
reduce brilliance / DIM
reduce to fine spray / ATOMIZE
reduce to fluid / LIQUEFY
reduce from full roundness / DEFLATE
reduce to lower rank / DEMOTE
reduce to a mean value / AVERAGE
reduce by plucking / THIN
reduce to powder / LEVIGATE
reduce to sail / REEF
reduce slowly / TAPER
reduce speed / SLOW; DE-CELERATE
reduce thickness of / THIN
reduce in value / LOWER
reduced / CUT; LOWERED
reducing / CHANGING
reducing regimen / DIET
reduction / CUT
redundancy / EXCESS; SUPER-FLUITY
redundant / EXCESS; COPIOUS
reduplicate / REPEAT
redwing / THRUSH; GADWALL
redwood / BIGTREE, SEQUOIA
ree / RUFF; ARIKARA, CHANNEL
reebok / PEELE; RHEBOK; ANTELOPE
reecho / RESOUND; REVERBERATE
reed / PIPE; GRASS; RATTAN
reed, c.f. / CALAMI
reed instrument / OBOE; BASSOON; CLARINET, WOODWIND
reed of loom / SLEY
reedbird / BOBOLINK
reedbuck / BOHOR, NAGOR
reeducate / RETRAIN
reef / LODE; MANGE, SHOAL
reef animal / CORAL
reefer / ROACH; JACKET
reek / FUG; FUME; NIDOR
reeking / FETID
reel / SPIN, SWAY; DANCE, WAVER, WHIRL. PIRN; SPOOL; BOBBIN
reel foot / CLUBFOOT
reem / OX; UNICORN

reembody / RESHAPE
reenlist / REUP
reenter / RECURVE
reessay / REATTEMPT
reestablish / REINSTATE
reeve / BAILIFF, STEWARD
reexamine / RECONSIDER
reexperience / RELIVE
refashion / REMAKE
refectory / DININGROOM
refer / CITE, HINT; POINT; ADVERT
refer to often / DIN; HARP
referable / IMPUTABLE
referee / JUDGE; UMPIRE; ARBITER
reference / HINT; ALLUSION
reference mark / DAGGER, DIESIS, OBELUS; OBELISK; ASTERISK
reference pages / INDEX, NOTES
referendum / POLL, VOTE; PLEBISCITE
refill / REPLENISH
refine / PURIFY; IMPROVE
refined / NEAT, NICE, PURE; CHASTE. POLITE
refinement / GRACE; POLISH; ELEGANCE
refit / RESTORE; RESUPPLY
reflect / MUSE; MIRROR, PONDER
reflect upon / RUMINATE
reflected sound / ECHO
reflection / GLARE, IMAGE
reflex / IMAGE. INVOLUNTARY
reflexed / FOLDED
reflorescence / REBLOSSOMING
refluence / EBB; REFLUX
reflux / EBB
reform / AMEND; CORRECT
reform effort / CRUSADE
reform school in Britain / BORSTAL
Reformation leader / LUTHER
reformatory / JUVENILEHALL
refracting lens / PRISM
refractor / LENS; PRISM; TELESCOPE
refractory / MULISH, UNRULY; PERVERSE
refrain / FORGO; DESIST; ABSTAIN. FALA, LALA; DITTY; CHORUS, MELODY
refreezing / REGELATION
refresh / CHEER, RENEW; REGALE
refreshed / RESTED; RESTORED
refreshing / COOL; TONIC
refreshments / FOOD; DRINKS
refrigerant / ICE; FREON; COOLER
refrigerate / COOL; FREEZE
refrigerator / ICEBOX; FREEZER
refrigerator car / REEFER; FREEZER
refringent / REFRACTIVE
reft / CLEFT; FORLORN
refuge / HAVEN; ASYLUM, HARBOR

refugee / EMIGRE; FUGITIVE
refulgence / SPLENDOR
refulgent / BRIGHT; BRILLIANT
refund / REPAY; REBATE
refurbish / REFINISH
refusal / NO; NAY; VETO;
  NEGATIVE
refusal to buy / BOYCOTT
refuse / DENY, NILL; REBUFF. ORT;
  LEES, MARC, SCUM, SLAG;
  DREGS, DROSS, OFFAL, SCRAP,
  TRASH, WASTE; SCORIA
refuse to agree / DISSENT
refuse approval / VETO
refuse to do business with /
  BOYCOTT
refuse from flax / POB
refuse of grapes / MARC
refuse heap / MIDDEN
refuse from melting metal /
  DROSS; SCORIA
refuse from ore smelting / SLAG
refuse from wool / COT; KEMP
refutable / DISPROVABLE
refutal / DISPROOF, ELENCHUS
refute / REBUT, REPEL; CONFUTE
refuting / ELENCTIC
regain / RECOVER; REPOSSESS
regal / ROYAL; STATELY;
  IMPERIAL
regale / TREAT; DELIGHT. FETE;
  FEAST; ENTERTAINMENT
regalia / FINERY; INSIGNIA
Regan's father / LEAR
Regan's sister / GONERIL;
  CORDELIA
regard / CARE, DEEM, HEED.
  RESPECT
regard with affection / LOVE
regard with favor / APPROVE
regard highly / ADMIRE, ESTEEM
regard with veneration / REVERE
regardant / WATCHFUL
regarding / RE; INRE; ANENT
regardless / RECKLESS
regards / RESPECTS;
  GOODWISHES
regatta / MEET, RACE
regenerate / RENEW; REFORM
regent / RULER; GOVERNOR
regime / RULE
regimen / MODE; SYSTEM
regimental component /
  BATTALION
reginal / QUEENLY
region / AREA, ZONE; SECTOR
region beyond darkness / EREBUS
region of delight / EDEN; HEAVEN
region of influence / ORBIT
regional / LOCAL; PROVINCIAL
register / FEEL; ENROL, ENTER,
  TALLY; RECORD. LIST, ROLL;
  SLATE; LEDGER

register of events / CHRONICLE
regius / ROYAL
regnant / REIGNING
regolith / MANTLE
regress / RETURN; WITHDRAW
regret / RUE; MOURN; LAMENT.
  GRIEF; SORROW; REMORSE
regretful / CONTRITE
regrettable / SAD; DEPLORABLE
regular / EVEN; FIXED; NORMAL,
  STEADY
regular attendant / BUFF
regular customer / CLIENT
regular task / JOB; CHORE, STINT
regular throb / PULSE
regularity / UNIFORMITY
regulate / RULE; GUIDE, ORDER
regulate action / PACE
regulate by easing / ALLEVIATE
regulation / LAW; RULE
regulations, pert. to / SUMPTUARY
regulus / MATTE; KINGLET
rehabilitate / REDEEM; RESTORE
rehash / ITERATE; RECAPITULATE
rehearsal / PREPARATION
rehearse / REPEAT; RECOUNT;
  PRACTICE
Rehoboam's father / SOLOMON
Rehoboam's mother / NAAMAH
Rehoboam's son / ABIJAH
Rehoboam's wife / MAACHAH
Reich / GERMANY
reign / RULE; GOVERN
reign, pert. to / REGNAL
reign of British in India / RAJ
reigning / DOMINANT; PREPOTENT
reimburse / REPAY; COMPENSATE
reimpression / REPRINT
rein / CURB, LINE, RULE; CHECK
reincarnation / REBIRTH
reindeer / CARIBOU
reins / LOINS
reinstate / REVEST; RESTORE
reinstate a deletion / STET
reiterate / HARP; RESAY; REPEAT;
  ITERATE
reject / DENY, NILL; REPEL,
  SPURN
reject a sweetheart / JILT
rejection / REBUFF;
  REPUDIATION
rejoice / JOY; EXULT, REVEL
rejoin / ANSWER; REUNITE
rejoinder / REPLY; ANSWER,
  RETORT
rejuvenate / REVIVE
rekindle / REVIVE; REINFUSE
rekindled / RELIT
relapse / REVERT
relate / TELL; DETAIL, RECITE
relate in detail / ITEMIZE
related / KIN; AKIN; COGNATE,
  GERMANE

related maternally / ENATE; ENATIC
related paternally / AGNATE
related to / CONNECTED
relating to / PERTINENT
relating to a league / FEDERAL
relation / KIN, SIB; KITH; STORY; REGARD; RELATIVE; NARRATION
relationship / AFFINITY, ALLIANCE
relative / SIS; AUNT; NIECE, UNCLE; COUSIN, FATHER, MOTHER, NEPHEW, PARENT, SISTER; BROTHER
relative amount / RATE
relative by marriage / INLAW
relative position / GRADE; STATUS
relative pronoun / WHO; THAT, WHAT
relative quality / CLASS
relative quantities / RATIO
relatively / COMPARATIVELY
relatives / KINDRED, KINSMEN; KINSFOLK
relativity formulator / EINSTEIN
relax / EASE, REST; ABATE, REMIT
relaxation / RECREATION
relay / SERVO; SUPPLY
release / FREE, UNDO; LOOSE; EXEMPT, LOOSEN, UNBIND
release from censure / ABSOLVE
release conditionally / PAROLE
relegate / REFER; CONSIGN
relent / RELAX, YIELD; SOFTEN
relentless / CRUEL, HARSH; PITILESS
relet / SUBLEASE
relevant / PROPER; GERMANE
reliable / HONEST, TRUSTY
reliance / HOPE; TRUST; DEPENDENCE
reliant / DEPENDENT
relic / TOKEN; MEMENTO, VESTIGE; KEEPSAKE, MEMORIAL, SOUVENIR
relict / WIDOW; SURVIVOR
relief / AID; EASE, HELP; SUCCOR
relieve / CURE, FREE; ABATE, ALLAY
religieuse / NUN
religion / LOVE; FAITH, PIETY; WORSHIP
religion of the Moslems / ISLAM
religious / NUN; MONK; FRIAR. HOLY; EXACT, GODLY, PIOUS; DEVOUT; CONVENTUAL
religious awakening / REVIVAL
religious belief / FAITH
religious brother / MONK; FRIAR; PRIEST
religious ceremony / MASS, RITE; SERVICE
religious circular / TRACT

religious community / CONGREGATION
religious denomination / SECT
religious dignitary / PRELATE
religious discipline / PENANCE
religious discourse / HOMILY, SERMON
religious doctrine / DOXY
religious dogma / TENET; DOCTRINE
religious festival / PURIM; EASTER; CHRISTMAS
religious festival of India / MELA
religious formula / CREED
religious holiday / FEAST
religious house / CHURCH, TEMPLE; SYNAGOGUE
religious image / ICON, IKON
religious law, pert. to / CANONIC
religious leader / POPE; HIERARCH
religious leader / POPE; HIERARCH
religious maxims / LOGIA
religious musical composition / HYMN; MOTET; ANTHEM; CANTATA; ORATORIO
religious object / ICON, IKON
religious observance / RITE
religious order / FELLOWSHIP
religious partisan / ZEALOT
religious pastorate / PARISH
religious recluse / NUN; MONK; HERMIT
religious service / MASS, RITE; OFFICE
religious solemn day / FAST
religious song / HYMN; CAROL, CHANT, PSALM; SPIRITUAL
religious songbook / HYMNAL; PSALTER
religious superior / ABBOT; MOTHER; PROVINCIAL
religious talk / SERMON
religious teacher of India / GURU
religious unorthodoxy / HERESY
religious war / JIHAD; CRUSADE
religious woman / NUN; SISTER
relinquish / CEDE, DROP, QUIT; LEAVE, WAIVE
relinquished / WAIVED; ABANDONED
reliquary / ARCA; APSIS, CHEST; CASKET
relish / LIKE; ENJOY, SAVOR. TANG, ZEST; GUSTO, TASTE, TWANG; FLAVOR, PALATE; PIQUANCY
relit / REIGNITED
relocate / MOVE
relucent / SPLENDID; REFULGENT
reluctance / AVERSION; RENITENCE

reluctance to move / INERTIA
reluctant / LOATH; AVERSE;
 HESITANT
relume / REKINDLE
rely / LEAN; TRUST; DEPEND
remain / LAST, STAY; ABIDE,
 TARRY
remainder / REST; BALANCE,
 REMNANT
remaining / LEFT, OVER;
 PERSISTING
remaining after deductions / NET
remaining thing / RELIC;
 MEMENTO
remaining trace / VESTIGE
remains / ASHES, RUINS; RELICS
remake / REDO; REBUILD
remand / RETURN; RECOMMIT
remanent / RESIDUAL
remark / SAY; HEED, NOTE; UTTER
remarkable / FAMOUS; EMINENT,
 NOTABLE; SINGULAR
remarry / REWED
remeasure / RETRACE
remedial / SANATORY;
 CORRECTIVE
remedial plant / AVENS; ARNICA;
 COMFREY, GENTIAN, VERVAIN
remedy / AID; CURE, HELP. BALM;
 TONIC; RELIEF; ANTIDOTE,
 MEDICINE
remedy for everything / ELIXIR;
 ARCANUM, PANACEA
remember / REST; RECALL,
 REGARD, RETAIN; RECOLLECT
remembrance / RELIC, TOKEN;
 MEMENTO
reminder / MEMO; TOKEN
reminisce / REVIEW; RECOLLECT
reminiscence / REFLECTION
remise / QUIT; RELEASE;
 SURRENDER
remiss / LAX; SLOW; LOOSE,
 SLACK
remissible / VENIAL
remission / PARDON; ABATEMENT
remit / ABATE, RELAX; LESSEN
remittal / PARDON; SURRENDER
remnant / END, ORT, RAG; DREG;
 PIECE, SHRED
remnant of fire / ASH; ASHES
remonstrance / PROTEST
remonstrate / OBJECT; PROTEST
remora / PEGA; LOOTSMAN,
 SUCKFISH
remorse / REGRET, SORROW;
 CONTRITION
remorseful / PENITENT
remorseless / CRUEL; SAVAGE;
 PITILESS, RUTHLESS
remote / FAR, OLD; AFAR; ALIEN;
 DISTANT, FOREIGN; INDIRECT
remote place / THULE

remote planet / PLUTO; NEPTUNE
remotely / AFAR
remotely ancestral / ATAVISTIC
remount / RESET; REHANG.
 REMUDA
remove / CUT, RID; DELE, DOFF,
 KILL, MOVE, OUST, PARE, PEEL;
 ABATE, CARRY, EJECT, ELIDE;
 CONVEY; DISMISS
remove air from / DEFLATE
remove bone from / BONE; FILLET
remove clothing / UNDRESS
remove color / BLEACH
remove a cover / UNCAP
remove to a distance / ELOIN;
 ELOIGN
remove hair / CUT; TRIM; PLUCK,
 SHAVE, SHEAR; EPILATE
remove ink / ERADICATE
remove interior / GUT; CORE
remove beyond jurisdiction /
 ELOIN; ELOIGN
remove by killing / OFF;
 EXTERMINATE
remove a limb / AMPUTATE
remove moisture / DRY
remove an obstruction / CLEAR
remove from office / OUST; RECALL
remove pencil mark / ERASE
remove in printing / DELE; DELETE
remove rind / PARE, PEEL
remove by rubbing / ABRADE
remove by suction / ASPIRATE
remove utterly / RAZE; LEVEL
remove whiskers / SHAVE
removed / AFAR; REMOTE
removed the center / CORED
remunerate / PAY; REPAY;
 REWARD
remuneration / PAY; REWARD;
 INDEMNITY
remunerative / YIELDING;
 LUCRATIVE
Remus' brother / ROMULUS.
 See Romulus
Remus' followers / FABII
renaissance / REVIVAL
Renaissance architect / BRAMANTE
Renaissance musician /
 PALESTRINA
Renaissance painter / RAPHAEL
Renaissance poet / PETRARCH
Renaissance scholar / ERASMUS
Renaissance sculptor / GHIBERTI
rend / RIP; RIVE, TEAR; BREAK,
 BURST
rend asunder / RIVE; SPLIT;
 CLEAVE
render / PAY, TRY; GIVE, RIVE,
 MAKE; YIELD; AFFORD, ASSIGN,
 BESTOW; DELIVER
render accessible / INVITE;
 WELCOME

render active / ANIMATE, ENLIVEN
render desolate / RUIN; DESTROY
render fat / TRY
render muddy / ROIL
render safe / SECURE
render suitable / FIX; ADAPT
render tame / GENTLE
render turbid / ROIL
render unconscious / KAYO
render useless / NULLIFY
render vocal selection / SING
render weak / ENERVATE
rendered hog fat / LARD
rendering / VERSION; EXECUTION
rendezvous / TRYST; MEETING
rendition / PERFORMANCE
renegade / RAT; REBEL; APOSTATE
renege / DENY; REVOKE
renew / REFIT; REPAIR, REVIVE
renew wine / STUM
renewal / REVIVAL;
   RESUBSCRIPTION
renitency / OPPOSITION,
   RESISTANCE
renitent / RECALCITRANT
rennet / COAGULANT
Reno specialty / DIVORCE
Reno's river / TRUCKEE
renounce / DENY, QUIT; LEAVE;
   ABJURE, DESERT, RECANT,
   REJECT; ABANDON
renovate / ALTER, CLEAN; REMAKE
renovation / RESTORATION
renown / REP; FAME, NAME, NOTE;
   GLORY
renowned / EMINENT, HONORED
rent / LET; HIRE; LEASE; CLEAVE.
   TEAR; BREACH, SCHISM. RIVEN
rental / RENT
rental contract / LEASE
rented car / CAB; TAXI
renter / LESSEE, TENANT
renunciation / REJECTION
rep / REPERTORY; REPUTATION;
   REPRESENTATIVE
repair / FIX; MEND, VAMP; REFIT;
   REMEDY
repair with another piece / PATCH
repair by stitching / DARN
repair thoroughly / OVERHAUL
repair unevenly / COBBLE
repairman / FIXER; DOCTOR
reparation / AMENDS;
   RESTITUTION
repartee / WIT; QUIP; REPLY;
   RETORT; RIPOSTE
repass / RETURN
repast / TEA; MEAL; FEAST;
   REFECTION
repay / AVENGE, REFUND;
   REQUITE
repeal / ANNUL; REVOKE;
   RESCIND; ABROGATE

repeat / ECHO; QUOTE, RECUR;
   PARROT
repeat someone's actions / MIMIC
repeat mindlessly / PARROT
repeat in music / BIS; DACAPO,
   ENCORE
repeat often / REITERATE
repeat sign in music / SEGNO
repeat a sound / ECHO
repeat tiresomely / DIN
repeated action / REPRISE
repeated knocking / RATATAT
repeatedly / OFTEN; FREQUENTLY
repeater / GARAND; RECIDIVIST
repeating / ITERANT
repeating bird / MYNAH; PARROT
repeating decimal / REPETEND
repel / CHECK, DETER, PARRY;
   REBUFF
repellent / REPULSIVE;
   DISGUSTING
repent / RUE; ATONE; GRIEVE
repentance / PENANCE,
   REMORSE
repentant / SORRY; PENITENT
repercussion / ECHO; EFFECT
repertoire / STOCK; REPERTORY
repetition / ECHO, ROTE;
   ITERANCE
repetitious / TIRESOME
repine / FRET; GRUMBLE;
   COMPLAIN
replace / STET; REPAY; REFUND;
   RESTORE
replace a string / RELACE
replacement / NEWCOMER;
   SUBSTITUTE
replenish / RENEW; REFILL
replete / FULL, RIFE; FILLED
repletion / SATIETY, SURFEIT;
   PLETHORA
replevin / BAIL; RETURN; RE-
   COVERY
replica / COPY; DUPLICATE,
   FACSIMILE
replicate / DUPLICATE
replication / COPY; REPLY
reply / ANSWER, RETORT; RE-
   SPOND
reply in kind / RETORT
report / TELL; NOTIFY, RECORD,
   RELATE. NOISE, RUMOR
reporter / NEWSMAN; STENOG-
   RAPHER
reporter's assignment / BEAT
repose / LIE; EASE, RELY, REST;
   SLEEP. PEACE, QUIET
reposeful / QUIET; SERENE
repository / SAFE; CACHE, DEPOT,
   VAULT; COFFER, GODOWN
repoussé / RELIEF
reprehend / BLAME, CHIDE
reprehensible / FAULTY; CULPABLE

reprehension / CENSURE, RE-PROOF

represent / ACT; SHOW; PAINT; DEPICT

representation / SHOW; IMAGE; EFFIGY; LIKENESS; NARRATION, SEMBLANCE

representation, pert. to / ICONIC

representation of the Last Supper / CENA

representative / TYPE; AGENT, PROXY; DEPUTY

repress / CALM, CURB; CHECK, CRUSH, QUELL, QUIET; REIRON, SUBDUE

reprieve / DELAY; RESPITE

reprimand / BLAME, CHIDE, SCOLD, SLATE; REBUKE

reprint / EDITION; FACSIMILE

reprisal / RETALIATION

reprise / REPEAT; DEDUCTION

reproach / SLUR; BLAME, SCORN, SHAME, TAUNT; ACCUSE, DE-FAME, REBUKE, REVILE, VILIFY

reproach accusingly / RECRIMI-NATE

reproach insultingly / TAUNT

reproach passionately / BERATE

reprobate / DETEST, DISOWN. WRETCH; CAITIFF, VILLAIN; SCALAWAG

reprobation / REJECTION; DIS-APPROVAL

reproduce / PRINT; REPEAT; GENERATE

reproductive cell / GERM; SPORE; GAMETE

reproof / REBUKE; CENSURE

reprove / FLAY; BLAME, SCOLD; BERATE

reproved / CHID

reptant / REPENT; CREEPING

reptile / ASP; GATER, GECKO, SNAKE; LIZARD, TURTLE; DINOSAUR

reptiles, pert. to / SAURIAN

reptilian / MALIGNANT

reptilian monster / DINOSAUR

republic / COMMONWEALTH

Republican Party / GOP

Republic's author / PLATO

republish / REPRINT

repudiate / DENY; DISOWN, RE-CANT

repudiate publicly / RECANT

repugnance / DISLIKE; AVERSION

repugnant / HOSTILE; INIMICAL

repulse / CHECK, REPEL; REBUFF

repulsive / UGLY; ODIOUS; FUL-SOME, HATEFUL

repulsive food / SLOP; SWILL

repulsive resin / ASAFETIDA

repulsive smell / STENCH

reputable / ESTEEMED; HONOR-ABLE

reputation / FAME, NAME; HONOR, IZZAT; CREDIT, ESTEEM, REPUTE

repute / FAME; STATUS

request / ASK, BEG; APPEAL; BE-SEECH. PLEA; PRAYER; EN-TREATY

request payment / DUN

requiem / MASS; DIRGE

requirable / NECESSARY

require / ASK, BEG; NEED, CLAIM

required usage / RITUAL

requirement / NEED; REQUISITE

requiring ceremony / FORMAL

requiring effort / DIFFICULT

requiring much money / EXPEN-SIVE

requisite / NEEDFUL; NECESSARY

requisition / CALL; ORDER; DE-MAND; REQUEST

requital / RETALIATION

requite / REPAY; AVENGE, REWARD

rerecord / RECUT; RETAPE

reredos / WALL; SCREEN

reremouse / BAT

res / POINT, THING

rescind / ANNUL, QUASH; CANCEL, REVOKE

rescission / ABROGATION

rescript / EDICT; DEGREE

rescue / FREE, SAVE; RANSOM, SUCCOR

reseal / REGLUE, RESHUT

research / STUDY; SEARCH; IN-QUIRY; SCRUTINY

reseda / MIGNONETTE

resemblance / IMAGE; ANALOGY; LIKENESS

resembling egg yolk / VITELLINE

resembling a pillar / STELAR

resembling in sound / ASSONANT

resent / BEGRUDGE

resentful / ENVIOUS

resentment / IRE; GALL; ANGER; UMBRAGE

reservation / CLAUSE; PROVISO

reservation store / TRADINGPOST

reserve / FUND; STORE; MODESTY; COLDNESS. SAVE; RETAIN

reserve one's energy / HUSBAND

reserve funds / SAVINGS

reserve price / MINIMUM

reserve supplies / STOCK

reserved / SHY; COLD; ALOOF

reserved in speech / RETICENT

reserves / MILITIA

reservoir / POOL, SUMP, TANK; HOLDER

resew / RESTITCH

reside / DIG; LIVE; ABIDE, DWELL; INHABIT

residence / HOME, SEAT; DOMICILE

residence of clergyman / MANSE

residence of envoy / EMBASSY

residence of farmer / FARM; GRANGE

residency / AGENCY

resident / ITE; TENANT; OCCUPANT

resident of, suffix / AN, ER; ENO, IAN, ITE

resident of convent / NUN; MONK

resident physician / INTERN

residing in / OF

residual / RELICT; REMAINING

residue / ASH, ORT; LEES, REST, SLAG; ASHES, DREGS, STRAW, WASTE; OVERAGE, REMNANT

resign / QUIT; DEMIT, LEAVE; RETIRE

resignation / CALM; PATIENCE; SUFFERANCE

resile / RECOIL, SPRING

resiliency / TONE; ELASTICITY

resilient / BUOYANT; STRETCHABLE

resin / GUM, LAC; ALOE, NARD; ANIME, COPAL, DAMAR, ELEMI, JALAP, MYRRH, ROSIN; BALSAM, CONIMA, MASTIC; PLASTIC, POLYMER; SANDARAC

resinous tree / FIR; PINE

resist / STEM; CHECK, REPEL; HINDER

resistance / CHECK; OPPOSITION

Resistance group / MAQUIS

resistance phenomenon / HEAT

resistance unit / OHM

resistance wire / NICHROME

resisting pressure / RENITENT

resistless / IRRESISTIBLE

resistor / GRIDLEAK, RHEOSTAT

resolute / BOLD, FAST, FIRM; FIXED; DOGGED

resolution / PLUCK; COURAGE; DECISION

resolution time / NEWYEARS

resolve / MELT, PASS; CLEAR; DECIDE, INTEND

resolved / FIRM; DETERMINED

resonance / ACCORD

resonant / RINGING; SOUNDING

resonator / SOUNDBOX

resorb / REABSORB

resort / HAUNT; REPAIR. SPA; SPOT; ASYLUM, REFUGE

resort in France / NICE; CANNES, TROPEZ; DEAUVILLE

resound / BOOM, ECHO, PEAL, RING

resource / ASSET, MEANS, MONEY

resourceful / ADROIT, CLEVER; INGENIOUS

resources / FUNDS; WEALTH

resow / RESEED

respect / HONOR, VALUE; ESTEEM, REVERE

respectable / DECENT, HONEST, WORTHY

respectful / DEFERENTIAL

respecting / INRE; ABOUT; APROPOS

respiration / BREATHING

respirator / MASK; PULMOTOR

respire / EXHALE, INHALE; BREATHE

respite / LULL, REST; DELAY, PAUSE, TRUCE

resplendence / GLORY, LIGHT; LUSTER

resplendent / GOLDEN; AUREATE; BRILLIANT

respond / SUIT; REACT, REPLY; ACCORD, ANSWER

respondent / DEFENDANT

response / REPLY; ANSWER; REFRAIN; ANTIPHON, SYMPATHY

responsible / LIABLE; ACCOUNTABLE

responsive / INFORMATIVE

respot / RESTIPPLE

rest / SIT; LEAN, STAY, STOP, WAIT; PAUSE, SLEEP; REPOSE. EASE; PEACE, QUIET; REMNANT, RESPITE, SILENCE, SUPPORT

rest day / SABBATH

rest in peace / RIP

restate as summary / RECAP

restaurant / CAFE; DINER, GRILL; BUFFET, EATERY, TAVERN

restaurant with no pretensions / BEANERY

restaurant with no waiters / CAFETERIA

restaurant show / CABARET

restaurant worker / CHEF, COOK; BUSBOY, WAITER; MAITRED; WAITRESS; MAITREDEE

rested / RELAXED; REFRESHED

restful / QUIET; PEACEFUL

resthouse / KHAN; SERAI

resting / ABED; DORMANT

resting place / GRAVE; LANDING

restitution / AMENDS; REQUITAL

restive / BALKY; UNEASY; FIDGETY

restless / ACTIVE; NERVOUS, RESTIVE

restlessness / ITCH; FIDGETS; AGITATION

restoration / REPAIR, RETURN; RENEWAL

restorative / SALTS, TONIC; BRACER, REMEDY
restore / CURE, HEAL; RENEW; REPAIR, REVIVE
restore to health / CURE
restore to power / REINSTATE
restore to strength / REINFORCE
restrain / DAM, TIE; BATE, BIND, CURB, DENY, REIN, RULE, STOP; CHAIN, CHECK, CRAMP, DETER, LIMIT
restrain by force / ARREST
restrain in scope / RESTRICT
restraining irons / SHACKLES
restraining rope / HOBBLE, TETHER
restraint / STINT; BRIDLE, FETTER; LIMITATION
restrict / HEM; CRAMP; CONFINE
restricted / NARROW, STRAIT
restriction / LIMITATION
restrictive / STYPTIC
result / ENSUE, ISSUE; FOLLOW. END; UPSHOT; OUTCOME
result of addition / SUM; TOTAL
result of a cause / EFFECT
result of division / QUOTIENT
result of multiplication / PRODUCT
result of subtraction / REMAINDER
result of a vote / MANDATE; ELECTION
resume / REOPEN, RETURN; CONTINUE. VITA; OUTLINE, SUMMARY
resurface / RETAR; REPAVE
resurface a tire / RECAP; RETREAD
resurge / REAPPEAR
resurrect / RESTORE; DISINTER
resurrection man / GRAVEROBBER
resuscitate / REVIVE
ret / ROT; SOAK; STEEP
retable / GRADINE, REREDOS; PREDELLA
retail / DEAL, SELL; DISPENSE
retailer / DEALER; SHOPKEEPER
retain / HAVE, HIRE, HOLD, KEEP, SAVE; EMPLOY
retainer / FEE; HENCHMAN; ATTENDANT
retaliate / AVENGE; REQUITE
retaliation / TALION; REVENGE
retaliative / VINDICTIVE
retard / CLOG, SLOW; CHECK, STALL; IMPEDE
retardation / LAG; DRAG; DELAY
retarded / DULL, SLOW; STUPID
retch / GAG; HEAVE, VOMIT; STRAIN
rete / PLEXUS; NETWORK
retention / GRASP; TENACITY
retiarius / GLADIATOR
retiary / NETLIKE; TELARIAN
reticella / NEEDLEPOINT

reticence / RESERVE
reticent / MIM, MUM; SILENT; SECRETIVE
reticle / LATTICE, NETWORK
reticular / COMPLEX; INTRICATE
reticulation / NETWORK
reticule / CABA, ETUI; CABAS; HANDBAG
retiform / NETLIKE
retinal organ / ROD; CONE
retinal spot / FOVEA
retinue / SUITE, TRAIN; ESCORT; CORTEGE
retire / QUIT; LEAVE; RECEDE, RESIGN
retired / ABED; ASLEEP; EMERITUS, SECLUDED
retirement / RETREAT; DEMISSION
retirement income / ANNUITY, PENSION
retiring / SHY; MODEST; BACKWARD
retold / REPEATED; RECOUNTED
retort / ARGUE, REPLY; RESPOND. VIAL; ALEMBIC, RIPOSTE; REPARTEE; REJOINDER
retortion / RETALIATION
retouch / PATCH; DOCTOR; IMPROVE
retrace / RECALL; BACKTRACK
retract / CANCEL, RECALL, RECANT REVOKE
retraction / PALINODE; DISAVOWAL
retreat / RECEDE, RETIRE; WITHDRAW. DEN; NEST, NOOK; HAVEN; ASYLUM, FLIGHT, REFUGE; SHELTER; SECLUSION
retreat in disorder / FLEE. ROUT
retrench / CLIP, PARE; PRUNE; LESSEN; CURTAIL; ECONOMIZE
retrenchment / ECONOMY; REDUCTION
retribution / PAY; NEMESIS; REQUITAL
retributive / CONDIGN
retrieve / REGAIN, RESCUE; RECOVER
retroactive / REGRESSIVE; REVERSIONARY
retrograde / INVERSE; BACKWARD
retrogression / ATROPHY
retro-rocket / DECELERATOR
retrospect / REVIEW, SURVEY
retrovert / INVERT
retund / DULL; BLUNT; DEADEN
return / RECUR, REPAY, REPLY; REVERT; REELECT. GAIN; YIELD
return to custody / REMAND
return to former state / REVERT
return to health / RECOVER
return on investment / PROFIT; DIVIDEND, INTEREST

return to mind / RECUR
return to office / REELECT
return a profit / NET, PAY
return punch / COUNTER
return thrust / RIPOSTE
return tit-for-tat / RETALIATE
returning / REDIENT; REPLACING
retuse / BLUNT; ROUNDED
Reuben's father / JACOB
reunion / MEETING; ASSEMBLY
reunite / REJOIN; RECONCILE
re-up / REENLIST
reus / DEFENDANT
revamp / REVISE; REWRITE; RENO-VATE
reveal / BARE, SHOW, TELL; EX-POSE, UNSEAL, UNVEIL; DIS-PLAY, DIVULGE
reveal without discretion / BLAB
reveille / CALL; DIANA, LEVET
revel / RIOT; CAROUSE, ROISTER. ORGY; FEAST, SPREE; DEBAUCH
revelation / ORACLE; APOCALYPSE
reveler / PLAYBOY; CELEBRANT
reveler's cry / EVOE
revelry / DEBAUCH; FESTIVITY
revenant / GHOST, SPOOK; EIDO-LON
revenge / REQUIT. MALICE; VEN-DETTA
revengeful / SPITEFUL; MALICIOUS
revenue / INCOME, RETURN, RE-WARD
reverberate / ECHO, RING, ROLL; RESOUND
reverberating / REBOANT; RESONANT
reverberation / REPERCUSSION
revere / ADORE, HONOR; ESTEEM
reverence / AWE; PIETY; HOMAGE, REGARD
reverend / CLERGYMAN
reverent / HUMBLE; RESPECTFUL
Revere's companion / DAWES
Revere's trade / ENGRAVING
reverie / MUSING; DAYDREAM
revers / LAPEL
reversal / UPSET; VOIDING
reverse / TURN; CHANGE, INVERT, REVOKE. CONTRARY, OPPOSITE
reverse curve / SCURVE
reverse English / DRAW
reverse fault / THRUST
reverse of the reverse / OBSERVE
reverse turn / IMMELMANN
reversed in order / CONVERSE
reverses / LOSSES
reversion / ATAVISM, ESCHEAT
revert / RETURN; REGRESS
revest / REINSTATE
review / REVISE, SURVEY. ESSAY; PARADE; JOURNAL; CRITIQUE

reviewer / CRITIC
revile / ABUSE, SCOFF; DEFAME, MALIGN, VILIFY
revise / EDIT; ALTER, AMEND, EMEND; CHANGE
reviser / EDITOR; PROOFREADER
revival / RENEWAL; RECOVERY; AWAKENING; REPRODUCTION
revive / CHEER, RALLY, ROUSE
reviver / RESUSCITATOR
revoke / ANNUL, RENIG; CANCEL, RECALL, RECANT, RENEGE, RE-PEAL
revoke a legacy / ADEEM
revolt / RISE; REBEL; NAUSEATE. MUTINY; INSURRECTION
revolting / REPELLENT; DISGUST-ING
revolution / CHANGE; ROTATION
Revolutionary general / LEE; GREENE
Revolutionary hero / HALE; ALLEN, STARK
Revolutionary leader / MARAT; DANTON
revolutions / REVS, RPMS; TURNS
revolve / BIRL, ROLL, SPIN, TURN; TWIRL
revolver / GAT, GUN, ROD; PISTOL
revolving body / PLANET; SATEL-LITE
revolving member / CAM, COG; ROTOR, WHEEL
revolving model of solar system / ORRERY
revue / MUSICAL
revulsion / DISGUST; REACTION
reward / FEE; MEED; BONUS, MEDAL, PRIZE, TOKEN; BOUNTY; GUERDON, PREMIUM
rewed / REMARRY
reword / PARAPHRASE
rex / KING
reynard / FOX
Reynard's enemy / ISENGRIN
rhabdoidal / RODLIKE
Rhadamanthus' brother / MINOS
Rhadamanthus' father / ZEUS
Rhadamanthus' mother / EUROPA
Rhadamanthus' wife / ALCMENE
rhamphoid / BEAKLIKE
rhapsodic / ECSTATIC
rhapsody / OUTPOURING
Rhea's child / HERA, ZEUS; HADES; DEMETER; POSEIDON
Rhea's father / URANUS
Rhea's husband / CRONOS
Rhea's mother / GE; GAEA
rhebok / PEELE; RHEEBOK
rhematic / VERBAL
rheostat / CONTROL; RESISTOR
rhesus / MACAQUE

rhetor / ORATOR
rhetoric / VERBIAGE
rhetorical / STYLISTIC
rheum / COLD; CATARRH, RHUBARB
rheumatism / LUMBAGO
rhexis / RUPTURE
rhinal / NASAL
Rhine branch / LEK; MAAS; IJSSEL
Rhine city / BONN; BASEL, MAINZ
Rhine tributary / ILL; AARE, NAHE, RUHR; LIPPE; MOSELLE
Rhine wine / HOCK; MOSELLE; RIESLING, TRAMINER
rhino / CASH; MONEY
rhinoceros / REEM; ABADA; BORELE; NASICORN
rhinoceros beetle / UANG
rhizome / ROOT, STEM; TUBER
Rhode Island bay / NARRAGANSETT
Rhode Island capital / PROVIDENCE
Rhode Island city / NEWPORT; CRANSTON
Rhode Island motto / HOPE
Rhode Island nickname / RHODY; PLANTATION
Rhode Island state flower / VIOLET
Rhode Island synagogue / TOURO
Rhode Island university / BROWN
Rhodes / RODI
Rhodes statue / COLOSSUS
Rhodesia capital / SALISBURY
Rhodesian falls / VICTORIA
Rhodesian ruins / ZIMBABWE
Rhone city / LYON, ARLES, LYONS
Rhone delta / CAMARGUE
Rhone tributary / AIN; ARVE; ISERE, SAONE
rhubarb / PIEPLANT
rhubline / LOXODROME
rhyme / VERSE; POETRY
rhymed toast / BRINDISI
rhyming game / CRAMBO
rhythm / BEAT, TIME; METER, TEMPO
rhythmic / CYCLIC; REGULAR
rhythmic beat / PULSE; ACCENT; CADENCE
rhythmic flow / LILT
rhythmic pause / BEAT, REST
rhythmical / CADENT
ria / INLET
rialto / MART; BRIDGE; BROADWAY
riancy / GAIETY
riant / GAY; BLITHE, BRIGHT
riata / LASSO, LARIAT
rib / PURL; COSTA; SUPPORT
rib of leaf / VEIN
ribald / COARSE, EARTHY, VULGAR
ribaldry / BAWDRY; OBSCENITY
ribbed / COSTATE

ribbed fabric / REP; CORD, REPP; PIQUE, TWILL; DIMITY, FAILLE; CORDUROY
ribbon / TAPE; BADGE, PRIZE, STRIP; CORDON, FILLET
ribbon, c.f. / TENE; TAENI
ribbon snake / GARTER
ribbonfish / GUAPENA, SERRANA
ribless / ECOSTATE
riblike / RIBBY
ribs, pert. to / COSTAL; COSTATE
ribwort / PLANTAIN
rice dish / PILAU, PILAW; RISOTTO
rice field / PADI; PADDY
rice grass / BARIT; CORDGRASS
rice heated before milling / SELA
rice in the husk / PADI; PADDY, PALAY
rice paste / AME
rice wine / SAKE, SAKI
ricebird / BOBOLINK
rich / FULL; AMPLE, SWEET, VIVID; COSTLY, MELLOW, SAVORY, SUPERB; COPIOUS, FERTILE, OPULENT
rich brown pigment / SEPIA
rich cake / TORTE; DARIOLE; MADELINE
rich cloth hanging / DORSAL, DOSSAL, DOSSER
rich in detail / ORNATE
rich fabric / LAME; PANNE
rich fur / ERMINE
rich king / MIDAS; CROESUS
rich man / NABOB
rich in oil / FAT; GREASY
rich ore deposit / LODE; BONANZA
rich part / FAT; CREAM
rich people / HAVES
rich silk fabric / BROCADE
rich soil / LOAM
rich tapestry / ARRAS
Richard I / LIONHEART
Richelieu's successor / MAZARIN
riches / PELF; WEALTH; OPULENCE
rick / HEAP, PILE; STACK; HAYCOCK
rickety / FEEBLE; UNSTEADY
ricochet / CAROM; REBOUND
rid / FREE; CLEAR
rid oneself of / DOFF
riddance / DELIVERANCE
riddle / REBUS, SIEVE; ENIGMA, PUZZLE; MYSTERY; CONUNDRUM. SIFT; PERFORATE
riddle cake / OATCAKE
ride / FLOAT, MOUNT
ride down / TRAMPLE
rideau / CURTAIN
rider / JOCKEY; ADDITION; AMENDMENT, PASSENGER

Rider Haggard hero / ALLAN; QUATERMAIN
Rider Haggard novel / SHE
rider's need / REINS; SADDLE
ridge / REEF, WALE; ARETE, CREST, SPINE; WRINKLE
ridge between moldings / ARRIS
ridge in cloth / RIB; WALE, WELT
ridge of earth / RIDEAU
ridge of glacial drift / OS; KAME, OSAR; ESKER, OESAR
ridge in ice field / HUMMOCK
ridge of rock / DIKE, REEF
ridge of sand / DENE, DUNE
ridicule / GUY, PAN; JEER, MOCK, RAZZ, TWIT; LAMPOON. BANTER, SATIRE
ridiculous / DROLL, FUNNY; AB-SURD
riding academy / MANEGE
riding breeches / JODHPURS
riding costume / HABIT
riding whip / QUIRT
rife / COMMON; PREVALENT
riff raff / MOB; RABBLE
riffle / SHUFFLE
rifle / ROB; SACK; STRIP; DESPOIL. KRAG; MINIE; GARAND, MAUSER, MUSKET
rifle ball / MINIE; BULLET
rifle blade / BAYONET
rifle firing pin / TIGE
rifleman / HUNTER; SOLDIER
rift / CLEFT, SPLIT; OPENING
rift valley / GRABEN
rift valley lake / NYASA; RUDOLF
rig / DRESS, EQUIP. GEAR; SAILS; TACKLE; DERRICK
rigamajig / DINGUS, GADGET
rigger / CLIMBER, LINEMAN; MANIPULATOR
rigging part / MAST, ROPE, SAIL, SPAR
right / TITLE, TRUTH; VIRTUE. FIT; FAIR, JUST, TRUE; EXACT
right away / ANON; PRONTO
right hand, pert. to / DEXTER
right hand man / AIDE; LIEU-TENANT
right hand page / RECTO
right of holding / TENURE
right minded / MORAL; UPRIGHT
right of suffrage / VOTE; FRAN-CHISE
right turn / GEE
right to use another's property / EASEMENT
right way / TAO
right-angled / RECTANGULAR
righteous / GODLY, MORAL; HONEST
rightful / DUE; LAWFUL

right-handed / DEXTRAL
rightly / HONESTLY, PROPERLY
rightness / TRUTH; RECTITUDE
rigid / SET; FIRM, HARD; HARSH, STARK, STIFF, TENSE
rigid hair / SETA; BRISTLE
rigidity / RIGOR
rigmarole / BABBLE; MUMMERY
rigolet / RIVULET
rigolette / SCARF, THROW
Rigoletto composer / VERDI
Rigoletto's daughter / GILDA
rigor / SEVERITY
rigorous / STERN; SEVERE, STRICT; SPARTAN
rigorously precise / EXACT; METICULOUS
rigors / HARDSHIPS
Rijeka / FIUME
Rikki-Tikki-Tavi / MONGOOSE
rile / VEX; STIR; ANGER, ANNOY
rill / STREAM; RIVULET
rille / VALLEY
rim / LIP; BRIM, EDGE; BRINK; BORDER, MARGIN
rim of cask / CHIME, CHINE
rim of wheel / FELLY, FELLOE
rima / CLEFT; FISSURE
rimaye / BERGSCHRUND
rime / RHYME; HOARFROST
rime giant / YMIR
Rimini notable / FRANCESCA
Rimini ruling family / MALATESTA
rimlike part / FLANGE
rimose / CHINKY; FISSURED
rimple / FOLD; WRINKLE
rimy / FROSTY
Rinaldo's cousin / ORLANDO
Rinaldo's horse / BAYARD; RABICAN
Rinaldo's sword / FUSBERTA
rind / HULL, HUSK, PEEL, SKIN; SHELL
rinderpest / MURRAIN
ring / PEAL, TOLL; CHIME. HOOP, RINK; ARENA; CIRCLE
ring activity / FISTICUFFS
ring finger / ANNULARY
ring to hold reins / TERRET, TERRIT
ring on lasso / HONDA
ring of light / HALO; GLORY; CORO-NA, NIMBUS; AUREOLA
ring off / HANGUP
ring official / JUDGE, TIMER; REFEREE
ring out / PEAL; SOUND
ring ouzel / AMSEL
ring recipient / BRIDE, GROOM; FIANCEE
ring in sail / GROMMET
ring bearing seal / SIGNET
ring slowly / TOLL

ringdove / CUSHAT
ringed boa / ABOMA
ringed planet / SATURN
ringent / GAPING
ringer / DOUBLE; FACSIMILE
ringhals / COBRA
ringleader / FIREBRAND
ringlet / CURL, LOCK; TRESS
ringneck / JACKAROO; GREEN-
 HORN
Ring's composer / WAGNER
ring-shaped / ANNULAR
ring-shaped Island / ATOLL
ring-shaped piece / QUOIT
ring-tailed cat / CACOMIXLE; CACO-
 MISTLE
ring-tailed mammal / LEMUR;
 RACCOON
ring-tailed roarer / BRAGGART
ringworm / ITCH; FAVUS, TINEA;
 FUNGUS, TETTER; MYCOSIS
rink / ARENA
rinse / LAVE, WASH; ELUTE;
 CLEANSE
Rio peak / CORCOVADO
Rio suburb / NICTEROI
Rio's bay / GUANABARA
Rio's beach / COPACABANA
Rio's mountain / SUGARLOAF
riot / ROW; FRAY, ORGY; BRAWL,
 MELEE; EMEUTE, TUMULT, UP-
 ROAR
riot act / WARNING
rioting / REVELRY; TRASHING
riotous / TURBULENT
riotous action / RAMPAGE
riotous party / ORGY; SPREE
rip / CUT; REND, TEAR. CHEAT,
 ROGUE
rip off / STEAL
ripa / BANK
riparian / BANKSIDE, RIVERINE
ripe / FIT; AGED; READY; MATURE
ripen / MATURE, MELLOW
ripeness / READINESS
riposte / RETORT; REPARTEE
ripper / SLASHER; MURDERER
ripping / FINE; REMARKABLE
ripple / LAP; RIFF; WAVELET
Rip's mountains / CATSKILLS
rise / GROW, LIFT, SOAR; CLIMB,
 MOUNT, OCCUR, REBEL.
 ASCENT
rise above / TOWER
rise abruptly / ZOOM; THRUST
rise again / RESURGE
rise from / STEM
rise of ground / HILL; HUMMOCK
rise in revolt / MUTINY
rise in sea level / EUSTASY
rise of ship's bow / SCEND
risen / UP; AWAKE
riser / STEAMPIPE

risible / COMIC, DROLL, FUNNY
rising / INSURRECTION
risk / DARE; CHANCE; VENTURE.
 PERIL; DANGER, HAZARD
risky / CHANCY, UNSAFE;
 DUBIOUS
ritardando / SLOWING
rite / FORM; USAGE; RITUAL
ritter / KNIGHT
ritual / LITURGY; CEREMONY
ritzy / RICH; SWELL
rival / FOE; ENEMY; OPPONENT.
 EMULATE
rivalry / CONTEST; COMPETITION
rive / REND, TEAR; SPLIT; CLEAVE
riven / TORN; CLEFT
river / RIO; STREAM
river, pert. to / RIPARIAN,
 RIVERINE
river in Africa / NILE, TANA;
 CONGO, NIGER
river in Alaska / YUKON
river in Argentina / CHUBUT
river in Asia / ILI; LENA; MEKONG
river in Austria / DANUBE
river to Baltic / ODER
river bank / RIPA
river bank, pert. to / RIPARIAN,
 RIVERAIN, RIVERINE
river barrier / DAM; WEIR
river bed / WADI; CHANNEL
river in Belgium / LYS; YSER
river boat / SCOW; BARGE, FERRY
river bottomland / HOLM
river in Brazil / AMAZON; TAPAJOS
river channel / BED, GAT
river of Charon / STYX
river in China / HO, SI; HAN;
 YANGTZE
river chute / RAPIDS
river crossed by Caesar / RUBICON
river deposit / SILT; DELTA
river dike / LEVEE
river dragon / CROCODILE
river drainage area / BASIN
river duck / TEAL
river of Eden / GIHON, PISON;
 EUPHRATES
river in England / CAM; AIRE;
 TRENT
river erosion / CORRASION
river in Europe / PO; ODER; RHINE;
 DANUBE
river feeder stream / TRIBUTARY
river fish / DACE; CATFISH
river of forgetfulness / LETHE
river in France / AIN, LYS; AIRE,
 EURE, OISE, ORNE, SAAR, YSER;
 ISERE, LOIRE, MARNE, MEUSE,
 RHONE, SAONE, SEINE, SOMME,
 VESLE
river front / DOCKSIDE
river gauge / NILOMETER

river in Germany / EMS; ELBE, ODER; RHINE, SPREE, WESER; NEISSE
river in Hades / STYX; LETHE
river horse / HIPPOPOTAMUS
river of ice / GLACIER
river in India / INDUS; GANGES
river in Indiana / WABASH
river inlet / RIA
river in Ireland / NORE; LIFFEY; SHANNON
river island / AIT; EYOT
river in Italy / PO; ARNO, LIRI; PIAVE, TIBER
river of Kubla Khan / ALPH
river land / FLATS
river of Mesopotamia / TIGRIS; EUPHRATES
river mouth / DELTA; ESTUARY
river in Munich / ISAR
river in Nebraska / PLATTE
river in Netherlands / MAAS
river in New Jersey / RARITAN
river in New York / HUDSON, MOHAWK; GENESEE
river nymph / NAIAD
river outlet / MOUTH
river passage / FORD
river path / COURSE
river in Pennsylvania / OHIO; GENESEE; ALLEGHENY; MONONGAHELA
river in Poland / BUG, SAN; VISTULA
river rat / SNEAKTHIEF
river in Russia / DON; NEVA, OREL, URAL
river in Scotland / AYR, DEE; DEVON
river shellfish / UNIO
river in Siberia / OB; LENA; YENISEI
river sluice / SASSE
river of song / SWANEE, WABASH
river source / RILL; CREEK; SPRING
river of Southwest U.S. / PECOS
river in Spain / EBRO
river of the underworld / STYX
river valley / DALE; STRATH
river in Venezuela / APURE
river in Vietnam / MEKONG
river's drainage area / WATERSHED
river's path / COURSE
rivers, pert. to / POTAMIC
riverside / BANK
riverside landing in India / GHAT; GHAUT
rivet / BOLT; FASTENER
Riviera city / NICE; CANNES
Riviera highway / CORNICHE
riviere / NECKLACE
rivose / GROOVED
rivulet / RILL; CREEK; STREAM

roach / HAIRROLL; COCKROACH
road / VIA, WAY; ITER, LANE, PATH; AGGER, ROUTE; STREET; FREEWAY, HIGHWAY
road across water / CAUSEWAY
road agent / HIGHWAYMAN
road end / CULDESAC
road machine / GRADER; SCRAPER
road shoulder / BERM; BERME
road surface / TAR; CEMENT; MACADAM
roadhouse / INN; TAVERN
roadside haven / INN; MOTEL, SERAI
roadside restaurant / DINER; TAVERN
roadstead / ANCHORAGE
roadwork / RUNNING
roam / GAD; ROVE, RANGE, STRAY
roamer / NOMAD; WANDERER
roan / BAY; LEATHER
roan tree / ROWAN
roar / CRY; BAWL, BRAY, YELL; BELLOW; THUNDER. DIN; NOISE
roar of breakers / RUT; ROTE
roarer / BULLY; SWAGGERER
roaring / HOWLING, IMMENSE
roast / PARCH; BANTER; CALCINA; RIDICULE. ROTI
roast chunk of meat / CABOB
roast in the open / BARBECUE
roasting fowl / CAPON
roasting iron / PIN; SPIT
rob / LOOT; REAVE, STEAL; BURGLE
Rob Roy / CANOE; COCKTAIL
robalo / SNOOK
robbed / REFT; RUBATO, STOLEN
robber / THIEF; BANDIT; BRIGAND, FOOTPAD
robber fly / BUMBLEBEE
robber of India / DACOIT
robbery / REIF; THEFT; PIRACY; LARCENY
robbery at sea / PIRACY
robe / ABA; COAT, TOGA; DRESS, SYRMA, TALAR; GARMENT
robe coming to ankles / TALAR
robe of office / TOGA
robe worn by bishop / SIMAR; CHIMER; ZIMARRA
robed / VESTED
robin / THRUSH; ROBINET; REDBREAST
Robin Goodfellow / PUCK
Robin Hood's beloved / MARIAN
Robin Hood's forest / SHERWOOD
Robin Hood's friar / TUCK
Robin Hood's refuge / GREENWOOD
robin snipe / KNOT; DOWITCHER
robin-run-in-the-hedge / IVY; BINDWEED, CLEAVERS
Robinson Crusoe author / DEFOE

Robinson Crusoe's companion /
XURY; FRIDAY

roborant / TONIC

roborate / RATIFY; STRENGTHEN

robot / SERVO; AUTOMATON

robot play / RUR

robots / AUTOMATA

robust / HALE; HARDY, LUSTY,
STOUT

robustious / ROUGH; VIGOROUS

roc / ANKA, RUKH; SIMURG;
SENMURI

rochelime / QUICKLIME

Rochester's wife, at last / JANE-
EYRE

rochet / GURNARD; SURPLICE

rock / SWAY; PITCH, SHAKE; TOT-
TER; VIBRATE. ORE; CRAG, REEF,
TRAP; STONE; BOULDER

rock with cavity / VUG; VUGG;
GEODE

rock of clay and mud / PELITE

rock crumblings / GEEST, SCREE,
TALUS; DETRITUS

rock crystal / QUARTZ

rock at earth's center / SIMA

rock in earth's mantle / SIAL

rock fragments / SAND; GRAVEL

rock material / SAND; GRAVEL

rock pile / JAIL

rock projection / TOR; CRAG;
NEEDLE

rock rabbit / HYRAX

rock salt / HALITE

rock shelter / ABRI

rock off Sicily / SCYLLA

rock snake / KRAIT; PYTHON

rock variety / SPAR, TRAP; AGATE,
CHERT, FLINT, PRASE, SHALE,
SLATE; BASALT, GABBRO,
GNEISS, SCHIST; DIORITE,
GRANITE

rock from volcano / LAVA, TUFA,
TUFF

rock whiting / KELPFISH

rock wool / INSULATION

rockcod / GROPER; GROUPER;
STONEFISH

rocker / CHAIR; CRADLE

rocket / JET; MISSILE; FIREWORK

rocket platform / PAD

rocket's goal / MARS, MOON;
PLANET

rockfish / BASS, RENA; REINA;
RASHER, TAMBOR; REDFISH,
ROCKCOD, STRIPER

Rockies peak / ELBERT

Rockies range / PARK; FRONT,
UINTA

rocking / OSCILLATING

rocking chair / ROCKER

rockweed / KELP; FOCUS

rocky / HARD, WEAK; SHAKY,
STONY; FLINTY

rocky desert / REG

rocky hill / TOR

Rocky Mountain park / ESTES;
JASPER; GLACIER

Rocky Mountain peak / ESTES,
PIKES; ELBERT

Rocky Mountain range / LEMHI,
TETON, UINTA; WASATCH

rococo / FLORID; BIZARRE; EX-
TRAVAGANT

roc's passenger / SINBAD

rod / GAD; AXLE, CANE, TWIG,
WAND; BATON, SHAFT; PISTOL

rod in basketry / OSIER

rod bundle / FASCES

rod for conductor / BATON

rod divination / DOWSING;
RHABDOMANCY

rod in fishing / POLE

rod holding flax / DISTAFF

rod of office / SCEPTER, SCEPTRE

rod used in punishment / FERULA,
FERULE

rode a bicycle / PEDALED

rodent / CUI, RAT; CAVY, CONY,
HARE, MARA, MOLE, PACA, PICA,
PIKA, VOLE; COYPU, HUTIA,
MOUSE, QUEMI; AGOUTI,
BEAVER, GOPHER, MARMOT,
RABBIT; TUCOTUDO

rodeo / CONTEST, ROUNDUP

Rodin statue / THINKER

rodlike / BACILLARY, VERGIFORM

rodomontade / RANT; BOAST

rod-shaped / VIRGATE

roe / OVA; DEER, EGGS; SPAWN;
CAVIAR

roe fish / SHAD; STURGEON

roebuck / HART

roentgen rays / XRAYS

rogation / LITANY; REQUEST

roger / OK; YES; FLAG

Roget's masterpiece / THESAURUS

rogue / IMP, WAG; CHEAT, KNAVE;
SCAMP

roguish / SLY; ARCH; PRANKY

roguish boy / ARAB; URCHIN

roil / VEX; RILE; MUDDY

roister / BRAG; BLUSTER,
SWAGGER

roisterer / MON; ROWDY; MOHOCK,
RIOTER

Roland / ORLANDO, PALADIN

Roland's companion / OLIVER

Roland's destroyer / GAN;
GANELON

Roland's horn / OLIFANT, OLIVANT

Roland's sword / DURANDAL

role / BIT; PART; CHARACTER
roll / FOLD, ROCK; DRIVE. BUN; LIST, ROTA; SCROLL
roll along / TRUNDLE
roll of cloth / BOLT
roll a flag / FURL
roll fried in deep fat / RISSOLE
roll of minced meat / MEATBALL
roll of parchment / PELL
roll of thread / COP; SPOOL
roll of tobacco / CIGAR, TWIST
roll up / FURL
rolled tea / CHA; CHAA, TSIA
rolled up / VOLUTE
roller / INKER; CASTER; TUMBLER
roller coaster / CHUTETHECHUTE
roller of typewriter / PLATEN
rollicking / JOVIAL
rolling / UNDULATING
rolling grassland / PRAIRIE
rolling stone / NOMAD, ROVER
rollway / SPILLWAY
rolypoly / DUMPY, PUDGY
rom / GYPSY
romaine / COS
Roman / LATIN; ITALIAN
Roman arena / COLOSSEUM
Roman armor / CATAPHRACT
Roman army leader / CENTURION
Roman assembly / FORUM; COMITIA
Roman author / CATO, LIVY, OVID; LUCAN, PLINY; CICERO, HORACE, SENECA
Roman basilica / LATERAN
Roman baths / THERMAE
Roman boot / CALIGA; CALCEUS
Roman boxing glove / CESTUS
Roman brassiere / STROPHIUM
Roman breastplate / LORICA
Roman bronze / AES
Roman camp settlement / CANABA
Roman citadel / ARX; CAPITOL
Roman civil citizenry / QUIRITES
Roman clan / GENS
Roman cloak / TOGA; PALLA; PAENULA
Roman coins / AS; SILIQUA, SOLI-DUS; DENARIUS, QUADRANS
Roman date / IDES; NONES; CALENDS
Roman dialect / LATIN. See also ITALIC
Roman district / SUBURA
Roman diviner / HARUSPEX
Roman emperor / NERO, OTHO; CARUS, GALBA, NERVA, TITUS; CAESAR
Roman fates / FATAE, NONES; PARCAE
Roman fiddler / NERO

Roman fountain / TREVI
Roman galley / BIREME; TRIREME
Roman gaming piece / TALUS; TES-SERA
Roman garment / TOGA; PALLA, STOLA, TUNIC; LACERNA, PAE-NILA, PLANETA; PLANETAE
Roman giant / CACA
Roman gladiator / SAMNITE; MIR-MILLO; RETIARIUS
Roman gladiator manager / LANISTA
Roman god / DI; LAR; DEUS, JOVE; AMMON; JUPITER
Roman god of dead / ORCUS
Roman god of death / MORS
Roman god of doors and gates / JANUS
Roman god of eloquence / MERCURY
Roman god of fire / VULCAN
Roman god of love / AMOR; CUPID
Roman god of metalworking / VULCAN; VOLCANUS
Roman god of sea / NEPTUNE
Roman god of sun / SOL
Roman god of underworld / DIS; PLUTO
Roman god of war / MARS
Roman god of woods and herds / PAN
Roman goddess / LUA; JUNO
Roman goddess of agriculture / CERES
Roman goddess of childbirth / LUCINA
Roman goddess of crops / ANNONA
Roman goddess of dawn / AURORA
Roman goddess of earth / OPS; CERES, TERRA
Roman goddess of fate / NONA; PARCA
Roman goddess of fields / FAUNA
Roman goddess of flowers / FLORA
Roman goddess of fruit / POMONA
Roman goddess of health / SALUS
Roman goddess of hearth / VESTA; HESTIA
Roman goddess of hope / SPES
Roman goddess of horses / EPONA
Roman goddess of love / VENUS
Roman goddess of moon / DIAN, LUNA; DIANA; PHOEBE
Roman goddess of night / NOX, NYX
Roman goddess of prosperity / SALUS
Roman goddess of wisdom / MINERVA
Roman greeting / AVE
Roman hall / SALA; ATRIA
Roman harvest festival / OPALIA

ROMAN NUMERALS

1	I	20	XX
2	II	30	XXX
3	III	40	XL
4	IV	45	VL
5	V	50	L
6	VI	60	LX
7	VII	70	LXX
8	VIII	80	LXXX or XXC
9	IX	90	XC
10	X	100	C
11	XI	200	CC
12	XII	300	CCC
13	XIII	400	CD
14	XIV	500	D
15	XV	600	DC
16	XVI	700	DCC
17	XVII	800	DCCC
18	XVIII	900	CM
19	XIX	1000	M

Roman helmet/ GALEA
Roman hill / CAELIAN, VIMINAL; AVENTINE, PALATINE
Roman historian / LIVY; SALLUST, TACITUS
Roman holiday / FERIA
Roman house gods / DI; LARES; PENATES
Roman house urn / CAPANNA
Roman javelin / PILUM
Roman law / JUS, LEX
Roman legal decree / DECRETE
Roman magistrate / EDILE; AEDILE, CONSUL, PRETOR; PRAETOR, TRIBUNE; DECEMVIR
Roman marketplace / FORUM
Roman marsh district / PONTINE
Roman meal / CENA; MERENDA; PRANDIUM
Roman naturalist / PLINY
Roman nose / AQUILINE
Roman official / EDILE; CENSOR, CONSUL, LICTOR; PRAETOR, TRIBUNE
Roman official in Judea / PILATE
Roman orator / CICERO
Roman pan / PATINA
Roman patriot / CATO; SCIPIO
Roman philosopher / SENECA; AURELLUS; LUCRETIUS
Roman pin / ACUS; FIBULA
Roman platter / LANX; PATERA
Roman plaza / FORUM
Roman poet / OVID; LUCAN; HORACE, VIRGIL; JUVENAL
Roman porridge / PULS
Roman priest / FLAMEN
Roman provincial governor / TETRARCH
Roman public games / LUDI

Roman road / VIA; ITER
Roman roof tile / TEGULA
Roman room / ALA; ATRIUM
Roman shield / PARMA; SCUTUM; CLIPEUS
Roman spear / HASTA, PILUM; JACULUM, TRAGULA
Roman sword / SPATHA; GLADIUS
Roman symbol of authority / FASCES
Roman temple / PANTHEON
Roman woodland spirit / FAUN
romance / TALE; FABLE, NOVEL; FICTION
romance language / FRENCH; CATALAN, ITALIAN, SPANISH; RUMANIAN
Romania / See RUMANIA
romano cheese / SARDO; CAPRINO; PECORINO
romantic / WILD; IDEAL; SENTIMENTAL
romantic novelist / HUGO
romantic poet / KEATS; SHELLEY
romantic song / BALLAD; SERENADE
romantic story / GEST, SAGA; NOVEL
romany / GYPSY
Rome's cathedral church / LATERAN
Rome's conqueror / ALARIC
Rome's founders / REMUS; ROMULUS
Rome's river / TIBER; TEVERE
romp / PLAY; FRISK; CAVORT. TOMBOY
Romulus' apotheosis / QUIRINUS
Romulus' brother / REMUS
Romulus' father / MARS

Romulus' grandfather / NUMITOR
Romulus' stepfather / FAUSTULUS
Romulus' stepmother / WOLF
Romulus' victim / REMUS
rood / CROSS; CRUCIFIX
rood goose / BRANT
roof / CANOPY, SLATES, SUMMIT; MANSARD
roof formation in cave / STALACTITE
roof material / TILE; SLATES; PANTILE
roof of mouth / PALATE
roof ornament / EPI
roof overhang / EAVE
roof tile/ PANTILE
roof of the world / PAMIRS
roofer's tool / SAX
roofing / TILES; SHAKES, SLATES; SHINGLES, TARPAPER
roofing member / PURLIN
roofing slab / RAG; SLAB, TILE; SLATE
roofing tin / TERNE; FLASHING
roofless / HOMELESS
rooflike cover / AWNING
rooftree / BEAM
rook / CROW; CASTLE. CHEAT
rook's cry / CAW
room / AULA, SALA; PLACE, RANGE, SCOPE, SPACE, SWEEP; EXTENT; BOUDOIR, CHAMBER
room for action / LEEWAY
room in harem / ODA
room for storage / CLOSET
roomer / LODGER; BOARDER
roominess / RANGE. EXPANSE
rooms / SUITE; APARTMENT
roomy / WIDE; RANGY; SPACIOUS
roomy boat / BARGE
roorback / LIE; CANARD
roost / SET, SIT; PERCH. POLE
rooster / COCK
root / STEM; BASIS, CAUSE, RADIX; ORIGIN, SOURCE. CHEER, PLANT
root, c.f. / RHIZO
root, pert. to / RADICULAR
root beer plant / GINGER; SASSAFRAS
root for condiment / GINGER; HORSERADISH
root out / PULL; EXTIRPATE; DERACINATE
root of some plants / BULB, CORM
root vegetable / POI, YAM; BEET, TARO; CARROT, POTATO, RADISH
root word / ETYMON
rooter / FAN, PIG; SUPPORTER
rootlet / RADICEL
rootstock / RHIZOME
rope / CORD, LAZO; CABLE, LASSO, LONGE, RIATA; HALTER, HAWSER, LARIAT; MARLINE

rope for animals / LEASH; HOBBLE, TETHER
rope fiber / DA; COIR, FERU, HEMP, IMBE, JUTE, RHEA; ABACA, ISTLE, IXTLE, SISAL; AMBARY
rope guide / WAPP
rope for hoisting / TYE
rope for leading horses / HALTER
rope loop / KNOT; BIGHT
rope with running knot / NOOSE
rope on ship / FOX, TYE; STAY, VANG; HAWSER, RATLIN
rope tied to cringle / LEEFANG
rope for training horse / LONGE
rope for tying boat / PAINTER
rope walker / FUNAMBULIST
rope on yardarm / SNOTTER
ropy / VISCOUS
roque / CROQUET
roral / DEW; DEWY, EOAN
rorqual / FINBACK
rorty / DRUNK, NOISY
Rosalind's friend / CELIA
Rosalind's lover / ORLANDO
Rosalind's pseudonym / GANYMEDE
Rosaline's admirer / ROMEO
rosary / BEADS; CHAPLET
rosary bead / AVE
rose / TEA; CLIMBER
rose, c.f. / RHODO
rose dye / EOSIN
rose essence / ATTAR; FRAGRANCE
rose fish / PERCH
rose fruit / HIP
rose oil / OTAR, OTTO; ATTAR, OTTAR
roseate / ROSY; BLOOMING
rosebud / LASS; BLOOM
roselike ornament / ROSETTE
Rosencrantz' fellow / GUILDENSTERN
Rosetta discovery / STONE
rosette / BOW; DECORATION
rosewood tree / JANCA; MOLOMPI
rosin / AMBER, RESIN
Rosinante / JADE
rosland / MOOR; HEATH
ross / SCALE, WASTE
rosser / PEELER
roster / LIST, ROLL, ROTA; MUSTER
rostrum / BEAK, PROW; PULPIT; PLATFORM
rosy / PINK; BRIGHT; ROSEATE; BLUSHING
rot / MOLD; DECAY; PUTREFY. RUBBISH, TWADDLE
rota / LIST; ROSTER; HURDYGURDY
rotary / TURNING
rotary engine / WANKEL; TURBINE
rotate / ROLL, SPIN, TURN; SWIRL, WHEEL; GYRATE

rotating / REVOLVING
rotating cylinder / ROLLER
rotating part / CAM; AXLE; ROTOR, WHEEL
rotating tool / DRILL, LATHE
rotation / SEQUENCE
rotche / AUK; DOVEKIE
rote / ROUTINE; REPETITION
rotisserie / GRILL
roto / WORKER; GRAVURE
rotten / PUTRID; UNSOUND
rotter / CAD
Rotterdam native / ERASMUS
rotting / DECOMPOSING
rotula / LOZENGE, PATELLA
rotund / SPHERICAL
rotunda / DOME
roue / RAKE; DEBAUCHEE
rouge / MAKEUP, POLISH; COSMETIC
rouged / FUCATE; RADDLED
rough / HARD, RUDE, WILD; BLUNT, CRUEL, GRUFF, HARSH, RAGGY, UNCUT, VAGUE; COARSE, RUGGED, SEVERE, STORMY
rough breathing / ASPER, RALES
rough exterior bark / ROSS
rough lava / AA
Rough Riders' leader / TR
rough sandstone / GRAYWACKE
rough shelter / SHED; SHACK; LEANTO
rough steep rock / CRAG
rough to touch / ASPERATE
rough tree bark / ROSS
roughhouse / NOISY, ROWDY, QUARREL
roughly outlined / SKETCHY
roughneck / GOON; ROWDY, TOUGH
rough-speaking / GRUFF
roulette bet / BAS; NOIR, PAIR; PASSE, ROUGE; MILIEU
Roumania / See RUMANIA
rounce / HANDLE
round / CYCLE, GLOBE; SPHERE, PLUMP, STOUT; ROTUND, SMOOTH
round appendage / LOBE
round body / ORB; BALL
round in music / ROTA; CANON, CATCH; ROTULA
round and oblong / ELLIPTICAL
round peg / MISFIT
round robin / PETITION
round room / ROTUNDA
Round Table knight / KAY, TOR; BORS, MARK; BALAN, BALIN, ECTOR, FLOLL; ACOLON, BOHORS, GARETH, GAWAIN, MODRED, SAGRIS; GALAHAD, PELLEAS

Round Table maker / MERLIN
Round Table site / WINCHESTER
round tipped / RETUSE
round up / HERD; GATHER, RODEO; CORRAL
roundabout / INDIRECT, DETOUR; TRAFFICCIRCLE
roundabout course / CIRCLE, DETOUR
rounded hill / KNOB; KNOLL, MORRO
rounded out / ROTUND
rounded projection / BOSS, KNOB, LOBE, LUMP, NODE
rounded roof / DOME; CUPOLA; ROTUNDA
rounder / RAKE, ROUE
roundhead / PURITAN
roundhouse / SHOP
roundup / DRAGNET
roundworm / NEMA; ASCARID, EELWORM, FILARIA; HOODWORM, NEMATODE, TRICHINA
roup / COLD; AUCTION
rouse / SPUR, STIR; DRIVE, WAKEN; BESTIR, EXCITE, KINDLE; ANIMATE
rousing / PEPPY; LIVELY
Rousseau novel / EMILE
roustabout / LABORER
rout / MOB; FLIGHT, UPROAR; DISORDER
route / WAY; PATH, ROAD; TRACK
route to another track / SHUNT; SWITCH
route easing traffic / BYPASS
route for planes / AIRLANE
routine / RUT; HABIT, REGULAR
rove / GAD; DRAW, ROAM; RANGE; WANDER
rover / NOMAD; PIRATE
roving / ERRANT; MIGRANT
row / OAR; FILE, LINE, RANK, RIOT, SPAT, TIER; BRAWL; FRACAS
rowan / ASH; TREE
rowboat / GIG; SCULL, SKIFF; CAIQUE, DINGHY, WHERRY
rowdy / RUDE; ROUGH, BHOY; RUFFIAN; HOOLIGAN, LARRIKIN; BLACKGUARD
rowel / GOAD, SPUR; PRICK
rowen / STUBBLE; AFTERMATH
Rowena's husband / IVANHOE
rower's bench / ZYGON; THWART
Roxane's secret lover / CYRANO
royal / NOBLE, REGAL; KINGLY, SUPERB
royal antelope / IPETE; KLEENEBOK
royal beast / LION
royal fur / ERMINE
royal mace / SCEPTER, SCEPTRE
royal residence / PALACE

royal seat / THRONE
royal shiner / DACE
royal touch / KINGSX
royalty / BONUS, SHARE
royalty in Hawaii / ALII
rub / BUFF, WIPE; ABRADE, POLISH; MASSAGE
rub gently / STROKE
rub with oil / ANOINT
rub out / ERASE
rub roughly / RASP; CHAFE, GRATE, SCOUR, SCRUB; SCRAPE
rubadub / DIN; BEAT; CLAMOR
Rubaiyat's author / OMAR; KHAYYAM
rubbed-in-dirt / GRIME
rubber / GUM; PARA; LATEX; ERASER, GALOSH; ELASTIC, MASSEUR; OVERSHOE; CAOUTCHOUC. PRY; PEER
rubber band / ELASTIC
rubber ring / LUTE; GASKET, WASHER
rubber tube / HOSE
rubberlike substance / GUTTA
rubberneck / SIGHTSEER
rubber-soled shoe / SNEAKER
rubbish / ROT; JUNK; CULCH, DROSS, TRASH
rubbish from mining / ATTLE
rubbish pile / DUMP
rubble / BRASH, TALUS; MOELLON
rubeola / MEASLES
rubescent / RED; FLUSHING
Rubicon crosser / CAESAR
rubicund / RUDDY
ruby / BALAS
ruby-like gem / GARNET, SPINEL
ruche / RUFF; FRILL
ruck / SQUAT; CREASE; WRINKLE. PACK; CROWD
ruckle / HEAP, PILE
ruction / ROW; UPROAR
rudder / HELM; GUIDE
rudder arm / TILLER
rudder fish / CHUB; CHOPS
ruddle / REDDEN. SIEVE
ruddy / RED; ROSY, RUBY; FLORID
rude / WILD; CRUDE, GRUFF, HARSH, ROUGH, SAUCY; CLUMSY, COARSE, ROBUST, RUGGED, SEVERE
rude building / HUT; SHED; SHACK; SHANTY
rude fellow / CAD; BOOR
rudely terse / CURT
rudeness / FERITY; INCIVILITY
rudiment / GERM, ROOT; ANLAGE, EMBRYO
rudiments / ABE; ELEMENTS; PRINCIPIA

rue / LAMENT, REGRET, REPENT
rueful / SAD; DISMAL, WOEFUL
ruff / REE; PERCH, REEVE, SNIPE. TRUMP
ruffed grouse / PARTRIDGE
ruffian / THUG; BRUTE, BULLY; DACOIT, RASCAL, ROBBER, WRETCH; VILLAIN. HOOLIGAN
ruffle / VEX; FOLD, ROIL, TUCK; ANNOY, CRIMP; EXCITE. FRILL
ruffle at neck/ JABOT, RUCHE
rug / MAT; AGRA, BAKU, KALI, KUBA; HERAT, SENNA; CANARA, CARPET, HERATI, KANARA; DRUGGET
rugate / RIDGED, RUGOSE
rugged / HARD, RUDE; HARSH, ROUGH
rugged outcrop / TOR; CRAG
Ruhr city / ESSEN; BOCHUM; DORTMUND
ruin / MAR. HURT, UNDO; WRECK; RAVAGE; DESTROY; DEVASTATE. DOOM, FALL, LOSS; DEFEAT
ruined / LOST; KAPUT; FALLEN; DECAYED
ruinous / BANEFUL, NOISOME, NOXIOUS
ruins / DEBRIS; REMAINS
rule / LEAD; ORDER. REIGN; BRIDLE, DIRECT, GOVERN, MANAGE. LAW; LINE, SWAY; CANON, GUIDE, MAXIM; RE-GIME; FORMULA, PRECEPT
rule by a few / OLIGARCHY
rule by one / MONARCHY
ruler / KING; DYNAST. FERULE, GERENT, REGENT; EMPEROR, MONARCH; GOVERNOR
ruler in Afghanistan / EMIR; AMEER, EMEER
ruler of Indian state / MAHARAJAH
ruling authority / REGENT
ruling family of France / CAPET
rum / ODD; QUEER. TAFIA; TAFFIA; BACARDI, SPIRITS; DEMERARA
Rumania capital / BUCHAREST
Rumanian city / CLUJ, IASI; JASSY
Rumanian coin / BAN, LEU
Rumanian money / LEU
Rumanian province / BANAT; TRANSYLVANIA
Rumanian river / OLT; PRUT; TIMIS; DANUBE
Rumanian seaport / CONSTANTA
rumble / ROAR; FIGHT, NOISE, SOUND
rumen / CUD
rum-flavored cake / BABA
ruminant / COW; DEER, GOAT; CAMEL, LLAMA, SHEEP; ANTELOPE

ruminant stomach / RUMEN,
  TRIPE; OMASUM
ruminate / CHEW, MULL, MUSE;
  REFLECT
rummage / SEARCH; RANSACK
rummage sale / CLEARANCE;
  FUNDRAISER
rummy / SOT; TOPER
rummy game / GIN, RUM; STOPS
rumor / TALK; NOISE, STORY; GOS-
  SIP, REPORT; HEARSAY
rumor personified / FAMA
rump / BEHIND; BUTTOCKS
rumple / MUSS; TOUSLE;
  CRUMPLE
rumpus / FRACAS; DISTURBANCE
run / FLY; DART, FLEE, FLOW,
  FUSE, MELT, MOLD, MOVE,
  PUSH, RACE, RISK, RUSH, SAIL,
  STAB, TEND; EVADE, HURRY,
  SPEED
run aground / MOOR; BEACH;
  STRAND
run away / FLEE; SCRAM; DE-
  CAMP
run away to marry / ELOPE
run between ports / PLY
run in cricket / BYE
run down / DECRY. EXHAUSTED
run effortlessly / LOPE
run full speed / SPRINT
run off / BOLT; ELOPE, SPILL
run in panic / STAMPEDE
run rapidly / SCUD; SPRINT
run with the wind / SCUD
runagate / FUGITIVE
runaway / AWOL; FUGITIVE
rune / MAGIC
runic alphabet / FUTHORC
runnel / BROOK; STREAMLET
runner / SKI; MILER, RACER,
  SCARF; STOLON
running knot / NOOSE; SLIPKNOT
run-of-the-mill / ORDINARY;
  UNSELECTED
runt / DWARF; STUMP
runway / RAMP; STRIP; CHANNEL
rupture / REND; BREAK. BREACH;
  QUARREL
rural / RUSTIC; BUCOLIC;
  PASTORAL
rural deity / PAN; FAUN; SILENUS
rural poem / ECLOGUE, GEORGIC;
  PASTORAL
rusalka / NAIAD
ruse / WILE; DODGE, TRICK
rush / RUN; DASH, MOVE, ROLL;
  HURRY. REED; HASTE, SPART;
  BULRUSH, CATTAIL
rush about wildly / RAMPAGE

rush out / SALLY
rushed / HIED, SPED
Rushmore sculptor / BORGLUM
rusk / BUN; TOAST; BISCUIT;
  ZWIEBACK
russet / APPLE. COARSE; HOME-
  SPUN
Russia / MUSCOVY
Russian / RED; IVAN, RUSS, SLAV;
  KULAK; SOVIET
Russian author / FET; BLOK;
  BUNIN, GOGOL, GORKI, GORKY;
  LESKOV, CHEKHOV, PUSHKIN,
  TOLSTOI, TOLSTOY; PASTERNAK
Russian beer / KVAS, KVASS,
  QUASS
Russian cheese / TWOROG
Russian city / DNO, OSA, UFA;
  BAKU, KIEV, OREL, TULA;
  MINSK, SOCHI; MOSCOW,
  ODESSA, SAMARA; KHARKOV;
  LENINGRAD
Russian community / MIR
Russian composer / CUI; RIMSKY
Russian cooperative / ARTEL
Russian council / DUMA; SOVIET
Russian court favorite / RASPUTIN
Russian decree / UKASE
Russian drink / VODKA
Russian emperor / CZAR, TSAR,
  TZAR
Russian empress / CZARINA, TSAR-
  INA; CZAREVNA, TSAREVNA
Russian guitarlike instrument /
  DOMRA
Russian hemp / RINE
Russian horseman / COSSACK
Russian hut / IZBA
Russian inland sea / ARAL, AZOF,
  AZOV
Russian isthmus / PEREKOP
Russian leader / LENIN; STALIN
Russian liquor / VODKA
Russian log hut / ISBA
Russian measure / VERST; ARSHIN
Russian monarch / CZAR, TSAR
Russian money / ALTIN, COPEK,
  KOPEK, RUBLE; KOPECK
Russian mountains / URAL; ALTAI;
  PAMIRS; STANOVOI
Russian name / AKIM, IGOR, IVAN
Russian news agency / TASS
Russian novelist / TOLSTOY
Russian oboe / SZOPELKA
Russian peasant / MUJIK; MOUJIK,
  MUZHIK, MUZJIK
Russian peninsula / KOLA; KANIN;
  TAIMYR
Russian plain / STEPPE
Russian plane / MIG

Russian poet / PUSHKIN
Russian prince / CZAREVITCH, TSAREVITCH
Russian princess / CZAREVNA, TSAREVNA
Russian river / AI, IK, OB; DON, NER, OKA, ROS, YUG; AMUR, DUNA, ILET, KARA, LENA, NEVA, URAL; DVINA, VOLGA; IRTYSH
Russian rude vehicle / KIBITKA
Russian secret police / NKVD, OGPU
Russian urn / SAMOVAR
Russian vehicle / ARBA; ARABA; TROIKA
Russian village / MIR
Russian whip / PLET; KNOUT
Russian wolfhound / BORZOI
Russian writer / CHEKHOV
rust / ERODE; CORRODE, OXIDIZE. SMUT; BLIGHT, CANKER, PATINA; EROSION; CORROSION
Rustam's father / ZAL
rustic / BOOR, CARL, LOUT; CARLE, HODGE, YOKEL; PEASANT. RURAL; SYLVAN; BUCOLIC. COUNTRY
rustic lover / SWAIN

rustic pipe / REED
rusticate / BANISH; SUSPEND
rustle / GET, ROB; MOVE, STIR; HASTE, HURRY
rustler / CATTLETHIEF
Rustum's son / SOHRAB
rut / WAY, HOLE, PATH; TRACK; FURROW, GROOVE
rutabaga / TURNIP
ruth / PITY, COMPASSION
ruthless / CRUEL; SAVAGE; PITILESS
Ruth's dead husband / MAHLON
Ruth's forte / HOMER
Ruth's husband / BOAZ
Ruth's mother-in-law / NAOMI
ruttish / WANTON; LUSTFUL
Ruy Diaz de Bivar / CID; ELCID
Rwanda capital / KIGALI
Rwandese language / KINYAR-WANDA
Rwandese people / BATWA, TUTSI; BAHUTU, WATUSI; BATUTSI
rye / BOOZE, ERGOT; GENTLEMAN
rye grass / RIE
Ryukyu island / AMAMI; OSHIMA; OKINAWA
Ryukyus capital / NAHA

S

S curve / ESS
Saadi poem / GULISTAN
Saba / SHEBA
sabal / PALMETTO
sabalo / TARPON
sabaoth / HOSTS; ARMIES
sabbat assemblers / COVEN
sabbath, pert. to / SABBATICAL
sabbatical / FURLOUGH
sabeline / FUR; SABLE
saber / BLADE, SABRE, SWORD; SIDEARM
saber-tooth / CAT; TIGER; SMILODON
sabino / CYPRESS; MAGNOLIA
sable / COAT; SOBOL; MARTEN. EBON; BLACK; SOMBER
sabotage / DAMAGE, INJURY
sabra / ISRAELI, OPUNTIA
Sabra's father / PTOLEMY
Sabra's rescuer / STGEORGE
Sabrina's father / LOCRINE
sabuline / SANDY; GRITTY; FRIABLE
sac / BAG; CYST; BURSA, POUCH
sacaton / BUNCHGRASS
saccade / CHECK
saccadic / JERKY, JUMPY
saccate / POUCHLIKE
saccharine / SWEET; SUGARY

sacerdotal / CLERICAL; PRIESTLY
sachem / CHIEF
sachet / BAG; SCENT; CUSHION
sachet scent / OTTO; LAVENDER
sack / FIRE, LOOT; RAVAGE; PILLAGE. BAG; BASE; CLOAK, POUCH
sackbut / TROMBONE
sacking / JUTE; GUNNY; BURLAP
sacrament / OATH, RITE; OBLIGATION
Sacramento tribe / YANA
sacred / HOLY; DIVINE; HALLOWED
sacred animal / LAMB; TOTEM
sacred asp emblem / URAEUS
sacred bamboo / NANDIN
sacred bark / CASCARA
sacred bean / LOTUS
sacred boat / ARK
sacred book of Buddhists / DHAMMAPADA
sacred book of Hindus / SHASTRA
sacred book of Islam / KORAN, QURAN
sacred book of Parsis / ZENDA-VESTA
sacred books of India / VEDAS
sacred books of Japan / KOJIKI; NIHONGI
sacred books of Judaism / BIBLE

sacred bull / APIS, HAPI, ZEBU
sacred chest / ARCA
sacred city / MECCA; MEDINA; BENARES
Sacred College member / CARDINAL
sacred disease / EPILEPSY
sacred dung beetle / SCARAB
sacred fig tree / PIPAL, PIPUL
sacred goblet / GRAIL
sacred image / ICON, IDOL, IKON; EIKON
Sacred isle / IRELAND
sacred language / PALI
sacred Moslem book / KORAN; ALCORAN
sacred musical composition / HYMN; MOTET, PSALM; CANTATA, CHORALE; ORATORIO
sacred offering / CORBAN
sacred place / SHRINE
sacred precinct / NAOS; CELLA, SEKOS
sacred Sikh book / GRANTH
sacred song / HYMN; PSALM
sacred syllable / OM
sacred tower / TOPE; STOPA; PAGODA
sacred tree / BO; PIPAL
sacred vessel / ARK, PIX, PYX; CHALICE
sacred weed / VERVAIN
sacred well of Mecca / ZEMZEM
sacred word / OM
sacred writing / BIBLE; SCRIPTURE
sacred Zoroastrian book / AVESTA
sacrifice / OFFERING; IMMOLATION
sacrifice by burning / HOLOCAUST
sacrifice in expiation / PIACULUM
sacrifice of liquid / LIBATION
sacrifice of many / HECATOMB
sacrifice place / ALTAR
sacrifice of something not alive / OBLATION
sacrificial drink / SOMA
sacrificial offering / OBLATION
sacrificial platform / ALTAR
sacrilegious / IMPIOUS, PROFANE
sacring bell / SQUILLA
sacristan / SEXTON
sacrum, pert. to / SACRAL
sac-shaped / SACCULATE
sad / DARK; HEAVY; DISMAL, GLOOMY, SOMBER, WOEFUL; DOLEFUL; DEJECTED, DOWNCAST
sad, c.f. / TRAGI
sad exclamation / WOE; ALAS; ALACK
sadden / GRIEVE; DEPRESS
saddle / LOAD; BURDEN; ENCUMBER. SEAT; FUSTE; LINTEL
saddle animal / ASS; MULE; HORSE

saddle attachment / STIRRUP
saddle cloth / MANTA; TILPAH
saddle horse / PAD; PALFREY
saddle knob / PIG; HORN; POMMEL
saddle reef / PHACOLITH
saddle tie / CINCH, GIRTH; LATIGO
saddle's rear / CANTLE
sadiron / FLATIRON
sadistic / CRUEL
sadness / SORROW; MELANCHOLY
safari / TREK; EXPEDITION
safe / SURE; SOUND; SECURE. VAULT; COFFER; STRONGBOX
safe conduct / PASS
safe place / PORT; HAVEN; SHELTER
safeguard / DEFEND; PROTECT. ESCORT, SHIELD
safekeeping / CUSTODY, STORAGE
safety / SECURITY
safety lamp for mine / DAVY
safety pin / CLASP; FIBULA
safflower / KUSUM
saffron / CROCUS, YELLOW
sag / SINK; DROOP; DECLINE
saga / EDDA, MYTH, TALE, LEGEND
saga of Norway's kings / HEIMSKRINGLA
saga writer / SNORRI
sagacious / KEEN, WISE; ACUTE; ASTUTE, SHREWD; INTELLIGENT
sagacity / SENSE; ACUMEN; PRUDENCE
sagamore / CHIEF; SACHEM
sage / SEER; SOLON; SALVIA; PROPHET; ARTEMISIA. WISE; PRUDENT, SAPIENT
sage of Chelsea / CARLYLE
sage of Concord / EMERSON
sage of Ferney / VOLTAIRE
sage hen / GROUSE
Sage Hen / NEVADAN
sage of Monticello / JEFFERSON
Sagebrush State / NEVADA
sagene / SEINE; FISHNET
sageness / WISDOM; SAGACITY
sagest / SOUNDEST; SHREWDEST
sagging / WEAK; SLUMPING
Sagittarius / ARCHER
Sagittary / CENTAUR
sagoin / MARMOSET
Sahara / DESERT
Saharan wind / GIBLEH; KHAMSIN, SIROCCO; HARMATTAN
sai monkey / CAPUCHIN
saic / KETCH
said / TOLD; SPOKE. PREVIOUS
said to be / REPUTED
sail / GLIDE; CRUISE, VOYAGE. JIB, LUG; ROYAL; LATEEN
sail back and forth / PLY
sail close to the wind / CONFORM
sail extended by spar / SPRITSAIL

sail nearer the wind / LUFF
sail part / BUNT, CLEW, FOOT, HEAD; SHEET
sailboat / CAT; YAWL; KETCH, SLOOP; LUGGER
sailing race / REGATTA
sailing vessel / BARK, BRIG, SAIC; SETEE, XEBEC; GALLEON
sailor / GOB, TAR; SALT; LASCAR, SEADOG, SEAMAN; MARINER
sailor's biscuit / HARDTACK
sailor's call / AHOY; AVAST
sailor's carving / SCRIMSHAW
sailor's dance / JIG; HORNPIPE
sailor's drink / GROG
sailor's furlough / LEAVE
sailor's patron / ELMO
sailor's song / SHANTY; CHANTEY
sailor's stew / LOBSCOUSE
sail's edge / LEECH
sail's lower corner / CLEW
saim / LARD
saint / CANONIZE, SANCTIFY
St. Andrew's cross / SALTIRE
Saint Andrews sport / GOLF
St. Anthony's cross / TAU
St. Anthony's fire / ERYSIPELAS
saint of Buddhism / ARHAT; ARAHAT
St. Elmo's fire / HELENA; CORPOSANT
St. George's sword / ASKELON
St. George's victim / DRAGON
saint of Islam / PIR
St. John's bread / CAROB
Saint Kitts capital / BASSETERRE
St. Lawrence canal / WELLAND
St. Lawrence rapids / LACHINE
"St. Louis Blues" composer / HANDY
St. Nicholas / SANTA
St. Paul's companion / SILAS
St. Vitus's dance / CHOREA
sainted / DEAD, HOLY; PIOUS
saintly / HOLY, PURE; PIOUS
saint's memento / RELIC
saints' lives / HAGIOLOGY; HAGIOGRAPHY
sake / SCORE; BEHALF; ACCOUNT
Sakhalin gulf / TATARY
Sakhalin strait / SOYA; TATAR
Sakhmet's husband / PTAH
Sakhmet's son / NEFERTEM
Sakuntala's husband / DUSHYANTA
Sakuntala's son / BHARATA
Sakyamuni / BUDDHA; SIDDHARTHA
sal / SALT
salaam / SALUTE; OBEISANCE
salable / VENDIBLE
salacious / IMPURE; LECHEROUS
salad / GREENS, SALLET
salad days / YOUTH

salad herb / COS, UDO; CRESS; ENDIVE; CHICORY, LETTUCE
saladang / GAUR
Saladin's foes / CRUSADERS
salamander / EFT; NEWT; POKER; TRITON; URODELA
salamander wool / ASBESTOS
Salamis victor / THEMISTOCLES
salary / PAY; WAGES; STIPEND; EARNINGS
sale / DEAL; MARKET; AUCTION, BARGAIN
sale announcemount / AD; NOTICE
Salem / JERUSALEM
Salem phobia / WITCHES
Salem preoccupation / WITCHHUNT
saleratus / BAKINGSODA
saleratus weed / GLASSWORT
salesman / AGENT; VENDOR; DRUMMER
salient / STRIKING; PROMINENT
salient trait / POINT; FEATURE
salina / SALTPOND
saline / SALTY
saline astringent / ALUM
saline solution / BRINE
salinity / SALTNESS; SALTINESS
saliva / SPIT; RHEUM; SPITTLE
saliva, pert. to / SIALIC
saliva-like / SIALOID
salivary gland / PAROTID; SUBLINGUAL
salix / OSIER; WILLOW
sallet / HELMET
sallow / WAN; PALE; SICKLY
sally / RUSH; SORTIE; OUTBURST. ISSUE
Sally Lunn / TEACAKE
salmagundi / HASH, OLIO; MEDLEY; FRICASSEE
salmi / STEW; RAGOUT
salmon / CHUM, COHO; CHINOOK, KOKANEE, SOCKEYE; OUANANICHE
Salome's brother / HEROD
Salome's mother / HERODIAS
salon / HALL; PARLOR; GALLERY
salon hostess / RECAMIER
saloon / BAR; CAFE; BARROOM
salt / SAL, WIT; FLAVOR, SAILOR. SEASON; MARINATE
salt, pert. to / SALINE
salt of the earth / ELECT; WEALTHY
salt efflorescence / REH; ALKALI
salt factory / SALTERN, SALTERY
salt lake / SHAT; SALIN, SHOTT; SALINA, SALINE
salt marsh / SALINA
salt marsh in Algeria / CHOTT, SHOTT
salt meat / SALAME, SALAMI
salt pan / PLAYA; SALINA
salt plain / SALADA

salt pond / SALINA
salt rheum / ECZEMA
salt from sea / BRINE
salt solution / BRINE; PICKLE
salt spring / LICK; SALINE
salt tax / GABELLE
salt tree / ATLE
salt water / SEA; BRINE, OCEAN
saltant / DANCING, LEAPING
saltarello / DANCE
saltcellar / SALER; SHAKER
salted / ALAT; CURED; CORNED
saltern / SALINA
saltine / CRACKER
saltless / INSIPID
saltpeter / NITER, NITRE; ANA-
TRON
saltworks / SALINA; SALTERN
saltwort / KALI
saltwort ashes / BARILLA
salty / RACY; BRINY, SPICY;
EARTHY
salty drop / TEAR
salty liquid / BRINE
salty sauce / SOY; SOYA
salubrious / TONIC; SANITARY
salutary / HEALTHY; BENEFICIAL
salutation / AVE, BOW; ALOHA
HELLO, KOTOW; KOWTOW, SA-
LAAM, SALUTE; WELCOME;
GREETING
salute / BOW; HAIL, KISS; GREET;
WELCOME. SALVO; COMPLI-
MENT
salute with song / SERENADE
salvage / SAVE; REDEEM
salvation / RESCUE; REDEMPTION;
PRESERVATION
Salvation Army founder / BOOTH
salve / BALM; OINTMENT. PAL-
LIATE
salver / TRAY
salvia / CHIA, SAGE; CLARY
salvo / SHOT; BURST, ROUND;
PROVISO; DISCHARGE
Salzburg's favorite son / MOZART
Samar native / BIKOL
samara / KEY; PUGNOSE
Samaria / ISRAEL
Samaria's founder / OMRI
samaritan / KIND; CHARITABLE
samba / ARERE, DANCE; OBECHE;
CANASTA
Sambal language / TINO
sambar / MAHA
same / ONE; LIKE, SELF; ALIKE,
EQUAL. IBID, IDEM; DITTO
same, c.f. / HOMO
same age / COEVAL
same in social rank / PEER
sameness / IDENTITY, MONOTONY
Samhain / HALLOWEEN

Samian sage / PYTHAGORAS
samiel / SIMOOM
samite / SILK
samlet / PARR
sammy / SODDEN, WATERY
Samoan bird / IAO; MANUAO
Samoan city / APIA; PAGOPAGO
Samoan island / UPOLU; SAVAII;
TUTUILA
Samoan mountain / PIUA, VAEA
Samoan nationalists / MAU
Samoan owl / LULU
Samoan political council / FONO
Samoan warrior / TOA
Sámoa's discoverer / ROGGEVEEN
samoon / SIMOOM
samovar / URN
samp / HOMINY; PORRIDGE
sampan / SKIFF
sample / MODEL, TASTE; SPECI-
MEN
sample of fabric / SWATCH
sampler / TASTER; EMBROIDERY
Samson's father / MANOAH
Samson's paramour / DELILAH
Samuel's mentor / ELI
Samuel's mother / HANNAH
Samuel's son / JOEL; ABIAH
Samuel's victim / AGAG
samurai / GENTRY; WARRIOR
San Antonio shrine / ALAMO
Sanaa's port / HODEIDA
sanable / CURABLE
sanative / CURATIVE; HEALTHFUL
sanatorium / RESORT; RETREAT;
HOSPITAL
sanatory / HYGIENIC, REMEDIAL
Sancho Panza's mount / DAPPLE
sanctification / CONSECRATION
sanctified / HOLY; BLESSED
sanctify / HALLOW, PURIFY
sanction / BAN; ABET; ALLOW;
APPROVE, CONFIRM. FIAT;
ASSENT
sanctitude / HOLINESS
sanctity / PURITY; SACREDNESS
sanctuary / DEN; BEMA, FANE,
NAOS; CELLA; ADYTUM,
ASYLUM, REFUGE, TEMPLE;
SHELTER
sanctum / DEN; STUDY
sand / GRIT; BEACH; SILICA;
COURAGE
sand bank / BAR; REEF; SHOAL
sand bar / SPIT; SHOAL
sand bird / SNIPE; PLOVER;
SANDPIPER
sand dune / DENE; BARCHAN,
HUMMOCK
sand flea / CHIGOE
sand grouse / GANGA; PINTAIL
sand island / BAR

sand lark / SANDERLING
sand launce / AMMODYTE
sand region / ERG; AREG
sand ridge / OS; DUNE, KAME, SEIF
sand and small stones / GRAVEL
sandal / SLIPPER; HUARACHE
sandal fastener / THONG
sandalwood tree / MAIRE; SANTAL
sandarac / RESIN; REALGAR
sandarac powder / POUNCE
sandarac tree / ARAR
sandarac wood / ALERCE, THYINE
sand-blind / BLEARY; PURBLIND
sandbox tree fruit / REGMA
sand-carrying wind / SAMIEL,
   SIMOOM, SIMOON
sanddab / BOTHID; FLOUNDER
sandiness / ARENOSITY
sandman's gift / SLEEP
sandpaper / SAND; POLISH
sandpiper / REE; KNOT, RUFF, STIB;
   REEVE, STINT, TEREK
sandroller / TROUTPERCH
sandstone / GRIT; WACKE; GRAY-
   WACKE, GREENSAND
sandstone deposit / PAAR
sandstorm / HABOOB; DUST-
   STORM
sandwich / HERO; SUBMARINE
Sandwich Islands / HAWAII
Sandwich Islands discoverer /
   COOK
sandwich meat / HAM; SPAM;
   COLDCUT
sandy / ARENOSE; SABULINE
sandy sea bottom / PAAR
sandy shore / BEACH
sandy waste / DESERT
San Francisco hill / NOB; RUSSIAN
San Francisco subway / BART
San Joaquin River dam / FRIANT
San Marino money / LIRA, LIRE
San Marino's mountain / TITANO
sane / LUCID, SOUND; RATIONAL
sang Swiss style / YODELED
sangfroid / COOL; NONCHALANCE
Sangreal / GRAIL
sangrel / SNAKEROOT
sanguinary / GORY; BLOODY;
   MURDEROUS; BLOODTHIRSTY
sanguine / WARM; ARDENT,
   BLOODY; CONFIDENT;
   OPTIMISTIC
sanitary / CLEAN; SALUBRIOUS
sanitation / HYGIENE
sanity / HEALTH, REASON,
   WISDOM
sans gêne / INFORMAL; UNCON-
   VENTIONAL
sans souci / CAREFREE
sansculotte / REVOLUTIONARY
Sanskrit dialect / PALI

Sanskrit dialogue / SUTRA
Sanskrit school / TOL
Sanskrit scripture / VEDA
Sanskritic language / URDU;
   HINDI; BIHARI, SINDHI;
   MARATHI
Santa Barbara island / ANACAPA
Santa Catalina resort / AVALON
Santa Claus' burden / TOYS
Santa Cruz island / NDENI
Santo Domingo / HISPANIOLA
Santorin / THERA
Santos export / COFFEE
Santuzza's lover / TURIDDU
Sao Paulo plain / YPIRANGA
sap / WEAKEN; ENERVATE. COSH,
   FOOL, MILK; FLUID, JUICE,
   LATEX; TRENCH; BLACKJACK
sap spout / SPILE
sapajou / CAPUCHIN
saphead / FOOL; CHUMP, NODDY
sapid / TASTY; SAVORY; PIQUANT
sapidity / FLAVOR; SAVORINESS
sapience / WISDOM
sapient / SAGE, WISE; SHREWD;
   SENSIBLE
sapiutan / ANOA
sapling / YOUTH
sapodilla / CHICO; SAPOTA,
   SAPOTE
saponaceous / SOAPY
sapor / GUSTO, SAVOR, TASTE
saporous / LUSCIOUS; FLAVOR-
   SOME
sapota / ACANA; SAPODILLA
sapper / UNDERMINER
sapphire / BLUE; CORUNDUM
Sappho's island / LESBOS
Sapporo's bay / OTARU
sappy / JUICY; SUCCULENT
sapsucker / WOODPECKER
sapwood / ALBURNUM
Saracen / ARAB; PAGAN; MOSLEM
Saracen chief / SALADIN
Sarah's handmaid / HAGAR
Sarah's husband / ABRAHAM
Sarah's son / ISAAC
Sarajevo assassin / PRINCIP
Sarasvati's father / RAMA
Sarasvati's husband / BRAHMA
Saratoga victor / GATES
Sarawak ruling family / BROOKE
Sarawak town / MIRI, SIBU
sarcasm / GIBE; TAUNT; RIDICULE
sarcastic / SHARP; BITING; MOR-
   DANT, SATIRIC
sarcodinian / AMEBA; AMOEBA
sarcoma / TUMOR; CANCER
sarcophagous / CARNIVOROUS
sarcophagus / TOMB; COFFIN
sard / CARNELIAN; CHALCEDONY
Sardinian capital / TURIN

Sardinian town / CAGLIARI
sardonic / BITTER; SCORNFUL;
  HEARTLESS
sardonyx / RED; ONYX
Sarg production / PUPPET
sargasso / GULFWEED
sargassum fish / ANGLER; FROG-
  FISH
sargo / GRUNT
Sargon's kingdom / AKKAD
Sargon's successor / SENNA-
  CHERIB
sarigue / GAMBA; CHUCHA
sark / SHIRT
sarlak / YAK
Sarmatian / POLE
sarmentum / RUNNER
sarong / KAIN; WRAPAROUND
Sarpanitum's husband / MARDUK
Sarpedon's brother / MINOS
Sarpedon's father / ZEUS
Sarpedon's kingdom / LYCIA
Sarpedon's mother / EUROPA
Sarpedon's slayer / PATROCLUS
sarrazin / BUCKWHEAT
sarsen / DRUIDSTONE, GREY-
  WETHER
sarwan / CAMELEER
sash / OBI; BAND, BELT; GIRDLE;
  CUMMERBUND
sashay / STRUT; CHASSE
sasin / BLACKBUCK
Saskatchewan capital / REGINA
sass / BACKTALK
sassafras tree / AGUE; SALOOP
Sassenach / ENGLISHMAN
sassy / PERT; SAUCY
sat / MET
Satan / DEVIL; BELIAL; LUCIFER
Satan of Arabs / EBLIS; AZAZEL
satanic / CRUEL; DIABOLIC,
  INFERNAL
satchel / BAG; CABAS; VALISE
sate / FILL, GLUT; SATIATE, SUR-
  FEIT
sated / BLASE
satellite / MOON, ZOND; ATLAS,
  LUNIK, TIROS; APOLLO, PLANET,
  VOSTOK; SPUTNIK, TELSTAR;
  VANGUARD
satellite's path / ORBIT
satiate / CLOY, FILL, GLUT, PALL,
  SATE
satiety / REPLETION
satin fabric / PEKIN; ETOILE;
  SATINET
satin imitation / RAYON; SATEEN
satin spar / CALCITE
satinpod / HONESTY
satire / IRONY; RIDICULE
satirical / BITTER; CUTTING
satirist / WIT; CRITIC
satirize / LAMPOON; TRAVESTY

satisfaction / CRO, UTU; AMENDS,
  REWARD; COMFORT, PAYMENT,
  REDRESS
satisfy / MEET, SUIT; SERVE; FUL-
  FIL, PLEASE; CONTENT, GRATIFY
satrap / RULER; DESPOT, TYRANT
saturate / SOP, WET; SOAK; IMBUE,
  SOUSE, STEEP; DRENCH
saturated / SODDEN
Saturn satellite / RHEA; DIONE,
  MIMAS, TITAN; PHOEBE, TETHIS,
  THEMIS; IAPETUS; HYPERION;
  ENCELADUS
saturnalia / ORGY; REVEL
Saturnian / GOLDEN; PROSPEROUS
saturnine / DULL; GLOOMY,
  MOROSE
Saturn's rings / ANSA
Saturn's son / JUPITER
Saturn's wife / OPS; CYBELE
satyr / FAUN; BUTTERFLY
satyrs' instrument / SYRINX
sauce / SASS; GRAVY; PERTNESS
sauce for eggs / MORNAY
sauce for fish / TARTAR
sauce for fowl / VELOUTE
sauce for greens / MAYONNAISE
sauce for meat / GRAVY
sauce for oriental food / SOY
sauce for salad / VINAIGRETTE
sauce for spaghetti / MARINARA
sauce for vegetables / BECHAMEL
saucepan / POSNET; SKILLET
saucer-shaped bell / GONG; TAM-
  TAM
saucy / BOLD, PERT; BRASH; FOR-
  WARD; IMPUDENT, MALAPERT
saucy backtalk / LIP
saucy miss / MINX
Saudi Arabia capital / RIYADH
Saudi Arabia city / HOFUF, JIDDA,
  MECCA; MEDINA
Saudi Arabia desert / RUBALKHALI
Saudi Arabia money / RIYAL
Saudi Arabia province / ASIR, NEJD;
  HEJAZ
Saul / PAUL
Saul's chief herdsman / DOEG
Saul's concubine / RIZPAH
Saul's daughter / MICHAL
Saul's father / KISH
Saul's general / ABNER
Saul's grandfather / NER; ABIEL
Saul's harpist / DAVID
Saul's son / JONATHAN
Saul's successor / DAVID
Saul's uncle / NER
sault / JUMP, LEAP
Sault Ste. Marie / SOO
saunter / LAG; DELAY; DAWDLE,
  RAMBLE, STROLL
saurel / SCAD
saurian / LIZARD; DINOSAUR

sausage / FRANK, WURST; SA-
LAME, WEINER, WEINIE;
BOLOGNA
sauté / FRY
sauterne / WINE
sauterne vineyard / YQUEM
sauve qui peut / ROUT
savage / RUDE, WILD; CRUEL,
FERAL, BRUTAL, FIERCE; UN-
TAMED. GOTH; BEAST, YAHOO
Savage Island / NIUE
savagery / FEROCITY; BARBARISM
savanna / CAMPO, PLAIN; MEADOW
savant / SAGE; SCIENTIST
save / HOLD, KEEP; HOARD, SPARE.
BUT; EXCEPT
save from ruin / SALVAGE
savin / CEDAR; JUNIPER
saving / FRUGAL; CAREFUL,
THRIFTY
savior / MESSIAH; REDEEMER
savoir-faire / TACT; URBANITY
savor / AROMA, SCENT, SMACK,
TASTE
savory / SAPID; PIQUANT;
LUSCIOUS
savory herb / MINT; ANISE; ROSE-
MARY, TARRAGON
savory jelly / ASPIC
savory sauce / DIP
savoy / CABBAGE, SPINACH
savvy / KNOWHOW
saw / TOOL; ADAGE, AXIOM,
MAXIM, MOTTO; BYWORD, SAY-
ING
sawbill / MERGANSER
sawbones / DOCTOR; SURGEON
sawfish / PRISTIS
sawhorse / TRESTLE
saw-leaved centaury / BEHN;
BEHEN
sawmill gate / SASH
saw-toothed / SERRATE
saw-whet / OWL
saxhorn / TUBA
saxifrage / SESELI
Saxon / ENGLISH. SESSENACH
Saxon king / ALFRED, EGBERT
Saxon kingdom / ESSEX; SUSSEX,
WESSEX
Saxon capital / DRESDEN
Saxony city / PLAUEN
Saxony native / SORB, WEND
say / AVER, TELL; SPEAK, STATE,
UTTER, VOICE
say again / ITERATE
say also / ADD
say no / REFUSE
say under oath / VOW; DEPOSE
say over / REPEAT
say uncle / SURRENDER
say yes / ACCEPT

saying / MOT, SAW; ADAGE, AXIOM,
MAXIM
sayings / LOGIA
say-so / DICTUM; COMMAND
scab / CRUST; STRIKEBREAKER
scabbard / SHEATH
scabby / LOW; MEAN, VILE;
SCURVY
scabies / ITCH; MANGE
scabious / FLEABANE
scabrous / SCALY; DOTTED, UN-
EVEN
scad / SAUREL; GOGGLER; CIGAR-
FISH
scads / LOTS; LOADS
scaffold / STAGE; GIBBET;
TRESTLE; PLATFORM
scalawag / KNAVE, SCAMP
scald / BURN; BLANCH. BARD
scaldic metaphor / KENNING
scale / CLIMB, WEIGH. FLAKE,
GAMUT; LAMINA; BALANCE
scale, c.f. / LEPIS; SQUAMO
scale duck / MERGANSER, SHEL-
DRAKE
scale fish / CLEAN; SCRAPE
scale insect / LAC; COCHINEAL
scale on plant / BRACT, PALEA
scalene / TRIANGLE
Scales / LIBRA
scaling tool / LADDER
scallion / LEEK; SHALLOT
scallop / ARC; CRENA, SHELL; PEC-
TEN. PINK
scalloped / WAVY; CRENATE
scalp / DENUDE. TOUPEE, TROPHY
scalp disease / FAVUS; ALOPECIA
scalpel / KNIFE
scaly / MEAN; CADDISH, LAMINAR
scaly anteater / MANIS; PANGOLIN
scamble / MESS. PUSH; JOSTLE
scamp / IMP; RASCAL; GROUPER;
SCALAWAG. SKIMP
scamper / FLY, RUN; DART;
SCURRY
scan / CON; SKIM; STUDY; SURVEY
scandal / ODIUM, SHAME; CAL-
UMNY, OBLOQUY; IGNOMINY.
FALSE
scandalize / DECRY, SHOCK; DE-
FAME, OFFEND, REVILE, VILIFY;
DISGUST, LAMPOON, TRADUCE
scandent / CLIMBING
Scandinavian / NORSE; DANISH;
SWEDISH. See also Norse
Scandinavian boat / PRAM; PRAAM
Scandinavian chronicle / SAGA
Scandinavian country / NORWAY,
SWEDEN; DENMARK, FINLAND,
ICELAND
Scandinavian demon / TROLL
Scandinavian legislature / THING

Scandinavian measure / FOD; ALEN

Scandinavian minstrel / SCALD, SKALD

Scandinavian Mongol / LAPP

Scandinavian monster / KRAKEN; GRENDEL

Scandinavian name / OLE;/ ERIC, SVEN

Scandinavian poet / SKALD

Scandinavian poetic group / EDDA

Scandinavian snack table / SMORGASBORD

Scandinavian voyager / ERIC

Scandinavians in Russia / ROS, RUS; RUSS

scant / MEAGER, SKIMPY, SLIGHT, SPARSE; LIMITED

scantling / STUD; SCRAP

scanty / BARE, POOR; SMALL, SPARE

scanty skirt / MINI

scape / VIEW; SHAFT; COLUMN; PEDUNCLE

scapegoat / PATSY

scapegrace / WRETCH; RAPSCALLION

scaphoid / NAVICULAR

scar / ARR; MARK, SPOT; CLIFF; BLEMISH CICATRIX

scarab / AMULET, BEETLE

scarab-headed god / KHEPRI

scarb tree / CRABAPPLE

scarce / RARE; SPARSE; UNCOMMON

scarcely / HARDLY, SELDOM

scarcely any / FEW

scarcely visible / DIM

scarceness / DEARTH; PAUCITY

scarcity / LACK, WANT; FAMINE

scare / ALARM, DAUNT; TERRIFY, PANIC; FRIGHT

scare away / TERRORIZE

scare off / INTIMIDATE

scare up / FIND; GATHER

scarecrow / GUY; BUGABOO; RAGAMUFFIN

scarf / BOA, TIE; ASCOT, FANON, ORALE, STOLE; MUFFLER

scarflike garment / TIPPET

scarfskin / CUTICLE; EPIDERMIS

scarify / FLAY; INCISE; SCRATCH

scarlet / RED; CARDINALATE

scarlet bird / TANAGER

scarlet fever / SCARLATINA

Scarlet Letter author / HAWTHORNE

scarlet macaw / ARACANGA

Scarlett O'Hara's home / TARA

scarlike / ULOID

scarp / CLIFF, SLOPE

scat / AWAY, SHOO; BEGONE

scathe / HARM, HURT; INJURY

scatheless / SOUND, WHOLE

scathing / BITTER; MORDANT

scatter / DOT, SOW, TED; REPEL, STREW; DISPEL, SPREAD

scatter chaotically / ROUT

scatter for drying / TED

scatter illegally / LITTER

scatter seeds / SOW

scatterbrained / GIDDY; FLIGHTY

scattered / SPORADIC

scattered in heraldry / SEME

scattered rubbish / LITTER

scenario / SCRIPT; LIBRETTO

scene / VIEW; SIGHT, VISTA; DISPLAY

scene of action / ARENA, STAGE; SPHERE

scene of first miracle / CANA

scenery / DROPS; FLATS; PANORAMA; LANDSCAPE

scenery, pert. to / SCENIC

sceneshifter / GRIP

scenic / DRAMATIC

scenic view / SCAPE

scenite / NOMAD

scent / ODOR; AROMA, FETOR, SMELL, TRAIL; PERFUME

scent bag / SACHET

scent of burnt food / NIDOR

scented / OLENT, AROMATIC

scepter / ROD; MACE

sceptic / SKEPTIC UNBELIEVER

Schamir's master / SOLOMON

schedule / LIST; CALENDAR; ITINERARY, TIMETABLE

scheduled / DUE; SLATED

schema / PLAN; DIAGRAM

scheme / PLAN, PLOT; CABAL; DEVICE

scheming / ARTFUL, TRICKY

schism / RENT; SPLIT; DIVISION

schismatic / HERETIC, SECTARY

schizoid / WITHDRAWN

schlemiel / FOOL; SILLY

schlepp / DRAG

schmaltz / CORN; SENTIMENTALITY

schnorrer / BEGGAR

scholar / PEDANT, PUNDIT, SAVANT; STUDENT; PHILOMATH

scholarly / ERUDITE, LEARNED

scholarly essay / THESIS; TREATISE; MONOGRAPH

scholarly Moslem group / ULAMA, ULEMA

scholar's hat / MORTARBOARD

scholarship / LORE; BURSE; LEARNING; ERUDITION

scholarship donor / RHODES

scholastic / ACADEMIC, PEDANTIC

scholastic degree / GRADE; INCEPTOR

scholastic estimate / MARK; GRADE

scholiast / ANNOTATOR

school / TRAIN, TUTOR. ECOLE, LYCEE; ACADEMY, COLLEGE; SEMINARY
school book / PRIMER
school cap / BERET; BEANIE
school dance / HOP; PROM
school of eels / SWARM
school exercise / TASK; LESSON
school of fish / SHOAL
school grounds / QUAD; CAMPUS
school group / PTA
school jacket / ETON
school marks / GRADES
school mistress / DAME; SCHOOLMARM
school preparation / HOMEWORK
school of seals / HERD
school session / TERM; SEMESTER
school subject / READING, WRITING; ARITHMETIC
school of trout / HOVER
school of whales / GAM, POD; HERD
schoolcraft / LEARNING
schooling / TRAINING
schoolman / SCHOLASTIC
schoolmaster / TEACHER; PEDAGOGUE
schoolroom need / DESK; CHALK; PENCIL; BLACKBOARD
schoolteacher / EDUCATOR; PEDAGOGUE
schooner / SHIP; GLASS
schorl / TOURMALINE
science / ART; OLOGY, SKILL; METHOD; KNOWLEDGE. See also under study for further ologies
science of ancient life / PALEONTOLOGY
science of animal behavior / ETHOLOGY
science of animal life / ZOOLOGY
science of being / ONTOLOGY
science of birds / ORNITHOLOGY
science of body tissue / HISTOLOGY
science of caves / SPELEOLOGY
science of cells / CYTOLOGY
science of customs / ETHOLOGY
science of disease origins / ETIOLOGY
science of diseases / PATHOLOGY
science of drugs / PHARMACOLOGY
science of the earth / GEOLOGY
science of earthquakes / SEISMOLOGY
science of the earth's surface / PHYSIOGRAPHY
science of environment / ECOLOGY
science fiction / SF; SPACEOPERA
science fiction novelist / VERNE, WELLS

science of final causes / TELEOLOGY
science of fruit-growing / POMOLOGY
science of fungi / MYCOLOGY
science of the heart / CARDIOLOGY
science of the heavens / ASTRONOMY
science of human relationships / SOCIOLOGY
science of human remains / ARCHEOLOGY
science of insects / ENTOMOLOGY
science of language / PHILOLOGY; LINGUISTICS
science of last things / ESCHATOLOGY
science of lice / ACAROLOGY
science of life / BIOLOGY
science of light / PHOTOLOGY
science of mankind / ANTHROPOLOGY
science of the mind / PSYCHOLOGY
science of minerals / MINERALOGY
science of mosses / BRYOLOGY
science of mountains / OROLOGY
science of old age / GERONTOLOGY
science of origins / EPISTEMOLOGY
science of peoples / ETHNOLOGY
science of plants / BOTANY
science of poisons / TOXICOLOGY
science of rocks / PETROLOGY
science of shells / CONCHOLOGY
science of the skin / DERMATOLOGY
science of structures / MORPHOLOGY
science of the universe / COSMOLOGY
science of water / HYDROLOGY
science of weather / METEOROLOGY
science of wines / OENOLOGY
scientific / EXPERT; SYSTEMATIC
scientific farmer / AGRONOMIST
scientist / SAVANT
scientist's shop / LAB
scilicet / NAMELY
scimitar / SABER, SWORD; CUTLASS
scintilla / BIT; ATOM, WHIT; SPARK; SMIDGEN
scintillate / SPARKLE, TWINKLE
sciolism / SUPERFICIALITY
sciolist / DABBLER; DILETTANTE
scion / BUD, SON; CION, HEIR; GRAFT
scission / SPLIT; SCHISM
scissors / GRIP; SHEARS
scleroid / HARD; INDURATED
sclerous / HARD; HORNY, THICK
scoff / GIBE, JEER, MOCK, RAIL; FLEER, LAUGH, SNEER; DERIDE

scold / JAW, NAG; FRAB, RANT, RATE; BLAME, CHIDE; CENSURE, REPROVE. SHREW; VIRAGO; XANTIPPE
scolded / BERATED
sconce / HEAD, SEAT; SKULL; BULWARK
scone / CAKE, FARL
scoop / DIP; LADLE; SHOVEL; SCUTTLE. DIG; BEAT
scoot / RUN; DART
scopate / BRUSHSHAPED
scope / END; AREA, ROOM; AMBIT
scope of activity / ORBIT
scorbutic / SCURVIED
scorch / BURN, CHAR, SEAR; PARCH, SINGE
scorching / HOT; CAUSTIC
score / MARK; NOTCH, POINT, TALLY; GROOVE, TWENTY; ACCOUNT
score in archery / HIT
score in baseball / RUN
score in basketball / BASKET
score in cribbage / PEG
score in football / TOUCHDOWN
score in hockey / GOAL
scoria / LAVA, SLAG; DROSS; CINDER
scoring card combination / MELD
scorn / MOCK; SCOFF, SCOUT, SPURN. DISDAIN; CONTEMPT
scorned / IGNOBLE; DESPISED
scornful / HAUGHTY, DERISORY
scorpion / LIZARD; SCORPIO; SCOURGE; CATAPULT; VINEGAROON
scorpion fish / LAPON; LIONFISH, ROCKFISH
scorpion-headed god / SELKET
Scorpio's bright star / ANTARES
scot / TAX; GAEL; SCOTSMAN; SCOTCHMAN; CALEDONIAN, HIGHLANDER
scotch / CUT; NOTCH, WEDGE; WHISKY. BALK. See also Scottish
Scotch cap / TAM
Scotch gaelic / ERSE
Scotch mist / MIZZLE
Scotch plaid / TARTAN
scoter / COOT; BLACKDUCK
scot-free / SAFE; CLEAR, LOOSE
Scotia / SCOTLAND
Scotland / SCOTIA; CALEDONIA. See also Scottish
Scotland capital / EDINBURGH
Scotland city / AYR; DUNDEE; GLASGOW
Scotland hills / CHEVIOT
Scotland island / BUTE, MULL, SKYE
Scotland mountain / NEVIS
Scotland mountains / GRAMPIANS

Scotland river / DEE, TAY; AFTON, CLYDE
Scotland Yard department / CID
Scotland's patron saint / ANDREW
Scotsman / SCOT; SANDY; CALEDONIAN
Scott novel / IVANHOE; WAVERLEY
Scottish alder / ARN
Scottish anchorage / RADE
Scottish author / DUNBAR
Scottish biographer / BOSWELL
Scottish cake / SCONE
Scottish child / BAIRN
Scottish church / KIRK
Scottish costume / KILT, KILTS; TARTAN
Scottish dance / REEL
Scottish dialect / LALLAN; LALLAND; LAWLANTS
Scottish dramatist / BARRIE
Scottish emblem / THISTLE
Scottish entertainer / LAUDER
Scottish fiord / LOCH; FIRTH
Scottish garment / KILT; PLAID; DAIDLY; FILIBEG; PHILIBEG
Scottish girl / LASSIE
Scottish harvest home / KIRN
Scottish Highlander / GAEL
Scottish hill / KNOW, KNOWE
Scottish inventor / WATT
Scottish king / BRUCE; ROBERT
Scottish lake / LOMOND
Scottish landowner / LAIRD
Scottish liberator / BRUCE
Scottish magistrate / BAILIE
Scottish musical instrument / PIPES; BAGPIPE
Scottish musician / PIPER
Scottish novelist / SCOTT
Scottish peak / BEN
Scottish peer / THANE
Scottish philosopher / HUME, MILL
Scottish pine / RIGA
Scottish poet / BURNS; RAMSAY
Scottish pouch / SPORRAN
Scottish royal family / STUART
Scottish saint / COLUMBA
Scottish sword / CLAYMORE
Scottish water spirit / KELPY; KELPIE
scoundrel / CAD; CHEAT, KNAVE, ROGUE, SCAMP; RASCAL, VARLET; VILLAIN
scour / RUB; SAND; SCRUB
scourge / BANE, WHIP; SWITCH. FLOG
Scourge of God / ATTILA
scouring pad / STEELWOOL
scourings / SCUM; DROSS, OFFAL
scout / SPY; INFORMER. SCORN, SPURN
scout unit / TROOP
scow / BARGE; LIGHTER

scowl / FROWN, LOWER; GLOWER
scrabble / CRAWL; SCRATCH
scrag / THIN; SCRAWNY. CHOKE
scraggy / BONY, LANK; GAUNT; MEAGER, SKINNY
scram / GIT; IMSHI; BEATIT, IM-SHEE
scramble / MIX, RUN; CRAWL; GATHER; CLAMBER
scrambled word / ANAGRAM
scran / SCRAP; MORSEL
scrannel / HARSH
scrap / BIT, ORT, RAG; BITE; CRUMB, FIGHT, SHRED; MORSEL
scrape / RASP, GRATE; SCUFFLE
scrape by / EKE; SQUEEZE
scrape off / ABRADE
scrape together / ACCUMULATE
scraped linen / LINT
scraping implement / HOE; FILE, RAKE; PLANE
scrappy / FEISTY; PARTIAL
scraps of literature / ANA
scratch / MAR; CLAW, RAKE, RIST, TEAR
scratching the ground / RASORIAL
scrawl / SCRATCH; SCRIBBLE
scrawny / THIN; GAUNT; SCRAGGY
scray / TERN
screak / CREAK; SQUEAK, SQUEAL
scream / CRY; ROAR, YELL; SCREECH
screamer / CHAJA, LINER; KAMICHI
scree / TALUS
screed / TIRADE; HARANGUE
screen / HIDE, MASK, SIFT; COVER, SHADE. SIEVE; FILTER, RIDDLE
screen of altar / REREDOS
screen siren / VAMP
screening / SHOWING; ELIMINA-TION
screenings / REFUSE; RUBBISH
screenplay / SCRIPT; SCENARIO
screw / FORCE, TWIST; DISTORT
screw bean / TORNILLO
screwball / NUT; CRACKPOT
screwed / DRUNK; SOZZLED
screwpine / ARA; PANDANUS
scribble / DODDLE, SCRAWL
scribe / CLERK; NOTARY, PENMAN; COPYIST
scrimmage / ROW; PLAY; TUSSLE
scrimp / STINT; CURTAIL
scrimper / MISER; TIGHTWAD
scrimshaw / INCISE
scrip / SATCHEL, WRITING; SHIN-PLASTER
script / HAND, TEXT; MANUSCRIPT
scripture / TEXT; BIBLE; TESTA-MENT
scripture reading / TEXT; LESSON
scrivener / NOTARY, SCRIBE

scrofula / KINGSEVIL
scroll / ROLL; CURLICUE, FLOURISH
scrooge / MISER
Scrooge's clerk / CRATCHIT
Scrooge's partner / MARLEY
scrouge / SQUEEZE
scrounge / CADGE
scrub / RUB; CHAFE, SCOUR; ABRADE
scrubby / SMALL; STUNTED
scruff / NAPE, SCUM; SCURF
scrumptious / FINE; SPLENDID
scruple / DOUBT, PAUSE, WAVER
scrupulous / NICE; EXACT; CARE-FUL, PRECISE
scrutable / PENETRABLE
scrutinize / EYE, PRY, SPY; SCAN, SIFT; PROBE, STUDY
scrutinous / STRICT; PRECISE
scrutiny / SEARCH; INSPECTION
scuffle / FIGHT, MELEE; TUSSLE
scull / CAR; ROWBOAT
scullion / MENIAL
sculpin / POGGE
sculptor / RODIN; HOUDON; PHIDIAS
sculptor's frame / ARMATURE
sculptor's tool / GRAVER; GRADINE; SPATULA
sculpture / STATUE; CARVING
sculpture leaving background / RELIEF
sculpture from Melos / VENUS
sculptured female column / CARY-ATID
sculptured head and shoulders / BUST
sculptured male column / ATLAS; TELAMON
sculptured representation / STATUE
sculptured Victory / NIKE
sculpturing in wood / XYLOGLYPHY
scum / FILM, SILT; REFUSE
scum on molten metal / DROSS
scum of society / CANAILLE, RIFF-RAFF
scup / BREAM, PORGY
scuppernong / MUSCADINE
scurf / SCABS; DANDRUFF
scurrility / ABUSE; DERISION
scurrilous / LOW; FOUL, MEAN; GROSS; COARSE, RIBALD
scurry / RUN; HURRY; SCAMPER
scurvy / MEAN; SCABBY. SCORBUTUS
scutate / SCALY; PLATED
scuttle / RUN; HIDE, SINK; HURRY. HOD
scye / SEY; ARMHOLE
Scylla's father / NISUS; PHORCYS
Scylla's mother / CRATAIS
scythe / SY; SYE

scythe handle / SNATH, SNEAD, SNEED

Scythian antelope / SAIGA

Scythian people / ALANS, SACAE

sea / ZEE, DEEP, MAIN, SURF, WAVE; OCEAN

sea, c.f. / THALASS; THALASSO

sea, pert. to / NAVAL; MARINE; THALASSIC

sea near Alaska / BERING

sea anemone / POLYP; OPELET; ACTINIAN

sea animal / CORAL; ANEMONE

sea of Antarctica / ROSS; WEDDELL

sea near Arabia / RED

sea in Asia / ARAL

sea of Australia / CORAL, TIMOR; TASMAN

sea bass / SERRANIDA

sea bird / AUK, ERN; ERNE, GULL, SKUA, TERN; SCAUP, SOLAN; FULMAR, GANNET, PETREL, PUFFIN, SCOTER

sea near Bosporus / MARMARA

sea calf / SEAL

sea in California / SALTON

sea cow / DUGONG; MANATEE

sea near Crimea / AZOV

sea crow / COOT, SKUA; CHOUGH; CORMORANT

sea cucumber / TREPANG; BECHEDEMER

sea deity / LER; NEREUS, TRITON; NEPTUNE; POSEIDON

sea dog / TAR; SEAL; PIRATE

sea duck / EIDER, SCAUP; SCOTER; POCHARD; MERGANSER

sea dyak / IBAN

sea eagle / ERN; ERNE

sea ear / ABALONE

sea of eastern Europe / BALTIC

sea fennel / SAMPHIRE

sea foam / MEERSCHAUM

sea food / CLAM, CRAB, FISH; OYSTER, SHRIMP

sea force / NAVY

sea fox / THRESHER

sea god / TRITON; NEPTUNE

sea goddess / INO; THETIS; AMPHITRITE

sea goose / SOLAN

sea near Greece / AEGEAN, IONIAN

sea green / CELADON

sea gull / COB, MEW; SKUA, TERN; FULMAR

sea hog / PORPOISE

sea horse / WALRUS

sea near Italy / ADRIATIC

sea lawyer / SAILOR; SNAPPER

sea life / HALOBIOS

sea mile / KNOT, NAUT

sea mollusk / CLAM; MUSSEL, OYSTER

sea monster / KRAKEN

sea nymph / NAIAD, SIREN; NEREID; MERMAID

sea of Palestine / DEAD

sea pheasant / PINTAIL

sea power advocate / MAHAN

sea raider / PIRATE, VIKING

sea robber / PIRATE

sea rover / PIRATE, VIKING

sea sandstone / PAAR

sea shell / CONCH; TRITON

sea of Siberia / KARA; LAPTEV

sea slug / TREPANG; NUDIBRANCH

sea snail / WHELK; TRITON

sea soldier / MARINE

sea spray / FOAM; SPUME; SPINDRIFT

sea squirt / TUNICATE

sea star / STARFISH

sea swallow / TERN; PETREL

sea water / BRINE

sea worm / SAO; LURG; NEREIS; ANNELID

seacoast / SHORE

sea-going vessel / SHIP; LINER

seal / SET; CERE, SIGN; STAMP; FASTEN. OTARY, SIGIL; CACHET, SIGNET

seal on document / BULLA

seal herd / POD

seal with oakum / CALK

seal pelt / SCULP

seal ring / SIGNET

seal young / PUP

sealed instrument / ESCROW

seals' breeding place / ROOKERY

seam / SEW; JOIN. SUTURE; STRATUM

seam of coal / BED

seam of ore / LEAD, LODE, VEIN

seaman / TAR; SALT; RATING, SAILOR; MARINER

seamanship / NAVIGATION

seamark / BUOY; BEACON

seamed / SUTURED; WRINKLED

seamlike fold / RAPHE; SPLICE

seamy / DISREPUTABLE

séance / SESSION; CONCLAVE

séance agent / MEDIUM

séance visitor / GHOST; SPIRIT

seaplane pontoon / FLOAT

seaport / PORT; HAVEN; HARBOR

sear / CHAR; PARCH; SCORCH. DRY

sear meat / BRAISE

search / HUNT, SEEK; PROBE, QUEST. ZETETIC; SCRUTINY

search blindly / GROPE

search carefully / COMB

search critically / EXAMINE

search diligently / HUNT

search in a disorderly way / RANSACK, RUMMAGE

search for facts / DELVE
search for food / FORAGE
search for / SEEK; PROBE, QUEST
search nosily / PRY; FERRET
search for pearls / DIVE
search by questioning / INQUIRY
search through / COMB
search by visiting / EXPLORE
seashore / BEACH, COAST
seashore recreation / BATHING, BOATING, FISHING, SUNNING; SWIMMING
seasickness / MALDEMER
season / AGE; INURE, SPICE; MODERATE. FALL, TERM, TIDE, TIME; AUTUMN, PERIOD, SPRING, SUMMER, WINTER; WEATHER
season of church year / LENT; EPIPHANY; PENTECOST
season of joy / JUBILEE; FESTIVAL
season until mature / AGE; RIPEN
seasonable / PROPER; OPPORTUNE
seasonal goddesses / HORAE
seasoned dish / OLLA
seasoning / SAGE, SALT; SPICE, THYME; RELISH; CONDIMENT
seasoning berry / CAPER
seasoning herb / SAGE; BASIL, THYME; OREGANO; ROSEMARY
season's yield / CROP; HARVEST
seat / FIX; PLACE. PEW; SITE; BENCH, CHAIR, PERCH, STOOL
seat of Arthur's court / CAMELOT
seat of bishop / SEE
seat in chancel / SEDILE
seat in church / PEW; BENCH
seat on elephant's back / HOWDAH
seat of eminence / THRONE
seat of government / CAPITAL
seat of intellect / BRAIN
seat worm / PINWORM
seated on horse / MOUNTED
seatless theatergoer / STANDEE
seatless traveler / STRAPHANGER
seaweed / ORE; AGAR, ALGA, KELP, LIMU, NORI; DULSE, LAVER, VAREC, WRACK
seaweed fertilizer / VRAIC
sebaceous / OILY; GREASY
sebaceous cyst / WEN
sebaceous gland blockage / MILIUM
sebaceous gland plug / COMEDO; BLACKHEAD
Seb's consort / NUT
Seb's daughter / ISIS
Seb's father / SHU
Seb's mother / TEFNUT
Seb's son / SET; OSIRIS
sec / DRY; BRUT
secede / QUIT; RETIRE; WITHDRAW
secern / SECRETE
secession / SEPARATION

seck / BARREN
seclude / HIDE; REMOVE, SCREEN
secluded / REMOTE, SECRET; ISOLATED
secluded corner / DEN; NOOK
secluded inlet / COVE
seclusion / PRIVACY, SECRECY
second / ABET; ASSIST. AIDE; BACKER
second childhood / DOTAGE
second coming / ADVENT
second copy / CARBON
second day / MONDAY
second fiddle / UNDERLING; SUBORDINATE
second growth crop / ROWEN; AFTERMATH
second helping / REFILL
second lieutenant / SHAVETAIL
second nature / HABIT
second person pronoun / YE; YOU; THOU, YOUR
second self / PAL; CHUM; ALTEREGO
second showing / RERUN
second sight / CLAIRVOYANCE
second team / SCRUB; JAYVEES
second of two / LATTER
secondary / BYE; LESS; MINOR; INFERIOR
secondary road / FEEDER
secondary school / PREP; GYMNASIUM
second-class / INFERIOR
second-generation / ADVANCED
secondhand / USED, WORN
second-rate poet / RIMESTER; POETASTER, RHYMESTER, VERSIFIER
second-story man / BURGLAR
second-string / SUBSTITUTE
second-stringer / SCRUB
secrecy / STEALTH; VELATION
secret / HID; CLOSE, INNER, PRIVY; ARCANE, COVERT, HIDDEN, OCCULT, UNSEEN. RUNE; MYSTERY
secret action / STEALTH
secret agent / SPY; SCOUT; DETECTIVE
secret assembly / CONCLAVE
secret doctrine / ESOTERY
secret initiate / EPOPT
secret meeting / TRYST
secret retreat / DEN; SANCTUM
secret service / INTELLIGENCE
secret society / PORO; MAFIA; CAMORRA
secret writing / CODE; CIPHER
secretary / DESK; AMANUENSIS
secrete / HIDE; EXUDE; CONCEAL
secreting body / GLAND
secreting hormones / ENDOCRINE
secretive / EVASIVE; RETICENT

secretly / SUBROSA; PRIVATELY
secrets / ARCANA
sect / CULT; PARTY; FACTION
sectarian / NARROW; EXCLUSIVE
sectile / CUTTABLE
section / AREA, PART; PIECE, SLICE
section of a circle / SECTOR
section of a city / ZONE; QUARTER
section of a pie / SLICE
section of a race / LEG
section of a trip / STAGE
sectional / LOCAL; PAROCHIAL.
 SOFA
sector / AREA, PART; FRONT
secular / LAY; LAIC; CIVIL; LAICAL;
 PROFANE; TEMPORAL. LAYMAN
secund / UNILATERAL
securable / AVAILABLE
secure / FIX, GET, PIN; FASTEN.
 FAST, FIRM, SAFE, SURE;
 STABLE
secure against entry / LOCK
secure on loan / BORROW
secure a sail / TRICE
secure by tying / STRAP
secure a vessel / MOOR; ANCHOR
security / TIE; BAIL, BOND, EASE,
 GAGE, PAWN; PLEDGE, SAFETY
sedan / CAR; LITTER
sedate / CALM; QUIET, SOBER,
 STAID, STILL; DEMURE, PLACID
sedative / OPIATE; ANODYNE.
 LENIENT; ASSUASIVE;
 PALLIATIVE
sedentary / SESSILE; INACTIVE
sedge / FLAG, IRIS; GRASS
sedge of Nile / PAPYRUS
sediment / LEES, SILT; DREGS;
 GROUNDS
sedimentary rock / CHALK, CHERT,
 FLINT, SHALE; DOLITE, GYPSUM,
 JASPER, PELITE; BRECCIA; DO-
 LOMITE; LIMESTONE, SAND-
 STONE
sedition / MUTINY, REVOLT,
 RISING; TREASON
seditious / FACTIOUS; INSURGENT
seduce / DECOY, TEMPT; ALLURE,
 ENTICE
seductive woman / VAMP; SIREN;
 COQUETTE
sedulous / BUSY; DILIGENT;
 ASSIDUOUS
see / EYE, SPY; ESPY, LOOK,
 MARK, NOTE, VIEW; VISIT,
 WATCH; BEHOLD, DESCRY,
 NOTICE; DISCERN, OBSERVE,
 WITNESS, DIOCESE
seed / OVA, PIP, PIT; GERM; GRAIN,
 OVULE, SPORE; KERNEL
seed case / POD
seed coat / ARIL, HULL, HUSK;
 TESTA; TEGMEN; TEGUMEN

seed container / BUR, POD;
 ACHENE, LEGUME, LOMENT;
 SILIQUE
seed of flowerless plant / SPORE
seed for food / PEA; BEAN, CORN;
 LENTIL, PINOLE, SESAME
seed leaf / COTYLEDON
seed of legume / PEA; BEAN
seed of maple tree / KEY; SAMARA
seed meal / PINOLE
seed of opium poppy / MAW
seed oyster / SPAT
seed plant / HERB; ENDOGEN
seed pod / LOMENT
seed remover / GIN
seed of sycamore / ACHENE
seed-bearing organ / OVULE;
 PISTIL
seeded / RATED; RANKED
seeding / SOWING
seedless mandarin orange /
 CLEMENTINE
seedless plant / FERN; FUNGUS
seedtime / YOUTH; SPRING
seedy / SHABBY; WRETCHED
seeing / SINCE; CONSIDERING
seek / ASK, TRY; HUNT, LOOK;
 TRACE; PURSUE, SEARCH
seek after / SUE; PURSUE
seek to attain / ASPIRE, STRIVE
seek to catch / FOLLOW
seek earnestly / ASPIRE
seek as a favor / COURT
seek knowledge / STUDY
seek manually / GROPE
seek to master / ATTEMPT
seek to persuade / SOLICIT
seel / WINK; BLIND, HEAVE
seem / LOOK; APPEAR
seeming / QUASI; APPARENT
seeming contradiction / PARADOX
seemly / FIT; FAIR, MEET; DECENT,
 PROPER
seen / VISUAL
seen on a screen / MOVIES, SLIDES
seep/ OOZE; DRAIN; PERCOLATE
seep out / EXUDE
seep through / LEACH; PERCOLATE
seep through a membrane /
 TRANSUDE
seepy / SODDEN; DRENCHED
seer / SAGE; ORACLE; PROPHET
seeress / SIBYL; PROPHETESS
seesaw / TEETER. ALTERNATE
seethe / SOP; BOIL, FUME, SOAK,
 STEW
segment / PART; SECTION;
 DIVISION
segment, pert. to / TORIC
segment of chain / LINK
segment of curve / ARC; BEND
segment of geometric solid /
 FRUSTUM

segment of lobster / TELSON
segment of vertebrate / SOMITE
segregate / ISOLATE; SEPARATE
segue / ATTACCA; TRANSITION
sei / RORQUAL
seine / NET; TRAP; SAGENE
seism / QUAKE; TEMBLOR
seize / NAB; GRAB, GRIP, HOLD, TAKE; CATCH, CLASP, GRASP; ARREST
seize avidly / CLUTCH
seize as booty / REAVE
seize illegally / USURP
seize for official purpose / COMMANDEER
seize violently / WREST
seized by enemy / CAPTURED
seizure / ARREST, ATTACK
seladang / GAUR; SALADANG
Selangor town / KLANG
seldom / RARELY; UNCOMMONLY
select / CULL, PICK; ELECT; CHOOSE. GOOD, RARE
select body / QUORUM; BLUE-RIBBON
select part / BEST; ELITE; FLOWER
selection / CHOICE, OPTION
selectman / ALDERMAN; COUNCILOR
Selene's father / HYPERION
Selene's mother / THEA
self / EGO; IDENTITY; PERSONALITY
self, c.f. / AUTO
self, pert. to / PERSONAL
self-assertion / EGOTISM
self-assurance / APLOMB
self-assured / CONFIDENT
self-centered / EGOTISTIC
self-conceit / EGO; VANITY; EGOTISM
self-confidence / APLOMB
self-conscious / UNEASY
self-conscious smile / SMIRK
self-contradiction / PARADOX
self-defense / JUDO; KARATE
self-denying / ASCETIC; TEMPERATE
self-effacing / RETIRING
self-esteem / PRIDE; VANITY; CONCEIT
self-government / AUTONOMY
self-identity / IPSEITY
selfish / MEAN; EGOISTIC; EGOTISTICAL
self-luminous body / SUN; STAR
self-moving car / AUTOMOBILE
self-opinionated / VAIN; CONCEITED
self-possessed / CALM; COMPOSED
self-respect / PRIDE; DIGNITY
self-righteous / PHARISAIC

self-sacrifice / ALTRUISM
selfsame / VERY; IDENTICAL
self-service cafeteria / HOMOTERIA
self-styled / SOIDISANT
self-sufficiency / AUTARKY
self-taught / AUTODIDACTIC
self-willed / DOGGED; STUBBORN
sell / VEND, BARTER; DISPOSE
sell direct / RETAIL
sell house-to-house / PEDDLE
sell out / HIT. BETRAY
seller / COSTER. HAWKER
seltzer / PLAIN, VICHY
selvage / EDGE; BORDER
semantic unit / RHEME; SEMEME
semaphore / SIGNAL
sematic / EMBLEMATIC, INDICATORY
semblance / GUISE; LIKENESS
seme / SOWN; STREWN
Semele's father / CADMUS
Semele's lover / ZEUS
Semele's mother / HARMONIA
Semele's sister / INO; AGAVE
Semele's son / DIONYSUS
semester / TERM; SESSION
semicentennial / JUBILEE
semicircular bench / EXEDRA
semicircular device / DIODE; TRANSISTOR
semicircular ell / APSE
semidiameter / RADIUS
semifinal / PENULT; PENULTIMATE
seminal / RADICAL; ORIGINAL
seminar / CONFERENCE, ROUND-TABLE
seminary / SCHOOL; ACADEMY, COLLEGE
semination / IMPREGNATION
seminivorous / SEEDEATING
Seminole chief / OSCEOLA
semiprecious stone / ONYX, SARD; AGATE; GARNET
Semiramis' husband / NINUS, ONNES
Semiramis' mother / DERCETO
Semite / JEW; ARAB; HEBREW; ISRAELITE
Semitic deity / BAAL; MOLOCH
Semitic goddess / ALLAT; ISHTAR, NINGAL; ASTARTE
Semitic language / GEEZ; ARABIC, HEBREW; ARAMAIC; PHOENICIAN
senate / CURIA; CHAMBER, COUNCIL
Senate delaying action / FILIBUSTER
Senate employee / PAGE
senator / SOLON; LAWMAKER
send / CAST, EMIT, HURL, SHIP, TOSS

send as agent / DEPUTE
send back / REMIT; REMAND, RETURN
send bill / RENDER; INVOICE
send down / DEMIT
send forth / EMIT; ISSUE, UTTER
send forward / DRIVE, IMPEL
send message / WIRE; TELEGRAPH
send on / FORWARD
send out / UTTER; DIFFUSE
send out of country / DEPORT, EXPORT
send in return / REMIT
send with speed / EXPRESS
Senegal capital / DAKAR
Senegal city / THIES
Senegal river / SALUM
Senegal tribe / WOLOF; FULANI
Senegambian gazelle / KORIN
senesce / AGE; WITHER
senescent / RIPE; AGING
seneschal / STEWARD; MAJOR-DOMO
senile / OLD; AGED; INFIRM
senile person / DOTARD; GRAY-BEARD
senility / AGE; DOTAGE
senior / ELDER, OLDER; SUPERIOR
seniority / STATUS; PRIORITY
Senlac's battle / HASTINGS
senna / SENE; CASSIA
sennet / SPET; BARRACUDA
sennight / WEEK
senor / MR; SIR
senora / MRS; MADAM
senorita / MISS
sensation / FEELING; PERCEPTION
sensational / LURID; DRAMATIC
sense / WIT; IDEA, VIEW; IMPORT, NOTION, REASON, WISDOM; FEELING, PERCEIVE
sense of contact / TOUCH
sense of duty / CONSCIENCE
sense of hearing / EAR
sense of humor / PLAYFULNESS
sense of modesty / SHAME
sense of obligation / GRATITUDE
sense of one's worth / PRIDE
sense organ / RECEPTOR
sense of propriety / TACT
sense of sight / EYE
sense of smell / NOSE
sense of taste / PALATE
senseless / MAD; INANE, SILLY; ABSURD, STUPID
sensibility / FEELING; DELICACY
sensible / SANE, WISE; SOBER
sensitive / RAW; KEEN, SORE; TENDER
sensitive to mental forces / PSYCHIC
sensitive plant / MIMOSA
sensory / AFFERENT

sensual / ANIMAL, CARNAL; DISSOLUTE
sensuous / ESTHETIC, MATERIAL
sent / MAILED; BROADCAST
sent a message / WIRED; SIGNALED
sentence / SAW; FUTWA; DECREE; OPINION, VERDICT, DOOM; CONDEMN
sentence balance / PARISON
sentence part / CLAUSE, PHRASE
sententia / SAW; PROVERB; APHORISM
sententious / SHORT, TERSE
sentient / AWARE; PERCEPTIVE
sentient body / BEING
sentiment / REGARD; EMOTION
sentimental / ROMANTIC
Sentimental Journey author / STERNE
sentinel / GUARD, WATCH; SENTRY; VEDETTE
sepal / LEAF; CALYX
separable / MOVABLE; DIVISIBLE
separate / CUT; PART, SORT, SIFT; SEVER; DIVIDE, ALONE; DE-TACHED, DISTINCT
separate accounting item / ENTRY
separate from others / SINGLE
separate part / LOT
separate thing / ITEM
separated / APART; ESTRANGED
separation / SCHISM; DISSOCIA-TION
separation into elements / ANALYSIS
separatrix / SOLIDUS, VIRGULE
sepiment / FENCE, HEDGE
sepiolite / MEERSCHAUM
seppuku / HARAKIRI
seps / LIZARD; SERPENT
sepsis / INFECTION
sept / CLAN; TRIBE; FAMILY
September birthstone / SAPPHIRE; CHRYSOLITE
septenary / SEPTET; SEPTENNIAL
septentrional / NORTHERN
septicemia / PYEMIA
Septuagint / LXX
sepulcher / TOMB; CRYPT, GRAVE
sepulchral / CHARNEL
sepulture / BURIAL; INTERMENT
sequacious / PLIANT; LOGICAL
sequel / EVENT, ISSUE; RESULT, UPSHOT
sequela / RESULT; CONSEQUENCE
sequence / RESULT, SERIES; EPISODE
sequence of five cards / STRAIGHT
sequence of three / TIERCE
sequester / ISOLATE; SEPARATE; SEGREGATE
sequestered / HIDDEN; PRIVATE

sequin / SPANGLE
seraglio / HAREM, SERAI; ZENANA
serape / SHAWL; BLANKET
seraph / ANGEL, SAINT
seraphic / ANGELIC, SUBLIME
Serb / SLAV; YUGOSLAV
Serbia / See Yugoslavia
Serbian capital / BELGRADE
Serbian city / NIS
Serbian cheese / MANUR, SIRAZ
Serbian hero / KARAGEORGE
Serbian measure / RIF
Serbian parliament / SKUPSHTINA
Serbian patriotic group / BLACK-
  HAND
sere / DRIED; EFFETE; WITHERED
serenade / NOCTURNE, SHIVAREE
Serendib / CEYLON
serene / CALM, COOL, FAIR;
  QUIET; IRENIC, PLACID
serenity / PEACE, QUIET;
  PLACIDITY
serf / ESNE, PEON; COLONA;
  THRALL, VASSAL; VILLEIN
serf in ancient Sparta / HELOT
serfage / BONDAGE, SLAVERY
sergeant fish / COBIA, SNOOK;
  ROBALO
serial / PERIODICAL
serial radio drama / SOAPOPERA
sericeous / SILKY
series / ROW, SET; ORDER;
  SEQUENCE
series of bets / PARLAY
series of ecological changes / SERE
series of eight / OCTAD
series of fence steps / STILE
series of forebears / LINEAGE;
  ANCESTRY
series of games in tennis / SET
series of gears / TRAIN
series in a line / RANK
series of links / CHAIN
series of military moves /
  CAMPAIGN
series of miracle plays / CYCLE
series of notes / SCALE
series of steps / FLIGHT; STAIR-
  CASE
series of syllogisms / SORITES
serigraphy / SILKSCREEN
serious / BAD; GRIM; GRAVE,
  SOBER, STAID, STERN
serious attention / CARE; APPLICA-
  TION
serious discourse / SERMON
serious disease / CANCER;
  CHOLERA
serious offense / SIN; CRIME;
  FELONY
serious student / SCHOLAR
seriousness / IMPORT; GRAVITY
sermon / HOMILY; ADDRESS

sermon's subject / TEXT
serous / WATERY
serow / GORAL, JAGLA
serpent / ASP; NAGA; ADDER,
  SNAKE
serpent, c.f. / OPHI, OPHIO
serpent, pert. to / OPHIC
serpent emblem / URAEUS;
  CADUCEUS
serpent lizard / SEPS
serpent woman / LAMIA
serpent worship / OPHISM;
  OPHIOLATRY
serpent-headed god / BUTO
serpentine / SNAKY; OPHITE;
  SINUOUS
serpentine mineral / ASBESTOS
serpentlike monster / NAGA;
  BASILISK
serpents' king / SESHA
serrated / NOTCHED, SAWLIKE
serration / TOOTH
serried / CROWDED
serum, pert. to / SEROUS
servant / BOY, MAN; MAID; HAMAL,
  VALET; BUTLER, FERASH,
  FLUNKY
servants, pert. to / MENIAL
servants' uniform / LIVERY
serve / AID; HELP, OBEY, WAIT;
  ATTEND
serve scantily / STINT
serve the purpose / SUFFICE
serve a summons / SUBPOENA
server / TRAY; ACOLYTE
Servian / SERBIAN
service / USE; DUTY, RITE; LABOR
service in church / MASS; OFFICE
service stripe / HASHMARK
service tree / SORB
service utensil / TRAY; SERVER
serviceable / SOUND; USEFUL
serviceman / GI; VET; SAILOR;
  SOLDIER
serviette / NAPKIN
servile / LOW; BASE, MEAN;
  ABJECT
servile follower / MINION
servility / BONDAGE; BASENESS
serving boy / PAGE; BELLHOP
serving girl / MAID
servingman / HENCHMAN
servingwoman / HANDMAID
servitor / WAITER; SERVANT
servitude / BONDAGE, SLAVERY
sesame / TIL; SEMSEM
sesame confection / HALVA;
  HALVAH, HALWAH
sesame oil / BENNE
sesame seed / GINGILI
sesquipedalian / MULTISYL-
  LABLED
sessile / FIXED; SEDENTARY

session / SEANCE; MEETING
set / FIX, LAY, PUT, RUN; RATE;
  MOUNT, PLACE, PLANT, STAKE;
  HARDEN. GROUP; CLIQUE,
  SERIES; COTERIE. FIRM, HARD;
  FORMAL; CONCRETE
set apart / ISOLATE. TABU; TABOO
set of articles / KIT; OUTFIT
set aside / REJECT; OVERRULE
set back / RECESS
set bounds / LIMIT
set of bowls / NEST
set of boxes /INRO
set of co-workers / TEAM
set on fire / IGNITE
set in a fixed position / POSE
set forth / GO; SAIL; DESCRIBE
set forth particulars / DETAIL
set of four / TETRAD; QUARTET
set free / DELIVER, RELEASE
set in / INDENTED
set of laws / CODE; CANON
set at liberty / FREE
set limits to / BOUND; CONFINE
set in motion / START
set off / BECOME; EMBELLISH
set of organ pipes / STOP
set of ornaments / PARURE
set out / START; EMBARK
set of plants / BED
set of records / ALBUM
set right / CORRECT, REDRESS
set to rights / SETTLE
set sail / LEAVE; EMBARK
set solidly / FIRM; FIXED
set of stables / MEWS
set into a surface / INLAY
set of three / TRIO
set time / DATE, HOUR;
  APPOINTMENT
set of twelve / DOZEN
set of two / DUO; DUET, PAIR
set up / LIFT; ERECT
set value on / RATE; ASSAY
seta / TELA; SPINE; BRISTLE
setal / HAIRY; BRISTLY
setback / LOSS; RELAPSE,
  REVERSE
Seth's brother / ABEL, CAIN
Seth's mother / EVE
Seth's son / ENOS
seton / THREAD; BRISTLE,
  FISTULA
setose / BRISTLY
Set's brother / OSIRIS
Set's father / SEB
Set's mother / NUT
Set's sister / ISIS; NEPHTHYS
Set's son/ ANUBIS
settee /SOFA; DAVENPORT
setter/ BIRDDOG
setting / SCENE; MILIEU
setting, as a hen / BROODY

setting for gems / PAVE; BEZEL;
  CHATON
setting of a play / MISEENSCENE
settle / FIX, PAY, SAG; CALM
settled / SEDATE; COMPOSED
settled course / RUT; ROUTINE
settlement / COLONY; HOMESTEAD
settler / BOOMER; PIONEER;
  COLONIST
settlings / LEES;   DREGS;   SEDI-
  MENT
set-to / BOUT; FIGHT, MELEE
setup / PLAN; MAKEUP
seven, c.f. / HEPTA
seven, pert. to / SEPTENARY
seven, pref. / SEPT
seven days / WEEK; HEBDOMAD
Seven Sisters / PLEIADES
seven stars / DIPPER
seven-hilled city / ROME
seven-night / WEEK; SENNIGHT
seven-sided figure / HEPTAGON
seventh / SEPTENARY; SAB-
  BATICAL
seventh day / SABBATH
seventh heaven / ECSTASY;
  PARADISE
sever / CUT. LOP; DETACH,
  SUNDER
sever violently / SLASH
several / FEW; SOME; DIVERS,
  SUNDRY
severally / SEPARATELY
severance / SCHISM; SPLITTING
severe / HARD; CRUEL, HARSH,
  RIGID; BITTER, STRICT;
  RIGOROUS; INCLEMENT
severe cold / GELIDITY
severe in judgment / CRITICAL
severe stiffness / AUSTERITY
severely criticize / ROAST, SLATE
severely strict / STERN; STRINGENT
severity / RIGOR; INCLEMENCY
Seville building / ALCAZAR,
  GIRALDA
Sèvres / PORCELAIN
sew / HEM; MEND; STITCH;
  HEMSTITCH
sew ornamentally / EMBROIDER
sew temporarily / BASTE
sewan /WAMPUM
Seward's Folly / ALASKA
sewed edge / HEM; SEAM
sewer / DITCH, DRAIN; CONDUIT
sewing aid / NEEDLE, THREAD;
  THIMBLE
sewing case / ETUI
sewing party / BEE
sex / KIND; GENDER; FEMALES
sexless / NEUTER; EPICENE
sexton / SHAMAS, SHAMES;
  SACRISTAN
sexy / BLUE; EROTIC

SEVEN AGAINST THEBES

TYDEUS
ADRASTUS
CAPANEUS
POLYNICES
AMPHIARAUS
HIPPOMEDON
PARTHENOPAEUS

SEVEN DWARFS
(in Walt Disney's Snow White and the Seven Dwarfs)

DOC
DOPEY
HAPPY
GRUMPY
SLEEPY
SNEEZY
BASHFUL

SEVEN GODS OF LUCK, JAPANESE

EBISU
HOTEI
BENTEN
DAIKOKU
JUROJIN
FUKUROKUJU
BISHAMONTEN

SEVEN HILLS OF ROME

CAELIAN
VIMINAL
AVENTINE
PALATINE
QUIRINAL
ESQUILINE
CAPITOLINE

SEVEN SAGES OF GREECE

BIAS
SOLON
CHILON
THALES
PITTACUS
CLEOBULUS
PERIANDER

Seychelles island / MAHE
sha / URIAL
shabby/ MEAN, WORN; SEAMY, SEEDY; RAGGED
shabby woman / DOWD, SLUT; FRUMP
shack / HUT; SHED; CABIN; SHANTY
shackle / BOND, GYVE, IRON; MANACLE. TIE; FETTER; TRAMMEL

shad / ALOSA; ALLICE; ALEWIFE, THWAITE
shadbird / SNIPE; SANDPIPER
shadbush / SERVICEBERRY
shaddock / POMELO; GRAPEFRUIT
shade / DIM; HIDE; CLOUD; DARKEN. HUE; TINT, TONE
shade of blue / NAVY; ALICE
shade of brown / TAN; COCOA, HENNA
shade of difference / NUANCE

shade of green / KELLY, LODEN
shade of orange / APRICOT
shade of purple / LILAC; VIOLET
shade of red / RUBY; CORAL
shade tree / ASH, ELM, LIN
shade of yellow / CANARY, CITRON
shaded / COVERED; SHADOWED
shaded promenade / MALL;
  ARCADE; ALAMEDA
shaded retreat / ARBOR, BOWER
shading line / HATCH
shadlike fish / HILSA
shadoof / WELLSWEEP
shadow / TAIL; DARKEN, GHOST,
  SHADE; DETECTIVE;
  SILHOUETTE
shadow in eclipse / UMBRA;
  PENUMBRA
shadowless man / ASCIAN
shadowy / DIM; DARK; MURKY;
  GLOOMY; GHOSTLY
shady / DUBIOUS; EQUIVOCAL
shady bower / ARBOR
shady place / COVERT
shady side / AUTUMN, OLDAGE
SHAEF's area / ETO; EUROPE
shaft / ROD; POLE; ARROW;
  CHIMNEY
shaft of column / FUST; SCAPE,
  VERGE
shaft of a feather / SCAPE
shaft horse / THILLER
shaft of light / RAY; GLEAM
shaft of a wagon / THILL
shafted weapon / LANCE, SPEAR;
  JAVELIN
shaggy / BUSHY, FUZZY, HAIRY,
  NAPPY
shaitan / DEVIL, SATAN
shake / BOB, JAR, WAG; JOLT,
  ROCK; QUAKE; DODDER,
  JABBLE, QUIVER; TREMBLE,
  VIBRATE. TREMOR; SHINGLE
shake back and forth / OSCILLATE
shake with cold / SHIVER
shake convulsively / SHUDDER
shake defiantly / BRANDISH
shake with fear / TREMBLE
shake fitfully / AGITATE
shake the head / DENY; REFUSE
shake jarringly / JOLT
shake a leg / HURRY
shake off / RECOVER; DISLODGE
shake in the wind / FLAP
shakedown / BLACKMAIL
shaken / AFRAID, SPRUNG
Shakespeare's daughter / JUDITH
Shakespeare's son / HAMNET
Shakespeare's wife / ANNE
Shakespearian actor / KEAN;
  BURBAGE, GARRICK, OLIVIER
Shakespearian actress / TERRY;
  SIDDONS; WOFFINGTON

Shakespearian character / NYM;
  IAGO, IRAS; ROMEO; ANTONY,
  HAMLET, OBERON
Shakespearian elf / PUCK
Shakespearian forest / ARDEN
Shakespearian heroine / KATE;
  IMOGEN, JULIET, PORTIA;
  JESSICA; ROSALIND
Shakespearian theater / GLOBE
shakeup / CHANGE; REORGANIZA-
  TION
shaking / ASPEN; TREPID
shaking disease / PALSY; TREMOR
shaky / FEEBLE; UNSOUND
shale / HUSK; PELITE; SANDSTONE
shall / CAN; MUST, WILL; OUGHT
shallow / FLIMSY, SLIGHT,
  TRASHY, TRIVIAL. SANDS,
  SHOAL
shallow box in trunk / TRAY
shallow dish / BASIN; SAUCER;
  PLATTER
shallow lake / LAGOON, LAGUNE
shallow utensil / PAN; SKILLET
shallow-minded / NARROW; SUPER-
  FICIAL
shalom / HELLO, PEACE;
  FAREWELL
sham / FRAUD, TRICK; HUMBUG.
  FAKE; FALSE
shaman / PRIEST; MAGICIAN
Shamash / UTU
Shamash's father / SIN
Shamash's sister / ISHTAR
Shamash's wife / AI; AYA
shamble / RAMBLE; SHUFFLE
shame / ABASH; MORTIFY.
  ODIUM; INFAMY
shamefaced / MODEST; BASHFUL
shamefast / SHY; DEMURE;
  DIFFIDENT
shameful / BASE, VILE; WICKED
shameless / ARRANT, BRAZEN;
  CORRUPT
shampoo / RINSE; CLEANSE
shamus / EYE; DETECTIVE
shanghai / KIDNAP, RAVISH
Shanghai section / CHAPEI;
  HONGKEW
Shanghai street / BUND
Shangri-la / UTOPIA
shank / END; CRUS, SHIN
Shantung city / CHEFOO, TSINAN
shanty / HUT; CHANTEY
shantyman / LOGGER; LUMBER-
  MAN
shape / CAST, FORM, MOLD;
  FASHION. FRAME; FIGURE; CON-
  TOUR, PATTERN
shape concepts / IDEATE
shape generally / OUTLINE
shape with a knife / WHITTLE
shape a loaf / KNEAD

shape on a mold / MODEL
shape up / DEVELOP
shaped like an arrowhead / SAGITTATE
shaped with an ax / HEWN; HEWED
shaped like an earlobe / AURICULATE
shaped like an egg / OVATE
shaped like a halberd / HASTATE
shaped like a hand / PALMATE
shaped like a hood / CUCULLATE
shaped like a kidney / RENIFORM
shaped mass / LOAF
shaped like a pine cone / PINEAL
shaped like a shield / PELTATE
shaped like a spearhead / LANCEOLATE
shaped like a sword / ENSIFORM
shaped like a triangle / DELTOID
shapeless / CHAOTIC; AMORPHOUS
shapely / COMELY; WELLMADE
shapeshifter / NAGUAL; WEREWOLF
shaping machine / LATHE
shaping tool / GOUGE, SWAGE
shard / SHELL; FRAGMENT, POTSHERD
share / DOLE; ALLOT; DIVIDE, IMPART, RATION. BIT; PART; QUOTA; PORTION
share in common / PARTICIPATE
sharer / PARTNER; ASSOCIATE
shark / GATA, MAKO, TOPE; REQUIN; TIBURON; PORBEAGLE
shark sucker / REMORA
sharp / EDGY, KEEN, TART; ACERB, ACUTE, EAGER, NIPPY, QUICK; SHRILL; CUTTING
sharp blow / RAP; PUNCH
sharp branch / SNAG, TINE, TWIG
sharp crest / ARETE
sharp cry / OUCH, YELL, YELP
sharp end / POINT, PRICK; PRICKLE
sharp flavor / BITE, TANG; TARTNESS
sharp growth / BURR; SPINE, THORN
sharp ice pinnacle / SERAC
sharp knock / RAP
sharp pain / PANG; STING; TWINGE
sharp and piercing / SHRILL
sharp point / BARB, CUSP
sharp poke / JAB; STAB
sharp rejoiner / QUIP; RETORT
sharp reply / RIPOSTE
sharp slap / SMACK; THWACK
sharp sound / POP; CLAP, SNAP; CRACKLE
sharp sound of disapproval / HISS
sharp terminal / EPI; SPIRE; FINIAL

sharp twist / KINK
sharpen / SET; HONE, WHET; STROP
sharpened / EDGED; POINTED
sharpening tool / HONE; STROP; GRINDER
sharply biting / NORDANT, PUNGENT
sharply pointed / ACUTE; ACULEATE
sharpness / EDGE; ACUMEN
sharpshooter / JAGER; SNIPER
sharp-tailed duck / PINTAIL; OLDSQUAW
sharp-tasting / ACID, TART; TANGY
sharp-tempered / EDGY
shatter / DASH; SMASH; SHIVER
shave / PARE; RAZOR, SLICE
shave leather / SKIVE
shaveling / LAD; MONK; PRIEST
shaven head / TONSURE
shaver / YOUNGSTER
shaving implement / PLANE, RAZOR
shaw / COPSE; THICKET
shawl / MAUD, WRAP; SERAPE; PAISLEY; MANTILLA
she / WOMAN; FEMALE
she cat / TABBY
she fowl / HEN
she fox / VIXEN
she goat / NANNY
she rabbit / DOE
she sheep / EWE
shea tree / KARITE
sheaf / GERB; BUNDLE, FASCES, PENCIL
shear / CUT; CLIP, POLL, TRIM; FLEECE
sheath / CASE; THECA; QUIVER; SCABBARD
sheath of petiole / OCREA
Sheba's queen / AAZIZ; BALKIS
shebang / SHOP; THING; BUSINESS
shebeen / SPEAKEASY
shed / CAST, MOLT; SPILL. ABRI, COTE; CABIN
shed copiously / RAIN
shed dead tissue / SLOUGH
shed from a surface / SCALE
shee / FAIRIES
sheen / GLOSS, SHINE; LUSTER, POLISH
sheep / EWE, RAM, TUP
sheep, pert. to / OVINE
sheep of Africa / ARUI, ZENU; AOUDAD
sheep of Asia / SHA; RASSE, URIAL; ARGALI, BHARAL, NAHOOR
sheep breed / MERINO, ROMNEY; CHEVIOT

sheep cry / BAA; BLEAT
sheep disease / COE, GID, ROT; RESP; ANTHRAX
sheep dog / COLLIE
sheep guardian / SHEPHERD
sheep hair / WOOL
sheep laurel / LAMBKILL
sheep leather / BOCK, ROAN
sheep marking clay / SMIT; REDDLE
sheep meat / MUTTON
sheep oil / LANOLIN
sheep once sheared / GIMMER; DINMONT
sheep pelt / WOOL; FLEECE
sheep pen / COTE, FOLD
sheep before shearing / HOGG; HEDER
sheep tick / KED
sheep two years old / TEG; BIDENT
sheepfold / REE; COTE
sheepish / SHY; TIMID; ABASHED
sheep-killing parrot / KEA
sheep's eyes / OGLES; GLANCES
sheepshead / SALEMA
sheepskin / FELL; DIPLOMA; PARCHMENT
sheer / MERE, PURE, THIN; CLEAR, STEEP, UTTER. SWEEP
sheer fabric / LAWN, LENO; NINON, TOILE; BEMBERG, CHIFFON, ORGANZA
sheet / PAGE; SURFACE; NEWSPAPER
sheet of metal / FOIL, LEAF
sheet of metal for printing / PLATE
sheet once folded / FOLIO
sheet of stamps / PANE
sheet of tissue / MEMBRANE
sheet twice folded / QUARTO
sheets / LINEN
sheik / CHIEF, LOVER; HEADMAN
shekel / COIN; WEIGHT
shela / MUSLIN
sheldrake / MERGANSER
shelf / BANK, REEF; LEDGE
shelf above fireplace / MANTEL
shelf behind altar / GRADINE, RETABLE
shell / BOMB, HUSK, SHOT, TEST; CONCH, CRUST; CHITON, LORICA, TRITON, TUNICA
shell beads / PEAG; SEWAN; WAMPUM
shell carving / CAMEO
shell casing / GAINE
shell fragments / SHRAPNEL
shell game / MONTE; SWINDLE; THIMBLERIG
shell hole / CRATER
shell used as horn / CONCH
shell money / ULLO; SEWAN, UHLLO; COWRIE, SEAWAN

shell not exploded / DUD
shell out / PAY
shell savagely / STRAFE
shellac / LAC; RESIN
shellback / TAR; SALT; SEAMAN
Shelley novel / FRANKENSTEIN
Shelley poem / ADONAIS, ALASTOR
shellfish / CLAM, CRAB; PRAWN; LIMPET; ABALONE, LOBSTER, MOLLUSK, SCALLOP
shellfish young / SPAT
shell-hurling gun / MORTAR
shelter / HIDE; SCONCE, SHIELD; CONCEAL. LEE; ABRI, ROOF; COVER, HAVEN; ASYLUM, REFUGE
shelter for animal / DEN; BARN, COTE, LAIR; STALL; STABLE
sheltered bay / COVE
sheltered corner / DEN; NOOK
sheltered side / LEE
sheltered from wind / ALEE
shelve / SHUNT, SLOPE; DISMISS
shelved / TABLED
Shem descendant / SEMITE
Shem's brother / HAM; JAPHETH
Shem's father / NOAH
Shem's mother / NAAMAH
Shem's son / LUD; ARAM, ELAM
shenanigan / TRICK; HORSEPLAY
shend / DISGRACE
Shensi capital / SIAN
Shensi mountains / CHINLING
Sheol / HADES
shepherd / PASTOR; HERDSMAN
shepherd kings of Egypt / HYKSOS
shepherd's club / MULLEIN
shepherd's needle / LADYSCOMB, VENUSCOMB
shepherd's patron / PAN
shepherd's pipe / OAT; REED; CHANTER
shepherd's staff / CROOK
sherbet / ADE, ICE; SORBET
sherd / SHARD, SHELL; POTSHERD
sheriff / MARSHAL, SHRIEVE
sheriff's band / POSSE
sheriff's deputies / POSSE
sheriff's deputy / BAILIFF
Sherlock Holmes author / DOYLE
Sherlock Holmes' friend / WATSON
sherry / XERES; OLOROSO; AMONTILLADO
She's author / HAGGARD
Shetland inlet / VOE
Shetlands court officer / FOUD
Shetlands island / UIST, YELL; MAINLAND
Shetlands judge / FOUD, FOWD
Shetlands measure / URE
Shetlands pasture tax / SCAT
shibboleth / SLOGAN; WATCHWORD

shield / ECU; EGIS; AEGIS, PAVIS, TARGE; SCUTUM; BUCKLER; ESCUTCHEON
shield of Australian aborigine / MULGA
shield border / ORLE
shield corner / CANTON
shield division / ENTE
shield straps / GUIGES; ENARMES
shielded / HIDDEN; PROTECTED
shield-shaped / PELTATE; CLYPEATE
shift / MOVE, TURN; ALTER. SWING; CHEMISE; ARTIFICE; EXPEDIENT, GRAVEYARD, MOONLIGHT
shift course / JIBE, VEER
shift position / JIBE
shifting / AMBULANT
shiftless / LAZY; PRODIGAL; IMPROVIDENT
shifty / TRICKY; EVASIVE
Shigatse edifice / TASHILUMPO
Shiite champion / MAHDI
shikari / HUNTER
shilelagh / CANE; STICK; CUDGEL; KIPPEEN
shill / STEERER
shilling mark / SOLIDUS, VIRGULE
shilly-shally / DEMUR, WAVER
shim / FILL; WEDGE
shimmer / FLICKER, TREMBLE
shimmy / WIGGLE; VIBRATE
shin / SCALE, SHANK
shinbone / TIBIA; CNEMIS
shindig / PARTY; BLOWOUT
shindy / SPREE; UPROAR
shine / BEAM, GLOW; EXCEL, GLARE, GLEAM; GLISTEN, RADIATE. GLOSS; LUSTER
shiner / CHUB; MINNOW; MENHADEN
shingle / SIGN; BEACH, TOAST
shingles / ZONA; HERPES
shining / AGLOW, NITID; BRIGHT, LUCENT
Shinto gateway / TORII
Shinto goddess / AMATERASU
Shinto gods / KAMI
Shinto priest / KANNUSHI
Shinto sacred tree / SAKAKI
Shinto sect / TENRIKYO
shinty / HOCKEY
shiny / BRIGHT, GLOSSY; LUSTROUS
ship / MAIL, SEND; EMBARK; FORWARD. KEEL; LINER, PLANE; TANKER, VESSEL
ship anchor chain / CABLE
ship biscuit / HARDTACK
ship carrying cargo / MERCHANTMAN
ship carrying oil / TANKER

ship channel / GAT
ship of Columbus / NINA; PINTA
ship crew's tour of duty / WATCH
ship with decks reduced / RAZEE
ship of the desert / CAMEL; DROMEDARY
ship dairy / LOG
ship fever / TYPHUS
ship moved by oars / BIREME, GALLEY; TRIREME
ship with one mast / SLOOP
ship with three masts / BARK
ship with two masts / BRIG, SNOW
ship used as prison / HULK
shipbuilder's prop / THWART
shipload / CARGO; LADING
shipman / SAILOR; SKIPPER
shipmaster / CAPTAIN
shipment / CARGO; FREIGHT
shipping box / CRATE; CARTON
shipping document / WAYBILL
ship's anchorage / BERTH; MOORING
ship's armor / PLATING
ship's beam / KELSON; KEELSON
ship's biscuit / HARDTACK
ship's body / HULL
ship's bottom / BILGE
ship's bow / PROW
ship's capacity / TONNAGE, TUNNAGE
ship's captain / MASTER
ship's compartment / HOLD; CABIN; STATEROOM; FORECASTLE
ship's compass stand / BINNACLE
ships' crane / DAVIT
ship's deck / POOP; ORLOP
ship's deck drain / SCUPPER
ship's deck opening / HATCH
ship's floor / DECK
ship's front / BOW; PROW, STEM
ship's hauling device / CAPSTAN
ship's jail / BRIG
ship's keel extension / SKEG
ship's kitchen / GALLEY
ship's load / CARGO; LADING
ship's long timber / KEEL
ship's main cabin / SALOON
ship's measure / LAST
ship's midsection / WAIST
ship's navigation aid / RADAR, SONAR
ship's officer / MATE; PURSER; CAPTAIN
ship's officers' deck / BRIDGE
ship's part / RIB; DECK, HULL, KEEL, MAST; RUDDER
ship's personnel / CREW
ship's plank's curve / SNY
ship's rear / AFT; STERN
ship's rigging / CORDAGE
ship's rope / GUY, TYE; SHROUD

ship's sail / CANVAS
ship's side / BEAM
ship's stairs / COMPANIONWAY
ship's station / BERTH; MOORING;
  ANCHORAGE
ship's tiller / HELM
ship's timber / MAST, SPAR
ship's track / WAKE
ship's waiter / STEWARD
shipshape / NEAT; ORDERLY
shipworm / TEREDO
shipwreck / RUIN; DISASTER
shipwrecked sailor / CRUSOE;
  CASTAWAY
shire / COUNTY
Shires / MIDLANDS
shirk / SHUN; AVOID, EVADE
shirker / SLACKER; GOLDBRICK
shirr / RUFFLE; GATHERING
shirt / SARK; KAMIS; BLOUSE,
  CAMISE, SKIVVY; CHEMISE
shirt of mail / BYRNIE; HAUBERK;
  HABERGEON
shirtwaist / BLOUSE
shirty / ANGRY, UPSET
shishkebab / SHASHLIK
shivaree / CHARIVARI
shive / SLICE; SPLINTER
shiver / QUAKE, SHAKE; QUIVER;
  SHUDDER
shiver with fear / GRUE; SHUDDER
shivery / SHAKY; AGUISH; BRITTLE
shizoku / SAMURAI
shoal / BAR; REEF; SCHOOL;
  SHALLOW
shoat / HOG; SHOTE
shock / JAR; STUN. BRUNT, CLASH,
  ONSET; TRAUMA
shock with alarm / STARTLE
shock with horror / APPAL
shocking / FOUL; HORRIBLE; RE-
  VOLTING
shod / CALCED. TAP
shoddy / BOGUS; INFERIOR
shoe / BOOT; BROGAN, LOAFER
shoe bottom / SOLE
shoe fastener / LACE; LATCHET
shoe leather strip / RAND, WELT
shoe part / HEEL, LAST, RAND,
  SOLE, WELT; UPPER; INSOLE
shoe spike / CLEAT
shoe stretcher / TREE
shoe upper / VAMP
shoeblack / BOOTBLACK
shoelace / LACET
shoelace tip / AGLET
shoemaker / SUTTER; COBBLER
shoemaker's form / LAST, TREE
shoemaker's patron / CRISPIN
shoemaker's thread / LINGEL,
  LINGLE
shogun / TYCOON

shoo / SCAT; BEATIT, BEGONE
shook / KIT; SHOCK
shoot / BEG; POT; DART, EMIT,
  FIRE, HURL, TALK. CION; SPRIG
shoot from ambush / SNIPE
shoot at / ESSAY; UNDERTAKE
shoot out / DART; SPROUT;
  BURGEON
shoot of plant / BINE, CION; GEM-
  MA, SPRIG, SPRIT; RATOON;
  SPROUT, STOLON
shooting iron / PISTOL; SIXGUN
shooting marble / TAW
shooting match / TIR
shooting star / LEONID, METEOR;
  PERSEID; FIREBALL
shoot-off / TIEBREAKER
shop / STORE; OFFICE; ATELIER,
  FACTORY
shop talk / CANT
shopkeeper / RETAILER; TRADES-
  MAN
shoplift / STEAL; PILFER
shopping area / MALL, MART
shop's sign / FACIA
shopworn / FADED; DAMAGED.
shore / BRACE; SUPPORT. LAND,
  STAY; BEACH, COAST
shore, pert. to / LITTORAL
shore below high tide / STRAND
shore bird / REE; RAIL, SORA;
  SNIPE, STILT, WADER; AVOCET,
  PLOVER; SANDPIPER
shore dinner / SQUANTUM
shore leave / LIBERTY
shore up / PROP; BUTTRESS
shore-inhabiting / LIMICOLINE
shoreless / BOUNDLESS, UN-
  LIMITED
shoreline / COASTLINE
shorn / CLIPPED, FLEECED
short / CURT; BLUNT, BRIEF,
  TERSE
short aria / ARIETTA
short article / PARAGRAPH
short bombardment / RAFALE
short bout / SETTO
short cloak / TALMA
short club / BILLY
short coat / JACKET, JERKIN,
  TOPPER; WAISTCOAT
short conversation / WORD
short cut / BYWAY; BEELINE
short distance / SPAN, STEP
short doze / CATNAP
short drapery / VALANCE
short flight / HOP
short haircut / BOB; TRIM
short intermission / RECESS
short jacket / ETON; BOLERO
short, jerky movement / BOB
short letter / MEMO, NOTE; BILLET

short line under staff / LEDGER
short and the long / PITH; ESSENCE
short look / GLANCE; GLIMPSE
short missile / DART; JAVELIN
short musical play / OPERETTA
short narrative / STORY; ANECDOTE
short note / LINE; BILLET
short notice / HASTE
short of / LACKING, WITHOUT
short open spout / LIP
short pencil / STUB
short play / SKIT; SKETCH
short projection/STUB
short race / DASH; SPRINT
short runner on sled / BOB
short seller / BEAR
short shrift / HASTE, PAUSE
short skirt / KILT, MINI; KIRTLE
short sleep / NAP; DOZE; SIESTA
short sonata / SONATINA
short song / LAY; DITTY
short stop / BREAK, PAUSE
short story / TALE; ANECDOTE
short surplice / COTTA
short and sweet / BRIEF; SUCCINCT
short syllable / MORA
short tail / SCUT
short and thick / DUMPY, SQUAT; STOCKY
short time / TICK; SPELL, TRICE
short and to the point / CURT; TERSE
short trip / OUTING; EXCURSION
short underground stem / TUBER
short visit / CHAT, COZE
short vowel mark / BREVE
shortage / DEFICIT
short-breathed / PURSY; WINDED
shortchange / SWINDLE
shortcircuit / MAR; SPOIL; BYPASS
shortcoming / WANT; FAILURE; INADEQUACY
shorten / DOCK; ELIDE; LESSEN, REDUCE; ABRIDGE
shorten sail / REEF
shortening / LARD, SUET
short-focus / WIDEANGLE
shorthand / STENOGRAPHY
shorthand system / GREGG; PITMAN
shorthorn / NEWCOMER
short-legged dog / BASSET
short-legged horse / COB
short-legged stocking / SOCK
short-lived / EPHEMERAL
shortly / ANON, SOON; QUICKLY
short-nap fabric / RAS
shortness / BREVITY
shorts / TRUNKS; DRAWERS

short-sighted / MYOPIC; PURBLIND
shortstop / INFIELDER
short-tailed rodent / MARMOT; HAMSTER
short-tempered / FIERY; TOUCHY
short-visored cap / ETON
Shoshonean Indian / UTE; HOPI, KOSO, MOKI, MONO; MOQUI, PIUTE, UINTA; PAIUTE
shot / SHELL; BULLET; MISSILE
shot in billiards / BANK, DRAW; CAROM; MASSE
shoulder / CARRY; JOSTLE. SHELF
shoulder, c.f. / OMO
shoulder, pert. to / SCAPULAR
shoulder blade / SCAPULA
shoulder ornament / BARS, LOOP; EPAULET
shoulder of road / BERM
shoulder wrap / CAPE; MANTA, SHAWL
shout / CRY; BAWL, CALL, ROAR, YELL
shout applause / CHEER
shout of encouragement / BIS, OLE, CHEER
shout of exultation / HURRAH
shout for / ROOT
shout for more / BRAVO; ENCORE
shouting / HUBBUB, OUTCRY
shove / PUSH; THRUST
shovel / SCOOP, SPADE; BACKHOE
show / ARRAY, GUIDE, PROVE, TEACH; EVINCE. SIGHT; PAGEANT; CEREMONY
show approval / NOD; SMILE
Show Boat author / FERBER
Show Boat captain / ANDY
Show Boat composer / KERN
show contempt / SNEER
show disapproval / BOO; HISS
show disparity / CONTRAST
show as evidence / EXHIBIT
show fondness / HUG, PET; DOTE
show friendliness / GREET; WELCOME
Show Me State / MISSOURI
show mercy / PITY; SPARE; PARDON; FORGIVE
show off / FLAUNT, PARADE
show to one's place / USHER
show openly / EVINCE; DISPLAY
show pleasure / SMILE
show to be false / DISPROVE
show to be true / PROVE
showboat / SHOWOFF
showdown / CLIMAX; EXPOSURE
shower / RAIN; SPRAY; DOUCHE
shower of ice / SLEET
showing judgment / SAGE, WISE
showing off / SWAGGER
showplace / MUSEUM; THEATER

showy / GAY; AIRY, FINE, LOUD; GAUDY
showy attitude / POSE; ARABESQUE
showy clothing / FINERY
showy exhibition / SPLURGE
showy flower / MUM; LILY; CALLA, CANNA, PEONY; ORCHID
showy ornament / SEQUIN; SPANGLE
showy trappings / REGALIA
Shqipni / ALBANIA
shred / RAG; SNIP, WISP, SCRAP; TATTER
shreddy / RAGGED; RAGGEDY
shrew / ERD; VIXEN; VIRAGO; TERMAGANT
shrewd / SLY; CAGY, KEEN, WILY; ACUTE, CANNY, SHARP
shrewdness / ACUMEN; CUNNING
shrewlike / SORICINE
shriek / YELP; SCREAM
shrift / SHRIVING; CONFESSION
shrill / PIPY; ACUTE, SHARP
shrill bark / YELP
shrill cry / SQUEAL; SCREECH
shrill as an insect / STRIDULATE
shrill noise / SCREECH, STRIDOR
shrill tone / SKIRL; SHRIEK
shrill-voiced / FALSETTO
shrimp / DWARF, PRAWN
shrimp dish / SCAMPI
shrine / NAOS; ALTAR; GROTTO
shrink / WANE; CRINGE, LESSEN
shrink from danger / COWER, QUAIL
shrink and dry out / SHRIVEL
shrink in loathing / RECOIL
shrinkage / LOSS; DECREASE
shrinking / COY, SHY
shrive / PARDON; CONFESS
shrivel / PARCH, WIZEN; WITHER
shroff / MONEYCHANGER
Shropshire / SALOPIA
shroud / HIDE, MASK, VEIL; SCREEN. ROPE; SHEET; BANDAGE. CEREMENT
shrub / BUSH, TITI ALDER, DRINK, ELDER. GORSE. LILAC, SALAL, SENNA, SUMAC; LAUREL, SPIREA
shrug / JACKET, WIGGLE
shrug off / DISMISS. MINIMIZE
shrunken / WRINKLED; ATROPHIED
shrunken head / TSANTSA
shuck / HUSK; SHELL
shucks / PSHAW
shudder / QUAKE, SHAKE; SHIVER
shuffle / MIX; SHIFT; CONFUSE
shuffling gait / SHAMBLE
shun / AVOID, DODGE, ESCHEW
shunt / VEER, SHIFT; SWITCH. CONDUCTOR
shunted / SIDETRACKED

shut / CLOSE; ENCLOSE
shut down / STOP; CLOSE
shut in / HEM
shut out / BAN; DEBAR; EXCLUDE
shut tightly / SEAL
shut up / PENT. QUIET; IMMURE
shut-eye / SLEEP
shut-in / INVALID
shutout / BLANKING; SCHNEIDER
shutout bid / PREEMPTIVE
shutter / BLIND; SCREEN, SHIELD
shuttle / BOBBIN
shy / JIB; BALK. COY, MIM; WARY; TIMID; DEMURE
shylock / USURER
Shylock's daughter / JESSICA
shyness / RESERVE; DIFFIDENCE
shyster / PETTIFOGGER
Siam / THAILAND
Siamese / THAI
Siamese coin / AT; ATT; BAHT; TICAL
Siamese isthmus / KRA
Siamese measure / WA; NIU, RAI, SEN, SOK, WAH; KEUP
Siamese river / SI; MUN; PING
Siamese twin / ENG; CHANG
Siam's river / WEI
sib / AKIN. KIN
Siberian antelope / SAIGA
Siberian city / OMSK; ALMAATA
Siberian lake / BAIKAL
Siberian mountains / ANADYR
Siberian native / TATAR, YAKUT; KIRGHIZ
Siberian peninsula / TAIMYR
Siberian plain / STEPPE
Siberian river / OB, OM; AMUR, LENA
Siberian swamp-forest / URMAN
Siberian tent / YURT; YURTA
sibilant / HISSING
sibilant signal / PST; HIST
sibilate / HISS
sibling / SISTER; BROTHER
sibyl / SEERESS; PYTHONESS
siccative / DRYING
Sicilian city / ENNA; PALERMO
Sicilian secret society / MAFIA
Sicilian volcano / ETNA
sick / ILL; ABED; AILING
sick of / FEDUP, SATED
sick person / CASE; INVALID, PATIENT
sicken / LANGUISH, NAUSEATE
sickened / DISGUSTED
sickle / HOOK, SIVE; REAPHOOK
sickle-cell disease / ANEMIA
sickle-cell trait / SICKLEMIA
sickle-shaped / FALCATE
sickly / ILL; AILING
sickness / MAL; DISEASE
Siddhartha / BUDDHA; GAUTAMA

side / EDGE, SECT, TEAM; CAUSE, FLANK; ASPECT
side, pert. to / COSTAL; LATERAL
side arm / SABER, SWORD; PISTOL
side of building / WALL
side by side / ABREAST
side of coin / HEADS, TAILS; OBVERSE, REVERSE
side dish / ENTREE
side of doorway / JAMB
side drawing / PROFILE
side of gemstone / FACET
side of head / TEMPLE
side kick / PAL; PARTNER
side of leaf in book / PAGE; RECTO, VERSO
side opposite the wind / LEE
side post of door / JAMB
side road / LANE; BYWAY
side timber of ship / RIB
side of triangle / LEG
sideboard / BUFFET; CREDENZA
sideburns / WHISKERS; BURNSIDES
sidelight / ALLUSION
sideline / HOBBY; AVOCATION
sidelined / BENCHED; GROUNDED
sideling / OBLIQUE, INDIRECT
sidelong / SIDEWAYS, SLANTING
sidemen / MUSICIAN; INSTRUMENTALIST
sidereal / ASTRAL, STARRY; HEAVENLY
siderolite / METEORITE
sideslip / SKID
sidestep / DUCK; EVADE
sidetrack / DIVERT, SHELVE
sidewalk / FOOTPATH, PAVEMENT
sidewalk edge / CURB
sidewinder / RATTLER
sidewise / LATERAL, OBLIQUE
sidle / EDGE, SKEW
Sidon's goddess / ASHTAROTH
siege / LEAGUER; BLOCKADE
Siegfried's cloak / TARNKAPPE
Siegfried's mother / SIEGLINDE
Siegfried's slayer / HAGEN
Siegfried's sword / BALMUNG
Siegfried's wife / KRIEMHILD
Sienese painter / DUCCIO
sierra / CHAIN, RANGE
Sierra Leone capital / FREETOWN
Sierra Leone island / SHERBO
Sierra Leone money / LEONE
Sierra Leone river / MANO; ROKEL
Sierra Leone tribe / LIMBA, MENDE, TEMNE
Sierra Nevada lake / TAHOE
Sierra Nevada peak / WHITNEY
siesta / NAP; CATNAP
sieve / BOLTER, FILTER, RIDDLE, SCREEN; STRAINER. SIFT
sieve for clay / LAUN

sifaka / LEMUR
siffle / HISS; WHISTLE
Sif's husband / LOKI
Sif's son / ULLR
sift / BOLT; PROBE; SCREEN
sifter / SIEVE; INVESTIGATOR
sigh / SOB; MOAN, SOUF; SOUGH
sight / AIM. VIEW; VISION
sight, pert. to / VISUAL; OPTICAL
sight on gun / BEAD
sightless / BLIND; INVISIBLE
sightly / COMELY; PLEASING
sigil / SEAL, SIGN, REFERENCE
Sigmund's father / VOLSUNG
Sigmund's sister / SIGNY
Sigmund's son / SIGURD
Sigmund's wife / HJORDIS
sign / MARK, OMEN; BADGE, TOKEN, TRACE; EMBLEM
sign of addition / AND; PLUS
sign of agreement / OK; NOD
sign of a cold / SNEEZE
sign of hit play / SRO
sign of illness / FEVER; SYMPTOM
sign off / QUIT
sign of omission / CARET
sign of reference / ASTERISK
sign up / ENLIST, ENROLL
sign of victory / VEE
sign of the Zodiac / LEO; ARIES, LIBRA, VIRGO; CANCER, GEMINI, PISCES. TAURUS; SCORPIO; AQUARIUS; CAPRICORN; SAGITTARIUS
signal / WAVE; ALARM. EMINENT, NOTABLE
signal to actor / CUE
signal alarm / SIREN; FLASHER
signal bell / GONG
signal code / MORSE
signal fire / BEACON
signal for a parley / CHAMADE
signal on stage / CUE; SENNET
signal telegraph / SEMAPHORE
signalize / EXALT; CELEBRATE
signate / INDICATED
signature / MARK, NAME; STAMP
signature of approval / VISA, VISE
signboard / PLACARD
signet / SEAL SIGIL
significance / IMPORT; MEANING
significant / WEIGHTY
significant point / MILESTONE
signification / SENSE; MEANING
signified primarily / DENOTED
signified secondarily / CONNOTED
signify / MEAN; IMPLY; MATTER
signify agreement / NOD
signor / SIR; GENTLEMAN
signora / LADY; MADAM
signorina / MISS
signpost / GUIDE; POINTER
signs, pert. to / SEMIC; SEMIOTIC

Sigurd's father / SIGMUND
Sigurd's foster-father / REGIN
Sigurd's victim / FAFNIR
Sigurd's wife / GUDRUN
Sikkim pass / JELEPLA
sil / OCHER
silage / FEED; ENSILAGE
Silas Marner author / ELIOT
silence / GAG; HUSH; QUIET,
  STILL. CALM; PEACE; SECRECY.
  OYEZ
silenced / MUTED; STIFLED
silent / MUM; DUMB, MUTE; TACIT
silent signal / NOD; BECK, WINK
Silesian city / BRESLAU
Silesian river / ODER
silex / FLINT; SILICA
silhouette / OUTLINE, PROFILE
silica / SAND; SILEX; QUARTZ
silk / MOIRE, RUMAL
silk cotton / KAPOK
silk before dyeing / GREIGE
silk fabric / MOFF; PEKIN, SATIN,
  TULLE
silk fiber / BRIN
silk floss / SLEAVE
silk grass / KARATAS
silk hat / TOPPER
silk of leno weave / MARQUISETTE
silk screen print / SERIGRAPH
silk substitute / NYLON, ORLON,
  RAYON; DACRON
silk thread / BAVE, TRAM; FLOSS
silk weight / PARI
silk-cotton tree / CEIBA
silken / SERIC; GLOSSY
silk-stocking / WEALTHY
silkweed / MILKWEED
silkworm / ERI; ERIA; TASAR;
  BOMBYX
silkworm's covering / COCOON
silky / SOFT; SLEEK
silky fabric / ACCA; GROS; SURAH;
  PONGEE, SAMITE, TOBINE
sill / INTRUSION, THRESHOLD
silliness / INANITY
silly / WEAK; INANE; SIMPLE,
  STUPID; ASININE, FOOLISH.
  BOOBY
silly person / ASS; GOOSE;
  SIMPLETON
silly smile / SMIRK; SIMPER
silo / FOODPIT; ELEVATOR
silt / MUD; SAND. CHOKE;
  OBSTRUCT
silver / ARGENT, CHANGE;
  ARGENTUM
silver in alchemy / LUNA
silver braid / ORRIS
silver coin / PESO, TARA; SHILLING
silver fish / SARGO; MULLET,
  TARPON
silver in heraldry / ARGENT

silver ingots / SYCEE
silver ore / ARGENTITE
silver oxide compound / ARGYROL
silver paper / TINFOIL
silver screen / CINEMA, MOVIES
Silver State / NEVADA
silvered / COATED, TINNED
silver-sulfur alloy / NIELLO
silver-tongued / ELOQUENT
silvery / ARGENT
silviculture / FORESTRY
simar / CHEMISE
simian / APE; MONKEY. APELIKE
similar / AKIN, LIKE; ALIKE;
  ANALOGIC
similarity / ANALOGY; RE-
  SEMBLANCE
simile / METAPHOR; COMPARISON
similitude / LIKENESS; FACSIMILE
simmer / BOIL, STEW; SEETHE
simoleon / BUCK; DOLLAR
Simon / PETER
simon-pure / REAL; MCCOY; AMA-
  TEUR
simoom / STORM; SIMOON;
  KHAMSIN
simper / SMIRK
simple / EASY, MERE, OPEN; PLAIN,
  SILLY; FOOLISH. HERB;
  MEDICINE
simple animal / MONAD, MONAS;
  AMOEBA
simple inflorescence / RACEME
simple song / LAY; DITTY
simple in style / PURE; CHASTE
simple sugar / OSE; GLYCOSE
simple-hearted / SINCERE
simple-minded / ARTLESS;
  IMBECILE
simpleton / ASS, DAW, OAF, SAP;
  BOOB, COOT, DOLT, FOOL,
  GABY, GAWK, GOWK, SIMP;
  DUNCE, NINNY
simplex / ONEWAY, SINGLE
simplicity / NAIVETE; FRANKNESS
simplify / ELUCIDATE
simulacrum / IMAGE; PHANTOM;
  LIKENESS
simulate / ACT, APE; SHAM; FEIGN
simulation / SHAM; PRETENSE
simultaneous / SYNCHRONOUS
simultaneous discharge / SALVO
simurgh / ROC
sin / ERR; OFFEND; TRANSGRESS.
  EVIL; OFFENSE; INIQUITY
Sinai / SINA; HOREB
Sinai town / TOR; QANTARA
since / AS; AGO, FOR; SITH, SYNE;
  BECAUSE
since, pref. / CIS
sincere / OPEN, TRUE; FRANK;
  CANDID, DIRECT
sincerity / HONESTY; OPENNESS

sinciput / FOREHEAD
Sind city / KARACHI; HYDERABAD
Sindbad's bird / ROC
Sind's conqueror / NAPIER
sine / WITHOUT
sine die / INDEFINITELY
sine qua non / ESSENTIAL;
   REQUISITE
sinecure / SNAP; CINCH
sinew / THEW; TENDON;
   STRENGTH
sinewy / WIRY; TOUGH; BRAWNY
sinful / EVIL; WICKED; IMPIOUS
sing / LILT; CAROL, CHANT, TRILL
sing above correct pitch / SHARP
sing freely / CAROL, TRILL
sing gally / LILT
sing in high key / PIPE
sing in low tone / HUM; CROON
sing in monotone / CHANT; INTONE
sing in a murmur / HUM; CROON
sing below pitch / FLAT
sing sentimentally / CROON
sing like Swiss / JODEL, YODEL
sing tremulously / WARBLE
singable / MELODIC
Singapore's refounder / RAFFLES
singe / SEAR; SCORCH
singer / DIVA; VOCALIST;
   CHANTEUSE
singer of antiphons / PRECENTOR
singer of love songs / SERENADER
singer in synagogue / CANTOR
singers of liturgy / CHOIR
Singhalese / CEYLONESE
singing bird / LARK WREN; VEERY;
   CANARY, LINNET, WARBLER
singing birds / OSCINES; PAS-
   SERES
singing group / TRIO; CHOIR;
   CHORUS, SEXTET; QUARTET
singing syllable / FA, LA, MI: TRA
singing voice / ALTO, BASS; BASSO,
   MEZZO, TENOR; SOPRANO; BARI-
   TONE; CONTRALTO
single / ONE; LONE, MONO, SOLO,
   UNAL; ALONE, UNWED; SEPA-
   RATE. ACE; BILL, UNIT
single, c.f. / UNI; MONO
single article / ITEM
single block of stone / MONOLITH
single effort / TRICE
single item in a chronicle / ANNAL
single in kind / ONE; LONE;
   UNIQUE
single out / CHOOSE, SELECT
single person / ONE; BACHELOR,
   SPINSTER
single thickness / PLY
single thing / UNIT
single unit / IT; ANY, ONE
single-celled alga / DIATOM
single-celled organism / MONAD

single-chambered / UNICAMERAL
single-colored / MONOCHROMATIC
single-foot / RACK; AMBLE
single-handed / ALONE; UNAIDED
single-masted vessel / SLOOP;
   CUTTER
single-minded / OBSESSED
singleness / UNITY
single-stringed instrument / MONO-
   CHORD
singleton / ONE
single-track railway / MONORAIL
singly / ONCE, SOLO; ALONE
singsong / UNVARIED; MONOT-
   ONOUS
singular / ODD; RARE; QUEER;
   CURIOUS, EMINENT, STRANGE
singult / SOB; SIGN
singultus / HICCUP; HICCOUGH
sinister / BAD; EVIL, LEFT;
   OMINOUS
sinistral / LEFTHANDED; ILLEGITI-
   MATE
Sinitic / CHINESE
sink / DIP, EBB, SAG; FALL; ABASE.
   DRAIN; CENOTE, DOLINE
sink lower / DECLINE
sink in mud / MIRE; BEMIRE
sink slowly / SETTLE
sink into something / MERGE
sink suddenly / DROP; FAINT,
   SLUMP
sinker / DROP; PLUMMET; DOUGH-
   NUT
sinkhole / POTHOLE, SWALLOW
Sinkiang capital / URUMCHI
Sinkiang desert / TAKLAMAKAN
Sinkiang lake / LOPNOR
Sinkiang river / TARIM; YARKAND
Sinkiang town / KASHGAR
sinless / PURE, IMPECCABLE
sinner / OFFENDER
sinuate / WAVY
sinuosity / CURVE; WIGGLE
sinuous / WINDING; SERPENTINE
sinus / BAY; ANTRUM
Siouan Indian / KAW, OTO; CREE,
   CROW. IOWA, OTOE; KANSA,
   OMAHA OSAGE, PONCA; BILOXI,
   DAKOTA, LAKOTA, MANDAN; CA-
   TAWBA, HIDATSA
Sioux division / BRULE, TETON;
   OGLALA, SANTEE; HUNKPAPA;
   BLACKFOOT
sip / SUP; TASTE; IMBIBE
siphon / TUBE; SIPHUNCLE. DRAW;
   CONVEY
sipid / TASTY; FLAVORSOME
sippet / BIT; CROUTON
sire / BEGET; GENERATE. FATHER
siren / ALARM, ALERT; SIGNAL;
   MERMAID, WHISTLE
siren of the Rhine / LORELEI

siren suit / COVERALL
sirenian / DUGONG; MANATEE
sirenical / SEDUCTIVE
siriasis / SUNSTROKE
sirih / BETEL
sirocco / FOEHN, GLIBLI, LESTE;
  KHAMSIN, SANTANA; HARMAT-
  TAN
sirup / JUICE; TREACLE;
  MOLASSES
sisal / HEMP; HENEQUEN
sisel / SUSLIK; SQUIRREL
Sisera's slayer / JAEL
sisi / GRUNT; PORKFISH
siskin / FINCH
sissy / COWARD; MILKSOP
sister / NUN, SIS; NURSE
sister's son / NEPHEW
Sistine ceiling painter / MICHEL-
  ANGELO
Sistine Madonna painter / RAPHAEL
Sisyphus' father / AEOLUS
Sisyphus' kingdom / CORINTH
Sisyphus' wife / MEROPE
sit / POSE; BROOD, PERCH, ROOST
sit astride / STRADDLE
sit in / JOIN, PLAY
sit on to hatch / INCUBATE
sit up / WAIT; LOOKALIVE
Sita's father / JANAKA
Sita's husband / RAMA
sitatunga / NAKONG
sit-down / STRIKE
site / AREA; SCENE; POSITION
site of first moon landing / TRAN-
  QUILITY
site of pyramids / GIZA; GIZEH
site of Taj Mahal / AGRA
sitology / DIETETICS
sitting / SEANCE; MEETING,
  SESSION
situate / FIX; PLACE
situated at the back / POSTERN
situated on / ATOP
situation / JOB; CASE, POST, SEAT,
  SITE; BERTH, STATE; PLIGHT;
  STATION
situs / SITE
sitz bath / HIPBATH
Siva / HARA; SHIVA; DHARMA;
  MAHADEVA
Siva snake / COBRA
Siva worshipper / SAIVA
Siva's abode / KAILASU
Siva's son / SKANDA; KARTTIKEYA
Siva's wife / UMA; DEVI, KALI,
  SATI; DURGA, GAURI; AMBIKA;
  BHAVANI, PARVATI
six, c.f. / HEX; HEXA
six, pert. to / SENARY
six in dice / SICE, SISE
Six Nations / IROQUOIS
six-day fever / SEXTAN

six-line stanza / SESTET
six-pack beverage / BEER
six-part composition / SEXTET
sixpence / SICE; TANNER
six-shooter / GUN; REVOLVER
six-sided polygon / HEXAGON
six-stanza poem / SESTINA
sixteenth note / SEMIQUAVER
sixth canonical hour / SEXT
sixth part of a circle / SEXTANT
sixth sense / ESP; INTUITION
sixty grains / DRAM
sixty sixties / SAR; SAROS
sizable / BIG; BULKY; LARGE
size / AREA, BULK; EXTENT,
  VOLUME
size of book / OCTAVO, QUARTO
size of coal / EGG, PEA; BUCK
size of paper / CAP; DEMY, POTT;
  ATLAS, FOLIO
size of shot / BB; BUCK
size of type / GEM; PICA; AGATE,
  ELITE
sizing / GLAIR, GLAZE; FILLER
sizzle / FRY; HISS
Skanda / KUMARA; KARTTIKEYA
Skanda's father / AGNI, SIVA
Skanda's wife / DEVASENA
skat jack / BOWER
skat no trump / GRAND
skat player / ENDHAND
skate / RAY; RUNNER
skating arena / RINK
skean / KNIFE; DAGGER
skedaddle / RUN; BOLT, SCAT;
  SCOOT
skeet / DIPPER
skeet gunner / TRAPSHOOTER
skeet target / PIGEON; CLAY-
  PIGEON
skein of yarn / RAP; COIL, HANK
skeletal part / OS; RIB; BONE;
  SPINE
skeleton / ATOMY, BONES, FRAME;
  OUTLINE
skeleton of anthozoan / CORAL
skeleton key / MASTERKEY
skeleton staff / CADRE
skep / BASKET; BEEHIVE
skeptic / DOUBTER; AGNOSTIC
skepticism / INCREDULITY
skerry / PUNT; ISLET; POTATO
sketch / DRAW, LIMN; PAINT,
  TRACE; DEPICT, DESIGN. MAP;
  SKIT; DRAFT, ROUGH, STUDY;
  PASTEL; DRAWING
sketchy / INCOMPLETE, UN-
  FINISHED
skew / TURN; TWIST; DISTORT
skewbald / PIED; PINTO; PIEBALD
skewer / PEG, PIN. TRUSS
ski jumping ramp / INRUN
ski race / SLALOM; BIATHLON

ski racer's crouch / EGG
ski run / SCHUSS, SLALOM
ski wax / KLISTER
sklagraph / XRAY
skid / DRAG, SLEW, SLIP, SLUE, VEER; SLIDE
skid road / TRAVOIS; CORDUROY
skidoo / GO; SCAT; VAMOOSE
skier's hill / SLOPE
skiff / GIG; DINGHY
skiing jump / GELANDESPRUNG
skiing race heat / RUN
skiing run / SLOPE
skiing turn / CHRISTIE
ski-jump ramp / INRUN
skilful / APT; ABLE; ADEPT, DEDAL, HANDY; ADROIT, CLEVER, EXPERT, HABILE
skilful statesman / SOLON
skilful worker / ARTISAN; CRAFTSMAN
skilfully / WELL; DEFTLY
skill / ART; CRAFT, KNACK; ABILITY, FINESSE
skilled / TRAINED; DEXTEROUS
skilled bookkeeper / ACCOUNTANT
skilled contriver / DAEDALUS
skilled person / ADEPT, EXPERT
skilled rifleman / MARKSMAN
skilled trade / JOINERY, MASONRY
skilled work / SLOYD
skillet / PAN; FRYPAN, SPIDER
skim / FLIT; BRUSH; REMOVE
skimp / STINT; SLIGHT
skimpy / SCANT; FRUGAL, STINGY
skin / FLAY, PEEL; CHEAT. FUR; BARK, FELL, FILM, HIDE, PELT, RIND; BOTTLE; CUTICLE
skin, c.f. / DERM; DERMA, DERMO
skin, pert. to / DERMAL, DERMIC
skin blemish / WEN; MOLE, RASH, WART; COMEDO, PAPULE; BLISTER
skin blister / VESICLE
skin covering / FUR
skin disease / UTA; ACNE; HIVES, MANGE, PSORA, RUPIA, TINEA; ECZEMA, TETTER
skin divers' gear / FINS; SNORKEL
skin layer / CUTIS; CORIUM, DERMIS; EPIDERM; EPIDERMIS
skin opening / CUT; PORE
skin ornamentation / TATTOO
skin pouch / SPORRAN
skin spot / MOLE; FRECKLE
skinflint / MISER; NIGGARD
skink / ADDA; LIZARD
skinny / BONY, LEAN, THIN
skip / JUMP, LEAP, MISS, OMIT, SLUR; CAPER; FROLIC, GAMBOL
skip in pronouncing / ELIDE
skip along the surface / DAP; SKIT; SKITTER

skip on water / DAP
skipjack / BONITO, SAUREL
skipper / CAPTAIN; BUTTERFLY
skirl / SHRIEK, SHRILL
skirmish / FRAY; BRUSH, MELEE
skirr / WHIRR; SCURRY. TERN
skirt / EDGE; DRESS; BORDER
skirt of armor / FAULD, TASSE
skirt worn in ballet / TUTU
skirt edge / HEM
skirt inset / GORE; PANEL
skirt opening / PLACKET
skit / JIG; SKETCH; PLAYLET
skite / SCOOT; SQUIRT
skitter / SKIM; SCAMPER
skittish / SHY; TIMID
skittles /PLAY; NINEPINS
skive / PARE; SHAVE
skoal / HAIL; TOAST; HEALTH, PROSIT; SLAINTE
skookum / GOOD; EXCELLENT
skua / ALLAN; JAEGER
skulduggery / CHICANE; TRICKERY
skulk / LURK; SLINK, SNEAK
skull / MIND; CRANIUM; BRAINPAN
skull, pert. to / CRANIAL
skull bone / VOMER; CRANIUM
skull protuberance / INION; GLABELLA
skullbanker / TRAMP; LARRIKIN
skullcap / BEANIE, CALOTTE, CHECHIA; YARMULKE; ZUCCHETTO
skull-less / ACRANIAL
skunk / ZORIL; TELEDU; FITCHEW, POLECAT; CONEPATE
sky / BLUE; WELKIN; HEAVENS; FIRMAMENT
sky blue / AZURE; CERULEAN
sky pilot / CHAPLAIN
sky serpent / AHI
skylark / PIPIT. FROLIC, GAMBOL
skyline / HORIZON
skyscraper / HIGHRISE
slab / PIECE, SLICE, STELE
slab under column / PLINTH
slabby / SLOPPY
slab-sided / GAWKY
slack / LAX, IDLE, SLOW; REMISS
slacken / EASE, FLAG; ABATE, RELAX
slacken speed / SLOW
slacker / SHIRKER; GOLDBRICK
slackly joined / LOOSE
slacks / PANTS
slade / DEN; GLEN; PLOWSOLE
slag / DROSS; SCORIA
slake / ALLAY; QUENCH; HYDRATE
slalom passage / GATE
slam / BANG; BERATE. VOLE; BRICKBAT
slambang / VIOLENT

slander / ABUSE, BELIE, DECRY, LIBEL; DEFAME, MALIGN, REVILE, VILIFY. CALUMNY
slanderer / BACKBITER
slanderous remark / ASPERSION
slang / CANT; ARGOT; JARGON
slangy / VULGAR
slant / TIP; CANT, LEAN, TILT; BEVEL. BIAS; ANGLE
slanted / ARAKE; OPINIONATED
slanted passageway / RAMP
slanted type / ITALIC
slanting / ALIST, ARAKE, ASKEW; OBLIQUE
slantwise / SKEWED; SIDEWAYS
slap / CUFF; SPANK. BLOW
slapdash / QUICK; CARELESS
slapjack / PANCAKE; GRIDDLECAKE
slapping / ROBUST; STRAPPING
slap-up / FINE; FANCY
slash / CUT; GASH, SLIT. DEBRIS
slashing / BOLD; INCISIVE
slat / LATH, SLAB. FLAP
slate / LIST, TILE; DOCKET, TABLET; SCHEDULE; BLACKBOARD. CENSURE; REPRIMAND
slate cutter's tool / SAW, SAX, ZAT, ZAX
slatelike rock / SHALE
slather / DAUB; LAVISH
slathers / MUCH; PLENTY
slats / RIBS; REAREND
slatted frame / CRATE
slattern / SLUT; SLOVEN; TROLLOP
slaty / GRAY; LAMINATED
slaughter / CARNAGE, KILLING; BUTCHERY
slaughter house / ABATTOIR, BUTCHERY, KNACKERY
Slav / POLE, SERB, SORB, WEND; CROAT, CZECH
slave / ESNE, SERF; HELOT; MINION, THRALL, VASSAL; BONDMAN. DRUDGE
slave block / CATASTA
slave driver / LEGREE; TASKMASTER
slave quarters / ERGASTULUM
slave ship / BLACKBIRDER
slave in Sparta / HELOT
slaveholder / OWNER; MASTER
slaver / DROOL; DRIVEL; SLOBBER
slavery / BONDAGE; SERVITUDE
slavey / MAID; TWEENY
Slavic / SLAVONIC
slavish / BASE, MEAN; ABJECT
slaw / SALAD; COLESLAW
slay / KILL; MURDER; DESTROY
slayer of Abel / CAIN
slayer of Goliath / DAVID
slayer of Marat / CORDAY
slayer of seven / TAILOR
slayer of Sisera / JAEL

sleave / FLOSS; TANGLE
sleazy / LOW; CHEAP; FLIMSY
sled / LUGE, TODE; SLEIGH, SLEDGE; COASTER
sledge / SLED; HAMMER
sleek / SHINY; GLOSSY, SMOOTH
sleep / LIE, NAP, NOD; DROWSE
sleep, c.f. / HYPN; HYPNO
sleep fitfully / DOZE
sleep lightly / NAP; SNOOZE
sleep out / CAMP
sleep quietly / SLUMBER
sleep soundly / REST; REPOSE
sleeper / TIE; PULLMAN
sleeping / DORMANT
sleeping car / PULLMAN; WAGON-LIT
sleeping car accommodation / BERTH; ROOMETTE
sleeping chamber / BEDROOM
sleeping noise / SNORE
sleeping place / BED, COT, PAD; CRIB, DOSS; BERTH
sleeping sickness / NAGANA; ENCEPHALITIS
sleeping sickness vector / TSETSE
sleepless / UNQUIET, WAKEFUL
sleep-producing / NARCOTIC
sleepwalker / NOCTAMBULE; SOMNAMBULIST
sleepy / DROWSY; SOMNOLENT
Sleepy Hollow belle / KATRINA
Sleepy Hollow schoolmaster / ICHABOD
sleeve / ARM; DOLMAN, JACKET, RAGLAN; BUSHING
sleeveless / FUTILE; FRUITLESS
sleeveless garment / ABA; CAPE; TUNIC; CHIMER, DOLMAN, MANTLE, PONCHO, TABARD; SINGLET
sleigh / PUNG, SLED; SLEDGE
sleight / CUNNING; DEXTERITY
sleight of hand / LEGERDEMAIN
Sleipnir's owner / ODIN
slender / LANK, LEAN, SLIM, THIN; REEDY, SPARE; FEEBLE, FLIMSY, MEAGER, SLIGHT
slender fish / EEL, GAR; PIPEFISH
slender mark / LINE
slender metal piece / PIN; NEEDLE
slender plant organ / STOLON; TENDRIL; ROOTHAIR
slender spar / YARD
slender spine / SETA
slender stick / ROD; WAND
slender thread / FILM; FILAMENT
slender woman / SYLPH
slenderize / REDUCE
sleuth / EYE; SHAMUS; DETECTIVE
sleuthhound / BLOODHOUND
slew / BOG; INLET, MARSH; SLOUGH. VEER. KILLED

sley / LAY; REED; BATTEN
slice / CUT; PARE; CARVE, SHAVE, SPLIT. SLAB
slice of meat / COLLOP, RASHER
slice of pie / WEDGE
slice very thin / SHAVE
sliced chopped cabbage / SLAW
slick / CLEVER, SMOOTH; SLIPPERY. LOY
slicker / RAINCOAT
slide / SKID, SLIP, SLUE; SLITHER
slide fastener / ZIPPER
slide out of course / SKID, SLUE
slide to a stop / COAST
slide in trumpet / VALVE
slide trumpet / SACKBUT
slide-rule scale / LOGARITHMIC
sliding box / DRAWER
sliding knot / SLIPKNOT
sliding machine part / PISTON
sliding piece / CAM; PANEL
sliding receptacle / DRAWER
sliding step / GLIDE
slight / SPURN; IGNORE; DISDAIN. SLUR. MERE, SLIM; PETTY, SCANT, SMALL
slight amount / SIGN; TRACE
slight coloring / TINT; TINGE
slight depression / DENT
slight drink / SIP; TASTE
slight elevation of ground / RIDEAU
slight intentionally / SNUB
slight knowledge / SMATTERING
slight offense / FAULT; BLEMISH
slight rumor / BREATH
slight slip / LAPSE
slight sound / CREAK, TWEET
slight taste / PECK; NIBBLE
slightest / LEAST
slighting comment / SLUR
slightly / PARTLY; PARTIALLY
slightly crazy / DAFFY, DOTTY, GOOFY, POTTY, WACKY
slightly tart / ACIDULOUS
slim / SMALL; SLIGHT, SVELTE
slim down / REDUCE
slime / MUCK, OOZE; GLEET; SLUDGE
slimy / VISCID; GLUTINOUS
slimy mud / OOZE
slimy substance / MUCILAGE
sling / HURL; FLING. STRAP; HARNESS
slingshot / CATAPULT
slingstone / PELLET
slink / LURK; CREEP, SKULK
slinky / SLY; SNEAKY
slip / ERR; FALL, SKID; SLIDE. BONER, FAULT; PETTICOAT
slip away gradually / LAPSE
slip by / ELAPSE
slip from memory / ESCAPE
slip on / DON

slip of the tongue / LAPSE
slipcase for book / FOREL; FORREL
slipknot / NOOSE
slipper / MULE; MOYLE; SANDAL; CHINELA
slippery / EELY, GLIB; UNSAFE
slipshod / CARELESS, SLOVENLY
slip-up / BOOBOO; MISTAKE
slit / GASH; SLASH, SPLIT. FISSURE
slither / SLIDE; SHUFFLE
slitlike opening / RIMA, SLOT
slitter / CUTTER, OPENER
sliver / SPLINTER
sloat / SLOT; SLOTE
slob / CLOD; LUMMOX, SLOVEN
slobber / DROOL; DRIBBLE
sloe / PLUM
slog / PLOD, PLUG
slogan / CRY; MOTTO; CATCHWORD
slop / SPILL. TRASH
slope / DIP; SLANT; INCLINE. RAMP; SCARP; GLACIS; GRADIENT
slope of the land / VERSANT
slope of lode / HADE
slope of a road / GRADE
slope upward / RISE; CLIMB
sloping / ASLANT; SLANTWISE
sloping edge / BEVEL, BEZEL
sloping mound / BANK
sloping passageway / RAMP
sloping type / ITALICS
sloppy / WET; MUDDY; TEARFUL; SLOVENLY
slosh / SPLASH
slot / RUT; GROOVE; OPENING
sloth / AI; UNAU; IDLENESS; INDOLENCE
slothful / LAZY; TORPID; SLUGGISH
slothful person / SLUG; IDLER; LAZYBONES
slothfully / IDLY; SUPINELY
slouch / DROOP; SHAMBLE
slough / BOG; MIRE, SCAB; BAYOU, INLET, MARSH. MOLT, SHED
Slovakian city / BRATISLAVA
sloven / SLATTERN
Slovenian city / LJUBLJANA
slovenly / UNTIDY; CARELESS
slovenly person / SLOB
slow / DULL, LATE, POKY; GRADUAL
slow coach / POKE; SLUGGARD
slow dance / ADAGIO
slow disintegration / RUST; EROSION
slow even bell-ringing / TOLLING
slow flow / OOZE; TRICKLE
slow to learn / DULL; THICK
slow lemur / KOKAM, LORIS
slow mollusk / SNAIL

slow in music / LARGO, LENTO; ADAGIO; ANDANTE; LARGHETTO
slow reptile / TURTLE
slow speech / DRAWL
slow stately dance / MINUET
slowed / RETARDED; SLACKENED
slowing / RIT; RITARDANDO
slowing gradually / SLENTANDO
slowpoke / DAWDLER, LAGGARD
slow-witted / DOLTISH
slowworm / BLINDWORM
sludge / MUD; MIRE; SLUSH
slue / SKID, VEER; PIVOT
slug / POMMEL, STRIKE. BULLET; NUDIBRANCH
sluggard / DRONE, IDLER
slugger's forte / RBI; HOMERUN
sluggish / LOGY, SLOW; DOPEY, INERT
sluggishness / SLOTH
slugs, pert. to / LIMACINE
sluice / DAM; CLOW, GATE; FLUME, SASSE
slum / DUMP; TENEMENTS
slum area / BARRIO, GHETTO
slumber / SLEEP; REPOSE
slumber clothing / PJS; NIGHTIE
slumber music / LULLABY
slumber sound / SNORE
slump / FALL, SINK. SAG; RECESSION
slungshot / COSH; BLACKJACK
slur / BLUR, SOIL; STAIN, SULLY. STIGMA; INNUENDO
slur over / SKIP; ELIDE
slurry / MIXTURE
slush / SISH, SLOP; LOLLY
slushy / GUSHY; SENTIMENTAL
slut / HUSSY; SLATTERN
sluttish / UNTIDY, WANTON
sly / ARCH, FOXY, WILY; ARTFUL, ASTUTE, CRAFTY, SHREWD, SUBTLE; CUNNING
sly animal / FOX
sly glance / LEER; ONCEOVER
smack / BLOW, BUSS, KISS, SLAP; SAVOR. FLAVOR. SLOOP
smacking / BRISK
small / FEW, WEE; MEAN, PUNY, TINY; PETIT, PETTY; LITTLE, MINUTE, PALTRY, SLIGHT
small, c.f. / LEPT, MINI; LEPTO, MICRO
small, suffix / ING
small Abyssinian monkey / GRIVET
small African antelope / ORIBI; DUIKER
small amount / BIT; DRAM, MITE; MINIM
small anchor / KEDGE; GRAPNEL
small animal / SHREW
small arachnid / MITE
small area / PLOT; AREOLA

small area of painting / DETAIL
small armadillo / PEBA, PEVA
small article / ITEM; PARAGRAPH
small article of virtu / BIBELOT
small of the back / LOINS
small banner / PENNANT; BANNERET; BANDEROLE
small barrel / KEG
small bay / COVE
small beard / GOATEE
small bed / COT; CRIB
small beer / TRASH; TRIVIA
small beetle / WEEVIL; CURCULIO
small bird / TIT, TODY; FINCH, JUNCO, PEWEE, PIPIT; SPARROW
small bite / NIP; NIBBLE
small boat / DORY; CANOE; DINGHY; CORACLE
small body of water / MERE, POND, POOL
small bomb / GRENADE
small book / BOOKLET; PAMPHLET
small booth / KIOSK
small bottle / VIAL; PHIAL
small bouquet / NOSEGAY
small boy / LAD, TAD
small branch / TWIG; SPRIG
small brook / RUN; RILL
small brown bird / WREN
small bubble in glass / BOIL, SEED
small bud / PIP
small bunch / WISP
small Burmese gibbon / HOOLOCK
small cake / BUN; TART; COOKIE; MADELINE
small candle / TAPER
small canyon / CANADA
small cask / TUB
small cavity / PORE
small chapel / ORATORY
small chicken / BANTAM, PULLET
small child / TOT; BABY; INFANT
small chunk / GOB
small cloth inset / GUSSET
small clothes / BREECHES; UNDERWEAR
small coin / RAP, SOU; CENT, MITE; PENNY, SOLDO
small community / TOWN; VILLAGE
small container for liquid / CRUET
small convex molding / BEAD, REED
small cord / TWINE; STRING
small creature / MINIM
small crevice / CHINK
small crucifix / PAX
small dagger / PONIARD; STILETTO
small deer / ROE
small depression / DENT, DINT
small detached piece / RAG; SCRAP
small dirigible / BLIMP
small dog / POM, PUG, PUP; FICE, PEKE; FEIST; WAPPET

small drink / NIP, PEG, SIP; DRAM; SNORT
small drum / TABOR
small elevation / HILL; MOUND
small enclosure / PEN; COOP, FOLD
small engine / MULE
small European barracuda / SPET
small European country / ANDORRA; LUXEMBOURG, MONTE-CARLO
small European tree / HOLLY; MASTIC, MEDLAR
small explosion / POP
small falcon / MERLIN
small fillet / ANNULET
small finch / SERIN
small fish / FRY, IDE; DACE; SMELT, SPRAT; DARTER, MINNOW, SHINER; SARDINE, SMEELIN
small fishing boat / SMACK
small flag / PENNANT; BANNERET
small flat metal disk / WASHER
small flat molding / FILLET
small flock / COVEY
small flute / FIFE; PICCOLO
small fly / GNAT; MIDGE; NOSEEUM
small fortification / REDOUBT
small fruit / AKENE; ACHENE; ACHENIUM
small fry / KIDS; NOBODIES
small gibbon / HOOLOCK
small glass bottle / VIAL; CRUET, PHIAL
small gnat / MIDGE
small goby / MAPO
small groove / STRIA
small harmonium / MELODEON
small hat / CAP, TAM; TOQUE
small hawk / KESTREL
small heron / BITTERN
small herring / SPRAT; ALEWIFE
small hill / TUMP; HILLOCK
small hole / PORE; EYELET
small horse / COB, TIT; PONY; GENET; JENNET
small house / COT, HUT; CABIN; COTTAGE
small insect / ANT; FLEA, MITE; APHID, MIDGE
small interstice / AREOLE
small island / CAY; ISLE; ISLET
small kitchen / KITCHENETTE
small lake / MERE, POND, POOL
small larklike bird / PIPIT
small lizard / EFT, EIT; GECKO
small loaf / BAP, BUN
small locomotive / DOLLY
small loop of thread / PICOT
small lump / NODULE
small machine part / COG, PIN; GEAR
small mallet / GAVEL

small marine animal / SALP; CORAL, SALPA; SALPID
small mark / IOTA; TITTLE
small mask / DOMINO
small mass / WAD; LUMP
small merganser / SMEE, SMEW; SMEATH
small military assignment / DETAIL
small monkey / TITI; MARMOSET
small mound of earth / TEE
small mug / NOGGIN
small musical instrument / OCARINA, PICCOLO; HARMONICA
small nail / BRAD
small narrow strait / GUT
small noise / POP, TAP
small note / MEMO; BILLET
small novel / NOVELETTE
small in number / FEW
small object / TRIFLE; TRINKET
small objet d'art / BIBELOT
small one-seeded fruit / ACHENE
small opening / GAP; PORE; CRANNY
small ornament / BEAD; TRINKET
small ornamental case / ETUI
small package / PACKET, PARCEL
small painting / MINIATURE
small part / BIT; SNIPPET
small part in play / BIT
small particle / MOTE
small particles / DUST, SAND; POWDER
small perforated sphere / BEAD
small perforation / PINHOLE
small pericarp / ACHENE
small person / FRY; RUNT; CHILD
small pest / BUG; GNAT
small pheasant / CHUKAR; BOBWHITE; FRANCOLIN
small piano / SPINET
small pickle / GHERKIN
small pie / TART; PASTY
small piece / CHIP; SCRAP; PARTICLE
small piece of cloth / STRIP; SWATCH
small piece of fire / EMBER, SPARK
small pieces of wood / KINDLING
small pile of earth / HILL; HILLOCK
small pill / GLOBULE
small pin / LILL
small plane surface / FACET
small planets / ASTEROIDS
small plug / SPILE
small pocket / FOB
small point / DOT, JOT; IOTA; TITTLE
small pointed instrument / AWL, PIN; SPRIG; NEEDLE
small portion / BIT, SIP; TASTE
small portrait / MINIATURE
small projection / TAB

small quantity/ BIT; BITE, IOTA; LITTLE; SMIDGEN
small quantity of liquid / DRAM, DROP
small quarrel / JAR; SPAT; RUNIN
small receptacle / INRO
small recess / NICHE
small report / POP
small restaurant / BISTRO; TEA-ROOM
small rich cake / TORTE; ECLAIR; MADELINE
small ring / ANNULET, CIRCLET
small river / BROOK, CREEK; RUNNEL
small room / DEN; CELL
small root / RADICEL
small rough dwelling / HUT; SHACK
small round bread / MUFFIN
small rug / MAT
small sac / SACCULE
small sandpiper / STINT; DUNTIN
small seedless raisin / CURRANT
small shallow dish / SAUCER
small share / MOIETY
small shark / TOPE; DOGFISH
small shield / ECU; BUCKLER
small shining particle / SPARK
small shoot / TWIG; SPRIG
small shot / PELLET
small spar / SPRIT
small speck / DOT, NIT
small sphere / DROP
small spirit heater / ETNA
small spotted cat / OCELOT
small stalk / PEDICEL
small stand / TABORET
small stipule / STIPEL
small store / SHOPPE
small stove / ETNA
small stream / RILL; RILLET
small strip of paper / SLIP
small sturgeon / STERLET
small swine / PIG
small table / STAND
small table mat / DOILY
small talk / CHAT; GOSSIP; PRATTLE
small tarred line / MARLINE
small taste / SIP
small tilthammer / OLIVER
small timber / SCANTLING
small tin cup / PANNIKIN
small toe / MINIMUS
small tower / TURRET
small town / HAMLET
small tree / SEEDLING
small tuft of hair / TATE
small tumor / WEN
small type size / AGATE, PEARL
small valley / DALE, VALE

small vial / AMPULE; AMPOULE
small village / DORP
small violin / KIT
small wave / RIPPLE
small and weak / PUNY
small weight / DRAM, MITE
small wood / HOLT; COPSE; SPINNEY
small wooden peg / PIN; SPILE
small woodpecker / PICULET
smallage / CELERY
smaller / LESS
smaller of two groups / MINORITY
smallest / LEAST; TINIEST
smallest independent particle / ATOM
smallest integer / ONE
smallest major planet / MERCURY
smallest particle / ATOM, WHIT
smallest state / RI
smallpox / VARIOLA
smalls / BREECHES; UNDERWEAR
smalto / TESSERA
smaragd / EMERALD
smart / CHIC, KEEN, NEAT, TRIG, TRIM; BRISK, SHARP, SHOWY, WITTY; ASTUTE. STING
smart aleck / WISEGUY
smart blow / RAP; SLAP
smart money / DAMAGES
smart set / SOCIETY
smarten up / TITIVATE
smartly dressed / CHIC, TRIG; DAPPER
smartness / ALACRITY
smash / BASH; BREAK, CRUSH; SHATTER
smatter / DALLY; DABBLE
smatterer / DABBLER; SCIOLIST; DILETTANTE
smattering / TRIVIA
smear / BLOT, DAUB, SOIL; STAIN; SMIRCH, SMUDGE
smear with fat / LARD; GREASE
smeary / OILY; GREASY; VISCOUS
smeddum / SPIRIT; GUMPTION
smegmatic / SOAPY
smell / ODOR; AROMA, FETOR, SCENT
smell, pert. to / OLFACTORY
smeller / NOSE; PRYER
smelling bad / OLID; FETID
smelt / FLUX, FUSE. INANGA; EULACHON, SPARLING
smelting product / SLAG; DROSS, MATTE
smew / MERGANSER
smidgen / SMITCH, TRIFLE
smile / BEAM, GRIN; FAVOR
smile artificially / SMIRK
smile fatuously / SIMPER

smiling / RIANT

smirch / DIRTY, STAIN, SULLY; BLACKEN

smirk / GRIN, LEER; SNEER; SIMPER

smite / HIT; CUFF, SLAY; BUFFET

smith of myth / VULCAN

smith's metal block / ANVIL

smithy / FORGE; FURNACE

smitten / ENAMORED, STRICKEN

smock / FROCK, TUNIC; CHEMISE

smoke / BURN, FUME, PUFF, REEK. SMOG; SMUDGE

smoke flue / STACK; FUNNEL; CHIMNEY

smoke out / EXPOSE; UNCOVER

smoke particle / FLOC

smoke screen / COVER

smoked / CURED; DARKENED

smoked beef / PASTRAMI

smoked pork / BACON

smoked salmon / LOX

smokeless powder / CORDITE

smokes / MISTS

smokestack / FUNNEL; CHIMNEY

smoking / ANGRY, AREEK

smoking party / STAG; SMOKER

smoking pipe / BRIAR, BRIER; MEERSCHAUM

smoky / FUMID, MISTY, MURKY

smoky haze / FOG; SMOG; SMAZE

smoky quartz / CAIRNGORM

smolder / SEETHE, SIMMER

smoldering / LATENT; REEKING

smooch / PET; NECK

smooge / FAWN; FLATTER

smooth / CALM, EASE, IRON, SAND; ALLAY; POLISH. EVEN, FLAT, GLIB, LENE; BLAND, LEVEL, SLEEK, SUAVE; GLASSY

smooth and agreeable / SUAVE

smooth with the beak / PREEN

smooth a board / PLANE

smooth breathing / LENE

smooth and connected / LEGATO

smooth and glossy / SLEEK

smooth glossy fabric / SATIN

smooth over / PLASTER

smooth and polished / LEVIGATE

smooth and self-satisfied / SMUG

smooth and shining / WAXEN

smooth speech sound / LENIS

smooth the way / PAVE

smoothed / PLANED; MOLLIFIED

smoothing implement / IRON; PLANE; SCRAPER

smoothly separable / SECTILE

smooth-skinned fruit / PLUM; GRAPE

smooth-spoken / GLIB

smote / STRUCK

smother / CHOKE; STIFLE; STRANGLE

smothered laugh / SNICKER

smudge / SMEAR, SMOKE, STAIN; BLACKEN

smug / PRIM; COMPLACENT

smug person / PRIG

smuggler / CONTRABANDIST

smut / CROCK; POLLUTE

smutty / SOILED; OBSCENE

Smyrna fig / ELEME, ELEMI

Smyrna today / IZMIR

sna / URIAL; NAHOOR

snack / BITE; MORSEL

snack between meals / NOSH; BEVER

snaffle / BIT; BRIDLE; HARNESS

snafu / MUDDLED, SNARLED

snag / PROBLEM; OBSTACLE. TEAR

snail / HELIX, SHELL, WHELK; TRITON; ABALONE; GASTROPOD; PERIWINKLE

snail's pace / CRAWL

snake / ASP, BOA; ABOMA, ADDER, KRAIT, MAMBA, RACER, VIPER; BONGAR, PYTHON; SERPENT; ANACONDA

snake, c.f. / OPHI; OPHIO

snake eyes / TWO; DEUCE

snake in the grass / TRAITOR

snakebird / DARTER; ANHINGA

snakebite antidote / GUACO; CEDRON; ANTIVENIN

snake-charm herb / MUNGO

snake-haired woman / GORGON, MEDUSA

snakehead / BISTORT

snake-like / SINUOUS, WINDING

snake-like fish / EEL; CONGER; LAMPREY

snakeroot / BLOLLY, STEVIA

snakes, pert. to / OPHIOID

snakestone / AMMONITE

snakewort / BISTORT

snaky / SLY; CUNNING; SERPENTINE

snaky wand / CADUCEUS

snap / BITE, FLIP; BREAK, CRACK. PEP, VIM; WAFER; COOKIE

snap with finger / FILLIP

snapper / SESI; BREAM, PARGO; ELATER, TAMURE, TURTLE

snappish / EDGY; TESTY; TOUCHY

snappy / BRISK, SHARP; LIVELY

snapshot / PHOTO

snare / GIN, NET, WEB; DRUM, TRAP; BENET, NOOSE; SPRINGE

snarl / ARR; GNAR, KNOT, YARR; GROWL, SCRAP; TANGLE

snarling / CYNICAL; SNAPPISH

snarly / CROSS, SURLY

snatch / NAB; GRAB, PULL; CLUTCH
snatcher / THIEF
snatchy / PEEVISH; SPASMODIC
snath / SNEAD; SNATHE
sneak / LURK; CREEP, SKULK, SLINK, STEAL
sneakers / GYMSHOES
sneaky / MEAN; FURTIVE
sneck / LATCH
sned / LOP; TRIM; PRUNE
snee / DIRK
sneer / JEER, MOCK; FLEER, TAUNT
sneezewort / PTARMICA; HELLEBORE
sneezing / STERNUTATION
sneezing charm / GESUNDHEIT
snell / KEEN; SEVERE. LOOP
snicker / GIGGLE, NICKER, TITTER
snickersnee / KNIFE
snide / MEAN. TRICKY
sniff / NOSE; SCENT, SMELL, WHIFF
snifter / DRAM; SNORT
snigger / SNICKER
snip / CLIP; SHRED
snipe / BUTT, KNOT; PHALAROPE
sniper / MARKSMAN; SHARP-SHOOTER
snippy / MEAN; SNAPPISH
snitch / INFORM, PILFER
snivel / CRY; WHINE; SNUFFLE
snob / APER; UPSTART
snood / NET; SNELL; FILLET
snook / GAR; ROBALO; BARRACUDA
snoop / PRY, SPY; PEER
snoot / NOSE; GRIMACE
snooze / NAP; DOZE
snore / STERTOR
snorter / BRAGGART
snout / NOSE; MUZZLE; PROBOSCIS
snow / SNA; NEVE; FLAKE; COCAINE
snow, pert. to / NIVAL
snow fall / AVALANCHE
snow field / FIRN, NEVE
snow grouse / PTARMIGAN
snow hut / IGLU; IGLOO
snow leopard / OUNCE
snow mouse / VOLE; LEMMING
snow runner / SKI; SLED
snowball / VIBURNUM; GUELDER-ROSE
snowbird / JUNCO
snowdrop / ANEMONE
snowy / PURE; NIVEOUS; SPOTLESS
snub / REBUFF, SLIGHT
snub nose / PUG
snub-nosed / SIMOUS
snuff / SNIFF, SNORT. RAPPEE
snuffbox / MULL; PUFFBALL
snuffbox bean / CACOON

snug / COZY, WARM; CLOSE
snug room / DEN; NEST
snuggery / RETREAT
snuggle / HUG; CUDDLE, NESTLE
so / ERGO, LIKE, THUS, TRUE; HENCE
so be it / AMEN
so much / TANTO
soak / DIP, RET, SOP, WET; SOUSE, STEEP; DRENCH. DRUNKARD
soak in brine / MARINATE
soak flax / RET
soak hides / BATE
soak in liquid / SEETHE
soak to a pulp / MACERATE
soak thoroughly / SATURATE
soaked / SOGGY; SODDEN
soaked crackers / PANADA
soaked with moisture / SOGGY; SODDEN
soap frame bar / SESS
soap froth / SUDS
soap plant / AMOLE
soap substitute / DETERGENT
soap vine / GOGO
soapberry tree / GUARA
soapstone / TALC; STEATITE
soapy mineral / TALC
soar / FLY; RISE; ASCEND
sob / SIGH; LAMENT
sober / CALM, COOL, DARK; GRAVE
sober-minded / STEADY; SERIOUS
sobriety / TEMPERANCE
sobriquet / ALIAS; AGNAME; NICKNAME
soccer / FOOTBALL
sociable / GENIAL; AFFABLE; FRIENDLY
social / AFFABLE; GREGARIOUS
social affair / TEA; BALL; PARTY
social appointment / DATE
social call / VISIT
social class / CASTE
social climber / ARRIVISTE
social custom / MOS; CODE; MANNER
social error / GAFFE; FIASCO
social group / CLAN, CLUB, SEPT; CASTE, TRIBE
social insect / ANT, BEE; TERMITE
social outcast / LEPER; PARIAH; ISHMAELITE
social sewing group / BEE
social standing / CASTE
socially prominent person / NOB; SWELL
society / CLUB; LODGE; COMPANY
society, c.f. / SOCIO
society beginner / DEBUTANTE
Society Islands city / PAPEETE
sock / CONE, TABI; SLIPPER
sockdolager / QUIETUS
socket / PLUG; HOLDER

socks / HOSE
socle / PEDESTAL
Socrates' poison / HEMLOCK
Socrates' pupil / PLATO; PHAEDO
Socrates' wife / XANTIPPE
Socratic method / DIALOGUE
sod / TURF; DIVOT, EARTH, GLEBE, SWARD
soda / POP; PHOSPHATE
soda accessory / STRAW
soda ash / ALKALI
sodality / CLUB; BROTHERHOOD
sodden / WET; SOGGY; SOAKED
sodium bicarbonate / SALERATUS
sodium carbonate / TRONA; NATRON
sodium chloride / SAL; SALT
sofa / DIVAN; LOUNGE, SETTEE; DAVENPORT
soft / LOW; EASY, MILD, WEAK; BLAND, DOWNY, PIANO; GENTLE
soft cake / BUN
soft candy / CREAM, FUDGE
soft cheese / BRIE
soft copal / ANIME
soft drink / ADE, POP; COKE, SODA; ROOTBEER
soft felt hat / FEDORA
soft food / PAP; MUSH; JELLY
soft hairs / DOWN
soft ice / LOLLY
soft leather / NAPA, ROAN
soft leather slipper / MOCCASIN
soft light fabric / LENO
soft limestone / MALM; CHALK
soft mass / WAD; PULP
soft murmuring tone / COO
soft muslin / MULL
soft ointment / SALVE
soft palate / VELA; VELUM
soft palate pendant / UVULA
soft part / PULP
soft and pulpy / PAPPY
soft in quality / TENDER
soft and ripe / MELLOW
soft rock / SOAPSTONE
soft shade / TINT; PASTEL
soft silk / FLOSS
soft silk fabric / SURAH
soft and smooth / VELVETY
soft snap / SINECURE
soft soap / FLATTERY
soft spot on bill / CERE
soft, sticky mud / MUCK; SLIME
soft in temper / EASY; FLEXIBLE
soft in tint / PASTEL
soft watery mud / MIRE; SLUDGE
soft wool / BOTANY; MERINO
soften / TAW; MELT; ABATE; LENIFY, MELLOW, RELENT; MOLLIFY; INTENERATE
soften by soaking / BATE; MACERATE

soften in temper / RELENT
soften in tone / MUTE; LOWER
soft-hearted / KIND; TENDER
softly colored / QUIET
soft-spoken / BLAND, SUAVE
soggy / HEAVY; SODDEN
soggy mass / MUD, SOP; MIRE
Sohrab's father / RUSTUM
soi-disant / WOULDBE; SOCALLED
soignée / SLEEK; ELEGANT
soil / MESS, MIRE, MOIL; SMEAR, STAIN, SULLY. DIRT, LAND; EARTH, GRIME; MANURE
soil, c.f. / AGRO
soil component / HUMUS
soil type / LOAM; PODZOL
soiree / PARTY; SOCIAL
sojourn / LIVE, STAY, STOP; TARRY
sol / SUN
solace / EASE; RELIEF; COMFORT
solan / GANNET
solar / HELIAC
solar atmosphere / CORONA
solar deity / RA; LUDD; HELIOS; SHAMASH
solar disc / ATEN, ATON
solatium / COMPENSATION
sold / VENDED
solder / FUSE; BRAZE; CEMENT
soldering cleanser / FLUX
soldering flux / ROSIN
soldering tool / IRON
soldier / GI; POILU, TROOP; PRIVATE, WARRIOR. SHIRK
soldier of American Revolution / BUCKSKIN
soldier of British army / TOMMY
soldier from Down Under / ANZAC
soldier of fortune / ADVENTURER
soldier in the ranks / PRIVATE
soldiers / ARMY; TROOPS
soldier's canvas bag / DUFFLE
soldier's hat / HELMET
soldier's lodging / TENT; BILLET; PUPTENT; BARRACKS, QUARTERS
soldier's shelter / TRENCH; FOXHOLE
soldiers side by side / RANK
soldier's weapon / GUN; LANCE, RIFLE, SABER; BAYONET, CARBINE, GRENADE
soldiery / MILITARY
sole / LONE, MERE, ONLY. VOLA; PELMA; FLATFISH
sole of foot, pert. to / VOLAR; PLANTAR
sole of plow / SLADE
solecism / BLUNDER; IMPROPRIETY
solely / ALONE; SINGLY
solemn / AWFUL, GRAND, GRAVE, STAID

solemn assent / AMEN
solemn assertion / VOW; OATH
solemnity / GRAVITY; CEREMONY
solicit / ASK, BEG, BID, SUE, WOO; PRAY, TOUT, URGE
solicit insistently / IMPORTUNE
solicit stubbornly / ENTREAT
solicit urgently / IMPLORE
solicit votes / CANVASS
solicitor / LAWYER; ATTORNEY
solicitor's chamber / INN
solicitous / ANXIOUS, CAREFUL
solicitude / CARE; ANXIETY, CONCERN
solid / FIRM, HARD; DENSE, GRAVE; STABLE. CONE, CUBE; PRISM
solid, c.f. / STEREO
solid alcohol / STERIN, STEROL
solid figure / CONE, CUBE; PRISM; CYLINDER; POLYHEDRON
solid food / MEAT; BREAD; POTATO
solidified fat / LARD, SUET; TALLOW
solidified mass / CAKE
solidify / GEL, SET; FREEZE, HARDEN
solidity / TRUTH; DENSITY
soliloquy / MONOLOGUE
solipsist / EGOIST
solitary / LONE, SOLE; LONELY, SINGLE. HERMIT
solitary, c.f. / EREM
solitary person / LONER
solitude / PRIVACY; SECLUSION
solo / ARIA. ALONE
Solomon's colleague / HIRAM
Solmons island / BUKA, SAVO; RENDOVA; GUADALCANAL
Solomon's successor / REHOBOAM
solon / SAGE; LAWMAKER
soluble / SOLVABLE; DISSOLUBLE
solution / KEY; ANSWER, LIQUID; MIXTURE
solution leached from ash / LYE
solution's strength / TITER
solve / UNFOLD; EXPLAIN, UNRAVEL
solvent / SOLID, SOUND
soma / BODY, HOMA; HAOMA
somalia capital / MOGADISHU
Somaliland gum / MATTI
somatic / CORPOREAL
somber / SAD; DARK; DUSKY, MURKY, SABLE
sombrero / HAT
sombrous / CLOUDY, GLOOMY
some / ANY, FEW; WHEEN
some person / ONE; SOMEBODY
somebody / VIP; SOMEONE
somehow / SOMEWAY
someplace different / ELSEWHERE
somersault / FLIP, LEAP; SOMERSET

something added / INSET; INSERT
something attached / TAG
something attractive / SHOW
something detrimental / SNAG; BLEMISH
something gratifying / BEAUTY
something that injures / DETRIMENT
something old / RELIC; ROUTINE
something owed / DEBT
something owned / ASSET
something to be done / AGENDUM
something unusual / NOVELTY
something urgent / MUST
something very easy / PIE; SNAP
sometime / ONCE; FORMER
somewhat / KIND OF, RATHER, SORT OF
somewhat vague / DIM; HAZY; OBSCURE
somewhere / ABOUT; NEARLY
somite / MEROSOME, METAMERE
somnambulist / SLEEPWALKER
somnolence / TRANCE
somnolent / DROWSY; OSCITANT
Somnus' aide / MORPHEUS
Somnus' father / EREBUS
Somnus' mother / NOX, NYX
son / HEIR; SCION; PROGENY; OFFSPRING
son of, pref. / AP; MAC; FITZ
son of Adam / ABEL, CAIN, SETH
son of Amram / AARON, MOSES
son of Bela / ARD
son of Belial / REBEL; RIOTER
son of Benjamin / BELA
son of Chaos / EREBUS
son of Gad / ERI
son of Isaac / ESAU; JACOB; ISRAEL
son of Japheth / GOMER, MAGOG, TUBAL
son of Joktan / UZAL; JERAH, OPHIR
son of Kohath / AMRAM
son of Noah / HAM; SHEM; JAPHETH
son of Odysseus / TELEGONUS; TELEMACHUS
son of Reuben / CARNI, PALLU
son of Seth / ENOS
son of Shem / ELAM
son of Simeon / SHAUL
sonance / SOUND
sonant / VOICED; SOUNDING
sonata movement / LARGO, RONDO; SCHERZO
song / AIR, LAY; ARIA, HYMN, LILT; CAROL, DITTY, LYRIC, MELOS, PSALM, TROLL; ANTHEM, BALLAD, STRAIN
song at awakening / AUBADE

song bird / TIT; LARK, WREN; VIREO; BULBUL, CANARY; WARBLER
song bird of India / SHAMA
song for Christmas / NOEL; CAROL
song for eight / OCTET
song for five / QUINTET
song for four / QUARTET; QUARTETTE
song of gaiety / LILT
song of grief / DIRGE
song for a group / CHORAL, CHORUS
song of joy / PAEAN; ANTHEM
song of a lover / SERENADE
song in opera / ARIA
song of praise / MAGNIFICAT
song for six / SEXTETTE
song for solo voice / AIR; ARIA
Song of Songs / CANTICLES
song for three / TRIO
song thrush / MAVIS; THROSTLE
song of triumph / PAEAN
song for two / DUO; DUET
song writer / COMPOSER
Songhai capital / TIMBUKTU
songlike / LYRICAL
songs / LIEDER
song's music / TUNE
song's words / LYRICS
songwriters' group / ASCAP
son-in-law / GENER
sonnet / LYRIC
sonnet division / OCTAVE, SESTET
sonnet pioneer / PETRARCH
sonnet series / SEQUENCE
Sonora tribe / JOVA, PIMA, SERI
sonorous / LOUD; CLEAR; RESONANT
sonorous instrument / BELL
sonship / FILIETY
soon / ANON; EARLY; BETIMES
Sooner State / OKLAHOMA
sooner than / ERE; BEFORE
soot / DIRT, SMUT; GRIME
sooth / TRUTH; REALITY
soothe / CALM, EASE, LULL; ALLAY
soothing / BALMY; LENITIVE
soothing agent / BALM; BALSAM
soothing drug / ANODYNE
soothing exclamation / AH; THERE
soothing treatment / RUB
soothing unguent / SALVE
soothsay / PREDICT; PROPHESY
soothsayer / SAGE, SEER; AUGUR; DIVINER; CHALDEAN
soothsaying / AUGURY; PROPHECY
sooty / INKY; BLACK; FULIGINOUS
sooty albatross / NELLY
sooty fumes / REEK; SMOKE
sop / DIP; SOAK; STEEP
sophism / FALLACY, QUIBBLE

sophisticate / SPOIL; DEBASE; VITIATE
sophisticated / ARTIFICIAL; WORLDLYWISE
Sophoclean hero / OEDIPUS
Sophoclean heroine / ELECTRA
sophomore / SOPH
sophomoric / SUPERFICIAL
Sophonisba's brother / HANNIBAL
Sophonisba's father / HASDRUBAL
Sophonisba's husband / SYPHAX
sopor / COMA; STUPOR
soporific / ANODYNE; NARCOTIC
soppy / WET; SOAKED
soprano / TREBLE
soprano / ALDA, BORI, PONS; SILLS; CALLAS; CABALLE
sora / RAIL
sorb / ROWAN; SERVICE
sorcerer / MAGUS; WIZARD; MAGICIAN
sorcerers / MAGI; MAGES
sorceress / HEX; CIRCE, LAMIA, WITCH
sorcery / OBE; MAGIC, OBEAH; VOODOO; GRAMARYE; ENCHANTMENT
sordid / BASE, FOUL, MEAN, VILE; SEAMY
sore / BOIL, HURT; ULCER; ABSCESS. TENDER, TOUCHY; PAINFUL
sorehead / GROUCH; MALCONTENT
soreness / VEXATION
sorghum / DARI, DURR, MILO; DURRA, SORGO; IMPHEE
sorites / ANA; HEAP; CHAIN
soroban / ABACUS
sorrel / BUCK; OXALIS
sorrow / RUE; MOURN; GRIEVE, REPINE, WOE; RUTH; DOLOR; REMORSE
sorrow for sin / PENANCE
sorrowful / SAD; BLUE; DOLENT
sorrowful cry / ALAS
sorrowful grievance / DISTRESS
sorrowful sinner / PENITENT
sorry / ABJECT; GRIEVED; CONTRITE
sorry state / WOE; DISTRESS
sort / CULL, SIFT; GRADE, ILK; KIND, TYPE
sortie / RAID, SALLY
sortilege / WITCHCRAFT
sorting process / TRIAGE
SOS call / MAYDAY
so-so / AVERAGE; MIDDLING; TOLERABLE
sot / TOPER; TIPPLER, TOSSPOT; DRUNKARD
Sotadic / PALINDROMIC
Sothis / SIRIUS

sottish / STUPID
sotto voce / SOFTLY
sou / COPPER
souari / BUTTERNUT
soubise / SAUCE
soubrette / COMIC; MAIDSERVANT
soucar / BANKER
souchong / TEA
souffle / FROTHY
sough / SIGH; RUSTLE
soul / FIRE, LIFE, MIND; ANIMA,
  ARDOR; PERSON, PNEUMA,
  SPIRIT
soul, c.f. / PSYCH
soulless / DULL; SPIRITLESS
sound / TRY; RING, TEST. TONE;
  NOISE. HALE, SANE; VALID;
  ENTIRE
sound, pert. to / SONIC
sound to attract attention / PST;
  AHEM
sound of automobile horn / BEEP,
  HONK
sound of bees / HUM; BUZZ; DRONE
sound of bell / DING, PEAL, TOLL
sound in body / HEALTHY
sound of contempt / HISS; WHISTLE
sound correspondence / RIME;
  RHYME
sound of disdain / SNORT
sound of loose piston / SLAP
sound loudly / BLARE, BLAST
sound of lung abnormality / RALE
sound measure / DB; PHON;
  DECIBEL
sound murmuringly / PUR; PURL,
  PURR
sound the ocean / PLUMB; FATHOM
sound of pain / MOAN; GROAN
sound ranging / SONAR
sound resemblance / ASSONANCE
sound of silk / RUSTLE
sound sonorously / RING
sound of a step / FOOTFALL
sound thought / LOGIC
sound of trumpet / BLARE
sound in Washington / PUGET
sound waves, pert. to / AUDIO,
  SONIC
sounding / SONANT; RESONANT
sounding device / SONDE
soundness / SANITY; STRENGTH
sound-sensing organ / EAR
soup / BISK; BROTH, PUREE;
  BISQUE; POTTAGE· BOUILLON
soup basis / OKRA; RICE; STOCK;
  BARLEY, POTAGE; CHICKEN
soup bowl / TUREEN
soup dipper / LADLE
soupçon / HINT; TASTE, TRACE
soupfin shark / TOPE
sour / BAD, SAD; ACID, TART;
  ACERB, ACRID, SHARP; ACIDIC

sour ale / ALEGAR
sour in aspect / DOUR
sour grass / OXALIS, SORREL
sour gum tree / TUPELO
sour milk beverage / LABAN,
  LEBEN; YOGURT; MATZOON
sour substance / ACID
source / FONT, ROOT, SEED;
  ORIGIN
source of cocaine / COCA
source of heat / GAS, SUN; COAL,
  ETNA, FIRE, FUEL; STEAM
source of help / AID; RESOURCE
source of iodine / KELP
source of light / SUN; LAMP
source of linen / FLAX
source of metal / ORE
source of ore / MINE
source of perfume / FLOWER
source of poi / TARO
source of power / ATOM; MOTOR;
  GENERATOR
source of sugar / CANE, BEET
source of vegetable oil / OLIVE;
  PEANUT
source of water / WELL; SPRING
source of wealth / MINE; GOL-
  CONDA
sourdough / OLDTIMER; PROS-
  PECTOR
soured wine / VINEGAR
sourish / ACESCENT
sourness / RANCOR
soursop / ANNONA
sour-tasting / ACERB, ACRID
sour-tempered / CROSS
souse / WET; DRENCH, PICKLE.
  SOT
South African / BOER
South African animal / KUDU;
  RATEL, ZORIL; ZORILLA;
  SURICATE
South African antelope / GNU;
  ELAND, ORIBI; GEMSBOK,
  SASSABY
South African armed troops / IMPI
South African bustard / PAAUW
South African club / KIRI; STICK;
  KNOBKERRIE
South African colonist / BOER
South African corn / MEALIE
South African dialect / TAAL
South African Dutch / BOER, TAAL
South African fish / ACARA
South African fox / ASSE; CAAMA
South African gazelle / SPRINGBOK
South African gold area / RAND
South African hill / KOP; BULT
South African hillock / KOPJE
South African legislature / RAAD
South African monkey VERVET
South African native / THO; ZULU;
  BANTU, KAFIR, SOTHO

South African novelist / PATON
South African open country / VELDT
South African parley / INDABA
South African plateau / KARROO
South African poet / CAMPBELL
South African province / TRANS-
VAAL
South African ravine / DONGA
South African rawhide / RIEM
South African skin garment /
KAROSS
South African snake / ELAPS;
BOOMSLANG
South African spear / ASSAGAI,
ASSEGAI
South African tree / ASSEGAI
South African tribesman / ZULU;
BANTU
South African village / DORP;
KRAAL
South African vulture / LAMMER-
GEIER
South African yoke bar / SKEY
South American animal / APAR,
CAVY; APARA, COATI, LLAMA,
TAPIR, TAYRA; JUPARA; KINKA-
JOU, TAMANDUA
South American armadillo / TATU
South American arrow poison /
CURARE
South American bat / DESMODUS
South American bean / TONKA
South American beverage / MATE;
YERBA
South American bird / ARA; COIN,
GUAN, JACU, MITU; AGAMI,
SYLPH, TURCO; CONDOR, JA-
BIRU; HOATZIN, SERIEMA, TINA-
MOU; CURASSOW, TERUTERO;
CHACHALACA
South American cape / HORN
South American cat / EYRA, PUMA;
KODKOD, MARGAY, OCELOT;
JAGUARONDI
South American city / ICA, ITA;
PARA; BAHIA, QUITO, SUCRE
South American country / PERU;
CHILE; BRAZIL, GUYANA; BO-
LIVIA, ECUADOR, SURINAM, URU-
GUAY; COLOMBIA; PARAGUAY;
ARGENTINA, VENEZUELA
South American cowboy / GAUCHO;
LLANERO
South American crocodile / CAI-
MAN, CAYMAN
South American dance / SAMBA,
TANGO
South American deer / PITA
South American dolphin / BOTO
South American drink / MATE
South American dry wind / PAM-
PERO
South American eel / CARAPO

South American estuary / PLATA
South American fish / ISPE, LISA;
ACARA; AIMARA, CARIBE, LAU-
LAU; PIRANHA; ARAPAIMA,
PIRARUCU
South American flightless bird /
EMU; RHEA
South American fox / CULPEO
South American guinea pig / CAVY
South American hat / JIPIJAPA
South American hawk / CARACARA
South American insectivore / AYRE
South American lake / MIRIM, POO-
PO; TITICACA
South American lapwing / TERU-
TERO
South American lasso / BOLAS
South American lizard / TEJU;
JACUARU
South American marmoset / TITI;
TAMARIN
South American medicine man /
MAMA, PAGI, PEAI, PIAY
South American monkey / TITI;
PREGO, SAJOU; NACHIN; OUA-
KARI, SAPAJOU
South American motmot / HOUTOU
South American mountains /
ANDES
South American ocelot / KUICHUA
South American opossum / GAMBA,
QUICA; SARIGUE
South American oxalis / OCA
South American palm / JIPIJAPA
South American peak / ACON-
CAGUA
South American pig / PECCARY
South American plains / LLANOS,
PAMPAS, SELVAS
South American rabbit / TAPETI
South American region / CHACO;
PATAGONIA
South American reptile / TEJU;
CAYMAN; ANACONDA, JARA-
RACA
South American river / APA, ICA;
ACRE, BENI, PARA; PLATA; AMA-
ZON, JAPURA; ORINOCO
South American rodent / CUI; CAVY,
DEGU, MARA, PACA; CUTTA,
JOCHI, RATEL, TAPIR; AGOUTI;
ABROCAMA, CAPYBARA, TUCO-
TUCO, VISCACHA
South American rubber / PARA
South American ruminant / LLAMA;
ALPACA, VICUNA; GUANACO
South American serpent / BOA;
ABOMA
South American shrub / JABO-
RANDI
South American sloth / PERICO
South American swampland /
CHACO

South American tick / CARRAPATO
South American tiger cat / MARGAY
South American tree / MORA, VERA;
  BALSA, CAROB, CEBIL, FOTUI
South American tribe / GE; ITE,
  JES, ONA, URO, URU, YAO;
  BORO, BOTO, CAME, CARA,
  CHOL, DIAU, DUIT, INCA, ITZA,
  IXIL, IXLI, LECA, LULE, MAKU,
  MAYA, MIXE, MOJO, MOXO,
  MURA, MUSO, MUZO, PANO,
  PAYA, PIRO, PURI, PURU, RAMA,
  TAMA, TOBA, TUPI, ULVA, URAN,
  VOTO; ACROA, ANDOA, ARAUA,
  CARIB, CHOCO, CHOLO, GUANA,
  INERI, KICHE, PIPIL, SIUSI; ARA-
  WAK, COLIMA, ZAPARO
South American tuber / OCA
South American turtle / MATAMATA
South American ungulate / TAPIR
South American vulture / URUBU;
  CONDOR
South American weasel / TAYRA;
  GRISON
South American wildcat / EYRA;
  YAGUARUNKI
South Arabian country / SHEBA
south Asian owl / UTUM
south Asian ox / KOUPREY
south Asian peninsula / MALAYA
south Asian vessel / PROA
South Australia capital / ADELAIDE
South Australia lake / EYRE
South Australia river / MURRAY
South Bend's pride / IRISH
South Carolina capital / COLUMBIA
South Carolina Indian / CATAWBA
South Carolina nickname / PAL-
  METTO
South Carolina river / EDISTO, PEE-
  DEE, SANTEE
South Carolina state tree / PAL-
  METTO
South Dakota capital / PIERRE
South Dakota mountain / HARNEY;
  RUSHMORE
South Dakota nickname / COYOTE;
  SUNSHINE
South Dakota state flower /
  PASQUE
South European / SERB; GREEK
South European peninsula / ITALY;
  GREECE
south of France / MIDI
South Italian peninsula / CALABRIA
South Pacific boat / PROA
South Pacific island / BALI; BIKINI,
  TAHITI; PITCAIRN; GUADAL-
  CANAL
South Seas albatross / MOLLY-
  MAWK
South Seas islander / KANAKA
South Seas megapode / MALEO

south wind / BISE; NOTUS; AUSTER
Southeast Treaty Organization /
  SEATO
southeast wind / EURUS; SOLANO
southerly / SOUTHWARD
southern / AUSTRAL; MERIDIONAL
Southern Alps peak / AORANGI
Southern California desert / MO-
  JAVE; COLORADO
Southern California Indian / MO-
  HAVE, MOJAVE
southern constellation / CRUX,
  VELA; DORADO
Southern Cross / CRUX
southern cuckoo / ANI
southern fruit / DATE; GUAVA,
  MANGO, PAPAW
southern pronoun / YALL; YOUALL
Southern Rhodesia capital / SALIS-
  BURY
Southern Rhodesia river / SABI;
  LIMPOPO
southern Slav / SLOVENE
Southern states / DIXIE; CON-
  FEDERACY
southpaw / LEFTY; LEFTHANDER
southwest wind / AFER
Southwestern Indian / HOPI; NAVA-
  HO, NAVAJO, PUEBLO
souvenir / RELIC; MEMENTO
sovereign / KING; QUID; CHIEF,
  POUND, RULER; PRINCE. REGAL,
  ROYAL; SUPREME; IMPERIAL
sovereign's decree / ARRET
sovereign's home / PALACE
sovereignty / EMPERY, EMPIRE;
  DOMINION
soviet / COUNCIL
Soviet news agency / TASS
Soviet newspaper / PRAVDA;
  IZVESTIA
Soviet Russia / USSR
sovietist / COMMUNIST
sow / SEED; PLANT, STREW. GILT;
  SWINE
sow bug / SLATER; WOODLOUSE
sowens / PORRIDGE
sown / SEME
spa / BATHS; SPRING
spa in England / BATH
spa in France / VICHY
spa in Germany / EMS; BADEN
space / AREA, ROOM, VOID; FIELD;
  EXTENT; EXPANSE; INTERVAL
space, pert. to / SPATIAL
space agency / NASA
space between beams / METOPE
space enough / ELBOWROOM
space exhausted of air / VACUUM
space filled with matter / PLENUM
space from place to place / DIS-
  TANCE
space in a sieve / MESH

SOVIET UNION, CONSTITUENT REPUBLICS OF, AND THEIR CAPITALS

Constituent Republic	Capital
Armenian	EREVAN (YEREVAN)
Azerbaijan	BAKU
Byelorussian	MINSK
Estonian	TALLINN
Georgian	TBILISI (TIFLIS)
Kazakh	ALMAATA
Kirghiz	FRUNZE
Latvian	RIGA
Lithuanian	VILNIUS (VILNA)
Moldavian	KISHINEV
Russian SSR	MOSCOW (MOSKVA)
Tadzhik	DUSHANBE
Turkmen	ASHKHABAD
Ukrainian	KIEV
Uzbek	TASHKENT

Autonomous Republic	Capital
Abkhaz	SUKHUMI
Adzhar	BATUMI
Bashkir	UFA
Buryat	ULANUDE
Chechen-Ingush	GROZNY
Chuvash	CHEBOKSARY
Dagestan	MAKHACHKALA
Kabardian-Balkar	NALCHIK
Kalmyk	ELISTA
Kara-Kalpak	NUKUS
Karelian	PETROZAVODSK
Komi	SYKTYVKAR
Mari	IOSHKAROLA
Mordvinian	SARANSK
Nakhichevan	NAKHICHEVAN
North Ossetian	ORDZHONIKIDZE
Tatar	KAZAN
Tuva	KYZYL
Udmurt	IZHEVSK
Yakut	YAKUTSK

---

space above stage / FLIES

space surrounding a home / LAWN, YARD

space of time / TERM

spacecraft / APOLLO, GEMINI; MARINER

spaceman / ASTRONAUT, COSMONAUT

spacious / VAST, WIDE; BROAD, ROOMY

spade / DIG. SPUD; SHOVEL

spade for peat / SLADE, SLANE

spade for post holes / LOY

spade-shaped / PALACEOUS

spaghetti / PASTA

spagyrist / ALCHEMIST

Spain / ESPANA, IBERIA. See also Spanish

spall / CHIP; SPLINTER

spalpeen / RASCAL

span / ARCH, AREA, PAIR, YOKE; BRIDGE

span of oxen / TEAM

span of years / AGE

spang / JUST; RIGHT; SQUARELY

spangle / SHINE; GLITTER

spaniel / COCKER; SPRINGER

Spanish / IBERIAN; CASTILIAN

Spanish admiral / CERVERA

Spanish area measure / VARA

Spanish ball game / PELOTA; JAI-ALAI

Spanish bay / BISCAY

Spanish bayonet / YUCCA

Spanish bean / HABA; FREJOL, FRIJOL

Spanish beard / MOSS

Spanish belle / MAJA

Spanish cape / NAO; TRAFALGAR

Spanish capital city / MADRID

Spanish card game / OMBRE, PEDRO

Spanish cards / NAIPES

Spanish castle / ALCAZAR

Spanish cathedral city / SEVILLE
Spanish cellist / CASALS
Spanish chaperone / DUENA; DUENNA
Spanish cheer / OLE
Spanish chief / CID; JEFE
Spanish city / IRUN; CADIZ; OVIEDO, TOLEDO
Spanish coin / PESO, REAL; PESETA; CENTAVO
Spanish composer / FALLA
Spanish conqueror of Mexico / CORTES, CORTEZ
Spanish conquistador / ALMAGRO, PIZARRO
Spanish council / JUNTA
Spanish cowboy / GAUCHO; LLANERO
Spanish dance / JOTA; BAILE, TANGO; BOLERO; FANDANGO, GUARACHA
Spanish dictator / FRANCO
Spanish dish / PAELLA
Spanish doggerel verse / COPLAS
Spanish epic / CID
Spanish exclamation / OLE
Spanish explorer / BALBOA, CORTEZ; CABRILLO, CORONADO
Spanish fabric / CREA, LINO, RASO, SEDA
Spanish farm / HACIENDA
Spanish fascist party / FALANGE
Spanish general / ALVA
Spanish gentleman / DON; SENOR; CABALLERO
Spanish grand inquisitor / TORQUEMADA
Spanish grass / ESPARTO
Spanish grippe / FLU; INFLUENZA
Spanish gypsy / GITANO; ZINCALO
Spanish gypsy music / FLAMENCO
Spanish hat / SOMBRERO
Spanish head covering / MANTILLA
Spanish hero / CID
Spanish hogfish / LADYFISH
Spanish holiday / FIESTA
Spanish iris / XIPHIUM
Spanish islands / CANARIES; BALEARICS
Spanish juice / LICORICE
Spanish king / ALFONSO
Spanish kingdom / LEON; CASTILE
Spanish lady / DAMA, DONA; SENORA
Spanish language / CASTILIAN
Spanish legislature / CORTES
Spanish mackerel / CERO; WAHOO; SIERRA
Spanish Main seaman / MORGAN, PIRATE; FILIBUSTER
Spanish man / SENOR; HOMBRE

Spanish matron / SENORA
Spanish mayor / ALCALDE
Spanish means of execution / GARROTE
Spanish measure of area / VARA
Spanish measure of length / VARA; LINEA, PALMO, SESMA
Spanish measure of volume / ARROBA, FANEGA; CANTARA
Spanish money / PESETA
Spanish moss / EPIPHYTE
Spanish mountains / PYRENEES
Spanish municipal officer / ALCALDE
Spanish musical instrument / GUITAR; CASTANET; TAMBOURINE
Spanish musical show / ZARZUELA
Spanish mystic / TERESA
Spanish nobleman / GRANDEE, HIDALGO
Spanish novelist / GONGORA; CERVANTES
Spanish oath / CARAMBA
Spanish oyster / PINNA
Spanish painter / DALI, GOYA, MIRO, SERT; PICASSO
Spanish palace / ESCORIAL
Spanish pear / AVOCADO
Spanish peninsula / IBERIA
Spanish pepper / CHILI; PIMENTO
Spanish pianist / ITURBI
Spanish plantation / HACIENDA
Spanish playwright / LOPE, VEGA; TIRSO; ALARCON
Spanish poet / LORCA; BECQUER, MACHADO, VALLEJO
Spanish police / RURALES
Spanish popular song / COPLA
Spanish pot / OLLA
Spanish province / AVILA; GRANADA
Spanish queen / ISABELLA
Spanish river / EBRO, MINO; DUERO, JICAR
Spanish saint / TERESA; DOMINIC; IGNATIUS
Spanish seaport / PALOS; MALAGA; ALICANTE
Spanish shepherd's coat / ZAMARRA
Spanish song of penitence / SAETA
Spanish soprano / BORI
Spanish soup / GAZPACHO
Spanish surrealist / DALI
Spanish sword / BILBO; TOLEDO
Spanish title of address / DON; SENOR; SENORA; SENORITA
Spanish waiter / MOZO
Spanish wine / LIRIA; MALAGA, RIOJAS, SHERRY; MANZANILLA; AMONTILLADO

Spanish young lady / SENORITA

Spanish-American barroom / CANTINA

Spanish-American corn cake / AREPA; TORTILLA

Spanish-American corn dish / TAMALE

Spanish-American farm / MILPA; CHACRA, RANCHO; ESTANCIA, HACIENDA

Spanish-American plain / LLANO, PAMPA

Spanish-American shawl / MANTA; SERAPE

Spanish-American war hero / TR; DEWEY; HOBSON

spank / SLAP, WHIP

spanned / UNITED; BRIDGED

spanner / WRENCH

spar / BOOM, GAFF, MAST, YARD; SPRIT; STEEVE. BOX; FIGHT

spar end / ARM

spar for flag / GAFF

spar to stow cargo / STEEVE

sparable / SHOENAIL

spare / GIVE, SAVE. LANK, LEAN, SLIM; GAUNT; MEAGER

spare time / LEISURE

sparge / ASPERGE; SPRINKLE

sparing / CHARY, FRUGAL

spark / ARC; BEAU, FUNK. FLASH

sparkish / GAY; GAUDY, SHOWY

sparkle / FLASH, GLEAM; GLISTEN, GLITTER; CORUSCATE; SCINTILLATE

sparkled / SHONE; TWINKLED

sparkler / DIAMOND; FIREWORK

sparkling / BUBBLY, STARRY; VIVACIOUS

sparkling wine / MOUSSEUX, SPUMANTE. CHAMPAGNE

sparoid fish / TAI; SCUP; BREAM, PORGY, SARGO

sparrow hawk / KESTREL

sparse / THIN; MEAGER, SCANTY

sparseness / SCARCITY

spart / BROOM; ESPARTO

Sparta / LACEDAEMON

Spartacist / LIEBKNECHT

Spartan / HARDY, STOIC; SEVERE

Spartan dog / BLOODHOUND

Spartan king / AGIS; LEONIDAS, MENELAUS

Spartan lawgiver / LYCURGUS

Spartan magistrate / EPHOR

Spartan serf / HELOT

Sparta's region / LACONIA

spasm / FIT, TIC; JERK; ICTUS, THROE

spasmodic / CONVULSIVE

spasmodic breath / GASP, PANT

spasmodic cramp / CRICK

spasmodic exhalation / COUGH; SNEEZE

spastic / TETANIC

spat / ROW; TIFF; GAITER

spate / RUSH; FLOOD; FRESHET

spatter / SPLASH; SPRINKLE

spatterdash / GAITER; LEGGING

spatula / KNIFE; TROWEL; SPREADER

spavined / LAME; BROKENDOWN

spawn / OVA, ROE; EGGS

spay / CASTRATE

speak / SAY; TALK; ORATE, UTTER, VOICE

speak abruptly to / SNAPAT

speak like an actor / EMOTE

speak affectedly / MINCE

speak angrily / SNARL

speak in behalf of / PLEAD

speak in command / DICTATE

speak with contempt / SNEER

speak in defense / PLEAD

speak didactically / PREACH

speak with emphasis / ACCENT, STRESS

speak first / GREET; ACCOST

speak haltingly / HAW; STAMMER, STUTTER

speak imperfectly / LISP

speak inaudibly / MUTTER

speak indistinctly / MUMBLE

speak injuriously / LIBEL; DEFAME

speak lazily / DRAWL

speak in low tones / MURMUR; WHISPER

speak from memory / RECITE

speak nasally / WHINE; SNUFFLE

speak of in passing / MENTION

speak of slightingly / DECRY; DISPARAGE

speak publicly / ANNOUNCE

speak quietly / MURMUR

speak in a showy manner / ORATE; DECLAIM

speak sibilantly / HISS; WHISPER

speak to / ADDRESS

speak together / CHAT; CONVERSE

speak very distinctly / ARTICULATE

speak violently / RAGE, RAVE

speaker / ORATOR; CHAIRMAN, LECTURER

speaker's platform / DAIS; STAGE

speaking affably / PHATIC

speaking art / RHETORIC

speaking several languages / POLYGLOT

speaking skill / ORATORY

speaking tube in plane / GOSPORT

spear / DART; LANCE; ASSAGAI, ASSEGAI, JAVELIN. STAB

spear a fish / GIG; GAFF

spear of grass / SPIRE, STALK

spear with three prongs / LEISTER, TRIDENT
spear thrower / ATLATL, WOMERA
spearfish / MARLIN; BILLFISH; SWORDFISH
spearlike weapon / PIKE
spear-shaped / HASTATE
spearwood / CURRAWANG
spearwort / CROWFOOT
special / EXPRESS; PARTICULAR
special ability / TALENT
special accomplishment / FORTE
special day / FEAST; HOLIDAY
special edition / EXTRA
special flavor / TANG
special group / ELITE; QUORUM
special management / TREATMENT
special support / PATRONAGE
special time / SEASON
special writer / COLUMNIST
specialize in / MAJOR
specially qualified / BLUERIBBON
specie / CASH, COIN; METAL, MONEY
species / KIND, SORT; CLASS
specific / DEFINITE; PARTICULAR
specific day / DATE, DDAY
specified epoch / AGE, ERA
specified time / DATE
specify / NAME; STATE; DEFINE
specimen / COPY, PART; MODEL; SAMPLE
specimen of cloth / SWATCH
specious / DECEPTIVE, PLAUSIBLE
speck / BIT, DOT, JOT; ATOM, MITE, MOTE, SOLE, SPOT; BACON, FLECK
speckle / DOT; STIPPLE
specs / EYEGLASSES
spectacle / SHOW; SCENE, SIGHT; PARADE; DISPLAY, PAGEANT
spectacles / SHADES; GLASSES; BIFOCALS
spectacular play / EXTRAVAGANZA
spectator / WITNESS; BYSTANDER
Spectator author / STEELE; ADDISON
specter / BOGY; GHOST, SHADE; SPIRIT, WRAITH; EIDOLON
spectral / WEIRD; GHASTLY, GHOSTLY
spectroscope lens / PRISM
spectrum / RANGE; RAINBOW
specular / METALLIC; REFLECTING
specular iron / OLIGIST; HEMATITE; SPIEGELEISEN
speculate / MUSE; TRADE; PONDER
speculation / RISK; SCHEME, THEORY; CONJECTURE
speculative / RISKY; THEORETICAL
speculative enterprise / VENTURE
speculum / MIRROR; DILATOR; REFLECTOR

sped / RAN; FLEW
speech / TALK; VOICE; ADDRESS
speech, c.f. / LALO, LOGO
speech, pert. to / VOCAL
speech of abuse / TIRADE
speech with an accent / DIALECT
speech center / CORTEX
speech defect / LISP; APHASIA, STAMMER, STUTTER; LALLATION
speech defect, c.f. / LALIA
speech disorder, c.f. / PHASIA
speech form / IDIOM
speech loss / APHASIA
speech of some length / SPIEL
speech sound / PHONE; PHONEME
speechify / HARANGUE
speechless / DUMB, MUTE; SILENT
speed / HIE, RUN; RACE, RUSH. HASTE; CELERITY, VELOCITY
speed car / RACER
speed contest / RACE
speed control / TIMING
speed regulator / GOVERNOR
speed of sound / MACHONE
speed up motor / REV; RACE
speed-checking device / RADAR
speedily / FAST; APACE
speedy / FAST; FLEET, QUICK
speer / ASK; INQUIRE, PROPOSE
spell / FORM; RELIEVE. CHARM; INCANTATION
spell of duty / SHIFT, TRICK, WATCH
spellbinder / ORATOR, RHETOR
spellbound / FASCINATED
spelling / ORTHOGRAPHY
spelling contest / BEE
spelt / EMMER, WHEAT
spelter / ZINC. SOLDER
spelunker / TROGLODYTE
spend / EXPEND, LAVISH; DISBURSE
spend as a cost / DISBURSE
spend fully / EXHAUST
spend futilely / WASTE
spend lavishly / POUR; SQUANDER
spend time idly / LOITER
spendthrift / WASTREL
Spenser character / UNA; GUYON; BRITOMART
spent / TIRED; EFFETE; EXHAUSTED
sperm whale / CACHALOT
spet / SENET; BARRACUDA
spew / EJECT, VOMIT
sphagnum bog / MUSKEG
sphenic / CUNEATE; WEDGE-SHAPED
sphere / ORB; AREA, BALL; GLOBE
sphere of action / ARENA, FIELD
sphere of contest / OVAL, RING, RINK; COURT; FIELD; DIAMOND; GRIDIRON

sphere of duty / PLACE; STATION
spherical / ROTUND; GLOBULAR
spherical particle / GLOBULE
sphericity / ROUNDNESS
spheroid / BALL
sphincter / VALVE
sphingine / INSCRUTABLE
sphinx / ORACLE; MONSTER
sphinx's test / RIDDLE
sphygmoid / PULSELIKE
Spica's constellation / VIRGO
spicate / SPIKED; POINTED
spice / HERB, MACE, ZEST; CLOVE, CUMIN; GINGER; SAFFRON; SEASONING
Spice Islands / MOLUCCAS
spice mixture / CURRY; PICKLE
spick and span / FRESH; BRAND-NEW
spicknel / MEU, MEW; MEUM
spicule of sponge / OXEA, TOXA; DESMA
spicy / GAMY, RACY; PUNGENT
spider / TRIVET; SKILLET; ARACHNID
spider home / WEB
spider monkey / QUATA; ATELES, COAITA, KOAITA
spider's nest / NIDUS
spider's web / NET
spider-web fluid / ARANEIN
spied / SAW; SEEN; PEERED
spiel / TALK; PITCH; BALLYHOO
spiffy / TRIM; SMART
spigot / TAP; COCK; SPILE; FAUCET
spike / EAR, GAD; BROB, HEEL, NAIL; TRENAIL
spike of an antler / TINE
spike of flowers / AMENT
spiked / TINED
spiked helmet of German army / PICKELHAUBE
spikelet / SPICULE
spikelet in barley / AWN
spikenard / NARD
spiketail / PINTAIL
spikewood / TRENAIL
spile / BUNG, PLUG
spill / SHED, SLOP; TUMBLE. PEG; PLUG
spill the beans / INFORM
spillage / LEAKAGE
spillikin / JACKSTRAW
spin / REEL, TURN; TWIRL, WHIRL
spin on axis / GYRATE, ROTATE
spin floating log / BIRL
spin out / LENGTHEN, PROTRACT
spinal / RACHIAL; VERTEBRAL
spinal bone / VERTEBRA
spinal column / BACKBONE
spinal cord, pert. to / MYELOID
spinal curvature / LORDOSIS, KYPHOSIS; SCOLIOSIS

spinal membrane / DURA
spindle / COP; AXIS, AXLE; ARBOR; MANDREL
spindle roll / COP
spindrift / SPRAY
spine / THORN; PRICKLE; BACK-BONE
spine of book / BACK
spine section / SACRUM
spinel / GEM; RUBY; BALAS, INKLE
spineless / WEAK; VACILLATING
spineless cactus / CHAUTE
spinet / VIRGINAL; HARPSICHORD
spine-tipped / ARISTATE
spinner / MAYFLY; HARVESTMAN
spinney / SHAW; COPSE; THICKET
spinning arrow / VIRE
spinning center / AXIS
spinning machine / MULE; JENNY
spinning mill / SPINNERY
spinning motion / TURN; SWIRL, TWIRL
spinning nets / TELARY; RETIARY
spinning shaft / AXLE
spinning spider / WEAVER
spinning toy / TOP
spinning wheel rod / SPINDLE
spinose / SPINY
spinster / OLDMAID; FEMESOLE
spiny / THORNY; PRICKLY
spiny animal / TENREC; ECHIDNA; HEDGEHOG; PORCUPINE
spiny cactus / CHOLLA
spiny fish / GOBY; PERCH
spiny plant / THORN; CACTUS; BRAMBLE
spiracle / BLOWHOLE
spiral / COIL; HELIX; CURLICUE
spiral nebula / GALAXY
spiral ornament / VOLUTE
spiral staircase / CARACOLE
spiral staircase tread / WINDER
spirate / BREATHED; VOICELESS
spire / WHORL; SUMMIT; MINARET, STEEPLE
spire's ornament / EPI
spirit / AIR, ELF, VIM; DASH, ELAN, FIRE, LIFE, SOUL; ARDOR, DEMON, FORCE, HEART, POWER, VIGOR; BREATH, ENERGY, METTLE, TEMPER
spirit away / ABDUCT
spirit of a community / ETHOS
spirit of an era / GENIUS
spirit of evil / MARA; DEMON, DEVIL
spirit in human form / FAIRY, GHOST
spirit lamp / ETNA
spirit level indicator / BUBBLE
spirited / BOLD; FIERY; ARDENT
spirited horse / ARAB; STEED; COURSER

spiritedly opposed / ATILT
spiritist / MEDIUM
spiritless / DULL, MOPY; AMORT, VAPID
spirits of the dead / MANES
spirits and water / GROG; TODDY
spirits of wine / ALCOHOL
spiritual / HOLY; DIVINE; GHOSTLY
spiritual being / ENS; ESSENCE
spiritual exegesis / ANAGOGE
spiritual father / CONFESSOR
spiritual nourishment / MANNA
spiritual overseer / PASTOR
spiritualist / MEDIUM
spiritualist meeting / SEANCE
spirituous / DISTILLED
spirituous liquor / WINE; BRANDY; WHISKEY
spiritus / ASPIRATE
spiritus frumenti / WHISKEY
spiry / CURLED; TAPERING
spissitude / DENSITY; VISCOSITY
spit / ROD; IMAGE, POINT; SALIVA
spite / THWART. VENOM; MALICE, RANCOR
spiteful / DEFIANT; MALIGNANT, SPLENETIC
spiteful gossip / CAT
spiteful temper / SPLEEN
spitfire / JIB; PLANE, VIXEN
Spitsbergen / SVALBARD
spitting snake / COBRA
spittle / SALIVA, SPUTUM
spittoon / CUSPIDOR
splanchnic / VISCERAL
splash / LAP; DAUB; SPATTER
splatter / DAB; SPLASH
splatterer / COOT
splay / BEVEL, SLOPE; EXPAND, SPREAD. CLUMSY
spleen / GALL, MILT; SPITE
splendid / BRAW; GRAND, LOFTY, NOBLE, SHOWY; BRIGHT, SUPERB; SHINING
splendor / POMP; ECLAT, GLORY; RENOWN
splenetic / PEEVISH; MELANCHOLY
splice / JOIN; MARRY, UNITE
splicing pin / FID
spline / KEY; FEATHER
splint / STRIP; SPLINTER
splint bone / FIBULA
splinter / SPLIT; SHIVER. SLIVER; FLINDER; FRAGMENT
split / CHOP, REND, RIVE; BURST, CRACK. CLEFT
split asunder / RIVEN
split the difference / SHARE; COMPROMISE
split one's ears / DEAFEN
split hairs / CAVIL; QUIBBLE
split leather / SKIVE. SKIVER
split personality / SCHIZOPHRENIA

split pulse / DAL
split up / SEPARATE
splotch / BLOT, FOUL; STAIN
splurge / FUSS, SHOW; DISPLAY
splutter / ADO; STIR. SPUTTER
spoil / MAR, ROT; RUIN; ADDLE, DECAY. LOOT; BOOTY
spoilage / WASTE
spoiled / RUINED; VITIATED
spoiled, as an egg / ADDLED
spoiled paper / SALLE
spoils / BOOTY; PILLAGE
Spokane's area / INLANDEMPIRE
spoke / SAID; UTTERED. BAR; RUNG
spoken / ORAL; PAROL, VOCAL
spoken word / AGRAPH
spokeshave / DRAWINGKNIFE
spokesman / AGENT; EMISSARY
spoliate / ROB; DESPOIL
spoliation / RAPINE; PILLAGE, PLUNDER
sponge / CADGE, ERASE; ABSORB, EFFACE. LOOF; LOOFA
sponge spicule / OXEA, TOXA
sponger / SYCOPHANT
sponges, pert. to / PORIFEROUS
spongewood / SOLA
spongy / POROUS, SOAKED; SPRINGY
sponsalia / BETROTHAL
sponsion / PLEDGE; PROMISE
sponsor / BACKER, PATRON
sponsorless samurai / RONIN
sponsorship / AEGIS; PROTECTION
spontaneity / FREEDOM
spontaneous / FREE; UNBIDDEN, VOLUNTARY
spontaneous action / IMPULSE
spontaneous generation / ABIO-GENESIS
spontoon / BILLY; HALFPIKE
spoof / HOAX; DECEIVE, MISLEAD
spook / GHOST; SPECTER. BALK
spookish / EERIE, WEIRD
spooky / SCARY; HAUNTED
spool / REEL; BOBBIN; MANDREL
spool for thread / COP
spoon / LABIS, LADLE; DIPPER. BILL, NECK; NESTLE
spoonflower / YAUTIA
spoony / FOND; WEAKMINDED
spoor / TRACK, TRAIL
sporadic / APART; ISOLATED
spore / GERM, SEED
spore case / ASCUS, THECA
spore fruit / ASCOCARP
sport / FUN; GAME, JEST, JOKE; FROLIC; DERISION. RUX; PLAY; FRISK; DIVERT, GAMBOL. See also game
sport shirt / TEE; POLO
sportful / GAY; MERRY; PLAYFUL

sportive / JOLLY; FRISKY, WANTON
sports arena / OVAL, RINK; FIELD; STADIUM
sports club / CREW, TEAM
sports hall / GYM; GYMNASIUM
sports jacket / BLAZER
sports official / JUDGE; UMPIRE; REFEREE
sports shoe / LOAFER; SNEAKER
sports squad / CLUB, TEAM; VARSITY
sports team costume / UNIFORM
sports trousers / SLACKS
sportsman / BETTER; HUNTER
sportsman's aide / GILLIE
sportsmanship / FAIRPLAY
sportula / FEE; GIFT; LARGESS
sporty / LOUD; FLASHY
spot / ESPY; STAIN; DETECT. BLOT, FLAW, MARK, SITE; MACLE
spot on playing card / PIP
spotless / PURE; IMMACULATE
spotlight / ARC; NOTORIETY. HIGHLIGHT
spots on face / FRECKLES
spotted / PIED; MACLED; DAPPLED
spotted amphibian / FROG, NEWT
spotted animal / PARD; JAGUAR; LEOPARD
spotted butterfly / SATYR
spotted cat / OCELOT
spotted cavy / PACA
spotted with colors / PIED; VARIEGATED
spotted cow / BRINDLE
spotted deer / AXIS; CHITAL, FALLOW
spotted dog / DALMATIAN
spotted fever / TYPHUS; RICKETTSIOSIS
spotted fish / DRUM
spotted insect / LADYBIRD
spotted ray / OBISPO
spotter / SPY; PINBOY
spotting / STIPPLE
spotty / MACLED; IRREGULAR
spouse / MATE, WIFE; HUSBAND
spout / JET; EMIT, GUSH, POUR. FAUCET
spout hole / BLOWHOLE
spout for maple sap / SPILE
spout words / ORATE; DECLAIM
spouted vessel / KETTLE, TEAPOT; SPRINKLER
spouting oil well / GUSHER
spouting spring / GEYSER
sprain / STRAIN, WRENCH
sprain remedy / ARNICA
sprat / HERRING
sprawl / LOLL; SPREAD; STRETCH
spray / ATOMIZE. FOAM; WREATH
spray of flowers / CHAPLET, GARLAND

spray gun / ATOMIZER
spray phenomenon / RAINBOW
spread / EMIT, OPEN; BRUIT, FLARE; EXPAND, EXTEND, UNFURL. FEAST
spread about / DIFFUSE
spread abroad / AIR, SOW
spread for examination / UNFOLD
spread hay to dry / TED
spread irregularly / SPRAWL
spread out / FAN; DEPLOY
spread outward / SPLAY
spread by rumor / NOISE; GOSSIP
spread in size / INCREASE
spread by word of mouth / BRUIT
spreader / SEEDER
spree / BAT; BOUT, LARK; BINGE, DRUNK; FROLIC; CAROUSAL
sprig / BRAD, TWIG; SCION, SHOOT
spright / SPRITE
sprightliness / VIVACITY
sprightly / PERT; AGILE, ALERT, BRISK; ELFIN
sprightly cadence / SWING
sprightly song / LILT
spring / HOP; DART, FLOW, JUMP, LEAP, RISE; BOUND, VAULT. SPA; SEASON, SOURCE
spring, pert. to / VERNAL
spring back / RESILE; REBOUND
spring bird / ROBIN
spring chicken / FLEDGLING
spring festival / EASTER, MAYDAY
spring fever / INERTIA, LANGUOR
spring flower / LILAC, TULIP; CROCUS
spring harvest in India / RABI; RUBBEE
spring a leak / CRACK; DETERIORATE
spring month / MAY; APRIL, MARCH
spring up / RISE; APPEAR
springboard / BATULE; TRAMPOLINE
springbok / GAZELLE
springe / GIN; TRAP; SNARE
springlet / SEEP
springlike / VERNAL
springtail / INSECT; COLLEMBOLAN
springtime of life / YOUTH
springy / SPONGY; ELASTIC
sprinkle / DEG, WET; RAIN; SPARGE; DRIZZLE, SPATTER
sprinkle flour on / DREDGE
sprinkled in heraldry / SEME
sprinkler / SPRAY; ASPERGILLUM
sprinkling / ASPERSION
sprinkling ceremony / ASPERGES
sprint / RUN; DASH, RACE
sprit / BUD; SPROUT. SPAR
sprite / ELF, FAY, HOB, IMP, NIX; PIXY, PUCK; ARIEL, FAIRY, PIXIE; GOBLIN

sprite in Shakespeare / PUCK; ARIEL
sproat / FISHHOOK
sprocket / COG; TOOTH
sprout / BUD; GROW, PUSH; RAMIFY. CION, TWIG; SHOOT
sprout from root / RATOON
spruce / NEAT, TIDY, TRIG, TRIM; NATTY
sprue / THRUSH
spry / AGILE, BRISK; NIMBLE
spud / NAIL; SPADE; POTATO
spudder / BARKER
spume / FOAM; FROTH, SPRAY
spumoni / MOUSSE
spun / BIRLED; ROTATED
spun wool / YARN
spunk / PLUCK, SPARK; METTLE, TINDER
spunky / GRITTY; SPIRITED
spur / GOAD, URGE; IMPEL, PRICK. GAD; GAFF; BRANCH, CALCAR
spur into action / ROUSE; INCITE
spur maker / SPURRIER
spur of mountain / ARETE
spur track / SIDETRACK
spur wheel / ROWAL, ROWEL
spurge / WARTWEED; EUPHORBIA
spurious / FAKE; BOGUS, FALSE, SNIDE; FORGED
spurn / SCORN; REJECT; CONTEMN
spurred / CALCARATE
spurt / JET; GUSH; SPOUT; SQUIRT
spurwing / PLOVER
sputter / SPIT
sputum / SALIVA; SPITTLE
spy / VIEW; SCOUT; DETECT. TOUT; AGENT; INFORMER
spy out / CASE; RECONNOITER
spyglass / TELESCOPE
Spyri novel / HEIDI
squab / SOFA; PIGEON; OTTOMAN
squabble / SPAT; DISPUTE
squabby / FAT; THICKSET
squad / CREW, GANG; GROUP
squadron / ESCADRILLE
squadron commander / MAJOR
squadron unit / FLIGHT; DIVISION
squalid / FOUL, POOR; MANGY, NASTY
squalid section / SLUM; GHETTO
squall / CRY; BAWL. GUST, WIND
squall clouds / SCUD, RACK
squally / NOISY; STORMY
squalor / DIRT; FILTH; FOULNESS
squama / ALULA, SCALE; TEGULA
squamate / SCALY
squander / SPEND, WASTE; MISUSE
square / JUST, TRUE; HONEST; RECTILINEAR. BLOCK; PLAZA
square building column / PILASTER
square dance / REEL; LANCERS; QUADRILLE

square ecclesiastical cap / BIRETTA
square measure / AR; ARE; ACRE; SECTION
square molding / LISTEL
square number / FOUR, NINE; HUNDRED, SIXTEEN
square peg / MISFIT
square sail / LUG
square shooter / GOODGUY; TRUE-PENNY
square of turf / SOD
squared circle / RING; PUGILISM
square-hewn stone / ASHLAR
square-holed lace / LACIS
square-toed / FORMAL; PRECISE
squarrose / ROUGH
squash / MASH; CRUSH. PEPO; RACKETS
squash plant / GOURD; CUCURBIT
squat / CROUCH. DUMPY, THICK
squatter / NESTER; SETTLER
squaw's mate / SANNUP
squeak / CRY; SHRILL; CONFESS
squeaked / CREAKED
squeal / TELL; INFORM
squeamish / FINICAL; FASTIDIOUS
squeamy / QUEASY; NAUSEOUS
squeegee / BLADE, WIPER; BRAYER
squeeze / HUG, NIP; CRUSH, GRIPE
squeeze with finger and thumb / PINCH
squelch / SILENCE; SUPPRESS
squib / LAMPOON; FIREWORK
squid / INKFISH; CUTTLEFISH
squint / LEER; STRABISMUS
squint-eyed / CROSSEYED
squire / ESCORT; ESQUIRE, GALLANT
squirearchy / GENTRY
squirm / WRITHE; WRIGGLE
squirrel / SISEL; CHIPPY, SUSLIK; CHICKAREE
squirrel food / ACORN
squirrel fur / VAIR; CALABAR, CALABER
squirrel monkey / TITI; MARMOSET
squirrel shrew / TANA
squirrel-like marsupial / PHALANGER
squirrel-like rodent / DORMOUSE
squirrels, pert. to / SCIURINE
squirrel's nest / DRAY, DREY
squirt / SPURT
squirt gun / WATERPISTOL
squish / JAM. SQUASH
Sri Lanka / CEYLON; SERENDIB; TAPROBANE. See also Ceylon, Ceylonese
Sri Lanka capital / COLOMBO
Sri Lanka city / KANDY
Sri Lanka mountain / ADAMSPEAK; PIDURUTALAGALA
SRO play / HIT; SELLOUT

S-shaped / SIGMOID
S-shaped curve / ESS
S-shaped molding / OGEE
S-shaped object / ESS
stab / GORE, PINK; KNIFE, SPEAR; PIERCE
stab at / LUNGE
stabile / STEADY. SCULPTURE
stability / FIRMNESS
stabilize / EVEN; STEADY
stabilizer / GYRO, TAIL
stabilizing weight / BALLAST
stable / FIRM; FIXED, SOLID; LAST-ING. BARN, MEWS
stable compartment / STALL
stable keeper / AVENER; LIVERY-MAN
stableman / GROOM; OSTLER; HOSTLER
staccato / ABRUPT
stack / PILE; SHOCK; CHIMNEY
stack of hay / RICK
stadium / BOWL, OVAL; FIELD
stactometer / DROPPER, PIPETTE
staff / BAR, ROD; MACE, POLE, WAND; CUDGEL
staff of bishop / BACULUS, CROSIER
staff of life / BREAD
staff of office / MACE
staff officer / ADC; AIDE
Stafford river / TRENT
Stafford town / STOKE
stag / HART, MALE; SMOKER
stag party / SMOKER
stage / DAIS; PHASE. PRODUCE
stage, pert. to / SCENIC
stage canvas / SCENE
stage cloth / BACKDROP
stage direction / EXIT; ENTER; EXEUNT
stage drapery / CURTAIN
stage extra / SUPER
stage failure / FLOP; TURKEY
stage fittings / PROPS; SCENERY
stage function / ROLE
stage of history / ERA; EPOCH
stage of insect development / IN-STAR
stage of life / AGE; YOUTH; MATU-RITY
stage offering / PLAY; DRAMA, RE-VUE; COMEDY; MUSICAL, RE-CITAL, TRAGEDY
stage play / DRAMA
stage player / ACTOR; ACTRESS
stage signal / CUE; SENNET
stage for speaker / DAIS; PLAT-FORM
stage whisper / ASIDE
stagecoach of a kind / CONCORD
stagehand / SCENESHIFTER
stager / ACTOR; VETERAN

stagger / REEL, STOT, STUN; LURCH; TOTTER
staggered formation / ECHELON
staggers / GID; MEGRIMS
staging / SCAFFOLDING
stagirite / ARISTOTLE
stagnant / STILL; TORPID; SLUG-GISH
stagnation / STASIS, TORPOR
stag's cry / ROAR
stagy / UNREAL; ARTIFICIAL
staid / GRAVE, SOBER; DEMURE, SEDATE
stain / DYE, MAR; BLOT, SLUR, SOIL, SPOT, TASH; SHAME. STIGMA
stained / DIRTY; MARKED; DEFILED
stainless / PURE; IMMACULATE
stair / STEP; STEPS, STILE
stair part / RISER, TREAD
stair post / NEWEL
staircase / FLIGHT
staircase part / BALUSTER
stairway / FLIGHT; STAIRCASE
stairway to front door / PERRON
stake / BET; ANTE, PALE, POLE, RISK; WAGER; HAZARD
stakes race / CUP; OAKS; DERBY
stakes wagered / POT
stalactite of water / ICICLE
stale / OLD; FLAT, WORN; TRITE, VAPID
stalemate / IMPASSE; DEADLOCK
stale-smelling / MUSTY
Stalingrad formerly / TSARITSYN
Stalingrad now / VOLGOGRAD
stalk / STEM; HAULM, STIPE
stalk of flower / SCAPE; PEDICEL
stalk of grass / CULM; STRAW
stalk of sugarcane / RATOON
stalking horse / AMBUSH; SEMBLANCE
stall / STOP; BLOCK, EVADE. BOX, PEW; LOGE; BOOTH; MANGER
stall in mud / MIRE, STOG
stallion / STUD; ENTIRE
stalwart / TALL; BRAVE; BRAWNY
stamen's end / ANTHER
stamin / TAMMY; SACKCLOTH
stamina / TONE; STRENGTH; EN-DURANCE
staminal / BASIC, TONIC
stammel / RED; STAMIN
stammer / HAW, HEM; MANT; FAL-TER; STUTTER
stammerer's sound / ER
stamp / MARK, MOLD; BRAND. DIE; SIGIL
stamp of approval / OK
stamp collecting / PHILATELY
stamp of merit / CACHET
stamp out / EXTINGUISH
stamp pad / INKER

stamp sheet section / PANE
stamp upon / TREAD; TRAMPLE
stampede / PANIC; FLIGHT
stamping device / DIE
stamping ground / HANGOUT
stamping instrument / DATER
stamping machine / DATER, PRESS
stance / POSE; POSITION
stanch / FAST, FIRM; LOYAL. STEM
stanchless / INSATIABLE
stanchly / CONSTANTLY
stand / BEAR, HALT, REST; ARISE.
  BOOTH, STALL; TABORET
stand against / OPPOSE, RESIST
stand in awe of / FEAR
stand for a child / SPONSOR
stand for finjan / ZARF
stand for / ENDURE; REPRESENT
stand for hot plate / TRIVET
stand opposite / FACE
stand up / LAST, RISE
stand up for / SUPPORT
standard / PAR; FLAG, RULE, TYPE;
  MODEL; BANNER. NORMAL;
  CLASSIC
standard of concentration / TITER
standard golf score / BOGY; BOGEY;
  BOGIE
standard of measurement / UNIT
standard of perfection / IDEAL;
  PARAGON
standard of Roman legion / EAGLE
standard zone for time / GREEN-
  WICH
standardize / REGULARIZE
standby / STAPLE; SUBSTITUTE
stand-in / SUBSTITUTE
standing / RANK; GRADE; STATUS.
  ERECT, FIXED, UNCUT
standing dislike / GRUDGE
standing in heraldry / STATANT
standing open / AJAR
standing orders / RULES; BYLAWS
standoff / TIE; DEADLOCK
standout / TOP; EXCELLENT
standpoint / IDEA; ANGLE
stannotype / TINTYPE
stannum / TIN
stanza / STAVE, VERSE; STROPHE
stanza of six lines / SESTINA
stanza of two lines / DISTICH
staple / CHIEF; REGULAR. COM-
  MODITY
star / SUN; NOVA; ASTERISK;
  CELEBRITY, PENTAGRAM. See
  also bright star
star, pert. to / ASTRAL; SIDEREAL
Star of David / MAGENDAVID
star of the day / SUN
star diviner / ASTROLOGER
star group / HYADES; PLEIADES
star grouping / GALAXY, NEBULA;
  CONSTELLATION

star in heraldry / ETOILE; ESTOILE
star mica / PHLOGOPITE
star worship / SABAISM
starboard / RIGHT
starboard's opposite / PORT; LAR-
  BOARD
starch / SAGO; FARINA; CASSAVA;
  ARROWROOT; CARBOHYDRATE
starch from cuckoopint / ARUM
starched / FORMAL; STIFFENED
starchy / STIFF; UNBENDING
starchy root / PIA; TARO
star-crossed / UNFORTUNATE
stare / GAPE, GAZE, OGLE
stare amorously / OGLE
stare angrily / GLARE
stargazer / DREAMER; ASTRON-
  OMER
stark / BARE; RIGID, STIFF
stark-naked / BARE, NUDE
starless / DARK; BLACK
starlet / ACTRESS
star-like / BRIGHT; STELLATE
starling / HUIA, MYNA, PILE;
  GRACKLE; BLACKBIRD
starlite / ZIRCON
starred lizard / HARDIM
starry / SIDEREAL; SPARKLING
stars, pert. to / ASTRAL; STELLAR
Stars and Stripes / OLDGLORY
star-shaped / STELLATE
star-shaped mask / ASTERISK
star-spotted / SEME
start / JUMP, OPEN; BEGIN. ALARM,
  ONSET
start auto by hand / CRANK
start suddenly aside / SHY
starting line / SCRATCH
starting point / GERM; ORIGIN
startle / ALARM, SCARE, SHOCK
startling / EXCITING
starvation / WANT; FAMINE
starve / FAMISH, FREEZE;
  DEPRIVE
starved / HUNGRY; FAMISHED;
  EMACIATED
starveling / HUNGRY, PAUPER
starwort / ASTER; CHICKWEED
stasis / STANDSTILL
state / SAY; AVER, AVOW; ASSERT;
  DECLARE. POMP, RANK; NATION
state, pert. to / CIVIL
state of affairs / SITUATION
state in another way / REPHRASE
state of aversion / DISGUST
state of bliss / EDEN; ECSTASY,
  RAPTURE; PARADISE
state of disorder / MESS; CHAOS
state of equality / PAR
state of fulfillment / FRUITION
state fully / SPECIFY
state by items / LIST
state of mind / MOOD; SPIRIT

state on oath / VOW; SWEAR; DE-
POSE
stated / REGULAR
statehouse / CAPITOL
stateliness / DIGNITY; SPLENDOR
stately / GRAND, NOBLE, REGAL;
AUGUST
stately home / PALACE; MANSION
stately lilies / CALLAS
statement / DICTUM; ASSERTION;
DECLARATION
statement of belief / CREDO,
CREED; ARTICLES
statement of goods shipped / IN-
VOICE, WAYBILL
state's chief executive / GOVERNOR
statesman / POLITICIAN
static / NOISE. MOTIONLESS
statim / ATONCE; IMMEDIATELY
station / BASE, POST, RANK;
CLASS, DEPOT, PLACE
stationary / FIXED, STILL; STABLE
stationary part / STATOR
stationed / BASED; ASSIGNED
stationery / PENS; PAPER; PENCILS
statistician / ACTUARY
statoscope / BAROMETER
statuary / SCULPTURE
statue / IMAGE; SCULPTURE
statue maker / SCULPTOR
statue by Michelangelo / DAVID,
PIETA
statue at Rhodes / COLOSSUS
statue by Rodin / KISS; THINKER
statue at Thebes / MEMNON
statue of the Virgin Mary /
MADONNA
statue's lover / PYGMALION
stature / RANK; HEIGHT; STAND-
ING
status / RANK; PLACE
statute / ACT, LAW; DECREE; ORDI-
NANCE
staunch / TRUE; STANCH
staurolite / CROSSTONE
stave / LAG; STAFF, STRIP, VERSE;
CUDGEL
stave off / STALL
stay / STOP, WAIT; ABIDE, CHECK.
BAR; PROP, TACK
stay for / WAIT; AWAIT
stay rope / GUY
staying power / STAMINA
stays / CORSET
stead / LIEU; PLACE
steadfast / FIRM, TRUE; STANCH
steadfastness / FIDELITY
steady / FIXED, SOBER; REGULAR
steady pace / TROT
steadying support / GUY; VANG
steak / CHUCK, FILET, ROUND,
SLICE, TBONE; SIRLOIN
steak hammer / TENDERIZER

steal / COP, ROB; GLOM, TAKE;
FILCH, SWIPE; PILFER, SNITCH,
THIEVE; PURLOIN
steal cattle / RUSTLE
steal game / POACH
steal a march on / FORESTALL
stealth / SECRECY
stealthy / SLY; FURTIVE
steam / OAM; MIST; FORCE, VAPOR;
ENERGY
steam, c.f. / ATMO
steam box / AGER
steam engine / TURBINE; EOLI-
PILE; LOCOMOTIVE
steam pipe / RISER
steamboat / PACKET
steamer / LINER; VESSEL
steamer chair / DECKCHAIR
steaming / FUMING; SMOKING
steamy / HOT; WARM; VAPOROUS
stearin / LARD; TALLOW
steatite / TALC; SOAPSTONE
steed / HORSE; CHARGER
steel / HARDEN. SWORD
steel band / TACE; TASSE
steel beam / IBAR; GIRDER
steel made in India / WOOTZ
steel process / BESSEMER
steel-clad / ARMORED
steelhead / TROUT
steely / HARD; PIERCING
steelyard / SCALE
steep / DIP, RET, SOP; SOAK; IM-
BUE. SHEER; ABRUPT
steep in brine / PICKLE
steep cliff / PRECIPICE
steep descent / CLIFF, SCARP
steep falls / CASCADE
steep jutting rock / CRAG
steep slope / SCARP; ESCARPMENT
steep in vinegar / MARINATE
steeple / SPIRE, TOWER; TURRET
steeple headdress / HENNIN
steeplechase / CROSSCOUNTRY
steeplejack / CLIMBER
steeple's point / EPI; FINIAL
steeps flax / RETS, ROTS
steep-sided hill / BUTTE
steer / CON; CONN, HELM; GUIDE,
PILOT. OX; STOT; BULLOCK
steering apparatus / HELM;
WHEEL; RUDDER, TILLER
steersman / COX; PILOT; HELMS-
MAN
steeve / LOAD, PACK, STOW
stein / MUG; TANKARD
steinbok / STEENBOK
stela / SLAB; GRAVESTONE
stellar / ASTRAL, STARRY
stellar emanation / BLAS
stem / DAM; STOP; CHECK;
BREAST. HALM, PROW; HAULM,
SCAPE, STALK

stem of climbing plant / BINE
stem decoration on goblet / KNOP
stem of flower / PEDICEL
stem from / DERIVE; DESCEND
stem of grass / CULM
stem of leaf / PETIOLE
stem of mushroom / STIPE
stem of palm / RATTAN
stem of plant / CAULIS
stem of rattan / CANE
stem of twining plant / BINE
stemless / SESSILE
stemple / STEP; CROSSBAR
stench / ODOR; FETOR, STINK
stenography / TYPING; SHORT-HAND
stenosis / NARROWING
stentorian / LOUD
step / PACE, WALK; TREAD. GAIT; PHASE, STAIR; DEGREE
step for crossing fence / STILE
step dance / CLOG; TAPDANCE
step in dancing / PAS; CHASSE
step heavily / TREAD; TRAMPLE
step of ladder / RIME, RUNG
step lightly / TIPTOE
step of rope ladder / RATLINE
step in a series / GRADE
step by step / SLOWLY; CAREFULLY
step up to the mark / TOE
step up a motor / REV
steppe / VELD; PLAIN; PRAIRIE; GRASSLAND
steppes storm / BURAN
stereo / HIFI
stereoscope / BINOCULAR
stereotyped / TRITE; HACKNEYED
steric / SPACIAL, SPATIAL
sterile / BARREN; UNFRUITFUL
sterile female calf / FREEMARTIN
sterilize / GELD, SPAY; NEUTER
sterilized man / EUNUCH
sterilizing operation / VASECTOMY
sterlet / STURGEON
sterling / PURE; SOUND; GENUINE
stern / GRIM; HARSH, RIGID; STRICT; AUSTERE
Sterne hero / SHANDY
sternmost / REARMOST
sternum / BREASTBONE
sternutatory / SNEEZING
sternutatory medicine / ERRHINE
sternway / BACKWARD
sterol / ALCOHOL
stertor / SNORE
stet / KEEP; RETAIN
stethoscope / AUSCULTATOR
stevedore / LOADER, PACKER, STOWER; LONGSHOREMAN
stew / BOIL, FRET; SEETHE, SIMMER. RAGOUT; GOULASH, PASHOFA; MULLIGAN
steward / MANAGER; CUSTODIAN

stewardess / HOSTESS
stewardship / TRUST; RESPONSI-BILITY
stewed / DRUNK; SEETHED
sthenia / STRENGTH
Stheno's sister / MEDUSA
stich / LINE; VERSE
stick / GLUE, HOLD, STAB, STAY, WAIT; PASTE; ADHERE. BAR, BAT, ROD; CANE, POLE, WAND; BATON
stick around / WAIT
stick by / SUPPORT
stick it out / PERSIST
stick in the mud / MIRE. TORY; DULLARD. SLOW
stick out / SHOW
stick tightly / ADHERE, COHERE
stick toy / POGO; JUMPINGJACK
stick used in hurling / CAMAN
stick used for wicket / STUMP
sticker / BURR, SEAL; LABEL, POSER, THORN
stickler / TAPIST; MARTINET
stickpin / TIEPIN
stickum / GLUE; PASTE; ADHESIVE
stickup / HOLDUP; ROBBERY
stickweed / RAGWEED
sticky / VISCOUS; ADHESIVE
sticky cake / TORTE
sticky mud / SLOP; GUMBO
sticky substance / GOO, GUM, TAR; GLUE
stiff / PRIM; RIGID; FORMAL. CORPSE; CADAVER
stiff cloth / CANVAS; BUCKRAM; CRINOLINE
stiff fabric / WIGAN
stiff high collar / RABATO, REBATO
stiffly proper / PRIM
stiffnecked / STUBBORN
stiffness / RIGOR
stifle / GAG; CHOKE; MUFFLE. KNEEBONE
stifling / CLOSE; CHOKING
stigma / MARK; BRAND
stigmatize / BRAND, SMEAR
stile / JAMB; STEPS
stiletto / AWL; DAGGER
still / CALM, DUMB, MILD, SOFT; QUIET; GENTLE, SERENE; IMMOBILE. BUT, YET. RETORT; ALEMBIC
stillicide / DRIPPING
stillness / HUSH; PEACE; SILENCE
stilly / CALM; QUIET
stilted / PEDANTIC, STRAINED
stilt-like bird / AVOCET
stimulant / SPUR; TONIC; BRACER
stimulate / FAN; FIRE, GOAD, SPUR, STIR, URGE, WHET; ROUSE
stimulative / TONIC
stimulus / MOTIVE; INCENTIVE

sting / BITE, GOAD; PRICK, SMART
stingaree / RAY; STINGRAY
stinger / BLOW; REMARK; ACULEUS
stinginess / STINT; PARSIMONY
stinging / PUNGENT; PIERCING
stinging ant / KELEP
stinging insect / BEE; GNAT, WASP; HORNET
stinging plant / NETTLE; BRAMBLE, THISTLE
stingy / MEAN; MISERLY, SPARING
stingy person / MISER
stink / ODOR; FETOR, SMELL; STENCH
stinker / SKUNK, SNAKE, ZORIL; FULMAR
stinking pheasant / HOATZIN
stint / STOP; CEASE, LIMIT, TASK; CHORE
stipe / STEM; STALK
stipend / FEE, PAY; HIRE; WAGES
stipendiary / PAID; HIRED; MERCENARY
stipple / SPECKLE
stipulate / SETTLE; ARRANGE, PREMISE
stipulation / AGREEMENT
stipule / OCREA; TENDRIL
stir / MIX; MOVE; BUDGE; AROUSE, BUSTLE; DISTURB, INSPIRE. ADO; JAIL, TODO; PRISON
stir calico color / TEER
stir up / RILE, ROIL; FOMENT
stirk / HEIFER; BULLOCK
stirpiculture / GNOTOBIOLOGY
stirps / RACE, ROOT; SOURCE
stirring / EXCITING; STIMULATING
stirring apparatus / MIXER; BLENDER
stirrup / STRAP; SUPPORT
stirrup bone / STAPES
stirrup cup / DOCHANDORRIS
stirrup leather / STRAP
stitch / SEW; TUCK; BASTE. KNOT, PAIN; CRICK; FURROW
stitch bird / IHI
stitch in the side / STEEK
stitched fold / HEM; TUCK
stitches / SUTURES
stithy / ANVIL, FORGE; SMITHY
stiver / BIT, RAP; PENNY
stoa / PORCH; PORTICO
stoat / ERMINE, WEASEL
stob / POST; STAKE
stoccado / THRUST
stochastic / RANDOM; IRREGULAR
stock / BASE, FUND, RACE; BREED, HOARD, TRUNK; ANIMALS. FILL; STORE
stock again / REPLENISH
stock dove / PIGEON
stock duck / MALLARD

stock exchange / BOURSE
stock farm / RANCH
stock food / ERS; FORAGE
stock market membership / SEAT
stock in trade / GEAR; CAPITAL
stockade / FENCE; BARRIER; ENCLOSURE
stockbroker / AGENT
stockfish / COD; HAKE, LING
stocking run / RAVEL; LADDER
stockings / HOSE; HOSIERY
stockish / STUPID
stockman / COWBOY; CATTLEMAN
stockstill / MOTIONLESS
stocky / HEAVY, SHORT; STUBBY; THICKSET
stocky horse / COB
stodge / CRAM; STUFF; OVEREAT
stodgy / DULL; HEAVY; STUFFY
stogy / CIGAR; BROGAN
stoic philosopher / ZENO
stoical IMPASSIVE; INDIFFERENT
stokehold / FIREROOM
stoker / FIREMAN
Stoker novel / DRACULA
stola-like robe / CHITON
stole / BAND; SCARF; ORARION. FILCHED
stolen goods / PELF, SWAG; MAINOR; PILLAGE
stolid / DULL; HEAVY; OBTUSE, WOODEN; PHLEGMATIC
stolidity / DENSITY; HEBETUDE
stolon / RUNNER
stoma / PORE; OPENING, OSTIOLE
stomach / BROOK; DIGEST. PAUNCH
stomach acidity / ACOR
stomach of bird / MAW; CRAW, CROA; GIZZARD
stomach of ruminant / RUMEN, TRIPE; OMASUM; MANYPLIES
stomachache / BELLYACHE
stomp / DANCE. KICK; STAMP
stone / GEM, PIT; ROCK; JEWEL, LAPIS; PEBBLE
stone, c.f. / LITH; LAPID
stone, pert. to / LITHIC
stone age / NEOLITHIC
stone age tool / CELT; EOLITH; HANDAXE, NEOLITH, SCRAPER
stone artisan / MASON
stone block / PAVER
stone brake / FERN
stone chamber / CIST; KISTVAEN
stone chip / SPALL
stone to death / LAPIDATE
stone debris / SCREE
stone of ephod / ONYX
stone flake / SPALL
stone fragments / BRASH, TALUS; RUBBLE
stone fruit / DRUPE

stone hammer / MASH; KEVEL; KNAPPER
stone medallion / CAMEO
stone monument / LECH; CAIRN; DOLMEN, MENHIR; CROMLECH
stone nodule / GEODE
stone for paving / SETT
stone pile / CAIRN
stone pillar / HERM; STELA, STELE
stone setter / PAVER
stone slab / STELE; MONOLITH
stone sling / ONAGER; TREBUCHET
stone tool / CELT
stone for writing / SLATE
stonecrop / ORPIN, SEDUM; OR-PINE; ROSEROOT
stonecutter / MASON
stonecutter's tool / SAX; DROVE; CHISEL
stonecutting worm of Hebrew tradition / SHAMIR
Stonehenge locale / SALISBURY
stone-mason's bench / BANKER
stone's throw / BOWSHOT
stonewall / DEFEND
stonework / MASONRY
stony / HARD; CRUEL, ROCKY
stony coral / MADREPORE
Stony Point victor / WAYNE
stood / PAUSED
stooge / PUPPET; CONFEDERATE
stook / SHEAF, SHOCK
stool / SEAT; COMMODE
stool pigeon / RAT; NARK; IN-FORMER
stoop / BOW; BEND; DEIGN. PORCH; STAIRS; VERANDA
stop / BAR, DAM, END; BALK, HALT, QUIT, REST, SEAL, STAY, STEM; CEASE, CHECK, DELAY, DETER. POINT; PERIOD; CONSONANT. HO; WHOA; AVAST
stop with a barrier / DAM
stop inadvertently / STALL
stop a leak / CALK, PLUG
stop light / RED
stop for a moment / PAUSE
stop with oakum / CALK
stop in organ / CLARION; DIA-PASON
stop short / BALK; BRAKE
stop trade in / EMBARGO
stop trade with / BOYCOTT
stop unintentionally / CONK
stop for a while / PAUSE; TAKEFIVE
stopcock / TAP; VALVE; SPIGOT
stope / MINE
stopgap / EXPEDIENT, MAKESHIFT
stopover / STAGE; STATION
stoppage / JAM; BLOCK
stopper / TAP; CORK, PLUG
stopwatch / TIMER
storage area / FILE; ATTIC; CELLAR

storage battery part / CELL
storage battery plate / GRID
storage bin / CRIB
storage building / BARN, SILO; WAREHOUSE
storage compartment / BIN; SAFE; CLOSET, DRAWER
store / SAVE, STOW, HOARD, STOCK. FUND, MART, SHOP; SUPPLY
store in the Army / PX, CANTEEN
store attendant / CLERK; SALES-MAN
store clothes / READYMADES
store display lights / NEONS
store event / SALE
store securely / REPOSIT
store up / AMASS, HOARD
stored fodder / SILAGE; ENSILAGE
storehouse / DEPOT, ETAPE; TREASURY; WAREHOUSE
storehouse for munitions / AR-SENAL
storekeeper / SHOPMAN; MER-CHANT
storeroom / GOLA; AMBRY; CLOSET
storied / LEGENDARY
stork / ARGALA, JABIRU; MAGUARI, MARABOU
storm / BLOW, FUME, HAIL, RAGE, RAVE. GALE; ORAGE; TEMPEST, TYPHOON
storm door / DINGLE
storm giantess / RAN
storm god of Babylon / ZU
storm god of India / MARUT, RUDRA
storm god of Mayans / CHAC
storm god of Slavs / STRIBOG
storm trooper / BROWNSHIRT
storm warning / FLAG; ALERT
stormy / FOUL; WINDY; SQUALLY
story / FIB, LIE; TALE, YARN; FABLE, FLOOR; LEGEND; AC-COUNT
story of family fortunes / SAGA
story that teaches / FABLE; PAR-ABLE; APOLOGUE
storyteller / LIAR; FABULIST
stot / BULL; STEER
stoup / FONT; BASIN; FLAGON
stour / TODO; TUMULT
stout / FAT; BRAVE, BURLY, LUSTY, OBESE, THICK; ROBUST. ALE; PORTER
stout burrowing rodent / MARMOT
stout silk fabric / GROS
stouthearted / BOLD; BRAVE
stoutness / STURDINESS
stove / ETNA, KILN, OVEN; RANGE; HEATER. STAVED; SMASHED
stove implement / POKER; LIFTER
stove part / LID; GRILL; BURNER

stovehouse / KILN, OAST; HOT-HOUSE

stovepipe / TOPPER; CAROLINE

stow / PACK; STORE, STUFF; STEEVE

Stowe character / EVA, TOM; TOPSY

strabismus / SQUINT; CROSSEYE

Strad / VIOLIN

straddle / BRACKET; BESTRIDE

strafe / RAKE; PUNISH; BOMBARD

straggle / ROAM, ROVE; RAMBLE

straggler / NOMAD, TRAMP; VAGABOND

straight / AROW, FAIR, JUST; ERECT, RIGHT, TIGHT; DIRECT

straight in horse racing / WIN; FIRST

straight line in a circle / CHORD; RADIUS

straight line touching a curve / TANGENT

straight man / STOOGE

straight in poker / SEQUENCE

straightaway / ANON. DIRECT

straightedge / RULER

straighten / ALIGN, ALINE; UNCOIL

straighten again / REALIGN

straightforward / OPEN; CANDID, DIRECT, HONEST

straightway / NOW, STAT; INSTANTER

strain / TAX; SIFT, TIRE, TOIL; EXERT, HEAVE; FILTER, PURIFY, SPRAIN. TUNE; STOCK; EFFORT, MELODY

strain to excess / OVERTAX

strain forward / PUSH; PRESS

strain to one's breast / HUG; EMBRACE

strained / TENSE

strainer / SIEVE; SCREEN, SIFTER

strainer of gauze / TAMIS

strait / NECK; NARROW; CHANNEL, DILEMMA. CLOSE, RIGID; STRICT

straiten / NARROW; CONSTRICT

straitened / DIFFICULT; DISTRESSED

straitjacket / CAMISOLE

Straits Settlements capital / SINGAPORE

strand / STOP; GROUND; ABANDON. BEACH; STRING

strand of metal / WIRE

stranded / BROKE; HELPLESS

strange / ODD; RARE, UNCO; ALIEN, NOVEL, WEIRD; EXOTIC, QUAINT

stranger / VISITOR; OUTSIDER

stranger, c.f. / XENO

strangle / CHOKE, MUFFLE, STIFLE

strangulate / OBSTRUCT; CONSTRICT

strangulation / GARROTE

strap / BELT; LEASH, STROP, THONG; FILLET

strap in falconry / JESS

strap for fettering / HOBBLE

strap in harness / BILLET

strap to hold a horse / HALTER

strap over horse's blanket / SURCINGLE

strap on a saddletree / LATIGO

straphanger / COMMUTER

strapping / STRONG; WELLMADE

strap-shaped / LORATE; LIGULATE

strass / GLASS, PASTE

stratagem /PLAN, PLOT, RUSE, WILE

strategic / CRUCIAL; CRITICAL

strategy / DESIGN; GENERALSHIP

Stratford notable / SHAKESPEARE

strath / VALLEY

stratum / BED; BAND, SEAM; LAYER; LAMINA

stratum, pert. to / ERIAL; TERRANE

straw / HAULM, STALK; TRIFLE

straw boss / SUBFOREMAN

straw broom / BESOM

straw hat / BOATER, PANAMA; SKIMMER

straw man / SETUP; PUPPET

straw mat / TATAMI

straw mattress / PALLET

straw vote / POLL; SAMPLE

strawberry / BRUISE; BIRTHMARK

strawberry bush / BUBBY, WAHOO

strawberry finch / AMADAVAT

strawboard / BOXBOARD

straw-colored / STRAMNEOUS

stray / ERR; ROVE; RAMBLE; DEVIATE. WAIF; NOMAD. LOST

stray calf / MAVERICK

stray horse / CAVY

streak / ROE; LINE, MARK, VEIN. RUN; STRIATE

streaked / STRIPED

streaked cow / BRINDLE

streaky / STRIPED; IRREGULAR

stream / RILL; BOURN, BROOK, CREEK, RIVER. RUN; FLOW, POUR

stream bank / LEVEE

stream of oblivion / LETHE

stream obstruction / DAM; WEIR

streamer / RAY; PENNON; PENNANT

stream-filled gorge / FLUME

streamlet / RILL; RUNNEL; RIVULET

streamlined / SLEEK; TRIMMED

street / WAY; LANE, ROAD; ALLEY; AVENUE

street arab / GAMIN; URCHIN

street covering / TAR; ASPHALT

street fight / MELEE

street organ / BARRELORGAN
street ruffian / MUN; MOHOCK, MUGGER
street show / RAREE
street singer / MINSTREL; TROUBADOUR
street transportation / BUS, CAB, CAR; TAXI
street in Venice / RIO; CANAL, CANALE
street zone / CURB, WALK; ISLAND
streetcar / TRAM; TROLLEY
streetcar operator / MOTORMAN
street-cleaner / SCAVENGER
strength / VIS; FORCE, MIGHT
strength of current / WATTAGE; AMPERAGE
strength of solution / TITER, TITRE
strengthen / PROP; BRACE, STEEL
strengthening / TONIC; ROBORANT
strengthening bracket / GUSSET
strengthening rod / RIB
strenuous / ARDENT, STRONG; EARNEST
strepitous / NOISY
streptomycin discoverer / WAKS-MAN
stress / FORCE, ICTUS; ACCENT; TENSION; PRESSURE
stressed syllable / ARSIS
stretch / BRAG, DRAW; EXPAND, EXTEND
stetch the legs / STROLL
stretch out / EKE; SPREAD
stretch over / SPAN; REACH
stretch a point / CONNIVE, DI-VERGE
stretch to see / CRANE
stretch tight / STRAIN
stretch the truth / EXAGGERATE
stretched / TAUT; PROLATE; EXTENDED
stretched out / CRANED; SPRAWLED
stretched tight / STIFF, TENSE
stretcher / DOOLY, DOOLIE, LITTER
stretching frame / TENTER; STENTER
strew / SOW; SPREAD; SCATTER
strewn in heraldry / SEME
striate / BANDED; STRIPED
striation / GROOVE; SCRATCH
stricken / ILL; WRETCHED
strict / NICE; EXACT, HARSH, RIGID, STERN; SEVERE, AUSTERE
strict disciplinarian / MARTINET, STICKLER
strictly / SEVERELY; PRECISELY
strictness / RIGOR; SEVERITY
stricture / BLAME; CENSURE
stride / GAIT, PACE, STEP
strident / HARSH; SHRILL; GRAT-ING

stridor / RAUCITY; HARSHNESS
stridulate / CHIRP, CRICK; SQUEAK
strife / WAR; FEUD; CONTEST, DIS-CORD, QUARREL, WRANGLE; STRUGGLE
strigate / SCALY; BRISTLY
strigil / SCRAPER
strigine / OWLLIKE
strigose / HISPID; GROOVED
strike / BAT, HIT, LAM, RAM; BANG, BEAT, BIFF, CONK CUFF, SLAP, SLOG, SLUG, SOCK, SWAT, WHAM
strike a balance / ADJUST; COM-PROMISE
strike like a bell / RING; CHIME
strike breaker / FINK, GOON, SCAB
strike gently / DAB, PAT, TAP; CHUCK
strike hands / GREET, SHAKE
strike hard / RAM; SLAM, SMITE, THUMP
strike with open hand / SLAP
strike out / FAN; DELE; CANCEL, DELETE, EFFACE; EXPUNGE
strike and rebound / CAROM; BOUNCE
strike it rich / HIT
strike sail / SURRENDER
strike sharply / RAP
strike with wonder / AMAZE; ASTOUND
striking / IMPRESSIVE
striking effect / ECLAT
striking success / HIT; COUP
strikingly odd / RUM; OUTRE; SINGULAR
Strindberg character / OLOF; JULIE
string / CORD, FILE, LINE; TWINE; THREAD
string along / FOOL; FLATTER
string bass / CONTRABASS
string bean / HARICOT; SNAPBEAN
string of cars / TRAIN; AUTOCADE
string figures / CATSCRADLE
string of horses / CAVVY; REMUDA, STABLE
string message of Incas / QUIPU
string up / HANG
stringed instrument / ASOR, HARP, LUTE, LYRE, VIOL; BANJO, CELLO, NABLA, REBAB, REBEC, ROCTA, SAROD, SITAR, VIOLA, CITHER, GUITAR, KISSAR, VIO-LIN, ZITHER; BANDORE, CITH-ARA, CITHERN, CITTERN, GIT-TERN, KITHARA, PANDORE; MAN-DOLIN; HURDYGURDY; VIOLIN-CELLO
stringed instrument accessory / BOW; BRIDGE; PLECTRUM
stringent / COGENT, STRICT; DRACONIAN
stringer / SLEEPER; REPORTER

stringy / ROPY; VISCID
strip / ROB; PEEL; DESPOIL. BAND; THONG; STRAKE, STRIPE
strip bark from / PEEL
strip blubber / FLENSE
strip of cloth / TAPE; FILLET
strip clothing from / DIVEST
strip cover from / BARE; DENUDE
strip of dough / NOODLE; LASAGNE
strip equipment from / DISMANTLE
strip of land / BELT, DOAB, DUAB
strip of leather / BELT, WELT; STRAP, THONG
strip of metal / SPLINE
strip needed parts from / CAN-NIBALIZE
strip of oxhide / RIEM
strip from the pod / SHELL
strip skin from / FLAY
strip of wood / LATH; SPLINT
stripe / BAR; BAND, WALE; STREAK
striped / LINED; STRIATED
striped antelope / BONGO
striped civet cat / ZIBET
striped equine / ZEBRA
striped fabric / SUSI; DORIA; MA-DRAS; GALATEA; SEERSUCKER
striped squirrel / CHIPMUNK
stripling / BOY, LAD; YOUTH
stripped of weapons / DISARMED
stripper / ECDYSIAST
strive / TRY, VIE; TOIL; LABOR; STRAIN
strive against / RESIST; CONTEND
strive to equal / APE; EMULATE
strive for / TRY; SEEK; SEARCH
strive to outdo / VIE; COMPETE
strobile / CONE
stroke / RUB; CARESS. FIT; BLOW
stroke of brilliance / COUP
stroke on letter / SERIF
stroke of luck / FLUKE, SMASH
stroll / ROVE; AMBLE; MEANDER, SAUNTER. TURN; JAUNT
stroll aimlessly / RAMBLE, WANDER
stroller / TRAMP; VAGRANT
strong / FIRM, HALE; HARDY; BIT-ING, BRAWNY, COGENT, RO-BUST; FORCEFUL, PUISSANT
strong affection / DEVOTION
strong blow / ONER
strong cord / ROPE; CABLE, TWINE
strong, dark cigar / MADURO
strong desire / LUST; HUNGER
strong drink / GIN; BRANDY; SPIRITS
strong fabric / DENIM, SISAL; CANVAS
strong fabric strip / WEBBING
strong feeling / EMOTION
strong fiber / BAST
strong language / PROFANITY
strong man / ATLAS; SAMSON

strong point / FORTE; BASTION
strong room / VAULT; COFFER
strong stream / SPATE; TORRENT
strong taste / BITE, TANG
strong thread / LISLE
strong tree / OAK
strong two-wheeled cart / DRAY
strong wind / BIRR, GALE, PUNA; TEMPEST, TYPHOON
strong wire / CABLE
strongarm / COERCE
strongbox / SAFE; CHEST, VAULT
strongheaded / SENSIBLE, STUB-BORN
stronghold / FORT; CITADEL; FORTRESS
strong-scented / GAMY, RANK; REDOLENT
strong-scented herb / RUE; MINT
strong-smelling / OLID; FETID
strong-willed / DOGGED; FROWARD
strop / HONE. SHARPEN
strophe / TURN; STANZA
struck / SMOTE
struck with horror / AGHAST
struck with wonder / AWED; AGAPE
structural order / TEXTURE
structurally safe / SOUND
structure / FRAME; FABRIC; EDIFICE
struggle / COPE; LABOR; COMBAT, STRIVE. TRIAL; EFFORT, STRIFE
struggle uncertainly / FLOUNDER
Struldbrugs' country / LUGGNAGG
struma / GOITER; SWELLING
strumpet / JADE; WENCH
strut / STEP; PRANCE; SWAGGER. BRACE; SUPPORT
struthian / RATITE
stub / FOIL; STUMP; RECEIPT
stubble field / ROWEN
stubbly / STIFF; BRISTLY
stubborn / DOGGED; OBSTINATE
stubborn beast / ASS; MULE; DONKEY
stubby / SHORT, THICK
stucco / OVERLAY, PLASTER; DECORATE
stuck / PASTED; BEMIRED
stuck on / INLOVE
stuck-up / VAIN; CONCEITED
stud / BOSS, KNOB; BUTTON. ADORN
stud horse / STALLION
stud horse's mate / BROODMARE
stud on sole / HOBNAIL
studding / SCANTLING
student / COED; PUPIL; LEARNER, SCHOLAR; DISCIPLE
student at Annapolis / MIDSHIP-MAN
student group / CLASS; SCHOOL; SEMINAR

student at West Point / CADET
studied / LEARNED; ELABORATE
studied hard / PORED
studio / ATELIER, STATION; WORK-ROOM
studious / DEVOTED; DILIGENT
studlike projection / BOSS, KNOP, KNOT
study / CON; BONE, CRAM, PORE, READ, SCAN; EXAMINE; RE-SEARCH. DEN; ROOM. See also under science
study of ancient continents / PALEOGEOGRAPHY
study of bells / CAMPANOLOGY
study of codes / CRYPTOLOGY
study of crime and punishment / PENOLOGY
study of dreams / ONEIROLOGY
study of eggs / OOLOGY
study of freshwater bodies / LIM-NOLOGY
study group / SEMINAR
study of handwriting / GRAPH-OLOGY
study of makeup / COSMETOLOGY
study of meanings / SEMANTICS; SEMASIOLOGY
study of mountains / OROLOGY
study of religious belief / THEOL-OGY
study of rocks / LITHOLOGY
study of the skull / PHRENOLOGY
study of stellar influence / ASTROL-OGY
study of temporal relations / CHRONOLOGY
study of timepieces / HOROLOGY
study of whales / CETOLOGY
study of word meanings / LEXI-COLOGY
study of word origins / ETYMOLOGY
stuff / PAD, RAM, WAD; CRAM, FILL, STOW; GORGE. CLOTH, TRASH; REFUSE
stuffed footstool / OTTOMAN
stuffing / BREAD, KAPOK; PAD-DING; FORCEMEAT
stuffy / CLOSE; SULTRY
stuggy / STODGY
stulm / ADIT; ENTRANCE
stultify / THWART; FRUSTRATE
stultiloquence / BABBLE; NON-SENSE
stum / MUST
stumble / ERR; FALL, STOT, TRIP
stumble on/ STRIKE
stumbling block / HITCH
stump / ROD; STUB. DEFEAT
stumping / CAMPAIGNING
stumpy / SHORT, THICK
stun / DAZE; SHOCK; CONFUSE
stung / TRICKED; DEFRAUDED

stunner / BEAUTY
stunning/ POWERFUL; BEAUTIFUL
stunt / FEAT; TRICK. DWARF
stunt man / DOUBLE
stunted animal / RUNT
stunted child / URF
stunted-looking / SCRUB; SCRUBBY
stupa / TOPE; SHRINE
stupe / PLEDGET; POULTICE
stupefaction / TORPOR
stupefy / DAZE, DULL, MAZE, STUN; BESOT
stupendous /HUGE, VAST; WON-DROUS
stupid / DULL, DUMB, FLAT; DENSE, INANE, SILLY; OBTUSE, STOLID; GLAIKIT
stupid mistake / BONER; BLUNDER
stupid person / ASS, OAF; CLOD, DOLT, LOUT, LOWN; DUNCE
stupidity / FOLLY; FATUITY
stupor / SOPOR; TORPOR; LETHARGY
sturdy / FIRM; HARDY, STOUT; ROBUST
sturdy fabric / DENIM
sturgeon / BELUGA, HAUSEN; STERLET
sturgeon eggs / CAVIAR
sturgeon gelatin / ISINGLASS
stuss / FARO
stutter / FALTER; STAMMER
Stuyvesant's farm / BOWERY
sty / PEN; PIMPLE; ENCLOSURE
stygian / GLOOMY, SOMBER
stylet / PEN; MODE, NAME, TYPE; MODEL, TITLE; MANNER, METH-OD; DICTION, FASHION
style of address / TITLE
style of architecture / DORIC, IONIC, TUDOR; GOTHIC
style of auto / COUPE, SEDAN; COMPACT
style of bridge / ARCH, DRAW; CANTILEVER
style of dress / MODE; FASHION
style of haircut / BOB; TONSURE
style of painting / GENRE
style of type / ROMAN; ITALIC; FRAKTUR
style of walking / GAIT, PACE
style of writing / DICTION; RHETORIC
stylet / AWL; PROBE; TROCAR; PONIARD; STILETTO
stylish / CHIC; CLASSY, MODISH
stylite / HERMIT; PILLARIST
styloid / PEGLIKE
stylus / TRACER; POINTER
stymie / BLOCK; IMPEDE
styptic / ALUM; MATICO; ASTRINGENT
Styrian city / GRAZ

Styx's father / OCEANUS
Styx's ferryman / CHARON
suable / LIABLE
suant / LEVEL; PLACID; UNIFORM
suasion / PERSUASION
suave / BLAND; UNCTUOUS
suavity / DECORUM; CIVILITY
sub / UNDERSTUDY;
    SECONDSTRINGER
sub rosa / SECRETLY
subadar / CAPTAIN
subaltern / INFERIOR
subalternant / UNIVERSAL
subbase / PLINTH
subcutaneous / HYPODERMIC
subdivide / SHARE; SEPARATE
subdivision / ARM; SECTOR
subdue / BEAT, FOIL, MELT, ROUT,
    TAME; CRUSH, LOWER, QUELL,
    WORST; DEFEAT, MASTER,
    MELLOW
subdued / QUIET; CONQUERED
subdued shade / PASTEL
suber / CORK
subfuscous / DUSKY
subgroup of genus / SPECIES
subjacent / BELOW, UNDER
subject / MIND, TEXT; POINT,
    THEME; THESIS, VASSAL;
    CITIZEN. PRONE; LIABLE
subject to analysis / ASSAY,
    PARSE; FACTOR
subject for discussion / TEXT;
    THEME, TOPIC; MATTER
subjective / MENTAL; PERSONAL
subjoin / ADD; AFFIX, ANNEX
subjugate / CONQUER; DOMINATE
sublease / RELET
sublimate / EXALT; PURIFY,
    REFINE
sublime / HIGH; GRAND, LOFTY;
    EXALTED
sublimity / MAJESTY; GRANDEUR
sublunary / EARTHLY, MUNDANE
subluxation / SPRAIN
submachine gun / TOMMY;
    TOMMYGUN
submarine / SUB; UBOAT;
    PIGBOAT
submarine device / PERISCOPE
submarine sandwich / HERO
submarine's weapon / TORPEDO
submerge / DIVE, SINK; PLUNGE
submerged ridge / REEF
submission / MEEKNESS;
    SURRENDER
submissive / MEEK, TAME;
    HUMBLE
submit / BOW; OBEY; YIELD
subordinate / LOWER; INFERIOR;
    SECONDARY
subordinate, pref. / VICE
subordinate item / DETAIL

subordinate matters / TRIVIA
subordinate part of building /
    ELL; WING; ANNEX
subordinate servant in India /
    MATY
suborn / BRIBE; INDUCE
subpoena / WRIT; SUMMONS
subrogate / SUBSTITUTE
subscribe / SIGN; CONSENT
subscript numeral / SUBINDEX
subsequent / LATER; FOLLOWING
subsequent vending / RESALE
subsequently / ANON; AFTER,
    SINCE
subserve / PROMOTE
subservient / OBEDIENT;
    SUBMISSIVE
subside / CALM, FALL, SINK;
    ABATE
subsidence / EBB; SINKING
subsidiary / ACCESSORY,
    AUXILIARY
subsidiary building / ANNEX
subsidiary currency / COINS;
    CHANGE
subsidiary's owner / CON-
    GLOMERATE
subsidize / AID; SUPPORT
subsidy / GRANT; ALLOWANCE
subsist / FEED, LIVE; ABIDE,
    EXIST
subsistence / ALLOWANCE;
    MAINTENANCE
subsistent / EXTANT
subsolar / MUNDANE; TROPICAL
subspecies / RACE; STRAIN
substance / BODY, GIST, PITH;
    MEANS, STUFF; MATTER;
    ESSENCE, PURPORT
substance, c.f. / HYLO
substandard speech /
    COLLOQUIALISM
substantial / FIRM, REAL, TRUE;
    BULKY, SOLID, SOUND, VALID;
    MASSIVE
substantially / MAINLY;
    ESSENTIALLY
substantiate / AFFIRM, VERIFY
substantiation / PROOF
substantive / REAL; ACTUAL
substantive word / NOUN;
    PRONOUN
substation / BRANCH
substitute / EXCHANGE. AGENT,
    PROXY, VICAR; DEPUTY. VICE;
    ERSATZ
substitute for butter / OLEO;
    MARGARINE
substituted spouse / PIRRAURA
substitution / REPLACEMENT
substrate / BASE
substructure / FOUNDATION
subsultus / TIC; TWITCH

subsume / CONTAIN; COMPREHEND
subtended section of circle / ARC
subterfuge / DODGE, SHIFT; PRETENSE
subterrane / CAVE, MINE
subterranean / HIDDEN; INFERNAL
subterranean being / GNOME; GOBLIN; TROGLODYTE
subterranean hollow / CAVE; CAVERN
subterranean world / HELL; TARTARUS
subtile / FINE; DELICATE
subtilize / REFINE; QUIBBLE
subtle / SLY; DEEP, WILY; ARTFUL, CRAFTY, SHREWD, TRICKY; CUNNING; PROFOUND
subtle emanation / AURA
subtle variation / NUANCE
subtlety / NICETY; FINESSE
subtonic note / SEVENTH
subtract / DEDUCT, REMOVE
subtraction answer / REMAINDER; DIFFERENCE
subtraction element / MINUEND; SUBTRAHEND
subtraction's inverse / ADDITION
subulate / TAPERING
suburban residence / MANOR, VILLA
suburbs / ENVIRONS; OUTSKIRTS
subvene / RELIEVE
subvention / GRANT; SUBSIDY
subversion / RUIN; OVERTHROW
subvert / RUIN; CORRUPT
subway / BMT, IND, IRT; BART, TUBE; METRO; UNDERPASS; UNDERGROUND
succedaneum / PROXY; SUBSTITUTE
succeed / WIN; GAIN; ENSUE; FOLLOW; PROSPER; FLOURISH
succeeding / NEXT; LATER
success / HIT; FORTUNE, VICTORY
successful / HAPPY, LUCKY; PROSPEROUS
succession / ORDER; LINEAGE; SEQUENCE
succession of rulers of a family / DYNASTY
succession of years / PERIOD
successive / SERIAL; CONSECUTIVE
successively / SERIATIM
succinct / SHORT, TERSE; LACONIC
succor / AID; HELP; ASSIST, RESCUE
succory / ENDIVE; CHICORY
succoth / BOOTHS

succubus / DEMON; HARLOT
succulent / JUICY, THICK; FLESHY
succulent fruit / PEAR; PEACH
succulent part of fruit / PULP
succulent plant / ALOE; AGAVE, SEDUM; KALANCHOE
succumb / DIE; SINK; COMPLY, YIELD; SUBMIT
succursal / SUBORDINATE
succussion / SHAKING
such / AS, SO; SIMILAR
suchness / ESSENCE
suck / DRAW; ABSORB, IMBIBE
suck in / IMBIBE; INVOLVE
sucker / FOIL; CATSPAW
sucker fish / PEGA; REMORA; PEGADOR
Sucker State / ILLINOIS
sudamen / MILIARIA
Sudan capital / KHARTOUM
Sudan people / FUR; ANAG, NUBA, NUER; DINKA; SHILLUK
Sudan river / NILE
Sudanese area / NUBIA
Sudanese early state / BORNU, MEROE; SONGHAI
Sudanese gazelle / DAMA
Sudanese lake / CHAD
Sudanese weapon / TRUMBASH
Sudanic language / EWE, IBO, KRU; EFIK, TSHI; YORUBA
sudation / SWEATING
sudden / HASTY, QUICK; ABRUPT
sudden attack / RAID; FORAY, ICTUS, SALLY
sudden collapse / DEBACLE
sudden convulsion / SPASM
sudden flight / STAMPEDE
sudden fright / PANIC
sudden leap / VOLT
sudden loud noise / POP; BANG
sudden movement / JERK; START
sudden outbreak / RIOT; MELEE
sudden outburst / SPATE
sudden raid / IRRUPTION
sudden rise / SPURT
sudden rush / DASH; SALLY
sudden rush of mob / STAMPEDE
sudden rush of wind / FLAW, GUST
sudden storm / SPATE
sudden stroke / CLAP
sudden thrust / LUNGE
sudden toss / FLIP, SNAP; FILLIP
suddenly / UNAWARES
sudor / SWEAT; PERSPIRATION
suds / BEER, FOAM; FROTH
sue / BEG, WOO; ENTREAT
suede finish / NAP
suet / FAT; LARD; GREASE, TALLOW
Suez Canal builder / DELESSEPS

Suez Canal lake / BITTER
suffer / AIL, LET; ACHE, BEAR,
   BIDE, DREE, FEEL; ALLOW;
   ENDURE
suffer from cold / PERISH, STARVE
suffer pain / ACHE, HURT
sufferance / PATIENCE;
   TOLERATION
suffering / PAIN; MISERY;
   DISTRESS
suffice / DO; SATISFY
sufficiency / ADEQUACY;
   COMPETENCY
sufficient / ENOW; AMPLE;
   ENOUGH; ADEQUATE
sufficient condition / CAUSE
suffix / ER, ES; ENT, EST, IAL,
   ISH, IST, ITE OUS; ANCE, TION
suffix denoting agency / URE
suffix denoting a doer / IST;
   STER
suffix denoting origin / OTE
suffix forming adjective / ENT,
   EST
suffix forming noun / ER; ING;
   TION
sufflate / DILATE; STRETCH
suffocate / CHOKE; STIFLE;
   SMOTHER
suffocating / CLOSE; STIFLING
suffragan / ASSISTING,
   AUXILIARY
suffrage / VOTE; BALLOT;
   FRANCHISE
suffragette / FEMINIST
suffuse / FILL, BLEND; SPREAD
suffuse with color / BLUSH
Sufist / MURID; MYSTIC; DERVISH
sugar / SWEET; SUCROSE
sugar burnt dark / CARAMEL
sugar container / BOWL
sugar house / REFINERY
sugar lump / CONE, CUBE, LOAF
sugar and molasses / MELADA
sugar server / TONGS
sugar solution / SYRUP
sugar source / BEET, CANE, CORN;
   MAPLE
sugar substitute / SACCHARIN
sugarcane liquor / TAFIA; TAFFIA
sugarcane refuse / BAGASSE,
   MEGASSE
sugarcane shoot / RATOON
sugar-coat / SWEETEN;
   CAMOUFLAGE
sugared / SWEET; SWEETENED
sugarplum / BONBON, COMFIT
sugary confection / CARAMEL
suggest / REFER; ALLUDE;
   INTIMATE
suggestible / PLIANT; YIELDING
suggestion / CUE, TIP; HINT

suggestive / BLUE; ALLUSIVE
suggestive glance / LEER
sui generis / UNIQUE; PECULIAR
suicide / FELODESE
suit / FIT; ADAPT, MATCH;
   ACCORD. CAUSE, DRESS;
   SERIES, WOOING; PETITION
suit at cards / CLUBS; HEARTS,
   SPADES; DIAMONDS
suit at law / CASE; LITIGATION
suit of mail / ARMOR
suitability / EXPEDIENCY
suitable / APT, FIT, PAT; GOOD,
   MEET; RIGHT; DECENT, PROPER
suitable for singing / MELIC
suitable time / SEASON
suitcase / BAG; VALISE
suite / CYCLE; RETINUE;
   APARTMENT
suite in music / PARTITA
suited / FIT; BECAME
suited for the occasion / BEFITTING
suiting / SERGE, TWEED
suitor / BEAU; SWAIN, WOOER
sulcate / GROOVED; FURROWED
sulcus / FISSURE
sulfa drug / ANTIBACTERIAL
sulfanilamide discoverer / DOMAGK
sulfur alloy / NIELLO
sulk / MOPE; GLOWER, GROUCH
sulky / MOODY, SURLY; SULLEN
sullage / SILT; SCORIA; SEWAGE
sullen / DOUR, GLUM; HEAVY;
   MOROSE
sully / SOIL, SPOT; DIRTY, STAIN
Sultan of Egypt / SALADIN
sultanate / OMAN; PORTE
sultan's decree / IRADE
sultan's harem member / KADEIN,
   KADINE; ODALISQUE
sultan's palace / SERAGLIO
sultans' realm / TURKEY
sultan's wife / SULTANA
sultry / HOT; CLOSE; TROPICAL
Sulu capital / JOLO
Sulu Moslem / MORO; JOLOANO
sum / TOTAL, WHOLE. ADD, TOT;
   FOOT; RESUME
sum invested / CAPITAL
sum up / ADD; RECAP, TOTAL
Sumatra fabric / IKAT
Sumatra feline / BALU
Sumatra lake / TOBA
Sumatra range / BARISAN
Sumatra squirrel shrew / TANA
Sumerian city / UR; LARSA;
   LAGASH
Sumerian deity / AN; ABU, UTU;
   ENKI, UTTU; LAHAR, NANNA;
   INANNA
Sumerian dialect / EMESAL
Sumerian hero / GILGAMESH

Sumerian king / GUDEA
Summa author / AQUINAS
summarize / SUM; EPITOMIZE
summary / BRIEF; DIGEST,
    PRECIS, RESUME; EPITOME,
    CURT; SHORT, TERSE
summary of belief / CREED,
    CREDO
summer / ETE; BEAM; LINTEL
summer, pert. to / ESTIVAL
summer annoyance / HEAT, RASH;
    SWEAT; SUNBURN
summer complaint / DIARRHEA
summer dish / SALAD
summer drink / ADE; JUICE
summer ermine / STOAT
summer flounder / PLAICE
summer hat / STRAW; PANAMA
summer house / ARBOR; GAZEBO;
    PERGOLA
summer period / DOGDAYS
summer retreat / CAMP, LAKE;
    BEACH; RESORT
summer squash / CYMLIN, SIMLIN;
    SCALLOP
summerset / TUMBLE; SOMER-
    SAULT
summertime fabric / SEERSUCKER
Summing Up author / MAUGHAM
summit / TIP, TOP; ACME, APEX,
    KNAP, PEAK, ROOF; CREST
summit conference locale / YALTA;
    POTSDAM
summon / BID; CALL, CITE, PAGE
summon together / CALL; MUSTER;
    CONVENE
summon up / RALLY; CONVOKE
summoned / BADE
summons / CALL; SUBPOENA
sump / PIT; WELL; DRAIN
sumpitan / BLOWGUN
sumpter / MULE; HORSE
sumption / PREMISE
sumptuary / FISCAL; LIMITING
sumptuous / RICH; SPLENDID;
    LUXURIOUS
sumptuous meal / FEAST
sums / MONIES; PROBLEMS
sun / SOL; HELIOS; DAYSTAR,
    BASK
sun, c.f. / SOLI; HELIO
sun, pert. to / SOLAR; HELIACAL
sun disk / ATEN
sun god / RA; SOL, TEM, TUM, UTU;
    AMEN, AMON, AMUN, ATMU,
    ATUM, FREY, INTI, UTUG; NI-
    NIB; APOLLO, BABBAR, HELIOS,
    OSIRIS, VARUNA; PHOEBUS,
    SHAMASH
sun goddess / AMATERASU
sun helmet / TOPI; TOPEE
sun phenomenon / HALO, SPOT;
    UMBRA; CORONA, FACULA

sun porch / SOLARIUM
sun shelter / VISOR; AWNING;
    PARASOL
sunbathe / BASK; APRICATE
sunbeam / RAY
sunbonnet / POKE
sunbow / IRIS; RAINBOW
sunburn / TAN
sunburnt / RED; ADUST
Sunda Island / BALI, JAVA;
    BORNEO
sundae ingredient / NUTS;
    CHERRY
Sunday / SABBATH
Sunday in Lent / LAETARE
sunder / CUT; PART, REND, RIVE,
    TEAR; SEVER; DIVIDE
sundial, pert. to / SKIATHERIC
sundial's pointer / GNOMON
sundog / PARHELION
sundown / EVE; SUNSET;
    EVENING
sundowner / HOBO; TRAMP
sun-dried brick / ADOBE, DOBIE
sundries / NOTIONS
sundry / DIVERS; SEVERAL,
    VARIOUS
sunfish / OPAH; BREAM; CRAPPIE;
    BLUEGILL, BUCK
sunflower / ASTER; MARIGOLD;
    HELIOTROPE
sunflower scale / PALEA
Sunflower State / KANSAS
sung alone / SOLO; ACAPELLA
sunglasses / SHADES
sunk / FALLEN; PERPLEXED
sunken fence / AHA; HAHA
sunken land / SAG; ATLANTIS
sunken reef / BOILER
sunless / DARK; UNLIT;
    SHADOWED
sunna / TRADITION
sunnite / ORTHODOX
sunny / WARM; CLEAR; BRIGHT
sunny-side-up / FRIED
sunrise / DAWN, EAST; ORIENT
sunset / WEST; SUNDOWN;
    TWILIGHT
sunshade / AWNING; PARASOL
Sunshine State / FLORIDA
sunspot / MACULA; FRECKLE
sunstone / AVENTURINE
suntans / KHAKIES
sunup / DAWN; MORN; SUNRISE;
    DAYBREAK
sup / EAT; DINE
supawn / MUSH; SUPPAWN
super / FINE; GREAT, LARGE
superable / FEASIBLE, POSSIBLE
superabundance / EXCESS;
    SURFEIT; PLETHORA
superannuated / AGED; ANILE,
    PASSE

superb / GRAND, NOBLE, PROUD, SHOWY; AUGUST; ELEGANT; GORGEOUS

supercargo / AGENT

supercilious / PROUD; HAUGHTY

superego / CONSCIENCE

supereminent / SUPREME; PRINCIPAL

supererogatory / EXTRA; NONESSENTIAL

superficial / OUTER; FLIMSY, SLIGHT

superficial cut / SCOTCH

superficial glitter / GILT; TINSEL

superficial wound / SCRATCH; ABRASION

superficies / OUTSIDE, SURFACE

superfine / EXTRA; CHOICE; EXCELLENT

superfluous / COPIOUS; EXCESSIVE, REDUNDANT

superhuman / DIVINE; MIRACULOUS

superhuman power / MANA, NGAI

superimpose / OVERLAY

superimposed melody / DESCANT

superincumbent / OPPRESSIVE

superinduce / SUPERADD

superintend / MANAGE; OVERSEE

superintendence / CHARGE; CONTROL

superintendent / BOSS; DIRECTOR

superior / TOP; UPPER; BETTER

superior capacity / TALENT

superior in quality / DELUXE

superiority / ADVANTAGE, SUPREMACY

superiority in competition / ADVANTAGE

superiority in office / SENIORITY

superlative / ELATIVE, SUPREME; PEERLESS; PREEMINENT

superlative suffix / EST

superman / OVERMAN; UBERMENSCH

Superman as a civilian / CLARK-KENT

superman patron / NIETZSCHE

Superman's girl friend / LOIS

Superman's home planet / KRYPTON

supernal / LOFTY; DIVINE; CELESTIAL

supernatant / FLOATING

supernatural / MAGIC; MIRACULOUS

supernatural being / GOD; ADARO, ANGEL, DEITY, FAIRY, TROLL

supernatural event / MIRACLE

supernumerary actor / EXTRA, SUPER

superscribe / DIRECT; ADDRESS

superscription / TITLE; ADDRESS

supersede / OUST; SUPPLANT

superseder / SUCCESSOR; SUBSTITUTE

supersensible / IDEAL; PSYCHIC

supersession / REPLACEMENT

supersonic transport / SST

superstition / IRRATIONALITY

supervene / FOLLOW, HAPPEN

supervise / DIRECT; OVERSEE

supervisor / BOSS; MANAGER

supinate / FELL; PROSTRATE

supine / LAZY; CARELESS, SLUGGISH

supineness / APATHY

suppawn / MUSH; CORNMEAL

supper / TEA; DINNER; BANQUET

supplant / REPLACE; SUPERSEDE

supple / AGILE, LITHE; LIMBER, PLIANT

supplement / ADD, EKE. ADDITION, APPENDIX

supplementary document / ANNEX

suppletory / ADDED; SUPPLE-MENTARY

suppliance / ENTREATY

suppliant / BEGGAR; PETITIONER

supplicant / SUITOR; PLEADER

supplicate / ASK, BEG, SUE; PRAY

supplication / PLEA, SUIT; PRAYER; ENTREATY

supplier / SUBCONTRACTOR

supplies / OUTFIT; PROVISIONS

supply / CATER, ENDUE, STOCK; PURVEY. FUND; STORE

supply in abundance / REPLENISH

supply again / REPLACE; REPLENISH

supply with comments / ANNO-TATE, FOOTNOTE

supply with a crew / MAN

supply of extra horses / RELAY; REMUDA

supply with food / FEED; CATER

supply with fuel / STOKE

supply with income / ENDOW

supply with resolution / NERVE

support / AID; ABET, BACK, HELP, PROP; BRACE, FAVOR; SECOND. GUY, RIB; BASE, REST, STAY

support allowance / ALIMONY

support for book / LECTERN

support for broken bone / SPLINT

support for canvas / SAIL; EASEL

support for chair / LEG

support in climbing / FOOTHOLD

support for column / PEDESTAL

support for compass / GIMBALS

support for lever / FULCRUM

support for millstone / RIND, RYND

support for oar / THOLE; ROWLOCK

support for pool cue / BRIDGE
support for statue / SOCLE; PLINTH
support with timbers / SHORE
support for tracks / TIE
support for vine / TRELLIS
support for wall / BUTTRESS
supported / SIDED; PIERED
supported a ticket / VOTED
supporter / ROOTER; BOOSTER; ADHERENT
supporter of institution / PATRON
supporter of world / ATLAS, KURMA
supporting bar / FID
supporting frame / EASEL; LATTICE, TRESSEL, TRESTLE; SCAFFOLD
supporting timbers / GIRDERS
supporting vitality / NERVE; COURAGE, STAMINA
supporting wire / GUY
suppose / WIS; DEEM, TROW; FANCY, JUDGE, OPINE, THINK; ASSUME; BELIEVE
supposed / PUTATIVE; THEORETICAL
supposition / GUESS; THEORY; SURMISE
supposititious / ASSUMED; HYPOTHETICAL
supposititious / FAKE; FRAUDULENT
suppress / STOP; CHECK, CRUSH, ELIDE, QUASH, QUELL; STIFLE; SMOTHER
suppressed desire / INHIBITION
suppressed laugh / GIGGLE; SNICKER
suppression / SILENCE; OMISSION; CENSORSHIP
suppuration / PUS
supra / ABOVE
supraliminal / SENSIBLE; CONSCIOUS
supremacy / DOMINANCE; ASCENDENCY
supreme / CHIEF, FIRST; UTMOST; HIGHEST
supreme being / GOD; ALLAH, DEITY; YAHWEH; CREATOR, JEHOVAH
Supreme Court justice / JAY; BLACK; TANEY; WARREN; MARSHALL
supreme ruler / MONARCH; IMPERATOR
supremely excellent / SUPERB
surbase / MOLDING
surcease / END; STOP; CESSATION
surcharge / OVERPLUS; OVERPRINT
surcingle / BELT; GIRTH; GIRDLE

surcoat / OVERCOAT
surd / DEAF; VOICELESS; IRRATIONAL
sure / FIRM, SAFE; SECURE, STABLE
sure ground / SAFETY; SECURITY
sure thing / CERT, PIPE
surefire / TRUSTY; RELIABLE
surefooted / ADROIT, NIMBLE
surely / YES; INDEED; CERTAINLY
surety / VAS; BAIL, BOND; PLEDGE; HOSTAGE
surf / SEA; FOAM; SPRAY
surf duck / COOT; SCOTER; SKUNKHEAD
surf noise / ROAR, ROTE
surface / AREA, FACE; OUTSIDE
surface car / TRAM; TROLLEYCAR
surface curve of liquid / MENISCUS
surface of a gem / BEZEL, FACET, TABLE
surface noise / POP; HISS
surface rib / LIERNE; CROSSRIB
surface a road / PAVE
surface of a solid / FACE
surfactant / DETERGENT
surfboard expert / KAHUNA
surfeit / CLOY, GLUT, PALL, SATE
surfeited / BLASE
surge / PUSH, RISE, ROLL, SLIP, TOSS; HEAVE, PITCH, SWELL; BILLOW
surgeon / MEDIC; DOCTOR; SAWBONES
surgeonfish / TANG
surgeon's thread / LIGATURE
surgical absorbent / SPONGE
surgical appliance / TRUSS; SPLINT
surgical compress / STUPE
surgical instrument / TENT; PROBE; ABLATOR, FORCEPS, LEVATOR
surgical knife / LANCET, STYLET, TROCAR; SCALPEL
surgical saw / TREPAN; TREPHINE
surgical stitch / SUTURE
surgical thread / SETON
surgical treatment / OPERATION
Surinam capital / PARAMARIBO
Surinam mineral export / BAUXITE
Surinam toad / AGUA, PIPA
surly / GLUM, SOUR; CROSS, GRUFF, HARSH
surly person / CRAB; CHURL
surmise / GUESS, INFER, OPINE; BELIEVE
surmount / CAP, TOP; RISE; EXCEED
surmounting / OVER; ABOVE
surname / EPONYM; COGNOMEN
surpass / CAP, TOP; BEAT, BEST; EXCEL, OUTDO

surpass in persistence / OUTSTAY
surpassed / LED; BEAT; OUTRAN
surpassing / EGREGIOUS, EXCESSIVE
surpassing in quality / EXCELLENT
surplice / ROBE; COTTA; PELISSE
surplus / EPACT, EXTRA; EXCESS; OVERAGE; REMAINDER
surplus of profits / MELON
surprise / ALARM, AMAZE; STARTLE
surprising / STRIKING; WONDERFUL
surrealist painter / ARP; DALI
surrealist writer / BRETON
surrebound / REECHO
surrender / CEDE; FORGO, YIELD; VACATE. CESSION
surrender by deed / REMISE
surreptitious / SLY; FURTIVE; UNDERHAND
surreptitiously / COVERTLY, SECRETLY
surrey / CARRIAGE
Surrey river / WEY; MOLE
Surrey town / EPSOM; DORKING
surrogate / LOCUM; DEPUTY; SUBSTITUTE
surround / HEM, MEW; BELT, GIRD; BESET, FENCE; BESIEGE, ENVELOP
surrounded / ENVIRONED
surrounded by the ocean / SEAGIRT
surrounding / ABOUT
surrounding area / ZONE; AREOLE; ENVIRON
surroundings / MILIEU; VICINITY
surtax / OVERTAX
surtout / HOOD; OVERCOAT
Surt's horde / GIANTS
Surt's road / RAINBOW
Surt's victim / FREY
surveillance / WATCH; SUPERVISION
survey / MAP; POLL, SCAN, VIEW; EXAMINE
surveying / GROMATICS
surveyor / LINEMAN; INSPECTOR
surveyor's aide / RODMAN
surveyor's instrument / ROD; LEVEL; STADIA; ALIDADE, TRANSIT; THEODOLITE
surveyor's tape / CHAIN
survival / RELIC; CONTINUANCE
survival of fittest advocate / EVOLUTIONIST
survive / REMAIN; OUTLAST, OUTLIVE
surviving / ENDURING, REMANENT
survivor's annuity / TONTINE
Surya's mother / ADITI, USHAS
Surya's son / KARNA
Susa in the Bible / SHUSHAN

Susa inhabitant / ELAMITE
Susanna's defender / DANIEL
Susanna's husband / JOIACHIM
susceptibility / ALLERGY
susceptible / EASY; TENDER; EXCITABLE
susceptive / SENSITIVE
suscitate / FAN; AROUSE; INFLAME
suslik / SPERMOPHILE
suspect / DOUBT, THINK; BELIEVE, IMAGINE; MISTRUST
suspend / HANG, STAY, STOP; DELAY
suspended animation / CATALEPSY
suspenders / BRACES; GARTERS
suspense / ANXIETY, SCRUPLE
suspension points / ELISION; OMISSION
suspensory bandage / SLING
suspicion / HINT; DOUBT; SURMISE
suspicious / LEERY; JEALOUS; DOUBTFUL
suspire / SIGH
Susquehanna island / QUE
Sussex river / ARUN, OUSE
Sussex town / RYE; LEWES; BRIGHTON
sustain / AID; BEAR, FEED, HELP, PROP
sustain life / FEED; NOURISH
sustaining / UNSPONSORED
sustenance / DIET, FOOD; BREAD, MANNA; ALIMENT
susurrate / RUSTLE
susurrus / SOUGH; SIGHING; WHISPERING
sutler / PROVISIONER
sutra / SAYING; PRECEPT
suttee / SUICIDE; IMMOLATION
suture / SEAM; SETON; STITCH
suture, c.f. / RRAPHY
suzerain / LIEGE; OVERLORD
suzerainty / DIGNITY; LORDSHIP
svelte / SLIM, TRIM; WILLOWY
swab / MOP; WIPE. CLOTH; LUBBER, SPONGE
Swabian city / ULM; FREIBURG
swacked / DRUNK; SOZZLED
swad / LUMP; BUNCH
swaddle / BIND, WRAP; SWATHE
swag / LOOT; BOOTY, SPOIL
swagbelly / POT; PAUNCH
swage / DOLLY; SHAPER
swagger / BOAST, STRUT; PRANCE
swaggerer / BULLY; FANFARON
swagman / HOBO; FENCE
Swahili dialect / KINGWANA
swain / CLOWN, LOVER, WOOER
swale / DIP; MEADOW
swallow / GULP; ABSORB. SWIFT; MARTIN

swallow hurriedly / BOLT, WOLF; GOBBLE
swallow in large draughts / QUAFF
swallow a liquid / DRINK
swallow up / DEVOUR, ENGULF
swallows, pert. to / HIRUNDINE
swallow-tails / DRESSCOAT
swallow-tailed duck / OLDSQUAW
swami / PUNDIT; TEACHER
swamp / BOG, FEN; SLUE; MARSH; DISMAL, MORASS, SLOUGH; POCOSIN; QUAGMIRE; EVER-GLADE. OVERWHELM
swamp fever / MALARIA
Swamp Fox / MARION
swamp rabbit / TAPETI
swamp tree / ALDER
swamp willow / PUSSYWILLOW
swamped / WRECKED; STRANDED
swampy area / TAIGA, TERAI; MUSKEG; EVERGLADE
swan / COB, PEN; CYGNET
Swan of Avon / SHAKESPEARE
swan genus / OLOR
swan herd / WEDGE
Swan Knight / LOHENGRIN
Swan Lake hero / SIEGFRIED
Swan Lake heroine / ODETTA
swan song / FAREWELL
swank / SWAGGER; OSTENTATION
swanky / POSH; SMART; CHICHI
swanpan / ABACUS; SUANPAN
swap / TRADE; BARTER; EX-CHANGE
swap horses / SWITCH
swap session / BOURSE
swaraj / HOMERULE
sward / SOD; LAWN, TURF; GRASS
swarf / GRINDINGS
swarm / NEST, TEEM; ABOUND. HOST, MASS; HORDE, PRESS; MYRIAD, THRONG
swarm of bees / BEIK, BYKE, HIVE
swarming / ALIVE; CROWDED
swart / DARK; GLOOMY
swarth / WRAITH
swarthy / DUN; DARK; DUSKY
swash / BRAG, DASH; SPLASH; BLUSTER. ORNATE. FLOURISH
swashbuckler / BRAVO; SWAG-GERER
swashy / WEAK
swastika / FYLFOT; GAMMADION
swat / HIT; SLAP; STRIKE
swatch / SAMPLE
swath / WINDROW
swathe / TIE; BIND, WRAP; BANDAGE
swathing / SWADDLING
Swat's ruler / AKHOOND
swatter / SLUGGER

sway / NOD, WAG; LEAN, REEL, ROCK, ROLL; LURCH; TEETER. RULE; CONTROL
sway loosely / FLOP; WOBBLE
sway from side to side / CAREEN, WADDLE
swayback / LORDOSIS
Swaziland capital / MBABANE
Swaziland language / SISWATI
Swaziland money / RAND
Swaziland river / USUTU
swear / VOW; AVER; CURSE; AFFIRM
swear falsely / PERJURE
sweat / TOIL; LABOR; PERSPIRE. SUDOR; DRUDGERY
sweating inflammation / MILIARIA; PRICKLYHEAT
Sweden / SVERIGE
Sweden capital / STOCKHOLM
Swedish actress / GARBO
Swedish airline / SAS
Swedish canal / GOTA
Swedish chemist / BERZELIUS
Swedish city / LUND; UPPSALA
Swedish clover / ALSIKE
Swedish dramatist / STRINDBERG
Swedish dynasty / VASA; FOLKUNG
Swedish explorer / HEDIN
Swedish farm / TORP
Swedish gymnast / LING
Swedish inventor / NOBEL
Swedish island / OLAND; GOTLAND
Swedish king / OSKAR; GUSTAF
Swedish lake / ASNEN; VATTERN
Swedish legal official / OMBUDS-MAN
Swedish money / ORE; DALER, KRONA
Swedish mountain / KEBNEKAISE
Swedish movie director / BERGMAN
Swedish mystic / SWEDENBORG
Swedish Nightingale / LIND
Swedish northland / LAPLAND
Swedish novelist / LAGERLOF
Swedish parliament / RIKSDAG
Swedish philanthropist / NOBEL
Swedish philosopher / SWEDEN-BORG
Swedish plain / SKANE
Swedish playwright / LAGERKVIST
Swedish poet / BELLMAN
Swedish river / UME; KLAR, LULE; TORNE
Swedish sculptor / MILLES
Swedish seaport / MALMO; OREBRO
Swedish strait / ORESUND
Swedish turnip / RUTABAGA
Swedish UN official / HAMMAR-SKJOLD

Swedish university / LUND; UPP-SALA
Swedish weight / LOD; STEN
Swedish women's leader / BREMER
Swedish writer / TEGNER
sweep / WIN; BRUSH, CLEAN, CURVE. SCOPE, SWATH; EXTENT
sweep away / DISPEL, REMOVE
sweep out / CLEAN
sweeper / BROOM, BRUSH; VACUUM
sweeping / BROAD; THOROUGH
sweepings / ORTS; LITTER
sweer / LAZY
sweet / KIND, MILD, PURE, SOFT; BALMY
sweet bag / SACHET
sweet bay / LAUREL; MAGNOLIA
sweet bread / STOLLEN
sweet cake / BUN; CRULLER
sweet cicely / CHERVIL
sweet clover / MELILOT
sweet corn / GOLDENBANTAM
sweet cumin / ANISE
sweet drink / ADE, POP; NECTAR
sweet to the ear / DULCET
sweet fern / POLYPODY
sweet flag / CALAMUS
sweet fluid / MEL; HONEY, SYRUP; NECTAR; MOLASSES
sweet gale / GAGEL
sweet grape / TOKAY
sweet grass / REED; MANNAGRASS
sweet liqueur / RATAFIA; ANISETTE
sweet pepper / PIMIENTO
sweet potato / YAM; BATATA, CAMOTE; OCARINA
sweet roll / BUN; DANISH
Sweet Singer of Israel / DAVID
sweet singer of myth / SIREN
sweet sound / MUSIC; MELODY
sweet wild cherry / MAZZARD
sweet wine / PORT; ANGELICA, MUSCATEL
sweetbread / RIS; THYMUS; PANCREAS
sweetbrier / EGLANTINE
sweeten / SUGAR
sweetened wine drink / NEGUS
sweetening / SACCHARIN
sweetfish / AYU
sweetgum / STORAX; LIQUIDAMBAR
sweetheart / JO; GRA; BEAU; LEMAN, LOVER; AMORET, FIANCE, SUITOR; FIANCEE; INAMORATA, VALENTINE
sweethearts / JACKANDJILL; DARBYANDJOAN
sweetie / LOVER
sweetmeat / CANDY; DRAGEE; NOUGAT; CONFECTION

sweet-smelling / OLENT
sweetsop / ATES, ATTA; ANNONA
swell / RISE; HEAVE, SURGE; DILATE. FOP; BULGE
swell of the sea / SURF, WAVE; SURGE
swelled head / PRIDE; CONCEIT
swellfish / PUFFER
swellhead / BOASTER, EGOTIST
swelling / BUBO, LUMP; EDEMA; STRUMA
swelling loudness / CRESCENDO
swelling on neck / GOITER
swelling on plant / GALL
swelling wave / ROLLER
swelter / HURRY; PERSPIRE
sweltry / HOT; SULTRY
swerve / SHY; TURN, VEER; SHEET
sweven / DREAM
swift / FAST; FLEET, RAPID; NIMBLE, PROMPT
swift horse / QUARTERHORSE
swift vessel / PACKET; CLIPPER
swifter / TAUTEN
swiftly / FAST; APACE; LICKETY-SPLIT
swiftness / SPEED; ALACRITY
Swift's friend / STELLA
Swift's hero / GULLIVER
Swift's pseudonym / BICKERSTAFF
swig / GULP, DRAFT; SWALLOW
swigger / TOPER; DRUNKARD
swill / DRINK. SLOPS; HOGWASH
swim / CRAWL, FLOAT; NATATE
swim along / CONCUR
swimming, pert. to / NATATORY
swimming aid / WATERWINGS
swimming bird / LOON; GREBE
swimming organ / FIN; NECTOPHORE
swimming pool / PLUNGE
swimming as a skill / NATATION
swimmingly / WELL; SMOOTHLY
swindle / GYP; BILK, DUPE, GULL; FLEECE
swindler / CHEAT, KNAVE, ROGUE; COZENER, SHARPER
swine / HOG, PIG, SOW; BOAR
swine, pert. to / PORCINE
swine breed / SPOT; DUROC; TAMNORTH
swine hunt / PIGSTICKING
swineherd / PIGMAN
swine's fat / LARD
swine's forage / PANNAGE
swine's pen / STY
swing / SWAY; DANGLE; VIBRATE
swing music / JAZZ, JIVE
swing musician / CAT; HEPCAT
swing to the side / SLEW, SLUE
swinge / WHIP; FORGE; THRASH
swinging barrier / DOOR, GATE

swinging door device / HINGE
swingle / SWIPLE. SCUTCH
swingletree / SINGLETREE
swinish / BESTIAL, PORCINE
swink / MOIL; DRUDGE
swipe / GLOM, TAKE; STEAL
swipes / BEER
swirl / EDDY, RUSH; GURGE, WHIRL
swirly / KNOTTED
swish / FLOG; WHISK
Swiss / see also Switzerland
Swiss cabin / CHALET
Swiss canton / URI, ZUG; VAUD;
  AARGAU, GLARUS
Swiss cheese / GRUYERE
Swiss city / BALE, BERN, GENF,
  SION; AARAU, BASEL, BASLE,
  BERNE; ZURICH; LOCARNO
Swiss cottage / CHALET
Swiss county / CANTON
Swiss falsetto song / YODEL
Swiss lake / URI; THUN; BRIENZ,
  GENEVA; LUCERNE; CONSTANCE
Swiss land measure / IMMI
Swiss language / LADIN;
  ROMANSCH
Swiss measure / ELLE, IMMI;
  LIGNE, STAAB
Swiss mountain / RIGI, TODI; JUNG-
  FRAU; MATTERHORN
Swiss mountain range / ALPS, JURA
Swiss novelist / MEYER; KELLER
Swiss patriot / TELL
Swiss river / AAR, INN; AARE;
  RHINE, RHONE
Swiss singer / YODELER
Swiss state / CANTON
switch / SHUNT; TOGGLE. FLOG,
  LASH
switch off / KILL; EXTINGUISH
switch on / LIGHT
switchback / ZIGZAG
switchboard / PBX; PLUGBOARD
switchboard girl / OPERATOR
Switzer / SWISS
Switzerland / SUISSE; SCHWEIZ;
  HELVETIA, SVIZZERA. See also
  Swiss
Switzerland capital / BERN
swivel / HINGE, PIVOT; FULCRUM
swiveleye / SQUINT
swivet / HASTE; EAGERNESS
swizzle / GUZZLE
swizzle stick / MIXER; STIRRER
swollen / TUMID; TURGID; PREG-
  NANT
swoon / FAINT; SYNCOPE;
  LIPOTHYMY
swoop / DIP; SWEEP; POUNCE
swop / SWAP; TRADE; EXCHANGE
sword / EPEE, PATA, TUCK; BILBO,
  BLADE, ESTOC, LANCE, SABER,

TACHI; KATANA, RAPIER, TO-
  LEDO; CLAYMORE, SCIMITAR
sword belt / BALDRIC, BAWDRIC;
  BALDRICK
sword case / SHEATH
sword of Charlemagne / FLAM-
  BERGE
sword contest / DUEL
sword for fencing / EPEE, FOIL;
  SABER
sword handle / HAFT, HILT
sword of India / PATA
sword of King Arthur / CALIBURN;
  EXCALIBUR
sword of Roland / DURANDAL
sword of Saint George / ASKELON
sword of Siegfried / GRAM; BAL-
  MUNG
sword-shaped / XIPHOID; ENSI-
  FORM
swordsman / FENCER; DUELIST
sworn / PLEDGED
sworn friends / BROTHERS
sworn statement / OATH; PLEDGE
sybarite / HEDONIST; SENSUALIST
sybaritic / LUXURIOUS; VOLUP-
  TUOUS
sycamore / PLANE; BUTTONWOOD
sycamore fig tree / DAROO
sycophancy / FLATTERY;
  SERVILITY
sycophant / LEECH, TOADY;
  HENCHMAN, PARASITE
Sycorax's son / CALIBAN
sye / SCYTHE
syllabic stress / TONE
syllabify / HYPHENATE
syllable / PHONE; DETAIL
syllable in music / DO, FA, MI
syllable in singing / LA; TRA
syllabus / OUTLINE; HEADNOTE
syllogism / ARGUMENT; DEDUC-
  TION, ENTHYMEME
syllogism series / SORITES
syllogist / LOGICIAN
syllogize / REASON
sylph / ELF; FAIRY
sylvan / SHADY, WOODY; RUSTIC,
  WOODED
sylvan deity / PAN; FAUN; SATYR;
  SILENUS
Sylvestrian monk / BENEDICTINE
symbol / SIGN; TOKEN; EMBLEM
symbol of authority / MACE
symbol of crusader / CROSS
symbol of Holy Spirit / DOVE
symbol of mourning / CREPE; ARM-
  BAND
symbol of pilgrimage / SCALLOP
symbol of victory / VEE; PALM
symbol of wedding / RING
symbolic / EMBLEMATIC

symbolic female figure / ORANT
symbolism / ICONOLOGY
symbolist poet / YEATS; RIMBAUD
symbolize / TYPIFY
symmetrical / REGULAR; HAR-
MONIOUS
symmetrize / BALANCE
symmetry / GRACE, ORDER;
BALANCE
sympathetic / CONGENIAL;
HARMONIOUS
sympathetic, as ink / INVISIBLE
sympathetic, as ink / INVISIBLE
sympathize / CONDOLE
sympathizer / IST, ITE; CONDOLER
sympathy / PITY; CONCERT; AFFIN-
ITY; COMPASSION
symphonic poem / TONEPOEM
symphony / ORCHESTRA
symphony composer / HAYDN; MO-
ZART; SCHUBERT
symposiarch / TOASTMASTER
symposium / BANQUET; MEETING;
CONFERENCE
symptom / MARK, SIGN; TOKEN;
INDICATION
symptom of illness / FEVER
symptomatic / INDICATIVE
symptomatology / SYNDROME
synagogue / SHUL; TEMPLE; CON-
GREGATION
synagogue official / PARNAS;
SHAMMAS
sync / SYNCHRONIZATION
synchronize / FIT
synchronous / COINCIDING
syncline / TROUGH; DOWNFOLD
syncopated music / RAG; JAZZ;
SWING
syncope / FAINT, SWOON; ELISION
syndetic / JOINING; CONNECTING
syndic / TRUSTEE; MAGISTRATE
syndicate / COMBINE; COMBINA-
TION. CONTROL
syndrome / SET; CONCURRENCE
syne / AGO. SINCE. THEN
Synge character / PLAYBOY
synod / SOBOR; COUNCIL, MEET-
ING; ASSEMBLY
synonym / METONYM; HETERONYM
synonymous / ALIKE; EQUIVALENT
synopsis / VIEW; TABLE; DIGEST;
EPITOME, OUTLINE, SUMMARY

synoptic gospel / LUKE, MARK;
MATTHEW
syntagma / GROUP
syntax / SYSTEM; RELATIONSHIP
synthesis / DEDUCTION; COMBINA-
TION
synthetic / ARTIFICIAL
synthetic fabric / NYLON, ORLON,
RAYON, SARAN, VINYL; DACRON,
OLEFIN, VINYON; ACETATE,
SPANDEX; POLYESTER; TRIACE-
TATE
synthetic language / RO; IDO
synthetic philosopher / SPENCER
synthetic resin / BAKELITE
synthetic rubber / BUNA
syntony / RESONANCE
syphilis / LUES
Syracusan scientist / ARCHIMEDES
Syracusan tyrant / HIERO
Syria / ARAM
Syria capital / DAMASCUS
Syrian cheese / LABNEH
Syrian city / HOMS; ALEPPO, BEI-
RUT; LATAKIA
Syrian deity / EL; BAAL
syringa / MOCKORANGE
syringe / PUMP; SPRAY; NEEDLE;
ATOMIZER
syrinx / PANPIPE
syrt / QUICKSAND
systaltic / PULSATING
system / ISM; PLAN; ORDER;
METHOD, SCHEME
system of laws / CODE
system of management / REGIME
system of measures / TROY;
METRIC
system of signals / CODE
system of worship / CLUT; RELI-
GION; DENOMINATION
systematic / TAXONOMIC;
METHODICAL
systematic attack / SIEGE
systematic instruction / PRACTICE
systematize / ARRANGE; ORGANIZE
systematized way of life / REGIMEN
systole / CONTRACTION
syzygy / DIPODY
Szechwan city / IPIN; CHUNGKING
Szechwan river / YANGTZE

T

T as a brand / THIEF
taa / PAGODA
taal / AFRIKAANS
tab / TAG; FLAP; CHECK, LABEL,
STRIP
tabanid fly / TAON; BREMSE
tabard / CAPE, COAT; MANTLE
tabasco / SAUCE

tabby / WAVY; BRINDLED. CAT
tabby cloth / MOIRE
tabefaction / EMACIATION
tabernacle / PYX; AMBRY, NICHE;
CHURCH, TEMPLE
Tabernacles festival / SUCCOS,
SUKKOT; SUCCOTH, SUKKOTH
tabes / ATROPHY, WASTING

tabid / ATAXIC
table / LIST, ROTA; BOARD STAND. POSTPONE
table centerpiece / EPERGNE
table linen / DAMASK, NAPERY
table of months / CALENDAR
table scarf / RUNNER
table utensil / DISH, FORK; KNIFE; SPOONS
tablecloth / DAMASK
tableland / MESA; BENCH; PLATEAU
tableland of central Asia / PAMIR
tableland of South Africa / KAROO
tableland of South America / ALTI-PLANO
tablet / PAD; PILL; SLATE; TROCHE; LOZENGE
tablet of stone / STELA, STELE
tableware / LINEN; SILVER
tabloid / NEWSPAPER. COM-PRESSED
taboo / BAN; TABU. INTERDICTED
taboo's opposite / NOA
tabor / DRUM; ATABAL, TABRET; TIMBREL
taborine / SIDEDRUM
tabula rasa / CLEANSLATE
tabular / FLAT; ARRANGED; LAMINATED
tabulation / LIST; SCHEDULE
tachygraphy / SHORTHAND
tacit / SILENT; INFERRED, UN-SPOKEN
taciturn / BRIEF; LACONIC; RETI-CENT
tack / BEAT; BASTE; FASTEN. BRAD, GEAR, NAIL
tackle / HOLD; GRASP. CAT; GEAR; ROPES; OUTFIT
tacky / UNTIDY; UNKEMPT
Tacoma's sound / PUGET
tact / KNACK, SKILL; ADDRESS, FINESSE
tactful / POLITE; AFFABLE
tactic / ORDERED, REGULAR
tactical pitfall / AMBUSH
tactics / PLANS; MANAGEMENT; GENERALSHIP
tad / BOY; GAMIN; URCHIN
tadpole / POLLIWOG
taenia / RIBBON; TAPEWORM
taffeta / LACY; ORNATE
taffy / CANDY; TOFFEE; WELSHMAN
tafia / RUM
tag / RAG; GAME, LAMB; AGLET, LABEL
tag player / IT
Tagalog / FILIPINO
Tagore play / CHITRA
tagrag / RIFFRAFF
Tahiti / OTAHEITE
Tahiti capital / PAPEETE

Tahitian deity / ORO; TAAROA
Tahitian peak / OROHENA
Tahiti's island group / SOCIETIES
tai / LAO
tail / TAG; TRACE. END; REAR; CAUDA; APPENDAGE
tail of rabbit / SCUT
tail-first / BACKWARDS
tailings / BRAN; CHAFF, FOOTS; RESIDUE
tailless cat / MANX
tailless rodent / PACA
taillike / CAUDAL
tailor /CUTTER, DRAPER, FITTER, SARTOR; BUSHELMAN
tailor's implement / HAM; GOOSE; NEEDLE, THREAD; SADIRON, THIMBLE
tails / VERSO
tain / TINFOIL; TINPLATE; CATTLE-RAID
Taino / ARAWAK
taint / ROT; SPOT; STAIN, SULLY; BLEMISH; DISGRACE
tainted / BAD; SPOILED; CONTAMI-NATED
Taipings' conqueror / GORDON
Taiwan / FORMOSA
Taj Mahal builder / JAHAN, JEHAN
Taj Mahal location / AGRA; INDIA
take / USE; HOLD, SNAP; ADOPT, CATCH, CLASP, GRASP; ACCEPT, CHOOSE, ENTRAP
take all tricks / CAPOT
take amiss / RESENT
take away / CUT; ADEEM; REMOVE; SUBTRACT
take back / RECANT, RETURN; RESCIND
take beforehand / PREEMPT
take a bite / SNACK; NIBBLE
take breath / REST; PAUSE
take captive / CATCH; ARREST
take care / HEED, MIND; NURSE; BEWARE
take care of a horse / GROOM
take on cargo / LADE, STOW
take a chair / SIT
take cognizance of / NOTICE
take to court / SUE
take delight / JOY
take dinner / SUP; DINE
take a direction / HEAD; STAND
take down / NOTE; HUMILIATE
take ease / REST; RELAX
take by force / SEIZE; RAVISH
take illegally / ROB; FILCH, POACH, STEAL; BURGLE, PILFER
take as likely / PRESUME
take the main meal / DINE
take movies of / FILM
take much delight / REVEL; WAL-LOW

take off / DOFF; LEAVE
take off weight / DIET; REDUCE
take for oneself / ADOPT
take out / DELE; ELIDE, ERASE; DE-
LETE
take part / SIDE; SHARE; CO-
OPERATE
take place / OCCUR; HAPPEN
take the place of / DISPLACE, SUP-
PLANT
take place regularly / RECUR
take precedence / OUTRANK, PRE-
CEDE
take root / LOCATE, SETTLE
take a seat / SIT
take as spoil / REAVE
take into stomach / EAT; SWALLOW
take supper / SUP; DINE
take a tenth / TITHE; DECIMATE
take as true/ POSIT
take umbrage / RESENT
talapoin / MONK; GUENON
talbot / HOUND
talc / POWDER; STEATITE; SOAP-
STONE
tale / YARN; FABLE, STORY; AC-
COUNT
tale of adventure / GEST; CONTE
talent / ART; GIFT; FLAIR, FORTE
talented / APT; CLEVER; SKILLED
Tales of Hoffman song / BAR-
CAROLE
talesman / JURYMAN
taleteller / GOSSIP; TATTLER
talipe / CLUBFOOT
talisman / AMULET, GRIGRI, MAS-
COT
talismanic inscription / ABRA-
CADABRA
talk / GAB, GAS; CHAT; HAVER,
ORATE, PRATE; GOSSIP, PARLEY;
CONSULT, PALAVER. RUMOR;
SPEECH; COLLOQUY, DIALOGUE
talk before curtain / PROLOGUE
talk dully / PROSE
talk familiarly / CHAT
talk foolishly / GAB; BABBLE,
DRIVEL; CHATTER
talk glibly / PATTER; CHATTER
talk idly / PRATE; GOSSIP
talk imperfectly / LISP; STAMMER,
STUTTER
talk inconsequentially / CHATTER
talk rapidly / GUSH; CHATTER
talk of trivia / SMATTER
talk wildly / RANT, RAVE
talk unintelligibly / PRATTLE
talkative / GARRULOUS; LOQUA-
CIOUS
talking / SPEAKING; CONVERSING
talking bird / MYNA; MYNAH;
PARROT

talking horse of Achilles / BALIOS;
XANTHOS
tall / HIGH; LOFTY; ELEVATED; EX-
AGGERATED
tall drink / HIGHBALL
tall edifice / TOWER; SKYSCRAPER
tall sedge / PAPYRUS
tall tale / BRAG, YARN; WHOPPER
tall timber / BACKWOODS, BOON-
DOCKS
tall tree / ELM, OAK; SEQUOIA
tall wine glass / FLUTE
tallage / TAX; TOLL; IMPOSITION
tallboy / HIGHBOY
Tallin / REVAL
tallit / PRAYERSHAWL
tallow / FAT; SUET; CANDLE,
GREASE
tallow, c.f. / STEAR; STEARO
tallow tree / CERA
tallowy / GREASY
tally / FIT; SUIT; AGREE. TAB;
SCORE; ACCOUNT
tallyho / COACH
talma / CAPE
Talmud / MISHNAH
Talmudic commentary / AGGADA,
GEMARA; HAGGADA, HALAKAH
Talmudic rabbi / AMDRA
talon / CLAW, NAIL, OGEE, SPUR
talpa / WEN; MOLE
talus / ANKLE, ASTRA, GALUS,
SCREE, SLOPE
tam / CAP; BERET
tamale wrapper / CORNHUSK
tamarack / LARCH
tamarin / MARMOSET
tamarisk / ATLE; ATLEE
Tamar's husband / ER
tambourine / DAIRA; TIMBREL
tame / DULL, FLAT, MILD, POOR;
GENTLE; INSIPID. SUBDUE; CON-
QUER; DOMESTICATE
tame animal / PET
tame cat / WEAKLING
tameless / WILD; FERAL
tamely / MEEKLY; QUIETLY
taminlike cloth / DUROY
tamis / TAMMY; STRAINER
tamp / PUG, RAM; PACK; POUND
tamper / BRIBE; DABBLE, MEDDLE,
TRIFLE
tampico fiber / HEMP; ISTLE
tampion / PLUG; STOPPER
tam-tam / GONG
tan / BARK, BUFF, ECRU; BEIGE;
BRONZE. TAW; BEAT
tanager / YENI; HABIA, LINDO;
REDBIRD
Tancred's cousin / BOHEMOND
tang / SHANK, TASTE; FLAVOR
tangent / TOUCHING

tangible / REAL; PLAIN, SOLID; EVIDENT
Tangier inhabitant / TANGERINE
tangle / MAT; KNOT; SNARL; SLEAVE. MOP; SHAG
tangleberry / HUCKLEBERRY
tangled bunch / MOP; SHAG
tanglefoot / WHISKEY; MOONSHINE
tangly / KNOTTED; ENTANGLED
tango / DANCE
tangy / SHARP; PUNGENT
tank / VAT; BASIN; BOILER; CISTERN
tankard / MUG; HANAP, STEIN
tanker / OILER
tanna / HOMILIST
Tannenberg victor / HINDENBURG
tanner / BATEMAN; SIXPENCE
tanning gum / KINO
tanning plant / AMLA, AMLI; ALDER
tantalize / IRK, NAG, VEX; TEASE; TORMENT
Tantalus' daughter / NIOBE
Tantalus' father / ZEUS
tantamount / EQUAL; EQUIVALENT
tantara / BLARE; FANFARE
tantivy / RUSH; GALLOP
tantra / TEXT; AGAMA; TREATISE
tantrum / FIT; RAGE; PAROXYSM
Tanzania capital / DARESSALAAM
Tanzanian island / PEMBA; ZANZIBAR
Tanzanian lake / NYASA; MALAWI; VICTORIA
Tanzanian language / SWAHILI
Tanzanian mountain / KILIMANJARO
Taoism's founder / LAOTSE, LAOTZE
tap / PLUG; FAUCET, SPIGOT. PAT; BROACH, SELECT, STRIKE
tap dance / STEPDANCE
tapa / BARKCLOTH
tape / BIND, SEAL; FASTEN, RECORD; MEASURE. STRIP
tape measure / TAPELINE
tape needle / BODKIN
taped / GAUGED; RECORDED
taper/ CANDLE. CONVERGE
taper a ship's timber / SNAPE
tapered / POINTED; DWINDLED
tapered piece / GORE, SHIM; GUSSET
tapering / CONIC; TERETE; LANCEOLATE
tapering figure / CONE
tapering pillar / OBELISK
tapestry / ARRAS, TAPIS; DOSSER; GOBELIN
tapeti / RABBIT

tapeworm / TAENIA
tapioca / SALEP; MANIOC; CASSAVA
tapir / ANTA; DANTA; SALADANG
tapoa / PHALANGER
Taprobane / CEYLON
tparoom / BAR, PUB; SALOON; BARROOM
taproot / FOUNDATION
taps / LIGHTSOUT
tapster / BARTENDER
Tapuya / GE; ACROA; BOTOCUDO, CAINGANG
tar / GOB; BREA; PITCH; SAILOR; ASPHALT. SMEAR
Tar Heel State / NORTH CAROLINA
taradiddle / FIB; FALSEHOOD
tarantula / SPIDER
Tara's mistress / SCARLETT
tarassis / HYSTERIA
tarboosh / FEZ; TURBAN
tardily / SLOWLY; DELIBERATELY
tardy / LATE, SLOW; REMISS; DILATORY
tare / WEED; VETCH; ALLOWANCE
targe / SHIELD. THRASH
target / BUTT, GOAL, MARK; BUCKLER
Targum / RESTATEMENT
tariff / TAX; DUTY, LEVY, RATE
tarin / SISKIN
Tarkington character / PENROD
tarlatan / MUSLIN
tarn / LAKE
tarnal / INFERNAL
tarnish / DULL, SOIL, SPOT; BEDIM, SULLY; DARKEN
taro / EDDO, GABE, KALO; AROID; DASHEEN
taro paste / POI
tarot / TRUMP; PLAYINGCARD
tarp / CANVAS, PAULIN; TARPAULIN
tarpon / SABALO; SILVERFISH
tarradiddle / FIB, LIE
tarriance / DELAY; DEFERRAL
tarrock / GULL; KITTIWAKE
tarry / LAG; BIDE, FLAG, STAY, WAIT; DELAY
Tarrytown resident / IRVING
tarsus / FOOT; ANKLE, MANUS
tart / ACID, KEEN, SOUR; ACRID, SHARP. PIE; PASTRY; STRUMPET
tartan / PLAID; HIGHLANDER
Tartar / TURK; ARGAL, ARGOL. See also Tatar
tartarus / ABYSS, HADES
Tartini's B flat / ZA
tartness / ACIDITY; ACERBITY
task / JOB; DUTY, BONUS, TOIL, CHORE, STENT, STINT
task as punishment / PENSUM

taskmaster / BOSS; OVERSEER
Tasmania capital / HOBART
Tasmanian cape / GRIM
Tasmanian crayfish / YABBIE
Tasmanian devil / DASYURE
Tasmanian lake / ECHO
Tasmanian river / TAMAR
Tasmanian wolf / YABBI; THYLA-CINE
tassel / TERCEL; GOSHAWK, PENDANT
taste / SIP, SUP; SAVOR. TANG, ZEST; SAPOR, SNACK, STYLE; PALATE; JUDGMENT
tasteful / NEAT; ELEGANT
tasteless / DULL, FLAT; VAPID
tastelessness / CRUDITY; VUL-GARITY
tasty / SAPID; ELEGANT
tat / JUTE, LACE; GUNNY
ta-ta / GOODBY
Tatar capital / KAZAN
Tatar dynasty / KIN, WEI
Tatar horseman / UHLAN; COSSACK
Tatar of northern China / HU
Tatar tribe / HUNS, SHOR; ALANI, HORDE
Tatler writer / STEELE; ADDISON
tatter / BIT, RAG; SHRED. REND
tatterdemalion / SLOPPY; DIS-REPUTABLE
tattle / BLAB, TELL; GOSSIP
tattler / GOSSIP; BLABBERMOUTH
tattletale / TELLTALE
tattletale gray / WHITISH
tattoo / PONY; POUNCH, RATTAT
tau / ANKH; CROSS
taught / EDUCATED, INFORMED
taunt / GIVE, JEER, JIBE, MOCK TWIT; SCOFF
taupe / MOLESKIN
taurine / BOVINE
tauromachy / BULLFIGHT
Taurus / BULL
taut / SNUG; TENSE, TIGHT
tautog / CHUB; BLACKFISH
tautology / PLEONASM; RE-DUNDANCY
tautophony / REPETITION
tavern / INN, PUB; HOTEL; CABA-RET, CANTINA
taw / ALLEY; MARBLE. TAN
tawdry / CHEAP, GAUDY, SHOWY; FLASHY
tawny / TAN; OLIVE, SWART
tawny antelope / ORIBI
tawny carnivore / LION
taws / FLOG, WHIP; THONG
tax / CESS, DUTY, GELD, LEVY, RATE, SCOT, SESS, TOLL; STENT, TITHE; CHARGE, EXCISE, IM-POST, OCTROI; GABELLE. STRAIN

taxi / CAB. START
Tchad / CHAD
tea / SHRUB; SOCIAL, TISANE
tea brewer / SAMOVAR
tea ceremony / CHANOYU
tea container / CADDY; CANISTER
tea powder / MATCHA
tea table / TEAPOY
tea utensils / MIZUYADOGU
tea variety / BOHEA, HISON, OOPAK, PEKOE; OOLONG
teach / DRILL, GUIDE, TRAIN, TUTOR; DIRECT, INFORM; EDUCATE
teacher / TUTOR; DOCENT, MEN-TOR; TRAINER; PEDAGOGUE
teacher of Alexander / ARISTOTLE
teacher of Samuel / ELI
teacher's association / NEA
teacher's helper / MONITOR
teaching / TRAINING; INSTRUC-TION
teaching aide / TA
teaching art / PEDAGOGY; PAIDEUTICS
teal / GARGANEY
team / RIG; BAND, CREW, GANG, SPAN; SQUAD, TROOP. JOIN
team of horses / SPAN
team supporters / FANS; ROOTERS
teamed / YOKED; GROUPED
teamster / CARTER, DRIVER; TRUCKMAN
teamster's command / GEE, HAW
teapot cover / COSY
teapoy / TEATABLE
tear / RIP; REND; SUNDER. JAG; RENT
tear apart / RIP; REND; TATTER; DESTROY
tear down / RAZE; WRECK; DE-MOLISH
tear gas / LACRIMATOR
tear out / PLUCK; EXTRACT
tear to bits / MINCE, SHRED
teardrop / LARME; LACHRYMA
tearful / MAUDLIN, WEEPING LACHRYMOSE
tearless / DRYEYED
tease / NAG, RAG, VEX; COMB, TWIT; BADGER, HARASS, HEC-TOR, PESTER
teaser / COMEON, PUZZLE, RIDDLE
technical vocabulary / GLOSSARY
technicality / DETAIL; LEGALISM
technique / ART; METHOD; SCIENCE
techy / FRETFUL, PEEVISH
tectiform / ROOFLIKE
tectonic / STRUCTURAL; DEFORMA-TION
ted / DRY; SPREAD

tedious / DRY; LONG, SLOW; PROSY
tedium / ENNUI; WEARINESS
tee / GOAL; MOUND, POINT
teem / POUR; ABOUND, THRONG
teeming / FULL; REPLETE; SWARMING
teemless / BARREN; CHILDLESS
teen / PAIN; SORROW. YOUTH
teenager / MINOR, YOUTH
teeny / TINY
teepee / TEPEE
teeter / SWAY; SEESAW
teeter-totter / SEESAW
teeth / BITE; BRUNT; DENTURE. See also tooth
teeth, pert. to / DENTAL
teeth coating / ENAMEL
teeth incrustation / PLAQUE, TARTAR
teeth protector / FLUORINE
teetotal / COMPLETE; ABSTINENT
teetotaler / DRY; ABSTAINER, RECHABITE
teetotum / TOP; DREIDEL
teg / SHEEP
tegular / TILELIKE
tegument / ARIL, SKIN; TESTA
tegument of a seed / TESTA
te-hee / TITTER
teil / LIME; LINDEN
tejon / COATI
tela / TISSUE
telamon / COLUMN
Telamon's brother / PELEUS
Telamon's father / AEACUS
Telamon's son / AJAX
telarian / SPIDER
telegram / WIRE; CABLE
telegraph / BUG; SIGNAL; SEMAPHORE
telegraph code / MORSE
telegraph inventor / MORSE
telegraph key / BUG; TAPPER
telegraph signal / DAH, DIT, DOT; DASH
telegrapher / OPERATOR
telegraphic / CONCISE, LACONIC
telegraphic speed unit / BAUD
telekinetic spirit / POLTERGEIST
Telemachus' father / ODYSSEUS
Telemachus' mother / PENELOPE
teleost / FISH
telepathist / MINDREADER
telepathy / ESP; MIND, WILL
telephone / CALL, DIAL, RING; PHONE
telephone exchange / CENTRAL; SWITCHBOARD
telephone inventor / BELL
telephone signal / BUZZ, RING
telephone wire / LINE
telescope / SPYGLASS; REFLECTOR

telescope inventor / GALILEO
television / TV; TUBE; VIDEO
television award / EMMY
television cable / CATV; COAXIAL
television equipment / CAMERA, SCREEN; ORTHICON
television gremlin / SNOW
television interference / SNOW; GHOST
television inventor / FARNSWORTH
television program / TELECAST
television recording / KINESCOPE
television tube / ICONOSCOPE
telic / FINAL; PURPOSEFUL
tell / COUNT, STATE, UTTER; IMPART, INFORM, RELATE
tell all / DEBUNK; CONFESS
tell all facts / RECOUNT
tell it to the Marines! / BOSH; BALONEY
tell off / RATE; ASSIGN
tell secrets / SPILL; GOSSIP, SNITCH, TATTLE
tell a story / YARN; REPORT; NARRATE
teller / CLERK; CASHIER; TALLYMAN
teller's post / CAGE
telling / COGENT; EFFECTIVE
telling blow / HIT; COUP, ONER; STROKE
Tell's canton / URI
Tell's oppressor / GESSLER
Tell's target / APPLE
telltale / BETRAYING. CUE; HINT; VALVE
tellurian / EARTHMAN
telpher / CABLECAR
telpherage / FUNICULAR
telson / PLEON; SEGMENT, TAILFAN
Telugu / GENTOO
tema / THEME
temblor / TREMOR; EARTHQUAKE
temerarious / RASH; IMPETUOUS
temerity / AUDACITY; PRECIPITANCY
temerous / CARELESS; INDISCREET
temescal / SWEATLODGE
Tempe vale mountain / OSSA; OLYMPUS
temper / CALM; ADAPT; ADJUST, ANNEAL, SOFTEN. MOOD, TONE; HUMOR; METTLE, SPIRIT
temper fit / PET; TANTRUM
temper glass / NEAL; ANNEAL
temperament / HABIT, HUMOR; NATURE
temperamental / EXCITABLE
temperance / SOBRIETY; MODERATION
temperate / CALM, COOL, SOBER; SEDATE

temperature / CALORICITY
temperature under freezing / FROST
tempered / HARDENED; MOLLIFIED
tempest / GALE, WIND; BLAST,
   ORAGE, STORM; COMMOTION
Tempest character / CALIBAN;
   PROSPERO
Tempest spirit / ARIEL
tempestive / TIMELY
tempestuous / GUSTY; TURBULENT
Templars' banner / BAUSEANT
template / MOLD; PATTERN, TEM-
   PLET
temple / VAT, WAT; FANE, NAOS,
   RATH; CELLA, MACAE; CHURCH,
   MOSQUE, PAGODA, SHRINE;
   SYNAGOGUE
temple porch / NARTHEX
temple room / NAOS; CELLA
temple tower / MINARET, SHIKARA
temple vestibule / PRONAOS
templed / ENSHRINED
tempo / TAKT, TIME; SPEED
temporal / LAY; CIVIL; SECULAR
temporalty / LAITY
temporarily / NONCE; MOMEN-
   TARILY
temporarily bright star / NOVA
temporary / PASSING, STOPGAP;
   PROVISIONAL
temporary abode / HOTEL, LODGE,
   MOTEL
temporary chairman / PROTEM
temporary device / STOPGAP
temporary drop / SLUMP
temporary expedient / JURY; MAKE-
   SHIFT
temporary fashion / FAD; FANCY
temporary gift / LOAN
temporary quarters / CAMP;
   BIVOUAC
temporary relief / RESPITE; RE-
   PRIEVE
temporary resident / TRANSIENT
temporary stage / PHASE
temporary stop / LULL, REST;
   PAUSE
temporize / TRIM; DELAY; COMPLY
temporizer / TIMESERVER
tempt / TRY; LURE, TEST; ENTICE
temptation / ALLURE, APPEAL
Tempter / DEVIL, SATAN
tempting / SEDUCTIVE; ATTRAC-
   TIVE
tempus / TIME
ten / DECADE, DENARY
ten, c.f. / DEC, DEK; DECA, DEKA
ten, suffix / TEEN
ten ares / DECARE
ten cents / DIME
Ten Commandments / DECALOGUE
ten decibels / BEL

ten dollar bill / SAWBUCK, TEN-
   SPOT
ten dollar gold piece EAGLE
ten million ergs / JOULE
ten million rupees / CRORE
ten as a quorum / MINYAN
ten thousand / MYRIAD
ten years / DECADE
tenable / DEFENSIBLE
tenacious / FIRM; STICKY; CLING-
   ING
tenacious substance / GLUE
tenacity / PLUCK; OBSTINACY
tenail / OUTWORK
tenancy / SOCAGE, TENURE
tenant / SAER; LESSEE, RENTER,
   VASSAL
tenant farm / CROFT
tend / CARE; GUARD, SERVE,
   TREND, VERGE, WATCH
tend a fire / STOKE
tend a garden / HOE; CULTIVATE
tend a horse / GROOM
tend to meet / CONVERGE
tend to rise / LEVITATE
tend toward / POINT; INCLINE
tendance / EMPLOY; SERVICE
tendency / BENT, BIAS; TREND
tender / KIND, MILD, SOFT, SORE;
   GENTLE; CAREFUL. BID; OFFER
tender feeling / SYMPATHY; SENTI-
   MENT
tenderfoot / TYRO; NOVICE,
   ROOKIE
tenderhearted / HUMANE; EMO-
   TIONAL
tenderly / SOFTLY; DELICATELY
tenderness / LOVE, PITY; PATHOS;
   DELICACY
tending / PRONE; LIKELY
tending to close / OCCLUSIVE
tending toward / FOR, PRO;
   MINDED
tendinous / SINEW
tendon / THEW; SINEW
tendon, c.f. / TENO
tendril / CILIUM, THREAD;
   CAPREOL
tenebrae / SERVICE, SHADOWS
tenebrific / SAD; GLOOMY
tenebrous / DARK; OBSCURE
tenement / FLAT; HOUSE; APART-
   MENT
tenent / HOLDING; GRASPING
Tenerife peak / TEYDE
tenet / VIEW; CREED, DOGMA,
   MAXIM; BELIEF; OPINION,
   PRECEPT
tenfold / DENARY; DECUPLE
ten-gallon hat / STETSON
tenné / ORANGE
Tennessee battlefield / SHILOH

Tennessee capital / NASHVILLE
Tennessee city / MEMPHIS
Tennessee dam / OCOEE; NORRIS
Tennessee lake / REELFOOT
Tennessee mountains / SMOKIES
Tennessee River rapids / MUSCLE-SHOALS
Tennessee state bird / MOCKING-BIRD
Tennessee state flower / IRIS
Tennessee state nickname / VOLUN-TEER
Tenniel subject / ALICE
tennis bat / RACKET
tennis cup / DAVIS
tennis match / DOUBLE, SINGLE
tennis point / ACE
tennis score / AD; SET; LOVE; DEUCE
tennis serve / ACE, JET; FAULT
tennis serve tipping net / LET
tennis shoes / SNEAKERS
tennis stroke / CUT, LOB; CHOP; VOLLEY
Tenno / MIKADO
Tennyson heroine / ENID, MAUD; ELAINE
Tenochtitlan / MEXICO
tenon / COG; COAK
tenor / GIST, MOOD, PART; DRIFT, TREND, VOICE; INTENT, SINGER
tenor mandolin / MANDOLA
tenor singer / CARUSO; MELCHIOR
tenor violin / VIOLA
tenoroon / OBOE
tenpennies / NAILS
ten-percenter / AGENT
tenpins / BOWLING
tense / TAUT; RIGID, TIGHT
tense of verb / PAST; AORIST; PER-FECT; PRETERIT
tensible / EXTENDABLE
ten-sided figure / DECAGON
tensile / DUCTILE
tension / RIGOR; STRAIN; STRETCH
ten-strike / STROKE; SUCCESS
tent / CANOPY, CANVAS; PAVILION
tent dweller / ARAB; CAMPER; SCENITE
tent flap / FLY; DOOR
tent show / CIRCUS; CARNIVAL
tentacle / PALP; FEELER; AN-TENNA
tentative / TRIAL; EXPERIMENT
tent-dwelling arabs / KEDAR
tented / ARCHED
tenter / STRETCHER
tenterhook / NAIL; SUSPENSE
tenth / TITHE. DECIMAL
tenth, pref. / DECI
tenth muse / SAPPHO
tenth nerve / VAGUS
tenth part / TITHE

tentmaker / OMAR; KHAYYAM
ten-twent-thirt / MELODRAMA
tenure / MANNER
tenuity / RARITY; THINNESS
tenuous / RARE, SLIM; SLENDER
tenure / RIGHT; HOLDING; POSSES-SION
teosinte / GRASS; FODDER
tepee / TENT; WIGWAM
tepid / WARM; LUKEWARM
tepidarium / WARMROOM
Terah's son / ABRAM, HARAN
teramorphous / DEFORMED
teraph / IMAGE; TALISMAN
teratism / ANOMALY, MONSTER
teratoid / ABNORMAL; MON-STROUS
tercel / FALCON; GOSHAWK
tercet / TRIPLET
terebinth / TURPENTINE
terebra / OVIPOSITOR
terebrate / BORE
teredo / SHIPWORM
terek / SANDPIPER
terella / EARTHKIN
terephah / TREF; UNCLEAN
Teresian / CARMELITE
terete / TAPERING
Tereus' son / ITYS
Tereus' wife / PROCNE
tergal / DORSAL
tergam / BACK; DORSUM
tergiversation / EVASION
tergiversator / TRIMMER; APOSTATE
term / DUB; CALL, NAME. TIME, WORD; LIMIT; TENURE; SEMESTER
term in arithmetic / ADD; DIVIDE; MULTIPLY
term in baccarat / BANCO
term in billiards / KISS; CAROM
term in geometry / CONE, CUBE; LOCUS; THEOREM
term in living / AGE
term mark / GRADE
term in music / ATONAL; MELODIC
term in office / TENURE
term in school / SEMESTER
term in tag / IT
term in trigonometry / SINE; CO-SINE, RADIAN, SECANT, SECTOR; TANGENT
termagant / SHREW; VIRAGO
terminable / LIMITABLE
terminal / END; DEPOT, LIMIT; FI-NALE. FINAL
terminal of battery / ANODE; CATH-ODE
terminal of nerve cell / AXITE
terminate / END; STOP; CEASE
termination / FINALE; CONCLUSION
termination of disease / LYSIS

terminology / CANT; NOMENCLA-
TURE
terminus / GOAL; LIMIT
termite / ANAI, ANAY
termites / ISOPTERA
termless / ENDLESS; INFINITE
terms / PROVISOS; CONDITIONS
tern / KIP; DARR, NOIO; SKIRR;
MEDRICK
ternal / THREEFOLD
ternary / THIRD; TRIPLE
ternate / TRIFOLIOLATE
terne / ALLOY. TIN
tern-like bird / GULL; SKIMMER
terpsichore / DANCE; DANCING
terra / EARTH
terra alba / GYPSUM, KAOLIN
terra cotta / CLAYWARE
terra firma / LAND
terra rosa / REDOCHER
terrace / BANK; PATIO; BALCONY
terrain / ARENA; MILIEU, REGION
terrane / FORMATION
terrapin / EMYD; POTTER, TURTLE
terrene / GEAL; EARTHLY, MUN-
DANE
terreplein / FOOTING
terrestrial / EARTHLY; SUBLUNARY
terret / RING
terrible / DIRE, GRIM; AWFUL; HOR-
RID, SEVERE
terrier / BULL, SKYE; CAIRN; AIRE-
DALE
terrific / HUGE; FEARFUL
terrified / AFRAID, SCARED
terrify / ALARM, DAUNT; DISMAY
terrifying / DIRE; AWFUL
terrifying person / OGRE;
BUGBEAR, MONSTER
terrine / STEW; TUREEN; EARTHEN-
WARE
territorial / RESERVIST; MILITIA-
MAN
territorial district / AMT; CANTON;
PROVINCE
territory / AREA, LAND; DOMAIN
territory ruled by a ban / BANAT
territory within another / ENCLAVE
terror / FEAR; PANIC; FRIGHT
terrorist / GOON, THUG
terrorize / COERCE; INTIMIDATE
terse / CURT; PITHY; CONCISE
tersely / BRIEFLY; SUCCINCTLY
terseness / BREVITY; ABRUPTNESS
tertial / TERTIARY
tertian / INTERMITTENT
terutero / LAPWING
tessellated / MOSAIC; CHECKERED
tessera / DIE; TILE; TOKEN
Tess's husband / CLARE
test / TRY; ASSAY, ESSAY, TEMPT;
EXAMINE. ORAL, QUIZ; CUPEL,
PROOF, TRIAL

test eggs / CANDLE
test grade / MARK
test match prize / ASHES
test ore / ASSAY; ANALYZE
test print / PROOF; GALLEY
test vessel / CUPEL; CRUCIBLE
testa / SHELL; INTEGUMENT
testament / WILL; COVENANT
testator / MAKER
tester / AWNING, CANOPY; EX-
AMINER
testifier / WITNESS; DEPONENT
testify / AVER, AVOW; AFFIRM, DE-
POSE
testify under oath / SWEAR; DE-
PONE
testimonial / TRIBUTE
testimony / EVIDENCE; DEPOSI-
TION
testiness / TEMPER; PROCACITY
testing / ASSAY, TRIAL
testudo / LYRE; SCREEN
testy / CROSS; TOUCHY; FRETFUL
tetanus / LOCKJAW
tete-a-tete / PRIVATE. CHAT; SET-
TEE
tether / ROPE. TIE; FASTEN
tethered / LEASHED
Teton peak / OWEN; MORAN
Tetons' discoverer / COLTER
tetrachord / INTERVAL
tetrachord note / MESE, NETE
tetrahedral / FOURSIDED
tetrapod / QUADRUPED
tetter / FRET; FAVUS; HERPES
tetterwort / PUCCOON, REDROOT
Teutoburg victor / ARMINIUS
Teuton / GOTH; GERMAN
Teutonic / See also Norse
Teutonic deities / AESIR, VANIR
Teutonic goddess of fate / NORN
Teutonic king / ALARIC
Teutonic letter / RUNE
Teutonic people / GEPIDAE
Teutonic war god / ER; ERR
Tevere / TIBER
tew / ADO; FUSS
tewel / BORE, VENT; TUYERE
Texas capital / AUSTIN
Texas city / WACO; AUSTIN, DAL-
LAS, ELPASO, LAREDO
Texas Indians / LIPAN, TEJAS
Texas leaguer / HIT
Texas national park / BIGBEND
Texas policeman / RANGER
Texas river / RED; BRAZOS
Texas shrine / ALAMO
Texas state bird / MOCKINGBIRD
Texas state flower / BLUEBONNET
Texas state motto / FRIENDSHIP
Texas state nickname / LONESTAR
Texas state tree / PECAN
text / TOPIC, VERSE; SUBJECT

textbook / MANUAL, PRIMER
textile / CLOTH; FABRIC. KNIT
textile cross-threads / WEFT, WOOF
textile manufacturer / WEAVER
textile from mulberry bark / TAPA
textile from raffia / RABANNA
textile screw pine / ARA; PANDAN
textile threads / WARP, WOOF
textile wholesaler / FACTOR
textual / VERBAL; LITERAL
texture / WEB; WALE; GRAIN
Thackeray hero / ESMOND
Thackeray heroine / BECKY
Thai / SIAMESE
Thailand / SIAM. See also Siam, Siamese
Thailand capital / BANGKOK
Thailand coin / ATT; BAHT; TICAL
Thailand isthmus / KRA
Thailand measure / RAI, SAT, SOK, WAH
Thailand people / LAO, TAI
Thailand temple / VAT, WAT
Thailand weight / PAI; CATTY, PICUL
Thais author / FRANCE
Thais composer / MASSENET
thalassian / TURTLE
thalassic / MARINE; OCEANIC
Thalia / MUSE; GRACE; NEREID; ASTEROID
thallophyte / ALGA; FUNGUS, LICHEN
Thames / ISIS
Thames battle victim / TECUMSEH
Thames bridge / TOWER; LAMBETH
Thames sandbank / NORE
Thames source / ISIS; CHURN
Thames-side section / FULHAM, PUTNEY
than / BUT; WHEN; EXCEPT
thana / POST; STATION
thanatos / DEATH
thane / CHIEF; SERVANT; HENCHMAN
thank / REQUITE; ACKNOWLEDGE
thank offering / FIRSTFRUITS
thankful / BEHOLDEN, GRATEFUL
thankfulness / GRATITUDE
thankless / NASTY; PROFITLESS
thankless person / INGRATE
thanks / PRAISE; GRATITUDE
thanks to / SINCE; BECAUSE
thanksgiving / GRATITUDE
that / IT; YON. WHICH
that is / IE; IDEST
that is to say / VIZ; NAMELY
that man / HE; HIM
that man's / HIS
that may be moved / PORTABLE
that one / HE, IT; HER, HIM, SHE
that specifically / THE
that thing / IT

that which, suffix / ER
that which attracts / LURE; LODE-STONE
that which is educed / EDUCT
that which follows / SEQUELA
that which is left / REST; RE-MAINDER
that which uncloses / KEY; OPEN-SESAME
that woman / HER, SHE
that woman's / HERS
thatch / HAIR, REED; COVER, STRAW
thatching / NETI, NIPA
thatness / EXISTENCE
thaumaturge / CONJURER, MAGI-CIAN
thaumaturgy / MAGIC; CONJURY
thaw / MELT; RELENT; LIQUEFY
the Bard of Avon / SHAKESPEARE
the Bear / URSA, WAIN; DIPPER
the Beloved Physician / LUKE
the choicest part / CREAM, ELITE; FLOWER
the Coast / CALIFORNIA
the cold months / WINTER
the colors / FLAG
thé dansant / TEADANCE
the deep / SEA; OCEAN
the devil / FIEND, SATAN; LUCIFER, OLDNICK
the dumps / DOLDRUMS
the East / ORIENT
the end / FINIS, OMEGA; THIRTY
the Eternal City / ROME
the Fair Penitent's deceiver / LO-THARIO
the Garden / EDEN; PARADISE
the gist / NUB
the Hunter / ORION
the Lion / LEO
the Lion of God / ALI
the Lord's Table / ALTAR
the masses / MOB; HOIPOLLOI
the Omnipotent / GOD
the one there / THAT
the Orient / EAST
the present / NOW; TODAY
the Ram / ARIES
the Sails / VELA
the same / IDEM; DITTO; ENCORE
the Tent Maker / OMAR
the Terrible / IVAN
the theatre / DRAMA
the Thin Man / WYNANT
the thing here / THIS
the thing there / THAT
the time being / PRESENT
T-head bolt / TOGGLE
theanthropos / CHRIST, GODMAN
thearchy / THEOCRACY
theater / DRAMA, ODEON, ODEUM, STAGE

theater actor / THESPIAN
theater attendant / PAGE; USHER
theater audience / HOUSE
theater award / TONY
theater company / CAST; TROUPE
theater curtain / DROP
theater district / RIALTO; DOWN-TOWN
theater floor / PIT; ORCHESTRA
theater group / ACT; ANTA
theater offering / DRAMA; COMEDY, REVUE
theater passage / AISLE
theater platform / STAGE; PODIUM
theater section / BOX; LOGE; BALCONY
theater set / SCENE
theater sign / SRO; MARQUEE
theater stall / LOGE
theater ticket / STUB
theater of war / FIELD, FRONT
theatergoer / SPECTATOR
theatergoers / AUDIENCE
theatrical / SHOWY, STAGY; DRAMATIC
theatrical acting / HISTRIONICS
theatrical exhibition / SPECTACLE
theatrical practice / HISTRIONISM
theatrical production / REVUE
theatrical profession / STAGE
theatrical reviewer / CRITIC
theatrical sketch / JIG; SKIT
theatrical success / HIT
theatrics / DRAMATICS; HISTRIONICS
theatron / STAGE
Theban acropolis / CADMEA
Theban god / AMUN
Theban hero / OEDIPUS
Theban king / CREON; OEDIPUS
Theban poet / PINDAR
Theban statue / MEMNON
Thebes founder / CADMUS
Thebes' name in Bible / NO
theca / SAC; CASE; SHEATH
theft / HAUL; FRAUD; LARCENY
thegn / THANE
thematic / TOPICAL; ESSENTIAL
theme / TEXT; ESSAY, LEMMA, MOTIF
theme in music / TEMA; MOTIF
then / ANON, ERGO, NEXT, THUS; HENCE
thenar / PALM
thenar eminence / MOUNTOF-VENUS
thence / THEREAFTER
Theocritean poem / IDYLL
theodolite / ALIDADE, TRANSIT
theologian / DIVINE; CLERGYMAN
theological school / SEMINARY; THEOLOGATE

theological virtues / HOPE; FAITH; CHARITY
theology / DIVINITY
theology of Christian unity / IRENICS
theomorphic / GODSHAPED
theophany / INCARNATION
theorbo / LUTE
theorem / AXIOM; PROPOSITION
theoretical / SPECULATIVE
theoretical force / OD; BIOD, ELOD, ODYL
theory / ISM; IDEA; SCHEME, SYSTEM
theory of evolution / DARWINISM
theory's proof / APAGOGE; REDUCTIO
theosophist / BESANT; BLAVATSKY
theosophy / MYSTICISM
therapeutic / HEALING; CURATIVE
therapeutic fluid / SERUM
therapy / CURE; HEALING
there / YON; THITHER
thereabout / SAY; NEARLY
thereafter / THENCE
thereby / SO; THUS
therefore / SO; ERGO, THEN, THUS
therein / WITHIN
thereupon / WHEN; WHEREAT
theriaca / TREACLE; ANTIDOTE
therm / BATHS; CALORIE
thermae / SPA; SPRINGS
thermal / HOT; WARM
thermal unit / BTU; DEGREE; CALORIE
thermometer / CALORIMETER
Thermopylae hero / LEONIDAS
thermostat / REGULATOR
thersitical / VULGAR; ABUSIVE
thesaurus / LEXICON; TREASURY
thesaurus compiler / ROGET
Theseus' city / ATHENS
Theseus' conquest / MINOTAUR
Theseus' father / AEGEUS
Theseus' friend / PIRITHOUS
Theseus' helper / ARIADNE
Theseus' stepmother / MEDEA
Theseus' victim / PROCRUSTES
Theseus' wife / ANTIOPE, PHAEDRA
thesis / ESSAY, PAPER; TREATISE
Thesmophoria celebrant / WOMAN
thespesia / BENDY, MAHOE
thespian / ACTOR. DRAMATIC
Thessalian king / AEOLUS
Thessalian mountain / OSSA; PELION
Thessalian vale / TEMPE
thetic / ARBITRARY
Thetis' husband / PELEUS
Thetis' son / ACHILLES
theurgic / MAGIC; MIRACULOUS
thews / BRAWN; SINEWS; MUSCLES

they / MEN; PEOPLE
thiamine / BONE
thiamine deficiency disease / BERIBERI
thick / FAT; DENSE, MISTY, MUDDY; STUPID, TORPID; COMPACT
thick board / BEAM; PLANK; TIMBER
thick bushy growth / TOD
thick covering / COVERT
thick fabric / DRAB; LODEN
thick growth / THICKET
thick gruel / LOBLOLLY
thick hair / BUSH, MANE
thick laying on of paint / IMPASTO
thick lubricant / GREASE
thick mixture / PASTE; SLURRY
thick ointment / SALVE; UNGUENT
thick part of sour milk / CURD
thick porridge / MUSH
thick silk / GROS; SATIN
thick slice / SLAB
thick soup / GUMBO, PUREE; POTAGE
thick of things / PRESS
thicken / GEL; JELL; CONGEAL; INSPISSATE
thickened juice / ROB; RHOB; SHRAB
thicket / BOSK, SHAW; COPSE, GROVE, SHOLA
thicketed country / CHAPARRAL
thickheaded / DENSE; STUPID
thickleaf / JADEPLANT
thick-lipped / LABROSE
thickly populated / DENSE; TEEMING
thickness / PLY; LAYER; DIAMETER
thickset / BULKY, BURLY, STOUT
thickset horse / COB
thickskinned / INSENSITIVE
thickskulled / DULL; STUPID
thickwitted / STUPID; DOLTISH
thief / CROOK; ROBBER; BURGLAR
thief trainer / FAGIN; KIDSMAN
thieve / GLOM; FILCH, STEAL; PILFER
thieves' jargon / ARGOT
thigh / HAM; HAUNCH
thigh, pert. to / CRURAL; FEMORAL
thighbone / FEMUR
thill / SHAFT
thimblerigger / CHEAT
thin / BONY, LANK, LEAN, RARE, SLIM; LANKY, SHEER; DILUTE, FLIMSY, SPARSE
thin, c.f. / SERO
thin board / LATH, SLAT
thin book / BOOKLET; PAMPHLET
thin cake / SCONE, WAFER; CRACKER
thin coating / FILM; PELLICLE
thin cotton cloth / JACONET

thin covering / VENEER
thin disk / PATEN, WAFER; SEQUIN
thin and dry / PAPERY
thin fabric / MULL; TULLE, VOILE; PONGEE; CHIFFON
thin fog / MIST
thin griddle cake / PANCAKE
thin layer / FILM; LAMELLA
thin layer of plywood / VENEER
Thin Man's dog / ASTA
thin metallic sound / TINKLE
thin muslin / MULL; TARLATAN
thin nail / BRAD
thin out / DILUTE; ATTENUATE
thin paper / PELURE, TISSUE; ONIONSKIN
thin part of soured milk / WHEY
thin porridge / GRUEL
thin rain / MIST; DRIZZLE
thin scale / LAMINA; LAMELLA
thin sheet of animal tissue / MEMBRANE
thin sheet of metal / FOIL
thin soup / BROTH
thin streak / LINE
thin tin plate / TAIN
thin in tone / REEDY
thin wooden fragment / SLIVER; SPLINTER
thine / THY; YOUR
thing / RES; ENTITY, MATTER, OBJECT; ASSEMBLY
thing added / INSET; ADDENDUM
thing differing / VARIANT
thing done / ACT; DEED
thing that exists / REALITY
thing found / TROVE
thing granted / AXIOM; PREMISE
thing hard to bear / MISERY, SORROW
thing in itself / NOUMENON
thing in law / RES; CHOSE
thing left out / OMISSION
thing of small value / BAUBLE
thing supposed / PREMISE
things / TRAPPINGS; BELONGINGS
things to be done / AGENDA; PROGRAM
things bought / ACATES
things done / ACTA; DEEDS
things owned / PROPERTY
things past / BYGONES
things to see / SIGHTS
things sensed / PHENOMENA
things of small value / TRIVIA
thingumbob / GIZMO; GADGET
think / WIS; DEEM, TROW, WEEN; FANCY, JUDGE, OPINE; BELIEVE
think about / CONSIDER
think back / REMINISCE
think better of / RECONSIDER
think deeply / PONDER; RUMINATE
think highly of / ADMIRE

think logically / REASON
think of / CONTEMPLATE
think out loud / BRAINSTORM
think over / MULL, MUSE
think over at length / BROOD
thinkable / CONCEIVABLE
Thinker sculptor / RODIN
thinly diffused / SCARCE, SPARSE
thinned out / DILUTED
thinner / LEANER; SKINNIER
thinness / RARITY; TENUITY
third / TIERCE
third, c.f. / TRIT
third base / HOTCORNER
third class / STEERAGE
third day / TERTIAN
third degree / TORTURE
third in degree / TERTIARY
third estate / COMMONS
third person / HE; HIM; THEM, THEY
third person ending / TH; ETH
third power / CUBE
Third Reich leader / HITLER;
   FUEHRER
thirlage / MULTURE
thirsting / SITIENT
thirsty / DRY; ADRY, AVID;
   PARCHED
thirteenth Hebrew month / VEADAR
thirty / END; FINISH
thirty masses / TRENTAL
this evening / TONIGHT
this minute / NOW; INSTANTLY
this place / HERE
this time / NOW
this way / SO; THUS
Thisbe's lover / PYRAMUS
thisness / REALITY; HAECCEITY
thistle / ASTER; DINDLE; HOGWEED
thistle bird / GOLDFINCH
thistle butterfly / PAINTEDLADY
thistledown / FLUFF
thither / THERE; YONDER
thole / PIN; OARLOCK. BEAR;
   SUFFER
tholos / SESE
Thomas / DOUBTER
Thomas opera / MIGNON
Thomism's expounder / AQUINAS
thong / LASH, RIEM, WHIP; BRAIL,
   QUIRT, STRAP
thong to toss javelin / AMENTUM
thong-shaped / LIGULATE
thooid / WOLFLIKE
thorax / CHEST; BREAST; CUIRASS
thorax crustacean / PEREION
Thoreau book / WALDEN
thorn / BRIAR, BRIER, SPINE;
   BRAMBLE
thorn apple / HAW; METEL;
   DATURA
thornback / RAY; ROKER
thorn-bearing / SPINATE

Thorne Smith character / TOPPER
thorny / SHARP, SPINY; BRAMBLY
thorny plant / BRIAR; CACTUS
thorny shrub / NABK, NUBK; BRIAR,
   BRIER
thorny tree / ACACIA
thorough / TOTAL; ARRANT, ENTIRE
thorough bass / HARMONY; CON-
   TINUO
thoroughbred /PURE; UNTAINTED
thoroughfare/ WAY; AVENUE,
   STREET; HIGHWAY
thoroughgoing / RANK; UTTER
thoroughly / FULLY; COMPLETELY
thoroughly bad / ARRANT
thoroughwort / BONESET
thorp / DORP; HAMLET
Thorpe's school / CARLISLE
Thor's father / ODIN
Thor's stepson / ULL; ULLR
Thor's weapon / HAMMER;
   MIOLNIR, MJOLNIR
Thor's wife / SIF
those against / CONS; ANTIS
those born in a country / NATIVES;
   INDIGENES
those in debt / OWERS
those for / PROS
those giving blood / DONORS
those in office / INS
those persons / THEM, THEY
those receiving gifts / DONEES
those receiving payments / PAYEES
those refused election / OUTS
those who are unemotional /
   STOICS
those who ask alms / BEGGARS;
   MENDICANTS
those who buy / CUSTOMERS
those who inherit / HEIRS
those who know / SAVANTS; IN-
   SIDERS
those who sell / AGENTS; SALES-
   MEN
Thoth's city / HERMOPOLIS
Thoth's divine client / OSIRIS
Thoth's forte / SCIENCE
though / IF; YET; HOWEVER
thought / CARE, IDEA; FANCY; NO-
   TION; OPINION
thought, c.f. / IDEO
thought transference / ESP;
   TELEPATHY
thoughtful / WARY; DREAMY; HEED-
   FUL, PENSIVE; PRUDENT,
   SERIOUS
thoughtful treatment / TLC
thoughtless / GAY; RASH; GIDDY;
   REMISS
thousand / GRAND; CHILIAD
thousand, c.f. / KILO; MILLI
thousand years / CHILIAD; MIL-
   LENNIUM

thousand-armed giant / BANA
thousands of years / AGE, EON; YUGA; KALPA
Thracian / GLADIATOR
Thracian city / SESTOS
Thracian deity / ZALMOXIS
Thracian mountain / PANGAEUS
Thracian musician / ORPHEUS
Thracians / BESSI, EDONI, GETAE
thrall / ESNE, SERF; HELOT, SLAVE
thralldom / BONDAGE; VASSALAGE
thrash / LAM; BEAT, DRUB, WHIP; FLAIL; DRUDGE; BELABOR
thrasher shark / THRESHER
thrasonical / BOASTFUL
thrave / BUNDLE
thrawn / TWISTED; PERVERSE
thread / REEVE, TWINE. CORD; FIBER, SENSE; FILAMENT
thread, c.f. / BYSS, MITO, NEMA
thread, pert. to / FILAR
thread ball / CLEW
thread of cotton / LISLE
thread feather / FILOPLUME
thread fragments / LINT
thread made of mesh / LACE
thread of metal / WIRE; CABLE
thread rope through a hole / REEVE
thread of silk / BAVE, TRAM
thread of a story / IDEA, PLOT
thread variety / LISLE, TWINE
threadbare / DULL, WORN; SEEDY, STALE
threaded bolt / SCREW
threaded fastener / NUT
threadfish / SHAD; COBBLER
threadlike / FILAR; LINEAR; STRINGY; NEMALINE
threadlike process / FIBER

threadlike ridge / LIRA
threadlike structure / HAIR; FILUM; CILIUM
threads / CLOTHES, SLEAVES
threads crossed by woof / WARP
threads crossing warp / WEFT, WOOF
threads strung vertically / WARP
threadworm / FILARIA
thready / SLIGHT; SLENDER
threat / OMEN; MENACE; WARNING
threaten / IMPEND; FOREWARN
threatened / MENACED; BLUSTERED
threatening / SINISTER; FOREBODING
three / TER; TRIO; TRIAD
three, c.f. / TER, TRI
three bears' guest / GOLDILOCKS
three at cards / TREY
three feet / YARD
three goddesses / FATES, NORMS
three hundredth anniversary / TERCENTENARY
three in one / TRIUNE
three Roman fates / PARCAE
three score and ten / SEVENTY
three-banded armadillo / APAR
three-base hit / TRIPLE
three-card gambling game / MONTE
three-cornered hat / TRICORN
three-cornered sail / LATEEN
three-cushion game / BILLIARDS
three-dimensional / SOLID; STEREO
threefold / TRINE; TREBLE, TRIPLE
threefold, c.f. / TER
three-horse team / RANDOM
three-legged figure / TRISKELION

THREE LITTLE MAIDS
(in Gilbert and Sullivan's **The Mikado**)

YUMYUM
PEEPBO
PITTISING

THREE MUSKETEERS°
(in Dumas' novel)

ATHOS
PORTHOS
ARAMIS

° D'ARTAGNAN became the "fourth Musketeer."

THREE WISE MEN (MAGI)

GASPAR
MELCHIOR
BALTHASAR

three-legged stand / TEAPOY, TRI-POD, TRIVET
three-masted schooner / TERN
three-masted vessel / BARK, SHIP; XEBEC, FRIGATE
three-oar boat / RANDAN
three-part composition / TRIO;. SONATA
three-pipped domino / TREY
three-pointer in rugby / TRY
three-pronged spear / TRIDENT
three-R's teacher / SCHOOLMARM
threescore / SIXTY
three-sided figure / TRIANGLE
threesome / TRIO
three-stringed musical instrument / REBEC
three-toed sloth / AI
threnody / DIRGE, ELEGY
thresh / FLOG; FLAIL; THRASH
thresh out / SIFT; PROBE
threshed / FLAILED
threshing implement / FLAIL
threshold / SILL; LIMEN; PORTAL; ENTRANCE
threw / FLUNG; LANCED, TOSSED
thrice / TREBLY
thrice, pref. / TER, TRE, TRI
thrift / ECONOMY; FRUGALITY
thriftless / LAVISH; WASTEFUL
thrifty / FRUGAL, SAVING; PRUDENT
thrill / KICK, QUIVER, TINGLE
thriller / YARN; WHODUNIT
thrilling / MOVING; EXCITING
thrips / THYSANOPTER
thrive / GROW; BATTEN, FATTEN
thriving / WELLTODO; PROSPEROUS
throat / MAW; GORGE; GULLET; WEASAND
throat, pert. to / GULAR
throat disease / CROUP; QUINSY; DIPHTHERIA
throat irritation / FROG
throat lozenge / TROCHE; PASTILLE
throat part / TONSIL; GLOTTIS, PHARYNX
throatwort / FOXGLOVE; BELL-FLOWER
throaty / THICK; GUTTURAL
throb / BEAT; PULSE; PALPITATE
throbbed / ACHED; PULSED
throe / PAIN, PANG
thrombosis / CLOT, PLUG
throne / ANGEL, ASANA, CHAIR
throng / MOB; HOST, MASS; HORDE
thronged / TEEMING; SWARMING
throstle / THRUSH; SPINNER
throttle / GAG; CHOKE; GARROTE
Throttlebottom / NONENTITY
through / BY; DIA, PER; ACROSS

through, pref. / DIA; TRANS
through and through / COMPLETELY
throughout / FULLY; ALWAYS. DURING
throve / BLOOMED; FLOURISHED
throw / CAST, HURL, TOSS; PITCH, SLING
throw away / WASTE; DISCARD
throw back / REPEL; RETORT
throw cold water on / CHILL; DAMPEN
throw of dice / MAIN
throw into disorder / PI; JUMBLE
throw down / RAZE; WRECK
throw a fit / RAGE; STORM
throw in with / JOIN
throw light on / CLARIFY; ILLUMINATE
throw lightly / LOB; FLIP
throw a monkey wrench / MAR; SCOTCH
throw off / DOFF, EMIT, SHED
throw out / RID; CONFUSE
throw over / JILT; DISCARD
throw a party / HOST
throw of six / SISE
throw stones / PELT; LAPIDATE
throw together / MIX; SKIMP; MINGLE
throw in the towel / QUIT; SURRENDER
throw of two / AMBSACE
throw up / NAG; VOMIT
throw in with / JOIN
throwback / ATAVISM; REVERSION
thrum / DRUM; STRUM; FRINGE
thrummy / ROUGH; SHAGGY
thrush / OMAO; MAVIS, OUSEL, ROBIN, SHAMA, VEERY; MISSEL, MISTLE, OLOMAO; STOMATITIS
thrust / POKE, PROD, PUSH, URGE, LUNGE
thrust back / REPEL; REPULSE
thrust in / PIERCE; INTERJECT
thrusting weapon / ESTOC, LANCE; BAYONET
thud / HIT; BEAT; THUMP; STRIKE
thug / GOON; HOODLUM, RUFFIAN
thuggee / ASSASSINATION
thuja / ARBORVITAE
thumb / POLLEX
thumbling / DWARF
thumb's base / BALL; THENAR
thumbs down verdict / DEATH
thumbstall / RUBBERFINGER
thump / BANG, THUD; POUND; STRIKE
thumping / TATTOO. LARGE
thunder / CLAP, PEAL, RAGE; STORM
thunder, c.f. / BRONTO
thunder, pert. to / CERAUNIC

thunder god / THOR; DONAR; JUPITER
thunderfish / RAAD; LOACH
thunderhead / CUMULUS; ANVIL-HEAD
thundering / HUGE; EXTREME
thunder-pumper / BITTERN
thunderstone / BELEMNITE
thunderstruck / ASTOUNDED
thurible / CENSER
thurifer / ACOLYTE
Thuringian city / JENA; ERFURT, WEIMAR
thus / SO; SIC; ERGO; HENCE
thus far / YET
thwack / RAP; THUMP; STRIKE
thwaite / ASSART, MEADOW
thwart / BALK, FOIL; CROSS; HIN-DER; ENCOUNTER, FRUSTRATE; CONTRAVENE. ACROSS; OBLIQUE; CROSSWISE
thy / YOUR; THINE
Thyestes' brother / ATREUS
Thyestes' father / PELOPS
Thyestes' victim / AGAMEMNON
thyine / SANDARAC
thylacine / DASYURE
Thymbra victor / CYRUS
thymiosis / YAWS
thymus / SWEETBREAD
thyroidism / GOITER
thyrsus / STAFF
thyrsus bearer / BACCHANTE
thysanopter / THRIPS
ti / PALM; TATAR
Tiamat's husband / APSU
tiara / CROWN, MITER; DIADEM; CORONET; GARDENIA
Tiber / TEVERE
Tiber port / OSTIA
Tiber tributary / NERA
Tiberius' adviser / SEJANUS
Tiberius' son / DRUSUS
Tiberius' wife / JULIA; VIPSANIA
Tibet capital / LHASA
Tibetan antelope / GOA; DZEREN, DZERON
Tibetan cereal food / TSAMBA
Tibetan city / SHIGATSE
Tibetan deer / SHOU
Tibetan headman / POMBO
Tibetan monastery / LAMASERY
Tibetan money / TANGA
Tibetan monk / LAMA
Tibetan ox / YAK
Tibetan palace / POTALA; TASHILUMPO
Tibetan people / CHAMPA, SHERPA, TANGUT
Tibetan pony / TANGUN
Tibetan religion / BON
Tibetan river / TSANGPO

Tibetan ruminant / SEROW, TAKIN, URIAL
Tibetan sheep / SNA; NAYAUR
Tibetan wildcat / MANUL
tibia / SHIN; FLUTE; CNEMIS
tic / TWITCH
Tichborne claimant / ORTON
tick / KED; MITE; CHECK; ACARID, CREDIT, MOMENT; MATTRESS
tick fever / RICKETTSIOSIS
ticker / HEART, WATCH; TELE-GRAPH
ticket / TAG; CARD; LABEL, SLATE; BALLOT, PERMIT; LICENSE, SUMMONS
ticket end / STUB
ticket-of-leave man / PAROLEE
tickle / AMUSE; GRATIFY; TITIL-LATE
tickle the palm / BRIBE; GREASE
tickled / PLEASED; THRILLED
tickler / COIL, FILE, MEMO
ticklish / CRITICAL, DELICATE
tickseed / TREFOIL
tick-tack-toe symbol / CROSS; NOUGHT
Ticonderoga's captor / ALLEN
Ticonderoga's fort / CARILLON
tidal flood / BORE; EAGRE, HYGRE
tidal inlet / ESTERO; ESTUARY
tidal wave / EAGRE; TSUNAMI
tidbit / CATE, TALE
tide / EBB, RIP; FLOW, NEAP, SURF, TIME; FLOOD, SURGE; SEASON. BEFALL
tidewater / COASTAL
tidily / NEATLY; SPRUCELY
tidiness / TRIM; ORDER; SYM-METRY
tidings / NEWS, WORD; REPORT
tidy / NEAT, TRIG, TRIM; SPRUCE. REDD. ANTIMACASSAR
tie / BIND, JOIN, KNIT, KNOT, LASH, LINK; TETHER. BOND, LACE; ASCOT; CRAVAT; DEAD-HEAT, LIGATURE
tie a bandage / LIGATE
tie game / DRAW; STALEMATE
tie the knot / MARRY
tie in roadbed / SLEEPER
tie up / TRUSS
tiebreaker / RUBBER
tied / EVEN; DRAWN, EQUAL
tie-in / CONDITION
Tien Shan sheep / OVISPOLI
tier / ROW; BANK, RANK
tierce / CASK; PARRY; THRUST
Tiergarten / ZOO
Tierra del Fuego Indian / ONA
tiff / FIT, PET; SPAT; SCENE
tiffany / GAUZE
tiffin / TEA; LUNCH

tige / PIN
tigella / HYPOCOTYL
tiger / SHER, SHIR; JAGUAR
tiger cat / CHATI
tigerish / BLOODTHIRSTY
Tigertown / DETROIT
tight / FAST, FIRM, TAUT; DRUNK;
 STINGY
tight spot / FIX, JAM; STRAIT
tight squeeze / CLOSESHAVE
tighten / FRAP; CONSTRICT
tightfisted / MISERLY
tight-fitting / SNUG
tight-fitting cap / COIF
tightly stretched / TENSE
tights / LEOTARD; BREECHES
tightwad / MISER, PIKER
Tigris River in Bible / HIDDEKEL
Tigris River city / MOSUL; BAGH-
 DAD
tiki / IMAGE; AMULET
til / SESAME
tile / SLATE; DOMINO; AZULEJO
tile design / MOSAIC
tile used in roofing / SLATE; PAN-
 TILE
tile-like / TEGULAR
tiler / ROOFER; DOORKEEPER
tiles, pert. to / TEGULAR
tilia / LINDEN; BASSWOOD
till / PLOW; CULTIVATE. DRAWER.
 UNTIL
tillable / ARABLE; CULTIVABLE
tillable land / ARADA, ARADO
tillage / CROPS; AGRICULTURE
tiller / HELM; PLOWMAN
tilmus / FLOCCILATION
tilt / TIP; CANT, LEAN, LIST; JOUST.
 TENT; CONTEST
tilt hammer / OLIVER
tilting / ALIST; SWAYING
timber / WOOD; TREES; LUMBER
timber bend / SNY; CAMBER
timber fault / CONK, WARP
timber for flooring / BATTEN
timber mill / SAWMILL
timber piece / TENON; MORTISE
timber pine / MATSU
timber rot / DOAT, DOTE
timber to tie the ropes / BITT
timber topper / HURDLER
timber tree / APA, ASH, OAK;
 BEECH, CEDAR
timber truck / WYNN
timber used as prop / CAVEL,
 KEVEL
timbered / WOODED; FORESTED
timberhead / BOLLARD
timberland / WOODS; FOREST
timberwolf / LOBO
timbre / QUALITY; RESONANCE
timbrel / TABOR; SISTRUM

time / AGE, ERA; BEAT, DATE,
 TERM; EPOCH, TEMPO, WHILE;
 PERIOD. MEASURE
time, pert. to / TEMPORAL
time and again / REPEATEDLY
time allowance / GRACE
time before / EVE
time being / NONCE
time between / RECESS; INTERIM;
 INTERLUDE
time clock / TELLTALE
time to come / FUTURE
time of day / HOUR
time of fasting / LENT
time free / LEISURE
time gone by / PAST, YORE
time of great power / HEYDAY
time immemorial / ANTIQUITY
time instrument / CLOCK, WATCH;
 SUNDIAL; CLEPSYDRA, HOUR-
 GLASS, SANDGLASS
time just before / EVE
time of life / AGE
time long ago / ELD; YORE
time out / LULL, REST; PAUSE; HIA-
 TUS, RECESS
time past / AGO; YORE; FORETIME
time shift / FLASHBACK
time unit / AGE, DAY, ERA; HOUR,
 WEEK, YEAR; MONTH; DECADE,
 MINUTE, SECOND; CENTURY
time of year / SEASON
time-honored / TRADITIONAL
timeless / ETERNAL; INFINITE;
 EVERGREEN
timely / APT, PAT; EARLY
timepiece / WATCH
timer / STOPWATCH
times / OFTEN
times to remember / EVENTS
timeserver / TOADY; TRIMMER
timetable / SCHEDULE
timeworn / OLD; AGED; TRITE
timid / SHY; PAVID; FEARFUL
timidity / FEAR; TIMOR; RESERVE
timing / TEMPO; COORDINATION
timon / CYNIC
Timor capital / DILI
Timor coin / AVO; PATACA
timorous / SHY; MEEK; TIMID;
 TREPID
timothy / HAY; GRASS
Timothy's grandmother / LOIS
Timothy's mother / EUNICE
timpani / KETTLEDRUMS
Timur / TAMERLANE
tin / CAN; STANNUM. PLATE
tin alloy / TERNE; PEWTER
tin can / DESTROYER
Tinu Can Island / NIUAFOO
tin container / CAN; BLICKEY
tin foil / TAIN

Tin Pan Alley product / POPTUNE
tinamou / YUTU; PARTRIDGE
tincal / BORAX
tinct / TINT. COLORED
tinction / DYEING; COLORING
tincture / DYE; DASH, TINT; COLOR
tincture in heraldry / OR; VERT;
 AZURE, GULES, SABLE; ARGENT
tincture of opium / PAREGORIC
tinder / PUNK; AMADOU
tinderbox / HOTSPOT
tine / SNAG; PRONG, TOOTH
tinea / RINGWORM
ting / CLINK
tinge / DYE; TINT; COLOR, STAIN.
 HUE; CAST; SHADE, TRACE
tinge deeply / IMBUE
tingle / SOO; RING; THRILL,
 TWINGE
tinhorn / CHEAP; FLASHY. MEDI-
 OCRITY
tinker / PATCH; MEDDLE.
 BUNGLER, WORKMAN
tinker's damn / RAP; STRAW
Tinker's teammate / EVERS;
 CHANCE
tinkle / CLINK; JINGLE
tinkling sound / TING
tinner / TINSMITH
tinny / THIN; EMPTY; SHODDY
tinplate / TERNE
tinsel / FALSE, GAUDY; TAWDRY
tint / HUE; CAST, TONE. DYE
tintinnabulation / RING; JINGLE
tintype / FERROTYPE
tiny / WEE; PUNY; LITTLE,
 MINUTE
tiny insect / FLEA, MITE; MIDGE
tiny mammal / BAT; SHREW
tiny particle / ATOM; ELECTRON
tiny piece / WHIT; MINIM; LITTLE
tip / END, FEE; APEX, CLUE, GIFT,
 HINT; VERTEX; FERRULE. HIT;
 CANT, TILT
tip over / UPEND, UPSET
tip of a pen / NEB, NIB; POINT
tip to the side / TILT; CAREEN
tip-off / KEY; CLUE; ADVICE
Tippecanoe victor / HARRISON
tippet / CAPE; AMICE, SCARF
tippler / SOT; SOAK; DRINKER
tipstaff / BAILIFF
tipster / TOUT; INFORMER
tipsy / DRUNK, MUZZY; EBRIOUS
tiptoe / EAGER; CAUTIOUS
tiptop / AONE, BEST
tirade / SCREED; DIATRIBE
tirailleur / SNIPER; RIFLEMAN
tire / FAG; BORE, JADE; WEARY.
 SHOE; RECAP
tire base / RIM
tire groove / SIPE
tire inventor / DUNLOP

tire part / SHOE, TUBE; CASING
tired / WEARY; FATIGUED
tireless / INDEFATIGABLE
Tiresias' bane / BLINDNESS, SEX-
 CHANGE
tiresome / DULL; HUMDRUM,
 TEDIOUS
tiresome person / BORE; SQUARE
tiresome work / GRIND
tirwit / LAPWING
tisane / TEA; PTISAN
tissue / WEB; TELA; FABRIC
tissue, pert. to / TELAR
tissue hardening / SCLEROSIS
tissued / VARIEGATED
tit / BIT, NAG; TITMOUSE
tit for tat / EXCHANGE, REPRISAL
titan / ATLAS, GIANT; PRO-
 METHEUS
titanate / RUTILE; ILMENITE
Titania's adored one / BOTTOM
Titania's husband / OBERON
titanic / HUGE; IMMENSE; COLOS-
 SAL
titanite / SPHENE
Titans' father / URANUS
Titans' mother / GE; GAEA
titbit / GOSSIP, MORSEL
titer / STRENGTH
tithable / ASSESSABLE
tithe / TAX; TEIND, TENTH, TIEND
tithingman / CONSTABLE
titian / AUBURN
titillate / EXCITE, TICKLE
titillation / THRILL; DELIGHT
titivate / SPRUCE; SMARTEN
titlark / PIPIT
title / BOOK, NAME; CLAIM, RIGHT;
 HEADING. TERM; STYLE
title of address / SIR; MADAM,
 SAHIB
title of baronet / SIR
title of Benedictine / DOM
title holder / OWNER; CHAMPION
title of honor / DAN, DON; SAYID
title of nobility in India / RAIA,
 RAJA; RAJAH
title of polite address in India /
 DEVI, MIAN; SAHIB; HUZOOR,
 SAHIBA
title to property / DEED
title of respect / DOM, DON, SIR,
 SRI; TUAN; MADAM, SENOR;
 SIGNOR; MONSIEUR
titled person / DAME, DUKE, LADY,
 LORD, PEER; BARON, NOBLE;
 PEERESS
titleholder / CHAMP; INCUMBENT
titmouse / MAG, NUN; YAUP; PA-
 RUS; TOMTIT, VERDIN; CHICKA-
 DEE, GOOSANDER
Tito / BROZ
titrate / DRIP; ANALYZE

titter / TEEHEE, GIGGLE
tittle/ ACE , JOT; IOTA; SPECK
tittle-tattle / GOSSIP, MURMUR
tittup / HOP; CAPER
titubate / STAGGER, STUMBLE
titular / TITLED; NOMINAL
titule / SPECIFY
Titus Andronicus' daughter / LAVINIA
Tityus' mother / GE
Tityus' slayer / APOLLO
Tityus' victim / LETO
Tiu / TYR; TIWAZ
tivoli / PINBALL; BAGATELLE
tizzy / STEW; TWITTER
Tlacapan ally / AZTEC; ACOLHUA
Tlingit Indian / AUK; HUNA; SITKA
tmesis / DIACOPE
to / FOR; INTO, TILL, UNTO; TO-WARD
to a T / PRECISELY
to any point / ANYWHERE
to be cautious / BEWARE
to be form / AM, IS; ARE, WAS; WERE
to be paid / DUE
to be sure / INDEED, VERILY
to become vapid / PALL
to boot / EKE, TOO; ALSO; ASWELL
to a degree / AS, SO; EVEN
to detect / DIVINE
to the end / UTTERLY; ABSOLUTELY
to the end that / SO
to and fro / RECIPROCAL
to go / LEFT; BAGGED
to a great degree / MOSTLY; LARGELY
to a higher place / UP
to the inside / INTO
to larboard / APORT
to the left / HAW; APORT
to let / RENTABLE
to no purpose / FUTILELY
to the nth degree / UTTERLY
to one side / ASIDE
to the order of / FOR
to the other side / OVER
to pieces / APART
to a point / SOSO; MIDDLING
to the point / APT; PERTINENT
to the point that / UNTIL
to the rear / AFT; ASTERN
to the right / GEE
to rights / SQUARELY. STRAIGHT
to same degree / AS
to the same extent / AS, SO; EVEN, SUCH
to sea / ASEA
to the second power / SQUARED
to shelter / ALEE
to some degree / PARTLY
to such extent / INSOFAR
to that / THERETO

to that extent / SO
to that place / THERE; THITHER
to that time / TILL; UNTIL
to the third power / CUBED
to this / HERETO
to this place / HERE; HITHER
to the time when / TILL; UNTIL
to what place / WHITHER
to wit / VIZ; NAMELY; VIDELICIT
to your health / SALUD; PROSIT, WASSAIL
toad / AGUA, PIPA; PADDOCK; NATTERJACK
toad-eater / SYCOPHANT
toadfish / SAPO; PUFFER
toadflax / LINARIA, RANSTED
toado / GLOBEFISH
toadsticker / JACKKNIFE
toadstool / FUNGUS; MUSHROOM
toady / FAWN; TRUCKLE. LICK-SPITTLE
toadysm / SYCOPHANCY
toast / SKOAL; PROSIT. WARM; BROWN
toast piece / SIPPET; CROUTON
toasting word / SALUD, SALUT, SKOAL, YASAS; CHEERS, PROSIT; SLAINTE, WASSAIL
toastmaster / MC
toasty / COZY, MILD, WARM
tobacco / WEED; LATAKIA; NICO-TINE
tobacco ash / DOTTEL, DOTTLE
tobacco box / FRIARBIRD
tobacco chaw / CUD; PLUG, QUID
tobacco disease / CALICO, MOSAIC
tobacco jar / HUMIDOR
tobacco juice / AMBEER
tobacco narcotic / NICOTINE
tobacco pipe / DUDEEN, HOOKAH; CHIBOUK; NARGHILE; MEER-SCHAUM
tobacco roll / TOBY; CIGAR, SEGAR; STOGIE
tobacco variety / CAPA, PIPE, SANA, SHAG; SNUFF; DUDEEN; CAPO-RAL, CAPOREL, LATAKIA, ORO-NOCO, PERIQUE; CIGARETTE
to-be / FUTURE
tobira / PITTOSPORUM
Tobit's angel / RAPHAEL
Tobit's son / TOBIAS
toboggan / SLED. DROP
toby / MUG
Toby's master / PUNCH
toccata / FANTASIA
tocher / DOT; DOWER, DOWRY
tock / HORNBILL
toco / FLOGGING; THRASHING
tocology / MIDWIFERY
tocsin / BELL, GONG; ALARM
tod / FOX, MAT; BUSH
today / NOW; NOWADAYS

toddle / WALK; DANCE; TOTTER
toddler / TOT; CHILD
toddy / GROG; JUICE
toddy palm sugar / GUR; JAGGERY
tode / SLED
to-do / ADO; FUSS, STIR; RACKET
toe / DIGIT; HALLUX; MINIMUS, SLANT
toe, c.f. / DACTYL
toe the mark / CONFORM
toe-and-heel / JIG, TAP; CLOG
toehold / CHANCE; OPENING
toes in ballet / POINTS
toff / DUDE; SWELL
toffee / TAFFY
toft / HOMESTEAD
tog / DRESS; CLOTHING
toga / GOWN; OFFICE
together / CONJOINTLY
together, pref. / CO; CON, SYN
together again / REUNITED
together with / AND
togetherness / UNITY; CLOSENESS
toggery / CLOTHES; TRAPPINGS
toggle / PIN; FROG; STRAP; BUTTON, COTTER; CROSSPIECE
toggle iron / HARPOON
Togo capital / LOME
Togoland capital / HO
togs / CLOTHES
tohubohu / CHAOS
tohunga / PRIEST; PROPHET
toil / WORK; LABOR, NET; RING, TRAP; EFFORT
toil wearisomely / MOIL; DRUDGE
toile / CLOTH, LINEN
toilet / WC; JOHN; PRIVY
toilet case / ETUI; ETWEE
toilet paper / TISSUE
toiletries / COSMETICS
toilsome / HARD; SEVERE; ONEROUS
toilworn / EXHAUSTED
Toison d'Or / GOLDENFLEECE
toit / DAWDLE
tokay / WINE; GRAPE
toke / FOOD
token / FARE, MARK, SIGN, SLUG; BADGE; EMBLEM, PLEDGE, SYMBOL
token of affection / KISS; EMBRACE
token of earnestness / GESTURE
token of friendship / KEEPSAKE
token payment / ACKNOWLEDGMENT
token of victory / PALM; MEDAL; LAUREL
tokened / SPOTTED
Tokyo district / GINZA; AKASAKA; YOSHIWARA
Tokyo river / SUMIDA
Tokyo's former name / EDO; YEDO
tolbooth / GAOL; PRISON

told in detail / RECITED
told a story / LIED; NARRATED
toldo / HUT
tole / TINWARE
toledo / BLADE, SWORD
tolerable / FAIR, SOSO; MIDDLING
tolerably / PRETTY; SOMEWHAT
tolerance / STAMINA; PATIENCE; VARIATION
tolerant / EASY; INDULGENT
tolerate / LET; BEAR, BIDE; ALLOW, BROOK
toll / DUE, FEE, TAX; DUTY, LEVY, RATE, PEAL, RING
toll road / TURNPIKE
tolling / KNELL
tolls / CUSTOMS
Tolstoi heroine / ANNA
Toltec hero / TOPILTZIN
Toltec site / TULA
tolu / BALSAM
tolypeutine / APAR; ARMADILLO
tom / CAT; MALE; TURKEY
Tom, Dick, and Harry / ANYONE
Tom Fool / CLOWN, NODDY
Tom Sawyer's aunt / POLLY
Tom Sawyer's pal / HUCK
Tom Thumb's impresario / BARNUM
tomahawk / HATCHET, ATTACK
tomato / LOVEAPPLE
tomato sauce / CATSUP; CATCHUP, KETCHUP
tomb / CRYPT, GRAVE, VAULT; MAUSOLEUM, SEPULCHER
tomb of ancient Egypt / MASTABA
tomb of Khufu / PYRAMID
tomb of a saint / SHRINE
tombac / ALLOY
tombola / LOTTO
tomboy / ROMP; HOYDEN
tombstone inscription / HICJACET
tomcat / GIB
tome / BOOK; VOLUME
tomentose / NAPPY; MATTED
tomfoolery / NONSENSE
Tommy / LIMEY; ENGLISHMAN
tommyrot / PIFFLE; POPPYCOCK
tomnoddy / FOOL
tomorrow / MANANA; NEXTDAY
tomtit / MIRO; WREN
tomtom / DRUM; BONGO; TAMTAM
ton / VOGUE; WEIGHT; FASHION
tonal language / BODO, LOCO, NAGA; MENDE, OTOMI; NAVAHO; CHINESE
tonality / KEY; SYSTEM
tone / AIR; MODE, MOOD, NOTE; COLOR, FORCE, PITCH, SOUND, TENOR, VIGOR; SPIRIT
tone, pert. to / TONAL
tone color / TIMBRE
tone down / SOFTEN

tone group / CHORD; CLUSTER
tone quality / TIMBRE; RESONAN
tone quality / TIMBRE; RESONANCE
tone succession / SCALE; MELODY, OCTAVE
tone variation / NUANCE
tong / SOCIETY
Tonga capital / NUKUALOFA
Tonga dynasty / TUPOU
Tonga money / PAANGA
tongue / TALK; IDIOM, LINGO; GLOSSA, SPEECH; DIALECT; LANGUAGE
tongue, c.f. / GLOSSO, LINGUI
tongue, pert. to / GLOSSAL, LIN-GUAL
tongue node/ PAPILLA
tongue of shoe / TAB; FLAP
tongue of wagon / COPE, NEAP, POLE
tonguebird / WRYNECK
tonguefence / DEBATE; DISPUTA-TION
tonguefish / SOLE
tongueflower / ORCHID; GLOSSID
tonguelash / RATE; SCOLD
tongueless / MUTE; UNHERALDED
tonguetied / SHY; MUTE
tonic / BRACER, ELIXIR; ROBO-RANT
tonic herb / ALOE; TANSY; ARTE-MISIA
tonic note / KEYNOTE
tonicity / TONE; TONUS
Tonkin capital / HANOI
Tonkin native / THO
Tonkin river / SONGKOI
tonnage / WEIGHT; CAPACITY
tonneau / BODY
tonous / SONOROUS
tonsils' companions / ADENOIDS
tonsorial / PARLOR; BARBERSHOP
tonsured / BALD; SHORN
tontine / ANNUITY
tony / STYLISH; FASHIONABLE
too / AND; ALSO, VERY; OVERLY
too bad / ALAS; ALACK
too early / PREMATURE
too late / BELATED
too much / EXCESS; NIMIETY
took a chair / SAT
took it easy / RELAXED
tool / DUPE; MINION; IMPLEMENT; INSTRUMENT
tool for boring / AWL, BIT; AUGER, DRILL
tool box / KIT; CHEST
tool used with brace / BIT
tool for cement work / TROWEL
tool for chopping / AX; AXE; HATCHET
tool for cutting / AX; ADZ, AXE, HOB, SAW, SAX, SYE; ADZE;

KNIFE; CHISEL, SCYTHE, SICKLE; HATCHET
tool for cutting meat / CLEAVER
tool for digging / PICK; SPADE; SHOVEL
tool for dressing wood / ADZE; PLANE
tool for engravery / BURIN; GRAVER; MATTOIR
tool for enlarging holes / REAMER
tool for farming / PLOW
tool for filing / FILE, RASP
tool for gardening / HOE; RAKE; SPADE; TROWEL
tool for grasping / PLIERS
tool for grass cutting / MOWER; SCYTHE, SICKLE
tool handle / HELVE
tool for molding / DIE
tool with a point / AWL, PIN; BROACH, NEEDLE
tool for post holes / LOY
tool for shaping metal / SWAGE
tool for shaping wood / ADZ; ADZE
tool to shave hides / SKIVER, SLATER
tool for splitting / FROE, FROW
tool to surface wood / PLANE
tool for threading / TAP; CHASER
tool to trim slate / SAX
tooling / ORNAMENTATION
tools for cutting / CUTLERY
toolsmith / TOOLMAKER
toot / BLOW; BLAST, SOUND
tooth / COG; FANG, TINE, TUSH, TUSK; MOLAR; CANINE, CUSPID; INCISOR; BICUSPID
tooth, c.f. / DENT; ODENT
tooth of a comb / DENT
tooth decay / CARIES, CAVITY
tooth of a gear pinion / LEAF
tooth of a gear wheel / COG; DENT
tooth gnashing / BRUXISM
tooth projection / CUSP
tooth puller / DENTIST, FORCEPS
tooth socket / ALVEOLUS
tooth substitute / BRIDGE; DEN-TURE
tooth surface / MENSA; DENTINE
tooth on wheel / COG; SPROCKET
toothache / DENTALGIA; ODON-TALGIA
toothed / DENTATE, NOTCHED, SERRATE
toothed formation / CRENELLATION
toothed instrument / SAW; COMB, RASP, ROWEL
toothed irregularly / EROSE
toothed perforation / ROULETTE
toothed wheel / COG; GEAR; ROWEL
toothless / EDENTATE
toothlike projection / DENTIL

toothsome / TASTY; PALATABLE
tooting / BRAGGING
too-too / ULTRA; EXTREMELY
tootsie / FOOT, ROSE; SWEET-
HEART
top / ACE, LID, NUN, TIP, TOY;
ACME, APEX; VERTEX. CAP; EX-
CEL; SURPASS. CHIEF; PROMI-
NENT
top of altar / MENSA
top of doorway / LINTEL
top of a dress / YOKE
top hat / BEAVER, TOPPER
top ornament / EPI; FINIAL;
FEATHER
top performer / ACE; STAR
topaz / CITRINE; SAPPHIRE
topaz hummingbird / AVA
topcoat / SURTOUT; TRENCHCOAT
tope / GROVE, SHARK, STUPA;
DOGFISH. SWIZZLE
topee / TOPI
toper / SOT; SOUSE; DRUNKARD
tophaceous / SANDY; GRITTY
top-heavy / OVERBALANCED
tophet / HEAT, HELL
top-hole / CHOICE, TIPTOP
topi / HELMET; PITHHAT
topi material / SOLA
topic / TEXT; POINT, THEME;
THESIS
topic of discourse / SUBJECT
topical / LOCAL; THEMATIC
topknot / TUFT; CREST
topknot on mask of tragedy /
ONKOS
toplofty / VAIN; POMPOUS
topmast crossbar / FID
topminnow / GUPPY, MOLLY; HEL-
LERI, PUPFISH, RIVULUS; GAM-
BUSIA; KILLIFISH, SWORDTAIL
topmost / HIGHEST
topnotch / AONE; CHOICE
topnotcher / ACE; ONER; TRUMP
topographer / MAPMAKER
toponymy / NOMENCLATURE
Topper author / SMITH
topping / TRIMMING. EXCELLENT
topple / FALL, UPSET; TUMBLE
toppled / DEFEATED; OVER-
THROWN
topsoil / SURFACE
topstone / CAPSTONE
topsy-turvy / CHAOTIC; CONFUSED
toque / HAT
tor / CRAG, ROCK
tora / HARTEBEEST
Torah / LAW; PENTATEUCH
torch / FIRE, LAMP, LINK; BRAND;
CRESSET, LANTERN; FLAMBEAU;
FLASHLIGHT
torchlight / DUSK; FIRELIGHT
tore / RENT; RIPPED; TATTERED

toreador / TORERO; BULLFIGHTER
to-rights / STRAIGHT
torment / NAG, TRY; BAIT, FRET,
RILE; ANNOY, HARRY, TAUNT,
TEASE, WORRY; BADGER, HA-
RASS; AFFLICT, HAGRIDE. PAIN;
ANGUISH
tormenter / GADFLY, LOOFAH;
STRIGIL
tormentil / PUCCOON; TURMERIC
tormina / COLIC
torn / REFT; RIVEN; JAGGED,
RAGGED
tornado / FUNNEL; CYCLONE,
TWISTER; WHIRLWIND
toro / BULL; COWFISH
Toronto's early name / YORK
torose / KNOBBY; MUSCULAR
torpedinous / STUPEFACIENT
torpedo / MINE; HOODLUM
torpid / DULL, NUMB; INERT
torpidity / STUPOR; LANGUOR
torpids / BOATRACES
torpor / COMA; LETHARGY
torque / TWIST; COLLAR
torrefy / PARCH, ROAST
torrent / FLOOD, SPATE; STREAM
torrid / HOT; SULTRY; PARCHED
torrid zone / TROPIC
torsion / TWISTING
torsk / COD; CUSK
torso / BODY; TRUNK
tort / WRONG; INJURY
torte / CAKE; PASTRY, SACHER
torticollis / WRYNECK
tortile / COILED
tortilla / PANCAKE; ENCHILADA
tortious / WRONGFUL
tortoise / EMYD; TURTLE; TER-
RAPIN
tortoise shell / CARAPACE
tortuous / CURVED; CROOKED,
SINUOUS
torture / RACK; MARTYR, PUNISH.
PAIN; AGONY; TORMENT
torture instrument / THUMB-
SCREWS
torture on a stake / IMPALE
torus / KNOB; DOUGHNUT
tory / DIEHARD; LOYALIST; CON-
SERVATIVE
Tosca composer / PUCCINI
Tosca villain / SCARPIA
tosh / NEAT; INTIMATE
toss / LOB; CAST, FLIP, HURL;
PITCH
tossed / THREW; TURNED
tosspot / SOT; DIPSO; DRUNKARD
tot / CHILD; SHAVER; TODDLER.
ADD
total / ADD, SUM. FULL; UTTER;
ENTIRE
total, c.f. / HOL; HOLO

total abstinence / NEPHALISM; TEE-TOTALISM
total destruction / HOLOCAUST
total in the poker pool / POT
total result / SUM; TEETOTAL
totalitarian / AUTOCRATIC; DICTATORIAL
totality / AGGREGATE; COMPLETENESS
totally / FULLY, QUITE; WHOLLY
totally confused / ASEA, LOST
tote / HAUL; CARRY
tote board / TOTALIZER; TOTALIZATOR
totem / EPONYM, PILLAR, SYMBOL; GUARDIAN
totem pole / XAT
totter / REEL, ROCK; FALTER
toucan / TOCO; ARIEL; ARACARI
touch / PAT; FEEL, PALP, STIR; GRAZE; BORROW, HANDLE; CONTACT. CONCERN
touch, pert. to / BAPTIC; TACTILE, TACTUAL
touch at edge / ABUT; ADJOIN
touch gently / NUDGE
touch in passing / GRAZE
touch softly / DAB, PAT
touch up / POLISH; REFURBISH
touch-and-go / PRECARIOUS
touchdown / GOAL
touched / MAD; MOVED
touchhole / VENT
touching / ANENT; TENDER; TANGENT; PATHETIC
touching at one point / TANGENT
touching part / PALP; FINGER
touching the wind / CLOSEHAULED
touch-me-not / LUPUS; BALSAM
touchstone / TEST; CRITERION
touchwood / PUNK; AMADOU
touchy / SORE; CROSS, TESTY; FRETFUL; CHOLERIC; IRRITABLE
tough / HARD, WIRY, CHEWY, HARDY; STRONG; RESISTANT. ROWDY
tough customer / ROUGH
tough guy / HOODLUM; PLUGUGLY
tough luck / MISFORTUNE
tough wood / ASH, ELM, OAK
toughen / TAN, TAW; STEEL; ANNEAL
toupee / WIG; HAIRPIECE
tour / TRIP; JAUNT; RAMBLE, SAFARI, VOYAGE; JOURNEY
tourbillion / DUSTDEVIL
tourelle / TURRET
tourist / TRAVELER; SIGHTSEER, TRANSIENT
tourmaline / ACHROITE; RUBELLITE
tournament / MEET; SERIES; JOUSTING

tourney / TILT; JOUST
Tours victor / MARTEL
tousle / PULL; RUMPLE
tout / SPY; TIPSTER
tow / TUG; DRAW, HAUL, PULL. FLAX
tow of flax / HARDS; CODILLA
tow truck / WRECKER
towai / KAMAHI
toward / AT, TO
toward, pref. / AD, OB
toward the back / RETRAD, RETRAL
toward the body / PROXIMAL
toward the center / ENTAD
toward the inside / INWARD
toward the left side / APORT
toward midday / NOONISH
toward the middle / MESAD, MESAL; MESIAD, MESIAL
toward the mouth / ORAD
toward the occident / WEST; WESTWARD
toward the outside / ECTAD
toward the rear / AFT; ABAFT; ASTERN
toward the rising sun / EAST; EASTWARD
toward shelter / ALEE; LEEWARD
toward the side / LATERAD, LATERAL
toward the top / UP; UPWARD
towardly / COMPLIANT
towboat / TUG
towel / CLOTH, DRIER, WIPER. DRY
towel on a roller / JACKTOWEL
toweling / HUCK; LINEN, TERRY; HUCKABACK
tower / PYLON, SPIRE; TURRET; CITADEL; MARTELLO, PINNACLE. SOAR
tower in the Bible / BABEL
tower to carry cables / PYLON
tower of ice / SERAC
tower of India / MINAR
Tower of London guard / BEEFEATER
tower of a mosque / MINARET
tower of silence / DOKHMA
towering / SOARING, VIOLENT
towerman / SWITCHMAN
towhead / BLOND; MERGANSER
towhee / BUNTING, CHEWINK
towing rope / HAWSER
towmont / YEAR
town / BURG; HAMLET; VILLAGE
town, pert. to / URBAN; OPPIDAN
town, pref. / TRE
town, suffix / BY; TON
townhouse / CITYHALL; RESIDENCE
township in ancient Greece / DEME
townsman / CIT; BURGHER, CITIZEN
towrow / UPROAR

towser / DOG
toxic / VENOMOUS; POISONOUS
toxic substance / ABRIN, TOXIN, VENIN
toxicant / POISON
toxophilite / ARCHER
toy / PLAY; SPORT; TRIFLE. TOP; DOLL, YOYO; BAUBLE, GEWGAW; TRINKET
toy dog / LAPDOG
toyed / DALLIED, SPORTED
toyon / HOLLY
trabea / TOGA
trabeated / BEAMED
trace / TRACK; DEDUCE, DERIVE. CLUE, IOTA, MARK, SIGN; TINGE, TOKEN; VESTIGE
trace out / SPELL
tracer / BULLET; INQUIRY; INQUIRER
tracery / LACEWORK
trachea / WINDPIPE
track / RUT, WAY; MARK; TRACE; COURSE
track of an animal / SLOT; SPOOR, TRAIL
track circuit / LAP
track of a ship / WAKE
track worn by wheel / RUT
track-and-field competition / MEET
tracker / GUIDE, PUGGI; SHIKAR
trackless / UNMARKED
tract / LOT; AREA, PLOT; ESSAY
tract of land / AREA; FIELD; REGION
tract of public land / PARK
tract for recreation / PARK; PLAYGROUND
tract between rises / VALE; VALLEY
tract between rivers / DOAB
tract of treeless land / PRAIRIE
tract of upland / DOWN
tractability / DOCILITY
tractable / TAME; DOCILE, PLIANT
tractate / ESSAY
tractile / DUCTILE
traction / FRICTION; TRANSPORTATION
tractor / CAB, CAT
trade / DEAL, SWAP, SWOP; BARTER. CRAFT; METIER; VOCATION
trade acceptance / DRAFT
trade agreement / CARTEL
trade association / GILD; GUILD, UNION
trade language / PIDGIN
trade off / BARGAIN; COMPROMISE
trade union / GILD; BROTHERHOOD
trade-last / TL; COMPLIMENT
trademark / BRAND; LOGOTYPE
trader / AGENT; DEALER; MONGER
trader to the army / SUTLER
tradescantia / SPIDERWORT

tradesman / AGENT; SHOPKEEPER
trading exchange / PIT; MARKET
trading league / HANSE
trading place / MART, SHOP; STORE; MARKET
trading post / PX; FORT; CANTEEN
tradition / LORE; USAGE; BELIEF, CUSTOM
traditional / RECEIVED; CONSERVATIVE
traditional American Indian exclamation / HOW, UGH
traditional story / MYTH, SAGA; FABLE; LEGEND; FOLKTALE
traduce / SLUR; DECRY; DEFAME, MALIGN
traducer / CALUMNIATOR
Trafalgar victor / NELSON
traffic / TRADE; EXCHANGE. FREIGHT; COMMERCE
traffic island / MEDIAN
traffic in sacred matters / SIMONY
traffic signal / LIGHT
traffic standstill / JAM; TIEUP
tragacanth / GUM
tragedian / ACTOR; PLAYWRIGHT
tragedy / PLAY; DRAMA; CALAMITY
tragic / FATAL; TERRIBLE; DISASTROUS
tragic lover / ROMEO
tragicomedy / DRAMA
tragopan / PHEASANT
trail / DRAG, FALL, HANG; TRACK. PATH; SPOOR
trail of a deer / SLOT
trail a pike / SOLDIER
trail of wild animal / SLOT; SCENT, SPOOR
trail-blazer / SCOUT; PIONEER
trailer / SEMI; MOVIE, TRUCK; CAMPER
trailing branch / RUNNER, STOLEN
train / DRAG, HAUL, TAME; DRILL, TEACH. LURE; SUITE; CORTEGE
train of attendants / SUITE; CORTEGE
train with berths / PULLMAN
train of followers / RETINUE
train making every stop / LOCAL
train the mind / EDUCATE
train of persons / PARADE
train of riders / CAVALCADE
train of thought / THREAD
train of wagons / CARAVAN
trained / SCHOOLED
trained an animal / TAMED
trainer of athletes / COACH; SECOND
trainer of gladiators / LANISTA
training / DRILL; SCHOOLING
trainman / FIREMAN; BRAKEMAN, ENGINEER; CONDUCTOR
traipse / ROAM, WALK

trait / LINE; FEATURE; CHARAC-TERISTIC

traitor / RAT; JUDAS; BETRAYER, BETRAYOR, QUISLING, TURN-COAT

traitorous / FALSE; DISLOYAL, RECREANT

traject / THROW. PASSAGE

trajectory / PATH; ORBIT

tralatition / TROPE; METAPHOR

tram / CABLECAR; STREETCAR

trammel / FETTER, HINDER, IM-PEDE. BOND

tramontane / FOREIGNER

tramp / HIKE, WALK; TREAD. HOBO; VAGABOND

tramp heavily / TRUDGE

trample / CRUSH; STEPON; DE-STROY

trample upon / IGNORE; OPPRESS

trampoline / SPRINGBOARD

trance / DAZE; SPELL; STUPOR

tranquil / CALM; PLACID, SERENE

tranquility / PEACE; CALMNESS

tranquilize / CALM; PACIFY, SE-DATE, SOOTHE

tranquilizer / DOWNER; LIBRIUM; PACIFIER, SEDATIVE

transact / TREAT; CONDUCT, PER-FORM

transaction / ACT; DEAL, SALE; AFFAIR

transanimation / METEMPSY-CHOSIS

transcend / CAP, TOP; PASS; EXCEL

transcendent / SUPREME; MATCH-LESS

transcendental / IDEALISTIC; NON-ALGEBRAIC

transcribe / COPY; REWRITE

transcript / RECORD; DUPLICATE

transept / ARM; SIDE; CROSSING

transfer / CEDE, DEED; ASSIGN, CONVEY; CONSIGN. DECAL; TICKET

transfer to another bottle / DECANT

transfer printing / OFFSET

transfer of property / GRANT

transfer of rights / DEMISE

transferee / ALIENEE

transferer / ALIENOR

transferrable print / DECALCO-MANIA

transferred / CHANGED; DE-LIVERED

transfigure / GLORIFY; TRANSMUTE

transfinite number / ALEF

transfix / PIN; IMPALE, PIERCE

transforation / PERFORATION

transform / ALTER; CHANGE; CON-VERT

transformation / WIG; AVATAR

transfuse / POUR; TRANSFER

transfusion / IV; BLOOD

transgress / ERR, SIN; BREAK; OFFEND

transgression / SIN; CRIME, ERROR

transgressor / FELON; CULPRIT

transient / BRIEF, HASTY; FLEET-ING

transient celestial body / METEOR

transient home / INN; HOTEL, MOTEL; HOSTEL

transient illumination / FLASH

transient interest / FAD

transient phenomena / EPHEMERA

transistor / FET; SEMICONDUCTOR

transistor radio / PORTABLE

transitory / BRIEF, HASTY; TEM-PORAL

transit / PASSAGE; THEODOLITE. CHANGE

transit facility / BUS; PLANE, TRAIN; SUBWAY; TROLLEY

transition / SHIFT; CHANGE; MOD-ULATION

transitive / TRANSFERRING

transitory / BRIEF; FLEETING

Transkeian capital / UMTATA

translate / DECODE, RENDER; CON-STRUE; INTERPRET

translation / PONY; VERSION

transliterate / DECODE

translucent / DIFFUSING

transmigration / REINCARNATION

transmission / GEARBOX, GEARING, SENDING

transmission gear / COG; IDLER

transmit / SEND; CONVEY; FOR-WARD

transmit by television / TELEVISE

transmitter / MIKE; ANTENNA, STA-TION

transmute / CHANGE; TRANSFORM

transoceanic / TRANSATLANTIC

transom / STERN, TRAVE; LINTEL, WINDOW

transparent / OPEN; CLEAR, LUCID; LIMPID; CRYSTAL

transparent acrylic/ LUCITE

transparent material / GLASS

transparent mineral /MICA; CAL-CITE

transparent quartz / CRYSTAL

transpicuous / LUCID; TRANS-PARENT

transpire / EXHALE, HAPPEN; DE-VELOP

transplant / REMOVE; REPLANT

transport / SEND; CARRY, FERRY; CONVEY. BOAT, CART; BLISS; RAPTURE

transport for stream / FERRY

transportation fee / FARE

transported / RAPT, SENT
transpose / SHIFT; INVERT; RE-VERSE
transposition / CHANGE; ANAGRAM
transposition of initials / SPOONERISM
transposition of letters / ANAGRAM
transudate / SWEAT
Transvaal capital / PRETORIA
Transvaal gold fields / RAND
Transvaal raider / JAMESON
Transvaal's flag / VIERKLEUR
transverse / ACROSS; ATHWART
transversely / ACROSS
Transylvanian monster / DRACULA
trap / NAB; TREE; SNARE; AMBUSH. GIN, NET, PIT, WEB; TOIL, WEIR; BUGGY, MOUTH; SPRINGE
trap door / DROP
trap for rabbits / TIPE
trapeze / SWING
trapezist / ACROBAT; AERIALIST
trapfall / GIN, PIT; PITFALL
trapped / CAUGHT, SNARED
trapper / MOUNTAINMAN
trappings / RIG; GEAR; LIVERY; REGALIA
Trappist / CISTERCIAN
traprock / WHIN
traps / CLOTHING; EQUIPMENT
trapshooting / SKEET
trash / DIRT, JUNK; DROSS, WASTE
trashy / TRIFLING; WORTHLESS
traulism / STAMMER
trauma / HURT; WOUND; INJURY
travail / LABOR, PAINS; ANGUISH
Travancore cape / COMORIN
travel / RIDE, TREK, TOUR. VOYAGE
travel, pert. to / VIATIC
travel by auto / RIDE; MOTOR
travel by boat / SAIL
travel on foot / HIKE; MARCH
travel by plane / FLY
travel by road / TREK; DRIVE
travel by train / RIDE
traveled / EXPERIENCED
traveler / PILGRIM; SALESMAN; PASSENGER
traveler's haven / HOTEL, MOTEL
traveling bag / GRIP; VALISE; SUIT-CASE
traveling group / SAFARI; CARAVAN
traveling salesman / DRUMMER
traveling show / CIRCUS; CARNIVAL
travelogue / LECTURE
traversary / INAUSPICIOUS
traverse / PASS; CROSS
travertine / TUFA; CALCITE
travesty / FARCE; PARODY; BURLESQUE
Traviata composer / VERDI
Traviata heroine / VIOLETTA
travois / SLED; POLES, SLING

trawl /TROLL; DRAGNET
trawler/ BOAT; TROLLER
tray / BOARD; SALVER, SERVER
treacherous / RECREANT; IN-SIDIOUS
treacherous area / QUICKSAND
treacherous disciple / JUDAS
treacherous killer / ASSASSIN
treachery / PERFIDY, TREASON
treacle / SYRUP; THERIAC; MO-LASSES
tread / STEP, WALK; TRAMPLE
tread the boards / ACT; PERFORM
tread on the heels of / ENSUE; FOLLOW
tread stealthily / SNEAK
treadle / LEVER, PEDAL; CHALAZA
treadle hammer / OLIVER
treadmill / ROUTINE
treason /PERFIDY; BETRAYAL; TREACHERY
treasonous offense / SABOTAGE, SEDITION
treasurable / EXQUISITE; INES-TIMABLE
treasure / GEM; CASH; HOARD, JEWEL; PLENTY, RICHES, WEALTH. LOVE; VALUE
treasure house / COFFER; THESAURUS
treasure ship / GALLEON
Treasure State / MONTANA
treasure trove / CACHE; WINDFALL
treasurer / BURSAR; PAYMASTER
treasury / EXCHEQUER
treasury agent / TMAN
treat / USE; TEND, TEST; MANAGE, REGALE; DISCUSS
treat with acid / BITE, ETCH
treat again / RENEW; REPEAT
treat with air / AERATE
treat boldly / BRAZEN; EMPHASIZE
treat carelessly / MISUSE; NEGLECT
treat deferentially / KOWTOW; VENERATE
treat gently / PET; CARESS
treat harshly / MISUSE
treat an illness / DOCTOR
treat improperly / BOTCH
treat indulgently / COCKER, PAM-PER
treat with iodine / PAINT
treat judiciously / WEIGH; DISCRIM-INATE
treat with malice / OUTRAGE, TOR-MENT
treat methodically / SYSTEMATIZE
treat a patient / NURSE
treat remedially / CURE; NURSE; BANDAGE
treat romantically / PET, WOO; COURT
treat roughly / MANHANDLE

treat rudely / INSULT, VILIFY; PUT-DOWN

treat slightingly / NEGLECT; OVER-LOOK

treat upon / HANDLE

treat a wound / DRESS; BANDAGE

treated opium / CHANDU; CHAN-DOO

treatise / ESSAY, TRACT; DISSER-TATION

treatment / USE; USAGE; MANAGE-MENT

treaty / PACT; COMPACT, EN-TENTE; COVENANT

treaty clause / PROVISION

treble / SHARP; SHRILL, TRIPLE

trebly / THREEFOLD

trebucket / SLING

treculia / BREADFRUIT

tree / IE, TI; AGA, DPA, ASH, BAY, CHE, ELM, FIR, GUM, HAW, HOP, LIN, OAK, TUI, ULE, YEW; AKEE, AMLI, ANAM, ANDA, ARAR, ASAK, ATLE, AULU, AUSU, AUZU, BARU, BIJA, BITO, BIWA, BOBO, BOGO, BRAB, BROM, CAJU, COCA, COLA, CORK, DALI, DILO, DOON, DOUM, DUKU, EBOE, EJOO, GOAI, GUAO, HINO, HOLM, IFIL, IPIL, KINO, KIRI, KOPI, KOZO, LIME, LING, LINN, MAKO, MYXA, NAIO, NEEM, NIOG, NIPA, ODUM, OHIA, PALM, PELU, PINE, POON, PUKA, RACK, RATA, RIMU, ROKA, SAUL, SHEA, SUPA, TALA, TARA, TAWA, TEAK, TEIL, TITI, TOON, TORO, TUNG, TUNO, TUTU, UPAS, WHAU, YATE, YAYA, YPIL; ALAMO, ALDER, ARECA, ASPEN, BALSA, BIRCH, CAROB, CEDAR, LARCH, MAPLE, PINON, PIPUL; ACACIA, BANYAN, BOOJUM, GINKGO, LAUREL, LIN-DEN, POPLAR; CATALPA

tree, c.f. / DRY; DRYO

tree, pert. to / ARBOREAL

tree abode / NEST; TREEHOUSE

tree afloat / SNAG

tree of Africa / AKEE, BAKU, COLA, OLAX, SHEA; AEGLE, ARTAR, SIRIS; BAOBAB; COPAIVA

tree of antiquity / FIG

tree of Asia / ACLE, ASAK, DITA; SIRIS

tree of Australia / KARRI, KAURI; JARRAH; BRIGALOW, EUCALYPT

tree of Buddha / BO

tree of California / REDWOOD

tree of China / KAYA; GINGKO; KUMQUAT

tree class / PALM; FRUIT; CITRUS, TIMBER

tree clump / SHAW; GROVE, MOTTE; THICKET

tree covering / TAN; BARK, ROSS

tree decay / PECK

tree exudation / GUM, SAP; AMBER, RESIN, ROSIN, SYRUP

tree farmer / FORESTER

tree fern / POLYPODY

tree foliage / LEAVES; LEAFAGE

tree frog / HYLA; PEEPER

tree group / TOPE; CLUMP, COPSE, GROVE, MOTTE; COPPICE, ORCHARD

tree of Guyana / MORA

tree of heaven / AILANTHUS

tree of India / DAR, SAJ, SAL; AMLI, DHAK, NEEM, POON, SHOQ; MAHUA; BANYAN, DEODAR

tree of Japan / UME; KAKI, KIRI, KUSU, KUWA, MOMO, SUGI; KIAKI; MOMIJI, SAKURA, YANAGI

tree juice / SAP

tree knot / BURL, KNAG

tree of Lebanon / CEDAR

tree limb / TWIG; BOUGH; BRANCH

tree limbs / RAMAGE

tree of Malaya / OHIA, UPAS; TERAP; DURIAN

tree of the Mediterranean / CAROB

tree moss / USNEA; LICHEN

tree moth / EGGER

tree of New Zealand / AKA, KIO; KOPI, MIRO, PELU, PUKA, RATA, RIMU TAWA, TORO; HINAU, KAURI, KAURY, NGAIO; KANUKA, KARAKA, TOTARA

tree of North America / HEMLOCK, HICKORY, REDWOOD; TAMA-RACK

tree pest / RUST; BEETLE

tree of the Philippines / DAO, IBA, TUA, TUI; BOGO, DITA, IPIL, SUPA; ANABO, LIGAS

tree plantation / LOT; STAND

tree pod / CAROB

tree product / NUTS, WOOD; FRUIT

tree shaft / BOLE; TRUNK

tree specialist / DENDROLOGIST

tree study / SILVICS; DENDROLOGY

tree tap / SPILE

tree that has died / STUMP; RAM-PIKE

tree tiger / JAGUAR; LEOPARD

tree tissue / BAST, PITH; XYLEM; PHLOEM; CAMBIUM

tree toad / HYLA

tree torso / TRUNK

tree of the tropics / EBOE, PALM; BALSA, MANGO; COLIMA, LEB-BEK, SAPOTA

tree trunk / BOLE

tree yielding chocolate / COLA, KOLA

treed / CORNERED

tree-dwelling marsupial / OPOSSUM
treeless plain / LLANO; PAMPAS, TUNDRA
treeless tract / STEPPE
tree-lined walk / MALL; ALAMEDA
treenail / NOG, PEG, PIN
trees / COPSE, GROVE; FOREST
trees, pert. to / SYLVAN
trees of a region / SILVA, SYLVA
tref / UNCLEAN
trefoil / LOTUS, MEDIC; CLOVER; MELILOT
trek / TRIP; MARCH; SAFARI
trellis / ARBOR; LATTICE; ESPALIER
tremble / ROCK; QUAKE, SHAKE; QUAVER, QUIVER
tremble with emotion / THROB; TINGLE
trembling / SHAKY; TREPID; NERVOUS
tremellose / VISCID
tremendous / HUGE; AWFUL; AWESOME, FEARFUL
tremendously / INTENSELY
tremolo / FLUTTERING
tremor / JAR; JOLT; SHAKE
tremor of excitement / THRILL
tremulous / SHAKY, TIMID; AGITATED
trench / PIT, SAP; DITCH, FOSSE; CHANNEL
trench gun / MORTAR
trench on / INVADE; OVERSTEP
trench at rear / PARADOS
trench surrounding fortification / MOAT
trench toward enemy position / SAP
trenchant / KEEN; ACUTE, SHARP
trenchant humor / SATIRE; SARCASM
trencher / PLATTER
trencherman / GLUTTON; GOURMAND
trend / BENT, BIAS; TENOR; COURSE
trepak step / PRISIADKA
trepan / SNARE; TREPHINE
trepang / BECHEDEMER
trepid / ALARMED; TIMOROUS
trepidant / TREMBLING
trepidation / ALARM; FRIGHT; FLUTTER
trespass / ERR; POACH, OFFEND; ENCROACH. CRIME, FAULT
trespass to hunt / POACH
trespasser / INTRUDER; KIBBITZER
tress / CURL, LOCK; RINGLET
trestle / BAR; BRIDGE; VIADUCT; FRAMEWORK
tret / TARE; ALLOWANCE
trews / TROUSERS
trey / THREE
triaconter / GALLEY

triad / TRIVALENT. TRIO; CHORD; TRINITY
triage / SORTING
trial / WOE; PAIN, SUIT, TEST; ESSAY; CONTEST, INQUIRY
trial impression / PROOF
triangle / AFFAIR, TRIGON
triangle variety / RIGHT; OBTUSE; SCALENE
triangle's side / LEG
triangular end of wall / GABLE
triangular facade / PEDIMENT
triangular flag / BURGEE, PENNON; PENNANT
triangular inset / GORE; GUSSET
triangular sail / JIB; LATEEN
triangular topsail / RAFFE
triangulate / SURVEY
trianon / VILLA
triarchy / TRIUMVIRATE
Triassic animal / DINOSAUR
triatonic / TRIVALENT
tribal / LINEAL; GENTILE
tribal division / CLAN, GENS, SEPT; CURIA
tribal symbol / TOTEM
tribe / CLAN, GENS, RACE; GROUP, TUATH
tribe of India / AO; AWAN, BHIL, TURI; BHEEL
tribulation / WOE; GRIEF, TRIAL
tribunal / BAR; BENCH, COURT, FORUM
tribune / PODIUM; MAGISTRATE
tributary / FORK; FEEDER. SUBJECT
tribute / TAX; DUTY, SCAT, TOLL; IMPOST, PRAISE
trice / LASH, PULL; JIFFY; INSTANT
triceps function / EXTENSION
trichinosis vector / PORK
trichold / CILIATE
trick / FOX; DUPE; CHEAT; JUGGLE; SWINDLE. FLAM, GAWD, JAPE, RUSE, WILE; DODGE, STUNT; DECEIT
trick in battle / GAMBIT; MANEUVER; STRATAGEM
tricked / FOOLED, HOAXED
trickery / FRAUD, GLAIK; KNAVERY; ARTIFICE; DECEPTION
trickle / DRIP, FLOW, SEEP
trickster / CHEAT, KNAVE; FOLKHERO
tricksy / SPORTIVE
tricky / SLY; WILY; SNIDE
tricorn / HAT; TRIANGULAR
tricot / CROCHET
tricycle / VELOCIPEDE
trident / FORK; SPEAR
Trieste's peninsula / ISTRIA
trifle / TOY; PLAY; SPORT. FIG, JOT; GEWGAW. STRAW

TRIBES OF ISRAEL, TWELVE

REUBEN
SIMEON
LEVI°
JUDAH
ISSACHAR
ZEBULUN
DAN
NAPHTALI
GAD
ASHER
JOSEPH (EPHRAIM, MANASSEH)
BENJAMIN

° Held no territory in Israel.

---

trifler / WASTREL; DILETTANTE
trifling / PETTY, SMALL; TRIVIAL
trifling amount / SOU; FICO, SNAP; PEANUTS
trifling objection / CAVIL; QUIBBLE
trifoliate / TERNATE
trifoliolate plant / OCA; MEDIC; CLOVER, OXALIS, SORREL; TREFOIL; NONESUCH, SHAMROCK
trig / NEAT, TIDY, TRIM
trigger / IGNITE, SETOFF
triggerfish / DURGON; OLDWIFE
triglyph / TABLET
trigon / LYRE; CUSPS; TRIANGLE
trigonometrical function / SINE; COSINE, SECANT; TANGENT
trilateral / THREESIDED
Trilby hero / BILLEE
Trilby villain / SVENGALI
trill/ SING; QUAVER, WARBLE
trillion, c.f. / TREG; TREGA
trillion's zeroes / TWELVE
trim / LOP; .ADORN; DECORATE. NEAT, SNUG, TIDY, TRIG
trim a coin / NIG; CLIP
trim up / NEATEN, POLICE
trimmed / SNOD; PRUNED, SMOOTH
trimmer / LAODICEAN
trimming / GIMP, LACE; RUCHE; EDGING, TINSEL; BEATING; PASSEMENTERIE
trimming shrubs, pert. to / TOPIARY
trimming tool / ADZE
trinal / THREEFOLD
trine / TRIPLE, TRIUNE; AUSPICIOUS. TRIGON
Trinidad dance / LIMBO
Trinidad music / CALYPSO
Trinidad tree / CYP
Trinidad's discoverer / COLUMBUS
Trinitarian / MATHURIN
trinitrotoluene / TNT
trinity / ATEST, TRIAD, TRINE; TRIUNE

trinket / GAUD; TRIFLE; BIBELOT
trio / THREESOME
trip / ERR; FALL, SLIP; DANCE. TOUR; ERROR; JOURNEY
trip hammer / OLIVER
tripartite / TRIPLE
tripe / GUT; ENTRAIL, RUBBISH; MARROWGUT
triplane builder / FOKKER
triple / TRINE; TREBLE. THREEBAGGER
triple crown / TIARA
triple goddess / HECATE
triplet / TRIO; TRIAD
tripletail / SAMA; BERRUGATE
tripod / CAT; EASEL, STAND; TRIVET; PYTHONESS
Tripoli measure / DRA, PIK; DRAA
Tripoli ruler / DEY
Tripoli's ancient name / OEA
tripper / TOURIST; TRAVELER
triptych / ALTARPIECE
trireme / GALLEY
trismus / LOCKJAW
Tristan's love / ISOLDE
triste / SAD; DISMAL
Tristram Shandy's author / STERNE
Tristram's love / ISOLT; ISEULT, YSEULT
trite / BANAL, CORNY, STALE; HACKNEYED
trite phrase / CLICHE; BROMIDE
trite remark /BANALITY; PLATITUDE
triton / EFT; EVET, NEWT; SALAMANDER
Triton's father / NEPTUNE
Triton's mother / AMPHITRITE
triturate / GRIND; LEVIGATE
triumph / OVATION, SUCCESS. WIN
triumphant / ELATED; JUBILANT
trivet / STAND; HOTPLATE
trivia / MINUTIAE
Trivia author / GAY
trivial / SMALL; COMMON, PALTRY
trivial verse /DOGGEREL

Troad city / TROY

trochal / ROTIFORM

troche / ROTULA; LOZENGE; PASTILLE

trochee / CHOREUS

trod / STEPPED

troglodyte / CAVEDWELLER

Troilus' father / PRIAM

Troilus' wife / CRESSIDA

Trojan / ILIAN. See also Troy

Trojan asteroid / PRIAM; AENEAS, HECTOR, NESTOR; TROILUS; ACHILLES, ANCHISES, DIO-MEDES

Trojan chieftain / AGENOR, HECTOR

Trojan countryside / TROAD, TROAS

Trojan hero / ENEAS, PARIS; AENE-AS, AGENOR, DARDAN, HECTOR

Trojan horse / HOAX; TRICK

Trojan horse maker / EPEIUS

Trojan prince / PARIS; AENEAS

Trojan prophet / HELENUS; CAS-SANDRA

troll / FISH, SING. GNOME

trolley / TRAM; CRANE

trollop / SLUT; SLATTERN

trombone / SACKBUT, SAMBUKE

trommel / SIEVE; SCREEN

trona / URAO

Trondheim crest / CORONATION

troop / BAND, GANG; SQUAD

troop array / ECHELON

troop maneuver / DEPLOYMENT

troop sally / SORTIE

trooper / CAVALRYMAN

troops / ARMY; SOLDIERS

troops at a fort / GARRISON

troopship / TRANSPORT

trope / HEADING; METAPHOR; CAN-TILLATION

trophy / CUP; PRIZE, SCALP, TOKEN; MEMENTO

tropic / ZONE. SOLAR

tropical / HOT; TORRID; EQUA-TORIAL

tropical American cat / PUMA; JAGUAR, OCELOT

tropical American fruit / GUAVA; PAPAYA

tropical American lizard / IGUANA

tropical American tree / DALI, DATE; ICICA; SAPOTA; SAPODILLA

tropical animal / EYRA; COATI

tropical bird / ANI, ARA; MOTMOT, PARROT, TOUCAN, TROGON; QUETZAL

tropical disease / BUBA, PIAN, YAWS; BUBAS, SPRUE; MALARIA; FRAMBESIA

tropical fever / AGUE; DENGUE

tropical fish / OPAH; GUASA, SAR-GO; ROBALO, SALEMA; MOJARRA

tropical food plant / TARO; ANAN-AS; DASHEEN

tropical fruit / DATE; GUAVA, MAN-GO, PAPAW; BANANA, PAPAYA, PAWPAW; PLANTAIN

tropical headgear / TOPI; TERAI, TOPEE

tropical herb / PIA; SIDA; TACCA

tropical hollow grass / BAMBOO

tropical lizard / AGAMA, GECKO

tropical mammal / COATI, TAPIR

tropical plant / DAL; ALOE, TARO; AGAVE, LIANA; IPECAC; LAN-TANA; HIBISCUS

tropical rodent / CAVY, PACA

tropical tree / AKEE, MABI, PALM; BALSA, BONGO, ZORRO; BANA-NA, BANYAN, BAOBAB; ANNATTO

trot / JOG; PADNAG

troth / FAITH, TRUTH; PLEDGE

trotter / FOOT

troubadour / POET; MINSTREL; MINNESINGER

trouble / AIL, VEX; ANNOY; HA-RASS, MOLEST, PESTER. WO; ADO, WOE; PAIN; GRIEF; SOR-ROW

troublemaker / FIREBRAND

troubles / ILLS; CARES

troublesome / HARD; ARDUOUS; TIRESOME

troublesome person / AGITATOR

troublous / TRYING; DISQUIETING

trough / HOD; CURL; BASIN; FEED-BOX

trough to cool ingots / BOSH

trough used in mining / SLUICE

trounce / BEAT, DRUB

troupe / COMPANY; ENSEMBLE

trousers / PANTS, TREWS; SLACKS; BREECHES

trousseau / OUTFIT; WARDROBE

trout / CHAR, PEAL; LONGE, SEWEN, SEWIN, TOGUE; GRILSE

trowel / DARBY, SCOOP; SPATULA

Troy / ILION, ILIUM. See also Trojan

Troy land / TROAS

Troy's epic / ILIAD

Troy's founder / ILUS

Troy's king / PRIAM

truant / IDLER; ABSENTEE

truce / PAUSE; ARMISTICE

truck / DEAL; TRADE; BARTER. VAN; LORRY; CAMION, PICKUP

truck driver / TEAMSTER

trucker / HAWKER; PEDDLER

truckle / STOOP, TOADY; CRINGE

truculence / CRUELTY; SAVAGE-NESS

truculent / RUDE; COARSE, FIERCE

trudge / PLOD, SLOG; TRAIPSE

true / REAL; EXACT, LOYAL; STANCH; CORRECT. SO
true copy / ESTREAT
true statement / AXIOM; POSTULATE
true to type / TYPICAL
true-blue / LOYAL; STEADFAST
truehearted / HONEST; SINCERE
trueness / HONESTY, LOYALTY
truepenny / STRAIGHTSHOOTER
truffle / TUBER; FUNGUS
truism / PLATITUDE
Truk Island / TOL; FEFAN, POLIE
trull / STRUMPET
truly / YEA; SOOTH; INDEED, REALLY
trummel / BREADBOX
trump / CAP; RUFF
trump nine in pinochle / DIX
trumpery / TRASH; TINSEL; RUBBISH
trumpet / HORN; BUGLE; BUCCINA, CLARION
trumpet call / DIAN; SENNET; CHAMADE, FANFARE; REVEILLE
trumpet creeper / TECOMA
trumpet shell / TRITON
trumpet sound / BLARE
trumpeter / AGAMI; BUGLER; PIGEON
trumpeter perch / MADO
truncate / LOP; SHORTEN
truncated roof / HIP
truncheon / STAFF; CUDGEL
trundle / ROLL; WHEEL
trunk / BOX; BODY, STEM; CHEST, TORSO
trunk line / MAINLINE
trunk of tree / BOLE
trunkfish / CHAPIN; BOXFISH
truss / TIE; BIND; SUPPORT
trust / RELY, TROW; EXPECT; CONFIDE. TICK; FAITH; LIPPEN
trustee / FIDUCIARY
trusting / RELIANT; UNSUSPECTING
trustless / UNFAITHFUL
trustworthy / TRUE; HONEST RELIABLE
trustworthy convict / TRUSTY; PAROLEE
trusty / FIRM; HONEST
trusty weapon / RIFLE; RAPIER
truth / TAO; FACT; RIGHT, SOOTH; VIRTUE
truth drug / PENTOTHAL
truth goddess / MA; MAAT; ALETHIA
truthful / OPEN; FRANK; CANDID; VERIDIC
truthfulness / VERACITY
truthless / FALSE, WRONG

try / AIM; DARE, TEST; ESSAY, PROBE; REFINE; ATTEMPT. CRACK; EFFORT
try to match / EMULATE
try out / RENDER. TRIAL
trying / DIFFICULT
tryst / DATE; RENDEZVOUS
tsamba / BARLEY
tsar / CZAR
tsar's wife / TSARINA
tsetse / KIVU
tsetse fly disease / NAGANA; ENCEPHALITIS
Tsashima victor / TOGO
Taameter Island / HAO; ANAA
tuatara / IGUANA; SPHENODON
tuatha de danaan / FAIRIES
tub / DAN, SOE, VAT; CASK, KNAP, KNOP; KEEVE, KIVER; FIRKIN
tuba / HELICON, SAXHORN
tubby / THICK
tube / TV; DUCT, PIPE; SUBWAY, TUNNEL
tube of glass / PIPETTE
tuber / BULB, EDDO, ROOT; JALAP
tuber eaten as delicacy / TRUFFLE
tuber variety / OCA, OKA, YAM; TARO; POTATO
tubercle / WEN; KNOB, NODE; TUMOR
tubercular person / LUNGER
tuberculosis TB; PHTHISIS; CONSUMPTION
tubfish / GURNARD
tubular part / SLEEVE
tuck / BLOW, FOLD; GATHER. RAPIER
tuckahoe / PORIA
tucker / WEARY. FOOD; KAIKAI
tuckered out / TIRED; POOPED
tufa / TUFF; TRASS; SCORIA
tuffet / HASSOCK
tuft / BUNCH, PLUME; CLUSTER
tuft of feathers / ALULA; CREST; AIGRET
tufthunter / SNOB; TOADY
tug / TOW; DRAG, DRAW, HAUL, JERK, PULL, TOIL, YANK. BOAT
tuition / FEE; TEACHING; DISCIPLINE
tule / REED; BULRUSH, SCIRPUS
tule root / WAPATOO
tulip tree / POPLAR
tulle / NET
tullibee / WHITEFISH
Tully / CICERO
tulsi / BASIL
tulwar / SCIMITAR
tumble / FALL, ROLL, SPIN, TURN; RUMPLE
tumble about / FLOP

tumbler / GLASS; PIGEON; ACRO-BAT

tumefaction / SWELLING

tumid / TURGID; POMPOUS, SWOLLEN

tummy / STOMACH

tumor / WEN, YAW; CANCER; NEOPLASM, SWELLING

tumor, c.f. / OMA; CELE

tumpline / HEADSLING

tumtum / DOGCART

tumulose / HILLY

tumult / ADO, DIN; RIOT, STIR; MELEE; HUBBUB, UPROAR

tumultuous / UNRULY; AGITATED

tumultuous flow / FLOOD; TORRENT

tumulus / TELL; MOUND; BARROW

tun / CASK; HOGSHEAD

tuna / ALBACORE; PRICKLYPEAR

tundra / PLAIN

tune / AIR; ARIA; MELODY, STRAIN. HARMONIZE

tuned / TEMPERED

tuneful / MUSICAL; MELODIOUS

tunic / COAT; GIPON, SMOCK, STOLA; CHITON

tunicate / BULB; SALPA

Tunisian capital / TUNIS

Tunisian cape / BON; BLANC

Tunisian city / SFAX, GAFSA; SOUSSE; BIZERTE

Tunisian gulf / GABES; HAMMAMET

Tunisian measure / SAAH; WHIBA

Tunisian money / DINAR

Tunisian river / MEDJERDA

Tunisian ruler / BEY, DEY

Tunisian weight / ROTL; UCKIA; KANTAR

tunnel / TUBE

tunnel in the Alps / CENIS; GOTHARD, SIMPLON

tunnel disease / BENDS

tunny / AMIA, TUNA

tup / RAM; HAMMER

tupelo / GUM; NYSSA

Tupian Indian / ANTA

turban / TURF; PATTA; MANDIL; SEERBAND

turbid / FOUL; MUDDY; ROILED

turbinal / SPIRAL

turbinate bone / CONCHA

turbine wheel housing / STATOR

turbit / PIGEON

turbot / BRET; BRILL; FLATFISH

turbulence / FURY; TUMULT

turbulent air / STORM; TYPHOON; HURRICANE

turbulent stream / TORRENT

tureen / TERRINE; CASSEROLE

turf / SOD; CLOD; SWARD, TRACK

turf slice / DIVOT

turf square / SOD

Turgenev novel / SMOKE

turgent / PUFFY; INFLATED

turgid / SWOLLEN

Turk / TATAR; TARTAR; OSMANLI, OTTOMAN

Turkestan lake / SHOR

Turkestan Moslem / SALAR

Turkestan trader / SART

turkey / GOBBLER. See also Turkish

turkey buzzard / AURA; VULTURE

Turkey capital / ANKARA

Turkey oak / CERRIS

Turkic speaker / OGOR; TATAR; TARTAR

Turkish administrative division / VILAYET

Turkish area / THRACE; ARMENIA; ANATOLIA

Turkish bath / HAMMAM

Turkish cap / FEZ; CALPAC; TARBUSH; TARBOOCH, TARBOOSH

Turkish city / ADANA, IZMIR; AINTAB; ISTANBUL, STAMBOUL; CONSTANTINOPLE

Turkish commander / AGA; AMIR; AMEER

Turkish constable / KAVASS

Turkish decree / IRADE

Turkish flag / ALEM

Turkish garment / DOLMAN

Turkish government / PORTE

Turkish governor / BEY; VALI, WALI; PASHA; KHEDIVE

Turkish hill / DAGH

Turkish horde / TATAR

Turkish inn / SERAI; IMARET; CARAVANSARY

Turkish judge / AGA; CADI, KADI; MULLA; MULLAH

Turkish lake / TUZ, VAN

Turkish magistrate / AGA; CADI

Turkish mansion / KONAK

Turkish measure / OKA; ALMUD, JERIB; ARSHIN

Turkish military chief / ZAIM

Turkish minister / VIZIER

Turkish money / LIRA, PARA; ASPER; MAHBUB, YUZLUK; PIASTER

Turkish mosque attendant / SOFTA

Turkish mountain / ARARAT

Turkish mountain range / ALAI; TAURUS

Turkish policeman / ZAPTIA

Turkish prayer rug / MELAS

Turkish province / BEYLIE

Turkish regiment / ALAI

Turkish ruler / KHAN; CALIPH, SULTAN

Turkish soldier / NIZAM; JANIZARY

Turkish standard / ALEM, TOUG

Turkish tobacco / LATAKIA

Turkmen desert / KARAKUM
turku / ABO
turmeric / REA; ANGO; OLENA; BLOODROOT
turmoil / ADO; BUSTLE, WELTER
turn / ACT, GEE; BEND, GYRE, STIR, VEER; ALTER, CURVE, PIVOT; CHANGE, ROTATE, SWERVE; DEVIATE. DEED, GIFT; TALENT
turn to account / UTILIZE
turn aside / VEER; SHUNT; DIVERT
turn away / SNUB; SIDETRACK
turn on axis / ROTATE
turn back / REPEL; REVERT
turn down / REFUSE, REJECT
turn inside out / EVERT
turn left / HAW
turn off / COOL
turn rapidly / WHIRL
turn right / GEE
turn the soil / TILL
turn into stone / PETRIFY
turn the tables / REQUITE, REVERSE
turn turtle / UPSET; INVERT
turn white / BLANCH
turn of year / SOLSTICE
turnabout / MERRYGOROUND
turncoat / RAT; TRAITOR; RENEGADE
turned aside / AVERTED
turned-back collar / REBATO
turner / ATHLETE, GYMNAST
turning, pref. / ROTO
turning handle / CRANK
turnip / NEEP; SWEDE; RUTABAGA
turnkey / JAILER, WARDEN
turnout / MEETING; EQUIPAGE
turnpike / ROAD; HIGHWAY
turnpike bar / TOLLGATE
turnsole / SUNFLOWER; HELIOTROPE
turpentine tree / TARATA; TEREBINTH
turpitude / BADNESS; DEPRAVITY
tursio / DOLPHIN
turtle / DOVE; JUNIATA, SNAPPER; TERRAPIN, TORTOISE; LOGGERHEAD
Tuscany city / PISA; SIENA; FLORENCE
Tuscany river / ARNO
tush / TUSK; SILENCE. TUT
tusk / IVORY, TOOTH; CANINE
tusk of boar / RAZOR
tusker / BOAR; ELEPHANT
Tussaud's museum / WAXWORKS
tussis / COUGH
tussle / SCUFFLE
tussock / TUFT
tut / HUSH; QUIET; REBUKE
Tutankhamen / PHARAOH
tutelage / GUARDIANSHIP

tutelary god / LAR; GENIUS; PROTECTOR
tutenag / ZINC; BIDRI
tutor / COACH, TEACH. MASTER; TRAINER
tutti / UNISON
Tutuila city / PAGOPAGO
TV / TUBE; TELEVISION
TV advertiser / SPONSOR
TV show / SITCOM
twaddle / JARGON; CHATTER, PRATTLE
twain / TWO
twang / SOUND; NASALITY. PULL
tweak / PINCH; TWITCH
tweezers / PINCERS
twelfth day / EPIPHANY
twelfth of a foot / INCH
Twelfth Night clown / FESTE
Twelfth Night heroine / VIOLA
twelve dozen / GROSS
twelve inches / FOOT
twelve o'clock / NOON; MIDNIGHT
twelvemonth / YEAR
twelve-point type / PICA
twenty / SCORE
twenty quires / REAM
twenty-four sheets of paper / QUIRE
twice, pref. / BI, DI; DIS
twice-born / REINCARNATED
twiddle / TWIRL, TWIST
twig / SHOOT, SPRAY, SPRIG
twilight / EVE; DUSK; GLOAMING
twilight sleep / NARCOSIS
twilled cloth / REP, CORD; DENIM, PIQUE, SERGE, SURAH
twin / PAIR; GEMEL
twin crystal / MACLE
twinberry / HONEYSUCKLE
twine / COIL, WIND; TWIST; EMBRACE. CORD; STRING
twinebush / HAKEA
twin-hulled vessel / CATAMARAN
twining plant / VINE
twining stem / BINE
twinkle / WINK; BLINK
twins of the Zodiac / GEMINI
twirl / SPIN, TURN; ROTATE
twist / COIL, ROLL, SKEW, SLUE, WARP; GNARL, KINK; QUIRK
twist out of shape / CONTORT, DISTORT
twist together / COIL; TWINE
twisted / AWRY; TORTILE
twister / TORNADO; WHIRLWIND
twit / JEER, JIBE; SCOFF, TEASE
twitch / JERK; TWEAK. TIC; PANG
twitching / TIC
twitter / CHIRP; GIGGLE
two / DUAD, PAIR; BRACE; COUPLE
two, pref. / BI
two cups / PINT

two hundred twenty yards / FUR-LONG

two hundredth anniversary / BICEN-TENNIAL

two rhyming lines / COUPLET

two thousand pounds / TON

two under par / EAGLE

two-edged sword / RAPIER; CLAY-MORE

two-faced / FALSE; DECEITFUL

two-handled Greek vessel / DIOTA; CRATER, KRATER; AMPHORA

two-horned / BICORN

two-hulled boat / CATAMARAN

two-masted vessel / BUM; BRIG, YAWL, ZULU; BRIGANTINE

two-quart vessel / FLAGON

two-sided / BILATERAL

twosome / PAIR

two-toed sloth / UNAU

two-wheeled vehicle / GIG; CART; BICYCLE

two-winged / DIPTERAL

two-year-old salmon / SMOLT

two-year-old sheep / TEG

Tyburn tree / GALLOWS

tycoon / NIP; GRANDEE

tyke / CHILD

type / KIND, NORM, SIGN, SORT; STAMP, TOKEN. TEST

type of art / DADA; GENRE

type of auto / COUPE, SEDAN; COMPACT

type bar / SLUG

type case / FONT

type of cloud / CIRRUS, NIMBUS; CUMULUS

type feature / KERN; SERIF, SWASH

type measure / EM, EN; PICA

type of orange / NAVEL; VALENCIA

type of pinafore / TIER

type of roof / HIP; GABLE; MAN-SARD

type size / PICA; AGATE; BREVIER; NONPAREIL

type of soil / LOAM

type for spacing / QUAD

type square / EM

type style / ROMAN; GOTHIC, ITALIC; SANSERIF

type of window / BAY; CASEMENT

typesetter / COMPOSITOR

typewriter roller / PLATEN

typewriter type / PICA; ELITE

typhlosis / BLINDNESS

typhoon / HURRICANE

typo / ERROR; MISPRINT

typographer / PRINTER; COM-POSITOR

tyrannical / CRUEL; DESPOTIC

tyrant / DESPOT; AUTOCRAT

Tyre's king / HIRAM

Tyrian princess / DIDO

tyro / NOVICE; NEOPHYTE

tyronic / AMATEURISH

Tyr's attacker / FENRIR

Tyr's father / ODIN

tzigane / GYPSY

U

ubiquity / OMNIPRESENCE

Uganda capital / ENTEBBE, KAM-PALA

Uganda language / LUO; LUGANDA

ugliness / DEFORMITY

ugly / CROSS, PLAIN; HOMELY

ugly building / EYESORE

ugly old woman / HAG; CRONE

ugly sprite / GOBLIN

Ugrian / MAGYAR, OSTYAK

ukase / EDICT; DECREE

Ukraine capital / KIEV

Ukraine coin / GRIVNA, SHAGIV

Ukraine legislature / RADA

Ukrainia / UKRAINE

ula / GUMS

ulcer / SORE

ulex / WHIN; FURZE, GORSE

ulexite / TIZA

ulnar / CUBITAL

Ulster capital / BELFAST

Ulster city / LONDONDERRY

ulterior / BEYOND; DISTANT

ultimate / LAST; FINAL; UTMOST

ultra / BEYOND; EXTREME

ultraconservative / TORY

ululant / HOWLING, WAILING

ululate / HOOT, HOWL, WAIL

ulva / SEAWEED

Ulysses / ULIXES; ODYSSEUS

Ulysses' dog / ARGUS

Ulysses' friend / MENTOR

Ulysses' kingdom / ITHACA

Ulysses' son / TELEMACHUS

Ulysses' swineherd / EUMAEUS

Ulysses' voyages / ODYSSEY

Ulysses' wife / PENELOPE

Uma / DEVI

umber / PIGMENT; GRAYLING

umbra / SHADOW; PHANTOM, SUN-SPOT

umbrage / PIQUE, SHADE; GRUDGE

umbrageous / SHADY; SHADED

umbrella / GAMP; CHATTA; PARA-SOL

umbrella part / RIB; COVER

umbrellalike finial / TEE

umpire / JUDGE; ARBITER, REFEREE

unabated / UNDIMINISHED

unable / HELPLESS, IMPOTENT
unable to hear / DEAF
unable to speak / DUMB, MUTE
unaccented / ATONIC
unaccented vowel sound / SCHWA
unaccompanied / LONE, SOLE, SOLO
unadorned / BALD, BARE; PLAIN
unadulterated / PURE; UNMIXED
unaffected / REAL; PLAIN; HONEST
unaided UNAL; ALONE; SINGLE
Unalaska inhabitant / ALEUT
unalterable / STABLE; IMMUTABLE
unanimous / UNITED; AGREEING
unanswerable / CONCLUSIVE, UN-DENIABLE; IRREFUTABLE
unaspirated / LENE
unassuming / HUMBLE, MODEST; NATURAL; RETIRING
unattached / FREE; ALONE, LOOSE
unavailing / VAIN; FUTILE
unaware / DULL; STUPID; IGNORANT
unbaked pottery / GREENWARE
unbalanced / UNSOUND; DE-RANGED
unbecoming / UNFIT; IMPROPER
unbelief / DOUBT; DISTRUST
unbeliever / DEIST; GIAOUR; DOUBTER, HERETIC, INFIDEL, SKEPTIC
unbending / RIGID, STERN; SERIOUS
unbind / UNDO; LOOSE, UNTIE
unbleached / ECRU; BEIGE; NATURAL
unblemished / PURE; CLEAN
unblushing / SHAMELESS, UN-ASHAMED
unbosom / AVOW; ADMIT; CONFESS
unbound / FREE; LOOSE
unbounded / VAST; ENDLESS, IM-MENSE; INFINITE; BOUNDLESS
unbranched antler / DAG
unbranded calf / MAVERICK
unbridled / LAX; FREE; LOOSE
unbroken / WHOLE; ENTIRE, IN-TACT
unburnt brick / DOBE; ADOBE
uncalled / UNCHOSEN; UNSUM-MONED
uncanny / EERY; EERIE, WEIRD
unceasing / ETERNAL; CONSTANT
unceremonious attire / NEGLIGEE
uncertain / ASEA; SHAKY, VAGUE
uncertainty / DOUBT; SUSPENSE
unchangeable / FAST; STEADY
uncharged particle / NEUTRON
unchaste / IMMODEST
unchecked / FREE; LOOSE; RAM-PANT
unchristian / PAGAN; BARBAROUS

uncinate / BENT; HAMATE, HOOKED
uncivil / MEAN, RUDE; BLUNT
uncivilized / SAVAGE
uncle / EAM, EME, OOM, TIO, ZIO
Uncle Tom's Cabin author / STOWE
Uncle Tom's Cabin character / EVA; LEGREE
unclean / FOUL, TREF, VILE; DIRTY, NASTY; FILTHY, IMPURE
unclose / OPEN; UNCOVER; UN-FASTEN
unclose, poet / OPE
unclothed / BARE, NUDE
unco / WEIRD; STRANGE, UNCANNY
uncoined metal / BULLION
uncombed / ROUGH; UNKEMPT
uncomely / UGLY; HOMELY; HATE-FUL
uncommon / ODD; RARE; QUEER
uncommunicative / RETICENT
uncompromising / FIRM; STERN
unconcerned / CALM, COOL, OPEN
unconfined / FREE; LOOSE
unconfirmed report / RUMOR
unconquerable / INVINCIBLE
unconscious state / COMA; SLEEP
unconstrained / EASY; UNTRAM-MELED
uncoordinated walking / LURCH; ABASIA
uncouth / ODD; RUDE; CLUMSY
uncouth fellow / CAD; BOOR
uncover / BARE, OPEN; STRIP
uncovered / BARE, OPEN; LIDLESS
unction / BALM; CONSECRATION
unctuous / OILY; BLAND, SUAVE
uncultivated / WILD; FALLOW
uncut / WHOLE
uncut glove leather / TRANK
uncut lumber / LOG; TIMBER
undaunted / BOLD; FEARLESS
undecorated / PLAIN
undefiled / PURE; SPOTLESS
undeniable / CERTAIN, EVIDENT
under / SUB; ALOW, LESS; BELOW
under age / MINOR
under ban / TABU; TABOO; VER-BOTEN
under obligation / INDEBTED
under part of hand / PALM
under severe strain / STIFF
underbrush / UNDERGROWTH
undercooked / RARE; UNDERDONE
undergird / FRAP
undergo / BEAR, DREE; ENDURE
undergo cell destruction / LYSE
undergo a decline / BOG; FALL
underground bud / BULB, CORM
underground chamber / CAVERN
underground dwarf / GNOME, TROLL

underground excavation / STOPE
underground passageway / TUBE;
    METRO; SUBWAY, TUNNEL
underground reservoir / CENOTE
underground river / STYX; PHLEGE-
    THON
underground room / CELLAR
underground shelter / ABRI
underground system of utilities /
    PIPES, SEWER; CONDUIT
underground tram / TUBE; METRO;
    SUBWAY
underground worker / MINER
underhand pitch / LOB
underhanded / SLY; MEAN
underhanded person / SLY; CHEAT
underling / SERF; SLAVE; SERVANT
undermine / DIG, SAP; WEAKEN
undermost / LOWEST
undern / AFTERNOON
underneath / BELOW; BENEATH
undernsong / TIERCE
underpin / PROP; FRAME; SUPPORT
underpinning / LEG; PROP
undersea dweller / MERMAN
undershirts / TSHIRTS; SINGLETS
undershot water wheel / NORIA
underside, pert. to / NEMAL
undersized animal / RUNT; SHRIMP
understand / SEE; KNOW; GRASP
understanding / KEN; MIND; SENSE
understanding, pert. to / NOETIC
understood / TACIT
understudy / STANDBY
undersurface of foot / SOLE
undertake / TRY; AGREE; ACCEPT
undertaker / MORTICIAN
undertaking / EFFORT; PROJECT
undertow / FLOW, TIDE; CURRENT
undervalue / DESPISE; MISPRIZE
underwater chamber / CAISSON
underwater concretion / PAAR
underwater detection device /
    SONAR
underwater diver / AQUANAUT
underwater ridge / REEF
underwater swimmer / FROGMAN
underwater tree stump / SNAG
underwater vessel / SUBMARINE
underwear / LINGERIE
underworld / DUAT; ARALU, HADES,
    SHEOL; AMENTI, EREBUS; ABAD-
    DON, GEHENNA, MICTLAN,
    XIBALBA
underworld denizen / IMP; DEVIL
underworld god / DIS; ADES; HA-
    DES, PLUTO; OSIRIS; SERAPIS
underworld goddess / HEL
underworld ruler / DEVIL, SATAN
underwrite / ENSURE, INSURE
undetermined quantity / ANY, FEW;
    SOME
undeveloped / EMBRYO, LATENT

undeveloped flower / BUD
undiluted /RAW; PURE; SHEER
undisclosed/ SECRET; ULTERIOR
undisturbed / CALM; QUIET, STILL
undivided / ONE; TOTAL, WHOLE
undivided whole /UNIT
undo/ OPEN, RUIN; ANNUL, LOOSE
undoing / RUIN
undomesticated / WILD; FERAL
undress / DISROBE
undressed fur / PELT
undressed kid / SUEDE
undressed skin / KIP
undue / IMPROPER; EXCESSIVE
undulant fever / BRUCELLOSIS
undulate / ROLL, WAVE; CRIMP
unduly / IMPROPERLY; EXCES-
    SIVELY
unduly dainty / FINICAL, FINICKY
undying / IMMORTAL; IMPERISH-
    ABLE
unearthly / EERIE; INHUMAN
uneasiness / UNREST; TROUBLE
uneasy / STIFF; ANXIOUS, AWK-
    WARD
uneducated / RUDE; IGNORANT
unemployed / IDLE; OTIOSE
unencumbered / COOL, FREE
unending / ETERNAL, FOREVER
unequal / UNEVEN, UNIQUE, UN-
    LIKE
unequal chances / ODDS
unequal triangle / SCALENE
unequaled / UNIQUE; PEERLESS
unequivocal / CLEAR; DIRECT
unerring / SURE; EXACT; CERTAIN
unescorted / ALONE
uneven / ODD; EROSE, ROUGH
uneven in color / STREAKY
uneven shingles / SHIMS
unexcited / CALM, COOL; SEDATE
unexciting / TAME
unexpected difficulty / SNAG
unexpected pleasure / TREAT
unexpected result / UPSET
unexpected stratagem / COUP
unexploded shell / DUD
unfadable / FAST
unfailing / SURE
unfair / FOUL, FALSE; UNJUST
unfaithful / FALSE; FICKLE
unfaltering / FIRM; STEADY
unfamiliar / NEW; UNCOMMON
unfashionable / PASSE; CARELESS
unfasten / RIP; UNDO; LOOSE
unfavorable / BAD, ILL; AVERSE
unfeeling / NUMB; CRUEL, HARSH
unfeigned / REAL, TRUE; CLEAR
unfermented grape juice / MUST,
    STUM
unfettered / FREE; LOOSE
unfilled cavity / VUG
unfit / IMPROPER

unfit to eat / ROTTED; SPOILED
unfitness / INCOMPETENCY
unflagging / UNWEARY; UN-
  WEARIED
unfledged / CALLOW
unflinching / UNSHRINKING
unfold / OPEN, TELL; CLEAR
unfold gradually / DEVELOP
unforced / EASY
unforested plain / STEPPE
unforged metal / PIG
unforgiving / CRUEL; IMPLACABLE
unforgotten / REMEMBERED
unfortunate / BAD, ILL; UNHAPPY
unfounded / IDLE, VAIN; FALSE
unfrequented / LONE; DESERTED
unfriendly / INIMICAL, UNGENIAL
unfrock / BARE; DIVEST; DEFROCK
unfruitful / BARREN; STERILE
unfulfilled / UNDONE
unfurl / OPEN; EXPAND, SPREAD
ungainly / GAWKY, STIFF; CLUMSY
ungenerous / MEAN; IGNOBLE
ungentlemanly person / CAD
ungirt / UNBELTED
ungodly / SINFUL, WICKED
ungovernable / UNRULY; FRANTIC
ungraceful / AWKWARD; UNGAINLY
ungrateful / THANKLESS
ungrateful person / INGRATE
unguent / BALM; SALVE; CEROMA
ungula / CLAW, HOOF, NAIL; TALON
ungulate / HOOFED. HERBIVORE
ungulate animal / DAMAN, HYRAX
unhallowed / WICKED; PROFANE
unhandy / INEPT; CLUMSY; AWK-
  WARD
unhappiness / WOE; BLUES;
  MISERY
unhappy / SAD; BLUE, DIRE, EVIL
unharmed / SAFE; UNHURT
unhealthy / SICKLY; NOXIOUS
unheeding / DEAF
unholy / PROFANE; UNSANCTIFIED
unhorse / FALL; UNSEAT
unhurried / EASY
unicellular animals / PROTOZOA
unicorn / REEM, URUS
unicorn fish / LIJA, UNIE
uniform / EVEN, SAME; ALIKE
unilateral / ONESIDED
unilocular / ONECELLED
unimaginative / LITERAL
unimaginative discourse / PROSE
unimpaired / WHOLE; INTACT
unimportant / MINOR, PETTY
uninjured / SAFE; INTACT
uninteresting / DRY; ARID, DULL
uninterrupted / ENDLESS
uninvited / UNASKED; UNSO-
  LICITED
union / BOND; ARTEL; FUSION

union / AFL, CIO, ILA, ITA, UAW,
  UMW; ILGWU
Union soldier / YANKEE
unique / ODD; LONE, RARE, SOLE
unique person / ONE; ONER
unique thing / ONER
uniqueness / UNICITY
unison / ACCORD; CONCORD
unit / ACE, ONE; ITEM; MONAD
unit of acceleration / NEWTON
unit of acoustics / BEL
unit of apothecaries' weight / DRAM
unit of army / SQUAD; PLATOON
unit of capacity / PINT; LITER,
  LITRE, QUART; GALLON
unit of color saturation / SATRON
unit of conductance / MHO
unit of discourse / WORD;
  PHONEME
unit of dry measure / PECK;
  BUSHEL
unit of electric charge / COULOMB
unit of electric current / VOLT
unit of electric light / PYR; WATT;
  LUMEN, WATTS
unit of electric power / WATT;
  HENRY
unit of electrical capacity / FARAD
unit of electrical inductance /
  HENRY
unit of electrical intensity / AMP;
  AMPERE
unit of electrical potential / VOLT
unit of electrical reluctance / REL
unit of electrical resistance / OHM
unit of electricity / AMP, WATT
unit of electrolics / ION
unit of electromagnetic resistance /
  ABOHM
unit of electromotive force / VOLT
unit of electrostatic quantity / ES
unit of energy / ERG, RAD; ERGON,
  JOULE; QUANTUM
unit of explosive force / KILOTON,
  MEGATON
unit of fluidity / RHE
unit of force / OD; DENE, DYNE,
  VOLT
unit of gravity / GAL
unit of heat / BTU; THERM;
  CALORY; CALORIE
unit of illumination / LUX; PHOT
unit of inductance / HENRY
unit of interstellar distance /
  PARSEC
unit of length / INCH, MILE, VARA,
  METER, VERST; PARSEC
unit of light / LUX, PYR; LUMEN;
  HEFNER
unit of light flux / LUMEN, LUMIN
unit of liquid measure / PINT;
  LITER, LITRE, QUART; GALLON

unit of magnetic flux / MAXWELL
unit of magnetic induction / GAUSS
unit of magnetic intensity / OERSTED
unit of magnetic potential / GILBERT
unit of mass / SLUG
unit of medicine / DOSE, DRAM
unit of metric system / GRAM; METER, STERE
unit of power / AMP, MIL, OHM, REL; DENE, DYNE, VOLT, WATT; FARAD, HENRY, WEBER; AMPERE
unit of power in ratio / BEL; DECIBEL
unit of pressure / BAR; BARAD, BARIE
unit of radiation / RAD; ROENTGEN
unit of reluctance / REL
unit of resistance / OHM
unit of scansion time / MORA
unit of score at bridge / TRICK
unit of sound loudness / DECIBEL
unit of square measure / ARE, ROD; ACRE
unit system / CGS
unit of time / DAY, ERA; HOUR, YEAR; MONTH; MINUTE, SECOND
unit of weight / TON, WEY; GRAM, KILO; CARAT, GRAIN, POUND
unit of wire measure / MIL
unit of work / ERG; ERGON, JOULE
unite / ADD, FAY, MIX, TIE, WED; ALLY, BAND, JOIN, KNIT, LINK, WELD, YOKE; BLEND, MERGE, UNIFY
unite closely / WED; WELD; SOLDER
unite edges / BUTT; RABBET
unite firmly / WED; KNIT; SOLDER
unite by fusing / WELD
unite in a league / FEDERATE
unite by weaving / SPLICE
united / ALLIED, JOINED
united brethren / MORAVIANS
united group / BAND, TEAM
United Kingdom area / WALES
United Nations arm / FAO, ILO, WHO; ICAO; UNESCO, UNICEF
united in opinion / UNANIMOUS
United States / see also American
United States capital / DISTRICT; WASHINGTON
United States citizen / AMERICAN
United States coin / CENT, DIME, HALF; NICKEL; QUARTER, TWO-BITS
United States emblem / EAGLE
United States forces World War I / AEF
United States monetary unit / DOLLAR

United States president's nickname / ABE, IKE
unity / ONE; UNION; UNISON
univalent radical / MONAD
univalve / SHELL; MOLLUSK
universal / TOTAL, WHOLE, WORLD; ENTIRE
universal knowledge / PANTOLOGY
universal language / RO; IDO; ESPERANTO
universal remedy / PANACEA
universe / WORLD; COSMOS, NATURE
universe, pert. to / COSMIC; UNIVERSAL
university in California / UC; USC; UCLA
university in Connecticut / YALE
university degree holder / DOCTOR; GRADUATE; LICENTIATE
university in Louisiana / TULANE
university in New York / NYU; CUNY, SUNY
university officer / DEAN; BURSAR, REGENT; PROVOST
university session / TERM; SEMESTER
university study group / SEMINAR
university teacher / PROFESSOR
unjust / BIASED, UNFAIR; HEINOUS, PARTIAL; ONESIDED, WRONGFUL
unkeeled / RATITE
unkempt / ROUGH; UNCOMBED
unknit / RAVEL; UNRAVEL
unknown / DARK; MYSTIC, OBSCURE
unknown god / KA
unknown person / ALIEN; IGNOTE
unlawful / BASTARD, ILLEGAL
unlawful outbreak / RIOT; MELEE
unlearned / IGNORANT; ILLITERATE
unless / BUT; NISI, SAVE; EXCEPT
unlimited authority / AUTOCRACY
unload / SELL; RELIEVE; DISCHARGE
unlock / OPEN; SOLVE; DECODE
unlucky / ILLFATED
unman / GELD; UNNERVE; EMASCULATE
unmanly / COWARDLY; EFFEMINATE
unmannered / RUDE; ROUGH
unmannered person / CAD; RUFFIAN
unmarried / SINGLE; CELIBATE
unmarried girl / MAID; MAIDEN; SPINSTER
unmarried man / BACHELOR
unmatched / ODD; UNMATED
unmethodical / UNRULY; CURSORY
unmistakable / CLEAR, PLAIN

UNITED STATES: STATES AND TERRITORIES

	Abbreviation		Capital
	U.S. Postal Service	Traditional	
Alabama	AL	ALA	MONTGOMERY
Alaska	AK	—	JUNEAU
American Samoa	—	SAMOA	PAGO PAGO
Arizona	AZ	ARIZ	PHOENIX
Arkansas	AR	ARK	LITTLE ROCK
California	CA	CALIF	SACRAMENTO
Canal Zone	—	CZ	BALBOA HEIGHTS
Colorado	CO	COLO	DENVER
Connecticut	CT	CONN	HARTFORD
Delaware	DE	DEL	DOVER
District of Columbia	DC	DC	WASHINGTON
Florida	FL	FLA	TALLAHASSEE
Georgia	GA	GA	ATLANTA
Guam	GU	—	AGANA
Hawaii	HI	—	HONOLULU
Idaho	ID	—	BOISE
Illinois	IL	ILL	SPRINGFIELD
Indiana	IN	IND	INDIANAPOLIS
Iowa	IA	—	DES MOINES
Kansas	KS	KANS	TOPEKA
Kentucky	KY	KY	FRANKFORT
Louisiana	LA	LA	BATON ROUGE
Maine	ME	—	AUGUSTA
Maryland	MD	MD	ANNAPOLIS
Massachusetts	MA	MASS	BOSTON
Michigan	MI	MICH	LANSING
Minnesota	MN	MINN	ST. PAUL
Mississippi	MS	MISS	JACKSON
Missouri	MO	MO	JEFFERSON CITY
Montana	MT	MONT	HELENA
Nebraska	NE	NEBR	LINCOLN
Nevada	NV	NEV	CARSON CITY
New Hampshire	NH	NH	CONCORD
New Jersey	NJ	NJ	TRENTON
New Mexico	NM	NMEX	SANTA FE
New York	NY	NY	ALBANY
North Carolina	NC	NC	RALEIGH
North Dakota	ND	NDAK	BISMARCK
Ohio	OH	—	COLUMBUS
Oklahoma	OK	OKLA	OKLAHOMA CITY
Oregon	OR	OREG	SALEM
Pennsylvania	PA	PA	HARRISBURG
Puerto Rico	PR	PR	SAN JUAN
Rhode Island	RI	RI	PROVIDENCE
South Carolina	SC	SC	COLUMBIA
South Dakota	SD	SDAK	PIERRE
Tennessee	TN	TENN	NASHVILLE
Texas	TX	TEX	AUSTIN
Utah	UT	—	SALT LAKE CITY
Vermont	VT	VT	MONTPELIER
Virginia	VA	VA	RICHMOND
Virgin Islands	VI	VI	CHARLOTTE AMALIE
Washington	WA	WASH	OLYMPIA
West Virginia	WV	WVA	CHARLESTON
Wisconsin	WI	WIS	MADISON
Wyoming	WY	WYO	CHEYENNE

unmitigated / ARRANT; UNABATED
unmixed / PURE; SHEER; SIMPLE
unnecessary / USELESS; NEEDLESS
unoccupied / IDLE; EMPTY; VACANT
unopened flower / BUD
unparalleled / ALONE; UNRIVALLED
unperturbed / CALM; SERENE
unplayed golf hole /BYE
unpleasant/ ODIOUS; IRKSOME
unplowed strip / HADE
unpolished / RAW; DULL, RUDE
unpredictable / ERRATIC, WAY-
    WARD
unprincipled / LAX; WICKED
unprincipled person / CAD; ROTTER
unproductive / BARREN; STERILE
unprofessional / LAY
unprofitable / POOR, SECK
unprogressive / BACKWARD
unpropitious / UNFAVORABLE
unqualified / MERE; SHEER, UNFIT
unquestionable / CERTAIN
unravel / FRAY; SOLVE; DIVEST
unreal / ROMANTIC; VISIONARY
unreasonable / SILLY; ABSURD
unreasonable fear / PANIC
unrefined / RAW; WILD; CRASS
unrelenting / FIRM, HARD, IRON
unreliable / UNSAFE, UNSURE
unremitting / CONTINUOUS
unreserved / FREE, OPEN; FRANK
unresponsive / COLD; PASSIVE
unrest / FERMENT
unrighteous / EVIL; SINFUL
unripe / RAW; GREEN; IMMATURE
unripe apple / CODLING
unrivaled / UNIQUE; PEERLESS
unroll / OPEN, UNDO; EVOLVE
unruffled / CALM, COOL; QUIET
unruly / RIOTOUS, VICIOUS
unruly child / BRAT
unruly crowd / MOB
unruly lock of hair / COWLICK
unruly outbreak / RIOT; MELEE
unruly person / REBEL; RANTIPOLE
unsafe / RISKY; EXPOSED
unscathed / UNHARMED; UN-
    INJURED
unseasonable / UNFIT; ILLTIMED
unseat / UNHORSE; DETHRONE
unseeable / UNSEEN; INVISIBLE
unseemly / UNFIT; INDECENT
unseen / INVISIBLE
unselfish / FREE; BROAD, NOBLE
unserviceable / USELESS
unsettle / UNFIX; RUFFLE
unsewed glove / TRANK
unshackled / FREE; FREED
unshadowed / CLEAR; BRIGHT
unshaped piece of metal / SLUG
unsightly / UGLY; UNPLEASING
unskilled / RAW; INAPT, INEPT
unskilled workman / LABORER

unskillful / INEPT, CLUMSY
unsmelted metal / ORE
unsophisticated / NAIVE; CALLOW;
    ARTLESS, NATURAL; INNOCENT
unsophisticated person / RUBE
unsorted wheat flour / ATA; ATTA
unsound / THIN, WEAK; FALSE
unspeakable / VILE; WICKED
unspoiled / RACY; FRESH; NATURAL
unspoken / MUTE; TACIT; APHONIC
unstable / ERRATIC; UNSTEADY
unsteady / FICKLE; MUTABLE
unstratified loam / LOESS
unstrung / WEAK; SHAKY; NER-
    VOUS
unstudied / UNPREPARED
unsubstantial / AERY, AIRY
unsuccessful / VAIN; FUTILE
unsuitable / INAPT, INEPT, UNAPT
unsullied / CLEAN
unsure / DOUBTFUL; UNCERTAIN
unsymmetrical / LOPSIDED
unsympathetic / CRUEL, STERN
untamed / WILD; FERAL; FERINE
untanned skin / PELT
untether / UNTIE; LOOSEN
untidiness / MESS, MUSS; JUMBLE
untidy / MESSY, MUSSY; UNKEMPT
untidy person / SLOB; SLOVEN
untidy state / MESS
until / TO; TIL, TILL, UNTO
untilled / FALLOW
unto / TO; TIL; TILL; UNTIL
untouchable / LEPER
untouched / PRISTINE
untrammeled / FREE
untranslated / ORIGINAL
untried / NEW; UNUSED
untrodden / PATHLESS; TRACKLESS
untroubled / CALM, COOL, EASY
untrue / FALSE; DISLOYAL
untruth / FIB, LIE; FICTION
untruthfulness / DECEPTION
untutored / RAW; CRUDE; IG-
    NORANT
untwist / RAVEL; UNCOIL; UN-
    RAVEL
untwisted silk / SLEAVE
unused / NEW; MINT; UNTRIED
unusual / RARE; CURIO; NOVEL;
    EXOTIC; CURIOUS
unusual person / ONER; CORKER
unusual thing / ONER; RARITY
unutterable / VILE; IMPURE
unvarying sound / MONOTONE
unvoiced / ASONANT
unwanted plants / WEEDS
unwary / CARELESS; INCAUTIOUS
unwavering / FIRM, SURE; STEADY
unwearied / CONSTANT, TIRELESS
unweave / RAVEL; UNCOIL, UN-
    WIND
unwell / ILL; SICK; SICKLY

unwieldy / BULKY, HEAVY, LARGE
unwieldy mass / HULK
unwilling / LOTH; LOATH; AVERSE
unwise / RASH; FOOLISH; IMPOLITIC
unwoven cloth / FELT
unwritten / ORAL; PAROL
unwritten belief / TRADITION
unwrought / RAW; CRUDE
unwrought inkle / SPINEL
unwrought metal / ORE
unyielding /PAT, SET; FAST
unyoke / SEVER; REMOVE
up / ATOP, HIGH, UPON; ABOVE
up, pref. / ANA
up above / ATOP
up to / TIL; TILL; UNTIL
up to date / NEW; MODERN
Upanishad / MA; ISA; ISHA, ITRI
upas tree poison / ANTIAR
upbeat / ARSIS
upbraid / TWIT; BLAME, CHIDE
upcountry / INLAND; INTERIOR
uphill / TOILSOME; ASCENDING
uphold / AID; ABET, BACK; DEFEND
upholster / COVER; CUSHION
upholstery fabric / TABARET
upholstery gimp / ORRIS
upkeep / COST; MAINTENANCE
upland plain / WOLD; PLATEAU
upon / ON, UP; EPI, SUR; ATOP
upon, poet. / OER
upon, pref. / EP; EPI
upper / GREATER; SUPERIOR
upper air / ETHER; ATMOSPHERE
upper arm bone HUMERUS
upper bract of grass / PALEA
upper classman / SENIOR
upper house / SENAT; SENATE
upper member of a pilaster / CAP
upper Nile people/MADI, NUER
upper part / TIP, TOP; SUMMIT
upper regions / ETHER; ATMOSPHERE
upper room / LOFT; ATTIC
upper throat / GULA
uppercase / CAPITAL
uppermost / TOP; HIGHEST
uppermost part / TOP; ACME, APEX
uppish / ARROGANT, ASSUMING
upright / FAIR, JUST, PURE, TRUE
upright column / STELE; PILLAR
upright doorway piece / JAMB
upright part of stairs / RISER
upright piece / JAMB, STUD
upright pole / MAST
upright post / STANCHION
uprightness / HONOR, WORTH
uprising / RIOT; MELEE; REVOLT
uproar / DIN; RIOT; BRAWL, NOISE
uproot / DESTROY; ERADICATE
upset / TIP; COUP, KEEL; SHOCK
upshot / END; EVENT, ISSUE

upstage / SNUB
upstart / SNOB; PARVENU; ARROGANT
upturned nose / PUG
upward, c.f. / ANO
upward movement of ship / SCEND
uraeus / ASP
uranic / CELESTIAL
Uranus / COELUS, HEAVEN, PLANET
Uranus' children / TITANS
Uranus' daughter / RHEA
Uranus' mother / GE; GAEA
Uranus' satellite / ARIEL; OBERON; MIRANDA, TITANIA, UMBRIEL
Uranus' son / SATURN
urban official / MAYOR; ALDERMAN
urban settlement / TOWN; VILLAGE
urbane / CIVIC, SUAVE; POLITE
urbanity / AMENITY, SUAVITY
urchin / BOY, IMP, TAD; ARAB
uredo / HIVES
urge / DUN, EGG, PLY, SUE, YEN; GOAD, PROD, PUSH, SPUR, STIR
urge importunately / DUN
urgency / NEED; PRESSURE
urgent / COGENT; EARNEST
urial / SHA; OORIAL
urn / VASE; SAMOVAR
Ursa Major / BEAR; DIPPER
ursoid / BEARLIKE
urticant / STINGING
urticaria / RASH; HIVES, UREDO
urus / OX; TUR; AUROCHS
urva / MONGOOSE
U.S. / AMERICA
usage / USE; WONT; HABIT; CUSTOM
use / DEAL; APPLY, AVAIL, EXERT, INURE, TRAIN, TREAT, WASTE. USAGE, WORTH; CUSTOM, PROFIT
use diligently / PLY; APPLY
use divining rod / DOWSE
use exertion / STRIVE; EXERCISE
use frugally / SPARE; BUDGET
use a lever / PRY
use a needle / SEW; STITCH
use trickery / PALTER
use up / EAT; SPEND; CONSUME
used / WORN; EMPLOYED; SECOND-HAND
used to be / WAS; WERE
used up / ATE; SPENT; CONSUMED
used for violin strings / GUT
useful / GOOD; UTILE; SUITED
useless / IDLE, VAIN; FUTILE
user of telephone / CALLER
usher / PAGE; ESCORT, HERALD
ustulate / CHARRED; SCORCHED
usual / COMMON, NORMAL, WONTED
usual custom / HABIT

usually / ORDINARILY
usurp / TAKE; SEIZE; ASSUME
uta/ TANKA
Utah capital / SALTLAKECITY
Utah Indian / UTE
Utah lake / SALTLAKE
Utah lily/ SEGO
Utah motto / INDUSTRY
Utah mountains/ LASAL, UINTA
Utah racing locale / BONNEVILLE
Utah river / WEBER
Utah state bird / GULL
Utah state emblem / BEEHIVE
Utah state flower / SEGO
Utah state nickname / MORMON;
  BEEHIVE, DESERET
utensil / TOOL; IMPLEMENT
utile / USEFUL; PRACTICAL
utility / USE; PROFIT; BENEFIT
utilize / USE
utmost / BEST, LAST; FINAL
utmost degree / TOPS
utmost limit / EXTREME

utopian / IDEAL; PERFECT
utter / SAY; PASS; SPEAK, STATE,
  VOICE; EXPRESS, PUBLISH.
  SHEER, STARK, TOTAL; ENTIRE
utter boisterously / BLUSTER
utter chaos / TOPHET
utter confusedly / SPLUTTER
utter greeting / BID
utter impulsively / BLURT
utter raucously / BLAT; BLAST
utter shrilly / PIPE; SKIRL
utter slight sound / PEEP, TOOT
utter sonorously / ROLL
utter suddenly / BLAST, BLURT
utter vehemently / THUNDER
utterance / SPEECH; EXPRESSION
uttered / ORAL; SPOKEN. SAID
utterly / QUITE, STARK; WHOLLY
uttermost / UTMOST; EXTREME
uva / GRAPE
uva ursi / BEARBERRY
uxorious / FOND; DOTING

V

V / VEE
V shaped indentation / NOTCH
V shaped part / WEDGE
vacancy / GAP; SPACE
vacant / FREE, IDLE, OPEN, VOID;
  EMPTY; HOLLOW; UNFILLED
vacate / QUIT, VOID; ANNUL,
  LEAVE; CANCEL
vacation / HOLIDAYS
vacation journey / TRIP
vacation spot / SPA; CAMP; RESORT
vacationing / OFF; AWAY
vaccinate / INOCULATE
vaccinia / COWPOX
vacillate / REEL, ROCK, SWAY;
  WAVER; SEESAW, TEETER,
  WOBBLE
vacillating / UNDECIDED
vacuity / VACANCY; EMPTINESS
vacuous / DULL, IDLE; EMPTY, IN-
  ANE; HOLLOW, STUPID, VACANT
vacuum / VOID
vacuum bottle / THERMOS
vacuum tube /DIODE, VALVE;
  TETRODE
vacuum's opposite / PLENUM
vade mecum / MANUAL; GUIDE-
  BOOK
vadium / BAIL; PLEDGE
vagabond / BUM, VAG; HOBO;
  SCAMP, TRAMP; BEGGAR; VA-
  GRANT; WANDERER
vagary / WHIM; ANTIC, FANCY
vagrant / VAGABOND
vague / DIM, LAX; HAZY; LOOSE;
  OBSCURE, SKETCHY, UNFIXED

vail / TIP; YIELD
vain / IDLE; EMPTY, FALSE, GAUDY,
  SHOWY; DREAMY, FUTILE, UN-
  REAL
vain person / FOP
vainglorious / BOASTFUL
vainglory / POMP; PRIDE; VANITY
vair / STOAT
vairagi / ASCETIC
valance / CANOPY, EDGING, PEL-
  MET
vale / DALE, DELL, GLEN; DINGLE,
  VALLEY
valentine / TOKEN; SWEETHEART
valet / MAN; SERVANT
valetudinarian / HYPOCHONDRIAC
Valhalla servants / VALKYRIES
Valhalla's owner / ODIN
valiance / VALOR; COURAGE
valiant / BOLD; BRAVE; DARING;
  GALLANT; FEARLESS, INTREPID
valiant man / HERO
valid / GOOD, JUST; GRAVE, LEGAL,
  SOUND; COGENT, STRONG;
  BINDING
validate / RATIFY; CONFIRM
Vali's father / ODIN
Vali's mother / RIND; RINDA
valise / BAG; ETUI, GRIP; HAND-
  BAG, SATCHEL; PORTMANTEAU
Valjean's nemesis / JAVERT
vallation / RAMPART
vallecula / FOSSA; FURROW
valley / DALE, DELL, DENE, GLEN;
  VAIL, VALE, WADI; GLADE;
  CANYON

valley on the moon / RILLE
valor / SPIRIT; BRAVERY, COURAGE
valorous / BOLD; BRAVE; HEROIC
valorous person / ACE; HERO
valuable / COSTLY, USEFUL,
   WORTHY; PRECIOUS; ESTIMABLE
valuable fur / MINK, SEAL; SABLE;
   ERMINE; ZIBELINE; CHINCHILLA
valuable thing / GOOD; ASSET
valuable violin / AMATI, STRAD
valuate / ESTIMATE
valuator / APPRAISER
value / RATE; REGARD; APPRAISE
value highly / PRIZE; ESTEEM
value received / CONSIDERATION
valued object / CURIO
valueless thing / TRIFLE
valve / GATE, TUBE; PISTON
vamoose / GO; CUT; LEAVE; DE-
   CAMP
vamp / FLIRT; VAMPIRE. SEDUCE
vampire / BAT; VAMP; DEMON,
   GHOST, GHOUL, LAMIA;
   DRACULA
vampire antidote / GARLIC
vampires' food / BLOOD
van / FORE; POINT, TRUCK, WAGON
Van Diemen's Land / TASMANIA
Vancouver Indian / NANAIMO
vandal / HUN; TEUTON; HOSTILE
vandalism / DESTRUCTION
vandalized / LOOTED; DEFACED
Vandals' leader / GENSERIC
Vandals' vanquisher / BELISARIUS
vandyke / BEARD
vane / BLADE; WEATHERCOCK
vang / ROPE; GUYROPE
vanguard / VAN; POINT, SCOUT
vanish / AWAY, FADE, FLEE
vanity / FOLLY, PRIDE; CONCEIT
vanity box / ETUI
Vanity Fair heroine / BECKY
vanquish / BEAT, FOIL, ROUT;
   CRUSH, QUELL, WORST; DEFEAT
vantage / ADVANTAGE
vantage place / COIGN
vanward / FORWARD
vapid / FLAT, TAME; PROSY, STALE;
   FEEBLE, JEJUNE
vapidity / INANITY; DULLNESS
vapor / AIR, FOG, GAS; FUME, MIST,
   REEK, ROKE, SMOG, WHIM
vapor, c.f. / ATMO
vapor in the air / FOG; HAZE, MIST;
   CLOUD
vaporer / BOASTER; BRAGGART
vaporize / ATOMIZE; VOLATILIZE
vaporized water / STEAM
vaporizer / SPRAY; ATOMIZER
vaporlike / AIRY; ETHEREAL
vaporosity / GASEITY
vaporous / VAIN; MISTY; STEAMY
vapors / MELANCHOLIA

vaquero / COWBOY; HERDSMAN
varan / LIZARD
varanian / MONITOR
Varangians / ROS, RUS
varec / KELP; WRACK; SEAWEED
variable / FICKLE, FITFUL; MUTA-
   BLE, PROTEAN; SHIFTING, UN-
   STEADY
variable star / MIRA, NOVA; ALGOL;
   CEPHEID
variance / SPAT; CHANGE;
   QUARREL
variant / SPORT; VARIETY
variate / MODIFY; DIVERSITY
variation / SHADE; CHANGE, NU-
   ANCE; MUTATION, VARIANCE
varicella / CHICKENPOX
varicose / SWOLLEN
varied tit / YAMAGARA
variegate / DIVERSIFY
variegated / PIED, SHOT; CALICO;
   DAPPLED, MOTTLED, SPOTTED
varietal / SPECIFIC; SUBSPECIFIC
variety / FORM, KIND, SORT, TYPE;
   CLASS, GENUS; CHANGE;
   SPECIES
variety, c.f. / VARI; VARIO
variety show / REVUE; MUSICAL
variola / SMALLPOX
variolate / INOCULATE
various / MANY; MEDLEY, SUNDRY;
   DIVERSE, SEVERAL; MANIFOLD
variet / CAD; CHURL, KNAVE
varnish / LAC; GLOSS, JAPAN
varnish ingredient / LAC; COPAL,
   ELEMI, RESIN
varnish vehicle / MEGILP
Varuna's gift / SOMA
Varuna's realm / WATER
varus / TALIPES; KNOCKNEE
vary / ALTER; CHANGE, DEPART
varying / DIFFERING, MODIFYING
vas / DUCT; VESSEL
Vasari's subject / PAINTERS
vascular / PASSIONATE
vase / URN; CONTAINER
vassal / SERF; LIEGE, SLAVE;
   TENANT; BONDSMAN, SUBJECT.
   SERVILE
vassalage / THRALL
vast / HUGE; ENORM, GREAT
vast age / EON; ETERNITY
vast amount / HOST, MINT
vast expanse / SEA
vast horde / HOST; LEGION
vast number / GOOGOL; ZILLION
vastness / BIGNESS; ENORMITY
vasty / HUGE; GIGANTIC
vat / AMA, BAC, TUB; GAAL, GAIL,
   GYLE, KEIR, KIER, KIVE; KEEVE;
   BARREL, VESSEL; CISTERN
vatic / ORACULAR; PROPHETIC
Vatican chapel / SISTINE

vaticinate / PREDICT; FORETELL
vaudeville / SHOW; COMEDY
vaudeville sketch / SKIT
vault / APSE, ARCH, CELL, SAFE
vaulted / ARCHED; CONCAVE
vaunt / PUFF; PARADE
vaunting / BOASTFUL; HIGHFLOWN
Vaya's son / HANUMAN
vector / CARRIER
vector rotator / VERSOR
Vedic deity / AGNI, SOMA, VAYU;
ADITI, DYAUS, INDRA, RUDRA,
USHAS; VARUNA; SAVITAR. See
also hindu gods and goddesses
Vedic god of love / BHAGA
Vedic goddess of dawn / USAS
Vedic language / PALI
veer / SHY, YAW; SLUE, TURN
veer off / WEAR; SHEER; SWERVE
vegetable / PEA; BEAN, BEET, CORN,
KALE, LEEK, OCRA, OKRA, OKRO;
CHARD, ONION, PEASE, ROOTS
vegetable exudation / RESIN
vegetable fiber / IXLE, PITA, PITO;
ISTLE, IXTLE
vegetable fuel / COAL, PEAT
vegetable of mustard family /
CRESS
vegetable organism / TREE; PLANT
vegetable retailer / GREENGROCER
vegetables in soup / JARDINIERE
vegetate / GROW; SPROUT
vegetating / PASSIVE; INACTIVE
vegetation / SUDD; GREENS
vehemence / FURY, HEAT, RAGE
vehement / HOT; KEEN; AMAIN
vehemently / AMAIN; FURIOUSLY
vehicle / CAR; AUTO, BIKE, CART,
SHIP, SLED; CYCLE, LORRY,
MOTOR
vehicle carrying a display / FLOAT
vehicle for heavy loads / VAN;
DRAY; LORRY, TRUCK
vehicle on runners / SLED; CUTTER,
SLEDGE
veil / HIDE; CLOAK, COVER. ORALE;
SHROUD; CURTAIN, YASHMAK
veil for Eucharist / AER
veiled / HID; VELATE
veiling material / VOILE
vein / RIB; VENA; GENUS, STYLE
vein of leaf / RIB
vein of ore / LEAD, LODE, REEF
vein in throat / JUGULAR
veined / STRIATED
velamen / MEMBRANE
velar / PALATAL; GUTTURAL
velate / HIDDEN, VEILED
velation / MYSTERY; COVERING
veld / PLAIN; GRASSLAND
vellicate / TWITCH
vellum / LAMBSKIN; PARCHMENT
velocity / RATE; SPEED; CELERITY

velours / PLUSH
velum / PALATE; MEMBRANE
velutinous / SILKY; VELVETY
velvet / PANNE
velvet grass / HOLCUS
velvetlike fabric / PLUSH
velvety / SILKY, SLEEK
venal / SORDID, VENOUS; SELFISH
venality / CORRUPTION, DIS-
HONESTY
vend / HAWK, SALE, SELL; RETAIL
vendee / BUYER
vendetta / FEUD; REVENGE
vendible / SALABLE; MARKETABLE
vendition / SALE
vendor / SELLER, VENDER; MER-
CHANT
vendue / SALE; AUCTION
veneer / COAT; GLOSS; POLISH
venenate / POISON
venerable / OLD; AGED, HOAR,
SAGE, WISH; AWFUL, GRAVE,
HOARY
venerable man / PATRIARCH
venerable monk / BEDE
venerate / ADORE, HONOR;
ESTEEM
veneration due God / LATRIA
veneration due saints / DULIA
veneration of saints / HAGIOLATRY
veneration due the Virgin / HYPER-
DULIA
Venetian beach / LIDO
Venetian blind / SHADE; JALOUSIE
Venetian boat / GONDOLA;
BUCENTAUR
Venetian boat operator / GONDO-
LIER
Venetian boat song / BARCAROLE
Venetian canals / RII; CANALI
Venetian magistrate / DOGE;
PODESTA
Venetian navigator / CABOT
Venetian red / SIENA; HEMATITE
Venetian section / RIALTO
Venezuela capital / CARACAS
Venezuelan city / MARACAIBO
Venezuelan Indian language / PAO;
MACU, PUME, PUMEH; WARRAU,
YARURO
Venezuelan lake / MARACAIBO
Venezuelan money / BOLIVAR
Venezuelan mountain / RORAIMA
Venezuelan plain / LLANO
Venezuelan port / LAGUAIRA
Venezuelan river / APURE;
ORINOCO
Venezuelan tree snake / LORA
vengeance / PUNISHMENT; RETALI-
ATION
vengeance goddess / ARA; FURY
vengeful / VINDICTIVE
veni, vidi, vici battle / ZELA

venial / EXCUSABLE; PARDONABLE
venin / TOXIN; POISON, VENENE
venireman / JUROR
venison / DEERMEAT
venom / GALL, HATE; SPITE, STING
venomous / SPITEFUL, VIPERINE
venomous serpent / ASP; COBRA, KRAIT, MAMBA; RATTLER; SIDEWINDER
venomous spider / TARANTULA
venose / VEINY; VENOUS
vent / GAP; FLUE, SALE; BREACH
ventilating airway / UPCAST
ventilating device / FAN; BLOWER
ventose / WINDY
ventral / FIN; HEMAD, HEMAL
ventricose / INFLATED, SWELLING
ventriloquist's partner / DUMMY
venture / DARE, RISK; STAKE, VAULT; CHANCE, HAZARD; PRESUME. LUCK; PERIL; DANGER
venture a guess / CONJECTURE
ventured / DARED, DURST; RISKED
venturesome / BOLD, RASH; RISKY; DARING; DOUGHTY; FEARLESS
venturous / BOLD; FEARLESS
venue / PLACE; LOCALITY
venule / VEINLET
Venus / ISHTAR; ASTARTE; APHRODITE
Venus' epithet / CYTHEREA
Venus as evening star / HESPER
Venus' father / JUPITER
Venus' island / MELOS
Venus' love / ADONIS
Venus' son / CUPID
veracious / TRUE; TRUTHFUL
veracity / TRUTH; CANDOR
veranda / LANAI, PORCH; LOGGIA
verb form / AM, BE, IS; ARE, WAS; WERE; TENSE
verbal / ORAL; VOCAL; SPOKEN
verbal adjective / GERUNDIVE
verbal ending / ED, ER, ES; ETH, ING
verbal examination / ORAL
verbal noun / GERUND
verbally / ALOUD; VERBATIM
verbatim / PRECISELY
verbiage / VERBOSITY
verbose / WORDY; DIFFUSE
verbosity / PROLIXITY
verd antique / PATINA; SERPENTINE
verdancy / GREENNESS
verdant / FRESH, GREEN; GULLIBLE
Verdi character / AIDA; AZUCENA
Verdi opera / AIDA; ERNANI, OTELLO; RIGOLETTO
verdict / ANSWER; FINDING
Verdun victor / PETAIN
verdure / GREENS; FOLIAGE;

GREENERY; GREENNESS; VEGETATION
verdurous / VIRESCENT
verge / EVE, ROD; BRIM, EDGE
Vergil's epic / ENEID; AENEID
Vergil's goatherd / DAMON
Vergil's hero / ENEAS; AENEAS
Vergil's poem / ENEID; AENEID
veridical / TRUTHFUL; VERACIOUS
verification / CONFIRMATION
verify / AVER; PROVE; FULFIL
verily / YEA; AMEN; TRULY; INDEED; CERTAINLY
verisimilar / LIKELY; PROBABLE
verisimilitude / PLAUSIBILITY
veritable / REAL; GENUINE
verity / FACT; SOOTH, TRUTH
verjuice / ACIDITY; SOURNESS
vermicelli / PASTA; WHORLS; SPIRALS; MACARONI
vermicular / WORMLIKE
vermifuge / ANTHELMINTIC
vermilion / RED; CARMINE
vermin / RAT; FLEA; ANIMAL
Vermont battle / BENNINGTON
Vermont capital / MONTPELIER
Vermont city / BARRE
Vermont hero / ALLEN; WARNER
Vermont lake / CHAMPLAIN
Vermont mountain / MANSFIELD
Vermont river / WINOOSKI
Vermont state flower / RED CLOVER
Vermont state nickname / GREENMOUNTAIN
Vermont tree / MAPLE
vernacular / NATIVE; IDIOMATIC
vernal / FRESH, GREEN
Verne character / NEMO; ROBUR
vernier / TRIMMER
vernile / SERVILE
veronica / BLUEBELL; SPEEDWELL
verruca / WART
Versailles villa / TRIANON
versant / SLOPE
versatile / READY; CLEVER, EXPERT, FICKLE, MOBILE; PLASTIC
verse / LINE, POEM, RANN, RIME; CANTO, RHYME, STAVE, STITCH; POETRY, STANZA
verse of five feet / PENTAMETER
verse form / ODE; POEM; RONDO; BALLAD, RONDEL, SONNET, TERCET
verse of four feet / TETRAMETER
verse pattern / LINES, METER
verse of six feet / HEXAMETER
verse of three feet / TRIMETER
verse of two feet / DIMETER
versed / ABLE, GOOD; CLEVER
versed in many languages / POLYGLOT
versicle / STITCH
versicolor / IRIDESCENT

versification / PROSODY
versifier / POET; LYRICIST
versify / POETIZE
version / READING; RENDITION
version of the scriptures / RSV;
    ITALA; VULGATE; SEPTUAGINT
versipel / WEREWOLF
verso / LEFT; REVERSE
verso, abbr. / VO
versus / AGAINST
vertebral / SPINAL; RACHIAL
vertex / TIP, TOP; APEX; CROWN
vertical / DOWN; ERECT, PLUMB
vertical support / PILLAR
vertical timber / BITT, MAST
vertical window in roof / DORMER
vertically in line / APEAK
verticil / WHORL
vertigo / DINUS; DIZZINESS
vertu / VIRTU; CURIOS; BRICABRAC
Vertumnus' wife / POMONA
vervain / VERBENA
verve / PEP; ELAN; ARDOR; ENERGY
very / SO; TOO; EXTREMELY; EX-
    CESSIVELY. HIGH, SAME; IDEN-
    TICAL
very abundant / LUXURIANT
very cold / GLACIAL
very fast / PRESTISSIMO
very good / VINTAGE
very hard mineral / EMERY; CORUN-
    DUM
very large / ENORM
very light mist / SEREIN
very loud / FF; DEAFENING; FOR-
    TISSIMO
very much / FAR; EXCESSIVE
very much, c.f. / ERI
very rich man / NABOB
very slow / LARGO
very small / WEE; MINUTE
very small amount / JOT; IOTA
very soft / PP; PIANISSIMO
Ve's brother / ODIN, VILI
Ve's victim / YMIR
vesicatory / BLISTERING
vesicle / SAC; BLISTER
vespers / PRAYER; EVENSONG
vespertine / EVENING
vespid / WASP
vessel / ARK, CAN, DOW, MUG,
    PAN, POT, TUB, TUG, URN, VAT;
    BARK, BOAT, DHOR, DRUM,
    MARU, SCOW, SHIP, TUBE, VASA
vessel, abbr. / SS
vessel for ashes of dead / URN
vessel for cooking / SKILLET
vessel for drinking / CUP, MUG
vessel of known capacity /
    MEASURE
vessel for liquids / CAN, CUP, POT,
    TUB; TANK, VIAL; CRUSE

vessel for liquors / FLASK; FLAGON;
    DECANTER
vessel of logs / RAFT
vessel for lubricants / OILCAN
vessel for oil / CRUSE
vessel for supply / OILER
vessel for vinegar / CRUET
vessel of war / BOMBER; CARRIER,
    CRUISER, TORPEDO; DESTROYER
vessel's bow / PROW
vessel's lowest deck / ORLOP
vessel's personnel / CREW
vest / GARMENT; WAISTCOAT
vest in / ASSIGN; ENTRUST
vesta / MATCH; GODDESS
vestal / PURE; CHASTE, SACRED
Vestal's handmaidens / VESTALS
vested / FIXED; COMPLETE
vestibule / HALL; ENTRANCE
vestige / MARK;   RELIC,   TRACE,
    TRACK; REMAINS
vestiture / COVERING
vestment / ALB; CAPE, COPE, ROBE
vestry / SACRISTY
vesture / CLOTHING, COVERING
Vesuvius-destroyed town / POMPEII
vet / EXGI; VETERAN
vetch / ERS; AKRA, TARE; PLANT
veteran / OLDTIMER; EXSOLDIER
veterinarian / VET; HIPPIATER
veto / FORBID, NEGATE, REFUSE
vex / IRK; FASH, FRET, GALL
vexation / PEST; PIQUE, WORRY;
    PLAGUE; CHAGRIN, TORMENT
vexatious / PESKY; PLAGUY; UNTO-
    WARD
vexed / RILY, SORE; PROVOKED
vexillum / COMPANY
vexing / PROVOKING
Via Lactea / GALAXY; MILKYWAY
via / BY; PER. WAY; HIGHWAY, PAS-
    SAGE
viable / FIT; CONSISTENT
viaduct / ROAD; BRIDGE; PASSAGE,
    TRESTLE
vial / PHIAL; BOTTLE
vials of wrath / ANGER; RANCOR
viands / FOOD; CATES, MEATS
viaticum / COMMUNION
viator / TRAVELER
Viaud pseudonym / LOTI
vibrancy / RESONANCE
vibrant / RESONANT; VIBRATING
vibrate / FAN, JAR; MOVE, ROCK,
    WAVE; SHAKE, SWING, WAVER
vibration / TRILL; TREMOR; TREM-
    OLO; RESONANCE; OSCILLATION
vibrationless point / NODE
vibrato / TREMOLO
vibratory motion / TREMOR
vibrio-caused disease / CHOLERA
vibrissa / WHISKER

VICE PRESIDENTS OF THE UNITED STATES

	Serving Under
John Adams	Washington
Thomas Jefferson	John Adams
Aaron Burr	Jefferson
George Clinton	Jefferson/Madison
Elbridge Gerry	Madison
Daniel D. Tompkins	Monroe
John Caldwell Calhoun	J. Q. Adams/Jackson
Martin Van Buren	Jackson
Richard Mentor Johnson	Van Buren
John Tyler	W. H. Harrison
George Mifflin Dallas	Polk
Millard Fillmore	Taylor
William Rufus Devane King	Pierce
John Cabell Breckinridge	Buchanan
Hannibal Hamlin	Lincoln
Andrew Johnson	Lincoln
Schuyler Colfax	Grant
Henry Wilson	Grant
William Almon Wheeler	Hayes
Chester Alan Arthur	Garfield
Thomas Andrews Hendricks	Cleveland
Levi Parsons Morton	Benjamin Harrison
Adlai Ewing Stevenson	Cleveland
Garret Augustus Hobart	McKinley
Theodore Roosevelt	McKinley
Charles Warren Fairbanks	Theodore Roosevelt
James Schoolcraft Sherman	Taft
Thomas Riley Marshall	Wilson
Calvin Coolidge	Harding
Charles Gates Dawes	Coolidge
Charles Curtis	Hoover
John Nance Garner	F. D. Roosevelt
Henry Agard Wallace	F. D. Roosevelt
Harry S Truman	F. D. Roosevelt
Alben William Barkley	Truman
Richard Milhous Nixon	Eisenhower
Lyndon Baines Johnson	Kennedy
Hubert Horatio Humphrey, Jr.	L. B. Johnson
Spiro Theodore Agnew	Nixon
Gerald Rudolph Ford	Nixon
Nelson Aldrich Rockefeller	Ford
Fritz Walter Mondale	Carter

vicar / FATHER, PRIEST; SUPERIOR; CLERGYMAN

vicarage / HOME; MANSE; BENE-FICE

vicarious / DEPUTED; SECOND-HAND

vicar's assistant / CURATE

vice / SIN; EVIL; CRIME, ERROR, FAULT, GUILT; DEFECT; BLEMISH

vice versa / CONVERSELY

viceregent / DEPUTY; DELEGATE

viceroy's wife / VICERINE

Vichy premier / LAVAL

Vichy water /SELTZER

vicinage / ENVIRONS, VICINITY; CLOSENESS; NEIGHBORHOOD. ADJOINING

vicious / BAD; EVIL, MEAN; CRUEL; FAULTY, IMPURE, SINFUL, UN-RULY

vicious person / BRUTE, YAHOO

viciousness / DEPRAVATION

vicissitude / CHANGE; REVERSE; ALTERNATION

Vicksburg victor / GRANT

victim / DUPE, PREY; MARTYR; CATSPAW, FALLGUY; SUFFERER

victimize / DUPE; BLAME; DECEIVE

victor / WINNER; CONQUEROR
victorfish / AKU; BONITO
Victoria capital / MELBOURNE
Victoria city / GEELONG; BALLARAT
Victoria region / GIPPSLAND
Victoria river / YARRA
Victor's crown / BAY; LAUREL
victory / NIKE; SUCCESS, TRIUMPH; CONQUEST
victory trophy / SCALP
victuals / DIET, FARE, FOOD, MEAT; BREAD, REPAST, SUPPLY, VIANDS; PROVISIONS, SUSTE-NANCE
vide / SEE; LOOK
videlicet / VIZ; NAMELY
video / TELEVISION
viduage / WIDOWS; WIDOWHOOD
vie / COPE; RIVAL; STRIVE; COM-PETE, CONTEND, CONTEST, EMULATE; ENDEAVOR
vielle / VIOL
Vienna woods / WIENERWALD
Vienna's palace / SCHONBRUNN
Vienna's park / PRATER
Vienna's river / DONAU; DANUBE
Vienna's royal family / HABSBURG
Vienna's white horses / LIPIZZANER
Viennese dance / WALTZ
Viennese musician / MOZART; STRAUSS
Vietnam / NAM
Vietnam capital / HANOI; SAIGON
Vietnam river / MEKONG
Vietnamese city / HUE; DANANG
Vietnamese money / DONG; PIASTRE
Vietnamese tunic / ODAI
view / EYE, SEE; LOOK, SCAN; STUDY; SURVEY; EXAMINE, EX-PLORE. DRIFT, SCENE, SCOPE, VISTA; BELIEF, DESIGN, NOTION, OBJECT
viewer / SPECTATOR
viewpoint / ANGLE, SLANT; VAN-TAGE
vigil / EYE; WATCH; DEVOTION, WATCHING
vigilance / CARE; CAUTION; WATCH-FULNESS
vigilance committee member / VIGI-LANTE
vigilant / WARY; ALERT, AWAKE
vignette / SKETCH; PICTURE
vigor / PEP, VIM, VIS, ZIP; ELAN; FORCE, POWER; ENERGY; STAMINA
vigorish / PIECE; INTEREST
vigorous / HALE; HARDY, LUSTY, SOUND; ROBUST, STRONG, STURDY
vigorously / LUSTILY

viking / ERIC, LEIF, OLAF; ROLLO, ROVER; PIRATE
Vila / FAIRY
vile / LOW; BASE, MEAN; CHEAP; ABJECT, FILTHY, IMPURE, PAL-TRY, SINFUL, SORDID, VULGAR, WICKED
vilification / ABUSE; DEFAMATION
vilify / SLUR; DECRY; ACCUSE, BERATE, DEBASE, DEFAME, MALIGN, REVILE; ASPERSE, BLACKEN, BLEMISH
Vili's brother / VE; ODIN
villa / COTTAGE
village / MIR, REW; DORP, STAD, VILL; DESSA, KRAAL, THORP, TOWN; HAMLET
village smithy's tree / CHESTNUT
villain / FIEND, KNAVE, ROGUE, SCAMP; RASCAL, WRETCH; RUFFIAN
villainous / BASE, MEAN, VILE
villainy / CRIME; KNAVERY; DE-PRAVITY; WICKEDNESS
villein / SERF; CEORL; TENANT
villous / DOWNY; HAIRY; SHAGGY
vim / PEP, ZIP; FORCE, VIGOR; ENERGY, SPIRIT
vimana / TOWER
vin ordinaire / TABLEWINE
Vincennes captor / CLARK
vincible / VULNERABLE; CONQUER-ABLE, SUSCEPTIBLE
vinculum / BAR, TIE; BOND
vindicate / CLEAR; PROVE; ASSERT, AVENGE, UPHOLD; CENSURE
vindication / EXCUSE; DEFENSE
vindictive / SPITEFUL; MALICIOUS, MALIGNANT, RANCOROUS, RE-SENTFUL
vindictive retaliation / REVENGE; VENDETTA
vindictiveness / SPITE
vine / AKA, HOP, IVY, IYO, PEA; BINE, CIPO; ABUTA, AMPEL, LIANA; LABLAB; CLIMBER, CREEPER; WISTERIA
vine, c.f. / VITI
vine cactus / OCOTILLO
vinegar / EISEL
vinegar, c.f. / ACETO
vinegar, pert. to / ACETIC
vinegar from ale / ALEGAR
vinegar bottle / CRUET
vinegar dregs / MOTHER
vinegar worm / EEL; NEMA
vinegarroon / SCORPION
vinegary / SOUR; ACRID; CRABBED, PEPPERY; ILLTEMPERED
vinegrowing / VINICULTURE
vineyard / CRU; WINERY
vingt-et-un / TWENTYONE

viniculture / VITICULTURE

vinification / FERMENTATION

Vinland discoverer / LEIF

vinous / WINY

vintage / CROP

vintner / ENOLOGIST; WINESELLER

vinyl / PLASTIC

viol / GUE, REBEC; SARANGI, SARINDA

viola / ALTO; VIOLET

violate / HURT; ABUSE; INJURE, RAVISH; DEBAUCH, DISTURB

violation of allegiance / TREASON

violation of confidence / BETRAYAL

violence / FURY, RAGE, RAPE; CRIME, FORCE; ASSAULT, OUT-RAGE

violent / HOT; WILD; ACUTE, RABID, SHARP; FIERCE, RAG-ING, RAVING, SEVERE, UNJUST; FURIOUS

violent behavior / RAMPAGE

violent blast of wind / GUST

violent dread / HORROR

violent effort / STRUGGLE

violent speech / TIRADE

violent storm / BURAN; TEMPEST, TORNADO, TYPHOON; HURRI-CANE

violent stream of water / TORRENT

violent woman / VIRAGO

violently / HARD; AMAIN

violet / VIOLA

violet-blue / INDIGO

violet-odored principle / IRONE; IONONE

violin / KIT; AMATI; REBAB, REBEC, STRAD; FIDDLE; CREMONA; STRADIVARI; STRADIVARIUS

violin maker / AMATI; GUARNER-IUS; STRADIVARIUS

violin peg / PIN

violinist / FIDDLER; MUSICIAN

violinist's implement / BOW

violoncello / CELLO

viper / ASP; ADDER, SNAKE; CERASTES; BACKBITER; SCAN-DALMONGER

viper genus / BITIS, ECHIS

viperine / BAD; CAUSTIC; SCATH-ING; MALIGNANT, SARCASTIC

viperish / BAD; MALIGNANT, POISONOUS

viper's bugloss / BLUEWEED

virago / TERMAGANT

virgate / ROD; WAND

Virgil / See Vergil

virgin / NEW; PURE; FRESH; CHASTE, MAIDEN, MODEST; UNMIXED. GIRL, MAID; DAMSEL

Virgin Islands island / TORTOLA

Virgin Mary mourning / PIETA

virginal / CHASTE

Virginia battle / YORKTOWN

Virginia capital / RICHMOND

Virginia city / NORFOLK

Virginia City lode / COMSTOCK

Virginia colonizer / RALEIGH

Virginia creeper / WOODBINE

Virginia mountains / BLUERIDGE

Virginia pioneer / SMITH

Virginia river / JAMES

Virginia state bird / CARDINAL

Virginia state flower / DOGWOOD

Virginia state nickname / OLD-DOMINION

virginity / PURITY; MAIDENHOOD

virgula / NEUME

virgule / COMMA; SOLIDUS

viridity / VERDURE; FRESHNESS, GREENNESS, SOUNDNESS

virile / MANLY; MATURE; VIGOR-OUS; MASCULINE; PROCREATIVE

virose / FETID; STINKING

virtu / CURIOS; QUALITY

virtual / PRACTICAL

virtue / MERIT, VALOR; CHASTITY, EFFICACY, STRENGTH; RECTI-TUDE

virtuoso / SKILLED

virtuous / GOOD, PURE; MORAL; CHASTE, HONEST, MODEST, WORTHY; UPRIGHT; BLAMELESS, EXEMPLARY, RIGHTEOUS

virulent / RABID; BITTER

virulent epidemic / PEST

virus / PHAGE, VENOM; POISON

visa / ENDORSEMENT

visage / FACE; ASPECT; APPEAR-ANCE; COUNTENANCE

viscera / GUTS; INNARDS

viscerate / DISEMBOWEL, EVIS-CERATE

viscid / STICKY; GLUTINOUS

viscose / RAYON

viscosity / GUMMINESS

viscount's child / HONOURABLE

viscous / LIMY, ROPY, SIZY; SLIMY; ADHESIVE; GLUTINOUS

viscous mud / SLIME

viscous substance / TAR; GLUE; GREASE

vise part / JAW

Vishnu / GOD; CREATOR; DE-STROYER, PRESERVER

Vishnu as soul of universe / VASU

Vishnu's bird / GARUDA

Vishnu's brother / INDRA

Vishnu's serpent / SESHA

Vishnu's wife / LAKSHMI, RUKMINI

visible / SEEN; CLEAR; PATENT; EVIDENT, OBVIOUS; APPARENT

visible trace / LINE, MARK

visible vapor / SPRAY, STEAM

VISHNU'S AVATARS

MATSYA	FISH
KURMA	TORTOISE
VARAHA	BOAR
NARASINGHA	MANLION
VAMANA	DWARF
RAMA	AXBEARER
RAMACHANDRA	
KRISHNA	COWHERD
BALARAMA	
BUDDHA	
KALKI	WHITEHORSE

Visigoth king / EURIC; ALARIC
vision / EYE; DREAM, GHOST, SENSE, SIGHT; CHIMERA, PHANTOM
vision, pert. to / OPTIC; OPTICAL, VISSIVE
visionary / FEY; AERY; AIRY; IDEAL; DREAMY, UNREAL; UTOPIAN; DELUSIVE, FANCIFUL, ROMANTIC
visit / SEE; CALL, COME, STAY; HAUNT; CHASTISE. GAM; INSPECTION
visit markets / SHOP
visitant / GUEST; CALLER; VISITOR
visitation / WOE; ATTACK; ILLNESS
visiting card / CALLINGCARD
visitor / GUEST; TRUSTEE; OVERSEER
vison / MINK; WEASEL
visor / MASK, PEAK; VIZARD
vista / MALL, VIEW; SCENE; AVENUE; OUTLOOK, SCENERY; PANORAMA
visual / OCULAR; OPTICAL
visualize / PICTURE; ENVISAGE
vital / LIFE; LIVING, MORTAL; ESSENTIAL, IMPORTANT, NECESSARY; INDISPENSABLE
vital juice / SAP; BLOOD, LATEX
vital organ / LUNG; HEART, LIVER, LUNGS
vital principle / LIFE, SOUL
vitality / PEP, SAP, VIM; LIFE; FORCE; STAMINA
vitalize / VIVIFY; ANIMATE, REFRESH
vitals / VISCERA
vitamin / BIOTIN, CITRIN, NIACIN; ADERMIN, ANEURIN, ARGUSIA, CHOLINE, TORULIN; THIAMINE; RIBOFLAVIN; BIOFLAVINOID
vitellus / YOLK
vitiate / VOID; ANNUL, SPOIL, TAINT; DEBASE, DEFILE, IMPAIR
vitiosity / DEPRAVITY
vitreous coating / ENAMEL
vitric / GLASSLIKE
vitrify / FUSE; GLAZE

vitrine / SHOWCASE
vitriol / SORY; CAUSTIC. PICKLE
vituperate / NAG; LASH; ABUSE, SCOLD; REVILE, STRAFE
viva / RAH; HURRAH, HURRAY
viva voce / ORALLY
vivacious / GAY; AIRY; BRISK, MERRY; BRIGHT, JOCUND, LIVELY
vivacity / ELAN, LIFE; GAIETY, SPIRIT; ANIMATION; LIVELINESS
vivandiere / CATERER
vivid / LIVE; CLEAR, LUCID, QUICK, SUNNY; ACTIVE, BRIGHT, LIVELY, STRONG; GLOWING, GRAPHIC
Vivien's victim / MERLIN
vivify / QUICKEN; ANIMATE
vixen / FOX, HAG; SHREW; VIRAGO
viz / TOWIT; VIDELICET
vizier / MINISTER
Vladivostok harbor / GOLDENHORN
vocabulary, pert. to / LEXICAL
vocal / ORAL
vocal composition / SONG; SPEECH; ORATION
vocal inflection / TONE; SOUND; QUALITY
vocal solo / ARIA, SONG, TUNE; ARIOSO
vocal sound / TONE
vocalist / ORATOR, SINGER
vocalize / SING; UTTER
vocalized hesitation / ER
vocation / ART; TRADE, CAREER, METIER, OFFICE; CALLING, MISSION
vocation of knight / CHIVALRY
vocational / TRADE; TECHNICAL
vociferate / BAWL, ROAR, YELL; UTTER; CLAMOR
vociferous / NOISY; BLATANT; CLAMOROUS
vodka base / WHEAT
vodka drink / SCREWDRIVER
vodun / VOODOO
vogue / TON, USE; MODE; FAVOR, USAGE; CUSTOM, REPUTE; FASHION

voice / SAY; EMIT; SOUND, UTTER; DIVULGE, EXPRESS; UTTERANCE

voice, pert. to / ORAL; VOCAL; PHONETIC

voice box / LARYNX

voice in music / ALTO, BASS, VOCE; TENOR; SOPRANO; BARITONE; CONTRALTO; COLORATURA

voiced speech sound / SONANT

voiceless / MUTE, SURD; SPIRATE

voiceless consonant / SURD

void / NUL; NULL, VAIN; EMPTY; DEVOID, UNREAL, VACANT; INVALID, LACKING, USELESS, WANTING. ANNUL, QUASH; CANCEL, VACATE. CASS; ABYSS, SPACE; VACUUM

voided escutcheon / ORLE

voided trial / MISTRIAL

voir dire / OATH

voivode / CHIEFTAIN

volador / GURNARD

volant / FLYING, NIMBLE

volatile / FICKLE, LIVELY; SPRIGHTLY; EVAPORABLE

volatile liquid / ETHER; ALCOHOL, LIGROIN

volcanic cinder / LAVE, TUFA, TUFF; SCORIA

volcanic deposit / TRASS

volcanic froth / PUMICE

volcanic island / FAROE; LIPARI; SURTSEY

volcanic lava / SLAG

volcanic matter / LAVE

volcanic rock / TUFA, TUFF; TRASS; BASALT, LATITE; OBSIDIAN, TEPHRITE

volcanic scoria / LAVA, SLAG, TUFF

volcano / ETNA, PELE; AETNA, HEKLA, PELEE; LASSEN; KILAUEA, VESUVIO; KRAKATAU, KRAKATOA, VESUVIUS; PARICUTIN, STROMBOLI

volcano crater / PIT; HOLE, MAAR

volcano hole / PIT; MAAR; CRATER

volcano island / IWO; LIPARI, SICILY

volcano mouth / PIT; MAAR; CRATER

volcano pit / HOLE, MAAR; CRATER

vole / SLAM; MOUSE

Volga tributary / OKA; KAMA, SURA

volition / WILL; CHOICE

volley / BURST, SALVO; DISCHARGE

volleyball stroke / SPIKE

Voltaire novel / ZADIG; CANDIDE

Voltaire play / ZAIRE; ALZIRE

Voltaire's real name / AROUET

volt-ampere / WATT

volte-face / REVERSAL

voluble / GLIB; FLUENT; TALKATIVE; LOQUACIOUS

volume / MO; BODY, BOOK, BULK, MASS, SIZE, TOME, TURN, WORK

voluntary / FREE; WILLING; DESIGNED, INTENDED, OPTIONAL; DELIBERATE; INTENTIONAL

voluntary forbearance / ABSTINENCE

volunteer / OFFER; BESTOW

Volunteer State / TENNESSEE

voluptuary / SYBARITE

voluptuous / FLESHLY; EXCITING, SENSUOUS; LUXURIOUS

volute / SHELL, WHORL

vomit / KECK; EJECT, HEAVE, RETCH

vomiting / EMESIS

voodoo charm / MOJO; OBEAH

voodoo snake deity / ZOMBI; ZOMBIE

voracious / HUNGRY; EDACIOUS, RAVENOUS; RAPACIOUS

voracious animal / HOG, PIG; GOAT; GLUTTON

voracious eel / MORAY

voracity / GREED

vortex / EDDY, GYRE; ROTATION; MAELSTROM, WHIRLPOOL

vorticose / WHIRLING

vorticose / SHRDL ETAOI

votary / DEVOTEE

vote / CAST, POLL; ELECT; CHOOSE. BALLOT; DECISION; FRANCHISE

vote into office / ELECT

voter / CITIZEN, ELECTOR; SUFFRAGIST

votes / AYES, NAYS, NOES, YEAS

voting ticket / SLATE; BALLOT

votive / GIVEN, VOWED; PROMISED

vouch / AVER, BACK; AFFIRM, ASSURE, ATTEST; CERTIFY, CONFIRM

vouch for / AVER; ASSURE, ATTEST; SPONSOR

voucher / CHIT, NOTE; RECEIPT; WITNESS

voucher acknowledging a debt / IOU; CHIT; DEBENTURE

vouchsafe / ALLOW, DEIGN, GRANT, STOOP, YIELD; ACCORD; CONCEDE

vow / OATH; PLEDGE; PROMISE

vowel accent / ACUTE, BREVE, GRAVE; MACRON; DIERESIS; CIRCUMFLEX

vowel mutation / UMLAUT

vowel suppression / ELISION, SYNCOPE

vox / VOICE

voyage / SAIL, TREK, TRIP; CRUISE, SAFARI, TRAVEL; JOURNEY

voyage record / LOG
Vulcan / MULCIBER
vulcanian / VOLCANIC
vulcanite / EBONITE
vulcanize / RECAP; REPAIR
Vulcan's ailment / LAMENESS
Vulcan's forge / ETNA
Vulcan's mother / JUNO
Vulcan's son / CUPID
Vulcan's wife / MAIA; VENUS
vulgar / LOW; MEAN, RUDE, VILE;
  COARSE, COMMON, RUSTIC;
  BOORISH, GENERAL, IGNOBLE;
  HOMESPUN
vulgar fellow / CAD

vulgarity / RUDENESS; COARSE-
  NESS
Vulgate's translator / JEROME
vulnerable / WEAK; LIABLE; UN-
  TENABLE; ASSAILABLE; SUS-
  CEPTIBLE
vulpine / FOXY; CUNNING
vulture / AURA; URUBU; CONDOR;
  BUZZARD
vulture-headed goddess / NEK-
  HEBET
vulturous / GREEDY; RAVENOUS;
  RAPACIOUS
vying / COMPETING, EMULATING

W

W / WEN
waag / GRIVET
Wabash city / TERREHAUTE
wabber / CONY
wabble / WOBBLE
wachna / COD
wacke / CLAY; SANDSTONE
wacky / FEY, MAD, ODD; WILD;
  SCREWY; ECCENTRIC
Waco university / BAYLOR
wad / CRAM; STUFF. LUMP, MASS;
  PENCIL; PLUMBAGO
wad of bills / BANKROLL
wadding / PADDING
waddy / CLUB; STICK; COWBOY
wade / FORD, WALK; CROSS
wade in / ATTACK, TACKLE
wade through / PLOW; DRUDGE
wader / CRANE, HERON, SNIPE
wadi / WADY, WASH; OASIS; VAL-
  LEY
wading bird / IBIS, RAIL, SORA;
  CRANE, EGRET, HERON, SNIPE
wading bird of Africa / UMBER
wafer / SNAP; BISCUIT, CRACKER
waff / INFERIOR. LOAFER
waffle iron / GRIDDLE
waft / BEAR, SAIL; CARRY, FLOAT.
  GUST, PUFF, WAVE; CURRENT
wag / SWAY; SHAKE; WIGGLE;
  OSCILLATE. WIT; JOKER; JESTER
wag the tongue / GAB; TALK
wage / PAY; PAYMENT, STIPEND
wager / BET; ANTE, GAGE; STAKE;
  HAZARD, PARLAY
wages / PAY; FEES, HIRE; REWARD;
  SALARY; STIPEND; CARRIAGE
waggery / WIT; SARCASM
waggish / ARCH; FUNNY, MERRY;
  JOCOSE, TRICKY; COMICAL,
  JOCULAR
waggle / WABBLE, WADDLE
Wagnerian / BUXOM, GRAND,
  PLUMP

Wagnerian character / ERDA;
  HAGEN; TRISTAN
Wagnerian cycle / RING
Wagnerian heroine / ELSA; SENTA;
  ISOLDE
Wagnerian theme / LEITMOTIV
Wagner's wife / COSIMA
wagon / VAN; CART, DRAY, TRAM,
  WAIN, ARABA, LORRY, TONGA,
  TRUCK; TELEGA
wagon body / BED
wagon builder / WAINWRIGHT
wagon pin / CLEVIS
wagon pole / TONGUE
wagon shaft / THILL
wagon side / RAVE
wagon tongue / NEAP, POLE;
  SHAFT, THILL
wagon track / RUT
wagon train / CARAVAN
wagoner / DRIVER
wagon-lit / SLEEPER
wagonload / FOTHER; FREIGHT
wagtail / BIRD, LARK; PIPIT
wah / PANDA
Wahabi / PURIST
wahine / WOMAN
wahoo / PETO; ROCKELM; BASS-
  WOOD
waif / ARAB; CHILD, GAMIN
wail / HOWL, KEEN; ULULATE
wailed / MOANED; LAMENTED
wailful / MOURNING
wailing / LAMENTING, SORROWING
wain / WAGON; DIPPER
wainscot / PANEL; LINING
waist / BODICE, CAMISA, CAMISE,
  MIDDLE, TAILLE; UNDER-
  GARMENT
waistcloth / LOINCLOTH
waistcoat / VEST; GILET; JERKIN,
  WESKIT
waister / NOVICE
waistline / GIRTH; MIDRIFF

wait / LAY, LIE; STAY, STOP
wait in ambush / LURK; WAYLAY
wait in expectation / BIDE
wait on / TEND; CATER, SERVE; ATTEND
wait-a-bit / GREENBRIER
waiter / GARCON; SERVANT
waiter in charge of wines / SOMMELIER
waiting line / QUEUE
waiting room / LOUNGE; GREENROOM
waits / CAROLERS
waive / FORGO, REMIT; DESERT
wake / STIR; AWAKE, ROUSE; AROUSE, AWAKEN, EXCITE, KINDLE, REVIVE; CAROUSE, PROVOKE
wake robin / ARUM; CUCKOOPINT; JACKINTHEPULPIT
wakeful / VIGILANT, WATCHFUL; OBSERVANT, SLEEPLESS
wakefulness / AHYPNIA; INSOMNIA
wakeless / UNBROKEN
waken / STIR; ROUSE; AROUSE, AWAKEN
waker / WATCH; SENTINEL
wakf / CHARITY
Walachian city / BRAILA; PLOESTI
Walden author / THOREAU
waldenses / VAUDOIS
waldgrave / FORESTER
wale / WELT; WHEAL; BRUISE. BELT, WHIP
Wales / CAMBRIA. See also Welsh
Wales, pert. to / WELCH, WELSH
Wales' animal emblem / DRAGON
Wales' herbal emblem / LEEK
walk / GAD; HIKE, MOVE, MUSH, PACE, PLOD, STEP, MARCH, STALK
walk about / AMBULATE
walk on air / EXULT, FRISK
walk all over / TYRANNIZE
walk around / CIRCLE; EXAMINE
walk artificially / MINCE, STRUT
walk in baseball / PASS
walk the chalk / CONFORM
walk like a crab / CRAWL, SIDLE
walk feebly / TOTTER
walk haltingly / LIMP
walk heavily / PLOD, PLOP, SLOG; TRAMP
walk with high steps / PRANCE
walk leisurely / LOITER, STROLL
walk of life / CAREER; PROFESSION
walk with long steps / STRIDE
walk with measured steps / PACE
walk out / LEAVE; STRIKE
walk out on / DESERT
walk out with / COURT
walk pompously / STALK, STRUT
walk the streets / PROWL

walk through / READ; REHEARSE
walk unsteadily / DADE; LURCH
walk in water / WADE
walk wearily / PLOD; TRUDGE
walked / TROD; STRODE
walker / PEDESTRIAN
walking / AFOOT; AMBULATING
walking mode / GAIT, PACE
walking papers / PINKSLIP
walking stick / CANE; STAFF, STILT; RATTAN; PHASMID, WHANGEE
walking trip / HIKE; TRAMP
walk-on / BIT
walkout / STRIKE
walkover / SWAP; CINCH
walk-up / APARTMENT
walkway / PATH; AISLE, ALLEY
wall / MURE, OGEE; RAMPART; PARTITION, STRUCTURE
wall, pert. to / MURAL; PARIETAL
wall border / DADO, OGEE
wall coating / STUCCO; PLASTER
wall column / PILASTER
wall covering / ARRAS, PAINT, PAPER; TAPESTRY
wall fern / POLYPODY
wall around fortress / RAMPART
wall grass / SEDUM
wall in / COOP; IMMURE
wall lizard / GECKO
wall material / COB; LIME; CEMENT, MARBLE, PANELS, STONES
wall painting / MURAL; FRESCO
wall paneling / WAINSCOT
wall of planks / BRATTICE
wall projecting into sea / MOLE, PIER
wall recesses / NICHES
wall section / DADO; PANEL
Wall Street / FINANCE
wallaba / APA
wallaby / KANGAROO
Wallace novel / BENHUR
Wallachian / VLACH
wallah / GUY; FELLOW
wall-beam support / TEMPLATE
wallboard / FIBERBOARD; PLASTERBOARD
walled / ENCASED; ENCLOSED
walled city / KUH; KANO; SCANNO
wallet / BAG; PURSE; KNAPSACK
walleye / EXOTROPIA
walleyed pike / DORE
wallflower / CHEIR, KEIRI
wall-like /MURAL
Walloon / HUGUENOT
Walloons' area / BRABANT
wallop / LAM; BEAT, BLOW, BOIL
walloping / HUGE; WHOPPING
wallow / ROLL, WADE; PLOUGH. PIT; MIRE, VICE; FILTH
walls / SEPTA; BARRIERS
Walpole character / HERRIES

Walpurgis Night celebrant / WITCH
walrus / MORSE; MUSTACHE; ROS-
MARINE
walrus herd / POD
Waltonian / ANGLER; FISHERMAN
waltz / DANCE, VALSE, WHIRL
wamble / MOVE; TWIST; SEETHE
wambly / SHAKY; OSCILLATING
wame / BELLY
wampum / PEAG; BEADS, PEAGE,
SEWAN; SEAWAN
wampum snake / HOOPSNAKE
wampus / MONSTER
wamus / CARDIGAN
wan / ASHY, PALE; ASHEN, FADED,
LIVID; PALLID, SALLOW, SICKLY
wan appearance / PALLOR
wand / ROD; POLE; BATON, OSIER
wander / ERR, GAD; HAAK, RAVE,
ROAM, ROVE; RANGE, STRAY;
DEPART
wander over / MEANDER; TRA-
VERSE
wanderer / VAG; ARAB; GYPSY,
NOMAD, ROVER, STRAY;
RAMBLER
wandering / ASTRAY, ERRANT,
ERRING, ROVING; NOMADIC,
VAGRANT
wandering cell / PHAGOCYTE
wandering domestic animal /
ESTRAY; MAVERICK
wandering from duty / TRUANT
Wandering Jew author / SUE
wandering in mind / DELIRIUM
wandering people / GYPSIES
wandering star / PLANET
wanderlust / RESTLESSNESS
wanderoo / MACAQUE
wandflower / GALAX
wane / EBB; FADE; LESSEN,
SHRINK
wane's opposite / WAX
waney / BEVELED
wanga / FETISH
wangle / TRICK; WIGGLE; CON-
TRIVE
wanigan / SHACK; SHANTY
wanion / CURSE
wankapin / LOTUS; CHINKAPIN
want / LACK, MISS, NEED, WISH;
CRAVE; DESIRE. DEARTH, DE-
FECT
want of appetite / ASITIA; AN-
OREXIA
want of energy / ATONY
want of success / FAILURE
want of tone / ATONY
want-ad section / CLASSIFIED
wantage / LACK
wanting brilliance / DULL, GRAY
wanting depth / SHALLOW
wanting elevation / LOW; FLAT

wanting good sight / PURBLIND
wanting good taste / INELEGANT
wanting knowledge / STUPID; IG-
NORANT, NESCIENT
wanting moisture / DRY; ARID
wanton / FREE, LEWD, RANK, WILD;
LOOSE; ROVING; LUSTFUL,
PLAYFUL
wanton destroyer / VANDAL
wap / LAP; STRIKE
wapentake / HUNDRED
wapiti / ELK; DEER, STAG
war / FIGHT; BATTLE, COMBAT,
ENMITY, STRIFE; CONTEST, CRU-
SADE
war, pert. to / MARTIAL
war bag / DUFFLEBAG
war bonnet / HEADDRESS
war club / MACE; POGAMOGGAN
war correspondent / PYLE;
LONDON
war cry / YELL; ALALA, WHOOP
war dog / HAWK; MILITANT
war fleet / NAVY; ARMADA
war games / MANEUVERS
war god / ARES, MARS, ODIN;
SKANDA
war god of Assyria / ASHUR; AS-
SHUR
war god of Babylonia / IRA; IRRA
war god of Egypt / SET; SETH
war god of Norsemen / TY; TIU,
TYR; ODIN, TYRR; WODEN
war god of Polynesia / TU
war god of Teutons / ER
war goddess of Babylonia / ISHTAR
war goddess of Celts / BADB, BODB;
MORRIGU; MORRIGAN
war goddess of Egypt / ANOUKE
war goddess of the Greeks / ENYO
war goddess of the Romans / BEL-
LONA
war hawk / JINGO; CHAUVINIST
war horse / STEED; CHARGER
war lock / SCALPLOCK
war paint / MAKEUP; REGALIA
war prize / MEDAL, SCALP
war theater / ETO
war vehicle / TANK; HALFTRACK
war vessel / WARSHIP
warble / SING; CAROL, CHIRP
warbler / CHAT; OVENBIRD, RED-
START; BECCAFICO
warcraft / STRATEGY
ward / ACT; FEND; AVERT, STAVE,
WATCH. GUARD; KEEPER;
CUSTODY
ward off / PARRY, REPEL
ward politician / HEELER; BELL-
RINGER
warden / KEEPER, RANGER; CURA-
TOR; GUARDIAN, OFFICIAL;
CUSTODIAN

warder / GUARD; TURNKEY; SENTINEL
wardrobe / CHEST, PRESS; CLOSET; CLOTHING
wardroom inhabitant / OFFICER
wardship / GUARDIANSHIP
ware / POTTERY
warehouse / LOFT, SILO; DEPOT, ETAPE, STORE; GODOWN; BUILDING
wares / GOODS; MERCHANDISE
warfare / HOSTILITIES
warl / MANCALA
warily / ALERTLY; CAUTIOUSLY
wariness / CAUTION; SHYNESS
warison / REWARD
warlike / FIERY; HOSTILE, MARTIAL; INIMICAL, MILITARY
warlike band / GUERRILLA
warlike Indian / APACHE; HOSTILE; COMANCHE
warlock / WIZARD; MAGICIAN
warm / MILD; CALID, EAGER, FIERY, SUNNY, TEPID; ARDENT, FERVID
warm air / OAM
warm and balmy / SUNNY; SUMMERY
warm the bench / SUB
warm comfortably / TOAST
warm compresses / STUPES
warm covering / BLANKET
warm drink / CAUDLE
warm dry wind / FOHN; FOEHN; CHINOOK
warm the heart / GLADDEN
warm and humid / MUGGY
warm over / REHEAT
warm room in baths / TEPIDARIUM
warm springs / THERMAE
warm up / REHEAT; PREPARE
warm-blooded / ARDENT; PASSIONATE
warmed-over / STALE, TRITE; SECONDHAND
warmhearted / CORDIAL; INTIMATE
war-monger / HAWK; JINGO
warmth / ELAN, GLOW, HEAT, ZEAL
warmth, pert. to / THERMITE
warmth of feeling / ARDOR; PASSION
warn / ALERT; NOTIFY, SIGNAL; CAUTION; ADMONISH; EXPOSTULATE
warn off / DEBAR; INHIBIT
warner / FLAGMAN, LOOKOUT
warning / BUOY, FLAG, OMEN, SIGN; ALARM, ALERT, LIGHT; ADVICE, ALARUM, AUGURY, BEACON, CAVEAT, NOTICE, SIGNAL
warning signal / SIREN; TOCSIN
warning system / DEW

warp / BIAS, CRAM, TURN; TWIST; SWERVE; ARRANGE, CONTORT
warp beam / LOOM; ROLLER
warp separator / DENT, REED; RAVEL; EVENER, RADDLE
warp threads / ABB; LEASE; STAMEN
warp and woof / BASIS; FABRIC
warped / WRY; AWRY
warplane / BOMBER; FIGHTER
warple / TWIST
warrant / MERIT, VOUCH; AFFIRM, ASSURE, ATTEST, INSURE, SECURE. BERAT; PLEVIN; PASSPORT; ASSURANCE, GUARANTEE
warranty / GUARANTY, SECURITY; GUARANTEE; AUTHORIZATION
warree / PECCARY
warren / PARK; ENCLOSURE
warrigal / DINGO
warrior / TOA; HERO; AMAZON, COHORT, FENCER; FIGHTER, SOLDIER
warrior of New Zealand / RAKAUKAWA
warrior's headpiece / HELMET
warrior's plating / ARMOR
Warsaw's river / VISTULA
warship / OILER, RAZEE; CARRIER, CRUISER, FLATTOP, FRIGATE, MONITOR; CORVETTE; DESTROYER, SUBMARINE; BATTLESHIP
warship part / TURRET
warship plating / ARMOR
warsle / WRESTLE
wart / WEN; TUMOR; VERRUCA
wartflower / CELANDINE
wartime agency / OSS, OWI
wartime allowance / RATION
wartorn / DEVASTATED
warty / BUMPY, NODED
Warwickshire town / RUGBY; STRATFORD
Warwickshire river / AVON, COLE
wary / SHY; CAGY; CHARY, LEERY; CAREFUL, GUARDED, HEEDFUL
was / WERE; EXISTED
was able / COULD
was carried / RODE
was concerned / CARED
was indignant / RESENTED
was insubordinate / DEFIED
was overfond / DOTED
was sorry / RUED; REGRETTED
was victorious / WON; PREVAILED
Wasatch peak / BELKNAP
wase / WISP
wash / WET; LAVE; BATHE, RENCH, RINSE; CLEANSE, LAUNDER, MOISTEN. WADI; GULCH; ARROYO, COULEE

wash basin / TUB; PISCINA
wash in clear water / RINSE
wash for gold / PAN
wash leather / LOSH; CHAMOIS
wash lightly / RINSE
wash out / ELUTE, FLUSH, PURGE
wash up / TERMINATE
washbowl / BASIN; LAVABO
washcloth / WASHRAG
washed-out / FADED, TIRED
washed-up / THROUGH; FINISHED
washerwoman / LAUNDRESS
washhouse / LAUNDRY
washing / COAT; LAVAGE; COATING
washing preparation / SOAP; DE-
  TERGENT
washing soda / SALSODA
washings / ELUATE
Washington / DISTRICT
Washington capital / OLYMPIA
Washington city / YAKIMA; SPO-
  KANE
Washington city planner / LENFANT
Washington mountain / RAINIER
Washington mountain range / CAS-
  CADES, OLYMPICS
Washington sound / PUGET
Washington state bird / GOLDFINCH
Washington state flower / RHODO-
  DENDRON
Washington state Indian / HOH;
  LUMMI, MAKAH
Washington state motto / ALKI
Washington state nickname / CHI-
  NOOK; EVERGREEN
Washington state tree / HEMLOCK
Washington team / REDSKINS,
  SENATORS
washingtonia / SEQUOIA
washout / CHASM, GULLY; FIZZLE
washroom / TOILET; LAVATORY
washy / PUNY; FEEBLE, SODDEN
wasn't / NAS
wasp / WHAMP; HORNET, INSECT
waspish / PEEVISH; PETULANT
wasp's nest / VESPIARY
wassail / DRINK; CAROUSE
wassailer / ORGIAST, REVELER
wast / WERT
wastage / OFFAL; DEBRIS
waste / KILL, LOSE, PINE, RUIN;
  DECAY, SPOIL; EXPEND, IMPAIR.
  LOSS; DROSS; DEBRIS, REFUSE.
  BARE, WILD; DISMAL; FORLORN
waste allowance / TRET
waste away / GNAW; REPINE;
  ATROPHY
waste bin / TRASHCAN; GARBAGE-
  CAN
waste fiber / NOIL
waste land / MOOR; HEATH;
  DESERT

Waste Land author / ELIOT
waste leaf / SMUTSHEET
waste matter / DREGS, DROSS
waste paper / BROKE
waste pipe / DRAIN, SEWER
waste silk / KNUB, NOIL; FRISON
waste time / LOAF, IDLE; DALLY
waste trench / CONDUIT
waste weir / SPILLWAY
wastebasket / FILETHIRTEEN
wasted / POOR, WORN; FRAYED,
  WILTED; DECREPIT
wasted with disease / TABID;
  FEEBLE, SICKLY; TABETIC
wasted effort / FUTILITY
wasteful / WEAK; LAVISH; PRO-
  FUSE, RUINOUS, WESTREL;
  PRODIGAL; SHIFTLESS, UN-
  THRIFTY. LOAFER, WASTER;
  SPENDER
waster / WASTREL; PRODIGAL
wasteyard / DUMP
wasting / ERODING; EMACIATING
wastrel / LOSEL; LOAFER;
  SPENDER; VAGABOND
watch / EYE, SEE, SPY; GLOM,
  TEND; GUARD, STARE. VIGIL;
  PATROL, SENTRY; VEDETTE;
  WATCHMAN
watch accessory / STRAP
watch chain / FOB
watch closely / EYE; GUARD
watch fire / BEACON; BONFIRE
watch for / AWAIT; EXPECT
watch one's step / CARE, MIND;
  BEWARE
watch one's weight / DIET
watch out / HEED; NOTICE
watch over / GUARD, NURSE
watch part / STUD; BEZEL, CROWN,
  JEWEL; ESCAPEMENT
watch pocket / FOB
watch ribbon / FOB
watch with satisfaction / GLOAT
watch secretly / SPY; SNOOP
watchdog / BANDOG; MASTIFF
watchdog of underworld / GARM;
  CERBERUS; HELLHOUND
watched over / NURSED, TENDED
watchet / SKYBLUE
watchful / WARY; AWAKE; CARE-
  FUL, HEEDFUL; CAUTIOUS
watchful guardian / ARGUS; CER-
  BERUS, HEIMDALL
watching / ALERT; OPENEYED
watchmaker / HOROLOGIST
watchman / GUARD; SENTRY,
  SERENO
watchman's rattle / GREGER
watchtower / SIGNAL; MIRADOR;
  MARTELLO; SIGNALTOWER
watchword / SLOGAN; PASSWORD

water / HOSE; DILUTE; IRRIGATE, SPRINKLE. EAU, SEA; AQUA, RAIN

water, c.f. / AQUA, AQUI, HYDR

water, pert. to / HYDRAULIC

water arum / CALLA

water barrier / DAM; MOLE

water bird / ERN; COOT, GULL, IBIS, LOON, RAIL, SWAN, TERN; BRANT, CRANE, EGRET, HERON, OUSEL, STILT; AVOCET, JACANA; PELICAN

water bottle / SKIN; CARAFE, FLAGON; DECANTER

water boy / BHEESTY; BHEESTEE

water brain of sheep / GID; ME-GRIMS; STAGGERS

water brash / PYROSIS; HEART-BURN

water buffalo / ARNA; ARNEE

water bug / BOATBUG; CROTON-BUG

water butt / BARREL

water around castle / MOAT

water channel / GUTTER, SLUICE

water chestnut / TRAPA; CALTROP

water chicken / GALLINULE

water chinkapin / WANKAPIN

water clock / CLEPSYDRA

water closet / WC; LATRINE

water cock / KORA; GALLINULE

water craft / ARK; BOAT, SHIP; BARGE, CANOE, LINER, YACHT; VESSEL

water dog / SPANIEL; HELL-BENDER

water duct / RACE; FLUME; GUTTER

water excursion / SAIL; CRUISE

water in fine drops / SPRAY

water flask / CANTEEN

water gap / GORGE; RAVINE

water gate / SLUICE

water gauge / NILOMETER

water gum / KANOOKA

water hole / POOL; OASIS; SPRING

water ice / ICES; SHERBET

water jar / EWER, LOTA, OLLA; BANGA; HYDRIA

water lily / LOTUS, WOCAS, WOKAS

water moccasin / VIPER

water nymph / NAIAD; NEREID, UN-DINE

water ousel / DIPPER

water passage / CANAL, SOUND

water in pharmacy / AQUA

water pipe / MAIN; HOOKA, SEWER; HOOKAH; CONDUIT, NARGILE; NARGHILE

water plant / LOTUS; ALISMA

water rat / VOLE; MUSKAM

water receptacle in church / FONT

water resort / SPA; SPRINGS

water scorpion / NEPA

water seeker / DOWSER

Water Snake / HYDRUS

water sound / LAP; DRIP, PURL

water spirit / NIS, NIX; KELP, NIXY; ARIEL, NISSE, NIXIE; KELPIE, SPRITE, UNDINE

water spout / GARGOYLE

water stream / RIA; BROOK, CREEK, RIVER

water stream obstruction / DAM; WEIR

water surface / RYME

water turkey / ANHINGA

water vessel / BOAT, LOTA, SAIL, SHIP; CANOE, FERRY, LINER, YACHT

water wagon / ABSTENTION; TEE-TOTALISM

water witch / GREBE; DOWSER; DABCHICK

Water-Bearer / AQUARIUS

waterbuck / KOB; KOBA

watercolor / GOUACHE, TEMPERA; AQUARELLE

water-cooled pipe / HOOKAH; NAR-GHILE; HUBBLEBUBBLE

watercourse / BED, RIA; LAKE; BROOK, CANAL, CREEK, RIVER; STREAM; CHANNEL

water-covered / AWASH

watercress / EKER

watered the lawn / HOSED

watered silk / MOIRE

waterfall / LIN, LYN; FOSS, LINN; SAULT; CASCADE, NIAGARA; CATARACT

watering can / SPRINKLER

watering place / SPA; OASIS

watering spout / ROSE; NOZZLE

waterless / DRY; ARID; ANHY-DROUS

water-lifting device / WHIM; NORIA, TABUT; SHADUF, TABOOT

water-lily leaf / PAD

water-lily tree / MAGNOLIA

waterline / TIDEMARK

waterlogged / FLOODED; SATU-RATED

Waterloo marshal / NEY

Waterloo victor / WELLINGTON

waterman / BARGEE; FERRYMAN

watermelon begonia / PEPEROMIA

waterpepper / SMARTWEED

waterproof / IMPERVIOUS. SLICKER; RAINCOAT

waterproof cloth / TARP; GOS-SAMER

waterscape / SEASCAPE

watershed / BASIN; CRISIS, DIVIDE

waterside / COAST, SHORE

waterskin / MATARA, MUSSUK

waterspout / SPATE; FUNNEL
watertight / DROPDRY; LEAKPROOF
waterway / BAYOU, CANAL; STRAIT, STREAM; CHANNEL
waterwheel / NORIA; PADDLE, SAKIEH; DANAIDE, TURBINE
waterwheel vane / LADLE
waterworks / TEARS; FOUNTAIN
waterworn gully / WASH; RAVINE
watery / WET; THIN; VAPID; SEROUS; AQUEOUS, TEARFUL
watery, c.f. / SERO
watery part / SERUM
watery vapor / FOG; HAZE, MIST
wattle / BRAID, PLAIT, TWIST. ROD; GILL, LOBE, TWIG; DEWLAP
wattle honeybird / IAO
wattle tree / BOREE, COOBA, MULGA; ACACIA, GIDGEE
wattlebird / HONEYBIRD
Watts' writings / HYMNS
watt-second / JOULE
waugh / WEAK
Waugh painting forte / WAVES
wave / FLY; WAFT; CRIMP; BECKON. SEA; BORE, SURF; SURGE; ROLLER; DECUMAN
wave, c.f. / ONDO
wave recorder / ONDOGRAPH
wave of surf / COMBER; BREAKER
wave to and fro / WAG; FLAP
wave top / CREST
waveguide / LINE
waveless / CALM; SMOOTH; TRANQUIL
wavelet / RIPPLE
waver / REEL, SWAY, VEER, WAVE; FLOAT; FALTER, TEETER, TOTTER
waver in opinion / DOUBT
waverer / LAODICEAN
wavering / FICKLE; UNSTEADY, VARIABLE; UNDECIDED, UNSETTLED
wavering sound / TREMOLO
Waverley author / SCOTT
wave's drop / PITCH
wave's rise / SEND; SCEND
waveson / FLOTSAM
wave-worn / BEATEN
wavey / SNOWGOOSE
wavy / REPAND, RISING; FALLING
wavy in heraldry / ONDE, ONDY, UNDE
wavy molding / CYMA
wawl / CRY; WAIL
wax / CERE, GROW; INCREASE. FIT; RAGE; CERATE; BEESWAX, CERUMEN
wax, pert. to / CERAL
wax bean / BUTTERBEAN
wax candle /TAPER; CIERGE
wax match/ VESTA

wax myrtle / BAYBERRY
wax plant / INDIANPIPE
wax and wane / PULSATE; FLUCTUATE
waxberry / BAYBERRY
waxed / GREW; INCREASED
waxen / ASHY, PALE; PALLID
waxlike substance / CERIN, CUTIN; SUBERIN; AMBERGRIS
waxworks owner / TUSSAUD
waxy / ANGRY, CERAL; CERATE
waxy ointment / CERATE
way / TAO, VIA; FORM, LANE, MODE, PATH, PLAN, ROAD, WILL, WONT; HABIT, MARCH, MEANS
way of acting / MANNER
way back / YORE; LANGSYNE
way in / ADIT; ENTRY, INLET
Way of All Flesh author / BUTLER
way out / EXIT; EGRESS
way over a fence / STILE
way of putting it / PRESENTATION
way station / LOCALSTOP
way through / OPENING, PASSAGE
way up or down / STAIRWAY; STAIRCASE
way of walking / GAIT, PACE
wayfarer / HIKER, TRAMP; DRIFTER, PILGRIM; TRAVELER
wayfaring / WENDING; TREKKING; JOURNEYING
way-going / LEAVING
Wayland's occupation / SMITH
waylay / LURK; AMBUSH
waymark / BLAZE
Wayne's epithet / MAD
way-out / FAROUT; AVANTGARDE
wayside / ROADSIDE
wayside haven / INN; HOTEL, MOTEL; HOSTEL, TAVERN; CARAVANSARY
wayside rest / KHAN; PARAO
wayward / UNRULY, WILFUL; ERRATIC, FORWARD, FROWARD; CONTRARY
waywise / BROKEN
wayworn / TIRED, WEARY
waywort / PIMPERNEL
wayzgoose celebrant / PRINTER
wazir / VIZIER
we / US; INGROUP; OURSELVES
weak / LOW, WAN; PUNY, SOFT, THIN; FAINT, FRAIL, SEELY, SILLY, SMALL; DEBILE, EFFETE, FEEBLE
weak cider / PERKIN; CIDERKIN
weak point / TAINT; BLEMISH
weak spot / FLAW; BLEMISH
weaken / DAP; FADE; LOWER, UNMAN; DEBASE, DILUTE, DISARM, LABEFY
weaken a drink / THIN; WATER

weaken gradually / SAP; PETER

weakening / LOOSENING; ENERVATION

weaker sex / WOMEN; WOMANKIND

weak-eyed / PURBLIND

weakfish / ACOUPA, MAIGRE; TOTUAVA

weakhearted / AFRAID; COWARDLY

weak-kneed / COWARDLY, UNSTEADY

weakling / WRIG; MILKSOP; MOLLYCODDLE

weakly / AILING, FEEBLE

weak-minded / DAFT, DULL, SLOW; DOTTY; STUPID; UNSOUND

weakness / ATONY, FAULT; DEFECT, FOIBLE; FAILING, FRAILTY

weal / WALE; WHEAL; PROFIT, STRIPE; UTILITY, WELFARE

weald / MOOR, VELD, WOLD

wealth / CASH, PELF; FUNDS, LUCRE, MEANS, MONEY, ASSETS, MAMMON, PLENTY, RICHES, CAPITAL

wealthy / RICH; FLUSH; MONIED; OPULENT; AFFLUENT

wealthy person / MIDAS, NABOB; MAGNATE

wean / CHILD. BREAK

weanling / CHILD

weapon / ARM, BOW, DAG, GUN; ARMS, BOLO, BOMB, CLUB, MACE, PATU; ARROW, LANCE, ONCIN, SPEAR, SWORD; BOMBER, DAGGER, MUSKET, PISTOL; FIREARM, GISARME, HALBERD, JAVELIN; CROSSBOW, STILETTO, TOMAHAWK; BOOMERANG

weapon of gaucho / BOLAS

weapon to throw missile / SLING; SLINGSHOT

wear / DON, USE; BEAR; CARRY, CHAFE; DISPLAY, EXHIBIT

wear away / EAT, RUB; FRAY, FRET, RUST; ABRADE; CONSUME

wear away slowly / ERODE; CORRODE

wear at the edges / FRAY

wear by friction / RUB; ERASE; ABRADE

wear off / FADE, PASS; VANISH

wear on / DRAG, PASS; CRAWL

wear ostentatiously / SPORT

wear out / FAG; TIRE; EXHAUST, FATIGUE

wear and tear / RAVAGES; DEPRECIATION

wearable / FIT; ADAPTED

wearied / BORED, TIRED; WORNOUT

weariful / BORING; TIRESOME

weariness / ENNUI; FATIGUE

wearing / TIRING; IRKSOME

wearing apparel / CLOTHING

wearing away / RUSTY; EROSIVE

wearing down / ATTRITION

wearing shoes / SHOD

wearisome / DREE, DULL; PROSY, WEARY; BORING, PLAGUY, PROLIX

wearisome person / BORE, DRIP, PEST; SQUARE

wearisome routine / TREADMILL

weary / FAG, IRK; BORE, JADE, TIRE; HARASS. WORN; SPENT, TIRED; IRKSOME; FATIGUED

Weary Willie / HOBO; TRAMP

wearying / TEDIOUS; TIRESOME

weary-worn / BEAT; BUSHED

weasand / GULLET, THROAT; WINDPIPE; ESOPHAGUS

weasel / VARE; OTTER, SABLE, STOAT; ERMINE, FERRET, MARTEN; MUSTELA

weasel cat / LINSANG

weasel spider / SOLPUGID

weasel words / CAVIL; QUIBBLE; DOUBLETALK; EQUIVOCATION

weaser / MERGANSER

weather / STORM; CONDITION. OUTLAST

weather condition / CLIMATE

weather eye / WATCH; LOOKOUT

weather forecaster / BAROMETER; METEOROLOGIST

weather gage / ADVANTAGE

weather indicator / BAROMETER; ANEMOMETER

weather satellite / ESSA; TIROS; NIMBUS

weather side / WINDWARD

weather a storm / STICK; ESCAPE

weather strip / WINDSTOP

weather word / DRY, FOG, ICY, WET; COLD, FAIR, RAIN, SNOW, WARM; HUMID; CLOUDY, WARMER; OVERCAST

weather-beaten / WORN; TIRED; TANNED; WEARIED; EXHAUSTED

weatherboard / WINDWARD. CLAPBOARD

weathercock / VANE; GIROUETTE

weathered / AGED; SEASONED

weatherglass / BAROMETER

weatherman / METEOROLOGIST

weather-tight / WATERPROOF

weave / KNIT, SPIN; BRAID, PLAIT, REEVE, TWIST; COMPOSE; FABRICATE

weave a rope / REEVE

weaverbird / BAYA, MAYA, TAHA; WHIDAH

weaver's hitch / SHEETBEND

WEDDING ANNIVERSARIES

	Old	New
1	PAPER	CLOCK
2	COTTON	CHINA
3	LEATHER	CRYSTAL, GLASS
4	SILK, FRUIT, FLOWERS, LINEN	APPLIANCES
5	WOOD	SILVERWARE
6	IRON, CANDY	WOOD
7	WOOL, COPPER	DESK SET
8	BRONZE, WOOL, POTTERY	LINEN, LACE
9	CHINA, POTTERY	LEATHER
10	TIN, ALUMINUM	DIAMOND JEWELRY
11	STEEL	FASHION JEWELRY
12	SILK, LINEN	PEARLS
13	LACE	TEXTILE, FURS
14	IVORY	GOLD JEWELRY
15	CRYSTAL	WATCH
20	CHINA	PLATINUM
25	SILVER	SILVER
30	PEARL	DIAMOND
35	CORAL	JADE
40	RUBY	RUBY
45	SAPPHIRE	GOLD
50	GOLD	EMERALD
60	EMERALD	DIAMOND
75	DIAMOND	DIAMOND

weaver's reed / SLEY
weaver's reel / PIRN
weaving harness / HEALD
weaving machine / LOOM
weaving term / LISSE
weaving tool / BATTEN, EVENER; SHUTTLE
weazen / LEAN, THIN; DRIED, SHARP; DRIEDUP, WIZENED
web / NET, PLY; TRAP; SNARE; FABRIC, TISSUE; NETWORK
web of paper / ROLL
web of a press / ROLL
webbing / STRAP
webbing on duck's feet / PALAMA
webby / PALMATE
weber / AMPERE
web-footed bird / DUCK, LOON, SWAN; GOOSE; AVOCET, GANNET; PELICAN, PENGUIN; CORMORANT
web-footed mammal / OTTER
web-like / TELAR
web-like membrane / TELA
webmaker / SPIDER
web-spinning / RETIARY
webwork / NET; MESH, RETE
webworm / CATERPILLAR
wed / MATE, SEAL, WIVE; MARRY, UNITE; ATTACH; ESPOUSE. MATED
wed secretly / ELOPE
wedded / INURED; ADDICTED

wedding / HYMEN; CEREMONY, ESPOUSAL, MARRIAGE; NUPTIALS
wedding band / RING
wedding finger / PRONUBIS
wedding gift / DOT; DOWRY
wedding missiles / RICE
wedding trip / HONEYMOON
wedge / CAM, GIB, KEY, PEG, VEE; COIN, FROE, GLUT, GORE, SHIM; CHOCK, CLEAT, COIGN, QUOIN
wedge in / JAM
wedgeshaped / SHIM; CUNEATE
wedlock / MARRIAGE; MATRIMONY
wee / PUNY, TINY; PETIT, SMALL
wee folk / FAIRIES
weed / DOCK, LOCO, TARE; CIGAR; DARNEL; TOBACCO
weed burner / FLAMETHROWER
weed out / PURGE; UPROOT
wedding implement / HOE; SPUD
weeds / CLOTHES
weedy / LANK, THIN; OVERGROWN
week / SENNET; HEBDOMAD, SENNIGHT
weekday / FERIA
weekly / AWEEK; HEBDOMADAL. JOURNAL
weel / CREEL; BASKET
ween / FANCY, THINK; CONJECTURE
weenie / WIENER, SAUSAGE; FRANKFURTER

weeny / PUNY, THIN, WEAK
weep / CRY, ORP, SOB; DRIP, MOAN; BEMOAN, BEWAIL, LAMENT; BLUBBER
weephole / DRAIN
weeping / TEARFUL; MOURNING
weeping monkey / CAPUCHIN
weeping mother of Greek myth / NIOBE
Weeping Philosopher / HERACLITUS
weepy / TEARFUL
weet / WRYNECK
weet-weet / SANDPIPER
weevil / TURK; BEETLE; CURCULIO
weft / WOOF
wehrwolf / WEREWOLF
weichsel / VISTULA
weigh / HEFT; BALANCE
weigh anchor / SAIL
weigh carefully / PONDER; CONSIDER
weigh down / BURDEN; TROUBLE
weigh heavily / OPPRESS
weigh in / ENTER; REPORT
weigh one's words / DELIBERATE
weigh with / EQUAL
weighing device / BEAM; SCALE, TRONE; BALANCE; STEELYARD
weighbridge / SCALE
weight / TON; DRAM, HEFT, LOAD, MASS, MITE, OBOL, ONUS; CARAT
weight, pert. to / BARIC
weight allowance / TARE, TRET
weight of ancient Rome / AS; BES
weight of ancient times / MINA; TALENT
weight of Arabia / KELLA; DIRHEM
weight of Asia / TA; CAN; TAEL; HUBBA
weight balance / RIDER
weight of Burma / KYAT
weight of China / LI; HAO, KIN, TAN; TAEL; CATTY, LIANG, PICUL
weight of Denmark / ES; LOD, ORT
weight in dream / INCUBUS
weight of Egypt / KAT; DEBEN
weight of England / STONE
weight on fishline / SINKER
weight of France / ONCE; LIVRE
weight of Greece / MINA
weight of Holland / WICHTSE; ESTERLIN
weight of India / SER; SEER, TOLA; POLLAM
weight of Italy / LIBBRA
weight of Japan / MO; FUN, RIN
weight for jewels / CARAT
weight of Libya / KELE
weight machine / SCALE, TRONE; BALANCE
weight of Mongolia / LAN
weight of Persia / SIR; ABBAS
weight in pile driver / RAM

weight of Russia / LOT; DOLA
weight on sash cord / MOUSE
weight of Siam / HAP, PAI; COYAN
weight of Spain / ARROBA
weight of Sweden / LOD, ORT
weight of Syria / COLA
weight system / TROY; AVOIRDUPOIS
weight of Turkey / OKA; DIRHEM
weight unit / GRAM, KILO; POUND
weight for wool / TOD; NAIL; CLOVE
weighted / ADJUSTED
weighted down / LADEN; BURDENED
weightiness / FORCE; HEAVINESS
weightless / FEATHERY
weighty / SOLID; SERIOUS
Weil's disease / JAUNDICE
weir / DAM, NET; TRAP; GARTH, LEVEE
weird / EERY; EERIE, ELFIN. FATE; CHARM, SPELL; DESTINY
Weird Sisters / FATES, NORNS
weirdly / PROSPEROUS
weirdo / ODDBALL; SCREWBALL
weirdy / NUT; ECCENTRIC
Weissnichtwo / UTOPIA; SHANGRILA
wejack / PEKAN
weka / WOODHEN
welch / WELSH
welcome / GREET; SALUTE; RECEIVE. HAPPY; GRATEFUL, PLEASING. PLEASURE; HOSPITALITY
weld / FUSE; UNITE; SOLDER
welfare / WEAL; PROFIT; BENEFIT, SUCCESS; ADVANTAGE, HAPPINESS
welkin / AIR, SKY; HEAVEN
well / SHAFT; SPRING; FOUNTAIN. AIN, FIT; HALE, JUST, TRIG; HAPPY, HARDY, RIGHT; HEARTY, USEFUL
well advised / PRUDENT
well along / ADVANCED
well armed / READY; PREPARED
well assured / CONFIDENT
well balanced / SOBER, SOUND
well behaved / GOOD, NICE
well being / HEALTH; WELFARE
well born / NOBLE; EUGENIC; BLUEBLOOD, PATRICIAN; ARISTOCRATIC
well bred / GENTEEL, REFINED; MANNERLY; CULTIVATED
well cooked / DONE
well defined / DEFINITE, DISTINCT
well disposed / FAVORABLE
well done / EUGE; BRAVO, BULLY
well educated / SOLID; INFORMED
well enough / RATHER; SOMEWHAT

well expressed / GRACEFUL; FELICITOUS
well favored / COMELY
well fed / PLUMP
well filled / FAT; REPLETE
well fitted / ABLE; COMPETENT
well found / EQUIPPED
well and good / FINE, OKAY
well groomed / SLEEK; UNRUFFLED
well grounded / SOLID, VALID
well heeled / RICH; FLUSH
well intentioned / KINDLY; AMIABLE
well judged / PRUDENT; SENSIBLE
well known / GREAT, NOTED; COMMON, FAMOUS; FAMILIAR, RENOWNED
well laid / SMART; CUNNING
well liked / POPULAR; FAVORITE
well lining / STEEN
well mannered / POLITE
well meant / FRIENDLY
well nigh / ALMOST, NEARLY
well off / WEALTHY; COMFORTABLE
well ordered / NEAT, TIDY
well out / OOZE, SEEP; EXUDE
well over / BRIM; WHELM
well pit / SUMP
well posted / INFORMED
well prepared / UPTO; PRIMED
well put / APPROPRIATE
well read / VERSED; LEARNED; LITERATE
well seasoned / SALTY; HARD-BOILED
well spent / REWARDING
well timed / OPPORTUNE
well trodden / EVERYDAY, ORDINARY
well up / SPRING
well wisher / ROOTER; SUPPORTER
welladay / WOE; ALAS; ALACK
well-boring device / JAR, RIG; DERRICK
well-bred people / GENTRY
well-bred woman / LADY
wellhead / SPRING
well-preserved corpse / MUMMY
wellspring / SOURCE
well-to-do / RICH; WEALTHY; PROSPEROUS
Welsh / CYMRIC
Welsh ambassador / CUCKOO
Welsh bard / TALIESIN; TALIESSIN
welsh on bet / CHEAT, WELCH; ABSCOND, DEFAULT
Welsh city / CARDIFF, RHONDDA
Welsh dog / CORGI
Welsh god of the sea / LLYR; DYLAN
Welsh magician / MERLIN
Welsh mountain / SNOWDON
Welsh musical congress / EISTEDDFOD

Welsh onion / CIBOL
Welsh rabbit / RAREBIT
Welsh river / DEG, USK
Welsh trout / POWAN; GWYNIAD
Welshman / CELT; TAFFY; CAMBRIAN
welt / LASH, WALE; PUNCH, RIDGE
welter / ROLL, SOAK; TUMBLE, WALLOW; FLOUNDER. BROIL; TURMOIL
wem / FLAW, SCAR
wen / CYST, MOLE, WART; TALPA, TUMOR; NODULE; VERRUCA, VERUCCA
wench / GIRL; SERVANT
wend / GO; PASS; DIRECT. SORB
wendigo / OGRE
went / GONE, LEFT; DEPARTED
went ahead / PROCEEDED
went ahead of / LED; PRECEDED
went by car / DROVE; MOTORED
went at easy gait / LOPED; TROTTED
went first / LED; POINTED
went in / ENTERED
wept / CRIED; SOBBED; LAMENTED
werewolf / MANWOLF, WERWOLF; UTURUNCU, VRYKOLAK, WEHRWOLF; LOUPGAROU; LYCANTHROPE
wergeld / CRO, ERIC; RANSOM; GALANAS, WERGILD; WEREGELD
weskit / VEST; WAISTCOAT
Wesleyan / METHODIST
Wessex author / HARDY
west / OCCIDENT
West African antelope / GUIB; GRIMME
West African anthropoid / KOOLOKAMBA
West African baboon / DRILL; MANDRIL; MANDRILL
West African buffalo / SAMOUSE
West African country / TOGO; GABON, GHANA
West African loris / POTTO
West African mammal / NAGOR, POTTO
West African monkey / PATAS; MANGABEY
West African people / IBO, KRU; FANG; BAULE, HAUSA; FULANI
West African seaport / ACCRA, DAKAR, LAGOS
West African tree / AKEE, ODUM; IROKO, ODOOM
West Australia capital / PERTH
West Australia park / YANCHEP
West Coast Indian / HUPA, POMO, SERI, YUKI; HOOPA, MAIDU
West Indian bird / TODY
West Indian drum / BONGO

West Indian fish / BOGA, CERO, PEGA, SESI, TANG; PELON, VORAZ

West Indian fruit / GENIPAP

West Indian insect / CHIGOE; CHICOGER

West Indian island / CUBA; ARUBA, HAITI, NEVIS; MARTINIQUE

West Indian liquor / RUM; TAFIA

West Indian lizard / ARBALO

West Indian mountain / PELEE

West Indian music / CALYPSO

West Indian pirate / FILIBUSTER

West Indian plant / ANIL

West Indian rodent / HUTIA

West Indian ruler / CACIQUE

West Indian shark / GATA

West Indian snake / FERDELANCE

West Indian sorcery / OBI; OBIA; OBEAH

West Indian toad / AGUA

West Indian tree / CERA, MABI; GENIP, YAGUA; ARALIE, BONACE

West Indian tribe / CARIB; BAYA-MO, CAHIBO

West Indian vessel / DROGER

West Indies / ANTILLES; CARIB-BEES

West Point / ARMY

West Point academy / USMA

West Point dance / HOP

West Point freshman / PLEB; PLEBE

West Point mascot / MULE

West Point sophomore / YEARLING

West Pointer / CADET

West Saxon earl / GODWIN

West Saxon king / INE; ALFRED

West Virginia capital / CHARLES-TON

West Virginia city / WHEELING

West Virginia river / KANAWHA

West Virginia state flower / RHODO-DENDRON

West Virginia state nickname / MOUNTAIN; PANHANDLE

west wind / AFER

Western alliance / NATO

Western Australia capital / PERTH

Western Australia city / KALGOOR-LIE

Western Australia desert / GIBSON

Western Australia river / SWAN

western division of Ossetians / DIGOR

western European / CELT, KELT; IBERIAN; SPANIARD

western gambling city / RENO; VEGAS; LASVEGAS

western hemisphere / AMERICA; AMERICAS

western Indian / UTE; NAVAHO, NAVAJO, PAIUTE; SHOSHONEAN

western novel author / GREY

Western Reserve state / OHIO

western shrub / SAGE; TOYON; CHAMISE; OCOTILLO

western state / UTAH; IDAHO; NE-VADA, OREGON; ARIZONA, MON-TANA, WYOMING; CALIFORNIA, WASHINGTON

Western's daughter / SOPHIA

Westminister section / MAYFAIR

Westphalia product / HAM

Westphalian city / HAMM; ESSEN

Westphalian river / EMS; RUHR

wet / SOP; SOAK; DRINK; DAMPEN; MOISTEN. ASOP, DAMP, DANK; HUMID, MISTY, MOIST, RAINY; HYDRIC, SOAKED, WATERY; SHOWERY

wet blanket / SOURPUSS; PARTY-POOPER

wet dressing / STUPE

wet earth / MUD; MIRE, OOZE

wet down hemp / RET

wet mess / MUCK, SLOP

wet sticky earth / MUD; CLAY, MIRE

wet thoroughly / SOAK; SOUSE

wetbird / CHAFFINCH

wether / RAM; EUNUCH; CASTRATO

wetting agent / SURFACTANT

wettish / DAMP, DANK; MOIST

whack / LAM; BEAT, BIFF, BLOW; STRIKE

whack down / FELL

whack up / DIVVY; DIVIDE

whacker / FIB, LIE; FALSEHOOD

whacking / HUGE; TITANIC

whale / BEAT, FLOG; THRASH. CET, ORC, ORK; CETE; SPERM; BE-LUGA, MAMMAL; GRAMPUS, NAR-WHAL; CACHALOT; LEVIATHAN

whale, c.f. / CET

whale, pert. to / CETIC, WHALY

whale diet / BRIT

whale fat / BLUBBER

whale herd / GAM, POD

whale oil / SPERMOIL

whale school / GAM, POD

whale skin / RIND

whaleback ship / LAKER

whalebird / PETREL

whaleboat / WHALER

whalebone / BALEEN; WHALEFIN

whalebone whale / RORQUAL

whaleman's spear / LANCE; HAR-POON

whale-oil cask / RIER

whale-oil derivative / SPERMACETI

whaler / LOLLOPER; SUNDOWNER

whale's carcass / KRANG, KRENG

whale's forelimb / PADDLE

whale's tail feature / FLUKE

whale's waxy secretion / AMBER-GRIS

whale's young / CALF

whaling / HUGE
whang / BANG, BLOW; CHUNK, THONG
whangdoodle / NONSENSE
whangee / CANE; BAMBOO
whap / FLAP, FLOP, MOVE; HURRY, BLOW, BUMP, FALL; WHAUP; STROKE
whare / HOUSE
whare-kura / SCHOOL
wharf / KEY; DOCK, PIER, QUAI, QUAY; HARBOR
wharf landing / STAITH
wharf rat / THIEF; LOADER, LOAFER
wharve / WHORL; PULLEY; SPINDLE
what / EH; HOW, WHO; WHEN; WHERE, WHICH; PRONOUN; WHATEVER
what? / ANAN, ANON
what one believes / CREDO
what means / HOW
what person / WHO
what place / WHERE
what reason / WHY
what time / WHEN
whatnot / ETAGERE; BOOKCASE, CREDENCE, CREDENZA
whaup / CURLEW
wheal / WALE, WEAL, WELT; STRIPE
wheat / SUJI; DURUM, EMMER, GRAIN, SPELT; CEREAL, EINKORN
wheat beard / AWN
wheat covering / BRAN
wheat disease / BUNT, SMUT; ERGOT
wheat head / EAR; SPIKE
wheat kernel / GRAIN
wheat middlings / SEMOLA; SEMOLINA
wheat storage place / SILO; ELEVATOR
wheatear / CHACK; CHACKLE
wheatena flour / ATTA
wheedle / COG; COAX, FAWN; COURT, HUMOR; CAJOLE, DELUDE, ENTICE
wheedling / BUTTERY; ENTICING
wheel / BIKE, DISC, DISK, REEL
wheel, pert. to / ROTAL
wheel about / SPIN, TURN
wheel animal / ROTIFER
wheel bar / AXLE; ARBOR; SPINDLE
wheel belt / STRAKE
wheel and block / SHEAVE
wheel of caster/ ROLLER
wheel center / HUB; NAVE
wheel check / SPRAD
wheel covering / TIRE
wheel and deal / CONTROL; OPERATE
wheel for furniture / CASTER

wheel groove / RUT; TRACK
wheel hub / HOB; NAVE
wheel mount / AXLE
wheel part / CAM, COG, HOB, HUB, RIM; TIRE; FELLY, SPOKE
wheel projection / CAM, COG
wheel radius / SPOKE
wheel shaft / AXLE
wheel spindle / AXLE; ARBOR
wheel spoke / RUNG; RADIUS
wheel on spur / ROWEL
wheel that swivels / CASTER, CASTOR
wheel with teeth / GEAR
wheel tooth / COG
wheel track / RUT
wheelbase / LENGTH
wheelchair / BATHCHAIR
wheeled vehicle / CAR, CART, PRAM; WAGON; BARROW; TUMBRIL
wheelhorse / WORKHORSE
wheelhouse / PILOTHOUSE
wheeling / BIKING
wheelman / HELMSMAN
wheelman in roulette/ TOURNEUR
wheel-rim band / TIRE
wheelsman / CYCLIST; BICYCLIST
wheelworks / GEARING
wheen / FEW; SOME
wheeze / PANG, RALE; BREATHE; CHESTNUT, RHONCHUS
whelk / PIMPLE MOLLUSK
whelm / FLOOD DELUGE, ENGULF
whelp / CUB, PUP PUPPY
when / WHILE; WHEREUPON
whence / HOW, ORIGIN, SOURCE
where / WHICH WHITHER
whereas / SINCE SEEING; INASMUCH FORASMUCH
whereat / WHEREUPON
whereby / HOW
wherefore / WHY; CAUSE; REASON
wherefrom / WHENCE
whereof / WHENCE
whereto / WHITHER
whereupon / THEN; WHEREON
wherever / WHEREER
wherewithal / WAY; CASH; MEANS
wheery / SCULL; ROWBOAT
whet / HONE, WARM; GRIND; AROUSE
whether / IF
whetstone / BUHR, HONE; SHARPENER
whey / SERA; SERUM
which one / WHO
which person / WHO; WHOM
which place / WHERE
which see / QV
which thing / WHAT
whicker / NEIGH; WHINNY
whid / SCUD; SCUTTLE
whidah / WEAVERBIRD

whiff / SIP; PUFF; SMOKE, SNIFF, TASTE; BREATH
whiffet / RUNT; NOBODY
whiffle / TURN, VEER; CHANGE
whiffler / TRIMMER; TURNCOAT
whig / JOG; WHEY
while / AS; YET; WHEN; ALBEIT
whiles / INTERIM; MEANTIME
whilom / AGO; PAST; FORMER
whilst / WHILE
whim / FAD, TOY; FREAK, HUMOR; NOTION, WHIMSY; CAPRICE
whimper / CRY; MEWL; PULE; WHINE
whimsey / ODD; FREAK; WHIMSY; CAPRICE; FANTASIA
whimsical / ODD; DROLL, QUEER
whimsical concept / FANCY
whimsical notion / VAGARY
whimsical quirk / CROTCHET
whimsicality / PRANK; WAGGERY
whim-whams / NERVES; JITTERS
whin / FURZE, GORSE; TRAPROCK
whine / PULE; SNIVEL; COMPLAIN
whinger / DIRK;/ HANGER
whinny / NEIGH; NICKER; WHICKER
whinstone / TRAP; CHERT
whinyard / SWORD; POCHARD
whip / SEW; BEAT, CANE, FLAY, CAT; PLET; KNOUT, QUIRT
whip hand / EDGE; POWER
whip handle / CROP
whip in / HERD; GATHER
whip mark / WALE, WEAL; WHEAL
whip off / DIVERT
whip into shape / CONDITION
whip and spur / POSTHASTE
whip of untanned skins / RAWHIDE
whipjack / BEGGAR; IMPOSTER
whipped cream / CHANTILLY
whippersnapper / JACKANAPES
whipping / BEATING; THRASHING
whipsocket / SNEAD
whir / BUZ; HISS; WHIZZ
whirl / EDDY, MOVE, REEL, SPIN
whirlblast / CYCLONE, TWISTER
whirligig / SPINNER; CARROUSEL
whirligig beetle / WEAVER
whirling motion / GYRE, SPIN
whirlpool / EDDY, GULF, WEEL, WIEL; GURGE; VORTEX; MAELSTROM
whirlwind / TORNADO
whirlwind of Faroe Islands / OE
whirring sound / BIRR, BUZZ, WHIZ
whisht / HUSH
whisk / BROOM, SWEEP. STIR
whiskbroom / WISP
whiskers / HAIR; BEARD, BRUSH
whiskey / RUM, RYE; ARRACK, POTEEN, SCOTCH; BOURBON, POTHEEN; MOONSHINE

whisper / BREATH, GOSSIP, MURMUR; SUSURRUS
whispered / ASIDE, FAINT
whist / HUSH. CARDS
whist declaration / MISERE
whist sweep / SLAM
whistle / BLOW, CALL, PIPE; SIREN; SIGNAL
whistle at / JEER, MOCK
whistle stop / HAMLET; TANKTOWN
whistler / MARMOT
whistlewood / ALDER; WILLOW
whistling swan / OLOR
whit / ACE, BIT, JOT; ATOM, DOIT, IOTA; TITTLE
Whitby event / SYNOD
Whitby monk / CAEDMON
white / WAN; ASHY, HOAR, PALE
white, c.f. / ALBO
white with age / HOAR; HOARY
white alert / ALLCLEAR
white alkali / SODA
white animal / ALBINO
white ant / ANAI, ANAY; TERMITE
white ball / CUEBALL; SPOTBALL
white beet / CHARD
white bent / FIORIN
white bird / EGRET, HERON, STORK
white bony substance / IVORY
white book / REPORT
white brain matter / ALBA
white brant / SNOWGOOSE
white cell / LEUCOCYTE
white cinnamon / CANELLA
white croaker / KINGFISH
white of egg / GLAIR; ALBUMEN
white elephant / ONUS; BURDEN
white elephant land / SIAM
white ermine / LASSET; MINIVER
white feather / COWARDICE
white fiber / SISAL
white flag / SURRENDER
white flecked / PIED, ROAN
white friar / CARMELITE
white frost / RIME
white game / PTARMIGAN
white gentian / FEVERROOT
white goods / LINENS
white grape / TOKAY; MALAGA; ALIGOTE, FURMINT, SULTANA; RIESLING
white grease / FAT; LARD
white heron / EGRET
white hot / CANDENT
White House / PRESIDENCY
white hunter / GUIDE
white iron / TINPLATE
white jade / ALABASTER
white lady / BANSHEE
white laurel / SWEETBAY
white lead / CERUSE
white lie / FIB; FALSEHOOD
white light / SUNLIGHT

white lightning / HOOCH; MOON-SHINE
white livered / COWARDLY
white man / PALEFACE; CAUCASIAN
white marble / CARRARA
white matter / BRAINS
white metal / PEWTER; BRITANNIA
white mice / MUSCOVITE
white mule / MOONSHINE
white oak / ROBLE; OVERCUP
white partridge/ PTARMIGAN
white plague / CONSUMPTION; TUBERCULOSIS
white playing marble / ALLEY
white poplar / ABELE, ASPEN
White Rabbit's possession / WATCH
white rose / YORK
White Russia / BYELORUSSIA
White Russia capital / MINSK
White Russia city / GOMEL; GRODNO
white scurf / DANDRUFF
White Sox' city / CHICAGO
white space / BLANKS, MARGIN
white spruce / EPINETTE
white sturgeon / BELUGA
white substance / IVORY
white vestment/ ALB; AMICE
white water / RAPIDS
white weasel / ERMINE
white whale / HUSE, HUSO; BE-LUGA; MOBYDICK
white whale's hunter / AHAB
white wine / GRAVES, MALAGA; CHABLIS, RIESLING; CHAM-PAGNE, SAUTERNES; CHAR-DONNAY
white yam / UBE, UBI, UVI
whitebait / SPRAT; ICEFISH
whitebeard / ANCIENT
whitebelly / WIDGEON; BALDPATE
whitebill / COOT
whitecap / WAVE; CREST
white-collar job / CLERK, STENO; OFFICEWORK
whited sepulcher / HYPOCRITE
whiteface / HEREFORD
white-faced / PALE; SHAKEN
whitefish / CISCO; LAVARET
white-flecked horse / ROAN
whitefriars / ALSATIA
whitegum / SWEETGUM
white-haired / HOARY, SNOWY
whitehead / MILIUM
white-headed boy / PET; FAVORITE
white-livered / ENVIOUS; COWARDLY
whitely / PALE
whiten / BLANCH, BLEACH; ETI-OLATE
whiteness / PALLOR, PURITY
whitening / BLEACH; CALCIMINE
whitesmith / TINSMITH

white-tailed bird / ERN; WHEATEAR
whitetop / FLEABANE
whiteware / CHINA; PORCELAIN
whitewash / CLEAR, GLOSS; PAR-GET; SHUTOUT; EXCULPATE
whiteweed / DAISY, OXEYE
whitewing / STREETCLEANER
whitewood / CANELLA; BASSWOOD
whither / WHERE
whiting / HAKE
whitish / HOARY; CHALKY
whitlow / FELON; AGNAIL; PARO-NYCHIA
Whitman's subject / MYSELF
Whitney invention / COTTONGIN
whitrack / STOAT; WEASEL
Whitsunday / PENTECOST
Whittier heroine / MAUD
Whittington's pet / CAT
whittle / CUT; DRESS, SHAVE
whittlings / CHIPS
whiz / HUM; HISS, PIRR, WHIR
whoa / HOLD, STOP; STAND
whodunit / MYSTERY
whoever / ANYONE
whole / ALL; HALE, WELL; SOUND
whole, c.f. / TOTI, TOTO
whole amount / SUM; GROSS, TOTAL
whole jury / PANEL
whole note / SEMIBREVE
whole number / INTEGER
whole-hearted / EARNEST, FERVENT
wholesome / MORAL, SOUND; STRONG
whole-souled / SINCERE; GEN-EROUS
wholetime / REGULAR; FULLTIME
wholistic / HOLISTIC
wholly / ALL; FULLY, QUITE
wholly occupied / RAPT
whomp / CRASH, THUMP
whoop / CRY; CALL, HOOP; SHOUT
whoop it up / CHEER
whooping cough / PERTUSSIS
whop / BEAT, FALL; THRASH
whopper / LIE; TARADIDDLE
whopping / VERY; GREAT, LARGE
whorl / VERTICIL, VOLUTION
whortleberry / BILBERRY; WHIN-BERRY
who's who / CREAM, ELITE
whoso / WHOEVER
whosoever / WHO
why / CAUSE; REASON; PURPOSE
wick / FUSE, FUZE, TOWN
wicked / BAD, ILL; DARK, EVIL
wicked person / FELON, FIEND
wickedness / SIN; EVIL, VICE
wicker / OSIER
wicker basket / KISH; CESTA, KIPSY
wicker hamper / CRATE, CREEL

wicker hut / JACAL
wicker-covered bottle / FIASCO
wickerwork / RATTAN; PLAITING
wicket / ARCH, GATE; GRILL, STICK, STUMP; WINDOW
wicket in cricket / PITCH; STICKS
wicket in croquet / HOOP
wickiup / HUT; LODGE; WIGWAM
Wickliffian / LOLLARD
wicopy / BASSWOOD
widdershins / BACKWARDS
widdy / GALLOWS
wide / VAST; BROAD, LARGE; REMOTE, DISTANT; EXPANDED
wide awake / KEEN, LIVE; ALERT
wide clear beach / OPENSTRAND
wide of the mark / ASTRAY, ERRANT
wide open / AGAPE; UNTRAMMELED
wide smile / GRIN
wide street / AVENUE; BOULEVARD
wide view / SURVEY; PANORAMA
wide-awake / TERN
widely / LARGELY
wide-mouth jar / OLA; EWER, OLLA
widen / SPREAD; AMPLIFY, ENLARGE
wideness / WIDTH; BREADTH
widespread / RIFE; GENERAL
widespread fear / PANIC
widespread tumult / RIOT; EMEUTE
widgeon / DUCK, SMEE, SMEW, WHIM
widgeon genus / MARECA
widow / RELICT; DOWAGER, RUNOVER
widow, pert. to / VIDUAL
widow in cards / SKAT
widow monkey / TITI
Widow of Windsor / VICTORIA
widower / RELICT
widowhood / VIDUAGE
widows / VIDUATE
widow's dower / TERCE
widow's income / DOWER
widow's mite / BIT
widow's right / SCOT; TERCE
widow's tears / SPIDERWORT
width / WIDENESS
wield / PLY, USE; SWAY, EXERT
wielded diligently / PLIED
wieldy / PLIANT; MANAGEABLE
Wien / VIENNA
wiener / HOTDOG, WEENIE; FRANKFURTER
wife / FEME, FRAU, MATE; BRIDE, FEMME; MATRON, SPOUSE; CONSORT, PARTNER; HELPMATE, HELPMEET
wife, pert. to / UXORIAL
wife of Bath / ALICE
wife of Boaz / RUTH

wife bound / HENPECKED
wife killing / UXORICIDE
wife of Lamech / ADAH; ZILLAH
wife of Osiris / ISIS
wife of Priam / HECUBA
wife of rajah / RANI; RANEE
wife of Shakespeare / ANNE
wife of Tyndareus / LEDA
wife of Ulysses / PENELOPE
wife of uncle / AUNT
wife's property / DOS, DOT; DOWRY
wife's self-immolation / SUTTEE
wig / RUG; JASEY; PERUKE, TOUPEE
wigging / SCOLDING
wiggle / WAG; WRIGGLE
wiggletail / TADPOLE
wiggy / HAUGHTY
wight / PERSON; CREATURE
wigs on the green / DONNYBROOK
wigwag / FLAG, WAVE; SIGNAL
wigwam / TIPI; TEPEE; TEEPEE; WICKIUP
wild / FERAL, LOOSE, GIDDY
wild alder / GOUTWEED
wild allspice / SPICEBUSH
wild animal collection / ZOO; MENAGERIE
wild animals / ZIIM
wild animal's trail / SLOT; SPOOR, TRACK
wild apple / CRAB; DOUCIN
wild ass / KULAN; ONAGER, QUAGGA
wild banana / FEI
wild beet / PIGWEED
wild brier / DOGROSE
wild celery / SMALLAGE
wild cherry / GEAN; MARASCA
wild cranberry / PEMBINA
wild dog / DHOLE, DINGO; TANATE
wild duck / SCAUP; MALLARD
Wild Duck author / IBSEN
wild East Indian buffalo / ARNA, ARNI, GAUR; ARNEE, SLADANG; SALADANG, SELADANG
wild flax / TOADFLAX
wild flight / ROUT; STAMPEDE
wild flower / BUGLE; COWSLIP, GENTIAN; PRIMROSE; BUTTERCUP
wild fright / PANIC; TERROR
wild game hunt / SAFARI
wild garlic / MOLY
wild ginger / ASARUM
wild goat / TUR; IBEX, TAHR, THAR
wild goose / BRANT, BRENT, GRAYLAG; BARNACLE
wild hog / BENE, BOAR; PECCARY, WARTHOG; BABIRUSA
wild honeybee / DINGAR
wild horse / BRONCO, BRUMBY, RUSSAR, TARPAN; MUSTANG

wild hunt / GABBLERATCHET
wild hyacinth / CAMAS
wild indigo / TUMBLEWEED
wild lime / COLIMA
wild mandrake / MAYAPPLE
wild marjoram / ORIGAN
wild mustard / CHARLOCK
wild oats / FOLLIES; DISSIPATION
wild olive / OLEASTER
wild onion / GARLIC
wild ox / ANOA, URUS; BANTENG
wild pansy / HEARTSEASE
wild parsley / KECK; LOVAGE
wild pig / BOAR
wild plant / FERN, TARE, WEED
wild plum / SLOE; ISLAY
wild region / HEATH, WASTE;
    DESERT
wild revelry / ORGY; SPREE
wild rice / ZIZANIA
wild rose / SWEETBRIER
wild sheep / SHA; ARUI, UDAD;
    URIAL; AOUDAD, ARGALI
wild shrub / SAGE; GORSE, HEATH
wild stretch of land / HEATH
wild swan / WHOOPER
wild swine / BOAR
wild thyme / HILLWORT
wild turnip / NAVEW, SWEDE
wild vanilla / LIATRIS
Wild West show / RODEO
wild and wooly / UNRULY
wild yam / COLICROOT
wild yeast / ANAMITE
wildcat / BALU, EYRA, LYNX;
    CHAUS, MANUL; BOBCAT,
    OCELOT
Wilde play / SALOME
wildebeest / GNU
wilderness / WASTE; DESERT
Wilderness battle victor / GRANT
wild-eyed / HAGGARD; FRENZIED
wildfire / WILLOTHEWISP
wildfowl / DUCK; GOOSE
wild-goose chase / FUTILITY
wildly / SAVAGELY; FRANTICALLY
wildwood / BOWER; BOSCAGE
wile / LURE; CHEAT, TRICK. ART;
    RUSE; FRAUD; DECEIT
wilful / OBDURATE, PERVERSE
wilfully / PURPOSELY; INFLEXIBLY
will / WISH; ELECT; CHOOSE, DE-
    CREE, DEMISE, DESIRE, DIRECT.
    BEHEST, CHOICE; FACULTY
will addition / CODICIL
will inheritor / DEVISEE
will left and made / TESTATE
will maker / DEVISOR; TESTATOR
will power / FIRMNESS
willful / FROWARD; OBSTINATE
William Tell's canton / URI
willies / BLUES, DUMPS; JIMJAMS
willing / FAIN, LIEF; EAGER

willingly / LIEF; LIEVE; GLADLY,
    FREELY; READILY; CHEERFULLY
willingness / ASSENT; EAGERNESS
williwaw / STORM; WINDSTORM
willock / PUFFIN
will-o'-the-wisp / FATUUS; CORPO-
    SANT, FIREDRAKE
willow / BAT, GIN; ITEA, WOLF;
    OSIER, SALIX; CARDER, SALLOW
willow basketry / WICKER
willow flowers / AMENT, SPIKE
willow green / RESEDA
willow grove / HOLT
willow herb / EPILOBE; FIREWEED
willow twig / OSIER, WITHE, WITHY;
    SALLOW
willow wren / CHIFFCHAFF
willowy / SUPPLE; SLENDER
willy-nilly / PERFORCE
Wilson's thrush / VEERY
wilt / SAG; FADE; DROOP;
    LANGUISH
wilted / RUNDOWN
Wilton / CARPET
Wiltshire inhabitant / MOONRAKER
wily / SLY; ARCH, FOXY; ARTFUL
wimble / BORE; AUGER, BRACE
Wimbledon sport / TENNIS
wimple / FOLD; PLAIT. VEIL; GOR-
    GET
win / GET; BEAT, BEST, EARN
win advantage over / BEST
win of all tricks in bridge / SLAM
win of all tricks in pique / CAPOT
win over / PERSUADE
win through / ACHIEVE, TRIUMPH
win through effort / EARN
wince / REEL, TURN; QUAIL,
    TWIST
winch / WHIN; CRANK, HOIST
winch operator / DONKEYMAN
winchester / GUN; RIFLE
wind / BEND, COIL, TURN; CURVE.
    AIR; GALE; BREATH, BREEZE
wind, c.f. / ANEMO
wind, pert. to / EOLIAN; AEOLIAN
wind of the Adriatic / BORA
wind from Africa / SIROCCO; HAR-
    MATTAN
wind of the Alps / BISE, BIZE;
    FOEHN
wind around / TWINE
wind of Australia / BUSTER
wind into a ball / CLEW
wind band / BRASS
wind blast / FLAW, GUST
wind a chain / WOOLD
wind colic / BLOAT
wind cone / SOCK
wind diagram / WINDROSE
wind near the equator / TRADE
wind of the Faroes / OE
wind gap / NOTCH

wind gauge / VANE; ANEMOMETER, VENTOMETER
wind god of Ancient Greece / AEOLUS
wind god of Assyria / RAMMAN
wind god of Babylonia / ADAD, ADDA
wind god of the Hindu / VAYU
wind god of the Mayans / BACAB
wind god of the Slavs / STRIBOG
wind gust / FLAW; FLURRY
wind into a hank / SKEIN
wind indicator / CONE, SOCK, VANE; ANEMOMETER
wind instrument / HORN, OBOE, PIPE, REED, TUBA; BUGLE, FLUTE
wind in the Levant / ETESIAN
wind of Malta / GREGALE
wind of the Mediterranean / BUFERA, SOLANO; ETESIAN, MISTRAL, SIROCCO
wind of the Near East / KAMSIN, SAMIEL, SHAMAL, SIMOOM, SIMOON; KHAMSIN
wind of Peru / SUR; PUNA, PUNO
wind player / PIPER; OBOIST
wind road / AIRWAY; VENTILATOR
wind science / ANEMOLOGY
wind sock / CONE; SLEEVE
wind sound / SOB; MOAN; SOUGH
wind speed unit / KNOT
wind spirally / COIL
wind together / COIL; TWIST
wind up / END; STOP; CLOSE
wind vane / POINTER; WEATHERCOCK
windage / DEFLECTION
windbag / THRASO; BOBADIL, TATTLER; BLOWHARD, BRAGGART
windbreak / SHELTER; GREENBELT
windbreaker / JACKET
wind-broken / EMPHYSEMATIC
wind-deposited earth / LOESS
wind-driven clouds / SCUD
winder / HOIST, SPOOL, WINCH
windfall / GODSEND
windflower / ANEMONE
windhover / KESTREL
windiness / VERBOSITY; FLATULENCE
winding / SNAKY; SPIRAL; BENDING
winding sheet / SHROUD; CEREMENT
winding ways / AMBAGES
windjammer / SHIP; SCHOONER
windlass / WINCH; CAPSTAN
windless / CALM
windlestraw / PUPPET; MEDIOCRITY
windmill arm / VANE

windmill sail / AWE, FAN
window / FOIL; TINFOIL; CAMOUFLAGE
window box / PLANTER
window casing / FRAME
window compartment / PANE
window cover / BLIND; SCREEN; SHUTTER; STORMSASH
window decorator / TRIMMER
window divider / MULLION
window above door / TRANSOM
window dressing / FACADE; FALSEFRONT
window frame / SASH; CASING
window glass / PANE; LIGHT, SHEET
window lead / CAME
window ledge / SILL
window pane / LIGHT
window part / PANE, SASH, SILL
window plant / MESEMB
window in roof / DORMER; SKYLIGHT
window strip / CAME
window weight / MOUSE
window-glass setter / GLAZIER
windpipe / TRACHEA, WEASAND
windrow / SWATH; FURROW
windrose / POPPY
windstorm / OE; BISE, BLOW, BURA
windswept / RAW
windup / RESULT; OUTCOME
windward / EXPOSED
Windward Island / MOOREA; GRENADA; DOMINICA; MARTINIQUE
windy / EMPTY; BOASTFUL
Windy City / CHICAGO
wine / VIN; HOCK, PORT, ROSE, SACK, SOMA, VINO; MEDOC, SOAVE, TINTA, TOKAY, XERES; CANARY, CLARET, GRAVES, MAGGIE, MALAGA, MUSCAT, PONTAC, SHERRY; CATAWBA, CHABLIS, CHIANTI, MADEIRA, MALMSEY, MOSELLE, RETSINA; SAUTERNES
wine, c.f. / OENO, VINI
wine, pert. to / VINIC; VINOUS
wine berry / GRAPE; CURRANT
wine bottle / FLASK; MAGNUM; DECANTER, JEROBOAM
wine cask / TUN; BUTT; BARREL
wine container / TUN; CASK; FLASK
wine cooler / BUCKET
wine cup / AMULA; CHALICE
wine cup of legend / GRAIL
wine dealer / VINTNER
wine dregs / MARC; VINASSE
wine evaporation / ULLAGE
wine fermentation / CUVAGE
wine before fermenting / MUST
wine flavor / SEVE
wine of a given year / VINTAGE
wine glass / TULIP; RUMMER

wine grape / GAMAY, PINOT; VER-
DOT; CATAWBA, VINIFER
wine grape refuse / MARC
wine on hand / CELLAR
wine and honey drink / MULSE;
PEKMEZ; OENOMEL
wine list / CARTE
wine measure / AAM; ORNA, ORNE,
PIPE; BOTTLE
wine merchant / VINTNER
wine pitcher / OLPE
wine refuse / MARC
wine room / CELLAR
wine sediment / LEES
wine and spice drink / NEGUS;
SANGAREE
wine steward / CELLARER
wine study / ENOLOGY; EONOLOGY
wine syrup / SAPA
wine taint / CASSE
wine town of Italy / ASTI
wine used locally / VINDEPAYS
wine valley / NAPA; SONOMA
wine vessel / TUN, VAT; CASK,
CUVE, OLPE; FLASK; CHALICE
wine and water of eucharist /
KRAMA
wineberry / MAKO, TUTU; BIL-
BERRY
winebibber / WINO; TOPER; BOOZER
wine-cask deficiency / ULLAGE;
WANTAGE
winegrower / VITICULTURIST
winesap / APPLE
wineshop / CAFE; BISTRO, TAVERN
wineskin / OLPE
wing / EL; ALA; ALAE; ANNEX,
PENNA, PINNA; PINION; AIRFOIL
wing, pert. to / ALAR
wing of beetle / TEGMAN; TEG-
MINA
wing of building / EL; ELL; ANNEX
wing cover / SHARD; ELYTRUM
wing flap / AILERON
wing footed / ALIPED
wing membrane of bat / PETAGIUM
wing movement / BEAT, FLAP;
FLUTTER
wing nut / THUMBNUT
wing part / FLAP; AILERON
wing shaped / ALAR; ALARY, ALATE
wing tuft / ALULA
wingback / HALFBACK
wingcut / WOODCUT
wingding / SPREE
winged / ALAR; ALATE; ALATED
winged figure / IDOLON; EIDOLON
winged fruit / SAMARA
winged god / EROS; CUPID
winged goddess / NIKE
winged hat of Mercury / PETASUS
winged in heraldry / AILE
winged horse / PEGASUS

winged insect / FLY; MOTH, WASP
winged sandals of Mercury /
TALARIA
winged seed / KEY; SAMARA
winged serpent / DRAGON
winged spirit / KER
winged wolf / EAGLE, HARPY
wingless / APTERAL; APTEROUS
wingless bird / MOA; KIWI;
APTERYX
wingless invertebrates / APTERA
winglike / ALAR; PTERIC; PTEROID
winglike part / ALA; ALAE; ALULA
wingman / FORWARD
wings / ALAE
wings, pert. to / ALAR
wingspread / WIDTH
wingy / SWIFT; SOARING
wink / BAT; HINT; BLINK; CONNIVE
wink at / TOLERATE, TURNAWAY
wink eyes rapidly / FLUTTER
wink of sleep / SHUTEYE
winker / BLINDER, EYELASH
winkle / WHELK
winner / VICTOR; CONQUEROR
winning / LOVELY; ALLURING
winning numbers / TERNS
winnings / GAIN; PICKINGS
winnow / FAN, WIM; SIFT; SEPA-
RATE
winsome / CUTE; BONNY; PRETTY
winter / HIBERNATE
winter, pert. to / BOREAL, BRUMAL,
HIEMAL, HYEMAL, WINTRY
winter ailment / COLD; CHILBLAIN
winter apple / RUSSET; WINESAP
winter duck / SQUAW; PINTAIL
winter festival / SATURNALIA
winter garment / FURS; MACKINAW
winter hay / FODDER
winter hazard / ICE; SNOW; SLEET
winter resort / FLORIDA; SKILODGE
winter sport / SKIING; SKATING
winter squash / CUSHAW, TURBAN
winter tracery / FROST
winter vehicle / SLED; SLEDGE,
SLEIGH; TOBOGGAN
winter weather in person / JACK-
FROST
Winter's Tale character / PERDITA;
AUTOLYCUS
wintry / COLD; HARSH; BRUMAL
winy / VINOUS
winze / SHAFT; STAPLEPIT
wipe / MOP, RUB; DUST; SWAB
wipe clean / ERASE
wipe out / ERASE; FINISH; DE-
TROY
wiper / RAG; BLADE, BRUSH,
CLOTH
wire / TELEGRAM. BIND
wire coil / SPRING
wire fastener / CLIP; STAPLE

wire measure / MIL; GAUGE
wire netting / SCREENING
wire rope / GUY; CABLE
wire service / AP, UP, WU; INS, UPI
wiredrawn / ATTENUATED
wirehair / TERRIER
wireless / RADIO
wireless inventor / MARCONI
wirepuller / SCHEMER
wires crossed in eyepiece / RET-ICLE; RETICULE
wiretapper / SNOOPER
wire-toothed brush / CARD
wirewalker / FUNAMBULIST
wireway / CONDUIT
wireweed / KNOTGRASS
wireworm / MILLIPEDE
wirra / SORROW, WURRAH
wiry / LEAN, THIN; STIFF, TOUGH
wis / BELIEVE
Wisconsin capital / MADISON
Wisconsin city / RACINE; OSHKOSH
Wisconsin college / RIPON; BELOIT
Wisconsin Indian tribe / FOX, SAC; SAUK
Wisconsin motto / FORWARD
Wisconsin peninsula / DOOR
Wisconsin scenic area / DELLS
Wisconsin state animal / BADGER
Wisconsin state flower / VIOLET
Wisconsin state nickname / BADGER
Wisconsin state tree / MAPLE
wisdom / LORE, PIETY, SENSE
wisdom book / PROVERBS
wisdom god of Babylonia / NABU, NEBO; MARDUK
wisdom god of the Hindus / GANESHA
wisdom god of Japan / DAINICHI
wisdom god of the Norsemen / BRAGI
wisdom goddess of ancient Greece / ATHENA, PALLAS
wisdom goddess of the Hindus / USHAS; SARASVATI
wisdom goddess of ancient Rome / MINERVA
wisdom tooth / MOLAR
wise / DEEP, SAGE, SANE; CLEVER, CRAFTY, EXPERT, SUBTLE; ERU-DITE
wise adviser / MENTOR
wise answer / ORACLE; PROPHECY
wise bird / OWL
wise guy / SMARTY; WITLING
wise man / SAGE; SOLON, WITAN
wise men / MAGI
wise saying / SAW; ADAGE; ORACLE
wise scholar / DOCTOR, SAVANT
wise to / ONTO; AWARE
wise up / ADVISE, INFORM
wise woman / ALRAUN; MIDWIFE

wiseacre / SMARTALECK
wisecrack / GAG, PUN, WIT; JOKE
wisely / SOUNDLY; SAGACIOUSLY
wisenheimer / FOOL; WISEGUY
wisent / BISON; AUROCHS
wish / HOPE, WANT; COVET, CRAVE; DESIRE, DIRECT
wish for / BID; LONG; YEARN
wish on / IMPOSE
wishbone / FURCULUM; MERRY-THOUGHT
wisher / ASPIRANT
wishful / HOPEFUL, LONGING
wishing well token / COIN
wishing-cap owner / FORTUNATUS
Wishram / CHINOOK
wishwash / SLOPS
wishywashy / PUNY, THIN, WEAK
wisket / BASKET
wisp / TUFT; BUNDLE; HANDFUL
wisp of smoke / FLOC
wisp of straw / WAP
wistful / LONGING, PENSIVE
wistiti / MARMOSET
wit / GAG, WAG; SALT; HUMOR, SENSE; ACUMEN, BANTER, SATIRE
witan / COUNCIL
witan member / EALDORMAN
witch / HAG, HEX; CIRCE, ENDOR, HECAT, LAMIA, NIMUE; HECATE
witch city / SALEM
witch doctor / HEX; GOOFER, SHA-MAN; OBEAHMAN
witch of Faerie Queene / DUESSA
witch hazel / ROWAN; WYCHELM
witch hunt / INQUISITION
witch stick/ WAND
witchcraft / MAGIC, OBEAH; VOO-DOO; GLAMOUR, SORCERY; GRAMARYE
witchery / SPELL; GLAMOUR; SOR-TILEGE; RAVISHMENT
witches' assembly / SABBAT
witches' brew / CONCOCTION
witches' broom / STAGHEAP
witches' gathering / SABBAT
witches' group / COVEN
witch-hunt victim / DISSENTER
witchlike / THAUMATURGIC
witch's familiar / CAT; TOAD
witch's transport / BROOM
witchy / EVIL; MALEVOLENT
with / NEAR; ALONG; NEARNESS
with, pref. / COM, CON, SYN
with the bow / CA; ARCO
with difficulty / EDGEWISE
with one end raised / ATILT
with full force / AMAIN; EAGERLY
with hand on hip / AKIMBO
with ice cream / ALAMODE
with it / GROOVY; RIGHTON
with this / HEREWITH

withal / ALSO; LIKEWISE
withdraw / EXIT, QUIT, WEAN
withdrawal / EBB; PULLOUT
withdrawal's priority / DEPOSIT
withdrawing / RECEDING
withdrawn / APART; ABSTRACTED
withe / TWIG; WITHY; WATTLE
wither / DIE, DRY; FADE, SEAR
withered / ARID, SERE
withered old woman / CRONE
withering / SHARP; SARCASTIC
withershins / COUNTERCLOCKWISE
withhold / DENY, HIDE, KEEP;
    SPARE; ARREST, DETAIN,
    HINDER
withhold business from / BOYCOTT
withhold food from / STARVE
within / IN; INTO; INNER; INSIDE
within, c.f. / END, ENT, ESO; ENDO,
    ENSO, ENTO; INTRA, INTRO
within, pref. / ENDO, ENSO; INTRA
within the walls / INTRAMURAL
withindoors / IN; ATHOME
without / SANS; OUTSIDE
without, c.f. / ECT; ECTO
without, pref. / IN
without accent / ATONIC
without breeding / CADDISH
without charge / FREE
without clothing / NUDE
without company / LONE; ALONE
without deduction / CLEAR
without discomfort / PAINLESS
without drapery / BARE
without effort / EASILY
without elevation / FLAT
without end / EVER; FOREVER
without family / LORN
without feeling / NUMB; CALLOUS
without feet / APOD
without foliage / LEAFLESS
without life / DEAD; AMORT
without luster / MAT; FLAT
without a mate / SINGLE
without moral stain / SINLESS
without parents / ORPHAN
without purpose / IDLE; AIMLESS
without remainder / ALIQUOT
without reserve / FREE; FREELY
without result / BLANK
without a saddle / BAREBACK
without a score / RUNLESS
without a sense of reason / IN-
    SENSATE
without sound / DUMB; SILENT
without teeth / EDENTATE
without title / NAMELESS
without ventilation / CLOSE
withoutdoors / OUTSIDE
withstand / LAST, STEM; ENDURE
withstand use / WEAR
withy / TWIG

witless / STUPID; SENSELESS
witless chatter / GAB, MAG; GAB-
    BLE; BLETHER, PRATTLE,
    TWADDLE
witling / FOOL
witloof / ENDIVE
witness / SEE; MARK, NOTE;
    PROVE. PROOF; AFFIANT; DE-
    PONENT
witness stand / BOX
witnessed / SAW; SEEN
witnessing clause of a writ / TESTE
wits / HEAD; BRAINS
Wittenberg resident / LUTHER
witter / BARB; TARGET
witticism / FUN, MOT, PUN; JOKE,
    QUIP; HUMOR, SALLY
witting / AWARE; CONSCIOUS
wittingly / PURPOSELY
wittol / CUCKOLD
witty / DROIT, DROLL, FUNNY
witty person / WAG, WIT; COMIC
witty remark / MOT; SALLY
witty reply / RETORT; REPARTEE
witty saying / EPIGRAM
witwall / ORIOLE; WOODPECKER
wivern / DRAGON, WYVERN
wizard / MAGE, SEER; SHAMAN
wizardry / MAGIC; SORCERY
wizen / DRY; WEAZEN; WITHER
wizened / SERE; DRIED; WITHERED
woad / BLUE; ISATIS
woadwaxen / WHIN; DYERSBROOM
wobble / SWAY; SHAKE; TEETER
wobbly / UNSURE; HESITANT
Wodehouse character / JEEVES
Woden / ODIN
wodge / LUMP
woe / ILL; BANE; AGONY, GRIEF
woe is me / ALAS
woe to the conquered / VAEVICTIS
woebegone / SAD; MEAN; WOEFUL
woeful /SAD ; MEAN; WOFUL
wold / DOWNS, WEALD, WOODS
wolf / LOBO, RAKE; COYOTE
wolf, pert. to / LUPINE
wolf at the door / POVERTY
wolf of fable / ISENGRIM
wolf of Odin / GERI; FREKI
wolf-headed god / UPUAUT
wolfhound / BORZOI
wolfish / LUPINE
wolflike / THOOID
wolflike mammal / HYENA
wolf-man / WEREWOLF
wolfram / TUNGSTEN
wolframite / CAL
wolf's foot / PAD
wolfsbane / ACONITE; MONKS-
    HOOD
wolverine / GULO; GLUTTON
Wolverine State / MICHIGAN

woman / MS; MRS; FRAU, LADY, MISS, WIFE; FEMME; FEMALE
woman, c.f. / GYN; GYNE
woman adviser / EGERIA
woman with bad temper / FURY; SHREW, VIXEN; BELDAM, VIRAGO
woman family ruler / MATRIARCH
woman graduate / ALUMNA
woman hater / MISOGYNE; MISOGYNIST
woman inheriting husband's property / DOWAGER
woman lawyer / PORTIA
woman who leaves a will / TESTATRIX
woman in Polynesia / VAHINE, WAHINE
woman under religious vows / NUN; SISTER
woman who rules / QUEEN; CZARINA; MAHARANI, PRINCESS
woman warrior / AMAZON
womanhood / WOMEN
womanish / FEMININE, MULEBRAL
womanly / FEMININE; EFFEMINATE
woman's club / SOROSIS; SORORITY
woman's collar / BERTHA
woman's domain / HOME; DISTAFF
woman's garment / GOWN; DRESS, JUPON, SIMAR, SKIRT, STOLE; BODICE, MANTUA
woman's handbag / CABAS, PURSE
woman's headdress / TIARA
woman's marriage portion / DOWRY
woman's name / ADA, AMY, ANN, EVA, EVE, FAY, IDA, INA, MAE, MAY, NAN, RAE; ALIX, ALMA, ALYS, ANNA, ANNE, AVIS, BONA, CARA, CLOE, CORA, DORA, EDNA, ELLA, ELSA, ELSI, EMMA, ENID, ERMA, ETTA, INEZ, JANE, JEAN, JOAN, JUNE, LIDA, LILA, LOIS, LORA, LUCY, MARY, MAUD, MYRA, NONA, NORA, OLGA, RITA, RONA, ROSA, ROSE, RUTH, SARA; ALICE, ANITA, CLARA, CLARE, DELIA, DIANA, ELSIE, ETHEL, FAITH, GRACE, IRENE, LUCIA, MARGO, MARIA, SARAH, SELMA, SUSAN, VELMA
woman's nickname / CAT, DEB, DOM, EVE, FLO, JAN, KIT, LIZ, LOU, MAB, MAG, MED, MEG, PEG, REG, SAL, SUE; ABBY, ADDY, ALLI, BENA, BESS, BETH, CARA, CATH, DINA, DORA, EMMI, FRAN, GAIL, JILL, JOSY, JUDY, JULE, KATE, KATH, KATY, LENA, LINA, LISA, LIZA, LORA, LULU, MARG, MART, MIMI, MINA, MOLL, NELL,

NINA, RONA, ROXY, SUSY, TAVE, TAVY, TESS, TINA, XINA; BETSY, BETTY, KATHY, OLLIE, PEGGY, PHEBE, SANDY
woman's suffrage leader / MOTT; ANTHONY
woman's work basket / CABAS
womb / MATRIX; UTERUS
wombat / KOALA; MARSUPIAL
wombed / HOLLOW
women's quarters / HAREM; ZENANA; SERAGLIO, THALAMUS
women's rights militant / LIBBER
womera / THROWINGSTICK
won / PROFITED; CONQUERED
won through effort / EARNED
wonder / AWE; MARVEL, RARITY; MIRACLE, PRODIGY; AMAZEMENT
Wonder State / ARKANSAS
wonder of the world / PRODIGY
wonderful / AWFUL; AMAZING, STRANGE; STRIKING; ADMIRABLE
wondering fear / AWE
wonderland / COCKAIGNE, DREAMLAND
wonderland visitor / ALICE
wonderless / BLASE
wonderment / SURPRISE
wonderstruck / AMAZED; BEWILDERED
wonderwork / MAGIC; MIRACLE
wondrous / MIRACULOUS
wonky / SHAKY
wont / HABIT, USAGE; CUSTOM; PRACTICE
wonted / USUAL
woo / SUE; COURT; INVITE; SOLICIT
wood / ELM, FIR, OAK; ALOE, CLUB, HOLT, PINE, TEAK, WOLD; BALSA, BEECH, BIRCH, CAHUY, CEDAR, COPSE, EBONY, GROVE, MAPLE, TREES, XYLEM
wood c.f. / HYL; HYLO, LIGN, XYLO
wood adder / GECKO
wood alcohol / METHANOL
wood ant / TERMITE; CARPENTER
wood ash substance / POTASH
wood betony / LOUSEWORT
wood bin / CRIB
wood binder / EDDER
wood coal / LIGNITE; CHARCOAL
wood deity / NAT; FAUN
wood of East Indian tree / ENG, SAL; TEAK
wood fiber / BAST
wood fragments / COOM; COOMB; SAWDUST
wood in growth / TREE
wood gum / XYLAN
wood hen / WEKA

wood hyacinth / SQUILL; HAREBELL
wood ibis / STORK
wood joint / TENON; MORTISE
wood knot / KNAG
wood layer/ PLY; VENEER
wood louse / SLATER, SOWBUG; PILLBUG
wood nymph / MOTH; DRYAD, DRYAS, NAPEA, OREAD, SATYR; SPRITE; HAMADRYAD
wood ox / ANOA
wood partridge / GROUSE
wood pigeon / RINGDOVE
wood pore / LENTICEL
wood prop / SPRAG
wood pulp product / NEWSPRINT
wood pussy / SKUNK
wood of the sandarac tree / ALERCE
wood sorrel / OCA, OCE, OKA; OXALIS
wood spike / PEG; TRENAIL
wood spirit / NAT; FAUN
wood striping / ROE
wood used as a brake /SPRAG
woodbine/ HONEYSUCKLE
woodblock / WOODCUT
wood-boring larva / SAWYER
woodchopper / LOGGER; FORESTER
woodchuck / MARMOT; MOONACK
woodcock /GULL; SIMPLETON
woodcraft/ TRACKING
woodcut/ XYLOGRAPH
woodcutter / FELLER, SAWYER
wood-dwelling /NEMORAL
wood-eating / LIGNIVOROUS
wood-eating insect / TERMITE
wooded / BOSKY; SYLVAN; ARBORED
wooded countryside / BOSCAGE
wooded hill / HOLT
wooden / STIFF, TREEN; STOLID
wooden bar / ROD
wooden bench / SETTEE
wooden brick / NOG; DOOK
wooden bucket / SOE
wooden cleat / BATTEN
wooden collar / CANG; CANGUE
wooden container / BOX, TUB
wooden cup / NOGGIN
wooden fastener / FID, NOG, PEG; DOWEL
wooden golf club / SPOON; DRIVER; BRASSIE
wooden hammer / MALLET
wooden horse / STRATAGEM
wooden horse's builder / EPEIUS
wooden implement / CLUB
wooden Indian's merchandise / CIGARS
wooden nickel / TOKEN
wooden pail / SOE; BUCKET
wooden peg / NOG, PIN; SKEG

wooden pin / FID, NOG, PEG; COAG, COAK; DOWEL, SPILE, THOLE
wooden pole / ROD; STAFF
wooden shoe / GETA; SABOT; PATTEN
wooden statue in Guildhall / GOG; MAGOG
wooden strip / LATH; BATTEN
wooden vessel / CASK; BUCKET
wooden walls / SHIPS; PALISADE
wooden wedding / FIFTH
woodenhead / BLOCKHEAD
wooden-soled shoe / CLOG
woodland / TREES, WOODS; FOREST
woodland bird / TANAGER
woodland path / TRAIL
woodland space / GLADE
woodland spirit / PAN; FAUN; DRYAD, SATYR; SILENUS; HAMADRYAD
woodlot / WOODFARM
woodman / CUTTER, HUNTER
woodnote / BIRDSONG
woodpecker / CHAB; FLICKER
woodpeckers, pert. to / PICINE
woodpile / CORDWOOD
woods / COPSE, GROVE, TREES; FOREST; WOODLAND
wood-shaping tool / ADZ; ADZE
woodsman / FORESTER
wood-turning machine / LATHE
woodwind / OBOE; FLUTE; BASSOON, PICCOLO; CLARINET
woodwork / MOLDING; WAINSCOTING
woodwork fastener / FID, NOG, PEG; NAIL; DOWEL, SCREW
woodworker / JOINER; CARPENTER
woodworking class / SHOP
woodworking tool / ADZ; ADZE
woodworm / BORER; WEEVIL
woody coal / LIGNITE
woody grass stem / REED
woody plant / TREE
woody shoot / ROD; TWIG
woody spike of corn / COB
woody tissue of a plant / XYLEM
wooer / SUER; SUITOR
woof / ABB; WEFT; TEXTURE
wooing / COURTSHIP
wooingly / SEDUCTIVELY
wool / HAIR, LANA; ANGORA
wool cap / TUQUE
wool colored / BEIGE
wool fat / LANOLIN
wool grader / CLASSER
wool grease / LANOLIN; LANOLINE
wool knot / NEP; BURL, NOIL
wool measure / TOD; HEER
wool package / BALE; FADGE
wool surface / NAP, NEP; PILE

wool tree / CEIBA
wool variety / ALPACA, ANGORA, MERINO; CHALLIS
wool wave / CRIMP
wooled / UNSHORN
woolen blanket material / YERGA
woolen fabric / LAIN; BEIGE, SERGE, TAMIN, TAMIS, TWEED; FRISCA, KERSEY, MERINO, MOREEN, RATINE, TAMINE, TAMINY, TAMISE, TARTAN; CHALLIS, DELAINE, ESTAMIN, ETAMINE, STAMMEL, TABINET; ESTAMINE, PRUNELLA
woolen refuse / FUD; MUNGO
woolen shawl / PAISLEY
woolen sieve / TAMIS, TAMMY
woolen singlet / JERSEY
woolen thread / YARN
woolfell / PELT
woolgathering / WANDERING
woolhead / BUFFLEHEAD
woolies / UNDERWEAR
woolpack / BALE
woolsorter's disease / ANTHRAX
Woolworth store / FIVEANDTEN
wooly / FLEECY, LANATE, LANOSE
wooly bear / CATERPILLAR
wooly clouds / CUMULUS
wooly hair / SHAG; SHAGGY
wooly herb / POLY
wooly pyrol / URD
woozy / DRUNK; BEFUDDLED
word / IDEA, TERM; ORDER; PHRASE, REPORT, SIGNAL, SPEECH; ACCOUNT
word, c.f. / ONOMATO
word of affirmation / YEA, YES; AMEN
word background / CONTEXT
word blindness / ALEXIA
word book / LEXICON; GLOSSARY
word to call cows / BOS
word deafness / APHASIA
word of excuse / SORRY
word game / CRAMBO; ANAGRAMS
word of God / LOGOS
word in handwriting on the wall / MENE; TEKEL; UPHARSIN
word of honor / PAROL; PAROLE, PLEDGE; PROMISE
word imitating a sound / ONOMATOPE
word indicating action / VERB
word indicating choice / OR
word of lamentation / ALAS
word of misuse/ MALAPROPISM
word of mouth / PAROL
word of negation / NO; NAY, NOT
word of opposed meaning / ANTONYM
word of pity / ALAS
word play / PUN

word of promise / PLEDGE
word in psalm / SELAH
word puzzle / REBUS; ANAGRAM, CHARADE; ACROSTIC; CROSSWORD
word of recognition / PASSWORD; SHIBBOLETH
word repetition / PLOCE
word of similar meaning / SYNONYM
word of similar sound / HOMOMORPH
word of similar spelling / HETERONYM
word square / PALINDROME
word to the wise / TIP; CLUE
word by word / VERBATIM
word for word / LITERAL
wordage / VERBIAGE; VOCABULARY
wording / PHRASEOLOGY
wordless / MUM; TACIT; SILENT
wordless acting / MIME
wordless play / DUMBSHOW
words of assent / IDO; AMEN; AYEAYE
words of play / SIDE; LINES
Wordsworth flower / DAFFODIL
Wordsworth poem / SONNET; PRELUDE
wordy / PROLIX; DIFFUSE, TEDIOUS
work / DO, GO; ACT, SEW; MOIL, TOIL; CHARE, LABOR; DRUDGE, MANAGE, REMARK; OPERATE, PERFORM. JOB; DEED, DUTY, FEAT, OPUS, TASK; CHORE; EFFORT; BUSINESS. See also composition
work aimlessly / POTTER, PUTTER
work appearing in successive parts / SERIAL
work of art / GEM; ETCHING
work at / DO
work at continually / PLY
work basket / CABAS
work clothes / OVERALLS; COVERALLS
work crew / GANG
work dough / KNEAD
work at an extra job / MOONLIGHT
work for / SERVE
work gang / CREW
work group / CREW, GANG, HIVE
work with hands / KNEAD
work hard / PEG, PLY, TEW; MOIL
work with head / STUDY
work of Homer / ILIAD
work horse / DRUDGE
work in / INCLUDE; INTERJECT
work inefficiently / PUTTER
work the land / FARM

work with a loom / WEAVE
work measurement unit / JOULE
work of music / OPUS
work on / PERSUADE, PRESSURE
work out / DO; SOLVE; TRANSLATE
work out in detail / TRACE
work over / REDO; RENEW; REHASH
work over to new form / RECAST
work party / BEE; SOCIAL
work persistently / PLY; TOIL
work and press into a mass /
  KNEAD
work superficially / PLAY; DABBLE,
  POTTER, PUTTER
work task / JOB; CHORE, STINT
work together / TEAM; COLLABO-
  RATE
work unit / ERG; ERGON
work up /RILE; ANGER, SHAPE;
  SKETCH
workable / FEASIBLE
workaday / PROSAIC; EVERYDAY
workbag / KIT; CABAS; TOOLBAG
worker /ANT; BEE; HAND; TOILER
worker insect/ ERGATES
worker in rattan / CANER
workers / MEN; CREW, GANG
worker's group/ ILO; UNION
worker's union / AUM, CIO, UMW
workfellow/ MATE
workhouse / ALMSHOUSE; RE-
  FORMATORY
working/ INUSE; TWITCHING
working agreement / CODE
working automaton / ROBOT
working for /UNDER. EARNING
working hours / WORKDAY
working implement / TOOL
working place /PLANT; OFFICE
workless / IDLE; UNEMPLOYED
workman /HAND; TOILER; ARTI-
  SAN, LABORER; MECHANIC; AR-
  TIFICER
workmanship / SKILL; EXECUTION
workout / EXERCISE, PRACTICE
works / ALL; WHOLE
workshop / LAB; STUDIO; ATELIER
world / LIFE; EARTH, GLOBE; COS-
  MOS, DOMAIN, PEOPLE, PLANET
world, pert. to / TEMPORAL
world beyond / HEREAFTER
world fair / EXPOSITION
world organization / UN; LEAGUE
world war agency / OPA, OSS, OWI
World War I battle / MARNE,
  SOMME, YPRES; VERDUN
World War I group / AEF
World War II agency / OPA
World War II theatre / ETO
world wide / GLOBAL; PANDEMIC
worldling / MATERIALIST

worldly / HUMAN; SORDID;
  EARTHLY
worldly-wise / SOPHISTICATED
world-weary / BORED
worm / ASP, EIS, ESS, IPO, LOA;
  BAIT, ERIA, LURG; CADEW,
  TINEA; MAGGOT; ANNELID
worm eaten / MAGGOTY; IMPAIRED
worm grass / PINKROOT
worm larva / LOA
worm out / PUMP
worm-eating mammal / TENREC
wormer / ANGLER
wormil / BOTFLY, MAGGOT
wormlike / VERMIFORM
wormlike form / LARVA
wormseed / SANTONICA
worms / BAIT
wormwood / MOXA; SAGEBRUSH
wormy / ACRAWL; CRAWLING
worn / USED; MAGGED, SECOND
worn down / TIRED; ERODED
worn garment / DUD
worn out / OLD; JADED, PASSE,
  SPENT, TIRED, WEARY; EFFETE
worn into shreds / TORN; FRAYED,
worn-out horse / NAG; HACK, JADE,
  PLUG
worricow / BUGBEAR
worried / IRKED, TIRED; WEARIED
worriment / TROUBLE
worry / IRK, NAG, RUX, VEX; BAIT,
  CARE, CARK, FRET, GALL, STEW;
  ANNOY, CHAFE, FEEZE, TEASE;
  BOTHER
worse / BAD; LESS; POORER
worsen / DETERIORATE
worsened / DISPARAGED
worship / ADORE, DEIFY, EXALT,
  HONOR; REVERE; IDOLIZE, RE-
  SPECT. DULIA; HOMAGE, LATRIA
worshiped animal / TOTEM
worshiper of false gods / IDOLATOR
worshiper of Siva / SAIVA
worshipful / REVERENT
worst / BEAT, BEST; UPSET; DE-
  FEAT; OVERTHROW. LEAST;
  POOREST
worst way / INTENSELY
worsted / DEFEATED. WOOL, YARN
worsted cloth / SERGE; TAMINE;
  ETAMINE
worsted yarn / CADDIS
wort / HERB; PLANT
worth / USE; RATE; MERIT, PRICE
worth having / DESIRABLE
worthiness / EXCELLENCE
worthless / NG; BAD; RACA, VILE
worthless bit / ORT, RAP; SCRAP;
  STIVER
worthless dog / CUR

worthless fellow / BUM; IDLER, LOSEL, LOSER; LOAFER
worthless hand at cards / BUST
worthless horse / JADE
worthless part / HUSK; CHAFF, DREGS; GANGUE
worthless scrap / ORT
worthless shell / HUSK
worthless thing / TRIPE
worthlessness / NUGACITY
worthwhile / REWARDING
worthy / NOBLE; EMINENT; LAUD-ABLE, VALUABLE; ESTIMABLE
worthy of mention / DESERVING
wot / KNOW; KNOWS
Wotan / ODIN; WODEN
woubit / WOOLYBEAR
would-be / PARVENU, UPSTART
wound / BREACH, INJURY, TRAUMA; LACERATION. HURT; SCATHE
wound in heraldry / VULN
wound covering / SCAR, TAPE; BAN-DAGE; DRESSING
wound exudation / PUS; ICHOR, SERUM; SANIES
wound the feelings / PUTOUT; SCATHE
wound with a horn / GORE
wound mark / CUT; SCAR
wounded / HURT; INJURED
woundless / UNHURT; INVULNER-ABLE
wound's crust / SCAB
woven / TEXTILE
woven cloth / MESH; FABRIC
woven fabric / WEB; ARRAS, CLOTH; TISSUE; BLANKET, TEXTILE, TEX-TURE
woven mesh / NET
wow / SUCCESS; KNOCKOUT
wrack / RUIN; CLOUD, VAPOR; SEA-WEED; DESTRUCTION
wrack and ruin / SMITHEREENS
wraith / GHOST; APPARITION
wraithlike / SPOOKY; SPECTRAL
wrangle / JAR; SPAR; BRAWL
wrangler / COWBOY
wrap / CERE, ROLL, COVER; EN-FOLD. SHAWL, STOLE; WRAPPER
wrap a dead body / CERE
wrap up / COVER; FINISH
wraparound / SARI; SHAWL; SARONG
wrapper / SHAWL; JACKET; HOUSE-COAT
wrapping / SHEATH; ENVELOPE
wrapping paper / KRAFT
wrasse / BALLAN
wrath / IRE; FURY, RAGE; ANGER; PASSION; RESENTMENT; INDIG-NATION

wrathful / HOT; ANGRY, IRATE; RAGING; ENRAGED, FRETFUL, FURIOUS; INDIGNANT; INFURI-ATED
wraxen / STRAINED
wreak / EXACT; GRATIFY, INFLICT
wreath / LEI; BAYS; CROWN, GREEN, TORSE; ANADEM; CHAP-LET, CIRCLET
wreath in heraldry / ORLE; TORSE
wreath of olive / IRESINE
wreathe / COIL, WIND; TWINE, TWIST; INFOLD; ENCIRCLE
wreathy / SPIRAL
wreck / RUINS; DEBRIS; REMAINS, RUBBISH; SHIPWRECK; DESOLA-TION; DESTRUCTION. RAZE, RUIN; WASTE
wrecked ship / HULK
wrecker / TOWTRUCK
wrecking ball / SKULLCRACKER
wrecking bar / PRY; LEVER
wrecking company / SALVAGERS
Wren edifice / STPAULS
wrench / BEND; TWIST, WREST, WRING; SPRAIN. SPANNER
wrest / REND, TURN; EXACT, TWIST WRING; SNATCH; DISTORT
wrest from / USURP
wrest illegally / EXTORT
wrestle / STRIVE, TUSSLE; CON-TEND, GRAPPLE; STRUGGLE
wrestler's cushion / MAT
wrestler's grip / NELSON; CHAN-CERY, SCISSORS; WRISTLOCK
wrestling champion in Japan / YOKOZUNA
wrestling as combat / JUDO; JUJITSU
wrestling in Japan / SUMO
wrestling throw / HIPE, HYPE, THRAW
wretch / KNAVE, ROGUE, SCAMP; PARIAH; CAITIFF, CULLION, OUT-CAST
wretched / BAD, ILL, SAD; MEAN, POOR, VILE; DREAR; DISMAL, PALTRY, SHABBY; FORLORN, UNHAPPY
wretchedly / FEEBLY
wretchedness / WOE; GRIEF; MIS-ERY, SORROW; DISTRESS; AFFLICTION
wriggle / TWIST; SQUIRM
wriggling / EELY; WRIGGLY
wright / ARTISAN, WORKMAN
Wright invention / AIRPLANE
wring / PAIN; TWIST, WREST; EX-TORT, HARASS, WRENCH; DIS-TORT
wringer / ORDEAL

wringing wet / SOAKED; SOPPING

wrinkle / FOLD, RUCK; CRIMP, CREASE, FURROW, RIMPLE; CRINKLE. RUGA, SEAM; RIDGE, TRICK; DEVICE

wrinkled / RUGATE, RUGOSE, RUGOUS; CREASED; CORRUGATED

wrinkles / RUGAE

wrinkly / GROOVED; PUCKERED

wrist / CARPUS

wrist bone / SCAPHOID

wrist guard / BRACE

wristband / CUFF; BRACELET

writ / BIBLE; DOCUMENT, SUBPOENA

writ to arrest / CAPIAS

writ of execution / ELEGIT

writ including delay / NISI

writ to a lower court / CERTIORARI

writ to show cause / PRECIPE

writ summoning a jury / VENIRE

write / PEN; DRAW; FRAME; INDITE, INVENT, SCRAWL, SCRIBE, SCRIVE

write carelessly / SCRAWL

write down / NOTE; RECORD

write marginal notes / GLOSS; POSTIL

write music / NOTATE; COMPOSE

write one's name / SIGN

write off / ANNUL; CANCEL

write poorly / SCRAWL

write up / TICKET; DESCRIBE; PUBLICIZE

writer / POET; DITER; AUTHOR, PENMAN, SCRIBE; COMPOSER

writer of fiction / NOVELIST

writer of verse / BARD, POET; ELEGIST; LYRICIST, SONGSTER

write-up / PUFF; STORY; ARTICLE

writhe / TWIST; SQUIRM; DISTORT, PERVERT

writhen / CONTORTED

writing / HAND; DOCUMENT

writing art / RHETORIC; PENMANSHIP; CALLIGRAPHY

writing character / WEDGE; LETTER, UNCIAL

writing flourish / CURLICUE

writing fluid / INK

writing implement / PEN; CHALK; PENCIL, STYLUS; BALLPOINT

writing machine / TYPEWRITER

writing paper / STATIONERY

writing paper package / REAM

writing paper size / CAP; DEMY

writing surface / PAPER; BLACKBOARD

writing table / DESK; ESCRITOIRE

writing tablet / PAD; SLATE

writing on the wall / MENE; TEKEL; UPHARSIN

written afterthought / PS; POSTSCRIPT

written agreement / PACT; CARTEL, TREATY

written below the line / SUBSCRIPT

written communication / MEMO, NOTE; LETTER; MEMORANDUM

written discourse / PAPER; THESIS; DISSERTATION

written exposition / TREATISE

written instrument / DEED; LEASE

written law / STATUTE

written promise to pay / IOU; NOTE

written reminder / MEMO; MEMORANDUM

written in seven languages / HEPTAGLOT

wrong / ERR, SIN; ABUSE; HARASS, INJURE; OPPRESS, VIOLATE. TORT; CRIME, ERROR; MISTAKE. BAD; EVIL; FALSE, UNFIT; FAULTY. OFF, OUT; AMISS

wrong, pref. / MAL; MIS

wrong act / TORT, MISDEED

wrong font / PI

wrong legally / GUILT; GUILTY

wrong move / MISSTEP

wrong name / MISNOMER

wrongdoer / FELON; SINNER; CULPRIT; CRIMINAL, EVILDOER

wrongdoing / SIN; EVIL; CRIME; FELONY; SINNING; INIQUITY

wronged / HURT; INJURED

wrongful / WRONG; SINFUL, UNFAIR, UNJUST, WICKED; CONTRARY

wrongful act / TORT

wrong-headed / OBSTINATE

wrongly / IMPROPERLY, MISTAKENLY

wrote / PENNED; INDITED, SCRIBED

wroth / ANGRY, IRATE; INCENSED

wrought / DONE; SHAPED, WORKED; EFFECTED, PRODUCED; PERFORMED; ELABORATED; MANUFACTURED

wrought up / FLUSHED; AGITATED

wry / BEND; TWIST, WREST; WRITHE; DEVIATE, DISTORT. FALSE; TURNED, WARPED; TWISTED; DISTORTED

wry face / MOUE; GRIMACE

wryneck / LOXIA; WHIPLASH; WOODPECKER; TORTICOLLIS

wryneck genus / JYNX

wud / MAD

wunderkind / PRODIGY

wurst / SAUSAGE

Wurttemberg measure / IMI

wych-elm / WITCHHAZEL

Wycliffite / LOLLARD

wye / INTERSECTION

wynd / ALLEY
Wyoming capital / CHEYENNE
Wyoming city / CODY; CASPER
Wyoming mountain / MORAN, TETON
Wyoming mountain range / TETON
Wyoming national park / YELLOW-STONE

Wyoming peak / GANNETT
Wyoming river / PLATTE; BIGHORN
Wyoming state flower / PAINT-BRUSH
Wyoming state nickname / EQUALITY
Wyoming Valley fort / FORTYFORT

X

x / EX, TEN
xanthic / YELLOW, YELLOWISH
Xanthippe / SCOLD, SHREW
Xanthippe's spouse / SOCRATES
Xanthos / SCAMANDER
xebec / BOAT; CHEBEC, VESSEL
xenodochium / INN; HOTEL; HOSTEL
xenodochy / HOSPITALITY
Xenophon's book / ANABASIS
xeransis / XERASIA; DESICCATION
xeres / JEREZ; SHERRY

xerophyte / CACTUS; SUCCULENT
xerotic / DRY
x-ray / ROENTGEN; TOMOGRAPH
x-ray discoverer / ROENTGEN
xylem / WOOD
xylograph / WOODCUT
xylophone / SARON; MARIMBA; GIGELIRA; INSTRUMENT
xyst / STOA; XYSTUS; PORTICO, TERRACE
xyster / SCRAPER

Y

y / WYE, YOD, YOK; YOGH
yabber / JABBER
yacht / SAIL
yacht basin / MARINA
yacht pennant / BURGEE
yachting / SAILING; CRUISING
yager / JAGER
yahoo / CUR, YAP; LOUT; BRUTE, CLOUT, CLOWN; RUSTIC, SAV-AGE; GREENHORN. BRUTAL, COARSE; VICIOUS; IGNORANT
Yahweh / JEHOVAH
yak / OX; SARLAK, SARLYK
Yale blue / RAMESES
Yale men / ELIS
yaller / LOW; VULGAR, YELLOW; COWARDLY; DESPICABLE; CON-TEMPTIBLE. BETRAYER, IN-FORMER
Yalta's peninsula / CRIMEA
Yalta's sea / BLACK
yam / HOI, UBE, UBI, UVE, UVI, POTATO
yammer / SHOUT, WHINE; QUAR-REL; COMPLAIN
yang's opposite / YIN
Yangtze above Suchow / KINSHA
Yangtze tributary / WU; HAN
yank / JERK; TWIST
Yankee / RUTH; MANTLE; AMER-ICAN, DIMAGGIO
yap / BARK, YELP. HICK, RUBE. SILLY; WORTHLESS
Yap stone money / FEI
yard / QUAD, SPAR; CROFT, GARTH,

VERGE; AREAWAY, VIRGATE. PEN; STORE
yard grass / POA
yarn / CLEW, FLAX, GARN, KNOP, SLUB, TALE, WARP; STORY; CREWEL
yarn count / TYPP
yarn fiber / LINT; STRAND
yarn measure / LEA; HANK; SKEIN
yarn for warp / ABB
yarran / SHRUB; ACACIA, WATTLE. WILD; UNCULTIVATED
yarrow / MILFOIL
yashmak / VEIL
yataghan / BALAS, SABER; DAGGER
yaup / CRY; GAPE, PAIN; DISTRESS. TITMOUSE
yaupon / HOLLY; CASSENA, CAS-SINE
yaw / BREW, RISE; FROTH, STEER; DEVIATE
yawl / JOLLYBOAT
yawn / GANE, GANT, GAPE, CHASM
yawning / AGAPE; DROWSY, GAP-ING; OSCITANT
yawning hollow / CHASM
yaws / PIAN; FRAMBESIA
yclept / NAMED; CALLED
Ye / YOU; THEE, THOU
yea / PRO, YES; TRULY; AFFIRMA-TIVE
yean / EAN; LAMB
year / TIME; ANNUM; PERIOD; VIN-TAGE
year of the reign / AR

yearbook / ANNUAL; ALMANAC; ALMANACK
yearling sheep / TAG
yearly / ANNUAL; ETESIAN; ANNUALLY, PERANNUM
yearly celebration / ANNIVERSARY
yearn / ACHE, LONG, PANT, PINE; EMOTE; ASPIRE, DESIRE, HANKER
yearn for / COVET, CRAVE
yearning / WISTFUL
years after Christ / AD
year's crops/ ANNONA
years between eleven and twenty / TEENS
years of one's life / AGE
year's record / ANNAL; ANNALS
yeast / BARM, BEES, FOAM; FROTH, SPUME; LEAVEN; FERMENT; LEAVENING
yeasty / LIGHT; FROTHY; FRIVOLOUS
yegg / BURGLAR; SAFECRACKER
yell / CRY; BAWL, GOWL, HOWL, ROAR, YOWL; SHOUT, UTTER; SCREAM, SHRIEK, SQUEAL; SCREECH
yell guide / CHEERLEADER
yellow / BUFF, YOLK; AMBER, OCHER, OCHRE, XANTH; CHROME, GOLDEN, MELINE; CITRINE, SAFFRON, XANTHIC; JAUNDICED
yellow, c.f. / XANTH
yellow alder / SAGEROSE
yellow arsenic / ORPIMENT
yellow bark / CALISAYA
yellow bill / SCOTER
yellow bird / CANARY, ORIOLE; GOLDFINCH, SQUAWFISH
yellow brown / DUN, TAN; TOPAZ; SORREL
yellow bugle / EVE, IVA
yellow dye / WELD, WOLD; URANIN
yellow fish / IDE, ORF; ORFE
yellow fossilized resin / AMBER
yellow like gold / GILT
yellow gray color / DRAB
yellow green chrysolite / EPIDOTE, PERIDOT
yellow iris / SEDGE
yellow ocher / SIL; LIMONITE
yellow pigment / SIL; CHROME; ETIOLIN
yellow pond lily / NUPHAR
yellow potato / YAM
yellow race / MONGOL; CHINESE; ORIENTAL; MONGOLIAN
yellow river / HWANGHO
yellow sea / HWANGHAI
yellow toadflax / RANSTEAD
yellow weed / RAPE; GOLDENROD
yellowback / NOVEL; MUSSEL

yellowbelly / BREAM; COWARD; SQUAWFISH
yellowgowan / CROWFOOT; DANDELION
yellowhammer / YITE; AMMER; FLICKER; WOODPECKER
yellowish / SALLOW; XANTHIC; ICTERINE; LUTESCENT
yellowish brown / TAN; ALOMA
yellowish green / OLIVE; ONDINE
yellowish red / AMBER, CORAL, SANDY
yellowlegs / SANDPIPER
yellows / ICTERUS; JAUNDICE
yellowthroat / WARBLER
yelp / YAP, YIP; BARK, KIYI, YOUP
Yemen capital / SANA; SANAA
Yemen city / DAMAR, MOCHA; DHAMAR; HODEIDA
Yemen ruler / IMAM
Yemen seaport / ADEN; MOCHA
Yemenite / ARAB; YEMENI
yen / DESIRE; LONGING; DESIRING
yeoman / FARMER; FREEHOLDER
yes / AY; AYE, IDO, YEA; GRANTED; AFFIRMATIVE
yesterday, pert. to / YESTER; HESTERNAL
yet / BUT, EEN; THUS, STILL, WHILE; THOUGH; BESIDES, FURTHER, HOWEVER; MOREOVER; EVENTUALLY, ULTIMATELY; NEVERTHELESS; NOTWITHSTANDING. SOFAR; ATLAST; THUSFAR
yew / BOW; CONIFER
yew, pert. to / TAXINE
yew genus / TAXUS
Yiddish / JEWISH
yield / BOW, NET; BEAR, BEND, CEDE, GIVE, OBEY; FORGO, RELAX, WAIVE; ACCEDE, AFFORD, ASSENT, COMPLY, RELENT, RETURN, SUBMIT, SUPPLY; CONCEDE, FURNISH, PRODUCE, SUCCUMB; ACQUIESCE, SURRENDER; RELINQUISH
yield gold / PAN
yield point/STRAIN, STRESS
yield under pressure/ GIVE; RELENT
yielded / CEDED; RENDERED, SOFTENED
yielding / SOFT; SUPPLE; COMPLIANT, CONCEDING, PRODUCING; SUBMISSIVE; UNRESISTING; ACCOMMODATING. COMPLIANCE
yielding point/ STRAIN, STRESS
yielding temporarily / TEMPORIZING
yip / YAP; YELP
yodel / SING; WARBLE
yoga/ JNANA; BHAKTI
Yogi /FAKIR, SWAMI; ASCETIC

yoke / JOIN; ATTACH, COUPLE; CON-FINE, CONJOIN, CONNECT, EN-SLAVE, HARNESS; ASSOCIATE. BAR, TIE; BOND, LINK, TEAM; CANGUE; SERVICE, SLAVERY; FASTENER; SERVITUDE; RUD-DERHEAD

yoke of animals / SPAN

yoked / TEAMED; CONNECTED

yoked animals / OXEN

yokefellow / PAL; MATE; ASSOCI-ATE, COMPANION

yokel / OAF; HICK, RUBE; RUSTIC; BUMPKIN

yolk / YELLOW; VITELLUS

Yom Kippur / HOLIDAY

yon / THAT; THERE; YONDER; DIS-TANT

yonder / YON; THERE; OVERTHERE

yoni / SAKTI; SHAKTI

yore / AGO, ELD, OLD; PASSED

yorker / TICE

Yorkshire city / HULL; LEEDS; SHEFFIELD

Yorkshire river / URE; AIRE, OUSE; SWALE; DERWENT

you / YE; THEE, THOU; PRONOUN

you and I / US, WE

you and me / US, WE

you people / YE

young / RAW; FRESH; JUVENILE, VIGOROUS, YOUTHFUL; INEXPE-RIENCED. YOUTH; OFFSPRING

young actress / STARLET

young animal / CUB, KID, PUP; COLT; WHELP

young animals / BROOD; LITTER

young antelope / KID

young barracuda / SPET

young bear/ CUB

young bird / NESTLING

young bird of prey / EYAS; EAGLET

young bluefish / SNAPPER

young boy / LAD; SHAVER

young cat / KIT; KITTEN

young chicken / FRYER; PULLET

young child / TAD; TOT; BABY; IN-FANT

young cod / SCROD, SPRAG

young cow / CALF: HEIFER

young deer / FAWN

young demon / IMP

young dog / PUP; PUPPY

young eel / ELVER

young fish / FRY; PARR; ALEVIN

young flower / BUD

young fox / CUB

young frog / TADPOLE

young girl / LASS; MISSY; MAIDEN

young goat / KID

young hare / LEVERET

young hawk / EYAS; BRANCHER

young hen / CHICK; PULLET; CHICKEN

young herring / BRIT

young hog / SHOAT, SHOTE; PIGLET

young horse / COLT, FOAL

young kangaroo / JOEY

young lad / GOSSOON

young lady / LASS; BELLE; DAM-SEL, MAIDEN

young lion / CUB; LIONET

young mackerel / SPIKE

young man / BOY, LAD; CHAP; LADDY; ADONIS, FELLOW

young mare / FILLY

young mature salmon / GRILSE

young menhaden / SARDINE

young men's group / YMCA

young oak / ACORN

young owl / OWLET

young oyster / SPAT

young pig / ELT; GILT; GRICE; SHOAT; SHOATE

young pigeon / SQUAB

young plant / SET; SHOOT; SEED-LING

young rabbit / LEVERET

young reporter / CUB

young salmon / MERT, PARR; SMOLT, SPROD; GRILSE; ESS-LING; LASPRING

young seal / PUP

young sheep / LAMB

young socialite / DEB; DEBUTANTE

young sow / GILT

young swan / CYGNET

young swine / PIG; GILT; SHOAT, SHOATE

young tree / SAPLING

young turkey / POULT

young woman / GIRL; NYMPH; MAIDEN

young women's group / YWCA

young zebra / COLT

younger / TOT; CADET; JUNIOR

youngest son / CADET

youngster / BOY, KID, LAD, TAD, TOT; GIRL; SHAVER; SPALDEEN

younker / STRIPLING

your / THY; THINE

yours and mine / OUR; OURN, OURS

youth / BOY, LAD, TAD; TEEN; MINOR; BOYHOOD, GOSSOON; NEOPHYTE, TEENAGER; STRIP-LING, YOUNGSTER

youth shelter / HOSTEL

youthful / EARLY, FRESH, YOUNG; BOYISH, CALLOW, NEANIC, UN-RIPE; PUERILE, TEENAGE; CHILD-ISH, IMMATURE, JUVENILE, VIG-OROUS. MINORITY; JUVENILITY; ADOLESCENCE

youthful years / TEENS

youze / CHEETAH
yowl / CRY; HOWL, YELL
Yseult / ISOLDE
Yseult's husband / MARK
Yseult's lover / TRISTRAM
Yucatan Indian / MAYA
yucca fiber / ISOTE, ISTLE, IXTLE, IXTLI, IZOTE
yucca-like plant / SOTOL
Yugoslav / SERB; CROAT; SERBIAN, SLOVENE
Yugoslavia capital / BELGRADE
Yugoslavian city / ZAGREB; SKOPLJE
Yugoslavian money / PARA; DINAR
Yugoslavian partisan leader / MIKHAILOVITCH

Yugoslavian premier / TITO
Yugoslavian province / BANAT
Yugoslavian river / UNA; IBAR, SAVA; DRINA
Yugoslavian town / STIP; VELES
Yukian Indian / TATU
Yukon Indian / TAKU
Yukon mountain peak / LOGAN
Yukon tributary / PELLY
Yule / YULETIDE; CHRISTMASTIDE
Yuman Indian / MOHAVE; YAVAPAI
Yum-Yum's friend / KOKO; PEEPBO; NANKIPOO; PITTISING
Yuncan Indian / CHIMU
yungan / DUGONG
yurga / YABOO
yurt / TENT; YURTA

Z

Z / ZED, ZEE; IZZARD
zac / IBEX
zacatilla / COCHINEAL
Zaire / CONGO
Zaire capital / KINSHASA
zalophus / SEAL; SEALION
zamang / RAINTREE
Zambia capital / LUSAKA
Zambia first president / KAUNDA
Zambia lake / KARIBA
Zambia monetary unit / KWACHA
zany / CLOWN; BUFFOON. FOOLISH
Zarathustra / ZOROASTER
zayat / HUT; SHELTER
zeal / ELAN; ARDOR; FERVOR, WARMTH; PASSION; DEVOTION, FERVENCY, INTEREST; EAGERNESS, INTENSITY; CORDIALITY, ENTHUSIASM; DEVOTEDNESS, EARNESTNESS
zealot / BIGOT; DEVOTEE, DREAMER, FANATIC; VISIONARY; ENTHUSIAST
zealous / AVID, KEEN, WARM; EAGER, READY, SWIFT; ARDENT, FERVID, PROMPT; DEVOTED, EARNEST, FERVENT, GLOWING; DILIGENT; STEADFAST; PASSIONATE; ENTHUSIASTIC
zealous advocate / PARTISAN
zealous follower / SECTARY
Zebec / XEBEC
Zebedee's son / JOHN; JAMES
zebrawood / ARAROBA
zebu-yak hybrid / ZO; ZOH; ZOBO
zed / ZEE
zenana / HAREM
zenith / TOP; ACME, APEX, PEAK; HEIGHT, SUMMIT; HIGHEST, MAXIMUM; MERIDIAN, PINNACLE; CULMINATION
zenith's opposite / NADIR; LOWEST

Zeno's follower / STOIC
zephyr / AIR; WIND; BREEZE
zeppelin / BLIMP; AIRSHIP, BALLOON
zero / NIL; CIPHER, NAUGHT, NOUGHT; NOTHING
zest / ELAN, GUST, TANG; GUSTO, SAUCE, SAVOR, SMACK, SPICE, TASTE; FLAVOR, RELISH; APPETITE, PLEASURE; ENJOYMENT
zesty / SAPID; PIQUANT
zetetic / SEARCHER; INQUIRING
Zeus / ZAN; JOVE; DYAUS; JUPITER
Zeus' birthplace / IDA
Zeus' brother / AIDES, HADES; POSEIDON
Zeus' daughter / ATE; HEBE; IRENE; ATHENA; ARTEMIS
Zeus' epithet / AMMON, SOTER
Zeus' father / KRONOS; CHRONUS
Zeus' first wife / METIS
Zeus' guardians / CURETES
Zeus' love / IO; LEDA; EUROPA; CALLISTO
Zeus' mother / RHEA
Zeus' realm / SKY; OLYMPUS
Zeus' sister / HERA; HESTIA
Zeus' son / ARES; ARCAS, ARGUS; MINOS; AEACUS, APOLLO, HERMES; PERSEUS; DIONYSUS, HERCULES
Zeus' symbol / BOLT; AEGIS
Zeus' wife / HERA, LETO, MAIA; DIONE, METIS; THEMIS; DEMETER; EURYNOME; MNEMOSYNE
zigzag ski race / SLALOM
Zilpah's son / GAD; ASHER
zinc / SPELTER; GALVANIZE
zinc ore / BLENDE
zinc slab / SPELTER
zinclike / ZINCOID

zingano / GYPSY
Zion / HILL, SION; ISRAELITES
zip / PEP; TANG; SPEED, VIGOR;
  BULLET; HISSING; IMITATIVE
zipper / TALON; FASTENER
zircon / JACINTH
zobo / OX; YAK; ZEBU
zodiac / **see** constellations and
  principal stars
zodiac sign / LEO; ARIES, LIBRA,
  VIRGO; CANCER, GEMINI, PIS-
  CES, TAURUS; SCORPIO; AQUA-
  RIUS; CAPRICORN; SAGIT-
  TARIUS
Zola novel / NANA
zonal / REGIONAL
zone / AREA, BELT; PLANE; GIRDLE,
  REGION, SPHERE; DISTRICT, DI-
  VISION; TERRITORY. ENGIRDLE
zone of action / SECTOR
zone of ecologic struggle / REGION;
  ECOTONE
zoo / PARK; MENAGERIE
zoo ship / ARK
zoogonous / BEGETTING, PRODUC-
  ING; VIVIPAROUS
zoogony / ZOOGENY
zoom / HUM
zoophagous / CARNIVOROUS

zoophyte / CORAL
Zophah's son / BEERA
zoril / POLECAT, ZORILLA
Zoroastrian / PARSI; GHEBER,
  PARSEE
Zoroastrian angel / AMESHAS-
  PENTA
Zoroastrian commentary / ZEND
Zoroastrian deity / ORMAZD; AHRI-
  MAN; AHURAMAZDA
Zoroastrian holy books / AVESTA
zorrillo / SKUNK
zorro / FOX
zounds / OONS
zucchetto / CALOTTE; SKULLCAP
zucchini / SQUASH
Zulu chief / CHAKA; DINGAAN;
  CETEWAYO; CETSHWAYO
Zulu headman / INDUNA
Zulu king / DINIZULU
Zulu language / BANTU
Zulu military force / IMPI
Zulu people / MATABELE
Zulu spear / ASSEGAI
Zululand capital / EKOWE; ESHOWE
zwieback / RUSK; BISCUIT
zylonite / CELLULOID
zymosis / FERMENTATION

AARGAU	ACTIVE	AFRICA	ALLIUM	ANEMIA	APOGEE
AARHUS	ACTUAL	AGARIC	ALLUDE	ANEMIC	APOLLO
ABACAY	ACUATE	AGENCY	ALLURE	ANGAUR	APOLOG
ABACUS	ACUITY	AGENDA	ALMOND	ANGELS	APPALL
ABADAN	ACUMEN	AGENOR	ALMOST	ANGINA	APPEAL
ABARIS	ACURIA	AGENTS	ALPACA	ANGLER	APPEAR
ABASIA	ADAGIO	AGGADA	ALPINE	ANGOLA	APPEND
ABATIS	ADDICT	AGHAST	ALRAUN	ANGORA	APPLES
ABBACY	ADDING	AGLAIA	ALSACE	ANIMAL	APPOSE
ABBESS	ADDLED	AGNAIL	ALSIKE	ANIMUS	APSARA
ABDUCT	ADDUCE	AGNAME	ALTAIR	ANITRA	APTERA
ABIJAH	ADELIE	AGNATE	ALTHEA	ANKARA	APTOTE
ABIJAN	ADENIA	AGOROT	ALUDEL	ANLACE	AQUILA
ABJECT	ADHERE	AGOUTI	ALUMNA	ANLAGE	ARABIA
ABJURE	ADIPIC	AGRAPH	ALUMNI	ANNALS	ARABIC
ABNAKI	ADJOIN	AGREED	ALVINE	ANNATS	ARABIN
ABOARD	ADJURE	AGUISH	ALWAYS	ANNEAL	ARABLE
ABOMEY	ADJUST	AIDING	ALZIRE	ANNONA	ARAGON
ABORAD	ADMIRE	AIGLET	AMADOU	ANNUAL	ARAHAT
ABORAL	ADNATE	AIGRET	AMANIA	ANOINT	ARALIE
ABOUND	ADONAI	AIKIDO	AMAZED	ANOMMA	ARAMIS
ABRADE	ADONIS	AILING	AMAZON	ANONYM	ARANDA
ABROAD	ADORER	AIMARA	AMBARI	ANOUKE	ARANGO
ABRUPT	ADRIAN	AINTAB	AMBARY	ANSCAR	ARARAS
ABSENT	ADRIFT	AIRING	AMBEER	ANSELM	ARARAT
ABSORB	ADROIT	AIRWAY	AMBIKA	ANSHAR	ARAWAK
ABSURD	ADVENT	AKIMBO	AMBLER	ANSRAK	ARCADE
ACACIA	ADVERB	ALALIA	AMBUSH	ANSWER	ARCANA
ACACIN	ADVERT	ALARIC	AMENDE	ANTCOW	ARCANE
ACADIA	ADVICE	ALARUM	AMENDS	ANTHEM	ARCARO
ACARID	ADVISE	ALASKA	AMENTI	ANTHER	ARCHED
ACATES	ADYTUM	ALATED	AMERCE	ANTIAR	ARCHER
ACCEDE	AEACUS	ALBANY	AMIDIC	ANTICS	ARCHIE
ACCENT	AECIUM	ALBERT	AMIDST	ANTLER	ARCHON
ACCEPT	AEDILE	ALBINO	AMIENS	ANTLID	ARCTIC
ACCESS	AEETES	ALBION	AMOEBA	ANTONY	ARDENT
ACCORD	AEGEAN	ALBITE	AMORAL	ANTRUM	AREOLA
ACCOST	AEGEUS	ALBOIN	AMORET	ANTUCO	AREOLE
ACCRUE	AENEAS	ALCOVE	AMOUNT	ANTUNG	ARETAS
ACCUSE	AENEID	ALCUIN	AMPERE	ANUBIS	ARGALA
ACEDIA	AEOLIA	ALECTO	AMPULE	ANURAN	ARGALI
ACETIC	AEOLIC	ALEGAR	AMRITA	ANYONE	ARGENT
ACHATE	AEOLIS	ALEPPO	AMULET	AONACH	ARGIVE
ACHENE	AEOLUS	ALERCE	AMUSIA	AORIST	ARGOSY
ACHETA	AERATE	ALETTE	ANABAS	AOSMIC	ARGUER
ACHETE	AERIAL	ALEVIN	ANACES	AOUDAD	ARINOS
ACHING	AESTII	ALEXIA	ANADEM	APACHE	ARIOSO
ACHISH	AETION	ALFRED	ANADYR	APATAN	ARISTA
ACIDIC	AFFAIR	ALGATE	ANAKES	APATHY	ARJUNA
ACINIC	AFFECT	ALIBLE	ANALOG	APELLA	ARMADA
ACINUS	AFFIRM	ALIGHT	ANANAS	APEMAN	ARMIES
ACKACK	AFFORD	ALIPED	ANANDA	APEPSY	ARMLET
ACOLON	AFFRAY	ALISMA	ANANYM	APEREA	ARMORY
ACOMIA	AFGHAN	ALITER	ANARCH	APIARY	ARMPIT
ACOUPA	AFLAME	ALKALI	ANCHOR	APICAL	ARNHEM
ACQUIT	AFLOAT	ALLATU	ANCONA	APIECE	ARNICA
ACROSS	AFRAID	ALLEGE	ANDREA	APIOLE	AROUET
ACTING	AFREET	ALLICE	ANDREW	APLOMB	AROUND
ACTION	AFRESH	ALLIED	ANDROS	APODAL	AROUSE

ARPENT	ATHENA	AZRAEL	BARBEL	BECHIC	BETTER
ARRACK	ATHENE	BAASHA	BARBER	BECKET	BETTOR
ARRANT	ATHENS	BABBAR	BARBET	BECKON	BETULA
ARREAR	ATHOME	BABBLE	BARDIC	BECOME	BEULAH
ARREST	ATINGA	BABISM	BARELY	BEDBUG	BEWAIL
ARRIDE	ATLAST	BABOON	BARGEE	BEDECK	BEWARE
ARRISH	ATLATL	BACKER	BARITE	BEDLAM	BEWEEP
ARRIVE	ATOMIC	BACKUP	BARITO	BEETLE	BEYLIE
ARROBA	ATONAL	BADGER	BARKED	BEFALL	BEYOND
ARROYO	ATONCE	BAFFLE	BARKER	BEFOOL	BEZOAR
ARSHIN	ATONED	BAGDAD	BARLEE	BEFORE	BHADON
ARTERY	ATONIC	BAGGED	BARLEY	BEFOUL	BHAKTI
ARTFUL	ATOSSA	BAGNIO	BARLOW	BEGGAR	BHARAL
ARTHUR	ATREUS	BAHUTU	BARNUM	BEGGED	BHARAT
ARTIST	ATRIUM	BAIKAL	BAROCO	BEGIRD	BHUTAN
ARUNTA	ATSINA	BAILIE	BAROLO	BEGONE	BIASED
ASARUM	ATTACH	BAILLY	BARONE	BEHALF	BIBBER
ASCEND	ATTACK	BAIRAM	BARONG	BEHAVE	BICEPS
ASCENT	ATTAIN	BAITER	BARRED	BEHEAD	BICHIR
ASCIAN	ATTEND	BAJREE	BARREL	BEHEST	BICKER
ASGARD	ATTEST	BAKERY	BARREN	BEHIND	BICORN
ASHBEL	ATTICA	BAKSHI	BARRIE	BEHOLD	BIDENT
ASHDOD	ATTILA	BALAAM	BARRIO	BEINGS	BIDPAI
ASHLAR	ATTIRE	BALATA	BARROW	BEIRUT	BIETLE
ASHORE	ATTLEE	BALBOA	BARSOM	BELAMI	BIFOLD
ASITIA	ATYPIC	BALCON	BARTER	BELDAM	BIFORM
ASKANT	AUBADE	BALDER	BARTON	BELFRY	BIGTOP
ASKARI	AUBURN	BALEEN	BARUCH	BELGAE	BIGWIG
ASLANT	AUGURY	BALIOL	BASALT	BELIAL	BIHARI
ASLAUG	AUGUST	BALIOS	BASHAW	BELIEF	BIKINI
ASLEEP	AUHUHU	BALKAN	BASKET	BELIKE	BIKING
ASMARA	AURINE	BALKIS	BASSET	BELIZE	BILALO
ASOSAN	AURIST	BALLAD	BASTET	BELLOW	BILDAD
ASPECT	AURORA	BALLAN	BATATA	BELOIT	BILLEE
ASPIRE	AUSTER	BALLET	BATEAU	BELONG	BILLET
ASSACA	AUSTIN	BALLOT	BATHOS	BELUGA	BILLOW
ASSAIL	AUTHOR	BALSAM	BATTAN	BEMIRE	BILOXI
ASSART	AUTUMN	BALSAS	BATTEN	BEMOAN	BIMINI
ASSENT	AVAILS	BALTIC	BATTER	BEMUSE	BINARY
ASSERT	AVALON	BALTIS	BATTIK	BENGUI	BINATE
ASSESS	AVATAR	BALZAC	BATTLE	BENHUR	BINDER
ASSETS	AVENER	BAMAKO	BATULE	BENIGN	BIOBIO
ASSHUR	AVENGE	BAMBOO	BAUBLE	BENNET	BIOTIC
ASSIGN	AVENUE	BANANA	BAUCIS	BENTEN	BIOTIN
ASSIST	AVERSE	BANDED	BAWDRY	BENTON	BIRDIE
ASSIZE	AVESTA	BANDIT	BAYAMO	BENTSH	BIREME
ASSORT	AVIARY	BANDOG	BAYARD	BENUMB	BIRLED
ASSUME	AVIATE	BANGED	BAYLOR	BERATE	BIRLER
ASSURE	AVITAL	BANGKA	BAYRUM	BERBER	BISCAY
ASTERN	AVOCET	BANGLE	BAZAAR	BEREAN	BISECT
ASTRAL	AVOWAL	BANGUI	BEACON	BEREFT	BISHOP
ASTRAY	AVOWED	BANIAN	BEADLE	BERGEN	BISQUE
ASTUTE	AVULSE	BANISH	BEAGLE	BERGUT	BISSAU
ASWELL	AWAKEN	BANKER	BEAKER	BERING	BISTER
ASYLUM	AWNING	BANKUL	BEALAH	BERLIN	BISTRO
ATABAL	AXILLA	BANNER	BEAMED	BERTHA	BITING
ATAMAN	AXUNGE	BANQUO	BEANIE	BESANT	BITTER
ATAVUS	AYEAYE	BANTAM	BEATEN	BESIDE	BLADUD
ATAXIA	AYESHA	BANTER	BEATER	BESTIR	BLANCH
ATAXIC	AYMARA	BANYAN	BEATIT	BESTOW	BLANKS
ATBARA	AZALEA	BANZAI	BEAUTY	BETHEL	BLARED
ATEASE	AZAZEL	BAOBAB	BEAVER	BETIDE	BLATTA
ATELES	AZORES	BARADA	BECAME	BETRAY	BLAZER

BLAZON	BOSSED	BROGUE	BUSTLE	CAMATA	CARIBE
BLEACH	BOSTON	BROKEN	BUTANE	CAMBER	CARIES
BLEARY	BOTANY	BROKER	BUTLER	CAMERA	CARINA
BLENCH	BOTFLY	BROLGA	BUTTER	CAMION	CARLET
BLENDE	BOTHER	BROMUS	BUTTON	CAMISA	CARMEL
BLENNY	BOTHID	BRONCO	BYBLOS	CAMISE	CARMEN
BLIGHT	BOTIGO	BRONTO	BYLAWS	CAMLAN	CARNAL
BLINDS	BOTTLE	BRONZE	BYPASS	CAMLET	CARONE
BLITHE	BOTTOM	BROOCH	BYRNIE	CAMOTE	CARPEL
BLOLLY	BOUGIE	BROODY	BYWORD	CAMPER	CARPET
BLONDE	BOUNCE	BROOKE	CABALA	CAMPUS	CARPUS
BLOODY	BOUNDS	BROWZE	CABANA	CANAAN	CARROT
BLOTCH	BOUNTY	BRUGES	CABELL	CANABA	CARTEL
BLOUSE	BOURNE	BRUGGE	CABRAL	CANADA	CARTER
BLOWER	BOURSE	BRUISE	CABREE	CANALE	CARTON
BOATEL	BOVINE	BRUMAL	CABRET	CANALI	CARUSO
BOATER	BOWELS	BRUMBY	CABRIE	CANAPE	CARVER
BOBBIN	BOWERY	BRUNCH	CABRIT	CANARA	CASABA
BOBBLE	BOWFIN	BRUNEI	CACHET	CANARD	CASALS
BOBCAT	BOWLER	BRUTAL	CACHOU	CANARY	CASAUN
BOCCIE	BOWMAN	BRUTUS	CACKLE	CANCEL	CASBAH
BOCHUM	BOXCAR	BUBBLE	CACOON	CANCER	CASEIC
BODICE	BOXING	BUBBLY	CACTUS	CANDIA	CASEIN
BODILY	BOYISH	BUCKET	CADDIS	CANDID	CASERN
BODKIN	BRACER	BUDDHA	CADENT	CANDLE	CASHEW
BODONI	BRACES	BUDGET	CADGED	CANDOR	CASING
BOGOTA	BRAHMA	BUDGIE	CADGER	CANGIA	CASINO
BOHEME	BRAILA	BUFANO	CADMEA	CANGUE	CASIRI
BOHORS	BRAINS	BUFERA	CADMUS	CANINE	CASKET
BOILED	BRAISE	BUFFER	CAESAR	CANKER	CASPAR
BOILER	BRANCH	BUFFET	CAFILA	CANNAE	CASPER
BOKORO	BRANDY	BUFFON	CAFTAN	CANNEL	CASSIA
BOLERO	BRAQUE	BUGLER	CAHIBO	CANNES	CASTER
BOLIDE	BRASSE	BUKSHI	CAHILL	CANNON	CASTLE
BOLTER	BRAWNY	BULBUL	CAIMAN	CANNOT	CASTOR
BOMARC	BRAYER	BULLET	CAIQUE	CANOPY	CASUAL
BOMBAY	BRAZEN	BUMMER	CAIRNS	CANQUE	CATENA
BOMBER	BRAZIL	BUMPER	CAJOLE	CANTAL	CATGUT
BOMBUS	BRAZOS	BUMPPO	CALAIS	CANTED	CATHAY
BOMBYX	BREACH	BUNDLE	CALAMI	CANTER	CATION
BONACE	BREAST	BUNGLE	CALASH	CANTLE	CATKIN
BONBON	BREATH	BUNION	CALCAR	CANTON	CATNAP
BONGAR	BREEZE	BUNKER	CALCED	CANTOR	CATNIP
BONITO	BREEZY	BUNSEN	CALDEN	CANUCK	CATSUP
BONNET	BREHON	BUNTON	CALDER	CANVAS	CATTLE
BONOBO	BREMEN	BURBOT	CALICO	CANYON	CAUCHO
BOOBOO	BREMER	BURDEN	CALIGA	CAPIAS	CAUCHY
BOOJUM	BREMSE	BUREAU	CALIGO	CAPONE	CAUCUS
BOOKIE	BRETON	BURGEE	CALIPH	CAPOTE	CAUDAL
BOOMER	BREVET	BURGLE	CALLAO	CAPPER	CAUDLE
BOOTHS	BREWER	BURIAL	CALLAS	CAPRIC	CAUGHT
BOOZER	BREWIS	BURIAT	CALLED	CARAFE	CAULIS
BOPPLE	BRIDAL	BURIED	CALLER	CARAPO	CAUSAL
BORDER	BRIDGE	BURLAP	CALLID	CARBON	CAUSED
BOREAL	BRIDLE	BURNER	CALLON	CARBOY	CAUTER
BOREAS	BRIENZ	BUROAK	CALLOT	CARCEL	CAVEAT
BORELE	BRIGHT	BURROW	CALLOW	CARDER	CAVEIN
BORGIA	BRIGIT	BURSAR	CALLUS	CARDOL	CAVERN
BORGES	BRIGUE	BURTON	CALOOL	CAREEN	CAVIAR
BORING	BRINIE	BUSBOY	CALORY	CAREER	CAVITY
BORNEO	BRITON	BUSHED	CALPAC	CAREME	CAVIYA
BORROW	BROACH	BUSHEL	CALUSA	CARESS	CAVORT
BORZOI	BROGAN	BUSTER	CAMASS		CAYMAN

CAYUGA	CHATON	CICADA	COAITA	COMMIT	COSTAL
CAYUSE	CHATTA	CICALA	COALER	COMMON	COSTER
CECITY	CHAUTE	CICERO	COARSE	COMPEL	COSTLY
CEDRAT	CHEBEC	CIERGE	COATED	COMPLY	COTORO
CEDRON	CHEEKY	CIGALE	COATEE	CONCHA	COTTER
CELERY	CHEERS	CIGARS	COATES	CONCUR	COTTON
CELLAR	CHEERY	CILICE	COBALT	CONDOR	COTTUS
CELTIC	CHEESE	CILIUM	COBBLE	CONFAB	COUGAR
CEMENT	CHEESY	CINDER	COBDEN	CONFER	COULEE
CENOTE	CHEFOO	CINEMA	COBNUT	CONGEE	COUNTY
CENSER	CHELAE	CIPHER	COCCYX	CONGER	COUPLE
CENSOR	CHEOPS	CIRCLE	COCHIN	CONICS	COURSE
CENSUS	CHEQUE	CIRCUS	COCKAL	CONIMA	COUSIN
CENTAL	CHERRY	CIRQUE	COCKER	CONINE	COUTER
CENTER	CHERUB	CIRRUS	COCKUP	CONMAN	COVERT
CERATE	CHETTY	CITHER	COCOON	CONNLA	COWARD
CERCUS	CHEVIN	CITOLE	CODDLE	CONOPS	COWBOY
CEREAL	CHICLE	CITRIN	CODGER	CONRAD	COWLED
CEREUS	CHIGOE	CITRON	CODIFY	CONSOL	COWPOX
CERIGO	CHILLY	CITRUS	CODRUS	CONSUL	COWRIE
CERISE	CHIMAR	CLAMMY	COELUS	CONTEX	COXCOX
CERIUM	CHIMED	CLAMOR	COERCE	CONTRA	COYOTE
CEROMA	CHIMED	CLAQUE	COEVAL	CONVEX	CRABBY
CERRIS	CHIMER	CLARET	COFFEE	CONVEY	CRACOW
CERTES	CHINAR	CLAROS	COFFER	CONVOY	CRADLE
CERUSE	CHININ	CLASSY	COFFIN	COOKED	CRAFTY
CERVID	CHINKY	CLAUDE	COGENT	COOKIE	CRAGGY
CERVUS	CHINSE	CLAUSE	COGNAC	COOLER	CRAMBO
CESIUM	CHINTZ	CLAVUS	COHEIR	COOLIE	CRANED
CESTUS	CHIPPY	CLAYEY	COHERE	COOPER	CRANNY
CESURA	CHIRAL	CLEAVE	COHORT	COPLAS	CRATER
CESURE	CHIRON	CLECHE	COILED	COPPER	CRAVAT
CESUTH	CHISEL	CLERGY	COINER	COPTIC	CRAVEN
CETANE	CHITAL	CLERIC	COLADA	CORBAN	CRAYON
CEYLON	CHITIN	CLEVER	COLANE	CORDAY	CRAZED
CHACMA	CHITON	CLEVIS	COLDLY	CORDON	CREASE
CHACRA	CHITRA	CLIACK	COLETA	CORIOT	CREATE
CHAETA	CHOCHO	CLICHE	COLEUR	CORIUM	CRECHE
CHAFED	CHOICE	CLIENT	COLEUS	CORKER	CREDIT
CHAFER	CHOKER	CLIMAX	COLIMA	CORNEA	CREMOR
CHAINS	CHOKWE	CLINCH	COLLAR	CORNED	CRENEL
CHAISE	CHOLER	CLINIC	COLLET	CORNEL	CREOLE
CHALET	CHOLLA	CLIQUE	COLLIE	CORNER	CRESOL
CHALKY	CHONDR	CLIVIS	COLLIN	CORNET	CRESPI
CHAMAL	CHOOSE	CLOCHE	COLLOP	CORONA	CRESSY
CHAMPA	CHOPIN	CLOOTS	COLONA	CORPSE	CRETAN
CHANCA	CHORAL	CLOSER	COLONY	CORRAL	CRETIN
CHANCE	CHOREA	CLOSET	COLORS	CORRIE	CREUSA
CHANCY	CHOROS	CLOTEN	COLTER	CORSAC	CREVAS
CHANDU	CHORUS	CLOTHE	COLUGO	CORSAK	CREVET
CHANEL	CHOSEN	CLOTHO	COLUMN	CORSET	CREWEL
CHANGA	CHOUAN	CLOUDY	COMATE	CORTES	CRIMEA
CHANGE	CHOUGH	CLOUET	COMBAT	CORTEX	CRINET
CHAPEI	CHOUKA	CLOUGH	COMBER	CORTEZ	CRINGE
CHAPEL	CHRIST	CLOVER	COMEDO	CORVUS	CRISIS
CHAPIN	CHROME	CLOVES	COMEDY	CORYMB	CRITIC
CHARAS	CHROMO	CLOVIS	COMELY	CORYZA	CROCUS
CHARGE	CHUBUT	CLUMSY	COMEON	COSHER	CRONOS
CHARIS	CHUCHA	CLUPEA	COMFIT	COSIMA	CRONUS
CHARON	CHUKAR	CLUTCH	COMHAL	COSINE	CROTCH
CHASER	CHUNGA	CLUTHA	COMING	COSMIC	CROTON
CHASSE	CHURCH	CNEMIS	COMINO	COSMOS	CROUCH
CHASTE	CIBOLA	CNIDUS	COMITY	COSSET	CROUSE

CROWDS	DAEMON	DEADEN	DEMOTE	DIBBLE	DOLENT
CROWED	DAGGER	DEADLY	DEMURE	DICKEY	DOLINE
CRUISE	DAGABA	DEAFEN	DENARY	DICTUM	DOLITE
CRUNCH	DAHLIA	DEALER	DENGUE	DIDYMA	DOLLAR
CRURAL	DAHOON	DEALIN	DENIAL	DIESEL	DOLLEY
CRUSET	DAIDLY	DEARTH	DENIER	DIESIS	DOLMAN
CRUSOE	DAIKON	DEBARK	DENOTE	DIGEST	DOLMEN
CRUSTY	DAIMIO	DEBASE	DENSER	DIGGER	DOMAGK
CRYING	DAINTY	DEBATE	DENTAL	DIKDIK	DOMAIN
CUBOID	DAIREN	DEBILE	DENTED	DILATE	DOMINO
CUCKOO	DAISEN	DEBORD	DENTIL	DILUTE	DONALD
CUDDLE	DAITYA	DEBRIS	DENUDE	DIMITY	DONATE
CUDGEL	DAKOTA	DEBTEE	DENVER	DIMPLE	DONEES
CUIABA	DAKSHA	DEBTOR	DEODAR	DIMWIT	DONKEY
CULLET	DALASI	DEBUNK	DEPART	DINDLE	DONORS
CULPEO	DALETH	DECADE	DEPEND	DINERO	DOODLE
CULTCH	DALLAS	DECAMP	DEPICT	DINGAR	DOOLIE
CULTUS	DAMAGE	DECANT	DEPLOY	DINGHY	DOOMED
CULVER	DAMARA	DECARE	DEPONE	DINGLE	DORADO
CUMBER	DAMASK	DECEIT	DEPORT	DINGUS	DORCAS
CUNEAL	DAMIER	DECENT	DEPOSE	DINNER	DORMER
CUPOLA	DAMINE	DECIDE	DEPUTE	DIPODY	DORSAL
CUPRIC	DAMNED	DECKLE	DEPUTY	DIPPER	DORSUM
CURARE	DAMPEN	DECOCT	DERAIN	DIRECT	DOSAGE
CURARI	DAMPER	DECODE	DERIDE	DIREST	DOSSAL
CURATE	DAMSEL	DECREE	DERIVE	DIRHEM	DOSSER
CURIOS	DAMSON	DECUMA	DERMAL	DIRIGO	DOSSIL
CURLED	DANANG	DEDUCE	DERMIC	DIRNDL	DOTAGE
CURLER	DANAUS	DEDUCT	DERMIS	DISARM	DOTARD
CURLEW	DANDER	DEEPEN	DESCRY	DISAWA	DOTING
CURSED	DANGER	DEEPER	DESERT	DISCAL	DOTTED
CURTSY	DANGLE	DEEPLY	DESIGN	DISCUS	DOTTEL
CURVED	DANIEL	DEFACE	DESIRE	DISHED	DOTTLE
CURVET	DANISH	DEFAME	DESIST	DISHES	DOUALA
CUSCUS	DANITE	DEFEAT	DESMAN	DISMAL	DOUBLE
CUSHAT	DANTES	DEFECT	DESMID	DISMAS	DOUCIN
CUSHAW	DANTON	DEFEND	DESPOT	DISMAY	DOULOS
CUSPED	DANUBE	DEFIED	DETACH	DISOWN	DOURAH
CUSPID	DANZIG	DEFILE	DETAIL	DISPEL	DOWLAS
CUSTOM	DANZON	DEFINE	DETAIN	DISUSE	DOWNER
CUTLER	DAPHNE	DEFLEX	DETECT	DITALI	DOWSER
CUTLET	DAPPER	DEFORM	DETENT	DITHER	DOZENS
CUTOFF	DAPPLE	DEFRAY	DETEST	DIVERS	DRAGEE
CUTTER	DARDAN	DEFTLY	DETOUR	DIVERT	DRAGON
CUVAGE	DARIEN	DEGREE	DEVICE	DIVEST	DRAPER
CYBELE	DARING	DEIMOS	DEVISE	DIVIDE	DRAPES
CYCLIC	DARIUS	DEINOS	DEVOID	DIVINE	DRAWER
CYGNET	DARKEN	DEJECT	DEVOIR	DIWALI	DREAMT
CYMLIN	DARNEL	DELATE	DEVOTE	DOCENT	DREAMY
CYMRIC	DARNER	DELEON	DEVOUR	DOCILE	DREARY
CYPRUS	DARTER	DELETE	DEVOUT	DOCKER	DREDGE
CYRANO	DARWIN	DELICT	DEWALI	DOCKET	DRENCH
CYREME	DARYAL	DELISK	DEWLAP	DOCMAC	DREXEL
DABBER	DASHER	DELOUL	DEXTER	DOCTOR	DRINKS
DABBLE	DASSIE	DELPHI	DHAMAR	DODDER	DRIVEL
DABOIA	DASTUR	DELUDE	DHARMA	DODGER	DRIVER
DABOYA	DATARY	DELUGE	DHOOTI	DODONA	DROGER
DACAPO	DATIVE	DELUXE	DIABLO	DOGANA	DROGUE
DACHAU	DATURA	DEMAND	DIADEM	DOGATE	DROMON
DACOIT	DAVIES	DEMEAN	DIALED	DOGGED	DRONGO
DACRON	DAWDLE	DEMENE	DIALOG	DOGGER	DROPSY
DACTYL	DAZZLE	DEMENT	DIAPER	DOGLET	DROUTH
DAEDAL	DEACON	DEMISE	DIATOM	DOKHMA	DROVER

DROWSE	ECZEMA	EMILIA	EQUATE	EVENER	FARRAR
DROWSY	EDDISH	EMMETT	EQUINE	EVENTS	FARROW
DRUDGE	EDENIC	EMPERY	EQUITY	EVENUS	FASCES
DRUSUS	EDESSA	EMPIRE	ERASER	EVINCE	FASCIA
DRYING	EDGING	EMPLOY	EREBUS	EVOLVE	FASTEN
DRYROT	EDIBLE	EMPTOR	ERENOW	EXCEED	FATHEN
DUALIN	EDISON	ENABLE	ERINYS	EXCEPT	FATHER
DUBBED	EDISTO	ENALID	ERITES	EXCESS	FATHOM
DUBLIN	EDITOR	ENAMEL	ERIVAN	EXCISE	FATIMA
DUCCIO	EEBREE	ENAMOR	ERMINE	EXCITE	FATTEN
DUDAIM	EECATL	ENATIC	ERNANI	EXCUSE	FATUUS
DUDEEN	EELPOT	ENCAMP	EROICA	EXEDRA	FAUCET
DUDLEY	EFFACE	ENCASE	EROTIC	EXEMPT	FAUCRE
DUELLO	EFFECT	ENCINA	ERRAND	EXEUNT	FAULTY
DUENNA	EFFETE	ENCLOSE	ERRANT	EXHALE	FAUNUS
DUESSA	EFFIGY	ENCORE	ERRATA	EXHORT	FAUVES
DUFFER	EFFLUX	ENDING	ERRING	EXHUME	FAVOSE
DUFFLE	EFFORT	ENDITE	ERSATZ	EXISTS	FAWNER
DUGONG	EGBERT	ENDIVE	ESCAPE	EXODOS	FEALTY
DUGOUT	EGERIA	ENDMEN	ESCARP	EXODUS	FECUND
DUIBNE	EGOIST	ENDURE	ESCHEW	EXOTIC	FEDORA
DUIKER	EGRESS	ENERGY	ESCORT	EXPAND	FEEBLE
DULCET	EIFFEL	ENFOLD	ESCROW	EXPECT	FEEBLY
DULUTH	EIGHTH	ENGAGE	ESCUDO	EXPEND	FEEDER
DUMDUM	EIGHTY	ENGEDI	ESDRAS	EXPERT	FEELER
DUMOSE	EIRENE	ENGELS	ESHBAN	EXPIRE	FEISTY
DUNBAR	EITHER	ENGINE	ESHOWE	EXPORT	FELINE
DUNCAN	ELAINE	ENGULF	ESKIMO	EXPOSE	FELLAH
DUNDEE	ELANET	ENIGMA	ESMOND	EXTANT	FELLOE
DUNLIN	ELAPSE	ENISLE	ESPANA	EXTEND	FELLOW
DUNLOP	ELATED	ENJOIN	ESPIAL	EXTENT	FELONY
DUNTIN	ELATER	ENLACE	ESPIED	EXTERN	FEMALE
DUPLEX	ELBERT	ENLINK	ESSENE	EXTORT	FENCER
DURANI	ELBRUS	ENLIST	ESSOIN	EYELET	FENDER
DURBAR	ELBRUZ	ENMESH	ESTATE	FABRIC	FENNEC
DURESS	ELDEST	ENMITY	ESTEEM	FACADE	FENNEL
DURHAM	ELEGIT	ENNEAD	ESTERO	FACIAL	FENRIR
DURIAN	ELEVEN	ENODAL	ESTHER	FACILE	FENRIS
DURING	ELFISH	ENOUGH	ESTRAY	FACING	FERASH
DUSCLE	ELICIT	ENRAGE	ETALIA	FACTOR	FERBER
DUSTER	ELISHA	ENRAPT	ETCHED	FACULA	FERGUS
DUSTUP	ELISOR	ENRICH	ETCHER	FAFNIR	FERINE
DUTIES	ELISSA	ENROLL	ETHANE	FAILLE	FERITY
DVORAK	ELIXIR	ENROOT	ETHICS	FAIRER	FERMAT
DYEING	ELLECK	ENSATE	ETHIOP	FAKEER	FERRET
DYNAMO	ELOHIM	ENSIGN	ETHNIC	FAKERY	FERRIC
DYNAST	ELOIGN	ENSURE	ETHROG	FAKOFO	FERRUM
DZEREN	ELOPED	ENTAIL	ETOILE	FALCON	FERULA
DZERON	ELPASO	ENTICE	ETUDES	FALLEN	FERULE
EABANI	ELUARD	ENTIRE	ETYMON	FALLER	FERVID
EAGLET	ELUATE	ENTITY	EUCHRE	FALLOW	FERVOR
EARING	EMBALM	ENTOMB	EUCLID	FALTER	FESCUE
EARLAP	EMBARK	ENTRAP	EUGENE	FAMILY	FESTER
EARNED	EMBERS	ENTREE	EULOGY	FAMINE	FETIAL
EARTHY	EMBLEM	ENZYME	EUNICE	FAMISH	FETISH
EASILY	EMBODY	EOCENE	EUNUCH	FAMOUS	FETTER
EASTER	EMBOSS	EOLIAN	EUREKA	FANEGA	FETTLE
EATERY	EMBRYO	EOLITH	EUROPA	FANNEL	FEWEST
ECARTE	EMERGE	EOSINE	EUROPE	FANNIA	FEWMET
ECHOIC	EMESAL	EPARCH	EUSDEN	FANTAN	FEZZAN
ECLAIR	EMESIS	EPEIUS	EUTAXY	FARFEL	FIACRE
ECTOMY	EMEUTE	EPONYM	EUXINE	FARINA	FIANCE
ECTYPE	EMIGRE	EPOPEE	EVELYN	FARMER	FIASCO

FIBBER	FLUENT	FRILLS	GAMBIT	GEORGE	GOANNA
FIBRIN	FLUNKY	FRINGE	GAMBLE	GERBIL	GOATEE
FIBULA	FLURRY	FRISCA	GAMBOL	GERENT	GOBBET
FICHTE	FLYING	FRISKY	GAMEST	GERMAN	GOBBLE
FICKLE	FLYWAY	FRISON	GAMETE	GERRIS	GOBLET
FIDDLE	FODDER	FRIVOL	GAMMON	GERUND	GOBLIN
FIDGET	FOGRAM	FRIZZY	GANDER	GETTER	GOBNIU
FIERCE	FOIBLE	FROGGY	GANDUM	GEWGAW	GOCART
FIESTA	FOKKER	FROLIC	GANGES	GEYSER	GODIVA
FIGARO	FOLDED	FRONDE	GANGUE	GEYSIR	GODKIN
FIGURE	FOLDER	FROSTY	GANNET	GHAZAL	GODLET
FIJIAN	FOLIUM	FROTHY	GAPING	GHAZNI	GODMAN
FILLED	FOLLOW	FROZEN	GARAGE	GHEBER	GODOWN
FILLER	FOMENT	FRUGAL	GARAND	GHETTO	GODWIN
FILLET	FONDLE	FRUNZE	GARBED	GHURKA	GOETHE
FILLIP	FONDUE	FUCATE	GARBLE	GIANTS	GOFFER
FILTER	FOOLED	FUDDLE	GARCON	GIAOUR	GOITER
FILTHY	FORAGE	FULANI	GARDEN	GIBBER	GOLDEN
FINALE	FORATI	FULFIL	GARETH	GIBBET	GOMART
FINALS	FORBID	FULHAM	GARGET	GIBBON	GOMERA
FINERY	FORCED	FULMAR	GARISH	GIBLEH	GOMUTI
FINEST	FOREST	FUMBLE	GARLIC	GIBLET	GOOBER
FINGER	FORGED	FUMING	GARNER	GIBSON	GOODBY
FINIAL	FORGER	FUNEST	GARNET	GIDEON	GOOFER
FINISH	FORGET	FUNGUS	GARRAN	GIDGEE	GOOGLY
FINITE	FORINT	FUNNEL	GARRET	GIGGLE	GOOGOL
FINJAN	FORMAL	FURIES	GARTER	GIGOLO	GOONCH
FIORIN	FORMAT	FURORE	GARUDA	GILDED	GOONEY
FIRKIN	FORMED	FURROW	GASCON	GILEAD	GOPHER
FISCAL	FORMER	FUSILE	GASKET	GILLIE	GORDON
FISHER	FORREL	FUSION	GASPAR	GILLOT	GORGET
FISTIC	FORTIS	FUSTET	GASPER	GIMLET	GORGON
FITFUL	FOSSIL	FUSTIC	GATHAS	GIMMER	GORHEN
FITTED	FOSTER	FUSUMA	GATHER	GINGER	GOSHEN
FITTER	FOTHER	FUTILE	GAUCHE	GINKGO	GOSPEL
FIZZLE	FOUGHT	FUTURE	GAUCHO	GIOTTO	GOSSIP
FLABBY	FOURTH	FYLFOT	GAUGED	GIRDER	GOTHAM
FLAGON	FOUSSA	GABBLE	GAVIAL	GIRDLE	GOTHIC
FLAMEN	FRACAS	GABBRO	GAWAIN	GITANO	GOUNOD
FLANGE	FRANCE	GABELL	GAYETY	GIVEUP	GOURDE
FLASHY	FRANCO	GADFLY	GAYYOU	GLACED	GOVERN
FLAUNT	FRAPPE	GADGET	GAZEBO	GLACIS	GOWPEN
FLAVOR	FRATER	GADOID	GDANSK	GLADLY	GRABEN
FLAWED	FRAYED	GAELIC	GEBANG	GLAIVE	GRACED
FLEDGE	FREELY	GAFFER	GEEZER	GLANCE	GRADED
FLEECE	FREERS	GAGGLE	GEFION	GLARUS	GRADER
FLEECY	FREEZE	GAIETY	GEIGER	GLASSY	GRADES
FLENSE	FREJOL	GAINER	GEISHA	GLAZED	GRADIN
FLESHY	FRENCH	GAINLY	GELADA	GLIDER	GRAFFE
FLETCH	FRENZY	GAITER	GELATE	GLIOMA	GRAHAM
FLEXED	FRESCO	GALAGO	GEMARA	GLOBAL	GRAIAE
FLEXOR	FRESNO	GALAXY	GEMINI	GLOOMY	GRAINY
FLIGHT	FREYJA	GALENA	GENDER	GLOSSA	GRAMPS
FLIMSY	FRIANT	GALLET	GENEPI	GLOSSO	GRANGE
FLINCH	FRIDAY	GALLEY	GENERA	GLOSSY	GRANNY
FLINTY	FRIDGE	GALLON	GENEVA	GLOVES	GRANTH
FLORAL	FRIEND	GALLOP	GENIAL	GLOWER	GRATER
FLORET	FRIEZE	GALLUP	GENIPI	GNARLY	GRATIS
FLORID	FRIGGA	GALOIS	GENIUS	GNATHO	GRAVEL
FLORIN	FRIGHT	GALOOT	GENOVA	GNEISS	GRAVER
FLOURY	FRIGID	GALORE	GENTLE	GNOMIC	GRAVES
FLOWER	FRIJOL	GALOSH	GENTOO	GNOMON	GREASE
FLUANT	FRIKKO	GALWAY	GENTRY	GOALIE	GREASY

GREAVE	GUSTAF	HARMED	HERATI	HOOKED	ICHANG
GREECE	GUTTER	HARMON	HERDER	HOOKER	ICHING
GREEDY	GUYANA	HARNEY	HEREIN	HOOKUP	ICICLE
GREENE	GUZZLE	HAROLD	HEREOF	HOOPOE	ICONIC
GREENS	GYMPIE	HAROUN	HERESY	HOOTER	IDALIA
GREGAL	GYNECO	HARPER	HERETO	HOOVER	IDEATE
GREGER	GYPSUM	HARRIS	HERIOT	HORACE	IDIOCY
GREIGE	GYRATE	HARROW	HERMES	HORMOS	IDOLON
GRIEVE	HABANA	HASLET	HERMIA	HORNED	IDOLUM
GRIFFE	HABILE	HASSLE	HERMIT	HORNET	IGERNE
GRIGRA	HABOOB	HASTEN	HERMON	HORRID	IGNERI
GRIGRI	HACKEE	HATHOR	HERMUS	HORROR	IGNITE
GRILLE	HACKIE	HATRED	HEROIC	HOSTEL	IGNORE
GRILSE	HACKLE	HATTER	HEROIN	HOTDOG	IGNOTE
GRIMME	HADITH	HAUNCH	HERPES	HOUDAH	IGOROT
GRINGO	HAEMAL	HAUSEN	HERWIG	HOUDON	IGRAIN
GRIPPE	HAEMIC	HAVANA	HESIOD	HOUTOU	IGUANA
GRIQUA	HAGBAI	HAWAII	HESPER	HOWDAH	IGUAZU
GRISLY	HAGGAI	HAWKER	HESTIA	HOWLER	IJSSEL
GRISON	HAGGLE	HAWSER	HETMAN	HOYDEN	ILIAHI
GRITTY	HAIRDO	HAZARD	HEYDAY	HUBBUB	ILLANA
GRIVET	HALITE	HEADER	HIATUS	HUBCAP	ILLIPI
GRIVNA	HALLEL	HEALER	HICCUP	HUDSON	ILLUME
GROATS	HALLOO	HEALTH	HIDDEN	HULGUL	ILLUSE
GROCER	HALLOW	HEARSE	HIEMAL	HUMANE	ILOILO
GRODNO	HALLUX	HEARST	HIGHLY	HUMANS	IMARET
GROMEL	HALTER	HEARTH	HIJACK	HUMBLE	IMBIBE
GROOVE	HALVAH	HEARTS	HINDER	HUMBUG	IMBRUE
GROOVY	HALWAH	HEARTY	HINLIL	HUNGER	IMMUNE
GROPED	HAMATE	HEATED	HIRAME	HUNGRY	IMMURE
GROPER	HAMITE	HEATER	HISPID	HUNTER	IMOGEN
GROTTO	HAMLET	HEAUME	HITHER	HURDLE	IMPACT
GROUCH	HAMLIN	HEAVEN	HITLER	HURLEY	IMPAIR
GROUND	HAMMAM	HEBERT	HITTER	HURRAH	IMPALA
GROUSE	HAMMER	HEBREW	HIVAOA	HURRAY	IMPALE
GROVEL	HAMNET	HEBRON	HOARSE	HURTLE	IMPART
GROVES	HECATE	HECKLE	HOAXED	HUSSAR	IMPEDE
GROWTH	HAMPER	HECTOR	HOBART	HUSTLE	IMPEND
GRUACH	HAMSUN	HECUBA	HOBBES	HUZOOR	IMPHAL
GRUDGE	HANDAX	HEDERA	HOBBLE	HYADES	IMPHEE
GRUMPY	HANDEL	HEEHAW	HOBSON	HYBRID	IMPOFO
GUDRUN	HANDLE	HEELED	HOCKEY	HYDRIA	IMPORT
GUEMAL	HANGAR	HEELER	HOIDEN	HYDRIC	IMPOSE
GUEMUL	HANGER	HEFNER	HOLCAD	HYDRUS	IMPOST
GUENON	HANGUL	HEGARI	HOLCUS	HYEMAL	IMPUGN
GUESTS	HANGUP	HEGIRA	HOLDER	HYETAL	IMPURE
GUFFAW	HANHAI	HEIFER	HOLDUP	HYGEIA	IMPUTE
GUIDON	HANIWA	HEIGHT	HOLGER	HYKSOS	IMSHEE
GUIGES	HANKER	HEINIE	HOLLOW	HYMNAL	INAGUA
GUILTY	HANKOW	HELENA	HOLMES	HYPHEN	INANGA
GUINEA	HANNAH	HELIAC	HOMAGE	HYSSOP	INANNA
GUITAR	HANSOM	HELIOS	HOMBRE	IAMBIC	INBORN
GUITRY	HAOKAH	HELIUM	HOMELY	IAMBUS	INBRED
GUIZOT	HAPPEN	HELLAS	HOMILY	IASION	INCISE
GULDEN	HAPTEN	HELLEN	HOMINY	IATRIC	INCITE
GULLET	HARASS	HELMET	HONDOO	IBERIA	INCOME
GULPIN	HARBIN	HELPER	HONEST	IBERIS	INDABA
GUNNEL	HARBOR	HEMERO	HONORS	ICARUS	INDEED
GUNYAH	HARDEN	HENNIN	HONSHU	ICEAGE	INDIAN
GURGLE	HARDIM	HENSON	HOODED	ICEBAG	INDICT
GURKHA	HARDLY	HEPTAD	HOODOO	ICEBOX	INDIGO
GUSHER	HARKEN	HERALD	HOOFED	ICECAP	INDITE
GUSSET	HARLOT	HERATI	HOOKAH	ICEMAN	INDUCE

INDUCT	ISAIAH	JESSIS	KADIJA	KHALKA	KUMISS
INDUNA	ISATIS	JESTER	KADINE	KHANUM	KUMMEL
INFAMY	ISCHIA	JETHRO	KAFFIR	KHATIB	KUNLUN
INFANT	ISEULT	JETSAM	KAFTAN	KHATTI	KURGAN
INFARE	ISHTAR	JETSET	KAGERA	KHEPRI	KURNAI
INFECT	ISLAND	JEWISH	KAHUNA	KHONSU	KUVASZ
INFIRM	ISLENO	JIGGER	KAIBAB	KHYBER	KUVERA
INFLUX	ISMENA	JIGSAW	KAIKAI	KIBLAH	KUWAIT
INFOLD	ISMENE	JILTED	KAINYN	KIDNAP	KVASTR
INFORM	ISNARD	JINGLE	KAISER	KIDNEY	KWACHA
INFUSE	ISOBAR	JINNAH	KAKKAK	KIGALI	KYUSHU
INGRES	ISOGON	JINNEE	KALAKH	KIKUYU	LAAGER
INHALE	ISOLDE	JITNEY	KALGAN	KILHIG	LABEFY
INHERE	ISRAEL	JOCKEY	KALIUM	KILLED	LABIAL
INHUME	ISSUED	JOCOSE	KALONG	KILLER	LABIUM
INJURE	ISTRIA	JOCUND	KAMAHI	KILTER	LABLAB
INJURY	ITALIA	JOGGLE	KAMBAN	KIMONO	LABNEH
INKNEE	ITALIC	JOHNNY	KAMETS	KINDLE	LABRET
INLAND	ITASCA	JOHORE	KAMSIN	KINDLY	LACHES
INLOVE	ITHACA	JOINED	KANAKA	KINGLY	LACKEY
INMATE	ITHUNN	JOINER	KANARA	KINGSX	LACTIC
INMOST	ITURBI	JOKTAN	KANGLI	KINNAH	LACUNA
INNATE	IWAIWA	JOLIBA	KANGTE	KINSHA	LADDER
INNING	IXCHEL	JOLIET	KANMON	KIRSCH	LADING
INNUIN	IZZARD	JOLYON	KANSAN	KIRTLE	LADINO
INNUIT	JABBER	JONSON	KANSAS	KISHON	LADOGA
INROAD	JABBLE	JOPLIN	KANTAR	KISLEV	LAGASH
INSANE	JABIRU	JORDAN	KANTEN	KISMET	LAGOON
INSECT	JACANA	JOSEPH	KANUKA	KISSAR	LAGUNE
INSERT	JACARE	JOSHUA	KAOLIN	KISSEL	LAHORE
INSIDE	JACKAL	JOSIAH	KARAKA	KISUMU	LAICAL
INSOLE	JACKET	JOSIAN	KARATE	KITCAT	LAKOTA
INSTAR	JACOBY	JOSTLE	KARIBA	KITTEN	LALLAN
INSTEP	JAEGER	JOUNCE	KARITE	KLATCH	LAMBDA
INSULT	JAFFNA	JOVIAL	KAROSS	KLAXON	LAMECH
INSURE	JAGHIR	JOYFUL	KARROO	KNIGHT	LAMEDH
INTACT	JAGUAR	JOYOUS	KASHER	KNIVES	LAMENT
INTEND	JAHVEH	JUDAIC	KASHGA	KNOBBY	LAMINA
INTENT	JAILED	JUDITH	KATANA	KNOTTY	LAMPAS
INTERN	JAILER	JUDSON	KATIPO	KOAITA	LANATE
INTONE	JALOPY	JUGGLE	KATMAI	KOBOLD	LANCED
INURED	JALUIT	JUICER	KATUKA	KOCHEL	LANCER
INVADE	JAMUNA	JUJUBE	KAUNAS	KODIAK	LANCET
INVENT	JANAKA	JULIET	KAUNDA	KODKOD	LANCHA
INVERT	JANGLE	JUMADA	KAVASS	KOHATH	LANDAU
INVEST	JAPURA	JUMALA	KAWAKA	KOHUHU	LANGUR
INVITE	JARGON	JUMBLE	KEENER	KOJIKI	LANIER
INVOKE	JARRAH	JUNEAU	KEEPER	KOKOON	LANNER
INWARD	JASPER	JUNGLE	KELIMA	KOODOO	LANOSE
IODINE	JATAKA	JUNIOR	KELLER	KOPECK	LANSEH
IOLITE	JAUNTY	JUNKER	KELOID	KORDAX	LAOTSE
IONIAN	JAVALI	JUNKET	KELPIE	KOREAN	LAOTZE
IONONE	JAVERT	JUNKIE	KELSON	KORUNA	LAPDOG
IPECAC	JEEVES	JUPARA	KELTIC	KOSHAR	LAPTEV
IRAQIS	JEJUNE	JUPATI	KENNEL	KOSHER	LAPUTA
IRENIC	JEMIMA	JUSTLY	KERMES	KOWHAI	LARDER
IRIDAL	JENNET	KABALA	KERMIS	KOWHIA	LAREDO
IRISED	JERBOA	KABAYA	KERNEL	KOWTOW	LARIAT
IRITIS	JEREED	KABERU	KERSEY	KRAKEN	LARINE
IRONER	JERKIN	KABUKI	KESHWA	KRATER	LARRIE
IRTYSH	JEROME	KABYLE	KETONE	KRONOS	LARRUP
IRVING	JERSEY	KACHIN	KETTLE	KRUMAN	LARSEN
ISAGON	JESSIE	KADEIN	KEYNES	KUMARA	LARYNX

LASCAR	LEMBUS	LINTER	LOUVRE	MAGGOT	MANTLE
LASHIO	LENAPE	LIONET	LOVAGE	MAGNET	MANTUA
LASKER	LENDER	LIPARI	LOVELY	MAGNUM	MANUAL
LASSEN	LENGTH	LIPOID	LOVING	MAGPIE	MANUAO
LASSET	LENIFY	LIPOMA	LOWELL	MAGUEY	MANURE
LASSIE	LENITY	LIPPEN	LOWEST	MAGURO	MAPACH
LATEEN	LENORE	LIPPER	LOWING	MAGYAR	MAQUIS
LATELY	LENTEN	LIQUID	LOYOLA	MAHBUB	MARACA
LATENT	LENTIL	LIQUOR	LUANDA	MAHLON	MARAUD
LATEST	LEONID	LISBOA	LUBBER	MAHONE	MARBLE
LATHER	LEPTON	LISBON	LUBECK	MAHORI	MARCID
LATIGO	LESAGE	LISTEL	LUCAYO	MAHOUT	MARDUK
LATINO	LESBOS	LISTEN	LUCENT	MAHSIR	MARECA
LATITE	LESKOV	LISTER	LUCERN	MAHSUR	MARGAY
LATONA	LESSEE	LITANI	LUCINA	MAHZOR	MARGIN
LATRIA	LESSEN	LITANY	LUCITE	MAIDAN	MARIAN
LATTEN	LESSER	LITCHI	LUDWIG	MAIDEN	MARICA
LATTER	LESSON	LITHIA	LUGGAR	MAIGRE	MARINA
LATTIC	LESSOR	LITHIC	LUGGER	MAILED	MARINE
LAUDER	LETHAL	LITTER	LUMBER	MAINLY	MARION
LAUFER	LETTER	LITTLE	LUMMOX	MAINOR	MARIUS
LAULAU	LETTIC	LIVELY	LUNACY	MAJLIS	MARKED
LAUNCH	LEVANT	LIVERY	LUNATE	MAJONG	MARKER
LAUREL	LEVIER	LIVING	LUNGED	MAKEUP	MARKET
LAVABO	LEVITY	LIZARD	LUNGER	MAKLUK	MARKKA
LAVAGE	LIABLE	LLANOS	LUNULA	MAKWAR	MARLEY
LAVANT	LIBATE	LOADER	LUNULE	MALADY	MARLIN
LAVIER	LIBBER	LOADUP	LUPINE	MALAGA	MARMOT
LAVISH	LIBBRA	LOAFER	LUSAKA	MALAWI	MAROON
LAWFUL	LICHAM	LOATHE	LUSORY	MALAYA	MARRAM
LAWYER	LICHEE	LOCALE	LUSTER	MALICE	MARRON
LAXITY	LICHEN	LOCATE	LUSTRE	MALIGN	MARROW
LAYMAN	LICTOR	LOCKER	LUTHER	MALINE	MARSHY
LAYMEN	LIEDER	LOCKET	LUXATE	MALLEE	MARTEL
LAYOUT	LIERNE	LOCKUP	LUXURY	MALLET	MARTEN
LAYSAN	LIFFEY	LOCUST	LYCEUM	MAMMAL	MARTHA
LAZULI	LIFTER	LODGED	LYDIAN	MAMMEE	MARTIN
LEADEN	LIGATE	LODGER	LYRICS	MAMMON	MARTYR
LEADER	LIGEIA	LOGGER	LYRIST	MAMTOU	MARVEL
LEAGUE	LIGHTS	LOGGIA	LYSINE	MANADA	MARXES
LEANER	LIGNIN	LOIMIC	LYSSIC	MANAGE	MASADA
LEANTO	LIGULA	LOITER	MACACA	MANAMA	MASCOT
LEASER	LIKELY	LOMENT	MACACO	MANANA	MASERU
LEAVEN	LIKING	LOMITA	MACHAN	MANAPE	MASHIE
LEAVES	LILIOM	LOMOND	MACHIN	MANAUS	MASJID
LEBBEK	LILITH	LONDON	MACHIR	MANCHU	MASKED
LECAMA	LILLIL	LONELY	MACKLE	MANDAN	MASQUE
LECHEE	LIMBER	LONGER	MACLED	MANDIL	MASSES
LECHWE	LIMPET	LOOFAH	MACRON	MANDRA	MASSYS
LECTOR	LIMPID	LOOKED	MACULA	MANEGE	MASTER
LEDGER	LINAGA	LOOSEN	MADAME	MANGAS	MASTIC
LEEWAY	LINDEN	LOOTED	MADCAP	MANGEL	MATACO
LEGACY	LINEAL	LOPNOR	MADDEN	MANGER	MATCHA
LEGATE	LINEAR	LOQUAT	MADDER	MANGLE	MATICO
LEGATO	LINENS	LORATE	MADMAN	MANIAC	MATINS
LEGEND	LINGEL	LORCHA	MADRAS	MANILA	MATRIS
LEGENT	LINGER	LORDLY	MADRID	MANIOC	MATRIX
LEGION	LINGLE	LORICA	MADURA	MANITO	MATRON
LEGIST	LINGUI	LORIOT	MADURO	MANNAR	MATSYA
LEGMAN	LINING	LOSSES	MAENAD	MANNER	MATTED
LEGREE	LINKED	LOTION	MAFFIA	MANOAH	MATTER
LEGUME	LINNET	LOUNGE	MAGGED	MANTEL	MATURE
LEIPOA	LINTEL	LOUTRE	MAGGIE	MANTIS	MATZOS

MAUGIS	MERELY	MINION	MONTRE	MUMINA	NAPIER
MAUGRE	MERINA	MINNOW	MOOREA	MUMMER	NAPKIN
MAUMAU	MERINO	MINORS	MOORED	MUMPER	NAPLES
MAUSER	MERIST	MINUET	MOORUP	MUNCIE	NAPOLI
MAYDAY	MERLIN	MINUIT	MOPANE	MUNSEE	NAPPED
MAYFLY	MERLON	MINUTE	MOPISH	MURDER	NAPPIE
MAYHAP	MERMAN	MINYAN	MOPSUS	MURINE	NARAKA
MAYHEM	MERMEN	MIRAGE	MORALE	MURMUR	NARDOO
MAZAME	MEROPE	MIRIAM	MORALS	MURRAY	NARGIL
MAZUMA	MERSEY	MIRROR	MORASS	MUSANG	NARIAL
MEADOW	MESABI	MISERE	MORBID	MUSCAT	NARINE
MEAGER	MESCAL	MISERY	MOREEN	MUSEUM	NARROW
MEALIE	MESETA	MISFIT	MORGAN	MUSING	NASHUA
MEATUS	MESHED	MISHAP	MORION	MUSJID	NASSAU
MECATE	MESIAD	MISKAL	MORMON	MUSKAM	NATANT
MEDDLE	MESIAL	MISLAY	MORNAY	MUSKEG	NATATE
MEDIAL	MESJID	MISLED	MOROSE	MUSKET	NATHAN
MEDIAN	MESPIL	MISSAL	MORPHO	MUSKIE	NATION
MEDICI	METATE	MISSEL	MORRIS	MUSLIM	NATIVE
MEDICK	METEOR	MISTER	MORSEL	MUSLIN	NATRON
MEDICO	METHOD	MISTIC	MORTAL	MUSSEL	NATURE
MEDINA	METHYL	MISTLE	MORTAR	MUSSET	NAUGHT
MEDIUM	METIER	MISUSE	MORVEN	MUSSUK	NAUSEA
MEDIUS	METOPE	MITTEN	MOSAIC	MUSTEE	NAVAHO
MEDLAR	METRIC	MIZZLE	MOSCOW	MUSTER	NAVAJO
MEDLEY	METTLE	MNESIS	MOSKVA	MUTINY	NAYAUR
MEDUSA	MEUDON	MNEVIS	MOSLEM	MUTTER	NCHEGA
MEEKLY	MEXICO	MOANED	MOSQUE	MUTTON	NEANIC
MEGARA	MIAMIA	MOBILE	MOSTLY	MUTUAL	NEARBY
MEGHNA	MIASMA	MOBULA	MOTHER	MUUMUU	NEARER
MEGILP	MICHAL	MODENA	MOTILE	MUZHIK	NEARLY
MEHARI	MICRON	MODERN	MOTION	MUZJIK	NEATEN
MEKONG	MIDDAY	MODEST	MOTIVE	MUZZLE	NEATLY
MELADA	MIDDEN	MODIFY	MOTLEY	MYOPIC	NEBIIM
MELANO	MIDDIE	MODISH	MOTMOT	MYRCIA	NEBRIS
MELENE	MIDDLE	MODIST	MOTTLE	MYRIAD	NEBULA
MELINE	MIDGET	MODRED	MOUJIK	MYRTLE	NEBULE
MELLOW	MIDRIB	MOHAIR	MOUSER	MYSELF	NECTAR
MELODY	MIDWAY	MOHAVE	MOUSSE	MYSTES	NEEDLE
MELOTE	MIGHTY	MOHAWK	MOVIES	MYSTIC	NEEMBA
MELTED	MIGNON	MOHELI	MOVING	MYTHIC	NEGATE
MELTON	MIKADO	MOHOCK	MOWGLI	NAAMAH	NEISSE
MEMBER	MILADY	MOIETY	MOWING	NABOTH	NELSON
MEMNON	MILANO	MOIRAI	MOZART	NACHIN	NEMEAN
MEMOIR	MILCAH	MOJAVE	MUCKLE	NAEVUS	NEPHEW
MEMORY	MILDEW	MOLARS	MUCOSA	NAGANA	NEPOTE
MENACE	MILEDH	MOLDAU	MUDCAT	NAGUAL	NERCID
MENAGE	MILIEU	MOLEST	MUDDLE	NAHOOR	NEREID
MENHIR	MILIUM	MOLINE	MUDHEN	NAIPES	NEREIS
MENIAL	MILLAY	MOLOCH	MUERMO	NAKHOD	NEREUS
MENRFA	MILLER	MOMENT	MUFFIN	NAKONG	NERGAL
MENRVA	MILLES	MOMIJI	MUFFLE	NAMELY	NEROLI
MENTAL	MILLET	MONACO	MUGGER	NAMMAD	NERUDA
MENTHA	MILTON	MONDAY	MUKDEN	NANDIN	NERVES
MENTOR	MIMBAR	MONGER	MUKLUK	NANIMO	NESSEL
MENTUM	MIMOSA	MONGOL	MUKTAR	NANISM	NESTER
MERAPI	MINBAR	MONIED	MULETA	NANKIN	NESTLE
MERARI	MINDED	MONIES	MULISH	NANOID	NESTOR
MERCER	MINDEL	MONISM	MULLAH	NANSEN	NETCHA
MERCIA	MINGLE	MONKEY	MULLER	NANTES	NETHER
MERDLE	MINIES	MONODY	MULLET	NAPALM	NETTED
MERELS	MINING	MONROE	MUMBLE	NAPERY	NETTLE

NEURAL	NOTION	OGLERS	ORIOLE	PADNAG	PARODY
NEURON	NOUGAT	OGMIOS	ORISON	PAEKTU	PAROLE
NEUTER	NOUGHT	OGRISH	ORKHON	PAELLA	PARROT
NEVADA	NOUMEA	OHENRY	ORLOFF	PAGODA	PARSEC
NEWARK	NOVENA	OHIOAN	ORMAZD	PAHANG	PARSEE
NEWEST	NOVIAL	OILCAN	ORMOLU	PAILOU	PARSON
NEWISH	NOVICE	OILLET	ORNATE	PAINED	PARTLY
NEWMAN	NOZZLE	OILPAN	OROIDE	PAIRED	PARURE
NEWTON	NUANCE	OLDAGE	OROZCO	PAIUTE	PARVIS
NIACIN	NUBIAN	OLDEST	ORPHAN	PAKEHA	PASCAL
NIAMEY	NUBILE	OLEASE	ORPINE	PALACE	PASCHA
NIBBLE	NUCHAL	OLEFIN	ORRERY	PALAMA	PASQUE
NICAEA	NUGGET	OLIVER	ORTIVE	PALATE	PASSED
NICENE	NULLAH	OLIVET	OSHIMA	PALEST	PASSER
NICETY	NULLED	OLOMAO	OSIRIS	PALILA	PASSUS
NICHES	NUMBAT	OMASUM	OSPREY	PALING	PASTED
NICKEL	NUMBER	OMELET	OSSIAN	PALLAS	PASTEL
NICKER	NUPHAR	OMITIS	OSSIFY	PALLET	PASTER
NICOLO	NURSED	ONAGER	OSTEAL	PALLID	PASTIL
NICOYA	NUTANT	ONDINE	OSTEND	PALLOR	PASTOR
NIDIFY	NUTMEG	ONEIDA	OSTIUM	PALMER	PASTRY
NIELLO	NUTRIA	ONEWAY	OSTLER	PALMUS	PATACA
NIIHAU	OAXACA	ONTOUR	OSTYAK	PALTER	PATCHY
NILGAI	OBECHE	ONWARD	OTALGY	PALTRY	PATENT
NIMBLE	OBELUS	OODLES	OTELLO	PAMIRS	PATERA
NIMBUS	OBERON	OOLITE	OTHERS	PAMPAS	PATESI
NIMROD	OBISPO	OOLOGY	OTIOSE	PAMPER	PATHOS
NINGAL	OBITER	OOLONG	OTITIS	PANACE	PATINA
NIOBES	OBJECT	OOMIAK	OTSEGO	PANADA	PATLID
NIPPER	OBLATE	OORALI	OTTAWA	PANAMA	PATOIC
NIPPLE	OBLIGE	OORIAL	OUSTED	PANDAN	PATOIS
NIPPON	OBLONG	OPALIA	OUSTER	PANDER	PATRAS
NISNAS	OBOIST	OPAQUE	OUTCRY	PANDIT	PATRIA
NISSEN	OBOLUS	OPELET	OUTFIT	PANELS	PATROL
NITWIT	OBSESS	OPENED	OUTING	PANISC	PATRON
NIVOSE	OBTAIN	OPENER	OUTLAW	PANISK	PATTEN
NOBODY	OBTUSE	OPENLY	OUTLAY	PANTOD	PATTER
NOCAKE	OCCULT	OPHISM	OUTLET	PANTRY	PATZER
NOCENT	OCCUPY	OPHITE	OUTPUT	PANTUN	PAULIN
NODDLE	OCEANA	OPIATE	OUTRAN	PANUCO	PAUNCH
NODOSE	OCELOT	OPORTO	OUTRUN	PAPAGO	PAUPER
NODULE	OCTANE	OPPOSE	OUTSET	PAPAYA	PAUSED
NOESIS	OCTANT	OPPUGN	OUTWIT	PAPERY	PAVING
NOETIC	OCTAVE	OPTICS	OVERDO	PAPHOS	PAVIOR
NOGAKU	OCTAVO	OPTIME	OVERLY	PAPULE	PAWNEE
NOGGIN	OCTROI	OPTION	OVIBOS	PARADE	PAWPAW
NOMIUS	OCULAR	ORACHE	OVIEDO	PARADO	PAYEES
NONAGE	ODDITY	ORACLE	OWYHEE	PARANG	PAYING
NONCOM	ODENSE	ORALLY	OXALIS	PARAPH	PEAHEN
NONEGO	ODESSA	ORANGE	OXFORD	PARCAE	PEANUT
NOODLE	ODETTA	ORATOR	OXHIDE	PARCEL	PEAVEY
NORATE	ODIOUS	ORCHID	OXSLIP	PARDON	PEBBLE
NORDIC	OECIST	ORDAIN	OXWORT	PARENT	PECTEN
NORMAL	OENEUS	ORDEAL	OXYGEN	PAREVE	PECTIN
NORMAN	OENGUS	OREBRO	OYSTER	PARGET	PEDANT
NORRIS	OENONE	OREGON	OZARKS	PARIAH	PEDATE
NORWAY	OFFEND	ORGEAT	PAANGA	PARISH	PEDDLE
NOSALE	OFFICE	ORIANA	PACHIS	PARITY	PEDLAR
NOTARY	OFFSET	ORIENT	PACIFY	PARLAY	PEDULE
NOTATE	OFLATE	ORIGAN	PACKER	PARLEY	PEEDEE
NOTICE	OGDOAD	ORIGEN	PACKET	PARLOR	PEELER
NOTIFY	OGLALA	ORIGIN	PADDLE	PARNAS	PEEPBO

PEEPER	PHAROS	PINKED	PODIUM	POTATO	PTERIC
PEERED	PHASIA	PINKIE	PODZOL	POTEEN	PTISAN
PEEVER	PHATIC	PINOCH	POETRY	POTENT	PTOSIS
PEEVEY	PHEDRE	PINOLE	POGROM	POTION	PUBLIC
PEIPUS	PHELIM	PINTLE	POINTS	POTOSI	PUCKER
PEKING	PHENOL	PINUPS	POIROT	POTTER	PUDDLE
PEKMEZ	PHILIP	PINZON	POISON	POUNCE	PUEBLO
PELAGE	PHLEGM	PIPING	POLACK	POUNCH	PUFFED
PELEUS	PHLOEM	PIPKIN	POLDER	POWDER	PUFFER
PELIKE	PHOBIA	PIPPIN	POLEAX	POWWOW	PUFFIN
PELION	PHOBOS	PIRACY	POLEYN	POYANG	PULLET
PELITE	PHOEBE	PIRATE	POLICE	PRAGUE	PULLEY
PELLET	PHONED	PIRENE	POLICY	PRAISE	PULPER
PELMET	PHONEY	PISACA	POLISH	PRANCE	PULPIT
PELOPS	PHONIC	PISCES	POLITE	PRANKY	PULQUE
PELOTA	PHOOEY	PISGAH	POLITY	PRASEO	PUMELO
PELTRY	PHRASE	PISHON	POLLAM	PRATER	PUMICE
PELUDO	PHRYNE	PISTIC	POLLAN	PRAVDA	PUNDIT
PELURE	PHYLUM	PISTIL	POLLEN	PRAYER	PUNISH
PELVIS	PHYSIC	PISTOL	POLLEX	PREACH	PUNKAH
PENANG	PHYTON	PISTON	POLLUX	PRECIS	PUNKIE
PENATE	PIATTI	PITMAN	POMACE	PRECUT	PUNTER
PENCIL	PIAZZA	PITPAN	POMADE	PREFER	PUPPET
PENEST	PICINE	PLACER	POMELO	PREFIX	PURIFY
PENEUS	PICKET	PLACID	POMMÉE	PREPAY	PURIRI
PENMAN	PICKLE	PLAGUE	POMMEL	PRESTO	PURIST
PENNED	PICKUP	PLAGUY	POMONA	PRETER	PURITY
PENNON	PICNIC	PLAICE	POMPEY	PRETOR	PURLIN
PENROD	PICUDA	PLAINS	POMPOM	PRETTY	PURSER
PENSUM	PIDGIN	PLAINT	POMPON	PREYED	PURSUE
PENTAD	PIECES	PLANED	PONAPE	PRICED	PURVEY
PENULT	PIEGAN	PLANET	PONCHO	PRIENE	PUSHER
PENURY	PIERCE	PLANTS	PONDER	PRIEST	PUSHKA
PEOPLE	PIERED	PLAPER	PONGEE	PRIMAL	PUTELI
PEPLOS	PIERIA	PLAQUE	PONTAC	PRIMED	PUTNEY
PEPPER	PIERIS	PLASMA	PONTIL	PRIMER	PUTOFF
PEPSIN	PIERRE	PLATED	PONTON	PRINCE	PUTOUT
PEQUOD	PIFFLE	PLATEN	POODLE	PRIORY	PUTRID
PERICO	PIGEON	PLATER	POOKOO	PRISON	PUTTEE
PERIOD	PIGLET	PLATTE	POOPED	PRIVET	PUTTER
PERISH	PIGMAN	PLAUEN	POORER	PROBER	PUZZLE
PERKIN	PIGNUT	PLAYER	POPLAR	PROCNE	PYEMIA
PERMIT	PIGSTY	PLEACH	POPLIN	PROFIT	PYGARG
PERNIO	PILAGA	PLEASE	POPPER	PROLIX	PYMENT
PERRIN	PILATE	PLEDGE	POROSE	PROMPT	PYRENE
PERRON	PILEUS	PLENTY	POROUS	PRONTO	PYRITE
PERSIA	PILFER	PLENUM	PORTAL	PROPEL	PYROPE
PERSON	PILLAR	PLEVIN	PORTAS	PROPER	PYRRHA
PERUKE	PILLOW	PLEXOR	PORTER	PROREB	PYTHIA
PERUSE	PILORI	PLEXUS	PORTIA	PROSIT	PYTHON
PESACH	PILOSE	PLIANT	PORTLY	PROTEM	QISHON
PESADE	PILPAY	PLIERS	PORVOO	PROTON	QUACKS
PESETA	PILPUL	PLIGHT	POSNET	PROUST	QUADRI
PESTER	PILSEN	PLINTH	POSOLE	PROVED	QUAGGA
PESTLE	PIMPLE	PLOUGH	POSSET	PRUNED	QUAHOG
PETAIN	PINANG	PLOVER	POSSUM	PRUNUS	QUAINT
PETARD	PINBOY	PLUCKY	POSTAL	PRUTAH	QUAKER
PETREL	PINCER	PLUNGE	POSTER	PRYING	QUALMS
PETROL	PINCHE	PLURAL	POSTIL	PSALMS	QUARRY
PEWTER	PINDAR	PLUTOS	POTAGE	PSEUDO	QUARTE
PEYOTE	PINEAL	PNEUMA	POTALA	PSOCID	QUARTO
PHAEDO	PINERO	POCKED	POTARO	PSYCHE	QUARTZ
PHAGUN	PINION	POCKET	POTASH	PSYCHO	QUAVER

QUEASY	RANCHO	RECORD	REMUDA	REVERT	ROCKER
QUEBEC	RANCID	RECOUP	REMULA	REVEST	ROCKET
QUEENS	RANCOR	RECTOR	RENAME	REVIEW	ROCOCO
QUEMOY	RANDAN	REDACT	RENARD	REVILE	RODENT
QUENCH	RANDEM	REDBUD	RENDER	REVISE	RODMAN
QUEZON	RANDOM	REDCAP	RENEGE	REVIVE	ROGERS
QUICHE	RANGER	REDDEN	RENNES	REVOKE	ROILED
QUICHU	RANINE	REDDLE	RENNET	REVOLT	ROLAND
QUINCE	RANKED	REDDOG	RENNIN	REWARD	ROLLER
QUINOA	RANKIN	REDEEM	RENOIR	REWORD	ROMANO
QUINSY	RANKLE	REDMAN	RENOWN	RHEBOK	ROMANY
QUITCH	RANSOM	REDOWA	RENTER	RHESUS	ROMMEL
QUIVER	RAPIDS	REDUCE	REOPEN	RHETOR	ROMNEY
QUOKKA	RAPIER	REECHO	REPAIR	RHEXIA	RONDEL
QUORUM	RAPINE	REEFER	REPAND	RHINAL	ROOFER
QUOTED	RAPPEE	REFILL	REPAST	RHODES	ROOKIE
QUOTES	RAPPEL	REFINE	REPAVE	RHONDA	ROOMER
RAAMAH	RAPPEN	REFLEX	REPEAL	RHYTHM	ROOTED
RABATO	RAPPER	REFLUX	REPEAT	RHYTON	ROOTER
RABBET	RAREFY	REFORM	REPENT	RIALTO	ROSARY
RABBIT	RARELY	REFUGE	REPINE	RIBALD	ROSCOE
RABBLE	RARITY	REFUND	REPORT	RIBBON	ROSEAU
RABIES	RASCAL	REFUSE	REPOSE	RIBOSE	ROSIER
RACEME	RASHER	REFUTE	REPUTE	RICHES	ROSMER
RACHEL	RASURE	REGAIN	REQUIN	RICHET	ROSSET
RACIAL	RATHER	REGALE	REQUIT	RIDDEN	ROSTER
RACINE	RATIFY	REGARD	RESALE	RIDDLE	ROTATE
RACKET	RATINE	REGENT	RESCUE	RIDEAU	ROTCHE
RADDLE	RATING	REGIME	RESEDA	RIDENT	ROTTED
RADIAL	RATION	REGINA	RESEED	RIDGED	ROTTEN
RADIAN	RATITE	REGION	RESELL	RIENZI	ROTTER
RADISH	RATLIN	REGLUE	RESENT	RIGGER	ROTULA
RADIUM	RATOON	REGNAL	RESHUT	RIGORS	ROTUND
RADIUS	RATTAN	REGRET	RESIDE	RIJEKA	ROUNCE
RADOME	RATTAT	REGULA	RESIGN	RILLET	ROVING
RADULA	RATTLE	REHANG	RESILE	RIMOSE	ROXANE
RAFALE	RAVAGE	REHASH	RESIST	RIMPLE	RRAPHY
RAFAYA	RAVINE	REHEAT	RESITE	RIMSKY	RRHAGE
RAFFIA	RAVING	REIRON	RESORT	RINGER	RRHINE
RAFFLE	RAVISH	REJECT	RESTED	RINNEN	RUBATO
RAFTER	READER	REJOIN	RESTER	RIOJAS	RUBBED
RAGGED	REALLY	RELACE	RESULT	RIOTER	RUBBEE
RAGGEE	REALTY	RELAIS	RESUME	RIPEST	RUBBER
RAGING	REAMER	RELATE	RETAIL	RIPPED	RUBBLE
RAGLAN	REAPER	RELENT	RETAIN	RIPPLE	RUBENS
RAGOUT	REARED	RELICS	RETAMA	RISING	RUDDER
RAGTAG	REARER	RELICT	RETAPE	RISKED	RUDDLE
RAHULA	REASON	RELIEF	RETARD	RITTER	RUDOLF
RAIDER	REBATE	RELINK	RETENE	RITUAL	RUEFUL
RAISED	REBATO	RELISH	RETEST	RIVERA	RUFFLE
RAISER	REBUFF	RELIVE	RETINA	RIVOSE	RUGATE
RAISIN	REBUKE	REMADE	RETIRE	RIYADH	RUGGED
RAJANG	RECALL	REMAIN	RETORT	RIZPAH	RUGOSE
RAKSHA	RECANT	REMAKE	RETRAD	ROARER	RUGOUS
RAMAGE	RECAST	REMAND	RETRAL	ROBALO	RUINED
RAMBLE	RECEDE	REMARK	RETREE	ROBBED	RULING
RAMIFY	RECENT	REMEDY	RETURN	ROBBER	RUMBLE
RAMMAN	RECESS	REMIND	REUBEN	ROBBIN	RUMMAGE
RAMMED	RECIFE	REMISE	REURGE	ROBERT	RUMMER
RAMOSE	RECIPE	REMISS	REVAMP	ROBSON	RUMPLE
RAMOUS	RECITE	REMORA	REVEAL	ROBUST	RUMPUS
RAMROD	RECKON	REMOTE	REVERE	ROCCUS	RUNNEL
RAMSAY	RECOIL	REMOVE	REVERS	ROCHET	RUNNER

RUPERT	SALTON	SAVORY	SEAMAN	SEREIN	SHASTA
RURIKS	SALUTE	SAWYER	SEANAD	SERENA	SHAVER
RUSHED	SALVER	SAXONY	SEANCE	SERENE	SHEARS
RUSSAR	SALVIA	SAYING	SEARCH	SERENO	SHEATH
RUSSET	SAMARA	SAYYID	SEASON	SERIAL	SHEAVE
RUSSIA	SAMBAR	SBRINZ	SEATER	SERIES	SHEBAT
RUSTED	SAMEKH	SCABBY	SEAWAN	SERMON	SHECAT
RUSTIC	SAMIEL	SCALAR	SEBAGO	SEROUS	SHEENY
RUSTLE	SAMITE	SCALED	SECANT	SERVAL	SHEETS
RUSTUM	SAMOAN	SCALER	SECKEL	SERVER	SHEKEL
RUTILE	SAMPAN	SCALES	SECOND	SESAME	SHELAH
SABALO	SAMPLE	SCAMPI	SECRET	SESELI	SHELLY
SABBAT	SAMSON	SCANNO	SECTOR	SESTET	SHELTY
SABINE	SANAGA	SCANTY	SECURE	SESTOS	SHELVE
SABINO	SANCHO	SCARAB	SEDATE	SETOFF	SHEOAK
SABLON	SANDAL	SCARCE	SEDILE	SETOSE	SHERIF
SACHEM	SANEST	SCARED	SEDUCE	SETTEE	SHERPA
SACHET	SANGAY	SCARID	SEEDER	SETTER	SHERRY
SACRAL	SANGHO	SCARPE	SEEING	SETTLE	SHIELD
SACRED	SANIES	SCATHE	SEEMLY	SEURAT	SHIFTY
SACRUM	SANITY	SCENIC	SEESAW	SEVERE	SHIITE
SADDEN	SANNUP	SCHEME	SEESEE	SEVIER	SHIKAR
SADDLE	SANSEI	SCHIPA	SEETHE	SEVRES	SHIKRA
SADIST	SANTAL	SCHISM	SEIDEL	SEWAGE	SHILOH
SADITE	SANTEE	SCHIST	SEINER	SEWARD	SHINER
SAFARI	SANTIM	SCHOOL	SEISIN	SEWERS	SHINTO
SAFETY	SANTIR	SCHUSS	SEIZED	SEWING	SHIRAZ
SAGENE	SANTON	SCIPIO	SEIZIN	SEXTAN	SHIRRA
SAGGER	SANTOS	SCLAFF	SELDOM	SEXTET	SHIVER
SAGOIN	SAPOTA	SCLERA	SELECT	SEXTON	SHOATE
SAGRIS	SAPOTE	SCONCE	SELENA	SEXTUS	SHODDY
SAHARA	SAPPER	SCORCH	SELENE	SFORZA	SHOFAR
SAHIBA	SAPPHO	SCORIA	SELKET	SHABAN	SHOGUN
SAIGON	SARADA	SCOTCH	SELLER	SHABBY	SHOPPE
SAILOR	SARDIS	SCOTER	SELVAS	SHADED	SHORTS
SAIMAA	SARDOU	SCOTIA	SEMELE	SHADES	SHOULD
SAIPAN	SAREMA	SCOTTI	SEMEME	SHADOW	SHOVEL
SAITHE	SARGON	SCOVEL	SEMENI	SHADUF	SHOWER
SAKAKI	SARLAK	SCRAPE	SEMERU	SHAGGY	SHOWME
SAKIEH	SARLYK	SCRAPS	SEMITE	SHAGIV	SHREWD
SAKURA	SARONG	SCRAWL	SEMOLA	SHAHIN	SHRIEK
SALAAM	SARRAS	SCREAM	SEMSEM	SHAKEN	SHRIKE
SALADA	SARTOR	SCREED	SENARY	SHAKER	SHRILL
SALAME	SARTRE	SCREEN	SENATE	SHAKES	SHRIMP
SALAMI	SARWAN	SCREWY	SENECA	SHAKTA	SHRINE
SALARY	SASEBO	SCRIBE	SENILE	SHAKTI	SHRINK
SALEMA	SASSAK	SCRIMP	SENIOR	SHAMAL	SHRIVE
SALENA	SATEEN	SCRIPT	SENNET	SHAMAN	SHROFF
SALIAN	SATING	SCRIVE	SENORA	SHAMAS	SHROUD
SALINA	SATIRE	SCROLL	SENRYU	SHAMES	SHUCKS
SALINE	SATRAP	SCRUFF	SENSED	SHAMIR	SHUTUP
SALISH	SATRON	SCRYER	SENTRY	SHAMMA	SIALIC
SALIVA	SATTEE	SCURRY	SENUFO	SHAMUS	SICILY
SALLET	SATURN	SCURVE	SENUSI	SHANDY	SICKEN
SALLOO	SAUCER	SCURVY	SEPTET	SHANSI	SICKLE
SALLOW	SAUGER	SCUTCH	SEPTUM	SHANTY	SICKLY
SALMON	SAUREL	SCUTUM	SEQUEL	SHAPED	SIDDUR
SALOME	SAVAGE	SCYLLA	SEQUIN	SHAPER	SIDING
SALOON	SAVAII	SCYTHE	SERAFF	SHARED	SIENNA
SALOOP	SAVANT	SEACAR	SERAIL	SHARER	SIERRA
SALPID	SAVATE	SEADOG	SERAPE	SHARIA	SIESTA
SALTED	SAVING	SEAFIG	SERAPH	SHARJA	SIFAKA
SALTEN	SAVIOR	SEALER	SERBET	SHARON	SIFTER

SIGHTS	SLAMET	SOCKET	SPIDER	STAPES	STRASS
SIGNAL	SLATED	SODDEN	SPIGOT	STAPLE	STRATH
SIGNED	SLATER	SODIUM	SPIKED	STARCH	STREAK
SIGNET	SLATES	SOFANE	SPIKES	STARRY	STREAM
SIGNOR	SLAVER	SOFTEN	SPINAL	STARVE	STREEP
SIGURD	SLAVEY	SOFTER	SPINEL	STASIS	STREET
SIKKIM	SLAYER	SOFTLY	SPINET	STATER	STREGA
SILAGE	SLEAVE	SOHRAB	SPIRAL	STATIC	STRESS
SILENT	SLEDGE	SOILED	SPIREA	STATOR	STREWN
SILICA	SLEEPY	SOIREE	SPIRIT	STATUE	STRICT
SILVAN	SLEEVE	SOKARI	SPLASH	STATUS	STRIDE
SILVER	SLEIGH	SOLACE	SPLEEN	STAVED	STRIFE
SIMEON	SLEUTH	SOLANO	SPLICE	STEADY	STRIKE
SIMIAN	SLIDER	SOLDER	SPLINE	STEAMY	STRING
SIMILE	SLIDES	SOLELY	SPLINT	STEARO	STRIPE
SIMLIN	SLIGHT	SOLEMN	SPOILS	STEELE	STRIVE
SIMMER	SLIPON	SOLLAR	SPOKEN	STEEVE	STROKE
SIMONY	SLIVER	SOLLER	SPONGE	STELAR	STROLL
SIMOOM	SLOGAN	SOMATO	SPONGY	STELLA	STROMO
SIMOON	SLOPPY	SOMBER	SPOOKY	STELLE	STRONG
SIMOUS	SLOUCH	SOMITE	SPOONS	STENCH	STRUCK
SIMPER	SLOUGH	SONANT	SPORTS	STEPPE	STRUMA
SIMPLE	SLOVAK	SONATA	SPORTY	STEREO	STUART
SIMPLY	SLOVEN	SONNET	SPOUSE	STERIN	STUBBY
SIMURG	SLOWLY	SONOMA	SPRAIN	STERNE	STUCCO
SINAIC	SLOWUP	SOONER	SPRAWL	STEROL	STUDIO
SINBAD	SLUDGE	SOOSOO	SPREAD	STEVEN	STUFFY
SINDHI	SLUDGY	SOOTHE	SPRING	STEVIA	STUPES
SINEWS	SLUICE	SOPHIA	SPRINT	STHENO	STUPID
SINEWY	SMALTO	SORDID	SPRITE	STICKS	STUPOR
SINFUL	SMARTY	SOREST	SPROUT	STICKY	STURDY
SINGER	SMEATH	SORREL	SPRUCE	STIFLE	STYLED
SINGLE	SMELLY	SORROW	SPRUNG	STIGMA	STYLET
SINGLY	SMILER	SORTED	SPUNKY	STIMIE	STYLUS
SINKER	SMILEY	SORTES	SPURGE	STINGY	STYMIE
SINNER	SMIRCH	SORTIE	SPUTUM	STIPEL	SUBDUE
SINTER	SMITCH	SOTHIS	SQUALL	STITCH	SUBMIT
SIPPET	SMITHY	SOTNIK	SQUAMA	STITHY	SUBTLE
SIRCAR	SMOKER	SOURCE	SQUAMO	STIVER	SUBURA
SIRDAR	SMOOTH	SOUSSE	SQUARE	STMALO	SUBURB
SIRENE	SMUDGE	SOVIET	SQUASH	STOCKS	SUBWAY
SIRIUS	SMYRNA	SOWBUG	SQUEAK	STOCKY	SUCCOR
SIRRAH	SNAPAT	SOWDER	SQUEAL	STODGY	SUCCOS
SIRUPY	SNAPON	SOWING	SQUILL	STOGIE	SUCKER
SISERA	SNARED	SPACED	SQUINT	STOICS	SUDDEN
SISKIN	SNASTE	SPADES	SQUIRE	STOKER	SUDDIE
SISLEY	SNATCH	SPADIX	SQUIRM	STOLEN	SUFFER
SISSOO	SNATHE	SPALAX	SQUIRT	STOLID	SUFFIX
SISTER	SNEAKY	SPARGE	SQUONK	STOLON	SUGARY
SITCOM	SNEEZE	SPARKS	STABLE	STONED	SUISSE
SITTER	SNEEZY	SPARSE	STACTE	STONES	SUISUN
SIXGUN	SNIPER	SPARTA	STADIA	STOOGE	SUITED
SKANDA	SNITCH	SPATHA	STAGER	STORAX	SUITOR
SKETCH	SNIVEL	SPAVIN	STAIRS	STORGE	SUKKOT
SKEWED	SNOOTY	SPECIE	STAITH	STORMY	SULCUS
SKEWER	SNOOZE	SPEECH	STALAG	STOWER	SULFUR
SKIING	SNORED	SPEEDY	STALER	STPAUL	SULLEN
SKIMPY	SNORRI	SPENCE	STALIN	STRABO	SULTAN
SKINNY	SOAKED	SPERRY	STAMEN	STRAFE	SULTRY
SKIVER	SOAMES	SPHENE	STAMIN	STRAIN	SULUNG
SKIVVY	SOBBED	SPHERE	STANCE	STRAIT	SUMERU
SLACKS	SOCAGE	SPHINX	STANCH	STRAKE	SUMIDA
SLALOM	SOCIAL	SPICED	STANZA	STRAND	SUMMER

SUMMIT	TACTIC	TARPAN	TENDON	THORIA	TIRANA
SUMMON	TAENIA	TARPON	TENNIS	THORNY	TIRING
SUMTER	TAFFIA	TARSIA	TENREC	THORPE	TIRWIT
SUNDAE	TAGGED	TARSUS	TENSON	THOUGH	TISANE
SUNDAY	TAGORE	TARTAN	TENSOR	THRACE	TISHRI
SUNDER	TAHITI	TARTAR	TENTER	THRALL	TISSOT
SUNDEW	TAILED	TARTAR	TENURE	THRASH	TISSUE
SUNDRY	TAILER	TASMAN	TERATO	THRASO	TISWIN
SUNKEN	TAILLE	TASSEL	TERCEL	THREAD	TITANO
SUNNAH	TAILOR	TASSET	TERCET	THREAT	TITANS
SUNSET	TAIMYR	TASTER	TERCIO	THREED	TITIAN
SUPARI	TAIPEH	TATAMI	TEREDO	THRESH	TITLED
SUPAWN	TAIPEI	TATARS	TEREFA	THRIFT	TITTER
SUPERB	TAIWAN	TATARY	TERESA	THRILL	TITTLE
SUPINE	TAKAHE	TATTER	TERETE	THRIPS	TIVOLI
SUPPED	TAKING	TATTLE	TERMED	THRIVE	TIZONA
SUPPLE	TALBOT	TATTOO	TERMES	THROAT	TLALOC
SUPPLY	TALCUM	TAURUS	TERRAL	THRONE	TMESIS
SURELY	TALENT	TAUTEN	TERRET	THRONG	TOBIAS
SUREST	TALION	TAUTOG	TERRIT	THRUMS	TOBINE
SURETE	TALKER	TAVERN	TERROR	THRUSH	TOCSIN
SURETY	TALLER	TAWDRY	TESTER	THRUST	TODDAO
SURFER	TALLIN	TAXINE	TETANY	THWACK	TODDLE
SURREY	TALLIT	TAYLOR	TETARD	THWART	TOFFEE
SURVEY	TALLOW	TEACUP	TETCHY	THYINE	TOGGLE
SUSLIK	TALMUD	TEAGUE	TETHER	THYMUS	TOILER
SUSSEX	TAMALE	TEAMED	TETHIS	TIAMAT	TOILET
SUTLER	TAMAYO	TEANAU	TETHYS	TICKET	TOLEDO
SUTTEE	TAMBAC	TEAPOT	TETRAD	TICKLE	TOLTEC
SUTTER	TAMBOR	TEAPOY	TETTER	TIDBIT	TOMATO
SUTURE	TAMEST	TEASEL	TEUTON	TIDILY	TOMBOY
SVELTE	TAMINE	TEASER	TEVERE	TIEDUP	TOMCAT
SWAMPY	TAMINY	TEBETH	TEXOMA	TIEDYE	TOMCOD
SWANEE	TAMISE	TECOMA	THALER	TIEPIN	TOMTIT
SWATCH	TAMMUZ	TEDDER	THALES	TIERCE	TOMTOM
SWATHE	TAMPER	TEDEUM	THALIA	TIERED	TONGUE
SWEATY	TAMPON	TEDIUM	THALLO	TIFFIN	TONITE
SWEDEN	TAMTAM	TEEPEE	THAMES	TIFLIS	TONSIL
SWEETS	TAMURE	TEETER	THANKS	TIGHTS	TONSOR
SWERVE	TANAIS	TEETSE	THEBES	TIGRIS	TOOLED
SWIPLE	TANATE	TEFNUT	THEINE	TILAKA	TOOTOO
SWITCH	TANDEM	TEGMEN	THEIRS	TILDEN	TOPDOG
SYDNEY	TANGLE	TEGNER	THEIST	TILLER	TOPEKA
SYLLID	TANGUN	TEGULA	THEMIS	TILPAH	TOPHAT
SYLVAN	TANGUT	TEHRAN	THENAR	TIMBAL	TOPHET
SYMBOL	TANIST	TELARY	THENCE	TIMBER	TOPPER
SYNTAX	TANKER	TELEDU	THEORY	TIMBRE	TOPPLE
SYPHAX	TANNED	TELEGA	THERIO	TIMELY	TORERO
SYRINX	TANNER	TELEME	THERME	TIMING	TORINO
SYRTOS	TANTRA	TELIAL	THERMO	TINCAL	TOROSE
SYSTEM	TAOISM	TELIUM	THESAN	TINDER	TOROUS
SYZYGY	TAOYAN	TELLER	THESIS	TINGLE	TORPID
SZEGED	TAPAGE	TELLUS	THETIC	TINIAN	TORPOR
TAAROA	TAPETI	TELSON	THETIS	TINKER	TORQUE
TABARD	TAPIST	TEMIAK	THIEVE	TINKLE	TORRID
TABLED	TAPPER	TEMPER	THIMPU	TINNED	TORULA
TABLES	TAPPET	TEMPLE	THIRST	TINSEL	TOSSER
TABLET	TARATA	TEMUCO	THIRTY	TINTED	TOSSUP
TABOOT	TARAWA	TENACE	THISBE	TIPPET	TOTARA
TABRET	TARGET	TENANT	THOMAS	TIPPLE	TOTTER
TABRIZ	TARGUM	TENARU	THONGA	TIPTOE	TOUCAN
TACKLE	TARIFF	TENDED	THOOID	TIPTOP	TOUCHE
TACOMA		TENDER	THORAX	TIRADE	TOUCHY

TOULON	TSESIS	ULETIC	UPROOT	VENOUS	VOLUTE
TOUPEE	TSETSE	ULITIS	UPSHOT	VERBAL	VOODOO
TOUSLE	TSINAN	ULIXES	UPUAUT	VERDIN	VORMSI
TOWARD	TUAREG	ULLAGE	UPWARD	VERDOT	VORTEX
TOWHEE	TUCKER	ULSTER	URAEUS	VERDUN	VOSGES
TOWSER	TUCSON	ULTIMA	URANIA	VEREIN	VOSTOK
TRACER	TULANE	ULTIMO	URANIC	VERGER	VOTARY
TRADER	TUMBLE	UMLAUT	URANIN	VERGIL	VOYAGE
TRAGUS	TUMTUM	UMPIRE	URANUS	VERIFY	VRITRA
TRALEE	TUMULT	UMTATA	URBANE	VERILY	VUELTA
TRANCE	TUNDRA	UNABLE	URCHIN	VERNAL	VULCAN
TRASHY	TUNEUP	UNAMEE	URGENT	VERONA	VULGAR
TRAUMA	TUNICA	UNBIND	URSULA	VERSAL	VULPES
TRAVEL	TUNNEL	UNCIAL	URTICA	VERSED	WABASH
TREATY	TUPAIA	UNCOIL	USANCE	VERSOR	WABBER
TREBLE	TUPELO	UNDINE	USEFUL	VERSUS	WABBLE
TREBLY	TURARA	UNDONE	USURER	VERTEX	WACHNA
TREMOR	TURBAN	UNEASE	UTERUS	VERVET	WADDLE
TRENCH	TURBID	UNEASY	UTMOST	VESPER	WADERS
TRENTO	TURBOT	UNESCO	UTOPIA	VESSEL	WAFFLE
TREPAN	TURDUS	UNEVEN	VACANT	VESTAL	WAGERS
TREPID	TUREEN	UNFAIR	VACATE	VESTED	WAGGLE
TREVAT	TURGID	UNFOLD	VACUUM	VESTRY	WAGNER
TREVET	TURKEY	UNFURL	VAGARY	VIANDS	WAGRAM
TRIAGE	TURNED	UNGUAL	VAHINE	VIATIC	WAHABI
TRICED	TURNER	UNGUIS	VAISYA	VICTIM	WAHELA
TRICHO	TURNIP	UNHAND	VALERY	VICTOR	WAHINE
TRICKY	TURPIN	UNHOLY	VALGUS	VICUNA	WAILER
TRICOT	TURRET	UNHURT	VALINE	VIDUAL	WAITER
TRIFLE	TURTLE	UNIATE	VALISE	VIELLE	WAIVED
TRIGON	TUSCAN	UNICEF	VALLEY	VIENNA	WALDEN
TRIPLE	TUSSIS	UNIQUE	VALLUM	VIHARA	WALKER
TRIPOD	TUSSLE	UNISON	VALOIS	VIKING	WALLET
TRIPOS	TUXEDO	UNITED	VALUED	VILIFY	WALLIS
TRISTE	TUYERE	UNIVAC	VAMANA	VILLON	WALLOW
TRITON	TWEENY	UNJUST	VAMOSE	VIMANA	WALLUP
TRIUNE	TWELVE	UNKIND	VANDAL	VINATA	WALNUT
TRIVAT	TWENTY	UNLESS	VANISH	VINOUS	WALRUS
TRIVET	TWIBIL	UNLIKE	VANITY	VINYON	WALTON
TRIVIA	TWINED	UNLOAD	VANNER	VIOLET	WAMARA
TRIVOT	TWINGE	UNMASK	VARAHA	VIOLIN	WAMPEE
TROCAR	TWISTED	UNPAID	VARLET	VIRAGO	WAMPUM
TROCHE	TWITCH	UNREAL	VARUNA	VIRGIL	WANDER
TROGON	TWOROG	UNREST	VASHTI	VIRGIN	WANKEL
TROIKA	TYCOON	UNRIPE	VASSAL	VIRILE	WANNER
TROOPS	TYDEUS	UNRULY	VASSEL	VIRTUE	WANTON
TROPEZ	TYLOMA	UNSAFE	VASTLY	VISAGE	WAPITI
TROPHY	TYLTYL	UNSEAL	VEADAR	VISCID	WAPPET
TROPIC	TYPHON	UNSEAT	VECTOR	VISCUM	WARBLE
TROUGH	TYPHUS	UNSEEN	VEDDAH	VISHNU	WARDEN
TROUPE	TYPIFY	UNSURE	VEILED	VISION	WARHOL
TROWEL	TYPING	UNTIDY	VELATE	VISUAL	WARMED
TRUANT	TYPIST	UNTRUE	VELLUM	VITALS	WARMER
TRUDGE	TYRANT	UNUSED	VELVET	VITRIC	WARMLY
TRUISM	TYRIAN	UNVEIL	VENDED	VIVIAN	WARMTH
TRUMPS	TZETZE	UNWELL	VENDEE	VIVIFY	WARNER
TRUNKS	UBASTI	UNWIND	VENDER	VIZARD	WARPED
TRUSTY	UBERTY	UNWISE	VENDUE	VIZIER	WARRAU
TRUTHS	UFFIZI	UPCAST	VENEER	VLTAVA	WARREN
TRYING	UGARIT	UPHOLD	VENENE	VOICED	WARSAW
TSAMBA	UGLIER	UPKEEP	VENIAL	VOLANT	WARTON
TSCHIL	UJJAIN	UPLAND	VENICE	VOLLEY	WASHER
TSERIN	UKIYOE	UPROAR	VENIRE	VOLUME	WASTER

WATERY	WHEELS	WINGED	WOUWOU	YANKEE	ZAGROS
WATSON	WHENCE	WINKLE	WOVOKA	YARDER	ZAMANG
WATTLE	WHERRY	WINNER	WRAITH	YARMUK	ZAPARO
WATUSI	WHIDAH	WINNOW	WRASSE	YARROW	ZAPTIA
WAYLAY	WHILOM	WINTER	WREATH	YARURO	ZAYNAB
WEAKEN	WHIMSY	WISDOM	WRENCH	YAUPON	ZEALOT
WEAKLY	WHINNY	WISENT	WRETCH	YAUTIA	ZEEKOE
WEALTH	WHISKY	WITHAL	WRIGHT	YCLEPT	ZEMZEM
WEAPON	WHITEN	WITHEN	WRITER	YEARLY	ZENANA
WEASEL	WHOLLY	WITHER	WRITHE	YEASTY	ZENITH
WEASER	WHORLS	WITHIN	WURLEY	YELLOW	ZEPHYR
WEAVER	WICKED	WITHIT	WURRAH	YEMENI	ZEUXIS
WEAZEN	WICKER	WIZARD	WYCLIF	YEOMAN	ZIGZAG
WEDDED	WICKET	WOBBLE	WYNANT	YESTER	ZILLAH
WEENIE	WIDELY	WOEFUL	WYVERN	YETAPA	ZILPAH
WEEVIL	WIDEST	WOMBAT	XAVIER	YEZIDI	ZINNIA
WEIGHT	WIELDY	WOMERA	XCHAIR	YGERNE	ZIPPER
WEIMAR	WIENER	WONDER	XERXES	YOGURT	ZIRCON
WEINER	WIGGLE	WONGAR	XIMENA	YOICKS	ZITHER
WEINIE	WIGLET	WONTED	XYLOID	YONDER	ZODIAC
WEJACK	WIGWAM	WONTON	XYSTER	YORKER	ZOMBIE
WELAND	WILFUL	WOODED	XYSTUS	YORUBA	ZOPHAR
WELDED	WILLOW	WOODEN	YABBIE	YOUALL	ZOUAVE
WELKIN	WILTED	WOOFER	YACARE	YOUTHY	ZURICH
WELTER	WILTON	WOOING	YADAVA	YSEULT	ZYGOMA
WENZEL	WIMBLE	WOOLLY	YAHGAN	YUMYUM	ZYGOTE
WESKIT	WIMPLE	WORKED	YAHOOS	YUNCAN	ZYKLON
WESLEY	WIMSEY	WORKER	YAHWEH	YUZLUK	
WESSEX	WINDED	WORRAL	YAKIMA	ZABABA	
WESTER	WINDER	WORSEN	YAKSHA	ZACHUN	
WETHER	WINDOW	WORTHY	YAMASI	ZAFTIG	
WHALER	WINERY	WOUBIT	YANAGI	ZAGREB	

Seven-Letter Words

ABADDON	ABSOLVE	ACTRESS	AFFRONT	AKASAKA
ABALONE	ABSTAIN	ACTUARY	AFGHANI	AKETOUN
ABANDON	ABTRUSE	ACTUATE	AGAINST	AKHOOND
ABASHED	ABUBAKR	ACULEUS	AGELESS	AKLAVIK
ABATING	ABUSIVE	ADAMANT	AGENDUM	AKVAVIT
ABATTIS	ABYSSAL	ADAMITE	AGEUSIS	ALADDIN
ABDOMEN	ACADEMY	ADAPTED	AGILITY	ALAMEDA
ABELARD	ACADIAN	ADDISON	AGITATE	ALAMEIN
ABETTOR	ACASTUS	ADDRESS	AGNOMEN	ALAMODE
ABEYANT	ACCOUNT	ADELPHO	AGNOSIA	ALARCON
ABIDING	ACCRUAL	ADENOID	AGONIZE	ALASHAN
ABIDJAN	ACCUSED	ADERMIN	AGRIOPE	ALASKAN
ABIGAIL	ACERATE	ADIPOSE	AGROUND	ALASTOR
ABILENE	ACETATE	ADJOURN	AHAGGAR	ALBANIA
ABILITY	ACETONE	ADJUDGE	AHRIMAN	ALBORAK
ABISTON	ACHARYA	ADMETUS	AILERON	ALBUMEN
ABITIBI	ACHATES	ADMIRAL	AILETTE	ALCAEUS
ABLATOR	ACHERON	ADONAIS	AILMENT	ALCALDE
ABOLISH	ACHIEVE	ADULATE	AILURUS	ALCAZAR
ABOLONE	ACHIOTE	ADVANCE	AIMLESS	ALCHEMY
ABOULIA	ACIDITY	ADVERSE	AIRFOIL	ALCHERA
ABRAHAM	ACOLOUS	ADVISER	AIRHOSE	ALCMENE
ABREAST	ACOLYTE	ADVISOR	AIRIEST	ALCOHOL
ABRIDGE	ACONITE	AEOLIAN	AIRLANE	ALCORAN
ABSALOM	ACQUIRE	AERATOR	AIRPORT	ALEMBIC
ABSCESS	ACRASIA	AFFABLE	AIRSHIP	ALENCON
ABSCOND	ACREAGE	AFFIANT	AISLING	ALERTLY
ABSENCE	ACROBAT	AFFLICT	AJACCIO	ALETHIA

ALFALFA	AMPHORA	APATITE	ARMORER	ATTRACT
ALFHEIM	AMPLIFY	APELIKE	ARMSEYE	ATTUNED
ALFONSO	AMPOULE	APELLES	ARRAIGN	ATTUNER
ALGEBRA	AMPULLA	APHASIA	ARRANGE	AUCTION
ALGERIA	AMUSING	APHEMIA	ARREARS	AUDIBLE
ALGIERS	ANACAPA	APHONIA	ARRIGHI	AUDIBLY
ALGIFIC	ANAGOGE	APHONIC	ARRIVAL	AUDITOR
ALIBABA	ANAGRAM	APOLOGY	ARSENAL	AUGMENT
ALIDADE	ANALOGY	APOSTLE	ARSENIC	AUGUSTA
ALIENEE	ANALYZE	APOTHEM	ARTEGAL	AUMAKUA
ALIENOR	ANAMITE	APPAREL	ARTEMIS	AURARIA
ALIGOTE	ANANIAS	APPEASE	ARTICLE	AURELIA
ALIMENT	ANAPEST	APPLAUD	ARTISAN	AUREOLA
ALIMONY	ANAPHIA	APPOINT	ARTISTE	AUREOLE
ALIQUOT	ANARCHY	APPOSED	ARTLESS	AURICLE
ALIZARI	ANATINE	APPRISE	ARUNDEL	AUROCHS
ALKORAN	ANATRON	APPROVE	ASCARID	AUSONIA
ALLEGRO	ANCHOVY	APRICOT	ASCETIC	AUSPICY
ALLENBY	ANCIENT	APRIORI	ASCITES	AUSTERE
ALLERGY	ANDANTE	APROPOS	ASCRIBE	AUSTRAL
ALMAATA	ANDIRON	APTERAL	ASEPTIC	AUTARKY
ALMAGRO	ANDORRA	APTERYX	ASHANTI	AUTEUIL
ALMANAC	ANDROID	APTNESS	ASIATIC	AUTOPSY
ALMONER	ANEMONE	AQUAVIT	ASININE	AVARICE
ALODIUM	ANEROID	AQUEOUS	ASKELON	AVELLAN
ALREADY	ANEURIN	AQUIFER	ASONANT	AVENAGE
ALSATIA	ANGELIC	AQUINAS	ASPASIA	AVENGER
ALSORAN	ANGELIN	ARABIAN	ASPERGE	AVERAGE
ALTHING	ANGELUS	ARACARI	ASPERSE	AVERTED
ALTJIRA	ANGUISH	ARAMAIC	ASPHALT	AVIATOR
ALUMNAE	ANGULAR	ARANEIN	ASSAGAI	AVOCADO
ALUMNUS	ANHINGA	ARAPAHO	ASSAULT	AVODIRE
ALVEARY	ANILINE	ARAROBA	ASSEGAI	AWEBAND
ALYSSUM	ANIMALS	ARBITER	ASSIZER	AWELESS
AMALAKA	ANIMATE	ARBUTUS	ASSUMED	AWESOME
AMALGAM	ANNATES	ARCADIA	ASTARTE	AWKWARD
AMANITA	ANNATTO	ARCANUM	ASTASIA	AXOLOTL
AMATEUR	ANNELID	ARCHAIC	ASTHORE	AZIMUTH
AMATIVE	ANNUITY	ARCHEAN	ASTOUND	AZUCENA
AMATORY	ANNULAR	ARCHERY	ASTRAEA	AZULEJO
AMAUMAU	ANNULET	ARCHIVE	ASUNDER	AZURITE
AMAZING	ANODYNE	ARDUOUS	ATACAMA	BAALBEK
AMBAGES	ANOMALY	AREAWAY	ATARAXY	BAALISM
AMBOINA	ANTACID	ARENOSE	ATAVISM	BABCOCK
AMBROSE	ANTAEUS	AREOLAR	ATELIER	BABIECA
AMBSACE	ANTARES	ARGOLIS	ATHALIA	BABRIUS
AMENITY	ANTENNA	ARGUSIA	ATHALIE	BACALAO
AMENTIA	ANTHOID	ARGYLES	ATHAMAS	BACARDI
AMENTUM	ANTHONY	ARGYROL	ATHANOR	BACCHIC
AMERCED	ANTHRAX	ARIADNE	ATHEIST	BACCHUS
AMERICA	ANTIGUA	ARICULA	ATHENAI	BACILLI
AMERIND	ANTIOPE	ARIDITY	ATHLETE	BACKBAY
AMESACE	ANTIQUE	ARIETTA	ATHWART	BACKHOE
AMHARIC	ANTLION	ARIKARA	ATITLAN	BACKING
AMHERST	ANTONIO	ARIOSTO	ATLANTA	BACULUS
AMIABLE	ANTONYM	ARISTON	ATOMIZE	BADNESS
AMMETER	ANTWERP	ARIZONA	ATROPHY	BAGANDA
AMNERIS	ANXIETY	ARMBAND	ATROPOS	BAGASSE
AMNESIA	ANXIOUS	ARMENIA	ATTACCA	BAGGAGE
AMNESTY	ANYBODY	ARMHOLE	ATTACHE	BAGHDAD
AMONGST	ANYTIME	ARMIGER	ATTALID	BAGPIPE
AMOROUS	AORANGI	ARMOIRE	ATTEMPT	BAHRAIN
AMPHION	APAGOGE	ARMORED	ATTIRED	

BAILIFF	BEARCAT	BETWEEN	BLOSSOM	BOUQUET
BAISAKH	BEARING	BETWIXT	BLOTTER	BOURBON
BALANCE	BEARISH	BEVELED	BLOWFLY	BOWLING
BALANGA	BEATIFY	BEWITCH	BLOWGUN	BOWSHOT
BALATON	BEATING	BEYOGLU	BLOWOUT	BOXFISH
BALCONY	BEATLES	BEZIQUE	BLUBBER	BOYCOTT
BALDRIC	BEBEERU	BHARATA	BLUEEYE	BOYHOOD
BALDWIN	BECAUSE	BHAVANI	BLUEGUM	BRABANT
BALEFUL	BECQUER	BHEESTY	BLUEHEN	BRACKEN
BALLADE	BEDIGHT	BIBELOT	BLUFFER	BRACKET
BALLAST	BEDIZEN	BICYCLE	BLUNDER	BRAHMAN
BALLOON	BEDOUIN	BIDARKA	BLURRED	BRAHMIN
BALMUNG	BEDROOM	BIGBEND	BLUSTER	BRAHOES
BALONEY	BEEHIVE	BIGHORN	BOARDER	BRAIDED
BANANAS	BEELINE	BIGNESS	BOASTER	BRAILLE
BANDAGE	BEESWAX	BIGOTED	BOATBUG	BRAMBLE
BANDANA	BEGGARS	BIGSHOT	BOATING	BRAMBLY
BANDORE	BEGGING	BIGTREE	BOBADIL	BRANDES
BANDUNG	BEGONIA	BIGWIGS	BOCHICA	BRANWEN
BANEFUL	BEGUILE	BILIMBI	BOGLAND	BRASSIE
BANGKOK	BELABOR	BILIOUS	BOGOMIL	BRAVADO
BANLIEU	BELASCO	BILLION	BOHEMIA	BRAVERY
BANQUET	BELATED	BILTONG	BOILING	BREADTH
BANSHEE	BELDAME	BIMARIS	BOKCHOY	BREAKAX
BANTENG	BELFAST	BINDERY	BOLETUS	BREAKER
BANTING	BELGIUM	BINDING	BOLIVAR	BREATHE
BAPTIZE	BELIEVE	BINGHAM	BOLIVIA	BRECCIA
BARBATE	BELINUS	BIOLOGY	BOLLARD	BRENNER
BARBUDA	BELKNAP	BIPEDAL	BOLOGNA	BRESLAU
BARCHAN	BELLHOP	BIPLANE	BOLSTER	BREVIER
BARENTS	BELLMAN	BIRDDOG	BOMBARD	BREVITY
BARGAIN	BELLONA	BIRETTA	BOMBAST	BRIBERY
BARILLA	BELOVED	BIRLING	BONADEA	BRIDGED
BARISAN	BELTANE	BISCUIT	BONANZA	BRIDGES
BARLAAM	BEMBERG	BISMARK	BONDAGE	BRIGAND
BARONET	BEMIRED	BISTORT	BONDMAN	BRILLIG
BAROQUE	BENARES	BITTERN	BONESET	BRINDLE
BARRAGE	BENCHED	BITUMEN	BONFIRE	BRISKET
BARRENS	BENDING	BIVALVE	BONNETS	BRISKLY
BARRIER	BENEATH	BIVOUAC	BOOKISH	BRISSOT
BARROOM	BENEFIT	BIZARRE	BOOKLET	BRISTLE
BASCULE	BENGALI	BIZERTE	BOORISH	BRISTLY
BASHFUL	BENISON	BLACKEN	BOOSTER	BRISTOL
BASINET	BENTLEY	BLADDER	BORDENS	BRITISH
BASSOON	BENZENE	BLANKET	BOREDOM	BRITTEN
BASTARD	BENZINE	BLARNEY	BORGLUM	BRITTLE
BASTION	BENZOIN	BLATANT	BORNEOL	BROCADE
BATAVIA	BEOWULF	BLATHER	BOROUGH	BROCKEN
BATEMAN	BEQUEST	BLAZING	BORSTAL	BROGLIE
BATFISH	BERATED	BLEEDER	BOSCAGE	BROMIDE
BATHING	BEREAVE	BLEMISH	BOSWELL	BROMINE
BATISTE	BERGMAN	BLENDER	BOTARGO	BRONCHO
BATTERY	BERSERK	BLERIOT	BOTCHED	BROTHEL
BATTLED	BERTRAM	BLESSED	BOTCHER	BROTHER
BATUTSI	BESAIEL	BLETHER	BOTHNIA	BROWNIE
BAUHAUS	BESEECH	BLEWITS	BOTTEGA	BRUITED
BAUXITE	BESIDES	BLICKEY	BOTTOMS	BRUSQUE
BAWDRIC	BESIEGE	BLINDER	BOUCHER	BRUTISH
BAYLYNX	BESTIAL	BLINKER	BOUDOIR	BRUXISM
BAYONET	BETHUEL	BLISTER	BOULDER	BUBALIS
BEACHED	BETIMES	BLOCKER	BOUNDED	BUBONIC
BEAMING	BETOKEN	BLOOMED	BOUNDEN	BUCCINA
BEANERY	BETROTH	BLOOPER	BOUNDER	BUCKEYE

BUCKLER	CAJUPUT	CAPITAL	CASSENA	CESSION
BUCKRAM	CALABAR	CAPITOL	CASSINE	CETINJE
BUCOLIC	CALABER	CAPORAL	CASSINO	CEZANNE
BUDDING	CALAMUS	CAPOREL	CASSIUS	CHABLIS
BUFFALO	CALAPAN	CAPREOL	CASSOCK	CHACKLE
BUFFOON	CALCEUS	CAPRICE	CASTANA	CHACTAS
BUGABOO	CALCHAS	CAPRINE	CASTERS	CHAFFER
BUGBEAR	CALCINA	CAPRINO	CASTILE	CHAGRIN
BUILDER	CALCITE	CAPSIZE	CASTOFF	CHALAZA
BULGING	CALDERA	CAPSTAN	CASTRAL	CHALICE
BULIMIA	CALDRON	CAPSULE	CATALAN	CHALLIS
BULLBAT	CALENDS	CAPTAIN	CATALOG	CHAMADE
BULLDOG	CALGARY	CAPTION	CATALPA	CHAMBER
BULLION	CALIBAN	CAPTIVE	CATARRH	CHAMFER
BULLOCK	CALIBER	CAPTURE	CATASTA	CHAMISE
BULLPEN	CALIBRE	CAPUCHE	CATAWBA	CHAMISO
BULLRUN	CALICUT	CAPULET	CATCALL	CHAMOIS
BULRUSH	CALIPER	CARABAO	CATCHER	CHAMPAC
BULWARK	CALLING	CARABID	CATCHUP	CHANCEL
BUMPKIN	CALLOUS	CARACAL	CATECHU	CHANCES
BUNGLER	CALOMEL	CARACAS	CATERER	CHANDOO
BUNTING	CALORIC	CARACOL	CATFISH	CHANELV
BUOYANT	CALOTTA	CARADOC	CATHBAD	CHANGED
BURBAGE	CALOTTE	CARAMBA	CATHODE	CHANGES
BURBANK	CALOYER	CARAMEL	CATLIKE	CHANNEL
BURBARK	CALTROP	CARAVAN	CATMINT	CHANOYU
BURBUSH	CALUMET	CARAVEL	CATSEAR	CHANTER
BURETTE	CALUMNY	CARAWAY	CATSPAW	CHANTEY
BURGAGE	CALVARY	CARBINE	CATTAIL	CHANTRY
BURGEON	CALVERT	CARCASS	CATTALO	CHAOTIC
BURGHER	CALYPSO	CARDIAC	CAUBEEN	CHAPEAU
BURGLAR	CAMBIUM	CARDIFF	CAUSTIC	CHAPLET
BURNING	CAMBRIA	CAREFUL	CAUTION	CHAPMAN
BURNISH	CAMBRIC	CARIBOO	CAVEMAN	CHAPOTE
BUSHING	CAMELOT	CARIBOU	CAVILER	CHAPTER
BUSHIRE	CAMELUS	CARIOCA	CAYENNE	CHARADE
BUSHMAN	CAMERAL	CARIOLE	CAYSTER	CHARBON
BUSTARD	CAMMOCK	CARLINE	CEDILLA	CHARCOT
BUTCHER	CAMOENS	CARLTON	CELADON	CHARDIN
BUTTERY	CAMOODI	CARLYLE	CELAENO	CHARGED
BUTTOCK	CAMORRA	CARMINE	CELEBES	CHARGER
BUZZARD	CAMPHOL	CARNAGE	CELESTE	CHARIOT
BUZZING	CAMPHOR	CARNOSE	CELLINI	CHARITY
BYGONES	CAMPION	CAROLER	CELLIST	CHARLES
CABALLE	CANASTA	CAROTID	CELOSIA	CHARMED
CABALLO	CANDENT	CAROTTE	CEMBALO	CHARMER
CABARET	CANDIDE	CAROUSE	CENACLE	CHARNEL
CABBAGE	CANDIOT	CARPING	CENSURE	CHARPOY
CABINDA	CANDIRU	CARRARA	CENTARE	CHARQUI
CABINET	CANELLA	CARRIED	CENTAUR	CHARRED
CABOOSE	CANEPIN	CARRIER	CENTAVO	CHARTER
CACIQUE	CANONIC	CARRION	CENTIME	CHASSIS
CADAVER	CANOPUS	CARROLL	CENTNER	CHASTEN
CADDISH	CANTARA	CARTAGE	CENTRAL	CHATEAU
CADELLE	CANTATA	CARTAGO	CENTURY	CHATTEL
CADENCE	CANTEEN	CARTIER	CEPHEID	CHATTER
CADENZA	CANTINA	CARTOON	CEPHEUS	CHAUCER
CAEDMON	CANTRAP	CARVING	CERAMIC	CHAUPER
CAELIAN	CANTRIP	CASCADE	CERTAIN	CHECHEN
CAESURA	CANVASS	CASCARA	CERTIFY	CHECHIA
CAFFEIN	CAPABLE	CASEOUS	CERUMEN	CHEDDAR
CAISSON	CAPANNA	CASHIER	CERVERA	CHEECHA
CAITIFF	CAPELLA	CASSAVA	CERVINE	CHEETAH

CHEKHOV	CLABBER	COLLEGE	CONFUTE	CORVINE
CHELSEA	CLAMBER	COLLIDE	CONGEAL	COSSACK
CHEMISE	CLANGED	COLLIER	CONGEST	COSTATE
CHENIER	CLARIFY	COLLUDE	CONICAL	COSTIVE
CHERISH	CLARION	COLOBUS	CONIFER	COSTUME
CHEROOT	CLARITY	COLOGNE	CONIINE	COTERIE
CHERVIL	CLASSER	COLOMBA	CONJOIN	COTONOU
CHESTER	CLASSIC	COLONEL	CONJURE	COTTAGE
CHEVIOT	CLATTER	COLONNA	CONNECT	COULOMB
CHEVRON	CLAUDEL	COLONUS	CONNIVE	COULTER
CHEWINK	CLAVATE	COLORED	CONNOTE	COUNCIL
CHIANTI	CLEANER	COLUMBA	CONQUER	COUNSEL
CHIASMA	CLEANSE	COLUMBO	CONSENT	COUNTER
CHIBOUK	CLEARED	COMBINE	CONSIGN	COUNTRY
CHICAGO	CLEARER	COMFORT	CONSOLE	COUPLET
CHICANE	CLEAVER	COMFREY	CONSORT	COURAGE
CHICANO	CLEMENT	COMICAL	CONSULT	COURIER
CHICKEN	CLIMATE.	COMITIA	CONSUME	COURSER
CHICORY	CLIMBER	COMMAND	CONTACT	COURTLY
CHIEFLY	CLINTON	COMMEND	CONTAIN	COUTURE
CHIFFON	CLIPEUS	COMMENT	CONTEMN	COVERED
CHIGGER	CLIPPED	COMMODE	CONTEND	COWFISH
CHIGNON	CLIPPER	COMMONS	CONTENT	COWHIDE
CHIKARA	CLOSELY	COMMUNE	CONTEST	COWLICK
CHILIAD	CLOSEST	COMORIN	CONTEXT	COWNOSE
CHILLED	CLOSING	COMPACT	CONTORT	COWPENS
CHILUNG	CLOTHED	COMPANY	CONTOUR	COWSLIP
CHIMERA	CLOTHES	COMPARE	CONTROL	COXCOMB
CHIMERE	CLOUDED	COMPASS	CONVENE	COZENER
CHIMNEY	CLUSTER	COMPEER	CONVENT	CRABBED
CHINELA	CLUTTER	COMPETE	CONVERT	CRACKER
CHINESE	CLYMENE	COMPILE	CONVICT	CRACKLE
CHINNED	COALOIL	COMPLEX	CONVOKE	CRAMPON
CHINOOK	COASTAL	COMPORT	COOKERY	CRANACH
CHIWERE	COASTER	COMPOSE	COPAIVA	CRANIAL
CHLAMYS	COATING	COMPOST	COPIOUS	CRANIUM
CHLORIS	COAXIAL	COMPOTE	COPPERY	CRANMER
CHOCTAW	COBBLER	COMPUTE	COPPICE	CRAPPIE
CHOLERA	COCAINE	COMRADE	COPYCAT	CARSSUS
CHOLINE	COCHISE	CONAKRY	COPYIST	CRATAIS
CHONDRO	COCKADE	CONCAVE	CORACLE	CRAVING
CHOPPER	COCKNEY	CONCEAL	CORDAGE	CRAWDAD
CHORALE	COCONUT	CONCEDE	CORDATE	CRAWLER
CHOREUS	COCTEAU	CONCEIT	CORDIAL	CREAKED
CHORTLE	CODFISH	CONCEPT	CORDITE	CREAMER
CHRONIC	CODICES	CONCERN	CORDOBA	CREASED
CHRONUS	CODICIL	CONCERT	CORINTH	CREATED
CHUCKLE	CODILLA	CONCISE	CORKOAK	CREATOR
CHUKKER	CODLING	CONCOCT	CORNISH	CREEPER
CHUKREE	COGNATE	CONCORD	COROLLA	CREMATE
CIBONEY	COHABIT	CONDEMN	CORONAL	CREMONA
CILIATE	COINAGE	CONDIGN	CORONER	CRENATE
CINEAST	COITION	CONDOLE	CORONET	CRESSET
CIPANGO	COLCHIS	CONDONE	CORONIS	CRESTED
CIRCLET	COLDCUT	CONDUCT	CORRECT	CREVICE
CIRCUIT	COLDEST	CONDUIT	CORRIDA	CRICKET
CISTERN	COLETTE	CONFESS	CORRODE	CRIMSON
CITADEL	COLGATE	CONFIDE	CORRUPT	CRINKLE
CITHARA	COLIBRI	CONFINE	CORSAGE	CRIPPEN
CITHERN	COLLAGE	CONFIRM	CORSAIR	CRIPPLE
CITIZEN	COLLATE	CONFLUX	CORSICA	CRISPEN
CITRINE	COLLECT	CONFORM	CORTEGE	CRISPIN
CITTERN	COLLEEN	CONFUSE	CORUNNA	CRITTER

CROCHET	CUTTING	DECODER	DESPITE	DISCERN
CROESUS	CYCLIST	DECORUM	DESPOIL	DISCOID
CROFTER	CYCLOID	DECREED	DESPOND	DISCORD
CROOKED	CYCLONE	DECRETE	DESSERT	DISCUSS
CROONER	CYCLOPS	DECUMAN	DESTINE	DISDAIN
CROQUET	CYMBALS	DECUPLE	DESTINY	DISEASE
CROSIER	CYNICAL	DEDUCED	DESTROY	DISGUST
CROSSED	CYNTHIA	DEFACED	DETAILS	DISLIKE
CROUTON	CYPRESS	DEFAMER	DETENTE	DISMISS
CROWBAR	CYPRIAN	DEFAULT	DETOURS	DISPLAY
CROWDED	CYPSELA	DEFENSE	DETRACT	DISPOSE
CROZIER	CZARDAS	DEFIANT	DETROIT	DISPUTE
CRUCIAL	CZARINA	DEFICIT	DETRUDE	DISROBE
CRUDITY	CZIGANY	DEFILED	DEVELOP	DISRUPT
CRUELLY	DABBLER	DEFILER	DEVIATE	DISSECT
CRUELTY	DACOSTA	DEFLATE	DEVILED	DISSENT
CRUISER	DAIKOKU	DEFLECT	DEVIOUS	DISTAFF
CRULLER	DAKHINI	DEFRAUD	DEVISEE	DISTANT
CRUMBLE	DALLIED	DEFROCK	DEVISOR	DISTEND
CRUMPLE	DAMAGED	DEFUNCT	DEVOLVE	DISTICH
CRUPPER	DAMAGES	DEGRADE	DEVOTED	DISTORT
CRUSADE	DAMKINA	DEIRDRE	DEVOTEE	DISTURB
CRUSHED	DAMPEST	DELAINE	DEWCLAW	DITMARS
CRYPTIC	DANAIDE	DELAYED	DEXTRAL	DITTANY
CRYSTAL	DANCING	DELIGHT	DIABASE	DIURNAL
CRYSTIC	DANITES	DELILAH	DIACOPE	DIVERGE
CTESIAS	DAPHNIA	DELISLE	DIAGRAM	DIVERSE
CUBITAL	DAPIFER	DELIVER	DIALECT	DIVINER
CUCKOLD	DAPPLED	DELPHIC	DIAMOND	DIVORCE
CUEBALL	DARIOLE	DELTOID	DIARIST	DIVULGE
CUIRASS	DARLING	DEMERIT	DICEROS	DOCTORS
CUISINE	DASHEEN	DEMESNE	DICKENS	DODGERS
CULEBRA	DASHIKI	DEMETER	DICTATE	DODGSON
CULLION	DASYURE	DEMIGOD	DICTION	DOENITZ
CULPRIT	DATHEMA	DEMOTIC	DIDACHE	DOGBOLT
CULTURE	DAUMIER	DEMPSEY	DIDYMUS	DOGCART
CULVERT	DAWDLER	DENMARK	DIEHARD	DOGDAYS
CUMULUS	DAYSTAR	DENOTED	DIETARY	DOGEATE
CUNEATE	DEADEND	DENSIFY	DIFFUSE	DOGFISH
CUNNING	DEADPAN	DENSITY	DIGAMMA	DOGROSE
CUPRITE	DEADSEA	DENTATE	DIGGING	DOGWOOD
CURABLE	DEALING	DENTINE	DIGNIFY	DOLEFUL
CURACAO	DEBACLE	DENTIST	DIGNITY	DOLLARS
CURATOR	DEBATER	DENTURE	DIGRAPH	DOLPHIN
CUREALL	DEBAUCH	DEPLETE	DIGRESS	DOLTISH
CURETES	DEBEERS	DEPLORE	DILATOR	DOMINIC
CURIOUS	DEBORAH	DEPOSIT	DILEMMA	DOMINIE
CURLING	DEBRIDE	DEPRESS	DILUTED	DOMREMY
CURRANT	DEBUSSY	DEPRIVE	DIMETER	DONATOR
CURRENT	DECAGON	DEPUTED	DINETTE	DONEFOR
CURSIVE	DECANAL	DERANGE	DINGAAN	DONJOHN
CURSORY	DECATUR	DERBENT	DINMONT	DOORWAY
CURTAIL	DECAYED	DERCETO	DIOCESE	DORKING
CURTAIN	DECEIVE	DERRICK	DIOCLES	DORMANT
CUSHION	DECENCY	DERVISH	DIOPTER	DORNICK
CUSPATE	DECIBEL	DERWENT	DIORITE	DOSOJIN
CUSTARD	DECIDED	DESCANT	DIPLOMA	DOSSIER
CUSTODY	DECIMAL	DESCEND	DIPTOTE	DOUBTER
CUSTOMS	DECKLED	DESCENT	DIREFUL	DOUGHTY
CUTAWAY	DECLAIM	DESERET	DISABLE	DOUGLAS
CUTICLE	DECLARE	DESERVE	DISAVOW	DOVECOT
CUTLASS	DECLASS	DESPAIR	DISBAND	DOVEKIE
CUTLERY	DECLINE	DESPISE	DISCARD	DOWAGER

DOWERAL	EASIEST	EMANATE	EPERGNE	ETAMINE
DOWSING	EASTEND	EMANENT	EPHELIS	ETCHING
DRACHMA	EASTERN	EMBARGO	EPHESUS	ETERNAL
DRACULA	EATABLE	EMBASSY	EPHRAIM	ETESIAN
DRAFTEE	EBBETTS	EMBAUBA	EPICEDE	ETHICAL
DRAGNET	EBONITE	EMBLAZE	EPICENE	ETIOLIN
DRAGOON	EBRIOUS	EMBRACE	EPICURE	ETRURIA
DRASTIC	ECHELON	EMBROIL	EPIDERM	EUGENIC
DRAUGHT	ECHIDNA	EMERALD	EPIDOTE	EUGENIE
DRAWERS	ECHOING	EMERGED	EPIGRAM	EULALIA
DRAWING	ECLIPSE	EMERSON	EPILATE	EUMAEUS
DREAMER	ECLOGUE	EMINENT	EPILOBE	EUNOMIA
DREIDEL	ECOLOGY	EMOTION	EPIOTIC	EURASIA
DRESDEN	ECONOMY	EMPEROR	EPIROTE	EUROTAS
DRESSED	ECOTONE	EMPIRIC	EPISODE	EURYALE
DRESSER	ECSTACY	EMPOWER	EPISTLE	EUSTASY
DRIBBLE	ECTASIA	EMPRESS	EPITAPH	EUTERPE
DRIEDUP	ECUADOR	EMULATE	EPITHET	EVANGEL
DRIFTER	EDACITY	EMULOUS	EPITOME	EVASION
DRINKER	EDAPHIC	ENARMES	EPOCHAL	EVASIVE
DRIPDRY	EDIFICE	ENCASED	EPSILON	EVENING
DRIZZLE	EDITING	ENCHANT	EPSTEIN	EVEREST
DROMOND	EDITION	ENCHASE	EQUATOR	EVERETT
DROPOUT	EDITORS	ENCLASP	ERASMUS	EVERNIA
DROPPER	EDOMITE	ENCLAVE	ERASURE	EVIDENT
DROSSER	EDUCATE	ENCLOSE	ERECTOR	EVILEYE
DROUGHT	EELLIKE	ENCRUST	EREMITE	EXACTLY
DRUGGET	EELPOUT	ENDGAME	ERGATES	EXALTED
DRUKYUL	EELSKIN	ENDHAND	ERINITE	EXAMINE
DRUMLIN	EELWORM	ENDLESS	ERINOSE	EXAMPLE
DRUMMER	EERIEST	ENDOGEN	ERINYES	EXCERPT
DRUNKEN	EFFECTS	ENDORSE	ERISTIC	EXCITED
DRYEYED	EGOTISM	ENDOWER	ERITREA	EXCLAIM
DRYNESS	EGOTIST	ENFORCE	ERLKING	EXCLUDE
DUBBING	EIDOLON	ENGAGED	ERMELIN	EXCRETE
DUBIOUS	EINKORN	ENGLAND	ERODENT	EXECUTE
DUCHESS	ELAMITE	ENGLISH	EROSION	EXEGETE
DUCTILE	ELASTIC	ENGRAVE	EROSIVE	EXERGUE
DUDGEON	ELATION	ENHANCE	EROTICA	EXHAUST
DUELIST	ELATIVE	ENLARGE	ERRABLE	EXHIBIT
DULLARD	ELBERTA	ENLIVEN	ERRATIC	EXIGENT
DUNGEON	ELDERLY	ENNOBLE	ERRATUM	EXISTED
DURABLE	ELEATIC	ENOLOGY	ERRHINE	EXPANSE
DURAMEN	ELEAZAR	ENPLANE	ERUDITE	EXPENSE
DURANCE	ELECTOR	ENRAGED	ESCAPED	EXPIATE
DURANGO	ELECTRA	ENROUTE	ESCHEAT	EXPLAIN
DURAZZO	ELEGANT	ENSLAVE	ESCOLAR	EXPLODE
DUSTING	ELEGIAC	ENSNARE	ESOTERY	EXPLOIT
DUTIFUL	ELEGIST	ENSUING	ESPARTO	EXPLORE
DWELLER	ELEMENT	ENTASIS	ESPOUSE	EXPOSED
DWINDLE	ELEPAIO	ENTEBBE	ESQUIRE	EXPRESS
DYNAMIC	ELEPHAS	ENTENTE	ESSENCE	EXPUNGE
DYNASTY	ELEVATE	ENTERED	ESSLING	EXSLAVE
EAGERLY	ELHANAN	ENTITLE	ESTAFET	EXTINCT
EANLING	ELIPHAZ	ENTRAIL	ESTAMIN	EXTRACT
EARACHE	ELISION	ENTRANT	ESTHETE	EXTREME
EARDROP	ELKHORN	ENTREAT	ESTIVAL	EYEBALL
EARLIER	ELLIPSE	ENTRUST	ESTOILE	EYELASH
EARNEST	ELYSIAN	ENVELOP	ESTRADE	EYELESS
EARNING	ELYTRON	ENVIOUS	ESTREAT	EYESORE
EARRING	ELYTRUM	ENVIRON	ESTUARY	EZEKIEL
EARSHOT	ELZEVIR	EPAGOGE	ETAERIO	FACIEND
EARTHLY	EMANANT	EPAULET	ETAGERE	FACIENT

FACTION	FETLOCK	FLORIST	FREEMAN	GALLOON
FACTORY	FETTERS	FLOTSAM	FREEWAY	GALLOWS
FACTUAL	FIANCEE	FLOUNCE	FREEZER	GALVANI
FACULTY	FICTION	FLOWERS	FREIGHT	GALWAYS
FAEROES	FIDDLER	FLOWERY	FREMONT	GAMBLER
FAIENCE	FIDELIO	FLOWING	FRESHER	GAMBOGE
FAILING	FIDGETS	FLUSHED	FRESHET	GAMBREL
FAILURE	FIDGETY	FLUSTER	FRETFUL	GAMELAN
FAIREST	FIEDLER	FLUTIST	FRIABLE	GAMELIN
FAIRIES	FIGHTER	FLUTTER	FRIENDS	GANELON
FALANGE	FIGMENT	FODIENT	FRIGATE	GANESHA
FALBALA	FIGURED	FOLIAGE	FRINGED	GANGWAY
FALCATE	FILARIA	FOLIATE	FRISKET	GANJIFA
FALERNO	FILBERT	FOLKUNG	FRITTER	GANNETT
FALLACY	FILCHED	FOLLIES	FRIZZLE	GARANCE
FALLGUY	FILIBEG	FONDANT	FROGMAN	GARBAGE
FALLING	FILIETY	FOOCHOW	FRONTAL	GARBILL
FALSIFY	FILLING	FOODPIT	FRONTON	GARDENS
FANATIC	FINALLY	FOOLISH	FROSTED	GARLAND
FANFARE	FINANCE	FOOTING	FROWARD	GARMENT
FANTASY	FINBACK	FOOTMAN	FRUSTUM	GARONNE
FANTINE	FINDING	FOOTPAD	FUCHSIN	GARRICK
FARMING	FINESSE	FOPPISH	FUEHRER	GARROTE
FARRAGO	FINGENT	FORBEAR	FULCRUM	GARTERS
FARRIER	FINICAL	FORCEPS	FULLAMS	GASEITY
FARSAKH	FINICKY	FOREARM	FULLEST	GATEWAY
FARTHER	FINIKEN	FOREIGN	FULSOME	GATWICK
FASCINE	FINLAND	FOREMAN	FUMBLER	GAULISH
FASCIST	FIREARM	FORERAN	FUNCHAL	GAUTAMA
FASHION	FIREBUG	FORESEE	FUNERAL	GAUTIER
FATBACK	FIREDOG	FOREVER	FURBISH	GAVARNI
FATEFUL	FIREFLY	FORFEIT	FURCATE	GAVOTTE
FATHEAD	FIREMAN	FORGERY	FURIOUS	GAZELLE
FATHERS	FIRENZE	FORGIVE	FURLONG	GEARBOX
FATIGUE	FISCHER	FORLORN	FURMINT	GEARING
FATIMID	FISHING	FORMANT	FURNACE	GEELONG
FATUITY	FISHNET	FORMING	FURNISH	GEHENNA
FATUOUS	FISSURE	FORMOSA	FURRIER	GELATIN
FAUSTUS	FISTULA	FORMULA	FURSEAL	GELDING
FAVORED	FITCHEW	FORREST	FURTHER	GEMSBOK
FAWNING	FITNESS	FORSAKE	FURTIVE	GENERAL
FEARFUL	FITTING	FORSETI	FUSILLI	GENERIC
FEATHER	FLACCID	FORTIFY	FUSTIAN	GENESEE
FEATURE	FLAGMAN	FORTRAN	FUTHORE	GENESIS
FEBRILE	FLAILED	FORTUNA	GABRIEL	GENETIC
FEDERAL	FLASHER	FORTUNE	GADAMES	GENETTE
FEEDBOX	FLATTER	FORWARD	GADROON	GENGHIS
FEELING	FLATTOP	FOUETTE	GADSDEN	GENIPAP
FEENJON	FLEABAG	FOULEST	GADWALL	GENIPAX
FELSPAR	FLEECED	FOULING	GAGARIN	GENTEEL
FELUCCA	FLEMING	FOUNDER	GAHERIS	GENTIAN
FEMORAL	FLENSER	FOVEATE	GAILLOT	GENTILE
FENCING	FLESHLY	FOXHOLE	GAINFUL	GENUINE
FENIANS	FLEURON	FOXTAIL	GAITERS	GEOLOGY
FERMENT	FLICKER	FOXTROT	GALAHAD	GEORGIA
FERRARA	FLIGHTY	FRAGILE	GALANAS	GEORGIC
FERROUS	FLINDER	FRAILTY	GALATEA	GEPIDAE
FERRULE	FLIPPER	FRAKTUR	GALEATE	GERANOS
FERTILE	FLOATER	FRANKLY	GALILEO	GERENUK
FERVENT	FLOODED	FRANTIC	GALIPOT	GERMANE
FESTIVE	FLOORED	FRAUGHT	GALLANT	GERMANY
FESTOON	FLOREAL	FRECKLE	GALLEON	GERSHON
FESTUCA	FLORIDA	FREEDOM	GALLERY	GESSLER

GESTURE	GODSEND	GRIDDLE	HALAKAH	HEADING
GEWGAWS	GOGGLER	GRIEVED	HALBERD	HEADMAN
GHAFFIR	GOGGLES	GRIFFON	HALCYON	HEALTHY
GHASTLY	GOHANNA	GRILLEE	HALFWAY	HEARING
GHERKIN	GOIBNIU	GRIMACE	HALIBUT	HEARKEN
GHOSTLY	GOLDBUG	GRINDER	HALIFAX	HEARSAY
GIALLAR	GOLIARD	GRISKIN	HALLWAY	HEATHEN
GIBBOUS	GOLIATH	GRISTLE	HALOGEN	HEATHER
GILBERT	GONDOLA	GRIZZLE	HALTING	HEATING
GILBLAS	GONERIL	GRIZZLY	HAMBURG	HEAVENS
GILDING	GONGORA	GROLIER	HAMMADA	HEBRAIC
GIMBALS	GONZAGA	GROMMET	HAMSTER	HECKLER
GIMMICK	GOODBYE	GROOMER	HAMULUS	HECTARE
GINGHAM	GOODGUY	GROOVED	HANALEI	HEDDLES
GINGILI	GOODIES	GROUCHO	HANAPER	HEDEOMA
GINSENG	GORDIAN	GROUCHY	HANDAXE	HEDERIC
GIRAFFE	GORILLA	GROUNDS	HANDBAG	HEDONIC
GIRALDA	GOSHAWK	GROUPED	HANDFUL	HEEDFUL
GIRASOL	GOSPORT	GROUPER	HANDLER	HEGUMEN
GIRDERS	GOSSIPY	GROWING	HANDOUT	HEINOUS
GISARME	GOSSOON	GROWLER	HANDSEL	HEIRESS
GITTERN	GOTHARD	GROWNUP	HANGING	HELENUS
GIUDICE	GOUACHE	GRUMBLE	HANGMAN	HELICON
GIZZARD	GOULASH	GRUMMET	HANGOUT	HELLCAT
GLACIAL	GOURMET	GRUYERE	HANOVER	HELLENE
GLACIER	GRACKLE	GRYLLUS	HANSARD	HELLERI
GLADDEN	GRADINE	GSTRING	HANUKKA	HELLHAG
GLADIUS	GRADUAL	GUANACO	HANUMAN	HELLISH
GLAIKIT	GRAINNE	GUAPENA	HAPENNY	HELMAND
GLAMOUR	GRAMMAR	GUAPORE	HAPLESS	HELOISE
GLANCES	GRAMPUS	GUARABU	HAPTENE	HELPFUL
GLASGOW	GRANADA	GUARANI	HAPUIII	HEMIOPE
GLASSES	GRANARY	GUARDED	HARDHAT	HEMLOCK
GLASSIE	GRANDAM	GUARIBA	HARDTOP	HEMMING
GLAUCOS	GRANDEE	GUAYABA	HARELIP	HENBANE
GLAZIER	GRANDMA	GUDGEON	HARICOT	HENLIKE
GLEEFUL	GRANDPA	GUERDON	HARMFUL	HENNERY
GLIMMER	GRANGER	GUIDING	HARMONY	HENOTIC
GLIMPSE	GRANITE	GUILDER	HARNESS	HEPATIC
GLISTEN	GRANNOS	GUMSHOE	HARPIES	HERBERT
GLISTER	GRANTED	GUNGNIR	HARPOON	HERDING
GLITNIR	GRANTEE	GUNLOCK	HARRIER	HEREDIA
GLITTER	GRAPHIC	GUNWALE	HARVARD	HERETIC
GLOBULE	GRAPNEL	GURNARD	HARVEST	HERITOR
GLONOIN	GRAPPLE	GUSHING	HASBEEN	HERNDON
GLORIFY	GRATIFY	GUTRUNE	HASHISH	HEROINE
GLOSSAL	GRATING	GUYROPE	HASSOCK	HERRIES
GLOSSID	GRAVITY	GWYDION	HASTATE	HERRING
GLOTTIS	GRAVURE	GWYNIAD	HASTILY	HERRITE
GLOWING	GRAYLAG	GYMNAST	HATCHEL	HESHVAN
GLUCOSE	GREATER	GYMNURE	HATCHET	HESSIAN
GLUTTON	GREATGO	GYOKURO	HATEFUL	HETAERA
GLYCOSE	GREATLY	GYPSIES	HAUBECK	HETCHEL
GNARLED	GRECIAN	HABITAT	HAUBERK	HEXAGON
GNOCCHI	GREENER	HABITUE	HAUGHTY	HIBACHI
GNOSTIC	GREGALE	HACKMAN	HAULAGE	HICKORY
GOATGOD	GREGORY	HACKNEY	HAUNTED	HIDALGO
GOBELIN	GREMIAL	HADDOCK	HAUTBOY	HIDATSA
GODDESS	GRENADA	HAGGADA	HAVEREL	HIDEOUS
GODHAVN	GRENADE	HAGGARD	HAWKEYE	HIDEOUT
GODHEAD	GRENDEL	HAGRIDE	HAYCOCK	HIGHBOY
GODLESS	GREYLAG	HAIRNET	HAYFORK	HIGHEST
GODLIKE	GRIBBLE	HAIRPIN	HAYSEED	HIGHWAY

HIKICHA	HOWLING	IMPASSE	INTRUST	JEZEBEL
HILLARY	HUICHOL	IMPASTO	INVALID	JEZREEL
HILLOCK	HUMBABA	IMPEACH	INVERSE	JIMGRIM
HIMILCO	HUMBLED	IMPERIL	INVOICE	JIMJAMS
HIPBATH	HUMDRUM	IMPETUS	INVOLVE	JINGASA
HIPBONE	HUMERUS	IMPIOUS	IPSEITY	JITTERS
HIRCINE	HUMIDOR	IMPLANT	IRACUND	JOCASTA
HIRSUTE	HUMMING	IMPLORE	IRELAND	JOCULAR
HIRUNDO	HUMMOCK	IMPOUND	IRENICS	JOHNSON
HISSING	HUNCHED	IMPRESS	IRESINE	JOINING
HISTORY	HUNDRED	IMPRINT	IRKSOME	JOKSHAN
HISTRIO	HUNTING	IMPROVE	ISAGOGE	JOLLIET
HITTITE	HURACAN	IMPULSE	ISFAHAN	JOLLITY
HJORDIS	HURDLER	INANITY	ISHMAEL	JOLOANO
HOARDER	HURLING	INCENSE	ISLAMIC	JONQUIL
HOARIER	HURRIED	INCISOR	ISODENT	JOURNAL
HOATZIN	HURTFUL	INCITED	ISOLANI	JOURNEY
HOBBEMA	HURUBUH	INCLINE	ISOLATE	JOYEUSE
HOBNAIL	HUSBAND	INCLUDE	ISOMERE	JUBILEE
HODEIDA	HWANGHO	INCUBUS	ISOTOPE	JUGULAR
HOECAKE	HYALINE	INDIANA	ISRAELI	JUJITSU
HOGBACK	HYALITE	INDIANS	ITALIAN	JUJUTSU
HOGGISH	HYANNIS	INDITED	ITALICS	JUMBLED
HOGNOSE	HYDRANT	INDULGE	ITEMIZE	JUNIATA
HOGWASH	HYDRATE	INERTIA	ITERANT	JUNIPER
HOGWEED	HYGIENE	INEXACT	ITERATE	JUPITER
HOISTED	HYPATIA	INFANCY	ITCHING	JURYMAN
HOLBEIN	HYPATON	INFIDEL	IVANHOE	JUSTICE
HOLDING	IABADAN	INFIELD	IVORIES	JUTLAND
HOLIDAY	IAPETUS	INFLAME	IZUIZUE	JUTTING
HOLLAND	IBERIAN	INFLATE	JACINTH	JUVENAL
HOLSTER	ICARIUS	INFLICT	JACKASS	KADDISH
HOLYDAY	ICEBERG	INGENUE	JACKDAW	KADJERI
HOMERUN	ICEFISH	INGRATE	JACKSON	KAILASU
HOMONYM	ICELAND	INGRESS	JACKTAN	KAIRUNI
HONESTY	ICEROOT	INGROUP	JACOBIN	KALIMAH
HONEYED	ICHABOD	INHABIT	JACONET	KALMUCK
HONGKEW	ICHNITE	INHERIT	JACUARU	KAMICHI
HONORED	ICHTHOS	INHIBIT	JACULUM	KAMPALA
HOODLUM	ICTERUS	INHUMAN	JADEITE	KANAWHA
HOOGHLY	IDEALLY	INITIAL	JAGGERY	KANCHIL
HOOLOCK	IDOLIZE	INJURED	JAIALAI	KANOOKA
HOOSIER	IDUMEAN	INKFISH	JAKARTA	KANTAKA
HOPEFUL	IDYLLIC	INNARDS	JALOPPY	KANTELE
HOPHEAD	IGNEOUS	INQUIRE	JAMAICA	KARACHI
HOPKILN	IGNITED	INQUIRY	JAMESON	KARAGAN
HOPLITE	IGNOBLE	INSIDES	JANITOR	KARAKUL
HORATIO	IGRAINE	INSIGHT	JANUARY	KARAKUM
HORDEUM	IGRAYNE	INSIPID	JAPHETH	KARATAS
HORICON	IGUASSU	INSOFAR	JARKATA	KARBALA
HORIZON	ILLBRED	INSOLID	JARRING	KARELIA
HORMONE	ILLEGAL	INSPECT	JASMINE	KASHGAR
HORNERO	ILLICIT	INSPIRE	JAVELIN	KASYAPA
HORRORS	ILLNESS	INSTALL	JAWBONE	KATOGLE
HOSANNA	ILLWILL	INSTANT	JAYHAWK	KATRINA
HOSTAGE	ILOCANO	INSTEAD	JAYVEES	KATURAI
HOSTESS	ILOKANO	INSULAR	JEALOUS	KATYDID
HOSTILE	IMAGINE	INSULIN	JEHOVAH	KEARNEY
HOSTLER	IMBECILE	INTEGER	JELEPLA	KEELSON
HOTCAKE	IMITATE	INTENSE	JERICHO	KENNEDY
HOTSEAT	IMMENSE	INTERIM	JESSAMY	KENNING
HOTSPOT	IMMERSE	INTERNE	JESSICA	KERATIN
HOWEVER	IMMORAL	INTRUDE	JESUITS	KERMESS

KERMISS	KOREISH	LARGESS	LENGTHY	LOAFING
KESTREL	KOSSUTH	LARGEST	LENIENT	LOBELIA
KETCHUP	KOUPREY	LARIGOT	LENTIGO	LOBSTER
KEYNOTE	KOWLOON	LASAGNA	LENTISK	LOCARNO
KHAKIES	KRATION	LASAGNE	LEOFRIC	LOCATOR
KHALKHA	KRAUSEN	LASALLE	LEONINE	LOCKAGE
KHAMSIN	KREMLIN	LASCALA	LEOPARD	LOCKJAW
KHANKAH	KREUZER	LASHING	LEOTARD	LOCRINE
KHARKOV	KRISHNA	LASTING	LEPORID	LOCULUS
KHAYYAM	KRUPNIK	LATAKIA	LEPROSE	LOCUSTA
KHEDIVE	KRYPTON	LATCHET	LESOTHO	LODGING
KHITANS	KUICHUA	LATERAD	LETDOWN	LOFOTEN
KHOISAN	KUMQUAT	LATERAL	LETTERS	LOGBOOK
KHUTBAH	KURBASH	LATERAN	LETTUCE	LOGICAL
KIANGSI	KWANNON	LATRANT	LEUMMIM	LOKSHEN
KIBBUTZ	LABIATE	LATRINE	LEVATOR	LOLLARD
KIBITKA	LABORED	LATTICE	LEVERED	LONDRES
KICKOFF	LABORER	LAUNDER	LEVERET	LONGEST
KIDSMAN	LABROSE	LAUNDRY	LEXICAL	LONGING
KIKUMON	LACERNA	LAUTREC	LEXICON	LOOKOUT
KILAUEA	LACERTA	LAVARET	LIAFAIL	LOOMING
KILLING	LACHINE	LAVINIA	LIAISON	LORELEI
KILOTON	LACKING	LAVROCK	LIATRIS	LORENZO
KINDRED	LACONIA	LAWLESS	LIBERAL	LOTTERY
KINGDOM	LACONIC	LAWSUIT	LIBERTY	LOUNGER
KINGLET	LACQUER	LAYETTE	LIBRATE	LOURDES
KINSHIP	LACTOSE	LAZARET	LIBRIUM	LOVABLE
KINSMAN	LACUNAR	LAZIEST	LICENSE	LOWERED
KINSMEN	LADYBUG	LEACOCK	LIDLESS	LOYALTY
KIPCHAK	LAERTES	LEADING	LIETUVA	LOZENGE
KIPLING	LAETARE	LEAFAGE	LIFFREY	LUCANIA
KIPPEEN	LAGARTO	LEAFLET	LIGGING	LUCAYAN
KIRGHIZ	LAGGARD	LEAGUED	LIGHTED	LUCERNE
KIRIMON	LAKSHMI	LEAGUER	LIGHTER	LUCIFER
KIRUNDI	LALLAND	LEAKAGE	LIGNITE	LUCIOLA
KITCHEN	LALLATE	LEANDER	LIGNOSE	LUGANDA
KITHARA	LAMBENT	LEANING	LIGROIN	LUGGAGE
KITSUNE	LAMBERT	LEAPING	LIKABLE	LULLABY
KIWANIS	LAMBETH	LEARNED	LIMITED	LUMBAGO
KLAMATH	LAMBOIL	LEARNER	LIMOGES	LUMBINI
KLISTER	LAMELLA	LEASHED	LIMOSIS	LUNARIA
KLOMPEN	LAMINAR	LEATHER	LIMPKIN	LUNATIC
KNACKER	LAMPOON	LEAVING	LIMPOPO	LUNETTE
KNAPPER	LAMPREY	LEBANON	LIMULUS	LUPULUS
KNAVERY	LANCERS	LECLERC	LINARIA	LUSTFUL
KNEADER	LANCHOW	LECTERN	LINCOLN	LUSTILY
KNEEPAN	LANCIER	LECTUAL	LINEAGE	LUSTRUM
KNELLER	LANDING	LECTURE	LINEMAN	LUTETIA
KNESSET	LANGUID	LEEFANG	LINGCOD	LYDDITE
KNICKER	LANGUOR	LEEWARD	LINGUAL	LYINGIN
KNOCKER	LANIARD	LEGASPI	LINKAGE	LYRICAL
KNOSSOS	LANISTA	LEGATEE	LINKING	MAACHAH
KNOTTED	LANOLIN	LEGBAND	LINSANG	MACADAM
KNOWHOW	LANSING	LEGBONE	LINSEED	MACABRE
KNOWING	LANTANA	LEGGING	LIPLIKE	MACAQUE
KNUCKLE	LANTERN	LEGHORN	LIQUEFY	MACBETH
KNURLED	LAPITHS	LEGIBLE	LIQUEUR	MACDUFF
KOELLIA	LAPLAND	LEISTER	LISSOME	MACHADO
KOKANEE	LAPLATA	LEISURE	LITERAL	MACHETE
KOKONER	LAPWING	LEMMING	LITURGY	MACHINE
KONGONI	LARCENY	LEMPIRA	LIVEOAK	MACHONE
KOOMKIE	LARDNER	LEMURIA	LIVORNO	MACRAME
KOOMRIE	LARGELY	LENFANT	LLANERO	MADDEST

MEDEIRA	MANSARD	MATINEE	METOPIC	MOISTEN
MADISON	MANSION	MATISSE	MEVROUW	MOJARRA
MADNESS	MANTRAP	MATRASS	MICHAEL	MOLDING
MADONNA	MANUMIT	MATREED	MICIPSA	MOLIERE
MADRASA	MANWOLF	MATTERS	MICROBE	MOLLIFY
MADRONA	MANXMAN	MATTHEW	MICTLAN	MOLLUSC
MAENADS	MANZONI	MATTOCK	MIDGARD	MOLLUSK
MAESTRO	MAPPING	MATTOIR	MIDIRON	MOLOKAI
MAEWEST	MARABOU	MATZOON	MIDRIFF	MOLOMPI
MAFIOSO	MARACAN	MATZOTH	MIGRANT	MOMBASA
MAGENTA	MARACAS	MAUDLIN	MIGRATE	MONARCH
MAGGOTY	MARANON	MAUGHAM	MILEAGE	MONARDA
MAGNATE	MARANTA	MAXILLA	MILETUS	MONGREL
MAGNETO	MARASCA	MAXIMUM	MILFOIL	MONITOR
MAGNIFY	MARATHI	MAXWELL	MILITIA	MONKISH
MAGUARI	MARCEAU	MAYFAIR	MILKSOP	MONOCLE
MAHAJAN	MARCHEN	MAYOTTE	MILLING	MONSOON
MAHATMA	MARCONI	MAZARIN	MILLION	MONSTER
MAHICAN	MARENGO	MAZZARD	MILREIS	MONTAGE
MAHJONG	MARGATE	MBABANE	MINARET	MONTALE
MAHOMET	MARIANA	MEANDER	MINDFUL	MONTANA
MAHOUND	MARIMBA	MEANING	MINERAL	MONTANE
MAHSEER	MARINER	MEASLES	MINERVA	MONTERO
MAIGRET	MARINES	MEASURE	MINGLED	MONTHLY
MAILLOT	MARISTS	MEATPIE	MINIMUM	MOOCHER
MAILMAN	MARITAL	MECENAS	MINIVER	MOONACK
MAITRED	MARITSA	MECHLIN	MINSTER	MOONLIT
MAJESTY	MARKHOR	MEDDLER	MINUEND	MOORHEN
MAJORCA	MARLINE	MEDIATE	MINUTES	MOORING
MAKASAR	MARLOWE	MEDRICK	MIOCENE	MOORISH
MAKINGS	MARMARA	MEDULLA	MIOLNIR	MORAINE
MALABAR	MARMITE	MEERKAT	MIRACLE	MORAVIA
MALACHI	MARMOSA	MEETING	MIRADOR	MORDANT
MALARIA	MAROTTE	MEGAERA	MIRANDA	MORDRED
MALAYAN	MARPLOT	MEGASSE	MISDEED	MORELLO
MALECON	MARQUEE	MEGATON	MISERLY	MORGANA
MALEFIC	MARQUIS	MEGRIMS	MISHNAH	MORGLAY
MALINES	MARSALA	MEGUILP	MISLAID	MORISCO
MALLARD	MARSHAL	MEISSEN	MISLEAD	MORNING
MALMSEY	MARSIAN	MELANGE	MISRULE	MOROCCO
MALTESE	MARTIAL	MELILOT	MISSILE	MORONIC
MALTOSE	MARTIAN	MELISSA	MISSING	MORPHIA
MALVERN	MARTINI	MELKITE	MISSION	MORRIGU
MAMMOTH	MARVELL	MELODIC	MISSIVE	MORSELS
MANACLE	MASCARA	MEMANUS	MISSTEP	MORTIER
MANAGER	MASCERA	MEMENTO	MISTAKE	MORTIFY
MANAGUA	MASKING	MEMINNA	MISTRAL	MORTISE
MANAMEH	MASONRY	MEMPHIS	MITOSIS	MORWONG
MANATEE	MASPERO	MENACED	MITTENS	MOSELLE
MANCALA	MASSAGE	MENORAH	MIXTURE	MOSHESH
MANDATE	MASSEUR	MENOTTI	MJOLNIR	MOSLEMS
MANDOLA	MASSIVE	MENTION	MNESTIC	MOTORED
MANDORE	MASTABA	MERAMEC	MOABITE	MOTTLED
MANDREL	MASTERY	MERCURY	MOBSTER	MOUNTED
MANDRIL	MASTIFF	MERENDA	MOCKERY	MOUNTIE
MANGLER	MASTIKA	MERMAID	MODELED	MOUSTOC
MANHOLE	MATADOR	MERMNAD	MODERNS	MOVABLE
MANIKIN	MATALAN	MESHACH	MODESTY	MOVIOLA
MANIPLE	MATAPAN	MESSAGE	MODISTE	MOYTURA
MANITOU	MATCHED	MESSIAH	MODULAR	MUDDLED
MANKIND	MATERIA	MESTIZO	MOELLON	MUDFISH
MANNERS	MATILDA	METHANE	MOHEGAN	MUDLARK
MANOWAR	MATINAL	METONYM	MOHICAN	MUEZZIN

MUFFLED	NEPHELE	NOURISH	OLELBIS	ORONTES
MUFFLER	NEPOTAL	NOVELET	OLIFANT	OROTUND
MULATTO	NEPOTIC	NOVELLA	OLIGIST	ORPHEUS
MULLEIN	NEPTUNE	NOVELTY	OLIVANT	ORPHREY
MULLION	NEREIDS	NOWHERE	OLIVIER	ORTHROS
MULTURE	NEREITE	NOXIOUS	OLIVINE	ORTOLAN
MUMMERY	NERISSA	NUCLEUS	OLOROSO	ORVIETO
MUMMIFY	NERTHUS	NUDISTS	OLYMPIA	OSCEOLA
MUNDANE	NERVOUS	NUGSUAK	OLYMPUS	OSCINES
MUNJEET	NESIOTE	NULLIFY	OMICRON	OSHKOSH
MUNSTER	NESTEGG	NUMERAL	OMINOUS	OSMANLI
MUNTJAC	NESTING	NUMIDIA	OMNIBUS	OSMOSIS
MURAENA	NETLIKE	NUMITOR	OMPHALE	OSSEOUS
MURDRUM	NETSUKE	NUMMARY	ONENESS	OSSICLE
MURGEON	NETTING	NUNATAK	ONEOVER	OSTIARY
MURNGIN	NETTLED	NUNNERY	ONEROUS	OSTIOLE
MURRAIN	NETWORK	NUPTIAL	ONESTEP	OSTRICH
MUSCLES	NEUTRAL	NURSERY	ONOMATO	OTALGIA
MUSCOVY	NEUTRON	NURTURE	ONSTEAD	OTHELLO
MUSETTE	NEVADAN	NUTGALL	ONTARIO	OTHRIEL
MUSICAL	NEWGATE	OARLOCK	OPACITY	OTOLITH
MUSKRAT	NEWPORT	OARSMAN	OPALINE	OTTOMAN
MUSLIMS	NEWSMAN	OATCAKE	OPENAIR	OUAKARI
MUSTANG	NEWYORK	OATMEAL	OPENING	OUTARDE
MUSTARD	NIAGARA	OATSEED	OPERAND	OUTCAST
MUSTELA	NIBBLED	OBELISK	OPERATE	OUTCOME
MUTABLE	NIBLICK	OBLIGED	OPEROSE	OUTFACE
MYCENAE	NICOSIA	OBLIQUE	OPHELIA	OUTGROW
MYCOSIS	NIDDICK	OBLOQUY	OPHIOID	OUTLAST
MYELOID	NIGGARD	OBSCENE	OPINION	OUTLINE
MYRMECO	NIGHTIE	OBSCURE	OPOSSUM	OUTLIVE
MYSTERE	NIHONGI	OBSERVE	OPPIDAN	OUTLOOK
MYSTERY	NIMIETY	OBTRUDE	OPPOSED	OUTPOST
NACARAT	NINEVEH	OBVERSE	OPPRESS	OUTRAGE
NACELLE	NINURTA	OBVIOUS	OPTICAL	OUTRANK
NAIROBI	NIPIGON	OCARINA	OPTIMAL	OUTSIDE
NAIVETE	NIPPERS	OCCIPUT	OPTIMUM	OUTSTAY
NAMAQUA	NIRVANA	OCEANIC	OPULENT	OUTWARD
NANKEEN	NITPICK	OCEANID	OPUNTIA	OUTWORK
NANKING	NITRATE	OCEANUS	ORARION	OVATION
NANSHAN	NIUAFOO	OCTAGON	ORATION	OVERACT
NAPHTHA	NIVEOUS	OCTOPUS	ORATORY	OVERAGE
NAPKINS	NOCTULE	OCULIST	ORCHARD	OVERALL
NARGILE	NOISOME	OCYPETE	ORDERED	OVERAWE
NARRATE	NOMADIC	ODDBALL	ORDERLY	OVERCUP
NARTHEX	NOMINAL	ODOROUS	ORDINAL	OVERDUE
NARWHAL	NOMINEE	ODYSSEY	OREGANO	OVEREAT
NASCENT	NONAGON	OEDIPUS	ORESTES	OVERLAY
NASTIKA	NONUPLE	OENOMEL	ORESUND	OVERMAN
NATCHEZ	NOONDAY	OERSTED	ORGANIC	OVERRUN
NATIVES	NOONISH	OFFENSE	ORGANZA	OVERSEE
NATURAL	NORFOLK	OFFHAND	ORIFICE	OVERTAX
NAYARIT	NORIMON	OFFICER	ORIGAMI	OWLLIKE
NEAREST	NORTHER	OILBIRD	ORINASE	OXIDIZE
NEEDFUL	NOSCEUM	OJIBWAY	ORINOCO	OXONIAN
NEGLECT	NOSEEUM	OKINAWA	ORIOLES	PABULUM
NEGRITO	NOSEGAY	OLALLIE	ORIONID	PACELLI
NEITHER	NOSTRIL	OLDADAM	ORLANDO	PACHISI
NELUMBO	NOSTRUM	OLDLINE	ORLEANS	PACIFIC
NEMESIS	NOTABLE	OLDMAID	OROGENY	PACKAGE
NEMORAL	NOTCHED	OLDNICK	OROHENA	PACKERS
NEMUNAS	NOTHING	OLDUVAI	OROLOGY	PACKING
NEOLITH	NOTIONS	OLDWIFE	ORONOCO	PADDING

PADDOCK	PARETIC	PELORUS	PHOEBUS	PITHHAT
PADRINO	PARISON	PELTATE	PHOENIX	PITIFUL
PADRONE	PARNELL	PEMBINA	PHONEME	PITTING
PADUCAH	PAROLEE	PENALTY	PHORCYS	PITUITE
PAENILA	PAROTIC	PENANCE	PHRENIC	PIZARRO
PAENULA	PAROTID	PENATES	PHRIXUS	PLACARD
PAGEANT	PARSLEY	PENCILS	PHRYGIA	PLACATE
PAINFUL	PARSNIP	PENDANT	PHTHALO	PLACKET
PAINTED	PARTAKE	PENDENT	PHTHSIS	PLAINLY
PAINTER	PARTIAL	PENGUIN	PIANIST	PLAITED
PAIRING	PARTITA	PENNAME	PIASTER	PLANATE
PAISLEY	PARTNER	PENNANT	PIASTRE	PLANETA
PAKCHOI	PARVATI	PENNATE	PIBROCH	PLANNER
PALADIN	PARVENU	PENNIES	PICASSO	PLANTAR
PALATAL	PASCHAL	PENSION	PICCOLO	PLANTER
PALAVER	PASHOFA	PENSIVE	PICTURE	PLANTIN
PALERMO	PASHTUN	PENTAIL	PICULET	PLASTER
PALETOT	PASSAGE	PEPPERY	PIDDOCK	PLASTIC
PALETTE	PASSING	PERCALE	PIEBALD	PLATEAU
PALFREY	PASSION	PERCEPT	PIERIAN	PLATING
PALLIUM	PASSIVE	PERDITA	PIGBOAT	PLATOON
PALMATE	PASTERN	PEREION	PIGLIKE	PLATTEN
PALMIST	PASTEUR	PEREKOP	PIGMENT	PLATTER
PALOMAR	PASTILE	PERFECT	PIGSKIN	PLAUTUS
PALPATE	PASTIME	PERFIDY	PIGTAIL	PLAYBOY
PALSIED	PASTURE	PERFORM	PIGWEED	PLAYFUL
PALUDAL	PATAMAR	PERFUME	PILGRIM	PLAYING
PALUDIC	PATELLA	PERGOLA	PILINGS	PLAYLET
PAMLICO	PATIENT	PERHAPS	PILLAGE	PLAYPEN
PAMPERO	PATOLLI	PERIAPT	PILLBUG	PLEADED
PANACEA	PATRICK	PERIDOT	PILLORY	PLEADER
PANACHE	PATRIOT	PERIGEE	PIMENTO	PLEASED
PANARIS	PATTERN	PERIQUE	PIMLICO	PLEDGED
PANCAKE	PAUCITY	PERIWIG	PIMPLES	PLEDGET
PANDECT	PAYABLE	PERJURE	PINBALL	PLEIONE
PANDORA	PAYMENT	PERJURY	PINCERS	PLENARY
PANDORE	PAYSAGE	PERMIAN	PINCHED	PLESSOR
PANGAEA	PEACHUM	PERPLEX	PINHEAD	PLIABLE
PANGASI	PEACOCK	PERSEID	PINHOLE	PLIANCY
PANNAGE	PEANUTS	PERSEIS	PINKEYE	PLICATE
PANNIER	PEARLIE	PERSEUS	PINNACE	PLOESTI
PANNOSE	PEASANT	PERSIAN	PINTADO	PLOVDIV
PANPIPE	PEASOUP	PERSICO	PINTAIL	PLOWMAN
PANTHER	PEBBLES	PERSIST	PINTANO	PLUMAGE
PANTILE	PECCARY	PERSONS	PINWORM	PLUMMET
PANTING	PECONIC	PERUSAL	PIONEER	PLUMULE
PAPEETE	PEDALED	PERVERT	PIPETTE	PLUNDER
PAPILLA	PEDDLER	PETASUS	PIQUANT	POCHARD
PAPRIKA	PEDICEL	PETIOLE	PIRAEUS	POCOSIN
PAPYRUS	PEERAGE	PETRALE	PIRAGUA	PODAGRA
PARABLE	PEERESS	PETRIFY	PIRANHA	PODARGE
PARACME	PEEVISH	PETTISH	PIRATES	PODESTA
PARADOS	PEGADOR	PFENNIG	PIROGUE	POETIZE
PARADOX	PEGADOT	PHAEDRA	PISCINA	POINTED
PARAGON	PEGASUS	PHAETON	PISCINE	POINTER
PARANEE	PEGLIKE	PHALANX	PISHPEK	POLACRE
PARAPET	PEIPING	PHANTOM	PISMIRE	POLARIS
PARASOL	PELAGIC	PHARAOH	PISTOLA	POLECAT
PARCHED	PELELIU	PHARYNX	PISTOLE	POLEMIC
PARDNER	PELICAN	PHASMID	PITAPAT	POLLACK
PARELLA	PELISSE	PHIDIAS	PITCHER	POLLARD
PARELLE	PELLEAS	PHILTER	PITEOUS	POLLOCK
PARESIS	PELMENY	PHILTRE	PITFALL	POLLUTE

POLYBUS	PRELECT	PROSPER	PYRRHIC	RAMPIKE
POLYGON	PRELUDE	PROTEAN	PYTHIAS	RAMSONS
POLYMER	PREMIER	PROTECT	QANTARA	RAMSTAM
POMPANO	PREMISE	PROTEIN	QATTARA	RANGOON
POMPEIA	PREMIUM	PROTEST	QUAITSO	RANKEST
POMPEII	PREPARE	PROVERB	QUALIFY	RANKING
POMPOUS	PREPUCE	PROVIDE	QUALITY	RANSACK
PONIARD	PRESAGE	PROVINE	QUANTUM	RANSTED
PONTACQ	PRESENT	PROVISO	QUARREL	RAPANUI
PONTIFF	PRESIDE	PROVOKE	QUARTAN	RAPHAEL
PONTINE	PRESSER	PROVOST	QUARTER	RAPTURE
PONTIST	PRESSON	PROWESS	QUARTET	RAREBIT
PONTOON	PRESUME	PROWLER	QUASSIA	RARITAN
POOHBAH	PRETEND	PRUDENT	QUECHUA	RASORES
POOREST	PRETEXT	PRUDHOE	QUEENLY	RASPING
POPCORN	PREVAIL	PRYDERI	QUERCUS	RATABLE
POPOVER	PREVENT	PSALTER	QUETSCH	RATAFIA
POPTUNE	PRICKET	PSCHENT	QUETZAL	RATATAT
POPULAR	PRICKLE	PSILOPA	QUIBBLE	RATCHET
POPULUS	PRICKLY	PSYCHIC	QUICKEN	RATHLIN
PORCINE	PRIDWIN	PTERION	QUICKLY	RATLINE
PORRECT	PRIMACY	PTEROID	QUIESCE	RATTLER
PORTAGE	PRIMARY	PTOLEMY	QUIETLY	RAUCITY
PORTEND	PRIMATE	PUBLISH	QUIETUS	RAUCOUS
PORTENT	PRIMPER	PUCCINI	QUININE	RAVAGES
PORTHOS	PRINCIP	PUCCOON	QUINNAT	RAVELIN
PORTICO	PRINTED	PUCELLE	QUINTAL	RAVIOLI
PORTION	PRISTIS	PUERILE	QUINTET	RAWHIDE
PORTRAY	PRIVACY	PUFFERY	QUITTER	READILY
POSSESS	PRIVATE	PUGNOSE	QUIXOTE	READING
POSTAGE	PROBATE	PUKEAWE	QUIZZER	REALGAR
POSTERN	PROBITY	PUKHTUN	QUONDAM	REALIGN
POSTMAN	PROBLEM	PULASKI	QURAYSH	REALITY
POTABLE	PROCEED	PULLMAN	RABANNA	REALTOR
POTAMIC	PROCRIS	PULLOUT	RABBITS	REAREND
POTENCY	PROCURE	PULSATE	RABICAN	REARING
POTHEEN	PROCYON	PUMPKIN	RABUINO	REBECCA
POTHOLE	PRODIGY	PUNAKHA	RACCOON	REBEKAH
POTLACE	PRODUCE	PUNCHER	RACHIAL	REBIRTH
POTOMAC	PRODUCT	PUNGENT	RACKETS	REBOANT
POTSDAM	PROFANE	PUPFISH	RACLOIR	REBOUND
POTTAGE	PROFESS	PUPTENT	RADAMES	REBUILD
POTTERY	PROFFER	PURANAS	RADDLED	RECEIPT
POULTRY	PROFILE	PURANDI	RADIALE	RECEIVE
POVERTY	PROFITS	PURITAN	RADIANT	RECENCY
POWDERY	PROFUSE	PURLOIN	RADIATE	RECITAL
PRABANG	PROGENY	PURPORT	RADICAL	RECITED
PRAETOR	PROGRAM	PURPOSE	RADICEL	RECLAIM
PRAIRAL	PROJECT	PURSUIT	RAFFLES	RECLINE
PRAIRIE	PROLATE	PUSHING	RAGGEDY	RECLUSE
PRALINE	PROLONG	PUSHKIN	RAGWEED	RECOLOR
PRATTLE	PROMISE	PUSTULE	RAILING	RECOUNT
PREBEND	PROMOTE	PUTAMEN	RAIMENT	RECOVER
PRECEDE	PRONAOS	PUTDOWN	RAINBOW	RECRUIT
PRECEPT	PRONATE	PUTELEE	RAINIER	RECTORY
PRECIPE	PRONOUN	PUTREFY	RALEIGH	RECURVE
PRECISE	PROPHET	PUTTEES	RAMADAN	REDBIRD
PREDICT	PROPOSE	PUZZLER	RAMBLER	REDDISH
PREEMPT	PRORATA	PYRAMID	RAMEKIN	REDFISH
PREFACE	PRORATE	PYRAMUS	RAMESES	REDHEAD
PREFECT	PROSAIC	PYREXIA	RAMPAGE	REDIENT
PRELACY	PROSODY	PYRITES	RAMPANT	REDNECK
PRELATE		PYROSIS	RAMPART	REDOUBT

REDRESS	REREDOS	RIPOSTE	RUBBISH	SAMOYED
REDROOT	RESCIND	RISIBLE	RUBELLA	SAMPLER
REDSKIN	RESERVE	RISOTTO	RUBEOLA	SAMURAI
REDUCED	RESHAPE	RISSOLE	RUBICON	SANCTUM
REDUCER	RESIDED	RIVALRY	RUCHING	SANDALS
REDWING	RESIDUE	RIVETER	RUDERAL	SANDBAG
REDWOOD	RESOLVE	RIVIERA	RUDOLPH	SANDHOG
REEDING	RESOUND	RIVIERE	RUFFIAN	SANGRUR
REELECT	RESPECT	RIVULET	RUINOUS	SANJOSE
REENACT	RESPIRE	RIVULUS	RUKMINI	SANJUAN
REFEREE	RESPITE	ROANOKE	RUMFORD	SANTAFE
REFINED	RESPOND	ROASTER	RUNAWAY	SANTANA
REFLECT	RESTATE	ROBBERY	RUNDOWN	SAPAJOU
REFRAIN	RESTING	ROBERTS	RUNLESS	SAPIENT
REFRESH	RESTIVE	ROBINET	RUNNING	SAPLING
REFUGEE	RESTORE	ROCKCOD	RUNOVER	SAPPORO
REFUSAL	RESURGE	ROCKELM	RUPTURE	SAPSAGO
REGALED	RETABLE	ROCKIES	RUQAYYA	SARACEN
REGALIA	RETIARY	RODLIKE	RURALES	SARANGI
REGATTA	RETICLE	RODOLFO	RUSHING	SARAWAK
REGIMEN	RETINUE	ROGUISH	RUSSELL	SARCASM
REGNANT	RETIRED	ROISTER	RUSSIAN	SARDINE
REGRATE	RETITLE	ROLLTOP	RUSTLER	SARIGUE
REGRESS	RETRACE	ROLOWAY	RYUKYUS	SARINDA
REGULAR	RETRAIN	ROMAINE	SABAISM	SASHIMI
REJOICE	RETREAD	ROMANCE	SABAOTH	SASSABY
RELAPSE	RETREAT	ROMAUNT	SABATON	SASSARI
RELATED	RETRIAL	ROMBERG	SABBATH	SATANIC
RELATOR	RETSINA	ROMPERS	SABINES	SATCHEL
RELAXED	RETURNS	ROMULUS	SABRINA	SATIATE
RELEASE	REUNION	RONDEAU	SACADAS	SATIETY
RELIANT	REUNITE	RONSARD	SACCATE	SATINET
RELIEVE	REUTERS	ROOKERY	SACCULE	SATIRIC
REMAINS	REVELER	ROOSTER	SACKBUT	SATISFY
REMARRY	REVELRY	ROOTERS	SADIRON	SATRAPY
REMNANT	REVENGE	ROOTLET	SADNESS	SATYRUS
REMODEL	REVERIE	RORAIMA	SAFFRON	SAUNTER
REMORSE	REVERSE	RORQUAL	SAGUARO	SAURIAN
REMOTER	REVILER	ROSARIO	SAILING	SAUSAGE
REMOVAL	REVISER	ROSEATE	SAILORS	SAUTOIR
RENDOVA	REVIVAL	ROSETTA	SAINTLY	SAVANNA
RENEWAL	REVOLVE	ROSETTE	SAKERET	SAVANTS
REOCCUR	REWRITE	ROSSINI	SALABLE	SAVARIN
REPAINT	REYNARD	ROSTAND	SALADIN	SAVINGS
REPAPER	RHEEBOK	ROSTRUM	SALERNO	SAVIOUR
REPLACE	RHIZOME	ROTATED	SALIENT	SAVITAR
REPLANT	RHODOPE	ROTIFER	SALLUST	SAWBUCK
REPLETE	RHUBARB	ROTTING	SALOPIA	SAWDUST
REPLICA	RICINUS	ROTUNDA	SALSODA	SAWLIKE
REPOINT	RICKETS	ROUAULT	SALTERN	SAWMILL
REPOSIT	RICKSHA	ROUGHEN	SALTERY	SAXHORN
REPRESS	RICOTTA	ROUGHER	SALTIER	SCABIES
REPRINT	RIFLING	ROUGHLY	SALTIRE	SCADENT
REPRISE	RIGHTLY	ROULADE	SALVAGE	SCALADE
REPROOF	RIGHTON	ROUNDED	SALWEEN	SCALADO
REPROVE	RIKSDAG	ROUNDEL	SAMARIA	SCALAGE
REPTANT	RIMBAUD	ROUNDUP	SAMBUKE	SCALENE
REPTILE	RINALDO	ROUTINE	SAMHAIN	SCALING
REPULSE	RINGERS	ROWBOAT	SAMISEN	SCALLOP
REPUTED	RINGING	ROWLOCK	SAMMAEL	SCALPEL
REQUEST	RINGLET	RRHAGIA	SAMNITE	SCAMPER
REQUIEM	RIOTOUS	RUAPEHU	SAMOUSE	SCANDAL
REQUITE	RIPENED	RUBBERS	SAMOVAR	SCAPULA

SCARLET	SELKIRK	SHAPELY	SIGNORE	SLOVENE
SCARPIA	SELLOUT	SHARPEN	SIKIANG	SLOWING
SCARRED	SELTZER	SHARPER	SIKSIKA	SLUGGER
SCARRON	SELVAGE	SHASLIK	SILENCE	SLUMBER
SCATTER	SEMINAR	SHASTRA	SILENUS	SMALLER
SCENERY	SEMITIC	SHATTER	SILIQUE	SMARAGD
SCENITE	SENATOR	SHAWWAL	SILURES	SMARTED
SCENTED	SENDING	SHEITAN	SILVICS	SMARTEN
SCEPTER	SENEGAL	SHELLEY	SIMILAR	SMARTER
SCEPTRE	SENMARI	SHELTER	SIMPLON	SMASHED
SCHELDT	SENSATE	SHELVES	SIMURGH	SMATTER
SCHEMER	SENSUAL	SHEPPEY	SINAPIS	SMEELIN
SCHERIA	SENUSSI	SHERBET	SINCERE	SMELTER
SCHERZO	SEPPUKU	SHERBRO	SINEWED	SMIDGEN
SCHMELZ	SEPTIME	SHEREEF	SINGLET	SMITTEN
SCHOLAR	SEQUANI	SHERIFF	SINKING	SMOKIES
SCHWEIZ	SEQUELA	SHEVUOS	SINLESS	SMOKING
SCIATIC	SEQUOIA	SHIKARI	SINNING	SMOLDER
SCIENCE	SERAPIS	SHIKOKU	SINUOUS	SMOTHER
SCIRPUS	SERBIAN	SHILLUK	SIRLOIN	SMUDGED
SCOMBER	SERFDOM	SHINGLE	SIROCCO	SNAFFLE
SCOOTER	SERIATE	SHINING	SISTINE	SNAGGER
SCORPIO	SERIEMA	SHIPPED	SISTRUM	SNAPPER
SCOURGE	SERIOUS	SHIPPER	SISWATI	SNARLED
SCOUTER	SERPENT	SHIRKER	SITFAST	SNEAKER
SCRAGGY	SERRANA	SHIRLEY	SITIENT	SNEEZER
SCRAPER	SERRATE	SHOOTER	SITTING	SNICKER
SCRAPPY	SERRIED	SHOPHAR	SITUATE	SNIGGER
SCRATCH	SERVANT	SHOPMAN	SIXTEEN	SNIPPET
SCRAWNY	SERVICE	SHOPPED	SJAMBOK	SNOOKER
SCREECH	SERVILE	SHORTEN	SKATIKU	SNOOPED
SCRIBED	SERVITE	SHOTGUN	SKATING	SNOOPER
SCRIPPS	SESSILE	SHOWERY	SKEEZIX	SNORKEL
SCROOGE	SESSION	SHOWING	SKEPTIC	SNORTER
SCRUBBY	SESTINA	SHOWOFF	SKETCHY	SNOTTER
SCRUPLE	SETANTA	SHQIPNI	SKILLED	SNOWDON
SCUFFLE	SETEBOS	SHQIPRI	SKILLET	SNUFFLE
SCULLER	SETTING	SHRIEVE	SKIMMER	SNUGGLE
SCUPPER	SETTLED	SHRIVEL	SKIPPER	SOARING
SCUTARI	SETTLER	SHUDDER	SKIRLER	SOBERER
SCUTTLE	SEVENTH	SHUFFLE	SKITTER	SOCAGER
SEADUCK	SEVENTY	SHUSHAN	SKITTLE	SOCIETY
SEAGIRT	SEVENUP	SHUTEYE	SKOPLJE	SOCKEYE
SEALION	SEVERAL	SHUTOUT	SKYBLUE	SOLDIER
SEATTLE	SEVILLE	SHUTTER	SKYLARK	SOLICIT
SEAWEED	SEXLESS	SHUTTLE	SLACKEN	SOLIDUM
SECONDE	SEXTANT	SHYLOCK	SLADANG	SOLIDUS
SECRECY	SFOGATO	SHYNESS	SLAINTE	SOLOMON
SECRETE	SHABUOT	SHYSTER	SLANDER	SOLVEIG
SECTARY	SHACKLE	SIALOID	SLASHER	SOLVENT
SECTILE	SHADING	SIAMANG	SLATTED	SOMATIC
SECTION	SHADKAN	SIAMESE	SLAVERY	SOMEONE
SECULAR	SHADOWS	SIANGKI	SLAVISH	SOMEWAY
SECURED	SHAITAN	SIBLING	SLEAVES	SONCINO
SEDALIA	SHAKING	SICILIA	SLEEPER	SONGHAI
SEDUCER	SHALLOP	SIDDONS	SLEEVES	SONGKOI
SEERESS	SHALLOT	SIDEARM	SLEIGHT	SOPATOR
SEGMENT	SHALLOW	SIDECAR	SLENDER	SOPHISM
SEISMIC	SHAMASH	SIERRAS	SLICKER	SOPHIST
SEIZURE	SHAMBLE	SIGHING	SLIPPER	SOPPING
SEJANUS	SHAMMAS	SIGMOID	SLITHER	SOPRANO
SEKHMET	SHANNON	SIGMUND	SLIVING	SORCERY
SELFISH	SHAPASH	SIGNORA	SLOBBER	SORGHUM

SORITES	SPRINGY	STILTED	SUBURBS	SWEDISH
SOROBAN	SPUMONI	STILTON	SUBVERT	SWEEPER
SOROCHE	SPUTNIK	STINGER	SUCCEED	SWEETEN
SOROSIS	SPUTTER	STIPEND	SUCCESS	SWEETIE
SORTING	SQUALLY	STIPPLE	SUCCOTH	SWELTER
SOTTISH	SQUALOR	STIPULE	SUCCUMB	SWIFTLY
SOUFFLE	SQUALUS	STIRRUP	SUCROSE	SWIMMER
SOUNDER	SQUARED	STJOHNS	SUDETEN	SWINDLE
SOUNDLY	SQUEEZE	STOICAL	SUFFICE	SWINISH
SOUREST	SQUELCH	STOKERS	SUGGEST	SWIZZLE
SOUTHEY	SQUILLA	STOLLEN	SUGRIVA	SWOLLEN
SOZZLED	SRIMATI	STOMACH	SUICIDE	SYAGUSH
SPACIAL	STADIUM	STONING	SUKKOTH	SYBARIS
SPANDEX	STAGGER	STOOLIE	SULMONA	SYCOSIS
SPANGLE	STAINER	STOPGAP	SULPHUR	SYMPTON
SPANIEL	STAMINA	STOPPER	SULTANA	SYNAXIS
SPANISH	STAMMEL	STOPPLE	SUMATRA	SYNCOPE
SPANNER	STAMMER	STORAGE	SUMMARY	SYNONYM
SPARING	STANDBY	STORIES	SUMMERY	SYRINGA
SPARKLE	STANDEE	STOUTER	SUMMONS	SYRINGE
SPARROW	STANLEY	STPAULS	SUMPTER	SYSTOLE
SPARSER	STANNUM	STRANGE	SUNAPEE	TABANUS
SPARTAN	STANTON	STRATUM	SUNBURN	TABARET
SPARTOI	STARLET	STRAUSS	SUNDIAL	TABASCO
SPATIAL	STARTED	STREAKY	SUNDOWN	TABELLA
SPATTER	STARTLE	STRETCH	SUNFISH	TABETIC
SPATULA	STATANT	STRETTA	SUNGARI	TABINET
SPEAKER	STATELY	STRETTO	SUNNING	TABITHA
SPECIAL	STATICS	STRIATE	SUNNITE	TABLEAU
SPECIES	STATING	STRIBOG	SUNRISE	TABORET
SPECIFY	STATION	STRIDOR	SUNSPOT	TACITUS
SPECKLE	STATUTE	STRIGIL	SUPPAWN	TACTICS
SPECTER	STAUNCH	STRINGY	SUPPORT	TACTILE
SPEEDER	STAYMAN	STRIPED	SUPPOSE	TACTUAL
SPELTER	STCLOUD	STRIPER	SUPREME	TADPOLE
SPENCER	STEALTH	STRIPES	SURCOAT	TAGALOG
SPENDER	STEAMER	STRIVEN	SURFACE	TAGTAIL
SPENSER	STEARIN	STROPHE	SURFEIT	TAILEND
SPHERIC	STEEPLE	STRUDEL	SURGEON	TAILFAN
SPICULE	STEERED	STUBBLE	SURGERY	TAINTED
SPIELER	STEERER	STUDENT	SURINAM	TAKEOFF
SPILLER	STEEVED	STUDIED	SURMISE	TALARIA
SPINACH	STELLAR	STUMBLE	SURNAME	TALIERA
SPINATE	STENCIL	STUMPER	SURPASS	TALIPES
SPINDLE	STENTER	STUNNED	SURPLUS	TALIPOT
SPINNER	STENTOR	STUNTED	SURTOUT	TALLAGE
SPINNEY	STEPHEN	STUPEFY	SURTSEY	TALLBOY
SPINOZA	STEPPED	STUTTER	SURVIVE	TALLEST
SPIRALS	STERILE	STYLISH	SUSANOO	TALLITH
SPIRANT	STERLET	STYLIST	SUSPECT	TALLYHO
SPIRATE	STERNAL	STYPTIC	SUSPEND	TALONED
SPIRITS	STERNUM	SUALTAM	SUSTAIN	TAMARAC
SPITTLE	STERTOR	SUANPAN	SUTURED	TAMARIN
SPLURGE	STETSON	SUAVITY	SUTURES	TAMAROU
SPOILED	STETTIN	SUBDUED	SVERIGE	TAMBOUR
SPOKANE	STEVENS	SUBERIN	SWAGGER	TAMPANG
SPONDEE	STEWARD	SUBJECT	SWAHILI	TAMPERE
SPONGER	STEWPAN	SUBLIME	SWALLOW	TAMPICO
SPONSOR	STICKER	SUBROSA	SWANLET	TAMPION
SPORRAN	STICKUP	SUBSIDE	SWANPAN	TANAGER
SPOTTED	STIFFEN	SUBSIDY	SWARTHY	TANAROS
SPRINGE	STIFFLY	SUBSIST	SWAYING	TANCRED
SPRINGS	STIFLED	SUBTILE	SWEATER	TANGENT

TANGIER	TERPENE	TILLAGE	TRAMPLE	TRUNDLE
TANGLED	TERRACE	TILTING	TRANSIT	TRUSTEE
TANGRAM	TERRAIN	TIMARAU	TRANSOM	TRYSTED
TANKARD	TERRANE	TIMBREL	TRAPEZE	TSANGPO
TANTARA	TERRENE	TIMOTHY	TRAPPER	TSANTSA
TANTIVY	TERRIER	TIMPANI	TRAVAIL	TSARINA
TANTRAS	TERRIFY	TINAMOU	TRAVOIS	TSHIRTS
TANTRUM	TERRINE	TINFOIL	TRAWLER	TSIGANE
TAPAJOS	TERTIAN	TINIEST	TREACLE	TSONGDU
TAPAJOZ	TESSERA	TINTYPE	TREADLE	TSQUARE
TAPIOCA	TESTATE	TINWARE	TREASON	TSUNAMI
TAPSTER	TESTBAN	TIPPLER	TREFOIL	TUATARA
TARANTO	TESTIFY	TIPSTER	TRELLIS	TUBULAR
TARAPON	TESTUDO	TITANIA	TREMBLE	TUGHRIK
TARBUSH	TETANIC	TITANIC	TREMOLO	TUITION
TARENTE	TETANUS	TITLARK	TRENAIL	TUMBLER
TARHEEL	TETRODE	TITULAR	TRENTAL	TUMBREL
TARNISH	TEXTILE	TOASTER	TRENTON	TUMBRIL
TARSIER	TEXTURE	TOBACCO	TREPANG	TUMULUS
TARTUFE	THALASS	TODDLER	TRESSEL	TUNEFUL
TATOUAY	THALLUS	TOLLING	TRESTLE	TUNISIA
TATTING	THANATO	TOLSTOI	TRIANON	TUNNAGE
TATTLER	THEATER	TOLSTOY	TRIBUNE	TUNNELS
TAURET	THEATRE	TONIGHT	TRIBUTE	TUONELA
TAURINE	THEORBO	TONNAGE	TRICEPS	TURBINE
TAUTAUG	THEOREM	TONNEAU	TRICKED	TURIDDU
TAXICAB	THEREIN	TONSURE	TRICKLE	TURKISH
TEACAKE	THEREOF	TONTINE	TRICORN	TURMOIL
TEACHER	THERETO	TOOLBAG	TRIDENT	TURNING
TEARFUL	THERIAC	TOOLING	TRIESTE	TURNKEY
TEAROOM	THERMAE	TOPCOAT	TRIFLES	TUSSAUD
TEDIOUS	THERMAL	TOPIARY	TRIMMED	TUSSIVE
TEEMING	THERMIC	TOPICAL	TRIMMER	TUSSOCK
TEENAGE	THERMOS	TORMENT	TRINITY	TUTORED
TEGMINA	THESEUS	TORNADO	TRINKET	TUTUILA
TEGULAR	THESPIS	TORONTO	TRIOLET	TWADDLE
TEGUMEN	THEURGY	TORPEDO	TRIPLED	TWEENEY
TEHERAN	THIAMID	TORRENT	TRIPLET	TWEETER
TELAMON	THICKEN	TORSION	TRIPOLI	TWINKLE
TELAVIV	THICKET	TORTILE	TRIPPER	TWISTED
TELEOST	THILLER	TORTOLA	TRIREME	TWISTER
TELLING	THIMBLE	TORTURE	TRISECT	TWITTER
TELSTAR	THINKER	TORULIN	TRISMUS	TWOBITS
TEMBLOR	THINNER	TOSSPOT	TRISTAN	TWOFOLD
TEMPERA	THIRSTY	TOTALLY	TRITEST	TWOSTEP
TEMPEST	THISTLE	TOTUAVA	TRITIUM	TWOWOOD
TEMPLAR	THITHER	TOUGHEN	TRIUMPH	TYPHOON
TEMPLET	THOREAU	TOURACO	TRIVIAL	TYPICAL
TEMPURA	THORIUM	TOURIST	TROCHEE	TYRANNY
TENABLE	THOUGHT	TOWBOAT	TROILUS	TZIGANE
TENDRIL	THRIFTY	TOWPATH	TROLLEY	UBEROUS
TENIERS	THROUGH	TRACHEA	TROLLOP	UDOLPHO
TENPINS	THUMMIM	TRACING	TROODOS	UKRAINE
TENSEST	THUNDER	TRACTOR	TROOPER	UKULELE
TENSILE	THUSFAR	TRADUCE	TROPISM	ULALUME
TENSION	THWAITE	TRAGEDY	TROTTER	ULULANT
TENSIVE	THYROID	TRAGULA	TROUBLE	ULULATE
TENSPOT	TIBESTI	TRAINED	TROUNCE	ULYSSES
TENUITY	TIBETAN	TRAINEE	TRUANCY	UMBRAGE
TENUOUS	TIBURON	TRAINER	TRUCKEE	UMBRIAN
TEQUILA	TIDINGS	TRAIPSE	TRUCKLE	UMBRIEL
TERMITE	TIGRINA	TRAITOR	TRUFFLE	UNAIDED
TERNATE	TIJUANA	TRAMMEL	TRUMPET	UNASKED

UNAWARE	VACCINE	VIADUCT	WALKING	WHINING
UNBOUND	VACUITY	VIBGYOR	WALKWAY	WHIPPET
UNCANNY	VAGRANT	VIBRATE	WALLABY	WHISKER
UNCIALS	VALANCE	VIBRATO	WALLOON	WHISKEY
UNCIVIL	VALIANT	VICINAL	WANDERS	WHISPER
UNCLEAN	VALJEAN	VICIOUS	WANNESS	WHISTLE
UNCLEAR	VALLEJO	VICTORY	WANTAGE	WHITHER
UNCOUTH	VALMIKI	VICTUAL	WANTING	WHITISH
UNCOVER	VALVULE	VIDUAGE	WAPATOO	WHITLOW
UNDRESS	VAMOOSE	VIDUATE	WARBLER	WHITMAN
UNDYING	VAMPIRE	VIEQUES	WARLIKE	WHITNEY
UNFIXED	VANDALS	VIETNAM	WARMING	WHITTLE
UNGODLY	VANDYKE	VILAYET	WARNING	WHOEVER
UNGUENT	VANILLA	VILLAGE	WARRANT	WHOOPED
UNHAPPY	VANTAGE	VILLAIN	WARRIOR	WHOOPER
UNHINGE	VAQUERO	VILLEIN	WARSHIP	WHOPPER
UNHORSE	VARANUS	VILNIUS	WARTHOG	WICHITA
UNICITY	VARIANT	VILNYUS	WARWICK	WICHTSE
UNICORN	VARIETY	VIMINAL	WASATCH	WICKIUP
UNIFORM	VARIOLA	VINASSE	WASHING	WIDGEON
UNKEMPT	VARIOUS	VINEGAR	WASHRAG	WIDOWED
UNKNOWN	VARNISH	VINIFER	WASSAIL	WIGGLER
UNLUCKY	VARSITY	VINLAND	WASTING	WILDCAT
UNMANLY	VATICAL	VINTAGE	WASTREL	WILHELM
UNMARRY	VATICAN	VINTNER	WATCHES	WILLFUL
UNMATED	VATTERN	VIOLATE	WATERED	WILLIAM
UNMIXED	VAUDOIS	VIOLENT	WATTAGE	WILLIES
UNQUIET	VAULTED	VIOLONE	WAVELET	WILLOWY
UNRAVEL	VEDANTA	VIRELAI	WAVESON	WINDBAG
UNREADY	VEDETTE	VIRGATE	WAYBILL	WINDING
UNSHORN	VEHICLE	VIRGULE	WAYWARD	WINDROW
UNSOUND	VEINLET	VIRUSES	WEALTHY	WINDSOR
UNTAMED	VELOUTE	VISAVIS	WEAPONS	WINESAP
UNTRIED	VELVETY	VISAYAN	WEARIED	WINNING
UNTRUTH	VENETIA	VISCERA	WEASAND	WINSOME
UNUSUAL	VENEZIA	VISCOSE	WEATHER	WIREMAN
UNWEARY	VENISON	VISCOUS	WEAVING	WISEGUY
UPBRAID	VENTAGE	VISIBLE	WEBBING	WISEMEN
UPPSALA	VENTAIL	VISITOR	WEDDELL	WISTFUL
UPRIGHT	VENTOSE	VISSIVE	WEDLOCK	WISTITI
UPSILON	VENTRAL	VISTULA	WEEDING	WITCHES
UPSTART	VENTURE	VITAMIN	WEEPING	WITHOUT
UPTIGHT	VERANDA	VITIATE	WEIGHTY	WITLESS
UPWAWET	VERBENA	VITRINE	WELCHER	WITLING
URANIAN	VERBOSE	VITRIOL	WELCOME	WITLOOF
URANIUM	VERDANT	VOIDING	WELFARE	WITNESS
URGENCY	VERDICT	VOLAPUK	WELLAND	WIZENED
URODELA	VERDURE	VOLCANO	WENDING	WOLFISH
URUGUAY	VERIDIC	VOLSUNG	WERGELD	WOMANLY
URUMCHI	VERMONT	VOLTAIC	WERGILD	WOODCUT
USELESS	VERRUCA	VOLUBLE	WERWOLF	WOODHEN
USHABTI	VERSANT	VOUCHER	WESTERN	WOOMERA
USUALLY	VERSIFY	VULGATE	WESTREL	WOORALI
UTENSIL	VERSION	VULPINE	WETTEST	WORKDAY
UTILITY	VERTIGO	VULTURE	WHANGEE	WORKERS
UTILIZE	VERUCCA	WADDELL	WHATNOT	WORKMAN
UTOPIAN	VERVAIN	WAGGERY	WHEREAS	WORLDLY
UTRICLE	VESICLE	WAGGISH	WHEREAT	WORNOUT
UTRILLO	VESPERS	WAHHABI	WHEREER	WORSHIP
UTTERED	VESTALS	WAIKIKI	WHEREIN	WORSTED
UTTERLY	VESTIGE	WAILING	WHEREON	WOULDBE
UXORIAL	VESUVIO	WAKEFUL	WHICKER	WRANGLE
VACANCY	VETERAN	WAKSMAN	WHIMPER	WRAPPER

WREATHE	WYOMING	YANKTON	YODELED	ZINCALO
WRECKED	XANTHIC	YAOUNDE	YODELER	ZINCOID
WRECKER	XANTHOS	YARDAGE	YOUNGER	ZIZANIA
WRESTLE	XENOPUS	YARDARM	YUCATAN	ZOOGENY
WRIGGLE	XERASIA	YARKAND	ZAGREUS	ZOOLOGY
WRIGGLY	XIBALBA	YASHMAK	ZAMARRA	ZORILLA
WRINKLE	XIPHIUM	YASHMIK	ZEBULUN	ZULEIKA
WRITING	XIPHOID	YAVAPAI	ZENOBIA	
WRITTEN	YAKUTSK	YAWNING	ZETETIC	
WRYNECK	YANCHEP	YENISEI	ZILLION	
WYCHELM	YANGTZE	YIDDISH	ZIMARRA	

Eight-Letter Words

AARDVARK	ADDICTED	AIRINESS	AMENABLE	ANTERIOR
ABATTOIR	ADDITION	AIRPLANE	AMERICAN	ANTEROOM
ABATVENT	ADELAIDE	AIRTIGHT	AMERICAS	ANTIBODY
ABDULLAH	ADENAUER	AKAKANET	AMETHYST	ANTIDOTE
ABEDNEGO	ADENITIS	ALACRITY	AMFORTAS	ANTIETAM
ABLATIVE	ADENOIDS	ALBACORE	AMMODYTE	ANTIGONE
ABLUTION	ADEQUACY	ALBANIAN	AMMONITE	ANTILLES
ABNORMAL	ADEQUATE	ALBERICH	AMONASRO	ANTILOGY
ABORTION	ADHERENT	ALBURNUM	AMORTIZE	ANTIPHON
ABRASION	ADHESIVE	ALDERMAN	AMPERAGE	ANYWHERE
ABRASIVE	ADJACENT	ALEATORY	AMPUTATE	APERIENT
ABROCOMA	ADJUSTED	ALHAMBRA	AMUNDSEN	APERITIF
ABROCOME	ADJUSTER	ALICANTE	AMYGDALA	APHORISM
ABROGATE	ADJUTANT	ALIENATE	ANABASIS	APIDANUS
ABSAROKA	ADMONISH	ALIENIST	ANABATIC	APOLLYON
ABSCISSA	ADRIATIC	ALIZARIN	ANACONDA	APOLOGUE
ABSENTEE	ADROITLY	ALKALINE	ANAGLYPH	APOPLEXY
ABSINTHE	ADULTERY	ALKERMES	ANAGRAMS	APOSTATE
ABSOLUTE	ADVANCED	ALLCLEAR	ANALECTS	APOTHEGM
ABSTRACT	ADVISERS	ALLEGORY	ANALOGIC	APPARENT
ABSTRUSE	ADVOCATE	ALLERGEN	ANALYSIS	APPEASED
ABUNDANT	AEGYPTUS	ALLIANCE	ANASARCA	APPEASER
ACADEMIC	AERATION	ALLODIUM	ANATHEMA	APPENDIX
ACANTHUS	AFFECTED	ALLOWING	ANATOLIA	APPETITE
ACAPULCO	AFFERENT	ALLSPICE	ANATOMIC	APPLAUSE
ACCEPTED	AFFIANCE	ALLURING	ANCESTOR	APPLEPIE
ACCIDENT	AFFINITY	ALLUSION	ANCESTRY	APPOSITE
ACCOUTER	AFFLUENT	ALLUSIVE	ANCHISES	APPRAISE
ACCURACY	AFFORDED	ALLUVIUM	ANCHORET	APPROACH
ACCURATE	AFRASIAN	ALMANACK	ANCIENTS	APPROVAL
ACCUSTOM	AGALLOCH	ALMIGHTY	ANDESINE	APRICATE
ACELDAMA	AGANIPPE	ALOPECIA	ANECDOTE	APRICOTS
ACERBATE	AGARAGAR	ALOUATTA	ANGELENO	APTEROUS
ACERBITY	AGITATED	ALOUETTE	ANGELICA	APTITUDE
ACESCENT	AGITATOR	ALPHABET	ANGLICAN	AQUALUNG
ACHENIUM	AGNATHIC	ALTEREGO	ANGUILLA	AQUANAUT
ACHERNAR	AGNOSTIC	ALTERITY	ANIMATED	AQUARIUS
ACHILLES	AGNUSDEI	ALTHOUGH	ANIMATOR	AQUILINE
ACHROITE	AGRAPHIA	ALTRUISM	ANISETTE	ARABELLA
ACQUIRED	AGRARIAN	ALVEOLUS	ANNALIST	ARACANGA
ACRANIAL	AGRAVAIN	ALYATTES	ANNOTATE	ARACHNID
ACRIMONY	AGREEING	AMADAVAT	ANNOUNCE	ARBALEST
ACRISIUS	AGRIMONY	AMAETHON	ANNOYING	ARBOREAL
ACROSTIC	AGUACATE	AMARANTH	ANNUALLY	ARCADIAN
ACTINIAN	AGUEWEED	AMARILLO	ANNULARY	ARCHIVES
ACTIVATE	AIGRETTE	AMBIENCE	ANOREXIA	ARCHNESS
ACTIVITY	AIRBORNE	AMBROSIA	ANTEATER	ARCTURUS
ACULEATE	AIRDROME	AMBULANT	ANTEDATE	ARDENTLY
ADDENDUM	AIREDALE	AMBULATE	ANTELOPE	ARGENTUM

ARGONAUT	AUTOBAHN	BASEBALL	BIENNIAL	BRAKEMAN
ARGUMENT	AUTOCADE	BASEMENT	BIFOCALS	BRAMANTE
ARISTATE	AUTOCRAT	BASENESS	BILBERRY	BRANCHED
ARKANSAS	AUTOMATA	BASILICA	BILLFISH	BRANCHER
ARMAGNAC	AUTONOMY	BASILISK	BINDWEED	BRANCHES
ARMATURE	AVENTAIL	BASKETRY	BINNACLE	BRANDEIS
ARMINIUS	AVENTINE	BASSANIO	BIRDLIME	BRANDISH
ARMORICA	AVERAGED	BASSWOOD	BIRDSONG	BRANDNEW
AROMATIC	AVERAGES	BASTILLE	BISMARCK	BRASILIA
ARPEGGIO	AVERSION	BATHURST	BLACKBOY	BRASSHAT
ARRANGED	AVIATION	BAUSEANT	BLACKFLY	BRATTICE
ARRESTED	AVIATORS	BAYBERRY	BLAMABLE	BRAWLING
ARRESTER	AVIFAUNA	BAYSTATE	BLANDISH	BREADBOX
ARROGANT	AWAITING	BDELLIUM	BLANKING	BREADPAN
ARSONIST	AWEATHER	BDELLOID	BLEACHED	BREAKOUT
ARTERIAL	BABIRUSA	BEAKLESS	BLEEDING	BREATHED
ARTICLES	BABUSHKA	BEAKLIKE	BLESSING	BREECHES
ARTIFICE	BABYHOOD	BEANLIKE	BLESSYOU	BREVIARY
ASBESTOS	BACCARAT	BEANTOWN	BLINDERS	BRIAREUS
ASCIDIAN	BACHELOR	BEARABLE	BLISSFUL	BRICKBAT
ASCOCARP	BACILLUS	BEARLIKE	BLIZZARD	BRICKRED
ASHENDEN	BACKBONE	BEATRICE	BLOCKADE	BRIGALOW
ASMODEUS	BACKDOOR	BEAUMONT	BLOOMING	BRIGHTEN
ASPERATE	BACKDROP	BEAUVOIR	BLOTCHED	BRIGHTON
ASPERGES	BACKTALK	BECHAMEL	BLOWHARD	BRINDISI
ASPERITY	BACKWARD	BECOMING	BLOWHOLE	BRINDLED
ASPIRANT	BACTERIA	BEDSTRAW	BLUEBACK	BRISBANE
ASPIRATE	BACTRIAN	BEEFWOOD	BLUEBIRD	BRITCHES
ASSASSIN	BADINAGE	BEETLING	BLUEGILL	BROADWAY
ASSEMBLE	BAEDEKER	BEETROOT	BLUENOSE	BROCHURE
ASSEMBLY	BAGHEERA	BEGINNER	BLUEWEED	BROOKLYN
ASSESSED	BAIDARKA	BEGOTTEN	BLUSHING	BROTHERS
ASSHURIM	BAKELITE	BEGRUDGE	BLUSTERY	BROUGHAM
ASSIGNED	BAKEMONO	BEHAVIOR	BOASTFUL	BRUMAIRE
ASSONANT	BALARAMA	BEHEMOTH	BOATLOAD	BRUSSELS
ASSUMING	BALDHEAD	BEHOLDEN	BOBBYPIN	BRUTTIUM
ASTATINE	BALDNESS	BELGRADE	BOBOLINK	BRYOLOGY
ASTERISK	BALDPATE	BELITTLE	BOBWHITE	BUBBLING
ASTEROID	BALDRICK	BELLTAIL	BOHEMIAN	BUCKSKIN
ASTONISH	BALLARAT	BELMOPAN	BOHEMOND	BUDAPEST
ASTRAEUS	BALLROOM	BELPAESE	BOLDFACE	BUDDHISM
ASTYANAX	BALLYHOO	BELTAINE	BOLDNESS	BUILDING
ASUNCION	BALUSTER	BENAMINI	BONDSMAN	BULGARIA
ATALANTA	BANALITY	BENEDICT	BONEHEAD	BULLDOZE
ATHALIAH	BANDANNA	BENEFICE	BONHOMIE	BULLETIN
ATHEROMA	BANISTER	BENGHAZI	BONIFACE	BULLHEAD
ATLANTIS	BANKROLL	BENJAMIN	BOOKCASE	BULLINGS
ATOMIZER	BANKRUPT	BEQUEATH	BORDEAUX	BULLSEYE
ATROCITY	BANKSIDE	BERGAMOT	BORDELLO	BURDEKIN
ATROPINE	BANNERET	BERIBERI	BOTOCUDO	BURGLARY
ATTACKED	BARBECUE	BESOTTED	BOTSWANA	BURGUNDY
ATTENDED	BARBICAN	BESSEMER	BOUILLON	BURNOOSE
ATTICISM	BARBITOS	BESTOWER	BOUNDARY	BURSITIS
ATTITUDE	BARBIZON	BESTRIDE	BOUTIQUE	BURSTONE
ATTORNEY	BARGELLO	BETJEMEN	BOUZOUKI	BUSHBABY
AUDACITY	BAREBACK	BETRAYAL	BOXBOARD	BUSINESS
AUDIENCE	BARITONE	BETRAYER	BRACELET	BUSYBODY
AUDITION	BARNACLE	BEWILDER	BRACKETS	BUTCHERY
AUDITORY	BARNDOOR	BHEESTEE	BRADSHAW	BUTTOCKS
AUGUMENT	BARRACKS	BIAFRANS	BRAGGART	BUTTRESS
AURELLUS	BARRETTE	BIBULOUS	BRAGGING	CABESTRO
AURICULA	BARTLETT	BICONVEX	BRAIDING	CABLECAR
AUSPICES	BASCINET	BICUSPID	BRAINPAN	CABRILLA

CABRILLO	CARDIGAN	CERATOID	CHOLERIC	COLOPHON
CACHALOT	CARDINAL	CERAUNIC	CHOPSUEY	COLORADO
CADASTRE	CARDIOID	CERBERUS	CHORIOID	COLORING
CADILLAC	CAREFREE	CEREALIA	CHRISTEN	COLOSSAL
CADUCEUS	CARELESS	CEREBRAL	CHRISTIE	COLOSSUS
CAFFEINE	CARILLON	CEREMENT	CHURINGA	COLUMBIA
CAGLIARI	CARLISLE	CEREMONY	CIBORIUM	COLUMBUS
CAINGANG	CARLOMAN	CERNUOUS	CICATRIX	COMANCHE
CAJOLERY	CARLOTTA	CERULEAN	CICERONE	COMATOSE
CALABASH	CARNIVAL	CESSPOOL	CIDERKIN	COMBLIKE
CALABRIA	CAROLERS	CETEWAYO	CIMARRON	COMEDIAN
CALADIUM	CAROLINE	CETOLOGY	CINCTURE	COMMANDO
CALAMITE	CAROUSAL	CEVENNES	CINERAMA	COMMERCE
CALAMITY	CAROUSEL	CHAIRMAN	CINNABAR	COMMUTER
CALANGAY	CAROUSER	CHALDEAN	CIRCULAR	COMPILER
CALANTAS	CARRIAGE	CHAMORRO	CITATION	COMPLAIN
CALCULUS	CARTHAGE	CHAMPION	CITYHALL	COMPLETE
CALCUTTA	CARUCATE	CHANCERY	CIVILIAN	COMPLINE
CALENDAR	CARYATID	CHANFRON	CIVILITY	COMPOSED
CALIBURN	CASANOVA	CHANGING	CLAIMANT	COMPOSER
CALINCHE	CASCABEL	CHANUKAH	CLARINET	COMPOUND
CALISAYA	CASCADES	CHAPERON	CLASSIER	COMPRESS
CALLIOPE	CASCADIA	CHAPLAIN	CLASSIFY	COMSTOCK
CALLISTO	CASEMATE	CHARCOAL	CLAUDIUS	CONCEIVE
CALMNESS	CASEMENT	CHARITES	CLAVICLE	CONCERTO
CALYPTER	CASHMERE	CHARLOCK	CLAYMORE	CONCLAVE
CAMARGUE	CASSETTE	CHARMING	CLAYWARE	CONCRETE
CAMATINA	CASTANET	CHARTULA	CLEANSER	CONDENSE
CAMBALUC	CASTAWAY	CHASSEUR	CLEAVERS	CONDOLER
CAMBODIA	CASTRATE	CHASTISE	CLEMATIS	CONENOSE
CAMBRIAN	CASUALLY	CHASTITY	CLEMENCY	CONEPATE
CAMELEER	CASUALTY	CHASUBLE	CLERICAL	CONFETTI
CAMISARD	CATACOMB	CHATTELS	CLERMONT	CONFINED
CAMISOLE	CATALINA	CHAUSSES	CLEVERLY	CONFLICT
CAMOMILE	CATALYST	CHEAPEST	CLIMBING	CONFRONT
CAMPAIGN	CATAPULT	CHEATING	CLINGING	CONFUSED
CAMPBELL	CATARACT	CHECKERS	CLINKING	CONGRESS
CANADIAN	CATCHING	CHEERFUL	CLOISTER	CONJOINT
CANAILLE	CATENARY	CHERIBON	CLOTHING	CONJUGAL
CANARIES	CATENATE	CHERUBIM	CLUBFOOT	CONJURER
CANBERRA	CATHOLIC	CHESTNUT	CLUPEOID	CONJUROR
CANCELLI	CATULLUS	CHEYENNE	CLYPEATE	CONNACHT
CANDIOTE	CAUCASUS	CHICKENS	COACHMAN	CONNOTED
CANICULA	CAULKING	CHICOGER	COALDUST	CONQUEST
CANICULE	CAUSEWAY	CHICQUER	COALESCE	CONSERVE
CANISTER	CAUTIOUS	CHILDISH	COBBLING	CONSIDER
CANONIZE	CAVALIER	CHILIAST	COCKTAIL	CONSISTS
CANTHOOK	CAVESSON	CHILKOOT	COGNOMEN	CONSPIRE
CAPACITY	CELARENT	CHIMAERA	COHERENT	CONSTANT
CAPETOWN	CELERITY	CHINDWIN	COIFFEUR	CONSTRUE
CAPRIOLE	CELIBATE	CHINKARA	COIFFURE	CONSUMED
CAPSTONE	CELLARER	CHINLING	COLANDER	CONTEMPT
CAPTIOUS	CELLARET	CHIPMUNK	COLDNESS	CONTESSA
CAPTURED	CELLULAR	CHIPPEWA	COLESLAW	CONTINUE
CAPTURES	CEMETERY	CHIRIQUI	COLLAPSE	CONTINUO
CAPUCHIN	CENOBITE	CHIRRUPS	COLLARDS	CONTRACT
CAPULETS	CENOTAPH	CHIVALRY	COLLATOR	CONTRAIL
CAPYBARA	CENOZOIC	CHLOASMA	COLLIERY	CONTRARY
CARACARA	CENTAURS	CHLORIDE	COLLOQUY	CONTRAST
CARACOLE	CENTAURY	CHLORINE	COLOMBIA	CONTRITE
CARAPACE	CEPHALUS	CHOISEUL	COLONCHE	CONTRIVE
CARCANET	CERASTES	CHOKEDUP	COLONIST	CONVENED

CONVERGE	CRITIQUE	DEATHCUP	DEROGATE	DISCOUNT
CONVERSE	CROCKERY	DEBILITY	DESCRIBE	DISCOVER
CONVINCE	CROMLECH	DEBONAIR	DESERTED	DISGRACE
COQUETTE	CROSSBAR	DEBUTANT	DESERTER	DISGUISE
CORDELIA	CROSSBOW	DECAMPED	DESERVED	DISHONOR
CORDUROY	CROSSEYE	DECANTER	DESIGNED	DISINTER
CORDWOOD	CROSSING	DECEASED	DESIGNER	DISJOINT
CORKWOOD	CROSSRIB	DECEIVER	DESIRING	DISLODGE
CORMORAN	CROTCHET	DECEMVIR	DESMODUS	DISLOYAL
CORNCAKE	CROUPIER	DECHTIRE	DESOLATE	DISMOUNT
CORNELIA	CROWDING	DECIMATE	DESPISED	DISORDER
CORNERED	CROWFOOT	DECISION	DESPOINA	DISPATCH
CORNHUSK	CROWNING	DECISIVE	DESPOTIC	DISPENSE
CORNICHE	CRUCIBLE	DECORATE	DESTINED	DISPERSE
CORNMEAL	CRUCIFIX	DECREASE	DETACHED	DISPLACE
CORONADO	CRUISING	DECREPIT	DETECTOR	DISPLAYS
CORONARY	CRUZEIRO	DECRETAL	DETHRONE	DISPOSED
CORPORAL	CUCUMBER	DEDICATE	DETONATE	DISPROOF
CORRIDOR	CUCURBIT	DEEMSTER	DETRITUS	DISPROVE
CORSICAN	CULDESAC	DEERLIKE	DEVASENA	DISRAELI
CORUNDUM	CULPABLE	DEERMEAT	DEVILISH	DISSOLVE
CORVETTE	CULVERIN	DEFEATED	DEVILTRY	DISSUADE
COSMETIC	CUPBOARD	DEFENDER	DEVOTION	DISTANCE
COSTUMER	CUPIDITY	DEFERENT	DEXTROSE	DISTASTE
COTENTIN	CURASSOW	DEFIANCE	DIABETES	DISTINCT
COTQUEAN	CURATIVE	DEFILING	DIABOLIC	DISTRAIT
COTTABUS	CURCULIO	DEFINITE	DIADOCHI	DISTRESS
COUCHANT	CURLICUE	DEFORMED	DIAGONAL	DISTRICT
COUGHING	CURRENCY	DEGRADED	DIALOGUE	DISTRUST
COUNTESS	CUSPIDOR	DEJECTED	DIAMETER	DIVIDEND
COUNTING	CUSTOMER	DELAWARE	DIAMONDS	DIVIDIVI
COUPLING	CUTTABLE	DELEGATE	DIANTHUS	DIVINITY
COURTESY	CUYAHOGA	DELETION	DIAPASON	DIVISION
COURTIER	CYLINDER	DELICACY	DIARRHEA	DIVORCEE
COUSCOUS	CYNOSURE	DELICATE	DIASPORA	DJAKARTA
COVENANT	CYTHEREA	DELIRIUM	DIASTOLE	DJELLABA
COVERALL	CYTOLOGY	DELMARVA	DIATRIBE	DOCILITY
COVERING	CZAREVNA	DELUSION	DICTATOR	DOCKSIDE
COVERTLY	CZARITZA	DELUSIVE	DIDACTIC	DOCTRINE
COVETOUS	DABCHICK	DEMEANOR	DIERESIS	DOCUMENT
COWARDLY	DAEDALUS	DEMENTED	DIGESTED	DOGGEREL
CRACKNEL	DAFFODIL	DEMERARA	DILATION	DOGHOUSE
CRACKPOT	DAIBUTSU	DEMIURGE	DILATORY	DOGMATIC
CRANSTON	DAINICHI	DEMOLISH	DILIGENT	DOGOODER
CRANTARA	DAINTILY	DEMONIAC	DIMAGGIO	DOKMAROK
CRATCHIT	DAMASCUS	DEMOPHIL	DIMINISH	DOLDRUMS
CRATINUS	DAMIETTA	DEMURRER	DINIZULU	DOLOMITE
CRAWLING	DAMNABLE	DENARIUS	DINOSAUR	DOMESTIC
CREATION	DAMPNESS	DENOUNCE	DIOMEDES	DOMICILE
CREATIVE	DANDRUFF	DENTAGRA	DIONYSUS	DOMINANT
CREATURE	DANSEUSE	DENTURES	DIPLOMAT	DOMINATE
CREDENCE	DARKENED	DEPARTED	DIPSTICK	DOMINEER
CREDENZA	DARKNESS	DEPLETED	DIPTERAL	DOMINICA
CREDIBLE	DAUGHTER	DEPONENT	DIRECTLY	DOMINION
CREEPING	DAVISCUP	DEPRAVED	DIRECTOR	DOMINOES
CRESCENT	DAYBREAK	DEPUTIZE	DISABLED	DONATION
CRESSIDA	DAYDREAM	DERANGED	DISARMED	DOOMSDAY
CRETONNE	DAZZLING	DERISION	DISASTER	DORMANCY
CREVASSE	DEADBEAT	DERISIVE	DISBURSE	DORMOUSE
CRIMINAL	DEADHEAT	DERISORY	DISCIPLE	DORTMUND
CRIPPLED	DEADLOCK	DEROGATE	DISCLOSE	DOTTEREL
CRITICAL	DEALINGS		DISCOLOR	DOUBLING
				DOUBTFUL

DOUGHNUT	EDUCATED	ENSEHADA	ETHNARCH	FALDEROL
DOVELIKE	EDUCATOR	ENSHEATH	ETHOLOGY	FALLIBLE
DOWNCAST	EFFECTED	ENSIFORM	ETIOLATE	FALSETTO
DOWNFOLD	EFFICACY	ENSILAGE	ETIOLOGY	FALSTAFF
DOWNPOUR	EFFLUVIA	ENTANGLE	EUCALYPT	FAMILIAR
DOWNTOWN	EGOISTIC	ENTHRALL	EULACHON	FAMISHED
DRAGOMAN	EGYPTIAN	ENTICING	EULOGIZE	FANCIFUL
DRAGONET	EINSTEIN	ENTIRELY	EUPEPSIA	FANDANGO
DRAGSTER	EJECTION	ENTRACTE	EUPHORIA	FANFARON
DRAINAGE	ELAPHINE	ENTRAILS	EUPHUISM	FANTASIA
DRAMATIC	ELAPHURE	ENTRANCE	EURYDICE	FARCICAL
DRAUGHTS	ELATERID	ENTREATY	EURYNOME	FAREWELL
DRAUPADI	ELDORADO	ENTRESOL	EVENSONG	FARRAGUT
DRAWBACK	ELDRITCH	ENVELOPE	EVENTFUL	FARSIGHT
DRAWNOUT	ELECTION	ENVIRONS	EVERYDAY	FARTHING
DREADFUL	ELECTRON	ENVISAGE	EVERYMAN	FASHIONS
DRENCHED	ELEGANCE	EOLIPILE	EVERYONE	FASTENER
DRESSING	ELEMENTS	EONOLOGY	EVICTION	FATHERLY
DRIFTING	ELENCHUS	EPHEMERA	EVIDENCE	FATIGUED
DRIPPING	ELENCTIC	EPIDEMIC	EVILDOER	FAVIFORM
DROOLING	ELEPHANT	EPIGRAPH	EXAMINER	FAVORITE
DROOPING	ELEVATED	EPILEPSY	EXAMINES	FAWNSKIN
DRUDGERY	ELEVATOR	EPINASTY	EXCAVATE	FEARLESS
DRUGGIST	ELLIPTIC	EPINETTE	EXCHANGE	FEARSOME
DRUMBEAT	ELOQUENT	EPIPHANY	EXCITING	FEASIBLE
DRUMFISH	ELSINORE	EPIPHYTE	EXCLUDED	FEATHERS
DRUMMING	EMACIATE	EQUALITY	EXECRATE	FEATHERY
DRUNKARD	EMBEZZLE	EQUIPAGE	EXEGESIS	FEATURED
DUCKBILL	EMBITTER	EQUIPPED	EXEGETIC	FECHSTAL
DUCKWEED	EMBOSSED	EREMITIC	EXEMPLAR	FEDAYEEN
DULCINEA	EMERGENT	ERICSSON	EXEQUIES	FEDERATE
DULKAADA	EMERITUS	ERIGERON	EXERCISE	FELDSPAR
DULLNESS	EMIGRANT	ERUPTION	EXERTION	FELICITY
DUMBSHOW	EMINENCE	ERUPTIVE	EXIGENCY	FELODESE
DUMPLING	EMISSARY	ERYTHEMA	EXISTING	FEMESOLE
DUNGHILL	EMPHASIS	ESCALADE	EXLIBRIS	FEMININE
DURANDAL	EMPHATIC	ESCALADO	EXORCISM	FEMINIST
DURANDEL	EMPLOYED	ESCAPIST	EXORDIAL	FENESTRA
DURATION	EMPLOYEE	ESCAROLE	EXORDIUM	FENSALIR
DWARFISH	EMPORIUM	ESCHALOT	EXPANDED	FEROCITY
DWELLING	ENAMELER	ESCORIAL	EXPEDITE	FERRYMAN
DWINDLED	ENAMORED	ESCULENT	EXPENSES	FERVENCY
DYNAMICS	ENCAENIA	ESOTERIC	EXPIABLE	FERVIDOR
DYNAMITE	ENCEINTE	ESPALIER	EXPLICIT	FESTIVAL
EARNINGS	ENCIRCLE	ESPOUSAL	EXPONENT	FEVERISH
EARRINGS	ENCLOSED	ESQUIMAU	EXPOSURE	FIDCHELL
EARSHELL	ENCOMIUM	ESTACADE	EXTENDED	FIDELITY
EARTHIER	ENCROACH	ESTAMINE	EXTERIOR	FIENDISH
EARTHKIN	ENCUMBER	ESTANCIA	EXTERNAL	FIGHTING
EARTHMAN	ENDANGER	ESTEEMED	EXULTANT	FILAMENT
EARTHNUT	ENDEAVOR	ESTERLIN	EXULTING	FILIGREE
EARTHPEA	ENDURING	ESTHETIC	EYEPIECE	FILIPINO
EASEMENT	ENERVATE	ESTIMATE	EYETOOTH	FINANCER
EASTWARD	ENFEEBLE	ESTONIAN	FABULIST	FINISHED
EASYMARK	ENFILADE	ESTOPPEL	FABULOUS	FIRDAUSI
EAUDEVIE	ENGENDER	ESTRANGE	FACECARD	FIREBALL
ECCLESIA	ENGINEER	ESTROGEN	FACILELY	FIRELIKE
ECLECTIC	ENGIRDLE	ESURIENT	FACTIOUS	FIREROOM
ECOSTATE	ENGRAVED	ETCETERA	FACTOTUM	FIRESIDE
ECSTATIC	ENIWETOK	ETEOCLES	FAIRNESS	FIREWEED
EDACIOUS	ENMESHED	ETERNITY	FAIRPLAY	FIREWORK
EDENTATE	ENORMITY	ETHEREAL	FAITHFUL	FIRMNESS
EDGEWISE	ENORMOUS	ETHIOPIA	FALCONRY	FISHHAWK

FISHHOOK	FORTRESS	GARGOYLE	GONCOURT	GYNARCHY
FISSURED	FORTUITY	GARMENTS	GONFALON	HABAKKUK
FIVEFOLD	FOUNTAIN	GARRISON	GOODHOPE	HABITUAL
FLAGRANT	FOURFOLD	GARROTER	GOODLUCK	HABSBURG
FLAMBEAU	FOURSOME	GASOLINE	GOODNESS	HACHIMAN
FLAMENCO	FOURWOOD	GAUNTLET	GOOSEEGG	HACIENDA
FLAPJACK	FOXGLOVE	GAZPACHO	GORGEOUS	HAIPHONG
FLASHING	FRACTION	GELASTIC	GOSSAMER	HAIRLESS
FLATBOAT	FRACTURE	GELIDITY	GOURMAND	HAIRROLL
FLATFISH	FRAGMENT	GEMINATE	GOUTWEED	HAKIMONO
FLATHEAD	FRAGRANT	GENDARME	GOVERNOR	HALFBACK
FLATIRON	FRANKLIN	GENERATE	GRACEFUL	HALFMAST
FLATNESS	FREAKOUT	GENEROUS	GRADIENT	HALFNOTE
FLATTERY	FRECKLES	GENESSEE	GRADUATE	HALFPIKE
FLAUBERT	FREEPORT	GENITIVE	GRAMARYE	HALIOTIS
FLAUTIST	FREEREIN	GENOCIDE	GRANDEUR	HALLOWED
FLAWLESS	FREETOWN	GENSERIC	GRANDMAL	HALOBIOS
FLAXSEED	FREEZING	GENTILES	GRANTING	HAMILCAR
FLEABANE	FREIBURG	GEOMANCY	GRAPHITE	HAMILTON
FLEETING	FREMITUS	GEOMETER	GRASPING	HAMMAMET
FLETCHER	FRENZIED	GEOPHAGY	GRATEFUL	HANDBILL
FLEXIBLE	FREQUENT	GEORGIAN	GRATTOIR	HANDBOOK
FLINFLON	FRESHMAN	GERMINAL	GRATUITY	HANDCART
FLIPPERS	FRICTION	GERONIMO	GRAVAMEN	HANDMAID
FLOATING	FRIENDLY	GERONTIC	GRAYBACK	HANDMILL
FLOGGING	FRIGHTEN	GERSHWIN	GRAYLING	HANDSOME
FLORENCE	FRIMAIRE	GERTRUDE	GREATAUK	HANDYMAN
FLOTILLA	FROGFISH	GHANAIAN	GREATEST	HANGERON
FLOUNDER	FRONTIER	GHIBERTI	GREENERY	HANIFITE
FLOURISH	FROSTING	GIGANTIC	GREETING	HANNIBAL
FLUORINE	FRUCTOSE	GIGELIRA	GRENACHE	HAPSBURG
FLUORITE	FRUITFUL	GILLETTE	GRETCHEN	HAQUETON
FLUSHING	FRUITION	GIMCRACK	GRIDIRON	HARAKIRI
FOGFRUIT	FUCHSINE	GINSBERG	GRIDLEAK	HARANGUE
FOLDEROL	FUGITIVE	GIOCONDA	GRIEVOUS	HARDENED
FOLKHERO	FULLNESS	GIOVANNI	GRIFFITH	HARDSHIP
FOLKTALE	FULLTIME	GLABELLA	GRIMALDI	HARDTACK
FOLLOWER	FUMAROLE	GLABROUS	GRINNELL	HARDWARE
FONDNESS	FUNNIEST	GLADGAME	GRISELDA	HAREBELL
FOOTBALL	FURBELOW	GLANDERS	GRISETTE	HARELIKE
FOOTFALL	FURCULUM	GLASSFUL	GROGGERY	HARIKIRI
FOOTHOLD	FURFURAL	GLAUCOMA	GROGSHOP	HARMONIA
FOOTNOTE	FURLOUGH	GLEIPNIR	GROMWELL	HARMONIC
FOOTPACE	FURROWED	GLESSITE	GROSBEAK	HARRISON
FOOTPATH	FURTHEST	GLOAMING	GROUNDED	HARTFORD
FOOTSORE	FUSBERTA	GLOBULAR	GUACHARO	HARUSPEX
FORCEFUL	FUTILELY	GLOOSCAP	GUARACHA	HASHMARK
FORCIBLE	FUTILITY	GLORIANA	GUARANTY	HASTINGS
FORECAST	GABORONE	GLORIOUS	GUARDIAN	HATTERAS
FOREHEAD	GADHELIC	GLORYPEA	GUARNERI	HAWAIIAN
FORELOCK	GALACTIC	GLOSSARY	GUERNSEY	HAWKLIKE
FOREMOST	GALLATIN	GLOSSINA	GUINEVER	HAWKSHAW
FORENSIC	GAMBLING	GLUTTONY	GUJARATI	HAWKWEED
FORESTER	GAMBUSIA	GOATFISH	GULFWEED	HAWTHORN
FORESTRY	GAMELION	GODTHAAB	GULISTAN	HAZELNUT
FORETELL	GANGLION	GOETHITE	GULLIBLE	HEADACHE
FORETIME	GANGRENE	GOGETTER	GULLIVER	HEADLAND
FORETOLD	GANGSTER	GOKURAKU	GULLLIKE	HEADLONG
FOREWARN	GANYMEDE	GOLCONDA	GULLTOPP	HEADNOTE
FOREWORD	GARBANZO	GOLDFISH	GUMPTION	HEADSMAN
FORMERLY	GARDENER	GOLGOTHA	GUTTATIM	HEATHROW
FORSAKEN	GARDENIA	GOMBROON	GUTTURAL	HEAVENLY
FORTLAMY	GARGANEY	GOMORRAH	GYMSHOES	HEBDOMAD

HEBETUDE	HOLINESS	IDLENESS	INFERNAL	ISTANBUL
HECATOMB	HOLISTIC	IDOLATOR	INFERRED	ITEMIZED
HEDGEHOG	HOLLANDS	IDOLATRY	INFINITE	ITERANCE
HEDONIST	HOLSTEIN	IGNATIUS	INFLATED	IZVESTIA
HEEDLESS	HOMELAND	IGNOMINY	INFORMAL	JACARACA
HEIGHTEN	HOMELESS	IGNORANT	INFORMED	JACKAROO
HEIMDALL	HOMERULE	ILITHYIA	INFORMER	JACKBOOT
HEIRLOOM	HOMESPUN	ILLATIVE	INFRADIG	JACKPINE
HEIRSHIP	HOMEWORK	ILLFATED	INFRINGE	JACOBITE
HELIACAL	HOMICIDE	ILLIMANI	INIMICAL	JACQUARD
HELLENIC	HOMILIST	ILLINOIS	INIQUITY	JAILBIRD
HELMSMAN	HONDURAS	ILLTIMED	INJECTOR	JALOUSIE
HELPLESS	HONESTLY	ILLUSION	INKERMAN	JAMBOREE
HELPMATE	HONEYDEW	ILLUSIVE	INNATELY	JANEEYRE
HELPMEET	HONGKONG	ILLUSORY	INNOCENT	JANIZARY
HELSINKI	HONOLULU	ILMENITE	INNUENDO	JAPANESE
HELVETIA	HONORARY	IMAGINED	INQUIRER	JAPONICA
HEMATITE	HOODWINK	IMBECILE	INSANITY	JARARACA
HEMATOID	HOODWORM	IMITATED	INSECURE	JAUNDICE
HENCHMAN	HOOLIGAN	IMITATOR	INSERTED	JELERANG
HENEQUEN	HOOPSTER	IMMATURE	INSIDERS	JEOPARDY
HEPATICA	HOOSEGOW	IMMOBILE	INSIGNIA	JEREMIAH
HEPTAGON	HOPALONG	IMMODEST	INSOLENT	JEROBOAM
HERACLES	HOPEDALE	IMMORTAL	INSOMNIA	JIMCRACK
HERCULES	HOPELESS	IMMUNITY	INSPIRIT	JIPIJAPA
HERDSMAN	HORATIAN	IMPAIRED	INSTANCE	JIUJITSU
HEREDITY	HORNBILL	IMPASTED	INSTITUT	JODHPURS
HEREFORD	HORNLESS	IMPERIAL	INSTRUCT	JOHNBULL
HEREUPON	HORNPIPE	IMPETIGO	INSULATE	JOIACHIM
HEREWITH	HOROLOGY	IMPOLITE	INTAGLIO	JONATHAN
HERITAGE	HORRIBLE	IMPOSING	INTARSIA	JOUSTING
HERMETIC	HORSEFLY	IMPOSTER	INTENDED	JOYSTICK
HERMIONE	HORSEMAN	IMPOSTOR	INTEREST	JUBILANT
HERODIAS	HOSPITAL	IMPOTENT	INTERIOR	JUDGMENT
HERRIMAN	HOTHOUSE	IMPROPER	INTERMIT	JUDICIAL
HESITANT	HOTPLATE	IMPUDENT	INTERNAL	JUGURTHA
HESITATE	HOWITZER	IMPURITY	INTERVAL	JUMPROPE
HESPERIA	HROTHGAR	INACTION	INTIMACY	JUNCTION
HERPERIS	HRVATSKA	INACTIVE	INTIMATE	JUNGFRAU
HESPERUS	HUARACHE	INASMUCH	INTREPID	JUNKPILE
HIAWATHA	HUGUENOT	INCENSED	INTRIGUE	JURASSIC
HIBERNIA	HUMANITY	INCENSIA	INTRUDER	JUVENILE
HIBISCUS	HUMBLEST	INCEPTOR	INUNDATE	JUVENTAS
HICCOUGH	HUMIDITY	INCHOATE	INVASION	KAFFIYEH
HICJACET	HUMOROUS	INCIDENT	INVENTED	KAIETEUR
HIDDEKEL	HUNKPAPA	INCISIVE	INVESTIA	KAKARALI
HIERARCH	HUNTSMAN	INCLINED	INVITING	KAKEMONO
HIGHBALL	HWANGHAI	INCREASE	INVOLVED	KALADLIT
HIGHLIFE	HYACINTH	INCUBATE	INWARDLY	KALAHARI
HIGHRISE	HYDROGEN	INDEBTED	IRISHMAN	KALANTAS
HILARITY	HYDROMEL	INDECENT	IRONGATE	KALEVALA
HILLSIDE	HYGIENIC	INDENTED	IRONWOOD	KAMADEVA
HILLWORT	HYPERION	INDIAMAN	IROQUOIS	KAMIKAZE
HINAYANA	HYPNOSIS	INDICATE	IRRIGATE	KANGAROO
HINDMOST	HYSTERIA	INDIGENT	IRRITATE	KANNUSHI
HIRELING	IATRICAL	INDIRECT	ISABELLA	KATAHDIN
HITHERTO	ICEPLANT	INDOLENT	ISCARIOT	KATAKANA
HOBBLING	ICHTHYAL	INDUCING	ISENGRIN	KATMANDU
HOCKSHOP	ICHTHYIC	INDUSTRY	ISHIKARI	KATTEGAT
HOEDRILL	ICTERINE	INEFFABLE	ISOGONAL	KEDGEREE
HOGSHEAD	IDEALIST	INFAMOUS	ISOLATED	KEELBOAT
HOKKAIDO	IDEATION	INFANTRY	ISOPTERA	KEEPSAKE
HOLIDAYS	IDENTITY	INFERIOR	ISSACHAR	KELPFISH

KENTUCKY	LAMENTED	LEWDNESS	LOVELORN	MANDALAY
KEROSENE	LAMINATE	LIASTUNG	LOYALIST	MANDAMUS
KEWEENAW	LANCELOT	LIBATION	LUCIDITY	MANDARIN
KEYBOARD	LANDLORD	LIBELLER	LUCULITE	MANDIBLE
KEYSTONE	LANDSLIP	LIBERATE	LUGGNAGG	MANDOLIN
KHARTOUM	LANDWEHR	LIBRETTO	LUKEWARM	MANDRAKE
KICKBACK	LANGSHAN	LICORICE	LUMINARY	MANDRILL
KICKSHAW	LANGSYNE	LIFEBUOY	LUMINOUS	MANEUVER
KILLDEER	LANGUAGE	LIFELESS	LUNCHEON	MANGABEY
KINABULU	LANGUISH	LIFELINE	LUNGFISH	MANGROVE
KINDLING	LANNERET	LIGATURE	LUPICIDE	MANIACAL
KINDNESS	LANOLINE	LIGULATE	LUSCIOUS	MANIFEST
KINETICS	LAOMEDON	LIKENESS	LUSTRATE	MANIFOLD
KINGCRAB	LAPIDARY	LIKEWISE	LUSTROUS	MANNERLY
KINGFISH	LAPIDATE	LILLIPUT	LUTEOLIN	MANOFWAR
KINGSTON	LARBOARD	LILYTREE	LYCURGUS	MANTEVIL
KINGWANA	LARGESSE	LIMABEAN	LYNCHING	MANTILLA
KINKAJOU	LARRIGAN	LIMACINE	LYREBIRD	MANUCODE
KINSFOLK	LARRIKIN	LIMASSOL	LYRICIST	MAPMAKER
KINSHASA	LASPRING	LIMERICK	LYSANDER	MARABOUT
KISHINEV	LASTGASP	LIMITING	MACANESE	MARASMUS
KISKADEE	LASVEGAS	LIMONITE	MACARONI	MARATHON
KISTVAEN	LATERITE	LINGERIE	MACERATE	MARAUDER
KIYOODLE	LATINIST	LINGUIST	MACHEATH	MARGARET
KLAIPEDA	LATTERLY	LINIMENT	MACHETTE	MARGRAVE
KLIETSCH	LAUDABLE	LINOLEUM	MACHINES	MARIANAS
KLONDIKE	LAUGHTER	LINOTYPE	MACKEREL	MARIANNE
KNACKERY	LAVATORY	LIONFISH	MACKINAW	MARIGOLD
KNAPSACK	LAVENDER	LIONSKIN	MADELINE	MARINADE
KNEEBONE	LAWGIVER	LIPIZZAN	MADHOUSE	MARINARA
KNITTING	LAWLANTS	LIPSTICK	MAECENAS	MARINATE
KNOCKNEE	LAWMAKER	LISTENED	MAGAZINE	MARITIME
KNOCKOUT	LAXATIVE	LISTENER	MAGELLAN	MARIVAUX
KNORHAAN	LAZINESS	LISTLESS	MAGGIORE	MARJORAM
KNOTTING	LAZULITE	LITERATE	MAGICIAN	MARKSMAN
KNOTWEED	LEACHING	LITERATI	MAGNOLIA	MARMOSET
KOHINOOR	LEAFLESS	LITHARGE	MAGWITCH	MARONITE
KOHLRABI	LEAPFROG	LITIGATE	MAHADEVA	MARQUESS
KRAKATAU	LEARNING	LITTERED	MAHARANI	MARRIAGE
KRAKATOA	LECTURER	LITTORAL	MAHJONGG	MARSHALL
KRASICKI	LECYTHUS	LOBLOLLY	MAHOGANY	MARTELLO
KREPLACH	LEFTHAND	LOBSTICK	MAINLAND	MARTINET
KREUTZER	LEGALIST	LOCALITY	MAINLINE	MARYJANE
KUKULCAN	LEGATION	LOCALIZE	MAINSTAY	MARYTODD
KUNAPIPI	LEGGINGS	LOCATION	MAJESTIC	MARZIPAN
KYPHOSIS	LEINSTER	LOCATIVE	MAJOLICA	MASONITE
LABORDAY	LEMONADE	LODESTAR	MAJORITY	MASSACRE
LABRADOR	LENGTHEN	LODGINGS	MAKASSAR	MASSENET
LACERATE	LENITIVE	LOGICIAN	MALACOID	MASSETER
LACEWORK	LENTANDO	LOGOTYPE	MALAPERT	MASTODON
LACHESIS	LENTICEL	LOITERER	MALDEMER	MASTWOOD
LACHRYMA	LEONARDO	LOLLOPER	MALEMUIT	MATABELE
LACROSSE	LEONIDAS	LONESOME	MALEMUTE	MATAMATA
LADYBIRD	LEOPARDI	LONESTAR	MALINGER	MATERIAL
LADYFISH	LEPORINE	LONGHORN	MALLARME	MATERNAL
LAGERLOF	LEPROTIC	LOOPHOLE	MALLORCA	MATHURIN
LAGUAIRA	LETHARGY	LOOTSMAN	MALTREAT	MATTHIAS
LALLEGRO	LETTERED	LOPSIDED	MALVASIA	MATTRESS
LAMASERY	LEVANTER	LORDOSIS	MAMPALON	MATURITY
LAMBASTE	LEVERAGE	LORIKEET	MANABUSH	MAUNALOA
LAMBKILL	LEVIGATE	LOTHARIO	MANACLES	MAUSOLUS
LAMBSKIN	LEVITATE	LOUISDOR	MANANNAN	MAVERICK
LAMENESS	LEVULOSE	LOVELACE	MANASSES	MAYAPPLE

MCINTOSH	MILKYWAY	MORDECAI	NARRATED	NOSINESS
MCKINLEY	MILLINER	MOREOVER	NASALITY	NOSTRILS
MCLENNAN	MINATORY	MOREPORK	NASICORN	NOUMENAL
MEANTIME	MINDANAO	MORESQUE	NATALITY	NOUMENON
MEATBALL	MINIMIZE	MORGAUSE	NATATION	NOVELIST
MEATIEST	MINISTER	MORGAWSE	NATATORY	NOWADAYS
MECHANIC	MINORITE	MOROCCAN	NATIVITY	NUGACITY
MEDDLING	MINORITY	MORPHEUS	NAUPLIUS	NUGATORY
MEDELLIN	MINOTAUR	MORPHINE	NAUSEATE	NUISANCE
MEDIATOR	MINSTREL	MORRIGAN	NAUSEOUS	NUKUHIVA
MEDICINE	MINUTELY	MORTGAGE	NAUSICAA	NUMEROUS
MEDIEVAL	MINUTIAE	MOSQUITO	NAUTICAL	NUMSKULL
MEDITATE	MIRMILLO	MOSSBACK	NAUTILUS	NUPTIALS
MEDJERDA	MIRTHFUL	MOTHERLY	NAZARETH	NUTATION
MEEKNESS	MISANDRY	MOTORMAN	NEARNESS	OAKAPPLE
MEGALITH	MISCARRY	MOTORIST	NECKLACE	OBDURATE
MEGAPODE	MISCHIEF	MOULMEIN	NECROSIS	OBEAHMAN
MELANION	MISERERE	MOUNTAIN	NEEDLESS	OBEDIENT
MELANITE	MISJUDGE	MOURNFUL	NEFERTEM	OBITUARY
MELCHIOR	MISNOMER	MOURNING	NEFERTUM	OBJECTOR
MELEAGER	MISOGYNE	MOUSSEUX	NEGATION	OBLATION
MELINITE	MISPLACE	MOVABLES	NEGATIVE	OBLIVION
MELODEON	MISPRINT	MOVEMENT	NEGLIGEE	OBSESSED
MELVILLE	MISPRIZE	MUCILAGE	NEMALINE	OBSIDIAN
MEMBRANE	MISQUOTE	MUHAMMAD	NEMATODE	OBSOLETE
MEMORIAL	MISSOURI	MUHARRAM	NEOPHYTE	OBSTACLE
MEMORIZE	MISTAKEN	MUIRFOWL	NEOPLASM	OBSTRUCT
MENACING	MISTAKES	MULCIBER	NEOTERIC	OBTUNDED
MENELAUS	MISTREAT	MULETEER	NEPHRITE	OCCASION
MENHADEN	MISTRESS	MULLIGAN	NEPHTHYS	OCCIDENT
MENILITE	MISTRIAL	MULLOWAY	NEPOTISM	OCCUPANT
MENISCUS	MISTRUST	MULTIPLY	NERITOID	OCOTILLO
MENTALLY	MITIGATE	MULVANEY	NESCIENT	ODOMETER
MEPHISTO	MNEMONIC	MUNIMENT	NESTLING	ODYSSEUS
MERCATOR	MOBYDICK	MURDERER	NEURITIS	OENOLOGY
MERCHANT	MOCCASIN	MUSCATEL	NEUSTRIA	OFFENDED
MERCIFUL	MODERATE	MUSCULAR	NEWCOMER	OFFENDER
MEREDITH	MOGOLLON	MUSHROOM	NEWDELHI	OFFERING
MERIDIAN	MOHAMMED	MUSICALE	NEWLYWED	OFFICIAL
MERMAIDS	MOHNSEED	MUSICIAN	NEWPENNY	OIKOLOGY
MEROSOME	MOISTURE	MUSKOGEE	NEWYEARS	OILSKINS
MESOZOIC	MOLASSES	MUSTACHE	NICHROME	OINTMENT
MESQUITE	MOLECULE	MUSTELID	NICKLAUS	OKLAHOMA
MESSIDOR	MOLESKIN	MUTATION	NICKNAME	OLDFIELD
METALLIC	MOLINARY	MUTINEER	NICOTINE	OLDGLORY
METAMERE	MOLINIST	MYCOLOGY	NICTEROI	OLDNORTH
METAPHOR	MOLUCCAS	MYRIAPOD	NIDULATE	OLDSQUAW
METHANOL	MOMENTUM	MYTHICAL	NIGHTJAR	OLDTIMER
MEXICALI	MONALISA	MYTILENE	NINEPINS	OLEANDER
MEZEREON	MONARCHY	NACREOUS	NITROGEN	OLEASTER
MICHIGAN	MONASTIC	NAINSOOK	NOBILITY	OLIBANUM
MIDDLING	MONETARY	NAISMITH	NOBLEMAN	OLYMPIAS
MIDLANDS	MONGOOSE	NAMELESS	NOBODIES	OLYMPICS
MIDNIGHT	MONOLITH	NAMESAKE	NOCHARGE	OMISSION
MIJNHEER	MONORAIL	NANCHANG	NOCTURNE	OMPHALOS
MILANION	MONOTONE	NANKIPOO	NODICORN	ONCEOVER
MILDEWED	MONOTONY	NAPHTALI	NODICORN	ONESIDED
MILDNESS	MONROVIA	NAPOLEON	NOMINATE	ONONDAGA
MILESIAN	MONSIEUR	NARCOSIS	NONACUTE	ONTOLOGY
MILIARIA	MONTREAL	NARCOTIC	NONESUCH	OOLOGIST
MILITANT	MOQUETTE	NARGHILE	NONFATAL	OPENEYED
MILITARY	MORALITY	NARGILEH	NONSENSE	OPENNESS
MILKWEED	MORATORY	NARIFORM	NORTHERN	OPERATED

OPERATIC	OVERSEER	PARTISAN	PERSONAL	PLANETAE
OPERATOR	OVERSHOE	PARZIVAL	PERSPIRE	PLANKTAR
OPERETTA	OVERSTAY	PASADENA	PERSUADE	PLANKTON
OPPONENT	OVERSTEP	PASIPHAE	PERTNESS	PLANTAIN
OPPOSING	OVERTAKE	PASSBOOK	PERUVIAN	PLASTRON
OPPOSITE	OVERTIME	PASSERES	PERVERSE	PLATBAND
OPPOSSUM	OVERTURE	PASSHICO	PESHITTA	PLATEASM
OPTIMIST	OVERTURN	PASSPORT	PETAGIUM	PLATELET
OPTIONAL	OVERWORN	PASSROPE	PETECHIA	PLATFORM
OPULENCE	OVISPOLI	PASSWORD	PETERPAN	PLATONIC
ORACULAR	PACIFIER	PASTILLE	PETITION	PLATYPUS
ORATORIO	PADDLING	PASTORAL	PETRARCH	PLEASANT
ORDAINED	PADMELON	PASTRAMI	PETULANT	PLEASING
ORDINARY	PAGOPAGO	PATERNAL	PETUNTSE	PLEASURE
ORDINATE	PAHOEHOE	PATHETIC	PEZIZOID	PLEBEIAN
ORGANISM	PAINLESS	PATHLESS	PHAEDRUS	PLECTRUM
ORGANIST	PAINTERS	PATIENCE	PHALANGE	PLEDGING
ORGANIZE	PAINTING	PAULDRON	PHANTASM	PLEIADES
ORIENTAL	PALATINE	PAVEMENT	PHARISEE	PLEONASM
ORIGANUM	PALEFACE	PAVILION	PHEASANT	PLETHORA
ORIGINAL	PALGRAVE	PAVONINE	PHILEMON	PLIOCENE
ORNAMENT	PALINODE	PEACEFUL	PHILIBEG	PLOWSOLE
OROMETER	PALISADE	PECORINO	PHILOMEL	PLUCKILY
OROVILLE	PALLIATE	PECTORAL	PHONETIC	PLUGUGLY
ORPIMENT	PALLMALL	PECULATE	PHRYGIAN	PLUMBAGO
ORTHERIS	PALMETTO	PECULIAR	PHTHISIS	PLUMBISM
ORTHICON	PALMLEAF	PEDAGOGY	PHYSETER	PLUTARCH
ORTHODOX	PALOMINO	PEDANTIC	PHYSICAL	PLUTONIC
OSCITANT	PALPABLY	PEDESTAL	PIACULUM	PLUVIOSE
OSCULATE	PALUDINE	PEDIGREE	PICKINGS	PNOMPENH
OTAHEITE	PALUDISM	PEDIMENT	PICKLOCK	POITIERS
OUACHITA	PAMPHLET	PEDIPALP	PICKMEUP	POKEWEED
OUTBURST	PANATELA	PEDUNCLE	PIEPLANT	POLESTAR
OUTDATED	PANCREAS	PEEPHOLE	PIERCING	POLISHER
OUTGOING	PANDANUS	PEEPSHOW	PIERIDES	POLITICS
OUTHOUSE	PANDAVAS	PEERLESS	PILASTER	POLLIWOG
OUTLINER	PANDECTS	PEIGNOIR	PILEATED	POLOCHIC
OUTMODED	PANDEMIC	PEKINESE	PILFERED	POLOCYTE
OUTSIDER	PANGAEUS	PELLAGRA	PILFERER	POLONIUS
OUTSTRIP	PANGOLIN	PELLICLE	PILLIGAN	POLTROON
OUTWEIGH	PANNIKIN	PELLMELL	PIMIENTO	POLYGLOT
OVENBIRD	PANORAMA	PELLUCID	PINAFORE	POLYMATH
OVERALLS	PANTHEON	PEMBROKE	PINDARIC	POLYMNIA
OVERCAME	PANTHERA	PEMMICAN	PINETREE	POLYPNEA
OVERCAST	PAQUEBOT	PENDULUM	PINKROOT	POLYPODY
OVERCOAT	PARABOLA	PENELOPE	PINKSLIP	POMOLOGY
OVERCOME	PARADIGM	PENITENT	PINNACLE	PONTIFEX
OVERDONE	PARADISE	PENOLOGY	PINOCHLE	POOHBEAR
OVERDOSE	PARAGOGE	PENSTOCK	PIPEFISH	POOLROOM
OVERFLOW	PARAGUAY	PENTAGON	PIPETUNE	POPULACE
OVERHANG	PARAKEET	PENUMBRA	PIPEVINE	POPULATE
OVERHAUL	PARALLEL	PERANNUM	PIQUANCY	POQUELIN
OVERHEAR	PARAMOUR	PERCEIVE	PIRARUCU	PORKFISH
OVERLAID	PARASANG	PERENTIE	PIRRAURA	PORPOISE
OVERLOOK	PARASITE	PERFORCE	PISANDER	PORRIDGE
OVERLORD	PARAVANE	PERIANTH	PISCATOR	PORTABLE
OVERNICE	PARIETAL	PERICARP	PITCAIRN	PORTIERE
OVERPASS	PARJANYA	PERICLES	PITCHMAN	PORTOLAN
OVERPLUS	PARMESAN	PERIODIC	PITILESS	PORTRAIT
OVERRATE	PAROXYSM	PERIPLUS	PLAGIARY	PORTUGAL
OVERRIPE	PARSIFAL	PERMEATE	PLAITING	POSEIDON
OVERRULE	PARTICLE	PERRAULT	PLANARIA	POSITION
OVERSEAS	PARTIMEN	PERSHING	PLANCHET	POSITIVE

POSSIBLE	PRONUBIS	QUOTIENT	REEDMACE	RESOLUTE
POSSIBLY	PROPERLY	RABELAIS	REELFOOT	RESONANT
POSTPONE	PROPERTY	RADIANCE	REENLIST	RESOURCE
POTATION	PROPHECY	RADIATOR	REFINERY	RESPECTS
POTERIUM	PROPHETS	RADISSON	REFINISH	RESPIRED
POTIPHAR	PROPOUND	RAFFAELE	REGARDED	RESPONSE
POTLATCH	PROSPECT	RAGNAROK	REGICIDE	RESTITCH
POTSHERD	PROSPERO	RAILROAD	REGIMENT	RESTLESS
POULTICE	PROTOCOL	RAINCOAT	REGIONAL	RESTORED
POWERFUL	PROTOZOA	RAINTREE	REGISTER	RESTRAIN
POWERSAW	PROTRACT	RAMAYANA	REGISTRY	RESTRICT
POWHATAN	PROTRUDE	RAMBLING	REGULARS	RESTROOM
PRACTICE	PROVERBS	RAMENTUM	REGULATE	RESUPPLY
PRANDIUM	PROVIDER	RAMICORN	REHEARSE	RETAILER
PREACHER	PROVINCE	RAMIFIED	REHOBOAM	RETAINER
PREAMBLE	PROVISOS	RAMULOSE	REIGNING	RETAKING
PRECEDED	PROVOKED	RANGELAW	REINDEER	RETARDED
PRECINCT	PROXIMAL	RANGIFER	REINFUSE	RETICENT
PRECIOUS	PRUDENCE	RANSTEAD	REKINDLE	RETICULE
PRECLUDE	PRUNELLA	RAPACITY	RELATION	RETIRING
PREDELLA	PRURIENT	RAPIDITY	RELATIVE	RETRENCH
PREMIERE	PRURITUS	RASCALLY	RELAXING	RETURNED
PRENATAL	PRUSSIAN	RASHNESS	RELENTED	REUNITED
PREPARED	PTARMICA	RASORIAL	RELIABLE	REVEILLE
PREPENSE	PTOMAINE	RASPUTIN	RELIANCE	REVENANT
PRESENCE	PUCKERED	RATAPLAN	RELIEVED	REVEREND
PRESERVE	PUFFBALL	RATIONAL	RELIGION	REVERENT
PRESSING	PUGILIST	RATTLING	RELOCATE	REVERSAL
PRESSMAN	PUISSANT	RAVENOUS	REMANENT	REVISION
PRESSURE	PULITZER	RAWBONED	REMARKED	REVOLVER
PRESTIGE	PULMONIC	REABSORB	REMEDIAL	RHAPSODY
PRETENSE	PULMOTOR	REACTION	REMEMBER	RHEOSTAT
PRETERIT	PULSIFIC	READABLE	REMOLADE	RHETORIC
PRETORIA	PUNCTURE	REAPHOOK	RENDERED	RHIANNON
PREVIOUS	PUNITIVE	REAPPEAR	RENEGADE	RHINITIS
PRIBILOF	PURBLIND	REARMOST	RENIFORM	RHONCHUS
PRIEDIEU	PURCHASE	REASSERT	RENITENT	RICEBIRD
PRIESTLY	PURSLANE	REASSURE	RENOUNCE	RICHMOND
PRIMATES	PURULENT	REBUTTAL	RENOVATE	RICHNESS
PRIMEVAL	PURVEYOR	RECAMIER	RENOWNED	RICKSHAW
PRIMROSE	PUTATIVE	RECEDING	RENTABLE	RICOCHET
PRINCELY	PUZZLING	RECEIVED	REPARTEE	RIDICULE
PRINCESS	PYRENEES	RECEIVER	REPEATED	RIESLING
PRINTING	PYRIFORM	RECENTLY	REPEATER	RIFFRAFF
PRIORESS	PYTHONIC	RECEPTOR	REPELLED	RIFLEMAN
PRIORITY	QUADRANS	RECKLESS	REPENTED	RIGHTFUL
PRISONER	QUADRANT	RECLINER	REPETEND	RIGHTIST
PRISTINE	QUADRIGA	RECOMMIT	REPHRASE	RIGIDITY
PRITHIVI	QUAGMIRE	RECORDED	REPLEVIN	RIGOROUS
PROBABLE	QUANDARY	RECOVERY	REPORTED	RIMESTER
PROBABLY	QUANTITY	RECREANT	REPORTER	RINGDOVE
PROCLAIM	QUARRIAN	REDACTOR	REPRIEVE	RINGHALS
PRODIGAL	QUARRIER	REDEEMED	REPRISAL	RINGLIKE
PRODUCED	QUARTERS	REDEEMER	REQUITAL	RINGWORM
PROFITED	QUECHUAN	REDENIAL	RESEALED	RIPARIAN
PROFOUND	QUEEQUEG	REDOCHER	RESEARCH	RISKIEST
PROGRESS	QUESTION	REDOLENT	RESEMBLE	RIVERAIN
PROHIBIT	QUICKSET	REDOUBLE	RESENTED	RIVERINE
PROLAPSE	QUIDNUNC	REDSHIRT	RESERVED	ROADSIDE
PROLIFIC	QUIRINAL	REDSKINS	RESIDENT	ROBORANT
PROLOGUE	QUIRINUS	REDSTART	RESIDUAL	ROCKFISH
PROMISED	QUIRITES	REDSTONE	RESIGNED	ROCKWOOL
PROMOTED	QUISLING	REDUCTIO	RESISTOR	RODERICK

ROEBLING	SANDBURG	SEASHORE	SHASHLIK	SLEIPNIR
ROENTGEN	SANDWORM	SEASONED	SHELVING	SLEUTHED
ROMANOVS	SANGAREE	SECLUDED	SHEPHERD	SLIMIEST
ROMANSCH	SANGRAAL	SECRETLY	SHEPHERT	SLIMNESS
ROMANTIC	SANGUINE	SECURELY	SHERLOCK	SLIPKNOT
ROOFLIKE	SANITARY	SECURITY	SHERWOOD	SLIPPERS
ROOMETTE	SANSERIF	SEDATIVE	SHIELDED	SLIPPERY
ROOMMATE	SANSKRIT	SEDIMENT	SHIFTING	SLOVAKIA
ROORBACK	SANTAREM	SEDITION	SHIGATSE	SLOVENLY
ROOTBEER	SANTIAGO	SEDULOUS	SHILLALA	SLOWDOWN
ROOTHAIR	SAPOROUS	SEEDLING	SHILLING	SLUGGARD
ROSALIND	SAPPHIRE	SEERBAND	SHINGLES	SLUGGISH
ROSEBOWL	SARDINIA	SELADANG	SHIPMATE	SLUGLIKE
ROSEFISH	SARDONIC	SELECTED	SHIPWORM	SLUMLORD
ROSEMARY	SARDONYX	SELENITE	SHIVAREE	SLUMPING
ROSEROOT	SARGASSO	SELFHEAL	SHOENAIL	SMALLAGE
ROSEWOOD	SASSANID	SELFSAME	SHOETREE	SMALLEST
ROSTRATE	SATANISM	SEMANTIC	SHOULDER	SMALLPOX
ROTATION	SATIRIZE	SEMESTER	SHOWBOAT	SMELTING
ROTIFORM	SATURATE	SEMINARY	SHOWCASE	SMILODON
ROULETTE	SAUCIEST	SEMINOLE	SHRAPNEL	SMOOTHER
ROUSSEAU	SAUROPOD	SEMIOTIC	SHRIMATI	SMOOTHLY
RUCKSACK	SAVAGELY	SEMOLINA	SHRIVING	SNAPBEAN
RUDENESS	SAVAGERY	SENATORS	SHRUNKEN	SNAPPERS
RUDIMENT	SAWBONES	SENILITY	SHUTTING	SNAPPILY
RUMANIAN	SCABBARD	SENNIGHT	SIBELIUS	SNAPPISH
RUMINANT	SCAFFOLD	SENORITA	SIBILANT	SNAPSHOT
RUMINATE	SCALAWAG	SENSIBLE	SICILIAN	SNEAKERS
RUSHMORE	SCALPHOID	SENSUOUS	SICKNESS	SNEAKING
RUSTLING	SCAPULAR	SENTENCE	SIDEDRUM	SNEEZING
RUTABAGA	SCARCITY	SENTIENT	SIDEREAL	SNOBBISH
RUTHLESS	SCARLETT	SENTINEL	SIDERITE	SNOWBIRD
RUYLOPEZ	SCATHING	SEPARATE	SIDESHOW	SOAPBARK
SAAREMAA	SCENARIO	SEQUENCE	SIDEWAYS	SOBRIETY
SABOTAGE	SCHEDULE	SERAGLIO	SIDEWISE	SOCALLED
SABULINE	SCHOLION	SERAPHIC	SIGNALED	SOCIABLE
SACRISTY	SCHOOLED	SERENADE	SILKWORM	SOCRATES
SADDENED	SCHOONER	SERENATA	SILLABUB	SODALITY
SAGACITY	SCHUBERT	SERENDIB	SILVANUS	SOFTENED
SAGAMORE	SCILICET	SERENITY	SIMULATE	SOLARIUM
SAGEROSE	SCIMITAR	SERGEANT	SINAPINE	SOLDIERS
SAILBOAT	SCIOLIST	SERIATIM	SINCIPUT	SOLDIERY
SAINFOIN	SCISSORS	SERIFORM	SINECURE	SOLECISM
SALADANG	SCIURINE	SEROTINE	SINGLETS	SOLENOID
SALESMAN	SCOLDING	SERPENTS	SINGSING	SOLIDAGO
SALESMEN	SCORCHED	SERRANID	SINGULAR	SOLITARY
SALONIKA	SCORNFUL	SERVANTS	SINISTER	SOLITUDE
SALTFISH	SCORPION	SERVITES	SITOLOGY	SOLLERET
SALTLAKE	SCOTLAND	SESTERCE	SIXPENCE	SOLOMONS
SALTNESS	SCOTSMAN	SEVERITY	SIZZLING	SOLPUGID
SALTPOND	SCRAMBLE	SEXTETTE	SKELETON	SOLSTICE
SALTWORT	SCRAPPLE	SFORZATO	SKILLFUL	SOLUTION
SALUTARY	SCRIBBLE	SHACKLES	SKILODGE	SOLUTORY
SALVADOR	SCROFULA	SHADDOCK	SKINBOAT	SOLVABLE
SALZBURG	SCRUPLES	SHADOWED	SKIPJACK	SOMBRERO
SAMENESS	SCRUTINY	SHADRACH	SKIRMISH	SOMEBODY
SAMPHIRE	SCULLERY	SHAGBARK	SKITTLES	SOMERSET
SANATORY	SCULPTOR	SHALEOIL	SKIVVIES	SOMETIME
SANCARLO	SCURVIED	SHALIMAR	SKULLCAP	SOMEWHAT
SANCTIFY	SEAPLANE	SHAMEFUL	SKYLIGHT	SONATINA
SANCTION	SEAPOWER	SHAMROCK	SLANTING	SONGBIRD
SANCTITY	SEARCHER	SHANGHAI	SLATTERN	SONGSTER
SANDARAC	SEASCAPE	SHANTUNG	SLAVONIC	SONOROUS

SOOTHING	SQUATTER	STRICKEN	SWELLING	TEENAGER
SORBONNE	SQUELCHY	STRIDENT	SWIMMING	TELARIAN
SORCERER	SQUIRREL	STRIGINE	SWINDLED	TELECAST
SOREHEAD	SRILANKA	STRIKING	SWINDLER	TELEGRAM
SORICINE	SRINAGAR	STRINGUP	SYBARITE	TELEVISE
SORORITY	STAGGERS	STRIPPER	SYCAMORE	TELIPINU
SOULLESS	STAGHEAP	STROBILE	SYMMETRY	TELLTALE
SOUNDBOX	STAGLINE	STROLLER	SYMPATHY	TEMERITY
SOUNDEST	STAGNATE	STRUGGLE	SYMPHONY	TEMPERED
SOUNDING	STAIRWAY	STRUMMER	SYNCLINE	TEMPLATE
SOURNESS	STALLION	STRUMPET	SYNDROME	TEMPORAL
SOURPUSS	STALWART	STUBBORN	SYNOPSIS	TEMPTING
SOUTHERN	STAMBOUL	STUFFING	SYPHILIS	TENACITY
SOUTHPAW	STAMPEDE	STURGEON	SYRACUSE	TENDENCY
SOUVENIR	STANDARD	SUBINDEX	SYSTEMIC	TENEBRAE
SPACIOUS	STANDING	SUBLEASE	SYSTOLIC	TENEMENT
SPADILLA	STANDISH	SUBMERGE	SZOPELKA	TENNYSON
SPALDEEN	STANDOFF	SUBPOENA	TABULATE	TENPENNY
SPANIARD	STANFORD	SUBSERVE	TACAUTAC	TENRIKYO
SPARKING	STANOVOI	SUBTLETY	TACITURN	TENTACLE
SPRALING	STARFISH	SUBTRACT	TACLOBAN	TEOCALLI
SPEAKING	STARLING	SUCCINCT	TAHITIAN	TEOSINTE
SPECIFIC	STARTING	SUCCUBUS	TAILLAGE	TEPHRITE
SPECIMEN	STAYLACE	SUCKFISH	TAILLESS	TERAGLIN
SPECIOUS	STEALING	SUDDENLY	TAJMAHAL	TERATISM
SPECTRAL	STEALTHY	SUFFERER	TALAPOIN	TERCELET
SPECULUM	STEAMIER	SUITABLE	TALESMAN	TERMINAL
SPEEDIER	STEATITE	SUITABLY	TALIESIN	TERMINUS
SPELAEAN	STEELERS	SUITCASE	TALISMAN	TERRAPIN
SPELLING	STEENBOK	SULLIVAN	TALLTALE	TERRELLA
SPERMOIL	STEEPEST	SUMERIAN	TALLYMAN	TERRIBLE
SPILLWAY	STEEPLED	SUNLIGHT	TAMANDUA	TERRIFIC
SPINNERY	STEERAGE	SUNSHADE	TAMARACK	TERTIARY
SPINNING	STEGODON	SUNSHINE	TAMATAVE	TERUTERO
SPINSTER	STELLATE	SUPERADD	TAMNORTH	TESTAMUR
SPIRACLE	STENDHAL	SUPERIOR	TAMWORTH	TESTATOR
SPIRITED	STGEORGE	SUPERNAL	TANGENCY	TESTIEST
SPITEFUL	STHELIER	SUPINATE	TANGIBLE	TESTTUBE
SPLENDID	STICKLER	SUPINELY	TANKTOWN	TETRAGON
SPLENDOR	STIFLING	SUPPLANT	TANTALUS	TETRAPOD
SPLINTER	STILETTO	SUPPOSED	TAPDANCE	TETRARCH
SPLUTTER	STINGING	SUPPRESS	TAPELINE	TEXTILES
SPOONING	STINGRAY	SURABAYA	TAPERING	THADDEUS
SPORADES	STINKING	SUREFIRE	TAPESTRY	THAILAND
SPORADIC	STIRRING	SURICATE	TAPEWORM	THALAMUS
SPORTIVE	STOCKADE	SURPLICE	TARASSIS	THALASSO
SPOTBALL	STOCKING	SURPRISE	TARBOOCH	THALLOID
SPOTLESS	STOTINKA	SURROUND	TARBOOSH	THANKFUL
SPRAWLED	STRADDLE	SURVEYOR	TARLATAN	THEMATIC
SPREADER	STRAIGHT	SURVIVED	TARPAPER	THEOLOGY
SPRINGER	STRAINED	SURVIVOR	TARRAGON	THERBLIG
SPRINKLE	STRAINER	SUSPENSE	TARTARUS	THEREFOR
SPRINTER	STRANDED	SUSURRUS	TARTUFFE	THERMITE
SPROCKET	STRANGER	SUVLABAY	TASMANIA	THEROPOD
SPUMANTE	STRANGLE	SVALBARD	TATTERED	THESPIAN
SPURIOUS	STRATEGY	SVENGALI	TAXONOMY	THIAMINE
SPURRIER	STRATIFY	SVIZZERA	TAYGETUS	THICKSET
SPYGLASS	STRAYING	SWARMING	TEACHING	THINNESS
SQUADRON	STREAKED	SWASTIKA	TEADANCE	THIRTEEN
SQUAMOUS	STREAMER	SWEATING	TEAMSTER	THOROUGH
SQUANDER	STRENGTH	SWEETBAY	TEATABLE	THRALDOM
SQUANTUM	STREYMOY	SWEETGUM	TECUMSEH	THREATEN
SQUARELY	STRIATED	SWEETSOP	TELARIAN	THRENODY

THRESHER	TRAGOPAN	TURNOVER	UTURUNCU	VITIATED
THRIVING	TRAINING	TURNPIKE	UXORIOUS	VITIATOR
THROMBUS	TRAMINER	TUTELARY	VACATION	VITILEVU
THROSTLE	TRANQUIL	TVASHTRI	VAGABOND	VITREOUS
THROTTLE	TRANSFER	TWILIGHT	VALENCIA	VIVACITY
THUMBNUT	TRANSMIT	TWINKLED	VALERIAN	VIVAVOCE
THURIBLE	TRANSUDE	TWISTING	VALHALLA	VOCALIST
THYESTES	TRAPROCK	UDOMETER	VALIDITY	VOCATION
TIBERIAS	TRASHCAN	UGLINESS	VALLETTA	VOLATILE
TIDELAND	TRASHING	ULCEROUS	VALOROUS	VOLCANIC
TIDEMARK	TRAVELER	ULLAGONE	VALUABLE	VOLCANUS
TIDEOVER	TRAVERSE	ULTERIOR	VAMBRACE	VOLITANT
TIENTSIN	TRAVESTY	ULTIMATE	VANGUARD	VOLPLANE
TIGHTWAD	TRAVOISE	UMBRELLA	VANQUISH	VOLTAIRE
TILELIKE	TREASURE	UNABATED	VAPOROUS	VOLUTION
TILLICUM	TREASURY	UNAWARES	VARIABLE	VORACITY
TILTYARD	TREATISE	UNBELIEF	VARIANCE	VOTESFOR
TIMBERED	TREENAIL	UNBELTED	VAUNTING	VRYKOLAK
TIMBUKTU	TREKKING	UNBIASED	VEGETATE	WAGONLIT
TIMELESS	TREPHINE	UNBIDDEN	VEHEMENT	WAINSCOT
TIMIDITY	TRESPASS	UNBROKEN	VELATION	WAITRESS
TIMOROUS	TREUTARO	UNCHASTE	VELOCITY	WALLAROO
TINCTURE	TRIANGLE	UNCHOSEN	VENDETTA	WANDERER
TINPLATE	TRIASSIC	UNCLESAM	VENDIBLE	WANDEROO
TINSMITH	TRICHINA	UNCOMBED	VENDIDAD	WANKAPIN
TIPSHEET	TRICKERY	UNCOMELY	VENERATE	WARDANCE
TIRELESS	TRIDACNA	UNCOMMON	VENOMOUS	WARDROBE
TIRESIAS	TRIFLING	UNCTUOUS	VERACITY	WARMROOM
TIRESOME	TRIGLYPH	UNCURBED	VERACRUZ	WARRANTY
TITHONUS	TRIMETER	UNDEVOUT	VERBATIM	WARSZAWA
TITICACA	TRIMMING	UNDULATE	VERBIAGE	WARTWEED
TITIVATE	TRIMURTI	UNENDING	VERBOTEN	WASHROOM
TITMOUSE	TRIPLANE	UNERRING	VERLAINE	WASTEFUL
TITOGRAD	TRISTRAM	UNFADING	VERONICA	WATCHDOG
TOADFISH	TROMBONE	UNFASTEN	VERTEBRA	WATCHFUL
TOADFLAX	TROPICAL	UNFILLED	VERTICAL	WATCHING
TOBOGGAN	TROTLINE	UNGAINLY	VERTICIL	WATCHMAN
TOILSOME	TROTTERS	UNGENIAL	VESPIARY	WATERLOO
TOKUGAWA	TROUBLED	UNGUIDED	VESTMENT	WATLINGS
TOLERANT	TROUNCED	UNGULATE	VESUVIUS	WAVERING
TOLERATE	TROUSERS	UNHARMED	VEXATION	WAVERLEY
TOLLGATE	TROUVERE	UNIVERSE	VIATICUM	WAXWORKS
TOMAHAWK	TRUCHMAN	UNKEELED	VIBURNUM	WAYFARER
TOMMYGUN	TRUCKMAN	UNLAWFUL	VICERINE	WEAKFISH
TOMMYROT	TRUMBASH	UNLIKELY	VICINITY	WEAKLING
TOMORROW	TRUMPERY	UNMARKED	VICTORIA	WEAKNESS
TONELESS	TRUMPETS	UNSHAVED	VICTUALS	WEHRWOLF
TONEPOEM	TRUNCATE	UNSOUGHT	VIGILANT	WELLMADE
TONLESAP	TRUTHFUL	UNSPOKEN	VIGOROUS	WELLTODO
TOPONYMY	TSAREVNA	UNSTABLE	VIOLENCE	WELSHGELD
TOREADOR	TSARITZA	UNSTEADY	VIOLETTA	WEREGILD
TORNILLO	TSUSHIMA	UNTENDED	VIPERINE	WEREGILD
TORSHAVN	TUAMOTUS	UNTETHER	VIPSANIA	WEREWOLF
TORTILLA	TUBERCLE	UNTILLED	VIRGINAL	WESTPORT
TORTOISE	TUBEWORM	UNTIMELY	VIRGINIA	WESTWARD
TOUCHING	TUCOTUCO	UNTITLED	VIRTUOUS	WHALEFIN
TOURNEUR	TUCOTUDO	UNTOWARD	VIRULENT	WHATEVER
TOWELING	TUMPLINE	UNVARIED	VISCACHA	WHEATEAR
TOWNSMAN	TUNGSTEN	UNWIELDY	VISCERAL	WHEELING
TOWTRUCK	TUNICATE	UPHARSIN	VISCONTI	WHENEVER
TOXICITY	TURMERIC	URBANITE	VISCOUNT	WHIMBREL
TRACHOMA	TURNAWAY	URBANITY	VITALITY	WHIPLASH
TRACKING	TURNCOAT		VITELLUS	WHIPPING

WHIRLING	WINOOSKI	WOODLAND	XANTIPPE	YPIRANGA
WHISKERS	WIRELESS	WOODSAGE	XENOPHON	YULETIDE
WHITTIER	WISEACRE	WOODWIND	YAMAGARA	ZALMOXIS
WHODUNIT	WISTARIA	WORDBOOK	YARMULKE	ZALOPHUS
WHOPPING	WISTERIA	WORKADAY	YARRAMAN	ZAMINDAR
WICHITAS	WITCHERY	WORKROOM	YATAGHAN	ZANZIBAR
WICKEDER	WITHDRAW	WORKSHOP	YEARBOOK	ZARZUELA
WIDENESS	WITHERED	WORMLIKE	YEARLING	ZEPPELIN
WILDCATS	WITHHOLD	WORMWOOD	YEARNING	ZIBELINE
WILDROSE	WOLFBANE	WORRYING	YELLOWER	ZIGGURAT
WINDFALL	WOLFLIKE	WRANGLER	YIELDING	ZIMBABWE
WINDPIPE	WOMANISH	WRECKAGE	YOKOHAMA	ZIPPORAH
WINDROSE	WONDROUS	WRETCHED	YOKOZUNA	ZOONOSES
WINDSTOP	WOODBINE	WRINKLED	YORITOMO	ZOOPHILE
WINDWARD	WOODCOAL	WRINKLES	YORKTOWN	ZUGZWANG
WINGLIKE	WOODFARM	WRITHING	YOSEMITE	ZULKADAH
WINNIPEG	WOODIBIS	WRONGFUL	YOUTHFUL	ZWIEBACK

Nine-Letter Words

ABANDONED	AFROASIAN	AMBIGUITY	APARTHEID
ABATEMENT	AFTERMATH	AMBIGUOUS	APARTMENT
ABOLITION	AFTERNOON	AMBITIOUS	APHRODITE
ABOMINATE	AFTERSONG	AMENDMENT	APOLOGIZE
ABORIGINE	AFTERWORD	AMORPHOUS	APPALLING
ABSTAINER	AGAMEMNON	AMPERSAND	APPALOOSA
ABSTINENT	AGGREGATE	AMPHIBIAN	APPARATUS
ABUNDANCE	AGINCOURT	AMPLIFIER	APPEARING
ABYSSINIA	AGITATION	AMPLITUDE	APPENDAGE
ACAPPELLA	AGREEABLE	AMSTERDAM	APPERTAIN
ACAROLOGY	AGREEMENT	AMUSEMENT	APPETIZER
ACCESSORY	AGRIPPINA	ANACLITIC	APPLEJACK
ACCIPITER	AHASUERUS	ANACRUSIS	APPLICANT
ACCLIMATE	AILANTHUS	ANALGESIC	APPRAISER
ACCOMPANY	ALABASTER	ANARCHIST	APROSEXIA
ACCORDANT	ALBATROSS	ANCESTORS	AQUARELLE
ACCORDING	ALCHEMIST	ANCESTRAL	AQUILEGIA
ACCORDION	ALDEBARAN	ANCHORAGE	AQUITAINE
ACCRETING	ALECTORIA	ANCHORITE	ARABESQUE
ACIDULOUS	ALEUTIANS	ANCILLARY	ARABINOSE
ACONCAGUA	ALEXANDER	ANCIPITAL	ARBITRARY
ACQUIESCE	ALGARROBA	ANDROMEDA	ARBITRATE
ACROPOLIS	ALGECIRAS	ANEMOLOGY	ARENICOLE
ACTUALITY	ALGONQUIN	ANGKORWAT	ARENOSITY
ADAMSPEAK	ALIGHIERI	ANGLESITE	AREOPAGUS
ADIPOCERE	ALLEGHENY	ANHYDROUS	ARGENTINA
ADJACENCY	ALLEGORIC	ANIMATION	ARGENTITE
ADJECTIVE	ALLEMAGNE	ANIMOSITY	ARISTIDES
ADJOINING	ALLEVIATE	ANNAPOLIS	ARISTOTLE
ADMIRABLE	ALLOWANCE	ANNEALING	ARMADILLO
ADMIRABLY	ALMAMATER	ANNOTATOR	ARMISTICE
ADMISSION	ALMANDITE	ANNOUNCER	ARMSTRONG
ADORATION	ALMSHOUSE	ANNULMENT	ARRIVISTE
ADVANTAGE	ALOPECOID	ANONYMOUS	ARROGANCE
ADVENTURE	ALPENHORN	ANOPHELES	ARROWROOT
ADVERSARY	ALTERNATE	ANTARCTIC	ARTEMISIA
AEGIALEIA	ALTIMETER	ANTHOLOGY	ARTIFICER
AEGISTHUS	ALTIPLANO	ANTIPASTO	ARTILLERY
AFFECTING	AMATERASU	ANTIPATHY	ASAFETIDA
AFFECTION	AMAUROSIS	ANTIPODAL	ASCENDING
AFFIANCED	AMAZEMENT	ANTIPODES	ASCERTAIN
AFORESAID	AMBERFISH	ANTIQUITY	ASHTAROTH
AFRIKAANS	AMBERGRIS	ANTIVENIN	ASHTORETH

ASPERSION	BANDICOOT	BLACKFISH	BRUSHWOOD
ASSERTION	BANDSTAND	BLACKFOOT	BRUTALITY
ASSIDUOUS	BARBARISM	BLACKHAND	BRUXELLES
ASSISTANT	BARBAROUS	BLACKHEAD	BRYNHILDE
ASSISTING	BARCAROLE	BLACKHOLE	BRYOPHYTE
ASSOCIATE	BARKCLOTH	BLACKJACK	BUCCANEER
ASSONANCE	BARNSTORM	BLACKMAIL	BUCENTAUR
ASSUASIVE	BAROMETER	BLACKPOOL	BUCHAREST
ASSURANCE	BARRACUDA	BLACKWOOD	BUCKWHEAT
ASSUREDLY	BARRISTER	BLAMELESS	BUJUMBURA
ASSYRIANS	BARTENDER	BLAVATSKY	BULLFIGHT
ASTEROIDS	BARTHOLDI	BLEMISHED	BUMBLEBEE
ASTOUNDED	BASTINADO	BLINDNESS	BURLESQUE
ASTROLOGY	BATHCHAIR	BLINDWORM	BURNSIDES
ASTRONAUT	BATHSHEBA	BLOCKHEAD	BURROWING
ASTRONOMY	BATTALION	BLOODCELL	BUSHELMAN
ATAHUALPA	BEACHHEAD	BLOODLESS	BUSHWHACK
ATAVISTIC	BEANSTALK	BLOODLINE	BUTTERCUP
ATENOPAIC	BEARBERRY	BLOODROOT	BUTTERFLY
ATONEMENT	BEAUMAINS	BLOODSHED	BUTTERINE
ATROCIOUS	BEAUTEOUS	BLUEBEARD	BUTTERNUT
ATROPHIED	BEAUTIFUL	BLUEBERRY	BYSTANDER
ATTENDANT	BECCAFICO	BLUEBLOOD	BYZANTIUM
ATTENTION	BEDIZENED	BLUEGRASS	CABALLERO
ATTENTIVE	BEDLAMITE	BLUERIDGE	CACOETHES
ATTENUATE	BEEFEATER	BLUNDERER	CACOMIXLE
ATTRITION	BEEKEEPER	BOATRACES	CACOPHONY
AUDACIOUS	BEELZEBUB	BOCCACCIO	CAESARION
AURICULAR	BEERSHEBA	BOLSHEVIK	CAFETERIA
AUSTERITY	BEFITTING	BOMBASTIC	CAIRNGORM
AUSTRALIA	BEFUDDLED	BOOKMAKER	CALABOOSE
AUTHENTIC	BEGETTING	BOOKSTAND	CALAVERAS
AUTHORITY	BEGINNING	BOOMERANG	CALCARATE
AUTHORIZE	BELEAGUER	BOOMSLANG	CALCIMINE
AUTOCRACY	BELEMNITE	BOONDOCKS	CALCULATE
AUTOLYCUS	BELGRAVIA	BOOTBLACK	CALEDONIA
AUTOMATIC	BELLICOSE	BORINQUEN	CALIBOGUS
AUTOMATON	BELLTOWER	BOSPOROUS	CALORIFIC
AUXILIARY	BELLYACHE	BOULEVARD	CALPURNIA
AVAILABLE	BELVEDERE	BOUNDLESS	CAMBRIDGE
AVALANCHE	BENIGHTED	BOUNTEOUS	CAMERAMAN
AVOCATION	BERRUGATE	BOUNTIFUL	CAMPANILE
AVOIDANCE	BERSERKER	BOURGEOIS	CANAVERAL
AWAKENING	BERZELIUS	BRABANTIO	CANDIDATE
AWARENESS	BETHLEHEM	BRAHMANAS	CANDLEMAS
AXMINSTER	BETRAYING	BRANCHING	CANDLENUT
BABYLONIA	BETROTHAL	BREADLINE	CANONICAL
BACCHANTE	BETROTHED	BREADPULP	CANTALOUP
BACILLARY	BICYCLIST	BREAKNECK	CANTELOPE
BACKBITER	BILATERAL	BREATHING	CANTICLES
BACKTRACK	BILLIARDS	BRICABRAC	CANTONESE
BACKWARDS	BINOCULAR	BRIDEWELL	CAPACITOR
BACKWOODS	BINTURONG	BRILLIANT	CAPITULUM
BAGATELLE	BIOGRAPHY	BRISKNESS	CAPPISTOL
BALAKLAVA	BIRDHOUSE	BRISTLING	CAPRICORN
BALDACHIN	BIRTHMARK	BRITANNIA	CAPTIVATE
BALEARICS	BISHOPRIC	BRITISHER	CARBONATE
BALLERINA	BISMILLAH	BRITOMART	CARBUNCLE
BALLPOINT	BLACKBIRD	BROADCAST	CAREFULLY
BALTHASAR	BLACKBUCK	BROADSIDE	CARETAKER
BALTHAZAR	BLACKDAMP	BROODMARE	CARIBBEES
BALTIMORE	BLACKDUCK	BROOKLINE	CARMELITE
BANDEROLE	BLACKFACE	BROTHERLY	CARNATION

CARNELIAN	CHARACTER	COINTREAU	CONSTANTA
CARNIVORE	CHARIVARI	COLERIDGE	CONSTRAIN
CARPENTER	CHARLATAN	COLICROOT	CONSTRICT
CARRAPATO	CHARYBDIS	COLLATION	CONSULTED
CARROUSEL	CHATTERER	COLLEAGUE	CONTAINED
CARRYOVER	CHAUFFEUR	COLLECTOR	CONTAINER
CARTILAGE	CHECKERED	COLLISION	CONTINENT
CARTRIDGE	CHECKMATE	COLLUSION	CONTORTED
CARTWHEEL	CHELICERA	COLONNADE	CONTRALTO
CARYOPSIS	CHEONGSAM	COLOSSEUM	CONTUSION
CASSANDRA	CHERBOURG	COLPORTER	CONUNDRUM
CASSAREEP	CHERNOZEM	COLUMBARY	CONVIVIAL
CASSEROLE	CHICKADEE	COLUMBINE	COOPERATE
CASSOWARY	CHICKAREE	COLUMNIST	COPYRIGHT
CASTALIAN	CHICKWEED	COMBATANT	CORCOVADO
CASTANEAN	CHIHUAHUA	COMBATIVE	CORDGRASS
CASTIGATE	CHILBLAIN	COMMANDER	COREOPSIS
CASTILIAN	CHILDLESS	COMMENCED	CORIANDER
CATACLYSM	CHIEFTAIN	COMMITTEE	CORMORANT
CATALEPSY	CHINKAPIN	COMMODITY	CORNCRAKE
CATALOGUE	CHLORIDIA	COMMOTION	CORNEMUSE
CATAMARAN	CHLOROSIS	COMMUNION	COROLLARY
CATCHWEED	CHOCHOSAN	COMMUNIST	CORPOREAL
CATCHWORD	CHOCOLATE	COMPANION	CORPOSANT
CATHARTIC	CHORISTER	COMPETENT	CORPULENT
CATHERINE	CHRISTENS	COMPETING	CORRASION
CATSKILLS	CHRISTIAN	COMPLETED	CORRELATE
CATTLEMAN	CHRISTMAS	COMPLIANT	CORROSION
CAUCASIAN	CHRONICLE	COMPONENT	CORROSIVE
CAUSATIVE	CHRYSALIS	COMPOSITE	CORRUGATE
CAVALCADE	CHUNGKING	CONCEALED	CORUSCATE
CAVALIERO	CHURCHILL	CONCEDING	COSMETICS
CAVECANEM	CIGARETTE	CONCEITED	COSMOLOGY
CAVERNOUS	CIGARFISH	CONCIERGE	COSMONAUT
CEASELESS	CIGUATERA	CONDEMNED	COSTARICA
CELANDINE	CIOCIOSAN	CONDENSED	COTILLION
CELEBRANT	CIREPERDU	CONDENSER	COTTONGIN
CELEBRATE	CIRRHOSIS	CONDIMENT	COTYLEDON
CELEBRITY	CLAMOROUS	CONDITION	COUNCILOR
CELESTIAL	CLAPBOARD	CONDUCIVE	COUNSELOR
CELLULOID	CLARIFIED	CONDUCTOR	COUNTLESS
CELLULOSE	CLARKKENT	CONESTOGA	COUPDETAT
CENTENARY	CLASSROOM	CONFESSOR	COURTESAN
CENTERING	CLEANSING	CONFIDENT	COURTSHIP
CENTURION	CLEARANCE	CONFIRMED	COURTYARD
CERATODUS	CLEMATITE	CONFUCIUS	COVERALLS
CERTAINLY	CLEOPATRA	CONFUSION	COWARDICE
CERTAINTY	CLEPSYDRA	CONGENIAL	CRABAPPLE
CERUSSITE	CLERGYMAN	CONGERIES	CRAFTSMAN
CERVANTES	CLIMACTIC	CONGRUITY	CRANBERRY
CESSATION	CLINCHING	CONJUGATE	CREDULOUS
CETSHWAYO	CLOISONNE	CONJURING	CREMASTER
CEYLONESE	CLOSENESS	CONNAUGHT	CREPITANT
CHAFFINCH	COAGULANT	CONNECTED	CRESCENDO
CHALCIOPE	COAGULATE	CONNUBIAL	CRINOLINE
CHALUMEAU	COALITION	CONQUERED	CRITERION
CHAMELEON	COASTLINE	CONQUEROR	CRITICISM
CHAMPAGNE	COCHINEAL	CONSCIOUS	CROCODILE
CHAMPLAIN	COCKAIGNE	CONSCRIPT	CROSSEYED
CHANTEUSE	COCKLEBUR	CONSONANT	CROSSTONE
CHANTILLY	COCKROACH	CONSTABLE	CROSSWISE
CHAPARRAL	COCKSCOMB	CONSTANCE	CROSSWORD
CHAPERONE	COFFEEPOT	CONSTANCY	CROSSWORK

CROSTARIE	DELIVERED	DISBELIEF	EACHOTHER
CROTONBUG	DELPHINUS	DISCHARGE	EAGERNESS
CRUSADERS	DEMISSION	DISCORDIA	EALDORMAN
CTESIPHON	DEMOPHILE	DISCOURSE	EARTHWORM
CUCHULAIN	DENIGRATE	DISCOVERY	EASTLYNNE
CUCULLATE	DENTALGIA	DISCREDIT	EASYGOING
CULMINATE	DEPARTING	DISEMBARK	EAVESDROP
CULTIVATE	DEPARTURE	DISFIGURE	ECCENTRIC
CUPBEARER	DEPENDENT	DISGUISED	ECDYSIAST
CUPSHAPED	DEPLETION	DISGUSTED	ECONOMICS
CURRAWANG	DEPRAVITY	DISHONEST	ECONOMIZE
CURRAWONG	DEPRECATE	DISINFECT	ECTOPLASM
CUSTODIAN	DEPRESSED	DISLOCATE	EDELWEISS
CUSTOMARY	DERRYDOWN	DISMANTLE	EDINBURGH
CUSTOMERS	DESCARTES	DISPARAGE	EDUCATION
CUTANEOUS	DESDEMONA	DISPLAYED	EFFECTIVE
CUTTHROAT	DESERTION	DISREGARD	EFFULGENT
DALMATIAN	DESERVING	DISSENTER	EGGSHAPED
DALTONISM	DESIGNATE	DISSIPATE	EGLANTINE
DANDELION	DESIRABLE	DISSOLUTE	EGOTISTIC
DANGEROUS	DESMOINES	DISTEMPER	EGREGIOUS
DANNUNZIO	DESPOTISM	DISTENDED	EIGHTFOLD
DAREDEVIL	DESSICATE	DISTILLED	ELABORATE
DARMSTADT	DESTITUTE	DISTILLER	ELASTOMER
DARTAGNAN	DESTROYED	DISTORTED	ELBOWROOM
DARTMOUTH	DESTROYER	DIVERGING	ELEGANTLY
DARWINISM	DESUETUDE	DIVERSIFY	ELEMENTAL
DASARATHA	DESULTORY	DIVERSION	ELEUTHERA
DAVENPORT	DETECTIVE	DIVISIBLE	ELEVATION
DEAFENING	DETERGENT	DIXIELAND	ELIMINATE
DEAUVILLE	DETERMINE	DIZZINESS	ELIZABETH
DEBAUCHED	DETRIMENT	DOCTRINAL	ELLIPSOID
DEBAUCHEE	DEUCALION	DOCUMENTS	ELOCUTION
DEBENTURE	DEUTERIUM	DODECAGON	ELOQUENCE
DEBUTANTE	DEVADATTA	DOGMATIST	ELSEWHERE
DECADENCE	DEVASTATE	DOGMATIZE	ELUCIDATE
DECALOGUE	DEVELOPER	DOGSALMON	EMACIATED
DECAMERON	DEVIATION	DOMINANCE	EMANATION
DECEBALUS	DEXTERITY	DOMINIQUE	EMBARRASS
DECEITFUL	DEXTEROUS	DONATELLO	EMBELLISH
DECENNIUM	DIABLERIE	DONKEYMAN	EMBRASURE
DECEPTION	DIABOLISM	DOVETAILS	EMBROIDER
DECEPTIVE	DIACRITIC	DOWITCHER	EMERGENCY
DECIDEDLY	DIANCECHT	DRACONIAN	EMOLLIENT
DECKCHAIR	DIAPHRAGM	DRAMATICS	EMOLUMENT
DECLINING	DIDELPHIS	DREAMLAND	EMOTIONAL
DECOMPOSE	DIDJERIDU	DRESSCOAT	EMPHASIZE
DECORATOR	DIETETICS	DRINKABLE	EMPHYSEMA
DECUMBENT	DIFFERENT	DROMEDARY	EMPIRICAL
DEDUCTION	DIFFICULT	DRUGSTORE	EMPTINESS
DEDUCTIVE	DIFFIDENT	DUBROVNIK	EMULATING
DEFECTION	DIFFUSING	DUFFLEBAG	ENACTMENT
DEFECTIVE	DIFFUSION	DULCAMARA	ENCAUSTIC
DEFENDANT	DIGITALIS	DUNGAREES	ENCELADUS
DEFERENCE	DIGNIFIED	DUPLICATE	ENCHANTER
DEFICIENT	DIGNITARY	DUPLICITY	ENCHILADA
DEFORMITY	DIONYSIAC	DUSHYANTA	ENCIRCLED
DEFRAUDED	DIRECTING	DUSTDEVIL	ENCLOSURE
DEJECTION	DIRECTION	DUSTSTORM	ENCOMPASS
DELESSEPS	DIRECTORY	DUTYBOUND	ENCOUNTER
DELICIOUS	DIRIGIBLE	DYSEGENIC	ENDOCRINE
DELIGHTED	DISAPPEAR	DYSENTERY	ENDOWMENT
DELIRIOUS	DISAVOWAL	DYSPEPSIA	ENDURANCE

ENERGETIC	EXCURSION	FLAMBERGE	GALLANTRY
ENGRAVING	EXCUSABLE	FLASHBACK	GALLINULE
ENGROSSED	EXECUTION	FLATTENED	GALVANIZE
ENIGMATIC	EXEMPLARY	FLEDGLING	GAMBOLING
ENJOYMENT	EXEMPTION	FLINTLOCK	GAMMADION
ENPASSANT	EXERCISES	FLOORSHOW	GANDHARVA
ENSHRINED	EXHAUSTED	FLORESTAN	GARAVANCE
ENTANGLED	EXISTENCE	FLUCTUATE	GARDENING
ENTHYMENE	EXONERATE	FLUORSPAR	GARIBALDI
ENTRANCED	EXOTROPIA	FOLIOLATE	GARRETEER
ENTRECOTE	EXPANSION	FOLLOWING	GARRULITY
ENUMERATE	EXPATIATE	FOOTSTALK	GARRULOUS
ENUNCIATE	EXPEDIENT	FORASMUCH	GASTRITIS
ENVIRONED	EXPENSIVE	FORCEMEAT	GASTROPOD
EPHEMERAL	EXPERTISE	FOREBEARS	GAVELKIND
EPHEMERID	EXPIATION	FOREIGNER	GAZETTEER
EPHEMERIS	EXPIATORY	FORENAMED	GELIGNITE
EPHIALTES	EXPLOSION	FORESIGHT	GEMCUTTER
EPIDAURUS	EXPOSITOR	FORESTALL	GENEALOGY
EPIDERMIS	EXPULSION	FORFEITED	GENERALLY
EPITOMIZE	EXQUISITE	FORFICULA	GENERATOR
EQUIPMENT	EXSOLDIER	FORGETFUL	GENTLEMAN
EQUIVOCAL	EXTEMPORE	FORMAGGIO	GENUFLECT
ERADICATE	EXTENDING	FORMATION	GEOLOGIST
ERIECANAL	EXTENSION	FORTHWITH	GEOPHAGIA
ERRONEOUS	EXTENSIVE	FORTITUDE	GERIATRIC
ERSTWHILE	EXTENUATE	FORTUNATE	GERMICIDE
ERUDITION	EXTIRPATE	FORTYFORT	GERUNDIVE
ESCALATOR	EXTORTION	FOUNDLING	GESTATION
ESDRAELON	EXTREMELY	FOURSIDED	GEYSERITE
ESOPHAGUS	EXTRINSIC	FRAGRANCE	GIBBERISH
ESOTERICS	EXTROVERT	FRAMBESIA	GIBRALTAR
ESPERANTO	EYELASHES	FRAMEWORK	GIDDINESS
ESQUILINE	FABIANISM	FRANCESCA	GILGAMESH
ESSENTIAL	FABRICATE	FRANCHISE	GIPPSLAND
ESTABLISH	FACSIMILE	FRANCOLIN	GIRONDIST
ESTAMINET	FAIRYLAND	FRANKFORT	GIROUETTE
ESTIMABLE	FALSEHOOD	FRANKNESS	GLADIATOR
ESTRANGED	FALTERING	FRATERNAL	GLADIOLUS
ETERNALLY	FANCYFREE	FRAUENLOB	GLADSTONE
ETHELBERT	FATIGUING	FREELANCE	GLASSLIKE
ETHNOLOGY	FAUSTULUS	FREESTATE	GLASSWORT
ETTUBRUTE	FAVORABLE	FREESTONE	GLOBEFISH
ETYMOLOGY	FEATHERED	FREIGHTER	GLOSSITIS
EUCHARIST	FEBRIFUGE	FRENCHMAN	GLUTINOUS
EUMENIDES	FELIBRIGE	FRESHNESS	GODMOTHER
EUPHORBIA	FERROTYPE	FRIARBIRD	GODSHAPED
EUPHRATES	FERTILITY	FRICASSEE	GOLDBRICK
EURIPIDES	FESTIVITY	FRIGIDITY	GOLDENAGE
EVAPORATE	FETISHISM	FRIVOLITY	GOLDENEYE
EVERGLADE	FEVERROOT	FRIVOLOUS	GOLDENROD
EVERGREEN	FIDUCIARY	FROCKCOAT	GOLDFINCH
EVERYBODY	FILOPLUME	FRUCTIDOR	GONDOLIER
EXCALIBUR	FIMBRIATE	FRUGALITY	GOODTIMES
EXCELLENT	FINANCIAL	FRUITLESS	GOOSANDER
EXCELSIOR	FIREBRAND	FRUSTRATE	GOSSIPING
EXCESSIVE	FIREDRAKE	FULMINATE	GOVERNING
EXCHEQUER	FIREFIGHT	FUNICULAR	GRADATION
EXCITABLE	FIRMAMENT	FUSILLADE	GRAMPIANS
EXCLUSION	FISHERMAN	GABERDINE	GRASSLAND
EXCLUSIVE	FLABELLUM	GALAPAGOS	GRATITUDE
EXCULPATE	FLAGEOLET	GALEIFORM	GRAVEYARD

GRAYBEARD	HARLEQUIN	HOMOTERIA	IMPLEMENT
GRAYWACKE	HARMATTAN	HONEYBEAR	IMPOLITIC
GREATDANE	HARMONICA	HONEYBIRD	IMPORTANT
GREENBELT	HARMONIZE	HONEYMOON	IMPORTUNE
GREENHORN	HARQUEBUS	HONORABLE	IMPOSTURE
GREENLAND	HARSHNESS	HONORABLY	IMPOTENCE
GREENNESS	HARUSPICY	HOOPSKIRT	IMPROMPTU
GREENROOM	HASDRUBAL	HOOPSNAKE	IMPROVISE
GREENSAND	HASHBROWN	HOPSCOTCH	IMPRUDENT
GREENWARE	HASHEMITE	HORDEOLUM	IMPUDENCE
GREENWICH	HATCHBACK	HORSEMINT	IMPUTABLE
GREENWOOD	HAWTHORNE	HORSEPLAY	INAMORATA
GRENADINE	HEADCLOTH	HORSESHOE	INAMORATO
GRIEVANCE	HEADDRESS	HOSTILITY	INCARNATE
GRIMALKIN	HEADLINER	HOTCORNER	INCENTIVE
GRIMHILDE	HEADSLING	HOURGLASS	INCEPTION
GRINDINGS	HEALTHFUL	HOUSEBOAT	INCESSANT
GROMATICS	HEARTBURN	HOUSECOAT	INCIDENCE
GROOMSMAN	HEARTLESS	HOUSEHOLD	INCIPIENT
GROTESQUE	HEARTWOOD	HOUSEMAID	INCLEMENT
GROUNDNUT	HEAUTARIT	HUASCARAN	INCOMMODE
GROVELING	HEAVINESS	HUCKABACK	INCORRECT
GRUFFNESS	HEDERATED	HUMILIATE	INCREMENT
GUACAMOLE	HELLEBORE	HUNCHBACK	INCUBATOR
GUANABARA	HELLHOUND	HUNDREDTH	INCUMBENT
GUARANTEE	HELVETIAN	HUNGARIAN	INDEMNITY
GUARNIERI	HEMSTITCH	HURRICANE	INDENTURE
GUATEMALA	HENPECKED	HURRIEDLY	INDICATED
GUERRIERE	HEPATITIS	HUSBANDRY	INDIGENCE
GUERRILLA	HEPTAGLOT	HYDERABAD	INDIGENES
GUIDEBOOK	HERBIVORE	HYDRAULIC	INDIGNANT
GUILLEMET	HEREAFTER	HYDROLOGY	INDOLENCE
GUILLEMOT	HERMITAGE	HYPERBOLA	INDONESIA
GUINEVERE	HERODOTUS	HYPERBOLE	INDUCTION
GUMMINESS	HESTERNAL	HYPHENATE	INDULGENT
GUTENBERG	HETERONYM	HYPNOTISM	INDURATED
GYMNASIUM	HEXAMETER	HYPOCOTYL	INEBRIETY
HABERGEON	HIBERNATE	HYPOCRISY	INELEGANT
HACKAMORE	HIBERNIAN	HYPOCRITE	INERTNESS
HACKNEYED	HIGHFLOWN	ICHNEUMON	INFANTILE
HAECCEITY	HIGHLIGHT	ICINGOVER	INFATUATE
HAGIOLOGY	HILARIOUS	ICONOLOGY	INFECTION
HAIRPIECE	HIMALAYAS	IDENTICAL	INFERENCE
HAIRSTYLE	HINDRANCE	IDIOCRASY	INFIELDER
HALEAKALA	HINDUKUSH	IDIOMATIC	INFIRMITY
HALFBREED	HINDUSTAN	IGNORANCE	INFLUENCE
HALFCASTE	HIPPIATER	ILLOGICAL	INFLUENZA
HALFPENNY	HIPPOCRAS	IMAGINARY	INFURIATE
HALFSTAFF	HIPPOLYTA	IMBROGLIO	INGENIOUS
HALFTRACK	HIRUNDINE	IMITATION	INGLENOOK
HALLOWEEN	HISTAMINE	IMITATIVE	INHERITED
HALMAHERA	HISTOLOGY	IMMELMANN	INHERITOR
HAMADRYAD	HISTORIAN	IMMERSION	INJURIOUS
HAMBURGER	HOARFROST	IMMIGRANT	INNERMOST
HAMMURABI	HOBGOBLIN	IMMOVABLE	INNISFAIL
HANDCLASP	HOIPOLLOI	IMMUTABLE	INNKEEPER
HANDCUFFS	HOLLERITH	IMPASSIVE	INNOCUOUS
HAPLOLOGY	HOLOCAUST	IMPELLING	INOCULATE
HAPPENING	HOLYGHOST	IMPERATOR	INQUIRING
HAPPINESS	HOMESTEAD	IMPERFECT	INSENSATE
HARBINGER	HOMOMORPH	IMPERIOUS	INSERTING
HARDSHIPS	HOMOPHONE	IMPETUOUS	INSIDIOUS

INSOLENCE	JELLYFISH	LEICESTER	LUDICROUS
INSPECTOR	JELLYLEAF	LEITMOTIF	LUMBERMAN
INSPIRING	JEQUIRITY	LENINGRAD	LUNATIONS
INSTANTER	JERUSALEM	LESHALLES	LUSITANIA
INSTANTLY	JETTATURA	LEUCOCYTE	LUTESCENT
INSTIGATE	JEWELCASE	LEVANTINE	LUXEMBURG
INSTITUTE	JICARILLA	LEVIATHAN	LUXURIANT
INSULATOR	JOANOFARC	LEXINGTON	LUXURIOUS
INSULTING	JOEMILLER	LIABILITY	MACEDONIA
INSURANCE	JOLLYBOAT	LIBERALLY	MACERATOR
INSURGENT	KALANCHOE	LIBERATOR	MACHINIST
INTELLECT	KARAKORAM	LIBERTINE	MADAROSIS
INTELSTAT	KASSERINE	LIBRATION	MADREPORE
INTENSELY	KIBBITZER	LIFEGUARD	MAELSTROM
INTENSITY	KILLIFISH	LIGHTNESS	MAGNETITE
INTENSIVE	KILOMETER	LIGHTROOM	MAGNIFIER
INTERDICT	KINESCOPE	LIGHTSOUT	MAGNITUDE
INTERJECT	KINGJAMES	LIGHTYEAR	MAHARAJAH
INTERLOCK	KINGSEVIL	LIMBURGER	MAHARANEE
INTERLUDE	KITTIWAKE	LIMESTONE	MAHLSTICK
INTERMENT	KLEENEBOK	LIMITABLE	MAIDSTONE
INTERNIST	KLIEGEYES	LIMNOLOGY	MAITREDEE
INTERPOSE	KNOTGRASS	LINDBERGH	MAJORDOMO
INTERPRET	KNOWINGLY	LINEAMENT	MAKESHIFT
INTERRUPT	KNOWLEDGE	LIONHEART	MALATESTA
INTERSECT	KOBENHAVN	LIPOTHYMY	MALICIOUS
INTERVENE	KRASINSKI	LIPPITUDE	MALIGNANT
INTERVIEW	KRIEMHILD	LISTENING	MALLEABLE
INTESTATE	KRITARCHY	LITERATIM	MALLEOLUS
INTESTINE	KSHATRIYA	LITHOLOGY	MAMMALOGY
INTRICACY	KURRAJONG	LITIGIOUS	MANABOZHO
INTRICATE	KWANGCHOW	LIVERPOOL	MANEUVERS
INTRINSIC	LABYRINTH	LIVERYMAN	MANGAREVA
INTRUSION	LACINIATE	LIXIVIATE	MANHANDLE
INTRUSIVE	LADYSCOMB	LJUBLJANA	MANHATTAN
INTUITION	LAGNIAPPE	LOADSTONE	MANIFESTO
INVECTIVE	LALLATION	LOATHSOME	MANSFIELD
INVENTION	LAMBARENE	LOBSCOUSE	MANYPLIES
INVENTIVE	LAMBSWOOL	LOCALSTOP	MAPLELEAF
INVISIBLE	LAMINARIA	LODESTONE	MARACAIBO
IPHIGENIA	LAMINATED	LODGEPOLE	MARCHPANE
IRASCIBLE	LAMPBLACK	LOGARITHM	MARESMILK
IRONSIDES	LANCASTER	LOGOGRIPH	MARGARINE
IRRADIATE	LANCEWOOD	LOGOMACHY	MARIHUANA
IRRAWADDY	LANDSCAPE	LOHENGRIN	MARIJUANA
IRREGULAR	LANGUEDOC	LOINCLOTH	MARIVELES
IRRITABLE	LAODICEAN	LONGEVITY	MARMALADE
IRRUPTION	LAPLANDER	LONGITUDE	MARMALADY
ISINGLASS	LARGHETTO	LONGJOHNS	MARMOREAL
ISLAMABAD	LASSITUDE	LONGRANGE	MARQUETRY
ISOLATION	LASTSTRAW	LOOSENESS	MARROWGUT
ISRAELITE	LATESCENT	LOOSENING	MARSEILLE
ITINERANT	LAUGHABLE	LORGNETTE	MARSUPIAL
ITINERARY	LAUNDRESS	LOTOPHAGI	MARVELOUS
JABORANDI	LAZARETTO	LOUDMOUTH	MASCULINE
JACKFROST	LAZYBONES	LOUISIANA	MASOCHIST
JACKKNIFE	LAZZARONE	LOUPGAROU	MASTERKEY
JACKSTONE	LEAKPROOF	LOUSEWORT	MASTICATE
JACKSTRAW	LEASEHOLD	LOVEAPPLE	MATCHLESS
JACKTOWEL	LEAVENING	LOXODONTA	MATCHLOCK
JADEPLANT	LECHEROUS	LOXODROME	MATERNITY
JAUNDICED	LEGENDARY	LUCRATIVE	MATRIARCH
JEFFERSON	LEGISLATE	LUCRETIUS	MATRICIDE

MATRIMONY	MOLLYMAWK	NESCIENCE	OSWEGOTEA
MATUTINAL	MOMENTOUS	NEWJERSEY	OTHERWISE
MAULSTICK	MONASTERY	NEWSPAPER	OTOLOGIST
MAUSOLEUM	MONGOLIAN	NEWSPRING	OURSELVES
MAYFLOWER	MONKEYPOD	NEWSSTAND	OUTLINING
MCPHERSON	MONKSHOOD	NICARAGUA	OUTRIGGER
MEANWHILE	MONOCHORD	NIETZSCHE	OUTSKIRTS
MEATEATER	MONOGRAPH	NIGHTGOWN	OUTWARDLY
MECHANISM	MONOLOGUE	NIGHTMARE	OVERGROWN
MEDALLION	MONOTREME	NILOMETER	OVERNIGHT
MEDIATING	MONSTROUS	NOCTURNAL	OVERPOWER
MEDICINAL	MONTAIGNE	NONENTITY	OVERPRINT
MEGAHERTZ	MOONLIGHT	NONPAREIL	OVERPRIZE
MEGAPHONE	MOONRAKER	NORTHSTAR	OVERSHOES
MEHETABEL	MOONSCAPE	NOTORIETY	OVERTHERE
MEKOMETER	MOONSHINE	NOTREDAME	OVERTHROW
MELBOURNE	MOONSTONE	NOURISHED	OVERWHELM
MELODIOUS	MOORGRASS	NOVELETTE	PACHAMAMA
MELODRAMA	MORAVIANS	NUKUALOFA	PACHYDERM
MELPOMENE	MORTGAGED	NUMERATOR	PAGLIACCI
MEMORANDA	MORTICIAN	NUSANTARA	PAILLASSE
MENAGERIE	MOTHEATEN	NUTRIMENT	PALACEOUS
MENDICANT	MOUSTACHE	OBEISANCE	PALATABLE
MENNONITE	MOUTHWASH	OBJECTION	PALESTINE
MENTIONED	MOZARELLA	OBLIGATED	PALISADES
MERCENARY	MRSGRUNDY	OBNOXIOUS	PALLIASSE
MERCILESS	MUDEATING	OBSCENITY	PALLYULLY
MERGANSER	MULETRESS	OBSCURELY	PALMISTRY
MERRIMENT	MULTIFORM	OBSCURITY	PALOVERDE
MESCALINE	MULTITUDE	OBSEQUIES	PALPEBRAL
MESMERISM	MUNICIPAL	OBSERVANT	PALPITATE
MESSENGER	MURCHISON	OBSESSION	PALUDINE
METEORITE	MURDEROUS	OBSTINACY	PANAMINTS
METHEGLIN	MURDSTONE	OBSTINATE	PANHANDLE
METHODIST	MUSCADINE	OCCASIONS	PANTOLOGY
MIDDLEMAN	MUSCOVITE	OCCLUSIVE	PANTOMIME
MIDEWIWIN	MUSKMELON	ODALISQUE	PAPERBACK
MIDWIFERY	MUSSOLINI	OFFENSIVE	PARACHUTE
MILESIANS	MUTINEERS	OFFICIOUS	PARADOXIC
MILESTONE	MYITKYINA	OFFSPRING	PARAGRAPH
MILLBOARD	MYRMIDONS	OLDCOLONY	PARALLELS
MILLEPORE	MYSTICISM	OLFACTORY	PARALYSIS
MILLINERY	NAMAYCUSH	OLIGARCHY	PARALYTIC
MILLIPEDE	NARCISSUS	OMBUDSMAN	PARALYZED
MILLSTONE	NARRATION	ONDOGRAPH	PARAMATTA
MILTIADES	NARROWING	ONECELLED	PARASITIC
MINCEMEAT	NASHVILLE	ONIONSKIN	PARCHMENT
MINIATURE	NAVICULAR	ONOMASTIC	PAREGORIC
MINIMIZED	NEBRASKAN	ONOMATOPE	PARENTAGE
MINNESOTA	NECESSARY	OPERATION	PARHELION
MINUSCULE	NECESSITY	OPERATIVE	PARICUTIN
MINUTEMAN	NECROLOGY	OPERCULUM	PARIETARY
MINUTIOSE	NECTARINE	OPPORTUNE	PAROCHIAL
MISCREANT	NEFARIOUS	ORANGUTAN	PAROTITIS
MISMANAGE	NEGLECTED	ORCHESTRA	PARRICIDE
MISRENDER	NEGLIGENT	ORDINANCE	PARSIMONY
MISTLETOE	NEGOTIATE	ORIENTATE	PARSONAGE
MNEMOSYNE	NEKHEEBET	ORIGINATE	PARTHENON
MOBILEBAY	NEOLITHIC	OROGRAPHY	PARTIALLY
MODIFYING	NEOLOGISM	OSCILLATE	PARTITION
MODULATED	NEOLOGIST	OSTEOPATH	PARTRIDGE
MOGADISHU	NEPHALISM	OSTIARIUS	PASDEDEUX
MOLLIFIED	NEOPHOBIA	OSTRACISM	PASSENGER

PASTERNAK	PESTHOUSE	POORHOUSE	PROFESSOR
PASTORATE	PETROGRAD	POPLITEUS	PROFUSION
PASTURAGE	PETROLEUM	POPPYCOCK	PROGNOSIS
PATAGONIA	PETRUCHIO	PORBEAGLE	PROLIXITY
PATCHWORK	PETTICOAT	PORCELAIN	PROMINENT
PATERNITY	PETTITOES	PORCUPINE	PROMOTING
PATHETLAO	PETULANCE	PORRINGER	PROMOTIVE
PATHOLOGY	PHACOLITH	PORTFOLIO	PRONGHORN
PATIENTLY	PHAGOCYTE	PORTLOUIS	PRONOUNCE
PATRIARCH	PHALANGER	PORTOLANO	PROPAGATE
PATRICIAN	PHALAROPE	PORTONOVO	PROPHETIC
PATRICIDE	PHARISAIC	POSSESSES	PROPONENT
PATRIMONY	PHENOMENA	POSTERITY	PROPRIETY
PATRIOTIC	PHILATELY	POSTHASTE	PROSELYTE
PATROCLUS	PHILOLOGY	POSTULANT	PROSTRATE
PATRONAGE	PHILOMATH	POSTULATE	PROTECTED
PATRONESS	PHILOMELA	POTCHEESE	PROTECTOR
PATZCUARO	PHNOMPENH	POTENTIAL	PROTOZOAN
PEACEPIPE	PHOSPHATE	POTPOURRI	PROVENCAL
PEACHWORT	PHOTOLOGY	POTTERIES	PROVIDENT
PECUNIARY	PHYSICIAN	POUCHLIKE	PROVINCES
PEDAGOGUE	PICTORIAL	PRACTICAL	PROVISION
PEDICULUS	PIERRETTE	PRAJAPATI	PROVOKING
PEEVISHLY	PILCOMAYO	PREACHING	PROXIMITY
PELLINORE	PILLARIST	PREAKNESS	PSEUDONYM
PELLITORY	PIMPERNEL	PRECEDENT	PSORIASIS
PENDRAGON	PINEAPPLE	PRECEDING	PSYCHOTIC
PENETRATE	PIPISTREL	PRECENTER	PTARMIGAN
PENITENTE	PIRITHOUS	PRECIPICE	PTOLEMIES
PENSIONER	PIROUETTE	PRECISELY	PUBLICITY
PENTAGRAM	PISCATORY	PRECISIAN	PUBLICIZE
PENTECOST	PITEOUSLY	PRECISION	PUBLISHED
PENTHOUSE	PITTISING	PREDATORY	PUISSANCE
PENTOTHAL	PITUITARY	PREDICATE	PULSATING
PEPEROMIA	PLACEMENT	PREEMPTED	PULSATION
PERCHANCE	PLAINTEXT	PREFATORY	PULSELIKE
PERCHERON	PLAINTIFF	PREGNANCY	PULVERIZE
PERCIVALE	PLANETARY	PREJUDICE	PUNCTILIO
PERCOLATE	PLANETOID	PREMATURE	PUNCTUATE
PEREGRINE	PLATELIKE	PREPOTENT	PUPPETEER
PERENNIAL	PLATITUDE	PRESENTLY	PURCHASER
PERFECTER	PLAUSIBLE	PRESERVER	PURGATIVE
PERFECTLY	PLAYPARTY	PRESIDENT	PURGATORY
PERFORATE	PLAYTHING	PRETERITE	PURPOSELY
PERFORMED	PLENILUNE	PREVALENT	PYGMALION
PERFORMER	PLENTIFUL	PRINCEDOM	PYONGYANG
PERIANDER	PLOWSHARE	PRINCETON	PYRETHRUM
PERIMETER	PLUGBOARD	PRINCIPAL	PYROXYLIN
PERIPHERY	PLUTOCRAT	PRINCIPIA	PYTHONESS
PERISCOPE	PLUTONIUM	PRINCIPLE	QUADRILLE
PERMANENT	PNEUMATIC	PRINTEMPS	QUADRUPED
PERMEABLE	PNEUMONIA	PRISIADKA	QUARTERON
PERMITTED	POETASTER	PRIVATEER	QUARTETTE
PERPETUAL	POETICULE	PRIVATELY	QUASIMODO
PERPLEXED	POIGNANCY	PRIVATION	QUERULOUS
PERSECUTE	POISONOUS	PRIVILEGE	QUICKLIME
PERSICARY	POKERFACE	PROBOSCIS	QUICKNESS
PERSONNEL	POLEVAULT	PROCACITY	QUICKSAND
PERTINENT	POLICEMAN	PROCEDURE	QUIESCENT
PETROLOGY	POLLINATE	PROCEEDED	QUOTATION
PETTICOAT	POLLUTION	PROCREATE	QUOTIDIAN
PERTUSSIS	POLYESTER	PRODUCING	RACKETEER
PERVASIVE	POLYNICES	PROFANITY	RADICULAR

RAKAUKAWA	REMISSION	ROUNDHEAD	SCREWPINE
RAMILLIES	RENASCENT	ROUNDNESS	SCRIMSHAW
RANCHERIA	RENDITION	RUBELLITE	SCRIPTURE
RANCOROUS	RENITENCE	RUBRICATE	SCROLLSAW
RANGATIRA	REPAIRMAN	RUNNYMEDE	SCRUBBING
RANTIPOLE	REPELLENT	RUSTICATE	SCULPTURE
RAPACIOUS	REPENTANT	SACCHARIN	SCUTIFORM
RAPTORIAL	REPERTORY	SACCULATE	SEASONING
RASPBERRY	REPLACING	SACKCLOTH	SEAWORTHY
RATIONALE	REPLENISH	SACRAMENT	SECESSION
READINESS	REPLETION	SACRIFICE	SECLUSION
READYMADE	REPOSSESS	SACRISTAN	SECONDARY
REALISTIC	REPRESENT	SAGACIOUS	SECRETARY
REANIMATE	REPRIMAND	SAGEBRUSH	SECRETIVE
REARRANGE	REPULSIVE	SAGITTATE	SECTIONAL
REATTEMPT	REPUTABLE	SALERATUS	SEDENTARY
RECAPTURE	REQUISITE	SALESLADY	SEDITIOUS
RECEPTION	REREBRACE	SALISBURY	SEDUCTIVE
RECESSION	RESENTFUL	SALTINESS	SEEMINGLY
RECHABITE	RESERVIST	SALTPETER	SEGREGATE
RECIPIENT	RESERVOIR	SALVAGERS	SELECTION
RECKONING	RESIDENCE	SALVATION	SEMANTICS
RECLINING	RESILIENT	SANCTUARY	SEMAPHORE
RECOLLECT	RESISTANT	SANDBLIND	SEMBLANCE
RECONCILE	RESONANCE	SANDGLASS	SEMIBREVE
RECONDITE	RESORTING	SANDPIPER	SEMICOLON
RECOUNTED	RESPECTED	SANDSTONE	SEMILEGAL
RECTITUDE	RESPIRING	SANGFROID	SEMIRAMIS
RECUMBENT	RESTIPPLE	SANTONICA	SENIORITY
RECURRENT	RESTRAINT	SAPODILLA	SENSELESS
REDBREAST	RESURFACE	SARASVATI	SENSITIVE
REDCLOVER	RETALIATE	SARCASTIC	SENTIMENT
REDUCTION	RETENTION	SARTORIUS	SEPTENARY
REDUNDANT	RETENTIVE	SASSAFRAS	SEPULCHER
REFECTION	RETIARIUS	SASSENACH	SERENADER
REFERABLE	RETICULAR	SATELLITE	SERIGRAPH
REFERENCE	RETRAHENT	SATIRICAL	SERVILITY
REFLECTOR	RETRIEVER	SATISFIED	SERVITUDE
REFRESHED	REVERENCE	SATURATED	SEVERALLY
REFULGENT	REVERSION	SAUTERNES	SEXCHANGE
REFURBISH	REVOLTING	SCALLOPED	SFORZANDO
REGARDING	REVOLVING	SCALPLOCK	SHAMELESS
REGISTRAR	REWARDING	SCAMANDER	SHANACHIE
REGULARLY	REYKJAVIK	SCANTIEST	SHANGRILA
REGULATOR	RHAPSODIC	SCANTLING	SHAPELESS
REICHSTAG	RHEINGOLD	SCAPEGOAT	SHARPENER
REIGNITED	RHYMESTER	SCARECROW	SHARPNESS
REINFORCE	RICHELIEU	SCAVENGER	SHAVETAIL
REINHARDT	RIGHTEOUS	SCHADCHEN	SHEEPLIKE
REINSTATE	RIGMAROLE	SCHATCHEN	SHEEPSKIN
REITERATE	RIGOLETTO	SCHILLING	SHEETBEND
REJECTION	RINTINTIN	SCHMALTZY	SHEFFIELD
REJOINDER	RIPUARIAN	SCHNORRER	SHELDRAKE
RELATIONS	ROBINHOOD	SCHOLARLY	SHELTERED
RELEASING	ROCHESTER	SCHOOLING	SHEREKHAN
RELIGIOUS	ROCINANTE	SCIENTIST	SHIFTLESS
RELIQUARY	ROGGEVEEN	SCLEROSIS	SHIMMERED
RELUCTANT	ROGUISHLY	SCOLIOSIS	SHIPWRECK
REMAINDER	ROKESMITH	SCORBUTUS	SHOEMAKER
REMAINING	ROSINANTE	SCOTCHMAN	SHORTHAND
REMBRANDT	ROSMARINE	SCRAPBOOK	SHREWDEST
REMINGTON	ROTTERDAM	SCRAPHEAP	SHUFFLING
REMINISCE	ROUGHNESS	SCREENING	SHWEDAGON

SIBILANCE	SPECTATOR	STRIKEOUT	TAMERLANE
SICKENING	SPEEDWELL	STRINGENT	TANGALUNG
SICKLEMIA	SPELUNKER	STRIPLING	TANGERINE
SIDETRACK	SPHENODON	STROMBOLI	TANTATARA
SIEGFRIED	SPHERICAL	STRONGBOX	TAPROBANE
SIEGLINDE	SPICEBUSH	STROPHIUM	TARANTULA
SIGHTSEER	SPIKENARD	STRUCTURE	TARNKAPPE
SIGNATURA	SPINDLING	STUPIDITY	TARPAULIN
SIGNATURE	SPINDRIFT	STYLISTIC	TAXIMETER
SILLINESS	SPINNAKER	SUBJOINED	TAXONOMIC
SIMPLETON	SPIRITUAL	SUBJUGATE	TECHNICAL
SINGAPORE	SPLENETIC	SUBLUNARY	TEENICIDE
SINHALESE	SPLITTING	SUBMARINE	TELEGONUS
SIPHUNCLE	SPOKESMAN	SUBSCRIPT	TELEGRAPH
SIQUEIROS	SPORTSCAR	SUBSTANCE	TELEMETER
SITUATION	SPOTLIGHT	SUCCESSOR	TELEOLOGY
SKAGERRAK	SPRIGHTLY	SUCCULENT	TELEPATHY
SKINFLINT	SPRINGBOK	SUFFOCATE	TELEPHONE
SKUNKHEAD	SPRINKLER	SUFFUSIVE	TELESCOPE
SLACKENED	SPRITSAIL	SUGARLOAF	TELLURIDE
SLANTWISE	SQUAWFISH	SUMMATION	TEMPERATE
SLAUGHTER	SQUEAMISH	SUMPTUARY	TEMPORARY
SLEEPLESS	STABILITY	SUMPTUOUS	TENEMENTS
SLENTANDO	STAGEHAND	SUNDOWNER	TENNESSEE
SLINGSHOT	STAGHOUND	SUNFLOWER	TENTATIVE
SMARTWEED	STAIRCASE	SUNSTROKE	TEREBINTH
SMUTSHEET	STALEMATE	SUPERSEDE	TEREBRATE
SNAKEEYES	STANCHION	SUPERVISE	TERMAGANT
SNAKELIKE	STAPLEPIT	SUPPORTED	TERMINATE
SNAKEROOT	STATEROOM	SUPPORTER	TERPANDER
SNAKEWEED	STATIONED	SUPPURATE	TERRIFIED
SNOWGOOSE	STATUETTE	SUPREMACY	TERRITORY
SOAPOPERA	STEADFAST	SURCINGLE	TERRORIST
SOAPSTONE	STEAMIRON	SURMULLET	TERRORIZE
SOCIETIES	STEAMPIPE	SURPRISED	TERSENESS
SOCIOLOGY	STEAMSHIP	SURRENDER	TESTAMENT
SOFTENING	STEELWOOL	SURROGATE	TESTATRIX
SOIDISANT	STEELYARD	SURVEYING	TESTIMONY
SOLEMNIZE	STEERSMAN	SUSPENDED	THALASSIC
SOLICITOR	STEINBECK	SUSPICION	THANKLESS
SOLILOQUY	STEPDANCE	SWADDLING	THEOCRACY
SOLITAIRE	STEVEDORE	SWAGGERER	THEOMANCY
SOMEWHERE	STIFFENED	SWEETENED	THERAPIST
SOMMELIER	STIFFNESS	SWEETLIPS	THEREFORE
SOMNOLENT	STIMULANT	SWEETMEAT	THERMIDOR
SOPHOCLES	STITCHING	SWIFTNESS	THESAURUS
SOPHOMORE	STOCKHOLM	SWITCHMAN	THIGHBONE
SORROWFUL	STOCKINGS	SWORDFISH	THOLOBATE
SORROWING	STONECROP	SWORDSMAN	THOROFARE
SORTILEGE	STONEFISH	SWORDTAIL	THRASHING
SORTILEGY	STONEWARE	SYCOPHANT	THREEFOLD
SOUFRIERE	STOPWATCH	SYLLOGISM	THREESOME
SOUNDNESS	STOREROOM	SYNAGOGUE	THRESHOLD
SOURGRASS	STORMSASH	SYNDICATE	THROWAWAY
SOUTHWARD	STRAPPING	SYNTHETIC	THYLACINE
SOVEREIGN	STRASBERG	TABLELAND	TIDALWAVE
SPAGHETTI	STRATAGEM	TABLEWARE	TIMETABLE
SPARETIME	STRATFORD	TABLEWINE	TIRNANOG
SPARKLING	STREAMLET	TACAMAHAC	TISIPHONE
SPASMODIC	STREETCAR	TAILGATER	TITFORTAT
SPEAKEASY	STRETCHER	TALIESSIN	TITILLATE
SPECTACLE	STRICTURE	TALKATIVE	TOADSTOOL

TOLERABLE	TYNDAREUS	VARICELLA	WAREHOUSE
TOLERANCE	TYRANNIZE	VARIEGATE	WARRANTED
TOMBIGBEE	ULANBATOR	VASECTOMY	WASHBASIN
TOMBSTONE	ULIGINOSE	VASSALAGE	WATCHWORD
TOMOGRAPH	ULSTERMAN	VATICINAL	WATERFALL
TOOLMAKER	UNANIMOUS	VEGETABLE	WATERLILY
TOOTHACHE	UNASHAMED	VEHEMENCE	WATERMARK
TOOTHLESS	UNBENDING	VELVETEEN	WATERSHED
TOOTHSOME	UNCERTAIN	VENERABLE	WEARINESS
TOPIARIST	UNCLOTHED	VENEZUELA	WEARISOME
TOPILTZIN	UNCONCERN	VENTRICLE	WEBFOOTED
TOPMINNOW	UNCOVERED	VENUSCOMB	WELLBEING
TORPIDITY	UNDECIDED	VERACIOUS	WELLSWEEP
TOSCANINI	UNDERDONE	VERBOSITY	WEROWANCE
TOTALIZER	UNDERHAND	VERDAGUER	WHEATCAKE
TOUCHDOWN	UNDERLING	VERDIGRIS	WHEREUPON
TOUGHNESS	UNDERMINE	VERGIFORM	WHETSTONE
TOUSSAINT	UNDERPASS	VERMIFORM	WHIMSICAL
TOWHEADED	UNDERTAKE	VERMILION	WHINBERRY
TRACKLESS	UNDERWEAR	VERSATILE	WHIRLIGIG
TRACTABLE	UNDERWENT	VERSIFIER	WHIRLPOOL
TRADESMAN	UNDIVIDED	VERSLIBRE	WHIRLWIND
TRADITION	UNEQUALED	VERTEBRAL	WHITEFISH
TRAFALGAR	UNFEELING	VESICULAR	WHITEOAKS
TRAILERED	UNFLEDGED	VESTIBULE	WHITEWASH
TRANSCEND	UNFOUNDED	VEXATIOUS	WHOLESALE
TRANSFORM	UNGUARDED	VIBRATING	WIDEANGLE
TRANSIENT	UNHEALTHY	VICTUALER	WIDOWHOOD
TRANSLATE	UNIFORMLY	VIDELICIT	WILLINGLY
TRANSMUTE	UNINJURED	VIENTIANE	WINDSTORM
TRANSPORT	UNITARIAN	VIERKLEUR	WISCONSIN
TRANSVAAL	UNIVERSAL	VIGILANCE	WITCHETTY
TRAPEZIST	UNLEARNED	VIGILANTE	WITCHHUNT
TRAPEZIUS	UNLIMITED	VINCENNES	WITHDRAWN
TRAPPINGS	UNMARRIED	VINDEPAYS	WOLVERENE
TRASIMENO	UNMOVABLE	VINDICATE	WOLVERINE
TREACHERY	UNREFINED	VIOLATION	WOMANKIND
TREADMILL	UNRELATED	VIOLENTLY	WONDERFUL
TREASURER	UNSETTLED	VIRACOCHA	WOODCHUCK
TREATMENT	UNSKILLED	VIRESCENT	WOODLOUSE
TREBUCHET	UNSNARLED	VIRGINITY	WOOLYBEAR
TREMATODE	UNTENABLE	VIRILOCAL	WORKHORSE
TREMBLING	UNTHRIFTY	VISCOSITY	WORLDWIDE
TRIBUTARY	UNTOUCHED	VISIGOTHS	WORSHIPER
TRICHOSIS	UNWEARIED	VISIONARY	WORTHLESS
TRICKSTER	UNWILLING	VITELLINE	WRANGLING
TRILOBITE	UNWRITTEN	VIVACIOUS	WRESTLING
TRIMMINGS	UPPERMOST	VIVANDIER	WRISTLOCK
TRITURATE	URSAMAJOR	VOICELESS	WYANDOTTE
TRIVALENT	URSAMINOR	VOLGOGRAD	XYLOGRAPH
TROUSSEAU	URTICARIA	VOLTMETER	YACHTRACE
TROVATORE	UTTERANCE	VOLUNTARY	YANKEEISM
TRUEPENNY	UTTERMOST	VOLUNTEER	YASODHARA
TRUNCHEON	UXORICIDE	VORACIOUS	YELLOWISH
TSARITSYN	VADEMECUM	VULGARITY	YERBAMATE
TURBULENT	VAEVICTIS	WADDYWOOD	YGGDRASIL
TURNTABLE	VAINGLORY	WAISTCOAT	YOMKIPPUR
TURPITUDE	VALENTINE	WAKEROBIN	YOSHIWARA
TURQUOISE	VALKYRIES	WALDGRAVE	YOUNGSTER
TWENTYONE	VANCOUVER	WALPURGIS	ZOROASTER
TWITCHING	VARIATION	WANDERING	ZUCCHETTO

ABERRATION	APPARITION	BANGLADESH	BRIDGEPORT
ABROGATION	APPEARANCE	BARBERSHOP	BRIDGETOWN
ABSOLUTELY	APPENNINES	BARCAROLLE	BRIGANTINE
ABSOLUTION	APPLESAUCE	BASKETBALL	BRILLIANCE
ABSTENTION	APPRENTICE	BASSETERRE	BROKENDOWN
ABSTINENCE	AQUAFORTIS	BASUTOLAND	BROWNSHIRT
ABSTRACTED	AQUAMARINE	BATONROUGE	BUCCINATOR
ACCELERATE	ARBORVITAE	BATTLESHIP	BUCEPHALUS
ACCESSIBLE	ARCHBISHOP	BECHEDEMER	BUDGERIGAR
ACCIDENTAL	ARCHEOLOGY	BELISARIUS	BUFFLEHEAD
ACCOUNTANT	ARCHIMEDES	BELLADONNA	BUFFOONERY
ACCUMULATE	ARISTOCRAT	BELLFLOWER	BUNCHGRASS
ACCURATELY	ARITHMETIC	BELLRINGER	BURDENSOME
ACCUSATION	ARMAGEDDON	BELLWETHER	BUTTERBEAN
ACROPHOBIA	ARTAXERXES	BELONGINGS	BUTTONHOLE
ACROTERIUM	ARTICULATE	BENEFACTOR	BUTTONWOOD
ADDISABABA	ARTIFICIAL	BENEFICIAL	CAGLIOSTRO
ADDITIONAL	ASCENDANCY	BENNINGTON	CALCULATOR
ADMONITION	ASPHYXIANT	BENZEDRINE	CALEDONIAN
ADULTERATE	ASPIDISTRA	BERNADETTE	CALIFORNIA
ADVENTURER	ASPIRATION	BERNADOTTE	CALORICITY
AFFLICTION	ASSAILABLE	BEWILDERED	CAMELOPARD
AGGRESSIVE	ASSESSABLE	BIBLIOPEGY	CAMOUFLAGE
AGRONOMIST	ASSESSMENT	BIBLIOPOLE	CAMPESTRAL
AHURAMAZDA	ASSIGNABLE	BILLETDOUX	CANDELABRA
ALANGALANG	ASSISTANCE	BILLOFFARE	CANDYSTORE
ALBIGENSES	ASSOCIATED	BINOCULARS	CANTALOUPE
ALCHERINGA	ASSUMPTION	BIRTHRIGHT	CANTERBURY
ALGOPHOBIA	ASTRINGENT	BITTERROOT	CANTILEVER
ALLEGATION	ASTROLOGER	BLACKBERRY	CANTONMENT
ALLEGIANCE	ASTROMANCY	BLACKBOARD	CANVASSING
ALLHALLOWS	ASTRONOMER	BLACKGUARD	CAOUTCHOUC
ALTARPIECE	ATMOSPHERE	BLACKHILLS	CAPABLANCA
ALTERATION	ATTACHMENT	BLACKSMITH	CAPITOLINE
ALTOPHOBIA	ATTAINMENT	BLACKWATER	CAPRICIOUS
AMANUENSIS	ATTENDANCE	BLACKWIDOW	CARBURETOR
AMATEURISH	ATTENDANTS	BLANKVERSE	CARDIALGIA
AMBASSADOR	ATTENUATED	BLISTERING	CARDIOLOGY
AMERCEMENT	ATTRACTIVE	BLOODAPPLE	CARICATURE
AMNEMACHIN	ATTUNEMENT	BLOODHOUND	CARPHOLOGY
AMPHITRITE	AUDITORIUM	BLOODSTONE	CARSONCITY
ANDROMACHE	AURICULATE	BLOOMSBURY	CARTOMANCY
ANECDOTIST	AUSPICIOUS	BLOSSOMING	CASSIOPEIA
ANEMOMETER	AUSTERLITZ	BLUEBONNET	CATAFALQUE
ANESTHESIA	AUSTRALIAN	BLUEBOTTLE	CATAPHRACT
ANIMALCULE	AUTHORIZED	BLUEGROTTO	CATSCRADLE
ANNIHILATE	AUTHORLESS	BLUEPENCIL	CATTLERAID
ANSWERABLE	AUTHORSHIP	BLUERIBBON	CAUTIOUSLY
ANTARCTICA	AUTOCRATIC	BLUSTERING	CAVALRYMAN
ANTECEDENT	AUTOMOBILE	BOBADILISM	CENSORSHIP
ANTHRACITE	AVANTGARDE	BOISTEROUS	CENTENNIAL
ANTHROPOID	AVENTURINE	BOLLWEEVIL	CEREMONIAL
ANTICIPATE	BACKGAMMON	BONNEVILLE	CERTIORARI
ANTICLIMAX	BACKSTITCH	BOOTLICKER	CHACHALACA
ANTIQUATED	BAFFLEMENT	BRAINSTORM	CHALCEDONY
ANTISEPSIS	BAKINGSODA	BRATISLAVA	CHALCIDICE
ANTISEPTIC	BALDERDASH	BREADFRUIT	CHANGEABLE
APOCALYPSE	BALLOONIST	BREASTBONE	CHANGELING
APOTHECARY	BALUSTRADE	BRICKLAYER	CHARDONNAY
APPARENTLY	BANDEROLLE	BRIDEGROOM	CHARITABLE

CHARLESTON	CONCLUSION	CROSSPIECE	DISASTROUS
CHARTREUSE	CONCLUSIVE	CROSSROADS	DISCIPLINE
CHATTERING	CONCOCTION	CRYPTOLOGY	DISCOBOLUS
CHAUVINIST	CONDESCEND	CUCKOOPINT	DISCOLORED
CHEERFULLY	CONDITIONS	CULTIVABLE	DISCOMFORT
CHEMISETTE	CONFECTION	CULTIVATED	DISCONCERT
CHERSONESE	CONFERENCE	CUMMERBUND	DISCREPANT
CHESAPEAKE	CONFESSION	CUMULATION	DISCRETION
CHEVROTAIN	CONFIDENCE	CUNCTATION	DISCURSIVE
CHICKENPOX	CONFLUENCE	CURTAILING	DISDAINFUL
CHIFFCHAFF	CONFOUNDED	CUTTLEFISH	DISEMBOWEL
CHILDBIRTH	CONGENITAL	CZAREVITCH	DISENCHANT
CHIMPANZEE	CONJECTURE	DASKAPITAL	DISGUSTING
CHINAGRASS	CONJOINTLY	DAVIDHARUM	DISHONESTY
CHINCHILLA	CONNECTING	DEBAUCHERY	DISHWASHER
CHIROMANCY	CONNECTION	DECELERATE	DISORDERED
CHITARRONE	CONNIPTION	DECORATION	DISORDERLY
CHITTAGONG	CONSCIENCE	DECORATIVE	DISPARAGED
CHRONICLES	CONSECRATE	DEFAMATION	DISPENSARY
CHRONOLOGY	CONSISTENT	DEFAMATORY	DISPERSION
CHRYSOLITE	CONSONANCE	DEFENSIBLE	DISSENSION
CHURCHLAND	CONSPIRACY	DEFLECTION	DISSOLUBLE
CHURCHYARD	CONSTANTLY	DELECTABLE	DISSOLVING
CINCINNATI	CONTAGIOUS	DELIBERATE	DISTRESSED
CIRCUMFLEX	CONTESTANT	DELICATELY	DIVERGENCE
CISTERCIAN	CONTIGUITY	DELIGHTFUL	DIVINATORY
CLASSIFIED	CONTINGENT	DELINQUENT	DOMINATION
CLAYPIGEON	CONTINUOUS	DEMOBILIZE	DOMINICKER
CLEANSLATE	CONTRABASS	DEMOLITION	DONNYBROOK
CLEMENTINE	CONTRACTOR	DEMURENESS	DOODLESACK
CLOSESHAVE	CONTRAVENE	DENDROLOGY	DOORKEEPER
CLOUDBURST	CONTRIBUTE	DEPARTMENT	DOUBLETALK
COARSENESS	CONTRITION	DEPENDENCE	DRAWBRIDGE
COCKAMAROO	CONTROLLER	DEPLORABLE	DRESSMAKER
COEXISTENT	CONVENTUAL	DEPLOYMENT	DROSOPHILA
COINCIDING	CONVERSELY	DEPORTMENT	DRUIDSTONE
COLLECTION	CONVERSING	DEPOSITION	DUMFOUNDED
COLLECTIVE	CONVEYANCE	DEPRECIATE	DYERSBROOM
COLORATURA	CONVULSIVE	DEPRESSION	EARTHQUAKE
COMMANDEER	COPACABANA	DERACINATE	EFFEMINATE
COMMERCIAL	COPENHAGEN	DERMATITIS	EFFERVESCE
COMMISSION	COPPERHEAD	DEROGATORY	EISTEDDFOD
COMPARISON	COPYHOLDER	DESCENDING	ELABORATED
COMPASSION	COQUETTISH	DESIGNEDLY	ELASTICITY
COMPATIBLE	CORDIALITY	DESOLATION	ELECTORATE
COMPENDIUM	CORINTHIAN	DESPICABLE	ELEMENTARY
COMPENSATE	CORNFLOWER	DESSALINES	ELLIPTICAL
COMPETENCY	CORNHUSKER	DETACHMENT	ELSALVADOR
COMPETITOR	CORNUCOPIA	DETERMINED	EMACIATING
COMPLACENT	COROMANDEL	DETESTABLE	EMACIATION
COMPLETELY	CORONATION	DETONATION	EMANCIPATE
COMPLETION	CORPULENCE	DEVASTATED	EMASCULATE
COMPLEXION	CORRECTIVE	DHAMMAPADA	EMBANKMENT
COMPLIANCE	CORREGIDOR	DIASKEUAST	EMBLEMATIC
COMPLIMENT	CORRELATED	DICTIONARY	EMBODIMENT
COMPOSITOR	CORROBOREE	DIFFERENCE	EMBROIDERY
COMPREHEND	CORRUGATED	DIFFICULTY	EMPIRICISM
COMPRESSED	COUNTERACT	DIFFIDENCE	ENCAMPMENT
COMPROMISE	COURAGEOUS	DILETTANTE	ENCYCLICAL
COMPULSION	COWCATCHER	DIMINUTION	ENERVATION
COMPULSORY	CRAPULENCE	DIMINUTIVE	ENGAGEMENT
CONCERNING	CRENELLATE	DININGROOM	ENGLISHMAN
CONCHOLOGY	CROSSHAIRS	DIPHTHERIA	ENTHUSIASM

ENTHUSIAST	FEUILLETON	GRAPEFRUIT	HULLABALOO
ENTOMOLOGY	FIANCHETTO	GRAPHOLOGY	HURDYGURDY
EPIMETHEUS	FIBERBOARD	GRASSROOTS	HYETOMETER
EPISCOPATE	FIGURATIVE	GRAVESTONE	HYGROMETER
EQUANIMITY	FILIBUSTER	GREENBRIER	HYPERDULIA
EQUATORIAL	FINGERROOT	GREGARIOUS	HYPODERMIC
EQUESTRIAN	FISTICUFFS	GREYWETHER	HYPOPHYSIS
EQUIVALENT	FIVEANDTEN	GUADELOUPE	HYPOTHESIS
ERGASTULUM	FLASHLIGHT	GUARANTEED	ICONOCLAST
ERUCTATION	FLATULENCE	GUARNERIUS	ICONOSCOPE
ERYSIPELAS	FLAVORSOME	GUMBOLIMBO	IDEALISTIC
ESCADRILLE	FLEURDELIS	GYNOPHOBIA	ILLITERATE
ESCAPEMENT	FLEURDELYS	HABITUATED	ILLUMINATE
ESCARPMENT	FLICKERING	HACKMATACK	ILLUSTRATE
ESCRITOIRE	FLOCCULENT	HAGIOLATRY	IMBECILITY
ESCUTCHEON	FLOURISHED	HALFSHADOW	IMMACULATE
ESPECIALLY	FLUTTERING	HALLELUJAH	IMMODERATE
ESSENTIALS	FOREBODING	HAMILTRUDE	IMMOLATION
EUCALYPTUS	FORECASTER	HAPHAESTUS	IMPECCABLE
EUPHROSYNE	FORECASTLE	HARDBOILED	IMPEDIMENT
EUTHANASIA	FORECOURSE	HARMONIOUS	IMPERVIOUS
EVALUATION	FOREORDAIN	HARRISBURG	IMPLACABLE
EVANGELIST	FORERUNNER	HARTEBEEST	IMPOSITION
EVAPORABLE	FORESHADOW	HARVESTMAN	IMPREGNATE
EVENTUALLY	FORFEITURE	HASMONEANS	IMPRESARIO
EVERGLADES	FORTISSIMO	HEARTSEASE	IMPRESSIVE
EVERYTHING	FORTUITOUS	HEBDOMADAL	IMPRIMATUR
EVERYWHERE	FORTUNATUS	HELICOPTER	IMPROPERLY
EVISCERATE	FORTYNINER	HELIOPOLIS	INACTIVITY
EXAGGERATE	FOUNDATION	HELIOTROPE	INADEQUACY
EXASPERATE	FRANCISCAN	HELLBENDER	INADEQUATE
EXCAVATION	FRATRICIDE	HELLESPONT	INCAPACITY
EXCELLENCE	FRAUDULENT	HEMOPHILIA	INCAUTIOUS
EXCITEMENT	FREEFORALL	HEMORRHAGE	INCENDIARY
EXECRATION	FREEHOLDER	HEPHAESTUS	INCIDENTAL
EXECUTIVES	FREEMARTIN	HEPHAISTOS	INCINERATE
EXPEDIENCY	FREQUENTLY	HEPTAMERON	INCIVILITY
EXPEDITION	FRIENDSHIP	HENCEFORTH	INCLEMENCY
EXPERIMENT	FRUITARIAN	HERACLITUS	INCOHERENT
EXPOSITION	FULIGINOUS	HEREDITARY	INCOMPLETE
EXPRESSION	FUNDRAISER	HERESIARCH	INCREDIBLE
EXPRESSIVE	FUSSBUDGET	HERETOFORE	INDEFINITE
EXTENDABLE	GARBAGECAN	HERMOPOLIS	INDIANPIPE
EXTINCTION	GASTRONOME	HESPERIDES	INDICATION
EXTINGUISH	GENERALISM	HIGHLANDER	INDICATIVE
EXTRACTION	GENETHLIAC	HIGHSCHOOL	INDICATORY
EXTRANEOUS	GEORGESAND	HIGHWAYMAN	INDICTMENT
EXUBERANCE	GEORGETOWN	HINDENBURG	INDIGENOUS
EYEGLASSES	GESUNDHEIT	HINDUSTANI	INDISCREET
FAIRHEADED	GETHSEMANE	HINTERLAND	INDISPOSED
FALLACIOUS	GETTYSBURG	HIPPOCRENE	INDISTINCT
FALSEFRONT	GIBICHÜNGS	HIPPODAMIA	INEVITABLE
FANATICISM	GLITTERING	HIPPOLYTUS	INEXORABLE
FARNSWORTH	GLUTTONOUS	HIPPOMENES	INFATUATED
FARSIGHTED	GOLDDIGGER	HISPANIOLA	INFECTIOUS
FASCINATED	GOLDENCALF	HODGEPODGE	INFLEXIBLE
FASTIDIOUS	GOLDENHORN	HONOURABLE	INFLEXIBLY
FEDERATION	GOLDILOCKS	HORIZONTAL	INFRACTION
FEDERATIVE	GOODWISHES	HOROLOGIST	INFURIATED
FELICITOUS	GOOSEBERRY	HORSELAUGH	INFUSORIAN
FELLOWSHIP	GOOSEFLESH	HORSESENSE	INHABITANT
FERDELANCE	GOOSEGRASS	HOSPITABLE	INHIBITION
FERTILIZER	GOVERNMENT	HUCKLEBONE	INHUMANITY

INHUMATION	LEGITIMATE	MEDITATION	NATTERJACK
INIGOJONES	LENGTHWISE	MEERSCHAUM	NAVIGATION
INORDINATE	LEPRECHAUN	MELANCHOLY	NEAPOLITAN
INSATIABLE	LEXICOLOGY	MELLOPHONE	NECROMANCY
INSPECTION	LIBERALITY	MEMORANDUM	NECROPHAGE
INSPISSATE	LIBERTYCAP	MENDACIOUS	NECROPOLIS
INSTRUMENT	LIBIDINOUS	MENDICANTS	NECTOPHORE
INSULATION	LIBREVILLE	MERCANTILE	NEEDLEFISH
INTANGIBLE	LICENTIATE	MERIDIONAL	NEGLIGENCE
INTEGUMENT	LIEBKNECHT	MERITBADGE	NEHALENNIA
INTENERATE	LIEUTENANT	METAPHRAST	NESSELRODE
INTERESTED	LIGHTHOUSE	METHODICAL	NETHERMOST
INTERLOPER	LIGNESCENT	METHUSELAH	NEWSCASTER
INTERSTICE	LIMICOLINE	METICULOUS	NIGHTSHADE
INTERWEAVE	LIMICOLOUS	METROPOLIS	NIGHTSHIRT
INTERWOVEN	LIMITATION	MICKIEWICZ	NIGHTSTICK
INTIMIDATE	LIMIVOROUS	MICROSCOPE	NOCTAMBULE
INTOLERANT	LINEBACKER	MICROSPORE	NOMANSLAND
INTOXICATE	LIPIZZANER	MIDSHIPMAN	NOMDEPLUME
INTRAMURAL	LIPPIZANER	MIGNONETTE	NOUAKCHOTT
INUNDATION	LITERATURE	MILITIAMAN	NOURISHING
INVETERATE	LITIGATION	MILLENNIUM	NUDIBRANCH
INVINCIBLE	LITTLEROCK	MINDREADER	NULLANULLA
IRIDESCENT	LITURGICAL	MINERALOGY	NUMEROLOGY
IROQUOIANS	LIVELIHOOD	MIRACULOUS	OBLIGATION
IRRATIONAL	LIVELINESS	MISCELLANY	OBLIGATORY
IRRELEVANT	LOCOMOTIVE	MISCONDUCT	OBLITERATE
IRRITATION	LOGANBERRY	MISERICORD	OBSERVANCE
ISHMAELITE	LOGGERHEAD	MISFORTUNE	OCCASIONAL
ISRAELITES	LOQUACIOUS	MISOGAMIST	OCCIDENTAL
JACKANAPES	LORNADOONE	MISOGYNIST	ODONTALGIA
JAGUARONDI	LOSANGELES	MISTAKENLY	OFFICEWORK
JARDINIERE	LOVELETTER	MIZUYADOGU	OHSUSANNAH
JINRIKISHA	LUXEMBOURG	MOCKORANGE	OKEECHOBEE
JOURNALIST	LYOPHILIZE	MODERATION	OKEFINOKEE
JOURNEYING	MADAGASCAR	MODULATION	OMNIPOTENT
JUVENILITY	MAGENDAVID	MOHAMMEDAN	OMNISCIENT
KALGOORLIE	MAGISTRATE	MONEGASQUE	ONEIROLOGY
KARAGEORGE	MAGNIFICAT	MONILIASIS	OPENSESAME
KARTTIKEYA	MAIDENHAIR	MONOPOLIZE	OPENSTRAND
KEBNEKAISE	MAIDENHOOD	MONOTONOUS	OPHIOLATRY
KIMBERLITE	MALCONTENT	MONSTRANCE	OPPOSITION
KNOBKERRIE	MALEVOLENT	MONTCERVIN	OPPRESSIVE
KNOCKERRIE	MANAGEABLE	MONTECARLO	OPTIMISTIC
KONIGSBERG	MANAGEMENT	MONTEGOBAY	ORDINARILY
KOOKABURRA	MANAWYDDAN	MONTGOMERY	ORIGINALLY
KOOLOKAMBA	MANCHESTER	MONTICELLO	ORIGINATED
KRONSHTADT	MANGOSTEEN	MONTMARTRE	ORIGINATOR
LABORATORY	MANIPULATE	MONTPELIER	OSTENSIBLE
LACEDAEMON	MANNAGRASS	MONTSERRAT	OSTROGOTHS
LACERATION	MANUSCRIPT	MORPHOLOGY	OUANANICHE
LACERTIDAE	MANZANILLA	MOTIONLESS	OUTLANDISH
LACHRYMOSE	MARIONETTE	MOUNTEBANK	OUTPOURING
LACRIMATOR	MARSHALSEA	MOZAMBIQUE	OVERORNATE
LACUSTRINE	MARTINIQUE	MULTIPLIER	OVERTHROWN
LAGERKVIST	MASANIELLO	MUNIFICENT	OVERWORKED
LANCEOLATE	MASQUERADE	MUSOPHOBIA	OVIPOSITOR
LANDLUBBER	MATOGROSSO	MUTABILITY	PADEREWSKI
LASCIVIOUS	MATTATHIAS	MYSTAGOGUE	PAIDEUTICS
LEBENSRAUM	MATTERHORN	MYSTERIOUS	PAINTBRUSH
LEFTHANDED	MAYONNAISE	NARASINGHA	PALESTRINA
LEFTHANDER	MECHANICAL	NARCISSIST	PALIMPSEST
LEGISLATOR	MEDIOCRITY	NASTURTIUM	PALINDROME

PALLIATIVE	PINEMARTEN	PROPHETESS	REORGANIZE
PANTAGRUEL	PITCHPENNY	PROPORTION	REPEATEDLY
PANTALOONS	PLAGIARISM	PROPRIETOR	REPERTOIRE
PARAMARIBO	PLANTATION	PROSECUTOR	REPETITION
PARAMECIUM	PLANTLOUSE	PROSERPINA	REPUBLICAN
PARAPHRASE	PLASMODIUM	PROSERPINE	REPUTATION
PARDONABLE	PLAYGROUND	PROSPECTOR	RESEMBLING
PARIMUTUEL	PLAYWRIGHT	PROSPERITY	RESENTMENT
PARLIAMENT	PLEASANTLY	PROSPEROUS	RESISTANCE
PARONYCHIA	PLEASINGLY	PROTECTION	RESOUNDING
PARROTBILL	PLEBISCITE	PROTESTANT	RESPECTFUL
PARTICIPLE	PLUTOCRACY	PROTRACTED	RESTAURANT
PARTICULAR	PODIATRIST	PROTRUSION	RETRACTION
PASSIONATE	POGAMOGGAN	PROVIDENCE	REVELATION
PAWNBROKER	POIGNANTLY	PROVINCIAL	REVELATORY
PEARSHAPED	POLITENESS	PROVISIONS	REVIVALIST
PEASHOOTER	POLITICIAN	PSYCHOLOGY	REVOLUTION
PEDESTRIAN	POLYCHROME	PUERTORICO	RIBOFLAVIN
PEJORATIVE	POLYDEUCES	PUGNACIOUS	RIDICULOUS
PENETRABLE	POLYHEDRON	PUNISHMENT	RITARDANDO
PENMANSHIP	POLYHYMNIA	PURPOSEFUL	ROADRUNNER
PENTAMETER	POLYNESIAN	PYROMANIAC	ROUNDABOUT
PENTAPOLIS	POMERANIAN	PYTHAGORAS	ROUNDROBIN
PENTATEUCH	PONDICHERY	QUARANTINE	ROUNDTABLE
PEPPERCORN	PONTICELLO	QUATERMAIN	RUBALKHALI
PEPPERIDGE	POPULARITY	RACECOURSE	RUDDERHEAD
PERCEPTION	POPULATION	RAGAMUFFIN	SABBATICAL
PERCEPTIVE	PORIFEROUS	RAVISHMENT	SABRETOOTH
PERCOLATOR	PORTENTOUS	RAWALPINDI	SACRAMENTO
PERCUSSION	POSSESSION	READYMADES	SACRECOEUR
PEREMPTORY	POSTMORTEM	REALESTATE	SACREDNESS
PERFIDIOUS	POSTSCRIPT	REASONABLE	SADDLETREE
PERIODICAL	PRAIRIEDOG	RECEPTACLE	SALAMANDER
PERIOSTEUM	PRAXITELES	RECIDIVIST	SALUBRIOUS
PERIWINKLE	PRECARIOUS	RECIPROCAL	SANANDREAS
PERMISSION	PRECAUTION	RECITATIVE	SANCTIONED
PERMISSIVE	PRECEPTIVE	RECOGNIZED	SANDERLING
PERORATION	PRECURSORY	RECOMPENSE	SANGUINARY
PERSEPHONE	PREDACIOUS	RECONSIDER	SANITATION
PERSEPOLIS	PREDISPOSE	RECREATION	SANTACLAUS
PERSISTENT	PREEMINENT	RECUPERATE	SANTAMARIA
PERSISTING	PREEMPTIVE	REDEMPTION	SATURATION
PERSONALLY	PREFERENCE	REDUNDANCY	SATURNALIA
PERSUASION	PREFERMENT	REFINEMENT	SATYAGRAHA
PERVERSION	PREJUDICED	REFLECTING	SAUERKRAUT
PETITIONER	PRESBYOPIA	REFLECTION	SAVAGENESS
PETITPOINT	PRESCIENCE	REFRACTIVE	SAVORINESS
PHARMACIST	PRESIDENCY	REFUTATION	SCANDALOUS
PHLEBOTOMY	PREVALENCE	REGARDLESS	SCARLETINA
PHLEGETHON	PRINCIPLES	REGELATION	SCATOPHAGA
PHLEGMATIC	PROCEEDING	REGENERATE	SCHISMATIC
PHLOGOPITE	PROCLAIMED	REGRANTING	SCHOLASTIC
PHOENICIAN	PROCRUSTES	REGRESSIVE	SCHONBRUNN
PHONOGRAPH	PRODUCTIVE	REGULARITY	SCHOOLMARM
PHOSPHORUS	PROFESSION	REGULARIZE	SCHWEITZER
PHRENOLOGY	PROFICIENT	REGULATION	SCRATCHING
PHYLLOXERA	PROFITABLE	RELATIVITY	SCRIPTURAL
PHYSIOCRAT	PROFITLESS	RELINQUISH	SCRUTINIZE
PIANISSIMO	PROFLIGATE	REMARKABLE	SCURRILOUS
PIANOFORTE	PROGENITOR	REMEDIABLE	SEAMSTRESS
PICKPOCKET	PROJECTION	REMEMBERED	SECONDHAND
PILOTHOUSE	PROMETHEUS	RENASCENCE	SEEDEATING
PINAKOTHEK	PROPENSITY	RENDEZVOUS	SEERSUCKER

SEISMOLOGY	STOCKYARDS	TARANTELLA	TYPEWRITER
SELFWILLED	STOMATITIS	TASHILUMPO	TYPOGRAPHY
SEMIQUAVER	STONEBRAKE	TASKMASTER	UBERMENSCH
SEMPSTRESS	STONEHENGE	TEETOTALER	ULTIMATELY
SENIORPROM	STRABISMUS	TELEMACHUS	UNAFFECTED
SENSUALIST	STRADIVARI	TELEVISION	UNBEARABLE
SENSUALITY	STRAIGHTEN	TEMPERANCE	UNBELIEVER
SEPARATELY	STRAMNEOUS	TEMPORALLY	UNCOMMONLY
SEPARATION	STRASBOURG	TENDERFOOT	UNCULTURED
SEPTENNIAL	STRAWBERRY	TENDERIZER	UNDENIABLE
SEPTICEMIA	STREETARAB	TENPOUNDER	UNDERMINER
SEPTUAGINT	STRENGTHEN	TEPIDARIUM	UNDERSCORE
SERPENTINE	STRIDULATE	TERREHAUTE	UNDERSTATE
SHAWINIGAN	STRINDBERG	TERRIFYING	UNDERSTOOD
SHERBROOKE	STRINGBEAN	TETRAMETER	UNDERSTUDY
SHIBBOLETH	STRINGHALT	THEOCRITUS	UNDERTAKER
SHIFTINESS	STRONGHOLD	THEODOLITE	UNDERWORLD
SHILLELAGH	STRUCTURAL	THEOLOGATE	UNDULATING
SHOESTRING	STRULDBRUG	THEREAFTER	UNEMPLOYED
SHOPKEEPER	STRYCHNINE	THIMBLERIG	UNEXPECTED
SHOREDITCH	STURDINESS	THORNAPPLE	UNEXPLODED
SHOSHONEAN	SUBFOREMAN	THOUGHTFUL	UNEXPLORED
SHREVEPORT	SUBLINGUAL	THREADLIKE	UNFAITHFUL
SHREWDNESS	SUBMISSION	THREESIDED	UNFASTENED
SIDDHARTHA	SUBMISSIVE	THROUGHOUT	UNFINISHED
SIDEWINDER	SUBSTITUTE	THUCYDIDES	UNFRUITFUL
SILHOUETTE	SUBTRAHEND	THUMBSCREW	UNGOVERNED
SILKSCREEN	SUBVERSION	TIEBREAKER	UNGRACEFUL
SILVERFISH	SUCCESSFUL	TIMBERLINE	UNHERALDED
SIMFEROPOL	SUCCESSIVE	TIMBERWOLF	UNICAMERAL
SIMILARITY	SUCCINCTLY	TIMESERVER	UNIFORMITY
SIMPLICITY	SUFFERANCE	TINKERBELL	UNILATERAL
SINGLETREE	SUFFRAGIST	TOLERATION	UNIVERSITY
SKIATHERIC	SUGGESTION	TOMFOOLERY	UNPLEASANT
SKUPSHTINA	SUNGLASSES	TONGUELIKE	UNPLEASING
SKYSCRAPER	SUPERVISOR	TOPSYTURVY	UNPREPARED
SLIVOVITSA	SURFACTANT	TORQUEMADA	UNRAVELING
SMARTALECK	SURROUNDED	TOUCHSTONE	UNRIVALLED
SMATTERING	SUSPENDERS	TOURMALINE	UNSELECTED
SNEAKTHIEF	SUSPICIOUS	TOXICOLOGY	UNSKILLFUL
SOMERSAULT	SUSTENANCE	TRAGACANTH	UNSUMMONED
SOOTHSAYER	SWALLOWING	TRAMPOLINE	UNTIDINESS
SPACEOPERA	SWEATLODGE	TRANSDUCER	UNTRUTHFUL
SPECIALIST	SWEDENBORG	TRANSGRESS	UNYIELDING
SPECTACLES	SWEETBREAD	TRANSCIENCE	VACATIONER
SPEECHLESS	SWEETBRIER	TRANSISTOR	VALPARAISO
SPELEOLOGY	SWEETHEART	TRANSITION	VARIEGATED
SPERMACETI	SYCOPHANCY	TRANSITORY	VEGETABLES
SPIDERWORT	SYMBOLICAL	TRANSLATOR	VEGETARIAN
SPIRITLESS	SYMPATHIZE	TRAVERTINE	VEGETATION
SPOONERISM	SYSTEMATIC	TRENCHCOAT	VELOCIPEDE
SPOONRIVER	TABLECLOTH	TRIACETATE	VENDEMAIRE
STALACTITE	TABLEDHOTE	TRIANGULAR	VENERATION
STALAGMITE	TABULARASA	TRISKELION	VENTILATOR
STANDSTILL	TABULATION	TROGLODYTE	VENTOMETER
STARGAZING	TACNAARICA	TROLLEYCAR	VERNACULAR
STARVATION	TAKLAMAKAN	TROUBADOUR	VERNISSAGE
STATIONERY	TALETELLER	TROUTPERCH	VERROCCHIO
STENTORIAN	TAMBOURINE	TSAREVITCH	VILLALOBOS
STEPHANITE	TANANARIVE	TUBERCULIN	VILLARRICA
STEPLADDER	TANNHAUSER	TUMBLEWEED	VINDICATOR
STEREOTYPE	TANTAMOUNT	TURPENTINE	VINDICTIVE
STEWARDESS	TARADIDDLE	TYPESETTER	VINEGAROON

VIVANDIERE	WASHINGTON	WHITSUNDAY	WOODPECKER
VIVIPAROUS	WATERCOLOR	WICKEDNESS	WORDSWORTH
VOCABULARY	WATERPROOF	WIDESPREAD	WORKINGMAN
VOCIFERATE	WATERWHEEL	WIENERWALD	WORLDSFAIR
VOLATILITY	WATERWINGS	WILDEBEEST	WRAPAROUND
VOLATILIZE	WEAKMINDED	WILMINGTON	XENOPHOBIA
VOLUPTUOUS	WEAVERBIRD	WINCHESTER	XYLOGLYPHY
VORACIOUS	WELLINGTON	WINESELLER	YAGUARUNKI
VULNERABLE	WENCESLAUS	WITCHCRAFT	YARRAYARRA
WAHWAHLUNG	WHISPERING	WITCHHAZEL	ZENDAVESTA
WAINWRIGHT	WHITEFIELD	WOFFINGTON	ZIGZAGGING
WALLFLOWER	WHITEWATER	WONDERLAND	

COMMON WORDS

IN

SIX LANGUAGES

COMMON WORDS IN SIX LANGUAGES

English	French	German
AIRPLANE	AVION	FLUGZEUG
ALL	TOUT	ALLE, ALLES, GANZ
ALWAYS	TOUJOURS	IMMER
AND	ET	UND
APRIL	AVRIL	APRIL
AUGUST	AOUT	AUGUST
AUNT	TANTE	TANTE
BE	ETRE	SEIN
BED	LIT	BETT
BEE	ABEILLE	BIENE
BEFORE	AVANT	VORHER
BELL	CLOCHE	GLOCKE
BLACK	NOIR	SCHWARZ
BOOK	LIVRE	BUCH
BOY	GARCON	KNABE, JUNGE
BREAD	PAIN	BROT
BROTHER	FRERE	BRUDER
BUT	MAIS	ABER
CAT	CHAT	KATZE
CHEESE	FROMAGE	KASE
CHILD	ENFANT	KIND
CHRISTMAS	NOEL	WEIHNACHTEN
CITY	VILLE	STADT
CROSS	CROIX	KREUZ
DAUGHTER	FILLE	TOCHTER
DAY	JOUR	TAG
DEAD	MORT	TOT
DECEMBER	DECEMBRE	DEZEMBER
DEVIL	DIABLE	TEUFEL
DO	FAIRE	TUN, MACHEN
DOG	CHIEN	HUND
DOOR	PORTE	TUR
EARTH	TERRE	ERDE
EAST	EST	OSTEN
EIGHT	HUIT	ACHT
EYE	OEIL	AUGE
FACE	VISAGE	GESICHT
FALL	AUTOMNE	HERBST
FATHER	PERE	VATER
FEBRUARY	FEVRIER	FEBRUAR
FIVE	CINQ	FUNF
FLOWER	FLEUR	BLUME
FOUR	QUATRE	VIER
FRIDAY	VENDREDI	FREITAG
GASOLINE	ESSENCE	BENZIN
GIRL	FILLE	MADCHEN
GOD	DIEU	GOTT
GOOD	BON	GUT
GREEN	VERT	GRUN
HALF	DEMI	HALB
HAND	MAIN	HAND
HEAD	TETE	KOPF
HEART	COEUR	HERZ
HERE	ICI	HIER
HORSE	CHEVAL	PFERD
HOT	CHAUD	HEISS
HUNDRED	CENT	HUNDERT
HUSBAND	MARI	MANN

Italian	Latin	Spanish
AEREO	———	AVION
TUTTO	OMNIS	TODO
SEMPRE	SEMPER	SIEMPRE
E	ET, ETQUE	Y
APRILE	APRILIS	ABRIL
AGOSTO	SEXTILIS	AGOSTO
ZIA	AMITA, MATERTERA	TIA
ESSERE	ESSE	ESTAR, SER
LETTO	LECTUS	CAMA
APE	APIS	ABEJA
PRIMA	ANTE, PRIUS	ANTES
CAMPANA	TINTINNABULUM	CAMPANA
NERO	ATER, NIGER	NEGRO
LIBRO	LIBER	LIBRO
RAGAZZO	PUER	MUCHACHO
PANE	PANIS	PAN
FRATELLO	FRATER	HERMANO
MA	PRAETER, NISI, SED	PERO
GATTO	FELES, FELIS	GATO
FORMAGGIO	CASEUS	QUESO
FANCIULLO	INFANS, PUERI	NINO
NATALE		NAVIDAD
CITTA	URBS	CIUDAD
CROCE	CRUX	CRUZ
FIGLIA	FILIA	HIJA
GIORNO	DIES	DIA
MORTO	MORTUUS	MUERTO
DICEMBRE	DECEMBER	DICIEMBRE
DIAVOLO	DIABOLUS	DIABLO
FARE	FACERE	HACER
CANE	CANIS	PERRO
PORTA	OSTIUM, IANUA	PUERTA
TERRA	TERRA	TIERRA
EST	ORIENS	ESTE
OTTO	OCTO	OCHO
OCCHIO	OCULUS	OJO
FACCIA	OS, FACIES	CARA
AUTUNNO	AUTUMNUS	OTONO
PADRE	PATER	PADRE
FEBBRALO	FEBRUARIUS	FEBRERO
CINQUE	QUINQUE	CINCO
FLORE	FLOS	FLOR
QUATTRO	QUATTUOR	CUATRO
VENERDI	———	VIERNES
BENZINA	———	GASOLINA
RAGAZZA	PUELLA	MUCHACHA
DIO	DEUS	DIOS
BUONO	BONUS	BUENO
VERDE	VIRIDIS	VERDE
MEZZO	DIMIDIUS	MEDIO
MANO	MANUS	MANO
TESTA, CAPO	CAPUT	CABEZA
CUORE	COR	CORAZON
QUI	HIC	AQUI
CAVALLO	EQUUS	CABALLO
CALDO	CALIDUS	CALIENTE
CENTO	CENTUM	CIENTO
MARITO	VIR, MARITUS	MARIDO

English	French	German
ICE	GLACE	EIS
IN	DANS	IN
INK	ENCRE	TINTE
INSANE	FOU	WAHNSINNIG
JANUARY	JANVIER	JANUAR
JULY	JUILLET	JULI
JUNE	JUIN	JUNI
KEY	CLEF	SCHLUSSEL
KING	ROI	KONIG
LADY	DAME	DAME
LAUGH	RIRE	LACHEN
LEFT	GAUCHE	LINK
LITTLE	PETIT	KLEIN
LOVE	AMOUR	LIEBE
LUCK	CHANCE	GLUCK
MAN	HOMME	MANN
MARCH	MARS	MARZ
MAY	MAI	MAI
MILK	LAIT	MILCH
MISS	MADEMOISELLE	FRAULEIN
MONDAY	LUNDI	MONTAG
MONKEY	SINGE	AFFE
MONTH	MOIS	MONAT
MOON	LUNE	MOND
MOTHER	MERE	MUTTER
MR.	MONSIEUR	HERR
MRS.	MADAME	FRAU
NEIGHBOR	VOISIN	NACHBAR
NEVER	JAMAIS	NIEMALS
NINE	NEUF	NEUN
NO	NON	NEIN
NOON	MIDI	MITTAG
NORTH	NORD	NORDEN
NOTHING	RIEN	NICHTS
NOVEMBER	NOVEMBRE	NOVEMBER
OCTOBER	OCTOBRE	OKTOBER
OLD	VIEUX	ALT
ONE	UN, UNE	EIN, EINE
OWL	HIBOU	EULE
PEN	PLUME	FEDER
PENCIL	CRAYON	BLEISTIFT
PIG	COCHON	SCHWEIN
POOR	PAUVRE	ARM
QUEEN	REINE	KONIGIN
RAIN	PLUIE	REGEN
RED	ROUGE	ROT
RICE	RIZ	REIS
RIGHT	DROIT	RECHT
RIVER	FLEUVE	FLUSS
ROOM	CHAMBRE	ZIMMER
RUBBER	CAOUTCHOUC	GUMMI
SALT	SEL	SALZ
SATURDAY	SAMEDI	SAMSTAG
SEPTEMBER	SEPTEMBRE	SEPTEMBER
SEVEN	SEPT	SIEBEN
SHE	ELLE	SIE
SHEEP	MOUTON	SCHAF
SILVER	ARGENT	SILBER
SISTER	SOEUR	SCHWESTER
SIX	SIX	SECHS
SMALL	PETIT	KLEIN

Italian	Latin	Spanish
GHIACCIO	GLACIES	HIELO
IN	IN	EN
INCHIOSTRO	ATRAMENTUM	TINTA
PAZZO	DEMENS	LOCO
GENNAIO	IANUARIUS	ENERO
LUGLIO	QUINCTILIS	JULIO
GIUGNO	IUNIUS	JUNIO
CHIAVE	CLAVIS	LLAVE
RE	REX	REY
SIGNORA	MATRONA	SENORA
RIDERE	RIDERE	REIR
SINISTRO	LAEVUS, SINISTER	IZQUIERDO
PICCOLO	PARVUS	PEQUENO
AMORE	AMOR	AMOR
FORTUNA	FORS	SUERTE
UOMO	HOMO	HOMBRE
MARZO	MARTIUS	MARZO
MAGGIO	MAIUS	MAYO
LATTE	LAC	LECHE
SIGNORINA	VIRGO	SENORITA
LUNEDI	—	LUNES
SCIMMIA	SIMIA	MONO
MESE	MENSIS	MES
LUNA	LUNA	LUNA
MADRE	MATER	MADRE
SIGNORE	DOMINUS	SENOR
SIGNORA	DOMINA	SENORA
VICINO	VICINUS	VECINO
MAI	NUNQUAM	NUNCA
NOVE	NOVEM	NUEVE
NO	NON, MINIME	NO
MEZZOGIORNO	MERIDIES	MEDIODIA
NORD	SEPTENTRIO	NORTE
NIENTE	NIHIL	NADA
NOVEMBRE	NOVEMBRIS	NOVIEMBRE
OTTOBRE	OCTOBER	OCTUBRE
VECCHIO	VETUS	VIEJO
UN, UNA	UNUS, UNA, UNUM	UN, UNA
GUFO	ULULA, STRIX	BUHO
PENNA	CALAMUS	PLUMA
MATITA, LAPIS	STILUS	LAPIZ
PORCO	SUS, PORCUS	PUERCO
POVERO	PAUPER	POBRE
REGINA	REGINA	REINA
PIOGGIA	PLUVIA	LLUVIA
ROSSO	RUBER	ROJO
RISO	ORYZA	ARROZ
DESTRO	DEXTER	DERECHO
FLUME	FLUMEN	RIO
CAMERA	CONCLAVE	CUARTO
GOMMA		CAUCHO
SALE	SAL	SAL
SABATO	—	SABADO
SETTEMBRE	SEPTEMBER	SEPTIEMBRE
SETTE	SEPTEM	SIETE
ESSA	ILLA	ELLA
PECORA	OVIS	OVEJA
ARGENTO	ARGENTUM	PLATA
SORELLA	SOROR	HERMANA
SEI	SEX	SEIS
PICCOLO	PARVUS	PEQUENO

English	French	German
SON	FILS	SOHN
SOUTH	SUD	SUDEN
SPRING	PRINTEMPS	FRUHLING
STAMP	TIMBRE	BRIEFMARKE
STAR	ETOILE	STERN
STORE	MAGASIN	LADEN
STREET	RUE	STRASSE
SUMMER	ETE	SOMMER
SUN	SOLEIL	SONNE
SUNDAY	DIMANCHE	SONNTAG
TEA	THE	TEE
TEACHER	MAITRE	LEHRER
TEN	DIX	ZEHN
THANK YOU	MERCI	DANKE
THE	LE, LA, LES	DER, DIE, DAS
THOUSAND	MILLE	TAUSEND
THREE	TROIS	DREI
THURSDAY	JEUDI	DONNERSTAG
TODAY	AUJOURDHUI	HEUTE
TOO	AUSSI	AUCH
TOWN	VILLE	STADT
TREE	ARBRE	BAUM
TUESDAY	MARDI	DIENSTAG
TWELVE	DOUZE	ZWOLF
TWO	DEUX	ZWEI
UNCLE	ONCLE	ONKEL
VERY	TRES	SEHR
VOICE	VOIX	STIMME
WATER	EAU	WASSER
WEDNESDAY	MERCREDI	MITTWOCH
WEEK	SEMAINE	WOCHE
WEST	OUEST	WESTEN
WHITE	BLANC	WEISS
WIFE	FEMME	FRAU
WINTER	HIVER	WINTER
WOOD	BOIS	HOLZ
YEAR	AN	JAHR
YES	OUI	JA

Italian	Latin	Spanish
FIGLIO	FILIUS	HIJO
SUD	MERIDIES	SUR
PRIMAVERA	VER	PRIMAVERA
FRANCOBOLLO	———	SELLO
STELLA	STELLA, ASTRUM	ASTRO
NEGOZIO	TABERNA	TIENDA
VIA	VIA, VICUS	CALLE
ESTATE	AESTAS	VERANO
SOLE	SOL	SOL
DOMENICA	———	DOMINGO
TE	———	TE
MAESTRO	MAGISTER	MAESTRO
DIECI	DECEM	DIEZ
GRAZIE	BENIGNE	GRACIAS
IL, LA, LO, I, GLI, LE		EL, LA, LOS, LAS
MILLE	MILLE	MIL
TRE	TRES	TRES
GIOVEDI	———	JUEVES
OGGI	HODIE	HOY
ANCHE	ETIAM	TAMBIEN
CITTA	URBS	CIUDAD
ALBERO	ARBOR	ARBOL
MARTEDI	———	MARTES
DODICI	DUODECIM	DOCE
DUE	DUO	DOS
ZIO	PATRUUS, AVUNCULUS	TIO
MOLTO	SUMME, MAXIME	MUY
VOCE	VOX	VOZ
ACQUA	AQUA	AGUA
MERCOLEDI	———	MIERCOLES
SETTIMANA		SEMANA
OVEST	OCCIDENS	OESTE
BIANCO	ALBUS, CANDIDUS	BLANCO
MOGLIE	UXOR, CONIUNX	MUJER
INVERNO	HIEMS	INVIERNO
LEGNO	LIGNUM	MADERA
ANNO	ANNUS	ANO
SI	ITA, CERTE, VERO, AIO	SI

Bantam provides essential companions for any puzzle-doer, game player or trivia buff.

THE BANTAM CROSSWORD DICTIONARY

With over 50,000 clues, 160,000 answers, 40 special tables, plus exclusive 6, 7, 8, 9, and 10-letter word finder. This is the newest, biggest, most authoritative crossword dictionary there is.

❑ 26375-7 $4.50/$4.95 in Canada

THE COMPLETE BOOK OF SOLITAIRE AND PATIENCE GAMES

by Albert H. Morehead & Geoffrey Mott-Smith

In addition to all of the most frequently enjoyed games of solitaire—Canfield, Klondike, Patience—the authors have added over 225 brand-new games to make this the most comprehensive book of its kind.

❑ 26240-8 $4.95/$5.95 in Canada

BOBBY FISCHER TEACHES CHESS

by Fischer, Margulies, and Mosenfelder

An extraordinary opportunity to learn the secrets of great chess playing from "the profoundest student of chess who ever lived." (*Life*)

❑ 26315-3 $5.95/$6.95 in Canada